CASES AND PROBLEMS IN CRIMINAL PROCEDURE: THE COURTROOM
Fifth Edition

Cases & Problems in Criminal Procedure: The Courtroom

Fifth Edition

by

Myron Moskovitz
Professor of Law
Golden Gate University

 LexisNexis

Library of Congress Cataloging-in-Publication Data

Moskovitz, Myron.
   Cases & problems in criminal procedure : the courtroom / by Myron Moskovitz. — 5th ed.
      p. cm.
Rev. ed. of: Cases and problems in criminal procedure. 4th ed. c2004.
   Includes index.
   ISBN 978-1-4224-7046-6 (hardbound)
   1. Criminal procedure--United States--Cases. I. Moskovitz, Myron. Cases and problems in criminal procedure. II.
Title. III. Title: Cases and problems in criminal procedure.
   KF9619.M67 2004
   345.73'05--dc22
                                                                                  2009038363

NOTE TO USERS
To ensure that you are using the latest materials available in this area, please be sure to periodically check the LexisNexis Law School web site for downloadable updates and supplements at www.lexisnexis.com/lawschool.

Editorial Offices
121 Chanlon Rd., New Providence, NJ 07974 (908) 464-6800
201 Mission St., San Francisco, CA 94105-1831 (415) 908-3200
www.lexisnexis.com

MATTHEW◆BENDER

(2009–Pub.043)

Preface

This book is the second part of *Cases & Problems in Criminal Procedure*. The first book, subtitled *The Police*, focuses on Fourth, Fifth, and Sixth Amendment issues, which tend to arise in relations between the police and the community. The stories involved in the problems are inherently interesting, as they involve the cops and robbers scenarios students (and others) tend to enjoy.

The cases in this book are a bit more prosaic. Nevertheless, they have their own charm, following the criminal case as it proceeds through the court system. They deal with the fairness of each procedural mechanism and, on a practical level, these issues may be more important to the student who ends up practicing some criminal law.

Like the first book, this book is based on the problem method. Each chapter opens with a problem, with the cases in the chapter to be read with an eye towards "solving" the problem. This approach is designed to help law professors teach students to do what lawyers do: analyze problems. When a client comes to a lawyer with a difficult legal problem, the lawyer usually researches the legal issues, finding a cluster of authorities. In order to advise the client (and — if necessary — litigate the case), the lawyer must analyze, distinguish, reconcile, and interrelate the authorities in the cluster, seeing them as a group indicating the direction of the law as well as seeing them separately.

This book is an attempt to recreate that experience for the law student and to help the student learn how to handle it. To learn to do something practical requires three things: a task, the appropriate tools, and a teacher. This book supplies the task and the tools. The task is the problem at the outset of each chapter. The tools are the statutes and cases that follow. Following many cases are notes giving the student hints as to how the cases might be used to help analyze the problems.

Analyzing problems is useful in itself — this is what lawyers do. But equally important, problem analysis can encourage the student to understand each case on a deeper level. One cannot apply a principle to a new set of facts unless one truly understands the principle and its underlying rationale.

Because the book focuses on how the United States Constitution affects criminal procedure, most of the cases are from the United States Supreme Court. However, on many issues, statutes and rules are intertwined with the constitutional issues, so I have included them too. I tried to select cases that deal with issues which criminal attorneys are likely to see fairly often, rather than esoteric issues which appellate judges sometimes find attractive. For this reason, I included some lower court cases that cover issues which arise in practice with some frequency, but which have thus far escaped the attention of the United States Supreme Court.

Keeping reading assignments for students to a reasonable length forced me to restrict the number of issues and cases I was able to include. I tried, however, to select fairly recent and well-written cases that address fundamental issues in each area. (My editing of the cases often omits the usual asterisks, brackets, and the like. My object was to make the cases as readable as possible for weary law students, and I hope the authors of those opinions will forgive the minor liberties I have taken.)

When I attended Boalt Hall in the early 1960's, I took a one-semester, 3-unit course called "Criminal Law & Procedure." This short course gave us ample time to cover all the major issues in both fields. Within a few years thereafter, however, the Warren Court — and the subsequent reactions of the Burger and Rehnquist courts — expanded the law of criminal procedure exponentially. The size of this book reflects that explosion.

While I believe that the approach taken by this book is pedagogically sound, I have another, more selfish reason for using this approach in my teaching: It is fun to play lawyer. Students usually agree, and I think this in itself enhances their learning. This approach does demand more work from them. Not only must they read the cases, but they must try to apply them to the problem. It helps if they prepare an outline of an analysis of the problem, based on the authorities in the chapter. All this takes more time and effort, but they do it and seem to enjoy doing it. They know that they are reading the cases as a lawyer would, for a specific purpose: to "solve" the problem.[1]

I hope you enjoy it too.

Myron Moskovitz

---

[1] A more complete presentation of my views on the problem method appears in M. Moskovitz, *Beyond the Case Method: It's Time to Teach With Problems*, 42 Journal of Legal Education 241 (1992).

Preface to Fifth Edition

Things move fast in Criminal Procedure. New cases come down every day, and some make pretty big changes in the law. This edition includes several important cases that have been issued since the earlier editions of this book.

Since one of the virtues of the last edition was its relatively manageable length (compared to some other casebooks in this field), I tried to keep the overall length of this edition about the same length.

The Problems are the essence of this Book, and they have retained their prominence at the outset of each Chapter. I have modified a few of the Problems, however, to take into account some new cases, or to make the Problems a bit "closer."

M.M.

Introduction

AN OVERVIEW OF THE CRIMINAL COURTROOM PROCESS

Each chapter in this book deals with only a part of the criminal courtroom process. Sometimes, it might be hard to see how each part fits into the whole. So here is a brief overview of the whole process in felony cases, as it usually operates in federal courts and most state courts.

Suppose the police believe that Dan has committed a series of four bank robberies. They arrest Dan and "book" him (write the charges and biographical data about Dan in a book), and they send a report of the case to the prosecutor's office ("United States Attorney" in the federal system, "District Attorney" in most states). The prosecutor considers the strength of the evidence against Dan and other factors in determining what charges to file, and then files a complaint against Dan in court. The complaint is similar to a complaint in a civil case. Each *count* (i.e., each separate charge) in the complaint states that on a certain date, Dan committed certain acts which violated a specified penal statute, at a location within the jurisdiction of the court.

Within a few days, Dan will be arraigned before a magistrate of the court (who does not have as much authority as the *judge* who will later preside at the *trial* of the case). At the arraignment, the magistrate will read the charges to Dan and ask him to enter a *plea* of guilty, not guilty, not guilty by reason of insanity, or "*nolo contendere*" (i.e., a default), to each charge. If Dan does not have a lawyer with him to advise him on what plea to enter, the magistrate will usually give Dan some time to hire one, or, if Dan is indigent, time to arrange for the services of a public defender. If Dan pleads guilty to any charge, the magistrate will sentence him or refer him to a judge for sentencing.

Suppose that, after consulting with counsel, Dan pleads not guilty to all charges. The magistrate will then set a date for a *preliminary hearing* (sometimes called a *preliminary examination*), to be held before the magistrate, unless Dan waives his right to a preliminary hearing. The magistrate will also consider whether Dan should be released on *bail* (or on his "own recognizance"), pending the preliminary hearing.

The preliminary hearing is intended to permit the magistrate to decide whether there is "probable cause" to hold Dan for trial on each count. This is a screening device, meant to save Dan the expense and anxiety of a trial on a weak case, and meant to save the courts the expense of a trial which is unlikely to lead to a conviction. At the preliminary hearing, the prosecutor will put on a somewhat skeletal case, with a minimum of witnesses - enough to show probable cause but not enough to let defense counsel see the whole prosecution case. The defense will seldom put on witnesses of its own, but will cross-examine prosecution witnesses in an effort to undermine probable cause and to try to "discover" as much of the prosecutor's case as possible, in preparation for trial.

The magistrate's decision may take several forms. She may dismiss some or all charges against Dan. She may also reduce some or all charges to "lesser-included" crimes. (For example, she may find probable cause to believe that Dan stole the money, but no probable cause to believe that he used force or threats — so a robbery charge should be reduced to larceny.) If the magistrate finds probable cause as to any charge which is a felony, she will "hold the defendant to answer" the charges at trial, and she will order the defendant "bound over" to the court for trial on these charges. The prosecutor will then file an *information* in the trial court. The information is similar to the complaint, setting out the remaining charges.

In federal court and in a few states, the prosecutor must obtain an *indictment* from a grand jury (unless Dan waives indictment, in which case an information may be filed). The grand jury may indict only if it finds probable cause to believe that Dan committed the crimes, based on evidence presented in secret by the prosecutor to the grand jury. (Defense counsel is not present before the grand jury, and no cross-examination of witnesses occurs.) Usually, if the prosecutor obtains the indictment before the date set for the preliminary hearing, the preliminary hearing will not be held, as the purpose of the preliminary hearing to determine "probable cause" will already have been served.

After the indictment or information is filed, Dan will be arraigned before a trial court judge, and Dan will enter a plea of guilty or not guilty to the remaining charges. If Dan pleads not guilty, the judge will set a date for the trial. The judge may also decide whether Dan should be released on bail pending trial. Before trial, both the prosecutor and defense counsel may be given certain rights to *discover* each other's case - although these rights are much more limited than discovery rights in civil cases.

Before trial, defense counsel may file certain *pretrial motions*, such as motions for discovery and motions to suppress evidence which is the result of an illegal search or interrogation.

At any point in this process, but usually before the trial begins, the parties may engage in *plea bargaining*. Each defendant has a right to a *speedy trial* (*i.e.*, a trial which begins fairly soon after the arrest or indictment), but the prosecutor and the court do not have the resources to give a speedy trial to every defendant. So the prosecutor must induce most defendants to plead guilty. This is done by offering to dismiss or reduce some charges or to recommend certain sentences. Before accepting a guilty plea, the judge will make sure that the defendant knows what he has been promised and not promised, and that he is giving up the right to trial by jury on the charges.

At trial, if both parties agree, the case may be tried by the judge. Usually, however, the defendant demands a jury trial, as it is generally assumed that a group of lay people is less likely to convict than a "case-hardened" judge. In most cases, the jury's verdict must be unanimous, which makes it less likely that the prosecutor will obtain a guilty verdict from a jury.

The case begins with *voir dire*, the questioning of prospective jurors by the two lawyers and/or the judge. If any prospective juror displays improper bias, a lawyer may challenge that person "for cause," and if the judge finds improper bias, that person will be dismissed. Each lawyer also has a limited number of *peremptory* challenges, allowing the dismissal of several prospective jurors for any (almost) or no reason.

After the jury is selected and sworn, each lawyer may make an *opening statement* to the jury, summarizing the evidence to be presented. Then the prosecution puts on its witnesses, who are subject to cross-examination by the defense. When the prosecution rests its case, defense counsel may move for a *directed verdict* of acquittal, on the ground that the prosecution evidence, even if believed by the jury, does not show all of the elements of the crime(s) charged in the information or indictment. If such a motion is denied or not made, the defense then puts on its case, and its witnesses are subject to cross-examination by the prosecutor. The defendant has a constitutional right not to testify, but if he does testify, he too is subject to cross-examination by the prosecutor. When the defense rests, the prosecutor may introduce rebuttal evidence, and sometimes the defense may introduce surrebuttal evidence.

Introduction

After each side rests its case, each attorney submits to the judge proposed *jury instructions*, containing the rules of law which apply to the case. Some of these instructions will be standard instructions taken from appellate court opinions and form books, and others will be devised by the lawyers. After hearing and ruling on any objections to proposed instructions, the judge will inform the lawyers as to which instructions will be given. Each lawyer then delivers a *summation* (sometimes called *closing argument*) to the jury. Because the prosecutor has the burden of proof (beyond a reasonable doubt), she will go first, then the defense lawyer will argue, and then the prosecutor is allowed a final rebuttal. Since each lawyer then knows what instructions the judge will give the jury, the lawyers will usually argue that the law contained in the instructions, when applied to the evidence heard by the jury, dictates a result favorable to that side.

After the summations, the judge reads the jury instructions to the jury. The jury then deliberates and returns with its verdict. If the jury is unable to decide any of the charges by the required majority (usually unanimity), the judge will declare a *mistrial* as to those charges and, if the prosecutor so requests, set the case for re-trial before a new jury. If the jury acquits the defendant, the defendant will be released and case is over - the prosecutor has no right to appeal an acquittal. If the jury convicts the defendant on any charge, the jury is then discharged, in most cases. Usually, the jury plays no role in the next phase, sentencing, unless the jury convicted the defendant of a capital crime and the prosecutor is seeking the death penalty.

Statutes control what the judge may consider in sentencing the defendant. Some statutes set low and high limits on the sentence, but allow the judge wide discretion as to any sentence within these limits (*e.g.*, "2 to 10 years"). Such statutes often allow the judge to consider just about any factor in choosing the sentence. Other statutes confer the authority to select the actual sentence on some other board or agency. Some statutes set the sentence at specific terms of years, depending on certain factors the judge must find (*e.g.*, 2 years for a robber with no criminal record and who injured no one, 6 years for a robber with a record who injured someone, and 4 years for an in-between robber). Before sentencing the defendant, the judge will usually request a *pre-sentence report* from the court's probation department or similar agency. These officials will investigate the defendant's background and recommend a sentence to the judge. At the sentencing hearing, defense counsel may object to all or parts of the presentence report, and may present evidence on the appropriate sentence. The sentence may also include a fine. In some cases, the judge may grant *probation* to the defendant, perhaps on condition that the defendant serve a few months in a local jail.

After selecting the appropriate sentence for the defendant, the judge will enter a *judgment*, which states both the conviction and the sentence. From this judgment, defendant may file a *notice of appeal* to the appellate court which oversees the trial court. Filing this notice does not stay the sentence, and the defendant will have to seek a stay of the sentence and bail on appeal in order to avoid incarceration during the appeal.

A defendant will often obtain a new attorney on appeal, one who specializes in appellate work. The prosecutor often does the same. Copies of the pleadings and other documents are compiled (usually into a volume called the "clerk's transcript"). A court reporter's transcript of all of the oral testimony and argument is also prepared. Using these transcripts and any exhibits submitted as evidence at trial, the defendant's lawyer writes and files an "Appellant's Opening Brief," the prosecutor's attorney writes and files a "Respondent's Brief," and the defendant's lawyer then writes and files an "Appellant's Reply Brief." The appellate court then sets the case for oral argument, the case is argued, and it is submitted for decision. The appellate court then decides the case, usually issuing a written opinion, which may or may not be published in the official reports. The court may affirm the trial court judgment, reverse it (usually for retrial, but sometimes with instructions to dismiss certain charges), or modify it (*e.g.*, by reducing the sentence). If either side is unhappy with the appellate court's ruling, that party may seek review from the next highest court (usually the state supreme court or United States Supreme Court), but that court usually has discretion to grant or deny a hearing in the case.

An appeal must be based on the *record* - the transcripts and exhibits from the trial court - and no other evidence will be considered by the appellate court. If a defendant claims that evidence outside of these transcripts and exhibits warrants relief, he must file a petition for a writ of *habeas corpus*. For example, if Dan claims that one of the jurors who convicted him was threatened during jury deliberations, evidence of this claim is unlikely to appear in the trial transcripts, and Dan must prove it by submitting affidavits attached to his petition for writ of habeas corpus. If Dan claims that a state court denied him his constitutional rights, he may sometimes seek habeas corpus relief in federal court.

If all else fails, Dan must pay his debt to society.

ON PROBLEM ANALYSIS

Each chapter of this book begins with a Problem, which simulates a case a lawyer might be called on to analyze, in order to advise a client or to prepare some litigation document.

Analyzing these Problems is not easy, even if you think you know "the law" in the chapter. Just as cases in real life are seldom simple, one-issue cases, each Problem raises several issues. The key to analyzing these Problems is good organization of the issues. Once you arrange the issues into a proper framework for analysis, the rest is - well, not easy, but manageable.

Organization of the issues is done by preparation of an outline. A typical outline will break down something like this:

    I.

        A.

            1.

            2.

        B.

    II.

        A.

            1.

                a.

                b.

            2.

        B.

What goes into these blank spaces? The following principles usually work pretty well:

- The issues in the "first level" of the outline (*i.e.*, the roman numerals I, II, etc.) come from *the question*; raised by the Problem. You need not know *any* law to write in these issues — just read the Problem, find the question, and read it carefully.[1]

- The issues in the lower levels of the outline (the A's and B's, 1's and 2's, etc.) come from *the rules of law* which appear in the cases in the chapter. To write in these issues properly, you will have to learn the rules of law - in some detail.

Let's apply these principles to a sample Problem.

Problem X

To: My law clerk

From: Dee Fence, Esq.

Re: *State v. Blemish*

A jury just convicted my client, Bill Blemish, of forcible rape.

The key prosecution witness was Gail Wind, an 18-year old woman. Before the trial began, the prosecutor moved for an order excluding from the courtroom the defendant and every spectator except members of Wind's family (four of them), while Wind testified. He presented an affidavit from a doctor who treated Wind, stating that she "could be psychologically damaged" if she ever saw her assailant again, and that "she became very upset when she thought she might have to talk about the rape in front of strangers." I objected, but the court granted the motion.

The judge allowed me to remain while Wind testified, and to cross-examine her. She identified Blemish as the rapist during her direct examination, but in my cross-examination, I got her to admit that she didn't get a very good look at her assailant and couldn't be positive that it was Blemish. So I decided not to put Blemish on the witness stand, and I rested. During closing argument, the prosecutor said to the jury, "I think Wind told the truth when she identified Blemish. Her admitting that she wasn't positive just shows that she is careful and honest. Besides, If Blemish didn't do it, he must have been somewhere else. But where? The defense hasn't told us." I objected and asked the judge to declare a mistrial and start over, but he denied my motion.

Tomorrow, I plan to move for a new trial on the grounds that the judge erred in granting the prosecutor's pretrial motion and in denying my motion for mistrial. Please read the attached authorities and write a memo advising me of what reasonable arguments I can make and how the judge is likely to rule on them.

___

United States Constitution, Fifth Amendment

No person . . . shall be compelled in any criminal case to be a witness against himself. . . .

___

United States Constitution, Sixth Amendment

In all criminal prosecutions, the accused shall have the right to a speedy and public trial . . . [and] to be confronted with the witnesses against him. . . .

___

[1] You might try this out by turning to any Problem in the book — now, before you have even read any of the chapters. Knowing no law, you should nevertheless be able to write out the major issues for an outline of a memo on the Problem — simply by finding the *question* in the Problem.

United States v. Drek

This case holds that, during closing arguments to the jury, a prosecutor may not comment on the defendant's failure to testify, for this would indirectly compel the defendant to testify. The prosecutor may, however, argue that the defendant failed to produce evidence rebutting the prosecution case.]

United States v. Disgusto

[This case holds that the right to public trial is intended to restrain courts from abusing defendants' rights, by exposing their proceedings to review by the public. Therefore, "every court proceeding which might significantly affect a defendant's rights" — including a motion to suppress evidence — must be held in public. However, "the public" does not mean everyone; so long as a reasonable number of spectators is allowed, the trial is considered "public."]

State v. Rifiuti

[This case holds that a prosecutor's closing argument was improper where she said, "In my 20 years as a prosecutor, I've never seen a stronger case for conviction than this one." The court stated that, while an attorney may characterize the evidence, she may not state a personal belief or experience during argument, because an attorney is not a sworn witness subject to cross-examination, and the defendant has a 6th Amendment right to confront all witnesses against him.]

People v. Schmutz

[This case holds that the right to be confronted with witnesses includes the right to cross-examine all prosecution witnesses in court in front of the jury, and that taped police interviews with such witnesses may not be admitted in lieu of live testimony.]

State v. Blech

[This case holds that the right to public trial is not absolute, and must be balanced against other interests, such as the need to protect the privacy of certain witnesses where the need for privacy is high, to ensure the emotional health of the witness and to enable the witness to testify freely. But the judge must consider and adopt reasonable alternatives to excluding the public, and the exclusion must be no broader than necessary. In *Blech*, the court upheld a trial court ruling clearing the courtroom of spectators and reporters while a 5-year old girl testified that she was sexually molested.]

United States v. Merde

[This case holds that the right to confront includes not just the right to cross-examine, but also the right of the defendant to be present and "confront" a witness while she testifies, because an accuser is less likely to lie if the lie must be stated in the presence of the person who will suffer from the lie. The court also created an exception to this rule, in a sex abuse trial, where the judge allowed a child witness to testify by one-way closed circuit television, because the judge found that this child would suffer extreme emotional trauma if faced with the defendant.]

After reading the above material, you have probably spotted some issues which should be discussed in your draft brief. Did the prosecutor's argument infringe on Blemish's right to remain silent? Was he denied his right to a public trial? Was he denied his right to confront a witness against him?

Good issues, but how do you present them? As they occur to you? In the order in which they appear in the testimony? Case by case? Unless you find some coherent way to organize your issues, your presentation will be less effective and persuasive than it should be, and it might even descend into an incoherent mess.

Preparing an outline pursuant to the two principles mentioned above may help you write a good memo. Also, it should help you to find *all* of the relevant issues.

Let's begin our outline. First, specify the major issues — the roman numerals. These come directly from the *question*, which appears somewhere in the problem. In this one, you'll find it in the last paragraph, where lawyer Fence directs you to write a memo advising her of reasonable arguments supporting her motion for a new trial based on two grounds - and your prediction of how the court will rule on these. Our major issues, then, should reflect this direction:

    I. Did the judge err by granting the prosecutor's pretrial motion?

    II. Did the judge err by denying the motion for a mistrial?

Usually, the major issues should appear in the same order that they arose in the facts, chronologically. This will minimize the need for repetition and allow you to refer back (rather than ahead) to facts or issues discussed elsewhere, producing a more readable memo.

Next, fill in the "submajor" issues, where they belong. This requires you to learn, understand, and organize the correct *rules of law*, and then fit these rules into the outline in their proper places. Often, a rule of law consists of several *elements*, each of which must be satisfied, and each of which should be a submajor issue in your outline.

    I. Did judge err by granting prosecutor's pretrial motion?

        A. Denial of right to public trial, under 6th Amendment?

            1. Was Wind's testimony "a proceeding which might significantly affect a defendant's rights?" *See United States v. Disgusto.*

            2. Did allowing Wind's family to stay make the trial sufficiently "public"? *See United States v. Disgusto.*

            3. If trial not "public," was order nevertheless justified by need to protect Wind's privacy?

                a. Was need high enough? *See State v. Blech.*

                b. Did judge consider alternatives or narrower order? *See State v. Blech.*

        B. Denial of right to confront witness, under 6th Amendment?

            1. Generally, is right to have defense attorney cross-examine enough, or

must defendant be present? *See People v. Schmutz* and *United States v. Merde.*

    2. Does exception apply? *Compare United States v. Merde.*

  II. Did judge err by denying motion for mistrial?

    A. Violation of privilege against self-incrimination, under 5th Amendment? *See United States v. Drek*: Was this comment on defendant's failure to testify, or just on his failure to produce evidence?

    B. Improper statement of personal belief, under Sixth Amendment? *See State v. Rifiuti*: Was this a statement of personal belief or just characterization of the evidence?

Now our outline is about as good as we can make it. Our assignment is not done yet — we still have to write the memo. Our memo will carefully apply each of the above issues to the facts. But we have laid the groundwork for a well-organized memo which covers all of the relevant issues.

When you come to each new chapter of this book, try to write an outline for the Problem in that chapter. This might seem difficult at first, but it should become easier as you gain some experience with it. The skills you learn from doing this may prove useful to you when taking exams — and when practicing law.

After writing the outline, you might wish to finish the job and write the memo. In writing the memo, try to follow the following principles: (1) focus on the *question* posed by the Problem; (2) stay organized, following your outline; (3) for each issue, briefly state the correct rule of law[2] and then apply that rule to the *facts*, discussing the facts in some depth; (4) spend more time on issues on which reasonable people might disagree, presenting the best arguments on *both* sides before reaching a conclusion; and (5) end the discussion of each issue with a *conclusion*- a prediction of what the court will rule and why- before moving on to the next issue.

For Problem X, the final memo might look something like this:

  To: Dee Fence, Esq.

From: Your faithful law clerk

  Re: *State v. Blemish*

I. The Judge's Order Granting the Prosecutor's Pretrial Motion.

There are two reasonable arguments we should make in urging that the judge erred in granting that motion:

A. First, we should argue that the order denied Blemish his 6th Amendment right to a public trial.

This right applies to any court proceeding which might significantly affect the defendant's rights. *United States v. Disgusto*. This clearly includes Wind's testimony, as she was the key witness against Blemish.

The trial is considered "public" if a reasonable number of spectators is allowed. *United States v. Disgusto*. Here, only four spectators were allowed, a fairly small number. Also, they were all members of the alleged victim's family, presumably hostile to Blemish, so they were unlikely to fulfill the purpose of the public trial requirement: to restrain courts

---

[2] For some Problems in this book, your explanation of the correct rule of law will have to be more lengthy, because the holdings of some of the cases in these chapters might be a bit murky.

from abusing defendants' rights. *United States v. Disgusto*. So I predict that the court will find that the trial was not "public."

Even if this part of the trial was not "public" the order would be justified if needed to protect Wind's privacy. This exception is satisfied only if (1) the need was high, and (2) the judge considered alternative remedies or a narrower order, but these would not do the job. *State v. Blech*.

Was the need high enough here? On the one hand, Wind's doctor said that she thought she would become upset if she had to talk about the rape in front of strangers, which seems to justify excluding all but family members from the courtroom. On the other hand, the doctor did not give his expert opinion as to whether this was true, or whether this could have any lasting effects on Wind. In addition, note that *Blech* involved a 5-year old girl, who was probably much more vulnerable than 18-year old Wind. This is a very close issue, and it is hard to predict what the court will do. I conclude, however, that the court will probably hold that the need was not high enough, because of the weakness of the doctor's affidavit and Wind's age.

From what you told me, I can't tell whether the judge considered alternatives or a narrower order. If he didn't, then his order was erroneous under *State v. Blech*. If he did, then his order was still erroneous if the possibilities he rejected were reasonable. Here, the judge might have satisfied Wind's need to avoid talking in front of strangers by asking if she knew anyone in the courtroom in addition to her relatives, and allowing only people she knew to stay.

In sum, I think the court will grant your motion on the public trial issue, because Wind's need for privacy was not shown to be high enough to justify excluding the public.

B. Second, we should argue that Blemish was denied his Sixth Amendment right to confront witnesses against him.

The right to confront includes the right to cross-examine (*People v. Schmutz*), which was not denied here. The right also includes the right to have the defendant himself present in front of the witness while she testifies. *United States v. Merde*. But *Merde* also allowed an exception to this rule where a child witness in a sex abuse case was allowed to testify without seeing the defendant. This too is a sex case, and here too we have some evidence that Wind might suffer psychological harm from seeing Blemish. On the other hand, however, *Merde* is probably distinguishable, as Wind was not a child, and her doctor's affidavit did not go so far as to state the doctor's opinion that she would suffer "extreme emotional trauma" if she saw him. The circumstances here are probably not strong enough to outweigh the policy underlying the constitutional right to confront: to ensure that the witness tells the truth. For this reason, I think the judge will buy our argument.

II. The Judge's Denial of Your Motion for Mistrial

There are also two reasonable arguments we should make in urging that the judge erred in denying this motion.

First, we should argue that the prosecutor's closing argument was a comment on Blemish's failure to take the witness stand, which violated his 5th Amendment privilege against self-incrimination. *United States v. Drek*; holds that the prosecutor may comment on the defendant's failure to produce evidence, but not on his failure to testify. The prosecutor's statement that "The defense hasn't told us" where Blemish was at the time of the rape doesn't clearly say whether he means "Blemish hasn't testified" or "Defense attorney hasn't put on any alibi witnesses." The first would be improper, and the second would be OK. We should argue that since the person most likely to know where Blemish was would be Blemish himself, the first meaning is the one probably inferred by the jury. This is a very close issue, however, and it is tough to predict how the court will rule. Because the prosecutor used the word "defense" instead of "Blemish," I think the court will probably rule against us.

Second, we should argue that the prosecutor improperly stated his personal belief when he said, "I think Wind told the truth. . . ." *State v. Rifiuti* holds that while an attorney may characterize the evidence, he may not tell the jury about his own personal belief. This too is a close issue. "I think" literally sounds like a statement of personal belief, but in this context it might instead be construed as "I think you should find that . . . ," which is just argument that her testimony is believable. Since the prosecutor did not mention his experience or elaborate on "I think" — as the prosecutor in *Rifiuti* did — I predict that the court will probably rule against us on this issue.

In sum, I think the judge will probably rule against us on the mistrial issue.

. . . .

In reading over this memo, note that "easy" issues are dealt with only briefly, while "hard" issues take more care. An "easy" issue is one on which reasonable people cannot really disagree — there is only one reasonable answer. A "hard" issue has two reasonable sides. Your job as a law student taking an exam, a law clerk working for a lawyer, or a lawyer working for a client, is pretty much the same: distinguish the easy issues from the hard issues, and construct arguments *on both sides* of the hard issues ("on the other hand, . . .") before coming to a conclusion.

Note also that this memo spends a lot of time *carefully* examining *the facts* of the case, and explains how the rules of law apply to them. This too is one of the main jobs of a good law student taking an exam and of a good lawyer representing a client.

One final suggestion: when you work on these Problems, try not to get emotionally involved with the characters, the events, or the charges. While working on Problem X, for example, if you have strong feelings regarding rape cases or the privilege against self-incrimination, you should look to see if your concerns are reflected in some way in the policies underlying the applicable rules of law (as explained in the cases). If they are, you might mention these concerns as a way of strengthening your legal arguments. But do *not* let your concerns dictate the *result* you want to reach *before* you do your legal analysis. Such "result-oriented prejudging" usually leads to weak analysis and poor representation for your client.

When you begin practicing law, you might decide not to take such cases. Many clients in criminal cases (and some civil cases) have done things which are not very nice. But once you take a case, you have an ethical duty to do your best for your client- no matter how you feel about him or her.

While you are doing these Problems, pretend that you have taken the case, and then do your best for the client. This will help you to develop the skills you will need to help the clients you *want* to represent. (It might help to remind yourself that none of these characters, events, or ridiculous names is real. They are all figments of the author's rather bizarre imagination.)

THE BILL OF RIGHTS

THE FIRST TEN AMENDMENTS TO THE UNITED STATES CONSTITUTION

FIRST AMENDMENT

Congress shall make no law respecting an establishment of religion, or prohibiting the free exercise thereof; or of the press; or the right of the people peaceably to assemble, and to petition the Government for a redress of grievances.

SECOND AMENDMENT

A well regulated Militia, being necessary to the security of a free State, the right of the people to keep and bear Arms, shall not be infringed.

THIRD AMENDMENT

No soldier shall, in time of peace be quartered in any house, without the consent of the Owner, nor in time of war, but in the manner to be prescribed by law.

FOURTH AMENDMENT

The right of the people to be secure in their persons, houses, papers, and effects, against unreasonable searches and seizures, shall not be violated, and no Warrants shall issue, but upon probable cause, supported by Oath or affirmation, and particularly describing the place to be searched, and the persons or things to be seized.

FIFTH AMENDMENT

No person shall be held to answer for a capital, or otherwise infamous crime, unless on a presentment or indictment of a Grand Jury, except in cases arising in the land or naval forces, or in the Militia, when in actual service in time of War or public danger; nor shall any person be subject for the same offense to be twice put in jeopardy of life or limb; nor shall be compelled in any criminal case to be a witness against himself, nor be deprived of life, liberty, or property, without due process of law; nor shall private property be taken for public use, without just compensation.

SIXTH AMENDMENT

In all criminal prosecutions, the accused shall enjoy the right to a speedy and public trial, by an impartial jury of the State and district wherein the crime shall have been committed, which district shall have been previously ascertained by law, and to be informed of the nature and cause of the accusation; to be confronted with the witnesses against him; to have compulsory process for obtaining witnesses in his favor, and to have the assistance of Counsel for his defence.

SEVENTH AMENDMENT

In Suits at common law, where the value in controversy shall exceed twenty dollars, the right of trial by jury shall be preserved, and no fact tried by a jury shall be otherwise re-examined in any Court of the United States, than according to the rules of the common law.

EIGHT AMENDMENT

Excessive bail shall not be required, nor excessive fines imposed, nor cruel and unusual punishments inflicted.

NINTH AMENDMENT

The enumeration in the Constitution, of certain rights, shall not be construed to deny or disparage others retained by the people.

TENTH AMENDMENT

The powers not delegated to the United States by the Constitution, nor prohibited by it to the States, are reserved to the States respectively, or to the people.

Summary Table of Contents

Preface iii
Preface to the Fifth Edition v
Introduction vii

Chapter 1:   The Decision to Prosecute 1
Chapter 2:   Pretrial Release 53
Chapter 3:   Discovery 101
Chapter 4:   The Preliminary Hearing 173
Chapter 5:   The Grand Jury 217
Chapter 6:   The Right To Speedy Trial 285
Chapter 7:   Plea Bargaining 343
Chapter 8:   The Jury Venire 407
Chapter 9:   The Jury Panel 467
Chapter 10:   Joinder & Severance 577
Chapter 11:   Double Jeopardy 631
Chapter 12:   Sentencing 677
Chapter 13:   Appeals 783
Chapter 14:   The Right To Effective Assistance Of Counsel 833
Chapter 15:   Ethical Obligations Of Criminal Defense Lawyers 901
Chapter 16:   Habeas Corpus 969
Chapter 17:   A Comparative Perspective 1025

Table of Contents

Preface iii
Preface to the Fifth Edition v
Introduction vii
    I.   *An Overview of the Criminal Courtroom Process* vii
    II.   *On Problem Analysis* x
    III.   *Bill of Rights* xvii

Chapter 1   **THE DECISION TO PROSECUTE** **1**

    The Role of The Prosecutor 1
    Problem 1A 3
    American Bar Association Standards For Criminal Justice 3-1.2, 3-3.1, 3-3.8
    and 3-3.9 4
    Problem 1B 10
        Oyler v. Boles 11
        United States v. Steele 14
        People v. Superior Court [and Cynthia Hartway] 17
        United States v. Goodwin 24
        People v. Kail 32
        United States v. Armstrong 36
        United States v. Bass 51

Chapter 2   **PRETRIAL RELEASE** **53**

    The Importance Of Pretrial Release 53
    Some Background 54
    Problem 2 55
    The Bail Reform Act of 1984 56
        Stack v. Boyle 62
        United States v. Botero 66
        United States v. Motamedi 71
        United States v. Tortora 75
        United States v. Patriarca 86

Chapter 3   **DISCOVERY** **101**

    Civil vs. Criminal Discovery 101
    Problem 3A 102
    Problem 3B 103
    Problem 3C 104
    Federal Rules of Criminal Procedure Rules 12.1, 15, 16, 26.2 105
    18 U.S. Code § 3500 ("The Jencks Act") 111
        Brady v. Maryland 112
        United States v. Nobles 123

Table of Contents

United States v. Agurs 131

United States v. Brinkman 138

United States v. Feola 143

Arizona v. Youngblood 155

United States v. McDade 168

Chapter 4   **THE PRELIMINARY HEARING** **173**

The Purpose(s) of the Preliminary Hearing 173

Problem 4 175

Federal Rules of Criminal Procedure, Rules 5 and 5.1 176

Coleman v. Burnett 178

Hunter v. District Court 193

Whitman v. Superior Court 199

People v. Wimberly 209

Chapter 5   **THE GRAND JURY** **217**

Some Background 217

Problem 5 220

Federal Rules of Criminal Procedure, Rule 6 222

Costello v. United States 228

United States v. Estepa 242

United States v. Basurto 247

United States v. Udziela 252

United States v. Mandujano 259

United States v. Williams 273

Chapter 6   **THE RIGHT TO SPEEDY TRIAL** **285**

Problem 6 285

The Speedy Trial Act 287

Federal Rules of Criminal Procedure, Rule 48 292

Barker v. Wingo 293

Strunk v. United States 302

Moore v. Arizona 304

United States v. Lovasco 305

United States v. Loud Hawk 314

Doggett v. United States 325

Vermont v. Brillon 337

Chapter 7   **PLEA BARGAINING** **343**

Some Background 343

Problem 7A 346

Table of Contents

American Bar Association Standards for Criminal Justice 3-4.1, 4-6.1 and
14-3.2 347

Problem 7B 347

Federal Rules of Criminal Procedure, Rule 11 349

    Boykin v. Alabama 355

    Brady v. United States 359

    Santobello v. New York 368

    Blackledge v. Allison 375

    State v. Solano 381

    United States v. Melancon 391

    Barnes v. State 401

Chapter 8   THE JURY VENIRE 407

Some Background 407

Problem 8 410

United States Code, Title 28 (28 U.S.C. §§ 1861—1867) 411

1.   Exclusions From the Venire 418

    Taylor v. Louisiana 418

    Barber v. Ponte 426

    Walker v. Goldsmith 435

2.   Pretrial Publicity 437

    Murphy v. Florida 437

    Powell v. Superior Court 444

Chapter 9   THE JURY PANEL 467

Problem 9 467

1.   The Challenge For Cause 469

    United States v. Salamone 469

    State v. Logan 483

2.   The Peremptory Challenge 492

   a.   The Function of the Peremptory Challenge (as seen by the Courts) . . 492

   b.   The Function of the Peremptory Challenge
(as seen by *trial attorneys*) 494

   c.   *Batson* 500

    Batson v. Kentucky 500

   d.   What Is a "Cognizable Group"? 512

    J.E.B. v. Alabama 519

    United States v. Santiago-Martinez 542

   e.   Proving that a Challenge was Improper 543

    Purkett v. Elem 551

    Snyder v. Louisiana 558

   f.   Remedies 569

Table of Contents

    g.   Reconsidering the Peremptory Challenge 573

    3.   Reconsidering the Jury 574

Chapter 10   **JOINDER & SEVERANCE** **577**

    Problem 10 577

    Federal Rules of Criminal Procedure, Rules 8, 13 and 14 579

        Bruton v. United States 579

        Richardson v. Marsh 587

        Zafiro v. United States 598

        Unites States v. Andrews, et. al. 605

        Gray v. Maryland 619

Chapter 11   **DOUBLE JEOPARDY** **631**

    Problem 11 632

        Ashe v. Swenson 633

        Stephens v. Attorney General of California 646

        Brown v. Ohio 647

        Commonwealth v. Balog 666

Chapter 12   **SENTENCING** **677**

    The Judge's Role in Sentencing 677

    "Determinate" And "Indeterminate" Sentencing Systems 678

    The Federal Sentencing Guidelines 679

        United States v. Patillo 681

    Sentencing in California 690

    The Lawyer's Role in Sentencing 691

    ABA Standards for Criminal Justice 18-6.3 691

    Problem 12 693

    California Penal Code Sections re Sentencing 694

    California Rules of Court Rules re Sentencing 703

        United States v. Grayson 712

        People v. Smith 720

        People v. Takencareof 721

        People v. Bennett 731

        People v. McNally 734

        People v. Reyes 742

        Apprendi v. New Jersey 746

        Cunningham v. California 768

Table of Contents

Chapter 13   APPEALS **783**

    Problem 13 784
    Federal Rules of Criminal Procedure, Rule 52 786
        Chapman v. California 786
        Anders v. California 791
        Harrington v. California 800
        Arizona v. Fulminante 804
        Smith v. Robbins 819

Chapter 14   THE RIGHT TO EFFECTIVE ASSISTANCE OF
              COUNSEL **833**

    Problem 14 834
        Holloway v. Arkansas 836
        Strickland v. Washington 855
    American Bar Association Standards For Criminal Justice 4-4.1, 4-4.2 and
    4-8.6 873
        People v. Pozo 874
        Johnson v. State 882
        Government of the Virgin Islands v. Weatherwax 883

Chapter 15   ETHICAL OBLIGATIONS OF CRIMINAL DEFENSE
              LAWYERS **901**

    Problem 15A 901
    Problem 15B 903
    American Bar Association Model Code of Professional Responsibility . . 904
    American Bar Association, Standards For Criminal Justice 4-3.1, 4-3.2, 4-3.7,
    4-3.9, 4-4.3, 4-5.1, 11-4.1 908
        Nix v. Whiteside 913
        Matter of Nackson 934
        United States v. Locascio 942
        People v. Simac 948
    "How Can You Represent Criminals?" — New Answers to Old
    Questions 964

Chapter 16   HABEAS CORPUS **969**

    Problem 16A 970
    Problem 16B 971
    United States Code, Title 28 (28 U.S.C. §§ 2254—2255) 971
        Stone v. Powell 973
        Wainwright v. Sykes 985
        McCleskey v. Zant 995

Table of Contents

Withrow v. Williams 1009

Chapter 17   **A COMPARATIVE PERSPECTIVE** **1025**

The O.J. Inquisition: A United States Encounter With Continental Criminal
Justice 1025

CUMULATIVE PROBLEMS **1075**

Problem A 1075
Problem B 1076
Outline of Issues in Problem A 1078
Outline of Issues on Problem B 1079
Table of Cases TC-1
Index I-1

Chapter 1

THE DECISION TO PROSECUTE

THE ROLE OF THE PROSECUTOR

"In our criminal justice system, the Government retains broad discretion as to whom to prosecute. So long as the prosecutor has probable cause to believe that the accused committed an offense defined by statute, the decision whether or not to prosecute, and what charge to file or bring before a grand jury, generally rests entirely in his discretion."

Wayte v. U.S., 470 U.S. 598 (1985).

"You will wield an amount of power over people's lives entirely disproportionate to your age and experience. Don't let it go to your heads."

An experienced prosecutor's advice to new assistant district attorneys in New York City.[1]

This extraordinary power of the prosecutor stems, in part, from his or her very peculiar role as a lawyer. Like any lawyer, the prosecutor has the power to initiate lawsuits (in criminal cases) and to ask the court to exercise its powers over the other party. But while other lawyers may speak and act only for their clients, the prosecutor has no client. Or, perhaps more accurately, he *does* have a client — the most important client in society: society itself. Because this client is so amorphous, however, the prosecutor cannot consult with his client as other lawyers do. In a general way, he consults with his client on policy matters at election time. But he cannot readily consult with his client on specific decisions regarding specific cases.

Therefore — for all practical purposes — the prosecutor is both lawyer and client. He makes not only the tactical decisions a lawyer would make, but also the policy decisions a client would make. He has had 3 years of concentrated study to become a lawyer, but what training has he had to become the client? Does he know

---

[1] Described in Heilbroner, *Rough Justice*, p. 23 (Dell, 1990.) Heilbroner's book gives a "real world" perspective on many of the topics you will learn about in this book (including plea bargaining, grand juries, the right to speedy trial, and selecting a trial jury), from the point of view of a young prosecutor.

See also Steven Phillips, *No Heroes No Villains: The Story of a Murder Trial* (Random House, 1997). At p. 242, the author explains his decision to stop being a prosecutor:

> No one should be permitted to make a lifetime career out of prosecuting his fellow man. Over the years the investigations and trials cannot help but create a warped, pessimistic and self-righteous attitude toward humanity. Just as a woman who teaches kindergarten may in time unconsciously treat all the people she meets as if they were children, so do most veteran prosecutors, after years of viewing the world through a sewer of violence and depravity, unconsciously come to divide humanity into helpless victims and vicious perpetrators. It is an ugly and unfair view. Worse still is the arrogance that comes from wielding power too long. Good prosecution requires self-confidence and the ability to make painful and difficult decisions, but in the long run the decisions stop being difficult, and the self-confidence becomes arrogance and self-righteousness.

any more about why people commit crimes or how prosecution and punishment might stop crime than the average barber or ballplayer?

As the client, he should make not only intelligent decisions, but good faith decisions. In most jurisdictions, he does not have the resources to prosecute all cases to the fullest extent — there are just not enough deputy prosecutors and courtrooms to take all cases to trial on all possible charges. Nor does he *want* to prosecute all cases to the fullest extent — why turn a minor first offender into a career criminal by putting him into a prison full of hardcore crooks? So the prosecutor *must have discretion.* But this discretion could also give him the raw power to prosecute his personal enemies, his political opponents, and people he just doesn't like — and to look the other way when his friends and allies misbehave.

Federal judge Irving Younger described an incident that occurred when he was a young Assistant U.S. Attorney in Manhattan, in 1961. One morning, he was called in to meet with his bosses, Attorney General Robert Kennedy and U.S. Attorney Robert Morgenthau, to discuss a noted criminal defense lawyer — Roy Cohn. Morganthau said to Younger:

> The Department has a special interest in Roy Cohn. The Department thinks it would be a good idea to consolidate all of our Cohn activities in one assistant. I'm designating you. Review the files. Follow up. Go wherever you have to. Your job is to find out whether Cohn is guilty of something. The Department wants Cohn.

Younger replied, "I'll get him."

But he didn't get him. Younger reviewed the files, flew to Switzerland (at taxpayer expense) to interview witnesses, made deals with witnesses to testify against Cohn, and obtained 3 separate indictments against Cohn — for perjury, fraud, and bribery. Each indictment went to trial, and each time the jury acquitted Cohn.

Younger reflected on why he was ordered to investigate

Cohn:

> Immediately after his first indictment, Roy Cohn called a press confer-ence to denounce Morgenthau. "Ever since Morgenthau took office," he said, "there isn't a defendant or a criminal around who hasn't been offered a proposition to get something on me." Cohn thought that Morgenthau wanted to imprison him in retaliation for Cohn's investigation, under [Senator Joe] McCarthy, of Communist infiltration into the Treasury Department when Henry Morgenthau, Robert's father, was Secretary. I do not know whether there is any truth to this, nor do I know whether it is true, as I heard said in the U.S. Attorney's office, that Robert Kennedy hated Cohn since the day when, both of them working for McCarthy, they had quarreled and come to blows. I do know that Cohn's complaint of vendetta deserves attention. In 1961, the Department decided to "get" Cohn — I know because I was there — and 3 times over the next several years brought him to trial. It is one of the remarkable things in modern legal history that Cohn was never found guilty, for a maxim among prosecutors is that if you indict enough you will ultimately convict.

But Cohn's escape is beside the point. The point is the peril. A prosecutor's power to damage or destroy anyone he chooses to indict is virtually limitless. Grand juries almost always do the prosecutor's bidding. If the procedural niceties have been complied with, a judge can only order the case to trial. And then it will be up to the jury. Someone else, submitting himself 3 times to 12 citizens selected at random, might not have been so lucky or so able to bear the cost as Cohn. Someone else, the next person a prosecutor decides to "get", may be convicted or ruined in the process.

I can think of no institutional safeguard against such a possibility. Everything rests on the honor, temperament, and professionalism of the prosecutor. Given the right man or woman in the job, only those who have something to fear need be afraid. Put the wrong person in charge and we are all in danger.

Looking back, Younger concluded that he was "not proud" of what he had done. "It was the power of power. If I possibly could, I was going to be the one to do the job the Department wanted done. Not once did I stop to think what it was a Department of." Younger, "Memoir of a Prosecutor", *Commentary*, Oct. 1976, pp. 66–70.

Problem 1A

To: My law clerk

From: Nellie Novice, Deputy District Attorney

The police department just sent over a police report, and my boss — District Attorney Dewey — gave it to me and told me to draw up the charges. Here is the report.

This evening at 9 p.m., I received a call from the neighbors of Phil and Polly Anders, reporting that they were fighting loudly in their home at 123 4th St. I went to that residence. Both Polly and Phil smelled of liquor. Polly had a bruise on her cheek, which she said was inflicted by Phil hitting her. Phil said that Polly was his wife and that he hit her because she had admitted having sex with Juan Casanova, who lived in their basement. Polly then said that Casanova had raped her, and she insisted that I arrest Casanova.

I arrested Casanova, brought him upstairs, and confronted him with Polly's accusation. He was pretty upset. He denied raping her, and said that they had had consensual intercourse. I then searched him, and found two rocks of crack cocaine in his jacket pocket. He said Polly sold them to him for $40. I also arrested Phil for disturbing the peace and assault and battery, and I arrested Polly for disturbing the peace. After I took them to the station, they were all released on bail. The next day, Polly came back to see me. She said that Juan had not raped her, and she lied because she was afraid of Phil — and she still loved Phil. She asked me not to prosecute either of them. I told her that I would have to tell the D.A. about her lying about the rape, because it is a misdemeanor to file a false report about a crime.

This is the second time that the Anders' neighbors have called the police about their fighting. The first time we told them to stop and they did. Phil has a prior drunk driving conviction. Polly and Casanova have no priors.

Sergeant Connie Copp

All of the crimes Copp booked the Anders for are misdemeanors, giving the judge the discretion to impose a sentence of up to a year in county jail and/or a fine of up to $1,000. Possession of cocaine is a felony, carrying a mandatory 5-year term in state prison.

Mr. Dewey told me that the police chief said he wants us to come down hard on false crime reports, as they give his department a bad name when they arrest people on bum raps, and they take a lot of time. My boss also said that local feminist groups have been pushing his office to treat battered women more sympathetically and go after the batterers. And he said that the newspapers have accused him of going soft on drug dealers, and they might endorse his opponent in the election for D.A. next month.

After telling me all this, he said, "But it's your call"!

I just started this job last week, and I'm a little embarrassed to display my ignorance to my superiors. So I'm asking you: what should I charge these people with? Are the following ABA Standards helpful?

AMERICAN BAR ASSOCIATION STANDARDS FOR CRIMINAL JUSTICE (1992)

STANDARD 3-1.2: THE FUNCTION OF THE PROSECUTOR

* * * *

(c) The duty of the prosecutor is to seek justice, not merely to convict.

(d) It is an important function of the prosecutor to seek to reform and improve the administration of criminal justice. When inadequacies or injustices in the substantive or procedural law come to the prosecutor's attention, he or she should stimulate efforts for remedial action. * * * *

STANDARD 3-3.1: INVESTIGATIVE FUNCTION OF PROSECUTOR

(a) A prosecutor ordinarily relies on police and other investigative agencies for investigation of alleged criminal acts, but the prosecutor has an affirmative responsibility to investigate suspected illegal activity when it is not adequately dealt with by other agencies.

(b) A prosecutor should not invidiously discriminate against or in favor of any person on the basis of race, religion, sex, sexual preference, or ethnicity in exercising discretion to investigate or to prosecute. A prosecutor should not use other improper considerations in exercising such discretion.

(c) A prosecutor should not knowingly use illegal means to obtain evidence or to employ or instruct or encourage others to use such means.

(d) A prosecutor should not discourage or obstruct communication between prospective witnesses and defense counsel. A prosecutor should not advise any person or cause any person to be advised to decline to give to the defense information which such person has the right to give. * * * *

Commentary

The bulk of a prosecutor's work consists of cases in which a complaint has been made by a citizen or by a public agency or cases that develop subsequent to an arrest made by the police. But there are instances in which a citizen is reluctant to prosecute, from ignorance, fear, inertia, or other motive, or in which the police have not taken the initiative. This may be because the area of illegal activity in question is not one that attracts law enforcement interest, as in the case of certain commercial frauds, or where law enforcement officials are themselves involved.

It is important, therefore, that in some circumstances the prosecutor take the initiative to investigate suspected criminal acts independent of citizen complaints or police activity. As one court has stated: "With the vast extension of the field of criminal law made necessary by complex social and economic conditions, it is not only the right but the duty of the prosecutor in such cases to himself take the initiative."] Most prosecutors are no doubt willing to accept this responsibility, provided, of course, that they have adequate investigative resources to undertake this task. The implementation of this Standard, therefore, is directly related to fulfillment of Standard 3-2.4(b), providing that adequate professional investigative personnel be made available to the prosecutor.

STANDARD 3-3.8: DISCRETION AS TO NONCRIMINAL DISPOSITION

(a) The prosecutor should consider in appropriate cases the availability of noncriminal disposition, formal or informal, in deciding whether to press criminal charges which would otherwise be supported by probable cause; especially in the case of a first offender, the nature of the offense may warrant noncriminal disposition.

(b) Prosecutors should be familiar with the resources of social agencies which can assist in the evaluation of cases for diversion from the criminal process.

STANDARD 3-3.9: DISCRETION IN THE CHARGING DECISION

(a) A prosecutor should not institute, or cause to be instituted, or permit the continued pendency of criminal charges when the prosecutor knows that the charges are not supported by probable cause. A prosecutor should not institute, cause to be instituted, or permit the continued pendency of criminal charges in the absence of sufficient admissible evidence to support a conviction.

(b) The prosecutor is not obliged to present all charges which the evidence might support. The prosecutor may in some circumstances and for good cause consistent with the public interest decline to prosecute, notwithstanding that sufficient evidence may exist which would support a conviction. Illustrative of the factors which the prosecutor may properly consider in exercising his or her discretion are:

(i) the prosecutor's reasonable doubt that the accused is in fact guilty;

(ii) the extent of the harm caused by the offense;

(iii) the disproportion of the authorized punishment in relation to the particular offense or the offender;

(iv) possible improper motives of a complainant;

(v) reluctance of the victim to testify;

(vi) cooperation of the accused in the apprehension or conviction of others; and

(vii) availability and likelihood of prosecution by another jurisdiction.

(c) A prosecutor should not be compelled by his or her supervisor to prosecute a case in which he or she has a reasonable doubt about the guilt of the accused.

(d) In making the decision to prosecute, the prosecutor should give no weight to the personal or political advantages or disadvantages which might be involved or to a desire to enhance his or her record of convictions.

(e) In cases which involve a serious threat to the community, the prosecutor should not be deterred from prosecution by the fact that in the jurisdiction juries have tended to acquit persons accused of the particular kind of criminal act in question.

(f) The prosecutor should not bring or seek charges greater in number or degree than can reasonably be supported with evidence at trial or than are necessary to fairly reflect the gravity of the offense.

(g) The prosecutor should not condition a dismissal of charges, nolle prosequi, or similar action on the accused's relinquishment of the right to seek civil redress unless the accused has agreed to the action knowingly and intelligently, freely and voluntarily, and where such waiver is approved by the court.

Commentary

Necessity for Probable Cause

The charging decision is the heart of the prosecution function. The broad discretion given to a prosecutor in deciding whether to bring charges and in choosing the particular charges to be brought requires that the greatest effort be made to see that this power is used fairly and uniformly. By its very nature, however, the exercise of discretion cannot be reduced to a formula. Nevertheless, guidelines for the exercise of discretion should be established. This Standard is not intended to be a substitute for developing appropriate prosecution policies on a local level. At most, it illustrates basic factors that should be included or excluded in the exercise of discretion.

A prosecutor ordinarily should prosecute if, after full investigation, he or she finds that a crime has been committed, the perpetrator can be identified, and there is sufficient admissible evidence available to support a verdict of guilty. Consistent with ABA model ethical codes, this Standard suggests that it is unethical for a prosecutor to institute criminal proceedings where he or she knows probable cause is lacking. A probable cause standard, which is substantially less than sufficient admissible evidence to sustain a conviction, is sufficiently minimal that a prosecutor should not err in deciding whether the quantum of evidence is adequate to institute criminal proceedings. Section (a) also provides that "a prosecutor should not institute, cause to be instituted, or permit the continued pendency of criminal charges in the absence of sufficient admissible evidence to support a conviction."

There is continuing disagreement among prosecutors about the related question of whether it is proper for a prosecutor to accede to a guilty plea when he or she knows that conviction is no longer possible, e.g., a witness whose testimony was necessary to establish probable cause has died or is otherwise no longer available to testify at trial. This Standard takes no position on this question.

Factors That May Properly Be Considered

The breadth of criminal legislation necessarily means that much conduct that falls within its literal terms should not always lead to criminal prosecution. It is axiomatic that all crimes cannot be prosecuted even if this were desirable. Realistically, there are not enough enforcement agencies to investigate and prosecute every criminal act that occurs. Moreover, some violations occur in circumstances in which there is no significant impact on the community or on any of its members. A prosecutor should adopt a "first things first" policy, giving greatest attention to those areas of criminal activity that pose the most serious threat to the security and order of the community.

Nor is it desirable that the prosecutor prosecute all crimes at the highest degree available. Crimes are necessarily defined in broad terms that encompass situations of greatly differing gravity. Differences in the circumstances under which a crime took place, the motives behind or pressures upon the defendant, mitigating factors in the situation, the defendant's age, prior record, general background, and role in the offense, and a host of other particular factors require that the prosecutor view the whole range of possible charges as a set of tools from which to carefully select the proper instrument to bring the charges warranted by the evidence.

In exercising discretion in this way, the prosecutor is not neglecting his or her public duty or discriminating among offenders. The public interest is best served and evenhanded justice best dispensed, not by the unseeing or mechanical application of the "letter of the law," but by a flexible and individualized application of its norms through the exercise of a prosecutor's thoughtful discretion.

Subsections (b)(i)-(vii) provide a series of guidelines for the exercise of the prosecutor's discretion. In addition to the obvious reasonable doubt test, the extent of the harm caused by the offense is an important factor to be considered in deciding whether to charge and what charges to bring. If prosecution is sought by a private party out of malice or to exert coercion on the defendant, as is sometimes the case in matters involving debt collection, for example, the prosecutor may properly decline to prosecute.

Another relevant consideration is the refusal of the victim to testify. A prosecutor may have difficulty establishing a case if an indispensable witness declines to testify. This sometimes occurs when the case involves evidence that, if made public, will cause great pain or harm to the victim. In serious cases, however, the interests of the community may require that the prosecutor try to obtain the victim's cooperation and, in some instances, it may be the prosecutor's duty to use the subpoena power to compel attendance of the witness. In contrast, the prosecutor may justifiably decline to prosecute less serious offenses because of lack of witness cooperation. This discretion is commonly exercised in family conflicts where minor violence has occurred. Often the injured party who calls the police is later reluctant about prosecution, either because the dispute has been resolved or because of the harmful consequences of prosecution to the family. The prosecutor should, however, assure himself or herself that the reason a witness has become uncooperative is not because he or she is being intimidated to act in this way.

Prosecutors frequently and properly choose to pursue a lenient course with one participant in a criminal activity in order to bring other, more serious, offenders to justice. The underlying rationale is expressed in statutes, found in many jurisdictions, that permit the grant of immunity from prosecution in exchange for testimony. Consistent with subsection (b)(vi), the Pleas of Guilty chapter of these Standards suggests that charge and sentence concessions are appropriate for a defendant whose "cooperation has resulted or may result in the successful prosecution of other offenders engaged in equally serious or more serious conduct."

The broad span of federal criminal statutes presents many cases of overlapping federal and state jurisdiction. Particularly where federal laws are largely auxiliary to state laws, the federal prosecutor is faced with the problem that his or her power to prosecute may result in a defendant's being punished in two tribunals for the same conduct. Where overlapping federal and state jurisdiction is present, federal action is justified in the presence of one or more of the following circumstances: (1) when the states are unable or unwilling to act; (2) when the jurisdictional feature — for example, use of the mails — is not merely incidental or accidental to the offense but an important ingredient of its success; (3) when, although the particular jurisdictional feature is incidental, another substantial federal interest is protected by the assertion of federal power; (4) when the criminal operation extends into a number of states, transcending the local interests of any one; (5) when it would be inefficient administration to refer to state authorities a complicated case investigated and developed on the theory of federal prosecution.

When the possibility of double prosecution arises because the crime is punishable in more than one state, similar considerations should be taken into account in deciding whether to defer to the other jurisdiction's right to prosecute. Where the issues already have been tried in another state, in the interests of fairness the prosecutor should ordinarily not seek to relitigate the case by bringing a new prosecution.

Compelled Prosecution by a Supervisor

Subsection (b)(i) provides that a prosecutor exercising his or her professional discretion may properly choose not to prosecute when he or she has a reasonable doubt about the guilt of the accused, despite the fact that probable cause may otherwise appear to exist. Implicit in this consideration — and explicit in section (c) — is the concomitant rule that a prosecutor should not be compelled by his or her supervisor to prosecute such a case. Supervising prosecutors should create an atmosphere in the prosecution office where subordinate prosecutors feel free to disclose and discuss such doubts about the guilt of an accused; in order to create such an atmosphere, supervising prosecutors should respect the views of their subordinates even if they do not share them. Nonetheless, a case that a prosecutor seeks not to prosecute because of doubts about guilt may properly be reassigned for prosecution to another prosecutor in the prosecution office who does not share the first prosecutor's doubts about the guilt of the accused.

Personal Advantage Not to Be Considered

A prosecutor should avoid measuring his or her record by the "conviction rate" of the office. Accordingly, a prosecutor should never allow the decision to proceed in a particular case to be influenced by a desire to inflate the success record of the office in obtaining convictions. Nor should the prosecutor hesitate to reduce a charge or decline presentation of a case because of such consideration.

Community Indifference to Serious Crime

There are cases in which even if convictions seem quite unlikely, perhaps because of hostile community attitudes toward the victims, a prosecutor should nonetheless proceed in the interests of justice if satisfied that a serious crime has been committed, the offender can be identified, and the necessary evidence is available. Another instance in which conviction would be difficult is where there has been widespread corruption in government. A prosecutor may have the duty in such a situation to take the case to a grand jury, where available, and, if successful in obtaining an indictment, to proceed with trial even though conviction would be exceedingly difficult to obtain. These actions represent more than gestures on the part of the prosecutor, for such tactics can successfully alert the community to wrongdoing and create a community commitment to rectify the offending conditions.

Discretion in Selecting the Number and Degree of Charges

The structure of the substantive law of crimes is such that a single criminal event will often give rise to potential criminal liability for a number of different crimes. Defense counsel often complain that prosecutors charge a number of different crimes, that is, "overcharge," in order to obtain leverage for plea negotiations. Although there are many different conceptions of what "overcharging" actually is, the heart of the criticism is the belief that prosecutors have brought charges, not in the good faith belief that they fairly reflect the gravity of the offense, but rather as a harassing and coercive device in the expectation that they will induce the defendant to plead guilty.

From the prosecutor's point of view, the charging decision is one that must be made at a stage when all the evidence is not necessarily in the form it will take at trial. The prosecutor must make a preliminary evaluation in order to proceed, knowing that at later stages dismissal of charges or an election among charges may be necessary. If the facts fairly warrant multiple charges growing out of a single episode, the prosecutor is, of course, entitled to charge broadly. A defendant accused of breaking and entering, robbery, rape, and murder committed in a single course of conduct involving one victim can hardly complain of "overcharging" if there is evidence of conduct supporting each charge. At some stage, of course, a voluntary dismissal of one or more of the lesser charges may very well be necessary, but a prosecutor cannot fairly be criticized for charging on all tenable counts initially.

The line separating overcharging from the sound exercise of prosecutorial discretion is necessarily a subjective one, but the key consideration is the prosecutor's commitment to the interests of justice, fairly bringing those charges he or she believes are supported by the facts without "piling on" charges in order to unduly leverage an accused to forgo his or her right to trial.

Note from Nellie:

State law normally provides that District Attorneys are elected by the people of a *county*, but they file criminal cases on behalf of the people of the *state*. What should the DA do if the people of the state want certain cases pursued, but the people of the county don't?

The New York State Legislature enacted a statute permitting a jury to impose the death penalty in certain murder cases. But the DA of Bronx County, New York, ran for office promising to adopt a "blanket policy" *refusing* to seek the death penalty in all such cases. He was elected, and he carried out his promise. May the state's Governor *replace* him in such cases? Yes, held New York's highest court, in *Johnson v. Pataki*, 91 N.Y.2d 214 (1997):

> Whether or not District Attorneys must exercise their death penalty discretion on a case-by-case basis, clearly the Legislature did not allow one or all 62 District Attorneys to functionally veto the statute by adopting a "blanket policy," thereby in effect refusing to exercise discretion.

Justice Titone dissented:

> It is clear beyond question that the *only* reason for the Governor's superseder decision in this case was his desire to substitute his own policy choices for those of the Bronx County District Attorney. In my view, however, this motive flies in the face of the evident legislative intent that the fundamental policy choice as to whether or not to seek the death penalty be made solely by the locally elected District Attorney.

As you have seen in examining Problem 1A, there may be some political and ethical constraints on the prosecutor's exercise of discretion. Are there also *legal* constraints? Problem 1B will explore this question.

Problem 1B

To: My law clerk

From: District Attorney Izzy Gilty

I just met with a group of homeowners and merchants from the Westside neighborhood, who call themselves "Save Our Community" (or "SOC"). These people are all black, and Westside is a predominantly-black neighborhood. They are very concerned about a group of young black males who belong to a gang called "The Bad Boys." These guys hang around a liquor store at 4th and Vine Streets and sell drugs to people driving by — mainly "white boys" driving in from the suburbs. The SOC contingent claims that The Bad Boys are armed and occasionally violent, endanger the safety of the neighborhood, and drive away customers of their businesses. They are corrupting the local young people, ruining property values, and destroying any hope of revitalizing their community

SOC wants me to drive these guys out, and they don't care how. Conventional police surveillance and undercover operations result in occasional arrests and convictions, but it hasn't stopped them. They are smart, and they know when and how the police operate.

Here are some possibilities:

1. Pull all the narcotics cops away from other parts of the city and pour them into Westside. I talked to the police chief, and he is willing to do this for a limited period of time (two weeks or so). This would mean that drug sales in other parts of town, populated mainly by whites, Hispanics, and Asians, would go unpunished for that period.

2. Pull a bunch of regular cops from other parts of town and put them into Westside. This would be cheaper, because we have more regular cops than narcotics specialists. The regular cops could just hang around and hassle the Bad Boys. Since the Bad Boys usually cross the middle of the street when they make a sale, we could cite them for jaywalking a lot. We might also get them for littering and other minor crimes and infractions.

If we do either of these, then I would re-assign my deputies to prosecute all resulting charges.

Here's a related problem. When we do manage to prosecute a Bad Boy, we have trouble getting juries to convict them. Not many acquittals, but a lot of hung juries. I think some jurors are afraid of retaliation by the gang. I'd like to find some way of "encouraging" these defendants to waive a jury and go to trial before a judge. Any ideas?

Please give me your input on these issues, and give me any alternative ideas you can think of. But keep in mind that I don't want to violate any laws against "selective prosecution" or "vindictive prosecution" or the like. And — as an elected public official — I don't want to *get caught* violating any such laws. (We have some very smart, aggressive defense attorneys in this city, and they won't pass up any chance to get their clients off — and they'd love to make us look bad in the process.) Of course, as an upstanding member of the bar, I don't want to do anything unethical either. So please review the attached authorities and tell me what I should do.

Incidentally, SOC supported me in my last bid for re-election, so I owe them. Also, I don't want to lose their support next time. If I'm out of a job, so are you!

After you've read this memo, burn it.

OYLER v. BOLES
United States Supreme Court
368 U.S. 448 (1962)

MR. JUSTICE CLARK delivered the opinion of the Court.

The petitioners are serving life sentences imposed under West Virginia's habitual criminal statute. This Act provides for a mandatory life sentence upon the third conviction "of a crime punishable by confinement in a penitentiary." The increased penalty is to be invoked by an information filed by the prosecuting attorney immediately upon conviction and before sentence." Alleging that this Act had been applied and to only a minority of those subject to its provisions, in violation of the Equal Protection Clause of the Fourteenth Amendment, the petitioners filed petitions for writs of habeas corpus in the Supreme Court of Appeals of West Virginia. Both of their petitions were denied.

William Oyler was convicted of murder in the second degree on February 5, 1953, which offense carried a penalty of from 5 to 18 years' imprisonment. The Prosecuting Attorney was granted leave to file an information alleging that Oyler was the same person who had suffered three prior convictions in Pennsylvania which were punishable by confinement in a penitentiary. The court then determined that the defendant had thrice been convicted of crimes punishable by confinement in a penitentiary and sentenced him to life imprisonment. * * * *

Petitioners claim they were denied the equal protection of law guaranteed by the Fourteenth Amendment. In his petition for a writ of habeas corpus to the Supreme Court of Appeals of West Virginia, Oyler stated:

> Petitioner was discriminated against as an Habitual Criminal in that from January, 1940, to June, 1955, there were six men sentenced in the Taylor County Circuit Court who were subject to prosecution as Habitual offenders, Petitioner was the only man thus sentenced during this period. It is a matter of record that the five men who were not prosecuted as Habitual Criminals during this period, all had three or more felony convictions and sentences as adults, and Petitioner's former convictions were a result of Juvenile Court actions.

> The Petitioner was discriminated against by selective use of a mandatory State Statute, in that 904 men who were known offenders throughout the State of West Virginia were not sentenced as required by the mandatory Statutes, Chapter 61, Article 11, Sections 18 and 19 of the Code. Equal Protection and Equal Justice was (sic) denied.

Statistical data based on prison records were appended to the petition to support the latter allegation.

Thus, petitioners' contention is that the habitual criminal statute imposes a mandatory duty on the prosecuting authorities to seek the severer penalty against all persons coming within the statutory standards, but that it is done only in a minority of cases. This, petitioners argue, denies equal protection to those persons against whom the heavier penalty is enforced. We note that it is not stated whether the failure to proceed against other three-time offenders was due to lack of knowledge of the prior offenses on the part of the prosecutors or was the result of a deliberate policy of proceeding only in a certain class of cases or against specific persons. The statistics merely show that according to penitentiary records a high percentage of those subject to the law have not been proceeded against. There is no indication that these records of previous convictions, which may not have been compiled until after the three-time offenders had reached the penitentiary, were available to the prosecutors. Hence the allegations set out no more than a failure to prosecute others because of a lack of knowledge of their prior offenses. This does not deny equal protection due petitioners under the Fourteenth Amendment.

Moreover, the conscious exercise of some selectivity in enforcement is not in itself a federal constitutional violation. Even though the statistics in this case might imply a policy of selective enforcement, it was not stated that the selection was deliberately based upon an unjustifiable standard such as race, religion, or other arbitrary classification. Therefore grounds supporting a finding of a denial of equal protection were not alleged.

Affirmed.

Note from Izzy:

In *State v. Villas*, 55 P.3d 437 (N.Mex.App. 2002), Albuquerque police set up a "sobriety checkpoint" at which they stopped motorists to check for intoxication. Villas was stopped and thereafter convicted of driving while intoxicated. She claimed that prosecuting her violated the Equal Protection Clause, because another driver was also intoxicated but was released by his brother — an Albuquerque police officer. The court disagreed:

> To establish a claim of selective prosecution, a defendant must prove both a discriminatory effect and a discriminatory purpose. To establish a discriminatory effect, the defendant must prove that he or she was singled out for prosecution while others similarly situated were not. To establish a discriminatory purpose, a defendant must prove that he or she was selected for prosecution based on intentional, purposeful discrimination stemming from impermissible considerations, such as race, religion, or the exercise of a constitutionally protected right.

> Defendant recognizes that this case is the inverse of a typical selective prosecution case, where one person is prosecuted even though many others committed the same offense. Nonetheless, she argues that these facts establish a discriminatory effect. She asserts that the improper favorable treatment of one individual constitutes selective prosecution of all others who faced charges for their actions. We cannot agree. Our courts have consistently required that the individual in question be "singled out" for prosecution. Defendant was not singled out; she was one of many who were prosecuted based on breath alcohol test results proving that they had been driving while intoxicated. It was Brother who was singled out in this case.

> Even if we accepted Defendant's argument that the failure to charge Brother constituted a discriminatory effect, we do not agree that the police officers had a discriminatory purpose in charging Defendant with DWI. Defendant presented no evidence showing that the police had an invidious reason for charging her with DWI. She does not claim that the decision to charge her was based on her race, religion, or her attempt to exercise constitutional rights. Instead, Defendant asserts that she was charged because she was not related to an APD officer. We do not agree that this constitutes a discriminatory purpose on the part of the arresting officers. Defendant presented no evidence showing that she was charged with DWI for any reason other than the simple fact that her BAC was above the legal limit. The officers' reasons for failing to charge Brother do not alter the reasons for charging other drivers, including Defendant, who were in fact driving while intoxicated. Even if the alleged discrimination in this case did not occur — if Brother had been charged with DWI Defendant would still have faced DWI charges. We hold that there was no violation of Defendant's right to equal protection.

Compare, however, *Stemler v. City of Florence*, 126 F.3d 856 (6th Cir. 1997), where plaintiff alleged that police arrested her for drunk driving because they believed she was a lesbian:

> While a plaintiff in a selective-prosecution case must demonstrate that she was prosecuted because she was the member of some group, and not merely because the state actor prosecuted her out of purely personal

animosity, the availability of such a claim has never been limited only to those groups accorded heightened scrutiny under equal protection jurisprudence. Instead, a plaintiff makes out a selective-enforcement claim if she shows that the state based its enforcement decision on an "arbitrary classification," *Oyler v. Boles*, 368 U.S. 448, 456 (1962), that is to say, a classification that gives rise to an inference that the state intended to accomplish some forbidden aim against that group through selective application of the laws. A selective-enforcement claim such as this one is thus conceptually different from a claim that a statute violates equal protection; while almost every statute can be shown to have some conceivable rational basis, thereby surviving an equal protection challenge unless it is shown to discriminate against a group accorded heightened scrutiny, it will often be difficult to find a rational basis for a truly discriminatory application of a neutral law.

It is beyond cavil that Stemler has adequately alleged a selective-enforcement claim here. The record supports a finding that she was perceived to be a member of "an identifiable group," and that defendants sought to implement their animus against that group by arresting and seeking to prosecute her. The defendant officers are unable, and indeed have not even attempted, to demonstrate that there is any conceivable rational basis for a decision to enforce the drunk-driving laws against homosexuals but not against heterosexuals. The defendants can rely only on their assertion that discrimination on the basis of sexual orientation should be accorded no scrutiny whatsoever. We emphatically reject this assertion; the proposition that the state may constitutionally discriminate by enforcing laws only against homosexuals (or Centre College graduates or SAE members) is not now, and never has been, the law. Under the facts as we are obligated to construe them, the defendants violated the core principle of the Equal Protection Clause by choosing to exercise the power of the state against Stemler solely for the reason that they disapproved of her perceived sexual orientation. Thus, the dismissal of her complaint must be reversed.

UNITED STATES v. STEELE

U.S. Court of Appeals, 9th Circuit
461 F.2d 1148 (1972)

WRIGHT, CIRCUIT JUDGE:

After a trial to the court, appellant was convicted of violating 13 U.S.C. § 221(a) by refusing to answer questions on the Department of Commerce census form of 1970. The court sentenced him to pay a $50 fine. We reverse.

Steele claims the census authorities deliberately applied an unjustifiable standard in selecting offenders for prosecution under 13 U.S.C. § 221(a). Only four people in Hawaii were chosen for prosecution. All had participated in a census resistance movement, publicizing a dissident view of the census as an unconstitutional invasion of privacy and urging the public to avoid compliance with census requirements.

Steele held a press conference, led a protest march, and distributed pamphlets entitled "Big Brother is Snooping." David Watamull was the owner of radio station KTRG, which broadcast editorials on the census. Census authorities had complained to the Federal Communications Commission about them because they "were calculated to incite people to subvert the census law." Donald Dickinson spoke against the census as an announcer on station KTRG. William Danks headed the state chapter of a group called Census Resistance '70; he distributed pamphlets and publicly criticized the census.

Leland Gray, the Regional Technician for the census in Hawaii, described the four as "hard core resisters." He ordered his staff to compile special background dossiers on them, a discretionary procedure not followed with any other offenders. Gray testified that his organization had been very concerned about the census resistance movement.

Steele attempted to prove that many others in Hawaii had provided census officials with no more information than he had. In a motion for a bill of particulars, he asked the government how many others in Hawaii had committed the same offense. The United States Attorney's office replied that the information was not available. Steele himself located six other persons who had completely refused on principle to complete the census forms. None of those had taken a public stand against the census and none were recommended for prosecution.

Mr. Gray testified that, to the best of his recollection, the four men prosecuted were the only ones who completely refused to cooperate. Steele's evidence about the six others demonstrates that Mr. Gray's memory was faulty.

Yick Wo v. Hopkins, 118 U.S. 356 (1886), established the principle that equal protection of the law is denied when state officials enforce a valid statute in a discriminatory fashion. The Due Process Clause of the Fifth Amendment furnishes a federal defendant with the same guarantee against discriminatory federal prosecution. A defendant cannot be convicted if he proves unconstitutional discrimination in the administration of a penal statute.

Mere selectivity in prosecution creates no constitutional problem. *Oyler v. Boles*, 368 U.S. 448 (1962). To invoke the defense successfully, one must prove that the selection was deliberately based on an unjustifiable standard, such as race, religion, or other arbitrary classification. *Id.* at 456. Steele is entitled to an acquittal if his evidence proved that the authorities purposefully discriminated against those who chose to exercise their First Amendment rights.

Although hampered by the government's refusal to supply data on the number of like offenses, Steele did manage to show that at least six others had committed the same offense. The Regional Technician said he had never heard of any of the six. The trial judge concluded that Steele and his colleagues were the only violators known to the census officials. That finding is not supported by the record taken as a whole.

As Mr. Gray explained them, the census operating procedures would in the normal course of events furnish information about any person who failed to complete the questionnaire. A refusal would be reported in the chain of command, from the enumerator through a Crew Leader, a Field Supervisor, and a District Office Manager, to the Regional Technician, Mr. Gray. At least two officials would attempt to obtain the missing answers from the violator. The system would reveal the names of offenders, and visits by census officials would lay the factual foundation for proving specific criminal intent.

This information-gathering system should have apprised the Regional Technician of the names of all who refused to complete the questionnaire. Yet Mr. Gray recollected only four total refusals, while the evidence establishes a minimum of ten. That fact alone strongly suggests a questionable emphasis upon the census resisters. When one also considers that background reports were compiled only on persons who had publicly attacked the census, the inference of discriminatory selection becomes almost compelling. An enforcement procedure that focuses upon the vocal offender is inherently suspect, since it is vulnerable to the charge that those chosen for prosecution are being punished for their expression of ideas, a constitutionally protected right.

The government offered no explanation for its selection of defendants, other than prosecutorial discretion. That answer simply will not suffice in the circumstances of this case. Since Steele had presented evidence which created a strong inference of discriminatory prosecution, the government was required to explain it away, if possible, by showing the selection process actually rested upon some valid ground. Mere random selection would suffice, since the government is not obligated to prosecute all offenders. But no effort was made to justify these prosecutions as the result of random selection, and Steele's evidence was inconsistent with such a theory. Since no valid basis for the selection of defendants was ever presented, the only plausible explanation on this record is the one urged by Steele.

We conclude that Steele demonstrated a purposeful discrimination by census authorities against those who had publicly expressed their opinions about the census. The conviction is reversed.

Notes from Izzy:

1. Did Steele have a First Amendment right to urge people to violate the census law? Is this what the Court held (or assumed)?

2. *Who decides* whether the prosecutor brought the case for an improper purpose — the judge or the jury? In *U.S. v. Martha Stewart*, 2004 WL 113506 (SDNY 2004), the court held: "A selective prosecution claim must be directed to the court, not the jury, because it raises an issue that is independent of the question of the defendant's guilt or innocence."

3. In *U.S. v. Lindh*, 212 F.Supp.2d 541 (E.D.Va. 2002), Lindh was indicted for violating federal laws against terrorism, stemming from his alleged involvement with the al Qaeda organization and the Taliban government in Afghanistan. He claimed that "he is in a protected class of persons that has exercised its First Amendment rights by associating with the Taliban for religious reasons. He therefore claims he is the victim of selective prosecution because the government has chosen not to prosecute others who provided services to the Taliban for non-religious reasons, but to prosecute him for providing services for religious reasons." The court disagreed, finding that Lindh had failed to present evidence showing that persons who were *not* prosecuted were "similarly situated" to Lindh.

PEOPLE v. SUPERIOR COURT [and Cynthia Hartway]
California Supreme Court
19 Cal.3d 338 (1977)

CLARK, JUSTICE.

The People petition for a writ of prohibition to prevent respondent superior court from enforcing its order directing that a peremptory writ of prohibition issue restraining the Municipal Court for the Oakland-Piedmont Judicial District from proceeding with prosecution of defendants, real parties in interest herein.

Defendants are women charged with soliciting or engaging in prostitution.[1] Penal Code § 647(b).[2] They moved in municipal court for dismissal of the charges on the grounds that § 647(b) is unconstitutional on its face and as applied by the Oakland Police Department. The principal questions presented by the motion were: (1) whether the term "solicit" as used in the statute is unconstitutionally vague; and (2) whether the Oakland Police Department deliberately discriminates against women in enforcing the statute. After a thorough evidentiary hearing into the latter question, the municipal court filed comprehensive findings of fact and conclusions of law, resolving both questions against defendants, and denied the motion.

[The Court first held that the word "solicit" in the statute was not unconstitutionally vague.]

The Oakland Police Department, in enforcing section 647, subdivision (b), does not deliberately discriminate against women and thereby deny them equal protection of the law.

The Fourteenth Amendment to the United States Constitution and article I, § 7(a), of the California Constitution prohibit all state action denying any person "equal protection of the laws."

* * * * We have not had occasion to consider all of the classifications that may be arbitrary for the purposes of a discriminatory enforcement claim, but it is clear that in California sex is such a classification (see *Sail'er Inn, Inc. v. Kirby* (1971) 5 Cal.3d 1), and we do not understand the People to contend otherwise.

Like the ordinance in *Yick Wo*, the statute challenged here is "fair on its face and impartial in appearance." (*Yick Wo v. Hopkins, supra*, 118 U.S. at 373.) Section 647(b) by its terms applies to " *Every person . . .* who solicits or who engages in any act of prostitution." (Emphasis added.) The statute is clearly designed to punish specific acts without reference to the sex of the perpetrator. However, equal protection of the law may be denied by a statute fair on its face and impartial in appearance if it is applied "with an evil eye and an unequal hand." (*Yick Wo v. Hopkins, supra*, 118 U.S. at 373-374.) Defendants contend that the Oakland Police Department so applies this statute.

---

[1] Approximately 252 individual actions are joined in this proceeding.

[2] Penal Code § 647 provides: "Every person who commits any of the following acts is guilty of disorderly conduct, a misdemeanor: * * * * (b) Who solicits or who engages in any act of prostitution. As used in this subdivision, 'prostitution' includes any lewd act between persons for money or other consideration."

Because of the presumption that official duty has been properly, hence constitutionally, performed (Evid.Code § 664), the defendant has the burden of proof in establishing the defense of discriminatory enforcement of the law. The elements of the defense of discriminatory enforcement were set forth in *Murgia v. Superior Court*. To establish the defense, the defendant must prove: (1) "that he has been deliberately singled out for prosecution on the basis of some invidious criterion;" and (2) that "the prosecution would not have been pursued except for the discriminatory design of the prosecuting authorities." 15 Cal.3d at 298.

Defendants allege that the Oakland Police Department engages in the following practices which, defendants contend, manifest a policy of deliberate discrimination against women in enforcing § 647(b):

1. More men than women are employed as "decoys" for solicitation of acts of prostitution, with the result that more female prostitutes than male customers are arrested for that crime.

2. In "trick" cases, the female prostitute, but not the male customer, is arrested even if his culpability is as great as, or greater than, hers.[4]

Decoy Cases

The record establishes that the Oakland Police Department does employ more men than women as decoys for solicitation of acts of prostitution and that, as a result of this practice, the department does arrest more female prostitutes than male customers for this crime.[5] The critical question is whether the department adopted this practice — employing more men than women as decoys — with intent to discriminate against women. After a thorough evidentiary hearing into this matter of fact, the municipal court found that the practice was not adopted with such intent. It found, instead, that the practice is a consequence of the department's sexually unbiased policy of concentrating its enforcement effort on the "profiteer," rather than the customer, of commercial vice. This dispositive finding of fact is amply supported by substantial evidence. Therefore, under settled principles of review, neither the superior court nor this court may reweigh the evidence in order to come to the contrary conclusion.

The subdivision of the Oakland Police Department having special responsibility for the enforcement of § 647(b) is the vice control unit; this unit is also responsible for combating illegal narcotics and gambling. For the purposes of this discussion, each of these criminal subcultures — prostitution, narcotics and gambling — may be thought of as pyramidal in structure. In narcotics, for example, the base of the pyramid is formed by users of illicit narcotics. The remainder of the structure is composed of providers of the contraband. The providers, from the major distributor at the apex of the triangle to the street dealer, are "profiteers," in the parlance of the vice control unit, i.e., they profit financially from the illicit commerce. An analogous structure can be perceived in prostitution. The customer forms the base

---

[4] "Trick" may refer to either the act of prostitution or the customer. Trick cases are to be distinguished from decoy cases. In decoy cases, one of the parties to a solicitation, either the apparent prostitute or the apparent customer, is an undercover vice officer. In trick cases, neither party is an undercover vice officer.

[5] In 1973 and 1974, 1,160 women were arrested by means of male decoys and 57 men were arrested by means of female decoys.

of the triangle; the prostitute, male or female, constitutes the largest class of profiteers; and at the apex are the pimp, the panderer, and the bar, restaurant, hotel and motel proprietors who knowingly derive profit from the vicious trade.

In order to most efficiently utilize its limited resources, the vice control unit concentrates on the profiteers in each vice with special emphasis on those at the apex of the illicit commerce. It is a matter of common knowledge of which we may take judicial notice that most law enforcement agencies — federal, state and local — endorse this approach with respect to narcotics. Although both parties to an illicit narcotics transaction break the law, as do both parties to an act of prostitution, no one seriously suggests that it is inappropriate for a law enforcement agency to concentrate on the profiteer and to carry out this policy by, among other things, using its undercover officers as decoys to arrest sellers rather than buyers. The record supports the municipal court's conclusion that the Oakland Police Department adopted a profiteer-oriented approach to prostitution in good faith and not as a smokescreen for deliberate discrimination against women.

In terms of personnel hours expended, 60% of the time allotted to prostitution is devoted to investigating pimps, panderers, and bar, restaurant, motel and hotel proprietors. Prostitutes, male and female, receive 30% of the unit's attention, and customers are the subject of the remaining 10%. Because 95% of the pimps, etc., are male, as are 10% of the prostitutes and all of the customers, it is clear that the vice control unit devotes at least half of its resources to prosecuting men.

It is by no means certain that employing more male than female undercover officers as decoys for solicitation is the most efficient use of this limited resource in fighting prostitution. However, on the available evidence, the Oakland Police Department could in good faith come to this conclusion. Prostitutes, the municipal court found, average five customers per night; the average customer does not patronize prostitutes five times a year. Because of an effective grapevine, arrest of one prostitute by an undercover officer will deter others, at least for a time. Customers, on the other hand, are usually unknown to one another. Therefore, in the absence of widespread publicity, arrest of one customer will not deter others. Finally, using female decoys is twice as "expensive" as using males because an additional officer is required under current practice to ensure the female's safety.

Even assuming *arguendo* that using more male than female decoys is a manifestation of a policy of deliberate discrimination against women, defendants have not established the other element of a discriminatory enforcement defense — that they would not have been arrested but for this policy. To the contrary, substantial evidence supports the municipal court's conclusion that "the Oakland Police Department made arrests for violations of § 647(b) based upon probable cause to believe the arrestee has committed the offense and not on the basis of the sex of the arrestee."

Trick Cases

In trick cases, * * * defendants allege, the Oakland Police Department arrests the woman, but not the man, even if his culpability is as great as, or greater than, hers.

In support of this allegation, defendants introduce evidence of six trick cases in which the woman was arrested for solicitation while the man was set free. In rebuttal, the People introduce evidence of four trick cases in which the man was arrested. Having judged the credibility of the witnesses, resolved any conflicts in their testimony, weighed the evidence and drawn factual conclusions, the municipal court found there was "absolutely no sexual discrimination whatsoever." Having carefully reviewed the record, we conclude that ample evidence supports this conclusion.

Let the peremptory writ of prohibition issue as prayed.

TOBRINER, ACTING CHIEF JUSTICE, dissenting.

I believe that the majority err in two respects. First, the majority mistakenly equate concentration of law enforcement efforts on sellers of illegal narcotics with the similar focus of enforcement procedures on the "profiteer" in prostitution transactions. In the case of narcotics transactions, the Legislature itself has drawn a distinction between buyers and sellers, and has endorsed the policy of concentrating police resources on the apprehension of sellers. (See Health & Saf.Code § 11350 (possession); § 11351 (possession for sale); and § 11352 (sale).)

But the Legislature specifically refused to draw such a distinction between prostitutes and their customers in defining the offense of solicitation. Pen.Code § 647(b). As the Court of Appeal noted in *Leffel v. Municipal Court* (1976) 54 Cal.App.3d 569, 575–576:

> The words "every person . . . who solicits . . . any act of prostitution" are clear and unambiguous. "Every" means "each and all within the range of contemplated possibilities" (Webster's New International Dictionary (3d ed.1961) p. 788.) Thus the ordinary meaning of the statute is that *all persons*, customers as well as prostitutes, who solicit an act of prostitution are guilty of disorderly conduct. This interpretation is consistent with the legislative purpose and policy behind the statute. The Legislative purpose is to eliminate prostitution and its intended evils. *Subjecting the customer to prosecution will further the legislative purpose -probably more so than any other legislative remedy.* [Emphasis added.]

Despite the clear legislative mandate to arrest and prosecute customers as well as prostitutes, the Oakland police have adopted an enforcement policy that directly contravenes the judgment of the Legislature. Although the police unquestionably may exercise discretion in the allocation of scarce resources, such discretion is not so unbridled as to permit the police to carve out invidious exceptions to a statutory prohibition, exceptions which the Legislature has specifically declined to enact. As the court noted in *People v. Gray* (1967) 254 Cal.App.2d 256, at 266:

> The recognition of the discriminatory enforcement of a penal law as a defense to a criminal action is one of the few means the individual citizen has to force public officials to do their job properly. The availability of discriminatory enforcement as a defense serves a good purpose; it acts as a constant reminder to the executive that the will of the people, expressed through the legislative branch, should be obeyed.

Thus, just as the police "may not enforce a facially fair gambling statute as if it were explicitly directed only at blacks" (*Murgia v. Municipal Court*, 15 Cal.3d at 296) they may not enforce a facially fair solicitation statute as if it were directed only at women.

In addition to drawing an inappropriate analogy to the enforcement of drug laws, the majority err in accepting at face value the People's contention that the challenged "profiteer-oriented" enforcement policy bears no relation to traditional sex-based stereotypes, but instead simply represents the most efficient means of reducing the incidence of prostitution. Several centuries of law enforcement history belie any claim that a "profiteer"-directed enforcement program is an effective means of eliminating prostitution, and the record in the instant case demonstrates quite unmistakenly that the arrest of male customers in addition to female prostitutes is a singularly more effective law enforcement strategy than the approach traditionally employed by the police.

From February 26, 1975, through April 22, 1975, the Oakland police were compelled by order of the Alameda County Superior Court to employ female decoys and to arrest male customers guilty of § 647(b) violations. During this brief period of even-handed enforcement, the arrest of male customers, coupled with newspaper publicity surrounding the sex-neutral police procedures, resulted, according to the testimony of the senior vice squad officer, in a "devastating" reduction in observed levels of prostitution related offenses. Similar results have been achieved in other jurisdictions in which enforcement efforts have been directed at male customers as well as female prostitutes. See, e.g., *United States v. Moses* (D.C.Ct.App.1975) 339 A.2d 46; Kanowitz, *Women and the Law* (1969) p. 17.

In light of the demonstrated success of an enforcement policy which encompasses both customers and prostitutes, I cannot accept the suggestion that the police department's resumption of its traditional enforcement policy, directed primarily at women, is explicable by reference to legitimate law enforcement objectives. Although the majority discern no discriminatory intent in the action of the Oakland police, I agree with the American Bar Association's section of Individual Rights and Responsibilities which has characterized such police practices as "one of the most direct forms of discrimination against women in this country today. In accordance with society's double standard of sexual morality, the woman who sells her body is punished criminally and stigmatized socially while her male customer is left unscathed." ABA Section of Individual Rights and Responsibilities, Rep. No. 101B, p. 1 (1974).

More than a half century ago, a New York court observed: "The men create the market, and the women who supply the demand pay the penalty. It is time this unfair discrimination and injustice should cease." *People v. Edwards* (N.Y. Cty.Ct. 1920) 180 N.Y.S. 631, 634 635.) Hopefully, it will not be yet another half century before this discriminatory practice is eliminated.

I would deny the requested writ.

Notes from Izzy:

1. For a similar case (and outcome), see *Salaiscooper v. Eighth Judicial Dist. Court ex.rel County of Clark*, 34 P.2d 509 (Nev. 2001).

2. In *U.S. v. Redondo-Lemos*, 27 F.3d 439 (9th Cir.1994), defendant was charged with acting as a "mule" — one who is paid to carry narcotics across the border for others. The prosecutor entered into a plea bargain with the defendant, under which the prosecutor would recommend a sentence of 5 years. The judge noted that defendant was a male, and that the prosecutor had a pattern of recommending 5

year sentences for male mules and much lower sentences — or even dismissals — for female mules. The judge found that this established a *prima facie* case of intentional discrimination based on gender. The prosecutor tried to justify the difference in treatment:

> The Assistant United States Attorney testified that in a specific case where a husband and wife were arrested, the charges against the woman were dismissed while the man accepted a plea agreement and was sentenced accordingly, even though the evidence was probably stronger against the woman. While the Assistant United States Attorney stated that this decision was not based on favoritism for female defendants, he did agree that where a male and female defendant, who have some kind of a relationship where children are involved, are equally charged in a narcotics case, it is more common for men to agree to plead on behalf of their "paramour" than it is for women. When asked if such decisions were made by the United States Attorney's Office, whether pleas of men were requested over women, or whether such agreements were initiated by the defendants, the Assistant United States Attorney responded that in the present case, the plea offer was brought to him; in some cases he "expected them to do it." "It's not anything unusual when you have got husbands and wives and they have got kids and nobody to take care of them. It's usually the Mexican males that will stand and take it."

> When asked by the Court if this was based upon culture, the Assistant United States Attorney agreed that the general feeling is "that it is the man's responsibility if they have been in a crime together to take the rap."

The trial court found the prosecutor's explanations insufficient to rebut the presumption, and therefore intentional discrimination was shown. The court sentenced defendant to 18 months in prison.

The Court of Appeals reversed: "The government's compassionate practice of allowing one parent to stay with children who otherwise would be effectively orphaned is not rendered unconstitutional because the government allows the parents to decide which one is best suited to be the care-giver." The court stressed "the extreme deference" which courts must give to "the judgments exercised by officers of a coordinate branch of government", especially where "the government responds fully and promptly to the district judge's concerns by presenting live testimony from those who made the prosecutorial decisions."

3. In *People v. Owen*, 59 Cal.App.4th 798 (1998), Owen (a police officer) was charged with "operating an endless chain scheme." He had accepted $2,000 at a recruiting meeting for a "pyramid" scheme to which Owen already belonged. While 70 other people attended the meeting, Owen was the only person prosecuted.

> Appellant moved to dismiss the indictment as a discriminatory prosecution, arguing that he was prosecuted and required to plead to a felony only because he is a police officer. Although the trial court agreed that appellant's status as a police officer motivated both his prosecution and the felony charge, it denied the motion after concluding that it was "perfectly permissible" for the district attorney to distinguish between police officers and civilians in charging decisions. * * * *

Appellant identifies himself as a member of the class of public safety officers, and contends this is a suspect class because it impacts his right to practice his chosen profession. He argues that strict judicial scrutiny must be applied to the prosecutor's decision to initiate felony charges against police officers but not civilians because the decision impacts the fundamental right to personal liberty. Alternatively, appellant argues there is no rational basis for distinguishing between police officers and civilians in the enforcement of Penal Code § 327. He concludes that his disparate treatment violated the Fourteenth Amendment to the United States Constitution and article I, § 7 of the California Constitution.

Appellant's initial premise is incorrect. Public safety officers are not a suspect class for equal protection purposes because, among other things, "there is no constitutional right or fundamental interest in continued public employment." *Long Beach City Employees Assn. v. City of Long Beach* (1986) 41 Cal.3d 937, 950. "The right to pursue one's chosen profession is not a fundamental right for the purpose of invoking the strict scrutiny test." *Cunningham v. Superior Court* (1986) 177 Cal.App.3d 336, 348. Nor does appellant's fundamental right to personal liberty provide a basis for the application of strict scrutiny. California courts have never accepted the general proposition that "all criminal laws, because they may result in a defendant's incarceration, are perforce subject to strict judicial scrutiny." *People v. Silva* (1994) 27 Cal.App.4th 1160, 1167.

Because the district attorney's decision to distinguish between police officers and civilians neither infringes upon a fundamental interest nor creates a suspect classification, we review that decision under the rational basis test. Under that test, we will uphold the district attorney's decision to initiate felony prosecutions against police officers but not civilians if the distinction between police officers and civilians "bears a rational relationship to a legitimate state purpose." *County of Los Angeles v. Patrick* (1992) 11 Cal.App.4th 1246, 1253.

The trial court correctly found that a rational relationship existed. Like civilians, police officers are required to refrain from committing crimes. Unlike civilians, they are also expected to prevent others from committing crimes, to assist in the investigation of crime, and to use their law enforcement authority to maintain the trust of the public in its criminal justice system.

Appellant failed to discharge those obligations when he joined the pyramid scheme and recruited new members for it. As a result, he is morally culpable to a greater extent than the civilian participants in the endless chain scheme. This provides a rational basis for the decision to prosecute appellant on a felony charge.

The fact that appellant was "off-duty" when he attended the July 13, 1995 meeting is irrelevant. Police officers are routinely disciplined for off-duty conduct that is inconsistent with their special obligations. * * * *

We also note that the prosecution of a police officer may have a greater deterrent effect because it might generate more media coverage and public interest in an otherwise unspectacular crime.

Appellant was singled out for felony prosecution because he is a police officer. There was nothing invidious, that is, arbitrary or unjustified, about this exercise of prosecutorial discretion. The judgment is affirmed.

UNITED STATES v. GOODWIN
United States Supreme Court
457 U.S. 368 (1982)

JUSTICE STEVENS delivered the opinion of the Court.

I

Respondent Goodwin was stopped for speeding by a United States Park Policeman on the Baltimore-Washington Parkway. Goodwin emerged from his car to talk to the policeman. After a brief discussion, the officer noticed a clear plastic bag underneath the armrest next to the driver's seat of Goodwin's car. The officer asked Goodwin to return to his car and to raise the armrest. Respondent did so, but as he raised the armrest he placed the car into gear and accelerated rapidly. The car struck the officer, knocking him first onto the back of the car and then onto the highway. The policeman returned to his car, but Goodwin eluded him in a high-speed chase.

The following day, the officer filed a complaint in the District Court charging respondent with several misdemeanor and petty offenses, including assault. Goodwin was arrested and arraigned before a United States Magistrate. The Magistrate set a date for trial, but respondent fled the jurisdiction. Three years later Goodwin was found in custody in Virginia and was returned to Maryland.

Upon his return, respondent's case was assigned to an attorney from the Department of Justice, who was detailed temporarily to try petty crime and misdemeanor cases before the Magistrate. The attorney did not have authority to try felony cases or to seek indictments from the grand jury. Respondent initiated plea negotiations with the prosecutor, but later advised the Government that he did not wish to plead guilty and desired a trial by jury in the District Court. * * * *

The case was transferred to the District Court and responsibility for the prosecution was assumed by an Assistant United States Attorney. Approximately six weeks later, after reviewing the case and discussing it with several parties, the prosecutor obtained a four-count indictment charging respondent with one felony count of forcibly assaulting a federal officer and three related counts arising from the same incident.[2] A jury convicted respondent on the felony count and on one misdemeanor count.

Respondent moved to set aside the verdict on the ground of prosecutorial vindictiveness, contending that the indictment on the felony charge gave rise to an

---

[2] By affidavit, the Assistant United States Attorney later set forth his reasons for this action: (1) he considered respondent's conduct on the date in question to be a serious violation of law, (2) respondent had a lengthy history of violent crime, (3) the prosecutor considered respondent's conduct to be related to major narcotics transactions, (4) the prosecutor believed that respondent had committed perjury at his preliminary hearing, and (5) respondent had failed to appear for trial as originally scheduled. The Government attorney stated that his decision to seek a felony indictment was not motivated in any way by Goodwin's request for a jury trial in District Court.

impermissible appearance of retaliation. The District Court denied the motion, finding that "the prosecutor in this case has adequately dispelled any appearance of retaliatory intent." * * * *

Although the Court of Appeals readily concluded that "the prosecutor did not act with actual vindictiveness in seeking a felony indictment," it nevertheless reversed. Relying on our decisions in *North Carolina v. Pearce* and *Blackledge v. Perry*, the court held that the Due Process Clause of the Fifth Amendment prohibits the Government from bringing more serious charges against a defendant after he has invoked his right to a jury trial, unless the prosecutor comes forward with objective evidence to show that the increased charges could not have been brought before the defendant exercised his rights. Because the court believed that the circumstances surrounding the felony indictment gave rise to a genuine risk of retaliation, it adopted a legal presumption designed to spare courts the "unseemly task" of probing the actual motives of the prosecutor.

II

To punish a person because he has done what the law plainly allows him to do is a due process violation "of the most basic sort." *Bordenkircher v. Hayes*, 434 U.S. 357, 363. In a series of cases beginning with *North Carolina v. Pearce* and culminating in *Bordenkircher v. Hayes*, the Court has recognized this basic — and itself uncontroversial — principle. For while an individual certainly may be penalized for violating the law, he just as certainly may not be punished for exercising a protected statutory or constitutional right.[3]

The imposition of punishment is the very purpose of virtually all criminal proceedings. The presence of a punitive motivation, therefore, does not provide an adequate basis for distinguishing governmental action that is fully justified as a legitimate response to perceived criminal conduct from governmental action that is an impermissible response to noncriminal, protected activity. Motives are complex and difficult to prove. As a result, in certain cases in which action detrimental to the defendant has been taken after the exercise of a legal right, the Court has found it necessary to "presume" an improper vindictive motive. Given the severity of such a presumption, however — which may operate in the absence of any proof of an improper motive and thus may block a legitimate response to criminal conduct — the Court has done so only in cases in which a reasonable likelihood of vindictiveness exists.

In *North Carolina v. Pearce*, the Court held that neither the Double Jeopardy Clause nor the Equal Protection Clause prohibits a trial judge from imposing a harsher sentence on retrial after a criminal defendant successfully attacks an initial conviction on appeal. The Court stated, however, that "it can hardly be doubted that it would be a flagrant violation (of the Due Process Clause) of the Fourteenth Amendment for a state trial court to follow an announced practice of imposing a heavier sentence upon every reconvicted defendant for the explicit purpose of punishing the defendant for his having succeeded in getting his original conviction set aside." 395 U.S. at 723-724. The Court continued:

---

[3] "For an agent of the State to pursue a course of action whose objective is to penalize a person's reliance on his legal rights is patently unconstitutional." *Bordenkircher v. Hayes*, 434 U.S. 357, 363.

Due process of law, then, requires that vindictiveness against a defendant for having successfully attacked his first conviction must play no part in the sentence he receives after a new trial. And since the fear of such vindictiveness may unconstitutionally deter a defendant's exercise of the right to appeal or collaterally attack his first conviction, due process also requires that a defendant be freed of apprehension of such a retaliatory motivation on the part of the sentencing judge. [*Id.* at 725]

In order to assure the absence of such a motivation, the Court concluded:

Whenever a judge imposes a more severe sentence upon a defendant after a new trial, the reasons for his doing so must affirmatively appear. Those reasons must be based upon objective information concerning identifiable conduct on the part of the defendant occurring after the time of the original sentencing proceeding. And the factual data upon which the increased sentence is based must be made part of the record, so that the constitutional legitimacy of the increased sentence may be fully reviewed on appeal. [*Id.* at 726]

In sum, the Court applied a presumption of vindictiveness, which may be overcome only by objective information in the record justifying the increased sentence. * * * *

In *Blackledge v. Perry*, 417 U.S. 21, the Court confronted the problem of increased punishment upon retrial after appeal in a setting different from that considered in *Pearce*. Perry was convicted of assault in an inferior court having exclusive jurisdiction for the trial of misdemeanors. The court imposed a 6-month sentence. Under North Carolina law, Perry had an absolute right to a trial de novo in the Superior Court, which possessed felony jurisdiction. After Perry filed his notice of appeal, the prosecutor obtained a felony indictment charging him with assault with a deadly weapon. Perry pleaded guilty to the felony and was sentenced to a term of five to seven years in prison. In reviewing Perry's felony conviction and increased sentence,[6] this Court first stated the essence of the holdings in *Pearce* and the cases that had followed it:

The lesson that emerges from *Pearce* is that the Due Process Clause is not offended by all possibilities of increased punishment upon retrial after appeal, but only by those that pose a realistic likelihood of "vindictiveness." [417 U.S. at 27]

The Court held that the opportunities for vindictiveness in the situation before it were such "as to impel the conclusion that due process of law requires a rule analogous to that of the *Pearce* case." *Ibid.* It explained:

A prosecutor clearly has a considerable stake in discouraging convicted misdemeanants from appealing and thus obtaining a trial de novo in the Superior Court, since such an appeal will clearly require increased expenditures of prosecutorial resources before the defendant's conviction becomes final, and may even result in a formerly convicted defendant's going free. And, if the prosecutor has the means readily at hand to discourage such appeals — by "upping the ante" through a felony

---

[6] The Court held that in pleading guilty Perry had not waived the right "not to be haled into court at all upon the felony charge." 417 U.S. at 30.

indictment whenever a convicted misdemeanant pursues his statutory appellate remedy — the State can insure that only the most hardy defendants will brave the hazards of a de novo trial. [*Id.* at 27-28.]

The Court emphasized in *Blackledge* that it did not matter that no evidence was present that the prosecutor had acted in bad faith or with malice in seeking the felony indictment. * * * * As in *Pearce*, the Court held that the likelihood of vindictiveness justified a presumption that would free defendants of apprehension of such a retaliatory motivation on the part of the prosecutor.[8]

Both *Pearce* and *Blackledge* involved the defendant's exercise of a procedural right that caused a complete retrial after he had been once tried and convicted. The decisions in these cases reflect a recognition by the Court of the institutional bias inherent in the judicial system against the retrial of issues that have already been decided. The doctrines of *stare decisis, res judicata,* the law of the case, and double jeopardy all are based, at least in part, on that deep-seated bias. While none of these doctrines barred the retrials in *Pearce* and *Blackledge*, the same institutional pressure that supports them might also subconsciously motivate a vindictive prosecutorial or judicial response to a defendant's exercise of his right to obtain a retrial of a decided question.

In *Bordenkircher v. Hayes*, 434 U.S. 357, the Court for the first time considered an allegation of vindictiveness that arose in a pretrial setting. In that case the Court held that the Due Process Clause of the Fourteenth Amendment did not prohibit a prosecutor from carrying out a threat, made during plea negotiations, to bring additional charges against an accused who refused to plead guilty to the offense with which he was originally charged. The prosecutor in that case had explicitly told the defendant that if he did not plead guilty and "save the court the inconvenience and necessity of a trial," he would return to the grand jury to obtain an additional charge that would significantly increase the defendant's potential punishment.[9] The defendant refused to plead guilty and the prosecutor obtained the indictment. It was not disputed that the additional charge was justified by the evidence, that the prosecutor was in possession of this evidence at the time the original indictment was obtained, and that the prosecutor sought the additional charge because of the accused's refusal to plead guilty to the original charge.

In finding no due process violation, the Court in *Bordenkircher* considered the decisions in *Pearce* and *Blackledge*, and stated:

> In those cases, the Court was dealing with the State's unilateral imposition of a penalty upon a defendant who had chosen to exercise a legal right to attack his original conviction — a situation very different from the give-and-take negotiation common in plea bargaining between the prosecution and defense, which arguably possess relatively equal bargaining power.

---

[8] The presumption again could be overcome by objective evidence justifying the prosecutor's action. The Court noted: "This would clearly be a different case if the State had shown that it was impossible to proceed on the more serious charge at the outset."

[9] The prosecutor advised the defendant that he would obtain an indictment under the Kentucky Habitual Criminal Act, which would subject the accused to a mandatory sentence of life imprisonment by reason of his two prior felony convictions. Absent the additional indictment, the defendant was subject to a punishment of 2 to 10 years in prison.

The Court stated that the due process violation in *Pearce* and *Blackledge* "lay not in the possibility that a defendant might be deterred from the exercise of a legal right, but rather in the danger that the State might be retaliating against the accused for lawfully attacking his conviction." 434 U.S. at 363.

The Court held, however, that there was no such element of punishment in the "give-and-take" of plea negotiation, so long as the accused "is free to accept or reject the prosecution's offer." *Ibid.* The Court noted that, by tolerating and encouraging the negotiation of pleas, this Court had accepted as constitutionally legitimate the simple reality that the prosecutor's interest at the bargaining table is to persuade the defendant to forgo his constitutional right to stand trial. The Court concluded:

> We hold only that the course of conduct engaged in by the prosecutor in this case, which no more than openly presented the defendant with the unpleasant alternatives of forgoing trial or facing charges on which he was plainly subject to prosecution, did not violate the Due Process Clause of the Fourteenth Amendment. [*Id.* at 365]

The outcome in *Bordenkircher* was mandated by this Court's acceptance of plea negotiation as a legitimate process. * * * * In declining to apply a presumption of vindictiveness, the Court recognized that "additional" charges obtained by a prosecutor could not necessarily be characterized as an impermissible "penalty." Since charges brought in an original indictment may be abandoned by the prosecutor in the course of plea negotiation — in often what is clearly a "benefit" to the defendant — changes in the charging decision that occur in the context of plea negotiation are an inaccurate measure of improper prosecutorial "vindictiveness." * * * * An initial indictment — from which the prosecutor embarks on a course of plea negotiation — does not necessarily define the extent of the legitimate interest in prosecution. For just as a prosecutor may forgo legitimate charges already brought in an effort to save the time and expense of trial, a prosecutor may file additional charges if an initial expectation that a defendant would plead guilty to lesser charges proves unfounded.[12]

III

This case, like *Bordenkircher*, arises from a pretrial decision to modify the charges against the defendant. Unlike *Bordenkircher*, however, there is no evidence in this case that could give rise to a claim of *actual* vindictiveness; the prosecutor never suggested that the charge was brought to influence the respondent's conduct. * * * * The conviction in this case may be reversed only if a *presumption* of vindictiveness — applicable in all cases — is warranted.

There is good reason to be cautious before adopting an inflexible presumption of prosecutorial vindictiveness in a pretrial setting. In the course of preparing a case for trial, the prosecutor may uncover additional information that suggests a basis

---

[12] In rejecting a presumption of vindictiveness, the Court in *Bordenkircher* did not foreclose the possibility that a defendant might prove through objective evidence an improper prosecutorial motive. In the case before it, however, the Court did not find such proof in the fact that the prosecutor had stated explicitly that additional charges were brought to persuade the defendant to plead guilty. The fact that the prosecutor threatened the defendant did not prove that the action threatened was not permissible; the prosecutor's conduct did not establish that the additional charges were brought solely to "penalize" the defendant and could not be justified as a proper exercise of prosecutorial discretion.

for further prosecution or he simply may come to realize that information possessed by the State has a broader significance. At this stage of the proceedings, the prosecutor's assessment of the proper extent of prosecution may not have crystallized. In contrast, once a trial begins — and certainly by the time a conviction has been obtained — it is much more likely that the State has discovered and assessed all of the information against an accused and has made a determination, on the basis of that information, of the extent to which he should be prosecuted. Thus, a change in the charging decision made after an initial trial is completed is much more likely to be improperly motivated than is a pretrial decision.

In addition, a defendant before trial is expected to invoke procedural rights that inevitably impose some "burden" on the prosecutor. Defense counsel routinely file pretrial motions to suppress evidence; to challenge the sufficiency and form of an indictment; to plead an affirmative defense; to request psychiatric services; to obtain access to government files; to be tried by jury. It is unrealistic to assume that a prosecutor's probable response to such motions is to seek to penalize and to deter. The invocation of procedural rights is an integral part of the adversary process in which our criminal justice system operates.

Thus, the timing of the prosecutor's action in this case suggests that a presumption of vindictiveness is not warranted. A prosecutor should remain free before trial to exercise the broad discretion entrusted to him to determine the extent of the societal interest in prosecution. An initial decision should not freeze future conduct.[14] As we made clear in *Bordenkircher*, the initial charges filed by a prosecutor may not reflect the extent to which an individual is legitimately subject to prosecution. * * * *

The nature of the right asserted by the respondent confirms that a presumption of vindictiveness is not warranted in this case. After initially expressing an interest in plea negotiation, respondent decided not to plead guilty and requested a trial by jury in District Court. In doing so, he forced the Government to bear the burdens and uncertainty of a trial. This Court in *Bordenkircher* made clear that the mere fact that a defendant refuses to plead guilty and forces the government to prove its case is insufficient to warrant a presumption that subsequent changes in the charging decision are unjustified. Respondent argues that such a presumption is warranted in this case, however, because he not only requested a trial — he requested a trial by jury.

We cannot agree. The distinction between a bench trial and a jury trial does not compel a special presumption of prosecutorial vindictiveness whenever additional charges are brought after a jury is demanded. To be sure, a jury trial is more burdensome than a bench trial. The defendant may challenge the selection of the venire; the jury itself must be impaneled; witnesses and arguments must be prepared more carefully to avoid the danger of a mistrial. These matters are much less significant, however, than the facts that before either a jury or a judge the State must present its full case against the accused and the defendant is entitled to offer

---

[14] We recognize that prosecutors may be trained to bring all legitimate charges against an individual at the outset. Certainly, a prosecutor should not file any charge until he has investigated fully all of the circumstances surrounding a case. To presume that every case is complete at the time an initial charge is filed, however, is to presume that every prosecutor is infallible — an assumption that would ignore the practical restraints imposed by often limited prosecutorial resources. Moreover, there are certain advantages in avoiding a rule that would compel prosecutors to attempt to place every conceivable charge against an individual on the public record from the outset.

a full defense. As compared to the complete trial de novo at issue in *Blackledge*, a jury trial — as opposed to a bench trial — does not require duplicative expenditures of prosecutorial resources before a final judgment may be obtained. Moreover, unlike the trial judge in *Pearce*, no party is asked "to do over what it thought it had already done correctly." * * * * A prosecutor has no "personal stake" in a bench trial and thus no reason to engage in "self-vindication" upon a defendant's request for a jury trial. * * * * Perhaps most importantly, the institutional bias against the retrial of a decided question that supported the decisions in *Pearce* and *Blackledge* simply has no counterpart in this case.[18]

There is an opportunity for vindictiveness. The cases demonstrate, however, that a mere opportunity for vindictiveness is insufficient to justify the imposition of a prophylactic rule. As *Blackledge* makes clear, "the Due Process Clause is not offended by all possibilities of increased punishment, but only by those that pose a realistic likelihood of vindictiveness." 417 U.S. at 27. The possibility that a prosecutor would respond to a defendant's pretrial demand for a jury trial by bringing charges not in the public interest that could be explained only as a penalty imposed on the defendant is so unlikely that a presumption of vindictiveness certainly is not warranted.

IV

In declining to apply a presumption of vindictiveness, we of course do not foreclose the possibility that a defendant in an appropriate case might prove objectively that the prosecutor's charging decision was motivated by a desire to punish him for doing something that the law plainly allowed him to do.[19] In this case, however, the Court of Appeals stated: "On this record we readily conclude that the prosecutor did not act with actual vindictiveness in seeking a felony indictment." Respondent does not challenge that finding. Absent a presumption of vindictiveness, no due process violation has been established.

The judgment of the Court of Appeals is reversed. The case is remanded for further proceedings consistent with this opinion.

---

[18] Indeed, there is a strong tradition in this country in favor of jury trials, despite the additional burdens that they entail for all parties. In many cases — and for many reasons — both the judge and the prosecutor may prefer to have a case tried by jury. In *Singer v. United States*, 380 U.S. 24, this Court held that a criminal defendant does not have a constitutional right to waive a jury trial and to have his case tried before a judge alone. The Court stated: "Trial by jury has been established by the Constitution as the normal and preferable mode of disposing of issues of fact in criminal cases."

[19] As the Government states in its brief:

"Accordingly, while the prosecutor's charging decision is presumptively lawful, and the prosecutor is not required to sustain any burden of justification for an increase in charges, the defendant is free to tender evidence to the court to support a claim that enhanced charges are a direct and unjustifiable penalty for the exercise of a procedural right. Of course, only in a rare case would a defendant be able to overcome the presumptive validity of the prosecutor's actions through such a demonstration."

JUSTICE BRENNAN, with whom JUSTICE MARSHALL joins, dissenting.

* * * *

The Court does not contend that *Blackledge* is inapplicable to instances of pretrial as well as post-trial vindictiveness. But after examining the record before us for objective indications of such vindictiveness, the Court concludes that "a presumption of vindictiveness is not warranted in this case." With all respect, I disagree both with the Court's conclusion and with its reasoning. In my view, the question here is not one of "presumptions." Rather, I would analyze respondent's claim in the terms employed by our precedents. Did the elevation of the charges against respondent "pose a realistic likelihood of vindictiveness?" Is it possible that "the fear of such vindictiveness may unconstitutionally deter" a person in respondent's position from exercising his statutory and constitutional right to a jury trial? The answer to these questions is plainly "Yes."

The Court suggests that the distinction between a bench trial and a jury trial is unimportant in this context. Such a suggestion is demonstrably fallacious. Experienced criminal practitioners, for both prosecution and defense, know that a jury trial entails far more prosecutorial work than a bench trial. Defense challenges to the potential-juror array, *voir dire* examination of potential jurors, and suppression hearings all take up a prosecutor's time before a jury trial, adding to his scheduling difficulties and caseload. More care in the preparation of his requested instructions, of his witnesses, and of his own remarks is necessary in order to avoid mistrial or reversible error. And there is always the specter of the "irrational" acquittal by a jury that is unreviewable on appeal. Thus it is simply inconceivable that a criminal defendant's election to be tried by jury would be a matter of indifference to his prosecutor. On the contrary, the prosecutor would almost always prefer that the defendant waive such a "troublesome" right. And if the defendant refuses to do so, the prosecutor's subsequent elevation of the charges against the defendant manifestly poses a realistic likelihood of vindictiveness.

The truth of my conclusion, and the patent fallacy of the Court's, is particularly evident on the record before us. The practical effect of respondent's demand for a jury trial was that the Government had to transfer the case from a trial before a Magistrate in Hyattsville to a trial before a District Judge and jury in Baltimore, and had to substitute one prosecutor for another. The Government thus suffered not only administrative inconvenience: It also lost the value of the preparation and services of the first prosecutor, and was forced to commit a second prosecutor to prepare the case from scratch. Thus, just as in *Blackledge*, respondent's election had the effect of "clearly requiring increased expenditures of prosecutorial resources before the defendant's conviction" could finally be achieved. And, to paraphrase *Blackledge*, "if the prosecutor has the means readily at hand to discourage such elections — by 'upping the ante' through a felony indictment — the State can insure that only the most hardy defendants will brave the hazards of a jury trial."

I conclude that the facts of this case easily support the inference of "a realistic likelihood of vindictiveness."

The Court discusses *Bordenkircher v. Hayes*, 434 U.S. 357 (1978) and suggests some analogy between that case and the present one. In my view, such an analogy is quite inapt. *Bordenkircher* dealt only with the context of plea bargaining and with the narrow situation in which the prosecutor "openly presented the defendant with the unpleasant alternatives of forgoing trial or facing increased charges." *Bordenkircher* did not remotely suggest that a pretrial increase in charges, made as a response to a demand for jury trial, would not present a realistic likelihood of vindictiveness when the demand put the prosecution to an added burden such as that imposed in this case. * * * *

The facts in this case plainly fit within the pattern of *Pearce* and *Blackledge*, not of *Bordenkircher*. There was no ongoing "give-and-take negotiation" between respondent and the Government, and there was the "unilateral imposition of a penalty" in response to respondent's choice "to exercise a legal right."

Because it seems clear to me that *Blackledge* requires it, I would affirm the judgment of the Court of Appeals.

Notes from Izzy:

1. While the majority rejects a *presumption* of "prosecutorial vindictiveness" here, the Court does say (in the text near footnote 19) that the defendant "in an appropriate case might prove objectively that the prosecutor's charging decision was motivated by a desire to punish him for doing something that the law plainly allowed him to do." What type of evidence would prove this — in light of what the Court permitted in *Bordenkircher* and *Goodwin*? Suppose the prosecutor had told Goodwin, "Too many defendants are demanding jury trials, and this is straining the resources of our office. If you demand a jury, I will increase the charges against you." Would this have raised the presumption?

2. In *State v. Phipps*, 959 S.W.2d 538 (Tenn.1997), the court held that "the State's pursuit of the death penalty following a successful appeal of a conviction for which the death penalty originally was not sought gives rise to a rebuttable presumption of prosecutorial vindictiveness."

PEOPLE v. KAIL
Illinois Appellate Court
501 N.E.2d 979 (1986)

JUSTICE WEBBER delivered the opinion of the court:

Defendant was charged by information in the circuit court of Champaign County with the offense of unlawful possession with intent to deliver more than 30 but not more than 500 grams of a substance containing cannabis in violation of section 705(d) of the Cannabis Control Act. * * * * At the conclusion of the trial, the court found defendant guilty and sentenced her to a term of 12 months. * * * *

The operative facts, briefly recapitulated, showed that on October 3, 1985, at approximately 10:47 p.m., defendant was riding a bicycle on a business sidewalk in the city of Champaign. According to the testimony of Officer Seeley, the arresting officer, she stopped defendant under a police-department policy requiring strict enforcement of all laws against suspected prostitutes, she suspected defendant to be a prostitute, and she would not have stopped defendant if she did not so suspect. After stopping defendant, Officer Seeley noticed that defendant's bicycle lacked a bell. Riding a bicycle on a business sidewalk and failing to equip the bicycle with a bell are violations of the Champaign city ordinances. Officer Seeley then charged defendant with failing to have a bell on her bicycle but did not charge her with riding a bicycle on a sidewalk. Because defendant lacked both adequate proof of identification and $50 to post bond, Officer Seeley arrested her, performed a "pat-down" search, handcuffed defendant and drove her to the police station where she was to be jailed until she could produce bond or proof of identification.

Preliminary to placing her in a cell, defendant was subjected to an inventory search during the course of which police uncovered the cannabis. * * * *

Because we find that defendant's right to equal protection was violated we do not address the other issues raised by her on appeal.

The State contends that the police department's policy of enforcing all ordinances against individuals it suspects of being prostitutes, but not against individuals not so suspected, furthers its legitimate goal to eradicate prostitution from the community.

We begin our analysis by stating what this case is and is not about. We are here confronted with the constitutionality of an administrative policy under which an otherwise constitutional ordinance is selectively enforced. This case does not involve a police officer's discretion to determine whether under the circumstances enforcement was warranted. Nor does this case involve the enforcement of a law the purpose of which is to combat prostitution. Rather, the law involved is an obscure minor ordinance the purpose of which is to assure a modicum of safety in warning of the approach of a bicycle.

While the State has broad discretion to enforce its laws, that discretion may not be exercised on the basis of an arbitrary classification. Claims of selective enforcement of the laws are appropriately judged according "to ordinary equal protection standards." *Wayte v. United States* (1985) 470 U.S. 598, 608. Where heightened scrutiny is inappropriate, the challenged State action is presumed to be valid and will be sustained where the classification is rationally related to a legitimate State interest. *Cleburne v. Cleburne Living Center* (1985) 473 U.S. 432. However, the State "may not rely on a classification whose relationship to an asserted goal is so attenuated as to render the distinction arbitrary or irrational." *Ibid.*

It is the duty of the courts to decide whether classifications bear a rational relationship to the law being enforced. The enforcement of an ordinance adopted by a city's governing body must satisfy the same requirement that is applicable to the enforcement of a statute enacted by the General Assembly. See *Chicago National League Ball Club, Inc. v. Thompson* (1985) 108 Ill.2d 357, 368.

The record in this case is clear. Officer Seeley testified that she stopped defendant pursuant to a police department policy to strictly enforce all ordinances against suspected prostitutes, that she suspected defendant of being a prostitute, and that she would not have stopped defendant but for her suspicion and the department's policy. Moreover, Officer Seeley acknowledged on cross-examination that she had, during the course of her three years of employment with the Champaign police department, seen literally hundreds, if not thousands of bicycles without bells around the Champaign university campus, but had not arrested anyone, prior to her arrest of defendant, for that offense.

While we recognize the State's right to legislate and enforce laws designed to combat prostitution, the law before us is of a different character. The purpose of the ordinance requiring a bell on a bicycle clearly does not envision the eradication of prostitution.

There is no conceivable set of facts which would establish a rational relationship between the class of suspected prostitutes and the State's legitimate interest in enforcing the ordinance requiring bells on bicycles. We can conceive of no such set of facts, and the State has failed to propound any. To suggest that the requirement of a bell on one's bicycle should be enforced only against suspected prostitutes because it helps combat prostitution is clearly so attenuated as to render the classification arbitrary or irrational.

Reversed.

JUSTICE GREEN, dissenting:

The majority correctly holds that the classification created by the policy of selective enforcement against suspected prostitutes is not a suspect classification requiring strict scrutiny but one subject to the rational basis test. A difficult question arises as to whether the rational basis must apply to the relationship between the enforcement policy and the law being enforced as the majority holds or between the enforcement policy and a legitimate governmental policy. A highly respected text discusses this question and indicates that the courts have not focused sharply upon the question. (LaFave & Israel, 2 *Criminal Procedure*, § 13.4 (1984).) I conclude that the better rule is to merely require the relationship between the selective policy and legitimate governmental policy to have a rational basis. Here, I would affirm.

In regard to selective prosecutions not subject to a direct scrutiny test, LaFave and Israel state in part:

> Yet another important issue regarding the meaning of the "rational relationship" test in this context concerns the subject matter against which the classification must appear to be rational. That is, is it sufficient "that the classification bear a rational relationship to a permissible governmental purpose," or must the classification be "rationally related to the purposes of the criminal law under which the defendant is charged"? More particularly, is it permissible to select out a person for prosecution under a particular law because of an unprovable belief that this individual is guilty of other criminal conduct? Though the propriety of such a charging policy has been vigorously debated by the commentators, the courts have given little attention to the question of whether such a policy is vulnerable on equal protection grounds. It would seem, however, that the extent of vulnerability depends upon the nature of the statute under which the prosecution is brought. Consider, for example, *United States v. Sacco* (9th Cir.1970), 428 F.2d 264, where the defendant objected that he was singled out, "based on his suspected role in organized crime," for investigation and prosecution under the alien registration laws.

> That this was the basis of selection was not disputed, yet the court unhesitantly held that it "cannot be said that that standard for selection is not rationally related to the purposes of the alien registration laws." In other words, it is quite rational, considering the purposes underlying the alien registration statute, to focus upon those aliens suspected not to be

law-abiding. One might well doubt whether the result would be the same were Sacco singled out on the same basis for prosecution under a generally nonenforced criminal adultery statute; there is nothing relating to the policies underlying that law which would explain a focus upon those suspected of organized crime. Yet, authority is to be found which would seemingly produce the same result on those facts. Illustrative in *People v. Mantel* (N.Y.Crim.Ct.1976), 388 N.Y.S.2d 565, where a task force of fire, safety and health inspectors made intensive and frequent inspections only of "sex related" businesses in the Times Square area after more traditional efforts to curb vice in that vicinity had failed. Stating the test as being "whether a particular classification bears a rational relationship to the broad purposes of the criminal law," the court upheld the practice. Whether the court would have reached the same result under the *Sacco* approach is problematical." LaFave & Israel, 2 Criminal Procedure § 13.4 (1984).

Neither *Wayte* nor *Cleburne* speaks to the question of whether the rational basis must be applied to the relationship between the selective policy and the offense to which it is being applied. In *Wayte*, the court held that a selective policy of prosecuting only those suspected violators of Selective Service registration requirements who had reported the violations themselves or had been reported by others met constitutional muster. No issue was raised as to whether a rational relationship between the offense being selectively prosecuted and legitimate governmental interest would suffice. In *Cleburne*, the issue was whether an ordinance which prohibited operation of a group home for mentally retarded in a particular area was unconstitutional as applied to the owners of a site, because of the lack of rational relationship between the ordinance and the legitimate governmental interests of the municipality.

The invalidation of the selective enforcement policy here will be of little impact, but the precedent being established will have substantial impact. It will prohibit selective enforcement focusing on those thought to be guilty of organized crime when the selective enforcement involves an offense unrelated to the criminal conspiracies of which the accused are suspected. No cases adopting the view of the majority have been called to my attention, and the cited text indicates that few if any of such decisions by a court of review exist.

I recognize that LaFave and Israel indicate that little authority exists in support of a theory that the rational relationship need exist only between the offense being selectively prosecuted and legitimate governmental interest and I respect their conclusion that such a relationship is insufficient to justify selective prosecution. However, when the classification upon which the selective policy is based is not suspect within equal protection concepts and there is a legitimate governmental interest served by the prosecution, I do not deem one prosecuted upon a showing of probable cause to be unduly prejudiced by the prosecution. Such a prosecution should not be constitutionally impermissible.

The legitimate governmental interest in deterring prostitution justified the instant policy of selective prosecution.

Notes from Izzy:

1. Is the dissent right? Will adoption of the majority approach stop "selective enforcement" against organized crime figures? If so, is this a bad thing? Is it wrong

for the federal government to take a closer look at the income tax returns (if any) of Mafia bosses? Or would such a policy inevitably lead to the type of investigation of Roy Cohn described at the outset of this chapter?

2. The ordinance Ms. Kail was arrested for violating seems rather trivial, and perhaps this influenced the majority. But perhaps the police department's policy of going after prostitutes was not at all trivial to the people who lived in that neighborhood. If evidence of this was presented in *Kail*, should that have changed the result?

UNITED STATES v. ARMSTRONG
United States Supreme Court
517 U.S. 456 (1996)

CHIEF JUSTICE REHNQUIST delivered the opinion of the Court.

In this case, we consider the showing necessary for a defendant to be entitled to discovery on a claim that the prosecuting attorney singled him out for prosecution on the basis of his race. We conclude that respondents failed to satisfy the threshold showing: They failed to show that the Government declined to prosecute similarly situated suspects of other races.

In April 1992, respondents were indicted in the United States District Court for the Central District of California on charges of conspiring to possess with intent to distribute more than 50 grams of cocaine base (crack) and conspiring to distribute the same, in violation of 21 U.S.C. §§ 841 and 846, and federal firearms offenses. For three months prior to the indictment, agents of the Federal Bureau of Alcohol, Tobacco, and Firearms and the Narcotics Division of the Inglewood, California, Police Department had infiltrated a suspected crack distribution ring by using three confidential informants. On seven separate occasions during this period, the informants had bought a total of 124.3 grams of crack from respondents and witnessed respondents carrying firearms during the sales. The agents searched the hotel room in which the sales were transacted, arrested respondents Armstrong and Hampton in the room, and found more crack and a loaded gun. The agents later arrested the other respondents as part of the ring.

In response to the indictment, respondents filed a motion for discovery* or for dismissal of the indictment, alleging that they were selected for federal prosecution because they are black. In support of their motion, they offered only an affidavit by a "Paralegal Specialist," employed by the Office of the Federal Public Defender representing one of the respondents. The only allegation in the affidavit was that, in every one of the 24 § 841 or § 846 cases closed by the office during 1991, the defendant was black. Accompanying the affidavit was a "study" listing the 24 defendants, their race, whether they were prosecuted for dealing cocaine as well as crack, and the status of each case.

The Government opposed the discovery motion, arguing, among other things, that there was no evidence or allegation "that the Government has acted unfairly or has prosecuted non-black defendants or failed to prosecute them." The District

---

* [Ed.: Apparently, the discovery motion sought "documents . . . that discuss the government's strategy for cocaine cases."]

Court granted the motion. It ordered the Government (1) to provide a list of all cases from the last three years in which the Government charged both cocaine and firearms offenses, (2) to identify the race of the defendants in those cases, (3) to identify what levels of law enforcement were involved in the investigations of those cases, and (4) to explain its criteria for deciding to prosecute those defendants for federal cocaine offenses.

The Government moved for reconsideration of the District Court's discovery order. With this motion it submitted affidavits and other evidence to explain why it had chosen to prosecute respondents and why respondents' study did not support the inference that the Government was singling out blacks for cocaine prosecution. The federal and local agents participating in the case alleged in affidavits that race played no role in their investigation. An Assistant United States Attorney explained in an affidavit that the decision to prosecute met the general criteria for prosecution, because

> There was over 100 grams of cocaine base involved, over twice the threshold necessary for a ten year mandatory minimum sentence; there were multiple sales involving multiple defendants, thereby indicating a fairly substantial crack cocaine ring; there were multiple federal firearms violations intertwined with the narcotics trafficking; the overall evidence in the case was extremely strong, including audio and videotapes of defendants; and several of the defendants had criminal histories including narcotics and firearms violations.

The Government also submitted sections of a published 1989 Drug Enforcement Administration report which concluded that "large-scale, interstate trafficking networks controlled by Jamaicans, Haitians and Black street gangs dominate the manufacture and distribution of crack." J. Featherly & E. Hill, *Crack Cocaine Overview* 1989.

In response, one of respondents' attorneys submitted an affidavit alleging that an intake coordinator at a drug treatment center had told her that there are "an equal number of Caucasian users and dealers to minority users and dealers." Respondents also submitted an affidavit from a criminal defense attorney alleging that in his experience many nonblacks are prosecuted in state court for crack offenses, and a newspaper article reporting that Federal "crack criminals are being punished far more severely than if they had been caught with powder cocaine, and almost every single one of them is black," Newton, Harsher Crack Sentences Criticized as Racial Inequity, Los Angeles Times, Nov. 23, 1992, p. 1.

The District Court denied the motion for reconsideration. When the Government indicated it would not comply with the court's discovery order, the court dismissed the case.[2]

A divided three-judge panel of the Court of Appeals for the Ninth Circuit reversed, holding that, because of the proof requirements for a selective — prosecution claim, defendants must "provide a colorable basis for believing that others similarly situated have not been prosecuted" to obtain discovery. The Court

---

[2] We have never determined whether dismissal of the indictment, or some other sanction, is the proper remedy if a court determines that a defendant has been the victim of prosecution on the basis of his race. Here, "it was the government itself that suggested dismissal of the indictments to the district court so that an appeal might lie."

of Appeals voted to rehear the case en banc, and the en banc panel affirmed the District Court's order of dismissal, holding that "a defendant is not required to demonstrate that the government has failed to prosecute others who are similarly situated." We granted certiorari to determine the appropriate standard for discovery for a selective-prosecution claim. * * * *

Under Federal Rules of Criminal Procedure, Rule 16(a)(1), a defendant may examine documents material to his defense, but, under Rule 16(a)(2), he may not examine Government work product in connection with his case. If a selective-prosecution claim is a "defense," Rule 16(a)(1) gives the defendant the right to examine Government work product in every prosecution except his own. Because respondents' construction of "defense" creates the anomaly of a defendant's being able to examine all Government work product except the most pertinent, we find their construction implausible. We hold that Rule 16(a)(1) authorizes defendants to examine Government documents material to the preparation of their defense against the Government's case-in-chief, but not to the preparation of selective-prosecution claims. * * * *

A selective-prosecution claim is not a defense on the merits to the criminal charge itself, but an independent assertion that the prosecutor has brought the charge for reasons forbidden by the Constitution. Our cases delineating the necessary elements to prove a claim of selective prosecution have taken great pains to explain that the standard is a demanding one. These cases afford a "background presumption," that the showing necessary to obtain discovery should itself be a significant barrier to the litigation of insubstantial claims.

A selective-prosecution claim asks a court to exercise judicial power over a "special province" of the Executive. The Attorney General and United States Attorneys retain "broad discretion" to enforce the Nation's criminal laws. *United States v. Goodwin*, 457 U.S. 368, 380, n. 11 (1982). They have this latitude because they are designated by statute as the President's delegates to help him discharge his constitutional responsibility to "take Care that the Laws be faithfully executed." U.S. Const., Art. II, § 3. As a result, "the presumption of regularity supports" their prosecutorial decisions and "in the absence of clear evidence to the contrary, courts presume that they have properly discharged their official duties." *United States v. Chemical Foundation, Inc.*, 272 U.S. 1, 14–15 (1926). In the ordinary case, "so long as the prosecutor has probable cause to believe that the accused committed an offense defined by statute, the decision whether or not to prosecute, and what charge to file or bring before a grand jury, generally rests entirely in his discretion." *Bordenkircher v. Hayes*, 434 U.S. 357, 364 (1978).

Of course, a prosecutor's discretion is subject to constitutional constraints. One of these constraints, imposed by the equal protection component of the Due Process Clause of the Fifth Amendment, is that the decision whether to prosecute may not be based on "an unjustifiable standard such as race, religion, or other arbitrary classification," *Oyler v. Boles*, 368 U.S. 448, 456 (1962). A defendant may demonstrate that the administration of a criminal law is "directed so exclusively against a particular class of persons with a mind so unequal and oppressive" that the system of prosecution amounts to "a practical denial" of equal protection of the law. *Yick Wo v. Hopkins*, 118 U.S. 356, 373 (1886).

In order to dispel the presumption that a prosecutor has not violated equal protection, a criminal defendant must present "clear evidence to the contrary."

Chemical Foundation, supra, at 14–15. We explained in *Wayte v. U.S.* why courts are "properly hesitant to examine the decision whether to prosecute." 470 U.S. 598, 608 (1985). Judicial deference to the decisions of these executive officers rests in part on an assessment of the relative competence of prosecutors and courts. "Such factors as the strength of the case, the prosecution's general deterrence value, the Government's enforcement priorities, and the case's relationship to the Government's overall enforcement plan are not readily susceptible to the kind of analysis the courts are competent to undertake." *Id.* at 607. It also stems from a concern not to unnecessarily impair the performance of a core executive constitutional function. "Examining the basis of a prosecution delays the criminal proceeding, threatens to chill law enforcement by subjecting the prosecutor's motives and decisionmaking to outside inquiry, and may undermine prosecutorial effectiveness by revealing the Government's enforcement policy." Ibid.

The requirements for a selective-prosecution claim draw on "ordinary equal protection standards." *Id.* at 608. The claimant must demonstrate that the federal prosecutorial policy "had a discriminatory effect and that it was motivated by a discriminatory purpose." *Ibid.* To establish a discriminatory effect in a race case, the claimant must show that similarly situated individuals of a different race were not prosecuted. * * * *

Having reviewed the requirements to prove a selective-prosecution claim, we turn to the showing necessary to obtain discovery in support of such a claim. If discovery is ordered, the Government must assemble from its own files documents which might corroborate or refute the defendant's claim. Discovery thus imposes many of the costs present when the Government must respond to a prima facie case of selective prosecution. It will divert prosecutors' resources and may disclose the Government's prosecutorial strategy. The justifications for a rigorous standard for the elements of a selective — prosecution claim thus require a correspondingly rigorous standard for discovery in aid of such a claim.

The parties, and the Courts of Appeals which have considered the requisite showing to establish entitlement to discovery, describe this showing with a variety of phrases, like "colorable basis," "substantial threshold showing," "substantial and concrete basis," or "reasonable likelihood." However, the many labels for this showing conceal the degree of consensus about the evidence necessary to meet it. The Courts of Appeals "require some evidence tending to show the existence of the essential elements of the defense," discriminatory effect and discriminatory intent. *United States v. Berrios*, 501 F.2d 1207, 1211 (C.A. 1974).

In this case we consider what evidence constitutes "some evidence tending to show the existence" of the discriminatory effect element. The Court of Appeals held that a defendant may establish a colorable basis for discriminatory effect without evidence that the Government has failed to prosecute others who are similarly situated to the defendant. We think it was mistaken in this view. The vast majority of the Courts of Appeals require the defendant to produce some evidence that similarly situated defendants of other races could have been prosecuted, but were not, and this requirement is consistent with our equal protection case law. As the three-judge panel explained, "selective prosecution implies that a selection has taken place."[3]

---

[3] We reserve the question whether a defendant must satisfy the similarly situated requirement in a case involving direct admissions by [prosecutors] of discriminatory purpose.

The Court of Appeals reached its decision in part because it started "with the presumption that people of *all* races commit *all* types of crimes — not with the premise that any type of crime is the exclusive province of any particular racial or ethnic group." It cited no authority for this proposition, which seems contradicted by the most recent statistics of the United States Sentencing Commission. Those statistics show that: More than 90% of the persons sentenced in 1994 for crack cocaine trafficking were black, United States Sentencing Common, 1994 Annual Report 107 (Table 45); 93.4% of convicted LSD dealers were white, ibid.; and 91% of those convicted for pornography or prostitution were white, id., at 41 (Table 13). Presumptions at war with presumably reliable statistics have no proper place in the analysis of this issue.

The Court of Appeals also expressed concern about the "evidentiary obstacles defendants face." But all of its sister Circuits that have confronted the issue have required that defendants produce some evidence of differential treatment of similarly situated members of other races or protected classes. In the present case, if the claim of selective prosecution were well founded, it should not have been an insuperable task to prove that persons of other races were being treated differently than respondents. For instance, respondents could have investigated whether similarly situated persons of other races were prosecuted by the State of California, were known to federal law enforcement officers, but were not prosecuted in federal court. We think the required threshold — a credible showing of different treatment of similarly situated persons — adequately balances the Government's interest in vigorous prosecution and the defendant's interest in avoiding selective prosecution.

In the case before us, respondents' "study" did not constitute "some evidence tending to show the existence of the essential elements of" a selective-prosecution claim. The study failed to identify individuals who were not black, could have been prosecuted for the offenses for which respondents were charged, but were not so prosecuted. This omission was not remedied by respondents' evidence in opposition to the Government's motion for reconsideration. The newspaper article, which discussed the discriminatory effect of federal drug sentencing laws, was not relevant to an allegation of discrimination in decisions to prosecute. Respondents' affidavits, which recounted one attorney's conversation with a drug treatment center employee and the experience of another attorney defending drug prosecutions in state court, recounted hearsay and reported personal conclusions based on anecdotal evidence. The judgment of the Court of Appeals is therefore reversed, and the case is remanded for proceedings consistent with this opinion.

JUSTICE STEVENS, dissenting.

Federal prosecutors are respected members of a respected profession. Despite an occasional misstep, the excellence of their work abundantly justifies the presumption that "they have properly discharged their official duties." *United States v. Chemical Foundation, Inc.*, 272 U.S. 1, 14–15 (1926). Nevertheless, the possibility that political or racial animosity may infect a decision to institute criminal proceedings cannot be ignored. *Oyler v. Boles*, 368 U.S. 448, 456 (1962). For that reason, it has long been settled that the prosecutor's broad discretion to determine when criminal charges should be filed is not completely unbridled. As the Court notes, however, the scope of judicial review of particular exercises of that discretion is not fully defined.

The United States Attorney for the Central District of California is a member and an officer of the bar of that District Court. As such, she has a duty to the judges of that Court to maintain the standards of the profession in the performance of her official functions. If a District Judge has reason to suspect that she, or a member of her staff, has singled out particular defendants for prosecution on the basis of their race, it is surely appropriate for the Judge to determine whether there is a factual basis for such a concern. I agree with the Court that Rule 16 of the Federal Rules of Criminal Procedure is not the source of the District Court's power to make the necessary inquiry. I disagree, however, with its implicit assumption that a different, relatively rigid rule needs to be crafted to regulate the use of this seldom-exercised inherent judicial power.

The Court correctly concludes that in this case the facts presented to the District Court in support of respondents' claim that they had been singled out for prosecution because of their race were not sufficient to prove that defense. Moreover, I agree with the Court that their showing was not strong enough to give them *a right* to discovery, either under Rule 16 or under the District Court's inherent power to order discovery in appropriate circumstances. Like Chief Judge Wallace of the Court of Appeals, however, I am persuaded that the District Judge did not abuse her discretion when she concluded that the factual showing was sufficiently disturbing to require some response from the United States Attorney's Office. Perhaps the discovery order was broader than necessary, but I cannot agree with the Court's apparent conclusion that no inquiry was permissible.

The District Judge's order should be evaluated in light of three circumstances that underscore the need for judicial vigilance over certain types of drug prosecutions.

First, the Anti-Drug Abuse Act of 1986 and subsequent legislation established a regime of extremely high penalties for the possession and distribution of so-called "crack" cocaine. Those provisions treat one gram of crack as the equivalent of 100 grams of powder cocaine. The distribution of 50 grams of crack is thus punishable by the same mandatory minimum sentence of 10 years in prison that applies to the distribution of 5,000 grams of powder cocaine.[2] The Sentencing Guidelines extend this ratio to penalty levels above the mandatory minimums: for any given quantity of crack, the guideline range is the same as if the offense had involved 100 times that amount in powder cocaine. These penalties result in sentences for crack offenders that average three to eight times longer than sentences for comparable powder offenders.

Second, the disparity between the treatment of crack cocaine and powder cocaine is matched by the disparity between the severity of the punishment imposed by federal law and that imposed by state law for the same conduct. For a variety of reasons, often including the absence of mandatory minimums, the existence of parole, and lower baseline penalties, terms of imprisonment for drug offenses tend to be substantially lower in state systems than in the federal system. The difference

---

[2] Compare 21 U.S.C. s 841(b)(1)(A)(iii) with s 841(b)(1)(A)(ii). Similarly, a mandatory 5-year sentence is prescribed for distribution of 500 grams of cocaine or 5 grams of crack. Compare s 841(b)(1)(B)(ii) with s 841(b)(1)(B)(iii). Simple possession of 5 grams of crack also produces a mandatory 5-year sentence. The maximum sentence for possession of any quantity of other drugs is one year. s 844(a). With one prior felony drug offense, the sentence for distribution of 50 grams of crack is a mandatory 20 years to life. s 841(b)(1)(A). With two prior felony drug offenses, the sentence is a mandatory life term without parole. Ibid.

is especially marked in the case of crack offenses. The majority of States draw no distinction between types of cocaine in their penalty schemes; of those that do, none has established as stark a differential as the Federal Government. For example, if respondent Hampton is found guilty, his federal sentence might be as long as a mandatory life term. Had he been tried in state court, his sentence could have been as short as 12 years, less worktime credits of half that amount.[5]

Finally, it is undisputed that the brunt of the elevated federal penalties falls heavily on blacks. While 65% of the persons who have used crack are white, in 1993 they represented only 4% of the federal offenders convicted of trafficking in crack. Eighty-eight percent of such defendants were black. During the first 18 months of full guideline implementation, the sentencing disparity between black and white defendants grew from preguideline levels: blacks on average received sentences over 40% longer than whites. See Bureau of Justice Statistics, *Sentencing in the Federal Courts: Does Race Matter?* 6–7 (Dec.1993). Those figures represent a major threat to the integrity of federal sentencing reform, whose main purpose was the elimination of disparity (especially racial) in sentencing. The Sentencing Commission acknowledges that the heightened crack penalties are a "primary cause of the growing disparity between sentences for Black and White federal defendants." Special Report 163.

The extraordinary severity of the imposed penalties and the troubling racial patterns of enforcement give rise to a special concern about the fairness of charging practices for crack offenses. Evidence tending to prove that black defendants charged with distribution of crack in the Central District of California are prosecuted in federal court, whereas members of other races charged with similar offenses are prosecuted in state court, warrants close scrutiny by the federal judges in that District. In my view, the District Judge, who has sat on both the federal and the state benches in Los Angeles, acted well within her discretion to call for the development of facts that would demonstrate what standards, if any, governed the choice of forum where similarly situated offenders are prosecuted.

Respondents submitted a study showing that of all cases involving crack offenses that were closed by the Federal Public Defender's Office in 1991, 24 out of 24 involved black defendants. To supplement this evidence, they submitted affidavits from two of the attorneys in the defense team. The first reported a statement from an intake coordinator at a local drug treatment center that, in his experience, an equal number of crack users and dealers were Caucasian as belonged to minorities. The second was from David R. Reed, counsel for respondent Armstrong. Reed was both an active court-appointed attorney in the Central District of California and one of the directors of the leading association of criminal defense lawyers who practice before the Los Angeles County courts. Reed stated that he did not recall

---

[5] Hampton was charged with conspiracy to distribute, four counts of crack distribution, and the use or carrying of a firearm in relation to a drug crime. According to an information filed by the Government, Hampton had three prior convictions for felony drug offenses. Therefore, he potentially faces a mandatory life sentence on the drug charges alone.

Under California law at the time of the offenses, possession for sale of cocaine base involving 50 grams carried a penalty of imprisonment for either three, four, or five years. Cal. Health & Safety Code § 11351.5. If the defendant had no prior convictions, he could be granted probation. § 11370. For each prior felony drug conviction, the defendant received an additional 3-year sentence. § 11370.2. Thus, with three priors and the possibility of worktime reductions, see Cal.Penal Code § 2933, Hampton could have served as little as six years under California law. Since the time of the offenses, California has raised several of these penalties, but the new punishments could not be applied to respondents.

"ever handling a crack cocaine case involving non-black defendants" in federal court, nor had he even heard of one. He further stated that "there are many crack cocaine sales cases prosecuted in state court that do involve racial groups other than blacks."

The majority discounts the probative value of the affidavits, claiming that they recounted "hearsay" and reported "personal conclusions based on anecdotal evidence." But the Reed affidavit plainly contained more than mere hearsay; Reed offered information based on his own extensive experience in both federal and state courts. Given the breadth of his background, he was well qualified to compare the practices of federal and state prosecutors. In any event, the Government never objected to the admission of either affidavit on hearsay or any other grounds. It was certainly within the District Court's discretion to credit the affidavits of two members of the bar of that Court, at least one of whom had presumably acquired a reputation by his frequent appearances there, and both of whose statements were made on pains of perjury.

The criticism that the affidavits were based on "anecdotal evidence" is also unpersuasive. I thought it was agreed that defendants do not need to prepare sophisticated statistical studies in order to receive mere discovery in cases like this one. Certainly evidence based on a drug counselor's personal observations or on an attorney's practice in two sets of courts, state and federal, can "tend to show the existence" of a selective prosecution.

Even if respondents failed to carry their burden of showing that there were individuals who were not black but who could have been prosecuted in federal court for the same offenses, it does not follow that the District Court abused its discretion in ordering discovery. There can be no doubt that such individuals exist, and indeed the Government has never denied the same. In those circumstances, I fail to see why the District Court was unable to take judicial notice of this obvious fact and demand information from the Government's files to support or refute respondents' evidence. The presumption that some whites are prosecuted in state court is not "contradicted" by the statistics the majority cites, which show only that high percentages of blacks are convicted of certain federal crimes, while high percentages of whites are convicted of other federal crimes. Those figures are entirely consistent with the allegation of selective prosecution. The relevant comparison, rather, would be with the percentages of blacks and whites who commit those crimes. But, as discussed above, in the case of crack far greater numbers of whites are believed guilty of using the substance. The District Court, therefore, was entitled to find the evidence before her significant and to require some explanation from the Government.[6]

In sum, I agree with the Sentencing Commission that "while the exercise of discretion by prosecutors and investigators has an impact on sentences in almost all

---

[6] Also telling was the Government's response to respondents' evidentiary showing. It submitted a list of more than 3,500 defendants who had been charged with federal narcotics violations over the previous 3 years. It also offered the names of 11 nonblack defendants whom it had prosecuted for crack offenses. All 11, however, were members of other racial or ethnic minorities. The District Court was authorized to draw adverse inferences from the Government's inability to produce a single example of a white defendant, especially when the very purpose of its exercise was to allay the Court's concerns about the evidence of racially selective prosecutions. As another court has said: "Statistics are not, of course, the whole answer, but nothing is as emphatic as zero. . . ." *United States v. Hinds County School Bd.*, 417 F.2d 852, 858 (C.A.5 1969).

cases to some extent, because of the 100-to-1 quantity ratio and federal mandatory minimum penalties, discretionary decisions in cocaine cases often have dramatic effects." Special Report 138.[7] The severity of the penalty heightens both the danger of arbitrary enforcement and the need for careful scrutiny of any colorable claim of discriminatory enforcement. In this case, the evidence was sufficiently disturbing to persuade the District Judge to order discovery that might help explain the conspicuous racial pattern of cases before her Court. I cannot accept the majority's conclusion that the District Judge either exceeded her power or abused her discretion when she did so. I therefore respectfully dissent.

Notes from Izzy:

1. *U.S. v. Turner*, 104 F.3d 1180 (9th Cir.1997), black defendants charged with sale of crack cocaine sought discovery of government information regarding the race of people charged with this crime and government manuals showing policies regarding whom to arrest or prosecute for this crime. Opposing the motion, the prosecutor presented the affidavit of Ronald Iden, the FBI agent in charge of the Los Angeles office.

> Iden submitted data showing that within Los Angeles County much of the violent crime committed by street gangs, such as robbery, assault, and murder, was connected to illegal drug trafficking. He stated his own belief that "no single event has contributed more to the explosive growth of violent street gangs within the United States than the wide availability of cocaine base ('crack' or 'rock' cocaine) within American cities since the mid-to late 1980s." He identified two violent street gangs, the Bloods and the Crips, as the most notorious of the gangs, deriving tremendous profits by trafficking crack cocaine to other cities and expanding their activities throughout the United States.

> Iden explained federal prosecution policy by observing that "often, narcotics investigations are used to dismantle violent criminal gangs" and that the "enforcement of the federal laws regarding crack cocaine was one weapon in addressing the problem of gang-related violent crimes in the City of Los Angeles and elsewhere in the Central District." He filed under seal the composition of the enforcement groups investigating violent street gangs and the gangs that they were investigating. He declared: "At no time is race or ethnicity ever a factor in any decision by the FBI."

The trial court ordered discovery. The government declined to provide it, and the charges were dismissed. The government appealed, and the Court of Appeals reversed, relying on *Armstrong*.

> The defendants have shown no more than the consequences of the investigation of violent street gangs, not that they were targeted because of

---

[7] For this and other reasons, the Sentencing Commission in its Special Report to Congress "strongly recommended against a 100-to-1 quantity ratio." Special Report 198. The Commission shortly thereafter, by a 4-to-3 vote, amended the guidelines so as to equalize the treatment of crack and other forms of cocaine, and proposed modification of the statutory mandatory minimum penalties for crack offenses. In October 1995, Congress overrode the Sentencing Commission's guideline amendments. Nevertheless, Congress at the same time directed the Commission to submit recommendations regarding changes to the statutory and guideline penalties for cocaine distribution, including specifically "revision of the drug quantity ratio of crack cocaine to powder cocaine."

race. That such gangs should be targeted is a neutral, nonracial law enforcement decision; the distribution of cocaine by gang members inclined to violence makes the distribution more heinous and more dangerous than the single sale of cocaine by individuals. The appellees have offered no evidence whatsoever of an intent on the part of the prosecutors to prosecute them on account of their race, and the prosecutors and FBI investigators have under oath denied such motivation. No reason was given by the district court to doubt the "background presumption" that United States Attorneys are properly discharging their duties, no reason given to doubt the integrity of prosecutors and investigators whose honesty, good faith, and absence of racial bias are unimpaired by anything in evidence before the court. The district court seems to have neither given credence to the affidavits that the government placed before it nor explained why the affidavits were not credible. The government had not taken the posture attributed to it by the court that it had no obligation to provide the information on which its prosecutions rested. The government had provided precisely that information. The discovery requests failed to meet the sine qua non for discovery attendant on a selective prosecution claim. It was an abuse of discretion for the court to grant them.

The appellees offer this hypothetical: if the government set up a road block in Beverly Hills it would end up catching and prosecuting Caucasian criminals. Analogously, the government has set up the equivalent of a road block in South Central Los Angeles and so ends up catching and prosecuting African Americans. The thesis of the appellees is that selection of a particular community for a particular enforcement operation constitutes racial discrimination if it is foreseeable that because of the ethnic composition of the community one race will necessarily provide most of the government's targets.

The defendants' hypothetical has a superficial attraction but is seriously flawed. It is not entirely unnatural for an observer noting ethnic identity to come to the conclusion that when almost all the defendants charged with a particular offense have a certain skin color or ethnic identity that a racial or ethnic prejudice must be at work in the selection. Such an observer, however, must not be very familiar with the demographic and occupational patterns of the United States. Despite our reputation as a melting pot, different neighborhoods and different occupations often attract distinct racial or ethnic groups; so that if a particular kind of crime comes into vogue it may well be a feature of a neighborhood or of an occupation marked by one or another ethnic or racial characteristic.

In effect, as applied in this case, the defendants' hypothetical is an argument that the minorities of the inner city of Los Angeles must be denied the protection of law enforcement by the federal government because the likely suspects are overwhelmingly apt to be members of the minority living in that area. The defense is a grave perversion of proper sensitivity to the civil liberty of minorities. If any policy of government had a racially discriminatory effect, it would be to deny law enforcement on the grounds of a specious claim of racial discrimination.

2. In *U.S. v. Tuitt*, 68 F.Supp.2d 4 (D.Mass. 1999), Tuitt sought discovery to support his claim that the Government selected blacks and Hispanics to prosecute in federal

court for selling cocaine. Defense counsel contacted attorneys who represented defendants in *state* cases on similar charges in the same geographical area, learning that 10% of the defendants were white. None of the *federal* defendants were white. The population of the geographical area was 78% white and 10% black. The court noted that here, unlike *Armstrong*, defense counsel had "undertaken a comprehensive survey of local state courts in order to provide an appropriate comparison." The court granted the motion for discovery — even though the defense presented no direct evidence of discriminatory *intent*:

> When discussing selective prosecution, *Armstrong* speaks of both discriminatory effect and discriminatory intent. *Armstrong* also acknowledges the "degree of consensus" that courts of appeals have reached in establishing the requisite showing for discovery with respect to selective prosecution: " 'some evidence tending to show the existence of the essential elements of the defense,' discriminatory effect and discriminatory intent." However, in discussing the discovery issue, the Court claims to address the discriminatory effect element only. Thus, it is hard to tell what evidence of intent a defendant must produce in order to obtain discovery. As described above, prima facie evidence of effect is difficult enough to adduce.
>
> Given the Supreme Court's actual analysis of the evidence offered in *Armstrong*, however, which in some ways appears to conflate the elements of effect and intent, this court believes that the evidence proffered by Defendant in the present matter more than adequately meets the rigorous discovery standard imposed. A discriminatory effect which is severe enough can provide sufficient evidence of discriminatory purpose. See *Gomillion v. Lightfoot*, 364 U.S. 339 (1960); *Yick Wo v. Hopkins*, 118 U.S. 356 (1886). If the Supreme Court meant to hold defendants to actual knowledge of a discriminatory choice on the part of a prosecutor — which, after all, would encompass the underlying claim of selective prosecution — the discovery standard would be impossible to meet. It is exceedingly rare for a prosecutor to admit that the decision to prosecute was based on ethnicity or nationality.
>
> There can be no doubt that the sufficiency of evidence of both effect and intent for discovery purposes must be resolved on a case-by-case basis. This, of course, is easier said than done. For example, the evidence proffered by Defendant is not quite the same as the information suggested in the example offered by Justice Rehnquist in *Armstrong*, namely, "whether similarly situated persons of other races were prosecuted by the State of California and were known to federal law enforcement officers, but were not prosecuted in federal court." While Defendant clearly has met the first portion of the example, i.e., similarly situated whites prosecuted by the Commonwealth of Massachusetts, he offers no inside information, whether direct or anecdotal, of a deliberate choice on the part of the Government not to prosecute such individuals in federal court. Nonetheless, while Defendant's proffer may fall short of Justice Rehnquist's example, it more than adequately passes muster under the actual standard set by the Court. * * * *
>
> Defendant has taken up the gauntlet here and has provided the very information suggested. Relying on both federal and state court data for

comparable periods of time, Defendant has demonstrated not only that no whites have been prosecuted in federal court, as was the case in *Armstrong*, but that similarly situated whites have been prosecuted in state court. At bottom, it appears from Defendant's proffer, as described above, that whites are committing crack cocaine offenses in the western section of the district court but are not being prosecuted federally.

3. In *U.S. v. Jones*, 159 F.3d 969 (6th Cir.1998), black defendant Climmie Jones moved to dismiss his indictment on narcotics and weapons charges, claiming "race-based selective prosecution."

Jones contends that the district court erred in denying his motion to dismiss the indictment because of alleged race-based selective prosecution. In the alternative, Jones argues that the district court erred by denying his motion to compel discovery.[3] The district court held a hearing and concluded that Jones had not established a selective prosecution claim, nor entitlement to discovery on the issue. Jones argues on appeal that he was prosecuted based on his race, citing to the Government's decision to prosecute him in federal court instead of state court and the egregious and unprofessional conduct of the arresting local law enforcement officers, Kerry Nelson and Terry Spence.

The conduct of officers Nelson and Spence was undeniably shameful. Prior to the planned arrest of Jones and his wife, the two officers had t-shirts made with Jones's picture emblazoned on the front accompanied by the printed words, "See ya, wouldn't want to be ya" above the picture, and below, "going back to prison." On the back of the t-shirts appeared a picture of Jones's wife, a co-defendant, with the words, "wait on me, Slow[4], I am coming, too." The two officers were wearing the t-shirts when they arrested Jones in August of 1995.

Over one year later, while on a Caribbean cruise, Officer Spence mailed a postcard purchased in Jamaica to Jones while he was in custody awaiting trial. Jones regards Spence's mailing of the postcard, that pictured a black woman with a basket of bananas on her head, as a racial insult. On the postcard, postmarked from Cozumel, Mexico on October 24, 1996, appeared the following handwritten message:

> Climmie, Slow Motion. What's up? Haven't talked to you since you were in court and lost all your motions. Sorry, but life goes on. Just wanted to drop you a line and let you know that Cozumel, Mexico is beautiful. I'm on vacation and I'll be back Monday for trial, and chances

---

[3] Jones sought through discovery: (1) names and arrest reports from the Rutherford County Sheriff's Department for the past five years which concern non-African-American individuals charged with felonious possession or distribution of crack cocaine; (2) names and arrest records from the Drug Enforcement Agency office in Nashville that concern non-African-American individuals charged with felonious possession or distribution of crack cocaine; and (3) the names and docket numbers maintained by the U.S. Attorney's office in Nashville for the past five years which concern non-African-American individuals charged with felonious possession or distribution of crack cocaine. Because a selective prosecution claim is not a defense to the merits of a criminal charge but, instead, an independent assertion of misconduct, discovery is not available pursuant to Fed.R.Crim.P. 16. See *United States v. Armstrong*, 517 U.S. 456, 463 (1996). Thus, a defendant must make a showing that he is entitled to discovery. See *id.* at 464.

[4] One of the appellant's aliases, short for another alias, "Slow Motion."

are good you're going to jail for a long time. See ya, Officer Spence.

Spence testified that he sent the postcard to relieve "stress I was feeling while I was on the cruise." Regarding the t-shirts, Spence explained that "It was just — I took pride in arresting Jones." Nelson also testified that he wore the t-shirt to demonstrate "a great deal of pride in Mr. Jones's arrest."

In addition, there was testimony at the hearing with respect to Jones's claim that local law enforcement agents improperly referred his case for federal prosecution based on his race. The testimony showed that the Murfreesboro Police Department had referred fourteen defendants, including Jones and his Caucasian co-defendant, Donnie Billings, for federal prosecution in the preceding five years. Of those fourteen defendants, four were African-American, two were Columbian, two were Lebanese, one was Israeli and five were Caucasian. Of the cases referred for federal prosecution in the preceding five years, however, only Jones's and Billings's prosecutions involved crack cocaine. Further, Jones presented evidence of eight non-African-American defendants prosecuted for crack cocaine offenses who were not referred for federal prosecution.

Following the hearing, the district court found no evidence of a discriminatory motive or intent on the part of law enforcement personnel in investigating or prosecuting the case. The district court found that the primary reason that Jones was prosecuted in federal court was the danger that he posed to the community generally and law enforcement specifically, based on his previous arrest for drug trafficking and threats he had made to police officers. Although denying Jones's selective prosecution claim and his request for discovery on the claim, the district court expressed its outrage at the conduct of the local law enforcement officers:

> It is, in my view, highly unprofessional. The Murfreesboro and Rutherford County police officers need to quit acting like children and act like grownups.

> The fact that this police department would wear these t-shirts with Mr. Jones' face on them and his wife's face on them and send these kind of postcards, in my view, is absolutely outrageous, unprofessional, childish and generally disgusting, and without thinking of the dignity of the process or people, that is just not the way professional law enforcement people operate. The postcard particularly upsets me. We had a suppression hearing, we had some evidence about the t-shirts, everybody knew, I believe, that that was, in the least embarrassing, at the most could affect the case and generally was, I think, not a high point for the government to say that lightly. Then Mr. Spence after the suppression hearing and after knowing all that mails this postcard. So, it is, in my mind, just unbelievable that an adult would do that.

> I wanted to put my thoughts on the record so that the mayor or county executive or chief of police or anyone who should see fit for reviewing my comments and take appropriate action if necessary and if warranted.[6]

---

[6] As of oral argument, no action had been taken. The Murfreesboro Police Department's failure to

Jones now asks this court to reverse the district court's denial of his selective prosecution claim and dismiss the indictment. Alternatively, he asks that we remand the case to compel discovery on the issue.

Jones urges us to consider the postcard, t-shirts, his referral for federal prosecution and the fact that his Caucasian co-defendant was not originally a target of the investigation as prima facie evidence of selective prosecution. Because the determination of the merits of a selective prosecution claim is essentially a factual inquiry, we review such a determination for clear error.

To prevail on a selective prosecution claim, a defendant must show that the federal prosecutorial policy had both a discriminatory effect and a discriminatory intent. See *United States v. Armstrong*, 517 U.S. 456, 465 (1996). To establish discriminatory intent in a case alleging selective prosecution based on race, a claimant must show that the prosecutorial policy was motivated by racial animus; to establish discriminatory effect, the claimant must demonstrate that similarly situated individuals of a different race were not similarly prosecuted. *Id.* (noting that the requirements for such a claim draw on "ordinary equal protection standards").

We conclude that Jones has established a *prima facie* case of discriminatory intent. The conduct of Officers Spence and Nelson was not only outrageous and unprofessional, but also racially motivated. Although there were three individuals involved in this case (Jones, his wife and co-defendant Donnie Billings), only Jones and his wife were African-American. The officers made t-shirts for only those two. Moreover, any argument premised on the fact that Billings was not as involved in the crime as Jones fails, because Jones's wife was no more involved than Billings and yet a t-shirt was made with her picture. We also reject the officers' purported reason for making the t-shirts — that they took pride in the arrests. For some reason, this pride manifested itself in a way that the department had never done before, because this was the first time that such t-shirts were present at an arrest or a search scene.

Additionally, Spence's mailing of the postcard evidences racial animus. Even if we were to discount the obvious impropriety of mailing a postcard, any postcard, to a criminal defendant awaiting trial, we could not so easily disregard the nature of the postcard mailed to Jones. The officer sent to an African-American man a postcard of an African-American woman with bananas on her head, and did not choose any other available postcards such as the sunset or the beach. Jones testified at his sentencing hearing that to him the postcard meant "nigger, you're a monkey with bananas." Given the history of racial stereotypes against African-Americans and the prevalent one of African-Americans as animals or monkeys, it is a reasonable — perhaps even an obvious — conclusion that Spence intended the racial insult that Jones perceived in receiving the postcard. In addition, Officer Spence's testimony that he sent the postcard to relieve stress is irrational, if not incredulous [sic]. It is far more likely that Spence sent the postcard

---

reprimand or otherwise sanction the two officers is troubling, to say the least. The commanding officer, Major Mickey McCullough, testified that he did not see anything wrong with the t-shirts. "It was a way for the officers to celebrate spending months and sometimes years in planning and work."

to disparage Jones and his wife on the basis of their race. Accordingly, we believe that Jones has made the requisite showing of discriminatory intent.[7]

The second prong of a selective prosecution claim — discriminatory effect — creates a greater challenge for Jones. As we have stated, to establish discriminatory effect, a defendant must show that similarly situated individuals of a different race were not similarly prosecuted. See *Armstrong*, 517 U.S. at 465. The evidence that Jones has presented to this point does not establish that law enforcement failed to refer similarly situated non-African-Americans for federal prosecution. Accordingly, Jones thus far has not established a prima facie case of discriminatory effect.

Jones argues in the alternative that the district court erred by denying his request for discovery on his selective prosecution claim because, even if Jones's evidence is not enough to establish a *prima facie* case at this point, he has set forth "some evidence" warranting discovery. Jones asserts that discovery will enable him to establish a prima facie case of discriminatory effect. We review the denial of a motion for discovery regarding a selective prosecution claim for an abuse of discretion.

In *Armstrong*, the Supreme Court stated that in order for a defendant to obtain discovery in a selective prosecution case, there must be a showing of "some evidence tending to show the existence of the essential elements of the defense, discriminatory effect and discriminatory intent." 517 U.S. at 468. As we have stated, Jones has established a showing of discriminatory intent. With respect to discriminatory effect, we believe that Jones has set forth some evidence "tending to show the existence of discriminatory effect," despite the fact that Jones was unable to establish a prima facie case of discriminatory effect on the merits of his selective prosecution claim. Obviously, a defendant need not prove his case in order to justify discovery on an issue.

Jones has presented evidence that law enforcement referred only him and his co-defendant Billings for a federal prosecution that involved crack cocaine, and failed to refer for federal prosecution eight non-African-Americans who were arrested and prosecuted for crack cocaine. The harshness of the crack cocaine guidelines in federal court is certainly a factor that may have been considered in referring defendants for federal prosecution. The fact that law enforcement never considered foregoing the prosecution of Billings, Jones's white co-defendant, in federal court does not change our analysis. It would have been beyond foolish for law enforcement to have done such a thing, considering that Jones's and

---

[7] We cannot emphasize enough our sense of outrage regarding officers Spence's and Nelson's egregious actions. Law enforcement officials are expected to enforce the law, and their satisfaction in apprehending a suspect, especially one with a criminal background and history of confrontations with such officials, comes as no surprise. However, law enforcement officials must act with integrity, professionalism and fairness. Officers such as Spence and Nelson, whose behavior does not even minimally reflect these attributes, diminish public confidence in law enforcement. The taunting of a defendant by the mailing of a racially charged postcard, and the wearing of custom-made shirts with inappropriate personalized language and pictures, undermines the integrity of our legal system and indeed a defendant's confidence that his case will be handled justly.

Billings's cases involved the same events.

Accordingly, Jones has set forth "some evidence" tending to show the existence of discriminatory effect that warrants discovery on his selective prosecution claim. Thus, the district court abused its discretion in denying Jones's request for discovery. We therefore remand the case to the district court to compel discovery on Jones's selective prosecution claim. If Jones is able to obtain evidence that establishes a prima facie case of discriminatory effect, Jones may renew his motion to dismiss the indictment.

4. Take another look at the incident recounted at the beginning of this Chapter, where the Justice Department was out to "get" Roy Cohn. If Cohn had moved to dismiss one of his indictments and was able to prove the facts described by Younger, should the court have granted his motion — based on the cases you have read in this Chapter?

UNITED STATES v. BASS
U.S. Supreme Court
536 U.S. 862 (2002)

PER CURIAM.

A federal grand jury sitting in the Eastern District of Michigan returned a second superseding indictment charging respondent with, *inter alia*, the intentional firearm killings of two individuals. The United States filed a notice of intent to seek the death penalty. Respondent, who is black, alleged that the Government had determined to seek the death penalty against him because of his race. He moved to dismiss the death penalty notice and, in the alternative, for discovery of information relating to the Government's capital charging practices. The District Court granted the motion for discovery, and after the Government informed the court that it would not comply with the discovery order, the court dismissed the death penalty notice. A divided panel of the United States Court of Appeals for the Sixth Circuit affirmed the District Court's discovery order. We grant the petition for a writ of certiorari and now summarily reverse.

In *United States v. Armstrong*, 517 U.S. 456, 465 (1996), we held that a defendant who seeks discovery on a claim of selective prosecution must show some evidence of both discriminatory effect and discriminatory intent. We need go no further in the present case than consideration of the evidence supporting discriminatory effect. As to that, *Armstrong* says that the defendant must make a "credible showing" that "similarly situated individuals of a different race were not prosecuted." The Sixth Circuit concluded that respondent had made such a showing based on nationwide statistics demonstrating that "the United States charges blacks with a death-eligible offense more than twice as often as it charges whites" and that the United States enters into plea bargains more frequently with whites than it does with blacks.* Even assuming that the *Armstrong* requirement can be satisfied by a nationwide showing (as opposed to a showing regarding the record of the

---

* In January 1995, the Department of Justice (DOJ) instituted a policy, known as the death penalty protocol, that required the Attorney General to make the decision whether to seek the death penalty once a defendant had been charged with a capital-eligible offense. The charging decision continued to be made by one of the 93 United States Attorneys throughout the country, but the protocol required that

decisionmakers in respondent's case), raw statistics regarding overall charges say nothing about charges brought against *similarly situated defendants*. And the statistics regarding plea bargains are even less relevant, since respondent *was* offered a plea bargain but declined it. Under *Armstrong*, therefore, because respondent failed to submit relevant evidence that similarly situated persons were treated differently, he was not entitled to discovery.

The Sixth Circuit's decision is contrary to *Armstrong* and threatens the "performance of a core executive constitutional function." *Armstrong, supra*, at 465. For that reason, we reverse.

---

the United States Attorneys submit for review all cases in which they had charged a defendant with a capital-eligible offense. *Ibid.*

Chapter 2

PRETRIAL RELEASE

"Excessive bail shall not be required. . . ."

8th Amendment, United States Constitution

Judge to Defendant (at arraignment): Do you have any questions?

Defendant: Yes, Judge. You said I was presumed innocent, right?

Judge: Yes, that's right.

Defendant: Then what am I doing in jail?

From a transcript in an Indiana case.[1]

THE IMPORTANCE OF PRETRIAL RELEASE

If the defendant cannot obtain release pending trial, he may face considerable hardships — even if he is ultimately acquitted. He might lose his job, and this loss of income might force his family to go on welfare. He will also be cut off from family and friends who might give him emotional support. So a defense attorney can help the client directly by obtaining his release.[2]

Obtaining pretrial release might also affect the outcome of the case. Sometimes a released defendant can assist in the investigation of the case by locating witnesses, and if the defendant can continue his employment, he might be able to

---

[1] 26 California Attorneys for Criminal Justice *Forum*, p. 81 (1999).

[2] *See also* Steven Phillips, *No Heroes No Villains: The Story of a Murder Trial* (Random House, 1997), p. 51:

> The consequences of pre-trial detention are particularly grim. The anxiety and uncertainty that preys on the mind of any incarcerated man are acute enough. Add to this the ever-present prospect of either acquittal and freedom, or conviction and a lengthy sentence, and you have created an emotional hell for the accused. There is the anguish of separation from one's family and the special torment of being unable to assist in the preparation of a defense. An accused person desperately needs to go out into his community and help his attorney (usually a mistrusted outsider in that community) to find the witnesses who will bolster the defense. This cannot be done from a jail cell. Statistics have long shown that a jailed defendant is far more likely to be convicted and sent to prison than a defendant who makes bail.
>
> In addition, the conditions in prisons for pre-trial detainees are generally far worse than those for convicted and sentenced prisoners. Opportunities for education and rehabilitation, such as they are, are far fewer for the more transitory population of pre-trial prisoners. Sentenced prisoners at least are aware of the terms that they face, and can begin to adjust emotionally to the realities of their situation. For those awaiting trial, anxiety and uncertainty become contagious, and adjustment or resignation become impossible. The crowning irony, of course, is that these men are presumed to be innocent.

help pay for his legal expenses. A defendant in custody is accessible to "jailhouse informants," who might testify that the defendant made certain admissions to them. Remaining in custody might demoralize a defendant, making him less helpful in preparing his defense and less attractive during the trial. If the prosecutor offers a plea bargain whereby the defendant obtains early release from custody in return for a guilty plea, the defendant's desire to get out of jail quickly might overwhelm his judgment regarding the life-long effect of a felony conviction on his record. If the defendant is released pretrial and behaves himself, this might impress the judge at a later sentencing hearing.

Bail issues arise at the beginning of the case, when the defense attorney is trying to gain the client's confidence. Winning a bail motion can provide "instant gratification" to the defendant, which can form the basis for a good attorney-client relationship throughout the case.

For all these reasons, defense attorneys consider pretrial release a potentially important phase of the criminal courtroom process.

Prosecutors, however, fear two potential consequences of pretrial release. First, the defendant might flee the jurisdiction or hide in order to escape trial and punishment. Second, the defendant might commit other crimes while out on bail.

The judge faced with an application for release should balance these interests, with the guidance of statutes and cases.

SOME BACKGROUND

In this chapter, we will focus on the federal Bail Reform Act of 1966 and its successor, the federal Bail Reform Act of 1984. What did these Acts "reform"?

Earlier, our county's pretrial release system was considered by many to be a "national disgrace". It was plagued by three interrelated problems. First, judges had virtually unbridled discretion regarding when to allow pretrial release, with few guidelines to follow. Second, the legally-recognized purpose of "bail" — a promise to pay money (usually backed up by collateral) to be forfeited if the defendant did not show up for trial — was to assure the defendant's appearance at trial. But in fact many judges were more concerned about the possibility that the defendant would commit new crimes if released, and they would set high bail or deny bail to prevent any release from custody. And third, as few defendants could post the cash bail required, they turned to private bail bondsmen for help, and these people often held real control (and reaped most of the rewards) of the bail system. The system (which still exists in many places) was described in Schlesinger, *Bail Reform: Protecting The Community And The Accused*, 9 Harvard Journal of Law & Public Policy 173, 174–175 (1986):

> Bail represents one of an accused's first encounters with the criminal justice system. Typically, shortly after arrest, a defendant is brought before a magistrate or judge, who sets an amount of bail that must be deposited with the court in order for him to obtain release. Cash bail, in which the defendant deposits the full amount of bail in cash with the court, is refunded to the defendant upon his court appearance. Because few defendants have available the cash necessary to post the entire amount, this form of bail is seldom used. A few states and the federal courts allow a defendant to deposit 10% of the amount of bail set with the court. Most

states allow a defendant or his family or friends to post property as collateral, which is forfeited if the defendant fails to appear. Because most courts require the equity in the property to be twice the amount of the bail set, property bonds are rarely used.

The judge may use a fixed bail schedule to determine the amount of bail for a defendant who has been charged with a criminal offense. The bail schedule is a statement of exactly how much bail is required to release the person charged with a particular crime; its use allows for rapid processing of defendants. In the District of Columbia and other jurisdictions, a court-approved bail schedule is available, and a defendant may post the scheduled amount at the police station with no judicial intervention. This is true even for serious felonies.

Although bail schedules are sometimes available for serious offenses, a judge will more often use his discretion in setting the amount of bail. The judge considers many factors in determining how much bail to set; however, in practice, only two criteria appear to be critical: the seriousness of the crime charged and the defendant's prior criminal record. In a study of bail practices in seventy-two cities, Paul Wice found that eighty-six percent of the judges believed that the seriousness of the charge was the most important release criterion. Wice comments that the criteria into which the judge inquires least frequently — the defendant's financial condition, the amount of bail that the defendant thinks he can raise, and whether the defendant appeared previously (if he was released prior to trial) — have the greatest effect on whether the defendant will in fact gain release. In other words, those criteria that are most directly relevant to the only question that bail's putative purpose raises — "How much bail is necessary to ensure the defendant's appearance for trial?" — are exactly the factors with which the judge is least likely to be concerned.

Because most defendants lack ready cash and do not own sufficient property, they turn to professional bondsmen, who purchase surety bonds from insurance companies. Although the practice varies by state, the accused pays only a percentage (generally 10%) of the amount of bail set to secure his pretrial freedom. The bondsman accepts responsibility for the defendant's court appearance, and the accused's fee is not refundable upon his appearance. Because the accused does not recover this fee if he appears at trial, there is no economic incentive for him to appear.

Congress enacted The Bail Reform Acts in an effort to cure the ills of the past, and many states followed suit with similar legislation.

Problem 2

To: My Law Clerk

From: Pete Moss, Esq.

Re: *U.S. v. Jose Canusi*

My client, Jose Canusi, has been indicted by a federal grand jury in El Paso on one count of smuggling about 40 kilograms of marijuana into the United States, in violation of 21 U.S.C. § 960, which allows for a prison term up to 5 years. He is in custody, and he would like to be released pending trial.

The U.S. Attorney has evidence that Jose and his brother, Benito, were stopped by Border Patrol officers a few miles on this side of the Mexican border. Jose ran off, but was caught in a few minutes and brought back. They were searched, and the marijuana was found in their backpacks. They were questioned, and they admitted that they smuggle marijuana and cocaine across the border on a regular basis. A gang in Mexico gives them the drugs, tells them where to deliver the drugs, and pays when they return. Jose crosses the border legally, with an immigration card, but he hides drugs on his person or in his car. By this means, they bring in large quantities about once a week.

Benito's lawyer moved to suppress the marijuana and the statements against him in his case, arguing that they were obtained from an illegal stop. His motion was granted, his indictment was dismissed, and the government has appealed. The appeal is still pending. I made a similar motion, but it has not yet been heard.

Jose told me the following. He is a farmworker, who lives with his family in Mexico. However, he crosses the border (legally) about 3 months of the year in order to do farm work in Texas, usually near El Paso, where his brother Benito lives. Jose usually stays at his brother's house when he is in Texas. Through his brother Benito, Jose knows many people in the Mexican-American community around El Paso and goes to church with his brother. The priest says that Jose is an upstanding member of the community. Jose's criminal record consists of one conviction for drunk driving 10 years ago and one for assault with a deadly weapon (knife) 5 years ago.

I am considering asking the judge to release Jose on the following conditions: (1) that a bail bond of $30,000 be posted, secured by Benito's home (which has been appraised at $50,000), (2) that Jose surrender his immigration card while the case is pending, (3) that Jose report to his priest once a day.

Please read the attached authorities and let me know what arguments I might make, whether there is any other evidence I should try to get, and what conditions I should propose. Also, what are my chances of getting Jose out?

Bail Reform Act of 1984
(United States Code, Title 18)

§ 3141. Release and detention authority generally

(a) **Pending trial.** A judicial officer authorized to order the arrest of a person under section 3041 of this title before whom an arrested person is brought shall order that such person be released or detained, pending judicial proceedings, under this chapter.

(b) **Pending sentence or appeal.** A judicial officer of a court of original jurisdiction over an offense, or a judicial officer of a Federal appellate court, shall order that, pending imposition or execution of sentence, or pending appeal of conviction or sentence, a person be released or detained under this chapter.

§ 3142. Release or detention of a defendant pending trial

(a) **In general.** Upon the appearance before a judicial officer of a person charged with an offense, the judicial officer shall issue an order that, pending trial, the person be —

(1) released on personal recognizance or upon execution of an unsecured

appearance bond, under subsection (b) of this section;

(2) released on a condition or combination of conditions under subsection (c) of this section;

(3) temporarily detained to permit revocation of conditional release, deportation, or exclusion under subsection (d) of this section; or (4) detained under subsection (e) of this section.

(b) Release on personal recognizance or unsecured appearance bond. Release on personal recognizance or unsecured appearance bond. The judicial officer shall order the pretrial release of the person on personal recognizance, or upon execution of an unsecured appearance bond in an amount specified by the court, subject to the condition that the person not commit a Federal, State, or local crime during the period of release and subject to the condition that the person cooperate in the collection of a DNA sample from the person if the collection of such a sample is authorized pursuant to section 3 of the DNA Analysis Backlog Elimination Act of 2000 (42 U.S.C. 14135a), unless the judicial officer determines that such release will not reasonably assure the appearance of the person as required or will endanger the safety of any other person or the community.

(c) Release on conditions.

(1) If the judicial officer determines that the release described in subsection (b) of this section will not reasonably assure the appearance of the person as required or will endanger the safety of any other person or the community, such judicial officer shall order the pretrial release of the person —

(A) subject to the condition that the person not commit a Federal, State, or local crime during the period of release and subject to the condition that the person cooperate in the collection of a DNA sample from the person if the collection of such a sample is authorized pursuant to section 3 of the DNA Analysis Backlog Elimination Act of 2000 (42 U.S.C. 14135a); and

(B) subject to the least restrictive further condition, or combination of conditions, that such judicial officer determines will reasonably assure the appearance of the person as required and the safety of any other person and the community, which may include the condition that the person

(i) remain in the custody of a designated person, who agrees to assume supervision and to report any violation of a release condition to the court, if the designated person is able reasonably to assure the judicial officer that the person will appear as required and will not pose a danger to the safety of any other person or the community;

(ii) maintain employment, or, if unemployed, actively seek employment;

(iii) maintain or commence an educational program;

(iv) abide by specified restrictions on personal associations, place of abode, or travel;

(v) (v) avoid all contact with an alleged victim of the crime and with a potential witness who may testify concerning the offense;

(vi) report on a regular basis to a designated law enforcement agency, pretrial services agency, or other agency;

(vii) comply with a specified curfew;

(viii) refrain from possessing a firearm, destructive device, or other dangerous weapon;

(ix) refrain from excessive use of alcohol, or any use of a narcotic drug or other controlled substance, as defined in § 102 of the Controlled Substances Act, without a prescription by a licensed medical practitioner;

(x) undergo available medical, psychological, or psychiatric treatment, including treatment for drug or alcohol dependency, and remain in a specified institution if required for that purpose;

(xi) execute an agreement to forfeit upon failing to appear as required, such designated property, including money, as is reasonably necessary to assure the appearance of the person as required, and post with the court such indicia of ownership of the property or such percentage of the money as the judicial officer may specify;

(xii) execute a bail bond with solvent sureties in such amount as is reasonably necessary to assure the appearance of the person as required;

(xiii) return to custody for specified hours following release for employment, schooling, or other limited purposes; and

(xiv) satisfy any other condition that is reasonably necessary to assure the appearance of the person as required and to assure the safety of any other person and the community.

(2) The judicial officer may not impose a financial condition that results in the pretrial detention of the person.

(3) The judicial officer may at any time amend the order to impose additional or different conditions of release.

* * * *

(e)   **Detention.** If, after a hearing pursuant to the provisions of subsection (f) of this section, the judicial officer finds that no condition or combination of conditions will reasonably assure the appearance of the person as required and the safety of any other person and the community, such judicial officer shall order the detention of the person before trial. In a case described in subsection (f)(1) of this section, a rebuttable presumption arises that no condition or combination of conditions will reasonably assure the safety of any other person and the community if such judicial officer finds that —

(1) the person has been convicted of a Federal offense that is described in subsection (f)(1) of this section, or of a State or local offense that would have been an offense described in subsection (f)(1) of this section if a circumstance giving rise to Federal jurisdiction had existed;

(2) the offense described in paragraph (1) of this subsection was committed while the person was on release pending trial for a Federal, State, or local offense; and

(3) a period of not more than five years has elapsed since the date of conviction, or the release of the person from imprisonment, for the offense described in paragraph (1) of this subsection, whichever is later.

Subject to rebuttal by the person, it shall be presumed that no condition or combination of conditions will reasonably assure the appearance of the person as required and the safety of the community if the judicial officer finds that there is probable cause to believe that the person committed an offense for which a maximum term of imprisonment of ten years or more is prescribed in the Controlled Substances Act, the Controlled Substances Import and Export Act, section 1 of the Act of September 15, 1980, or an offense under 18 U.S.C. § 924(c).

(f) **Detention hearing.** The judicial officer shall hold a hearing to determine whether any condition or combination of conditions set forth in subsection (c) of this section will reasonably assure the appearance of such person as required and the safety of any other person and the community —

(1) upon motion of the attorney for the Government, in a case that involves —

(A) a crime of violence;

(B) an offense for which the maximum sentence is life imprisonment or death;

(C) an offense for which a maximum term of imprisonment of ten years or more is prescribed in the Controlled Substances Act, the Controlled Substances Import and Export Act, or chapter 705 of title 46;

(D) any felony if such person has been convicted of two or more offenses described in subparagraphs (A) through (C) of this paragraph, or two or more State or local offenses that would have been offenses described in subparagraphs (A) through (C) of this paragraph if a circumstance giving rise to Federal jurisdiction had existed, or a combination of such offenses; or

(E) any felony that is not otherwise a crime of violence that involves a minor victim or that involves the possession or use of a firearm or destructive device, or any other dangerous weapon, or involves a failure to register; or

(2) Upon motion of the attorney for the Government or upon the judicial officer's own motion, in a case that involves —

(A) a serious risk that such person will flee; or

(B) a serious risk that such person will obstruct or attempt to obstruct justice, or threaten, injure, or intimidate, or attempt to threaten, injure, or intimidate, a prospective witness or juror.

The hearing shall be held immediately upon the person's first appearance before the judicial officer unless that person, or the attorney for the Government, seeks a continuance. . . . At the hearing, such person has the right to be represented by counsel, and, if financially unable to obtain adequate representation, to have counsel appointed. The person shall be afforded an opportunity to testify, to present witnesses, to cross-examine witnesses who appear at the hearing, and to present information by proffer or otherwise. The rules concerning admissibility of evidence in criminal trials do not apply to the presentation and consideration of information at the hearing. The facts the judicial officer uses to support a finding pursuant to subsection (e) that no condition or combination of conditions will reasonably assure the safety of any other person and the community shall be supported by clear and convincing evidence.

* * * *

(g) **Factors to be considered.** The judicial officer shall, in determining whether there are conditions of release that will reasonably assure the appearance of the person as required and the safety of any other person and the community, take into account the available information concerning —

(1) the nature and circumstances of the offense charged, including whether the offense is a crime of violence, a violation of section 1591, a Federal crime of terrorism, or involves a minor victim or a controlled substance, firearm, explosive, or destructive device;

(2) the weight of the evidence against the person;

(3) the history and characteristics of the person, including

(A) the person's character, physical and mental condition, family ties, employment, financial resources, length of residence in the community, community ties, past conduct, history relating to drug or alcohol abuse, criminal history, and record concerning appearance at court proceedings; and

(B) whether, at the time of the current offense or arrest, the person was on probation, on parole, or on other release pending trial, sentencing, appeal, or completion of sentence for an offense under Federal, State, or local law; and

(4) the nature and seriousness of the danger to any person or the community that would be posed by the person's release. In considering the conditions of release described in subsection (c)(1)(B)(xi) or (c)(1)(B)(xii) of this section, the judicial officer may upon his own motion, or shall upon the motion of the Government, conduct an inquiry into the source of the property to be designated for potential forfeiture or offered as collateral to secure a bond, and shall decline to accept the designation, or the use as collateral, of property that, because of its source, will not reasonably assure the appearance of the person as required.

(h) **Contents of release order.** In a release order issued under subsection (b) or (c) of this section, the judicial officer shall —

(1) include a written statement that sets forth all the conditions to which the release is subject, in a manner sufficiently clear and specific to serve as a guide for the person's conduct; and

(2) advise the person of —

(A) the penalties for violating a condition of release, including the penalties for committing an offense while on pretrial release;

(B) the consequences of violating a condition of release, including the immediate issuance of a warrant for the person's arrest; and

(C) sections 1503 of this title (relating to intimidation of witnesses, jurors, and officers of the court), 1510 (relating to obstruction of criminal investigations), 1512 (tampering with a witness, victim, or an informant), and 1513 (retaliating against a witness, victim, or an informant).

(i) **Contents of detention order.** In a detention order issued under subsection (e) of this section, the judicial officer shall —

(1) include written findings of fact and a written statement of the reasons for the detention;

(2) direct that the person be committed to the custody of the Attorney General for confinement in a corrections facility separate, to the extent practicable, from persons awaiting or serving sentences or being held in custody pending appeal;

(3) direct that the person be afforded reasonable opportunity for private consultation with counsel; and

(4) direct that, on order of a court of the United States or on request of an attorney for the Government, the person in charge of the corrections facility in which the person is confined deliver the person to a United States marshal for the purpose of an appearance in connection with a court proceeding.

The judicial officer may, by subsequent order, permit the temporary release of the person, in the custody of a United States marshal or another appropriate person, to the extent that the judicial officer determines such release to be necessary for preparation of the person's defense or for another compelling reason.

(j) Presumption of innocence. Nothing in this section shall be construed as modifying or limiting the presumption of innocence.

§ 3145.   Review and appeal of a release or detention order

(a) Review of a release order. If a person is ordered released by a magistrate, or by a person other than a judge of a court having original jurisdiction over the offense and other than a Federal appellate court —

(1) the attorney for the Government may file, with the court having original jurisdiction over the offense, a motion for revocation of the order or amendment of the conditions of release; and

(2) the person may file, with the court having original jurisdiction over the offense, a motion for amendment of the conditions of release.

The motion shall be determined promptly.

(b) Review of a detention order. If a person is ordered detained by a magistrate, or by a person other than a judge of a court having original jurisdiction over the offense and other than a Federal appellate court, the person may file, with the court having original jurisdiction over the offense, a motion for revocation or amendment of the order. The motion shall be determined promptly.

(c) Appeal from a release or detention order. An appeal from a release or detention order, or from a decision denying revocation or amendment of such an order, is governed by the provisions of § 1291 of title 28 and § 3731 of this title. The appeal shall be determined promptly.

Note: In *U.S. v. Singleton*, 182 F.3d 7 (D.C. Cir. 1999), the court stated:

Under the Bail Reform Act, 18 U.S.C. § 3141 et seq., a person awaiting trial on a federal offense may either be released on personal recognizance or bond, conditionally released, or detained. See 18 U.S.C. § 3142(a). The Act establishes procedures for each form of release, as well as for temporary and pretrial detention. Detention until trial is relatively difficult to impose. First, a judicial officer must find one of six circumstances triggering a detention hearing. See 18 U.S.C. § 3142(f). Absent one of these circumstances, detention is not an option. Second, assuming a hearing is appropriate, the judicial officer must consider several enumerated factors to determine whether conditions short of detention will "reasonably assure the appearance of the person as required and the safety of any other person and the community." 18 U.S.C. § 3142(g). The judicial officer may order detention if these factors weigh against release.

The court held that Congress intended that a determination of whether a crime is a "crime of violence" under subsection (f) shall be made "categorically," i.e., by reference to the elements of the offence, and not on a case-by-case basis. The court also held that possession of a firearm by a convicted felon is not a "crime of violence." (Contra on this point: *U.S. v. Dillard*, 214 F.3d 88 (2nd Cir. 2000).

STACK v. BOYLE
United States Supreme Court
342 U.S. 1 (1951)

Mr. Chief Justice Vinson delivered the opinion of the Court.

Indictments have been returned in the Southern District of California charging the twelve petitioners with conspiring to violate the Smith Act, 18 U.S.C. §§ 371, 2385. Upon their arrest, bail was fixed for each petitioner in the widely varying amounts of $2,500, $7,500, $75,000 and $100,000. On motion of petitioner Schneiderman following arrest in the Southern District of New York, his bail was reduced to $50,000 before his removal to California. On motion of the Government to increase bail in the case of other petitioners, bail was fixed in the District Court for the Southern District of California in the uniform amount of $50,000 for each petitioner.

Petitioners moved to reduce bail on the ground that bail as fixed was excessive under the Eighth Amendment.[1] In support of their motion, petitioners submitted statements as to their financial resources, family relationships, health, prior criminal records, and other information. The only evidence offered by the Government was a certified record showing that four persons previously convicted under the Smith Act in the Southern District of New York had forfeited bail. No evidence was produced relating those four persons to the petitioners in this case. At a hearing on the motion, petitioners were examined by the District Judge and cross-examined by an attorney for the Government. Petitioners' factual statements stand uncontroverted.

After their motion to reduce bail was denied, petitioners filed applications for habeas corpus in the same District Court. Upon consideration of the record on the motion to reduce bail, the writs were denied. The Court of Appeals for the Ninth Circuit affirmed. * * * *

From the passage of the Judiciary Act of 1789, to the present Federal Rules of Criminal Procedure, Rule 46(a)(1), federal law has unequivocally provided that a person arrested for a non-capital offense shall be admitted to bail. This traditional right to freedom before conviction permits the unhampered preparation of a defense, and serves to prevent the infliction of punishment prior to conviction. Unless this right to bail before trial is preserved, the presumption of innocence,

---

[1] "Excessive bail shall not be required, nor excessive fines imposed, nor cruel and unusual punishments inflicted." U.S.Const., Amend. VIII.

secured only after centuries of struggle, would lose its meaning.

The right to release before trial is conditioned upon the accused's giving adequate assurance that he will stand trial and submit to sentence if found guilty. Like the ancient practice of securing the oaths of responsible persons to stand as sureties for the accused, the modern practice of requiring a bail bond or the deposit of a sum of money subject to forfeiture serves as additional assurance of the presence of an accused. Bail set at a figure higher than an amount reasonably calculated to fulfill this purpose is "excessive" under the Eighth Amendment.

Since the function of bail is limited, the fixing of bail for any individual defendant must be based upon standards relevant to the purpose of assuring the presence of that defendant. The traditional standards as expressed in the Federal Rules of Criminal Procedure[3] are to be applied in each case to each defendant.

In this case, petitioners are charged with offenses under the Smith Act and, if found guilty, their convictions are subject to review with the scrupulous care demanded by our Constitution. Upon final judgment of conviction, petitioners face imprisonment of not more than five years and a fine of not more than $10,000. It is not denied that bail for each petitioner has been fixed in a sum much higher than that usually imposed for offenses with like penalties and yet there has been no factual showing to justify such action in this case. The Government asks the courts to depart from the norm by assuming, without the introduction of evidence, that each petitioner is a pawn in a conspiracy and will, in obedience to a superior, flee the jurisdiction. To infer from the fact of indictment alone a need for bail in an unusually high amount is an arbitrary act. Such conduct would inject into our own system of government the very principles of totalitarianism which Congress was seeking to guard against in passing the statute under which petitioners have been indicted.

If bail in an amount greater than that usually fixed for serious charges of crimes is required in the case of any of the petitioners, that is a matter to which evidence should be directed in a hearing so that the constitutional rights of each petitioner may be preserved. In the absence of such a showing, we are of the opinion that the fixing of bail before trial in these cases cannot be squared with the statutory and constitutional standards for admission to bail.

The Court concludes that bail has not been fixed by proper methods in this case and that petitioners' remedy is by motion to reduce bail, with right of appeal to the Court of Appeals. Accordingly, the judgment of the Court of Appeals is vacated and the case is remanded to the District Court with directions to vacate its order denying petitioners' applications for writs of habeas corpus and to dismiss the applications without prejudice. Petitioners may move for reduction of bail in the criminal proceeding so that a hearing may be held for the purpose of fixing reasonable bail for each petitioner.

---

[3] Rule 46(c): "_Amount._ If the defendant is admitted to bail, the amount thereof shall be such as in the judgment of the commissioner or court or judge or justice will insure the presence of the defendant, having regard to the nature and circumstances of the offense charged, the weight of the evidence against him, the financial ability of the defendant to give bail and the character of the defendant." [Ed. — This rule has been replaced by the Bail Reform Act of 1984.]

Mr. Justice Jackson, whom Mr. Justice Frankfurter joins.

The practice of admission to bail, as it has evolved in Anglo-American law, is not a device for keeping persons in jail upon mere accusation until it is found convenient to give them a trial. On the contrary, the spirit of the procedure is to enable them to stay out of jail until a trial has found them guilty. Without this conditional privilege, even those wrongly accused are punished by a period of imprisonment while awaiting trial and are handicapped in consulting counsel, searching for evidence and witnesses, and preparing a defense.

Admission to bail always involves a risk that the accused will take flight. That is a calculated risk which the law takes as the price of our system of justice.

It is complained that the District Court fixed a uniform blanket bail chiefly by consideration of the nature of the accusation and did not take into account the difference in circumstances between different defendants. If this occurred, it is a clear violation of Rule 46(c). Each defendant stands before the bar of justice as an individual. Even on a conspiracy charge, defendants do not lose their separateness or identity. While it might be possible that these defendants are identical in financial ability, character and relation to the charge — elements Congress has directed to be regarded in fixing bail — I think it violates the law of probabilities. Each accused is entitled to any benefits due to his good record, and misdeeds or a bad record should prejudice only those who are guilty of them. The question when application for bail is made relates to each one's trustworthiness to appear for trial and what security will supply reasonable assurance of his appearance.

Complaint further is made that the courts below have been unduly influenced by recommendations of very high bail made by the grand jury. It is not the function of the grand jury to fix bail, and its volunteered advice is not governing. Since the grand jury is a secret body, ordinarily hearing no evidence but the prosecution's, attended by no counsel except the prosecuting attorneys, it is obvious that it is not in a position to make an impartial recommendation. Its suggestion may indicate that those who have heard the evidence for the prosecution regard it as strongly indicative that the accused may be guilty of the crime charged. It could not mean more than that without hearing the defense, and it adds nothing to the inference from the fact of indictment. Such recommendations are better left unmade, and if made should be given no weight.

But the protest charges, and the defect in the proceedings below appears to be, that, provoked by the flight of certain Communists after conviction, the Government demands and public opinion supports a use of the bail power to keep Communist defendants in jail before conviction. Thus, the amount is said to have been fixed not as a reasonable assurance of their presence at the trial, but also as an assurance they would remain in jail. There seems reason to believe that this may have been the spirit to which the courts below have yielded, and it is contrary to the whole policy and philosophy of bail. This is not to say that every defendant is entitled to such bail as he can provide, but he is entitled to an opportunity to make it in a reasonable amount. I think the whole matter should be reconsidered by the appropriate judges in the traditional spirit of bail procedure.

Note from Pete:

Stack held that the purpose of bail is to assure the defendant's appearance at trial. Does this mean that if the magistrate is convinced that the defendant will appear at trial, she must release the defendant on bail — even if she believes that he might commit more crimes while out on bail? As you can see from reading the Bail Reform Act of 1984, § 3142(e) permits the magistrate to deny release on bail where no release conditions will reasonably assure the safety of the community. Is this constitutional, under *Stack*?

In *U.S. v. Salerno*, 481 U.S. 739 (1987), the Supreme Court upheld this provision, noting that Congress had been responding to "the alarming problem of crimes committed by persons on release." Salerno claimed that the statute denied him due process of law, as it *punished* him without the normal protections of a criminal trial (trial by jury, proof beyond a reasonable doubt, etc.). But the Court held that Congress intended the statute to *regulate*, not to *punish*: "Preventing danger to the community is a legitimate regulatory goal." The Court noted that the statute operates only in limited circumstances, provides for a prompt hearing, limits the time of confinement, and provides for confinement separate from convicts. The Court also relied on cases allowing detention without conviction in various special circumstances (war, insurrection, incompetents, juveniles). The Court said that the government's interest in preventing crime by arrestees is "overwhelming." The Court admitted that the individual's interest in liberty is fundamental, but held that this interest may "be subordinated to the greater needs of society."

I'm not sure I understand the difference between "regulation" and "punishment". Suppose Congress were to provide that anyone guilty of a federal crime should not be "punished", but should be confined in a pleasant institution until rehabilitated, and sincere efforts should be made to rehabilitate him. Under *Salerno*, could such confinement be ordered by a magistrate after a hearing similar to the one provided by 18 U.S.C. § 3142 — i.e., without giving defendant the right to a jury, proof beyond a reasonable doubt, and the like?

In *Salerno*, the defendant also claimed that the statute is invalid under the 8th Amendment's proscription against "excessive bail," citing the language in *Stack v. Boyle* that says that the purpose of bail is to assure defendant's presence at trial, and any amount higher than this is "excessive." The Court held, however, that refusal to release the defendant on *any* amount of bail does not constitute *excessive* bail, and the "dicta" from *Stack* does not compel a contrary conclusion. Justice Marshall's dissent called this illogical, as the same result is achieved by denial of bail as by excessive bail.

Justice Marshall also found the majority's ruling inconsistent with the presumption of innocence, by some ingenious reasoning. If the prosecutor shows at a pretrial detention hearing that defendant is dangerous, and defendant is confined, and then defendant is *acquitted* on the underlying charges (because the prosecutor failed to prove its case beyond a reasonable doubt), may he still be confined? Of course not, as this would make the acquittal meaningless. But under the presumption of innocence, defendant is just as innocent *before* the acquittal as *after* it. The majority must be holding, therefore, that the fact of the indictment means that defendant is *not* presumed innocent. But the indictment shows only that there is enough probable cause to try defendant, not that he is presumed guilty.

UNITED STATES v. BOTERO

U.S. District Court, Southern District of Florida
604 Fed.Supp. 1028 (1985)

SPELLMAN, DISTRICT JUDGE.

This is an appeal of a pretrial detention order issued by the Honorable Samuel J. Smargon, United States Magistrate. For the reasons detailed below, this Court agrees with Magistrate Smargon's conclusion that the Defendant, Hernan Botero, poses a serious risk of flight and that no condition or combination of conditions would reasonably assure his appearance at trial. Accordingly, this Court affirms the order of pretrial detention.

Background

The defendant, Hernan Botero, is a fifty-two year old Colombian citizen. He was educated in the United States and, prior to the instant indictment, frequently traveled to the United States for business and for pleasure. In February 1981, a federal grand jury, sitting in Miami, Florida, returned an eighteen count indictment charging Hernan Botero and others with a "money laundering" scheme involving some fifty-seven million dollars. At the time that the indictment was returned, Mr. Botero was in Colombia.

Mr. Botero has acknowledged, through counsel, that he was aware of the indictment shortly after it was returned. He refused, however, to return to the United States voluntarily to face these charges. At one point in 1981, it appears that he was willing to return to the United States pursuant to an agreement that he would be permitted to be released on bond. The negotiations for his return broke down when the government insisted that as a condition of his bond, he would not be permitted to leave the United States.

The United States Government formally requested the Government of the Republic of Colombia to extradite Hernan Botero pursuant to the Treaty of Extradition of 1979. Mr. Botero was arrested in Colombia in May 1984, pursuant to the request for extradition, and was detained by his country of origin without bond. He successfully resisted extradition on ten counts of the indictment because the offenses charged in those counts were not subject to extradition under the treaty. Thus, when Mr. Botero was returned by the Colombian Government to the United States in January 1985, he faced seven counts — one count of conspiracy, one count of false statements and five counts of mail fraud. Mr. Botero has continued to challenge his extradition and the jurisdiction of this Court to try him even on the seven counts that he is presently facing. At his arraignment, he refused to enter any plea as to the seven counts that are before this Court.

The Government moved for pretrial detention pursuant to the Bail Reform Act of 1984, and a detention hearing was held on January 16, 1985 before Magistrate Smargon. In an Order issued the following day, Magistrate Smargon, applying the factors enumerated in 18 U.S.C. § 3142(g), found that Mr. Botero posed a serious risk of flight and that no condition or combination of conditions would reasonably assure his appearance at trial. He therefore ordered that Mr. Botero be detained without bond.

Mr. Botero moved for reconsideration, and on February 12, 1985 further hearings were held before Magistrate Smargon. At that time, counsel for Mr. Botero presented additional conditions of release which he argued would reasonably assure Mr. Botero's appearance at trial. Magistrate Smargon, however, again found that these conditions were inadequate and that pretrial detention was warranted.

Mr. Botero argues that even if the statute can constitutionally be applied to him, the Magistrate erred in finding that he posed a substantial risk of flight and that no conditions of release could reasonably assure his appearance at trial.

Section 3142(g) sets forth the factors a Court must consider in determining whether a defendant should be detained pretrial. These factors are: (1) the nature and circumstances of the offense charged including whether the offense is a crime of violence or involves a narcotic drug; (2) the weight of the evidence against the person; (3) the history and characteristics of the person, including — (A) his character, physical and mental condition, family ties, employment, financial resources, length of residence in the community, community ties, past conduct, history relating to drug or alcohol abuse, criminal history, and record considering appearances at court proceedings; and (B) whether, at the time of the current offense or arrest, he was on probation, on parole, or on other release pending trial, sentencing, appeal or completion of sentence for an offense under Federal State or local law; and (4) the nature and seriousness of the danger to any person or the community that would be posed by the person's release.

When these factors are considered, it is plain to this Court that Mr. Botero poses a serious risk of flight.

Nature and Circumstances of the Offense

The defendant is charged with a "money laundering" scheme involving some 57 million dollars over a ten month period. According to the Government, Hernan Botero entered into an agreement with employees at the Landmark First National Bank to open five fictitious accounts. Large amounts of cash, in excess of $10,000 for each deposit, were to be deposited in these accounts. Hernan Botero and his brother Roberto allegedly directed the distribution of these funds through wire transfers and conversion into cashier's checks. No currency transaction reports were ever filed with the Internal Revenue Service.

The maximum sentence Hernan Botero could receive if he were convicted on all seven counts he is presently facing is thirty-five years.

The defendant is not charged with any violations of the narcotics laws which would give rise to the presumption of § 3142(e). Section 3142(e) provides, in part, that there is a rebuttable presumption that "no condition or combination of conditions will reasonably assure the appearance of the person and the safety of the community if the judicial officer finds there is probable cause to believe that the person committed an offense for which a maximum term of imprisonment of ten years or more is prescribed under the Controlled Substances Act (21 U.S.C. § 801 et. seq.), the Controlled Substances Import and Export Act (21 U.S.C. § 951 et seq.) or section 1 of the Act of September 15, 1980 (21 U.S.C. § 955a)." However, the Government has consistently maintained — and this Court agrees — that "money laundering" is an integral part of the narcotics business. The same factors which create an unusually high risk of flight in narcotics offenses and which form the basis for the statutory presumption are present here — the business is extremely lucrative and those involved have established substantial ties outside the United States. Thus, persons involved in money laundering, just as those involved in narcotics trafficking, have the resources and foreign contacts to escape to other countries to avoid prosecution.

Weight of the Evidence

The weight of the evidence against Hernan Botero is strong. Hernan Botero's brother, Roberto Botero, was tried and convicted on substantially the same evidence that the Government will offer against Hernan Botero. During the trial, the Government's two main witnesses testified that Hernan Botero was the mastermind of the entire laundering scheme. Moreover, even Roberto Botero acknowledged that Hernan was involved with the five fictitious accounts used to transfer the 57 million dollars.

History and Characteristics of the Person

Hernan Botero is a prominent Colombian citizen of enormous wealth and stature. He has no previous arrests and until this case, enjoyed a fine reputation in Colombia.

Physical and Mental Condition

Mr. Botero does not have a history of physical or mental problems.

Family Ties

The only family ties that Hernan Botero has in the United States are his brother, Roberto Botero, and Hernan's family that recently relocated to South Florida to be near him during these proceedings. As pointed out above, Roberto Botero has been convicted of crimes charged in the same indictment and is presently released on bond pending appeal.

Employment

Hernan Botero has never been employed in the United States. His businesses and other financial resources are all based in Colombia.

Financial Resources

The Botero family has vast financial resources in Colombia. They own a grain importing business, a fashionable Medellin hotel and a professional soccer team. Although these assets are in corporate or family names, Hernan Botero testified that he "controlled" a number of these interests. The only property Mr. Botero owns in the United States is the subject of a tax lien.

Length of Residence in the Community

Prior to the instant indictment, Mr. Botero and his immediate family would come to South Florida three or four times a year. He has not been in the United States since the instant indictment was returned in 1981.

Community Ties

At this time, Mr. Botero has no ties to this community.

Past Conduct and Record of Past Appearances

Mr. Botero admits that he has known about the charges pending against him and has purposely absented himself from this country because of these charges. He has resisted extradition and continues to dispute the validity of the extradition process. He has refused to enter a plea and refuses to recognize this Court's jurisdiction. Because Mr. Botero was only extradited on seven counts of the indictment, he continues to be a fugitive on the remaining ten counts.

Mr. Botero strenuously argues that his fight against extradition cannot be used by this Court in considering whether there is a serious risk that he will flee prior to trial. The defendant points out that he did not leave the United States when the indictment was returned — he was already in his native Colombia and simply sought to avail himself of his legal rights in Colombia. According to Mr. Botero, when he learned the Government of Colombia was going to comply with the request by the United States for his extradition, he contacted an attorney who advised him to fight the extradition. The attorney advised him that a waiver of extradition would expose him to trial on all seventeen counts of the indictment, whereas even if the extradition treaty were enforced, Mr. Botero would face fewer charges if he resisted extradition.

While Mr. Botero may now have entirely legitimate tactical reasons for resisting extradition, the fact remains that the defendant has absented himself from this jurisdiction and has refused to answer these charges. This Court recognizes that Colombia is Mr. Botero's native country. But prior to the indictment in this case, the defendant frequently travelled to the United States for business and travel. It is clear that Mr. Botero was aware of the charges pending in this country and that his motivation for not voluntarily returning over the past few years was to avoid facing these charges. Certainly, these facts can and should be considered by this Court in determining whether he poses a serious risk of flight. At a minimum, Mr. Botero's refusal to voluntarily return is indicative of a mental state which could easily rationalize flight on legal, moral or intellectual grounds.

In the context of determining whether a defendant poses a substantial risk of flight, this Court does not find any meaningful distinction between a person who left the country when he learned of pending charges and one who already outside the country refuses to return to face these charges. The intent is the same — the avoidance of prosecution.

Nature and Seriousness of the Danger to the Community

This Court does not find that Mr. Hernan Botero poses a danger to the community if he were released pending trial. The Government has suggested that it has reason to believe that Mr. Botero's personal safety may be in danger and therefore his presence in the community could be potentially dangerous to those in proximity to him. Because the Court is convinced of its conclusion without considering this factor, it has declined to require any details of this alleged danger.

Conclusion as to Risk of Flight

When all of these factors are considered, it is clear that Hernan Botero poses a substantial risk of flight. Notwithstanding his past history of good character, he is a man facing serious charges with possible penalties of thirty-five years imprisonment. The evidence against him apparently is strong — his brother was convicted on substantially the same evidence. He has not been in the United States since 1981 and even then he did not have significant ties to this country. For three years he attempted to avoid prosecution by not returning to this country. Even after his extradition, he continues to challenge the jurisdiction of this Court as to seven counts. As to the remaining counts, he continues to be a fugitive. He has considerable means and foreign connections which would make it possible for him to escape to other countries with relative ease in order to avoid prosecution for offenses punishable by lengthy prison sentences.

Finding that Mr. Botero poses a serious risk of flight does not, however, end this Court's inquiry. Pretrial detention can only be ordered if the Court finds that no condition or combination of conditions will reasonably assure the appearance of the defendant at trial.

The Proposed Conditions

The defendant has proposed a combination of conditions of release which include the following: a two million dollar personal surety bond secured by commercial property in Florida and Colombia, the home of his daughter-in-law's parents in Massachusetts and Mr. Botero's home in Medellin, Colombia; release to the custody of a person approved by the United States Attorney and deputized by this Court who shall maintain around the clock custody of Mr. Botero; a curfew which would be tantamount to house arrest; an electronic monitoring device; and execution of a waiver of extradition applicable to any country to which he may flee.

Given the serious risk of flight posed by Mr. Botero, these conditions are inadequate to reasonably assure his appearance at trial. The property in the United States offered to collateralize the bond may be worth a considerable amount of money, but a man of Mr. Botero's means could flee the jurisdiction and then reimburse those persons whose property would be forfeited. Repaying those family and friends would be an incidental cost compared to his freedom. This Court will not consider property outside the jurisdiction of the Court of the United States as collateral.

Similarly, the defendant's proposal of a strict curfew and house arrest, even under twenty-four hour guard and an electronic tracking system is inadequate to reasonably assure this Court of Mr. Botero's future appearance. It must be remembered that wherever Mr. Botero stays in the Miami area, he will be only minutes away from a private airfield. Thus, even a short delay in notifying the authorities would permit Mr. Botero to successfully flee. Mr. Botero need only wait for the appropriate time — when his guard was out of the room, asleep or had his attention elsewhere — to get the head start he would need. Moreover, it is not entirely clear what authority and what duty a private guard would have to prevent Mr. Botero's flight. Certainly, this Court would be reluctant to hold such a guard in contempt if it appeared that he was unable to physically prevent Mr. Botero's flight.

Finally, this Court doubts that a waiver of extradition executed by Mr. Botero under these circumstances could ever be considered voluntary and enforceable. Mr. Botero contests the jurisdiction of this Court to conduct these proceedings. Any waiver he executes here in an effort to secure his release would have to be considered suspect.

In sum, at this point, the Court finds that even the stringent conditions proposed by the defense would not be sufficient to reasonably assure Mr. Botero's appearance at trial. The order of pretrial detention is therefore affirmed.

Note from Pete:

Can the detention of Hernan be reconciled with the release of Roberto?

UNITED STATES v. MOTAMEDI
U.S. Court of Appeals, 9th Circuit
767 F.2d 1403 (1985)

KENNEDY, CIRCUIT JUDGE:

The Government moves for reconsideration of our reversal of the district court's pretrial detention order. Because the Government has failed to establish by a preponderance of the evidence that Motamedi poses a flight risk, the motion for reconsideration must be denied.

Motamedi was arrested on charges of conspiracy to export items without a license, in violation of the Arms Export Control Act, 22 U.S.C. § 2778. The United States Magistrate conditioned his pretrial release upon the posting of a $400,000 secured appearance bond, with special conditions including intensive Pretrial Services supervision, travel restrictions, and surrender of both passport and greencard. Motamedi complied with these conditions and was released.

A month and a half elapsed, and Motamedi was indicted on one count of conspiracy under 18 U.S.C. § 371, and fourteen counts of unlicensed exportation of items attended by false shipper's declarations, under 22 U.S.C. § 2778(c), 18 U.S.C. § 2(b). The maximum sentence on the conspiracy count is five years, and the maximum sentence on each of the exportation counts is two years.

Motamedi voluntarily appeared for arraignment, at which time the Government requested a detention order on the ground that Motamedi posed a serious risk of flight. Based on the information presented, the magistrate found that Motamedi, an Iranian citizen, was acting as a de facto purchasing agent for the current Iranian government and could return to Iran with impunity; that he maintained large foreign bank accounts with most, if not all, of the deposits being made by the Iranian government; that he persisted in his allegedly illegal exporting activities despite warnings by agents of the United States Customs and Federal Bureau of Investigation that it was illegal to export the items in question; and that the nature and circumstances of the offenses charged are serious. Based on her findings, the magistrate concluded that the Government had demonstrated by a preponderance of the evidence that no condition or combination of conditions would reasonably assure the appearance of Motamedi for further proceedings in the case, and ordered him detained.

Faced with detention, Motamedi moved the district court, pursuant to § 3145(b) of the Bail Reform Act of 1984, * * * to revoke the detention order and to set bail. A second hearing was held at which the parties presented the same information that was before the magistrate. The court concluded that the magistrate's factual findings were not clearly erroneous and that it would reach the conclusion that no condition or combination of conditions would reasonably assure Motamedi's appearance, regardless of whether the applicable burden of proof was preponderance of the evidence or clear and convincing evidence. The district court affirmed the detention order, and this appeal followed.

We reversed and ordered release on the same financial terms and conditions as had been granted prior to revocation of bail. The Government moved for reconsideration and clarification of our release order. Without passing on the arguments presented in the Government's motion, we authorized the district court to increase the monetary amount of the bond, with the condition that it be an amount that Motamedi could post. The bond is set at $750,000. Because the parties raise issues of first impression under the Bail Reform Act of 1984, concerning the applicable burden of proof to be met in the district court and the proper standard of review in this court, we heard oral argument and now issue this opinion in support of our order.

In determining the applicable standard of review, we bear in mind that federal law has traditionally provided that a person arrested for a noncapital offense shall be admitted to bail. *Stack v. Boyle*, 342 U.S. 1, 4 (1951). Only in rare circumstances should release be denied. *Sellers v. United States*, 89 S.Ct. 36, 38 (1968) (Black, J., in chambers); *United States v. Schiavo*, 587 F.2d 532, 533 (1st Cir.,1978). Doubts regarding the propriety of release should be resolved in favor of the defendant. *Herzog v. United States*, 75 S.Ct. 349, 351 (1955) (Douglas, J., in chambers); *United States v. McGill*, 604 F.2d 1252, 1255 (9th Cir.,1979).

Release pending trial is governed by the Bail Reform Act of 1984 which, like its predecessor, the Bail Reform Act of 1966, 18 U.S.C. §§ 3146–3152 (repealed October 12, 1984), mandates release of a person facing trial under the least restrictive condition or combination of conditions that will reasonably assure the appearance of the person as required. 18 U.S.C. § 3142(c)(2). The Fifth and Eighth Amendments' prohibitions of deprivation of liberty without due process and of excessive bail require careful review of pretrial detention orders to ensure that the statutory mandate has been respected.

We hold that the applicable standard of review for pretrial detention orders is one of deference to the district court's factual findings, absent a showing that they are clearly erroneous, coupled with our right of independent examination of the facts, the findings, and the record to determine whether an order of pretrial detention may be upheld.

We must further determine the Government's burden of proof in establishing risk of flight under the 1984 Act. If the Government may establish such risk by a mere preponderance of the evidence, it is entitled to know that we rule against it in what has become a close case. In the trial court and in this court, the Government must establish risk of flight by a clear preponderance of the evidence, not by the higher standard of clear and convincing evidence. We reach this conclusion from the language and structure of the present statute, considered in light of the rules which pertained at the time of the enactment.

The Bail Reform Act of 1966 authorized pretrial detention without bail only in those cases where conditions could not reasonably assure the defendant's presence at trial. See 18 U.S.C. § 3146(a) (repealed 1984). In contrast, the 1984 Act permits the pretrial detention of a defendant without bail where it is demonstrated either that there is a risk of flight or no assurance that release is consistent with the safety of another person or the community. Danger to another or to the community is a statutory addition that constitutes a significant departure from the previous law.

Under the 1984 Act, a finding that a person presents a danger to the community must be supported by clear and convincing evidence. 18 U.S.C. § 3142(f). The statute, however, is silent with regard to the burden of proof governing the finding that a person poses a risk of flight. The language and structure of the 1984 Act lead us to conclude that the flight risk determination is governed by a standard other than that of clear and convincing evidence.

We must presume that Congress acts with deliberation, rather than by inadvertence, when it drafts a statute. The statute's silence regarding the burden of proof for flight risk determinations should be considered in light of its explicit edict that the heavy burden of clear and convincing evidence applies to a finding of danger to an individual or to the community. The most plausible interpretation for this statutory pattern is that Congress intended the two inquiries to be governed by different standards.

This determination does not, however, conclude the analysis, for we must now ascertain the standard of proof properly applicable to findings of flight risk under the 1984 Act. Presumably, the congressional silence on this point evinces a legislative intent to incorporate the standard applicable to this determination under the 1966 Act. Although the old Act did not include an express statement regarding the standard which governed findings of flight risk, its language strongly suggested the applicability of the preponderance standard. * * * * Finally, because the standard of proof usually applicable to pretrial proceedings is the preponderance of the evidence, we conclude that the congressional silence with regard to the applicable standard of proof in demonstrating risk of flight is the preponderance of the evidence.

Such differential treatment comports with the congressional recognition of danger to another or to the community as a discrete, independent basis for the denial of pretrial release. Since bail was determined under the former law by the likelihood of defendant's appearance at trial, and without explicit recognition of the need to protect the community, it is reasonable to subject the Government to a higher standard of proof when the second purpose is added as an explicit statutory category. Further, a finding of danger to the community is likely to involve more specific and quantifiable evidence than is a finding of risk of flight. For instance, prior convictions, police reports, and other investigatory documents are, as a matter of course, used to show past histories of violence. From these objective sources, trial judges may infer a present danger to the community. Such data is not often available regarding the risk of flight. Thus, it is wholly feasible for the Government to satisfy the higher burden in showing danger to the community.

In concluding that the Government's burden in denying bail on the basis of flight risk is that of the preponderance of the evidence, we are not unmindful of the presumption of innocence and its corollary that the right to bail should be denied only for the strongest of reasons. This rule, however, pertains to the nature of the permissible factors to be utilized in denying an application for bail, not to the quantum of proof required to establish the presence of such factors.

Having determined both the applicable standard of review and the proper burden of proof, we must consider whether the Government has demonstrated by a preponderance of the evidence that no condition or combination of conditions will reasonably assure Motamedi's appearance. Section 3142(g) specifies the various factors to be considered by the court in determining whether conditions of release may be imposed that will reasonably assure the appearance of the person. The court must take into account available information concerning the nature and circumstances of the offense charged, the weight of the evidence against the person, the history and characteristics of the person, including his character, physical and mental condition, family ties, employment, financial resources, length of residence in the community, community ties, past conduct, history relating to drug and alcohol abuse, criminal history, record concerning appearance at court proceedings, and the nature and seriousness of the danger to any person or the community that would be posed by the person's release.

There are many factors listed in § 3142(g) which point toward the conclusion that Motamedi should be released. Motamedi is a 27-year old Iranian citizen who has been admitted for permanent residence in this country. He has been living in the Los Angeles area since 1976 and has applied for citizenship. He has approximately eighty-five relatives in the Los Angeles area, many of whom are citizens. His immediate family, including his wife, brothers, mother, and father, all reside in the area. His parents have posted their residence as security on the $750,000 bond. He has no prior criminal record, and no history of alcohol or drug abuse. He has not violated any conditions of his release, and has made all court appearances.

In denying Motamedi's motion for revocation of the detention order, the district court relied on the magistrate's findings that the charges against Motamedi are serious; that he exported military items after being warned that it was illegal to do so, and after telling the United States Attorney that he had ceased doing so; that he is an Iranian citizen who may return to Iran with impunity; and that he maintains large bank accounts in foreign countries. These findings appear to be drawn primarily from allegations contained in the indictment. The district court stated that it found most persuasive the fact that Motamedi is an Iranian citizen allegedly acting as an agent of the Iranian government who could return to Iran with impunity.

With all due respect for the district court's determinations, our independent review leads us to a contrary conclusion. It is apparent from the record below that the district court accorded great weight to the charges against Motamedi and the Government's assertions of his guilt. Our court has stated, however, that the weight of the evidence is the least important of the various factors. Although the statute permits the court to consider the nature of the offense and the evidence of guilt, the statute neither requires nor permits a pretrial determination that the person is guilty. These factors may be considered only in terms of the likelihood that the person will fail to appear or will pose a danger to any person or to the community. See 18 U.S.C. § 3142(g). Otherwise, if the court impermissibly makes a preliminary determination of guilt, the refusal to grant release could become in substance a matter of punishment. In the instant case, both parties present persuasive arguments regarding the weight of the evidence. Accordingly, we conclude that this factor does not tip the balance either for or against detention.

Similarly, the factor of alienage, upon which the district court also placed much weight, may be taken into account, but it does not point conclusively to a determination that Motamedi poses a serious risk of flight. Motamedi argues that because all of his family's property was confiscated after the fall of the Shah, and his family was forced to flee, he is not free to return to Iran. Moreover, he contends that evidence concerning the present existence of large foreign bank accounts is lacking. Again, both parties present strong arguments on the implications of Motamedi's alienage, and we conclude that the factor does not tip the balance either for or against detention.

The Government argues that Motamedi poses a serious risk of flight because of the additional charges contained in the indictment. Motamedi states that he has known of the investigation into his exporting activities since January, 1984. Moreover, he was informed upon his arrest that the Government would seek an indictment on the current charges, but he was nevertheless released on conditions for several weeks before issuance of the indictment. Accordingly, he argues, there is no greater risk that he will flee now than there has been since his arrest and release on conditions. We agree.

Having reviewed the facts, the findings, and the record, we conclude that the grounds upon which the district court based its determination that Motamedi poses a serious risk of flight, and that no condition or combination of conditions will reasonably assure his appearance as required, are insufficient. In this case, the Government has failed to establish by a preponderance of the evidence that Motamedi presents a serious risk of flight. For this reason, the Government's motion for reconsideration is denied.

Notes from Pete:

1. Can this case be reconciled with *Botero*?

2. How do *Botero* and *Motamedi* apply to our case?

UNITED STATES v. TORTORA
U.S. Court of Appeals, 1st Circuit
922 F.2d 880 (1990)

SELYA, CIRCUIT JUDGE.

The government appeals an order of the United States District Court for the District of Massachusetts releasing defendant-appellee Carmen A. Tortora from pretrial detention. The applicable bail statute provides in relevant part that if a "judicial officer finds that no condition or combination of conditions will reasonably assure . . . the safety of any other person and the community," the judicial officer shall order the defendant detained pending trial. 18 U.S.C. § 3142(e). * * * * We conclude that the district court erred in ordering Tortora's release.

I. *Statement of the Case*

On March 22, 1990, an indictment was returned which charged Tortora and seven others with various crimes, including violations of the Racketeer Influenced and Corrupt Organizations (RICO) statute, 18 U.S.C. §§ 1962(c),(d). The eight men were alleged to be members of the Patriarca Family of the Mafia.[2] Tortora, said to be a soldier, was charged with committing three predicate crimes in furtherance of the RICO enterprise: conspiring to collect an extension of credit by extortionate means; collecting an extension of credit through extortion; and traveling in aid of racketeering. Tortora was also charged with the commission of three substantive crimes, to wit: extortion, 18 U.S.C. § 894; violation of the Travel Act, 18 U.S.C. § 1952; and conspiracy to violate the Travel Act, 18 U.S.C. § 371.

At the arraignment, the government moved to have appellee detained pending trial pursuant to 18 U.S.C. § 3142. Detention hearings were conducted by a magistrate. * * * * He concluded that no set of conditions could reasonably assure the community's safety if appellee were freed. Because he determined pretrial detention to be warranted based on dangerousness, the magistrate did not reach the question of whether there was a sufficient risk of flight to justify detention on that ground as well.

Appellee engaged new counsel and asked the district court to modify or revoke the magistrate's order. A hearing was convened, but no new evidence submitted. The district judge requested that appellee produce a specific release proposal. The proposal was received subsequent to the hearing. The judge found that the suggested conditions reasonably assured the safety of the community and adopted them as the foundation for a release order.

Passing over the boilerplate — the conditions mandated, for example, that the appellee not violate the law, appear at scheduled proceedings, eschew possession of weapons and substance abuse, restrict his travel, etc. — the court's order required the appellee to (1) remain at home twenty-four hours a day, except for a reasonable number of visits to doctors and lawyers, wearing an electronic bracelet; (2) refrain from communicating with any person not approved by the prosecutor and defense counsel; (3) meet with codefendants only in the presence of counsel for the purpose of preparing a defense; (4) allow only one telephone line into his residence, hooking it up to a pen register; and (5) post the residence — a house owned by his brother (who, apparently, agreed to execute the necessary documents) — as security.

We stayed the release order and expedited the government's appeal.

II. *Standard of Review*

We approach our task mindful of our obligation to afford independent review, tempered by a degree of deference to the determinations made below. Recognizing that appellate courts are ill-equipped to resolve factbound disputes, this standard cedes particular respect, as a practical matter, to the lower court's factual

---

[2] The record reveals that the Mafia (sometimes called "La Cosa Nostra") is organized around regional mobs called "Families." The Patriarca Family is thought to reign in New England. At the top of the Family hierarchy is the "Boss," who has absolute authority within the Family. The underboss and the consigliere (counselor) are the Boss's principal deputies. The next echelon comprises capo regimes (captains) who are line officers. Soldiers (members) are individuals who are officially "made" or "baptized" into the Family. Associates perform duties for the organization, but are not members of it.

determinations. Hence, independent review represents an intermediate level of scrutiny, more rigorous than the abuse-of-discretion or clear-error standards, but stopping short of plenary or *de novo* review. "If upon careful review of all the facts and the trial judge's reasons the appeals court concludes that a different result should have been reached, the detention decision may be amended or reversed." *U.S. v. O'Brien*, 895 F.2d 810, 814 (1st Cir., 1990).

This case requires that we be clear about what it is that we are independently reviewing. The district court's release order comprised simply a handwritten notation on the face of the appellee's proposal, declaring that, "for reasons stated at the 18 October 1990 nonevidentiary hearing," the listed conditions "will reasonably assure the safety of the community." This conclusory language accomplished very little in the way of finding subsidiary facts or furnishing needed enlightenment to an appellate tribunal. The judge gave no explanation of why he believed the proposed conditions would prove adequate. Nor were these deficits ameliorated by the reference to the October 18 hearing; having reviewed the transcript of that session, we are unable to discover a meaningful articulation of the court's reasoning or discern its rationale.

Were this an appeal of a detention order rather than a release order, the lack of a written statement of particularized reasons would in all probability necessitate vacation of the order. See 18 U.S.C. § 3142(i). We believe that, although not specifically required by the statute, a similar statement of reasons should ordinarily accompany release orders in contested cases. Only in this way will the judicial officer's reasoning be clearly conveyed to the point where an appeals court can most effectively perform its independent review function.

While it would be possible for us merely to set aside the release order and remand for a statement of the lower court's reasons, we believe that step to be unnecessary in this case. It appears from the hearing transcript, albeit only translucently, that the district court did not base its release order on new or different factfinding. The court seems instead to have accepted the subsidiary facts as found by the magistrate, concluding only, for reasons not articulated, that a particular set of conditions never suggested to the magistrate could reasonably assure public safety.[4] It is this decision that we must review, in conjunction with the facts as presented in the record and as found by the magistrate, and taking due cognizance of the district court's failure to state its reasons for disturbing the detention order. Hence, appellate review can be satisfactorily accomplished on the existing record.

Should we independently determine that the release conditions do not reasonably assure community safety, we can either revise the conditions or reverse the order. The first of these options, however, may be more apparent than real. While we could, of course, modify the stated conditions if, on the record before us, there were minor, self-evident adjustments that would make the release conditions adequate, an appellate tribunal is at a considerable disadvantage. Unlike the district court, we do not have a *nisi prius* function and must, therefore, go very slowly in attempting to fashion neoteric conditions of release — particularly where, as here,

---

[4] Perhaps because of this configuration, no mention was made below of the standard by which a district court reviews the magistrate's findings in respect to pretrial detention or release orders. We believe that the proper approach is for the district court to engage in *de novo* review of the contested order.

there is little evidence of other alternatives and the court below has afforded us no cohesive explanation of its decision.

III. *Discussion*

A. *Detention for Dangerousness.*

The Bail Reform Act of 1984, 18 U.S.C. §§ 3141–3156, represented a watershed in the criminal law. It transformed preexisting practice in very significant ways, providing among other things for the pretrial detention of persons charged with certain serious felonies on the ground of dangerousness — a ground theretofore not cognizable. To arm this new weapon, the government was obliged to prove clearly and convincingly that no set of release conditions would reasonably assure the community's safety. 18 U.S.C. § 3142(e). In determining whether suitable conditions existed, a judicial officer was required to take into account the following: (1) the nature and circumstances of the offense charged; (2) the weight of the evidence as to guilt or innocence; (3) the history and characteristics of the accused, including past conduct; and (4) the nature and gravity of the danger posed by the person's release. See 18 U.S.C. § 3142(g). Danger, in this context, was not meant to refer only to the risk of physical violence.

Undoubtedly, the safety of the community can be reasonably assured without being absolutely guaranteed. Requiring that release conditions *guarantee* the community's safety would fly in the teeth of Congress's clear intent that only a limited number of defendants be subject to pretrial detention. Thus, we agree with the Eighth Circuit that the courts cannot demand more than an "objectively reasonable assurance of community safety." *U.S. v. Orta*, 760 F.2d 887, 892 (8th Cir.1985).

Against this backdrop, the inquiry we must make into the government's appeal of a release order is bifocal in nature. First, we must assay the statutory factors, giving due deference to the gloss placed upon them by the magistrate (and tacitly endorsed by the district judge) to see if the appellee was properly classified as dangerous. If not, and absent other grounds for detention (e.g., undue risk of flight), the release order should be allowed to operate. But if the finding of dangerousness withstands scrutiny, we must then look at the particular conditions imposed by the district court to determine the likelihood that, upon the defendant's release, public safety will nevertheless be reasonably assured.

B. *The Inquiry into Dangerousness.*

In this instance, the first part of our inquiry produces little in the way of serious controversy. The reliable evidence, obtained primarily through court-authorized electronic surveillance, paints a picture which closely conforms with the magistrate's factual findings and with the purposes undergirding Congress's decision to change the rules. We summarize the situation.

Carmen Tortora, 43 years of age, has a checkered criminal past, replete with violence and indications of a total commitment to a life of crime. In 1967, he was convicted of armed robbery and assault with a dangerous weapon and sentenced to 3-to-5 years in prison. In 1972 he was convicted of robbery and assault with a dangerous weapon. That same year, he was convicted on two counts of armed bank robbery and sentenced to fifteen years of incarceration. In 1981, while on parole, Tortora was found guilty of making extortionate loans and collecting credit obligations by extortionate means, receiving an eight year sentence. He was paroled in March 1986 and remained on parole for three years. During the parole period, he allegedly participated in the affairs of the RICO enterprise (the Patriarca Family) and undertook certain criminal activities described in the instant indictment.

In sum, Tortora's curriculum of criminal endeavors encompasses virtually his entire adult life. In addition to his nasty habit of committing crimes while on parole, Tortora has a demonstrated penchant for violence. For example, his 1981 extortion conviction came about after the authorities overheard Tortora threatening his selected victim as follows:

> I'm gonna split your motherfuckin' head open if I don't start getting some money! This fuckin' bullshit, fuckin' hidin', I'll cut your fuckin' throat! Now, you get me some motherfuckin' money down there! Or the next time I see ya, I'll send the guys out to split your fuckin' head open! I'll tell them to cut your motherfuckin' head off.

Tortora's arrest on this occasion was viewed by his Family superiors as merely a step in his professional development — a view which Tortora apparently shared. Before his case came to trial, Tortora visited two high-ranking members of the organization who gave him words of encouragement, advised him to plead guilty (advice which he heeded), and arranged some financial support.

Tortora's history and character go hand-in-hand with his lengthy involvement with La Cosa Nostra.[6] We have already discussed his 1981 conviction for extortion. Another predicate act involves a conspiracy to collect extortionate credit, the prime evidence of which is a recorded conversation between Tortora and his capo regime, Vincent M. Ferrara. The final predicate act is even more damning: Tortora is accused of violating the Travel Act by participating in a ritualistic ceremony inducting new members (Tortora included) into the Patriarca Family. During the meeting, Tortora swore lifelong allegiance to the Mafia and agreed to murder any individual who posed a threat to it. On inquiry, he vowed to kill his brother if the latter posed a danger to any member of the organization. In essence, Tortora made the Mafia his highest priority in life and pledged fealty to its needs, whatever the circumstances. As the district judge observed: "I think a fair reading of that meeting was that there was a commitment by all to do whatever was necessary, an oath, whatever it costs to whomever else was involved, to further the objectives of this so-called organization."

Applying the criteria of § 3142(g) to these facts leaves little doubt that Tortora is precisely the type of defendant Congress had in mind when it wrote of the "small but identifiable group of particularly dangerous defendants as to whom neither the imposition of stringent release conditions nor the prospect of revocation of release can reasonably assure the safety of the community or other persons." See S.Rep. No. 225, 1984 U.S.Code Cong. & Admin.News at 3189. The case for dangerousness,

---

[6] Appellee argues that federal courts may not consider associational ties as a factor in measuring a person's likely dangerousness. We find this asseveration specious. Tortora's association with a criminal cabal, his membership in a Family, and his avowals to further the Family's goals through illicit activity, are highly relevant considerations under 18 U.S.C. § 3142(g). Appellee is being judged, as he should be, as an individual, with one relevant characteristic being his devotion to the Mafia and his pledge to violate the law whenever necessary to further its ends.

we suggest, is so unarguable that we can simply superimpose Tortora's track record on the § 3142(g) mosaic in shorthand form:

1. Tortora was indicted for crimes of violence, see 18 U.S.C. § 3156(a)(4) (defining "crime of violence"); he has a long criminal history marked by thuggery; violence has been the hallmark of his substantive activities on the Mafia's behalf; and his statements during the induction ceremony reflected an abiding commitment to the use of deadly force.

2. There is no indication that Tortora is debilitated in any way that might hinder him in continuing to commit violent crimes.

3. The evidence of Tortora's guilt is both substantial and credible. The government's case is based in large part on direct evidence, including tape recordings. While the admissibility of the recordings may be an issue at trial, that circumstance does not preclude their use at a bail hearing.

4. We think it quite significant that Tortora's criminal activities persisted throughout most of his adult life, even while he was on supervised release. The offense underlying his 1981 conviction, as well as other acts attributed to him in this indictment, occurred while he was on parole. By any realistic measure, this history is a telling indicator that he cannot be trusted to abide by conditions of release.

5. Tortora has sworn an oath to kill informants and his past shows him to be capable of violent crime. Therefore, it is likely that the danger he would pose to society, if released, would be grave.

6. Certainly, Tortora's ties to home and hearth do not militate against his future criminal involvement. After all, he agreed to kill his brother and desert his mother on her death bed if in the Mafia's best interests. Put bluntly, there is every reason to believe that he will prefer Family over family.

In sum, the facts as found by the magistrate constitute clear and convincing evidence that Tortora is virtually a paradigm of the criminal who, within the contemplation of the Bail Reform Act, might plausibly be subjected to pretrial detention on grounds of dangerousness.[7]

C. *The Inquiry into the Release Conditions.*

We turn next to the other half of the equation: whether the conditions imposed by the district court were reasonably adequate to assure the community's safety, notwithstanding Tortora's dangerousness. We approach this inquiry mindful both of the respect due to the court below and of our responsibility to exercise independent oversight.

We have listed the salient conditions, and it would be pleonastic to recite them anew. They are admittedly elaborate and extensive. But they have an Achilles' heel: if there is a unifying theme in this intricate set of restrictions, it is that virtually all

---

[7] To be sure, there are integers in the § 3142(g) calculus which count in defendant's favor. He lives with his wife and children in Brockton, Massachusetts. He is employed at a video store owned by his wife. There is no evidence that he is a substance abuser. When released on bail in prior cases, he appeared for court dates on schedule. But, the factors favoring release are plainly outweighed by the factors favoring detention.

of them hinge on the defendant's good faith compliance.[8] To illustrate, electronic monitoring, while valuable in pretrial release cases (especially in allowing early detection of possible flight), cannot be expected to prevent a defendant from committing crimes or deter him from participating in felonious activity within the monitoring radius. Second, by allowing outside visits to doctors and lawyers, the conditions open up a sizeable loophole; there is no feasible way of assuring that Tortora, while en route to and from such appointments, will not make stops and take detours with a view toward continuing his criminal life. House arrest poses much the same problem; limiting visitors can only work, for example, if the appellee submits the names of potential guests for clearance. The only enforcement mechanism provided to ensure that Tortora properly restricts his contacts is a requirement that Tortora keep a record of those contacts — a mechanism which, itself, is honor-dependent. Finally, the monitoring of Tortora's sole telephone line can be easily evaded by, say, the surreptitious introduction into his home of a cellular telephone or stopping at a pay telephone while headed for an authorized appointment.

Consequently, we find that the conditions as a whole are flawed in that their success depends largely on the defendant's good faith — or lack of it. They can be too easily circumvented or manipulated. Such a flaw takes on great significance where, as in this case, little about the defendant or his history suggests that good faith will be forthcoming. If past is prologue, then promises to hew the straight and narrow will mean next to nothing to this defendant. In our estimation, the conditions fail to offer an objectively reasonable assurance of safety to the community.

At oral argument, it was hinted that, if dubiety reigned, we could simply tighten the vise by amending the conditions of release. We think such a course impracticable here. Given the breadth of human imagination, it will always be possible to envision some set of release conditions which might reasonably assure the safety of the community. For instance, agents could be posted by the government to watch Tortora at all times to ensure that he remains compliant; the guards could search all visitors, dog Tortora's footsteps en route to all appointments, and otherwise act as private jailers. But the Bail Reform Act, as we read it, does not require release of a dangerous defendant if the only combination of conditions that would reasonably assure societal safety consists of heroic measures beyond those which can fairly be said to have been within Congress's contemplation. * * * *

In asserting that the restrictions are satisfactory to justify his liberty, appellee makes five interrelated arguments. He claims that the conditions achieve a reasonable level of adequacy; that deference to the court below suggests that the release order be affirmed; that fundamental fairness supports his release because similarly situated individuals have been set free; that pretrial confinement will, in his case, likely last so long as to impact upon his constitutional rights; and that the public interest would be more poorly served by keeping him in prison. We find this

---

[8] The lone exception is the condition that the house be posted as security. Once this is accomplished, Tortora cannot easily evade its effect. The efficacy of the condition in achieving its purpose is, however, suspect. There is evidence that Tortora's allegiance to crime and the Patriarca Family are far more important to him than his allegiance to his brother (who owns the dwelling). Furthermore, there is considerable uncertainty as to whether the law would allow the house to be forfeited if Tortora kept his scheduled court dates but violated some other condition of his release by, say, committing a new crime. Real estate as security seems a much more effective condition of release in a "flight risk" case than in a "dangerousness" case.

asseverational array unconvincing in all its aspects. * * * *

As to the first, in a situation where a standard of independent review controls and where the judge (1) took no evidence, (2) accepted the magistrate's finding of dangerousness, and (3) gave no statement of reasons why he thought the release conditions proposed by Tortora's counsel would work effectively, the deference we can accord the release order is severely limited. This is especially true when, as here, the magistrate, who presided at the evidentiary hearing and made the pertinent factual determinations concluded unequivocally that "no reasonable condition or combination of conditions — short of pretrial detention — will reasonably assure the safety of the community as it relates to the defendant Tortora." The deference properly due to the district court's assessment is, we think, outweighed by the considerations we have mentioned.

The argument that the conditions are at least as confining as those imposed on two other alleged members of the Patriarca Family, Biagio DiGiacomo and Antonio L. Spagnolo (who were charged in a separate albeit comparable indictment and granted pretrial release by a different district judge in the interim between the magistrate's order detaining Tortora and the district court's order releasing him) misses the point.[9] Appellee stresses the DiGiacomo example on the thesis that DiGiacomo outranked Tortora in the Mafia hierarchy and thus, as a leader, posed a special threat to the community. For illustrative simplicity, we will slight Spagnolo, who was released by the same order and under the same conditions as DiGiacomo, and explain why we find appellee's reliance on the DiGiacomo example unpersuasive.

Detention determinations must be made individually and, in the final analysis, must be based on the evidence which is before the court regarding the particular defendant. The inquiry is factbound. No two defendants are likely to have the same pedigree or to occupy the same position.

Even a cursory comparison of the situations of DiGiacomo and Tortora hammers home these verities. There are at least two major differences. Tortora, a proven parole violator, had a busy and brutal criminal past. DiGiacomo, in contrast, had no previous criminal record. The second distinction is even more fundamental. The district court found that DiGiacomo would be likely to satisfy his legal obligations, such as release conditions. The magistrate in the instant case made exactly the opposite finding with respect to Tortora, stating that he (Tortora) "by his own words and deeds, has already demonstrated that conditions are not worth the paper on which they are written." The district judge did not pass upon, let alone explicitly overrule, this finding of fact. Thus, Tortora's case and DiGiacomo's case, despite what they may have in common, are not fair congeners.[10]

Appellee next implores us to consider the possible length of his pretrial confinement and the rigors attendant thereto. While we are not blind either to the passage of time — appellee has already been held for more than half a year and his trial (which may last up to eight months) is not likely to start until early 1991 — or

---

[9] Insofar as we are aware, the government elected not to appeal these release orders. At any rate, both DiGiacomo and Spagnolo have reportedly entered into plea agreements.

[10] Although each bail applicant must be screened individually, it is interesting to note that DiGiacomo's codefendant, Spagnolo, when compared to Tortora, is set apart equally well. Spagnolo had an arrest record, but no prior convictions. Moreover, Judge Wolf, who granted pretrial release to DiGiacomo and Spagnolo, wrote that the latter "constituted less of a threat to safety than DiGiacomo."

to the harshness which pretrial detention works in such circumstances, Congress was surely aware of this potential when it enacted 18 U.S.C. § 3142. Nevertheless, Congress conspicuously omitted any instruction to consider the potential length of detention as part of the pretrial release calculus. The Supreme Court has upheld § 3142 on its face against a constitutional attack. See *United States v. Salerno*, 481 U.S. 739 (1987). Since *Salerno*, it has been accepted that due process challenges to pretrial detention, as applied, must be resolved on a case-by-case basis. At this stage of the proceedings, Tortora's pretrial incarceration has not been so protracted as to support a due process claim. Because the duration of further immurement is still speculative, consideration of whether an appreciably longer incarcerative period would constitute a violation of constitutional or statutory law in Tortora's case is presently unripe.[11]

Appellee's last argument is mind-boggling in its implication. He cites to the principle stated in *Phillips*, 732 F.Supp. at 267, that the issue to "be addressed is whether the defendant's *release* would pose a danger to the community that would not exist if the defendant were held in pretrial preventive detention;" and contends that, even if the stated conditions are not adequate to assure the safety of the community in an objectively reasonable sense, the release order was justified because, if kept in prison, he will have at least as much ability to commit crimes as he would have if released. We find the *Phillips* principle perverse. The Bail Reform Act does not ordain that dangerousness upon release is to be measured relative to dangerousness if incarcerated, and for good reason: the ability of an incarcerated person to commit crimes while in jail is a problem for the Executive Branch to solve. The idea that someone who otherwise ought not to be released should be let loose by the courts because his jailers may not prevent him from committing crimes while in prison comprises a classic non sequitur, alien to the Bail Reform Act, to its legislative history, and to common sense.

IV. *Conclusion*

We need go no further. On independent review of the facts and determinations below, and with due regard to the decisions of the magistrate and the district judge, we conclude that Tortora should not be set at liberty at this stage of the proceedings. In our judgment, the safety of the community cannot reasonably be assured should the appellee be released subject to the proposed conditions or to any readily ascertainable combination of practicable restrictions.[12] We therefore sustain the government's appeal, vacate the release order, reinstate the magistrate's earlier order for pretrial detention, and remand for further proceedings not inconsistent herewith.

---

[11] Similarly, appellee's argument that his place of incarceration is so distant and inconvenient as to interfere with his ability to consult with his attorneys and prepare a defense consists at this juncture of rank supposition. In the absence of a concrete factual predicate — and none was offered below — the suggestion is too speculative to be evaluated in either constitutional or statutory terms. In any event, such geographic factors do not appear to be germane in considering pretrial release of dangerous defendants under the Bail Reform Act of 1984.

[12] We refuse to speculate about, and therefore take no view of, whether the district court, on a proper showing, could possibly devise some sort of special "pretrial house arrest" as suggested by our concurring brother, which might allow the defendant's release from pretrial detention.

BREYER, CHIEF JUDGE* (concurring).

I agree with the panel majority on three points:

1) The record makes clear that the appellee's release, under ordinary conditions of bail, would pose a serious threat to "the safety of other person[s] and the community." 18 U.S.C. § 3142(e). It reveals a past record of violent behavior; a likelihood that appellee swore the most solemn oaths committing him to silence, indeed to kill, witnesses and others at his confederates' bidding; and strong evidence of present crimes carrying severe penalties; all of which together demonstrate that judicial authorities cannot trust him and that he is the sort of person Congress had in mind when enacting the "preventive detention" provisions of the Bail Reform Act. See 18 U.S.C. § 3142(g). The magistrate so found. The district court did not find to the contrary. The record requires such a finding.

2) The record indicates that appellee's circumstances differ significantly from those of his alleged associates Biagio DiGiacomo and Antonio Spagnolo, whom the district court released on conditions similar to those involved here. In the case of DiGiacomo and Spagnolo, the court, prior to releasing them (to a form of house arrest), carefully analyzed the danger they posed. On the one hand, the court recognized that house arrest, compared with incarceration, would make it "at least marginally easier to direct criminal activity." On the other hand, the court noted that the two defendants had been fully aware for the previous three years of the government's forthcoming prosecution, the evidence that it would likely present, and the likely witnesses against them, yet they did not "directly or indirectly" threaten, injure, or attempt to intimidate any government agent or witness "in the three years prior to indictment." The district court in this case provided no such analysis, it pointed to no such offsetting feature, and the government says it could not have done so, for the appellee in this case was, in effect, surprised by the indictment.

3) There is no explanation at all in the record as to how the pre-trial conditions — the wearing of an electronic bracelet that would mark the appellee's where-abouts, a pen-register on his telephone, and appellee's promise not to contact unapproved persons-will prevent the appellee from engaging in the most obvious serious risk, namely his planning with others to silence witnesses. Of course, should the government *catch him* communicating with unapproved persons, his brother's house is forfeited. But, why could the appellee not communicate with visitors inside the house; why could he not obtain an unauthorized telephone; why could he not communicate at night through a window? After all, the electronic bracelet tells the government where he is, it helps prevent flight, but it does not tell the government who is with him, whom he speaks to or what he says. In other words, the record, while explaining that defendant promises not to plan crimes, is totally silent as to how the government can catch the defendant if he does so. It does not discuss the costs or obstacles involved in supervising compliance with the conditions.

I part company with the majority, however, if it means to imply that, given proper record evidence and findings, the district court lacks the legal power to create and to impose a kind of "pre-trial house arrest" upon a defendant such as this one. The statute says that if a "judicial officer finds that *no condition or combination of conditions* will reasonably assure the safety of any other person and the commu-

---

* Ed.: Now MR. JUSTICE BREYER, of the U.S. Supreme Court.

nity, such judicial officer shall order the detention of the person before trial." 18 U.S.C. § 3142(e) (emphasis added). I agree that the underlined language does not refer to outlandish conditions, such as requiring several government agents to follow a defendant wherever he goes. Yet, when describing conditions, the statute refers to the court's power to impose "any other condition that is *reasonably necessary* to assure the safety of any other person and the community." 18 U.S.C. § 3142(c)(B)(xiv) (emphasis added). It seems to me that what is "reasonably necessary" depends upon the circumstances. Where two or three years of pre trial detention is at stake, and detention is in a distant facility, requiring counsel to drive several hours to confer with his client, conditions that impose cost burdens upon the government might well seem more "reasonable" than in more usual circumstances. Indeed, if conviction follows, it may prove possible to recoup extra costs through a punitive fine. I should leave an evaluation of "house arrest" and the government's related claim that courts cannot impose conditions that (to secure "safety") work a "tremendous financial burden," all to a later time. It is sufficient here that the record fails to make even a minimal demonstration as to how the conditions imposed meet the threat revealed.

Notes from Pete:

1. In *U.S. v. Bellomo*, 944 F.Supp. 1160 (S.D.N.Y.1996), the acting boss of the Genovese family ("and one of the persons responsible for, among other things, resolving disputes among the five organized crime families in New York City") was charged with racketeering, murder, and other crimes. In his motion for pretrial release, he claimed that the "weight of the evidence" against him was not great, because two polygraph (lie detector) examiners had concluded that he was truthful when he denied involvement in murder. The court denied Bellomo's motion:

> The polygraph evidence is properly considered on this application, despite its long established inadmissibility in criminal trials, because the rules of evidence do not apply in detention hearings under the Bail Reform Act. 18 U.S.C. § 3142(f). It is important, however, to be clear as to its relevance.

> The issue now before the Court is whether there is a risk that Bellomo will flee the jurisdiction or endanger others before the trial can be held, not whether he is guilty or innocent of the charges in the indictment. The polygraph results therefore are relevant only to the extent they bear on whether Bellomo has an incentive to flee or poses a threat to the community.

> A major significance in a detention hearing of the strength of the government's case is its bearing on the extent to which the defendant has a motive to flee prosecution if released pending trial. All other things being equal, a defendant facing serious potential penalties in the event of conviction is more likely to disappear if the government's case is strong than if an acquittal appears likely.

> As noted, the government in this case has strong evidence of Bellomo's guilt on the murder and murder conspiracy charges. It evidently has an eyewitness who will testify to Bellomo's involvement in ordering or approving the charged murder, evidence that is quite likely to be received in evidence at trial.

Bellomo's polygraph evidence, even if it were persuasive as measured by the standard of polygraph tests generally, would not diminish the strength of the government's case sufficiently to mitigate Bellomo's strong incentive to flee. For one thing, as Bellomo's counsel conceded at argument, polygraph evidence never has been admitted in a federal trial in this Circuit, even in the three years since *Daubert v. Merrell Dow Pharmaceuticals, Inc.*, 509 U.S. 579 (1993). While the admissibility of polygraph evidence in light of *Daubert* perhaps is an open question, Bellomo confronts at least a significant possibility that the evidence will be excluded even if it is offered. Moreover, even if admitted, the polygraph results would not be conclusive, and Bellomo still would face the risk that the jury would accept the government's evidence rather than that of Bellomo's polygraphers. The polygraph evidence in the best of circumstances therefore would be of questionable value. It does not overcome the government's proof that Bellomo has powerful reasons to disappear.

2. In *U.S. v. Malloy*, 11 F.Supp.2d 583 (D.N.J.1998), Malloy was charged with violating the Arms Export Control Act. He moved to modify his bail conditions — from electronic monitoring to use of a "satellite tracking system." Noting that "Courts must endeavor to impose the least restrictive bail conditions that will assure both the defendant's appearance at trials as well as the public's safety. See 18 U.S.C. § 3142(c)," the court granted the motion:

The tracking system provides more freedom of movement than electronic monitoring/house arrest. The technology uses the Global Positioning System designed for military use in the 1970's and consists of twenty-four satellites orbiting Earth. Defendants monitored by the system wear a wrist or ankle band and carry a tracking unit that is about the size of laptop computer. Signals from the satellites and tracking unit are transferred to a communications center that plots where the defendant has been and at what time. In addition, certain "exclusion zones" can be created. When the defendant is not in close proximity to the tracking unit or enters an exclusion zone, Pretrial Services would be notified within minutes that a violation occurred.

UNITED STATES v. PATRIARCA
United States Court of Appeals, 1st Circuit
948 F.2d 789 (1991)

TORRUELLA, CIRCUIT JUDGE

According to the government, defendant-appellee Raymond J. Patriarca is the former Boss of the New England Mafia Family bearing his name (although named after his father). * * * * Patriarca assumed leadership of the Patriarca Family following the death of his father in July 1984 and held it until he was demoted following his indictment in this case. That indictment, handed down on March 22, 1990, charges Patriarca with two counts under RICO, 18 U.S.C. § 1962, and five counts of violating the Travel Act, 18 U.S.C. § 1952. The Travel Act violations also serve as predicate acts for the RICO charges.

The government moved for pretrial detention under the Bail Reform Act, 18 U.S.C. §§ 3142(e) and (f), contending that no condition or combination of conditions would reasonably assure Patriarca's appearance at trial and the safety of the community. The magistrate did not rule on risk of flight, but did hold that only pretrial detention would ensure public safety. More than one year later, following additional hearings, the district court ordered Patriarca's release. The government appeals that order. * * * *

Standard of Review

Our review of the district court's release order is not de novo, but, rather, independent, "giving deference to the determination of the district court." *United States v. O'Brien*, 895 F.2d 810, 814 (1st Cir.1990). * * * *

Dangerousness

The magistrate's detention order was based primarily on two conclusions drawn from subsidiary facts: first, that Raymond Patriarca's membership in the Mafia indicated a continuing commitment to a criminal way of life; second, that the evidence against Patriarca was strong, since a substantial portion of it consisted of his own tape-recorded words. The district judge did not specifically dispute either of these conclusions and agreed that they militated in favor of detention. But the court did not end its inquiry there. Instead, the judge conducted his own analysis of appellee's situation in light of the statutory factors set forth in 18 U.S.C. § 3142(g). His findings follow.

Nature and circumstances of the offense

Patriarca is charged with two RICO violations and five Travel Act violations. The court noted that at least two of the Travel Act violations related to extortion and credit transactions, which are crimes of violence, 18 U.S.C. § 3156(a)(4)(A), thus triggering the detention determination called for by 18 U.S.C. § 3142(f)(1)(A). On the other side of the balance, the court found that appellee was not charged with any personal acts of violence, nor with obstruction of justice, nor with any narcotics offense. The RICO charges rested essentially on appellee's leadership role in the Mafia, but the government had stipulated that Patriarca no longer held that position. Moreover, if convicted of the charges, the guideline sentence would be in the range of only five to six years, absent departure.

Weight of the evidence

The judge found that the evidence that Patriarca was the Boss of the Patriarca Family was strong, but characterized the evidence on the Travel Act violations as of uncertain weight. He also found significant the fact that all the evidence was documentary; there were no testimonial witnesses, thus no one for appellee to threaten if he were to be released.

History and characteristics of the defendant

The judge noted that Patriarca has strong family ties; legitimate employment as a real estate developer; no history of drug or alcohol abuse; a rational demeanor and an apparent ability to act in his own, enlightened, self-interest. Patriarca suffers from recurrent bladder cancer and requires hospitalization every three months.

Importantly, he has no criminal record. The court found, though, that the absence of a record was at least in part because Patriarca's position as Boss allowed him to rely on others to commit substantive crimes. The court characterized Patriarca as a reluctant and ineffective Mafia Boss, one who achieved his position by virtue of nepotism rather than merit. He had never been a strong leader and his power had diminished substantially, to the point where, in the summer of 1989, an underling had threatened to kill him if he did not step down. In response, Patriarca ceded considerable power to this individual. The court acknowledged that appellee had presided at a Mafia induction ceremony at which the inductees swore lifelong loyalty to the Mafia, and promised to kill any informants if instructed to do so. But, the judge also found that "no one is likely to order this defendant to kill anybody. He has no penchant or personal aptitude for violence."[2] Finally, Patriarca had been demoted from Boss, largely because the organization held him responsible for allowing the FBI to tape the induction ceremony. His tenuous status within the Mafia made it unlikely that he would be called upon to assist his replacement.

In sum, the facts as found by the district court indicate that Patriarca did not have a clean slate despite his lack of a criminal record. Nevertheless, the court found the evidence that Patriarca was so dangerous that no set of conditions could assure the safety of the community to be short of clear and convincing. See 18 U.S.C. § 3142(f) (imposing a clear and convincing burden on the government to prove dangerousness). Essentially, the judge found that although in theory a Mafia Boss was an intimidating and highly dangerous character, the government had not demonstrated that this Boss posed a significant danger, or at least not a danger that could not be overcome given appropriate conditions.

We cannot disagree with that conclusion. It was rendered after substantial consideration, by a judge with a great deal of familiarity with the case. The dangerousness inquiry thus shifts to the adequacy of the conditions imposed by the court. But first, we look at the district court's findings as to risk of flight.

Risk of Flight

The district court applied a similar analysis in evaluating the risk that Patriarca would flee rather than appear for trial. Significant here were appellee's ties to his family, making it unlikely that he would leave them (and jeopardize their homes under the forfeiture condition). Further, appellee's poor health rendered flight dangerous. If Patriarca escaped but was captured, he would likely face a substantial upward departure in his sentence. Given Patriarca's health, the judge noted that a longer term of imprisonment would amount to a sentence to die in prison. The court also found that, although Patriarca had known for some time that he was under FBI surveillance, he did not flee. He had appeared before several grand juries when subpoenaed. And he stayed put when confronted with rampant rumors of his imminent indictment.

On the other side of the flight risk equation, the court acknowledged that the Mafia had both the will and the way to facilitate flight. The Patriarca Family (the government argued that it was Patriarca himself) had once assisted a fugitive's

---

[2] To be sure, danger to the community does not refer only to the risk of physical violence. *See U.S. v. Tortora*, 922 F.2d 880, 884 (1st Cir. 1990). The comments of the trial judge indicate that he was well aware of this fact, and that he also considered the possible danger flowing from the continuing commission of crime and from assistance Patriarca might lend to his successor in the organization.

flight by supplying him with $100,000 cash; however, the court found that the government had not tied appellee personally to that episode. Moreover, as Patriarca no longer commanded significant power or respect in the organization, the court believed that he was not likely to receive support from the Mafia were he to flee.

Overall, the court found that the evidence of the likelihood of Patriarca's flight was minimal, not even enough to satisfy the preponderance burden of proof. The court's determination, while perhaps not inevitable, seems a supportable exercise of its factfinding function. The most compelling consideration — the Mafia's ability to aid flight — is not supplemented by evidence of this Mafia member's propensity to flee. Therefore, the adequacy of the conditions to assure appellee's presence at trial becomes relevant.

Adequacy of the Conditions

The district court devised an innovative and extensive group of conditions for appellee's release. In addition to the stock provisos, see 18 U.S.C. § 3142(a), the court required that Patriarca shall: (1) remain in his home 24 hours a day subject to electronic monitoring, except that he may leave his home for medical appointments and medical emergencies in the custody of one of his attorneys; (2) meet and/or communicate directly or indirectly only with his attorneys and individuals approved by the court, defendant being required to keep a record of his direct and indirect communications; (3) at his own expense, install and maintain 24-hour video camera surveillance directed at each entrance to his house; (4) have only one telephone and one telephone line at his residence; (5) execute an agreement to forfeit $4 million, collateralized by real estate held in the name of his wife and certain other relatives, upon a determination by the court that he has violated a condition of his release and that forfeiture should result; (6) be subject to unannounced searches (of the defendant, his residence, and his visitors) by agents or officers of the FBI, Pretrial Services or by other law enforcement agencies.

These conditions were devised to provide assurance against both aspects of the Bail Reform Act inquiry, danger to the community and risk of flight, and we find ourselves (with one reservation detailed below) unable to disturb the district court's conclusion that they suffice. First, Patriarca agreed that the forfeiture condition (number (5) above) would take effect upon the violation of any condition of release. This agreement, essentially a private contract, was intended to avoid the uncertainty noted in _Tortora_ as to whether under the Bail Reform Act forfeitures only apply to failure to appear at trial. We see no reason why such an agreement should not be valid and it adds considerably to the incentive value of the forfeiture condition. Without such a provision, forfeiture tends to be more effective against risk of flight than against danger to the community. See _Tortora_, 922 F.2d at 886 n. 8.

Second, the judge explicitly disclaimed reliance on Patriarca's good faith compliance, a fatal weakness of the conditions imposed in _Tortora_. This disclaimer has two parts. One is the video monitoring system which serves as an objective check on appellee's behavior. The other is the judge's explicit finding that Patriarca would comply because compliance was in his enlightened self-interest. Based on his assessment of Patriarca's ability to perceive the consequences of his own conduct, the judge considered the risk of forfeiture, the danger to Patriarca's health, and the possibility of a substantial upward departure at sentencing to be adequate assurance of compliance — wholly apart from good faith.

Third, appellee is financing the elaborate video monitoring system himself, and the other conditions are not extraordinarily burdensome to the government. The government is thus not going to "heroic measures," nor is it establishing a private jail at public expense. See *Tortora*, 922 F.2d at 887.

Taken together, we find the conditions are within the district court's "legal power to create and to impose a kind of 'pre-trial house arrest.'" See *id.* at 895 (Breyer, J., concurring). We cannot say these conditions do not provide reasonable assurance of public safety and of appellee's attendance at trial.

In urging us to vacate the release order, the government relies heavily on *Tortora*, claiming that as both Carmen Tortora and Raymond Patriarca are members of the Patriarca Family, they are painted with the same brush and merit the same treatment. *Tortora* itself provides our response: "Detention determinations must be made individually and, in the final analysis, must be based on the evidence which is before the court regarding the particular defendant." 922 F.2d at 888. And a comparison of the two cases reinforces the need for individualized analysis. The district court here gave careful consideration to the relevant statutory factors, considered new evidence, and provided us with a careful summary of its conclusions, all absent in *Tortora*. Carmen Tortora had a long criminal record; Raymond Patriarca has none. Tortora was a parole violator, had a penchant for violence, and no evidence pointed to his debilitation (or rehabilitation). Moreover, there was, in Tortora's case, a specific factual finding that he was likely to violate any conditions of release. Here, the court found just the opposite with respect to Patriarca. And here, in the interval between the magistrate's detention order and the district court's release order, a significant event occurred: Patriarca's demotion from his role as Boss of the Family. The two cases provide a vivid example of the error of lumping defendants together based solely on their alleged Mafia membership. They also demonstrate the nature of independent review, which can vary in intensity according to the care put into the decision below. We do not find the cases sufficiently comparable to change the result here.[4]

As we insinuated above, we do have one reservation related to the forfeiture condition. The Bail Reform Act provides that release conditions may include the requirement that the defendant: execute an agreement to forfeit upon failing to appear as required, such designated property, including money, as is reasonably necessary to assure the appearance of the person as required, and post with the court such indicia of ownership of the property or such percentage of the money as the judicial officer may specify. 18 U.S.C. § 3142(c)(1)(B)(xi). Plainly contemplated by this language is some exploration of a defendant's assets or net worth. Without such information we fail to see how a judicial officer could arrive at a forfeiture amount which would reasonably assure compliance. In *O'Brien*, for example, the

---

[4] Further distinctions can be drawn between the release conditions imposed upon the two defendants. Tortora was to be allowed to leave his home unaccompanied to visit his doctors and lawyers; Patriarca's lawyers must come to him, and they must accompany him to his doctor's appointments. Tortora was to be allowed to meet with co-defendants in the presence of counsel; Patriarca is forbidden to do so under any circumstances. Tortora was to post only one house, belonging to his brother, and the forfeiture may have taken place only upon Tortora's failure to appear; Patriarca will post significantly greater assets and has agreed to forfeiture for any violation. It does not appear that Tortora consented to random searches; Patriarca has done so. The video monitor is unique to Patriarca. Again, we find that comparing the two cases supports, rather than undermines, our holding here.

court was persuaded to release the defendant in part because the proposed surety was "so vital to defendant that he sought long and hard to avoid offering it." 895 F.2d at 816; see also *United States v. DiGiacomo*, 746 F.Supp. 1176, 1190 (D.Mass.1990) (requiring defendant to put all his assets up for forfeiture). By contrast, it appears here that the $4 million worth of real estate was freely offered up by Patriarca, and the record does not suggest what portion of appellee's worth the forfeiture represents. As the forfeiture provision is a crucial release condition, its effectiveness will be bolstered (or its inadequacy revealed) by additional factfinding on this point. For that purpose we shall remand the case to the district court.[5]

Conclusion

Membership in, and leadership of, a Mafia Family are undoubtedly "highly relevant considerations" in the pretrial detention analysis. *Tortora*, 922 F.2d at 885 n. 10. But mention of the Mafia is insufficient, in itself, to carry the day for the government, and we decline to disturb the district court's considered assessment that the other factors do not prove that Raymond Patriarca is such a danger to the community, or such a risk of flight, that no reasonable set of conditions on his release is conceivable. We are, however, concerned with the process by which the amount of property to be forfeited was determined. For that reason, we remand to the district court for further findings as to appellee's financial position.

HILL, SENIOR CIRCUIT JUDGE (concurring *dubitante*).

I concur in our judgment ordering a remand for additional factfinding on net worth. I concur in so much of the opinion and judgment approving the denial of pretrial detention because I feel especially deferential to the district judge's findings and conclusions.

I am troubled, nevertheless, by the direction we have taken and are taking. The appellee has not been tried under the indictment. When and if he is he will be entitled to the presumption of innocence and to a jury properly instructed on the burden of proof placed on the prosecution. However, we are given a record, on the question of pretrial detention, *vel non*, which identifies appellee as a committed member of La Cosa Nostra, pledged to do its bidding. That, alone, would substantiate a finding that he presents a danger of flight; he will flee if his sovereign tells him to flee and his master, La Cosa Nostra, may be endangered by disclosures at his trial. But that finding was not made by the district court.

I am troubled by the weight given to the finding that Patriarca can and will pay for much of the technologically exotic surveillance of himself. We must not announce that, in this country, a financially successful hood whose gotten gains permit him to imprison himself in comfort need not put up with our prison system, but one apprehended before the accumulation of great wealth will not be due our deference.

The ability of the defendant to pay should have nothing to do with the decision as to whether pretrial release conditions constitute the "heroic measures beyond those which can fairly be said to have been within Congress's contemplation" to

---

[5] We wish to emphasize that the evidence here was certainly sufficient to allow the trier to reach a contrary conclusion and order that Patriarca remain in pretrial detention. But as mentioned earlier, the independent review standard contemplates a certain deference to factbound determinations made by the district court. In our view, this deference must carry the day in the case at bar.

which we referred in *U.S. v. Tortora*, 922 F.2d 880, 887. The district court should first decide, without reference to who pays, whether the measures to be employed are within the meaning of 18 U.S.C. § 3142(c)(1). If they are, the court may also consider imposing the cost upon the defendant, but I suggest that they cannot be found to be within the contemplation of the Act because the defendant can afford to pay for them.

Had the district court found that pretrial detention was required, I have little doubt that its imposition would have received my concurrence.

Leaning heavily upon the better opportunity the district judge has had to evaluate the witnesses, and agreeing with the remand ordered, I concur.

Notes from Pete:

1. Can this case be reconciled with *Tortora*?

2. In *U.S. v. Goba*, 240 F.Supp.2d 242 (W.D.N.Y. 2003), defendants were charged with providing support to Al Qaeda, a foreign terrorist organization.

> During the spring and summer of 2001, Defendants traveled in two separate groups from the United States to Pakistan, and from Pakistan to Afghanistan, where they attended an al-Qaeda terrorist training camp. Defendants allegedly received firearms and other tactical training, underwent anti-American and anti-Israeli indoctrination, were lectured on martyrdom and the justification for using suicide as a weapon, and attended a speech personally given by Usama bin Ladin that, in part, emphasized the need to prepare and train for a "fight against the Americans." After several weeks, Defendants left the camp and returned to Lackawanna, New York. All resumed their regular lives until their arrests on or about September 13, 2002.

The court denied defendants' motion for pretrial release:

> I find that the charged offense, 18 U.S.C. § 2339B, is a "crime of violence," and that the Government has demonstrated by clear and convincing evidence that Defendants pose a danger to the community. Significantly, the Government has produced credible evidence that each defendant associated himself with al-Qaeda, a designated terrorist organization with the avowed aim of inflicting death and destruction on American citizens and interests. In reaching my decision, I note that the express purpose of a terrorist training camp such as al-Farooq is to make its participants more dangerous (and thus more useful to the terrorist group) than they were before they received the training. Given the well-known modus operandi of terrorist organizations such as al-Qaeda, the stated goals of Usama bin Ladin, and the evidence regarding the type of training that each Defendant received while at the camp, I find that no release condition or combination of release conditions will adequately safeguard the community.

> In addition, I find that the Government has proven by a preponderance of the evidence that each defendant poses a risk of flight if released. The Government proffered evidence indicating that each defendant has the ability to sustain himself abroad, either with his own resources or through

the use of an international support network. This ability, combined with Western New York's proximity to the Canadian border and the potential period of incarceration faced by each defendant, is sufficient to establish that no release condition or combination of conditions will assure the continued appearance of these Defendants.

Therefore, Defendants Goba, Mosed, Taher and Al-Bakri shall remain detained pending trial.

3. In *Oliver v. U.S.*, 682 A.2d 186 (D.C.Ct.App.1996), the court held that the trial court did not exceed its statutory authority or violate the Fourth Amendment when it ordered drug testing as a condition of pretrial release of drugs and weapons charges. The court affirmed Oliver's conviction for criminal contempt for violating the order.

4. In *U.S. v. Scott*, 424 F.3d 888 (9th Cir. 2005):

Scott was arrested for drug possession crimes under state law and released on his own recognizance. Among the conditions of his release was consent to "random" drug testing "anytime of the day or night by any peace officer without a warrant," and to having his home searched for drugs "by any peace officer anytime, day or night, without a warrant."

Based on an informant's tip, officers went to Scott's house and administered a urine test. The government concedes the tip did not establish probable cause. When Scott tested positive for methamphetamine, the officers arrested him and searched his house. The search ultimately turned up a shotgun.

The Government argued that Scott's pre-trial release was a "special need" that justified searching him on less than probable cause. The court disagreed:

The government argues here that searching pre-trial releasees by testing them for drugs serves two special needs: (1) protecting the community from criminal defendants released pending trial and (2) ensuring that defendants show up at trial. But — at most — only the second of these claimed needs is, as the special needs exception requires, "beyond the normal need for law enforcement." * * * *

The government's first identified purpose, protecting the community, presumably means protecting it from the criminal activities of pre-trial releasees. The dissent points out correctly that the "government's interest in preventing crime by arrestees is both legitimate and compelling." But the government's interest in preventing crime by *anyone* is legitimate and compelling. Crime prevention is a quintessential general law enforcement purpose and therefore is the exact opposite of a special need.

The second purpose, ensuring that pre-trial releasees appear in court, fares somewhat better: While it has a law enforcement component — a defendant's failure to appear in court when ordered to do so is a criminal offense, it also implicates the efficient functioning and integrity of the judicial system, a purpose separate from the general interest in crime control.

We assume for purposes of our analysis that the non-law-enforcement purpose — the interest in judicial efficiency — is "primary" in this case. It remains to determine whether this need is important enough to override the individual's acknowledged privacy interest and sufficiently vital to suppress the Fourth Amendment's normal requirement of individualized suspicion, and then weigh it against the intrusion on the individual's interest in privacy.

To begin with, the connection between the object of the test (drug use) and the harm to be avoided (nonappearance in court) is not obvious. The defendant may use drugs while on pre-trial release and be so overcome by the experience — he's in a drug-induced stupor or in a hospital emergency room — that he misses his court date. Or, having made it to court, he may be too mentally impaired to participate meaningfully in the proceedings. These are conceivable justifications, but they strike us as highly unlikely. The government has produced nothing to suggest these are common enough problems to justify intruding on the privacy rights of every single defendant out on pre-trial release. Drug use during pre-trial release may also result in a defendant's general unreliability or, more nefariously, an increased likelihood of absconding. Whether this is plausible depends on whether drug use is a good predictor of these harms — a case that must be established empirically by the government that seeks to impose the drug testing condition. * * * *

We are especially reluctant to indulge the claimed special need here because Scott's privacy interest in his home, where the officers came to demand the urine sample, is at its zenith. * * * * Unlike public school students, who have limited privacy interests because of the state's special custodial role, Customs employees, who occupy sensitive government positions, or drivers and railway employees, whose activities impose safety risks on others, pre-trial releasees are ordinary people who have been accused of a crime but are presumed innocent. We have already noted that Scott's assent to his release conditions does not by itself make an otherwise unreasonable search reasonable; to the extent his assent decreased his reasonable expectation of privacy, we hold that the decrease was insufficient to eliminate his expectation of privacy in his home. * * * *

Because the government has failed to make the requisite special needs showing, the police needed probable cause to test Scott for drugs. We thus cannot validate Scott's search under the special needs doctrine.

Judge Bybee dissented, opining that the Government's interests outweighed Scott's interests:

1. The State's Interests

a. *Protecting the public.* The majority rejects the state's interest in protecting the public as a "quintessential general law enforcement purpose which is the exact opposite of a special need," and argues that the presumption of innocence insulates the pretrial releasee from the claim that he is "more likely to commit crimes than other members of society."

First, the state's interest is not so easily dismissed by referring to the state's general duty to protect the public or the presumption of innocence. * * * * While protecting its citizens is the first duty of government,

Nevada's concern for the safety of the public is not "general law enforcement" when it is manifested in pretrial conditions tailored to this defendant.

Second, the accused enjoys the presumption of innocence as a *trial* right; an accused does not enjoy the same presumption with respect to ordinary civil rights of citizens, such as freedom of movement. *See, e.g.*, U.S. CONST. amend. VIII (" *Excessive* bail shall not be required"). * * * * Both courts and Congress have implicitly rejected the majority's argument by treating persons indicted for crimes differently than ordinary citizens. In *Wolfish*, the Supreme Court rejected a similar argument, concluding that "the presumption of innocence is a doctrine that allocates the burden of proof in criminal trials but it has no application to a determination of the rights of a pretrial detainee during confinement before his trial has even begun." 441 U.S. at 533. * * * *

The majority's lack of consideration for the state's expressed interests is especially irresponsible in cases involving "drugs or illegal weapons" where authorities supervising the convict "must be able to act based on a lesser degree of certainty than the Fourth Amendment would otherwise require in order to intervene before the person does damage to himself or society." *Griffin*, 483 U.S. at 879. Scott's status as a pre-trial releasee distinguishes him from the probationer considered in *Griffin*, but the distinction is not constitutionally relevant. The Court's analysis in *Griffin* and *Knights* should apply equally to the facts of this case. Scott was arrested for felony drug possession and the probation officers searched his home based on reasonable suspicion that he possessed firearms and drug paraphernalia. Perhaps the state has a lesser interest where conviction has not yet been established, but surely the state retained some interest in intervening before Scott did "damage to himself or society."

Moreover, "the government's interest in preventing crime by arrestees is both legitimate and compelling." *United States v. Salerno*, 481 U.S. 739, 749 (1987). By failing to recognize these interests, the majority grossly misrepresents the government's interest in protecting the public through supervising individuals on pretrial release.

b. *Securing attendance at trial.* With regard to Nevada's second articulated interest, ensuring that the defendant appears in court, the majority hypothesizes that the state is concerned that the defendant "may use drugs and be so overcome by the experience that he misses his court date" or "may be too mentally impaired to participate meaningfully in the proceedings." The majority writes this off as "highly unlikely" and asserts that the "government has produced nothing to suggest these are common enough problems to justify intruding on the privacy rights of every single defendant out on pre-trial release" and must do so "empirically."

Thus, without explanation, the majority requires that state governments empirically prove that drug use is preventing individuals from appearing in court before they can require consent to drug testing in exchange for pretrial release. There are other reasons a state might link drug testing with attendance at trial. Even if the state was not concerned with physical attendance, the state has a strong interest in preserving its judicial resources. Drug testing helps ensure that the accused is physically and mentally prepared for trial, so that there are no delays or claims that the defendant was unable to understand the proceedings or participate in his defense.

Even assuming that drug use does not generally affect a pretrial releasee's likelihood of appearing in court, the majority ignores the other state interests underlying the conditions. Although random drug tests "cannot be said to relate directly to the likelihood that a defendant will comply with his or her duty to attend subsequent court hearings," the conditions "clearly relate to the prevention and detection of further crime and thus to the safety of the public." *In re York*, 40 Cal.Rptr.2d 308. Requiring states to make an empirical showing before imposing a drug testing condition ties the hands of states in preventing crimes and protecting the public. Moreover, today's holding carries monumental implications for the numerous state governments that regularly require, where drug offenses are concerned, submission to drug testing in exchange for pretrial release.

2. Scott's Interests

As to Scott's interest, the searches were conducted at Scott's home, a location specially protected by the Fourth Amendment. No criminal judgment or sanction had been imposed on Scott at the time of the search. Further, at the time of arrest he was not carrying any dangerous weapons. Although all of these factors favor privacy protection, Scott's initial arrest was for felony possession of methamphetamine and two misdemeanors — possession of drugs and drug paraphernalia. Such drugs are frequently used or stored in the home. Thus, Scott's reasonable expectation of privacy may be somewhat greater than that of a probationer, parolee, or presentence releasee, but it is less than that of an "ordinary citizen."

Moreover, Scott's reasonable expectation of privacy is diminished somewhat by his agreement to place himself under the supervision of the Department of Alternative Sentencing and waive the warrant requirement in exchange for being released on OR. The search condition itself, a "salient circumstance" in the Fourth Amendment balance, allowed warrantless searches for controlled substances and alcohol, and implicitly waived the probable cause requirement by imposing "random" drug testing. The consent form clearly expressed the search condition and Scott was unambiguously informed of it.

The conditions on the form, to submit to random drug testing and warrantless searches of his home for alcohol and controlled substances, were also related to the felony and misdemeanor drug crimes with which he was charged. "The release condition thus significantly diminished Scott's reasonable expectation of privacy."

In my view, the *Knights* balance tips more favorably in the direction of the state's legitimate interests as it concerns the random drug testing condition. Scott knowingly consented to random drug testing in exchange for release from prison pending trial. I would hold that the state did not violate the Constitution by requiring Scott to submit to a random drug test based on reasonable suspicion. Once the state administered the drug test, and it came back positive, the officers had probable cause to arrest Scott, search his living room, and question him as to the presence of any weapons on the premises. Thus, I would hold that the guns were obtained during a lawful search. I find the Court's decisions in *Griffin* and *Knights* instructive in this regard.

The majority attempts to distinguish *Griffin* by stating that "pre-trial releasees are not probationers," and "people released pending trial, by contrast, have suffered no judicial abridgment of their constitutional rights." While technically I agree that pretrial releasees have not had a *judicial* abridgment of their constitutional rights, they have a lesser expectation of privacy than an ordinary citizen. A pretrial releasee suffers great burdens and is scarcely at liberty. A person facing pending charges and released on their own recognizance is required to appear in court at the state's command, is often subject, as in this case, to the condition that he seek formal permission from the court (at significant expense) before exercising what would otherwise be his unquestioned right to travel outside the jurisdiction. A defendant who could not post bail or obtain release on OR faces a much larger deprivation of liberty by being confined pending trial. Pretrial confinement may imperil the suspect's job, interrupt his source of income, and impair his family relationships. Detention may limit a defendant's preparation for trial by limiting his access to his attorney and potential witnesses. It may also "result in permanent stigma and loss of reputation to the defendant." *United States v. Motamedi*, 767 F.2d 1403, 1414 (9th Cir.1985) (Boochever, J., concurring and dissenting in part). As Judge Boochever explained:

> The magnitude of these concerns is increased by the fact that the injuries consequent upon pretrial confinement may not be reparable upon a subsequent acquittal. Society has no mechanism to recompense an individual for income lost or damages to a career due to pretrial confinement. Nor do we compensate the individual and his family for their mental suffering and loss of reputation due to pretrial incarceration.

Further, "his employment prospects may be diminished severely, he may suffer reputational harm, and he will experience the financial and emotional strain of preparing a defense." *Id.* Moreover, a defendant released on his own recognizance, even though he has not been charged with a crime, is considered to be "in custody" for some purposes. *Hensley v. Municipal Ct.*, 411 U.S. 345 (1973) (pretrial releasee is considered in custody for habeas purposes). Importantly, the common law seems to have regarded the difference between pretrial incarceration, bail, and other ways to secure a defendant's court attendance as different methods of retaining control over a defendant's person, which was in custody." Thus, those complying with release conditions are able to forgo a deprivation of liberty much greater than any release condition.

This is not to say that all release conditions should be deemed constitutional. In fact, there have been several instances where courts have found release conditions too constrictive on liberty. However, individuals charged with a crime and released before trial are not like ordinary citizens. While "pretrial releasees are not probationers," they are separated from confinement only by a few hundred dollars or a signature on a consent form.

This last point requires closer examination of the implications of the majority's ruling. The majority treats Scott's assent to the conditions of his OR release as a question of whether the Fourth Amendment permits Scott to waive his Fourth Amendment rights. This seems quite backwards to me. It seems to me that at the time Scott agreed to these conditions in exchange for release on OR he was in a much better position than we are to weigh the reasonableness of the government's proposed course of conduct. Unless we can find some irreducible right or moral imperative within the Fourth Amendment, one that absolutely forbids pretrial detainees from agreeing to *any* conditions before they are released, the majority's approach begs the question.

In one sense, the government has no more "induced" Scott to forgo his Fourth Amendment rights in exchange for his liberty, than Scott has "induced" the government to forgo its right to require bail in exchange for the right to search him at his home. The question is not inducement or not — although, ultimately, that is the way the majority treats the question — but whether the inducement is reasonable.

There are, of course, constitutionally irreducible rights — the right not to be a slave being the prime example. The Court has also suggested that government may not condition to receipt of government largesse, license, or privilege on the waiver of certain rights guaranteed by the Constitution, at least where the condition bears no plausible relationship to the receipt of the benefit. The receipt of a tax exemption cannot be conditioned, for example, on an express waiver of the privilege of criticizing the government. But no one has ever suggested that the rights of security and privacy in our "persons, houses, papers, and effects" cannot be infringed by statute or waived by agreement, at least when the infringement is related in some rational way to changes in the individual's legal status. *Griffin* and *Knights* are conclusive evidence to the contrary. I am not suggesting that there are no limits to what the government may demand from an OR releasee; I would hold in this case that the conditions Nevada exacted are not unreasonable.

The majority opinion may free Scott from the consequences of the state's discovery of a sawed-off shotgun in his home, but in the end today's opinion is not a liberty-enhancing decision. As the majority acknowledges, "many pre-trial detainees willingly consent to such conditions, preferring to give up some rights in order to sleep in their own beds while awaiting trial." Today's decision strikes down Nevada's practice of offering pretrial detainees the option of being released on OR and sleeping in their own beds in exchange for agreeing to a limited number of conditions that the state believes will protect the public and secure the attendance of the accused at trial. But the implications of the majority's new *per se* rule could hardly be more severe or far-reaching. * * * *

5. Now that you've read this Chapter, go back to the beginning. How would you answer the bewildered defendant who cannot understand how the same legal

system that purports to presume his innocence can use a contrary presumption to incarcerate him before trial? (Try to come up with something better than "You're right — I can't understand it either!")

Chapter 3

DISCOVERY

Civil vs. Criminal Discovery

In *civil* cases, courts and legislatures have been quite liberal in allowing parties pretrial discovery of the other side's case. They have allowed inspection of documents, things, and places, requests for admissions, written interrogatories, and — the most effective discovery device — the deposition.

But discovery in *criminal* cases has been more restricted. Several reasons have been advanced for this, and each reason has been criticized:

* "If the defendant is allowed to learn the prosecution's case before trial, he might tailor his testimony to meet it."

> ***Contra***: This presumes that the defendant is guilty and prone to commit perjury. Also, as the defendant testifies only after the prosecution presents its case, defendant may "tailor his testimony" even without pretrial discovery.

* "When defendant learns the identity of prosecution witnesses, he might try to intimidate or bribe them."

> ***Contra***: This is not a sufficient reason to deny discovery in *all* cases. If the prosecutor can show that a particular defendant might do this, then discovery should be denied or limited in that case.

* "Discovery in civil cases is equal for both sides, but it cannot be equal in criminal cases, because the defendant cannot be compelled to furnish information which might incriminate him, under the 5th Amendment. The prosecutor could not depose the defendant."

> ***Contra***: The 5th Amendment does protect the defendant's own statements, but not other evidence he might have. Also, in a criminal case the *investigative* resources of the parties are not equal, as the prosecutor and police have much more resources than the defendant. Defendant needs discovery to balance out this inequality.

* "In civil cases, the parties must pay for any discovery they use, and this cost limits the burden of discovery on the other side. Most criminal defendants are indigent, however, and the state pays their legal expenses. These defendants will overuse and abuse any right to discovery."

> ***Contra***: Most indigent criminal defendants are represented by public defenders, who have their own budgetary restrictions and high caseloads. They will not waste their time with useless discovery.

In the midst of this debate, criminal discovery has expanded somewhat in recent years, prodded by constitutional considerations and the example of Federal Rule 16 (set out below).

As you read this chapter, note that it is about *formal discovery*, the process of obtaining information from the other side through a formal motion. There are, however, *other* ways of obtaining information about your opponent's case which should not be overlooked. Sometimes counsel can get things just by asking. Many prosecutors will give a copy of a police report and other documents to defense counsel on a simple request, to avoid the trouble of dealing with a formal motion and to impress defense counsel with the strength of the prosecution case — which might help the prosecutor negotiate a favorable plea bargain. (If the prosecutor omits something, however, defense counsel might be in no position to complain about it if no formal discovery motion has been filed.)

The most important discovery device in civil cases, the deposition, is generally not allowed in criminal cases.[1] The 5th Amendment prevents the prosecutor from deposing the defendant, and other considerations (cost, delay, etc.[2]) have persuaded legislatures not to allow the defendant to depose prosecution witnesses. Nevertheless, there may be other ways for the defendant to obtain sworn testimony of prosecution witnesses. At a *preliminary hearing*, defense counsel may cross-examine prosecution witnesses and obtain a written transcript of their testimony. Transcripts of *grand jury testimony* of prosecution witnesses might be obtained by defense counsel. Transcripts of testimony of prosecution witnesses at a *motion to suppress evidence* might be useful to defense counsel to impeach those witnesses at trial. And finally, there is nothing to prevent either lawyer from sending investigators to *interview* witnesses for the other side, though they cannot compel anyone to speak to them or to give them written or sworn testimony outside the courtroom.

Problem 3A

To: My Law Clerk

From: Sue E. Generis, Esq.

Date: April 6

I am representing Don Dork, who has been charged in federal court with sale of cocaine. I interviewed Dork yesterday at the jail, and my notes of the interview say the following:

> Mr. Dork says that he was arrested last night at his home by Agent Nark of the Drug Enforcement Agency (DEA). Dork asked him what was going on, and Nark told him that they had a witness who had bought cocaine from Dork at 4th and Post Streets during the evening of March 1. Dork told him that he was out of town all day and night on March 1, at his mother's birthday party. He told me that he has a ticket stub for a bus ride he took that day to the town where his mother lives. He says he had a record of prior drug use, and he thinks that the DEA is out to get him because of this.

---

[1] In *McDole v. State*, 339 Ark. 391 (1999), the court rejected a contention that allowing depositions in civil cases but not in criminal cases violated a criminal defendant's right to equal protection of the laws.

[2] *See People v. Municipal Court (Runyan)*, 20 Cal. 3d 523, 2 A.L.R.4th 681 (1978).

I have a good relationship with the U.S. Attorney's Office, and they usually give me most of what I ask for on an informal basis. In this case, however, they said I would have to "go by the book." (Dork is the nephew of a local politician, so I think the prosecutor is afraid of accusations of favoritism.) I've gotten pretty used to the informal "softball" discovery we usually use day-to-day around her, so I guess I've forgotten a lot about "hardball" discovery — i.e., what to do when the parties refuse to give anything they aren't required to give. Please prepare a *discovery plan* for me.

In preparing a discovery plan, make a list of (1) what pieces of evidence might help us to win at trial, (2) which of these pieces of evidence we might obtain *from our opponents* (i.e., through *discovery*) — as contrasted with our own investigation. Read carefully the attached rules and cases to see what the law requires our opponents to give us. And (3): consider how we should *word* any discovery demand. Even if the law allows us to demand something, our opponents do not have to give it to us unless we clearly ask for it. And never forget that our opponents are "the enemy" — they do not *want* to help us, and therefore they might try to construe the language of our demand as narrowly as possible. And finally, consider whether any discovery demand might *cost* us something, i.e., whether it might somehow give the prosecutor something he might otherwise not get.

Oh, one more thing: let me know what the *prosecutor* might try to discover *from us*, and how we might avoid it, if possible.

Problem 3B

To: My Law Clerk

From: Sue E. Generis, Esq.

Date: May 28

Trial began yesterday in *U.S. v. Dork*. Assistant U.S. Attorney Wally Whitehat put on 2 witnesses.

First, Frank Fink testified that he occasionally did work for the police department, being paid by the case. The prosecutor asked him, "Did I promise to drop a pending marijuana possession charge against you if you cooperated with us in the present case?" Fink said, "Yes, you did." Fink said that on March 1, he met an acquaintance of his whom he called "Sleaze", at the corner of 4th and Post Streets. Sleaze pointed out a man wearing a knit cap, scarf, and parka and said, "That guy is a drug dealer. Sometimes he rips people off by selling sugar. He gets their money and takes off before they find out." Fink went over to the man and asked him to sell him a small amount of cocaine. The man gave him a small bag of white powder and asked for $100, which Fink gave him. Fink turned the bag over to DEA Agent Nark. Whitehat asked Fink if he saw in the courtroom the man who sold him the powder. Fink pointed to Dork and said, "I think that's the guy."

On cross-examination, I asked Fink whether he had ever been convicted of a felony, and he said no. I also asked him for Sleaze's real name, and Fink said that he knew it but did not want to reveal it, as he did not want to get Sleaze into trouble with drug dealers, and Sleaze might be useful in the future.

Then DEA lab analyst Bunson Berner testified that on March 2, Nark gave him a bag with Dork's name on it and asked him to analyze the contents. Berner did, and he determined that the contents were cocaine. On cross-examination, I asked Berner where this alleged cocaine and his written report were. He said that after he analyzed the powder, he left the lab to go to lunch and forgot to lock the lab. When he returned, the lab had been burglarized, and the bag containing the powder and his report had been stolen. He said his testimony that the powder was cocaine was based on his memory. He also said that he tests about 50 samples a day.

After the prosecution rested its case, I put on Dork, who testified that he was at his mother's birthday party on March 1. We introduced his bus ticket stub into evidence. On cross-examination, Whitehat had Dork admit that he had a prior conviction for possession of cocaine. I then put on Mama Dork, who testified that Dork was at her birthday party on March 1. On cross-examination, Whitehat asked her if she had made any notes about the party. She said that I had phoned her and asked her who was at the party, and then I asked her to write me a letter about what she remembered about the party, which she did.

Whitehat has moved for an order compelling me to show him Mama Dork's letter. Please advise me as to what arguments I should make in opposition to the motion, and tell me whether the judge is likely to grant it.

I have asked the court to compel Whitehat to disclose the true name and address of "Sleaze", and I have asked for a subpoena to compel "Sleaze" to come and testify. Whitehat objects, invoking the "informer's privilege." What arguments can I make, and are they likely to succeed?

Problem 3C

To: My Law Clerk

From: Sue E. Generis, Esq.

Date: June 7

Well, we lost. This morning, the jury deliberated for about 20 minutes and then convicted Dork.

At lunch, I saw a cop I know (Officer Krumkey) and mentioned the case to him, and he told me that about 10 years ago he had arrested Fink for felony drunk driving, and he was convicted. Krumkey had also handled Fink's recent marijuana arrest, and he was present when the prosecutor and Fink's lawyer (Frank) and prosecutor worked out their deal. Frank had said, "It's a fair deal. Fink doesn't like Dork anyway, because Dork burned him on a drug deal once."

I'd like to move for a new trial, based on what the cop told me at lunch, and on the prosecution's failure to preserve the alleged "cocaine" analyzed by the DEA lab, along with Berner's report. What arguments should I make, and are they likely to succeed?

Federal Rules of Criminal Procedure

Rule 12.1. Notice of an Alibi Defense

(a) Government's Request for Notice and Defendant's Response.

(1) Government's Request. An attorney for the government may request in writing that the defendant notify an attorney for the government of any intended alibi defense. The request must state the time, date, and place of the alleged offense.

(2) Defendant's Response. Within 10 days after the request, or at some other time the court sets, the defendant must serve written notice on an attorney for the government of any intended alibi defense. The defendant's notice must state:

(A) each specific place where the defendant claims to have been at the time of the alleged offense; and

(B) the name, address, and telephone number of each alibi witness on whom the defendant intends to rely.

(b) Disclosing Government Witnesses.

(1) Disclosure. If the defendant serves a Rule 12.1(a)(2) notice, an attorney for the government must disclose in writing to the defendant or the defendant's attorney:

(A) the name, address, and telephone number of each witness the government intends to rely on to establish the defendant's presence at the scene of the alleged offense; and

(B) each government rebuttal witness to the defendant's alibi defense.

(2) Time to Disclose. Unless the court directs otherwise, an attorney for the government must give its Rule 12.1(b)(1) disclosure within 10 days after the defendant serves notice of an intended alibi defense under Rule 12.1(a)(2), but no later than 10 days before trial.

(c) Continuing Duty to Disclose. Both an attorney for the government and the defendant must promptly disclose in writing to the other party the name, address, and telephone number of each additional witness if:

(1) the disclosing party learns of the witness before or during trial; and

(2) the witness should have been disclosed under Rule 12.1(a) or (b) if the disclosing party had known of the witness earlier.

(d) Exceptions. For good cause, the court may grant an exception to any requirement of Rule 12.1(a) — (c).

(e) Failure to Comply. If a party fails to comply with this rule, the court may exclude the testimony of any undisclosed witness regarding the defendant's alibi. This rule does not limit the defendant's right to testify.

(f) Inadmissibility of Withdrawn Intention. Evidence of an intention to rely on an alibi defense, later withdrawn, or of a statement made in connection with that intention, is not, in any civil or criminal proceeding, admissible against the person who gave notice of the intention.

Rule 15.   Depositions

(a)   When Taken.

(1)   In General. A party may move that a prospective witness be deposed in order to preserve testimony for trial. The court may grant the motion because of exceptional circumstances and in the interest of justice. If the court orders the deposition to be taken, it may also require the deponent to produce at the deposition any designated material that is not privileged, including any book, paper, document, record, recording, or data.

(2)   Detained Material Witness. A witness who is detained under 18 U.S.C. § 3144 may request to be deposed by filing a written motion and giving notice to the parties. The court may then order that the deposition be taken and may discharge the witness after the witness has signed under oath the deposition transcript.

(b)   Notice.

(1)   In General. A party seeking to take a deposition must give every other party reasonable written notice of the deposition's date and location. The notice must state the name and address of each deponent. If requested by a party receiving the notice, the court may, for good cause, change the deposition's date or location.

(2)   To the Custodial Officer. A party seeking to take the deposition must also notify the officer who has custody of the defendant of the scheduled date and location.

(c)   Defendant's Presence.

(1)   Defendant in Custody. The officer who has custody of the defendant must produce the defendant at the deposition and keep the defendant in the witness's presence during the examination, unless the defendant:

(A) waives in writing the right to be present; or

(B) persists in disruptive conduct justifying exclusion after being warned by the court that disruptive conduct will result in the defendant's exclusion.

(2)   Defendant Not in Custody. A defendant who is not in custody has the right upon request to be present at the deposition, subject to any conditions imposed by the court. If the government tenders the defendant's expenses as provided in Rule 15(d) but the defendant still fails to appear, the defendant — absent good cause — waives both the right to appear and any objection to the taking and use of the deposition based on that right.

(d)   Expenses.
If the deposition was requested by the government, the court may — or if the defendant is unable to bear the deposition expenses, the court must — order the government to pay:

(1) any reasonable travel and subsistence expenses of the defendant and the defendant's attorney to attend the deposition; and

(2) the costs of the deposition transcript.

(e) Manner of Taking. Unless these rules or a court order provides otherwise, a deposition must be taken and filed in the same manner as a deposition in a civil action, except that:

(1) A defendant may not be deposed without that defendant's consent.

(2) The scope and manner of the deposition examination and cross-examination must be the same as would be allowed during trial.

(3) The government must provide to the defendant or the defendant's attorney, for use at the deposition, any statement of the deponent in the government's possession to which the defendant would be entitled at trial.

(f) Use as Evidence. A party may use all or part of a deposition as provided by the Federal Rules of Evidence.

(g) Objections. A party objecting to deposition testimony or evidence must state the grounds for the objection during the deposition.

(h) Depositions by Agreement Permitted. The parties may by agreement take and use a deposition with the court's consent.

Rule 16.   Discovery and Inspection

(a) Government's Disclosure.

(1) Information Subject to Disclosure.

(A) Defendant's Oral Statement. Upon a defendant's request, the government must disclose to the defendant the substance of any relevant oral statement made by the defendant, before or after arrest, in response to interrogation by a person the defendant knew was a government agent if the government intends to use the statement at trial.

(B) Defendant's Written or Recorded Statement. Upon a defendant's request, the government must disclose to the defendant, and make available for inspection, copying, or photographing, all of the following:

(i) any relevant written or recorded statement by the defendant if:

the statement is within the government's possession, custody, or control; and

the attorney for the government knows — or through due diligence could know — that the statement exists;

(ii) the portion of any written record containing the substance of any relevant oral statement made before or after arrest if the defendant made the statement in response to interrogation by a person the defendant knew was a government agent; and

(iii) the defendant's recorded testimony before a grand jury relating to the charged offense.

(C) Organizational Defendant. Upon a defendant's request, if the defendant is an organization, the government must disclose to the defendant any statement described in Rule 16(a)(1)(A) and (B) if the government contends that the person making the statement:

(i) was legally able to bind the defendant regarding the subject of the statement because of that person's position as the defendant's director, officer, employee, or agent; or

(ii) was personally involved in the alleged conduct constituting the offense and was legally able to bind the defendant regarding that conduct because of that person's position as the defendant's director, officer, employee, or agent.

(D)   Defendant's Prior Record. Upon a defendant's request, the government must furnish the defendant with a copy of the defendant's prior criminal record that is within the government's possession, custody, or control if the attorney for the government knows — or through due diligence could know — that the record exists.

(E)   Documents and Objects. Upon a defendant's request, the government must permit the defendant to inspect and to copy or photograph books, papers, documents, data, photographs, tangible objects, buildings or places, or copies or portions of any of these items, if the item is within the government's possession, custody, or control and:

(i) the item is material to preparing the defense;

(ii) the government intends to use the item in its case-in-chief at trial; or

(iii) the item was obtained from or belongs to the defendant.

(F)   Reports of Examinations and Tests. Upon a defendant's request, the government must permit a defendant to inspect and to copy or photograph the results or reports of any physical or mental examination and of any scientific test or experiment if:

(i) the item is within the government's possession, custody, or control;

(ii) the attorney for the government knows — or through due diligence could know — that the item exists; and

(iii) the item is material to preparing the defense or the government intends to use the item in its case-in-chief at trial.

(G)   Expert witnesses. At the defendant's request, the government must give to the defendant a written summary of any testimony that the government intends to use under Rules 702, 703, or 705 of the Federal Rules of Evidence during its case-in-chief at trial. If the government requests discovery under subdivision (b)(1)(C)(ii) and the defendant complies, the government must, at the defendant's request, give to the defendant a written summary of testimony that the government intends to use under Rules 702, 703, or 705 of the Federal Rules of Evidence as evidence at trial on the issue of the defendant's mental condition. The summary provided under this subparagraph must describe the witness's opinions, the bases and reasons for those opinions, and the witness's qualifications.

(2)   Information Not Subject to Disclosure. Except as Rule 16(a)(1) provides otherwise, this rule does not authorize the discovery or inspection of reports, memoranda, or other internal government documents made by an attorney for the government or other government agent in connection with investigating or prosecuting the case. Nor does this rule authorize the discovery or inspection of statements made by prospective government witnesses except as provided in 18 U.S.C. § 3500.

(3) Grand Jury Transcripts. This rule does not apply to the discovery or inspection of a grand jury's recorded proceedings, except as provided in Rules 6, 12(h), 16(a)(1), and 26.2.

(b) Defendant's Disclosure.

(1) Information Subject to Disclosure.

(A) Documents and Objects. If a defendant requests disclosure under Rule 16(a)(1)(E) and the government complies, then the defendant must permit the government, upon request, to inspect and to copy or photograph books, papers, documents, data, photographs, tangible objects, buildings or places, or copies or portions of any of these items if:

(i) the item is within the defendant's possession, custody, or control; and

(ii) the defendant intends to use the item in the defendant's case-in-chief at trial.

(B) Reports of Examinations and Tests. If a defendant requests disclosure under Rule 16(a)(1)(F) and the government complies, the defendant must permit the government, upon request, to inspect and to copy or photograph the results or reports of any physical or mental examination and of any scientific test or experiment if:

(i) the item is within the defendant's possession, custody, or control; and

(ii) the defendant intends to use the item in the defendant's case-in-chief at trial, or intends to call the witness who prepared the report and the report relates to the witness's testimony.

(C) Expert witnesses. The defendant must, at the government's request, give to the government a written summary of any testimony that the defendant intends to use under Rules 702, 703, or 705 of the Federal Rules of Evidence as evidence at trial, if —

(i) the defendant requests disclosure under subdivision (a)(1)(G) and the government complies; or

(ii) the defendant has given notice under Rule 12.2(b) of an intent to present expert testimony on the defendant's mental condition.

This summary must describe the witness's opinions, the bases and reasons for those opinions, and the witness's qualifications.

(2) Information Not Subject to Disclosure. Except for scientific or medical reports, Rule 16(b)(1) does not authorize discovery or inspection of:

(A) reports, memoranda, or other documents made by the defendant, or the defendant's attorney or agent, during the case's investigation or defense; or

(B) a statement made to the defendant, or the defendant's attorney or agent, by:

(i) the defendant;

(ii) a government or defense witness; or

(iii) a prospective government or defense witness.

(c) Continuing Duty to Disclose. A party who discovers additional evidence or material before or during trial must promptly disclose its existence to the other party or the court if:

(1) the evidence or material is subject to discovery or inspection under this rule; and

(2) the other party previously requested, or the court ordered, its production.

(d) Regulating Discovery.

(1) Protective and Modifying Orders. At any time the court may, for good cause, deny, restrict, or defer discovery or inspection, or grant other appropriate relief. The court may permit a party to show good cause by a written statement that the court will inspect ex parte. If relief is granted, the court must preserve the entire text of the party's statement under seal.

(2) Failure to Comply. If a party fails to comply with this rule, the court may:

(A) order that party to permit the discovery or inspection; specify its time, place, and manner; and prescribe other just terms and conditions;

(B) grant a continuance;

(C) prohibit that party from introducing the undisclosed evidence; or

(D) enter any other order that is just under the circumstances.

Rule 26.2. Producing a Witness's Statement

(a) Motion to Produce. After a witness other than the defendant has testified on direct examination, the court, on motion of a party who did not call the witness, must order an attorney for the government or the defendant and the defendant's attorney to produce, for the examination and use of the moving party, any statement of the witness that is in their possession and that relates to the subject matter of the witness's testimony.

(b) Producing the Entire Statement. If the entire statement relates to the subject matter of the witness's testimony, the court must order that the statement be delivered to the moving party.

(c) Producing a Redacted Statement. If the party who called the witness claims that the statement contains information that is privileged or does not relate to the subject matter of the witness's testimony, the court must inspect the statement in camera. After excising any privileged or unrelated portions, the court must order delivery of the redacted statement to the moving party. If the defendant objects to an excision, the court must preserve the entire statement with the excised portion indicated, under seal, as part of the record.

(d)   Recess to Examine a Statement. The court may recess the proceedings to allow time for a party to examine the statement and prepare for its use.

(e)   Sanction for Failure to Produce or Deliver a Statement. If the party who called the witness disobeys an order to produce or deliver a statement, the court must strike the witness's testimony from the record. If an attorney for the government disobeys the order, the court must declare a mistrial if justice so requires.

(f)   "Statement" Defined. As used in this rule, a witness's "statement" means:

(1) a written statement that the witness makes and signs, or otherwise adopts or approves;

(2) a substantially verbatim, contemporaneously recorded recital of the witness's oral statement that is contained in any recording or any transcription of a recording; or

(3) the witness's statement to a grand jury, however taken or recorded, or a transcription of such a statement.

(g)   Scope. This rule applies at trial, at a suppression hearing under Rule 12, and to the extent specified in the following rules:

(1) Rule 5.1(h) (preliminary hearing);

(2) Rule 32(i)(2) (sentencing);

(3) Rule 32.1(e) (hearing to revoke or modify probation or supervised release);

(4) Rule 46(j) (detention hearing); and

(5) Rule 8 of the Rules Governing Proceedings under 28 U.S.C. § 2255.

18 U.S. CODE § 3500 ("THE JENCKS ACT")

§ 3500. Demands for production of statements and reports of witnesses

(a) In any criminal prosecution brought by the United States, no statement or report in the possession of the United States which was made by a Government witness or prospective Government witness (other than the defendant) shall be the subject of subpoena, discovery, or inspection until said witness has testified on direct examination in the trial of the case.

(b) After a witness called by the United States has testified on direct examination, the court shall, on motion of the defendant, order the United States to produce any statement (as hereinafter defined) of the witness in the possession of the United States which relates to the subject matter as to which the witness has testified. If the entire contents of any such statement relate to the subject matter of the testimony of the witness, the court shall order it to be delivered directly to the defendant for his examination and use.

(c) If the United States claims that any statement ordered to be produced under this section contains matter which does not relate to the subject matter of the testimony of the witness, the court shall order the United

States to deliver such statement for the inspection of the court in camera. Upon such delivery the court shall excise the portions of such statement which do not relate to the subject matter of the testimony of the witness. With such material excised, the court shall then direct delivery of such statement to the defendant for his use. * * * *

(e) The term "statement", as used in subsections (b), (c), and (d) of this section in relation to any witness called by the United States, means —

(1) a written statement made by said witness and signed or otherwise adopted or approved by him;

(2) a stenographic, mechanical, electrical, or other recording, or a transcription thereof, which is a substantially verbatim recital of an oral statement made by said witness and recorded contemporaneously with the making of such oral statement; or

(3) a statement, however taken or recorded, or a transcription thereof, if any, made by said witness to a grand jury.

[Enacted in 1957, with subsequent amendments.]

BRADY v. MARYLAND
United States Supreme Court
373 U.S. 83 (1963)

Opinion of the Court by MR. JUSTICE DOUGLAS, announced by MR. JUSTICE BRENNAN.

Petitioner and a companion, Boblit, were found guilty of murder in the first degree and were sentenced to death, their convictions being affirmed by the Court of Appeals of Maryland. Their trials were separate, petitioner being tried first. At his trial Brady took the stand and admitted his participation in the crime, but he claimed that Boblit did the actual killing. And, in his summation to the jury, Brady's counsel conceded that Brady was guilty of murder in the first degree, asking only that the jury return that verdict "without capital punishment." Prior to the trial, petitioner's counsel had requested the prosecution to allow him to examine Boblit's extrajudicial statements. Several of those statements were shown to him; but one dated July 9, 1958, in which Boblit admitted the actual homicide, was withheld by the prosecution and did not come to petitioner's notice until after he had been tried, convicted, and sentenced, and after his conviction had been affirmed.

Petitioner moved the trial court for a new trial based on the newly discovered evidence that had been suppressed by the prosecution. Petitioner's appeal from a denial of that motion was dismissed by the Court of Appeals. The petition for post-conviction relief was dismissed by the trial court; and on appeal the Court of Appeals held that suppression of the evidence by the prosecution denied petitioner due process of law and remanded the case for a retrial of the question of punishment, not the question of guilt. * * * *

We agree with the Court of Appeals that suppression of this confession was a violation of the Due Process Clause of the Fourteenth Amendment.

This ruling is an extension of *Mooney v. Holohan*, 294 U.S. 103, 112, where the Court ruled on what nondisclosure by a prosecutor violates due process:

It is a requirement that cannot be deemed to be satisfied by mere notice and hearing if a state has contrived a conviction through the pretense of a trial which in truth is but used as a means of depriving a defendant of liberty through a deliberate deception of court and jury by the presentation of testimony known to be perjured. Such a contrivance by a state to procure the conviction and imprisonment of a defendant is as inconsistent with the rudimentary demands of justice as is the obtaining of a like result by intimidation. * * * *

We now hold that the suppression by the prosecution of evidence favorable to an accused upon request violates due process where the evidence is material either to guilt or to punishment, irrespective of the good faith or bad faith of the prosecution.

The principle of *Mooney v. Holohan* is not punishment of society for misdeeds of a prosecutor but avoidance of an unfair trial to the accused. Society wins not only when the guilty are convicted but when criminal trials are fair; our system of the administration of justice suffers when any accused is treated unfairly. An inscription on the walls of the Department of Justice states the proposition candidly for the federal domain: "The United States wins its point whenever justice is done its citizens in the courts."[2] A prosecution that withholds evidence on demand of an accused which, if made available, would tend to exculpate him or reduce the penalty helps shape a trial that bears heavily on the defendant. That casts the prosecutor in the role of an architect of a proceeding that does not comport with standards of justice, even though, as in the present case, his action is not the result of guile. * * * *

Affirmed.

Notes from Sue:

1. Should *Brady* work *both ways*? The Constitution, of course, does not require the defendant to do anything, but I suppose the legislature could enact a *statute* that requires defense counsel to inform the prosecution of any *inculpatory* evidence in the possession of the defense (except defendant's own statements, to the extent that they are protected by the privilege against self-incrimination). Does this seem fair, or is there any problem with it?

2. **Suppose the prosecutor makes a "deal" with a witness.**

In *Giglio v. U.S.*, 405 U.S. 150 (1972), after Giglio was convicted at trial, defense counsel obtained evidence that the prosecutor had promised the key prosecution witness (Taliento) that he would not be prosecuted if he testified against the defendant. The prosecutor had failed to tell defense counsel of this promise before or during trial. The trial court denied defendant's motion for new trial, but the Supreme Court reversed:

---

[2] Judge Simon E. Sobeloff when Solicitor General put the idea as follows in an address before the Judicial Conference of the Fourth Circuit on June 29, 1954:

The Solicitor General is not a neutral, he is an advocate; but an advocate for a client whose business is not merely to prevail in the instant case. My client's chief business is not to achieve victory but to establish justice. We are constantly reminded of the now classic words penned by one of my illustrious predecessors, Frederick William Lehmann, that the Government wins its point when justice is done in its courts.

Whether the nondisclosure was a result of negligence or design, it is the responsibility of the prosecutor. The prosecutor's office is an entity and as such it is the spokesman for the Government. A promise made by one attorney must be attributed, for these purposes, to the Government. To the extent this places a burden on the large prosecution offices, procedures and regulations can be established to carry that burden and to insure communication of all relevant information on each case to every lawyer who deals with it.

Here the Government's case depended almost entirely on Taliento's testimony; without it there could have been no indictment and no evidence to carry the case to the jury. Taliento's credibility as a witness was therefore an important issue in the case, and evidence of any understanding or agreement as to a future prosecution would be relevant to his credibility and the jury was entitled to know of it.

In *U.S. v. Sudikoff*, 36 F.Supp.2d 1196 (C.D.Calif.1999), Sudikoff was charged with securities violations. One of his associates, McInnes, received immunity from the Government and was to testify at Sudikoff's trial. During pretrial discovery, the Government disclosed McInnes's immunity agreement. Sudikoff then moved to compel the Government to disclose all prior communications with the Government that led up to the agreement. The court granted the motion:

The Court has concluded that *Brady* is not narrowly limited to admissible evidence but neither is it so broad as to include evidence that would only assist in trial preparation. The Court therefore holds that *Brady* requires disclosure of exculpatory information that is either admissible or is reasonably likely to lead to admissible evidence. * * * *

The Court holds that proffers of an accomplice witness that led to a leniency agreement and information that reveals the negotiation pursuant to which that agreement was reached might reasonably be considered favorable to the defendant's case. This is for two reasons. First, to the extent the proffers and other information reveal that the witness's proposed testimony may have varied over time, they may reveal inconsistencies relevant to the accomplice witness's credibility and within the scope of *Brady*. Second, to the extent the proffers and other information reveal the accomplice witness's motives and desire to seek an immunity agreement, they are relevant to the witness's credibility and within the scope of *Giglio*.

A leniency agreement between the government and an accomplice witness is often the result of extensive discussion and negotiation between these two parties. The government understandably seeks to ensure that the accomplice witness has probative testimony before assenting to any agreement and the accomplice witness understandably seeks to ensure that his possible admissions are to some extent protected. In the present case, the discussions between the government and witness McInnes lasted for several months before an agreement was finally reached.

Because this process can be lengthy and because it often carries some of the typical negotiating give-and-take, it is possible, maybe even likely, that the witness's proposed testimony that was proffered at the beginning of the process differed in some respects from the testimony proffered at the end of the process. For example, it is likely that during initial contacts with the government the witness would proffer a less detailed version of his testimony than he would once it became more likely that an agreement would be reached. Though such variations could stem entirely from the nature of this process, a defendant implicated by the accomplice witness could reasonably argue that they stem from the accomplice witness's tendency to embroider on the truth. Thus, the existence of such variations might reasonably be held to be favorable to the defense.

Although the government might argue that all such variations are innocuous and lack probity, the Court cannot comfortably so hold. While many, if not most, of these differences probably do result only from the nature of the process, the Court cannot conclude that this is sufficient to prevent disclosure under *Brady*. Neither the government nor the Court is aware of the details of the defense strategy and therefore neither the government nor the Court can accurately determine which variations are important.

Moreover, while it may be reasonable to conclude that any differences are innocuous, because it might be reasonable to likewise conclude otherwise, the government should disclose the information. Where doubt exists as to the usefulness of evidence, the government should resolve such doubts in favor of full disclosure. This is consistent with the Court's conclusion that the proper standard under *Brady* is evidence "that might reasonably be considered favorable to the defendant's case." *Bagley*, 473 U.S. at 696. There is no requirement that the exculpatory nature of *Brady* material be indisputable.

Therefore, the Court finds that any variations in an accomplice witness's proposed testimony could be considered favorable to the defense and the existence of such differences should be disclosed under *Brady*.

In addition to revealing possible inconsistencies, the Court holds that witness proffers and other information fall within the scope of *Giglio*. In *Giglio*, the Supreme Court reaffirmed the notion that the fact that a witness is testifying pursuant to a leniency agreement is relevant to credibility. This conclusion is neither surprising nor novel.

When judging the credibility of testimony, a jury may properly consider a "witness' interest in the outcome of the case and any bias or prejudice." Ninth Circuit Manual of Model Jury Instructions: Criminal 37 (1997). Because accomplice witnesses who testify pursuant to immunity agreements may be motivated by more than just the desire to tell the truth, courts require specific jury instructions regarding their credibility. See e.g., *id.* at 65–66 (instructing jury to consider "with greater caution" testimony given pursuant to immunity agreement or by informant).

In *Hoffa v. United States*, 385 U.S. 293 (1966), the defendants had been convicted based in part on the testimony of an informant who received from the government incentives to testify. On appeal, these defendants argued that the use of such witnesses violated due process because it raised unacceptable risks of perjurious testimony. The Supreme Court rejected this argument and permitted the use of such testimony but only because "the established safeguards of the Anglo-American legal system leave the veracity of a witness to be tested by cross-examination, and the credibility of his testimony to be determined by a properly instructed jury." *Id.* at 311. Because the informant in *Hoffa* "was subjected to rigorous cross-examination, and the extent and nature of his dealings with federal and state authorities were insistently explored" and because the trial judge instructed the jury to carefully consider the informant's credibility, the Supreme Court found the testimony consistent with due process. * * * *

Consistent with *Hoffa's* conclusion that the use of informants is constitutional if the existence of any incentives is disclosed and considered by the jury, courts expect prosecutors and investigators to take all reasonable measures to safeguard the system against treachery. This responsibility includes the duty as required by *Giglio* to turn over to the defense in discovery all material information casting a shadow on a government witness's credibility.

Though *Giglio* concerned the suppression of the very existence of a leniency agreement, information that illuminates the process leading up to the agreement may "cast a shadow" on an accomplice witness's credibility in a manner that disclosure of only the agreement itself would not accomplish.

The motive behind an accomplice witness's agreement to testify may range from a simple *quid pro quo* to an earnest desire to disclose the truth. The defense cannot distinguish between such motives unless the government reveals information about the negotiation leading to the agreement.

This conclusion applies even if the negotiating process was short. Even if the witness made only one proffer of proposed testimony and the government immediately made an offer of leniency that was immediately accepted, such a proffer is the motivating force behind the leniency agreement and as such can reveal what the witness was willing to do in return for leniency. Again, this information is relevant to the witness's credibility.

Thus, the Court concludes that information that reveals the process by which an accomplice witness and the government reach a leniency agreement is relevant to the witness's credibility because it reveals the witness's motive to testify against the defendant. Therefore, such information is discoverable under *Brady* and *Giglio*.

In *State v. Lindsey*, 621 So.2d 618 (La. Ct.App. 1993), Lindsey and Pate were charged with robbery — Lindsey being the perpetrator and Pate being one of the planners. At Lindsey's trial, the prosecutor called Pate to the stand, and she testified that she had not helped plan the robbery, and that Lindsey committed the robbery suddenly, without Pate's prior knowledge that Lindsey had intended to do so. After the jury convicted Lindsey, he moved for a new trial, claiming that the prosecution had failed to disclose that it had entered into plea negotiations with Pate. At the hearing on the motion for new trial, the evidence disclosed that before Pate testified, the prosecutor had not entered into any firm plea agreement with Pate, but he had told Pate's attorney that he, the prosecutor, would give consideration in plea negotiations to Pate for testifying truthfully. The trial court granted the motion for new trial, and the appellate court affirmed, citing *Brady*.

The prosecutor failed to disclose to Lindsey that he promised favorable consideration if she testified and her testimony were deemed credible. The promise gave Pate a direct, personal stake in Lindsey's conviction. The fact that a specific reward was not guaranteed through a promise or a consummated plea agreement, but was expressly contingent on the state's good faith and satisfaction with Pate's testimony, served only to strengthen any incentive to testify falsely in order to secure Lindsey's conviction.

At a minimum, the assertions made by the state to Pate's attorney were sufficient to give Pate the impression that convincing testimony favorable to the state would benefit her in her own case. Indeed, such an impression would have been absolutely correct, as the state accepted a plea bargain [with Pate] immediately following the close of evidence, even before the jury had returned the verdict and the trial was concluded.

The court further noted that the prosecutor's failure to disclose was "exacerbated" by (1) the prosecutor's failure to correct Pate's testimony on cross-examination that she did not expect any favorable treatment from the prosecutor for her testimony, and (2) the prosecutor's closing argument to the jury, in which he argued that Pate "has nothing to gain or lose" by her testimony.

Two dissenting judges believed that Lindsey's attorney should have known the situation even without disclosure by the prosecutor.

Of course the witness hoped to receive consideration. That's obvious and apparent in any case in which any codefendant who has not been convicted testifies against another codefendant. Simple common sense makes it implicit in the circumstances. Importantly, the defense counsel argued to the jury the numerous asserted inconsistencies in Mrs. Pate's testimony and all that she had to benefit from her testimony against this defendant. . . . It seems to me that the record indicates that the defense was aware of the actual situation, had an opportunity to cross-examine the witness about it, and argued it to the jury. I would not hold that the state has to inform the defendant of the obvious and thus would not extend *Brady* and its progeny to the instant circumstances.

3. In *Spicer v. Roxbury Correctional Institute*, 194 F.3d 547 (4th Cir. 1999), Spicer was convicted of assaulting the manager of the Armadillo Bar by hitting him in the back of the head with a liquor bottle. The key witness at trial was Brown, who testified that he saw Spicer fleeing from the bar. After reading of the conviction in the newspaper, lawyer Christopher called Spicer's lawyer (Salkin). Christopher said that he had represented Brown on cocaine charges and that Brown had told him that Spicer had said things to him suggesting that he was involved in the assault. Christopher wanted to offer Brown's information to the prosecutor (Sindler) to get a favorable plea bargain for Brown, so Christopher pressed Brown for all information he had against Spicer. Brown never told Christopher that he had seen Spicer fleeing the bar. Christopher then told prosecutor Sindler what Brown had told him. Sindler then interviewed Brown (without Christopher being present), and Brown told Sindler that he had seen Spicer fleeing the bar. Sindler never told Spicer's attorney what Christopher had told him.

Spicer's attorney then filed a petition for habeas corpus, presenting evidence of these facts (via Christopher) and arguing that Sindler had violated *Brady* by failing to tell him about Brown's "prior inconsistent statement" to Christopher. The state court denied relief, because the prior inconsistent statement was not made directly by Brown to the prosecutor. The federal appeals court disagreed:

> Brown's prior inconsistent statement about whether he was an eyewitness clearly satisfies the first requirement of a *Brady* violation — that the evidence be "favorable" to the defendant. Evidence that can be used to impeach a witness is unquestionably subject to disclosure under *Brady*. * * * *
>
> The impeachment quality of the evidence is clear. Over the course of half a dozen meetings between Brown and his attorney, Christopher, during which Christopher emphasized "the need to present as much evidence as we could to the State in order to interest them in working out a deal," Brown consistently told Christopher that he had seen "Spicy" a few days before the assault and a few days after the assault, but not on the day of the assault. In fact, Christopher testified that he had "pressed" Brown on this point, advising him that "it would be very much to his benefit if he knew any other detail that could make the package more attractive." Even then, Brown insisted that he had not seen Spicer on the day of the assault.
>
> After some preliminary negotiations, Christopher conveyed to Sindler what Brown had told him about Brown's contacts with Spicer in the days before and after, but not the day of, the Armadillo's incident. When Sindler interviewed Brown outside the presence of his attorney, however, Brown, for the first time, claimed to have seen Spicer being chased by another man as he ran from Armadillo's on the day in question.
>
> Sindler confirmed Christopher's statement that Brown's story had changed from what Christopher had related to the prosecutor to what Brown told the prosecutor directly, and Sindler also acknowledged that he "recognized that what Mr. Christopher told me wasn't what Mr. Brown had told me." In fact, he specifically "recalled at the time knowing that there was the part about Spicer running away from Armadillos that was not said by Gary Christopher to me. Then I know that when I met with Larry Brown, he said that." In short, Christopher's and Sindler's compatible recollections confirm the inconsistency between the different versions of events offered by Brown.
>
> The discrepancy between Brown's testimony in court and his prior statements to his attorney would have provided Spicer with significant impeachment material aimed at the very heart of Brown's testimony — that he had been an eyewitness who could identify Spicer at the scene. The impeachment value of this information increases, because, of all the purported eyewitnesses, only Brown knew Spicer; the other witnesses had never seen him before and had difficulty identifying him.
>
> Accordingly, the fact that Brown told at least two different versions of what he did or did not see on the day of the assault, coupled with the significance of the distinction — whether or not Brown was an eyewitness — demonstrates that this information, if disclosed to the defense in Spicer's trial, could have been used to impeach Brown. As impeachment evidence, it was subject to disclosure under *Brady* and its progeny if it was material.

The second element of *Brady* requires us to determine whether the prosecution suppressed this impeaching evidence, irrespective of whether the suppression was willful or inadvertent. Suppressed evidence is "information which had been known to the prosecution but unknown to the defense." *United States v. Agurs*, 427 U.S. 97, 103 (1976).

There is no question that in this case the prosecution never informed Spicer's counsel that Brown's version of Spicer's involvement in the Armadillo's incident had changed. The state acknowledges that its prosecutor recognized that Brown's earlier statements to his attorney did not correspond to what Brown told prosecutors directly and that its prosecutors did not provide that information to Spicer's counsel before trial. The prosecutor's actions appear to have been based on a misunderstanding of his disclosure obligation under *Brady*. But this misunderstanding, or even his error in judgment about it, cannot justify releasing the prosecutor from the obligation. * * * *

We emphasize, however, that we do not hold that the prosecutor is obligated under *Brady* to seek out or to uncover inconsistencies in the versions of events that a witness presents to his own attorney in preparation for plea negotiations. The prosecution cannot be responsible for producing exculpatory material that flows in private discussions from a witness to his attorney. Nor do we hold that the prosecutor is obligated to disclose potentially exculpatory material contained in the back-and-forth hypothesizing that commonly occurs during plea negotiations between the prosecution and defense attorneys. But when the prosecutor receives information that he, as an objectively reasonable prosecutor, should recognize as exculpatory or of impeachment value, he is under a duty to disclose it to the defendant if it is material.

JUDGE KING dissented:

The prior statement that Sindler failed to disclose was not that of his witness, Brown, but that of Brown's lawyer. Nothing that Brown testified to before the grand jury or at Spicer's trial was inconsistent with anything that he had ever said in Sindler's presence; the purported discrepancy is instead between what Brown told Sindler directly, and what Christopher represented that Brown had said earlier.

The lack of identity between the speakers is crucial to this appeal, particularly considering that Christopher's statement was given in the context of a proffer to Sindler. Proffers by counsel attempting to negotiate a plea, immunity, or other benefit for their clients are, by their very nature, unreliable for ascertaining specific facts. The following is an apt description of the proffer process:

> Through incremental steps, we get information about what the witness can tell us, and we are willing to say at each step what our reaction is to the information we have received. Counsel will come in for a witness and advise us that he has a witness who is prepared to cooperate. At that point, we will usually take a hypothetical proffer from the attorney that identifies general areas of subject matter, timing, sometimes specifics, sometimes more general information. If, at that

point, the proffer is generally acceptable to the prosecutor, we will advise the attorney that if the testimony comes in along those lines, we would be interested in accepting a fuller proffer. [Robert E. Bloch, et al., *Representing Corporate Employees During an Antitrust Grand Jury Investigation*, 56 Antitrust L.J. 901, 920 (1988) (statement of Judy L. Whalley, Deputy Director of Operations, Antitrust Division, United States Department of Justice)]

Even after defense counsel has submitted a "fuller proffer," it is virtually always the case that the prosecutor requires the witness to make a personal statement. An examination of this process makes it clear that the preliminary, hypothetical representations of counsel are not considered to be those of the witness:

> There is no way that we can fully judge the candor, credibility, and cooperativeness of a witness without meeting with that witness directly. In order to grant such reassurances as we can in that situation, we use proffer letters. The proffer letter states that during the witness interview, we will agree not to use the statements of the witness directly against the witness in the future. [*Id.* at 920–21]

Obviously, if the parties to the negotiation process in any way imagined that the prior statements of counsel could potentially incriminate the client-witness, those statements would be included within the scope of the proffer letter. It therefore speaks volumes that the typical letter omits any reference to counsel's initial overtures.

It should be clear from the foregoing that proffers made by defense attorneys to prosecutors rarely encompass certainty. Most often, the proffer and negotiation process instead resembles a poker game, rife with understatement, bluff, and bluster. Lawyers for criminal defendants are understandably leery of turning up their hole cards, i.e., their clients' knowledge of other crimes, unless it is likely that they will garner a few chips in return. Most significantly, neither side contemplates that the informal proffer will ever be used by either side, or anyone else, for any purpose.

In practice, the process often does not entail even the limited structure and formality of the one described above. Many times the prosecutor and defense counsel will be familiar with each other from their past professional dealings. The attorneys may have developed a cordial relationship, and, away from the office, they may be friends. A chance encounter in the courthouse hallway can, in a matter of moments, migrate from amiable banter to discussion of a potential plea.

Any agreement arising out of this type of impromptu negotiation is bound to be sketchy, and may amount to nothing more than a tacit understanding to talk again later. Neither side will walk away from the meeting knowing precisely what it has bargained for, but each will be confident that it has given away little of substantive value.

Such are the realities of the modern plea negotiation process, and it was in light of these realities that the state habeas court specifically found that "Brown never made any inconsistent statement to the State regarding his being an eyewitness to the chase." This finding properly focuses on Brown's statements, and not those of Christopher in his proffer to Sindler, rendered unreliable by the context in which they were made.

The state habeas court concluded that "neither *Brady* nor the line of cases following *Brady* required the State to inform defense counsel of a potential discrepancy between what Brown's attorney indicated Brown knew and what Brown actually told the Prosecutor." The state court's application of the law to the facts before it was not only "reasonable" within the meaning of § 2254(d), it was unassailable. The Supreme Court has never invoked *Brady* to grant habeas relief on facts remotely similar to those in this case.

In characterizing the difference between the statements of Brown and his lawyer as a "potential discrepancy," the state habeas court acknowledged the reality that negotiation is something less than an exact science. Absent Christopher's eventual testimony to the contrary, it is easy to imagine that he might have held back key pieces of information in order to gauge Sindler's response to the tidbits already on the table. Under that likely scenario, Brown and Christopher would have shared a common understanding regarding the matters to which Brown could testify. Consequently, Christopher's proffer would have been, at most, an incomplete account of the truth related to him by his client. That being the case, it could not be credibly argued that Sindler would have any conceivable duty to disclose to Spicer or Salkin the details of the proffer.

Yet the majority holds that Sindler violated his duty in this case because, as it turned out, Brown's testimony did not comport with Christopher's understanding. Such Monday-morning quarterbacking unfairly makes a scapegoat of Sindler, who could quite reasonably assume that the story he was hearing from Brown was the same one that Christopher had been told, and that any variation between what Brown claimed to know and Christopher's account of the same was wholly attributable to the latter's negotiation tactics. Indeed, from Sindler's perspective, it would have made little sense for Brown to have told him more than Brown had revealed to his own lawyer.

There is simply no way that Sindler could have known of Brown's embellishment without investigating the matter further, i.e., contacting Christopher for the purpose of confronting Brown. It is well-established, however, that a prosecutor's duty to the defendant does not extend so far. See *United States v. Walker*, 559 F.2d 365, 373 (5th Cir.1977) ("While *Brady* requires the Government to tender to the defense all exculpatory evidence in its possession, it establishes no obligation on the Government to seek out such evidence.").

Without the necessary follow-up, it was impossible for Sindler to conclude that Brown's statements in his presence were in fact inconsistent with what Brown had told Christopher. Without the requisite inconsistency, Christopher's bare proffer had no impeachment value, and was therefore not "favorable" to Spicer's defense. Evidence that is not favorable to the accused need not be disclosed under *Brady*.

4. *When* must the prosecutor disclose " *Brady* material" to the defense?

When the defense requests it? No, held the court in *In re U.S.*, 267 F.3d 132 (2nd Cir. 2001):

> As long as a defendant possesses *Brady* evidence in time for its effective use, the government has not deprived the defendant of due process of law simply because it did not produce the evidence sooner. There is no *Brady* violation unless there is a reasonable probability that earlier disclosure of the evidence would have produced a different result at trial or at a plea proceeding.

The court also address the difficulty facing a prosecutor deciding whether and when to disclose certain evidence:

> Like the extent of the required disclosure, the timing of a disclosure required by *Brady* is also dependent upon the anticipated remedy for a violation of the obligation to disclose: the prosecutor must disclose "material" exculpatory and impeachment information no later than the point at which a reasonable probability will exist that the outcome would have been different if an earlier disclosure had been made. * * * *

> The linking of the scope of the disclosure obligation with the remedy for its breach creates both a responsibility and a problem for the prosecutor. An assessment of whether an outcome would have been different if undisclosed evidence had been disclosed is best made after a trial is concluded. At that point the significance of the undisclosed evidence can be considered in light of the strength of all the evidence indicating guilt. The prosecutor, however, cannot await the outcome and must therefore make a prediction before the trial as to how the nondisclosure of favorable evidence will be viewed after the trial. * * * *

> In some circumstances, the prosecutor's prediction of "reasonable probability" will be easily made. For example, if there are three eyewitnesses who have told investigators that the perpetrator is someone other than the defendant, there will almost always be a reasonable probability that the disclosure of such evidence would have resulted in a different outcome from a trial at which it was not disclosed, regardless of the strength of the prosecution's evidence. At the other extreme, an item of evidence with some arguably exonerating effect might be so trivial in significance to the entire trial evidence that there is no reasonable probability that its disclosure would have altered the outcome. But much evidence favorable to a defendant will lie between these extremes, obliging prosecutors to make a careful prediction as to when the point of "reasonable probability" is reached. Of course, a prosecutor anxious about tacking too close to the wind will disclose a favorable piece of evidence.

5. Does *Brady* apply to evidence held by the police? Yes, held the Court in *Kyles v. Whitley*, 541 U.S. 419, 438 (1995):

> To accommodate the view that the prosecution is not accountable for undisclosed evidence known only to the police would amount to a serious change of course from the *Brady* line of cases. In the State's favor it may be said that no one doubts that police investigators sometimes fail to inform a prosecutor of all they know. But neither is there any serious doubt that procedures and regulations can be established to carry the prosecutor's

burden and to insure communication of all relevant information on each case to every lawyer who deals with it. Since, then, the prosecutor has the means to discharge the government's *Brady* responsibility if he will, any argument for excusing a prosecutor from disclosing what he does not happen to know about boils down to a plea to substitute the police for the prosecutor, and even for the courts themselves, as the final arbiters of the government's obligation to ensure fair trials.

In *Commonwealth v. Burke*, 781 A.2d 1136 (Pa. 2001), the court held that the obligation imposed by *Kyles* requires prosecutors to obtain "exculpatory evidence in the files of police agencies of the same government bringing the prosecution." Therefore, a prosecutor representing the state in one county must obtain exculpatory evidence in the files of a police department of *another county* in the state.

6. What is the *penalty* for a *Brady* violation?

In *Government of Virgin Islands v. Fahie*, 419 F.3d 249 (3rd Cir. 2005), the court held:

> We conclude that dismissal for a *Brady* violation may be appropriate in cases of deliberate misconduct because those cases call for penalties which are not only corrective but are also highly deterrent. Deliberate misconduct is targeted for extra deterrence because we expect willful misbehavior to be the most effectively deterred by enhanced penalties. While retrial is normally the most severe sanction available for a *Brady* violation, where a defendant can show both willful misconduct by the government, and prejudice, dismissal may be proper.

UNITED STATES v. NOBLES
United States Supreme Court
422 U.S. 225 (1975)

MR. JUSTICE POWELL delivered the opinion of the Court.

In a criminal trial, defense counsel sought to impeach the credibility of key prosecution witnesses by testimony of a defense investigator regarding statements previously obtained from the witnesses by the investigator. The question presented here is whether in these circumstances a federal trial court may compel the defense to reveal the relevant portions of the investigator's report for the prosecution's use in cross-examining him. The United States Court of Appeals for the Ninth Circuit concluded that it cannot. We granted certiorari and now reverse.

I

Respondent was tried and convicted on charges arising from an armed robbery of a federally insured bank. The only significant evidence linking him to the crime was the identification testimony of two witnesses, a bank teller and a salesman who was in the bank during the robbery. * * * * Respondent offered an alibi, but his strongest defense centered around attempts to discredit these eyewitnesses. Defense efforts to impeach them gave rise to the events that led to this decision.

In the course of preparing respondent's defense, an investigator for the defense interviewed both witnesses and preserved the essence of those conversations in a written report. When the witnesses testified for the prosecution, respondent's counsel relied on the report in conducting their cross-examination. Counsel asked the bank teller whether he recalled having told the investigator that he had seen only the back of the man he identified as respondent. The witness replied that he did not remember making such a statement. He was allowed, despite defense counsel's initial objection, to refresh his recollection by referring to a portion of the investigator's report. The prosecutor also was allowed to see briefly the relevant portion of the report. * * * * The witness thereafter testified that, although the report indicated that he told the investigator he had seen only respondent's back, he in fact had seen more than that and continued to insist that respondent was the bank robber.

The other witness acknowledged on cross-examination that he too had spoken to the defense investigator. Respondent's counsel twice inquired whether he told the investigator that "all blacks looked alike" to him, and in each instance the witness denied having made such a statement. The prosecution again sought inspection of the relevant portion of the investigator's report, and respondent's counsel again objected. The court declined to order disclosure at that time, but ruled that it would be required if the investigator testified as to the witnesses' alleged statements from the witness stand. * * * * The court further advised that it would examine the investigator's report in camera and would excise all reference to matters not relevant to the precise statements at issue.

After the prosecution completed its case, respondent called the investigator as a defense witness. The court reiterated that a copy of the report, inspected and edited in camera, would have to be submitted to Government counsel at the completion of the investigator's impeachment testimony. When respondent's counsel stated that he did not intend to produce the report, the court ruled that the investigator would not be allowed to testify about his interviews with the witnesses. * * * *

The Court of Appeals for the Ninth Circuit, while acknowledging that the trial court's ruling constituted a "very limited and seemingly judicious restriction," nevertheless considered it reversible error. The court found that the Fifth Amendment prohibited the disclosure condition imposed in this case. The court further held that Fed.Rule Crim.Proc. 16, while framed exclusively in terms of pretrial discovery, precluded prosecutorial discovery at trial as well. In each respect, we think the court erred.

II

The dual aim of our criminal justice system is "that guilt shall not escape or innocence suffer," *Berger v. United States*, 295 U.S. 78, 88 (1935). To this end, we have placed our confidence in the adversary system, entrusting to it the primary responsibility for developing relevant facts on which a determination of guilt or innocence can be made. See *United States v. Nixon*, 418 U.S. 683, 709 (1974).

While the adversary system depends primarily on the parties for the presentation and exploration of relevant facts, the judiciary is not limited to the role of a reference or supervisor. Its compulsory processes stand available to require the presentation of evidence in court or before a grand jury. As we recently observed in *United States v. Nixon, supra*, 418 U.S. at 709:

We have elected to employ an adversary system of criminal justice in which the parties contest all issues before a court of law. The need to develop all relevant facts in the adversary system is both fundamental and comprehensive. The ends of criminal justice would be defeated if judgments were to be founded on a partial or speculative presentation of the facts. The very integrity of the judicial system and public confidence in the system depend on full disclosure of all the facts, within the framework of the rules of evidence. To ensure that justice is done, it is imperative to the function of courts that compulsory process be available for the production of evidence needed either by the prosecution or by the defense. Decisions of this Court repeatedly have recognized the federal judiciary's inherent power to require the prosecution to produce the previously recorded statements of its witnesses so that the defense may get the full benefit of cross-examination and the truth-finding process may be enhanced. See, e.g., *Jencks v. United States*, 353 U.S. 657 (1957).[5] At issue here is whether, in a proper case, the prosecution can call upon that same power for production of witness statements that facilitate full disclosure of all the relevant facts.

In this case, the defense proposed to call its investigator to impeach the identification testimony of the prosecution's eyewitnesses. It was evident from cross-examination that the investigator would testify that each witness' recollection of the appearance of the individual identified as respondent was considerably less clear at an earlier time than it was at trial. It also appeared that the investigator and one witness differed even as to what the witness told him during the interview. The investigator's contemporaneous report might provide critical insight into the issues of credibility that the investigator's testimony would raise. It could assist the jury in determining the extent to which the investigator's testimony actually discredited the prosecution's witnesses. If, for example, the report failed to mention the purported statement of one witness that "all blacks looked alike," the jury might disregard the investigator's version altogether. On the other hand, if this statement appeared in the contemporaneously recorded report, it would tend strongly to corroborate the investigator's version of the interview and to diminish substantially the reliability of that witness' identification.[6]

It was therefore apparent to the trial judge that the investigator's report was highly relevant to the critical issue of credibility. In this context, production of the report might substantially enhance "the search for truth," *Williams v. Florida*, 399 U.S. at 82. We must determine whether compelling its production was precluded by some privilege available to the defense in the circumstances of this case.

---

[5] The discretion recognized by the Court in Jencks subsequently was circumscribed by Congress in the so-called Jencks Act, 18 U.S.C. § 3500.

[6] 6 Rule 612 of the new Federal Rules of Evidence entitles an adverse party to inspect a writing relied on to refresh the recollection of a witness while testifying. The Rule also authorizes disclosure of writings relied on to refresh recollection before testifying if the court deems it necessary in the interests of justice. The party obtaining the writing thereafter can use it in cross-examining the witness and can introduce into evidence those portions that relate to the witness' testimony. As the Federal Rules of Evidence were not in effect at the time of respondent's trial, we have no occasion to consider them or their applicability to the situation here presented.

III

A

The Court of Appeals concluded that the Fifth Amendment renders criminal discovery "basically a one-way street." Like many generalizations in constitutional law, this one is too broad. The relationship between the accused's Fifth Amendment rights and the prosecution's ability to discover materials at trial must be identified in a more discriminating manner.

The Fifth Amendment privilege against compulsory self-incrimination is an "intimate and personal one," which protects "a private inner sanctum of individual feeling and thought and proscribes state intrusion to extract self-condemnation." *Couch v. United States*, 409 U.S. 322, 327. As we noted in *Couch*, the "privilege is a personal privilege: it adheres basically to the person, not to information that may incriminate him."[7]

In this instance, disclosure of the relevant portions of the defense investigator's report would not impinge on the fundamental values protected by the Fifth Amendment. The court's order was limited to statements allegedly made by third parties who were available as witnesses to both the prosecution and the defense. Respondent did not prepare the report, and there is no suggestion that the portions subject to the disclosure order reflected any information that he conveyed to the investigator. The fact that these statements of third parties were elicited by a defense investigator on respondent's behalf does not convert them into respondent's personal communications. Requiring their production from the investigator therefore would not in any sense compel respondent to be a witness against himself or extort communications from him.

We thus conclude that the Fifth Amendment privilege against compulsory self-incrimination, being personal to the defendant, does not extend to the testimony or statements of third parties called as witnesses at trial. The Court of Appeals' reliance on this constitutional guarantee as a bar to the disclosure here ordered was misplaced.

B

The Court of Appeals also held that Fed.Rule Crim.Proc. 16 deprived the trial court of the power to order disclosure of the relevant portions of the investigator's report.[8] Acknowledging that the Rule appears to control pretrial discovery only, the court nonetheless determined that its reference to the Jencks Act, 18 U.S.C. § 3500,

---

[7] "The purpose of the relevant part of the Fifth Amendment is to prevent compelled self-incrimination, not to protect private information. Testimony demanded of a witness may be very private indeed, but unless it is incriminating and protected by the Amendment or unless protected by one of the evidentiary privileges, it must be disclosed." *Maness v. Meyers*, 419 U.S. 449, 473–474 (1975) (White, J., concurring in result). Moreover, the constitutional guarantee protects only against forced individual disclosure of a "testimonial or communicative nature," *Schmerber v. California*, 384 U.S. 757, 761 (1966).

[8] Rule 16(b), which establishes the Government's reciprocal right of pretrial discovery, excepts "reports, memoranda, or other internal defense documents made by the defendant, or his attorneys or agents in connection with the investigation or defense of the case, or of statements made by the defendant, or by government or defense witnesses, or by prospective government or defense witnesses, to the defendant, his agents or attorneys." That Rule therefore would not authorize pretrial discovery of the investigator's report.

signaled an intention that Rule 16 should control trial practice as well. We do not agree.

Both the language and history of Rule 16 indicate that it addresses only pretrial discovery. Rule 16(f) requires that a motion for discovery be filed "within 10 days after arraignment or . . . such reasonable later time as the court may permit," and further commands that it include all relief sought by the movant. When this provision is viewed in light of the Advisory Committee's admonition that it is designed to encourage promptness in filing and to enable the district court to avoid unnecessary delay or multiplication of motions, the pretrial focus of the Rule becomes apparent. The Government's right of discovery arises only after the defendant has successfully sought discovery under subsection (a)(2) or (b) and is confined to matters "which the defendant intends to produce at the trial." Fed.Rule Crim.Proc. 16(c). This hardly suggests any intention that the Rule would limit the court's power to order production once trial has begun.[9] Finally, the Advisory Committee's Notes emphasize its pretrial character. Those notes repeatedly characterize the Rule as a provision governing pretrial disclosure, never once suggesting that it was intended to constrict a district court's control over evidentiary questions arising at trial. * * * *

We conclude, therefore, that Rule 16 imposes no constraint on the District Court's power to condition the impeachment testimony of respondent's witness on the production of the relevant portions of his investigative report. In extending the Rule into the trial context, the Court of Appeals erred.

IV

Respondent contends further that the work-product doctrine exempts the investigator's report from disclosure at trial. While we agree that this doctrine applies to criminal litigation as well as civil, we find its protection unavailable in this case.

The work-product doctrine, recognized by this Court of *Hickman v. Taylor*, 329 U.S. 495 (1947), reflects the strong "public policy underlying the orderly prosecution and defense of legal claims." *Id.* at 510. As the Court there observed:

> Historically, a lawyer is an officer of the court and is bound to work for the advancement of justice while faithfully protecting the rightful interests of his clients. In performing his various duties, however, it is essential that a lawyer work with a certain degree of privacy, free from unnecessary intrusion by opposing parties and their counsel. Proper preparation of a client's case demands that he assemble information, sift what he considers to be the relevant from the irrelevant facts, prepare his legal theories and plan his strategy without undue and needless interference. That is the historical and the necessary way in which lawyers act within the framework of our system of jurisprudence to promote justice and to protect their

---

[9] Rule 16(g) imposes a duty to notify opposing counsel or the court of the additional materials previously requested or inspected that are subject to discovery or inspection under the Rule, and it contemplates that this obligation will continue during trial. The obligation under Rule 16(g) depends, however, on a previous request for or order of discovery. The fact that this provision may have some effect on the parties' conduct during trial does not convert the rule into a general limitation on the court's inherent power to control evidentiary matters.

clients' interests. This work is reflected, of course, in interviews, state-ments, memoranda, correspondence, briefs, mental impressions, personal beliefs, and countless other tangible and intangible ways — aptly though roughly termed by the Circuit Court of Appeals in this case as the "work product of the lawyer." Were such materials open to opposing counsel on mere demand, much of what is now put down in writing would remain unwritten. An attorney's thoughts, heretofore inviolate, would not be his own. Inefficiency, unfairness and sharp practices would inevitably develop in the giving of legal advice and in the preparation of cases for trial. The effect on the legal profession would be demoralizing. And the interests of the clients and the cause of justice would be poorly served. [*Id.* at 510–511]

The Court therefore recognized a qualified privilege for certain materials prepared by an attorney "acting for his client in anticipation of litigation." *Id.* at 508.[11]

Although the work-product doctrine most frequently is asserted as a bar to discovery in civil litigation, its role in assuring the proper functioning of the criminal justice system is even more vital. The interests of society and the accused in obtaining a fair and accurate resolution of the question of guilt or innocence demand that adequate safeguards assure the thorough preparation and presentation of each side of the case. * * * *

At its core, the work-product doctrine shelters the mental processes of the attorney, providing a privileged area within which he can analyze and prepare his client's case. But the doctrine is an intensely practical one, grounded in the realities of litigation in our adversary system. One of those realities is that attorneys often must rely on the assistance of investigators and other agents in the compilation of materials in preparation for trial. It is therefore necessary that the doctrine protect material prepared by agents for the attorney as well as those prepared by the attorney himself. * * * * Moreover, the concerns reflected in the work-product doctrine do not disappear once trial has begun. Disclosure of an attorney's efforts at trial, as surely as disclosure during pretrial discovery, could disrupt the orderly development and presentation of his case. We need not, however, undertake here to delineate the scope of the doctrine at trial, for in this instance it is clear that the defense waived such right as may have existed to invoke its protections.

The privilege derived from the work-product doctrine is not absolute. Like other qualified privileges, it may be waived. Here respondent sought to adduce the testimony of the investigator and contrast his recollection of the contested statements with that of the prosecution's witnesses. Respondent, by electing to present the investigator as a witness, waived the privilege with respect to matters covered in his testimony.[14] Respondent can no more advance the work-product doctrine to sustain a unilateral testimonial use of work-product materials than he could elect to testify in his own behalf and thereafter assert his Fifth Amendment

---

[11] The work-product doctrine is distinct from and broader than the attorney-client privilege.

[14] What constitutes a waiver with respect to work-product materials depends, of course, upon the circumstances. Counsel necessarily makes use throughout trial of the notes, documents, and other internal materials prepared to present adequately his client's case, and often relies on them in examining witnesses. When so used, there normally is no waiver. But where, as here, counsel attempts to make a testimonial use of these materials, the normal rules of evidence come into play with respect to cross-examination and production of documents.

privilege to resist cross-examination on matters reasonably related to those brought out in direct examination.[15]

V

Finally, our examination of the record persuades us that the District Court properly exercised its discretion in this instance. The court authorized no general "fishing expedition" into the defense files or indeed even into the defense investigator's report. Rather, its considered ruling was quite limited in scope, opening to prosecution scrutiny only the portion of the report that related to the testimony the investigator would offer to discredit the witnesses' identification testimony. The court further afforded respondent the maximum opportunity to assist in avoiding unwarranted disclosure or to exercise an informed choice to call for the investigator's testimony and thereby open his report to examination.

The court's preclusion sanction was an entirely proper method of assuring compliance with its order. Respondent's argument that this ruling deprived him of the Sixth Amendment rights to compulsory process and cross-examination misconceives the issue. The District Court did not bar the investigator's testimony. It merely prevented respondent from presenting to the jury a partial view of the credibility issue by adducing the investigator's testimony and thereafter refusing to disclose the contemporaneous report that might offer further critical insights. The Sixth Amendment does not confer the right to present testimony free from the legitimate demands of the adversarial system; one cannot invoke the Sixth Amendment as a justification for presenting what might have been a half-truth. Deciding, as we do, that it was within the court's discretion to assure that the jury would hear the full testimony of the investigator rather that a truncated portion favorable to respondent, we think it would be artificial indeed to deprive the court of the power to effectuate that judgment. Nor do we find constitutional significance in the fact that the court in this instance was able to exclude the testimony in advance rather than receive it in evidence and thereafter charge the jury to disregard it when respondent's counsel refused, as he said he would, to produce the report. * * * *

The judgment of the Court of Appeals for the Ninth Circuit is therefore reversed.

Notes from Sue:

1. According to the Court, what statute or rule served as the trial court's authority to order discovery in this case?

2. Suppose the defense counsel had *not* planned to call his investigator as a witness in *Nobles*. What argument might the prosecutor have made to discover the

---

[15] We cannot accept respondent's contention that the disclosure order violated his Sixth Amendment right to effective assistance of counsel. This claim is predicated on the assumption that disclosure of a defense investigator's notes in this and similar cases will compromise counsel's ability to investigate and prepare the defense case thoroughly. Respondent maintains that even the limited disclosure required in this case will impair the relationship of trust and confidence between client and attorney and will inhibit other members of the "defense team" from gathering information essential to the effective preparation of the case. The short answer is that the disclosure order resulted from respondent's voluntary election to make testimonial use of his investigator's report. Moreover, apart from this waiver, we think that the concern voiced by respondent fails to recognize the limited and conditional nature of the court's order.

investigator's notes anyway? Would such an argument have succeeded?

3. In *U.S. v. Horn*, 811 F.Supp. 739 (D.N.Hampshire1992), defendant was charged with bank fraud. The government made 10,000 documents available to the defense for inspection and copying at a private company under contract with the government. When a defense attorney went to inspect the documents, an employee of the company offered to make copies of those documents the attorney wanted copied, and the attorney accepted. Unknown to the defense attorney, however, the lead prosecutor had instructed the employee to make an *extra* copy of each document requested by defense counsel, and give that extra copy to the prosecutor. The court held that this violated the defendant's work product privilege.

> During the course of preparing this case for trial, defense counsel had reviewed thousands of documents and had thousands of documents copied by an independent copier. However, what happened on November 9 was significantly different from what had occurred in the past. Counsel arrived at 18 Tremont Street to review documents. They wanted to copy a small number of documents, culled from thousands, for very specific purposes. One of those purposes which has been referred to by defense counsel was to develop a basis for impeaching a key government witness, Mr. Boire. In addition, they culled out several documents which specifically related to other defense tactics, strategies, and problems which were revealed to the court *ex parte* and which the court will not reveal here to avoid compounding the problem at hand. While some of the documents that were selected will be revealed at trial by the defense, others in all probability will not be revealed. Some of the documents are relevant to vital credibility issues that the defendants have demonstrated exist to the satisfaction of the court. The documents in question might never have been noticed or discovered by the government from among the approximately ten thousand documents or, if noticed, their significance might never have been apparent or recognized.

> The high degree of selectivity resulting in a relatively small number of documents being copied clearly reflected the thought processes of defense counsel. Taking into account all of the circumstances concerning the documents in question, the court finds and rules that the documents constitute a combination of ordinary and opinion work product. In view of the fact that this is a criminal proceeding where important constitutional rights of due process under the Fifth Amendment and effective assistance of counsel under the Sixth Amendment are at stake, along with the liberty interests of the defendants, this work product deserves special protection. See *Nobles*, 422 U.S. at 238.

The court also found that, after defense counsel learned of the scheme and moved to seal the documents, the lead prosecutor *used* one of the copied documents during a meeting with Mr. Boire to prepare him as a government witness. She also disregarded the court's later order to seal the documents. Defendant argued that dismissal was the appropriate remedy. Instead, the court ordered that: (1) before trial, the government must provide defendant with a written summary of each government witness, (2) defense counsel is allowed to *depose* Mr. Boire, (3) the government is prohibited from introducing any of the copied documents at trial, (4) the government must reimburse defendant for attorneys' fees incurred in litigating this issue, and (5) the lead prosecutor is ordered removed from the case. (The Court of Appeals later reversed the attorneys fees award, holding that it was barred by sovereign immunity. *U.S. v. Horn*, 29 F.3d 754 (1st Cir.1994).)

UNITED STATES v. AGURS
United States Supreme Court
427 U.S. 97 (1976)

Mr. Justice Stevens delivered the opinion of the Court.

After a brief interlude in an inexpensive motel room, respondent repeatedly stabbed James Sewell, causing his death. She was convicted of second-degree murder. The question before us is whether the prosecutor's failure to provide defense counsel with certain background information about Sewell, which would have tended to support the argument that respondent acted in self-defense, deprived her of a fair trial under the rule of *Brady v. Maryland*, 373 U.S. 83.

The answer to the question depends on (1) a review of the facts, (2) the significance of the failure of defense counsel to request the material, and (3) the standard by which the prosecution's failure to volunteer exculpatory material should be judged.

I

At about 4:30 p. m. on September 24, 1971, respondent, who had been there before, and Sewell, registered in a motel as man and wife. They were assigned a room without a bath. Sewell was wearing a bowie knife in a sheath, and carried another knife in his pocket. Less than two hours earlier, according to the testimony of his estranged wife, he had had $360 in cash on his person. About 15 minutes later, three motel employees heard respondent screaming for help. A forced entry into their room disclosed Sewell on top of respondent struggling for possession of the bowie knife. She was holding the knife; his bleeding hand grasped the blade; according to one witness, he was trying to jam the blade into her chest. The employees separated the two and summoned the authorities. Respondent departed without comment before they arrived. Sewell was dead on arrival at the hospital.

Circumstantial evidence indicated that the parties had completed an act of intercourse, that Sewell had then gone to the bathroom down the hall, and that the struggle occurred upon his return. The contents of his pockets were in disarray on the dresser and no money was found; the jury may have inferred that respondent took Sewell's money and that the fight started when Sewell re-entered the room and saw what she was doing.

On the following morning, respondent surrendered to the police. She was given a physical examination which revealed no cuts or bruises of any kind, except needle marks on her upper arm. An autopsy of Sewell disclosed that he had several deep stab wounds in his chest and abdomen, and a number of slashes on his arms and hands, characterized by the pathologist as "defensive wounds."

Respondent offered no evidence. Her sole defense was the argument made by her attorney that Sewell had initially attacked her with the knife, and that her actions had all been directed toward saving her own life. The support for this self-defense theory was based on the fact that she had screamed for help. Sewell was on top of her when help arrived, and his possession of two knives indicated that he was a violence-prone person. * * * * It took the jury about 25 minutes to elect a foreman and return a verdict.

Three months later, defense counsel filed a motion for a new trial, asserting that he had discovered (1) that Sewell had a prior criminal record that would have further evidenced his violent character; (2) that the prosecutor had failed to disclose this information to the defense; and (3) that a recent opinion of the United States Court of Appeals for the District of Columbia Circuit made it clear that such evidence was admissible even if not known to the defendant. * * * * Sewell's prior record included a plea of guilty to a charge of assault and carrying a deadly weapon in 1963, and another guilty plea to a charge of carrying a deadly weapon in 1971. Apparently both weapons were knives.

The Government opposed the motion, arguing that there was no duty to tender Sewell's prior record to the defense in the absence of an appropriate request; that the evidence was readily discoverable in advance of trial and hence was not the kind of "newly discovered" evidence justifying a new trial; and that, in all events, it was not material.

The District Court denied the motion. It rejected the Government's argument that there was no duty to disclose material evidence unless requested to do so, * * * assumed that the evidence was admissible, but held that it was not sufficiently material. The District Court expressed the opinion that the prior conviction shed no light on Sewell's character that was not already apparent from the uncontradicted evidence, particularly the fact that he carried two knives; the court stressed the inconsistency between the claim of self-defense and the fact that Sewell had been stabbed repeatedly while respondent was unscathed.

The Court of Appeals reversed. * * * * The court found no lack of diligence on the part of the defense and no misconduct by the prosecutor in this case. It held, however, that the evidence was material, and that its nondisclosure required a new trial because the jury might have returned a different verdict if the evidence had been received. * * * *

The decision of the Court of Appeals represents a significant departure from this Court's prior holding; because we believe that that court has incorrectly interpreted the constitutional requirement of due process, we reverse.

II

The rule of *Brady v. Maryland*, 373 U.S. 83, arguably applies in three quite different situations. Each involves the discovery, after trial of information which had been known to the prosecution but unknown to the defense.

In the first situation, typified by *Mooney v. Holohan*, 294 U.S. 103, the undisclosed evidence demonstrates that the prosecution's case includes perjured testimony and that the prosecution knew, or should have known, of the perjury. * * * * In a series of subsequent cases, the Court has consistently held that a conviction obtained by the knowing use of perjured testimony is fundamentally unfair, * * * and must be set aside if there is any reasonable likelihood that the false testimony could have affected the judgment of the jury. * * * * It is this line of cases on which the Court of Appeals placed primary reliance. In those cases the Court has applied a strict standard of materiality, not just because they involve prosecutorial misconduct, but more importantly because they involve a corruption of the truth-seeking function of the trial process. Since this case involves no misconduct, and since there is no reason to question the veracity of any of the prosecution witnesses, the test of materiality followed in the *Mooney* line of cases is not necessarily applicable to this case.

The second situation, illustrated by the *Brady* case itself, is characterized by a pretrial request for specific evidence. In that case, defense counsel had requested the extrajudicial statements made by Brady's accomplice, one Boblit. This Court held that the suppression of one of Boblit's statements deprived Brady of due process, noting specifically that the statement had been requested and that it was "material." * * * * A fair analysis of the holding in *Brady* indicates that implicit in the requirement of materiality is a concern that the suppressed evidence might have affected the outcome of the trial. * * * *

The test of materiality in a case like *Brady* in which specific information has been requested by the defense is not necessarily the same as in a case in which no such request has been made. * * * * Indeed, this Court has not yet decided whether the prosecutor has any obligation to provide defense counsel with exculpatory information when no request has been made. Before addressing that question, a brief comment on the function of the request is appropriate.

In *Brady*, the request was specific. It gave the prosecutor notice of exactly what the defense desired. Although there is, of course, no duty to provide defense counsel with unlimited discovery of everything known by the prosecutor, if the subject matter of such a request is material, or indeed if a substantial basis for claiming materiality exists, it is reasonable to require the prosecutor to respond either by furnishing the information or by submitting the problem to the trial judge. When the prosecutor receives a specific and relevant request, the failure to make any response is seldom, if ever, excusable.

In many cases, however, exculpatory information in the possession of the prosecutor may be unknown to defense counsel. In such a situation he may make no request at all, or possibly ask for "all *Brady* material" or for "anything exculpatory." Such a request really gives the prosecutor no better notice than if no request is made. If there is a duty to respond to a general request of that kind, it must derive from the obviously exculpatory character of certain evidence in the hands of the prosecutor. But if the evidence is so clearly supportive of a claim of innocence that it gives the prosecution notice of a duty to produce, that duty should equally arise even if no request is made. Whether we focus on the desirability of a precise definition of the prosecutor's duty or on the potential harm to the defendant, we conclude that there is no significant difference between cases in which there has been merely a general request for exculpatory matter and cases, like the one we must now decide, in which there has been no request at all. The third situation in which the *Brady* rule arguably applies, typified by this case, therefore embraces the case in which only a general request for "*Brady* material" has been made.

We now consider whether the prosecutor has any constitutional duty to volunteer exculpatory matter to the defense, and if so, what standard of materiality gives rise to that duty.

III

We are not considering the scope of discovery authorized by the Federal Rules of Criminal Procedure, or the wisdom of amending those Rules to enlarge the defendant's discovery rights. We are dealing with the defendant's right to a fair trial mandated by the Due Process Clause of the Fifth Amendment to the Constitution. Our construction of that Clause will apply equally to the comparable Clause in the Fourteenth Amendment applicable to trials in state courts.

The problem arises in two principal contexts. First, in advance of trial, and perhaps during the course of a trial as well, the prosecutor must decide what, if anything, he should voluntarily submit to defense counsel. Second, after trial a judge may be required to decide whether a nondisclosure deprived the defendant of his right to due process. Logically, the same standard must apply at both times. For unless the omission deprived the defendant of a fair trial, there was no constitutional violation requiring that the verdict be set aside; and absent a constitutional violation, there was no breach of the prosecutor's constitutional duty to disclose.

Nevertheless, there is a significant practical difference between the pretrial decision of the prosecutor and the post-trial decision of the judge. Because we are dealing with an inevitably imprecise standard, and because the significance of an item of evidence can seldom be predicted accurately until the entire record is complete, the prudent prosecutor will resolve doubtful questions in favor of disclosure. But to reiterate a critical point, the prosecutor will not have violated his constitutional duty of disclosure unless his omission is of sufficient significance to result in the denial of the defendant's right to a fair trial.

The Court of Appeals appears to have assumed that the prosecutor has a constitutional obligation to disclose any information that might affect the jury's verdict. That statement of a constitutional standard of materiality approaches the "sporting theory of justice" which the Court expressly rejected in *Brady*. * * * * For a jury's appraisal of a case "might" be affected by an improper or trivial consideration as well as by evidence giving rise to a legitimate doubt on the issue of guilt. If everything that might influence a jury must be disclosed, the only way a prosecutor could discharge his constitutional duty would be to allow complete discovery of his files as a matter of routine practice.

Whether or not procedural rules authorizing such broad discovery might be desirable, the Constitution surely does not demand that much. While expressing the opinion that representatives of the State may not "suppress substantial material evidence," former Chief Justice Traynor of the California Supreme Court has pointed out that "they are under no duty to report *sua sponte* to the defendant all that they learn about the case and about their witnesses." *In re Imbler*, 60 Cal.2d 554, 569 (1963). And this Court recently noted that there is "no constitutional requirement that the prosecution make a complete and detailed accounting to the defense of all police investigatory work on a case." *Moore v. Illinois*, 408 U.S. 786, 795. * * * * The mere possibility that an item of undisclosed information might have helped the defense, or might have affected the outcome of the trial, does not establish "materiality" in the constitutional sense.

Nor do we believe the constitutional obligation is measured by the moral culpability, or the willfulness, of the prosecutor. * * * * If evidence highly probative of innocence is in his file, he should be presumed to recognize its significance even if he has actually overlooked it. Conversely, if evidence actually has no probative significance at all, no purpose would be served by requiring a new trial simply because an inept prosecutor incorrectly believed he was suppressing a fact that would be vital to the defense. If the suppression of evidence results in constitutional error, it is because of the character of the evidence, not the character of the prosecutor.

As the District Court recognized in this case, there are situations in which evidence is obviously of such substantial value to the defense that elementary fairness requires it to be disclosed even without a specific request.[18] For though the attorney for the sovereign must prosecute the accused with earnestness and vigor, he must always be faithful to his client's overriding interest that "justice shall be done." He is the "servant of the law, the twofold aim of which is that guilt shall not escape or innocence suffer." *Berger v. United States*, 295 U.S. 78, 88. This description of the prosecutor's duty illuminates the standard of materiality that governs his obligation to disclose exculpatory evidence.

On the one hand, the fact that such evidence was available to the prosecutor and not submitted to the defense places it in a different category than if it had simply been discovered from a neutral source after trial. For that reason, the defendant should not have to satisfy the severe burden of demonstrating that newly discovered evidence probably would have resulted in acquittal. * * * * If the standard applied to the usual motion for a new trial based on newly discovered evidence were the same when the evidence was in the State's possession as when it was found in a neutral source, there would be no special significance to the prosecutor's obligation to serve the cause of justice.

On the other hand, since we have rejected the suggestion that the prosecutor has a constitutional duty routinely to deliver his entire file to defense counsel, we cannot consistently treat every nondisclosure as though it were error. It necessarily follows that the judge should not order a new trial every time he is unable to characterize a nondisclosure as harmless under the customary harmless-error standard. Under that standard, when error is present in the record, the reviewing judge must set aside the verdict and judgment unless his "conviction is sure that the error did not influence the jury, or had but very slight effect." *Kotteakos v. United States*, 328 U.S. 750, 764. Unless every nondisclosure is regarded as automatic error, the constitutional standard of materiality must impose a higher burden on the defendant.

The proper standard of materiality must reflect our overriding concern with the justice of the finding of guilt.[20] Such a finding is permissible only if supported by evidence establishing guilt beyond a reasonable doubt. It necessarily follows that if the omitted evidence creates a reasonable doubt that did not otherwise exist,

---

[18] The hypothetical example given by the District Judge in this case was fingerprint evidence demonstrating that the defendant could not have fired the fatal shot.

[20] It has been argued that the standard should focus on the impact of the undisclosed evidence on the defendant's ability to prepare for trial, rather than the materiality of the evidence to the issue of guilt or innocence. See Note, *The Prosecutor's Constitutional Duty to Reveal Evidence to the Defense*, 74 Yale L.J. 136 (1964). Such a standard would be unacceptable for determining the materiality of what has been generally recognized as " *Brady* material" for two reasons. First, that standard would necessarily encompass incriminating evidence as well as exculpatory evidence, since knowledge of the prosecutor's entire case would always be useful in planning the defense. Second, such an approach would primarily involve an analysis of the adequacy of the notice given to the defendant by the State, and it has always been the Court's view that the notice component of due process refers to the charge rather than the evidentiary support for the charge.

constitutional error has been committed. This means that the omission must be evaluated in the context of the entire record.[21] If there is no reasonable doubt about guilt whether or not the additional evidence is considered, there is no justification for a new trial. On the other hand, if the verdict is already of questionable validity, additional evidence of relatively minor importance might be sufficient to create a reasonable doubt.

This statement of the standard of materiality describes the test which courts appear to have applied in actual cases, although the standard has been phrased in different language.[22] It is also the standard which the trial judge applied in this case. He evaluated the significance of Sewell's prior criminal record in the context of the full trial which he recalled in detail. Stressing in particular the incongruity of a claim that Sewell was the aggressor with the evidence of his multiple wounds and respondent's unscathed condition, the trial judge indicated his unqualified opinion that respondent was guilty. He noted that Sewell's prior record did not contradict any evidence offered by the prosecutor, and was largely cumulative of the evidence that Sewell was wearing a bowie knife in a sheath and carrying a second knife in his pocket when he registered at the motel.

Since the arrest record was not requested and did not even arguably give rise to any inference of perjury, since after considering it in the context of the entire record the trial judge remained convinced of respondent's guilt beyond a reasonable doubt, and since we are satisfied that his firsthand appraisal of the record was thorough and entirely reasonable, we hold that the prosecutor's failure to tender Sewell's record to the defense did not deprive respondent of a fair trial as guaranteed by the Due Process Clause of the Fifth Amendment. Accordingly, the judgment of the Court of Appeals is reversed.

Notes from Sue:

1. The Court says that it does not like the standard of materiality applied by the Court of Appeals because it would require the prosecutor to disclose "any information which might affect the jury's verdict." The Court says that this goes too far, as the prosecutor has no duty to disclose all of its case. Why not? Wouldn't the quest for the truth be better served if D has a chance to examine *all* of P's evidence (even if P's "work product" — thoughts, etc. — are not disclosed)? Does some "sporting theory" of justice (which the Court purports to reject) underlie the Court's holding?

---

[21] "If, for example, one of only two eyewitnesses to a crime had told the prosecutor that the defendant was definitely not its perpetrator and if this statement was not disclosed to the defense, no court would hesitate to reverse a conviction resting on the testimony of the other eyewitness. But if there were fifty eyewitnesses, forty-nine of whom identified the defendant, and the prosecutor neglected to reveal that the other, who was without his badly needed glasses on the misty evening of the crime, had said that the criminal looked something like the defendant but he could not be sure as he had only had a brief glimpse, the result might well be different." Comment, 40 U.Chi.L.Rev. 112, 125.

[22] One commentator has identified three different standards this way: "In earlier cases, the following standards for determining materiality for disclosure purposes were enunciated: (1) evidence which may be merely helpful to the defense; (2) evidence which raised a reasonable doubt as to defendant's guilt; (3) evidence which is of such a character as to create a substantial likelihood of reversal." Comment, *Materiality and Defense Requests: Aids in Defining the Prosecutor's Duty of Disclosure*, 59 Iowa L.Rev. 433, 445 (1973).

2. In *Commonwealth v. Tucceri*, 412 Mass. 401 (1992), a rape victim described the rapist as clean-shaven. Defendant and his wife testified that he had a moustache at the time of the alleged crime, but he was convicted. Before trial, defendant had moved for disclosure of any exculpatory evidence, though he did not specifically ask for any photos taken of defendant after his arrest (even though he and his lawyer knew that such photos had been taken). Ten years after the conviction, defendant learned that the police had photos showing him with a moustache. The court held that he was entitled to a new trial, even though he had made no more than a general request, because there was a "substantial risk that the jury would have reached a different conclusion if the evidence had been admitted at the trial".

3. When is withheld evidence "material"?

In *Kyles v. Whitley*, 514 U.S. 419 (1995), the court held that a *Brady* error occurs only when the prosecution suppresses "material" evidence that is favorable to the accused, including evidence that would impeach the credibility of government witnesses. In most circumstances, exculpatory evidence is material "if there is a reasonable probability that, had the evidence been disclosed to the defense, the result of the proceeding would have been different." Where, however, the prosecutor knowingly used perjured testimony or knowingly failed to disclose that evidence used to convict the defendant was false, the standard is more favorable to the defendant: the conviction must be set aside "if there is any reasonable likelihood that the false testimony could have affected the judgment of the jury."

Compare *People v. Brown*, 660 N.E.2d 964 (Ill.1995). Brown was convicted of aggravated battery on a child, mainly on the testimony of 11-year old S.B. that Brown had given S.B. and his brother whiskey and had beaten and choked them. After trial, Brown petitioned for relief, attaching an affidavit from S.B. stating that he had lied on the witness stand, and that Brown had not furnished whiskey and had not beaten or choked the boys. There was *no* evidence that the *prosecutor had known* that the testimony was false. The Illinois Supreme Court rejected the petition. After discussing cases going each way on this issue, the Court stated:

> We find the better rule is one expressed in those cases requiring an allegation of knowing use of false testimony in order to establish a constitutional violation. In the absence of an allegation of the knowing use of false testimony, or at least some lack of diligence on the part of the State, there has been no involvement by the State in the false testimony to establish a violation of due process. Without such involvement, the action of a witness falsely testifying is an action of a private individual for which there is no remedy under the due process clause.

JUDGE HARRISON dissented:

> Patrick Brown sits in prison today based solely on evidence that may have been fabricated by the prosecution's witnesses. Although there is substantial precedent for the majority's holding that the use of perjured testimony does not offend the constitution unless prosecutors knew it was false when they presented it to the jury, I cannot adhere to this view. Rather, I agree with the position taken in *People v. Shannon* (1975), 28 Ill.App.3d 873, 878, which held that "the use of the State's judicial process to enforce a right of the People, the violation of which is based upon the perjured testimony of a private individual, constitutes State action whether

or not the State knew that the testimony was perjured. Known to the State or not, the use of its judicial process to convict and imprison on perjured testimony is a miscarriage of justice which is abhorrent to fundamental fairness and as such is intolerable. Perjury is the mortal enemy of justice, and the battle between them must be waged at every level, including the constitutional."

In *Wood v. Bartholomew*, 516 U.S. 1 (1995), the prosecutor failed to disclose that a polygraph examiner had determined that a key witness against defendant (Rodney) had lied about whether he had assisted defendant in a robbery-murder. Polygraph results were inadmissible as direct evidence and for impeachment. The Court of Appeals held that the failure to disclose was material, as defense counsel could have used the results when interviewing Rodney, and perhaps these results might have persuaded him to change his story. The Supreme Court disagreed, holding that "it is not 'reasonably likely' that disclosure of the polygraph results — inadmissible under state law — would have resulted in a different outcome at trial."

UNITED STATES v. BRINKMAN
U.S. Court of Appeals, 4th Circuit
739 F.2d 977 (1984)

MURNAGHAN, CIRCUIT JUDGE:

Robert Wilhelm Brinkman, also known as Robert H. Mausgrover, appeals from his conviction of violating the Extortionate Credit Transaction Act, 18 U.S.C. § 894(a)(1), and the Interstate Travel Act, 18 U.S.C. § 1952.

Brinkman, Manuel Kane and two others formed a company called Ultracept, for the purposes of marketing a machine that separated oil and water. Brinkman, who claimed to have invented the machine, served as a consultant and handled the sales end, while Kane acted as a major investor. Under the terms of the contract with Ultracept, Brinkman received a salary, together with a royalty based on a percentage of the sales; he also received stock in the corporation. Kane's official title was President and Treasurer, and his responsibilities included paying the bills. In his capacity, Kane handled the checking account and his was an authorized signature on the account. All the royalty payments to Brinkman were made in the form of checks drafted on Ultracept's account and signed by Kane.

The business had trouble getting off the ground, leading to significant losses to Kane, who blamed much of the difficulty on Brinkman's erratic sales effort. In July, 1981, after Kane indicated an unwillingness to make further investments, Brinkman agreed to waive his royalties until the company got back on its feet. Brinkman subsequently did procure a number of sales.

In late 1981, Kane decided to pull out. Brinkman, who had received his full salary and royalty payments through June, 1981, but no royalties since that time, confronted Kane; Kane, however, refused the demand for payment. Brinkman began a series of efforts to obtain payment, beginning with picketing, but moving to threats. In April, 1982, Defendant sent a funeral bouquet to Mrs. Kane, with a black-bordered tag stating "With deepest Sympathy — Soon." In March, 1983, Brinkman allegedly followed, in his car, Kane and a business associate, in what amounted to a high-speed chase through Charlotte, North Carolina.

Word of Brinkman's desire to hire a "hit man" led the FBI to arrange for an informant, known to Brinkman by the alias "Bob Nails," to meet with Brinkman. The meetings confirmed that Brinkman wanted a hit man, and Nails subsequently introduced Brinkman to FBI undercover agent Mike Hartman. Brinkman, in a recorded discussion, described to Hartman how he wanted Kane beaten up, and gave an exact description of where Kane's office was located. At other recorded meetings, Brinkman suggested a tougher course of action. Hartman thereafter called Brinkman to tell him that Kane had given him $5,000. He asked Brinkman to meet him at the Kentucky Fried Chicken on Carowinds Boulevard, one hundred yards over the North Carolina state line in South Carolina. Brinkman met Hartman, and Hartman gave him the $5,000, $800 of which Brinkman returned to Hartman as the collection fee.

Brinkman thereafter was arrested by FBI agents after his return to North Carolina. Brinkman's indictment, returned on July 7, 1983, charged him with two extortionate credit transaction counts in violation of 18 U.S.C. § 894(a)(1), and one count of interstate travel to facilitate extortion, 18 U.S.C. § 1952. Prior to trial, Brinkman moved for the disclosure of the identity and address of Bob Nails, the paid government informant; although the Magistrate ordered disclosure, the district court reversed the Magistrate's order. * * * *

Brinkman then filed, pursuant to Fed.R.Crim.P. 17(b), an ex parte application for a court order to subpoena certain witnesses, including Bob Nails. Although the court granted the application, the government learned of the names on the list and, two days prior to trial, successfully moved to quash the subpoena for Nails. * * * *

At the close of the government's evidence, at trial, Brinkman moved unsuccessfully for a judgment of acquittal. He was convicted of one of the two 18 U.S.C. § 894 counts and the Travel Act count. He was sentenced to five years' imprisonment for the § 894 count, and three concurrent years for the Travel Act count. On appeal, he challenges each of the court's rulings on his motions. * * * *

The next issue is whether the district court abused its discretion in denying Brinkman's motion for disclosure of the identity and whereabouts of the government informer known only by the alias "Bob Nails." The seminal case, *Roviaro v. United States*, 353 U.S. 53 (1957) reversed, on fundamental fairness grounds, a decision upholding the government's refusal to disclose the identity of an informant who was the only other person involved in an illegal heroin transaction. In reaching its result, the court stated:

> We believe that no fixed rule with respect to disclosure is justifiable. The problem is one that calls for balancing the public interest in protecting the flow of information against the individual's right to prepare his defense. Whether a proper balance renders nondisclosure erroneous must depend on the particular circumstances of each case, taking into consideration the crime charged, the possible defenses, the possible significance of the informer's testimony, and other relevant factors. [Id. at 62]

In *McLawhorn v. State of North Carolina*, 484 F.2d 1 (4th Cir.1973), the court applied *Roviaro* in reversing a conviction where the unrevealed informant, who was an undercover detective, and the defendant were the only parties to the drug sale. In so holding, the court stated that

The privilege of nondisclosure ordinarily applies where the informant is neither a participant in the offense, nor helps set up its commission, but is a mere tipster who only supplies a lead to law investigating and enforcement officers. [*Id.* at 5]

We face, however, a situation in which Nails, the informant, falls somewhere in between the role of a mere tipster and that of a participant in the offense. That Nails was more than a "mere tipster" is clear from the fact that he had two important discussions with Brinkman, established that Brinkman wanted a hit man, and introduced Brinkman to Hartman. On the other hand, it is equally inappropriate to label Nails a "participant" in the offense; the crux of the government's case came from the later, recorded discussions between Hartman and Brinkman, to which Nails was not a party.

That Nails was more than a mere tipster does not lead inexorably to a conclusion that the district court erred in denying the motion for disclosure. In *United States v. Diaz*, 655 F.2d 580, 588 (5th Cir.1981), for example, the court declined to apply the *Rovario* rule since, "while the informant here was more than a mere 'tipster,' his involvement in this drug transaction was not as an integral participant."

We therefore must focus not on the labels that may be attached to Nails, but on propriety of the district court's assessment of the *Rovario* balance in light of "the particular circumstances" of the case. *Rovario v. United States, supra,* at 62. The district court balanced the concerns as follows:

> This Court is persuaded that the public interest in maintaining the anonymity of an undercover agent who, according to the Government's statement, is currently involved in other investigations which would be virtually crippled by revealing the agent's true identity, outweighs the need for the Defendant to learn the true identity of an agent who was not a witness or a participant in the crime with which the Defendant has been charged, and was minimally involved with introducing the Defendant to a government agent.

We cannot conclude that the district court abused its discretion in applying the *Rovario* balance to the particular circumstances of the case, and therefore we affirm the decision denying Brinkman's motion for disclosure. * * * *

For the foregoing reasons, appellant's conviction is affirmed.

Notes from Sue:

1. In *Alvarado v. Superior Court*, 23 Cal.4th 1121 (2000), defendant was charged with murdering a snitch, on orders from the "Mexican Mafia", which had a reputation for killing witnesses who testified against their members. The trial court refused to order the prosecutor to disclose pretrial the names of three witnesses to the killing, and also ruled that the three witnesses could testify at trial anonymously (i.e., that defense counsel would not be allowed to question them at trial about their names and addresses). The California Supreme Court upheld the first ruling, but not the second:

> Whenever nondisclosure of a witness's identity will prevent the effective investigation and cross-examination of a crucial witness, the confrontation clause precludes the prosecution from relying upon the witness's testimony at trial while refusing to disclose the witness's identity. As the United

States Supreme Court has explained: "When the credibility of a witness is in issue, the very starting point in 'exposing falsehood and bringing out the truth' through cross-examination must necessarily be to ask the witness who he is and where he lives. The witness's name and address open countless avenues of in- court examination and out-of-court investigation. To forbid this most rudimentary inquiry at the threshold is effectively to emasculate the right of cross-examination itself." *Smith v. Illinois* (1968) 390 U.S. 129, 131.

Accordingly, we conclude that the challenged order must be vacated insofar as it authorizes, in advance of trial and without regard to the evidence and circumstances as they then may appear, the prosecution permanently to withhold the identity of these prosecution witnesses from the defense. At the same time, however, we emphasize that the trial court remains free to fashion a more limited order denying, restricting, or deferring disclosure of the identity of each witness before trial (including limiting disclosure to defendants' counsel), as long as that order does not impermissibly impair defendants' right to confront and cross-examine the witnesses effectively at trial.

2. In *Johnson v. State*, 811 A.2d 898 (Md.App. 2002), a police officer hid himself in a "covert location," from which he allegedly observed Johnson sell drugs. The court held that a covert location is similar to a secret government informant, because there is "a strong interest in protecting the person or persons who cooperated with police by consenting to the use of the covert location" and the court should consider "the safety of the cooperating citizens and the officers on duty" when deciding whether to order the prosecutor to disclose the location to the defense. These interests must be balanced, however, against the defendant's "right to confront witnesses by allowing cross-examination about what the officer could see from his location."

3. In *U.S. v. Moussaoui*, 333 F.3d 509 (4th Cir. 2003), the following occurred in the trial court:

On September 11, 2001, members of al Qaeda hijacked three passenger aircraft and flew them into the World Trade Center towers in New York City and the Pentagon in Virginia. A fourth plane, apparently headed for the Capitol Building in Washington, D.C., crashed in Pennsylvania after an heroic effort by passengers resisting the hijacking.

Moussaoui, an admitted al Qaeda member, was arrested approximately one month prior to September 11. He has been in pre-trial confinement since his arrest. A subsequently issued indictment alleges that until the time of his arrest, Moussaoui was a part of the planned attacks. He is charged with conspiracy to commit acts of terrorism transcending national boundaries, (Count One); conspiracy to commit aircraft piracy, (Count Two); conspiracy to destroy aircraft, (Count Three); conspiracy to use weapons of mass destruction, (Count Four); conspiracy to murder United States employees, (Count Five); and conspiracy to destroy property, (Count Six). The Government is seeking the death penalty on Counts One through Four.

In September 2002, Moussaoui moved for access to the enemy combat ant witness, asserting that this individual would be an important part of his defense. The Government opposed this request.

The district court granted the motion in part. Applying the procedures set forth in the Classified Information Procedures Act (CIPA), 18 U.S.C.A.App. 3 §§ 1–16, as a useful framework for decision, the court determined that testimony from the enemy combatant witness would be relevant and material to Moussaoui's planned defense to the charges. The court also concluded that Moussaoui and the public's interest in a fair trial outweighed the Government's national security interest in precluding access to the enemy combatant witness. However, the court ruled that the Government's national security concerns counseled against granting unfettered pretrial access to the enemy combatant witness and against requiring that the enemy combatant witness be produced for testimony at trial. The district court therefore issued a testimonial writ directing that the Government produce the witness for a Rule 15 deposition and setting conditions for the deposition.

The appellate court dismissed the Government's appeal of this order, as no final judgment had yet been entered. Subsequently, the Government refused to comply with the trial court's order. The Government expected the court to sanction the Government by *dismissing the indictment*, which would be an appealable ruling, enabling the Government to challenge the discovery order on appeal. But the trial court did not dismiss the indictment. Instead, the court ruled that the Government *could not seek the death penalty*. *U.S. v. Moussaoui*, 282 F.Supp.2d 480 (E.D.Va. 2003).

The government appealed this order. In *U.S. v. Moussaoui*, 382 F.3d 453 (4th Cir. 2004), the court held that the trial court erred in ordering the Government to produce the witnesses for depositions, as written summaries of their testimony would adequately protect the defendant's interests.

(4) In *Commonwealth v. Dias*, 886 N.E.2d 713 (Mass. 2008), the prosecutor argued that he should not be required to disclose the name of the informant, because the informant would refuse to testify anyway, invoking his privilege against self-incrimination. The court rejected this argument:

> Whether the informant could assert a valid Fifth Amendment privilege if called as a witness at trial is a distinct issue from whether the informant's identity must be disclosed before trial because it is apparent that he has information relevant and helpful to the defense. While calling the informant as a witness might be one way of putting that information to good use in this case, it is not the only way, and it may not be as useful to the defense as knowledge of his identity before trial. The ability to connect the information in the affidavit to the name of a person could prove to be invaluable to the effectiveness of the cross-examination of Belisle, and seriously affect the credibility of her testimony. It might also assist in highlighting other weaknesses in the Commonwealth's case, and in opening up an avenue of defense investigation and preparation for the cross-examination of other witnesses called by the Commonwealth (including Detective Bernardo), not otherwise apparent.

UNITED STATES v. FEOLA

U.S. District Court, Southern District of New York
651 F.Supp. 1068 (1987)

BRIEANT, CHIEF JUDGE.

Defendants in this case stand charged, by first superseding indictment filed on March 27, 1986, with having operated a cocaine and marijuana trafficking ring, centered in Westchester County and Manhattan, which distributed narcotics during 1985. * * * *

Defendants make numerous requests for discovery from the Government of certain documents and other items, each of which will be considered in turn by the Court. * * * *

Exculpatory Materials

Defendants call upon the Government to provide exculpatory evidence as mandated by *Brady v. Maryland,* 373 U.S. 83 (1963). Included in their request for exculpatory material are defendants' specific motions for disclosure of promises of preferential treatment, and of impeachment information pertaining to government witnesses.

The Government acknowledges its obligation to produce such information, and represents to this Court that it has already agreed to do so "in a fashion that will not prejudice the rights of the defendants." It contends, however, that to the extent defendants demand disclosure of information other than that which is exculpatory in nature, their demands plainly fall outside the scope of *Brady.*

To reiterate that obligation, the Supreme Court in *Brady* held that "the suppression by the prosecution of evidence favorable to an accused upon request violates due process where the evidence is material either to guilt or to punishment, irrespective of the good faith or bad faith of the prosecution." *Id.* at 87. As asserted by the Court of Appeals for this Circuit, "the heart of the holding in *Brady*" is the impermissibility of withholding evidence "favorable to the accused and material to the determination of guilt or to the appropriate punishment." *United States v. Leroy,* 687 F.2d 610, 618 (2d Cir., 1982). Moreover, the Government is under a continuing duty to preserve and disclose such *Brady* materials.

In addition, it has been determined that the failure of the prosecution to disclose information that would impeach a government witness may also deprive the defendant of a fair trial under the *Brady* rule. *Cantone v. Superintendent, New York Correctional Facility at Green Haven,* 759 F.2d 207 (2d Cir.1985). A defendant is entitled to exculpatory or mitigating evidence in the Government's possession, including evidence pertinent to a material witness's credibility or reliability. *Perkins v. LeFevre,* 642 F.2d 37, 40 (2d Cir.1981). Thus, the law requires that exculpatory statements of government witnesses be disclosed to the defendant, and that the jury be informed of all agreements between the Government and accomplice witnesses. *United States v. Buettner-Janusch,* 500 F.Supp. 1285 (S.D.N.Y. 1980). Failure of the Government to reveal evidence of an understanding with a witness that the witness will receive lenient treatment for his offenses in return for his testimony will violate due process and result in the need for a new trial. *United States v. Pfingst,* 477 F.2d 177, 191 (2d Cir.1973).

The Court deems this request to be sufficiently specific and detailed as to raise no problem under *United States v. Agurs*, 427 U.S. at 104, and its progeny (requisite "pretrial request for specific evidence").

Accordingly, the motion of defendants is granted and the Government is directed to disclose to defendants all exculpatory material encompassed by *Brady*. The Court notes that this is a continuing duty, and that the within materials must be provided by a "reasonable time" before trial, which is held to be thirty (30) days prior to the trial, in the context of this case. * * * *

Preservation of notes

Defendants' motion for preservation of any and all tape recordings or handwritten or typed notes of interviews or communications made in connection with this case by federal law enforcement personnel, and all other state and/or local law enforcement agencies, is hereby granted. The Government must comply with its obligation well established by case law and see to the preservation of such materials by all law enforcement personnel under its direct or indirect control.

In *United States v. Bufalino*, 576 F.2d 446, 450 (2d Cir.1978), the Court of Appeals held that:

> We emphatically second the district court's observation that any resulting costs in the form of added shelf space will be more than counterbalanced by gains in the fairness of trials and also by the shielding of sound prosecutions from unnecessary obstacles to conviction.

In *Bufalino*, the Court also announced that it would "look with an exceedingly jaundiced eye upon future efforts to justify non-production of a Rule 16 or Jencks Act "statement" by reference to "department policy" or "established practice" or anything of the like. There simply is no longer any excuse for official ignorance regarding the mandate of the law." *Id.* at 449.

It should be noted in complying with this order that government agencies must keep in mind the broad definition of discoverable "statements" incorporated in the governing texts. See Rule 16(a)(1)(A), F.R.Crim.P.; 18 U.S.C. § 3500. The Court in *Bufalino* expressed its concurrence with the District of Columbia Circuit that *Brady* envisions that "in framing their rules for evidence preservation investigative agencies must define discoverable evidence very broadly, including any materials that "might" be "favorable" to the accused." Id. at 450. Cf. *United States v. Anzalone*, 555 F.2d 317 (2d Cir., 1977) (recommending that FBI retain agents' handwritten notes of witness interviews).

The Government recognizes this obligation to preserve original notes and writings, as is apparent from reading its Memorandum of Law. However, it brings this Court's attention to certain field notes of the New York State Police Department investigation which the Government believes were destroyed after being fully incorporated into State Police reports in accordance with the practice of that department. The Government represents that no defendant would suffer any prejudice as a consequence.

The Court finds this situation to be regrettable, in light of *Bufalino*, but not likely to be prejudicial to the defendants if the notes were fully incorporated into the State Police reports. There is no evidence that they were not.

In *United States v. Grammatikos*, 633 F.2d 1013 (2d Cir.1980), decided after *Bufalino*, the Court held that the Government's failure to preserve consensual tape recordings of conversations between the defendant and a paid government informant, material which would have been discoverable, did not entitle defendant to dismissal of the indictment or to a new trial at which testimony of the informant could not be presented. This ruling was made in a situation where the culpability of the Government was not great, the circumstances surrounding the disposal of the tape recording tended to refute any suspicion of evil motive or foul play, and there were compelling reasons to believe that the tapes were inculpatory. The appropriateness and extent of sanctions in such situations depends on a case-by-case assessment of the Government's culpability for the loss (a point which in logic should have no relevance), together with a realistic appraisal of the significance of the lost evidence when viewed in light of its nature, its bearing on critical issues in the case, and the strength of the Government's untainted proof.

In the instant case, the destroyed notes did not rise to the level of significance of the evidence in *Grammatikos*, in that the information contained therein was fully incorporated in other materials. There does not appear to be any suggestion of bad intentions on the part of the state officials, nor complicity of the Federal Government, nor have the notes been shown, or even alleged, to be exculpatory in nature. * * * *

List of Government Witnesses

Defendants move this Court to require the United States Attorney to furnish defense counsel with a complete list of the names and addresses of the witnesses it intends to call in its case in chief, including "each and every cooperating witness, informant, or cooperating co-defendant who either is prepared to testify at trial or who was present and has relevant information as to the facts of this case which may be favorable to the defendant."

Such a sweeping request must be denied by this Court as far beyond the scope of Rule 16 and the precedential authority. However, the motion is granted as to any witnesses who are in federal custody or protective custody; such witnesses, if any, should be identified in order that defense counsel if they wish can make a request for an interview.

Nowhere in the United States Code or the Federal Rules of Criminal Procedure are the courts explicitly authorized or forbidden to order pre-trial disclosure of government witnesses in non-capital cases. The general discretion of district courts to compel the Government to identify its witnesses is widely acknowledged. See, e.g., *United States v. Cannone*, 528 F.2d 296, 301–2 (2d Cir.1975). The disclosure of the identity of the prosecution's witnesses is desirable on the one hand, to aid the defense in its preparation for trial and to mitigate against the detriment of surprise. On the other hand, especially in narcotics cases, the dangers of intimidation of witnesses, subornation of perjury, and even actual injury of witnesses, may necessitate concealment of their identities. It is the task of the court to perform this balancing function under the special circumstances of each case.

The Circuit Court in *United States v. Alessi*, 638 F.2d 466 (2d Cir.1980), found the prosecution to be under no obligation to give the defendant advance warning of the witnesses who would testify against him and not precluded from introducing evidence of a "surprise witness," particularly in light of the fact that the Government had furnished to defendant all impeachment-related material concerning the witness after the direct examination.

Moreover, the courts in this district have widely found that the defendant is not entitled to a witness list absent a particularized showing of need. See, e.g., *United States v. Wilson*, 565 F.Supp. 1416 (S.D.N.Y.1983). Where defendants make only an abstract, conclusory claim that disclosure is necessary to prepare for trial, the defendants fail to meet their burden and it would serve no legitimate purpose to require the Government to disclose the names of, and impeachment materials concerning, persons whom it intends to call as witnesses. As asserted by the Government, the dangers inherent in the disclosure of the names of government witnesses in the context of a narcotics case have been considered to be quite serious. See *United States ex rel. Lloyd v. Vincent*, 520 F.2d 1272, 1274 (2d Cir.1975) (interest of the state and of the witnesses in preserving the confidentiality of undercover agents in narcotics cases justified exclusion of public during witness testimony). In his concurrence, Circuit Judge Lumbard emphasized the danger to witnesses peculiar to narcotics cases: "In no area of law enforcement have murder, mayhem and terror more frequently been used against disclosure and testimony." *Id.* at 1275. The danger inherent in the very nature of the within narcotics case must of course be given serious consideration.

Here this Court is presented with very real dangers to the witnesses of the Government, while defendants do not make a particularized showing of the need for this information. The abstract, conclusory claim of defendants that such disclosure is necessary to the proper preparation of defense for trial will not suffice. Absent a strong showing that the benefits would outweigh the risks, and finding that such a showing has not been made by the moving defendants, this Court shall not order the disclosure of the Government's witnesses, except as to those who may be in federal or protective custody. * * * *

Early Production of Section 3500 Materials

Defendants move for the entry of an order directing the Government to furnish all reports and statements of government agents, police officers, and government witnesses no less than ten days (fourteen days by request of some of the defendants) prior to trial, pursuant to 18 U.S.C. § 3500. In support thereof, defendants state that such a disclosure order is necessary to prepare and present the defense, to protect the due process rights of defendants, and to prevent undue and burdensome delays at time of trial. Some defendants additionally invoke the arguments of effective assistance of counsel, equal protection, speedy trial, and meaningful access to courts. As much as this Court would like to assist the defendants in the preparation of their defense and at the same time avoid delays at trial, the Court cannot order the Government to produce these materials prior to trial by virtue of 18 U.S.C. § 3500 (hereinafter "Section 3500"). Section 3500(a) mandates that:

> In any criminal prosecution brought by the United States, no statement or report in the possession of the United States which was made by a Government witness or prospective Government witness (other than the defendant), shall be the subject of subpoena, discovery, or inspection until said witness has testified on direct examination in the trial of the case. * *
> * *

Neither the case law nor § 3500 require the Government to turn over such potential impeachment material at the time of pre-trial motions.

As discussed also in *United States v. Wallace*, 272 F.Supp. 838, 840 (S.D.N.Y., 1967), a pre-trial motion for production and inspection of statements or reports made by government witnesses or prospective government witnesses to an agent of the Government is premature since such material does not have to be produced by the Government until the conclusion at trial of direct testimony of the witnesses with respect to whom discovery is sought. The relevance to the subject matter of the direct examination is then determined by the court, after gathering the necessary materials, at the appropriate point in the trial. Although this Court may not require the Government to provide defendants with such § 3500 materials, it concurs with the encouragement of pre-trial disclosure of § 3500 materials suggested by the Second Circuit in *United States v. Percevault*:

> Although we hold that the government cannot be compelled to disclose statements of prospective witnesses prior to the time prescribed by the Jencks Act, we note that in most criminal cases, pre-trial disclosure will redound to the benefit of all parties, counsel, and the court. Indeed, sound trial management would seem to dictate that Jencks Act material should be transmitted prior to trial, especially in complex cases, so that those abhorrent lengthy pauses at trial to examine documents can be avoided and also, we should emphasize, to protect the government against post-conviction claims of prejudicial surprise or claims of suppression of material and favorable evidence. [490 F.2d 126, 132 (2d Cir.1974)]

Accordingly, this Court encourages the Government to meet this request with a spirit of cooperation.

Defendant's Statements

Defendants request that the Court order the Government to disclose any written or recorded statements made by the defendants or copies thereof, within the possession, custody or control of the Government, the existence of which is known, or by the exercise of due diligence may become known, to the Government. The Court notes that, in its letter to this Court dated December 9, 1986, the Government represents that it is unaware of any statements by defendant Tarantelli to any person known by him to be a Government agent, and that the Government will not seek to introduce any such statement against him at trial. It also states that statements were made by defendants Gumpricht, Acevedo and Cercena to law enforcement agents, and that these statements have been disclosed to their respective counsel.

This motion is granted as to those statements to which each defendant is entitled under Rule 16(a) of the F.R.Crim.P. Rule 16(a) provides, in pertinent part, that:

> Upon motion of a defendant the court may order the attorney for the government to permit the defendant to inspect and copy or photograph any relevant (1) written or recorded statements or confessions made by the defendant, or copies thereof, within the possession, custody or control of the government, the existence of which is known, or by the exercise of due diligence may become known, to the attorney for the government.

The case law has expanded upon this rule to authorize broad pre-trial discovery of the defendant's statements, whether made during or after the commission of the crimes charged; to a government agent, to a grand jury, or to anyone else; and whether obtained surreptitiously or voluntarily. *United States v. Percevault*, 490 F.2d 126, 129 (2d Cir., 1974). "Common sense and judicial experience teach that a defendant's prior statement in the possession of the Government may be the single most crucial factor in the defendant's preparation for trial." *Id.* at 130.

In accordance with its broad scope, courts have liberally construed the term "statement" as not limited to formal statements by defendants, and have held discoverable recordings of statements unwittingly made to government informants or to intended victims that had secured the cooperation of the police. Tapes of statements made by a defendant in the process of committing a crime are also within the scope of Rule 16.

Accordingly, this motion is granted for each defendant as to his own statements. Each defendant can discover and inspect copies of his *own* statements; whether a defendant will allow other defendants to examine his statements is subject to the discretion of that defendant and his counsel. The Government shall not at this stage of the proceedings be ordered to disclose statements of co-defendants, witnesses, or co-conspirators, as discussed below. * * * *

Production of Investigative Files

Defendants make motions for the production of the investigative files of the Government; the interview reports of law enforcement officials; the names and addresses of all persons who have knowledge regarding this case or who have been interviewed by the Government; any information known to government agents and which is not in writing; any statements by non-witnesses not being called by the Government to testify at trial regarding the defenses or the offenses charged; the names and addresses of other people under surveillance at defendants' property; the names and addresses of any government agent who was present or participated in any way; and other requests of the same all-encompassing character.

All motions of this nature must be categorically denied because prohibited from disclosure or inspection by Rule 16(a)(2), F.R.Crim.P., as "reports, memoranda or other internal government documents made by the attorney for the government or other government agents in connection with the investigation or prosecution of the case." As announced by the Court of Appeals in *United States v. Pfingst*, a defendant is not entitled to the disclosure of portions of memoranda prepared by a government attorney which contain summaries, evaluations of evidence and discussions of the legal and practical problems of prosecution. 477 F.2d 177 (2d Cir., 1973). To the extent that communications between the United States Attorney and any state or city official with respect to the defendant were embodied in reports, memoranda, or other internal government documents made by a government attorney or agent in connection with the case, these materials were not discoverable. *United States v. Goldman*, 439 F.Supp. 337 (S.D.N.Y.1977). See also *United States v. Warme*, 572 F.2d 57 (2d Cir.1978) (1978) (FBI agents' reports on ongoing investigation of person to whom defendant had provided counterfeit money); *United States v. Marshak*, 364 F.Supp. 1005 (S.D.N.Y.1973) (investigative reports of city police department exempt from discovery or inspection).

Even more broadly has this rule been construed by the courts, precluding disclosure of information which is neither expressly authorized by Rule 16 nor otherwise discoverable as exculpatory under *Brady* or as impeaching under § 3500. "Although Rule 16(a) provides a mechanism for liberal discovery, it was not intended to provide the defendant with access to the entirety of the government's case against him." *United States v. Percevault*, 490 F.2d at 130. In *United States v. Cafaro*, 480 F.Supp. 511, 520 (S.D.N.Y.1979), the court denied defense requests for all persons whom the Government asked about the narcotics activities of the defendants, as defendants have "no right to be apprised of all investigatory work on a case." See *United States v. Massino*, 605 F.Supp. 1565 (S.D.N.Y.1985), rev'd on other grounds 784 F.2d 153 (2d Cir.1986) (where information in witness lists was sought irrespective of whether exculpatory, and disclosure would amount to excessive pretrial display of government's investigative file).

Defendants' requests in effect for all information regarding the defendants must be denied. A criminal defendant is not entitled to know everything that the government investigation has unearthed when such information is not used against him at trial. Moreover, the Government has "no obligation to 'preview its case or expose its legal theory', nor must it disclose the 'precise manner in which the crime charged in the indictment is alleged to have been committed.' " *United States v. Shoher*, 555 F.Supp. 346, 349 (S.D.N.Y.1983).

In sum, the defendants are not entitled to complete disclosure of all evidence in the Government's files which might conceivably assist them in the preparation of their defense, but they are not to be denied access to exculpatory evidence known to the Government and unknown to them.

Production of Documents and Tangible Objects

Also requested by defendants are "such tangible objects which are in the possession, custody, or control of the government and which are material to the preparation of Defendants' defense or intended for use by the government as evidence in chief at the trial." Listed specifically are such items as any and all tangible objects obtained from the person or effects of defendants; documents, instrument, forms or any statements of any kind signed or purported to have been signed by any defendant; books, papers, documents or tangible objects the Government plans to offer into evidence; fingerprint impressions, clothing hair, fiber, or other materials obtained from the scene of the alleged offenses; hotel, motel, airline, other public transportation, telephone and/or other public or private communications records which the Government intends to use at trial; any narcotics or drug paraphernalia seized from defendants; and photographs the Government intends to use at trial.

The Government responds that, as it has informed all defendants, "the physical evidence relating to this case has been, and continues to be available for inspection upon reasonable notice."

The requested items are well within the discovery and inspection expressly permitted by Rule 16(a)(1)(C):

> Upon request of the defendant the government shall permit the defendant to inspect and copy or photograph books, papers, documents, photographs, tangible objects, buildings or places, or copies or portions

thereof, which are within the possession, custody or control of the government, and which are material to the preparation of his defense, or are intended for use by the government as evidence in chief at the trial, or were obtained from or belong to the defendant.

Thus, defendants are entitled to inspect or copy all of the materials herein which are material to the defense, as those requested appear to be; are intended to be used by the Government at trial; or were obtained from or belong to the defendants. For instance, in *United States v. Kaminsky*, 275 F.Supp. 365 (S.D.N.Y.1967), the defendants were entitled to inspection of the bonds which were the subject of the indictment and were entitled to see copies of fingerprints of defendants as alleged to appear on some of the bonds, as well as fingerprint reports or analysis of experts who studied the prints and rendered opinions thereon (defendants charged with possessing and pledging of stolen bonds). Similarly, *United States v. Acarino* held that defendant's counsel and any experts chosen by him were entitled to inspect and test an alleged narcotic belonging to defendant in the Government's possession. 270 F.Supp. 526 (E.D.N.Y.1967). So too should the fingerprint and narcotic information be subject to inspection in the instant case.

Logs of telephone conversations were found to be discoverable in *United States v. Konefal*, where the calls were placed by government agents to defendant at his home; the court ordered that, if such logs were unavailable, the Government was to make every effort to account for their whereabouts and to provide defendant with written explanations for their absence. 566 F.Supp. 698 (N.D.N.Y.1983). But see *United States v. Payden*, 613 F.Supp. 800 (S.D.N.Y.1985) (requests for analysis performed on toll records and other conclusions of investigative officers denied in that these were internal government documents made in connection with the investigation of the case). Here the telephone logs themselves are discoverable under Rule 16(a)(1)(C), but of course any work product exposing the theory of the Government is not. See Rule 16(a)(2).

Photographic identification, pen register tapes, and telephone records are clearly included under this rule as discoverable objects to which defendants are entitled.

In granting this motion, the Court holds that the Government should continue to insure that the material herein is made available for inspection and copying by the defendants.

Notice of Intention to Use

The defendants additionally request, pursuant to Rule 12(d)(2) of the F.R.Crim.P., that the Government notify all defendants of its intention to use any evidence which defendants may be entitled to discover under Rule 16 particularly as requested herein. Defendants further note that, pursuant to Rule 16(c), F.R.Crim.P., the Government's duty to disclose the materials requested herein which are required or come to the attention of the Government subsequently to the disposition of the present request be properly supplied to all defendants.

The Court hereby grants both requests of the within motion, as clearly enumerated in the Federal Rules of Criminal Procedure. Rule 12(d)(2) provides that:

> The defendant may request notice of the government's intention to use (in its evidence in chief at trial) any evidence which the defendant may be

entitled to discover under Rule 16 subject to any relevant limitations prescribed in Rule 16.

In addition, Rule 16(c) sets forth a continuing duty to disclose, as follows:

> If, prior to or during trial, a party discovers additional evidence or material previously requested or ordered, which is subject to discovery or inspection under this rule, he shall promptly notify the other party or his attorney or the court of the existence of the additional evidence or material.

Henceforth, all parties are under an extended duty to disclose all items to which the other party is entitled under the rules of discovery and inspection and as directed herein by this Court. * * * *

Copies of Reports of Examinations and Tests

In their motion for an order pursuant to Rule 16(a)(1) of the F.R.Crim.P., defendants ask the Government to provide defendants with copies of any results or reports of physical examinations and of scientific tests or experiments available which are within the possession, custody, or control of the Government, the existence of which is known, or by the exercise of due diligence may become known to the attorney for the Government, and which are material to the preparation to the defense or are intended for use by the Government as evidence at the trial. Among the specific requests are: any such results or reports concerning any and all drugs which are the subject of the instant indictment; the results of all fingerprint tests or experiments performed on any and all materials, objects, or property seized on any defendant's property; any and all comparisons of fingerprints, clothing, hair, fiber, or other materials made in connection with this case; and any and all results or reports of physical or mental examination(s). In a separate motion, defendants seek the report containing the results of any polygraph examination administered to anyone in connection with the Government's investigation of the case; the Court will consider this latter motion to be incorporated into the request herein for reports of examinations and tests.

Pursuant to Rule 16(a)(1)(D), F.R.Crim.P., the Court grants this motion insofar as it directs the Government to provide to defendants all reports of examinations and tests encompassed by this broad rule, which permits a defendant:

> to inspect and copy of photograph any results or reports of physical or mental examinations, of scientific tests or experiments, or copies thereof, which are within the possession, custody, or control of the government, the existence of which is known, or by the exercise of due diligence may become known, to the attorney for the government, and which are material to the preparation of the defense or are intended for use by the government as evidence in chief at the trial.

See, e.g., *United States v. Lumumba*, 741 F.2d 12 (2d Cir.1984) (government under obligation to disclose the results of scientific tests which it had intended to offer at trial as evidence); *United States v. Bel-Mar Laboratories, Inc.*, 284 F.Supp. 875 (E.D.N.Y.1968) (reports of experts, whether such experts were government employees or were specifically retained to test and analyze subject drugs, were subject to disclosure); *United States v. Willis*, 33 F.R.D. 510 (S.D.N.Y.1963) (defendant entitled to photographs, copies of plans of vessels, copies of medical reports, and reports of blood tests).

However, this motion is denied with respect to the polygraph information, which this Court does not consider to be a "scientific test or experiment" within the contemplation of this rule in that its reliability has not been sufficiently established in the scientific community, and which is not otherwise discoverable under Rule 16. No mention of such will be permitted at trial by any attorney, without first seeking leave in the absence of the jury.

Identification Session Information

Defendant Acevedo makes a motion for disclosure of the names and addresses of each person to whom a photograph alleged to be that of any defendant or to whom the person of any defendant was displayed for the purpose of identification; the time, date, and place of such display; the names and addresses of each person then and there present; and a copy of each and every photograph taken or displayed at that time and place.

The Court determines that the identity information regarding such identification witnesses should not be disclosed to defendants, because pre-trial release of the identity of government witnesses and informants is not required for the preparation of the defense, particularly when balanced against the potential danger to these witnesses in a narcotics case such as this. * * * *

Furthermore, the Government is not required to disclose to defendants the results of any photographing of defendants for identification purposes at a "show up" since such photography was not in contemplation of the rule concerning "scientific tests or experiments." *United States v. Callahan*, 300 F.Supp. 519 (S.D.N.Y.1969). Of course if such photographs will be presented by the Government at trial in its case in chief, however, they fall within the discovery and inspection of "tangible objects" mandated by Rule 16(a)(1)(C), above.

Writings to Refresh Memory

Also the subject of a motion for discovery by Defendant Acevedo are "all writings used to refresh the memory of any informant or co-conspirator", pursuant to Rule 612 of the F.R.Evid. The Court considers this motion to be premature, for it remains to be seen, at the testimony of such witnesses at trial, whether their memories will need to be refreshed, and what writings, if any, will be utilized therewith. This motion is denied without prejudice to its being renewed at the appropriate time at trial.

Prior Convictions of Defendants

Defendants request any information possessed by the Government regarding prior or subsequent "bad acts" or prior or subsequent criminal conduct of the defendants which is not charged in the indictment, and disclosure of the names and addresses of each witness who will testify to said activity.

Under the F.R.Crim.P, each defendant is permitted only to receive a copy of the record of his prior criminal convictions, pursuant to Rule 16(a)(1)(B):

> Upon request of the defendant, the government shall furnish to the defendant such copy of his prior criminal record, if any, as is within the possession, custody, or control of the government, the existence of which is

known, or by the exercise of due diligence may become known, to the attorney for the government.

Except as to a copy of his conviction record, if any, which must be provided to each defendant, this motion is denied. The identity of any witnesses to any prior bad acts need not be revealed to defendants in view of the prevailing risks associated with such disclosure. The bad acts which are not the subject of a prior conviction will not be ordered to be produced. Such information may be held inadmissible at trial, thereby rendering the within request premature. See *United States v. Deardorff*, 343 F.Supp. 1033 (S.D.N.Y.1971) (defendants under indictment for bribery were entitled to discover reports in custody of the Government setting forth the prior criminal records of persons named in the indictment as defendants, but would be denied discovery regarding the investigation made by the Government as to those persons).

Prior Bad Acts of Co-defendants and Co-conspirators

Defendants further request the criminal records and prior bad acts of any unindicted co-defendants or co-conspirators in these matters. To the extent not required to be produced in respect of a witness, such a request is hereby denied by this Court.

Record of Grand Jury Proceedings

Finally, defendants seek extensive details concerning the grand jury proceedings in this case, including, *inter alia*, the transcript testimony of any and all persons who testified before the grand jury; the identity of each of the grand jurors, and of those who voted to indict the defendants; the dates evidence was presented to any grand jury considering the offenses charged in the instant indictment; the names of witnesses who testified; the identities of any government attorney presenting evidence; any and all documents introduced; and any and all testimony of co-defendants or unindicted co-conspirators.

This Court categorically declines to order the release of any of this information beyond *Brady* material, and grants this motion only insofar as it requests the"recorded testimony of the defendant before a grand jury which relates to the offense charged", discoverable under Rule 16(a)(1)(A), F.R.Crim.P., as to each defendant. Of course, the testimony of witnesses may subsequently be available to the defendants pursuant to 18 U.S.C. § 3500. Rule 6 prohibits disclosure of matters occurring before a grand jury, except"upon a showing that grounds may exist for a motion to dismiss the indictment because of matters occurring before the grand jury." Rule 6(e)(3)-(C)(ii). A defendant is not entitled to disclosure of grand jury proceedings unless a showing of"particularized need" is made. *Dennis v. United States*, 384 U.S. 855 (1966). This Court finds that no such showing has been made with respect to any of the herein requested discovery of the grand jury proceedings.
* * * *

Conclusion

The foregoing constitutes the final resolution of the pending motions by this Court.

Note from Sue:

In *U.S. v. Cherry*, 876 F.Supp. 547 (S.D.N.Y.1995), Cherry was indicted for violations of the federal Racketeer Influenced & Corrupt Organizations (RICO) Act, based on certain "predicate" crimes Cherry was alleged to have committed: two homicides. The RICO prosecution resulted from a joint investigation conducted by federal officers and the New York City Police Department (NYCPD). The NYCPD had prepared arrest reports when Cherry had been arrested for the homicides, and Cherry now sought discovery of these reports in his federal RICO prosecution. The court denied the request, holding that the reports were protected by Rule 16(a)(2):

> I hold that in a federal prosecution based in part upon the investigative efforts of local or state law enforcement agents, Rule 16(a)(2) bars disclosure of reports generated by such agents; and that it makes no difference whether the local or state agents generated their reports as part of an independent investigation or during the course of a joint federal operation.

> I reach that conclusion because of the principle underlying Rule 16(a)(2), and the practical consequences of a contrary holding.

> The underlying principle is the"work product" doctrine, originally articulated by the Supreme Court as a bar to discovery in civil litigation, *Hickman v. Taylor*, 329 U.S. 495 (1947), but later characterized as playing an"even more vital" role"in assuring the proper functioning of the criminal justice system," *United States v. Nobles*, 422 U.S. 225, 238 (1975). Rule 16(a)(2)"contains two exemptions to disclosure, designed to preserve the secrecy of government files." 8 Moore's Federal Practice (2d ed. 1994) at 16–45. The first exception, upon which the motion at bar turns,"embodies the 'work product' rule, which protects from disclosure a litigant's theories and thought processes contained in internal notes and memoranda related to the case." *Id.* In *Nobles*, the Supreme Court said of the doctrine in a criminal context: At its core, the work-product doctrine shelters the mental process of the attorney, providing a privileged area within which he can analyze and prepare his client's case. But the doctrine is an intensely practical one, grounded in the realities of litigation in our adversary system. One of those realties is that attorneys often must rely on the assistance of investigators and other agents in the compilation of materials in preparation for trial. It is therefore necessary that the doctrine protect material prepared by agents for the attorney as well as those prepared by the attorney himself. 422 U.S. at 238–39.

> It is clear enough that this principle of work product secrecy will be undermined, indeed in the case at bar done away with entirely, if the protection of Rule 16(a)(2) is limited to reports prepared by federal investigators and agents. One should hesitate to eviscerate so important a principle, particularly where the language of the rule does not explicitly require it. Rule 16(a)(2) protects from disclosure reports by"government" agents"in connection with the investigation or prosecution of the case." The NYCPD files sought to be subpoenaed at bar fit within that description, unless the rule must be given the narrow construction for which Cherry contends. I accept that the rule may receive a broad or narrow reading. I prefer the broader reading because it vindicates the underlying legal

principle. The narrow reading serves no countervailing public policy; certainly Cherry suggests none. Cherry's purpose is simply to gain access to the government's entire file. The purpose is understandable, but not sanctioned by Rule 16. See *U.S. v. Feola*, 651 F.Supp. at 1143 (under Rule 16"criminal defendants are not entitled to complete disclosure of all evidence in the Government's files which might conceivably assist them in the preparation of their defense. . . .").

This federal prosecution is a direct outgrowth of investigations by local authorities. Those investigations covered the same conduct by the same defendants charged in the federal indictment. For all practical purposes, including the application of Rule 16(a)(2), this local investigation and federal prosecution should be considered one"case." To hold otherwise, thereby making underlying local or state investigatory files subject to pre-trial discovery by a subsequently federally indicted defendant, would in all likelihood inhibit cooperation between local and federal law enforcement agencies, to the benefit of criminals but to the detriment of the public good.

ARIZONA v. YOUNGBLOOD
United States Supreme Court
488 U.S. 51 (1988)

CHIEF JUSTICE REHNQUIST delivered the opinion of the Court.

Respondent Larry Youngblood was convicted by a Pima County, Arizona jury of child molestation, sexual assault, and kidnaping. The Arizona Court of Appeals reversed his conviction on the ground that the State had failed to preserve semen samples from the victim's body and clothing. We granted certiorari to consider the extent to which the Due Process Clause of the Federal Constitution requires the State to preserve evidentiary material that might be useful to a criminal defendant.

On October 29, 1983, David L., a 10-year-old boy, attended a church service with his mother. After he left the service at about 9:30 p.m., the boy went to a carnival behind the church, where he was abducted by a middle-aged man of medium height and weight. The assailant drove the boy to a secluded area near a ravine and molested him. He then took the boy to an unidentified, sparsely furnished house where he sodomized the boy four times. Afterwards, the assailant tied the boy up while he went outside to start his car. Once the assailant started the car, albeit with some difficulty, he returned to the house and again sodomized the boy. The assailant then sent the boy to the bathroom to wash up before he returned him to the carnival. He threatened to kill the boy if he told anyone about the attack. The entire ordeal lasted about 1 1/2 hours.

After the boy made his way home, his mother took him to Kino Hospital. At the hospital, a physician treated the boy for rectal injuries. The physician also used a"sexual assault kit" to collect evidence of the attack. The Tucson Police Department provided such kits to all hospitals in Pima County for use in sexual assault cases. Under standard procedure, the victim of a sexual assault was taken to a hospital, where a physician used the kit to collect evidence. The kit included paper to collect saliva samples, a tube for obtaining a blood sample, microscopic slides for making smears, a set of Q-tip like swabs, and a medical examination report. Here, the physician used the swab to collect samples from the boy's rectum and mouth. He then made a microscopic slide of the samples. The doctor also obtained samples of the boy's saliva, blood, and hair. The physician did not examine the samples at any time. The police placed the kit in a secure refrigerator at the police station. At the hospital, the police also collected the boy's underwear and T-shirt. This clothing was not refrigerated or frozen.

Nine days after the attack, on November 7, 1983, the police asked the boy to pick out his assailant from a photographic lineup. The boy identified respondent as the assailant. Respondent was not located by the police until four weeks later; he was arrested on December 9, 1983.

On November 8, 1983, Edward Heller, a police criminologist, examined the sexual assault kit. He testified that he followed standard department procedure, which was to examine the slides and determine whether sexual contact had occurred. After he determined that such contact had occurred, the criminologist did not perform any other tests, although he placed the assault kit back in the refrigerator. He testified that tests to identify blood group substances were not routinely conducted during the initial examination of an assault kit and in only about half of all cases in any event. He did not test the clothing at this time.

Respondent was indicted on charges of child molestation, sexual assault, and kidnaping. The State moved to compel respondent to provide blood and saliva samples for comparison with the material gathered through the use of the sexual assault kit, but the trial court denied the motion on the ground that the State had not obtained a sufficiently large semen sample to make a valid comparison. The prosecutor then asked the State's criminologist to perform an ABO blood group test on the rectal swab sample in an attempt to ascertain the blood type of the boy's assailant. This test failed to detect any blood group substances in the sample.

In January 1985, the police criminologist examined the boy's clothing for the first time. He found one semen stain on the boy's underwear and another on the rear of his T-shirt. The criminologist tried to obtain blood group substances from both stains using the ABO technique, but was unsuccessful. He also performed a P-30 protein molecule test on the stains, which indicated that only a small quantity of semen was present on the clothing; it was inconclusive as to the assailant's identity. The Tucson Police Department had just begun using this test, which was then used in slightly more than half of the crime laboratories in the country.

Respondent's principal defense at trial was that the boy had erred in identifying him as the perpetrator of the crime. In this connection, both a criminologist for the State and an expert witness for respondent testified as to what might have been shown by tests performed on the samples shortly after they were gathered, or by later tests performed on the samples from the boy's clothing had the clothing been properly refrigerated. The court instructed the jury that if they found the State had destroyed or lost evidence, they might "infer that the true fact is against the State's interest."

The jury found respondent guilty as charged, but the Arizona Court of Appeals reversed the judgment of conviction. It stated that "when identity is an issue at trial and the police permit the destruction of evidence that could eliminate the defendant as the perpetrator, such loss is material to the defense and is a denial of due process." The Court of Appeals concluded on the basis of the expert testimony at trial that timely performance of tests with properly preserved semen samples could have produced results that might have completely exonerated respondent. The

Court of Appeals reached this conclusion even though it did "not imply any bad faith on the part of the State."

The Supreme Court of Arizona denied the State's petition for review, and we granted certiorari. We now reverse.

Decision of this case requires us to again consider "what might loosely be called the area of constitutionally guaranteed access to evidence." *United States v. Valenzuela-Bernal*, 458 U.S. 858, 867 (1982). In *Brady v. Maryland*, 373 U.S. 83 (1963), we held "that the suppression by the prosecution of evidence favorable to the accused upon request violates due process where the evidence is material either to guilt or to punishment, irrespective of the good faith or bad faith of the prosecution." *Id.* at 87. In *United States v. Agurs*, 427 U.S. 97 (1976), we held that the prosecution had a duty to disclose some evidence of this description even though no requests were made for it, but at the same time we rejected the notion that a "prosecutor has a constitutional duty routinely to deliver his entire file to defense counsel." *Id.* at 111; see also *Moore v. Illinois*, 408 U.S. 786, 795 (1972) ("We know of no constitutional requirement that the prosecution make a complete and detailed accounting to the defense of all police investigatory work on a case").

There is no question but that the State complied with *Brady* and *Agurs* here. The State disclosed relevant police reports to respondent, which contained information about the existence of the swab and the clothing, and the boy's examination at the hospital. The State provided respondent's expert with the laboratory reports and notes prepared by the police criminologist, and respondent's expert had access to the swab and to the clothing.

If respondent is to prevail on federal constitutional grounds, then, it must be because of some constitutional duty over and above that imposed by cases such as *Brady* and *Agurs*. Our most recent decision in this area of the law, *California v. Trombetta*, 467 U.S. 479 (1984), arose out of a drunk driving prosecution in which the State had introduced test results indicating the concentration of alcohol in the blood of two motorists. The defendants sought to suppress the test results on the ground that the State had failed to preserve the breath samples used in the test. We rejected this argument for several reasons: first, "the officers here were acting in 'good faith and in accord with their normal practice," id. at 488; second, in the light of the procedures actually used the chances that preserved samples would have exculpated the defendants were slim; and, third, even if the samples might have shown inaccuracy in the tests, the defendants had "alternative means of demonstrating their innocence." *Id.* at 490. In the present case, the likelihood that the preserved materials would have enabled the defendant to exonerate himself appears to be greater than it was in *Trombetta*, but here, unlike in *Trombetta*, the State did not attempt to make any use of the materials in its own case in chief.*

---

* In this case, the Arizona Court of Appeals relied on its earlier decision in *State v. Escalante*, 153 Ariz. 55 (1986), holding that "when identity is an issue at trial and the police permit destruction of evidence that *could eliminate* a defendant as the perpetrator, such loss is material to the defense and is a denial of due process." The reasoning in *Escalante* and the instant case mark a sharp departure from *Trombetta* in two respects. First, *Trombetta* speaks of evidence whose exculpatory value is "apparent." 467 U.S. at 489. The possibility that the semen samples could have exculpated respondent if preserved or tested is not enough to satisfy the standard of constitutional materiality in *Trombetta*. Second, we made clear in *Trombetta* that the exculpatory value of the evidence must be apparent "*before* the evidence was destroyed." *Ibid.* (emphasis added). Here, respondent has not shown that the police knew the semen samples would have exculpated him when they failed to perform certain tests or to refrigerate

* * * *

The Due Process Clause of the Fourteenth Amendment, as interpreted in *Brady*, makes the good or bad faith of the State irrelevant when the State fails to disclose to the defendant material exculpatory evidence. But we think the Due Process Clause requires a different result when we deal with the failure of the State to preserve evidentiary material of which no more can be said than that it could have been subjected to tests, the results of which might have exonerated the defendant. Part of the reason for the difference in treatment is found in the observation made by the Court in *Trombetta* that "whenever potentially exculpatory evidence is permanently lost, courts face the treacherous task of divining the import of materials whose contents are unknown and, very often, disputed." Part of it stems from our unwillingness to read the "fundamental fairness" requirement of the Due Process Clause, as imposing on the police an undifferentiated and absolute duty to retain and to preserve all material that might be of conceivable evidentiary significance in a particular prosecution. We think that requiring a defendant to show bad faith on the part of the police both limits the extent of the police's obligation to preserve evidence to reasonable bounds and confines it to that class of cases where the interests of justice most clearly require it, i.e., those cases in which the police themselves by their conduct indicate that the evidence could form a basis for exonerating the defendant. We therefore hold that unless a criminal defendant can show bad faith on the part of the police, failure to preserve potentially useful evidence does not constitute a denial of due process of law.

In this case, the police collected the rectal swab and clothing on the night of the crime; respondent was not taken into custody until six weeks later. The failure of the police to refrigerate the clothing and to perform tests on the semen samples can at worst be described as negligent. None of this information was concealed from respondent at trial, and the evidence — such as it was — was made available to respondent's expert who declined to perform any tests on the samples. The Arizona Court of Appeals noted in its opinion — and we agree — that there was no suggestion of bad faith on the part of the police. It follows, therefore, from what we have said, that there was no violation of the Due Process Clause.

The Arizona Court of Appeals also referred somewhat obliquely to the State's "inability to quantitatively test" certain semen samples with the newer P-30 test. If the court meant by this statement that the Due Process Clause is violated when the police fail to use a particular investigatory tool, we strongly disagree. The situation here is no different than a prosecution for drunk driving that rests on police observation alone; the defendant is free to argue to the finder of fact that a breathalizer test might have been exculpatory, but the police do not have a constitutional duty to perform any particular tests.

The judgment of the Arizona Court of Appeals is reversed.

---

the boy's clothing; this evidence was simply an avenue of investigation that might have led in any number of directions. The presence or absence of bad faith by the police for purposes of the Due Process Clause must necessarily turn on the police's knowledge of the exculpatory value of the evidence at the time it was lost or destroyed.

Justice Stevens, concurring in the judgment.

Three factors are of critical importance to my evaluation of this case. First, at the time the police failed to refrigerate the victim's clothing, and thus negligently lost potentially valuable evidence, they had at least as great an interest in preserving the evidence as did the person later accused of the crime. Indeed, at that time it was more likely that the evidence would have been useful to the police — who were still conducting an investigation — and to the prosecutor — who would later bear the burden of establishing guilt beyond a reasonable doubt — than to the defendant. In cases such as this, even without a prophylactic sanction such as dismissal of the indictment, the State has a strong incentive to preserve the evidence.

Second, although it is not possible to know whether the lost evidence would have revealed any relevant information, it is unlikely that the defendant was prejudiced by the State's omission. In examining witnesses and in her summation, defense counsel impressed upon the jury the fact that the State failed to preserve the evidence and that the State could have conducted tests that might well have exonerated the defendant. More significantly, the trial judge instructed the jury:"If you find that the State has allowed to be destroyed or lost any evidence whose content or quality are in issue, you may infer that the true fact is against the State's interest." As a result, the uncertainty as to what the evidence might have proved was turned to the defendant's advantage.

Third, the fact that no juror chose to draw the permissive inference that proper preservation of the evidence would have demonstrated that the defendant was not the assailant suggests that the lost evidence was"immaterial." Our cases make clear that"the proper standard of materiality must reflect our overriding concern with the justice of the finding of guilt," and that a State's failure to turn over (or preserve) potentially exculpatory evidence therefore "must be evaluated in the context of the entire record." *United States v. Agurs*, 427 U.S. 97, 112 (1976). In declining defense counsel's and the court's invitations to draw the permissive inference, the jurors in effect indicated that, in their view, the other evidence at trial was so overwhelming that it was highly improbable that the lost evidence was exculpatory. In *Trombetta*, this Court found no due process violation because"the chances were extremely low that preserved breath samples would have been exculpatory." *Id.* at 489. In this case, the jury has already performed this calculus based on its understanding of the evidence introduced at trial. Presumably, in a case involving a closer question as to guilt or innocence, the jurors would have been more ready to infer that the lost evidence was exculpatory.

With these factors in mind, I concur in the Court's judgment. I do not, however, join the Court's opinion because it announces a proposition of law that is much broader than necessary to decide this case. It states"that unless a criminal defendant can show bad faith on the part of the police, failure to preserve potentially useful evidence does not constitute a denial of due process of law." In my opinion, there may well be cases in which the defendant is unable to prove that the State acted in bad faith but in which the loss or destruction of evidence is nonetheless so critical to the defense as to make a criminal trial fundamentally unfair. This, however, is not such a case. Accordingly, I concur in the judgment.

JUSTICE BLACKMUN, with whom Justice Brennan and Justice Marshall join, dissenting.

The Constitution requires that criminal defendants be provided with a fair trial, not merely a"good faith" try at a fair trial. Respondent here, by what may have been nothing more than police ineptitude, was denied the opportunity to present a full defense. That ineptitude, however, deprived respondent of his guaranteed right to due process of law. * * * *

I

* * * *

I also doubt that the "bad faith" standard creates the bright-line rule sought by the majority. Apart from the inherent difficulty a defendant would have in obtaining evidence to show a lack of good faith, the line between "good faith" and "bad faith" is anything but bright, and the majority's formulation may well create more questions than it answers. What constitutes bad faith for these purposes? Does a defendant have to show actual malice, or would recklessness, or the deliberate failure to establish standards for maintaining and preserving evidence, be sufficient? Does "good faith police work" require a certain minimum of diligence, or will a lazy officer, who does not walk the few extra steps to the evidence refrigerator, be considered to be acting in good faith? While the majority leaves these questions for another day, its quick embrace of a bad faith standard has not brightened the line; it only has moved the line so as to provide fewer protections for criminal defendants.

II

The inquiry the majority eliminates in setting up its "bad faith" rule is whether the evidence in question here was "constitutionally material," so that its destruction violates due process. The majority does not say whether "evidentiary material of which no more can be said than that it could have been subjected to tests, the results of which might have exonerated the defendant," is, for purposes of due process, material. But because I do not find the question of lack of bad faith dispositive, I now consider whether this evidence was such that its destruction rendered respondent's trial fundamentally unfair. * * * *

The exculpatory value of the clothing in this case cannot be determined with any certainty, precisely because the police allowed the samples to deteriorate. But we do know several important things about the evidence. First, the semen samples on the clothing undoubtedly came from the assailant. Second, the samples could have been tested, using technology available and in use at the local police department, to show either the blood type of the assailant, or that the assailant was a nonsecreter, i.e., someone who does not secrete a blood type "marker" into other body fluids, such as semen. Third, the evidence was clearly important. A semen sample in a rape case where identity is questioned is always significant. Fourth, a reasonable police officer should have recognized that the clothing required refrigeration. Fifth, we know that an inconclusive test was done on the swab. The test suggested that the assailant was a nonsecreter, although it was equally likely that the sample on the swab was too small for accurate results to be obtained. And, sixth, we know that respondent is a secreter.

If the samples on the clothing had been tested, and the results had shown either the blood type of the assailant or that the assailant was a nonsecreter, its constitutional materiality would be clear. But the State's conduct has deprived the defendant, and the courts, of the opportunity to determine with certainty the import of this evidence: it has "interfered with the accused's ability to create a defense by imposing on him a requirement which the government's own actions have rendered impossible to fulfill." *Hilliard v. Spalding*, 719 F.2d at 1446. Good faith or not, this is intolerable, unless the particular circumstances of the case indicate either that the evidence was not likely to prove exculpatory, or that the defendant was able to use effective alternative means to prove the point the destroyed evidence otherwise could have made.

I recognize the difficulties presented by such a situation. The societal interest in seeing criminals punished rightly requires that indictments be dismissed only when the unavailability of the evidence prevents the defendant from receiving a fair trial. In a situation where the substance of the lost evidence is known, the materiality analysis laid out in *Trombetta* is adequate. But in a situation like the present one, due process requires something more. Rather than allow a State's ineptitude to saddle a defendant with an impossible burden, a court should focus on the type of evidence, the possibility it might prove exculpatory, and the existence of other evidence going to the same point of contention in determining whether the failure to preserve the evidence in question violated due process. To put it succinctly, where no comparable evidence is likely to be available to the defendant, police must preserve physical evidence of a type that they reasonably should know has the potential, if tested, to reveal immutable characteristics of the criminal, and hence to exculpate a defendant charged with the crime.

The first inquiry under this standard concerns the particular evidence itself. It must be of a type which is clearly relevant, a requirement satisfied, in a case where identity is at issue, by physical evidence which has come from the assailant. Samples of blood and other body fluids, fingerprints, and hair and tissue samples have been used to implicate guilty defendants, and to exonerate innocent suspects. This is not to say that all physical evidence of this type must be preserved. For example, in a case where a blood sample is found, but the circumstances make it unclear whether the sample came from the assailant, the dictates of due process might not compel preservation (although principles of sound investigation might certainly do so). But in a case where there is no doubt that the sample came from the assailant, the presumption must be that it be preserved.

A corollary, particularly applicable to this case, is that the evidence embody some immutable characteristic of the assailant which can be determined by available testing methods. So, for example, a clear fingerprint can be compared to the defendant's fingerprints to yield a conclusive result; a blood sample, or a sample of body fluid which contains blood markers, can either completely exonerate or strongly implicate a defendant. As technology develops, the potential for this type of evidence to provide conclusive results on any number of questions will increase. Current genetic testing measures, frequently used in civil paternity suits, are extraordinarily precise. The importance of these types of evidence is indisputable, and requiring police to recognize their importance is not unreasonable.

The next inquiry is whether the evidence, which was obviously relevant and indicates an immutable characteristic of the actual assailant, is of a type likely to be independently exculpatory. Requiring the defendant to prove that the particular piece of evidence probably would be independently exculpatory would require the defendant to prove the content of something he does not have because of the State's misconduct. Focusing on the type of evidence solves this problem. A court will be able to consider the type of evidence and the available technology, as well as the circumstances of the case, to determine the likelihood that the evidence might have proved to be exculpatory. The evidence must also be without equivalent in the particular case. It must not be cumulative or collateral, and must bear directly on the question of innocence or guilt.

Due process must also take into account the burdens that the preservation of evidence places on the police. Law enforcement officers must be provided the option, as is implicit in *Trombetta*, of performing the proper tests on physical evidence and then discarding it. Once a suspect has been arrested the police, after a reasonable time, may inform defense counsel of plans to discard the evidence. When the defense has been informed of the existence of the evidence, after a reasonable time the burden of preservation may shift to the defense. There should also be flexibility to deal with evidence that is unusually dangerous or difficult to store.

III

Applying this standard to the facts of this case, I conclude that the Arizona Court of Appeals was correct in overturning respondent's conviction. The clothing worn by the victim contained samples of his assailant's semen. The appeals court found that these samples would probably be larger, less contaminated, and more likely to yield conclusive test results than would the samples collected by use of the assault kit. The clothing and the semen stains on the clothing therefore obviously were material.

Because semen is a body fluid which could have been tested by available methods to show an immutable characteristic of the assailant, there was a genuine possibility that the results of such testing might have exonerated respondent. The only evidence implicating respondent was the testimony of the victim.[8] There was no other eyewitness, and the only other significant physical evidence, respondent's car, was seized by police, examined, turned over to a wrecking company, and then dismantled without the victim's having viewed it. The police also failed to check the car to confirm or refute elements of the victim's testimony.[9]

---

[8] This Court "has recognized the inherently suspect qualities of eyewitness identification evidence." *Watkins v. Sowders*, 449 U.S. 341, 350 (1981) (Brennan, J., dissenting). Such evidence is "notoriously unreliable," *ibid*; see *United States v. Wade*, 388 U.S. 218, 228 (1967), and has distinct impacts on juries. "All the evidence points rather strikingly to the conclusion that there is almost nothing more convincing than a live human being who takes the stand, points a finger at the defendant, and says, 'That's the one!' " E. Loftus, *Eyewitness Testimony* 19 (1979). Studies show that children are more likely to make mistaken identifications than are adults, especially when they have been encouraged by adults. See generally Cohen and Harnick, *The Susceptibility of Child Witnesses to Suggestion*, 4 Law and Human Behavior 201 (1980). Other studies show another element of possible relevance in this case: "Cross-racial identifications are much less likely to be accurate than same race identifications." Rahaim and Brodsky, *Empirical Evidence versus Common Sense: Juror and Lawyer Knowledge of Eyewitness Accuracy*, 7 Law and Psychology Rev. 1, 2 (1982). These authorities suggest that eyewitness testimony alone, in the absence of corroboration, is to be viewed with some suspicion.

[9] The victim testified that the car had a loud muffler, that country music was playing on its radio, and that the car was started using a key. Respondent and others testified that his car was inoperative on the night of the incident, that when it was working it ran quietly, that the radio did not work, and that the

Although a closer question, there was no equivalent evidence available to the respondent. The swab contained a semen sample, but it was not sufficient to allow proper testing. Respondent had access to other evidence tending to show that he was not the assailant, but there was no other evidence that would have shown that it was physically impossible for respondent to have been the assailant. Nor would the preservation of the evidence here have been a burden upon the police. There obviously was refrigeration available, as the preservation of the swab indicates, and the items of clothing likely would not tax available storage space.

Considered in the context of the entire trial, the failure of the prosecution to preserve this evidence deprived respondent of a fair trial. It still remains "a fundamental value determination of our society that it is far worse to convict an innocent man than to let a guilty man go free." *In re Winship*, 397 U.S. 358, 372 (1970) (concurring opinion). The evidence in this case was far from conclusive, and the possibility that the evidence denied to respondent would have exonerated him was not remote. The result is that he was denied a fair trial by the actions of the State, and consequently was denied due process of law. Because the Court's opinion improperly limits the scope of due process, and ignores its proper focus in a futile pursuit of a bright-line rule, I dissent.

Notes from Sue:

1. In *Youngblood*, Justice Stevens opined that the jurors believed that "the other evidence at trial was so overwhelming that it was highly improbable that the lost evidence was exculpatory." Later, however, his conviction was vacated. See Tim O'Brien, "Reasonable Doubt & DNA", Washington Post, 9/7/00, p. A25:

> Three weeks ago Youngblood's conviction was vacated — thrown out by the Pima County Superior Court in Tucson. While the small amount of semen that was preserved was insufficient for reliable testing at the time of the appeal, new testing procedures that only recently became available were conducted by the Tucson police. They showed conclusively what attorneys Wittels and Davis knew all along: The police really did have the wrong man. It was a case of mistaken identity. * * * *

> The Tucson police have graciously conceded that it was "unfortunate" Youngblood spent so much time incarcerated for a crime he didn't commit, but they say they did what they thought was right at the time. Youngblood is angry to have been robbed of "the best part of my life," and he wants to sue the police. All agree it should not have happened.

> To prevent it from happening again, courts must be receptive to any credible claim that new tests might prove the actual innocence of one who has already been convicted. Had Larry Youngblood been charged with first degree murder, he'd probably be dead now.

2. Other cases where police destroyed evidence.

In *People v. Newberry*, 166 Ill.2d 310 (1995), a field test of a substance possessed by Newberry showed it not to be narcotics, but a "look-alike" substance. Newberry was then indicted for "possession of a look-alike." But a subsequent laboratory test

---

car could be started only by using a screwdriver. The police did not check any of this before disposing of the car.

showed that there was cocaine in the substance, so the indictment was dismissed and Newberry was re-indicted for possession of cocaine. A laboratory technician learned that the original indictment was dismissed (but not of the new indictment), so he destroyed the substance. The court held that, even though there was no evidence that this destruction was in bad faith, Newberry had been denied due process, and the indictment must be dismissed:

> *Youngblood* is distinguishable from the case before us today. In *Youngblood*, the disputed material was not essential for establishing the defendant's guilt or innocence. Its value was speculative, and it played no role in the prosecution's case. Because there was no bad faith on the part of the police, the defendant's due process challenge to his conviction was therefore denied. The situation in this case is markedly different. Here, the evidence in question is more than just "potentially useful." It is essential to and determinative of the outcome of the case. Newberry cannot be convicted of the drug possession charges absent proof of the content of the disputed substance, nor does he have any realistic hope of exonerating himself absent the opportunity to have it examined by his own experts. * * * *

In an effort to minimize the prejudice to Newberry's defense, the State wrongly asserts that the discarded substance here is no different than the breath sample that the police failed to preserve in *California v. Trombetta* (1984), 467 U.S. 479. In *Trombetta*, defendants charged with driving under the influence of intoxicating liquor unsuccessfully sought suppression of breath-analysis test results on the grounds that the police failed to preserve the breath samples, thereby limiting the defendants' ability to challenge the incriminating test results. The State appellate court set aside their convictions, holding that due process demanded that the arresting officers preserve the breath samples, but the United States Supreme Court reversed. The Court reasoned that due process was not violated because the police had acted in good faith and in accord with normal procedures when they failed to preserve the samples, and the testing device's high degree of accuracy made it extremely unlikely that further testing of the samples would have helped the defense. The Court further noted that the defendants were not without alternative means of demonstrating their innocence.

Here, by contrast, nothing in the record indicates that the laboratory procedures used to test the substance were especially reliable or that further testing would not have yielded different and more favorable results for Newberry. In addition, Newberry lacked alternative means for showing that he was not guilty. He could not "obtain comparable evidence by other reasonably available means." *Trombetta*, 467 U.S. at 489. The sole basis for bringing criminal charges against Newberry was the chemical content of the substance seized by the police, and when that substance was discarded, it was lost to Newberry forever. It is now impossible for him to meet or dispute the test results by evidence of equal integrity and persuasiveness.

The State asserts that Newberry is not without recourse because he can still assail the State's test results by introducing the conflicting field test results and by cross-examining the State's experts about the procedures they followed. While these opportunities may exist, the relief they offer is illusory. Whatever the actual reliability of the tests performed in the lab — and the reliability may not be great — the laboratory analysis of the evidence will carry great weight with the jury, and the jury will undoubtedly give such an analysis more deference than the initial field test procedures, which are inherently less precise and controlled.

Wholly aside from these considerations, there is a fundamental distinction between this case and those decisions cited by the State requiring a showing that the police acted in bad faith. Here, unlike *Youngblood* and *Trombetta*, the police destroyed the disputed substance after defense counsel had requested access to it in his discovery motion. Where evidence is requested by the defense in a discovery motion, the State is on notice that the evidence must be preserved, and the defense is not required to make an independent showing that the evidence has exculpatory value in order to establish a due process violation. If the State proceeds to destroy the evidence, appropriate sanctions may be imposed even if the destruction is inadvertent. No showing of bad faith is necessary.

JUSTICE MILLER dissented:

Like the defendant in *Youngblood*, the defendant in the present case asserts only that the unpreserved evidence might have proved to be exculpatory if it had been subjected to further testing. A laboratory test established the presence of cocaine in the substance allegedly found in the defendant's possession, though an earlier field test had been negative. There is no suggestion here that the authorities were aware, after the laboratory test conducted, that the evidence had any exculpatory value at the time it was destroyed. Of course, at trial the defendant could challenge the accuracy of the test conducted in the laboratory. The defendant could also refer to the negative result of the initial field test. The defendant does not argue that the negative field test was proof of the exculpatory value of the evidence.

Moreover, whatever duty there is to preserve evidence, that duty is limited to evidence likely to be important to the defense. "To meet this standard of constitutional materiality" the evidence must have an exculpatory value apparent prior to its destruction, and the defendant must be unable to obtain comparable proof elsewhere. *California v. Trombetta* (1984), 467 U.S. 479, 489. The present defendant has failed entirely to satisfy the initial step of that inquiry.

The majority, however, would require a defendant to show bad faith on the part of the State only when the lost or destroyed evidence was not "potentially useful" to the defense and the evidence was not a component of the State's case in chief. The majority's contention, however, runs directly counter to the Court's rationale for the bad faith rule and its rejection, in destruction cases, of the Brady rule which "makes the good or bad faith of the State irrelevant." *Youngblood*, 488 U.S. at 57. Indeed, accepting the majority's argument would not only reinstate the Brady rule in some destruction cases, but would do so not because of the exculpatory value of the evidence, but because of its inculpatory value to the government. To avoid that paradoxical result, I believe that the good faith of the authorities is a relevant consideration here even though the **evidence is important** to the State's case.

The majority also posits that good faith is irrelevant in this case because the evidence was destroyed after defense counsel requested, during discovery, that it be turned over to the defense. There is no indication in the record, however, that the technician who destroyed the evidence did so to frustrate the defendant's presentation of a defense, or that the technician was even aware of counsel's request. According to the representation made by the assistant State's Attorney, and not disputed by the defendant, the evidence technician destroyed the contraband in June 1991 because he saw that the original indictment, which alleged that the defendant was in possession of a look-alike substance, had been nol-prossed more than three months earlier and therefore believed that the case had been closed. Good faith remains relevant in these circumstances and should be sufficient to defeat the defendant's due process argument. At most, the record shows that the conduct in failing to preserve the evidence was negligence, which is not a violation of due process. See *Youngblood*, 488 U.S. at 58.

In *State v. Steffes*, 500 N.W.2d 608 (N.Dak.1993), a police officer stopped Steffes for drunk driving and gave him a field sobriety test. The officer recorded Steffes' performance on the test in the police patrol car's audio tape recorder. About 3 months later, before the trial, the officer *recorded over* the audio tape. At trial, the officer explained that he did this because he mistakenly believed that the case had been resolved and the tape would not be needed, and he needed a fresh tape for his patrol car. Steffes requested a jury instruction stating that the jury may infer that evidence on the tape would be unfavorable to the prosecution. The trial court refused to give the instruction, and Steffes was convicted. The North Dakota Supreme Court affirmed, holding that whether the officer's action was deemed negligent, reckless, or even intentional, it did not rise to the level of the "bad faith" required by *Youngblood*. The court relied on several similar holdings from other jurisdictions.

In *U.S. v. Cooper*, 983 F.2d 928 (9th Cir.1993), Drug Enforcement Agency (DEA) agents arrested Cooper for manufacture of methamphetamines. The agents searched Cooper's lab and confiscated his equipment. Cooper's lawyer then called the agents and told them that the lab was used not to make methamphetamines, but to make legal drugs, and that the equipment was very expensive and should be returned. The agents replied that it was being held for evidence. Instead, the agents had the equipment destroyed, on the ground that confiscated drug equipment might be contaminated (though they had no evidence that this equipment was in fact contaminated). The trial court found that the agents acted in bad faith, and ordered the indictment dismissed. On appeal, the government did not challenge the bad faith finding, but claimed that Cooper could obtain evidence "comparable in value" to the destroyed equipment — experts familiar with the properties of the lab equipment and the designer of the equipment. The court affirmed, finding the government's proposals unpersuasive. "General testimony about the possible nature of the destroyed equipment would be an inadequate substitute for testimony informed by its examination."

In *Commonwealth v. Henderson*, 411 Mass. 309 (1991), a police officer wrote down a robbery victim's description of the robber. The notes were then somehow lost or destroyed, though there was no evidence of bad faith. Following rulings in several other states, the court held that the due process clause of the Massachusetts Constitution set a standard *higher* than that set by the U.S. Supreme Court in *Youngblood*. The court adopted the standard set out in Justice Stevens' concurring opinion: even without bad faith, due process is denied if the lost evidence was "so critical to the defense as to make a criminal trial fundamentally unfair". Applying this standard, the court upheld the trial court's dismissal of the indictment.

3. In *Illinois v. Fisher*, 124 S.Ct. 1200 (2004),

Respondent was charged with possession of cocaine in the Circuit Court of Cook County in October 1988. He filed a motion for discovery eight days later requesting all physical evidence the State intended to use at trial. The State responded that all evidence would be made available at a reasonable time and date upon request. Respondent was released on bond pending trial. In July 1989, however, he failed to appear in court, and the court issued an arrest warrant to secure his presence. Respondent remained a fugitive for over 10 years, apparently settling in Tennessee. The outstanding arrest warrant was finally executed in November 1999, after respondent was detained on an unrelated matter. The State then reinstated the 1988 cocaine-possession charge.

Before trial, the State informed respondent that in September 1999, the police, acting in accord with established procedures, had destroyed the substance seized from him during his arrest. Respondent thereupon formally requested production of the substance and filed a motion to dismiss the cocaine-possession charge based on the State's destruction of evidence. The trial court denied the motion, and the case proceeded to a jury trial. The State introduced evidence tending to prove the facts recounted above. Respondent's case in chief consisted solely of his own testimony, in which he denied that he ever possessed cocaine and insinuated that the police had "framed" him for the crime. The jury returned a verdict of guilty, and respondent was sentenced to one year of imprisonment.

The Appellate Court reversed the conviction, holding that the Due Process Clause required dismissal of the charge. The Appellate Court reasoned:

Where evidence is requested by the defense in a discovery motion, the State is on notice that the evidence must be preserved, and the defense is not required to make an independent showing that the evidence has exculpatory value in order to establish a due process violation. If the State proceeds to destroy the evidence, appropriate sanctions may be imposed even if the destruction is inadvertent. No showing of bad faith is necessary.

The Appellate Court distinguished our decision in *Youngblood* on the ground that the police in *Youngblood* did not destroy evidence subsequent to a discovery motion by the defendant. While acknowledging that "there is nothing in the record to indicate that the alleged cocaine was destroyed in bad faith," the court further determined that, unlike in *Youngblood*, the destroyed evidence provided respondent's "only hope for exoneration," and was "essential to and determinative of the outcome of the case." Consequently, the court concluded that respondent "was denied due process when he was tried subsequent to the destruction of the alleged cocaine."

The Supreme Court disagreed:

> We have held that when the State suppresses or fails to disclose material exculpatory evidence, the good or bad faith of the prosecution is irrelevant: a due process violation occurs whenever such evidence is withheld. See *Brady v. Maryland*, 373 U.S. 83 (1963); *United States v. Agurs*, 427 U.S. 97 (1976). In *Youngblood*, by contrast, we recognized that the Due Process Clause "requires a different result when we deal with the failure of the State to preserve evidentiary material of which no more can be said than that it could have been subjected to tests, the results of which might have exonerated the defendant." We concluded that the failure to preserve this "potentially useful evidence" does not violate due process " *unless a criminal defendant can show bad faith on the part of the police.*"
>
> The substance seized from respondent was plainly the sort of "potentially useful evidence" referred to in *Youngblood*, not the material exculpatory evidence addressed in *Brady* and *Agurs*. At most, respondent could hope that, had the evidence been preserved, a *fifth* test conducted on the substance would have exonerated him. But respondent did not allege, nor did the Appellate Court find, that the Chicago police acted in bad faith when they destroyed the substance. Quite the contrary, police testing indicated that the chemical makeup of the substance inculpated, not exculpated, respondent, and it is undisputed that police acted in "good faith and in accord with their normal practice." Under *Youngblood*, then, respondent has failed to establish a due process violation.

UNITED STATES v. McDADE
U.S. District Court, Eastern District of Pennsylvania
1992 WL 382351 (1992)

GAWTHROP, DISTRICT JUDGE.

In this case, Joseph M. McDade, a United States Congressman of many years, is charged with conspiracy, racketeering, and accepting illegal gratuities. Discovery disagreements have arisen. The defense does not complain that the government has been improperly stingy in its offerings of documents and tangible objects under Federal Rule of Criminal Procedure 16(a)(1)(C), but rather, that the government has delivered so much documentation that it has virtually buried the defense under an avalanche of documentary and electronic outpourings, and has thus rendered the defense incapable of distilling that which is germane and relevant to the impending trial.

The defense has submitted pictures of discovery rooms in Philadelphia, New York, and Virginia. None of the rooms is small, and all of the rooms are chock full of apparently full file cabinets. The defense says that even though it has hired twelve people to try to dig into this substantial cubic yardage of discovery, the task is a long way from being completed, and the prospect of trial delay, as well as general unfairness to the defendant, is manifest.

The government counters that, at this stage, more than three and one-half months before trial, the defense has no right to discover what the government intends to produce and prove at trial, since such information is attorney work product. The government contends that to grant the defendant's requests for lists of witnesses and exhibits would, in effect, force the government to disgorge a blueprint of its trial strategy, which would be both unfair to the government and violative of at least the spirit of Rule 16(a)(2), which provides that the government need not disclose "reports, memoranda, or other internal government documents made by the attorney for the government or other government agents in connection with the investigation or prosecution of the case."

I find both sides' arguments to have some logical, legal, and equitable bases.

The leading Third Circuit case in the area is *United States v. Kenny*, 462 F.2d 1205 (3d Cir.1972). There the court considered a situation in which there was a discovery room, full of documents, kept open to the defendant six days per week before trial, and even on Sundays during trial. The magnitude of the tendered discovery engendered the same objection: that such an approach was so overly liberal that the defense could never make meaningful use of the myriad materials made available. The Third Circuit found no reversible error in the district court's approach, noting that the defendants were given adequate opportunity to view the evidence before trial and to examine any later-discovered evidence during trial. The court noted that the unavoidable nature of the Kenny case was that the alleged conspiracy had generated a great deal of tangible evidence. Indeed, that seems to be the situation at bar as well.

There is some contrary authority, notably *United States v. Poindexter*, 727 F.Supp. 1470 (D.D.C.1989), in which Judge Greene required the government to identify with much greater specificity those documents on which it intended to rely in its prosecution of Admiral Poindexter for his participation in an alleged conspiracy to conceal the National Security Council's Iran-Contra activities. The court held that the government could not meet its discovery obligations by broadly identifying several thousand pages, any of which it "may" rely on at trial.

I today prefer to take an intermediate approach. I understand the difficulty the defense is having in attempting to pull a probative needle or two out of the many large proverbial haystacks which the government has made available. Indeed, I recognize that whatever resolution I now reach, discovery in this case in inevitably going to be onerous for counsel and their staffs on both sides of the aisle. But I think that for me to force the government to set forth its trial plans in mid-December for a trial which starts at the end of March would be to compel too much. Therefore, I will not order the government to disclose lists of the exhibits and other documents on which it intends to rely at trial.

Rather, I will exercise my discretion by directing the government, to the best of its good-faith ability, to tell the defense of any discrete parcels of material that it does not plan to use at trial. In so doing, again I am expressly not telling the government to reveal to the defense exactly what it intends to use at trial. What I am directing is that, to continue with the trite, bucolic metaphor, if the government does in fact know that of the, say, 27 empirical haystacks which it has forked over to the defense, there are 11 haystacks, for example, which the government views as being so far afield from the focus of the trial that it does not intend to use them, then the cause of speedy and efficient justice would be furthered by the government's telling the defense about those 11 haystacks which contain no needles.

This negative-identification approach shall be undertaken not only with respect to written documents, but also with respect to the 2400 hours of tape-recorded conversations provided to the defense. Unlike written documents, tape recordings cannot be speed-read; they must be listened to in their entirety. It would take one person 100 very full days to listen to all these tapes. Or more realistically, it would take the entire twelve-person defense team at bar 20 ten-hour days listen to the tapes just once. And of course, this calculation is conservative, since tape recordings often must be monitored time and again in order to identify almost-inaudible words or faint, garbled voices. If the government knows of any tapes upon which it does not intend to rely at trial, it is to identify those tapes for the defense.

Obviously, this order does not affect in any way the government's conceded obligation to provide material to the defense under *Brady v. Maryland*, 373 U.S. 93 (1963), and its progeny. *Brady* material is discoverable per se, with the continuing duty to divulge it being on the government.

Finally, I invite the defense to notify the court of any governmental noncompliance with the letter or spirit of this order, for counsel are advised that should this method of attacking the mounds of materials prove ineffectual, the court may consider taking a more stringent, specific approach.

Notes from Sue:

1. When the court issued its ruling, trial was over 3 months away. Did that matter? Why?

2. Did the government violate Rule 16 (or any other discovery rule) by refusing to do as defense counsel asked? If not, where did the court get the authority to rule as it did?

3. While we have been focusing on federal discovery, it might be interesting to take a brief look at some *state* law. The history of criminal discovery in California has been turbulent.

Before 1990, the California Supreme Court established a broad inherent right in trial courts to order discovery for the *defendant*. But the Court also found *prosecution* discovery of *defense* material to be so complicated by the privilege against self-incrimination that the Court decided not to allow prosecution discovery under the court's inherent powers, and to wait until appropriate statutes were enacted.

In 1990, the California electorate enacted Proposition 115, which established an exclusive scheme for criminal discovery, covering both prosecution and defense. The resulting statutes appear in California Penal Code §§ 1054–1054.7.

Section 1054.1 requires the prosecutor to disclose to defense counsel the names and addresses of all witnesses he intends to call at trial, while § 1054.2 prohibits defense counsel from disclosing any such witnesses' address or phone number to the defendant himself (unless the court permits such disclosure, on a showing of good cause). Thus, while the Jencks Act tries to protect federal witnesses by concealing their statements (and presumably their identity) until after they testify, California protects witnesses in a different way: it requires disclosure of their statements pretrial, but bars defense counsel from telling the defendant their addresses and phone numbers.

Section 1054.1 also requires the prosecutor to disclose statements of all defendants, all "relevant real evidence" obtained during the investigation, the felony conviction record of any material witness, exculpatory evidence, and statements of witnesses the prosecutor intends to call at trial (including experts).

Section 1054.3 requires the defendant to disclose the names, addresses, and statements of witnesses she intends to call at trial (including experts), and any "real evidence" she intends to offer. Note that unlike Federal Rule 16, the prosecutor is entitled to discover these matters whether or not the defendant seeks or obtains any discovery from the prosecutor.

Section 1054.5 requires a party to make an "informal request" for desired information before seeking a court order for discovery. Section 1054.6 protects each attorney's "work product".

These provisions were upheld against various constitutional attacks in *Izazaga v. Superior Court*, 54 Cal.3d 356 (1991).

Chapter 4

THE PRELIMINARY HEARING

THE PURPOSE(S) OF THE PRELIMINARY HEARING

After the defendant is arrested, formal charges are filed in court against him (usually by a *complaint*), and then he is *arraigned* on these charges. At the arraignment, he must enter a *plea* to these charges (usually guilty, not guilty, or *nolo contendere*). If he pleads not guilty, a date will be set for a *preliminary hearing* (sometimes called a "preliminary examination").

Why provide a preliminary hearing? There is no comparable proceeding in *civil* cases.

In most states, the preliminary hearing is designed to enable the court — after arrest but before trial — to determine if there is "probable cause" to believe that the defendant is guilty of the crimes charged. This is meant to serve two purposes: (1) if there is little likelihood that defendant will be convicted at trial, he should be released from pretrial custody or bail conditions, and (2) "screening": if there is little likelihood of conviction on some or all of the charges, the court system should be relieved of the burden of trying these charges, and the defendant should be relieved of the emotional and (sometimes) financial burden of facing trial on these charges.

In jurisdictions that allow felonies to be prosecuted only after *grand jury indictments* (which includes the *federal* courts), the preliminary hearing serves only the first purpose. The grand jury's job is to look for probable cause. If they find it before the preliminary hearing is held, there is no longer any need for the preliminary hearing, and it will be cancelled.

The judge at the preliminary hearing is usually called a "magistrate" or "commissioner." If he or she finds probable cause as to certain charges, the defendant is then "bound over" to the trial court (with a different judge) for trial. The prosecutor will then file an *information* — a document which specifies the remaining charges — in the trial court.

As the police usually have probable cause to arrest the defendant, the prosecution usually has whatever evidence made up that probable cause — plus whatever their post-arrest investigation has turned up — to present at the preliminary hearing. Therefore, there is usually plenty of evidence to show probable cause as to at least *some* of the charges. Nevertheless, prosecutors sometimes "overcharge" — deliberately or mistakenly — and defense attorneys are sometimes able to convince the magistrate to dismiss or reduce some of the charges.

Defense counsel normally cannot do this by convincing the magistrate to believe defense witnesses rather than prosecution witnesses. The usual test for "probable cause" is whether the evidence, if believed, would permit a reasonable jury to find all the elements of the crimes charged. The magistrate is not supposed to resolve credibility battles — that is the jury's job.

Defense counsel must do a thorough job of cross-examining prosecution witnesses at the preliminary hearing — even if he has little chance of convincing the magistrate that there is no probable cause. If the witness becomes "unavailable" to testify at trial (e.g., due to death or loss of memory), the transcript of the preliminary hearing testimony of that witness (both on direct and on cross) will be admissible at trial, because the defendant had the *opportunity* to cross-examine that witness. *California v. Green*, 399 U.S. 149 (1970).

This right to cross-examine gives rise to another very useful purpose of the preliminary hearing for the defense. *Discovery* in criminal cases is much more limited than it is in civil cases. The most useful discovery device in civil cases — the *deposition* — is unavailable in criminal cases in most states (except where a witness will be unavailable at trial, e.g., because the witness is dying).

In a *civil* case, a deposition enables a lawyer to bring in his opponent's key witnesses, put them under oath, ask them questions, and follow up their answers with other questions — and have all the answers taken down by a court reporter. These answers might help the lawyer conduct his own investigation and preparation of his case for trial. Just as important, these answers tend to *nail down* the witness to one particular story: if the witness tries to change his story at trial, the lawyer may read to the jury the transcript of the deposition.

In a *criminal* case, defense counsel would love to depose the key civilian and police witnesses who will testify against defendant at trial — but he can't. Or can he? The *preliminary hearing* often gives him the opportunity to do essentially the same thing. The prosecutor has put the arresting officer on the witness stand, under oath, to show probable cause, and a court reporter is taking down everything the witness says. The prosecutor is asking his witness easy questions, and the transcript of the answers to these questions might be of limited value to the defense. But now it is defense counsel's turn to *cross-examine*! Now he can ask the penetrating questions he would have liked to ask at a deposition. What if the prosecutor calls only one witness and does not call other prosecution witnesses whom defense counsel would also like to "depose?" Defense counsel has the right to *subpoena* witnesses to testify at the preliminary hearing, so he may subpoena such witnesses, put them on the stand, and "depose" them too. (Seldom, however, will defense counsel put the defendant or other *defense* witnesses on the stand at the preliminary hearing. Why give the prosecutor the chance to "depose" *them*?)

Such "indirect discovery" is not the legally recognized purpose of the preliminary hearing, but it is often its true value to the defense.

This creates some tension. Defense counsel must justify his cross-examination and subpoenas of prosecution witnesses by arguing that the testimony is relevant to the question of probable cause — not by arguing that it will help him at trial. At some point, the magistrate might want to cut off defense counsel, saying: "Look, I understand that you want to depose these people, but I've already heard enough evidence to decide that there is probable cause here. The legally-recognized purpose of the preliminary hearing has been served, and I have a long calendar of cases waiting. If you want to take depositions in criminal cases, go ask the Legislature. Next case, please."

Keep this tension in mind as you read the Problem and cases in this chapter.

In fact, few cases go to trial after a preliminary hearing. Because the prelim gives both sides (and especially the defendant himself) a pretty good idea of what the prosecution evidence will look like at trial, both sides are usually prepared to "plea bargain" a disposition of the case without the need for a trial.

Problem 4

To: My law clerk

From: Augusta Wind, Esq.

My client, Robin Steele, was arrested by the FBI on a federal charge of bank robbery, in violation of 18 U.S.C. § 2113. At the preliminary examination, the prosecutor called only one witness — FBI Agent Phil Brick — who testified on direct examination as follows:

Q: Are you acquainted with Agent Edgar Heever's investigation of the Riggs Bank robbery on July 5?

A: Yes. I am Heever's supervisor. He is on another assignment today. I have read his report and spoken to him.

Q: What did he say?

Defense counsel: I object, your honor. The question calls for hearsay.

The Magistrate: Overruled. You may answer the question.

A: Heever spoke to Ms. Tillie Taylor, a teller at the bank. She said that a white male, about 6 foot 2 inches tall, with a dark beard and sheer pantyhose pulled over his face came up to her window. He pointed a gun at her and demanded all the cash in Tillie's till. She gave him $2,000 and he left.

Q: Did she later identify a photograph of the robber?

A: Yes. Heever showed her a bunch of photos, and saw her pick out one photo and say, "I think that's the one." The photo was attached to Heever's report.

Q: Do you see in court the man she picked out?

A: Yes. It's the defendant, the man sitting next to defense counsel.

The Prosecutor: I'd like the record to indicate that Defendant is a white male, 6 foot 2 inches tall, with a dark beard. That's all the questions we have for Agent Brick, your honor.

Defense counsel: Just a few questions, Agent Brick. How good is Ms. Taylor's eyesight?

A: Well, Heever said that she is quite nearsighted, but she usually wears glasses.

Q: Did the FBI recently set up a program to reward witnesses who could help convict bank robbers?

The Prosecutor: I object, your honor. I don't see the relevance of this line of questioning to the matter of probable cause.

Defense Counsel: Your honor, I am trying to develop testimony that Ms. Taylor had a motive to pick out one of the FBI's photos. I have several more questions for Agent Brick along this line. Also, I'd like to ask him the names of everyone who was in the bank at the time of the robbery — employees and customers.

The Magistrate: Counsel, I've already heard enough from this witness to decide that there is probable cause here. If what Agent Brick says is true, then a reasonable jury could convict the defendant. You will have plenty of opportunity at trial to present the evidence you want and make any arguments you want to the jury. Objection sustained.

Defense Counsel: Well then, your honor, I would like to subpoena several witnesses to testify here. I'd like to subpoena Ms. Taylor, and also each employee of the bank who was in the bank at the time of the robbery — the guards, tellers, and anyone else. Also, if I can get the names of any customers in the bank at the time of the robbery, I'd like to subpoena them too.

The Magistrate: I don't need to hear all that, Counsel. I've already decided that there is probable cause here. A preliminary examination isn't a trial, and I can't spend all day hearing witnesses in one preliminary examination when I have 10 prelims scheduled for today. Your request for subpoenas is denied. I find probable cause here.

All this just happened yesterday. Please read the attached authorities and give me some advice as to what I should do now. Keep in mind that I have only a limited amount of time to spend on this case, and I don't want to do anything unless it has a reasonable chance of success and helping our client in some significant way. Also, note that the prosecutor might obtain a grand jury indictment at any time.

Federal Rules of Criminal Procedure

Rule 5. Initial Appearance

(a) In General.

(1) Appearance Upon an Arrest.

(A) A person making an arrest within the United States must take the defendant without unnecessary delay before a magistrate judge, or before a state or local judicial officer as Rule 5(c) provides, unless a statute provides otherwise. * * * *

(b) Arrest Without a Warrant. If a defendant is arrested without a warrant, a complaint meeting Rule 4(a)'s requirement of probable cause must be promptly filed in the district where the offense was allegedly committed. * * * *

(d) Procedure in a Felony Case.

(1) Advice. If the defendant is charged with a felony, the judge must inform the defendant of the following:

(A) the complaint against the defendant, and any affidavit filed with it;

(B) the defendant's right to retain counsel or to request that counsel be appointed if the defendant cannot obtain counsel;

(C) the circumstances, if any, under which the defendant may secure pretrial release;

(D) any right to a preliminary hearing; and

(E) the defendant's right not to make a statement, and that any statement made may be used against the defendant.

(2) Consulting with Counsel. The judge must allow the defendant reasonable opportunity to consult with counsel.

(3) Detention or Release. The judge must detain or release the defendant as provided by statute or these rules.

(4) Plea. A defendant may be asked to plead only under Rule 10.

(e) Procedure in a Misdemeanor Case. If the defendant is charged with a misdemeanor only, the judge must inform the defendant in accordance with Rule 58(b)(2). * * * *

Rule 5.1. Preliminary Hearing

(a) In General. If a defendant is charged with an offense other than a petty offense, a magistrate judge must conduct a preliminary hearing unless:

(1) the defendant waives the hearing;

(2) the defendant is indicted;

(3) the government files an information under Rule 7(b) charging the defendant with a felony;

(4) the government files an information charging the defendant with a misdemeanor; or

(5) the defendant is charged with a misdemeanor and consents to trial before a magistrate judge.

(b) Selecting a District. A defendant arrested in a district other than where the offense was allegedly committed may elect to have the preliminary hearing conducted in the district where the prosecution is pending.

(c) Scheduling. The magistrate judge must hold the preliminary hearing within a reasonable time, but no later than 10 days after the initial appearance if the defendant is in custody and no later than 20 days if not in custody.

(d) Extending the Time. With the defendant's consent and upon a showing of good cause — taking into account the public interest in the prompt disposition of criminal cases — a magistrate judge may extend the time limits in Rule 5.1(c) one or more times. If the defendant does not consent, the magistrate judge may extend the time limits only on a showing that extraordinary circumstances exist and justice requires the delay.

(e) Hearing and Finding. At the preliminary hearing, the defendant may cross-examine adverse witnesses and may introduce evidence but may not object to evidence on the ground that it was unlawfully acquired. If the magistrate judge finds probable cause to believe an offense has been committed and the defendant committed it, the magistrate judge must promptly require the defendant to appear for further proceedings.

(f) Discharging the Defendant. If the magistrate judge finds no probable cause to believe an offense has been committed or the defendant committed it, the magistrate judge must dismiss the complaint and discharge the defendant. A discharge does not preclude the government from later prosecuting the defendant for the same offense.

(g) Recording the Proceedings. The preliminary hearing must be recorded by a court reporter or by a suitable recording device. A recording of the proceeding may be made available to any party upon request. A copy of the recording and a transcript may be provided to any party upon request and upon any payment required by applicable Judicial Conference regulations.

(h) Producing a Statement.

(1) In General. Rule 26.2(a)-(d) and (f) applies at any hearing under this rule, unless the magistrate judge for good cause rules otherwise in a particular case.

(2) Sanctions for Not Producing a Statement. If a party disobeys a Rule 26.2 order to deliver a statement to the moving party, the magistrate judge must not consider the testimony of a witness whose statement is withheld.

COLEMAN v. BURNETT
U. S. Court of Appeals, District of Columbia Circuit
477 F.2d 1187 (1973)

SPOTTSWOOD W. ROBINSON III, CIRCUIT JUDGE:

This appeal tenders for resolution questions as to the examinatorial entitlements of the criminally accused at federal preliminary hearings. Appellants, Lawrence D. Coleman, Jorge D. Dancis and Ronald Shepard, were arrested and charged * * * with the commission of unrelated crimes within the District of Columbia. Following arrest, each was brought before a judicial officer * * * for the proceedings prescribed by then Rule 5 of the Federal Rules of Criminal Procedure.[3] Coleman and Dancis each sought, and each was denied, a subpoena requiring the attendance at his preliminary hearing of the only apparent eyewitness to his alleged offenses. Shepard, during his preliminary hearing, was restricted in cross-examination of the complainant and a corroborating Government witness, and in the presentation of evidence of his own.

Subsequent to the preliminary hearings, the three appellants joined in a class-action complaint in the District Court. They sought declaratory judgments that the preliminary hearings were defective, writs of mandamus reopening them, and an injunction restraining, *pendente lite*, presentation of their cases for grand jury consideration. * * * * The District Court denied a preliminary injunction and dismissed the action, * * * and this appeal ensued. For reasons which follow, we

---

[3] Former Fed.R.Crim.P. 5(c), which is critically involved in this case, is quoted in note 54, infra. Former Rule 5 was recently amended. Fed.R.Crim.P. 5, 5.1 (effective Oct. 1, 1972). Now, Rule 5 deals with the accused's initial appearance before the magistrate and Rule 5.1 with his preliminary hearing.

reverse the District Court's judgment to the extent that it denied a declaration that Dancis' preliminary hearing was faulty and remand the case in order that the declaration may be made. In all other respects we affirm, but without prejudice to rectification in the criminal proceeding pending against Dancis of the error committed at his preliminary hearing. * * * *

II. Shepard's Appeal

Appellant Shepard was charged with assaulting a Deputy United States Marshal * * * while a prisoner in the cellblock * * * of the District of Columbia Court of General Sessions. * * * * A judge of that court, sitting as a committing magistrate, * * * presided over his preliminary hearing. The complaining witness, Deputy Marshal John H. Lonien, testified that while he was on duty in the cellblock, Shepard committed an unprovoked attack upon him, striking him above the right eye with a fist. Another Government witness, Herbert Rutherford, employed as a guard in the cellblock, corroborated Marshal Lonien's testimony.

Shepard's counsel was permitted considerable latitude in cross-examination of these witnesses as to matters they had testified to on direct examination. The judge, however, sustained the Government's objections to a number of inquiries directed to them on other topics. The specific complaint Shepard refers to us runs to the judge's rulings on eleven questions propounded to Marshal Lonien and four to Guard Rutherford. * * * * Those questions, in the main, solicited testimony as to disparaging remarks assertedly directed to cellblock personnel by prisoners other than Shepard, and to the nature and extent of any injuries inflicted by Shepard on Marshal Lonien and of injuries allegedly sustained by Shepard himself.[47] The judge also ruled out Shepard's proffer of photographs purporting to show his post-altercation physical condition, and inquiry of a defense witness as to whether cellblock personnel had tried to confiscate the photographs.

---

[47] The following questions were directed to Marshal Lonien on cross-examination and excluded:

Q: Did you lose any time from work because of this incident?

Q: Did you hear any of the other marshals making racial slurs and telling the prisoners to move faster?

Q: Isn't it true, Marshal Lonien, some other prisoners, beside Mr. Shepard, made disparaging remarks to you?

Q: Did you ever describe what happened on this day to Mr. Luke Moore as an escape attempt?

Q: Can you describe how you attempted to lead him?

Q: Did you see Mr. Shepard on the floor with other marshals?

Q: Did you know, Marshal Lonien, how Mr. Shepard was rendered unconscious?

Q: Did you see anybody kick Mr. Shepard in the eye?

Q: Did you ask anybody for help?

Q: Did you ever describe what took place in the cellblock as a riot?

Q: Did you receive medical treatment for your injuries?

Questions addressed to Guard Rutherford but excluded were:

Q: Do you know who took Mr. Shepard's handcuffs off?

Q: Mr. Rutherford, have you had any trouble with prisoners as they are being led in?

Q: Did you have a part in restraining Mr. Shepard on that date?

Q: Did you see Marshal Lonien attempt to place Mr. Shepard in solitary confinement?

The more common basis of the Government's objections to defense counsel's cross-examinatorial approach was that he was venturing beyond the boundaries of a hearing designed to explore probable cause and embarking on a quest for discovery of elements of the Government's case.[48] After some amount of prior ambivalence on the subject, Shepard now disclaims any attempt at discovery, as distinguished from refutation of probable cause. * * * * He further argues that the questions addressed to Marshal Lonien and Guard Rutherford bore a substantial relationship to the existence or nonexistence of probable cause.

A. Discovery at Preliminary Hearings

Former Rule 5(c) granted the accused, and its present counterpart continues to confer, the right to "cross-examine witnesses against him" at a preliminary hearing.[54] The true dimension of that right is bound to depend in considerable measure upon the degree to which discovery by the defense may be a purpose the preliminary hearing is designed to serve. That, in turn, is a topic upon which the judges of this court have expressed views which, to say the least, have not been entirely harmonious. * * * * One view has been that the sole objective of a preliminary hearing is to determine whether there is probable cause to believe that the accused has committed an offense, and that the accused may lay claim to the benefit of only so much discovery as may become incidental to a properly conducted inquiry into probable cause. * * * * That view has now been incorporated into federal jurisprudence by the Federal Magistrates Act.

This Act provides mandatorily, with exceptions later to be considered, * * * for "a preliminary hearing to determine whether there is probable cause to believe that an offense has been committed and that the arrested person has committed it." The reason the Act indulges the preliminary hearing no independent discovery role is evident from its legislative history. During hearings before the Senate Committee on the Judiciary, witnesses urged "that preliminary examination afforded a necessary and useful medium for defense counsel to obtain discovery of the

---

[48] There were other objections to specific questions, principally on the ground that they were outside the scope of the witness' direct examination.

[54] Former Fed.R.Crim.P. 5(c) provided:

> The defendant shall not be called upon to plead. If the defendant waives preliminary examination, the commissioner shall forthwith hold him to answer in the district court. If the defendant does not waive examination, the commissioner shall hear the evidence within a reasonable time. The defendant may cross-examine witnesses against him and may introduce evidence in his own behalf. If from the evidence it appears to the commissioner that there is probable cause to believe that an offense has been committed and that the defendant has committed it, the commissioner shall forthwith hold him to answer in the district court; otherwise the commissioner shall discharge him. The commissioner shall admit the defendant to bail as provided in these rules. After concluding the proceeding the commissioner shall transmit forthwith to the clerk of the district court all papers in the proceeding and any bail taken by him.

United States Magistrates now exercise the functions formerly committed to commissioners. 18 U.S.C. § 3060 (1970). Present Fed.R.Crim.P. 5.1(a) provides:

> If from the evidence it appears that there is probable cause to believe that an offense has been committed and that the defendant committed it, the federal magistrate shall forthwith hold him to answer in district court. The finding of probable cause may be based upon hearsay evidence in whole or in part. The defendant may cross-examine witnesses against him and may introduce evidence in his own behalf. Objections to evidence on the ground that it was acquired by unlawful means are not properly made at the preliminary examination. Motions to suppress must be made to the trial court as provided in Rule 12.

prosecution's evidence." * * * * The Committee, however, was "of the opinion that the problem of discovery should be treated separately from that of the preliminary hearing." * * * * Although the need for expanded pretrial discovery procedures was recognized, * * * the Committee felt that

> The preliminary hearing does not present an ideal opportunity for discovery. It is designed for another purpose; namely, that of determining whether there is probable cause to justify further proceedings against an arrested person. Thus, the degree of discovery obtained in a preliminary hearing will vary depending upon how much evidence the presiding judicial officer thinks is necessary to establish probable cause in a particular case. This may be quite a bit, or it may be very little, but in either event it need not be all the evidence within the possession of the Government that should be subject to discovery. * * * *

The Committee accordingly concluded[64] "that discovery procedure should remain separate and distinct from the preliminary examination." * * * *

That settles the matter, of course, for Shepard and others whose hearings took place *after* the effective date of the Act. The mission of the hearing is an investigation into probable cause for further proceedings against the accused. It does not include discovery for the sake of discovery. To be sure, the evidence the Government offers to establish probable cause is by nature also discovery for the accused. So also is information adduced on cross-examination of Government witnesses on the aspects of direct-examination testimony tending to build up probable cause. In those senses, some discovery becomes a by-product of the process of demonstrating probable cause. But in no sense is discovery a legitimate and unto itself.

B. Cross-Examination at Preliminary Hearings

To say merely that discovery is not a primary function of federal preliminary hearings is to respond only incompletely to the issue Shepard poses. As we have said, former Rule 5(c) conferred upon the accused the right to "cross-examine witnesses against him," * * * and that right he continues to enjoy. Moreover, in *Coleman v. Alabama*, 399 U.S. 1 (1970), the Supreme Court, in holding that a preliminary hearing to ascertain probable cause to bind an accused for additional proceedings is a critical stage of the criminal process at which the Sixth Amendment right to counsel obtains,[70] pointed out as one of the considerations supporting its holding that "the lawyer's skilled examination and cross-examination of witnesses may expose fatal weaknesses in the prosecution's case that may lead the magistrate to refuse to bind the accused over."[71] Since the right to counsel is the right to

---

[64] The Committee also specified another reason: "In addition, because its fundamental purpose is to prevent unjustified restraints of liberty, the preliminary examination should be held within a short time after an accused is first arrested. Discovery, on the other hand, can most usefully take place at a later stage, much closer to trial, when the evidence is more nearly complete and defense counsel is better prepared."

[70] The right to counsel at federal preliminary hearings is also statutorily granted. 18 U.S.C. § 3006A(b)-(c) (1970).

[71] "Plainly the guiding hand of counsel at the preliminary hearing is essential to protect the indigent accused against an erroneous or improper prosecution. First, the lawyer's skilled examination and cross-examination of witnesses may expose fatal weaknesses in the State's case that may lead the

effective assistance of counsel, *Coleman* requires us to evaluate Shepard's challenge with the increased solicitude appropriate when constitutional rights are at stake. * * * * This we have done, and we are led to the conclusion that the District Court's disposition of Shepard's grievance should not be disturbed.

According to Shepard's brief on appeal, the purpose of his counsel's questions on cross-examination of the two Government witnesses was to show that "(a) there were no physical injuries to the Marshals; (b) there were severe injuries to Mr. Shepard rendering him unconscious; (c) the assault charge was brought as a subterfuge for the Marshals' own conduct; (d) the Marshals were provoked by disparaging remarks by prisoners other than Mr. Shepard; (e) there was mass confusion in the cellblock seriously impeding the perception of the Marshals; and (f) there was evidence that Mr. Shepard acted in self-defense, if he acted at all." * * * * The first difficulty we have encountered is that the handling of the cross-examination made this understanding all too difficult to come by. Cross-examination at a preliminary hearing, like the hearing itself, is confined by the principle that a probe into probable cause is the end and aim of the proceeding, * * * and the line between refutation of probable cause and discovery into the prosecution's case ofttimes is thin. Here counsel's purpose in propounding the questions which the presiding judge excluded was unquestionably blurred by the fact that counsel frequently appeared to be off on an impermissible quest for discovery. At no time prior to the rulings complained of did counsel delineate for the judge's edification the factual thesis he was seeking to promote. Only as the hearing neared its close, and after the rulings had been made, did counsel broach anything remotely similar to the defensive theory now explained on appeal.[76] Our reading of conviction that the presiding judge, when ruling on counsel's questions, could hardly divine what counsel had in mind. Therefore, we cannot say that he committed error in barring responses to inquiries that seemed unrelated to the task of evaluating probable cause.

Moreover, cross-examination is properly to be limited at preliminary hearing, as at trial, to the scope of the witness' direct examination. To the extent that it is not — and here it was not — cross-examination ostensibly, even if undesignedly, becomes an effort at some sort of discovery. We do not suggest that magistrates may not indulge variations from the usual order of offering evidence, and during presentation of the Government's case permit the defense to get in elements of its own. But when cross-examination exceeds the range of direct examination unaccompanied by an elucidation of its connection with probable cause, it is small wonder that discovery is taken to be the examiner's goal.

---

magistrate to refuse to bind the accused over. Second, in any event, the skilled interrogation of witnesses by an experienced lawyer can fashion a vital impeachment tool for use in cross-examination of the State's witnesses at the trial, or preserve testimony favorable to the accused of a witness who does not appear at the trial. Third, trained counsel can more effectively discover the case the State has against his client and make possible the preparation of a proper defense to meet that case at the trial. Fourth, counsel can also be influential at the preliminary hearing in making effective arguments for the accused on such matters as the necessity for an early psychiatric examination or bail." 399 U.S. at 9.

[76] At that point, counsel stated: "If I could show in this preliminary hearing, Your Honor, that the reason this charge was brought was to cover up a wrongful assault on Mr. Shepard, and you would let me go into some of these questions as to who made the decision to charge and what Marshal Lonien (the witness) did afterwards, I think I could prove to Your Honor right now, before the case goes over to District Court, that an assault didn't take place and this was a cover up."

An even more important consideration stems from the difference between the objective of the preliminary hearing and that of the trial. While, of course, conviction necessitates proof at trial of all elements of a crime beyond a reasonable doubt, it suffices for purposes of a binding over for trial that the evidence show "probable cause to believe that an offense has been committed and that the defendant has committed it."[77] The preliminary hearing is not a minitrial of the issue of guilt, but is rather an investigation into the reasonableness of the bases for the charge, and examination of witnesses thereat does not enjoy the breadth it commands at trial. * * * * "A preliminary hearing," the Supreme Court has said, "is ordinarily a much less searching exploration into the merits of a case than a trial, simply because its function is the more limited one of determining whether probable cause exists to hold the accused for trial." * * * *

It is the contrast of probable cause and proof beyond a reasonable doubt that inevitably makes for examinatorial differences between the preliminary hearing and the trial. Probable cause signifies evidence sufficient to cause a person of ordinary prudence and caution to conscientiously entertain a reasonable belief of the accused's guilt. * * * * Proof beyond a reasonable doubt, on the other hand, connotes evidence strong enough to create an abiding conviction of guilt to a moral certainty. * * * * The gap between these two concepts is broad. A magistrate may become satisfied about probable cause on much less than he would need to be convinced. Since he does not sit to pass on guilt or innocence, he could legitimately find probable cause while personally entertaining some reservations. By the same token, a showing of probable cause may stop considerably short of proof beyond a reasonable doubt, and evidence that leaves some doubt may yet demonstrate probable cause. In the instance before us, the testimony of two witnesses on direct examination furnished more than an ample foundation for a finding of probable cause which the cross-examination allowed did not impair. By our appraisal, the convoluted defensive theory Shepard now says he wanted to develop * * * was not likely to change the result. Whatever its potency as a basis for a reasonable doubt at trial, its capability to dissolve enough of the Government's showing to negate probable cause strikes us as highly improbable. We speak not only of the cross-examination which was banned but also of the items of similar purport which on Shepard's presentation were excluded. * * * * In any event, the situation is far too cloudy to warrant a grant of the extraordinary relief which Shepard seeks.

Magistrates presiding over preliminary hearings, no less than judges presiding over trials, are endowed with broad powers to supervise examination of witnesses. * * * * Beyond that, they should be indulged some leeway in their resolution of probable cause issues. Courts should not upset these judgmatic exercises unless a supervisory excess or a decisional error is clearly shown, * * * and we do not perceive either here. Shepard's counsel was permitted to cross-examine each Government witness closely as to the elements of his direct testimony and, for the reasons stated, we cannot say that disallowance of the questions ruled out was improper. For similar reasons, we are unable to say that the photographs and the questions as to the defense witness possessed such a tendency to dissolve probable cause that their exclusion was erroneous. A writ of mandamus lies only to enforce a plain, positive duty; it is not available to exact a response to a dubious claim. * * * * At best, any obligation to reverse the rulings on the excluded evidence is entirely too unclear. We accordingly affirm as to Shepard.

---

[77] That is the standard specified both in former Rule 5(c) and present Rule 5.1(a).

III. Dancis' Appeal

Dancis, our third appellant, was charged with two violations of the Marijuana Tax Act. * * * * The charges came on for ventilation at a preliminary hearing over which a United States Magistrate presided. The magistrate denied his counsel's request for a subpoena requiring the attendance of an unnamed undercover agent, who apparently was the sole available eyewitness to the two marijuana transactions attributed to Dancis. The Government's only witness at the hearing was the agent's supervisor, whose testimony as to the alleged transactions was necessarily hearsay, and as to the transactor's identity was simply that the agent had identified Dancis from a six-year old photograph. The magistrate, on a finding of probable cause, held Dancis for grand jury action, and the District Court, in the case under review, held that the hearing was legally sufficient.

Dancis argues that each of two flaws vitiated his preliminary hearing. One is that the magistrate's refusal to allow him access to the undercover agent's testimony was prejudicial error. The other is that the Confrontation Clause[88] outlaws the magistrate's finding of probable cause solely upon the hearsay testimony of the agent's supervisor.[89] We deem it unnecessary to reach the constitutional issue posed by Dancis' second contention[90] because we agree that he is on sound ground in advancing the first.[91]

A. <u>Defensive Evidence at Preliminary Hearings</u>

Former Rule 5(c) confirmed the right of an accused to "introduce evidence in his own behalf" at his preliminary hearing. * * * * It also imposed the requirement that an affirmative decision on probable cause be reached "on the evidence." * * * * The specifications of present Rule 5.1(a) are identical. * * * * Thus a federal preliminary hearing is not only the occasion upon which the Government must justify continued detention by a showing of probable cause, but also an opportunity for the accused to rebut that showing.[95] Rule 5(c) made it clear that it is as much the arrestee's prerogative to endeavor to minimize probable cause as it is the Government's to undertake to maximize it, and that both sides must be indulged reasonably in their respective efforts. And the Government's demonstration on probable cause must

---

[88] "In all criminal prosecutions, the accused shall enjoy the right . . . to be confronted with the witnesses against him." U.S.Const. Amend. VI.

[89] The argument, as we understand it, is not that hearsay must be as totally excluded from preliminary hearings as it is from trials, but seems rather to be that the elements of probable cause dependent upon eyewitness observations cannot be established on a wholly hearsay basis. "Credible" hearsay may underlie an arrest warrant. *E.g.*, United States v. Harris, 403 U.S. 573, 579 (1971). Hearsay may support a grand jury indictment. *E.g.*, Costello v. United States, 350 U.S. 359, 363. Until recently, the question whether hearsay was admissible in preliminary hearings remained open with us (*see* Washington v. Clemmer, 339 F.2d 715 (1964)), as was the question whether a finding of probable cause to hold the accused to answer may be predicated on hearsay evidence alone (id. at 719). Now, however, Fed.R.Crim.P. 5.1(a) provides that the finding "may be based upon hearsay evidence in whole or in part."

[90] We cannot accept the argument that *Coleman v. Alabama* establishes the validity of that contention. *Coleman* vindicates the Sixth Amendment right to counsel at preliminary hearings. But *Coleman* did not touch the issue of right to confrontation at such hearings. As stated in text, we do not reach the question on this appeal.

[91] Constitutional questions are not to be resolved unless the need to do so is imperative. *See, e.g.*, Rosenberg v. Fleuti, 374 U.S. 449, 451 (1963).

[95] This the accused may undertake either by the production of witnesses of his own or by cross-examination of witnesses presented by the Government.

surmount not only difficulties of its own but also any attack the accused may be able to mount against it.[96]

In sum, "the evidence" which alone must guide resolution of the probable cause issue is the whole evidence — for the defense as well as for the prosecution. The magistrate must "listen to the versions of all witnesses and observe their demeanor and provide an opportunity to defense counsel to explore their account on cross-examination." *Ross v. Sirica*, 380 F.2d 557, 656 (1967). The magistrate "sits as a judicial officer to sift all the evidence before resolving the probable cause issue." *Ibid.* He "cannot decline to issue subpoenas on the ground that only the Government's evidence is probative." *Ibid.*

These provisions of the Rules and our interpretations of them are now reinforced by the holding in *Coleman v. Alabama* * * * that the Sixth Amendment secures for the accused the assistance of counsel at a preliminary hearing having for its purpose a determination on probable cause to hold him for further proceedings. * * * * Among counsel's potential contributions, the Court stated, is "skilled examination of witnesses which may expose fatal weaknesses in the prosecution's case that may lead the magistrate to refuse to bind the accused over." It cannot be gainsaid that what the Sixth Amendment mandated for Alabama's preliminary hearing it exacts equally for the federal preliminary hearing which, we repeat, is exclusively an exploration into probable cause to hold the accused to answer the prosecution further. * * * * Nor can it be doubted that *Coleman* demands more than the mere presence of counsel at the hearing. The right to counsel which *Coleman* declared would amount to no more than a pious overture unless it is a right to counsel able to function efficaciously in his client's behalf. The Sixth Amendment's guaranty of counsel is a pledge of effective assistance by counsel, * * * and *Coleman* makes it clear that federal preliminary hearings, as critical stages of criminal prosecutions, require no less. If the accused's counsel is reduced to a state of impotence in the discharge of this responsibility, it is evident that the accused is deprived of the very benefit which the Sixth Amendment's boon of counsel was designed to confer. * * * *

So, an accused is normally entitled to subpoenas compelling the attendance at his preliminary hearing of witnesses whose testimony promises appreciable assistance on the issue of probable cause. * * * * The test, our past utterances on the subject have indicated, couples the witness' materiality[107] with an absence of good cause for not requiring his presence,[108] and its operation does not depend upon which side

---

[96] While the standard of probable cause which the Government must meet at preliminary hearings is roughly equivalent to the standard required for issuance of an arrest warrant or for an arrest without a warrant, the procedure at preliminary hearings differs from that upon the issuance of a warrant or a warrantless arrest in at least one very important respect. That difference is the presence of the accused at the preliminary hearing and his right to cross-examine prosecution witnesses and introduce evidence in his own behalf. Arrest warrants, on the other hand, are issued upon the Government's *ex parte* presentation to a magistrate, and warrantless arrests are made on information communicated *ex parte* to arresting officers. The traditional function of the preliminary hearing is a second determination on probable cause, this time after according the accused a reasonable opportunity to rebut it. Unless the accused is indulged in that respect, the preliminary hearing is little more than a duplication of the probable cause decisions that foreran his arrest.

[107] Those likely to be called on this basis, in addition to alibi witnesses, are the complainant and other material witnesses named in the complaint who for some reason have not been called by the Government.

[108] Limitations on the right to subpoena witnesses have been recognized where the witness is physically or psychologically unable to testify, and where the witness' testimony could not, in light of

might have been expected to call the witness. * * * * Certainly an accused will not in every instance qualify for a subpoena for the production of a Government witness at his preliminary hearing, but where he succeeds in a plausible showing that that witness could contribute significantly to the accuracy of the probable cause determination, the request for the subpoena should be granted. "This," we have said, "is consistent with the principal purpose of the preliminary hearing as a mechanism to determine whether the evidence is adequate to establish probable cause." * * * *

We think the testimony of the undercover agent Dancis desired at his preliminary hearing met the standard of materiality. From aught that appears, he was the only available person who could testify to the two charged marijuana transfers from personal observation, and by the same token the only one who could directly identify the party responsible for them. Since probable cause to bind Dancis over for further prosecution depended on the caliber of the Government's showing that he was that party and that what he did on the two occasions under scrutiny was illegal, it seems clear that the witness he requested could have given testimony bearing critically upon those matters. In *Washington v. Clemmer* * * *, it was the complainant in a rape case who was sought, and in *Ross v. Sirica* * * *, the only three eyewitnesses to a murder. In both cases we held that denial of the accused's access to them was error, * * * and it appears to us that the sole eyewitness to the transgressions laid to Dancis was equally material.

As we admonished in *Ross*, "whatever the full reach of the accused's subpoena rights at a preliminary hearing, he is entitled to compel the attendance of eyewitnesses unless, of course, because of physical or psychological disability in a particular case such witnesses cannot attend." * * * * That seems the more so when the nature of the Government's presentation at Dancis' preliminary hearing is taken fully into account. The Government offered but one witness, and he could testify on the vital issues of offenses and identity only from hearsay, and it is evident that that weakened the showing. To the extent that hearsay is employed, the effort to establish probable cause becomes more prone to attack since the reliability of the absent hearsay declarant always becomes an added factor to be reckoned with. In *Ross*, where, similarly to Dancis' case, the Government's one witness at a preliminary hearing on a murder charge was a police officer who could merely relay what three eyewitnesses had told him about the crime, two judges of this court aptly observed, without dispute from the rest, that:

> A judicial officer engaged in a judicial determination of probable cause can hardly rest easy solely with the hearsay account of the policeman of what these eyewitnesses told him if the eyewitnesses can be available, so that he can listen to their versions and observe their demeanor, and provide an opportunity to defense counsel to explore their account on cross-examination. The presence of those witnesses impresses us as falling within the orbit of the rights conferred upon the accused by the fourth sentence of Rule 5(c).

Indeed, the problem addressed in *Ross* is compounded in the situation before us now. The Government's evidence at Dancis' preliminary hearing was not only hearsay, but also hearsay without any apparent means of refutation whatever. The undercover agent was not only absent from the hearing, but at the time was also

---

other evidence, negative probable cause, Ross v. Sirica, 380 F.2d 557, 565.

totally unidentified. He did not sign the complaint against Dancis, nor was he named in it, and the testimony at the hearing referred to him simply by his code name "John P." Defense counsel's inquiries on cross-examination as to his real name, and even as to generic characteristics,[116] drew objections from the Government which the magistrate sustained. There was little or nothing in the Government's presentation to lend credit to the reliability of either the agent or the observations purportedly incriminating and identifying Dancis. It is difficult to imagine a case wherein the accused was more helpless to defend against a hearsay attribution of probable cause.

To say, as we do, that the testimony of the absent witness was material does not mean necessarily that the refusal of the subpoena was error vitiating the preliminary hearing. A refusal may be justified, and if it is a finding of probable cause climaxing the hearing must stand. * * * * The record before us, however, is singularly devoid of any such justification. There is no hint that the undercover officer was physically unamenable to a subpoena or in any way disabled from responding to it. * * * * There is no suggestion that his information about the episodes under exploration was to any extent privileged from compulsory disclosure. * * * * Nor is there a basis for attributing the denial of the subpoena to the exigencies of any undercover operation. * * * * The magistrate did not predicate the denial upon any of these grounds, nor did the Government even urge any of them. And to the extent that the record may furnish indications that the magistrate was satisfied on probable cause without hearing from the undercover agent, * * * it suffices to repeat that the issue thereon cannot properly be resolved without accommodating reasonable demands of the prosecution and the defense for the production of evidence capable of shaping the outcome. * * *

B. Return of Indictment

Concluding as we do that the magistrate erred in refusing Dancis the benefit of the undercover officer's testimony, we are left to determine how the mistake should be corrected. The first question confronting that effort is whether the indictment returned against Dancis forecloses rectification of the error. It is well settled that an indictment itself establishes sufficient probable cause for holding the accused for trial, * * * and that explains why we have consistently held that he is not entitled to a preliminary hearing where he is indicted before a hearing is held. Typical situations are those wherein the accused is indicted prior to arrest on the charges, * * * or prior to the date set for preliminary hearing on the charges, * * * or where he is in custody on another charge when indicted. * * * * In none of these instances can a preliminary hearing serve a need to probe probable cause to detain the accused, for the indictment has fulfilled that need. * * * * Nor can the hearing be invoked merely as a device for obtaining discovery, for discovery independent of the ascertainment of probable cause is not one of its functions.

The case before us, however, is markedly different. Dancis was given a preliminary hearing on the pending charges prior to return of the indictment. At that hearing, by his allegation, he was denied the right then conferred by former Rule 5(c) to examine a witness in his own behalf. That contention, we think, keeps

---

[116] When defense counsel inquired of the undercover officer's supervisor on cross-examination, "Now, what is John P's full name?" "What is the officer's nationality?" "What is the officer's race?," the magistrate sustained objections from the Government to each question.

Dancis in court despite the post-hearing rendition of the indictment.

Where in terms of the requirements of the Rules, a preliminary hearing is defective, the accused is obviously entitled to a reopening of the hearing to enable remediation of the defect if that can be done before a grand jury acts in the matter. "To say that the preliminary hearing was defective is to say that the determination of probable cause was inadequate and should not operate to deprive the accused of his liberty pending grand jury consideration." Accordingly, we have not hesitated to direct a supplemental preliminary hearing on demonstration that at the original hearing the accused did not get his just due. * * * * That remedy, of course, is additional to the accused's prerogative to seek a dissolution of the commitment itself.

We have, moreover, adhered to the view that such a deprivation can be remedied by a reopening of the hearing even after return of an indictment. The indictment bars relitigation of the question of probable cause, of course, but the fact remains that save for disrespect of the accused's rights he would have enlarged his insight into the Government's case against him — as a by-product of efforts pro and con on probable cause in the course of the Government's submission. Since, however, a Rule 5(c) right was dishonored, the accused lost a part of that by-product, and we have held that the hearing should be reopened to afford the accused an opportunity to retrieve the part which has been lost. * * * *

That is the rationale of our past decisions respecting post-indictment supplemental preliminary hearings. The supplemental hearing was not an occasion for a reexamination of probable cause, for the indictment had settled that issue. Nor was its purpose discovery for its own sake, but only such discovery as would inexorably have accompanied scrupulous observance of the Rule 5(c) right. Reopening of the preliminary hearing, then, emerged as both an appropriate sanction for and remediation of Rule 5(c) violations. The effect of the supplemental hearing was to confer upon the accused the benefit of only so much incidental discovery as would have been his but for the infringement of Rule 5(c).

Since our development of this prophylactic doctrine, however, the Federal Magistrates Act was adopted, and the question becomes whether the Act has set the doctrine for naught. The Act lays down the broad mandate that an arrestee be offered a preliminary hearing, * * * the date for which must be fixed at his initial appearance before a judge or magistrate after his arrest. * * * * The hearing must be conducted "within a reasonable time following initial appearance, but in any event not later than" ten days where the arrestee remains in custody * * * or twenty days where he is enlarged in the interim. * * * * The act specifies, however, in § 303(e) that "no preliminary examination shall be required to be accorded an arrested person if at any time subsequent to the initial appearance of such person before a judge or magistrate and prior to the date fixed for the preliminary examination an indictment is returned."[140]

---

[140] "No preliminary examination in compliance with subsection (a) of this section shall be required to be accorded an arrested person, nor shall such arrested person be discharged from custody or from the requirement of bail or any other condition of release pursuant to subsection (d), if at any time subsequent to the initial appearance of such person before a judge or magistrate and prior to the date fixed for the preliminary examination pursuant to subsections (b) and (c) an indictment is returned or, in appropriate cases, an information is filed against such person in a court of the United States." 18 U.S.C. § 3060(e) (1970).

We need not ponder whether the Act erects a barrier to a post-indictment pretrial reopening of a preliminary hearing which is seriously defective under the criteria specified in the Rules. To be sure, the remedy we provided in *Ross v. Sirica*, 380 F.2d 557 (1967) in circumstances comparable to those here, was a remand to the magistrate for a supplemental hearing. But *Ross*, like other decisions in its day, rested on the theory that discovery was as much a function of the preliminary hearing as an investigation into probable cause to bind the accused for further prosecution. * * * * The Act was passed after *Ross* was decided, and whether or not it imposed an absolute ban on reopenings of preliminary hearings, it certainly destroyed discovery as a reason for ordering a reopening. * * * * Furthermore, nothing in *Ross* nor in any of our other holdings inexorably required a supplemental hearing when another procedure might do equal or superior service. On the contrary, it was our uniform practice to relegate the problem of remediation, not to the magistrate, but to the trial judge when the deficiency in the preliminary hearing first came to light after the accused had been convicted. * * * *

Even more importantly, *Ross* predated not only the Act but also the Supreme Court's decision in *Coleman v. Alabama*, 399 U.S. 1 (1970), and *Coleman* introduced an element of the remedy problem which this court has not hitherto had occasion to consider. To put in a nutshell what we later elucidate, *Coleman* identifies the constitutional right to effective assistance of counsel as an incident of preliminary hearings and assures vindication of that right. * * * * It is evident, then, that the return of an indictment against the accused cannot eliminate the need for procedures of some kind to redress violations of the *Coleman* right. * * * * On the other hand, the *Coleman*-type remedy, when invoked prior to trial, embraces an array of alternatives for dissipating potential prejudice. * * * * So, even if a reopening of the hearing survives the Act as one of these alternatives, Dancis cannot compel that particular choice.

Mandamus is an extraordinary remedy, available only to enforce a clear, unequivocal duty. It does not lie to control an exercise of judgment. Dancis, we say, is entitled, notwithstanding the indictment, to protection against injury resulting from the magistrate's mistake. But Dancis is not necessarily entitled to receive that protection through a supplemental hearing before the magistrate, assuming even that the Act leaves that course open as a possibility. Additionally, as we later discuss, a supplemental hearing suffers by comparison with other alternatives open in this case. It is unnecessary, then, for us to decide whether in any event such a hearing would be available after an indictment has issued, and that decision we pretermit to another day.

C. The Remedy

Coleman v. Alabama bestowed upon Dancis an inviolable right to protection against harmful consequences flowing from the magistrate's refusal to permit examination of the undercover agent at the preliminary hearing. *Coleman* also offers guidance as to the proper course to be taken where, following trial and conviction, the accused seeks to remedy a constitutional deficiency in his preliminary hearing. In *Coleman*, the Court could not determine from the record whether the absence of counsel from the accused's preliminary hearing actually worked prejudice at his trial, so it vacated the conviction and remanded the case to the Alabama courts for an inquiry on that score. In the event that prejudice was found, the remedy would be a new trial; but if, applying the test set out in *Chapman v.*

California, 386 U.S. 18 (1967)[158], it was found that the infirmity in the preliminary hearing was harmless, the conviction would be reinstated. Even prior to *Coleman,* as we have said, in our own post-conviction decisions we have settled upon the same remedial course where serious flaws in preliminary hearings left them infirm.

These decisions chart the route to be traveled when the error is judicially detected only after conviction. But that is not Dancis' situation, for while he has been indicted he has not yet been tried. Dancis could, of course, proceed to trial secure in the knowledge that should he encounter prejudice because of the refusal of the subpoena requested at his preliminary hearing, any conviction would have to be set for naught. But it would be senseless to require him to undergo trial and conviction before undertaking to repair the defect. On the contrary, we have emphasized that one deprived of his just due at a preliminary hearing not only may, but ordinarily must, seek rectification in court immediately. This position may reflect the undesirability of permitting an accused to withhold his complaint until after he has lost a gamble on the jury's verdict. In any event, it certainly reflects a decided preference to avert prejudice before it occurs rather than to wait and deal with it after the fact.

We think, too, that the problem of remediation arising pretrial, no less than when it emerges after conviction, is one to be addressed by the court itself. There is nothing to be gained, over and above handling by the judge, by sending the case back to the magistrate for a supplemental preliminary hearing after the accused has been indicted. The magistrate cannot reinvestigate probable cause, for the indictment establishes its existence, nor is there anything else that officer can do that the judge cannot do better. The concern is that the accused may suffer prejudice at his forthcoming trial by the infringement of his rights at the hearing, and avoidance of prejudice is the function and duty of the judge himself. Obviously the judge could not, by directing the magistrate to reopen the preliminary hearing, shift his own responsibility to the magistrate. In our view, where an unmitigated blunder at a preliminary hearing may infect the ensuing trial, the court is obligated to scrutinize the accused's claim of possible injury, and to take appropriate corrective action. We perceive no reason why, in the circumstances presented, the problem at hand cannot be fully accommodated within the framework of the criminal prosecution pending against Dancis. The judge who is to preside at Dancis' trial is amply equipped to dissipate whatever risk of prejudice was bred by Dancis' inability to call the undercover officer as a witness at his preliminary hearing. There are opportunities uniquely open to the trial judge, particularly with the cooperation of the parties, to seek remediation of the magistrate's error before any real damage is done, and the judge is free to draw upon his imagination in the kind of remedy-fashioning which traditionally has been a prerogative of the federal judiciary. Moreover, it would be advantageous to the prosecution and the accused alike to eliminate the problem from the realm of future litigation.

The indictment against Dancis named the undercover agent, and it may well be that he testified before the grand jury. If so, the trial judge might consider making the agent's grand jury testimony available to defense counsel. Alternatively, since after indictment the Government no longer has had an interest in keeping the agent's identity secret, and obviously will have to produce him as a witness at trial,

---

[158] In *Chapman,* it was held that before a federal constitutional error can be held "harmless," the court must be of the belief that it was harmless beyond a reasonable doubt. The court must find that there is no reasonable possibility that the error complained of might have contributed to the conviction.

a voluntary interview may be indicated. If need be, the judge might set appropriate bounds for an interview and arrange for the agent's participation therein. It may be that, by consent of the parties and approval of the judge, a deposition by written interrogatories to the agent would suffice as an expedient. Without any effort to exhaust the possibilities, we make these observations simply as suggestions of procedures calculated to safeguard Dancis against prejudice consistently with an orderly and expeditious progression of the case to trial. The point we do emphasize is that the judge is in a position to do anything the magistrate could now undertake, and indeed to do a great deal more. We leave for the trial judge, in the first instance, the decision on suitable relief.

The judgment appealed from is reversed insofar as it denied the requested declaration that Dancis' preliminary hearing was rendered defective by the magistrate's refusal to allow a subpoena commanding the appearance of the undercover agent as a witness, and the case is remanded to the District Court in order that such a declaration may be made. In all other respects, the judgment is affirmed, but without prejudice to steps in the criminal proceeding pending against Dancis which are designed to appropriately remedy the error committed at his preliminary hearing.

Fahy, Senior Circuit Judge, concurring in part and dissenting in part:

I concur in Part III (the Dancis case) of Judge Robinson's very careful and scholarly opinion. As to Part II (Shepard's appeal), I am of a different view. I think the cross-examination of the principal government witness was unduly restricted at the preliminary hearing. Unless subsequent events which are not considered by the court should lead to a different disposition of his case, I think he is entitled to a supplemental preliminary hearing.

I accept the position that the purpose of the preliminary hearing was to determine probable cause and not to obtain discovery, but the effort of defense counsel in the cross-examination was to elicit testimony which bore upon the issue of probable cause. Shepard had been identified by the principal government witness as the one who had made the involved assault upon him. The magistrate explicitly recognized that the cross-examination was designed to impeach this witness. Defense counsel was endeavoring to show a situation of pandemonium in a cellblock, in which the officer's identification of Shepard as the one who attacked him might have been mistaken due to a general melee following racial slurs and an attack upon Shepard himself, who was felled and rendered unconscious with a fractured skull. Moreover, in the cross-examination counsel was not only seeking to test the credibility of the complaining witness but, in a good faith and intelligent, lawyer-like manner, was seeking to bring before the magistrate a fair exposition of what occurred, which had by no means been adequately developed by the government's witnesses. Thus, after being repeatedly rebuffed, counsel stated:

Mr. Axelrod (defense counsel): If I could show in this preliminary hearing, Your Honor, that the reason this charge was brought was to cover up a wrongful assault on Mr. Shepard, and you would let me go into some of these questions as to who made the decision to charge and what Marshal Lonien (the complaining witness being examined) did afterwards, I think I could prove to Your Honor right now, before the case goes over to the District Court, that an assault didn't take place and this was a cover up.

The Court: Sir, you have heard what I said as to limitations I am placing on the evidence that will be admitted on this preliminary hearing. Within the scope of those limitations, you may proceed.

The limitations in my opinion deprived the defense of a fair opportunity to probe the issue of probable cause as contemplated by Rule 5, F.R.Crim.P. It is clear that in seeking to impeach a witness on cross-examination counsel may question him on matters affecting credibility, including his lack of knowledge or perceptive capacity, his bias or his adverse interest in the litigation, and including also any prior inconsistent statements or acts. Rule 611(b) of the proposed new Rules of Evidence explicitly grants the right to go beyond the scope of the direct in cross-examination of a witness in a jury trial, with discretion in the judge as indicated:

A witness may be cross-examined on any matter relevant to any issue in the case, including credibility. In the interests of justice, the judge may limit cross-examination with respect to matters not testified to on direct examination.

Here the witness was the complaining witness, and the cross-examination was not before a jury during a trial but before a judge at a preliminary hearing, during which both hearsay and otherwise inadmissible evidence may be presented. Rule 5.1, F.R.Crim.P., effective October 1, 1972. The overly restrictive limitations imposed upon counsel are not in keeping with these developments.

Moreover, "discovery" by the time-honored method of seeking the truth — proper cross-examination — provided at a preliminary hearing the discovery is incidental to the issue of probable cause, is in line with the modern trend for greater discovery in criminal proceedings. Unless intervening events which, as I have said, we have not considered, should preclude it, I would require that Shepard now be given a supplemental probable cause hearing. Only about an hour would be consumed.

Notes from Augusta:

1. In Dancis' case, the prosecutor did not call as a witness the undercover agent who allegedly *saw* the drug sales. Instead, he called the agent's supervisor, who could testify only as to what the agent told him — clearly hearsay, which will be inadmissible at trial. While Rule 5.1(a) does allow hearsay at the preliminary examination, he is taking a bit of a chance by using only hearsay to prove a crucial point, as the magistrate might be less impressed by hearsay than eyewitness testimony. Why would the prosecutor choose to take such a chance?

2. In reversing the judgment in Dancis' case, the Court suggested several possible remedies the trial court might adopt. I find it peculiar that the Court failed to mention the most obvious remedy, one which would give D the exact thing he wanted out of the prelim: allowing D to take the agent's oral deposition. Why didn't the Court mention this? Do you think the Court intended to preclude this remedy?

HUNTER v. DISTRICT COURT
Colorado Supreme Court
190 Colo. 48, 84 A.L.R.3d 800 (1975)

KELLEY, JUSTICE.

On July 28, 1975, the respondent district judge conducted a preliminary hearing in the criminal case of *People v. Jesus Romero*, pursuant to Crim.P. 7(h). The defendant had been charged with two counts of rape, § 18-3-401, C.R.S. 1973, and one count of second-degree kidnapping. § 18-3-302, C.R.S. 1973.

At the hearing, the testimony of the complaining witness, Louise Gonzales, was contradicted in several respects by the testimony of Eddie Quintana, a witness for the defense. Most of the discrepancies concerned the sequence of events occurring on the evening in question up to the time of the alleged kidnapping and rape. Mrs. Gonzales testified that she had never had sexual intercourse with the defendant prior to the alleged rape; that she attended a party on the evening in question escorted by the defendant; that the defendant verbally and physically abused her at the party; that Eddie Quintana, a friend, had given her a ride home after the party; that she did not realize that the defendant was following them; that when she left Quintana's car, the defendant abducted her against her will; that he took her in his van to an open field where twice he had non-consensual sexual intercourse with her after physically abusing her; and that she escaped to call the police.

Quintana, who works at the same plant with the defendant and Mrs. Gonzales, was called as a defense witness. He testified that the defendant and Mrs. Gonzales arrived at the party together; that the defendant had stated publicly at the party that they were out in the country together and that he had "balled" her; that Mrs. Gonzales became upset and said, "You fucker, that was just between us"; that the defendant then attempted to restrain Mrs. Gonzales on the floor, at which time she threatened to call the police; that Mrs. Gonzales sought a ride home with Quintana to which he agreed; that on the way home she noted that the defendant was following them; and that Quintana dropped her off at her home, telling her to get inside quickly in order to avoid trouble with the defendant.

The judge found that the testimony of the complaining witness had been contradicted in several material respects. Therefore, the judge chose to disregard the testimony of Mrs. Gonzales "in its entirety", because he could not distinguish between fact and fiction in her testimony. He therefore dismissed the information. The district attorney seeks a writ from this court directing the judge to reinstate the information.

There are two issues presented by this proceeding: (1) does a district court judge conducting a preliminary hearing have jurisdiction to consider the credibility of the witnesses in determining the existence or absence of probable cause; and (2) assuming such jurisdiction to exist, did the respondent judge abuse his discretion in this case?

The preliminary hearing in Colorado under Crim.P. 7(h) is not a minitrial, but rather is limited to the purpose of determining whether there is probable cause to believe that a crime was committed and that the defendant committed it. *Maestas v. District Court, Colo.,* 541 P.2d 889 (1975). It focuses upon a probable cause determination, rather than a consideration of the probability of conviction at the ensuing trial. See Note, *The Function of the Preliminary Hearing in Federal Pretrial Procedure*, 83 Yale L.J. 771 (1974). As a screening device, the preliminary hearing insures that the prosecution can at least sustain the burden of proving probable cause. It protects the accused by avoiding an embarrassing, costly and unnecessary trial and it benefits the interests of judicial economy and efficiency.

In light of its limited purpose, evidentiary and procedural rules in the preliminary hearing in Colorado are relaxed. Crim.P. 7(h)(3). While the bulk of testimony at a preliminary hearing may be hearsay, the prosecution may not totally rely on hearsay to establish probable cause where competent evidence is readily available. The prosecution need not produce all of its evidence against the defendant at the preliminary hearing, but only that quantum necessary to establish probable cause. Under our Rule 7(h)(3), the burden of proof is on the prosecution, and the defendant need not testify, while he has the right to cross-examine the witnesses called by the People.

The issue of whether a judge in a preliminary hearing may consider the credibility of witnesses in determining probable cause is one of first impression in Colorado. Other jurisdictions which have considered the matter have generally held that the credibility of witnesses as a preliminary hearing is a proper consideration for the judge in determining probable cause. *Wilson v. State*, 59 Wis.2d 269 (1973); *Jones v. Superior Court*, 4 Cal.3d 660 (1971); *Wrenn v. Sheriff*, 87 Nev. 85 (1971); *People v. Paille #2*, 383 Mich. 621 (1970); *People v. Bieber*, 100 N.Y.S.2d 821 (Mag.Ct. 1950). But the facts and the narrow basis of decision relied upon in these cases indicate that the general rule is limited.

In *Wilson, supra*, the Wisconsin Supreme Court held that a magistrate must assess the credibility of witnesses in preliminary hearings in order to determine if there is credible evidence to establish probable cause. However, the court restricted the inquiry of credibility to the "plausibility of the story and not general trustworthiness." As the preliminary hearing in Wisconsin is primarily for the purpose of determining probable cause of the arrest, and not for discovery, all that the prosecution needed to establish was a plausible, believable account of the crime committed by the defendant. In *Wrenn v. Sheriff, supra*, the Supreme Court of Nevada stated that when there is conflicting evidence at the preliminary hearing, the magistrate must determine the weight to be accorded the testimony of the witnesses. But the court qualified its holding:

> If an inference of criminal agency can be drawn from the evidence it is proper for the magistrate to draw it, thereby leaving to the jury at the trial the ultimate determination of which of the witnesses are more credible. The accused's explanation for the homicide, being in the nature of a defense (no specific intent to kill), whether true or false, reasonable or unreasonable, is for the trier of fact to consider at trial; and neither the preliminary examination nor the hearing upon petition for habeas corpus is designed as a substitute for that function.

In *People v. Paille #2, supra*, the Supreme Court of Michigan upheld the trial court's dismissal of an arrest warrant at the preliminary hearing, because the judge found that the testimony of the witnesses for the People was "incredible" and perjurious. Therefore, the judge had a "duty to pass judgment not only on the weight and competency of the evidence, but also the credibility of the witnesses."

In *People v. Bieber, supra,* a judge of the City Magistrate Court, held that at a preliminary hearing, the judge can resolve conflicts in testimony, but only "where the evidence is overwhelming."

Only in the *Jones* case does a state court hold that a judge in a preliminary hearing is always at liberty "to weigh the evidence, resolve conflicts and give or withhold credence to particular witnesses." That California Supreme Court decision indicates the fundamental difference between the function of a preliminary hearing in California and in the other above-cited jurisdictions, including Colorado.

The preliminary hearing in California is a "mini-trial", emphasizing the probability of conviction at trial on admissible evidence. In such a situation, the *Jones* decision properly allows the judge to act as a trier of fact. In Colorado, however, the preliminary hearing is not a "mini-trial", and the judge in such a role is not a trier of fact. Rather, his function is solely to determine the existence or absence of probable cause.

We hold that a judge in a preliminary hearing has jurisdiction to consider the credibility of witnesses only when, as a matter of law, the testimony is implausible or incredible. When there is a mere conflict in the testimony, a question of fact exists for the jury, and the judge must draw the inference favorable to the prosecution.

The conflicts in testimony in this case are not sufficient to support a finding by the judge that Mrs. Gonzales' testimony was implausible or incredible as a matter of law. We are not unmindful of the deference normally shown to findings of a judge who has the benefit of assessing the demeanor of the witness in person rather than on the basis of a cold record. Nevertheless, we believe that in this case the trial judge abused his discretion in disregarding the testimony of Mrs. Gonzales.

We order the information reinstated by the district judge.

ERICKSON, JUSTICE (dissenting):

I respectfully dissent. In my view, the majority opinion is not supported by, and is contrary to, this court's holding in *Maestas v. District Court, Colo.,* 541 P.2d 889 (1975). The majority ignores the manifest inconsistency of referring to a preliminary hearing as a screening device designed to test the sufficiency of the prosecution's case, and then foreclosing the trial judge from screening out, or dismissing the prosecution's case, when probable cause has not been established. As we said in *Maestas,* "a preliminary hearing is of value to the prosecution in that it offers a method for testing the complaints of prosecuting witnesses, and eliminating prosecutions actuated by prejudice or motives inconsistent with a fair administration of the criminal law."

The Commentary of The American Law Institute's Model Code of Pre-Arraignment Procedure offers the following recommendation as a means for determining probable cause at the preliminary hearing:

> The quantum of evidence or the screening standard applicable to the preliminary hearing is usually stated in terms of probable cause but is not further defined. Because the same term is used to state the standard applicable to arrests and because the hearing often serves the function of reviewing the legality of the arrest in addition to screening cases for trial, the two standards are often confused and many courts apply the arrest

standard to the preliminary hearing. Since the Code's view is that the function of the hearing is to screen out charges that should not go to trial, it adopts a standard that requires more evidence than is required for an arrest.

Since the purpose is to screen out cases that should not be tried, Subsection (3) formulates the standard in terms of evidence sufficient to support a verdict of guilty. The judge does not have to be persuaded of the defendant's guilt but should view the cases as if it were a trial and he were required to rule on whether there is enough evidence to send the case to the jury. This standard is thus familiar to trial judges and should prove less confusing in its application than the current applicable standards. [Model Code of Pre-Arraignment Procedure, pp. 596, 597]

Even though the preliminary hearing is not a mini-trial, the trial judge should be allowed to utilize his powers of evaluation and reason in the face of conflicting testimony.

The majority opinion charts a new course which is contrary to the great weight of authority and which virtually eliminates the screening function of the preliminary hearing. How is a judge to determine if a charge is "actuated by prejudice or motives inconsistent with a fair administration of criminal law" unless he assumes the responsibility of evaluating the credibility and claims of the witnesses appearing before him? Indeed, Mr. Justice Groves, speaking for a unanimous court in *Biddle v. District Court*, 183 Colo. 281 (1973), recognized that the screening function necessarily embraced a determination of the credibility of witnesses. This observation was consonant with the views of a majority of the jurisdictions that have addressed the same issue. *Wilson v. State*, 59 Wis.2d 269 (1973); *Jones v. Superior Court*, 4 Cal.3d 660 (1971); *Wrenn v. Sheriff*, 87 Nev. 85 (1971); *People v. Paille #2*, 383 Mich. 621 (1970); *People v. Bieber*, 100 N.Y.S.2d 821 (Mag.Ct. 1950).

The law is well settled that the prosecution bears the burden of proof at a preliminary hearing. The prosecution, in order to establish probable cause, must separate fact from fiction so that the court can evaluate the prosecution's case. If the prosecution's case, and the testimony offered in support of it, appear to be generated by motives other than candor and honesty, then the prosecution has simply failed to sustain its burden of proof.

In this case, the judge plainly indicated that he was unable to distinguish between fact and falsehood on the basis of the testimony of the prosecution's chief witness. Under these circumstances, to hold that the charges must be bound over for trial clearly undermines the law respecting the burden of proof at a preliminary hearing.

The majority holding will cause defense counsel to view the preliminary hearing as a useless charade. Under the majority view, it would be sheer folly for defense counsel to offer evidence or call witnesses. The preliminary hearing, under the majority decision, amounts to an *ex parte* proceeding where the defendant's attempt to explain his position is reduced to a meaningless gesture. Criminal charges, in the future, are to be bound over on the basis of a wooden comparison between the testimony of the prosecution's witness and the elements of the crime. Such a procedure undermines the true function of the preliminary hearing, which is to weed out the cases which should never have been filed.

Moreover, this court was never intended to sit as a super trial court, and to evaluate the credibility of witnesses whom it has neither seen nor heard. Questions concerning the credibility of witnesses and the weight to be given their testimony at a preliminary hearing are for the trial judge to resolve, and this court should not substitute its judgment for that of the trial court. The law was well stated by the Supreme Court of Illinois when it said:

> Questions concerning the credibility of witnesses and the weight to be given their testimony are matters for the court on the preliminary examination, or for the jurors when the witnesses testify before them, and this court will not substitute its judgment on such matters for that of the trial court or the jury. [*People v. Tilley*, 411 Ill. 473 (1952).]

Similarly, the Supreme Court of California correctly resolved the same issue:

> Credibility of witnesses at the preliminary examination, of course, is a question of fact within the province of the committing magistrate to determine, and neither the superior court nor an appellate court may substitute its judgment as to such question for that of the magistrate. The magistrate is not bound to believe even the uncontradicted testimony of a particular witness, especially where the statements are self-serving and the magistrate has reason to believe that other testimony of the witness is untruthful. [*DeMond v. Superior Court*, 57 Cal.2d 340 (1962)]

Massachusetts, in a decision that is to be commended for its analysis of the issue which is now before us, not only recognized that the trial judge has a right and a duty to weigh the credible evidence, but also clarified the quantum of proof that is required in a finding of probable cause at a preliminary hearing:

> The standard of probable cause to bind over must require a greater quantum of legally competent evidence than the probable cause to arrest finding to insure that the preliminary hearing's screening standard is defined in a way that effectuates its purpose. It is the magistrate who must determine whether the policeman's "reasonable belief", when made visible constitutes "probable cause" to believe a crime has been committed and sufficient evidence to warrant a jury's finding the accused guilty. Since the examining magistrate's determination of the minimum quantum of evidence required to find probable cause to bind over is somewhat analogous in function to the court's ruling on a motion for a directed verdict at trial as to whether there is sufficient evidence to warrant submission of the case to the jury, we have decided to adopt a "directed verdict" rule in defining the minimum quantum of credible evidence necessary to support a bind-over determination. The examining magistrate should view the case as if it were a trial and he were required to rule on whether there is enough credible evidence to send the case to the jury. Thus, the magistrate should dismiss the complaint when, on the evidence presented, a trial court would be bound to acquit as a matter of law. *People v. Bernstein*, 95 N.Y.S.2d 696, 699 (N.Y.C.Magis.Ct. 1950). The minimum quantum of evidence required by this bind-over standard is more than that for probable cause for arrest but less than would "prove the defendant's guilt beyond a reasonable doubt." *People v. Bieber*, 100 N.Y.S.2d 821, 823 (N.Y.C.Magis.Ct.). [*Myers v. Commonwealth*, 298 N.E.2d 819 (Mass.1973)]

In summary, I believe that the trial judge should be bound by a test that would be equivalent to the Massachusetts test and patterned upon the principles we established in *People v. Bennett*, 183 Colo. 125 (1973), to assess a motion for judgment of acquittal.

In my view, the record in this case does not reflect any abuse of discretion by the trial judge in his determination that probable cause was not established. The testimony of the prosecution's key witness was contradicted in several material respects by the defendant's witness, Edward R. Quintana. Quintana testified that Mrs. Gonzales struck out at the defendant during the party because the defendant was bragging about having "balled" her. Mrs. Gonzales became very upset, according to Quintana, and actually threatened to call the police. Quintana also heard Mrs. Gonzales say to the defendant, "You fucker, that was just between us." Other testimony established that Mrs. Gonzales may well have been embarrassed about going out with the defendant, inasmuch as she was married to another man. The trial judge was justified in considering whether the charges which Mrs. Gonzales made were "actuated by prejudice or motives inconsistent with a fair administration of the criminal law."

In my opinion, the majority opinion breeds inconsistency into an already troublesome area of the law. Though consistency has been said to be the "last refuge of the unimaginative", I prefer laws that are certain and predictable. For this reason, I would discharge the rule.

Notes from Augusta:

1. What makes the testimony of a prosecution witness "implausible"? I suppose that if Ms. Gonzales had testified that Romero had abducted her in his spaceship and raped her in outer space, this story would be "implausible" — even though she testified to all of the legal elements of rape.

Perhaps the more important question is, what evidence (if any) could the *defendant* ever present to show that her story is "implausible"? Unless his evidence tends to show this, it would not even seem to be admissible. As the test for probable cause is "plausibility", then only evidence that *attacks* "plausibility" is *relevant* to the preliminary hearing. Will the defendant's own testimony denying that he raped Ms. Gonzales attack the "plausibility" of her story? How about records showing that he was *in jail* at the time of the alleged rape?

2. How will this "plausibility" test affect the defendant's ability to use the preliminary hearing for *discovery*? On cross-examination, may Romero's attorney ask Ms. Gonzales if she *consented* to having sex with Romero? May he subpoena the police officer who interviewed Ms. Gonzales and ask him what she told him? Would such testimony affect the "plausibility" of her story?

3. As noted at the beginning of this chapter, there is a great deal of tension between the *ostensible* purpose of the preliminary hearing (to determine probable cause) and its usual *"real"* purpose for the defense (as a discovery device). A good example of this tension appears in California, which does not require a grand jury indictment, but permits it as an alternative to the information. Prosecutors would sometimes use the grand jury as a way to avoid the preliminary hearing. But in *Hawkins v. Superior Court*, 22 Cal.3d 584 (1978), the California Supreme Court held that it was a denial of equal protection (under California's state constitution) to

deny a preliminary hearing to a defendant just because he had been indicted by a grand jury. Even though the indictment made it no longer necessary to use the preliminary hearing to determine *probable cause*, the *discovery* opportunities for defense counsel at the preliminary hearing were held to be so important that they amounted to "fundamental rights", which could not be denied without a compelling state interest, which the prosecution failed to show. After *Hawkins*, prosecutors took their case to the people, and the California electorate made some changes, which are discussed in the next case, *Whitman*.

WHITMAN v. SUPERIOR COURT
California Supreme Court
54 Cal.3d 1063 (1991)

LUCAS, CHIEF JUSTICE.

In this case, we resolve some issues presented by the adoption in June 1990 of an initiative measure designated on the ballot as Proposition 115 and entitled the "Crime Victims Justice Reform Act." Petitioner herein raises various challenges under the federal and state Constitutions to the provisions of the measure that authorize the admission of hearsay evidence at preliminary hearings in criminal cases. He also contests the sufficiency and competency of the evidence presented at his preliminary hearing.

As will appear, we conclude that, properly construed and applied, the hearsay provisions of Proposition 115 are constitutionally valid. We also conclude, however, that the evidence admitted at petitioner's preliminary hearing, consisting entirely of hearsay testimony by a noninvestigating officer lacking any personal knowledge of the case, was insufficient and incompetent to constitute probable cause to bind petitioner over for trial, and that his motion to dismiss the charges should have been granted.

Facts

Petitioner was charged with one felony count of driving under the influence of alcohol and/or drugs with three or more prior similar convictions (Veh.Code § 23152), one felony count of driving with a blood-alcohol level of.08 percent or more (§ 23152), as well as misdemeanor counts of driving with a suspended of revoked license (§ 14601.2), and being under the influence of methamphetamine (Health & Saf.Code § 11550). These offenses were alleged to have occurred on August 8, 1990. A preliminary hearing was held on September 19, 1990, leading to the filing of an information containing these charges.

At the hearing, the People called only a single witness, Officer Bruce Alexander, who was not one of the arresting or investigating officers and who had no direct, personal knowledge of petitioner's alleged offenses. Over petitioner's continuing objection to the use of hearsay evidence, Alexander attested to his eight years of employment as a police officer, and thereupon recounted to the magistrate various entries made in the report of the investigating officer, Officer Navin. Alexander confirmed that he had never discussed Navin's report with that officer, was not personally acquainted with Navin, and first became aware of Navin's report, and of the case against petitioner, on the morning of the preliminary hearing after the district attorney handed him a copy of Navin's report.

In response to the prosecutor's questioning, Alexander indicated that, according to Navin's report, on August 8, while in a marked patrol car, Navin saw a 1969 Chevrolet traveling eastbound on Cherry Avenue. Navin heard someone shout and saw the driver of the Chevrolet lean out the window to raise his right fist. Navin watched as a white Ford quickly passed the Chevrolet. Navin paced the Chevrolet, which was traveling 50 miles per hour in a 40 miles per hour zone. Navin thereupon made a traffic stop.

Alexander further testified that, according to Navin's report, the driver of the car identified himself as Thomas Paul Whitman. Among other things, Navin noticed the strong odor of alcohol, bloodshot eyes, and dilated pupils. The driver's mood changed from passive to belligerent, leading Navin to believe that the driver might be under the influence of drugs. Alexander continued his "testimony," relating, according to Navin, that the driver successfully completed the finder-dexterity test and balanced on one foot, but swayed when asked to walk a straight line. Believing the driver was under the influence, Navin transported him to the station where a blood test was administered. Counsel stipulated that a blood test revealed a blood-alcohol level of 0.08 percent and was positive for the presence of methamphetamine.

Thereupon, Alexander was permitted to state his opinion, based solely on the information revealed in Navin's report, that petitioner had been under the influence of alcohol and "perhaps some type of stimulant."

Defense counsel moved to strike all of Alexander's direct testimony for lack of proper foundation regarding Navin's qualifications as a police officer. The magistrate denied the motion, after permitting Alexander to opine that because Navin's badge number was considerably lower than his, Navin probably had 12 years' experience as a police officer.

On cross-examination, Alexander admitted he did not know the time or circumstances of the preparation of Navin's report, or the various tests conducted to determine petitioner's sobriety. Additionally, Alexander was unable to explain certain discrepancies and omissions in the report. Counsel elicited the fact that although Navin's report indicated petitioner's eyes were brown, in fact they are green.

Despite petitioner's objections and his argument that Alexander could not personally identify him as the suspect stopped by Navin, the magistrate held petitioner to answer on the counts charged. The magistrate noted that the description of petitioner contained in Navin's report closely matched the description in the records of the Department of Motor Vehicles, which was also placed in evidence.

Thereafter, petitioner moved the superior court to dismiss the information (Pen.Code § 995), on the ground that the evidence elicited at the preliminary hearing was incompetent and insufficient to establish probable cause. The motion was denied, and the Court of Appeal summarily denied petitioner's application for mandate. We issued an alternative writ of mandate to consider the important constitutional and interpretive questions presented.

Petitioner raises a variety of arguments regarding the admissibility, and constitutional propriety, of Officer Alexander's hearsay testimony. Before we consider these contentions, we first review the new constitutional and statutory hearsay provisions added by Proposition 115.

Constitutional & Statutory Provisions

Proposition 115 added both constitutional and statutory language pertinent to our present inquiry. Section 30, subdivision (b), is added to article I of the state Constitution, declaring hearsay evidence admissible at preliminary hearings in criminal cases, as may be provided by law. ("In order to protect victims and witnesses in criminal cases, hearsay evidence shall be admissible at preliminary hearings, as prescribed by the Legislature or by the people through the initiative process.")

In addition, the measure amends § 872, subdivision (b), of the Penal Code to provide that a probable cause determination at a preliminary hearing may be based on hearsay statements related by a police officer with certain qualifications and experience. ("Notwithstanding § 1200 of the Evidence Code [the hearsay rule], the finding of probable cause may be based in whole or in part upon the sworn testimony of a law enforcement officer relating the statements of declarants made out of court offered for the truth of the matter asserted. Any law enforcement officer testifying as to hearsay statements shall either have five years of law enforcement experience or have completed a training course certified by the Commission on Peace Officer Standards and Training which includes training in the investigation and reporting of cases and testifying at preliminary hearings.")

Additionally, § 1203.1 is added to the Evidence Code to provide a preliminary hearing exception to the general requirement that all hearsay declarants be made available for cross-examination. ("§ 1203 is not applicable if the hearsay statement is offered at a preliminary examination, as provided in § 872 of the Penal Code.")

Further, Penal Code § 866, subdivision (a), is amended to give the magistrate discretion to limit the defendant's right to call witnesses on the defendant's behalf. ("The magistrate shall not permit the testimony of any defense witness unless the offer of proof discloses to the satisfaction of the magistrate, in his or her discretion, that the testimony of that witness, if believed, would be reasonably likely to establish an affirmative defense, negate an element of a crime charged, or impeach the testimony of a prosecution witness or the statement of a declarant testified to by a prosecution witness.")

Finally, Penal code § 866 (b), explains that "It is the purpose of a preliminary examination to establish whether there exists probable cause to believe that the defendant has committed a felony. The examination shall not be used for purposes of discovery." * * * *

Discussion

As previously indicated, in addition to contesting the sufficiency of the evidence elicited at the preliminary hearing, petitioner raises various constitutional challenges to the foregoing provisions of Proposition 115. He argues that the use of hearsay testimony without confrontation or cross-examination of the declarants violates his federal Sixth Amendment right to confrontation, his Fourteenth Amendment right to due process of law, and the separation of powers doctrine of article III of the state Constitution. * * * *

Before discussing the merits of petitioner's various remaining constitutional challenges, we first turn to his alternative argument to the effect that, as an interpretive matter, the hearsay provisions of Proposition 115 did not contemplate, and do not permit, reliance on hearsay of the kind involved in this case. Thereafter, we address petitioner's constitutional arguments.

1. Testimony of Noninvestigating Officers or "Readers"

* * * *

Petitioner's primary argument is that, as a matter of sound statutory interpretation, Office Alexander should not have been permitted to relate the contents of Officer Navin's investigative report because Alexander was not involved in the investigation of the case and had no personal knowledge of the circumstances under which Navin's report was prepared. We agree. Properly construed, Proposition 115 does not authorize a finding of probable cause based on the testimony of a non-investigating officer or "reader" merely reciting the police report of an investigating officer. We believe the probable intent of the framers of the measure was to allow a properly qualified investigating officer to relate out-of-court statements by crime victims or witnesses, including other law enforcement personnel, without requiring the victims' or witnesses' presence in court. The testifying officer, however, must not be a mere reader but must have sufficient knowledge of the crime or the circumstances under which the out-of-court statement was made so as to meaningfully assist the magistrate in assessing the reliability of the statement.

New Penal Code § 872(b), by its terms refers to "testimony of a law enforcement officer relating the *statements of declarants* made out of court." (Italics added.) A "declarant" is defined by Evidence Code § 135 as "a person who makes a statement." As the Legislative Analyst described it to the voters, the intent underlying this provision was to allow introduction of "out-of-court statements" at preliminary hearings if those statements are "introduced through the testimony of certain trained and experienced law enforcement officers." (Ballot Pamp., Proposed Stats. and Amends. to Cal. Const. with arguments to voters, Primary Elec. (June 5, 1990) p. 33.) As the People observe, the section and its use of the term "declarants" is not limited to the statements of civilian or citizen witnesses but would include the statements or reports of any persons, including other law enforcement officers such as Officer Navin herein.

But other provisions of the measure convince us that the use of mere "readers" such as Officer Alexander was not contemplated by the measure. To permit testimony by noninvestigating officers that merely recites the contents of the reports of the investigating officers would render largely meaningless or nugatory the new statutory provision, also added by Proposition 115, that require that the testifying officer have at least five years of law enforcement experience or have completed a training course covering the "investigating and reporting" of criminal cases. Pen.Code § 872(b). This provision undoubtedly was intended to enhance the reliability of hearsay testimony at preliminary hearings. Yet such reliability is not furthered if the only testimonial function of the "qualified" noninvestigating officer such as Officer Alexander is to parrot information contained in a report prepared by another officer who may lack such extensive experience or training.

As petitioner observes, the experience and training requirements of Penal Code § 872 (b) could be readily circumvented if prosecutors were permitted routinely to designate the same "qualified" officer as a "reader" of the reports of other officers, regardless of their own qualifications, or lack thereof. The alternate requirement of training in "investigating and reporting" crimes strongly supports petitioner's position that Proposition 115's hearsay provisions were intended to foreclose the testimony of a noninvestigating officer lacking personal knowledge of either the crime of the circumstances under which the out-of-court statements were made.

Thus, in permitting only officers with lengthy experience or special training to testify regarding out-of-court statements, Penal Code § 872(b), plainly contemplates that the testifying officer will be capable of using his or her experience and expertise to assess the circumstances under which the statement is made and to accurately describe those circumstances to the magistrate so as to increase the reliability of the underlying evidence.

Moreover, to allow testimony by noninvestigating officers or readers would seemingly sanction a form of double or multiple hearsay beyond the contemplation of the framers of, and voters for, Proposition 115. Although such multiple hearsay was not present in this case, we doubt that Proposition 115 was intended to sanction a procedure whereby a noninvestigating officer, lacking any personal knowledge of the matter, nonetheless would be permitted to relate not only what the investigating officer told him but also what the other witnesses told the investigating officer. It is noteworthy that although Proposition 115 created an exception to the basic hearsay rule contained in Evidence Code § 1200 (see new Pen.Code § 872(b)), the measure did not purport to create a similar exception for the multiple hearsay rule of Evidence Code § 1201.

In addition, an interpretation of Proposition 115 that would allow "reader" or multiple hearsay testimony would raise constitutional questions that we can and should avoid by limiting admissible hearsay testimony to testimony by qualified investigative officers. As discussed below, we believe that the latter, more limited, form of hearsay evidence satisfies federal requirements of reliability, and thus properly may be admitted at preliminary hearings despite the defendant's inability to confront and cross-examine the declarant witness or victim. But substantial additional objections to the reliability of the evidence might arise if multiple hearsay were involved, and the defendant were also deprived of the opportunity to meaningfully cross-examine the testifying officer regarding the circumstances under which the out-of-court statement was made.

In the present case, for example, on cross-examination, Officer Alexander was unable to answer potentially significant questions regarding the methods and circumstances of Officer Navin's investigation, including the time the report was written, the details of the sobriety test given the petitioner, and petitioner's pupil reaction and degree of dilation. Indeed, Alexander was even uncertain how long Navin had been employed on the force or even whether Navin was a male or female officer. Similar uncertainties are inherent in any procedure in which the testifying officer acts as no more than a "reader" of another officer's investigative report. * * * *

Thus, we conclude that the magistrate erred in allowing Officer Alexander to read or relate portions of Officer Navin's report, and that such error requires dismissal of the information. It appears, however, that the People will be entitled to refile the information (see Pen.Code § 1387), and a new preliminary hearing may be held. Accordingly, for purposes of guiding the lower courts during any such further proceedings, we will consider petitioner's alternative contentions.

2. Constitutional Right to Confrontation

In the foregoing discussion, we construe Proposition 115 to allow an investigating officer to relate at the preliminary hearing any relevant statements of victims or witnesses, if the testifying officer has sufficient knowledge of the crime or the circumstances under which the out-of-court statement was made so as to meaningfully assist the magistrate in assessing the reliability of the statement. The new measure would permit the magistrate to base a finding of probable cause entirely on that testimony. Pen.Code § 872(b). Petitioner asserts that such a procedure would violate his state and federal constitutional rights to confront his accusers. We disagree. * * * *

The Sixth Amendment to the federal Constitution recites in pertinent part that "In all criminal prosecutions, the accused shall enjoy the right . . . to be confronted with the witnesses against him. . . ."

The foregoing confrontation clause is not an absolute bar to all hearsay evidence or other procedures which may limit or preclude a direct face-to-face confrontation between accused and accuser. Thus far, at least, the clause has operated to exclude admission at trial of some otherwise admissible hearsay evidence, although many exceptions exist to that bar. See *Idaho v. Craig* (1990) 110 S.Ct. 3139 [admissibility at trial of hearsay statements by child victims of sexual abuse]; *Ohio v. Roberts*, 448 U.S. at pp. 63–65 [admissibility of testimony and unavailability of declarant are shown]; *Bourjaily v. United States* (1987) 483 U.S. 171, 182–184 [requirement of reliability of testimony satisfied by "firmly rooted" coconspirator exception to hearsay rule]; *United States v. Inadi* (1986) 475 U.S. 387, 394–400 [requirement of unavailability of declarant inapplicable to statements made by nontestifying coconspirator].

Petitioner, focusing on the foregoing "reliability" element for evaluating hearsay evidence, contends that new Penal Code § 872(b) "has no provision for guaranteeing the reliability of the hearsay." As we construe the section, however, it does not permit hearsay testimony by a noninvestigating officer lacking any personal knowledge of the circumstances under which the out-of-court statement, declaration or report was made. Additionally, the experience and training requirements of the section help assure that the hearsay testimony of the investigating officer will indeed be as reliable as appropriate in light of the limited purpose of the preliminary hearing, as discussed in greater detail below. Although the underlying reliability of the victim or witness may remain untested until trial, we think the evaluation and cross-examination of the testimony of the qualified investigating officer provides sufficient basis for a pretrial probable cause determination.

Finally, under new Penal Code § 866(a), the magistrate has authority to permit the defendant to call any witness whose proposed testimony would be reasonably likely to establish an affirmative defense, negate a crime element, or impeach prosecution evidence. Based on the foregoing safeguards or limitations, the new provisions appear to satisfy petitioner's reliability objections.

Moreover, aside from questions of reliability, it is doubtful that the federal confrontation clause operates to bar hearsay evidence offered at a preliminary hearing held to determine whether probable cause exists to hold the defendant for trial. * * * *

First, as petitioner acknowledges, other than the probable cause hearing held to justify continued detention of the accused (discussed below), there exists no federal constitutional right to a preliminary hearing to determine whether a case should proceed to trial. Instead, in the federal system, most felonies and capital offenses are prosecuted by indictment. Moreover, it is well established that hearsay is admissible in indictment proceedings before federal grand juries. *Costello v. United States* (1956) 350 U.S. 359, 363–364.

Indeed, the United States Supreme Court has repeatedly stated that "The right to confront is basically a trial right." *Barber v. Page* (1968) 390 U.S. 719, 725. As *Barber* explained (in the context of contrasting the utility of confrontation at a preliminary hearing), the confrontation right "includes both the opportunity to cross-examine and the occasion for the jury to weigh the demeanor of the witness. A preliminary hearing is ordinarily a much less searching exploration into the merits of a case than a trial, simply because its function is the more limited one of determining whether probable cause exists to hold the accused for trial." 390 U.S. at p. 725.

A few years later, the high court squarely held that the federal confrontation clause does not require that full adversarial safeguards, such as presentation of witnesses and cross-examination of their testimony, be made available for every pretrial probable cause hearing. *Gerstein v. Pugh* (1975) 420 U.S. 103, 119–124. *Gerstein* explained that, for purposes of Fourth Amendment analysis in determining whether probable cause exists to detain an arrestee for a significant time pending trial, a full adversarial hearing, together with confrontation and cross-examination of witnesses, need not be afforded so long as a "timely judicial determination" of probable cause is made as a prerequisite to continued detention.

The court in *Gerstein* contrasted Fourth Amendment detention hearings with the more formal preliminary hearings used in many states to determine whether the evidence justifies going to trial. The court observed that "adversarial procedures are customarily employed" during such formal hearings, but it avoided suggesting that such procedures are constitutionally mandated. Instead, *Gerstein* simply noted "that state systems of criminal procedure vary widely," encouraged such "experimentation," and concluded that "There is no single preferred pretrial procedure, and the nature of the probable cause determination usually will be shaped to accord with a State's pretrial procedure viewed as a whole."

Significantly, *Gerstein* observed that, by their very nature, probable cause determination do not involve "the fine resolution of conflicting evidence that a reasonable-doubt or even a preponderance standard demands, and credibility determinations are seldom crucial in deciding whether the evidence supports a reasonable belief in guilt. This is not to say that confrontation and cross-examination might not enhance the reliability of probable cause determinations in some cases. In most cases, however, their value would be too slight to justify holding, as a matter of constitutional principle, that these formalities and safeguards designed for trial must also be employed in making the Fourth Amendment determination of probable cause." 420 U.S. at 121–122.

The *Gerstein* court acknowledged that a prior decision (*Coleman v. Alabama* (1970) 399 U.S. 1) had held an Alabama preliminary hearing was a "critical stage" of the prosecution for which the presence of counsel was required. But the court noted that under the Alabama law involved in *Coleman*, not only was the purpose of the hearing to determine probable cause to charge an offense, but the suspect was specifically allowed to confront and cross-examine prosecution witnesses at such hearings, thus making it essential that the defendant have counsel's assistance. The *Gerstein* court continued by stating that "This consideration [need for counsel's assistance] does not apply when the prosecution is not required to produce witnesses for cross-examination." 420 U.S. at 23. *Gerstein's* implication seems to be that state limitations on the purpose and scope of the preliminary hearing may reduce the necessity for adversarial procedural safeguards such as right to counsel.

Assuming, based on the foregoing language in *Gerstein* and *Coleman* that the confines of the federal confrontation clause may vary depending on the purpose and scope of the hearing provided by state law, it seems reasonable to conclude that the federal clause is not violated by allowing hearsay testimony at post-Proposition 115 preliminary hearings in this state. Under that measure, the very purpose of the hearing has been considerably narrowed: "It is the purpose of a preliminary examination to establish whether there exists probable cause to believe that the defendant has committed a felony. *The examination shall not be used for purposes of discovery.*" Pen.Code § 866 (b), italics added.)

The foregoing statutory pronouncement marks a sharp contrast to this court's previous expansive concept of the preliminary hearing as a discovery and trial preparation device, allowing counsel the opportunity to "fashion" their impeachment tools for use in cross-examination at trial, to preserve testimony favorable to the defense, and to provide the defense "with valuable information about the case against the accused, enhancing its ability to evaluate the desirability of entering a plea or to prepare for trial." *Hawkins v. Superior Court* (1978) 22 Cal.3d 584, 588. Significantly, the utility of the preliminary hearing as a discovery tool has been cited in support of the minority position that the use of hearsay at such hearings violates the defendant's confrontation rights. See, e.g., *State v. Anderson* (Utah 1980) 612 P.2d 778, 784–786 [relying on confrontation clause of Utah Const.].

As Justice Puglia explained in his concurring opinion in *Herbert v. Superior Court*, 117 Cal.App.3d at 671–672, "The constitutional right of confrontation is 'basically a trial right' Although the federal Constitution requires a probable cause hearing to justify significant pretrial detention of defendant, that hearing need not include traditional adversary safeguards such as the right of confrontation. Moreover, the federal Constitution does not require a judicial hearing at all as a prerequisite to prosecution by information. A fortiori, when state procedure nevertheless provides for such a hearing, it would logically follow that the federal Constitution does not require the full panoply of procedural rights available at trial to be observed in the preliminary hearing."

We agree with Justice Puglia's analysis. We note that, under the express language of rule 5.1, subdivision (a), of the Federal Rules of Criminal Procedure, a magistrate at a federal preliminary examination may base his or her finding of probable cause in whole, or in part, on hearsay evidence. See Wright, *Federal Practice and Procedure* (2d ed.1982) Criminal, § 85. We think it would be anomalous to hold that the admission of such evidence at a comparable state proceeding violates federal confrontation clause principles. The wide majority of sister state courts agree. As stated in one of the cases representing the majority rule, "to impose the same rules of evidence at the preliminary hearing as at the trial stage would amount to the granting of a second trial and this would be judicial waste and delay. A preliminary hearing is not designed to be a dress rehearsal for the trial." *Wilson v. State* (Wyo.1982) 655 P.2d 1246, 1251.

We conclude that the new, limited form of preliminary hearing in this state sufficiently resembles the Fourth Amendment probable cause hearing examined in *Gerstein* to meet federal confrontation clause standards despite reliance on hearsay evidence. * * * *

Conclusion

Because the magistrate's finding of probable cause in this case was based on the improper and unauthorized use of "reader" testimony, we conclude that the superior court erred in denying petitioner's motion to set aside the information under Penal Code § 995. Accordingly, the order of the Court of Appeal denying such relief is reversed and the Court of Appeal is directed to issue a peremptory writ of mandate compelling the superior court to vacate its prior order and to enter a new order granting defendant's motion to set aside the information.

KENNARD, JUSTICE, concurring & dissenting.

* * * *

By permitting hearsay testimony in these circumstances, the majority fails to take into account Proposition 115's express purpose in permitting hearsay testimony at preliminary hearings, as described in article I, § 30(b).

Article I, § 30(b) explains that Proposition 115 permits hearsay at the preliminary hearing "to protect victims and witnesses in criminal cases." Although the provision does not explain what victims and witnesses are to be protected from, several possibilities come immediately to mind. Testifying causes victims and witnesses to relive an often stressful and traumatic experience, it disrupts their daily routines, and it provides an opportunity for harassment or retaliation by the defendant or friends of the defendant. If the recollections of victims and witnesses can be presented through the hearsay testimony of an officer, these hazards and inconveniences are avoided.

The objective of article I, § 30(b), can be achieved by applying its protections to victims and witnesses other than police officers. Compared to private citizens who are victims of or witnesses to a crime, officers testifying at a preliminary hearing are significantly less likely to be harassed or intimidated by criminal defendants, and less likely to be reliving an unusually stressful or traumatic experience. And although officers may have their daily routines disrupted by court appearances, such appearances are within the scope of their duties. An officer's job is not finished when a suspect is arrested; rather, it continues through conviction and punishment. Like prosecutors and judges, officers are an integral part of the criminal justice system. Attendance at court is an occupational hazard of a career in law enforcement.

In sum, protection of private citizens rather than police officer witnesses appears to have been the fundamental concern underlying the phrase "to protect victims and witnesses in criminal cases." as expressed in article I, § 30(b). Accordingly, § 872(b), which implements article I, § 30(b), should be construed as establishing a new general hearsay exception for the out-of-court statements of private citizens only, not those of police officers. Not only would this construction implement the purposes of Proposition 115, it would also create a clear, workable standard that would meaningfully assist magistrates and attorneys.

The majority opinion makes no attempt to explain how its interpretation of § 872(b) is consistent with the purpose of "protecting victims and witnesses" set forth in article I, § 30(b). It merely makes a broad and unsupported assertion that qualified officers may "relate out-of-court statements by crime victims or witnesses, including other law enforcement personnel." For the reasons I have expressed above, this assertion is inconsistent with the intent of Proposition 115.

Not only is the majority's holding unfaithful to the intent of Proposition 115, it is also likely to mire the criminal justice system in confusion.

The majority holds that an officer can testify based on another officer's report if the testifying officer's "knowledge of the crime or the circumstances" is sufficient to "meaningfully assist the magistrate" in determining reliability. This vague test contains no guidance whatsoever for magistrates and litigators, leaving them adrift on the flood of litigation likely to ensue from efforts to grasp the meaning of the majority's ill defined terminology regarding the testifying officer's "knowledge of the crime or the circumstances" and ability to "meaningfully assist the magistrate."

Can officers "meaningfully assist the magistrate" if they observed the preparation of the police report, but have no independent knowledge of the circumstances of the offense? Is the majority's "meaningful assistance" requirement met if, before testifying at the preliminary hearing, the testifying officer spoke to the officer who prepared the report and was assured of the reliability of the report, but the two officers did not discuss the contents of the report? What if the testifying officer's "knowledge of the crime" was gained from reading a number of police reports that had been prepared by various officers — can that officer then testify as to the contents of each of the reports he or she had read? And if, after the magistrate ruled the testimony to be inadmissible, the testifying officer telephones the officer who prepared the report and discusses its contents for five or ten minutes, can the testifying officer then resume the witness stand and read from the other officers' report?

Because the majority's vague and confusing test will not answer these questions, different magistrates presented with similar facts will make inconsistent rulings. To resolve the inconsistencies and uncertainties, the parties will be required to resort to the time-consuming pursuit of appellate remedies. Eventually the Courts of Appeal will provide content to the majority's empty formulation. In the meantime, however, the majority's failure to create a workable "bright line" rule for hearsay evidence at preliminary hearings will serve to obstruct, rather than to streamline, the criminal justice system, thereby frustrating the people's expressed purpose to create "a system in which justice is swift and fair" (Prop. 115, § 1(c)).

PEOPLE v. WIMBERLY
California Court of Appeal
5 Cal.App.4th 439 (1992)

WOODS, ASSOCIATE JUSTICE.

Dispositive of this appeal are two related Proposition 115 preliminary hearing issues: (1) was the officer who testified to hearsay statements qualified to do so and (2) were those multiple hearsay statements admissible pursuant to Penal Code § 872, subdivision (b)? We conclude that under *Whitman v. Superior Court* (1991) 54 Cal.3d 1063, the officer was § 872(b) qualified but the multiple hearsay statements he testified to were inadmissible. Accordingly, we affirm the order setting aside the information.

The district attorney charged respondent with committing a July 9, 1990, residential burglary and a contemporaneous grand theft. At the October 5, 1990, preliminary hearing the district attorney called a single witness, Detective Osman, a 12-year City of Monterey Park police officer.

Over objection, Detective Osman testified that the day after the burglary he did "a follow-up investigation," namely, he talked to the victim, read the crime report, and talked to its author, Officer Yahn. Detective Osman further testified to the victim's statements, his testimony apparently based upon his conversation with the victim rather than upon Officer Yahn's report. This part of Detective Osman's testimony established the corpus of both charged offenses but did not link respondent to either crime. To establish that link the district attorney elicited from Detective Osman the statements of a Mr. Schiro, someone Detective Osman had not spoken to. Mr. Schiro was the manager of the apartment complex in which the victim lived. Mr. Schiro had spoken to Officer Yahn and Officer Yahn included Mr. Schiro's statements in his crime report.

Detective Osman testified that "according to Officer Yahn, Mr. Schiro stated," in substance, that on the day of the burglary respondent asked to be let into the victim's apartment and that he, Mr. Schiro, unlocked the door for respondent because respondent was the victim's brother.

The magistrate held respondent to answer on both counts. In superior court, respondent's § 995 motion to set aside the information was granted. If the magistrate erred in permitting Detective Osman to testify to either the statements of the victim or the statements of Mr. Schiro, then the order setting aside the information was correct and must be affirmed.

The magistrate relied upon § 872(b), enacted as part of Proposition 115. This section provides: "Notwithstanding § 1200 of the Evidence Code [the hearsay rule], the finding of probable cause may be based in whole or in part upon the sworn testimony of a law enforcement officer relating the statements of declarants made out of court offered for the truth of the matter asserted. Any law enforcement officer testifying as to hearsay statements shall either have five years of law enforcement experience or have completed a training course certified by the Commission on Peace Officer Standards & Training which include training in the investigation and reporting of cases and testifying at preliminary hearings."

By its terms, this statute creates a special hearsay exception applicable only at preliminary hearings. To determine whether or not hearsay statements were properly admitted under § 872(b), two questions must be addressed: first, was the testifying officer qualified; second, if qualified, were the hearsay statements admissible?

1. Was Detective Osman qualified?

Because Detective Osman had been a City of Monterey Park police officer for 12 years, he satisfied the threshold requirement of § 872(b): "Any law enforcement officer testifying as to hearsay statements shall . . . have five years of law enforcement experience. . . ." As *Whitman* makes clear, five years law enforcement experience is a necessary but insufficient qualification. Officer Alexander, the testifying officer in *Whitman*, had eight years experience but was unqualified. But *Whitman* makes less clear just what, in addition to five years experience, constitutes § 872(b) officer qualification.

Officer Alexander illustrates what constitutes non-qualification. "Proposition 115 does not authorize a finding of probable cause based on the testimony of a noninvestigating officer or 'reader' merely reciting the police report of an investigating officer." *Whitman*, supra, 54 Cal.3d 1063, 1072. Officer Alexander was unqualified, *Whitman* states, because he was merely a "reader," an officer who had no involvement with the case before the preliminary hearing and whose information came only from the report he "read." Officer Alexander, in *Whitman* terminology, was a "noninvestigating officer."

Whitman further states: "We believe the probable intent of the framers of the measure was to allow a properly qualified investigating officer to relate out-of-court statements by crime victims or witnesses, including other law enforcement personnel, without requiring the victims' or witnesses' presence in court. The testifying officer, however, must not be a mere reader but must have sufficient knowledge of the crime or the circumstances under which the out-of-court statement was made so as to meaningfully assist the magistrate in assessing the reliability of the statement." *Id.* at pp. 1072–1073.

Thus, to be qualified, the testifying officer must be an investigating officer, "a properly qualified investigating officer."

But what is an "investigating officer"? *Whitman* does not define the term and we are unaware of any accepted, useful definition. Certainly, to merely say it is an officer who investigates is circular and unhelpful. In practice, the term, has almost as many meanings as there are law enforcement agencies which use it.

An investigating officer may be a Colombo-like homicide detective who studies the crime scene, personally and repeatedly interrogates witnesses and possible witnesses, conduct line-ups, questions suspects, requests and coordinates scientific studies, and gathers sufficient admissible evidence for a prosecution. But an investigating officer may also be little more than a bureaucratic paper shuffler, a veteran officer who collects police reports — crime report, arrest report, evidence report, perhaps a follow-up report — determines if they are sufficient for prosecution, and if so, presents them to the prosecutor.

Although not defining "investigating officer" *Whitman* does provide an example of one. The officer who saw the crime being committed (driving under the influence of alcohol and/or drugs) and arrested its perpetrator is characterized as "an investigating officer." *Id.* at 1072. *Whitman* further suggests that one may be an investigating officer by having "sufficient knowledge of the crime or the circumstances under which the out-of-court statement was made so as to meaningfully assist the magistrate in assessing the reliability of the statement. *Id.* at pp. 1072–1073.

We conclude that Detective Osman satisfied the *Whitman* requirements. He was not a mere "reader." In a relatively simple burglary case he personally interviewed the victim, the officer who took the crime report (Officer Yahn), and the defendant's parole officer. We hold that Officer Osman was a "properly qualified investigating officer."

2. Was Detective Osman's testimony relating the victim's statements properly admitted?

Detective Osman testified that he had personally talked to the victim the day after the burglary. The victim, Detective Osman testified, stated that on July 9, 1990, he left his locked residence at 6 a.m. and upon returning at 4:15 p.m. discovered about $3,000 worth of jewelry missing. He had not given permission to anyone to enter his house or take his property.

We are satisfied that these victim-hearsay-statements were properly admitted by the magistrate. Detective Osman, having personally interviewed the victim, had "sufficient knowledge of . . . the circumstances under which the . . . statement[s] [were] made so as to meaningfully assist the magistrate in assessing the reliability of the statements." *Id.* at pp. 1072–1073.

In fact, as is common with burglary victims, the magistrate required little if any assistance to assess the reliability of the victim-statements. Defense counsel, who cross-examined Detective Osman on other aspects of his testimony, asked no questions about the victim-statements.

3. Was Detective Osman's testimony relating Mr. Schiro's statements properly admitted?

Detective Osman testified to what Officer Yahn stated (in his report) that Mr. Schiro stated. Unlike his victim-statement testimony, this testimony was double hearsay. Detective Osman, not having spoken to Mr. Schiro, was not "capable of using his . . . experience and expertise to assess the circumstances under which the statement[s] [were] made and to accurately describe those circumstances to the magistrate so as to increase the reliability of the underlying evidence." *Id.* at p. 1074.

Although *Whitman* stops just short of flatly prohibiting § 872(b) double hearsay, we believe such prohibition is unavoidable. Double hearsay, like "reader" testimony, has "inherent" uncertainties. *Id.* at 1074–1075. The testifying officer, who has not interviewed the declarant, will inevitably be "unable to answer potentially significant questions regarding the . . . circumstances" (id. at 1074) under which the statement was made. For example, Detective Osman would have been unable to answer questions concerning Mr. Schiro's demeanor, certainty, apparent intelligence, possible bias, suggestibility, etc. Yet these "potentially significant" matters are the very ones which require the special witness qualifications specified in § 872(b) and elaborated by *Whitman*.

Moreover, a rule which would prohibit an officer who heard statements from testifying to them, such as one-year Officer Yahn, but permit an officer who did not hear them, to testify to them, such as Detective Osman, is, at best, constitutionally suspect.

* * * * *Whitman*, 54 Cal.3d at 1074.

We hold that because Detective Osman's testimony relating Mr. Schiro's statements was double hearsay, it was inadmissible. Since it was only that testimony which linked the defendant to the crimes, the error was prejudicial. The order setting aside the information is affirmed.

Notes from Augusta:

1. As noted in *Wimberly*, California's "Crime Victims Justice Reform Act" also added § 866, subdivision (a) to the California Penal Code, which provides:

> When the examination of witnesses on the part of the People is closed, any witness the defendant may produce shall be sworn and examined. Upon the request of the prosecuting attorney, the magistrate shall require an offer of proof from the defense as to the testimony expected from the witness. The magistrate shall not permit the testimony of any defense witness unless the offer of proof discloses to the satisfaction of the magistrate, in his or her sound discretion, that the testimony of the witness, if believed, would be reasonably likely to establish an affirmative defense, negate an element of a crime charged, or impeach the testimony of a prosecution witness or the statement of a declarant testified to by a prosecution witness.

What "offer of proof" is sufficient to satisfy the defense burden?

In *People v. Erwin*, 20 Cal.App.4th 1542 (1993), defendant was charged with child molesting, and the only witness at the preliminary hearing was the police detective who interviewed the child. Defense counsel asked to call the child and her mother as defense witnesses, making the following offer of proof:

> Respondent's trial counsel alleges that, if called to the stand, the victim's mother, Judy H., would testify, as follows: "1. She is the mother of the alleged child witness in this case. 2. At the relevant time, she was a present and percipient witness yet saw nothing akin to molestation occurring. 3. She can clarify and better establish both physical and communicative relationships of the participants at the relevant time to each other, rooms, furniture and other appurtenances of the house in question. 4. She can establish the extremely good morale [sic] character of defendant who personally denied to her that he had improperly touched her daughter in any manner whatsoever. 5. She can establish that at the time in question the alleged child witness had a large, recent colored bruise located high in the inner thigh of one leg clearly visible on that day. 6. She can establish that she and the alleged victim engaged in repeated question and answer demonstration sessions regarding the alleged detail of the touching, definitions of terminology used and versions of interaction among participants at the time in question. 7. She can establish that the alleged child victim was extremely tired and had been in a fast and deep sleep for a period of time immediately before the child allegedly made an accusation of molestation. 8. She can testify exactly what was said between her and the child at the time of making an initial alleged accusation. 9. In good faith it is further offered that the child's mother has a better memory of many of

the same day's events occurring before and after the alleged incident. 10. The mother can provide better historic details, facts and circumstances under which the alleged victim in this case had been previously molested in the past for which the child allegedly made highly similar if not identical accusations against another individual. 11. Taking into consideration the child's testimony, the child's mother may substantially impeach the testimony of the child witness in many respects, including but not limited to, statements of original complaint, nature and existence of the bruise, influence and circumstances of prior alleged molestation at the hands of another individual, occurrences at the location in question while the child was asleep and observances of the mother made while the child was asleep, not in the same room or reasonably unable to make the same observations.

The magistrate prohibited this testimony, holding that allow it would circumvent the intent underlying Proposition 115. But the appellate court reversed, holding that there was nothing in the new legislation that prevented defense counsel from calling any witness who might provide relevant evidence.

Suppose, however, that at the conclusion of the officer's testimony, the magistrate had said, "I find that his testimony furnishes probable cause, so it does not matter what these other witnesses might say. Therefore, their testimony is not relevant, and I will not hear it". Would (should) this have changed the result in *Erwin*?

Compare *People v. Eid*, 31 Cal.App.4th 114 (1994). Eid was charged with various sexual offenses on an unconscious victim, Heidi J. At the preliminary hearing, the sole prosecution witness was policewoman Jenkins, who had interviewed Heidi (who allegedly said that she had "passed out" from beer and marijuana and had not consented to sex with Eid), a doctor who had examined Heidi, and Eid and his co-defendants. Eid's counsel sought to call Heidi as a witness for the defense. Although Heidi had refused to speak to defense investigators, Eid's counsel claimed that "it's clear that Heidi consented to what went on here, and we believe that under oath she will tell the truth." The defense "believed Heidi would admit she was not unconscious, that she voluntarily went into the room, that she was making out in the front yard with one or more of the boys in question. If she tells the truth, she will definitely negate the elements of the crime, the entire crime." The magistrate refused to call Heidi. The superior court held that the magistrate had abused his discretion, and dismissed the case, but the court of appeal reversed:

> We note that if Heidi had testified the incident was consensual as the defense asserted she would, an affirmative defense would have been established. * * * * However, the defense failed to make an offer of proof which demonstrated Heidi would have so testified. * * * * The offer of proof was based on nothing more than optimistic expectation Heidi would admit her statements to Jenkins were false. That offer was insufficient to warrant cross-examination of her at the preliminary hearing under § 866, subdivision (a).

2. Consider *Newhouse v. Superior Court*, 42 Cal.App.4th 83 (1996). At the preliminary hearing, Officer Schultz testified for the prosecution that he executed a search warrant on Newhouse's warehouse and then arrested Newhouse and spoke to him. On cross-examination, the defense attorney asked Schultz what Newhouse said to him. Defense counsel made no offer of proof as to how Schultz would answer

the question. The magistrate refused to allow the question. The appellate court upheld the magistrate's ruling.

The court first held that a defendant may introduce hearsay statements at the preliminary hearing, so long as the hearsay comes from the testimony of a police officer who qualifies under Penal Code § 872(b):

> The People argue that our ruling today is inconsistent with the purpose and intent of Proposition 115, which was to restore a balance to a criminal justice system perceived as being too oriented to defendants' rights. Proposition 115 is a many faceted measure, working great changes in the law much more significant and in pursuit of its general purpose than the use of hearsay at preliminary hearings. The *Whitman* court observed that § 872(b) provided only a limited exception to the hearsay rule. All we say is that exception can only fairly be enjoyed by both sides to the adversarial process. We do not say that the defense can call witness after witness in a parade of self-serving hearsay in disregard of § 866. We hold only that if the People can elicit incriminating hearsay from a law enforcement officer, the defense can elicit exculpatory hearsay from a law enforcement officer. What's sauce for the People's goose is sauce for the defendant's gander.

> Any other conclusion would work an unfairness and a lack of balance in the criminal process, which we will not attribute to the voters. Suppose, for example, a defendant is arrested for a possessory crime, and gives a two-sentence statement to the arresting officer. In the first sentence the defendant admits access to and control over the premises, but in the second sentence he denies knowledge or awareness of the contraband because he has just returned from an extended trip out of the state and has not yet entered the premises since his return. Under the People's view, the officer could testify as to the first statement, which helps the People, but not the latter, which helps the defendant. We do not believe the voters who passed Proposition 115 intended to engraft into the law this kind of Kafkaesque compartmentalization of truth. * * * *

> Petitioner, however, is not himself entitled to the advantage of our ruling. Having failed to make an offer of proof before the magistrate, he has failed to properly establish for appellate review that his statements were in fact exculpatory, and to what extent. This court thus cannot determine whether petitioner was denied a substantial right at his preliminary hearing, and we cannot issue a writ.

Newhouse then noted that he was not seeking to call Officer Schultz as a defense witness, but was merely seeking to cross-examine him. The court held, however, that the question asked was not proper cross-examination: "Cross-examination is limited to the scope of the direct examination. Officer Schultz did not testify on direct examination concerning any conversations with petitioner nor any statements petitioner may have made. Petitioner's inquiry to Officer Schultz about his statements was therefore not proper cross-examination, but an attempt to offer affirmative evidence of his own."

3. In *Correa v. Superior Court*, 27 Cal.4th 444 (2002), Officer Bland testified at a preliminary hearing that she interviewed Gil, who spoke only Spanish, which Bland did not understand. A neighbor, Garcia, translated Gil's statements for Bland. Defendant argued that Bland's testimony regarding Garcia's alleged translation of

Gil's statements was "double hearsay" that should not be allowed into evidence at a preliminary hearing. The court disagreed, invoking a "language conduit theory" that is an exception to the hearsay rule.

Chapter 5

THE GRAND JURY

"No person shall be held to answer for a capital, or otherwise infamous crime, unless on a presentment or indictment of a Grand Jury. . . ."

5th Amendment, U.S. Constitution

SOME BACKGROUND

Consider the following descriptions of the grand jury:

1. From *Wood v. Georgia*, 370 U.S. 375 (1962):

> Historically, the grand jury has been regarded as a primary security to the innocent against hasty, malicious and oppressive persecution; it serves the invaluable function in our society of standing between the accuser and the accused, whether the latter be an individual, minority group, or other, to determine whether a charge is founded upon reason or was dictated by an intimidating power or by malice and personal ill will.

2. From *Hawkins v. Superior Court*, 22 Cal.3d 584 (1978):

> Unfortunately, grand jury proceedings today are structured in a manner that renders fulfillment of the ideal unattainable. The prosecuting attorney is typically in complete control of the total process in the grand jury room: he calls the witnesses, interprets the evidence, states and applies the law, and advises the grand jury on whether a crime has been committed. The grand jury is independent only in the sense that it is not formally attached to the prosecutor's office; though legally free to vote as they please, grand jurors virtually always assent to the recommendations of the prosecuting attorney, a fact borne out by available statistical and survey data. Indeed, the fiction of grand jury independence is perhaps best demonstrated by the following fact to which the parties herein have stipulated: between January 1, 1974, and June 30, 1977, 235 cases were presented to the San Francisco grand jury and indictments were returned in all 235.

> The pervasive prosecutorial influence reflected in such statistics has led an impressive array of commentators to endorse the sentiment expressed by United States District Judge William J. Campbell, a former prosecutor:

>> Today, the grand jury is the total captive of the prosecutor who, if he is candid, will concede that he can indict anybody, at any time, for almost anything, before any grand jury.

> Another distinguished federal jurist, Judge Marvin E. Frankel, put it this way:

The contemporary grand jury investigates only those whom the prosecutor asks to be investigated, and by and large indicts those whom the prosecutor wants to be indicted.[1]

Which view of the grand jury is more accurate?

The first view is enshrined in the Fifth Amendment, which requires that a federal felony prosecution be initiated only by a grand jury indictment (unless waived by the defendant). Perhaps implicitly recognizing that the other views have some merit, however, the Supreme Court has never extended that requirement to the states. (In *Hurtado v. California*, 110 U.S. 516 (1884), the Supreme Court held that the Fifth Amendment requirement of a grand jury indictment is not incorporated into the 14th Amendment Due Process clause, so states are free to use or not use grand juries. While most provisions of the Bill of Rights have long since been applied to the states, *Hurtado* has never been overruled.)

In the beginning, most states followed the Fifth Amendment's example and also required grand jury indictments. Over the years, however, most states have dropped the requirement, and permit the prosecutor to proceed by filing an "information" against the defendant. (Many states, however, *allow* the prosecutor to seek a grand jury indictment if he wishes.)

Why has the grand jury fallen by the wayside in most states? One reason is cost: it is cheaper to allow the prosecutor to go directly to court rather than through a group of 18 or so citizens whose expenses must be paid and who must be assembled, sometimes from a large rural area. Another reason is that the two original purposes of the grand jury are not seen as very important today. One purpose was to serve as a check on "over-zealous" and possibly corrupt private and government prosecutors. Today, in most states, prosecutors are elected, and the ballot box is seen as a sufficient check on their actions. And, as the above quotes from *Hawkins* and Tom Wolfe indicate, the modern grand jury is often seen as a tool of the prosecutor rather than as a useful check on his decisions to prosecute. The other main purpose of the grand jury was to investigate possible criminal activities in the community. Today, state law enforcement authorities have much better investigative resources than a group of citizens called to serve as grand jurors.

A few states, however (such as New York), have retained the requirement of a grand jury indictment, and that requirement is still in the 5th Amendment, so every federal felony prosecution must still begin with an indictment (unless waived). So the two original purposes of the grand jury might still be relevant in those jurisdictions.

These two purposes are sometimes called the "shield" function and the "sword" function.

As a "shield", the grand jury is supposed to protect potential defendants from unwarranted prosecutions. As the above quote from Judge Wachtler indicates, however, many people believe that the modern grand jury does not shield anyone very well. The grand jury operates in secret, in order to protect its sources, protect the reputations of people whom witnesses testify about, and prevent the escape of

---

[1] A popular author put it more succinctly:

> Mainly you used the grand jury to indict people, and in the famous phrase of Sol Wachtler, chief judge of the State Court of Appeals, a grand jury would "indict a ham sandwich," if that's what you wanted. [Tom Wolfe, *The Bonfire of the Vanities*, p. 629 (Bantam ed., 1987).]

people it might choose to indict. Therefore, only the prosecutor, a court reporter, and the witness may be in the grand jury room with the grand jurors. No defendant or defense counsel is present, so no cross-examination or presentation of adverse evidence occurs. As the grand jury hears only one side of the case, and that is presented by a professional prosecutor who often uses professional witnesses (such as FBI agents), it is not surprising that the grand jury seldom refuses to return a requested indictment.

As a "sword", the grand jury is supposed to investigate and ferret out crime. A group of lay people, however, can usually add little to the professional investigative forces of the police and prosecutor. But the grand jury does have an investigative tool which the police and prosecutor lack. If a witness to a crime chooses not to speak to law enforcement authorities, the authorities are helpless — they cannot compel anyone to talk. (This is not because of the privilege against self-incrimination. The police simply have not been given the legal authority to compel someone to talk to them.) The grand jury, however, does have this power. The grand jury may issue a *subpoena* to compel a person to come to the grand jury, take an oath, and answer questions posed by the prosecutor. The witness might assert certain evidentiary privileges — such as the 5th Amendment privilege against self-incrimination — but where no privilege applies, the witness must answer. Even if the witness properly asserts the 5th Amendment privilege, the prosecutor may obtain a court order granting the witness *immunity* from use of his answers (and the fruits of any answers) in any subsequent prosecution. With such immunity, the answers will no longer hurt the witness, so he must answer.

The grand jury might also issue a *subpoena duces tecum*, compelling a witness to bring specified documents to the grand jury. To obtain these documents through a search warrant, the police would have to show probable cause. No such showing is needed for a grand jury subpoena.

The cases in this chapter deal with the grand jury both as "shield" and as "sword."

For the average defendant, the most important benefit of the grand jury is neither shield nor sword, but *discovery*. After a prosecution witness testifies on direct examination at a federal trial, the defendant may obtain a copy of the *transcript* of any relevant grand jury testimony of that witness. This testimony will not be as complete as that of a witness at a preliminary hearing, as no cross-examination occurs at the grand jury hearing. Nevertheless, the transcript might be useful to impeach the trial testimony of a witness. Discovery is not, however, one of the legally-recognized purposes of the grand jury hearing. Also, sometimes prosecutors try to use the very liberal rules of evidence at grand jury hearings to diminish the value of the transcript to defense counsel. This chapter also raises this issue.

How does the grand jury compare to the *other* method of determining probable cause: the preliminary hearing? Consider, again, *Hawkins v. Superior Court*, 22 Cal.3d 584 (1978):

> It is undeniable that there is a considerable disparity in the procedural rights afforded defendants charged by the prosecutor by means of an information and defendants charged by the grand jury in an indictment. The defendant accused by information immediately becomes entitled to an impressive array of procedural rights, including a preliminary hearing

before a neutral and legally knowledgeable magistrate, representation by retained or appointed counsel, the confrontation and cross-examination of hostile witnesses, and the opportunity to personally appear and affirmatively present exculpatory evidence.

In vivid contrast, the indictment procedure omits *all* the above safeguards: the defendant has no right to appear or be represented by counsel, and consequently may not confront and cross-examine the witnesses against him, object to evidence introduced by the prosecutor, make legal arguments, or present evidence to explain or contradict the charge. The grand jury is not required to hear evidence for the defendant. If he is called to testify, the defendant has no right to the presence of counsel, even though, because of the absolute secrecy surrounding grand jury proceedings, he may be completely unaware of the subject of inquiry or his position as a target witness.

This remarkable lack of even the most basic rights is compounded by the absence from the grand jury room of a neutral and detached magistrate, trained in the law, to rule on the admissibility of evidence and insure that the grand jury exercises its indicting function with proper regard for the independence and objectivity so necessary if it is to fulfill its purported role of protecting innocent citizens from unfounded accusations, even as it proceeds against those who it has probable cause to believe have committed offenses.

Problem 5

To: My law clerk

From: Millie Meter, Esq.

My client, Carmela Corleone, has been indicted for conspiracy to sell cocaine.

The FBI has been investigating Ms. Corleone for some time. They call her "The Godmother," and they suspect her of being the "queenpin" of a large criminal organization involved in narcotics, prostitution, gambling, and extortion. FBI agents tried to interview many people, but most refused to speak to them. They went to Assistant U.S. Attorney Peter Peck, who suggested asking the federal grand jury to investigate the case. The grand jury agreed to do so.

At the grand jury hearing, Peck called FBI Agent Elliot Hess as a witness. Hess testified as follows:

> On July 5, Ms. Corleone told one of her sons, Sonny, to travel to Bolivia and buy a large quantity of cocaine. Sonny agreed to do so, and left immediately for Bolivia. I arrested him at the airport when he returned with 20 kilograms of cocaine in his luggage.

I obtained a copy of the FBI report that Hess prepared on the case. In it, he stated: "This morning, I interviewed Freddo Finco at his secured cell in federal prison. Finco told me that on July 5, he was present at a conversation at the Corleone home, where he heard Ms. Corleone tell Sonny to go to Bolivia and buy 100 kilograms of cocaine. Finco then saw Sonny drive to the airport."

The grand jury subpoenaed Ms. Corleone to testify. She arrived with her attorney, Tom Hooligan, but Hooligan was not allowed to come into the grand jury room with her. Hooligan objected, and said that the grand jury had no right to force his client to testify, as she was suspected of criminal activities. Peck called Ms. Corleone to the witness stand, and she took the oath. Peck asked her, "On July 5, did you tell Sonny to go to Bolivia?" She said, "Yes, but just to buy some *coffee*. He must have misunderstood me and thought I said 'cocaine'."

The grand jury issued its indictment, which reads as follows:

IN THE UNITED STATES DISTRICT COURT
THE SOUTHERN DISTRICT OF NEW YORK

UNITED STATES OF AMERICA,
      Plaintiff,

v.

CARMELA CORLEONE
      Defendant

No. CR 12345
INDICTMENT

The 1998 Grand Jury charges that:

I.

From January 1, 1989, until September 1, 1998, in New York City, New York, Defendant CARMELA CORLEONE did engage in a conpiracy to sell cocaine, without lawful authority, in violation of 21 United States Code, section 846.

II.

Said conspiracy was committed with unindicted co-conspirator SONNY CORLEONE and others.

III.

To carry out the objects of their conspiracy, Defendant and co-conspirators committed several overt acts, including the following: importation of cocaine from Bolivia to New York City during the month of July, 1998.

A TRUE BILL

Manuel Labor, Foreperson

Approved as to form:

Frederica Fedd
Assistant U.S. Attorney

After the grand jury indicted Ms. Corleone, I obtained the transcript containing the above testimony. I also received a call from Peck, who told me that he had just interviewed Finco himself, and Finco said that he had lied to Hess. Finco said that he was in fact not present on July 5 at the alleged conversation between Ms. Corleone and Sonny, but he knew that such a conversation had occurred, because Sonny had told him about it later.

I then filed a motion to dismiss the indictment, and a motion to prevent the prosecutor from introducing at trial Ms. Corleone's testimony before the grand jury. Please read the attached authorities and advise me as to what arguments to make and what chance of success I have.

Federal Rules of Criminal Procedure, Rule 6

Rule 6.   The Grand Jury

(a)   Summoning a Grand Jury.

(1)   In General. When the public interest so requires, the court must order that one or more grand juries be summoned. A grand jury must have 16 to 23 members, and the court must order that enough legally qualified persons be summoned to meet this requirement. * * * *

(b)   Objection to the Grand Jury or to a Grand Juror.

(1)   Challenges. Either the government or a defendant may challenge the grand jury on the ground that it was not lawfully drawn, summoned, or selected, and may challenge an individual juror on the ground that the juror is not legally qualified.

(2)   Motion to Dismiss an Indictment. A party may move to dismiss the indictment based on an objection to the grand jury or on an individual juror's lack of legal qualification, unless the court has previously ruled on the same objection under Rule 6(b)(1). The motion to dismiss is governed by 28 U.S.C. § 1867(e). The court must not dismiss the indictment on the ground that a grand juror was not legally qualified if the record shows that at least 12 qualified jurors concurred in the indictment. * * * *

(d)   Who May Be Present.

(1)   While the Grand Jury Is in Session. The following persons may be present while the grand jury is in session: attorneys for the government, the witness being questioned, interpreters when needed, and a court reporter or an operator of a recording device.

(2)   During Deliberations and Voting. No person other than the jurors, and any interpreter needed to assist a hearing-impaired or speech-impaired juror, may be present while the grand jury is deliberating or voting.

(e)   Recording and Disclosing the Proceedings.

(1)   Recording the Proceedings. Except while the grand jury is deliberating or voting, all proceedings must be recorded by a court reporter or by a suitable recording device. But the validity of a prosecution is not affected by the unintentional failure to make a recording. Unless the court orders otherwise, an attorney for the government will retain control of the recording, the reporter's notes, and any transcript prepared from those notes.

(2)   Secrecy.

(A) No obligation of secrecy may be imposed on any person except in accordance with Rule 6(e)(2)(B).

(B)   Unless these rules provide otherwise, the following persons must not disclose a matter occurring before the grand jury:

(i)   a grand juror;

(ii)   an interpreter;

(iii)   a court reporter;

(iv)   an operator of a recording device;

(v)   a person who transcribes recorded testimony;

(vi)   an attorney for the government; or

(vii)   a person to whom disclosure is made under Rule 6(e)(3)(A)(ii) or (iii).

(3) Exceptions.

(A)   Disclosure of a grand-jury matter — other than the grand jury's deliberations or any grand juror's vote — may be made to:

(i)   an attorney for the government for use in performing that attorney's duty;

(ii)   any government personnel — including those of a state, state subdivision, Indian tribe, or foreign government — that an attorney for the government considers necessary to assist in performing that attorney's duty to enforce federal criminal law; or

(iii)   a person authorized by 18 U.S.C. § 3322.

(B)   A person to whom information is disclosed under Rule 6(e)(3)(A)(ii) may use that information only to assist an attorney for the government in performing that attorney's duty to enforce federal criminal law. An attorney for the government must promptly provide the court that impaneled the grand jury with the names of all persons to whom a disclosure has been made, and must certify that the attorney has advised those persons of their obligation of secrecy under this rule.

(C)   An attorney for the government may disclose any grand-jury matter to another federal grand jury.

(D)   An attorney for the government may disclose any grand-jury matter involving foreign intelligence, counterintelligence (as defined in 50 U.S.C. § 401a), or foreign intelligence information (as defined in Rule 6(e)(3)(D)(iii)) to any federal law enforcement, intelligence, protective, immigration, national defense, or national security official to assist the official receiving the information in the performance of that official's duties. An attorney for the government may also disclose any grand jury matter involving, within the United States or elsewhere, a threat of attack or other grave hostile acts of a foreign power or its agent, a threat of domestic or international sabotage or terrorism, or clandestine intelligence gathering activities by an intelligence service or network of a foreign power or by its agent, to any appropriate Federal, State, State subdivision, Indian tribal, or foreign government official, for the purpose of preventing or responding to such threat or activities. * * **

(E)   The court may authorize disclosure — at a time, in a manner, and subject to any other conditions that it directs — of a grand-jury matter:

(i)   preliminarily to or in connection with a judicial proceeding;

(ii)   at the request of a defendant who shows that a ground may exist to dismiss the indictment because of a matter that occurred before the grand jury;

(iii)   at the request of the government, when sought by a foreign court or prosecutor for use in an official criminal investigation;

(iv)   at the request of the government if it shows that the matter may disclose a violation of State, Indian tribal, or foreign criminal law, as long as the disclosure is to an appropriate state, state-subdivision, Indian tribal, or foreign government official for the purpose of enforcing that law; or

(v)   at the request of the government if it shows that the matter may disclose a violation of military criminal law under the Uniform Code of Military Justice, as long as the disclosure is to an appropriate military official for the purpose of enforcing that law. * * * *

(4)   Sealed Indictment. The magistrate judge to whom an indictment is returned may direct that the indictment be kept secret until the defendant is in custody or has been released pending trial. The clerk must then seal the indictment, and no person may disclose the indictment's existence except as necessary to issue or execute a warrant or summons.

(5)   Closed Hearing. Subject to any right to an open hearing in a contempt proceeding, the court must close any hearing to the extent necessary to prevent disclosure of a matter occurring before a grand jury.

(6)   Sealed Records. Records, orders, and subpoenas relating to grand-jury proceedings must be kept under seal to the extent and as long as necessary to prevent the unauthorized disclosure of a matter occurring before a grand jury.

(7)   Contempt. A knowing violation of Rule 6, or of guidelines jointly issued by the Attorney General and the Director of National Intelligence pursuant to Rule 6, may be punished as a contempt of court.

(f)   Indictment and Return. A grand jury may indict only if at least 12 jurors concur. The grand jury — or its foreperson or deputy foreperson — must return the indictment to a magistrate judge in open court. If a complaint or information is pending against the defendant and 12 jurors do not concur in the indictment, the foreperson must promptly and in writing report the lack of concurrence to the magistrate judge.

(g)   Discharging the Grand Jury. A grand jury must serve until the court discharges it, but it may serve more than 18 months only if the court, having determined that an extension is in the public interest, extends the grand jury's service. An extension may be granted for no more than 6 months, except as otherwise provided by statute.

(h)   Excusing a Juror. At any time, for good cause, the court may excuse a juror either temporarily or permanently, and if permanently, the court may impanel an alternate juror in place of the excused juror.

Notes from Millie:

1. **May the defendant obtain *the transcript* of the grand jury proceeding that led to his indictment?** In Chapter 3 ("Discovery"), we saw that the defendant may obtain those portions of the transcript that contain his own testimony and the

testimony of witnesses who testify against him at trial (after they testify). What does Rule 6(e)(3)(C) add to this? Subsection (i) says the transcript may be disclosed "when so directed by the court," but gives no guidelines as to when the court should so direct. Subsection (ii) says the transcript may be disclosed "upon a showing that grounds may exist for a motion to dismiss the indictment because of matters occurring before the grand jury," but without first seeing the transcript, how can the defendant make such a showing?

Professor Wright addresses this problem in his Federal Practice & Procedure, v. 1, at § 108:

> Generally requests to see grand jury minutes under [Rule 6(e)(3)(C)(ii)] have been denied, on the ground that the defendant has not made a sufficiently strong showing that grounds for a motion to dismiss the indictment may exist. Of course such a showing is difficult to make until the minutes have been inspected, but given how unlikely it is that an indictment will be dismissed because of what occurred before the grand jury, the matter is not of great importance.
>
> Fortunately the purposes for which defendants may be given access to grand jury minutes are not as limited as Rule 6(e)(3)(C)(ii) would suggest. Rule 6(e)(3)(C)(i) . . . allows disclosure "when so directed by the court preliminarily to or in connection with a judicial proceeding," and thus empowers the court to order disclosure to defendant for purposes other than a motion to dismiss the indictment. In addition . . . both the discovery rules and the Jencks Act give defendants a right of access to portions of the grand jury minutes.
>
> In some states a defendant is given a copy of the grand jury testimony as a matter of right, and it has been argued that this should be the policy in the federal courts. This, however, has never been the rule. The leading case is the 1959 decision in *Pittsburgh Plate Glass v. U.S.*, 360 U.S. 395, in which it was held that defendant cannot have access to the grand jury minutes as a matter of right and that the burden is on defendant to show "a particularized need" for the minutes that outweighs the usual policy of secrecy. * * * *
>
> Thus a defendant may obtain his own grand jury testimony, the relevant testimony of government witnesses after they have testified at the trial, and, on a proper showing, grand jury minutes needed to support a motion to dismiss the indictment. Defendants have not fared well when they have sought to persuade courts to give them access to the grand jury testimony of witnesses to be called by the defense or witnesses who are not called at trial by either side. This smacks of inspecting the minutes purely for discovery, and this is a purpose about which the courts are not enthusiastic. A showing of "particularized need" is required before disclosure will be ordered.

2. **How much may prosecutors say about a pending investigation without violating Rule 6(e)?**

The court addressed this question in *In re Sealed Case No. 99-3091(Office of Independent Counsel Proceeding)*, 192 F.3d 995 (D.C. Cir. 1999):

On January 31, 1999, while the Senate was trying President William J. Clinton on articles of impeachment, the New York Times published a front page article captioned "Starr is Weighing Whether to Indict Sitting President." As is relevant here, the article reported:

> Inside the Independent Counsel's Office, a group of prosecutors believes that not long after the Senate trial concludes, Mr. Starr should ask the grand jury of 23 men and women hearing the case against Mr. Clinton to indict him on charges of perjury and obstruction of justice, the associates said. The group wants to charge Mr. Clinton with lying under oath in his Jones deposition in January 1998 and in his grand jury testimony in August, the associates added.

The next day, the Office of the President (the White House) and Mr. Clinton jointly filed in district court a motion for an order to show cause why OIC, or the individuals therein, should not be held in contempt for disclosing grand jury material in violation of Federal Rule of Criminal Procedure 6(e). The White House and Mr. Clinton pointed to several excerpts from the article as evidence of OIC's violations of the grand jury secrecy rule.

The court found no violation of Rule 6(e), because the article did not disclose "matters occurring before the grand jury":

> This phrase encompasses not only what has occurred and what is occurring, but also what is likely to occur, including the identities of witnesses or jurors, the substance of testimony as well as actual transcripts, the strategy or direction of the investigation, the deliberations or questions of jurors, and the like. In the earlier contempt proceeding against Independent Counsel Starr, however, we cautioned the district court about "the problematic nature of applying so broad a definition, especially as it relates to the 'strategy or direction of the investigation,' to the inquiry as to whether a government attorney has made unauthorized disclosures." *In re Sealed Case No.98 3077*, 151 F.3d at 1071 n. 12.

> We have never read Rule 6(e) to require that a veil of secrecy be drawn over all matters occurring in the world that happen to be investigated by a grand jury. Indeed, we have said that "the disclosure of information 'coincidentally before the grand jury which can be revealed in such a manner that its revelation would not elucidate the inner workings of the grand jury' is not prohibited." *Senate of Puerto Rico v. United States Dep't of Justice*, 823 F.2d 574, 582 (D.C.Cir.1987). Thus, the phrases "likely to occur" and "strategy and direction" must be read in light of the text of Rule 6(e) — which limits the Rule's coverage to "matters occurring before the grand jury" — as well as the purposes of the Rule.

> Rule 6(e) protects several interests of the criminal justice system: First, if preindictment proceedings were made public, many prospective witnesses would be hesitant to come forward voluntarily, knowing that those against whom they testify would be aware of that testimony. Moreover, witnesses who appeared before the grand jury would be less likely to testify fully and frankly, as they would be open to retribution as well as to inducements. There also would be the risk that those about to be indicted would flee, or would try to influence individual grand jurors to vote against

indictment. Finally, by preserving the secrecy of the proceedings, we assure that persons who are accused but exonerated by the grand jury will not be held up to public ridicule.

These purposes, as well as the text of the Rule itself, reflect the need to preserve the secrecy of the grand jury proceedings themselves. It is therefore necessary to differentiate between statements by a prosecutor's office with respect to its own investigation, and statements by a prosecutor's office with respect to a grand jury's investigation, a distinction of the utmost significance.

Information actually presented to the grand jury is core Rule 6(e) material that is afforded the broadest protection from disclosure. Prosecutors' statements about their investigations, however, implicate the Rule only when they directly reveal grand jury matters. To be sure, we have recognized that Rule 6(e) would be easily evaded if a prosecutor could with impunity discuss with the press testimony about to be presented to a grand jury, so long as it had not yet occurred. Accordingly, we have read Rule 6(e) to cover matters "likely to occur." And even a discussion of "strategy and direction of the investigation" could include references to not yet delivered but clearly anticipated testimony. But that does not mean that any discussion of an investigation is violative of Rule 6(e). Indeed, the district court's Local Rule 308(b)(2), which governs attorney conduct in grand jury matters, recognizes that prosecutors often have a legitimate interest in revealing aspects of their investigations "to inform the public that the investigation is underway, to describe the general scope of the investigation, to obtain assistance in the apprehension of a suspect, to warn the public of any dangers, or otherwise aid in the investigation."

It may often be the case, however, that disclosures by the prosecution referencing its own investigation should not be made for tactical reasons, or are in fact prohibited by other Rules or ethical guidelines. For instance, prosecutors may be prohibited by internal guidelines, see, e.g., United States Attorney Manual § 1 7.530, from discussing the strategy or direction of their investigation before an indictment is sought. This would serve one of the same purposes as Rule 6(e): protecting the reputation of innocent suspects. But a court may not use Rule 6(e) to generally regulate prosecutorial statements to the press. The purpose of the Rule is only to protect the secrecy of grand jury proceedings.

Thus, internal deliberations of prosecutors that do not directly reveal grand jury proceedings are not Rule 6(e) material. A discussion of actions taken by government attorneys or officials — e.g., a recommendation by the Justice Department attorneys to department officials that an indictment be sought against an individual — does not reveal any information about matters occurring before the grand jury. Nor does a statement of opinion as to an individual's potential criminal liability violate the dictates of Rule 6(e). This is so even though the opinion might be based on knowledge of the grand jury proceedings, provided, of course, that the statement does not reveal the grand jury information on which it is based.

It may be thought that when such deliberations include a discussion of whether an indictment should be sought, or whether a particular individual is potentially criminally liable, the deliberations have crossed into the realm of Rule 6(e) material. This ignores, however, the requirement that the matter occur before the grand jury. Where the reported deliberations do not reveal that an indictment has been sought or will be sought, ordinarily they will not reveal anything definite enough to come within the scope of Rule 6(e).

For these reasons, the disclosure that a group of OIC prosecutors "believe" that an indictment should be brought at the end of the impeachment proceedings does not on its face, or in the context of the article as a whole, violate Rule 6(e). We acknowledge, as did OIC, that such statements are troubling, for they have the potential to damage the reputation of innocent suspects. But bare statements that some assistant prosecutors in OIC wish to seek an indictment do not implicate the grand jury; the prosecutors may not even be basing their opinion on information presented to a grand jury.

COSTELLO v. UNITED STATES
United States Supreme Court
350 U.S. 359 (1956)

Mr. Justice Black delivered the opinion of the Court.

We granted certiorari in this case to consider a single question: "May a defendant be required to stand trial and a conviction be sustained where only hearsay evidence was presented to the grand jury which indicted him?"

Petitioner, Frank Costello, was indicted for willfully attempting to evade payment of income taxes due the United States for the years 1947, 1948 and 1949. The charge was that petitioner falsely and fraudulently reported less income than he and his wife actually received during the taxable years in question. Petitioner promptly filed a motion for inspection of the minutes of the grand jury and for a dismissal of the indictment. His motion was based on an affidavit stating that he was firmly convinced there could have been no legal or competent evidence before the grand jury which indicted him since he had reported all his income and paid all taxes due. The motion was denied.

At the trial which followed, the Government offered evidence designed to show increases is Costello's net worth in an attempt to prove that he had received more income during the years in question than he had reported. To establish its case, the Government called and examined 144 witnesses and introduced 368 exhibits. All of the testimony and documents related to business transactions and expenditures by petitioner and his wife. The prosecution concluded its case by calling three government agents. Their investigations had produced the evidence used against petitioner at the trial. They were allowed to summarize the vast amount of evidence already heard and to introduce computations showing, if correct, that petitioner and his wife had received far greater income than they had reported. We have held such summarizations admissible in a "net worth" case like this.

Counsel for petitioner asked each government witness at the trial whether he had appeared before the grand jury which returned the indictment. This cross-examination developed the fact that the three investigating officers had been the only witnesses before the grand jury. After the Government concluded its case, petitioner again moved to dismiss the indictment on the ground that the only evidence before the grand jury was "hearsay," since the three officers had no firsthand knowledge of the transactions upon which their computations were based. Nevertheless the trial court again refused to dismiss the indictment, and petitioner was convicted. The Court of Appeals affirmed, holding that the indictment was valid even though the sole evidence before the grand jury was hearsay.

Petitioner here urges: (1) that an indictment based solely on hearsay evidence violates that part of the Fifth Amendment providing that "No person shall be held to answer for a capital, or otherwise infamous crime, unless on a presentment or indictment of a Grand Jury" and (2) that if the Fifth Amendment does not invalidate an indictment based solely on hearsay we should now lay down such a rule for the guidance of federal courts.

The Fifth Amendment provides that federal prosecutions for capital or otherwise infamous crimes must be instituted by presentments or indictments of grand juries. But neither the Fifth Amendment nor any other constitutional provision prescribes the kind of evidence upon which grand juries must act.

The grand jury is an English institution, brought to this country by the early colonists and incorporated in the Constitution by the Founders. There is every reason to believe that our constitutional grand jury was intended to operate substantially like its English progenitor. The basic purpose of the English grand jury was to provide a fair method for instituting criminal proceedings against persons believed to have committed crimes. Grand jurors were selected from the body of the people and their work was not hampered by rigid procedural or evidential rules. In fact, grand jurors could act on their own knowledge and were free to make their presentments or indictments on such information as they deemed satisfactory. Despite its broad power to institute criminal proceedings, the grand jury grew in popular favor with the years. It acquired an independence in England free from control by the Crown or judges. Its adoption in our Constitution as the sole method for preferring charges in serious criminal cases shows the high place it held as an instrument of justice. And in this country as in England of old, the grand jury has convened as a body of laymen, free from technical rules, acting in secret, pledged to indict no one because of prejudice and to free no one because of special favor. As late as 1927, an English historian could say that English grand juries were still free to act on their own knowledge if they pleased to do so.

In *Holt v. United States*, 218 U.S. 245, this Court had to decide whether an indictment should be quashed because supported in part by incompetent evidence. Aside from the incompetent evidence, "there was very little evidence against the accused." The Court refused to hold that such an indictment should be quashed, pointing out that "The abuses of criminal practice would be enhanced if indictments could be upset on such a ground." *Id.* at 248. The same thing is true where as here all the evidence before the grand jury was in the nature of "hearsay." If indictments were to be held open to challenge on the ground that there was inadequate or incompetent evidence before the grand jury, the resulting delay would be great indeed. The result of such a rule would be that before trial on the merits a defendant could always insist on a kind of preliminary trial to determine the competency and adequacy of the evidence before the grand jury. This is not required by the Fifth Amendment. An indictment returned by a legally constituted and unbiased grand jury, like an information drawn by the prosecutor, if valid on its face, is enough to call for trial of the charge on the merits. The Fifth Amendment requires nothing more.

Petitioner urges that this Court should exercise its power to supervise the administration of justice in federal courts and establish a rule permitting defendants to challenge indictments on the ground that they are not supported by adequate or competent evidence. No persuasive reasons are advanced for establishing such a rule. It would run counter to the whole history of the grand jury institution, in which laymen conduct their inquiries unfettered by technical rules. Neither justice nor the concept of a fair trial requires such a change. In a trial on the merits, defendants are entitled to a strict observance of all the rules designed to bring about a fair verdict.

Defendants are not entitled, however, to a rule which would result in interminable delay but add nothing to the assurance of a fair trial. Affirmed.

MR. JUSTICE BURTON, concurring.

I agree with the denial of the motion to quash the indictment. In my view, however, this case does not justify the breadth of the declarations made by the Court. I assume that this Court would not preclude an examination of grand-jury action to ascertain the existence of bias or prejudice in an indictment. Likewise, it seems to me that if it is shown that the grand jury had before it no substantial or rationally persuasive evidence upon which to base its indictment, that indictment should be quashed. To hold a person to answer to such an empty indictment for a capital or otherwise infamous federal crime robs the Fifth Amendment of much of its protective value to the private citizen.

Here, as in *Holt v. United States*, 218 U.S. 245, substantial and rationally persuasive evidence apparently was presented to the grand jury. We may fairly assume that the evidence before that jury included much of the testimony later given at the trial by the three government agents who said that they had testified before the grand jury. At the trial, they summarized financial transactions of the accused about which they were not qualified to testify of their own knowledge. To use Justice Holmes' phrase in the *Holt* case, such testimony, standing alone, was "incompetent by circumstances," *id.* at 248, and yet it was rationally persuasive of the crime charged and provided a substantial basis for the indictment. At the trial, with preliminary testimony laying the foundation for it, the same testimony constituted an important part of the competent evidence upon which the conviction was obtained. To sustain this indictment under the above circumstances is well enough, but I agree with Judge Learned Hand that "if it appeared that no evidence had been offered that rationally established the facts, the indictment ought to be quashed; because then the grand jury would have in substance abdicated." 2 Cir., 221 F.2d 668, 677.

Notes from Millie:

1. How much evidence is needed to support an indictment?

In *U.S. v. O'Shea*, 447 F.Supp. 330 (S.D.Fla.1978), the court dismissed an indictment after reviewing the minutes of the grand jury hearing and finding that there was not sufficient evidence to support a finding of probable cause. "This is not a case which challenges an indictment because of the quality of the evidence. The problem is that there is simply no evidence sufficient to establish probable cause that the defendant committed any one of the three offenses of which he is charged." The court noted: "If the Grand Jury system is to survive, its intended purpose must not be prostituted by prosecutors who allegedly control the grand jury."

However, in *U.S. v. Short*, 671 F.2d 178 (6th Cir. 1982), the court stated that "As long as there is some competent evidence to sustain the charge issued by the Grand Jury, an indictment should not be dismissed." The court noted that *O'Shea* seems to be the only reported case in which a court has dismissed an indictment on the ground of lack of evidence before the grand jury.

Why is it so difficult for defense counsel to persuade a court to dismiss an indictment on the ground that the evidence before the grand jury failed to show "probable cause"? Hint: Take another look at Note #1 after Federal Rule 6, above.

In Andrew Leipold, *Why Grand Juries Do Not (And Cannot) Protect The Accused*, 80 Cornell L.Rev. 260 (1995), the author concludes:

> The barriers to a grand jury's ability to screen are not obvious, because its task seems so simple. Jurors listen to the prosecutor's case and then are asked to answer a single question: is there probable cause to believe that the suspect committed the specified crime?

> Stated simply, grand jurors are not qualified to answer this question. Whether probable cause exists is ultimately a legal determination about the sufficiency of the evidence: whether the prosecutor put forth enough information to surpass the legal threshold established by the probable cause standard. In submitting a case to the grand jury, we are asking nonlawyers with no experience in weighing evidence to decide whether a legal test is satisfied, and to do so after the only lawyer in the room, the prosecutor, has concluded that it has. Because jurors lack any experience or expertise in deciding whether probable cause exists, it becomes not only predictable but logical that the jurors will return a true bill. This is not because they are a rubber stamp, but because they have no benchmark against which to weigh the evidence, and thus no rational basis for rejecting the prosecutor's recommendation to indict.

2. May the grand jury *refuse* to indict even when it finds probable cause?

In *U.S. v. Navarro-Vargas*, 408 F.3d 1184 (9th Cir. 2005), defendant challenged an instruction that the district court judge had given to the grand jury that indicted defendant:

> The district court instructed the grand jury using the model charge recommended by the Judicial Conference of the United States. The grand jury charge included the following explanations and instructions:

> > [1] The purpose of a Grand Jury is to determine whether there is sufficient evidence to justify a formal accusation against a person. If law enforcement officials were not required to submit to an impartial Grand Jury proof of guilt as to a proposed charge against a person suspected of having committed a crime, they would be free to arrest and bring to trial a suspect no matter how little evidence existed to support the charge.

[2] As members of the Grand Jury, you in a very real sense stand between the government and the accused. It is your duty to see to it that indictments are returned only against those whom you find probable cause to believe are guilty and to see to it that the innocent are not compelled to go to trial.

[3] You cannot judge the wisdom of the criminal laws enacted by Congress, that is, whether or not there should or should not be a federal law designating certain activity as criminal. That is to be determined by Congress and not by you. Furthermore, when deciding whether or not to indict, you should not be concerned about punishment in the event of conviction. Judges alone determine punishment. [4] Your task is to determine whether the government's evidence as presented to you is sufficient to cause you to conclude that there is probable cause to believe that the accused is guilty of the offense charged. To put it another way, you should vote to indict where the evidence presented to you is sufficiently strong to warrant a reasonable person's believing that the accused is probably guilty of the offense with which the accused is charged.

[5] It is extremely important for you to realize that under the United States Constitution, the grand jury is independent of the United States Attorney and is not an arm or agent of the Federal Bureau of Investigation, the Drug Enforcement Administration, the Internal Revenue Service, or any governmental agency charged with prosecuting a crime. There has been some criticism of the institution of the Grand Jury for supposedly acting as a mere rubber stamp, approving prosecutions that are brought before it by governmental representatives. However, as a practical matter, you must work closely with the government attorneys. The United States Attorney and his Assistant United States Attorneys will provide you with important service in helping you to find your way when confronted with complex legal problems. It is entirely proper that you should receive this assistance. If past experience is any indication of what to expect in the future, then you can expect candor, honesty, and good faith in matters presented by the government attorneys.

Navarro-Vargas and Leon-Jasso contend that the grand jury's independence was compromised when it was instructed in paragraphs [3], [4], and [5] that it "should vote to indict" the accused in each case in which it believed probable cause exists, that it could not "judge the wisdom of the criminal laws enacted by Congress," and that government counsel would use "candor, honesty, and good faith." The Appellants argue that this error is structural and requires dismissal of the indictment. * * * *

Whether the model grand jury instructions violate the Grand Jury Clause depends on what the Clause's cryptic reference to "Grand Jury" means and whether independence (in the sense advocated by the Appellants) is an irreducible element of what it means to have a grand jury. And for that inquiry, our starting point must be the grand jury's history, recognizing that any recounting of a near-millennia of history will give us only the broadest contours of an ancient institution.

[The court then extensively discussed *the history* of the grand jury in England, in colonial America, and in modern times.] * * * *

With this in mind, we turn to the Appellants' arguments. They challenge three instructions that in their view "demean" the grand jury's historical responsibility. Appellants do not ask us to rewrite the instructions in any particular way, but they suggest that no instruction would be better than an incorrect instruction. We consider each challenged instruction in turn.

1. "The Wisdom of the Criminal Laws"

Navarro-Vargas and Leon-Jasso first challenge the passage that states:

> You cannot judge the wisdom of the criminal laws enacted by Congress, that is, whether or not there should or should not be a federal law designating certain activity as criminal. That is to be determined by Congress and not by you.

Appellants contend that this passage unconstitutionally misinstructs the grand jury as to its role and function. They assert that no authority supports the district court's decision to circumscribe the subject matter of the grand jurors' inquiries and deliberations. According to Appellants, this limitation "run[s] counter to the whole history of the grand jury institution, in which laymen conduct their inquiries unfettered by technical rules." In addition, Appellants argue that federal courts have limited powers to fashion rules of grand jury procedure and that they cannot use this power to reshape the grand jury institution, "substantially altering the traditional relationships between the prosecutor, the constituting court, and the grand jury itself." They further contend that since the grand jury has the power to charge greater or lesser offenses, it can surely judge the wisdom of a particular law in determining whether to indict. Appellants submit that this faulty instruction constitutes structural error requiring dismissal of the indictment.

We first wish to observe that the instruction is not contrary to any long-standing historical practice surrounding the grand jury. We know of no English or American practice to advise grand juries that they may stand in judgment of the wisdom of the laws before them. Indeed, there is strong evidence to support the current instruction. We have previously cited the attestation or oath required of grand jurors in an early and influential colonial constitution which enjoined the jurors to "diligently enquire and true presentment make, of all such matters and things as shall be given thee in charge, or come to thy knowledge." We have also cited evidence of charges given shortly after the adoption of the Bill of Rights in which federal judges charged grand juries with a duty to submit to the law and to strictly enforce it.

The phrase "wisdom of the laws" is not a term of art. We might assume that the phrase means that juries cannot question whether the law represents good policy. If a grand jury can sit in judgment of wisdom of the policy behind a law, then the power to return a no bill in such cases is the clearest form of "jury nullification." The "wisdom of the laws" might also refer to a broader power of substantive constitutional review — the power to determine that the law is unconstitutional and, therefore, void. We doubt that the grand jury is particularly well suited to make either of these judgments, although, as we discuss below, there is no check on the ability of the grand jury to do so. The grand jury can only choose to indict or not in the cases before it. It cannot make judgments about any other cases, and since the jurors' deliberations are secret, no judge, prosecutor, or grand jury can rely on its reasoning in the future. Furthermore, the grand jury has few tools for informing itself of the policy or legal justification for the law; it receives no briefs or arguments from the parties. The grand jury has little but its own visceral reaction on which to judge the "wisdom of the law."

By contrast, if the president or the attorney general determines that a law is either unwise or unconstitutional, he may decline to enforce the law and will do so systematically and, often, publicly. 28 U.S.C. § 530D(a) (requiring notice to Senate of Department of Justice's decision not to defend an act of Congress). And, as we have noted, he is answerable for his judgment. Similarly, if a court finds that a law is unconstitutional, the judgment extends to all cases within the court's jurisdiction, and the decision is public and subject to review. The grand jury is, by design, isolated from other influences. The prospect of a grand jury here and there deciding for itself that a law lacked "wisdom" is an invitation to lawlessness and something less than the equal protection of the laws.

We recognize and do not discount that some grand jurors might *in fact* vote to return a no bill because they regard the law as unwise at best or even unconstitutional. For all the reasons we have discussed, there is no *post hoc* remedy for that; the grand jury's motives are not open to examination. Moreover, there is no *ex ante* solution either; there is nothing to prevent a grand jury from engaging in nullification or substantive constitutional review, not even the model grand jury instructions. History demonstrates that grand juries do not derive their independence from a judge's instruction. Instead, they derive their independence from an unreviewable power to decide whether to indict or not.

The question before us is whether judging the wisdom of the law is so integral to the role of the grand jury that it is constitutional error for the district court to instruct against it. We cannot say that the instruction is so contrary to the grand jury's role that it violates the Fifth Amendment. Or, put another way, we cannot say that the grand jury's power to judge the wisdom of the laws is so firmly established that the district court must either instruct the jury on its power to nullify the laws or remain silent.

2. "Should" Indict if Probable Cause Is Found

Navarro-Vargas and Leon-Jasso also claim that the following passage misinstructs the grand jury:

> Your task is to determine whether the government's evidence as presented to you is sufficient to cause you to conclude that there is probable cause to believe that the accused is guilty of the offense charged. To put it another way, you should vote to indict where the evidence presented to you is sufficiently strong to warrant a reasonable person's believing that the accused is probably guilty of the offense with which the accused is charged.

Appellants claim that this passage is unconstitutional because it instructs grand jurors that they "should" indict if they find probable cause, but does not explain that they can refuse to indict even if they find probable cause. Further, Appellants argue that the instructions use the singular terms "purpose" and "task" in advising the grand jurors that their sole responsibility is to make probable cause determinations. Even though the instructions indicate that the jurors "should" indict if they find probable cause, Appellants believe that the model charge reasonably read, imposes upon the grand jury a *duty* to indict if they find probable cause. Appellants argue that this improper instruction deprives them of the "traditional functioning of the institution that the Fifth Amendment demands."

This instruction does not violate the grand jury's independence. The language of the model charge does not state that the jury "must" or "shall" indict, but merely that it "should" indict if it finds probable cause. As a matter of pure semantics, it does not "eliminate discretion on the part of the grand jurors," leaving room for the grand jury to dismiss even if it finds probable cause.

Even assuming that the grand jury should exercise something akin to prosecutorial discretion, the instruction does not infringe upon that discretion. The analogy that the Court recognized between the grand jury and the prosecutor is useful for understanding the source of both the grand jury's and prosecutor's discretion. Under Article II, § 3, the president "shall take Care that the Laws be faithfully executed." That duty can be delegated to subordinates, including the attorney general and the U.S. attorneys serving in each judicial district. U.S. attorneys, operating with limited resources, are literally incapable of seeing that each and every federal law is executed. Allocating their resources, they decide whether those resources are better put to prosecuting narcotraficantes, 21 U.S.C. § 1906; government fraud, 18 U.S.C. § 1031, and public corruption, 18 U.S.C. § 666; or to pursuing unlawful transportation of dentures, 18 U.S.C. § 1821; disruption of zoos, circuses, and rodeos, 18 U.S.C. § 43; or parking violations committed on federal lands, 36 C.F.R. § 4.13. It is also possible that an attorney general might decide not to enforce, or at least to underenforce, politically controversial laws or laws that, in the attorney general's view, are unconstitutional. In effect, a decision not to prosecute someone who would likely be indicted and could be convicted is a form of prosecutorial nullification.

Notwithstanding Article II's instruction to take care that the laws are faithfully executed, the president and those who represent him have broad independence in their prosecutorial decisions. The president's independence arises not out of any constitutional direction to exercise prosecutorial discretion, prosecutorial nullification, or substantive constitutional review, but out of the lack of any check on the president's ability to do so. The president operates virtually without check on decisions not to charge violations. There are, of course, long-term checks on the president. Congress has broad powers of inquiry and may, if necessary, impeach a president for his decisions. In extreme cases, courts may make judgments about selective prosecutions that violate the promise of due process or equal protection of the laws. The people have a check by bringing political pressure on the president and, if the president seeks a second term, to offer a referendum vote at the ballot box on the president's judgment in enforcing the laws.

In this respect, the grand jury has even greater powers of nonprosecution than the executive because there is, literally, no check on a grand jury's decision not to return an indictment. The grand jury has no accountability at the ballot box, before Congress, the President, or the courts. The grand jury's duty to follow the Constitution is no less than the President's duty to take care that the laws are faithfully executed. It is the grand jury's position in the constitutional scheme that gives it its independence, not any instructions that a court might offer.

Even though the terms "purpose" and "task" are singular, conveying that the grand jury has one purpose, these instructions do not undermine the grand jury's purpose and function. The instructions remind the grand jury that it has "extensive powers" and in "a very real sense stand[s] between the government and the accused." Admittedly, the instructions do not explain to the grand jury what its "extensive powers" are or have been in the past, including its power to refuse to indict even when a conviction can be obtained. However, the instructions remind the grand jury of its independence from the federal government and leave room for it to refuse to indict. Consequently, we conclude that this instruction is not inconsistent with the Fifth Amendment.

3. The "Candor, Honesty, and Good Faith" of Government Attorneys

Finally, Appellants claim that the following passage inappropriately instructs the grand jury:

> The United States Attorney and his Assistant United States Attorneys will provide you with important service in helping you to find your way when confronted with complex legal problems. It is entirely proper that you should receive this assistance. If past experience is any indication of what to expect in the future, then you can expect candor, honesty, and good faith in matters presented by the government attorneys.

Appellants claim that this vote of confidence by the judge to the honesty of the government attorneys further undermines the independence of the grand jury. They argue that the grand jury is told to independently evaluate probable cause but that this independence is diluted by this instruction that encourages deference to prosecutors.

We also reject this final contention and hold that although this passage may include unnecessary language, it does not violate the Constitution. The "candor, honesty, and good faith" language, when read in the context of the instructions as a whole, does not violate the constitutional relationship between the prosecutor and grand jury. The contested passage may be surplusage, but it is not unprecedented. Apparently, these laudatory comments about the prosecutor have been included in grand jury materials for some time. The instructions balance the praise for the government's attorney by informing the grand jurors that some have criticized the grand jury as a "mere rubber stamp" to the prosecution and reminding them that the grand jury is "independent of the United States Attorney."

We do not regard this reference in the same way that we do vouching for witnesses. The U.S. attorney is not testifying, but is presenting the testimony of others. The phrase is not vouching for the prosecutor, but is closer to advising the grand jury of the presumption of regularity and good faith that the branches of government ordinarily afford each other.

Again, the question before us is whether this language is unconstitutional, not whether it is overly deferential or unnecessary. This passage would be problematic if it misinstructed the grand jury that it was an agent of the U.S. attorney and not an independent body acting as a check to the prosecutor's power. However, it does not do this. It reminds the grand jury that it stands between the government and the accused and is independent. The laudatory language is likely unnecessary, but it surely does not threaten the constitutional relationship between the prosecutor and grand jury.

In upholding the model grand jury instructions against Appellants' constitutional challenge, we do not necessarily hold that the current instructions could not or should not be improved. We recognize the commentary pointing to discrete changes that tend to reduce the independence of the modern grand jury and the commentary urging reform in expanding the grand jury's duty and role in the criminal process. We even concede that there may be more done to further increase the shielding power of the modern federal grand jury. However, we are not a drafting committee for the grand jury instructions. We are not faced with the question of how to reform the modern grand jury but whether its model instructions are constitutional. To answer this question, we hold that the provisions of the model grand jury instructions challenged here are constitutional.

JUDGE HAWKINS dissented:

A. Improperly Limiting Grand Jurors to Probable Cause Determination

The instructions begin by telling the grand jurors that what would follow outlines their responsibilities. This prefatory emphasis is significant because the instructions go on to explain that "the purpose of the Grand Jury is to determine whether there is sufficient evidence to justify a formal accusation against a person." A grand juror paying close attention would conclude that the purpose of the grand jury is *singular* and that its discretion is constrained by the instruction.

This impression is confirmed again later in the charge: "Your task is to determine whether the government's evidence as presented to you is sufficient to cause you to conclude that there is probable cause." Once again, the instruction defines the purpose, or "task," singularly, and even the majority concedes that "the terms 'purpose' and 'task' are singular, conveying that the jury has a unique purpose." Once again, the unique purpose conveyed is determining probable cause. The instruction seems to compel the grand jury to indict as long as probable cause exists: "You should vote to indict where the evidence presented to you is sufficiently strong to warrant a reasonable person's believing that the accused is probably guilty of the offense with which the accused is charged."

The majority discounts the admonishment "should," arguing that it is distinct from "must" or "shall." Even "as a matter of pure semantics," the majority is incorrect to say that the use of the word "should" preserves the grand jury's discretion. The word "should" is used "to express a duty or obligation." THE OXFORD AMERICAN DICTION AND LANGUAGE GUIDE 931 (1999). The "should" and "shall" distinction is a lawyer's distinction, not a difference most lay people sitting as grand jurors would be likely to understand. The instruction's use of the word "should" is most likely to be understood as imposing an inflexible "duty or obligation" on grand jurors, and thus to circumscribe the grand jury's constitutional independence.

This "should" admonishment is at odds with the grand jury's broad independent role. As the Supreme Court held in *Vasquez v. Hillery*, 474 U.S. 254, 263 (1986), "the grand jury does not determine *only* that probable cause exists to believe that a defendant committed a crime, or that it does not." (emphasis added).

The grand jury's defining feature is its independence. The Fifth Amendment deliberately inserts a group of citizens between the government's desire to bring serious criminal charges and its ability to actually do so. "It is a constitutional fixture in its own right, belonging to no branch of the institutional Government, serving as a kind of buffer or referee between the Government and the people." United States v. Williams, 504 U.S. 36, 47 (1992). Indeed, "the Fifth Amendment's constitutional guarantee *presupposes* an investigative body acting independently of either the prosecuting attorney *or judge* " *Id.* at 49. The history of the adoption of the grand jury requirement in the Bill of Rights underscores its independent role, and its independence was noted by courts at the founding of the Republic.

B. Limiting Grand Jury's Protective Role

The grand jury's independence serves not only in the determination of probable cause, as these grand juries were instructed, but also to protect the accused from the other branches of government by acting as the "conscience of the community."

The significance of this second — and potentially protective — role should not be understated. Indeed, the strength of this understanding is emphasized in *Vasquez*. There, the Supreme Court said:

> In the hands of the grand jury lies the power to charge a greater offense or a lesser offense; numerous counts or a single count; and perhaps most significant of all, a capital offense or a noncapital offense — all on the basis of the same facts. * * * *

1. Questioning the Wisdom of the Law & Prosecutorial Discretion

The grand jury must have the power to consider the wisdom of a law because it performs what is undeniably a prosecutorial function. The Fifth Amendment's command that a felony prosecution simply cannot proceed without the approval of the grand jury permits it to act as a check on prosecutorial discretion by the simple act of refusing to return an indictment. The majority is concerned about this unfettered discretion, arguing that "if a grand jury can sit in judgment of wisdom of the policy behind the law, then the power to return a no bill in such cases is the clearest form of 'jury nullification.' " The majority doubts that the grand jury is well-suited to make such judgments on the wisdom of the law, though it appears to accept the concept of prosecutorial discretion in the hands of a United States Attorney: "a decision not to prosecute someone who would likely be indicted and could be convicted is a form of prosecutorial nullification."

Prosecutorial discretion — the decision whether and how to bring charges against a particular defendant — is an important, even critical component of the criminal justice system, whether it be exercised by prosecutors or grand jurors. Not every potential crime can (or should) be investigated or prosecuted, and an important part of the prosecutorial function is deciding which potential defendants to select for criminal prosecution, and how serious the charges should be. Prosecutors can, and often do, make such decisions based on their judgments as to how wise and important certain laws may be.

And herein lies the essential hypocrisy of the government's position. Standing firmly in the defense of its exercise of discretion (amounting at times to nullification), it just as firmly argues that grand jurors are without authority to make similar judgments about which laws deserve vigorous enforcement and which ones do not, in deciding whom to indict, and on what charges. In the government's eye, the grand jury is a mere instrument of prosecutorial will, a probable cause screening device obligated to act at the direction of the prosecutor and then only when the prosecutor has decided whom and how much to charge.

But grand jurors have been traditionally viewed as the "conscience of the community," a function that partakes far more of judgment and discretion than of the narrow ministerial role that the challenged instructions assign to them.

Because the *petit* jury may not take into account community values to decide whether to convict, it is even more important to foster this traditional function of the *grand* jury — a body not subject to the prohibition against double jeopardy or other procedural constraints that apply once the case proceeds to trial.

2. Severity of the Punishment

As to the severity of punishment, the Supreme Court in *Vasquez* stated that the grand jury has "the power to charge a greater offense or a lesser offense; numerous counts or a single count; and perhaps most significant of all, a capital offense or a non-capital offense, all on the basis of the same facts." If grand jurors can choose, per *Vasquez*, between capital and non-capital offenses, how could they not be influencing the determination of punishment? They are exerting such influence, and they should be able to continue to do so, not boxed in by jury instructions that seek to eradicate this important function.

3. Instructions as Structural Protections

After long historical exegesis, the majority apparently agrees that a grand jury has the power to refuse to indict someone even when the prosecutor has established probable cause that this individual has committed a crime.

We part company, however, when it comes to how to protect this power of the grand jury. The majority believes that the "structure" and "function" of the grand jury — particularly the secrecy of its proceedings and unreviewability of many of its decisions — sufficiently protects that power. But the majority fails to see that the instructions given a grand jury shape its structure and function. Typical grand juries, including the grand jury in these cases, hear evidence from the prosecutor and receive instructions from the judge. Those instructions do not include a reference to *Vasquez* or a discussion of the full range of the grand jury's powers, and include the language we have discussed, which jurors are likely to understand as *precluding* the authority to refuse to indict if there is probable cause. Conscientious grand jurors, instructed as were the jurors in these cases, will *believe* they lack any authority beyond that on which they are instructed, and will act accordingly.

Instructing a grand jury that it lacks power to do anything beyond making a probable cause determination thus unconstitutionally undermines the very structural protections that the majority believes saves the instruction. The power to deliberate in secret is valuable, but limiting the factors included in that deliberation circumscribes that power. Similarly, the power to make unreviewable decisions is a serious power indeed, but limiting the range of considerations that impact those decisions undermines that power. Given the "almost invariable assumption of the law that jurors follow their instructions," we must assume that grand jurors followed the instructions offered in this case and, therefore, that the instructions undermined the very structural factors on which the majority rests its decision.

Indeed, there is something supremely cynical about saying that it is fine to give jurors erroneous instructions because nothing will happen if they disobey them. Grand jurors come in with no knowledge of the system, but, one would hope, a desire to fulfill their assigned role, not to flout it. Indeed, our legal system assumes that jurors have this desire, an assumption embodied in the presumption that jurors will fulfill their role as instructed by those in authority.

C. Praising the Government Attorneys

Further invading the independence of the grand jury was the court's instruction that it could expect "candor, honesty, and good faith in matters presented by the government attorneys." In Leon-Jasso's case, the judge also told the grand jurors that the prosecutors were "wonderful public servants." What these instructions do not tell grand jurors is that prosecutors are free to deprive the grand jurors of exculpatory evidence, *Williams*, 504 U.S. at 45–47, to provide unconstitutionally seized evidence, *United States v. Calandra*, 414 U.S. 338 (1974), and to present evidence otherwise inadmissible at trial, *Costello v. United States*, 350 U.S. 359

(1956). How independent can a grand jury be when they are told how wonderful the prosecutors are? The majority concedes that the "candor, honesty, and good faith" instruction is "unnecessary language," but attempts to justify its constitutionality by demonstrating that this language has been included for some time and claiming that the laudatory remarks do not threaten the constitutional relationship between the prosecutor and grand jury. Appellants, however, have the better argument: the grand jury's independence is diluted by this instruction, which encourages deference to prosecutors. By undermining the grand jury's independence, this part of the grand jury instruction is also unconstitutional.

The Petit Jury Analogy

Arguing from a remedy not sought to an institution not involved, the majority relies upon the rejection of nullification instructions in the petit jury context. But this argument ignores an important distinction between the two groups: with petit juries, jeopardy attaches, whereas with grand juries, a new prosecution effort can begin. Because evidence can always be re-presented to a second grand jury, it is far from inevitable that justice will not be done if grand jurors were given a full disclosure instruction.

Because the Framers placed a high value on the kinds of powers articulated by *Vasquez* for grand juries, it would be unjustifiably paternalistic to fail to tell the grand jurors the scope of their constitutional powers over charging decisions specifically entrusted to their judgment. Finally, it is a mistake to conclude that a full disclosure instruction to a grand jury would subvert the rule of law. If our constitutional system permits the grand jury to act on its "conscience," then it hardly makes sense to say that a grand juror who chooses to not indict despite probable cause is acting lawlessly. Rather, that action lies fully within the discretion delegated by the Constitution.

The petit jury analogy not only fails, it also provides a powerful reason for allowing the grand jury the independence to consider, for example, the wisdom of the law under which a suspect is to be prosecuted: we no longer permit petit juries to exercise such discretion, for the perfectly sensible reason that petit jurors decide guilt or innocence in accordance with clearly established legal standards. If grand juries, too, cannot exercise such discretion, then considerations such as the wisdom of the law will be isolated from any citizen's review, subject only to the prosecutor's discretion.

If the majority's view of the grand jury prevails, then the prosecutor will have discretion over all matters concerning indictment, whereas the *constitutional institution* of the grand jury will not. The prosecutor, a "single employee of the state" not only should not have sole discretion, such sole discretion is not the system envisioned by the Fifth Amendment. Adopting a system where discretion is solely in the hands of the prosecutor would result in a "perilous decline" in the grand jury institution, analogous to the decline in the petit jury institution caused by judges determining sentencing factors that increase punishment beyond what is authorized by the jury verdict.

UNITED STATES v. ESTEPA
U.S. Court of Appeals
471 F.2d 1132 (1972)

FRIENDLY, CHIEF JUDGE:

Charles Estepa and Francis Vasquez appeal from their conviction on four counts of an indictment charging them, along with Jaime Vasquez, Rafael Perez and Jose Luis Dones, with distributing heroin, possessing it with an intent to distribute, and conspiring to do so, in violation of 21 U.S.C. §§ 812, 841 and 846. Although Estepa challenges the sufficiency of the evidence and Vasquez raises some other points, it is unnecessary to consider these, since we hold dismissal of the indictment to be required because of the nature of the presentation to the grand jury.

For purposes of this opinion, we can adopt the statement of facts in the Government's brief on Vasquez' appeal:[1]

In the late afternoon of October 14, 1971, Patrolman Jose Guzman of the New York Joint Task Force, acting in an undercover capacity, met with defendant Jaime Vasquez at approximately 5:30 p.m., at 878 Southern Boulevard, Bronx, New York, where they discussed the possibility of Patrolman Guzman purchasing one-eighth of a kilogram of heroin. When Vasquez suggested they see "Joe and Frank," referring to his brother, defendant Francis Vasquez, they proceeded to a house on Longfellow Avenue in the Bronx.

At that location, Patrolman Guzman met Francis Vasquez, who told him he could sell him an eighth of heroin for $3,100. Shortly thereafter, defendant Dones joined the conversation and was told by the Vasquez brothers that Patrolman Guzman was looking for some cocaine. Dones responded that for $7,000 he could supply him with one-half a kilogram of cocaine. Patrolman Guzman was then told to return later that evening. That evening, Guzman returned to 878 Southern Boulevard where he met Jaime Vasquez and showed him a roll of money which he then placed in the trunk of his automobile. A short time later, Frank Vasquez and Dones arrived in a Volkswagen. Jaime Vasquez had a short conversation with his brother and Dones after which he instructed Guzman to follow the Volkswagen. The two cars proceeded to Longwood Avenue where Dones exited his automobile, came over to Guzman's car and told the undercover patrolman that he would return in ten minutes with the "stuff". While Jaime Vasquez remained with Guzman, Dones returned to his automobile and was driven by Frank Vasquez to 149th Street where he and Vasquez entered a social club. A short time later, Dones and Vasquez left the club accompanied by defendant Charles Estepa, but did not enter the Volkswagen, which Vasquez had left double-parked in front of the club, proceeding instead on foot to 150th Street.

Approximately twenty-five minutes later, a blue Ford containing Dones, Frank Vasquez, Estepa (in the front passenger's seat) and driven by an unknown male, returned to Longwood Avenue and parked opposite Patrolman Guzman's automobile. Dones exited the Ford and told Guzman and Jaime Vasquez that he would return in thirty minutes. Approximately one hour later, the same Ford returned with the same passengers, passed Guzman's parked car, hesitating as it

---

[1] The only witnesses to give testimony at the trial were law enforcement officers.

did so, and parked around the corner. A few minutes later, Dones arrived alone on foot, entered Guzman's car and handed Guzman a tin foil package, inside of which was a plastic bag containing 128.73 grams of heroin hydrochloride. Guzman went to the trunk of his car, where he had placed the money, and dropped his keys as a signal to the surveillance agents. Dones and Jaime Vasquez, who had remained with Guzman during the evening, were then placed under arrest.

A few blocks away, other agents, who had kept the Ford containing Estepa and the unidentified driver under surveillance, received word of the arrest by radio. As the surveillance agents pulled alongside the Ford and identified themselves by showing their badges, the Ford made a quick U-turn and sped off. A high speed chase ensued. At the intersection of Garrison and Whorten Avenues, two packages were thrown out the front window of the Ford on the passenger side where Estepa was sitting. These packages were later retrieved and found to contain a total of 17.27 grams of heroin hydrochloride. The agents then pulled alongside the Ford and again ordered the car to stop after identifying themselves. The Ford, however, sped up, swerved to avoid a trunk and at 156th Street made a right turn, a maneuver the agents were unable to negotiate because of the speed of their automobile. The Ford stopped on 156th Street, and both occupants, Estepa and the driver, alighted. The driver escaped on foot and Estepa was placed under arrest. A search of the automobile revealed a packet containing 10.94 grams of heroin hydrochloride on the floor of the passenger side of the front seat where Estepa had been sitting.

Although the Ford in question was officially registered to one Joseph M. Medina, Estepa referred to the car after his arrest as "my car", and was in possession of the automobile's registration.

It is plain from this recitation that, except for the individuals named in the indictment, the person, and the only person, who was in a position to inform the grand jury of just what occurred up to the point of the arrest of Dones and Jaime Vasquez was Patrolman Guzman. Examination of the trial record shows that the persons (other than the defendants) in the best position to inform the grand jury of what occurred thereafter were Narcotics Agent Finnerty and New York City Policeman Walpole, and, with respect to Estepa's post-arrest statement, New York City Policeman Miller.

None of these men was called. The sole witness before the grand jury was New York City Policeman Twohill, whose observations of the appellants were both limited and remote. When we inquired at argument why Patrolman Guzman was not called to testify before the grand jury, we were told he was in the field doing other work that day; when we asked what reason prevented postponement of the presentation for a day or two, we were told there was none.

Despite Policeman Twohill's extremely limited personal knowledge, he spoke to the grand jury at length and in detail. He began with an incident on September 13, 1971, a month before the substantive crime with which the two appellants were charged.[2] He testified that Perez passed a package, later analyzed by the laboratory of the Bureau of Narcotics and Dangerous Drugs, to Jaime Vasquez who then passed it on to Patrolman Guzman, who paid $150. On this occasion, the Assistant United States Attorney interjected "you didn't observe the actual pass, but you did observe the meeting, is that correct?", to which Twohill responded "I did." Twohill

---

[2] The events of September 13 formed the basis of Count II, against Jaime Vasquez and Perez.

then testified that, on September 27, Jaime Vasquez passed a package, later determined to contain heroin, to Patrolman Guzman, who paid $120.[3] This time, the Assistant did nothing to alert the grand jury to any limitations on Twohill's knowledge. Moving on to the transaction on October 14, 1971, which constituted Counts IV, V and VI against these defendants (and also the principal — in Estepa's case the sole — basis for the conspiracy count), Twohill testified that Guzman requested Jaime Vasquez to furnish a one-eighth kilo of heroin and some cocaine and that Jaime Vasquez told Guzman to drive to Dones' home on Longfellow Avenue. Even if we assume that Twohill had witnessed this meeting from afar, there was nothing in his testimony or in the questions of the Assistant to inform the grand jury that he had not and could not have heard any such request or answer. He recounted to the grand jury what took place at Dones' house and a conversation between Frank Vasquez and Guzman in connection with the sale of a one-eighth kilo of heroin for $3,100, a conversation between Dones and Guzman for the sale of a half kilo of cocaine for $7,000, and an instruction by Frank Vasquez to Guzman to meet near Jaime Vasquez' home. Here again, even if we assume, perhaps overgenerously so far as the record goes, that Twohill saw something, he clearly heard nothing, but the grand jurors were not told this. There followed testimony about Guzman's having driven Jaime Vasquez back to his home, returning there, and showing him a roll of money, which Twohill might well have observed. He next described the meeting of the Vasquez brothers, Dones and Guzman. Here he failed to follow the script and said that Guzman, rather than Jaime Vasquez, directed that they follow Dones' car. The error was natural since, as we are aware but the grand jury was not, he had no personal knowledge whatever. Twohill then testified that Vasquez and Guzman, followed by Dones and his passengers, proceeded to a location on Longwood Avenue in the Bronx where Vasquez spoke with the individuals in Dones' car. Next came testimony of the arrival at and departure from the social club, which Twohill had in fact observed. He then proceeded to testify to the arrival of Dones, Frank Vasquez and Estepa in the blue Ford and to Guzman's being told to wait for half an hour for the defendants' return with the narcotics; nothing informed the grand jury that Twohill had not heard anything of the sort. Finally, and most egregiously, after relating the return of the blue Ford, the signal and the arrest, he described the chase, the throwing of the packets out of the Ford, the arrest of Estepa, and the discovery of a package under the front seat of the Ford, which he had not observed at all since, as he testified at trial, he had remained at the scene of the arrest.

We have previously condemned the casual attitude with respect to the presentation of evidence to a grand jury manifested by the decision of the Assistant United States Attorney to rely on testimony of the law enforcement officer who knew least, rather than subject the other officers, or himself, to some minor inconvenience, even if the motivation was merely this rather than the more sinister reason suggested in Judge Medina's dissent in *United States v. Beltram*, 388 F.2d 449, 451–452 (2d Cir.). When the framers of the Bill of Rights directed in the Fifth Amendment that "No person shall be held to answer for a capital, or otherwise infamous crime, unless on a presentment or indictment of a Grand Jury," they were not engaging in a mere verbal exercise. The importance of avoiding undue reliance upon hearsay before a grand jury is heightened by this circuit's view that an indictment constitutes a finding of probable cause and avoids the need for a preliminary hearing under

---

[3] This constituted Count III, against Jaime Vasquez.

F.R.Cr.P. 5(c). We have not gone so far as to apply to grand juries the proposal in the American Law Institute's Model Code of Pre-Arraignment Procedure §§ 330.4(4) and 340.5 (Tent.Draft No. 5, 1972), that hearsay may be received at a preliminary hearing or by a grand jury only "if the court determines that it would impose an unreasonable burden on one of the parties or on a witness to require that the primary source of the evidence be produced at the hearing, and if the witness furnishes information bearing on the informant's reliability and, as far as possible, the means by which the information was obtained," although we do not believe *Costello v. United States*, 350 U.S. 359 (1956), would prevent this exercise of our supervisory powers should we deem it wise. But we have insisted that, even though "there is no affirmative duty to tell the grand jury *in haec verba* that it is listening to hearsay," *United States v. Malofsky*, 388 F.2d 288, 289 (2 Cir.) (1968), the grand jury must not be "misled into thinking it is getting eye-witness testimony from the agent whereas it is actually being given an account whose hearsay nature is concealed." *United States v. Leibowitz*, 420 F.2d 39, 42 (2 Cir. 1969). That was what happened here.

The Government argues that the prosecutor discharged his obligation to enlighten the grand jury by bringing out that Twohill did not see "the actual pass" from Perez to Jaime Vasquez to Guzman on September 13, 1971, and by two other statements noted in the margin. But grand jurors cannot be supposed to possess sufficient astuteness to infer that, because Twohill on one occasion made clear the limited degree of his knowledge of a transaction occurring more than a month before the events of October 14, this carried through to all; indeed, the contrary inference would be quite as reasonable. The Government contends more broadly that, since Twohill never stated he was acting in an undercover capacity, the grand jurors should have known he was only a surveilling agent who could not have seen or heard the details of the occurrences and conversations to which he testified with such specificity. Grand jurors do not have this degree of familiarity with law enforcement techniques, and it would have been so easy for the Assistant United States Attorney to tell them what they are now claimed to have known. Moreover, this explanation does not at all explain Twohill's testimony about the chase, the throwing of the packets, and Estepa's arrest. This was something a surveilling agent could well have observed, yet the fact, presumably known to the Assistant, was that Twohill had not witnessed it at all.

The many opinions in which we have affirmed convictions despite the Government's needless reliance on hearsay before the grand jury show how loathe we have been to open up a new road for attacking convictions on grounds unrelated to the merits. We have been willing to allow ample, many doubtless think too ample, latitude in the needless use of hearsay, subject to only two provisos — that the prosecutor does not deceive grand jurors as to "the shoddy merchandise they are getting so they can seek something better if they wish," *United States v. Payton, supra*, 363 F.2d at 1000 (dissenting opinion), or that the case does not involve "a high probability that with eyewitness rather than hearsay testimony the grand jury would not have indicted." *United States v. Leibowitz*, 420 F.2d at 42. We had hoped that, with the clear warnings we have given to prosecutors, going back to *United States v. Umans*, 368 F.2d 725, 730 (2 Cir. 1966), and the assurances given by United States Attorneys, a reversal for improper use of hearsay before the grand jury would not be required. Here the Assistant United States Attorney, whether wittingly or unwittingly — we prefer to think the latter — clearly violated the first of these provisos. We cannot, with proper respect for the discharge of our duties, content ourselves with yet another admonition; a reversal with instructions to dismiss the indictment may help to translate the assurances of the United States Attorneys into consistent performance by their assistants. As Judge Medina said in his dissent in *United States v. Beltram, supra*, 388 F.2d at 453, "This would not let appellants go scot free, as there would be time to reindict them and have their guilt or innocence passed upon again on a record not tainted with irregularity."

The judgments of conviction are reversed, with instructions to dismiss the indictment.

Notes from Millie:

1. How can this case be reconciled with *Costello*?

2. The court in *Estepa* cited Judge Medina's dissent in *U.S. v. Beltram*. Here is part of it:

> I do not dispute the fact that there is no constitutional obstacle to the presentment of a case to the grand jury by means of hearsay evidence. Such a view is foreclosed by *Costello v. United States*, 350 U.S. 359 (1956). My point has a double aspect. As the grand jury may and often does refuse to indict, it seems to me that it is only just and fair to require the prosecutor at least to warn the grand jury that most or all of the proofs presented are at second hand. Of even greater significance, in my opinion, is the evil practice, especially in narcotics cases, of using before the grand jury only a peripheral witness, who recites in more or less narrative fashion what other narcotics agents have seen, heard or done. The key witness, in this case Scott, is not produced; nor is the grand jury told in any intelligible way that the principal witness to the commission of the crimes has not been produced. The inevitable consequence of this procedure is to make it impossible for the defense, by demanding production of the grand jury minutes at the trial, to use contradictions and misstatements of the principal witness under oath to impeach him.

> I remember the days when it was like pulling teeth to get a federal judge to hand over grand jury minutes to defense counsel for purposes of cross-examination. But those times have passed and, in a more enlightened age, it is thought more consistent with the accused's right to defend himself to permit his counsel, generally as a matter of course, at least in this Circuit, to see the grand jury testimony of trial witnesses for the prosecution and to permit the use on cross-examination of these witnesses of such parts of the grand jury testimony as counsel deems to be contradictory. What is the use of such a practice, established in the cause of truth and justice, if the prosecutor can in effect return to the old system by the simple expedient of withholding key witnesses from the grand jury hearing?

> These narcotics agents are not sacrosanct. The only way to make them mend their ways is, in the exercise of our supervisory powers, to reverse a few convictions obtained in this manner.

> Generally speaking, our Court has passed over this particular practice, as does the majority opinion in this case, by citing *Costello* and saying that we have never held that an indictment should be dismissed "because it was

secured by hearsay testimony." But in *United States v. Umans*, 368 F.2d 725 (2d Cir. 1966), the following was the unanimous view of a panel of this Court:

> While we are not condemning the procedure used here before the grand jury, we think it not amiss for us to state that excessive use of hearsay in the presentation of government cases to grand juries tends to destroy the historical function of grand juries in assessing the likelihood of prosecutorial success and tends to destroy the protection from unwarranted prosecutions that grand juries are supposed to afford to the innocent. Hearsay evidence should only be used when direct testimony is unavailable or when it is demonstrably inconvenient to summon witnesses able to testify to facts from personal knowledge.

With all due respect for my brothers, I cannot see how this is any test at all. It surely does not go to the point I am making in this dissent. How is one to know when the use of hearsay is "excessive"? In this very case it is claimed that direct testimony was unavailable and that it was demonstrably inconvenient to summon Scott as a witness before the grand jury, simply because he had been working late the night before the case was presented to the grand jury and because of the limited number of narcotics agents.

Moreover, in this case the failure to call Scott to testify before the grand jury might have brought about a conviction that otherwise would have been an acquittal. At the trial, Scott admitted he had not been able to identify the man who came into Beltram's room on the night of the second purchase of cocaine. But, in his recital to the grand jury of what Scott had seen, Smith unequivocally said that Scott did identify Colon. Had Scott given any such testimony before the grand jury, it would inevitably have been brought out on cross-examination at the trial, after perusal of the grand jury minutes, and, at the very least, Scott's credibility would have been impaired, especially as the testimony that he could and did identify Colon and that he could not and did not identify Colon given on the two occasions respectively was under oath. On the other hand, had Scott been produced and had he testified to the grand jury that he was unable to identify Colon, the grand jury might have refused to indict.

Accordingly, I would reverse the judgment below as against both appellants and dismiss the indictment. This would not let appellants go scot free, as there would be time to reindict them and have their guilt or innocence passed upon again on a record not tainted with irregularity.

UNITED STATES v. BASURTO
U.S. Court of Appeals, 9th Circuit
497 F.2d 781 (1974)

FERGUSON, DISTRICT JUDGE:

Appellants and 14 others were charged in a one-count indictment with conspiring to import and distribute marijuana, in violation of 21 U.S.C. §§ 176a, 841 and 952. The conspiracy was alleged to have occurred between February 1, 1971 and December 4, 1971, and to have involved smuggling marijuana from Mexico into the

United States by airplane. Following the denial of motions to suppress evidence and to dismiss the indictment, appellants were convicted of the charged offense after a jury trial. We reverse.

William Barron was named in the indictment as a co-conspirator but not a defendant. He testified as to appellants' activities in the conspiracy before the grand jury which brought the indictment. Prior to the commencement of trial, Barron informed the Assistant United States Attorney prosecuting the case that he had committed perjury before the grand jury in important respects. In particular, he told the prosecutor that all his grand jury testimony relating to his knowledge of appellants' activities in the conspiracy prior to May 1, 1971, was untrue. That date is significant, because effective then 21 U.S.C. § 176a was repealed by the Comprehensive Drug Abuse Prevention and Control Act of 1970, 21 U.S.C. § 801 et seq. Persons convicted of narcotics offenses under 21 U.S.C. § 176a were subject to a mandatory minimum sentence of five years, while those convicted under the new statute were not subject to such inflexible sentencing.

The only witness other than Barron to testify before the grand jury as to appellants' activities in connection with the conspiracy prior to May 1, 1971, was Thomas Waddill, a Customs agent. Both Barron's and Waddill's testimony was unrecorded. The parties dispute whether Agent Waddill, at the time of his grand jury appearance, had any knowledge of appellants' activities prior to May 1, 1971, other than what Barron had told Waddill.[1] Upon learning of Barron's perjured grand jury testimony, the prosecuting attorney informed opposing counsel. He did not, however, notify the court or the grand jury. In his opening statement at trial, he made reference to Barron's perjury before the grand jury, but sought to minimize its scope and importance:

> Mr. Barron did testify at the Grand Jury, but part of his testimony was a lie. Mr. Barron will take the stand and tell you that today, or excuse me, when he takes the stand. He will tell you he lied about where he met Buddy Wilson, Buddy Waggoner, the man seated here in the brown suit. He will tell you that the reason he told this lie is he was protecting a friend of his in Seattle, Washington. He will tell you that other than minute details which he has since recalled, such as a change in a date or a change in possibly who was present at exactly a particular moment, other than those details this is the only material lie that he told before the Grand Jury, but it was a lie. He will tell you that when he takes the stand in this trial he will tell the truth.

The conduct of the prosecutor in this case reinforces the expression by Professor Moore that, over the years, the government prosecutor has gained substantial influence over the grand jury, and subsequently that institution has lost much of its former independence. See 8 J. Moore, *Federal Practice*, ¶ 6.02(1).

The Fifth Amendment provides that "no person shall be held to answer for a capital, or otherwise infamous crime, unless on a presentment or indictment of a Grand Jury." The purpose of that requirement is to limit a person's jeopardy to offenses charged by a group of his fellow citizens acting independently of either the

---

[1] It is not necessary that the dispute be resolved, since it does not affect the holding of this court. The issue here is not one relating to the sufficiency of evidence before a grand jury to sustain an indictment, but rather, the duty of a prosecutor when he becomes aware that perjury as to a material matter has been committed.

prosecutor or the judge. *Stirone v. United States*, 361 U.S. 212 (1960).

It is clear, however, that when a duly constituted grand jury returns an indictment valid on its face, no independent inquiry may be made to determine the kind of evidence considered by the grand jury in making its decision. *Costello v. United States*, 350 U.S. 359 (1956). To do so would further invade the independence of the grand jury. The holding reached by this court does not affect that established rule. Today, the grand jury relies upon the prosecutor to initiate and prepare criminal cases and investigate which come before it. The prosecutor is present while the grand jury hears testimony; he calls and questions the witnesses and draws the indictment. With that great power and authority there is a correlative duty, and that is not to permit a person to stand trial when he knows that perjury permeates the indictment.

At the point at which he learned of the perjury before the grand jury, the prosecuting attorney was under a duty to notify the court and the grand jury, to correct the cancer of justice that had become apparent to him. To permit the appellants to stand trial when the prosecutor knew of the perjury before the grand jury only allowed the cancer to grow.

As we have noted above, the perjury before the grand jury was material because of the change in the law; all of Barron's grand jury testimony relating to the appellants' activities before May 1, 1971 was perjured. The grand jury, if it returned an indictment, might have done so under the Comprehensive Drug Abuse Prevention and Control Act of 1970 had it known of the perjury.

We also note that jeopardy had not attached at the time the prosecutor learned of the perjured testimony, nor had the statute of limitations for the offenses charged run. Under *Illinois v. Somerville*, 410 U.S. 458 (1973), if the prosecutor had brought the perjury to the court's attention before the trial commenced and the indictments had been dismissed, the Double Jeopardy Clause of the Fifth Amendment would not have barred trial under a new indictment.

We hold that the Due Process Clause of the Fifth Amendment is violated when a defendant has to stand trial on an indictment which the government knows is based partially on perjured testimony, when the perjured testimony is material, and when jeopardy has not attached. Whenever the prosecutor learns of any perjury committed before the grand jury, he is under a duty to immediately inform the court and opposing counsel — and, if the perjury may be material, also the grand jury — in order that appropriate action may be taken. * * * *

The judgments of convictions are reversed.

HUFSTEDLER, CIRCUIT JUDGE (concurring specially):

I concur in the result reached by the majority, but I find unsatisfactory the constitutional theory it advances to support its conclusion that the prosecutor had a duty to inform the grand jury of Barron's perjured testimony. Unlike the prosecutor in *Napue v. Illinois* (1959), 360 U.S. 264, who "did nothing to correct the witness' false testimony," the prosecutor in the case at bench notified both defense counsel and the trial court upon learning of the perjured testimony. I do not believe that the prosecutor's failure additionally to inform the grand jury was such a breach of his constitutional duty of good faith as to constitute a violation of defendants' due process rights.

Although the majority's constitutional analysis is not persuasive, it would be an appropriate exercise of our power to supervise the administration of criminal justice in the federal courts to impose upon federal prosecutors the duty to notify the grand jury described by the majority. An important function of our supervisory power is to guarantee that federal prosecutors act with due regard for the integrity of the administration of justice.

The grand jury serves important public interests, not only through its examination into the commission of crimes, but also by its ability "to stand between the prosecutor and the accused, and to determine whether the charge was founded on credible testimony or was dictated by malice or personal ill will." *Hale v. Henkel* (1906), 201 U.S. 43, 59. By failing to inform the grand jury of Barron's perjured testimony and thus precluding the opportunity to reconsider the indictment in light of the corrected version of the defendants' activities, the prosecutor effectively frustrated this vital function. A supervisory rule requiring a prosecutor who learns before trial that an indictment is based in some material way on perjured testimony to seek dismissal of the tainted indictment would safeguard the grand jury's role as mediator between prosecutor and potential defendant. Such a supervisory rule would also help insure that the prosecutor fulfills his responsibility to deal with the grand jury in a way that promotes the wise exercise of its investigatory and indictment powers. Even though breach of that prosecutorial duty may not constitute a violation of defendant's constitutional rights, the prosecutor is nevertheless responsible to the court for conduct that is potentially detrimental to the integrity of the judicial system. It is thus well within our supervisory jurisdiction to require that the United States Attorney shall move for dismissal of indictments based on perjured testimony. Whether measured by the supervisory rule I have suggested or the constitutional duty imposed by the majority, the response of the prosecutor in the case at bench to the discovery that a witness had perjured himself before the grand jury was inadequate. I therefore agree with the result reached by the majority in the first section of its opinion. I concur in the majority's treatment of the other issues raised by these appeals.

Notes from Millie:

1. What, exactly, did the prosecutor do wrong in *Basurto*, according to the court?

2. In *People v. Huston*, 88 N.Y.2d 400 (1996), the court set aside an indictment because of misbehavior by the prosecutor, which included telling the grand jury that *he personally believed* that the defendant was guilty.

3. In *U.S. v. Sigma International, Inc.* 196 F.3d 1314 (11th Cir. 1999), the court found that the prosecutor had behaved improperly in presenting a case to the grand jury — though the behavior was not so bad as to justify setting aside the indictment:

> We would be remiss in our responsibility to protect the integrity of the grand jury process, however, if we did not discuss [prosecutor] Rubinstein's conduct before the third grand jury. The first thing Rubinstein said to the grand jury after introducing himself was "I'm here to present to you this morning some evidence and some legal explanation about a case which we'll be asking you to vote on and consider tomorrow." He then told the jurors that he would screen their questions, answering them himself when possible, to speed up the process. At the beginning of day two, he again told the jurors that he wanted to rush them so they could vote at the end of the

day. Such statements were inappropriate. A prosecutor may not set the grand jury's schedule for it, nor may a prosecutor suggest that the grand jury has a limited amount of time in which to reach a decision. See ABA Standards for Criminal Justice Prosecution Function 3 3.5(a) (3d ed.1993) (stating that prosecutors should give due deference to the grand jury as an independent body). By telling a brand new grand jury that it would vote tomorrow, Rubinstein nearly foreclosed any serious questioning or deliberation by that body. Several times, however, he clarified that he did not want to rush the jurors unfairly; if they needed more time they were to let him know. In addition, at the end of the second day, he allowed the grand jury to make its own decision (without him in the room) about whether to vote that day.

Although in the end, the grand jury made an independent decision to indict, Rubinstein attempted to turn that independent decision into simply a rubber stamp decision. For instance, at various points during his presentation, Rubinstein told the grand jury how to interpret the evidence in order to find that the appellants acted knowingly (an element of the crimes charged) on specific occasions that were critical to the Government's case. A prosecutor's job is to present evidence of criminal activity to a grand jury. In so doing, the prosecutor may also explain why a piece of evidence is legally significant, but he may not tell the jury what inferences it should draw from the evidence. Factual questions are for the grand jury to determine on its own. See ABA Standards for Criminal Justice Prosecution Function 3 3.5(a) & cmt. (3d ed.1993) (stating that a prosecutor may explain the law and the legal significance of the evidence, but he must leave to the grand jury the determination of whether the evidence constitutes probable cause). Courts have recognized that grand juries, which are drawn from a pool of ordinary citizens, may need some assistance understanding criminal laws; thus, they allow prosecutors to explain the law and interpret the legal significance of evidence. But, courts have consistently emphasized that a prosecutor must temper his assistance in order to preserve the grand jury's independence. A prosecutor who informs the grand jury of both the legal and factual significance of the evidence he has presented risks infringing on the grand jury's independence and jeopardizing the integrity of its proceedings. Most of the inferences Rubinstein drew from the evidence were apparent. Therefore, his comments on what the evidence established, while out of line, were not so far out that they cause us seriously to doubt the grand jury's independence in this case.[2]

---

[2] The full court later granted a rehearing *en banc* in this case, whereupon the parties reached a plea agreement. *See* 291 F.3d 765 (11th Cir. 2002).

UNITED STATES v. UDZIELA
U.S. Court of Appeals, 7th Circuit
671 F.2d 995 (1982)

BAUER, CIRCUIT JUDGE.

Defendant-appellant Edward Udziela appeals from his conviction for conspiring to manufacture and distribute phencyclidine (PCP), in violation of 21 U.S.C. § 846, and for aiding and abetting in the manufacture of PCP, in violation of both 18 U.S.C. § 2 and 21 U.S.C. § 841(a)(1). This appeal raises the important question whether perjured grand jury testimony, discovered and disclosed by the government after dismissal of the grand jury but before trial, should trigger an *in camera* judicial hearing to determine the existence and sufficiency of other evidence supporting the indictment. We hold that such a hearing is required in the future, unless the government chooses to seek a new indictment based on other, untainted evidence. Nevertheless, we affirm for the reasons expressed below.

I

Bruce Nacker, Paul Udziela (Paul) and appellant Edward Udziela (appellant) played varying roles in a conspiracy to manufacture and distribute PCP, an illegal drug. * * * * The scheme started in December 1979 when Paul approached Nacker, his Chicago neighbor for approximately four years, and discussed the profitability of selling PCP. After considering the matter, they decided to work together. Nacker, who was educated in biochemistry and pharmacy, obtained the formula and chemical components needed to produce a small amount of PCP. He then prepared the first batch and delivered it to Paul, who eventually sold it for $1,500 and divided the proceeds with Nacker.

Shortly before the first batch was completed, the two neighbors decided to expand their production to accommodate a buyer seeking large quantities of PCP. They called several drug companies and ordered additional chemicals necessary for increased drug production, sometimes giving fictitious names of individuals or businesses, or the names of friends' businesses, to shield the purchasers' true identities. Appellant was aware of these clandestine activities, having occasionally sat in on conversations between his brother Paul and Nacker. * * * * Officials of one Chicago drug business, Lapine Scientific Company, became suspicious and contacted United States Drug Enforcement Administration (DEA) agents, who decided to monitor the activities of Nacker and Paul.

Although most of the companies' drug shipments were received by the conspirators, an order from Alfa Ventron Company in Massachusetts was inexplicably delayed. As a result, Nacker reordered the same quantity. Shortly thereafter, Nacker learned that his first Alfa Ventron Company order had been received, rendering the second unnecessary. Rather than cancel the second order, Nacker elected to obtain additional ingredients, which when mixed with his second order would yield double the initially anticipated amount of PCP.

Seeking additional chemicals, and unaware of DEA surveillance, appellant and his brother Paul drove to Precision Organic Chemical Company (Precision), a sham drug company operated by undercover DEA agents. Agent Mel Schabilion, posing as a Precision employee, greeted Paul, gave him a purchase order for three gallons of phenyl magnesium bromide, and then carried the chemical containers outside to appellant's car, where appellant was waiting. There Schabilion met appellant, exchanged pleasantries with him, loaded the three bottles of chemicals into appellant's car, and watched appellant and his brother depart.

Appellant then drove Paul from Precision to Nacker's garage, where the PCP was produced, and dropped off his brother and the chemicals. Later that day, appellant also drove his brother and Nacker to a store to buy a fish tank in which to mix the chemicals. In addition, appellant acted as a lookout during production and drove to a local store to purchase ice needed in the manufacturing process. That evening, agents searched Nacker's garage and seized drug containers and equipment. Nacker, Paul, and appellant were subsequently arrested.

Nacker ultimately appeared before the grand jury, where he attempted to minimize his role in the drug manufacturing conspiracy. He claimed that: (1) he never previously manufactured PCP; (2) he learned the PCP formula from Paul; (3) he only ordered chemicals twice; and (4) he and Paul were the only persons involved. He also admitted that he lied to federal agents about his role in the conspiracy, but claimed to be telling the true story to the grand jury because he was under oath.

The day before trial, after the grand jury was no longer sitting, Nacker revealed that he had lied to the grand jury. The government, taken by surprise, immediately disclosed this new information to appellant's counsel. The case proceeded to trial, and on direct examination, Nacker told a story greatly different from his grand jury version, directly implicating appellant in many respects. After three days at trial, appellant moved to dismiss the indictment because he claimed it was based, at least in part, on Nacker's perjured testimony. The motion was denied and appellant was eventually convicted. This appeal followed.

II

Appellant's sole contention on appeal is that the trial court erred in not dismissing his indictment. Although Nacker's perjury was not discovered until after the grand jury was dismissed, appellant argues that the government was obligated to seek dismissal of the flawed indictment and then, if it chose, attempt to secure a new indictment. The government, on the other hand, contends that dismissal is warranted only if the perjured testimony was introduced knowingly, which it claims was not the case. As authority for their positions in this case of first impression in this Circuit, both sides rely heavily on their respective interpretations of *United States v. Basurto*, 497 F.2d 781 (9th Cir.1974).

A

Before discussing *Basurto*, the problem raised in this appeal should be placed in perspective. Under the ancient English system, where criminal prosecutions were instituted by the King at the suit of private prosecutors, "the most valuable function of the grand jury was not only to examine into the commission of crimes, but to stand between the prosecutor and the accused, and to determine whether the charge was founded upon credible testimony or was dictated by malice or personal ill will." *Hale v. Henkel*, 201 U.S. 43, 59 (1906). In drawing this nation's charter, the drafters of the United States Constitution elevated the grand jury to constitutional status, embodied in the fifth amendment command that no federal prosecution shall occur "unless on a presentment or indictment of a Grand Jury." Indeed, the framers thought the grand jury essential to preserve our basic liberties. See *United States v. Calandra*, 414 U.S. 338, 343 (1974). Thus, "the grand jury performs the dual function of determining if there is probable cause to believe that a crime has been committed and of protecting citizens against unfounded criminal prosecutions." *Branzburg v. Hayes*, 408 U.S. 665, 686 87 (1972).

Despite its lofty place as an instrument of justice, as a practical matter the modern grand jury is greatly dependent on the United States Attorney "to present to it such evidence as it needs for its performance of its function and to furnish it with controlling legal principles." *United States v. Ciambrone*, 601 F.2d 616, 622 (2d Cir.1979). Recognizing this increasing dependency, federal courts in recent years have become more sensitive to allegations of governmental misconduct before the grand jury and have demonstrated greater willingness to curb prosecutorial abuse of such proceedings. Thus, in cases where over-zealous prosecutors have manipulated a grand jury by willfully misleading it or knowingly presenting false evidence, courts have not hesitated to exercise their power to dismiss indictments. See, e.g., *United States v. Samango*, 607 F.2d 877 (9th Cir.1979) (intentional suppression of favorable testimony); *United States v. McKenzie*, 524 F.Supp. 186 (E.D.La. 1981) (prosecutors placed undue pressure on the grand jury to indict policeman accused of murder and brutality); *United States v. Martin*, 480 F.Supp. 880 (S.D.Tex.1979) (failure to reveal both SEC agreement not to prosecute and alleged bribery scheme); *United States v. Gold*, 470 F.Supp. 1336 (N.D.Ill.,1979) (failure to divulge exculpatory evidence and other misconduct); *United States v. Phillips Petroleum Co.*, 435 F.Supp. 610 (N.D.Okla.1977) (withholding of exculpatory testimony); *United States v. Braniff Airways, Inc.*, 428 F.Supp. 579 (W.D.Tex.1977) (failure to present complete record of prior grand jury proceeding as well as statutory provision exempting airlines from antitrust laws); *United States v. DeMarco*, 401 F.Supp. 505 (C.D.Cal.1975) (failure to disclose information vital to the grand jury's informed and independent judgment); *United States v. Gallo*, 394 F.Supp. 310 (D.Conn.1975) (selective presentation of evidence from a prior grand jury proceeding); *United States v. Wells*, 163 F. 313 (D.Idaho1908) (prosecutor expressed his opinion that defendants were guilty and that the grand jury should return an indictment against them); *cf. Johnson v. Superior Court*, 15 Cal.3d 248 (1975) (California Penal Code imposes on prosecutor an implied duty to divulge exculpatory information).

Without necessarily endorsing these cases, we note that they generally involved fairly serious or blatant prosecutorial misconduct. The dismissals in those decisions, whether based on constitutional grounds or the federal courts' supervisory powers, reflected the courts' fundamental concern for protecting the integrity of the judicial process, "particularly the function of the grand jury, from unfair or improper prosecutorial conduct." *United States v. Chanen*, 549 F.2d 1306, 1309 (9th Cir.1977)).

In certain situations, we have shown similar willingness to exercise our supervisory power when the integrity of the judicial system was threatened or undermined by executive misconduct. See, e.g., *United States v. Cortina*, 630 F.2d 1207 (7th Cir.1980).

On the other hand, the federal supervisory power does not give "the federal judiciary a 'chancellor's foot' veto over law enforcement practices of which it does not approve." *Id.* at 1214. Strictly speaking, the grand jury is a constitutional fixture in its own right, belonging to neither the executive nor the judicial branch (*United*

States v. Chanen, 549 F.2d 1306, 1312 13 (9th Cir.1977)), though it often relies on both when performing its duties. In light of the subtle yet distinct relationships among these three constitutionally authorized entities, we must take care not to encroach on legitimate executive activities before the grand jury. It is with good reason, then, as Justice (then Judge) Blackmun put it, that "courts generally have been *most cautious* in invalidating indictments for alleged grand jury misconduct of the prosecutor." *Beatrice Foods Co. v. United States*, 312 F.2d 29, 39 (8th Cir.1963) (emphasis added).

B

With these thoughts in mind, we turn to the Ninth Circuit's decision in *United States v. Basurto*, 497 F.2d 781 (9th Cir.1974). In that case Ernest Basurto was charged with conspiracy to import and distribute marijuana. Prior to the commencement of Basurto's trial, the government's key witness, William Barron, informed the prosecution that all his grand jury testimony concerning Basurto's conspiratorial activities was perjured. The prosecutor informed Basurto's counsel of Barron's perjury, but failed to notify the court or the grand jury. At the trial's conclusion, Basurto was convicted on the conspiracy charge. On appeal, a panel of the Ninth Circuit reversed Basurto's conviction, holding that

> The Due Process Clause of the Fifth Amendment is violated when a defendant has to stand trial on an indictment which the government knows is based partially on perjured testimony, when the perjured testimony is material, and when jeopardy has not attached. Whenever the prosecutor learns of any perjury committed before the grand jury, he is under a duty to immediately inform the court and opposing counsel — and if the perjury be material, also the grand jury — in order that appropriate action may be taken. [*Id.* at 785 86]

Noting that the use of false testimony to obtain tainted convictions goes against "any concept of ordered liberty," the *Basurto* majority concluded, on constitutional grounds, that reversal of a conviction is required:

> When the government allows a defendant to stand trial on an indictment which it knows to be based in part upon perjured testimony. The consequences to the defendant of perjured testimony given before the grand jury are no less severe than those of perjured testimony given at trial, and in fact may be more severe. The defendant has no effective means of cross-examining or rebutting perjured testimony given before the grand jury, as he might in court. [497 F.2d at 781]

Judge Hufstedler, in a specially concurring opinion, agreed that the prosecutor's failure to disclose perjury undermined the grand jury's independence. She noted, however, that such a prosecutorial failure might not always amount to a violation of the defendant's constitutional rights. To remedy this shortcoming, she preferred to base the decision on the court's supervisory jurisdiction, under which the court could require the United States Attorney to move for dismissal of the tainted indictment independent of any constitutional challenge by a defendant.

Although a few subsequent decisions have followed *Basurto*, more recent opinions have "not only cut back on the reach of *Basurto*, but have also questioned its continuing validity." *United States v. Cathey*, 591 F.2d 268, 271 72 (5th Cir. 1979).

Indeed, a panel of the Ninth Circuit itself noted that prosecutorial misconduct must be "flagrant" to violate due process, a rather strict application of *Basurto*, if not an entirely new standard. See *United States v. Bettencourt*, 614 F.2d 214, 216 (9th Cir.,1980).

We also doubt the total validity of *Basurto* and, therefore, decline to follow its broad holding. The *Basurto* rationale suffers from a major flaw. It suggests that the "consequences to the defendant of perjured testimony given before the grand jury are no less severe than those of perjured testimony given at trial, and in fact may be more severe" because a defendant has no opportunity to cross-examine a grand jury witness. The *Basurto* court then cites several decisions involving perjury at trial as support for its position. This view misapprehends the limited function of the grand jury. Under the fifth amendment all that is required of an indictment is that it be "returned by a legally constituted and unbiased grand jury." *Costello v. United States*, 350 U.S. 359, 363 (1956). The grand jury "does not sit to determine the truth of the charges brought against a defendant, but only to determine whether there is probable cause to believe them true, so as to require him to stand trial." *Bracy v. United States*, 435 U.S. 1301, 1302 (1978) (Rehnquist, J., in chambers).

The effect of *Basurto*, to borrow the Supreme Court's language in *Costello*, "would be that before trial on the merits a defendant could always insist on a kind of preliminary trial to determine the competency and adequacy of the evidence before the grand jury." *Costello v. United States*, 350 U.S. at 363. The resulting delay from endless challenges would be unacceptable, especially in cases where the prosecution was unaware of or merely negligent in allowing perjured grand jury testimony and where the perjury constituted but a small portion of the evidence before the grand jury.

We think a more appropriate standard must be sensitive to the grand jury's independence yet strong enough to guard against outrageous or intentional prosecutorial misconduct.[3] In this case, however, no prosecutorial misconduct confronts us. The government was completely unaware of Nacker's perjured grand jury testimony and, upon discovering it, immediately informed defense counsel.

In light of the narrow issue this case presents, we exercise our supervisory power and hold, prospectively, that where perjured testimony supporting an indictment is discovered before trial, the government has the option of either voluntarily withdrawing the tainted indictment and seeking a new one before the grand jury when it reconvenes, unless it is already sitting, or of appearing with defense counsel before the district court for an *in camera* inspection of the grand jury transcripts for a determination whether other, sufficient evidence exists to support the indictment. If other, sufficient evidence is present so that the grand jury may have indicted without giving any weight to the perjured testimony, the indictment cannot be challenged on the basis of the perjury. See *United States v. DeLeo*, 422 F.2d 487, 496 97 (1st Cir.1970). Our rationale for these rules is simple enough: errors before the grand jury, such as perjured testimony, normally can be corrected at trial, where evidentiary and procedural rules safeguard the accused's constitutional

---

[3] We approach with care the delicate balance between grand jury independence and aggressive prosecution because, as one commentator aptly noted, "given the *Costello* ruling, a court that dismisses a validly returned indictment is more guilty of interfering with the independence of the grand jury than a prosecutor who presents a slanted case to the grand jury." Note, *Grand Jury: A Prosecutor Need Not Present Exculpatory Evidence*, 38 Wash. & Lee L.Rev. 110, 117 (1981).

rights. See *Loraine v. United States*, 396 F.2d 335, 339 (9th Cir.1968); but see *United States v. Serubo*, 604 F.2d 807, 817 (3d Cir. 1979) (while in theory a trial provides the defendant with a full opportunity to contest and disprove the charges against him, in practice, the handing up of an indictment will often have a devastating personal and professional impact that a later dismissal or acquittal can never undo). Put differently, grand jury proceedings need not be perfect.

After thoroughly reviewing the grand jury transcript in this case, we are convinced that ample evidence apart from Nacker's perjured testimony supported the indictment. For example, DEA Agent Lance Mrock told the grand jury of his firsthand observation of the transaction between Paul Udziela and Agent Schabilion at Precision Organic Chemical Company. Agent Mrock specifically noted appellant's presence at Precision, just as Agent Schabilion did at trial. Agent Mrock also noted that appellant and Paul proceeded directly to Nacker's garage, that appellant met with Nacker and Paul outside the garage, and that appellant unloaded the chemicals and then remained in the garage for a few minutes. Based on Mrock's testimony, the grand jury could see that appellant knowingly participated in a drug manufacturing conspiracy. Thus, regardless of Nacker's testimony, the grand jury was justified in determining that probable cause existed to indict appellant. Our independent review obviates the need for a hearing before the district court in this case. Because other, sufficient evidence was presented to the grand jury, appellant's motion to dismiss the indictment was properly denied.

Affirmed.

Notes from Millie:

1. In *United States v. Mechanik*, 475 U.S. 66 (1986), two witnesses testified at the same time before the grand jury. This violated Rule 6(d), which allows only one witness in the grand jury room at a time. The Court held that this violation did not warrant reversal of defendant's later conviction, even assuming that it would have been a good reason to dismiss the indictment before trial.

> The Rule protects against the danger that a defendant will be required to defend against a charge for which there is no probable cause to believe him guilty. But the petit jury's subsequent guilty verdict means not only that there was probable cause to believe that the defendants were guilty as charged, but also that they are in fact guilty as charged beyond a reasonable doubt. Measured by the petit jury's verdict, then, any error in the grand jury proceeding connected with the charging decision was harmless beyond a reasonable doubt. This holds true here. If the prosecutor erred in presenting evidence to the grand jury, that error was harmless. It is inappropriate to reverse the ensuing conviction.

Does this ruling make *Estepa, Basurto*, and *Udziela* meaningless, as a practical matter? After *Mechanik*, what could those defendants have done?

2. In *State v. Chong*, 86 Hawai'i 282, 949 P.2d 122 (1997), Chong moved to dismiss his indictment.

> In the course of the hearing on Chong's motion to dismiss the indictment, the deputy prosecutors' testimonies established that the prosecution had prepared the witnesses who testified before the grand jury by providing them with a list of questions that a deputy prosecutor expected

to ask them, along with the witnesses' anticipated answers, excerpted from the witnesses' own prior statements or reports. It was also the prosecution's practice to include with the questions and answers instructions for each witness to look over the predicate questions and answers and note any necessary corrections to the predicate answers. Witnesses were never told to memorize the predicate answers and testify accordingly. Rather, they were instructed to tell the truth.

According to the deputy prosecutors, the prosecution provided the grand jury witnesses with the predicate questions and answers for several reasons: (1) to prepare witnesses for the case by focusing them on the questions and those prior statements, which, in the prosecution's view, were necessary to show probable cause; (2) to determine from the witnesses whether the answers, as excerpted, were correct; and (3) to keep the grand jury proceedings focused on the key issues so that the proceedings could be handled as quickly and efficiently as possible. The deputy prosecutor who prepared the predicate questions and answers testified that "the answers that we send to the witnesses we get from the reports that we receive. Everything that we get is directly from the witnesses' reports or from talking to the witnesses. And that's what I did in this case."

The deputy prosecutors testified that grand jury witnesses who were given the predicate questions and answers usually were also given written instructions and specifically told to notify the prosecutors if the predicate answers were inconsistent with their recollection. The witnesses were also instructed to tell the truth. A comparison of the predicate answers with the witnesses' answers to the predicate questions during the grand jury proceedings reflects that the witnesses did not "memorize" the predicate answers and were not "rehearsed witnesses" or "scripted automatons." In numerous instances, the witnesses' answers during the grand jury proceedings were far more detailed and descriptive than the predicate answers. The evidence did not indicate that the testimonies of the witnesses were other than their own statements based on their own recollections. There is no evidence in the record to indicate that the predicate answers provided by the prosecution to the witnesses and the testimonies of the witnesses before the grand jury were a fabrication of facts.

The trial court held that the prosecutor had improperly invaded the province of the grand jury, and the court granted Chong's motion to dismiss the indictment. But the Hawai'i Supreme Court reversed:

We hold that the prosecution's use of pre-scripted questions and answers in connection with its grand jury witnesses, called in the proceeding as a result of which the indictment against Chong was returned, did not so clearly infringe upon the jury's decision-making function and was not so innately prejudicial that the practice — in and of itself — violated Chong's right to due process of law by invading the province of the grand jury or tending to induce action other than that which the grand jurors, in their uninfluenced judgment, deemed warranted on the evidence fairly presented before them. Pursuant to Rule 1.1 of the Hawai'i Rules of Professional Conduct, "a lawyer has a responsibility to thoroughly prepare his or her witnesses before calling them to the stand."[5]

3. See Peter J. Henning, *Prosecutorial Misconduct in Grand Jury Investigations*, 51 South Carolina Law Review 1 (1999).

UNITED STATES v. MANDUJANO
United States Supreme Court
425 U.S. 564 (1976)

MR. CHIEF JUSTICE BURGER announced the judgment of the Court, in an opinion in which MR. JUSTICE WHITE, MR. JUSTICE POWELL, and MR. JUSTICE REHNQUIST join.

This case presents the question whether the warnings called for by *Miranda v. Arizona*, 384 U.S. 436 (1966), must be given to a grand jury witness who is called to testify about criminal activities in which he may have been personally involved; and whether, absent such warnings, false statements made to the grand jury must be suppressed in a prosecution for perjury based on those statements.

During the course of a grand jury investigation into narcotics traffic in San Antonio, Tex., federal prosecutors assigned to the Drug Enforcement Administra-

---

[5] The record is devoid of any indication that the deputy prosecuting attorneys in this case comported themselves incompatibly with the American Bar Association's Standards for Criminal Justice Prosecution Function (3d ed.1993), most notably Standards 3-3.1 ("Investigative Function of Prosecutor"), 3-3.5 ("Relations With Grand Jury"), 3-3.6 ("Quality and Scope of Evidence Before Grand Jury"), and 3-5.6 ("Presentation of Evidence"). "A prosecutor in presenting a case to a grand jury should not intentionally interfere with the independence of the grand jury, preempt a function of the grand jury, or abuse the processes of the grand jury." Standard 3-3.6(f). "In general, the prosecutor should be guided by the standards governing and defining the proper presentation of the state's case in an adversary trial before a petit jury." ABA Standards § 3-3.5 commentary at 64. "It is not only proper but it may be the duty of the prosecutor to interview any person who may be called as a witness in the case," so long as "prospective witnesses are not treated as partisans," but, rather, "as impartial and as relating the facts as they see them." ABA Standards § 3-3.1 commentary at 50.

It is also proper to caution a witness concerning the need to exercise care in subscribing to a statement prepared by another person. In the event that a written statement is signed or otherwise acknowledged by the witness as a correct representation of facts known to the witness, a copy of the statement should be furnished to the witness upon request. *Id.* Moreover, after written statements are secured by investigators, it is proper under our system, and indeed wise, for the prosecutor to interview such witnesses personally, not only to verify the investigator's report but to become familiar with the personality of the witness in order to anticipate how the witness will react on the stand. *Id.* at 52.

On the other hand, we fully subscribe to the following principles and exhort the prosecutors in this state to abide by them on peril of undermining the fundamental fairness and integrity of the grand jury process: "A prosecutor must not take advantage of his or her role as the *ex parte* representative of the state before the grand jury to unduly or unfairly influence it in voting on charges brought before it." ABA Standards § 3-3.5 commentary at 64. "Since grand jury proceedings are generally secret and *ex parte*, it is particularly desirable that a record be made of the prosecutor's communications and representations to the jury." *Id.* Unless a prosecutor is prepared to forego impeachment of a witness by the prosecutor's own testimony as to what the witness stated in an interview or to seek leave to withdraw from the case in order to present the impeaching testimony, a prosecutor should avoid interviewing a prospective witness except in the presence of a third person. Standard 3-3.1(g).

And, finally, a prosecutor is barred from introducing evidence that he or she knows is false. This obligation applies to evidence that bears on the credibility of a witness as well as to evidence on issues going directly to guilt. Even if false testimony is volunteered by the witness and takes the prosecutor by surprise, if the prosecutor knows it is false, it is the prosecutor's obligation to see that it is corrected. ABA Standards § 3-5.6 commentary at 101–02.

tion Task Force learned of an undercover narcotics officer's encounter with respondent in March 1973. At that time, the agent had received information that respondent, who was employed as a bartender at a local tavern, was dealing in narcotics. The agent, accompanied by an informant, met respondent at the tavern and talked for several hours. During the meeting, respondent agreed to obtain heroin for the agent, and to that end placed several phone calls from the bar. He also requested and received $650 from the agent to make the purchase. Respondent left the tavern with the money so advanced to secure the heroin. However, an hour later respondent returned to the bar without the narcotics and returned the agent's money. Respondent instructed the agent to telephone him at the bar that evening to make arrangements for the transaction. The agent tried but was unable to contact respondent as directed. The record provides no explanation for respondent's failure to keep his appointment. No further action was taken by the agent, and the investigatory file on the matter was closed. The agent did, however, report the information to federal prosecutors. At that time, the Government was seeking information on local drug traffic to present to a special grand jury investigating illicit traffic in the area.

Respondent was subpoenaed to testify before the grand jury on May 2, 1973; this was approximately six weeks after the abortive narcotics transaction at the tavern where respondent was employed. When called into the grand jury room and after preliminary statements, the following colloquy occurred between the prosecutor and respondent:

Q: Now, you are required to answer all the questions that I ask you except for the ones that you feel would tend to incriminate you. Do you understand that?

A: Do I answer all the questions you ask?

Q: You have to answer all the questions except for those you think will incriminate you in the commission of a crime. Is that clear?

A: Yes, sir.

Q: You don't have to answer questions which would incriminate you. All other questions you have to answer openly and truthfully. And, of course, if you do not answer those questions truthfully, in other words if you lie about certain questions, you could possibly be charged with perjury. Do you understand that?

A: Yes, sir.

Q: Have you contacted a lawyer in this matter?

A: I don't have one. I don't have the money to get one.

Q: Well, if you would like to have a lawyer, he cannot be inside this room. He can only be outside. You would be free to consult with him if you so chose. Now, if during the course of this investigation, the questions that we ask you, if you feel like you would like to have a lawyer outside to talk to, let me know.

During the questioning, respondent admitted that he had previously been convicted of distributing drugs, that he had recently used heroin himself, and that he had purchased heroin as recently as five months previously. Despite this admitted experience with San Antonio's heroin traffic, respondent denied knowledge of the identity of any dealers, save for a street corner source named Juan. Respondent steadfastly denied either selling or attempting to sell heroin since the time of his conviction 15 years before.

Respondent specifically disclaimed having discussed the sale of heroin with anyone during the preceding year and stated that he would not even try to purchase an ounce of heroin for $650. Respondent refused to amplify on his testimony when directly confronted by the prosecutor:

Q: Mr. Mandujano, our information is that you can tell us more about the heroin business here in San Antonio than you have today. Is there anything you would like to add telling us more about who sells heroin?

A: Well, sir, I couldn't help you because, you know, I don't get along with the guys and I just can't tell you, you know.

Following this appearance, respondent was charged by a grand jury on June 13, 1973, in a two-count indictment with attempting to distribute heroin in violation of 21 U.S.C. §§ 841(a)(1), 846, and for willfully and knowingly making a false material declaration to the grand jury in violation of 18 U.S.C. § 1623.[1] The falsity of his statements was conceded; his sole claim was that the testimony before the grand jury should be suppressed because the Government failed to provide the warnings called for by *Miranda*. Following an evidentiary hearing, the District Court granted respondent's motion to suppress. The court held that respondent was a "putative" or "virtual" defendant when called before the grand jury; respondent had therefore been entitled to full *Miranda* warnings.[2]

The Court of Appeals affirmed. It recognized that certain warnings had in fact been given to respondent at the outset of his grand jury appearance. But the court agreed with the District Court that "full *Miranda* warnings should have been accorded Mandujano, who was in the position of a virtual or putative defendant." The essence of the Court of Appeals' holding is:

In order to deter the prosecuting officers from bringing a putative or virtual defendant before the grand jury, for the purpose of obtaining incriminating or perjurious testimony, the accused must be adequately apprised of his rights, *or all of his testimony, incriminating and perjurious, will be suppressed.* [Emphasis added.]

In so ruling, the court undertook to distinguish its own holding in *United States v. Orta*, 253 F.2d 312 (1958), in which Judge Rives, speaking for the court, stated:

---

[1] Count 2 of the indictment charged that the following declarations were materially false:

Q: Have you talked to anyone about selling heroin to them during the last year?

A: No, sir.

Q: And you have never told anyone that you would try to get heroin to sell to them?

A: No, sir.

Q: No one has ever given you any money

A: No.

Q: To go buy them heroin?

A: No, sir.

[2] Respondent was subsequently tried and convicted under Count 1 of the indictment for attempting to distribute heroin. The grand jury testimony was not utilized by the prosecution at that trial.

A grand jury witness might answer truthfully and thereafter assert the constitutional guaranty. *Under no circumstances, however, could he commit perjury and successfully claim that the Constitution afforded him protection from prosecution for that crime.* The immunity afforded by the constitutional guaranty relates to the past, and does not endow the person who testifies with a license to commit perjury.

The only debatable question is one of the supervision of the conduct of Government representatives in the interest of fairness. The mere possibility that the witness may later be indicted furnishes no basis for requiring that he be advised of his rights under the Fifth Amendment, when summoned to give testimony before a Grand Jury. There is no showing that the Grand Jury before which Orta testified was seeking to indict him or any other person already identified. [*Id.* at 314; emphasis added]

The Court of Appeals concluded that the "totality of the circumstances" commanded suppression of all the testimony on which the charge of perjury rested.

We agree with the views expressed by Judge Rives in *Orta* and disagree with the Court of Appeals in the instant case; accordingly, we reverse.

The grand jury is an integral part of our constitutional heritage which was brought to this country with the common law. The Framers, most of them trained in the English law and traditions, accepted the grand jury as a basic guarantee of individual liberty; notwithstanding periodic criticism, much of which is superficial, overlooking relevant history, the grand jury continues to function as a barrier to reckless or unfounded charges. "Its adoption in our Constitution as the sole method for preferring charges in serious criminal cases shows the high place it held as an instrument of justice." *Costello v. United States*, 350 U.S. 359, 362 (1956). Its historic office has been to provide a shield against arbitrary or oppressive action, by insuring that serious criminal accusations will be brought only upon the considered judgment of a representative body of citizens acting under oath and under judicial instruction and guidance.

Earlier we noted that the law vests the grand jury with substantial powers, because "the grand jury's investigative power must be broad if its public responsibility is adequately to be discharged." *United States v. Calandra*, 414 U.S. 338, 344. Indispensable to the exercise of its power is the authority to compel the attendance and the testimony of witnesses and to require the production of evidence.

When called by the grand jury, witnesses are thus legally bound to give testimony. This principle has long been recognized. In *United States v. Burr*, 25 Fed.Cas. 38 (CC Va., 1807), Mr. Chief Justice Marshall drew on English precedents, aptly described by Lord Chancellor Hardwicke in the 18th century, and long accepted in America as a hornbook proposition: "The public has a right to every man's evidence." This Court has repeatedly invoked this fundamental proposition when dealing with the powers of the grand jury. *United States v. Nixon*, 418 U.S. 683, 709 (1974). The grand jury's authority to compel testimony is not, of course, without limits. The same Amendment that establishes the grand jury also guarantees that "no person . . . shall be compelled in any criminal case to be a witness against himself." The duty to give evidence to a grand jury is therefore conditional; every person owes society his testimony, unless some recognized privilege is asserted.

Under settled principles, the Fifth Amendment does not confer an absolute right to decline to respond in a grand jury inquiry; the privilege does not negate the duty to testify, but simply conditions that duty. The privilege cannot, for example, be asserted by a witness to protect others from possible criminal prosecution. Nor can it be invoked simply to protect the witness' interest in privacy. "Ordinarily, of course, a witness has no right of privacy before the grand jury." *Calandra, supra,* 414 U.S. at 353.

The very availability of the Fifth Amendment privilege to grand jury witnesses, recognized by this Court in *Counselman v. Hitchcock,* 142 U.S. 547 (1892), suggests that occasions will often arise when potentially incriminating questions will be asked in the ordinary course of the jury's investigation. Probing questions to all types of witnesses is the stuff that grand jury investigations are made of; the grand jury's mission is, after all, to determine whether to make a presentment or return an indictment. "The basic purpose of the English grand jury was to provide a fair method for instituting criminal proceedings against persons believed to have committed crimes." *Costello v. United States, supra,* 350 U.S. at 362.

It is in keeping with the grand jury's historic function as a shield against arbitrary accusations to call before it persons suspected of criminal activity, so that the investigation can be complete. This is true whether the grand jury embarks upon an inquiry focused upon individuals suspected of wrongdoing, or is directed at persons suspected of no misconduct but who may be able to provide links in a chain of evidence relating to criminal conduct of others, or is centered upon broader problems of concern to society. It is entirely appropriate, indeed imperative, to summon individuals who may be able to illuminate the shadowy precincts of corruption and crime. Since the subject matter of the inquiry is crime, and often organized, systematic crime, as is true with drug traffic, it is unrealistic to assume that all of the witnesses capable of providing useful information will be pristine pillars of the community untainted by criminality.

The Court has never ignored this reality of law enforcement. Speaking for the Court in *Kastigar v. United States,* 406 U.S. 441 (1972), Mr. Justice Powell said:

> Many offenses are of such a character that the only persons capable of giving useful testimony are those implicated in the crime. [*Id.* at 446]

Moreover, the Court has expressly recognized that "the obligation to appear is no different for a person who may himself be the subject of the grand jury inquiry." *United States v. Dionisio,* 410 U.S. 1, 10 (1973). * * *

Accordingly, the witness, though possibly engaged in some criminal enterprise, can be required to answer before a grand jury, so long as there is no compulsion to answer questions that are self-incriminating; the witness can, of course, stand on the privilege, assured that its protection "is as broad as the mischief against which it seeks to guard." *Counselman v. Hitchcock,* 142 U.S. at 562. The witness must invoke the privilege, however, as the "Constitution does not forbid the asking of criminative questions." *United States v. Monia,* 317 U.S. 424, 433 (1943) (Frank-furter, J., dissenting).

The Fifth Amendment speaks of compulsion. It does not preclude a witness from testifying voluntarily in matters which may incriminate him. If, therefore, he desires the protection of the privilege, he must claim it or he will not be considered to have been "compelled" within the meaning of the Amendment. [*Id*. at 427]

Absent a claim of the privilege, the duty to give testimony remains absolute.

The stage is therefore set when the question is asked. If the witness interposes his privilege, the grand jury has two choices. If the desired testimony is of marginal value, the grand jury can pursue other avenues of inquiry; if the testimony is thought sufficiently important, the grand jury can seek a judicial determination as to the bona fides of the witness' Fifth Amendment claim, in which case the witness must satisfy the presiding judge that the claim of privilege is not a subterfuge. If in fact "there is reasonable ground to apprehend danger to the witness from his being compelled to answer," *Brown v. Walker*, 161 U.S. at 599, the prosecutor must then determine whether the answer is of such overriding importance as to justify a grant of immunity to the witness.

If immunity is sought by the prosecutor and granted by the presiding judge, the witness can then be compelled to answer, on pain of contempt, even though the testimony would implicate the witness in criminal activity. The reason for this is not hard to divine; Mr. Justice Frankfurter indicated as much in observing that immunity is the *quid pro quo* for securing an answer from the witness: "Immunity displaces the danger." *Ullmann v. United States*, 350 U.S. 422, 439 (1956). Based on this recognition, federal statutes conferring immunity on witnesses in federal judicial proceedings, including grand jury investigations, are so familiar that they have become part of our "constitutional fabric." *Lefkowitz v. Turley*, 414 U.S. 70, 81 82 (1973). Immunity is the Government's ultimate tool for securing testimony that otherwise would be protected; unless immunity is conferred, however, testimony may be suppressed, along with its fruits, if it is compelled over an appropriate claim of privilege. On the other hand, when granted immunity, a witness once again owes the obligation imposed upon all citizens the duty to give testimony since immunity substitutes for the privilege.

In this constitutional process of securing a witness' testimony, perjury simply has no place whatever. Perjured testimony is an obvious and flagrant affront to the basic concepts of judicial proceedings. Effective restraints against this type of egregious offense are therefore imperative. The power of subpoena, broad as it is, and the power of contempt for refusing to answer, drastic as that is and even the solemnity of the oath cannot insure truthful answers. Hence, Congress has made the giving of false answers a criminal act punishable by severe penalties; in no other way can criminal conduct be flushed into the open where the law can deal with it. * * * *

In this case, the Court of Appeals required the suppression of perjured testimony given by respondent, as a witness under oath, lawfully summoned before an investigative grand jury and questioned about matters directly related to the grand jury's inquiry. The court reached this result because the prosecutor failed to give *Miranda* warnings at the outset of Mandujano's interrogation. Those warnings were required, in the Court of Appeals' view, because Mandujano was a "virtual" or "putative" defendant that is, the prosecutor had specific information concerning Mandujano's participation in an attempted sale of heroin and the focus of the grand jury interrogation, as evidenced by the prosecutor's questions, centered on Mandujano's involvement in narcotics traffic. The fundamental error of the prosecutor, in the court's view, was to treat respondent in such a way as to "smack of entrapment";

as a consequence, the court concluded that "elemental fairness" required the perjured testimony to be suppressed.

The court's analysis, premised upon the prosecutor's failure to give *Miranda* warnings, erroneously applied the standards fashioned by this Court in *Miranda*. Those warnings * * * were aimed at the evils seen by the Court as endemic to police interrogation of a person in custody. * * * *Miranda* addressed extrajudicial confessions or admissions procured in a hostile, unfamiliar environment which lacked procedural safeguards. The decision expressly rested on the privilege against compulsory self-incrimination; the prescribed warnings sought to negate the "compulsion" thought to be inherent in police station interrogation. But the *Miranda* Court simply did not perceive judicial inquiries and custodial interrogation as equivalents: The compulsion to speak in the isolated setting of the police station may well be greater than in courts or other official investigations, where there are often impartial observers to guard against intimidation or trickery. [384 U.S. at 461]

The Court thus recognized that many official investigations, such as grand jury questioning, take place in a setting wholly different from custodial police interrogation. Indeed, the Court's opinion in *Miranda* reveals a focus on what was seen by the Court as police "coercion" derived from "factual studies relating to police violence and the 'third degree': physical brutality, beating, hanging, whipping and to sustained and protracted questioning incommunicado in order to extort confessions." *Id.* at 445 446. To extend these concepts to questioning before a grand jury inquiring into criminal activity under the guidance of a judge is an extravagant expansion never remotely contemplated by this Court in *Miranda*; the dynamics of constitutional interpretation do not compel constant extension of every doctrine announced by the Court.

The marked contrasts between a grand jury investigation and custodial interrogation have been commented on by the Court from time to time. Mr. Justice Marshall observed that the broad coercive powers of a grand jury are justified, because "in contrast to the police it is not likely that the grand jury will abuse those powers." *United States v. Mara*, 410 U.S. 19, 46 (1973) (dissenting opinion).

The warnings volunteered by the prosecutor to respondent in this case were more than sufficient to inform him of his rights and his responsibilities and particularly of the consequences of perjury. To extend the concepts of *Miranda*, as contemplated by the Court of Appeals, would require that the witness be told that there was an absolute right to silence, and obviously any such warning would be incorrect, for there is no such right before a grand jury. Under *Miranda*, a person in police custody has, of course, an absolute right to decline to answer any question, incriminating or innocuous, whereas a grand jury witness, on the contrary, has an absolute duty to answer all questions, subject only to a valid Fifth Amendment claim. And even when the grand jury witness asserts the privilege, questioning need not cease, except as to the particular subject to which the privilege has been addressed. Other lines of inquiry may properly be pursued.

Respondent was also informed that if he desired he could have the assistance of counsel, but that counsel could not be inside the grand jury room. That statement was plainly a correct recital of the law. No criminal proceedings had been instituted against respondent, hence the Sixth Amendment right to counsel had not come into play. *Kirby v. Illinois*, 406 U.S. 682 (1972). A witness "before a grand jury cannot insist, as a matter of constitutional right, on being represented by his counsel." *In re Groban*, 352 U.S. at 333. * * * * Under settled principles the witness may not insist upon the presence of his attorney in the grand jury room. Fed.Rule Crim.Proc. 6(d).

Respondent, by way of further explanation, was also warned that he could be prosecuted for perjury if he testified falsely. Since respondent was already under oath to testify truthfully, this explanation was redundant; it served simply to emphasize the obligation already imposed by the oath.

> Once a witness swears to give truthful answers, *there is no requirement to warn him not to commit perjury or, conversely to direct him to tell the truth.* It would render the sanctity of the oath quite meaningless to require admonition to adhere to it. [*United States v. Winter*, 348 F.2d 204, 210 (CA2 1965). (Emphasis added.)]

Similarly, a witness subpoenaed to testify before a petit jury and placed under oath has never been entitled to a warning that, if he violates the solemn oath to "tell the truth," he may be subject to a prosecution for perjury, for the oath itself is the warning. Nor has any case been cited to us holding that the absence of such warnings before a petit jury provides a shield against use of false testimony in a subsequent prosecution for perjury or in contempt proceedings.[7]

In any event, a witness sworn to tell the truth before a duly constituted grand jury will not be heard to call for suppression of false statements made to that jury, any more than would be the case with false testimony before a petit jury or other duly constituted tribunal.[8] In another context, this Court has refused to permit a witness to protect perjured testimony by proving a *Miranda* violation. In *Harris v. New York*, 401 U.S. 222 (1971), the Court held that, notwithstanding a *Miranda* violation: "The Fifth Amendment privilege cannot be construed to include the right to commit perjury." *Id.* at 225.

The fact that here the grand jury interrogation had focused on some of respondent's specific activities does not require that these important principles be jettisoned; nothing remotely akin to "entrapment" or abuse of process is suggested by what occurred here. Assuming, *arguendo*, that respondent was indeed a "putative defendant," that fact would have no bearing on the validity of a conviction for testifying falsely.

The grand jury was appropriately concerned about the sources of narcotics in the San Antonio area. The attempted heroin sale by respondent provided ample reason

---

[7] The fact that warnings were provided in this case to advise respondent of his Fifth Amendment privilege makes it unnecessary to consider whether any warning is required, as the Government asks us to determine. In addition to the warning implicit in the oath, federal prosecutors apparently make it a practice to inform a witness of the privilege before questioning begins.

[8] *Masinia v. United States*, 296 F.2d 871, 877 (CA8, 1961). Cases voiding convictions for perjury involved situations where the investigatory body was acting outside its lawful authority. *Brown v. United States*, 245 F.2d 549 (CA8, 1957); *United States v. Thayer*, 214 F.Supp. 929 (Colo.1963). For example, in *Brown v. United States, supra,* the Court of Appeals concluded that a federal grand jury in Nebraska had undertaken a "roving commission," investigating matters outside its lawful power. The District Court in that case had concluded that the grand jury's activities had come "perilously close to being a fraud on the jurisdiction of this court." 245 F.2d at 553. No such circumstances are presented by this case. We therefore have no occasion to address the correctness of the results reached by the courts in these inapposite instances.

to believe that he had knowledge about local heroin suppliers. It was, therefore, entirely proper to question him with respect to his knowledge of narcotics trafficking.[9] Respondent was free at every stage to interpose his constitutional privilege against self-incrimination, but perjury was not a permissible option. As the Tenth Circuit has held, the law provides "other methods for challenging the government's right to ask questions." *United States v. Pommerening*, 500 F.2d 92, 100 (1974).

The judgment of the Court of Appeals is therefore reversed, and the cause is remanded for further proceedings consistent with this opinion.

MR. JUSTICE BRENNAN, with whom MR. JUSTICE MARSHALL joins, concurring in the judgment.

I concur in the judgment of the Court, for "even when the privilege against self-incrimination permits an individual to refuse to answer questions asked by the Government, if false answers are given the individual may be prosecuted for making false statements." *Mackey v. United States*, 401 U.S. 667, 705 (1971) (Brennan, J., concurring in judgment). Although the Fifth Amendment guaranteed respondent the right to refuse to answer the potentially incriminating questions put to him before the grand jury, in answering falsely he took "a course that the Fifth Amendment gave him no privilege to take." *United States v. Knox*, 396 U.S. 77, 82 (1969). "Our legal system provides methods for challenging the Government's right to ask questions ? lying is not one of them." *Bryson v. United States*, 396 U.S. 64, 72. Further, the record satisfies me that the respondent's false answers were not induced by governmental tactics or procedures so inherently unfair under all the circumstances as to constitute a prosecution for perjury a violation of the Due Process Clause of the Fifth Amendment.

However, two aspects of the plurality opinion suggests a denigration of the privilege against self-incrimination and the right to the assistance of counsel with which I do not agree. * * * *

It is clear that the government may not, in the absence of an intentional and knowing waiver, call an indicted defendant before a grand jury and there interrogate him concerning the subject matter of a crime for which he already stands formally charged. *United States v. Calandra*, 414 U.S. at 345. The Fifth Amendment requires suppression of any statements of the accused that were so obtained. True, calling a person "who may himself be the subject of the grand jury inquiry" is not a violation *per se* of the Fifth Amendment. *United States v. Dionisio*, 410 U.S. 1, 10 (1973). This general proposition may be justified as necessary to the basic policy that the public has a right to every man's evidence, but in my view it must yield in situations risking vast potential for abuse in the absence of further safeguards calculated to preserve the policies underlying our adversary system.

It cannot be gainsaid that prosecutors often do call before grand juries persons suspected of criminal activity to testify concerning that activity, and the availability

---

[9] This is not to suggest that the questioning would have been improper if the principal aim of the grand jury's investigation had centered upon respondent's activities, rather than a general investigation into local narcotics traffic. As previously indicated, no impropriety results from summoning the target of its inquiry, *United States v. Dionisio*, 410 U.S. 1, 10 (1973); it is appropriate, in fact, to give that individual an opportunity to explain potentially damaging information before the grand jury decides whether to return an indictment.

of this device has often been fatally tempting to those aware of its potential for abuse. There can be no doubt that sanctioning unfettered discretion in prosecutors to delay the seeking of criminal indictments pending the calling of criminal suspects before grand juries to be interrogated under conditions of judicial compulsion runs the grave risk of allowing "the prosecution to evade its own constitutional restrictions on its powers by turning the grand jury into its agent." *United States v. Mara*, 410 U.S. 19, 29 (1973) (Douglas, J., dissenting).[12] In such situations, an individual's only protection against the mobilized power of the State is his Fifth Amendment privilege, but it is a protection of which there must be safeguards to make him aware. Careful measures are needed if the privilege is "still to stand guard when so much is attempted by inquisition, however subtle, at any stage of the criminal proceedings." *Wood v. United States*, 128 F.2d 265, 279 (1942).

Given the prosecutor's authority to choose the precise timing of a criminal indictment, it is not surprising that commentary uniformly decries the attempted distinction between a *de facto* and *de jure* defendant in the determination of the amount of protection accorded by the Fifth Amendment privilege.

> Distinctions based on status have created an incongruous grand jury witness, the *de facto* defendant who, though not formally accused, is marked for prosecution. Functionally indistinguishable from a *de jure* defendant, he enjoys only the protection of an unimplicated witness and must submit to interrogation without appraisal of the charge pending against him or of his fifth amendment rights. The prosecutor can take advantage of this anomalous treatment by deferring formal charge, summoning a *de facto* defendant before the grand jury and seeking disclosures which ensure indictment and may be used at trial. [Note, *Self Incrimination by Federal Grand Jury Witnesses: Uniform Protection Advocated*, 67 Yale L.J. 1271, 1276 1277 (1958).]

Indeed, it seems obvious that a *de facto* defendant's privilege is placed in much greater jeopardy than that of a *de jure* defendant, who has at least been informed of the charges against him and is more likely to have consulted with counsel and thereby have been made aware of his privilege.

Even more serious, the use by prosecutors of the tactic of calling a putative defendant before a grand jury and interrogating him regarding the transactions and events for which he is about to be indicted is, in the absence of an "intentional relinquishment or abandonment" of his "known" privilege against compulsory self-incrimination, *Schneckloth v. Bustamonte*, 412 U.S. 218, 235 (1973), a blatant subversion of the fundamental adversary principle that the State "establish its case, not by interrogation of the accused even under judicial safeguards, but by evidence independently secured through skillful investigation." *Watts v. Indiana*, 338 U.S. at 54. Where such prosecutorial tactics are employed, it borders on the absurd to say, as is said in justification of the *Monia* dictum, that the "government may assume that its compulsory processes are not eliciting" incriminating information. Rather, it is clear beyond question that the government is acutely aware of the potentially incriminatory nature of the disclosures sought, and thus one cannot avoid the

---

[12] Federal prosecutors, it has been asserted, have also taken advantage of the *de facto/de jure* distinction to postpone indictments and thereby utilize the subpoena power of the grand jury to obtain discovery in evasion of the strictures on Government discovery pursuant to Fed.Rule Crim.Proc. 16(c). Tigar & Levy, *The Grand Jury as the New Inquisition*, 50 Mich.St.B.J. 693, 700 (1971).

conclusion that in condoning resort to such tactics, the courts become partners in undermining the adversary system of criminal justice" by allowing prosecutors deliberately to seek to avoid the burdens of independent investigation by compelling self-incriminating disclosures. Such tactics by prosecutors are exemplars of the very evils sought to be prevented by the enshrinement of the Fifth Amendment privilege in the Constitution. In giving those tactics our stamp of approval, we turn our backs on our recognition heretofore that it is crucial that courts "be alert to repress any abuses of the investigatory power invoked, bearing in mind that the most valuable function of the grand jury has been not only to examine into the commission of crimes, but to stand between the prosecutor and the accused." *Hoffman v. United States*, 341 U.S. 479, 485 (1951). "A defendant's right not to be compelled to testify against himself at his own trial might be practically nullified if the prosecution could previously have required him to give evidence against himself before a grand jury." *Michigan v. Tucker*, 417 U.S. 433, 441 (1974).

Thus, I would hold that, in the absence of an intentional and intelligent waiver by the individual of his known right to be free from compulsory self-incrimination, the Government may not call before a grand jury one whom it has probable cause as measured by an objective standard to suspect of committing a crime, and by use of judicial compulsion compel him to testify with regard to that crime. In the absence of such a waiver, the Fifth Amendment requires that any testimony obtained in this fashion be unavailable to the Government for use at trial. Such a waiver could readily be demonstrated by proof that the individual was warned prior to questioning that he is currently subject to possible criminal prosecution for the commission of a stated crime, that he has a constitutional right to refuse to answer any and all questions that may tend to incriminate him, and by record evidence that the individual understood the nature of his situation and privilege prior to giving testimony.

> Some courts have reasoned that because of the investigative function and inquisitorial nature of the grand jury, it cannot be burdened with affording a witness the full panoply of procedural safeguards. However, it is *because* in a grand jury proceeding there is no right to other procedural safeguards that a witness should be told of his right to remain silent. [*In re Kelly*, 350 F.Supp. at 1202]

Certainly to the extent that our task is to weigh "the potential benefits" to be derived from this requirement against the "potential injury to the historic role and functions of the grand jury," *United States v. Calandra*, 414 U.S. at 349, we must come down on the side of imposing this requirement if subversion of the adversary process is to be avoided where suspected persons are ignorant of their rights. In no way does the requirement of a knowing waiver "interfere with the effective and expeditious discharge of the grand jury's duties," *id.* at 350, or "saddle a grand jury with minitrials and preliminary showings that would impede its investigation," *United States v. Dionisio*, 410 U.S. at 17, or "delay and disrupt grand jury proceedings," *Calandra, supra*, 414 U.S. at 349. And plainly the requirements of an effective warning and an intelligent waiver by a putative defendant prior to attempts to elicit potentially incriminating information impose no onerous duty on the prosecutor. The reported decisions of the lower federal courts are replete with examples of prosecuting officials proffering such warnings as an essential element of our fundamental liberties. Where uncertain whether the situation requires it, the prosecutor may safely err on the side of ensuring the knowing and intentional nature of the waiver, for he does no more than discharge his responsibility to safeguard a constitutional guarantee calculated to ensure the liberty of us all. Only when these safeguards are afforded a putative defendant called and interrogated before a grand jury may we truthfully proclaim that the Fifth Amendment "privilege is as broad as the mischief against which it seeks to guard." *Counselman v. Hitchcock*, 142 U.S. at 562.

II

A second and also disturbing facet of the plurality opinion today is its statement that "no criminal proceedings had been instituted against respondent, hence the Sixth Amendment right to counsel had not come into play." It will not do simply to cite, as does the plurality opinion, *Kirby v. Illinois*, 406 U.S. 682, (1972), for this proposition. *Kirby's* premise, so fundamental that it was "noted at the outset," was that "the constitutional privilege against compulsory self-incrimination is in no way implicated here." *Id.* at 687. In sharp contrast, the privilege against compulsory self-incrimination is inextricably involved in this case since a putative defendant is called and interrogated before a grand jury. Clearly, in such a case a defendant is "faced with the prosecutorial forces of organized society, and immersed in the intricacies of substantive and procedural criminal law." *Id.* at 689.

Accepted principles require scrutiny of any situation wherein a right to the assistance of counsel is claimed by "analyzing whether potential substantial prejudice to defendant's rights inheres in the particular confrontation and the ability of counsel to help avoid that prejudice." *United States v. Wade*, 388 U.S. 218, 227 (1967). And the question of whether the guidance of counsel is ordinarily required to enable an individual effectively to avoid prejudice to his Fifth Amendment privilege was clearly answered by this Court last Term.

> The assertion of a testimonial privilege, as of many other rights, often depends upon legal advice from someone who is trained and skilled in the subject matter, and who may offer a more objective opinion. A layman may not be aware of the precise scope, the nuances, and boundaries of his Fifth Amendment privilege. It is not a self-executing mechanism; it can be affirmatively waived, or lost by not asserting it in a timely fashion. [*Maness v. Meyers*, 419 U.S. 449, 466 (1975)]

Given the inherent danger of subversion of the adversary system in the case of a putative defendant called to testify before a grand jury, and the peculiarly critical role of the Fifth Amendment privilege as the bulwark against such abuse, it is plainly obvious that some guidance by counsel is required. This conclusion entertains only the "realistic recognition of the obvious truth that the average putative defendant does not have the professional legal skill to protect himself when brought before a tribunal wherein the prosecution is represented by experienced and learned counsel." *Johnson v. Zerbst*, 304 U.S. at 462 463.

> It is said that a witness can protect himself against some of the many abuses possible in a secret interrogation by asserting the privilege against self-incrimination. But this proposition collapses under anything more than the most superficial consideration. The average witness has little if any idea when or how to raise any of his constitutional privileges. In view of the intricate possibilities of waiver which surround the privilege he may easily

unwittingly waive it. [*In re Groban, supra*, 352 U.S. at 345 346 (Black, J., dissenting)]

Under such conditions, it "would indeed be strange were this Court" to hold that a putative defendant, called before a grand jury and interrogated concerning the substance of the crime for which he is in imminent danger of being criminally charged, is simply to be left to "fend for himself." *Coleman v. Alabama, supra*, 399 U.S. at 20 (Harlan, J., concurring and dissenting).

It may be that a putative defendant's Fifth Amendment privilege will be adequately preserved by a procedure whereby, in addition to warnings, he is told that he has a right to consult with an attorney prior to questioning, that if he cannot afford an attorney one will be appointed for him, that during the questioning he may have that attorney wait outside the grand jury room, and that he may at any and all times during questioning consult with the attorney prior to answering any question posed. See *United States v. Capaldo*, 402 F.2d 821, 824 (CA2, 1968).[22] At least if such minimal protections were present, a putative defendant would be able to consult with counsel prior to answering any question that he might in any way suspect may incriminate him. Thereafter, if the privilege is invoked and contested, a hearing on the propriety of its invocation will take place in open court before an impartial judicial officer, and the putative defendant will there have his counsel present. If the invocation of the privilege is disallowed, the putative defendant will then have the opportunity to answer the question posed prior to the imposition of sanctions for contempt. *Garner v. United States*, 424 U.S. at 663.

There is clearly no argument that a procedure allowing a putative defendant called to testify before a grand jury to consult at will with counsel outside the grand jury room prior to answering any given question would in any way impermissibly "delay and disrupt grand jury proceedings." *United States v. Calandra*, 414 U.S. at 349. This is clearly manifested by the plethora of reported instances in which just such procedures have been followed. Nor would such a procedure damage the constitutional "role and functions of the grand jury," for the only effect on its investigative function is to secure a putative defendant's Fifth Amendment privilege and thereby avoid subversion of the adversary system.

It is, of course, unnecessary in this case to define the exact dimensions of the right to counsel, since the testimony obtained by the grand jury interrogation was not introduced as evidence at respondent's trial on the charge concerning which he was questioned. I write only to make plain my disagreement with the implication in the plurality opinion that constitutional rights to counsel are not involved in a grand jury proceeding, and my disagreement with the further implication that there is a right to have counsel present for consultation outside the grand jury room but that it is not constitutionally derived and therefore may be enjoyed only by those wealthy enough to hire a lawyer. I cannot accede to a return to the regime of "squalid discrimination," *Griffin v. Illinois*, 351 U.S. 12, 24 (1956) (Frankfurter, J.,

---

[22] Contra, arguing that the presence of counsel *inside* the grand jury room is required, see Boudin, *The Federal Grand Jury*, 61 Geo.L.J. 1, 17.

Certainly there is no viable argument that allowing counsel to be present in the grand jury room for purposes of consultation regarding testimonial privileges would subvert the nature or functioning of the grand jury proceeding. Such a procedure is sanctioned by statute in several States. Kan.Stat.Ann. § 22 3009 (1974); S.D.Comp.Laws § 23 30 7 (1975); Utah Code Ann. § 77 19 3 (1975); Wash.Rev.Code § 10.27.120 (1974); Mich.Stat.Ann. § 28.943 (1972) (one-man grand jury).

concurring in judgment), where the justice "a man gets depends on the amount of money he has." *Id.* at 19 (opinion of Black, J.). Only recently, The Chief Justice reminded us of "the basic command that justice be applied equally to all persons," and further that "the passage of time has heightened rather than weakened the attempts (by this Court) to mitigate the disparate treatment of indigents in the criminal process." *Williams v. Illinois*, 399 U.S. 235, 241 (1970). If indeed there is, as the plurality opinion says, a right to have counsel present outside the door to the grand jury room, it is most assuredly in my view everyone's right, regardless of economic circumstance.

Note from Millie:

In *In re Melvin*, 546 F.2d 1 (1st Cir.1976), a federal prosecutor sought a court order compelling Melvin (who had not been arrested or charged with any crime) to appear in a lineup. While a grand jury had been investigating whether Melvin had committed bank robbery, the prosecutor made no showing of probable cause to believe that he had committed the crime. The trial court issued the order. On Melvin's appeal, the government argued that the prosecutor was justified in seeking the order, as the prosecutor was assisting the grand jury in obtaining evidence. The court disagreed:

> The United States Attorney short-circuited the usual procedure. Rather than subpoenaing Melvin, having the grand jury request his appearance in a lineup, and only on his refusal to comply seeking a court order, the United States Attorney, without showing a prior grand jury directive addressed to Melvin, went directly to court seeking the order compelling Melvin to appear in a lineup. This was no mere technical error, as the Government asserts, but an error affecting the proper roles of the prosecutor and the grand jury, since to endorse such a procedure would be to allow the United States Attorney to assume the powers of a grand jury so long as he merely adds the talismanic verbiage that what he seeks is "necessary" in furtherance of its investigations. * * * *

> Because of its special investigative function and the historically grounded obligation of every person to appear and give his evidence before the grand jury, a grand jury alone enjoys the inherent right to compel production of identification evidence in these circumstances. Grand jury subpoenas to testify are deemed not that kind of governmental intrusion on privacy against which the Fourth Amendment affords protection. The grand jury, at least in theory, exercises these broad investigative powers under the authority and supervision of the court, as a representative of the public.

> To be sure, the powers of the United States Attorney in connection with a grand jury investigation are substantial. He may, in practice, select the witnesses to be subpoenaed to appear before the grand jury and generally direct the investigation. The United States Attorney may obtain subpoenas issued in blank by the court, fill in the blanks, and have the witnesses served without consulting the grand jury.

> Still, he may not use his subpoena powers under Rule 17 to gather evidence without the participation of the grand jury. "The Constitution of the United States, the statutes, the traditions of our law, the deep rooted

preferences of our people speak clearly. They recognize the primary and nearly exclusive role of the Grand Jury as the agency of compulsory disclosure. They do not recognize the United States Attorney's office as a proper substitute for the grand jury room and they do not recognize the use of a grand jury subpoena, a process of the District Court, as a compulsory administrative process of the United States Attorney's office." *Durbin v. U.S.*, 221 F.2d 520, 522 (1954).

An order to appear in a lineup, addressed to someone as to whom probable cause to arrest has not yet been found, and requiring attendance outside the grand jury room at a proceeding not under the grand jury's immediate supervision, goes considerably beyond the routine issuance of subpoenas and other actions in which the United States Attorney has proceeded without specific direction of the grand jury. The order involves a major intrusion upon personal liberty which, if justified, is justified only upon the basis of the grand jury's unique investigative powers. Indeed, it has yet to be specifically established by the Supreme Court or a circuit court that a grand jury may compel an appearance in a lineup . . . In any event, the broadcast delegation of a power of this magnitude to the United States Attorney cannot be accepted if the grand jury's own role is to remain at all meaningful. Assuming without deciding that a directive to appear in a lineup is within the grand jury's power to issue, we think that the directive has to come from the grand jury itself and has to be conveyed by the grand jury to the witness in an appropriately formal fashion. Thereafter, if the witness will not comply, the court upon petition of the United States Attorney may in supplemental proceedings assist the grand jury in securing compliance.

Because the district court's order was not shown to have been in aid of an appropriate directive of the grand jury issued to Melvin, and was lacking any other basis of authority, we hold that the order was beyond its authority to issue.

See also *State v. Guido*, 698 A.2d 729 (R.I. 1997).

UNITED STATES v. WILLIAMS
United States Supreme Court
504 U.S. 36 (1992)

JUSTICE SCALIA delivered the opinion of the Court.

The question presented in this case is whether a district court may dismiss an otherwise valid indictment because the Government failed to disclose to the grand jury "substantial exculpatory evidence" in its possession.

I

On May 4, 1988, respondent John H. Williams, Jr., a Tulsa, Oklahoma, investor, was indicted by a federal grand jury on seven counts of "knowingly making a false statement or report for the purpose of influencing the action of a federally insured financial institution," in violation of 18 U.S.C. § 1014. According to the indictment, between September 1984 and November 1985 Williams supplied four Oklahoma banks with "materially false" statements that variously overstated the value of his current assets and interest income in order to influence the banks' actions on his loan requests.

Williams' misrepresentation was allegedly effected through two financial statements provided to the banks, a "Market Value Balance Sheet" and a "Statement of Projected Income and Expense." The former included as "current assets" approximately $6 million in notes receivable from three venture capital companies. Though it contained a disclaimer that these assets were carried at cost rather than at market value, the Government asserted that listing them as "current assets" — i.e., assets quickly reducible to cash was misleading, since Williams knew that none of the venture capital companies could afford to satisfy the notes in the short term. The second document — the Statement of Projected Income and Expense — allegedly misrepresented Williams' interest income, since it failed to reflect that the interest payments received on the notes of the venture capital companies were funded entirely by Williams' own loans to those companies. The Statement thus falsely implied, according to the Government, that Williams was deriving interest income from "an independent outside source."

Shortly after arraignment, the District Court granted Williams' motion for disclosure of all exculpatory portions of the grand jury transcripts, see *Brady v. Maryland*, 373 U.S. 83 (1963). Upon reviewing this material, Williams demanded that the District Court dismiss the indictment, alleging that the Government had failed to fulfill its obligation under the Tenth Circuit's prior decision in *United States v. Page*, 808 F.2d 723, 728 (1987), to present "substantial exculpatory evidence" to the grand jury. His contention was that evidence which the Government had chosen not to present to the grand jury — in particular, Williams' general ledgers and tax returns, and Williams' testimony in his contemporaneous Chapter 11 bankruptcy proceeding — disclosed that, for tax purposes and otherwise, he had regularly accounted for the "notes receivable" (and the interest on them) in a manner consistent with the Balance Sheet and the Income Statement. This, he contended, belied an intent to mislead the banks, and thus directly negated an essential element of the charged offense.

The District Court initially denied Williams' motion, but upon reconsideration ordered the indictment dismissed without prejudice. It found, after a hearing, that the withheld evidence was "relevant to an essential element of the crime charged," created "a reasonable doubt about respondent's guilt," and thus "rendered the grand jury's decision to indict gravely suspect." Upon the Government's appeal, the Court of Appeals affirmed the District Court's order, following its earlier decision in *Page*. It first sustained as not "clearly erroneous" the District Court's determination that the Government had withheld "substantial exculpatory evidence" from the grand jury. It then found that the Government's behavior "substantially influenced" the grand jury's decision to indict, or at the very least raised a "grave doubt that the decision to indict was free from such substantial influence." Under these circumstances, the Tenth Circuit concluded, it was not an abuse of discretion for the District Court to require the Government to begin anew before the grand jury. * * * * *

"Rooted in long centuries of Anglo American history," *Hannah v. Larche*, 363 U.S. 420, 490 (1960) (Frankfurter, J., concurring in result), the grand jury is mentioned in the Bill of Rights, but not in the body of the Constitution. It has not been textually assigned, therefore, to any of the branches described in the first three Articles. It "is a constitutional fixture in its own right." *United States v. Chanen*, 549 F.2d 1306, 1312 (CA9 1977). In fact the whole theory of its function is that it belongs to no branch of the institutional government, serving as a kind of buffer or referee between the Government and the people. Although the grand jury normally operates, of course, in the courthouse and under judicial auspices, its institutional relationship with the judicial branch has traditionally been, so to speak, at arm's length. Judges' direct involvement in the functioning of the grand jury has generally been confined to the constitutive one of calling the grand jurors together and administering their oaths of office. See *United States v. Calandra*, 414 U.S. 338, 343 (1974); Fed.Rule Crim.Proc. 6(a).

The grand jury's functional independence from the judicial branch is evident both in the scope of its power to investigate criminal wrongdoing, and in the manner in which that power is exercised. "Unlike a court, whose jurisdiction is predicated upon a specific case or controversy, the grand jury can investigate merely on suspicion that the law is being violated, or even because it wants assurance that it is not." *United States v. R. Enterprises*, 498 U.S. 292, 111 S.Ct. 722, 726 (1991). It need not identify the offender it suspects, or even "the precise nature of the offense" it is investigating. *Blair v. United States*, 250 U.S. 273, 282 (1919). The grand jury requires no authorization from its constituting court to initiate an investigation, nor does the prosecutor require leave of court to seek a grand jury indictment. And in its day to day functioning, the grand jury generally operates without the interference of a presiding judge. It swears in its own witnesses, Fed.Rule Crim.Proc. 6(c), and deliberates in total secrecy.

True, the grand jury cannot compel the appearance of witnesses and the production of evidence, and must appeal to the court when such compulsion is required. And the court will refuse to lend its assistance when the compulsion the grand jury seeks would override rights accorded by the Constitution, see, e.g., *Gravel v. United States*, 408 U.S. 606 (1972) (grand jury subpoena effectively qualified by order limiting questioning so as to preserve Speech or Debate Clause immunity), or even testimonial privileges recognized by the common law, see *In re Grand Jury Investigation of Hugle*, 754 F.2d 863 (CA9 1985) (same with respect to privilege for confidential marital communications). Even in this setting, however, we have insisted that the grand jury remain "free to pursue its investigations unhindered by external influence or supervision so long as it does not trench upon the legitimate rights of any witness called before it." *United States v. Dionisio*, 410 U.S. 1, 17 18 (1973). Recognizing this tradition of independence, we have said that the Fifth Amendment's "constitutional guarantee *presupposes* an investigative body acting independently of either prosecuting attorney *or judge*." *Id.* at 16; (emphasis added).

No doubt in view of the grand jury proceeding's status as other than a constituent element of a "criminal prosecution," U.S. Const., Amdt. VI, we have said that certain constitutional protections afforded defendants in criminal proceedings have no application before that body. The Double Jeopardy Clause of the Fifth Amendment does not bar a grand jury from returning an indictment when a prior grand jury has refused to do so. See *Ex parte United States*, 287 U.S. 241, 250 251 (1932). We have twice suggested, though not held, that the Sixth Amendment right to counsel does not attach when an individual is summoned to appear before a grand jury, even if he is the subject of the investigation. See *United States v. Mandujano*, 425 U.S. 564, 581 (1976); see also Fed.Rule Crim.Proc. 6(d). And although "the grand jury may not force a witness to answer questions in violation of the Fifth Amendment's constitutional guarantee" against self incrimination, *Calandra*, supra, 414 U.S. at 346, our cases suggest that an indictment obtained through the use of evidence previously obtained in violation of the privilege against self incrimination "is nevertheless valid." *Calandra, supra*, 414 U.S. at 346.

Given the grand jury's operational separateness from its constituting court, it should come as no surprise that we have been reluctant to invoke the judicial supervisory power as a basis for prescribing modes of grand jury procedure. Over the years, we have received many requests to exercise supervision over the grand jury's evidence taking process, but we have refused them all, including some more appealing than the one presented today. In *Calandra v. United States*, a grand jury witness faced questions that were allegedly based upon physical evidence the Government had obtained through a violation of the Fourth Amendment; we rejected the proposal that the exclusionary rule be extended to grand jury proceedings, because of "the potential injury to the historic role and functions of the grand jury." 414 U.S. at 349. In *Costello v. United States*, 350 U.S. 359 (1956), we declined to enforce the hearsay rule in grand jury proceedings, since that "would run counter to the whole history of the grand jury institution, in which laymen conduct their inquiries unfettered by technical rules." *Id.* at 364.

These authorities suggest that any power federal courts may have to fashion, on their own initiative, rules of grand jury procedure is a very limited one, not remotely comparable to the power they maintain over their own proceedings. It certainly would not permit judicial reshaping of the grand jury institution, substantially altering the traditional relationships between the prosecutor, the constituting court, and the grand jury itself. As we proceed to discuss, that would be the consequence of the proposed rule here.

B

Respondent argues that the Court of Appeals' rule can be justified as a sort of Fifth Amendment "common law," a necessary means of assuring the constitutional right to the judgment "of an independent and informed grand jury," *Wood v. Georgia*, 370 U.S. 375, 390 (1962). Respondent makes a generalized appeal to functional notions: Judicial supervision of the quantity and quality of the evidence relied upon by the grand jury plainly facilitates, he says, the grand jury's performance of its twin historical responsibilities, i.e., bringing to trial those who may be justly accused and shielding the innocent from unfounded accusation and prosecution. We do not agree. The rule would neither preserve nor enhance the traditional functioning of the institution that the Fifth Amendment demands. To the contrary, requiring the prosecutor to present exculpatory as well as inculpatory evidence would alter the grand jury's historical role, transforming it from an accusatory to an adjudicatory body.

It is axiomatic that the grand jury sits not to determine guilt or innocence, but to assess whether there is adequate basis for bringing a criminal charge. That has always been so; and to make the assessment it has always been thought sufficient to hear only the prosecutor's side. As Blackstone described the prevailing practice in 18th century England, the grand jury was "only to hear evidence on behalf of the prosecution, for the finding of an indictment is only in the nature of an enquiry or accusation, which is afterwards to be tried and determined." 4 W. Blackstone,

Commentaries 300 (1769). So also in the United States. According to the description of an early American court, three years before the Fifth Amendment was ratified, it is the grand jury's function not "to enquire upon what foundation the charge may be denied," or otherwise to try the suspect's defenses, but only to examine "upon what foundation the charge is made" by the prosecutor. *Respublica v. Shaffer*, 1 U.S. (1 Dall.) 236 (1788). As a consequence, neither in this country nor in England has the suspect under investigation by the grand jury ever been thought to have a right to testify, or to have exculpatory evidence presented.

Imposing upon the prosecutor a legal obligation to present exculpatory evidence in his possession would be incompatible with this system. If a "balanced" assessment of the entire matter is the objective, surely the first thing to be done — rather than requiring the prosecutor to say what he knows in defense of the target of the investigation — is to entitle the target to tender his own defense. To require the former while denying (as we do) the latter would be quite absurd. It would also be quite pointless, since it would merely invite the target to circumnavigate the system by delivering his exculpatory evidence to the prosecutor, whereupon it would have to be passed on to the grand jury — unless the prosecutor is willing to take the chance that a court will not deem the evidence important enough to qualify for mandatory disclosure. See, e.g., *United States v. Zimmerman & Schwartz, P.C.*, 738 F.Supp. 407, 411 (Colo.1990) (duty to disclose exculpatory evidence held satisfied when prosecution tendered to the grand jury defense provided exhibits, testimony, and explanations of the governing law).

Respondent acknowledges (as he must) that the "common law" of the grand jury is not violated if the grand jury itself chooses to hear no more evidence than that which suffices to convince it an indictment is proper. Thus, had the Government offered to familiarize the grand jury in this case with the five boxes of financial statements and deposition testimony alleged to contain exculpatory information, and had the grand jury rejected the offer as pointless, respondent would presumably agree that the resulting indictment would have been valid. Respondent insists, however, that courts must require the modern prosecutor to alert the grand jury to the nature and extent of the available exculpatory evidence, because otherwise the grand jury "merely functions as an arm of the prosecution." We reject the attempt to convert a nonexistent duty of the grand jury itself into an obligation of the prosecutor. The authority of the prosecutor to seek an indictment has long been understood to be "coterminous with the authority of the grand jury to entertain the prosecutor's charges." *United States v. Thompson*, 251 U.S. 407, 414 (1920). If the grand jury has no obligation to consider all "substantial exculpatory" evidence, we do not understand how the prosecutor can be said to have a binding obligation to present it.

There is yet another respect in which respondent's proposal not only fails to comport with, but positively contradicts, the "common law" of the Fifth Amendment grand jury. Motions to quash indictments based upon the sufficiency of the evidence relied upon by the grand jury were unheard of at common law in England. And the traditional American practice was described by Justice Nelson, riding circuit in 1852, as follows:

> No case has been cited, nor have we been able to find any, furnishing an authority for looking into and revising the judgment of the grand jury upon the evidence, for the purpose of determining whether or not the finding was founded upon sufficient proof, or whether there was a deficiency in respect

to any part of the complaint. [*United States v. Reed*, 27 Fed.Cas. 727, 738 (CCNDNY 1852).]

We accepted Justice Nelson's description in *Costello v. United States*, 350 U.S. 359 (1956), where we held that "it would run counter to the whole history of the grand jury institution" to permit an indictment to be challenged "on the ground that there was incompetent or inadequate evidence before the grand jury." *Id.* at 363 364. And we reaffirmed this principle recently in *Bank of Nova Scotia*, where we held that "the mere fact that evidence itself is unreliable is not sufficient to require a dismissal of the indictment," and that "a challenge to the reliability or competence of the evidence presented to the grand jury" will not be heard. 487 U.S. at 261. It would make little sense, we think, to abstain from reviewing the evidentiary support for the grand jury's judgment while scrutinizing the sufficiency of the prosecutor's presentation. A complaint about the quality or adequacy of the evidence can always be recast as a complaint that the prosecutor's presentation was "incomplete" or "misleading."[8] Our words in *Costello* bear repeating: Review of facially valid indictments on such grounds "would run counter to the whole history of the grand jury institution, and neither justice nor the concept of a fair trial requires it." 350 U.S. at 364.

Echoing the reasoning of the Tenth Circuit in *United States v. Page*, 808 F.2d at 728, respondent argues that a rule requiring the prosecutor to disclose exculpatory evidence to the grand jury would, by removing from the docket unjustified prosecutions, save valuable judicial time. That depends, we suppose, upon what the ratio would turn out to be between unjustified prosecutions eliminated and grand jury indictments challenged — for the latter as well as the former consume "valuable judicial time." We need not pursue the matter; if there is an advantage to the proposal, Congress is free to prescribe it. For the reasons set forth above, however, we conclude that courts have no authority to prescribe such a duty pursuant to their inherent supervisory authority over their own proceedings. The judgment of the Court of Appeals is accordingly reversed.

Justice Stevens, with whom Justice Blackmun and Justice O'Connor join, and with whom Justice Thomas joins as to Parts II and III, dissenting.

* * * *

Like the Hydra slain by Hercules, prosecutorial misconduct has many heads. Some are cataloged in Justice Sutherland's classic opinion for the Court in *Berger v. United States*, 295 U.S. 78 (1935):

> That the United States prosecuting attorney overstepped the bounds of that propriety and fairness which should characterize the conduct of such an officer in the prosecution of a criminal offense is clearly shown by the record. He was guilty of misstating the facts in his cross examination of

---

[8] In *Costello*, for example, instead of complaining about the grand jury's reliance upon hearsay evidence the petitioner could have complained about the prosecutor's introduction of it. See, e.g., *United States v. Estepa*, 471 F.2d 1132, 1136 1137 (CA2 1972) (prosecutor should not introduce hearsay evidence before grand jury when direct evidence is available); see also Arenella, *Reforming the Federal Grand Jury and the State Preliminary Hearing to Prevent Conviction Without Adjudication*, 78 Mich.L.Rev. 463, 540 (1980) ("Some federal courts have cautiously begun to use a revitalized prosecutorial misconduct doctrine to circumvent *Costello's* prohibition against directly evaluating the sufficiency of the evidence presented to the grand jury").

witnesses; of putting into the mouths of such witnesses things which they had not said; of suggesting by his questions that statements had been made to him personally out of court, in respect of which no proof was offered; of pretending to understand that a witness had said something which he had not said and persistently cross examining the witness upon that basis; of assuming prejudicial facts not in evidence; of bullying and arguing with witnesses; and in general, of conducting himself in a thoroughly indecorous and improper manner. The prosecuting attorney's argument to the jury was undignified and intemperate, containing improper insinuations and assertions calculated to mislead the jury. [*Id.* at 84 85.]

This, of course, is not an exhaustive list of the kinds of improper tactics that overzealous or misguided prosecutors have adopted in judicial proceedings. The reported cases of this Court alone contain examples of the knowing use of perjured testimony, *Mooney v. Holohan*, 294 U.S. 103 (1935), the suppression of evidence favorable to an accused person, *Brady v. Maryland*, 373 U.S. 83 (1963), and misstatements of the law in argument to the jury, *Caldwell v. Mississippi*, 472 U.S. 320, 336 (1985), to name just a few.

Nor has prosecutorial misconduct been limited to judicial proceedings: the reported cases indicate that it has sometimes infected grand jury proceedings as well. The cases contain examples of prosecutors presenting perjured testimony, *United States v. Basurto*, 497 F.2d 781, 786 (CA9 1974), questioning a witness outside the presence of the grand jury and then failing to inform the grand jury that the testimony was exculpatory, *United States v. Phillips Petroleum, Inc.*, 435 F.Supp. 610, 615 617 (ND Okla.1977), failing to inform the grand jury of its authority to subpoena witnesses, *United States v. Samango*, 607 F.2d 877, 884 (CA9 1979), operating under a conflict of interest, *United States v. Gold*, 470 F.Supp. 1336, 1346 1351 (ND Ill.1979), misstating the law, *United States v. Roberts*, 481 F.Supp. 1385, 1389, and n. 10 (CD Cal. 1980), and misstating the facts on cross examination of a witness, *United States v. Lawson*, 502 F.Supp. 158, 162, and nn. 6 7 (Md.1980).

Justice Sutherland's identification of the basic reason why that sort of misconduct is intolerable merits repetition:

The United States Attorney is the representative not of an ordinary party to a controversy, but of a sovereignty whose obligation to govern impartially is as compelling as its obligation to govern at all; and whose interest, therefore, in a criminal prosecution is not that it shall win a case, but that justice shall be done. As such, he is in a peculiar and very definite sense the servant of the law, the twofold aim of which is that guilt shall not escape or innocence suffer. He may prosecute with earnestness and vigor — indeed, he should do so. But, while he may strike hard blows, he is not at liberty to strike foul ones. It is as much his duty to refrain from improper methods calculated to produce a wrongful conviction as it is to use every legitimate means to bring about a just one. [*Berger v. United States*, 295 U.S. at 88.]

It is equally clear that the prosecutor has the same duty to refrain from improper methods calculated to produce a wrongful indictment. Indeed, the prosecutor's duty to protect the fundamental fairness of judicial proceedings assumes special importance when he is presenting evidence to a grand jury. As the Court of Appeals for the Third Circuit recognized, "the costs of continued unchecked prosecutorial misconduct" before the grand jury are particularly substantial because there

> the prosecutor operates without the check of a judge or a trained legal adversary, and virtually immune from public scrutiny. The prosecutor's abuse of his special relationship to the grand jury poses an enormous risk to defendants as well. For while in theory a trial provides the defendant with a full opportunity to contest and disprove the charges against him, in practice, the handing up of an indictment will often have a devastating personal and professional impact that a later dismissal or acquittal can never undo. Where the potential for abuse is so great, and the consequences of a mistaken indictment so serious, the ethical responsibilities of the prosecutor, and the obligation of the judiciary to protect against even the appearance of unfairness, are correspondingly heightened. [*United States v. Serubo*, 604 F.2d 807, 817 (CA3 1979).]

In his dissent in *United States v. Ciambrone*, 601 F.2d 616 (CA2 1979), Judge Friendly also recognized the prosecutor's special role in grand jury proceedings:

> As the Supreme Court has noted, "the Founders thought the grand jury so essential to basic liberties that they provided in the Fifth Amendment that federal prosecution for serious crimes can only be instituted by 'a presentment or indictment of a Grand Jury.' " *United States v. Calandra*, 414 U.S. 338, 343 (1974). Before the grand jury the prosecutor has the dual role of pressing for an indictment and of being the grand jury adviser. In case of conflict, the latter duty must take precedence. *United States v. Remington*, 208 F.2d 567, 573 74 (2d Cir.1953) (L. Hand, J., dissenting). The *ex parte* character of grand jury proceedings makes it peculiarly important for a federal prosecutor to remember that, in the familiar phrase, the interest of the United States "in a criminal prosecution is not that it shall win a case, but that justice shall be done." *Berger v. United States*, 295 U.S. 78, 88. [*Id.* at 628 629.][9]

* * * *

Although the grand jury has not been "textually assigned" to "any of the branches described in the first three Articles" of the Constitution, it is not an autonomous body completely beyond the reach of the other branches. Throughout its life, from the moment it is convened until it is discharged, the grand jury is subject to the control of the court. As Judge Learned Hand recognized over sixty years ago, "a grand jury is neither an officer nor an agent of the United States, but

---

[9] Although the majority in *Ciambrone* did not agree with Judge Friendly's appraisal of the prejudicial impact of the misconduct in that case, it also recognized the prosecutor's duty to avoid fundamentally unfair tactics during the grand jury proceedings. Judge Mansfield explained:

> On the other hand, the prosecutor's right to exercise some discretion and selectivity in the presentation of evidence to a grand jury does not entitle him to mislead it or to engage in fundamentally unfair tactics before it. The prosecutor, for instance, may not obtain an indictment on the basis of evidence known to him to be perjurious, *United States v. Basurto*, 497 F.2d 781, 785 86 (9th Cir.1974), or by leading it to believe that it has received eyewitness rather than hearsay testimony, *United States v. Estepa*, 471 F.2d 1132, 1136 37 (2d Cir.1972). We would add that where a prosecutor is aware of any substantial evidence negating guilt he should, in the interest of justice, make it known to the grand jury, at least where it might reasonably be expected to lead the jury not to indict. See ABA Project on Standards for Criminal Justice — The Prosecution Function, § 3.6. [601 F.2d at 623.]

a part of the court." *Falter v. United States*, 23 F.2d 420, 425 (CA2). This Court has similarly characterized the grand jury:

> A grand jury is clothed with great independence in many areas, but it remains an appendage of the court, powerless to perform its investigative function without the court's aid, because powerless itself to compel the testimony of witnesses. It is the court's process which summons the witness to attend and give testimony, and it is the court which must compel a witness to testify if, after appearing, he refuses to do so. [*Brown v. United States*, 359 U.S. 41, 49 (1959).]

This Court has, of course, long recognized that the grand jury has wide latitude to investigate violations of federal law as it deems appropriate and need not obtain permission from either the court or the prosecutor. See, e.g., *Costello v. United States*, 350 U.S. 359, 362 (1956). Correspondingly, we have acknowledged that "its operation generally is unrestrained by the technical procedural and evidentiary rules governing the conduct of criminal trials." *United States v. Calandra*, 414 U.S. at 343. But this is because Congress and the Court have generally thought it best not to impose procedural restraints on the grand jury; it is not because they lack all power to do so.

To the contrary, the Court has recognized that it has the authority to create and enforce limited rules applicable in grand jury proceedings. Thus, for example, the Court has said that the grand jury "may not itself violate a valid privilege, whether established by the Constitution, statutes, or the common law." *Id.* at 346. And the Court may prevent a grand jury from violating such a privilege by quashing or modifying a subpoena, id. at 346, n. 4, or issuing a protective order forbidding questions in violation of the privilege, *Gravel v. United States*, 408 U.S. 606, 628 629 (1972). Moreover, there are, as the Court notes, a series of cases in which we declined to impose categorical restraints on the grand jury. In none of those cases, however, did we question our power to reach a contrary result.

Although the Court recognizes that it may invoke its supervisory authority to fashion and enforce privilege rules applicable in grand jury proceedings, and suggests that it may also invoke its supervisory authority to fashion other limited rules of grand jury procedure, it concludes that it has no authority to "prescribe standards of prosecutorial conduct before the grand jury," because that would alter the grand jury's historic role as an independent, inquisitorial institution. I disagree.

We do not protect the integrity and independence of the grand jury by closing our eyes to the countless forms of prosecutorial misconduct that may occur inside the secrecy of the grand jury room. After all, the grand jury is not merely an investigatory body; it also serves as a "protector of citizens against arbitrary and oppressive governmental action." *United States v. Calandra*, 414 U.S. at 343. Explaining why the grand jury must be both "independent" and "informed," the Court wrote in *Wood v. Georgia*, 370 U.S. 375 (1962):

> Historically, this body has been regarded as a primary security to the innocent against hasty, malicious and oppressive persecution; it serves the invaluable function in our society of standing between the accuser and the accused, whether the latter be an individual, minority group, or other, to determine whether a charge is founded upon reason or was dictated by an intimidating power or by malice and personal ill will. [*Id.* at 390.]

It blinks reality to say that the grand jury can adequately perform this important historic role if it is intentionally misled by the prosecutor — on whose knowledge of the law and facts of the underlying criminal investigation the jurors will, of necessity, rely.

Unlike the Court, I am unwilling to hold that countless forms of prosecutorial misconduct must be tolerated — no matter how prejudicial they may be, or how seriously they may distort the legitimate function of the grand jury — simply because they are not proscribed by Rule 6 of the Federal Rules of Criminal Procedure or a statute that is applicable in grand jury proceedings. Such a sharp break with the traditional role of the federal judiciary is unprecedented, unwarranted, and unwise. Unrestrained prosecutorial misconduct in grand jury proceedings is inconsistent with the administration of justice in the federal courts and should be redressed in appropriate cases by the dismissal of indictments obtained by improper methods.[12]

III

What, then, is the proper disposition of this case? I agree with the Government that the prosecutor is not required to place all exculpatory evidence before the grand jury. A grand jury proceeding is an *ex parte* investigatory proceeding to determine whether there is probable cause to believe a violation of the criminal laws has occurred, not a trial. Requiring the prosecutor to ferret out and present all evidence that could be used at trial to create a reasonable doubt as to the defendant's guilt would be inconsistent with the purpose of the grand jury proceeding and would place significant burdens on the investigation. But that does not mean that the prosecutor may mislead the grand jury into believing that there is probable cause to indict by withholding clear evidence to the contrary. I thus agree with the Department of Justice that "when a prosecutor conducting a grand jury inquiry is personally aware of substantial evidence which directly negates the guilt of a subject of the investigation, the prosecutor must present or otherwise disclose such evidence to the grand jury before seeking an indictment against such a person." U.S. Dept. of Justice, United States Attorneys' Manual, pp. 9 11.233, 88 (1988).

Although I question whether the evidence withheld in this case directly negates respondent's guilt, I need not resolve my doubts because the Solicitor General did not ask the Court to review the nature of the evidence withheld. Instead, he asked us to decide the legal question whether an indictment may be dismissed because the prosecutor failed to present exculpatory evidence. Unlike the Court and the Solicitor General, I believe the answer to that question is yes, if the withheld evidence would plainly preclude a finding of probable cause. I therefore cannot endorse the Court's opinion.

---

[12] Although the Court's opinion barely mentions the fact that the grand jury was intended to serve the invaluable function of standing between the accuser and the accused, I must assume that in a proper case it will acknowledge — as even the Solicitor General does — that unrestrained prosecutorial misconduct in grand jury proceedings "could so subvert the integrity of the grand jury process as to justify judicial intervention.

Notes from Millie:

1. What effect does *Williams* have on *Estepa* and *Basurto*? Did the Supreme Court explicitly or implicitly disapprove of those decisions? What is footnote 12 of the dissent all about?

2. The dissent suggests that the prosecutor "intentionally misled" the grand jury. Is this correct, in the same sense that the prosecutor in *Estepa* misled the grand jury? If not, does this mean that *Estepa* is not inconsistent with *Williams*?

3. In *State v. Gaughran*, 615 A.2d 1293 (N.J.Super.Ct. 1992), defendant was indicted for forcible rape, by a state grand jury which was told that the alleged victim had a medical exam after the incident, but was not shown the medical report — which showed no signs of force. The court held that New Jersey's state constitution sets higher standards than the U.S. Constitution, and it refused to follow *Williams*.

> In order to assure an independent and fair Grand Jury system in the State of New Jersey, it is essential that the jurors be informed of the relevant facts. The evidentiary impact of the medical report should not be underestimated. It directly contradicts the victim's claim of anal and vaginal penetration and does not support her claim of a one and a half hour struggle. The Grand Jurors could not have been expected to ask for the results of the medical exam. They were skillfully misled by omission into believing that it had corroborated the victim's testimony. By withholding relevant and highly exculpatory evidence in its possession, the State treated this Grand Jury as its rubber stamp, its "playtoy". In fact, given the nature of the medical report and its devastating impact on the presentation, the failure to present it can be termed as intentional subversion of the process.

The court dismissed the indictment.

4. **May a grand jury hear evidence obtained by *an illegal search or seizure?***

In *U.S. v. Puglia*, 8 F.3d 478 (7th Cir. 1993), defendant was indicted on narcotics charges, and then successfully moved to suppress certain evidence from his trial. The prosecutor returned to the grand jury and used the suppressed evidence — along with other evidence — to procure a second indictment. Defendant claimed that this second indictment should be dismissed, but the court disagreed. The court said that the primary purpose of the exclusionary rule is to deter illegal searches and seizures. While this might work in the trial context, it is not likely to work when applied to the grand jury, as "prosecutors will not waste their time seeking indictments of individuals against whom they do not have enough evidence."

5. In *U.S. v. Myers*, 123 F.3d 350 (6th Cir.1997), Myers was subpoenaed to testify before a federal grand jury. He appeared and took the stand, and the assistant U.S. attorney asked him questions about his alleged possession of cocaine. The prosecutor had failed, however, to follow a Justice Department policy that required him to advise a grand jury witness who is a "target" of a grand jury investigation that he is such a "target." Myers answered the questions. After he was indicted, Myers moved to suppress from his trial his answers to the questions at the grand jury hearing. The court first held that Myers had no *constitutional* right to be advised that he was a "target", citing *U.S. v. Washington*, 431 U.S. 181 (1977). The court next held that "a violation by the government of its internal operating procedures, on its own, does not create a basis for suppressing Myers's grand jury testimony." The

court was "troubled" by the government's violations, but felt that *U.S. v. Williams* "essentially removed all general supervisory authority over the grand jury from the federal courts."

Chapter 6

THE RIGHT TO SPEEDY TRIAL

"In all criminal prosecutions, the accused shall enjoy the right to a speedy and public trial. . . ."

6th Amendment, U.S. Constitution

The Constitution contains no comparable right to a speedy trial in *civil* cases. Though federal and state statutes do include provisions helping to move civil cases to trial, clever defense attorneys often keep a civil case tied up in pretrial litigation for years. Why shouldn't the Constitution put a lid on these tactics too?

In many (perhaps most) cases, the defendant in a criminal case is in no hurry to go to trial. The passage of time usually hurts the prosecution more than the defense. Prosecution witnesses might forget details, move away, or die. True, the same might happen to defense witnesses; but the prosecution has the burden of proof, and loss of evidence usually hurts the prosecution more than the defense. In addition, as time goes on and the crime fades from public consciousness, the pressure on the prosecutor and the court for aggressive prosecution and severe punishment may also fade. For these reasons, the defendant usually agrees to waive any rights he has to a speedy trial.

But not always. If the defendant cannot obtain pretrial release, the right to speedy trial can be important. If the defendant has a reasonable chance of acquittal, he wants to get the trial over and get out of custody as soon as possible.

The right to speedy trial is important for another reason: its effect on plea bargaining. Neither the prosecutor nor the courts have the resources needed to take every case to trial "speedily" — there are just not enough prosecutors, judges, and courtrooms. In most jurisdictions, less than 20% of the cases go to trial. For the remaining 80+%, the prosecutor has two choices: dismiss the case or plea bargain. The right to speedy trial gives the defendant the power to say to the prosecutor: "Include me in the 20%, dismiss my case, or make me an offer I can live with." Usually, the prosecutor must opt for the latter. Thus, in a sense, the right to speedy trial is the engine that drives plea bargaining.

Problem 6

To: My law clerk

From: Assistant U.S. Attorney Warren Peace

Upsan Downs has been indicted by a federal grand jury for sale of cocaine and possession of heroin. His lawyer has moved to dismiss the indictment on speedy trial grounds. Here is what has happened so far.

Larry Looper was an undercover agent for the Drug Enforcement Agency during 2003. Looper says that on Monday, January 5, 2003, he bought some cocaine from Downs while Downs was standing on the corner of 1st and Mission Streets, an area known for high drug traffic. Looper stayed undercover all year, keeping a notebook of all of his drug buys. In December of 1996, he broke his cover and arrested about 30 people who allegedly sold drugs to him during the year.

On December 5, 2003, Looper went to Downs and told him that he had evidence against Downs and could arrest him, but would not do so if Downs helped him get evidence against Mr. Big, a wholesale drug dealer in town. Downs agreed, and he tried to get something on Mr. Big, but could not arrange to meet him. When he failed to come through, Looper found Downs sitting in his (Downs') car and arrested him, on May 5, 2004. Looper searched the car, and he found some heroin in the glove compartment. Downs was released on $50,000 bail, on condition that he not leave the city and that he report to a federal marshal once a week. A federal grand jury indicted Downs on June 1, 2004, for sale of cocaine and possession of heroin. His bail was continued.

Downs was arraigned, and trial was set for August 5, 2004. On August 1, 2004, he filed a motion to suppress the heroin, on the ground that Looper had no search warrant to search Downs' car. He asked to continue the trial so that the motion to suppress could be heard and decided. The judge continued the trial to November 5, 2004. He heard the motion to suppress on October 5, and he denied it that same day.

On November 1, 2004, I moved to continue the trial. I presented an affidavit showing that on October 6, 2004, Looper had been shot in the leg by one of the people he had deceived and arrested, and he was in the hospital recovering. The judge continued the trial until May 5, 2005. Downs objected to such a long continuance, but the judge said that his docket was full in December, and he would be on vacation in January, and he had a lot of cases to handle when he came back.

Downs had been on parole for a prior drug offense. On December 1, 2004, he was caught selling drugs again. His parole was revoked and he was sent to state prison to serve out his remaining term of one year.

Downs' lawyer told me that Downs claims that he never sold drugs to Looper. Downs doesn't really remember what he was doing on January 5, 2003, but he thinks he might have been home with a cold that day, and his mother was taking care of him. His mother thinks this is probably right. But she is 85 years old and her memory isn't what it used to be.

On May 1, 2005, Downs filed a motion to dismiss the indictment, on speedy trial grounds. It will be heard on the morning set for trial, May 5. If the motion is likely to be granted, I'll seriously consider offering Downs a plea bargain with reduced charges, just to make sure we convict him of something. Please read the attached authorities and let me know whether motion will be granted.

The Speedy Trial Act
Title 18, United States Code, § 3161
(adopted in 1975)

§ 3161. Time limits and exclusions

(a) In any case involving a defendant charged with an offense, the appropriate judicial officer, at the earliest practicable time, shall, after consultation with the counsel for the defendant and the attorney for the Government, set the case for trial on a day certain, or list it for trial on a weekly or other short-term trial calendar at a place within the judicial district, so as to assure a speedy trial.

(b) Any information or indictment charging an individual with the commission of an offense shall be filed within thirty days from the date on which such individual was arrested or served with a summons in connection with such charges. * * * *

(c)

(1) In any case in which a plea of not guilty is entered, the trial of a defendant charged in an information or indictment with the commission of an offense shall commence within seventy days from the filing date (and making public) of the information or indictment, or from the date the defendant has appeared before a judicial officer of the court in which such charge is pending, whichever date last occurs. If a defendant consents in writing to be tried before a magistrate on a complaint, the trial shall commence within seventy days from the date of such consent.

(2) Unless the defendant consents in writing to the contrary, the trial shall not commence less than thirty days from the date on which the defendant first appears through counsel or expressly waives counsel and elects to proceed pro se.

* * * *

(h) The following periods of delay shall be excluded in computing the time within which an information or an indictment must be filed, or in computing the time within which the trial of any such offense must commence:

(1) Any period of delay resulting from other proceedings concerning the defendant, including but not limited to:

(A) delay resulting from any proceeding, including any examinations, to determine the mental competency or physical capacity of the defendant;

(B) delay resulting from any proceeding, including any examination of the defendant, pursuant to § 2902 of title 28, United States Code;

(C) delay resulting from deferral of prosecution pursuant to § 2902 of title 28, United States Code;

(D) delay resulting from trial with respect to other charges against the defendant;

(E) delay resulting from any interlocutory appeal;

(F) delay resulting from any pretrial motion, from the filing of the motion through the conclusion of the hearing on, or other prompt disposition of, such motion;

(G) delay resulting from any proceeding relating to the transfer of a case or the removal of any defendant from another district under the Federal Rules of Criminal Procedure;

(H) delay resulting from transportation of any defendant from another district, or to and from places of examination or hospitalization, except that any time consumed in excess of ten days from the date an order of removal or an order directing such transportation, and the defendant's arrival at the destination shall be presumed to be unreasonable;

(I) delay resulting from consideration by the court of a proposed plea agreement to be entered into by the defendant and the attorney for the Government; and

(J) delay reasonably attributable to any period, not to exceed thirty days, during which any proceeding concerning the defendant is actually under advisement by the court.

(2) Any period of delay during which prosecution is deferred by the attorney for the Government pursuant to written agreement with the defendant, with the approval of the court, for the purpose of allowing the defendant to demonstrate his good conduct.

(3)

(A) Any period of delay resulting from the absence or unavailability of the defendant or an essential witness.

(B) For purposes of subparagraph (A) of this paragraph, a defendant or an essential witness shall be considered absent when his whereabouts are unknown and, in addition, he is attempting to avoid apprehension or prosecution or his whereabouts cannot be determined by due diligence. For purposes of such subparagraph, a defendant or an essential witness shall be considered unavailable whenever his whereabouts are known but his presence for trial cannot be obtained by due diligence or he resists appearing at or being returned for trial.

(4) Any period of delay resulting from the fact that the defendant is mentally incompetent or physically unable to stand trial.

(5) Any period of delay resulting from the treatment of the defendant pursuant to § 2902 of title 28, United States Code.

(6) If the information or indictment is dismissed upon motion of the attorney for the Government and thereafter a charge is filed against the defendant for the same offense, or any offense required to be joined with that offense, any period of delay from the date the charge was dismissed to the date the time limitation would commence to run as to the subsequent charge had there been no previous charge.

(7) A reasonable period of delay when the defendant is joined for trial with a codefendant as to whom the time for trial has not run and no motion for severance has been granted.

(8)

(A) Any period of delay resulting from a continuance granted by any judge on his own motion or at the request of the defendant or his counsel or at the request of the attorney for the Government, if the judge granted such continuance on the basis of his findings that the ends of justice served by taking such action outweigh the best interest of the public and the defendant in a speedy trial. No such period of delay resulting from a continuance granted by the court in accordance with this paragraph shall be excludable under this subsection unless the court sets forth, in the record of the case, either orally or in writing, its reasons for finding that the ends of justice served by the granting of such continuance outweigh the best interests of the public and the defendant in a speedy trial.

(B) The factors, among others, which a judge shall consider in determining whether to grant a continuance under subparagraph (A) of this paragraph in any case are as follows:

(i) Whether the failure to grant such a continuance in the proceeding would be likely to make a continuation of such proceeding impossible, or result in a miscarriage of justice.

(ii) Whether the case is so unusual or so complex, due to the number of defendants, the nature of the prosecution, or the existence of novel questions of fact or law, that it is unreasonable to expect adequate preparation for pretrial proceedings or for the trial itself within the time limits established by this section.

(iii) Whether, in a case in which arrest precedes indictment, delay in the filing of the indictment is caused because the arrest occurs at a time such that it is unreasonable to expect return and filing of the indictment within the period specified in § 3161(b), or because the facts upon which the grand jury must base its determination are unusual or complex.

(iv) Whether the failure to grant such a continuance in a case which, taken as a whole, is not so unusual or so complex as to fall within clause (ii), would deny the defendant reasonable time to obtain counsel, would unreasonably deny the defendant or the Government continuity of counsel, or would deny counsel for the defendant or the attorney for the Government the reasonable time necessary for effective preparation, taking into account the exercise of due diligence.

(C) No continuance under subparagraph (A) of this paragraph shall be granted because of general congestion of the court's calendar, or lack of diligent preparation or failure to obtain available witnesses on the part of the attorney for the Government.

* * * *

(j)

(1) If the attorney for the Government knows that a person charged with an offense is serving a term of imprisonment in any penal institution, he shall promptly:

(A) undertake to obtain the presence of the prisoner for trial; or

(B) cause a detainer to be filed with the person having custody of the prisoner and request him to so advise the prisoner and to advise the prisoner of his right to demand trial.

(2) If the person having custody of such prisoner receives a detainer, he shall promptly advise the prisoner of the charge and of the prisoner's right to demand trial. If at any time thereafter the prisoner informs the person having custody that he does demand trial, such person shall cause notice to that effect to be sent promptly to the attorney for the Government who caused the detainer to be filed.

(3) Upon receipt of such notice, the attorney for the Government shall promptly seek to obtain the presence of the prisoner for trial.

* * * *

Section 3162. **Sanctions**

(a)

(1) If, in the case of any individual against whom a complaint is filed charging such individual with an offense, no indictment or information is filed within the time limit required by § 3161(b) as extended by § 3161(h) of this chapter, such charge against that individual contained in such complaint shall be dismissed or otherwise dropped. In determining whether to dismiss the case with or without prejudice, the court shall consider, among others, each of the following factors: the seriousness of the offense; the facts and circumstances of the case which led to the dismissal; and the impact of a reprosecution on the administration of this chapter and on the administration of justice.

(2) If a defendant is not brought to trial within the time limit required by § 3161(c) as extended by § 3161(h), the information or indictment shall be dismissed on motion of the defendant. The defendant shall have the burden of proof of supporting such motion but the Government shall have the burden of going forward with the evidence in connection with any exclusion of time under § 3161(h)(3). In determining whether to dismiss the case with or without prejudice, the court shall consider, among others, each of the following factors: the seriousness of the offense; the facts and circumstances of the case which led to the dismissal; and the impact of a reprosecution on the administration of this chapter and on the administration of justice. Failure of the defendant to move for dismissal prior to trial or entry of a plea of guilty or nolo contendere shall constitute a waiver of the right to dismissal under this section.

(b) In any case in which counsel for the defendant or the attorney for the Government (1) knowingly allows the case to be set for trial without disclosing the fact that a necessary witness would be unavailable for trial; (2) files a motion solely for the purpose of delay which he knows is totally frivolous and without merit; (3) makes a statement for the purpose of obtaining a continuance which he knows to be false and which is material to the granting of a continuance; or (4) otherwise willfully fails to proceed to trial without justification consistent with § 3161 of this chapter, the court may punish any such counsel or attorney, as follows:

(A) in the case of an appointed defense counsel, by reducing the amount of compensation that otherwise would have been paid to such counsel pursuant to § 3006A of this title in an amount not to exceed 25 per centum thereof;

(B) in the case of a counsel retained in connection with the defense of a defendant, by imposing on such counsel a fine of not to exceed 25% of the compensation to which he is entitled in connection with his defense of such defendant;

(C) by imposing on any attorney for the Government a fine of not to exceed $250;

(D) by denying any such counsel or attorney for the Government the right to practice before the court considering such case for a period of not to exceed ninety days; or

(E) by filing a report with an appropriate disciplinary committee.

The authority to punish provided for by this subsection shall be in addition to any other authority or power available to such court. * * * *

Section 3164. **Persons detained or designated as being of high risk**

(a) The trial or other disposition of cases involving:

(1) a detained person who is being held in detention solely because he is awaiting trial, and

(2) a released person who is awaiting trial and has been designated by the attorney for the Government as being of high risk, shall be accorded priority.

(b) The trial of any person described in subsection (a)(1) or (a)(2) of this section shall commence not later than ninety days following the beginning of such continuous detention or designation of high risk by the attorney for the Government. The periods of delay enumerated in § 3161(h) are excluded in computing the time limitation specified in this section. * * * *

Section 3173. **Sixth amendment rights**

No provision of this chapter shall be interpreted as a bar to any claim of denial of speedy trial as required by amendment VI of the Constitution.

Section 3174. **Judicial emergency and implementation**

(a) In the event that any district court is unable to comply with the time limits set forth in § 3161(c) due to the status of its court calendars, the chief judge, where the existing resources are being efficiently utilized, may, after seeking the recommendations of the planning group, apply to the judicial council of the circuit for a suspension of such time limits as provided in subsection (b). The judicial council of the circuit shall evaluate the capabilities of the district, the availability of visiting judges from within and without the circuit, and make any recommendations it deems appropriate to alleviate calendar congestion resulting from the lack of resources.

(b) If the judicial council of the circuit finds that no remedy for such congestion is reasonably available, such council may, upon application by the chief judge of a district, grant a suspension of the time limits in § 3161(c) in such district for a period of time not to exceed one year for the trial of cases for which indictments or informations are filed during such one-year period. During such period of suspension, the time limits from arrest to indictment, set forth in § 3161(b), shall not be reduced, nor shall the sanctions set forth in § 3162 be suspended; but such time limits from indictment to trial shall not be increased to exceed one hundred and eighty days. The time limits for the trial of cases of detained persons who are being detained solely because they are awaiting trial shall not be affected by the provisions of this section.

Federal Rules of Criminal Procedure

Rule 48. Dismissal

   (a)   By the Government. The government may, with leave of court, dismiss an indictment, information, or complaint. The government may not dismiss the prosecution during trial without the defendant's consent.

   (b)   By the Court. The court may dismiss an indictment, information, or complaint if unnecessary delay occurs in:

   (1) presenting a charge to a grand jury;

   (2) filing an information against a defendant; or

   (3) bringing a defendant to trial.

Notes from Warren:

1. Most states have legislation similar to the Speedy Trial Act, imposing numerical time limits on various procedures between arrest and trial.

2. In *U.S. v. Hall*, 181 F.3d 1057 (9th Cir. 1999), Hall and Nelson were indicted on drug charges. Nelson moved to continue the joint trial of both defendants so that Nelson could engage in plea negotiations with the prosecutor. The court granted the motion, imposing the continuance on Hall under § 3161(h)(7) (above). This continuance caused the trial to begin beyond the 70 days allowed by § 3161(c)(1). Nelson's plea negotiations were successful: in return for a reduced sentence, he agreed to testify against Hall. He did, and Hall was convicted. The court of appeal reversed:

Under 18 U.S.C. § 3161(h)(7), "a reasonable period of delay [is excludable] when the defendant is joined for trial with a codefendant as to whom the time for trial has not run and no motion for severance has been granted." Excludability under this section is not automatic; the period of delay must be "reasonable." * * * *

Courts look particularly to whether the delay was necessary to achieve its purpose and to whether there was any actual prejudice suffered by the appellant. Applying that analytical framework here, we find that the 77-day delay from July 21 to October 6 was unreasonable. The general purpose of § 3161(h)(7) is to facilitate the efficient use of judicial resources by enabling joint trials where appropriate. See S. Rep. 38 (1974). In this case, however, a primary purpose of the continuances was to enable Nelson to pursue plea negotiations with the government. In her June 11 continuance motion, Nelson stated that a continuance was necessary in part because "the parties are engaged in plea negotiations which may or may not be fruitful, but additional time is needed to complete those negotiations." Thus, unlike other cases where carrying along a codefendant is necessary to insure a joint trial, here an underlying aim was to eliminate the need for a joint trial by achieving a plea agreement between Nelson and the government. It was neither necessary nor reasonable to delay Hall's trial for that purpose.

Moreover, the delay from July 21 to October 6 prejudiced Hall's defense. Throughout the pretrial delay, Hall was scheduled to be tried together with Nelson. Five days before the trial was to begin, however, Nelson reached a plea agreement with the government whereby she agreed to testify against Hall. Thus, in being carried along in Nelson's continuances, Hall was effectively prevented from going to trial until the government had secured Nelson as a witness against him. Seen in this light, the delay prejudiced Hall in the sense that it impaired his defense at trial.

BARKER v. WINGO
United States Supreme Court
407 U.S. 514 (1972)

MR. JUSTICE POWELL delivered the opinion of the Court.

Although a speedy trial is guaranteed the accused by the Sixth Amendment to the Constitution, * * * this Court has dealt with that right on infrequent occasions. See, e.g., *United States v. Marion*, 404 U.S. 307 (1971). The Court's opinion in *Kloper v. North Carolina*, 386 U.S. 213 (1967), established that the right to a speedy trial is "fundamental" and is imposed by the Due Process Clause of the Fourteenth Amendment on the States. * * * * In none of these cases have we attempted to set out the criteria by which the speedy trial right is to be judged. This case compels us to make such an attempt.

I

On July 20, 1958, in Christian County, Kentucky, an elderly couple was beaten to death by intruders wielding an iron tire tool. Two suspects, Silas Manning and Willie Barker, the petitioner, were arrested shortly thereafter. The grand jury indicted them on September 15. Counsel was appointed on September 17, and Barker's trial was set for October 21. The Commonwealth had a stronger case against Manning, and it believed that Barker could not be convicted unless Manning testified against him. Manning was naturally unwilling to incriminate himself. Accordingly, on October 23, the day Silas Manning was brought to trial, the Commonwealth sought and obtained the first of what was to be a series of 16 continuances of Barker's trial. * * * * Barker made no objection. By first convicting Manning, the Commonwealth would remove possible problems of self-incrimination and would be able to assure his testimony against Barker.

The Commonwealth encountered more than a few difficulties in its prosecution of Manning. The first trial ended in a hung jury. A second trial resulted in a conviction, but the Kentucky Court of Appeals reversed because of the admission of evidence obtained by an illegal search. At his third trial, Manning was again convicted, and the Court of Appeals again reversed because the trial court had not granted a change of venue. A fourth trial resulted in a hung jury. Finally, after five trials, Manning was convicted, in March 1962, of murdering one victim, and after a sixth trial, in December 1962, he was convicted of murdering the other.

The Christian County Circuit Court holds three terms each year — in February, June, and September. Barker's initial trial was to take place in the September term of 1958. The first continuance postponed it until the February 1959 term. The second continuance was granted for one month only. Every term thereafter for as long as the Manning prosecutions were in process, the Commonwealth routinely moved to continue Barker's case to the next term. When the case was continued from the June 1959 term until the following September, Barker, having spent 10 months in jail, obtained his release by posting a $5,000 bond. He thereafter remained free in the community until his trial. Barker made no objection, through his counsel, to the first 11 continuances. When on February 12, 1962, the Commonwealth moved for the twelfth time to continue the case until the following term, Barker's counsel filed a motion to dismiss the indictment. The motion to dismiss was denied two weeks later, and the Commonwealth's motion for a continuance was granted. The Commonwealth was granted further continuances in June 1962 and September 1962, to which Barker did not object.

In February 1963, the first term of court following Manning's final conviction, the Commonwealth moved to set Barker's trial for March 19. But on the day scheduled for trial, it again moved for a continuance until the June term. It gave as its reason the illness of the ex-sheriff who was the chief investigating officer in the case. To this continuance, Barker objected unsuccessfully.

The witness was still unable to testify in June, and the trial, which had been set for June 19, was continued again until the September term over Barker's objection. This time the court announced that the case would be dismissed for lack of prosecution if it were not tried during the next term. The final trial date was set for October 9, 1963. On that date, Barker again moved to dismiss the indictment, and this time specified that his right to a speedy trial had been violated. * * * * The motion was denied; the trial commenced with Manning as the chief prosecution witness; Barker was convicted and given a life sentence.

Barker appealed his conviction to the Kentucky Court of Appeals, relying in part on his speedy trial claim. The court affirmed. In February 1970, Barker petitioned for habeas corpus in the United States District Court for the Western District of Kentucky. The District Court rejected the petition. On appeal, the Court of Appeals for the Sixth Circuit affirmed the District Court. It ruled that Barker had waived his speedy trial claim for the entire period before February 1963, the date on which the court believed he had first objected to the delay by filing a motion to dismiss. In this belief the court was mistaken, for the record reveals that the motion was filed in February 1962. The Commonwealth so conceded at oral argument before this Court. * * * *

The court held further that the remaining period after the date on which Barker first raised his claim and before his trial — which it thought was only eight months but which was actually 20 months — was not unduly long. In addition, the court held that Barker had shown no resulting prejudice, and that the illness of the ex-sheriff was a valid justification for the delay.

II

The right to a speedy trial is generically different from any of the other rights enshrined in the Constitution for the protection of the accused. In addition to the general concern that all accused persons be treated according to decent and fair procedures, there is a societal interest in providing a speedy trial which exists separate from, and at times in opposition to, the interests of the accused. The inability of courts to provide a prompt trial has contributed to a large backlog of cases in urban courts which, among other things, enables defendants to negotiate more effectively for pleas of guilty to lesser offenses and otherwise manipulate the system. * * * * In addition, persons released on bond for lengthy periods awaiting trial have an opportunity to commit other crimes.[8] It must be of little comfort to the residents of Christian County, Kentucky, to know that Barker was at large on bail for over four years while accused of a vicious and brutal murder of which he was ultimately convicted. Moreover, the longer an accused is free awaiting trial, the more tempting becomes his opportunity to jump bail and escape. * * * * Finally, delay between arrest and punishment may have a detrimental effect on rehabilitation.[10]

If an accused cannot make bail, he is generally confined, as was Barker for 10 months, in a local jail. This contributes to the overcrowding and generally deplorable state of those institutions. * * * * Lengthy exposure to these conditions "has a destructive effect on human character and makes the rehabilitation of the individual offender much more difficult." * * * * At times the result may even be violent rioting. * * * * Finally, lengthy pretrial detention is costly. The cost of maintaining a prisoner in jail varies from $3 to $9 per day, and this amounts to millions across the Nation. * * * * In addition, society loses wages which might have been earned, and it must often support families of incarcerated breadwinners.

A second difference between the right to speedy trial and the accused's other constitutional rights is that deprivation of the right may work to the accused's advantage. Delay is not an uncommon defense tactic. As the time between the commission of the crime and trial lengthens, witnesses may become unavailable or

---

[8] In Washington, D.C., in 1968, 70.1% of the persons arrested for robbery and released prior to trial were re-arrested while on bail. Mitchell, *Bail Reform and the Constitutionality of Pretrial Detention*, 55 Va.L.Rev. 1223, 1236 (1969).

[10] "It is desirable that punishment should follow offence as closely as possible; for its impression upon the minds of men is weakened by distance, and, besides, distance adds to the uncertainty of punishment, by affording new chances of escape." J. Bentham, *The Theory of Legislation* 326 (Ogden ed. 1931).

their memories may fade. If the witnesses support the prosecution, its case will be weakened, sometimes seriously so. And it is the prosecution which carries the burden of proof. Thus, unlike the right to counsel or the right to be free from compelled self-in-crimination, deprivation of the right to speedy trial does not per se prejudice the accused's ability to defend himself.

Finally, and perhaps most importantly, the right to speedy trial is a more vague concept than other procedural rights. It is, for example, impossible to determine with precision when the right has been denied. We cannot definitely say how long is too long in a system where justice is supposed to be swift but deliberate.[15]

As a consequence, there is no fixed point in the criminal process when the State can put the defendant to the choice of either exercising or waiving the right to a speedy trial. If, for example, the State moves for a 60-day continuance, granting that continuance is not a violation of the right to speedy trial unless the circumstances of the case are such that further delay would endanger the values the right protects. It is impossible to do more than generalize about when those circumstances exist. There is nothing comparable to the point in the process when a defendant exercises or waives his right to counsel or his right to a jury trial.

The amorphous quality of the right also leads to the unsatisfactorily severe remedy of dismissal of the indictment when the right has been deprived. This is indeed a serious consequence because it means that a defendant who may be guilty of a serious crime will go free, without having been tried. Such a remedy is more **serious than an exclusionary** rule or a reversal for a new trial, * * * but it is the only possible remedy.

III

Perhaps because the speedy trial right is so slippery, two rigid approaches are urged upon us as ways of eliminating some of the uncertainty which courts experience in protecting the right. The first suggestion is that we hold that the Constitution requires a criminal defendant to be offered a trial within a specified time period. The result of such a ruling would have the virtue of clarifying when the right is infringed and of simplifying courts' application of it. Recognizing this, some legislatures have enacted laws, and some courts have adopted procedural rules which more narrowly define the right. * * * * The United States Court of Appeals for the Second Circuit has promulgated rules for the district courts in that Circuit establishing that the government must be ready for trial within six months of the date of arrest, except in unusual circumstances, or the charge will be dismissed. This type of rule is also recommended by the American Bar Association. * * * *

But such a result would require this Court to engage in legislative or rulemaking activity, rather than in the adjudicative process to which we should confine our efforts. We do not establish procedural rules for the States, except when mandated by the Constitution. We find no constitutional basis for holding that the speedy trial right can be quantified into a specified number of days or months. The States, of course, are free to prescribe a reasonable period consistent with constitutional

---

[15] "In large measure because of the many procedural safeguards provided an accused, the ordinary procedures for criminal prosecution are designed to move at a deliberate pace. A requirement of unreasonable speed would have a deleterious effect both upon the rights of the accused and upon the ability of society to protect itself." *United States v. Ewell*, 383 U.S. 116, 120 (1966).

standards, but our approach must be less precise.

The second suggested alternative would restrict consideration of the right to those cases in which the accused has demanded a speedy trial. Most States have recognized what is loosely referred to as the "demand rule," * * * although eight States reject it. * * * * It is not clear, however, precisely what is meant by that term. Although every federal court of appeals that has considered the question has endorsed some kind of demand rule, some have regarded the rule within the concept of waiver, * * * whereas others have viewed it as a factor to be weighed in assessing whether there has been a deprivation of the speedy trial right. * * * * We shall refer to the former approach as the demand-waiver doctrine. The demand-waiver doctrine provides that a defendant waives any consideration of his right to speedy trial for any period prior to which he has not demanded a trial. Under this rigid approach, a prior demand is a necessary condition to the consideration of the speedy trial right. This essentially was the approach the Sixth Circuit took below.

Such an approach, by presuming waiver of a fundamental right * * * from inaction, is inconsistent with this Court's pronouncements on waiver of constitutional rights. The Court has defined waiver as "an intentional relinquishment or abandonment of a known right or privilege." *Johnson v. Zerbst*, 304 U.S. 458, 464 (1938). Courts should "indulge every reasonable presumption against waiver," *Aetna Ins. Co. v. Kennedy*, 301 U.S. 389, 393 (1937), and they should "not presume acquiescence in the loss of fundamental rights," *Ohio Bell Tel. Co. v. Public Utilities Comm'n*, 301 U.S. 292, 307 (1937). In *Carnley v. Cochran*, 369 U.S. 506 (1962), we held:

> Presuming waiver from a silent record is impermissible. The record must show, or there must be an allegation and evidence which show, that an accused was offered counsel but intelligently and understandably rejected the offer. Anything less is not waiver. [*Id.* at 516]

The Court has ruled similarly with respect to waiver of other rights designed to protect the accused. See, e.g., *Miranda v. Arizona*, 384 U.S. 436, 475–476 (1966).

In excepting the right to speedy trial from the rule of waiver, we have applied to other fundamental rights, courts that have applied the demand-waiver rule have relied on the assumption that delay usually works for the benefit of the accused and on the absence of any readily ascertainable time in the criminal process for a defendant to be given the choice of exercising or waiving his right. But it is not necessarily true that delay benefits the defendant. There are cases in which delay appreciably harms the defendant's ability to defend himself. * * * * Moreover, a defendant confined to jail prior to trial is obviously disadvantaged by delay, as is a defendant released on bail but unable to lead a normal life because of community suspicion and his own anxiety.

The nature of the speedy trial right does make it impossible to pinpoint a precise time in the process when the right must be asserted or waived, but that fact does not argue for placing the burden of protecting the right solely on defendants. A defendant has no duty to bring himself to trial; * * * the State has that duty as well as the duty of insuring that the trial is consistent with due process. * * * * Moreover, for the reasons earlier expressed, society has a particular interest in bringing swift prosecutions, and society's representatives are the ones who should protect that interest.

It is also noteworthy that such a rigid view of the demand-waiver rule places defense counsel in an awkward position. Unless he demands a trial early and often, he is in danger of frustrating his client's right. If counsel is willing to tolerate some delay because he finds it reasonable and helpful in preparing his own case, he may be unable to obtain a speedy trial for his client at the end of that time. Since under the demand-waiver rule no time runs until the demand is made, the government will have whatever time is otherwise reasonable to bring the defendant to trial after a demand has been made. Thus, if the first demand is made three months after arrest in a jurisdiction which prescribes a six-month rule, the prosecution will have a total of nine months — which may be wholly unreasonable under the circumstances. The result in practice is likely to be either an automatic, pro forma demand made immediately after appointment of counsel or delays which, but for the demand-waiver rule, would not be tolerated. Such a result is not consistent with the interests of defendants, society, or the Constitution.

We reject, therefore, the rule that a defendant who fails to demand a speedy trial forever waives his right. * * * * This does not mean, however, that the defendant has no responsibility to assert his right. We think the better rule is that the defendant's assertion of or failure to assert his right to a speedy trial is one of the factors to be considered in an inquiry into the deprivation of the right. Such a formulation avoids the rigidities of the demand-waiver rule and the resulting possible unfairness in its application. It allows the trial court to exercise a judicial discretion based on the circumstances, including due consideration of any applicable formal procedural rule. It would permit, for example, a court to attach a different weight to a situation in which the defendant knowingly fails to object from a situation in which his attorney acquiesces in long delay without adequately informing his client, or from a situation in which no counsel is appointed. It would also allow a court to weigh the frequency and force of the objections as opposed to attaching significant weight to a purely pro forma objection.

In ruling that a defendant has some responsibility to assert a speedy trial claim, we do not depart from out holdings in other cases concerning the waiver of fundamental rights, in which we have placed the entire responsibility on the prosecution to show that the claimed waiver was knowingly and voluntarily made. Such cases have involved rights which must be exercised or waived at a specific time or under clearly identifiable circumstances, such as the rights to plead not guilty, to demand a jury trial, to exercise the privilege against self-incrimination, and to have the assistance of counsel. We have shown above that the right to a speedy trial is unique in its uncertainty as to when and under what circumstances it must be asserted or may be deemed waived. But the rule we announce today, which comports with constitutional principles, places the primary burden on the courts and the prosecutors to assure that cases are brought to trial. We hardly need add that if delay is attributable to the defendant, then his waiver may be given effect under standard waiver doctrine, the demand rule aside.

We, therefore, reject both of the inflexible approaches — the fixed-time period because it goes further than the Constitution requires; the demand-waiver rule because it is insensitive to a right which he have deemed fundamental. The approach we accept is a balancing test, in which the conduct of both the prosecution and the defendant are weighed.[29]

---

[29] Nothing we have said should be interpreted as disapproving a presumptive rule adopted by a court

IV

A balancing test necessarily compels courts to approach speedy trial cases on an ad hoc basis. We can do little more than identify some of the factors which courts should assess in determining whether a particular defendant has been deprived of his right. Though some might express them in different ways, we identify four such factors: Length of delay, the reason for the delay, the defendant's assertion of his right, and prejudice to the defendant. * * * *

The length of the delay is to some extent a triggering mechanism. Until there is some delay which is presumptively prejudicial, there is no necessity for inquiry into the other factors that go into the balance. Nevertheless, because of the imprecision of the right to speedy trial, the length of delay that will provoke such an inquiry is necessarily dependent upon the peculiar circumstances of the case.[31] To take but one example, the delay that can be tolerated for an ordinary street crime is considerably less than for a serious, complex conspiracy charge.

Closely related to length of delay is the reason the government assigns to justify the delay. Here, too, different weights should be assigned to different reasons. A deliberate attempt to delay the trial in order to hamper the defense should be weighted heavily against the government. * * * * A more neutral reason such as negligence or overcrowded courts should be weighted less heavily but nevertheless should be considered since the ultimate responsibility for such circumstances must rest with the government rather than with the defendant. Finally, a valid reason, such as a missing witness, should serve to justify appropriate delay.

We have already discussed the third factor, the defendant's responsibility to assert his right. Whether and how a defendant asserts his right is closely related to the other factors we have mentioned. The strength of his efforts will be affected by the length of the delay, to some extent by the reason for the delay, and most particularly by the personal prejudice, which is not always readily identifiable, that he experiences. The more serious the deprivation, the more likely a defendant is to complain. The defendant's assertion of his speedy trial right, then, is entitled to strong evidentiary weight in determining whether the defendant is being deprived of the right. We emphasize that failure to assert the right will make it difficult for a defendant to prove that he was denied a speedy trial.

A fourth factor is prejudice to the defendant. Prejudice, of course, should be assessed in the light of the interests of defendants which the speedy trial right was designed to protect. This Court has identified three such interests: (i) to prevent oppressive pretrial incarceration; (ii) to minimize anxiety and concern of the accused; and (iii) to limit the possibility that the defense will be impaired. * * * * Of these, the most serious is the last, because the inability of a defendant adequately to prepare his case skews the fairness of the entire system. If witnesses die or disappear during a delay, the prejudice is obvious. There is also prejudice if defense witnesses are unable to recall accurately events of the distant past. Loss of memory, however, is not always reflected in the record because what has been forgotten can rarely be shown.

---

in the exercise of its supervisory powers which establishes a fixed time period within which cases must normally be brought.

[31] For example, the First Circuit thought a delay of nine months overly long, absent a good reason, in a case that depended on eyewitness testimony. *United States v. Butler*, 426 F.2d 1275, 1277 (1970).

We have discussed previously the societal disadvantages of lengthy pretrial incarceration, but obviously the disadvantages for the accused who cannot obtain his release are even more serious. The time spent in jail awaiting trial has a detrimental impact on the individual. It often means loss of a job; it disrupts family life; and it enforces idleness. Most jails offer little or no recreational or rehabilitative programs. * * * * The time spent in jail is simply dead time. Moreover, if a defendant is locked up, he is hindered in his ability to gather evidence, contact witnesses, or otherwise prepare his defense. * * * * Imposing those consequences on anyone who has not yet been convicted is serious. It is especially unfortunate to impose them on those persons who are ultimately found to be innocent. Finally, even if an accused is not incarcerated prior to trial, he is still disadvantaged by restraints on his liberty and by living under a cloud of anxiety, suspicion, and often hostility.

We regard none of the four factors identified above as either a necessary or sufficient condition to the finding of a deprivation of the right of speedy trial. Rather, they are related factors and must be considered together with such other circumstances as may be relevant. In sum, these factors have no talismanic qualities; courts must still engage in a difficult and sensitive balancing process. * * * * But, because we are dealing with a fundamental right of the accused, this process must be carried out with full recognition that the accused's interest in a speedy trial is specifically affirmed in the Constitution.

V

The difficulty of the task of balancing these factors is illustrated by this case, which we consider to be close. It is clear that the length of delay between arrest and trial — well over five years — was extraordinary. Only seven months of that period can be attributed to a strong excuse, the illness of the ex-sheriff who was in charge of the investigation. Perhaps some delay would have been permissible under ordinary circumstances, so that Manning could be utilized as a witness in Barker's trial, but more than four years was too long a period, particularly since a good part of that period was attributable to the Commonwealth's failure or inability to try Manning under circumstances that comported with due process.

Two counterbalancing factors, however, outweigh these deficiencies. The first is that prejudice was minimal. Of course, Barker was prejudiced to some extent by living for over four years under a cloud of suspicion and anxiety. Moreover, although he was released on bond for most of the period, he did spend 10 months in jail before trial. But there is no claim that any of Barker's witnesses died or otherwise became unavailable owing to the delay. The trial transcript indicates only two very minor lapses of memory — one on the part of a prosecution witness — which were in no way significant to the outcome.

More important than the absence of serious prejudice, is the fact that Barker did not want a speedy trial. Counsel was appointed for Barker immediately after his indictment and represented him throughout the period. No question is raised as to the competency of such counsel. * * * * Despite the fact that counsel had notice of the motions for continuances, * * * the record shows no action whatever taken between October 21, 1958, and February 12, 1962, that could be construed as the assertion of the speedy trial right. On the latter date, in response to another motion for continuance, Barker moved to dismiss the indictment. The record does not show on what ground this motion was based, although it is clear that no alternative motion was made for an immediate trial. Instead the record strongly suggests that while he hoped to take advantage of the delay in which he had acquiesced, and thereby obtain a dismissal of the charges, he definitely did not want to be tried. Counsel conceded as much at oral argument:

> Your honor, I would concede that Willie Mae Barker probably — I don't know this for a fact — probably did not want to be tried. I don't think any man wants to be tried. And I don't consider this a liability on his behalf. I don't blame him.

The probable reason for Barker's attitude was that he was gambling on Manning's acquittal. The evidence was not very strong against Manning, as the reversals and hung juries suggest, and Barker undoubtedly thought that if Manning were acquitted, he would never be tried. Counsel also conceded this:

> Now, it's true that the reason for this delay was the Commonwealth of Kentucky's desire to secure the testimony of the accomplice, Silas Manning. And it's true that if Silas Manning were never convicted, Willie Mae Barker would never have been convicted. We concede this.[39]

That Barker was gambling on Manning's acquittal is also suggested by his failure, following the pro forma motion to dismiss filed in February 1962, to object to the Commonwealth's next two motions for continuances. Indeed, it was not until March 1963, after Manning's convictions were final, that Barker, having lost his gamble, began to object to further continuances. At that time, the Commonwealth's excuse was the illness of the ex-sheriff, which Barker has conceded justified the further delay.

We do not hold that there may never be a situation in which an indictment may be dismissed on speedy trial grounds where the defendant has failed to object to continuances. There may be a situation in which the defendant was represented by incompetent counsel, was severely prejudiced, or even cases in which the continuances were granted *ex parte*. But barring extraordinary circumstances, we would be reluctant indeed to rule that a defendant was denied this constitutional right on a record that strongly indicates, as does this one, that the defendant did not want a speedy trial. We hold, therefore, that Barker was not deprived of his due process right to a speedy trial.

The judgment of the Court of Appeals is affirmed.

Note from Warren:

Take another look at the Speed Trial *Act*. How does the approach taken by the *Act* differ from the approach taken by the Speedy Trial *Clause* — as interpreted by *Barker*? If they differ, which applies to our case — the Act, the Clause, or both?

---

[39] Hindsight is, of course, 20/20, but we cannot help noting that if Barker had moved immediately and persistently for a speedy trial following indictment, and if he had been successful, he would have undoubtedly been acquitted since Manning's testimony was crucial to the Commonwealth's case. It could not have been anticipated at the outset, however, that Manning would have been tried six times over a four-year period. Thus, the decision to gamble on Manning's acquittal may have been a prudent choice at the time it was made.

STRUNK v. UNITED STATES

United States Supreme Court
412 U.S. 434 (1973)

Opinion of the Court by Mr. Chief Justice Burger, announced by Mr. Justice Douglas.

Petitioner was found guilty in United States District Court of transporting a stolen automobile from Wisconsin to Illinois, in violation of 18 U.S.C. § 2312 and was sentenced to a term of five years. The five-year sentence was to run concurrently with a sentence of one to three years that petitioner was then serving in the Nebraska State Penitentiary pursuant to a conviction in the courts of that State.

Prior to trial, the District Court denied a motion to dismiss the federal charge, in which petitioner argued that he had been denied his right to a speedy trial. At trial petitioner called no witnesses and did not take the stand; the jury returned a verdict of guilty. The Court of Appeals reversed the District Court, holding that petitioner had in fact been denied a speedy trial. However, the court went on to hold that the "extreme" remedy of dismissal of the charges was not warranted; the case was remanded to the District Court to reduce petitioner's sentence to the extent of 259 days in order to compensate for the unnecessary delay which had occurred between return of the indictment and petitioner's arraignment.

Certiorari was granted on petitioner's claim that, once a judicial determination has been made that an accused has been denied a speedy trial, the only remedy available to the court is "to reverse the conviction, vacate the sentence, and dismiss the indictment." No cross-petition was filed by the Government to review the determination of the Court of Appeals that the defendant had been denied a speedy trial. The Government acknowledges that, in its present posture, the case presents a novel and unresolved issue, not controlled by any prior decisions of this Court. *
* * *

In the absence of a cross-petition for certiorari questioning the holding that petitioner was denied a speedy trial, the only question properly before us for review is the propriety of the remedy fashioned by the Court of Appeals.

Turning to the question of the power of the Court of Appeals to fashion what it appeared to consider as a "practical" remedy, we note that the court clearly perceived that the accused had an interest in being tried promptly, even though he was confined in a penitentiary for an unrelated charge. Under these circumstances,

> The possibility that the defendant already in prison might receive a sentence at least partially concurrent with the one he is serving may be forever lost if trial of the pending charge is postponed. [*Smith v. Hooey*, 393 U.S. 374, 378 (1969)]

The Court of Appeals went on to state:

> The remedy for a violation of this constitutional right has traditionally been the dismissal of the indictment or the vacation of the sentence. Perhaps the severity of that remedy has caused courts to be extremely hesitant in finding a failure to afford a speedy trial. Be that as it may, we know of no reason why less drastic relief may not be granted in appropriate cases. Here no question is raised about the sufficiency of evidence showing

defendant's guilt, and, as we have said, he makes no claim of having been prejudiced in presenting his defense. In these circumstances, the vacation of the sentence and a dismissal of the indictment would seem inappropriate. Rather, we think the proper remedy is to remand the case to the district court with direction to enter an order instruction the Attorney General to credit the defendant with the period of time elapsing between the return of the indictment and the date of the arraignment. Fed.R.Crim.P. 35 provides that the district court may correct an illegal sentence at any time. We choose to treat the sentence here imposed as illegal to the extent of the delay we have characterized as unreasonable.

It is correct, as the Court of Appeals noted, that *Barker* prescribes "flexible" standards based on practical considerations. However, that aspect of the holding in *Barker* was directed at the process of determining whether a denial of speedy trial had occurred; it did not deal with the remedy for denial of this right. By definition, such denial is unlike some of the other guarantees of the Sixth Amendment. For example, failure to afford a public trial, an impartial jury, notice of charges, or compulsory service can ordinarily be cured by providing those guaranteed rights in a new trial. The speedy trial guarantee recognizes that a prolonged delay may subject the accused to an emotional stress that can be presumed to result in the ordinary person from uncertainties in the prospect of facing public trial or of receiving a sentence longer than, or consecutive to, the one he is presently serving — uncertainties that a prompt trial removes. *Smith v. Hooey*, 393 U.S. at 379 (1966). We recognize that the stress from a delayed trial may be less on a prisoner already confined, whose family ties and employment have been interrupted,[2] but other factors such as the prospect of rehabilitation may also be affected adversely. The remedy chosen by the Court of Appeals does not deal with these difficulties.

The Government's reliance on *Barker* to support the remedy fashioned by the Court of Appeals is further undermined when we examine the Court's opinion in that case as a whole. It is true that *Barker* described dismissal of an indictment for denial of a speedy trial as an "unsatisfactorily severe remedy." Indeed, in practice, "it means that a defendant who may be guilty of a serious crime will go free, without having been tried." 407 U.S. at 522. But such severe remedies are not unique in the application of constitutional standards. In light of the policies which underlie the right to a speedy trial, dismissal must remain, as *Barker* noted, "the only possible remedy." *IbId.*

Given the unchallenged determination that petitioner was denied a speedy trial, the District Court judgment of conviction must be set aside. The judgment is therefore reversed, and the case remanded to the Court of Appeals to direct the District Court to set aside its judgment, vacate the sentence, and dismiss the indictment.

---

[2] It can also be said that an accused released pending trial often has little or no interest in being tried quickly; but this, standing alone, does not alter the prosecutor's obligation to see to it that the case is brought on for trial. The desires or convenience of individuals cannot be controlling. The public interest in a broad sense, as well as the constitutional guarantee, commands prompt disposition of criminal charges.

Notes from Warren:

1. Was the Court dealing with a violation of the Speedy Trial *Act* or the Speedy Trial *Clause*? Does it matter? Is the remedy the same under both?

2. In *U.S. v. Furey*, 514 F.2d 1098 (2nd Cir.1975), the court held that where "a defendant's Sixth Amendment right to a speedy trial has been denied, the remedy invariably is dismissal of the charges or indictment with prejudice."

MOORE v. ARIZONA
United States Supreme Court
414 U.S. 25 (1973)

Per Curiam

Almost three years after he was charged and 28 months after he first demanded that Arizona either extradite him from California, where he was serving a prison term, or drop a detainer against him, petitioner was tried for murder in Arizona. Prior to trial, he filed a state habeas corpus application, alleging a deprivation of his Sixth and Fourteenth Amendment right to a speedy trial. In affirming the denial of the petition, the Arizona Supreme Court ruled that under this Court's decision in *Barker v. Wingo*, 407 U.S. 514 (1972), a showing of prejudice to the defense at trial was essential to establish a federal speedy trial claim. The state court found no such prejudice here because petitioner was afforded a preliminary hearing and allowed to subpoena witnesses.

The state court was in fundamental error in its reading of *Barker v. Wingo* and in the standard applied in judging petitioner's speedy trial claim. *Barker v. Wingo* expressly rejected the notion that an affirmative demonstration of prejudice was necessary to prove a denial of the constitutional right to a speedy trial:

> We regard none of the four factors identified above (length of delay, reason for delay, defendant's assertion of his right, and prejudice to the defendant) as either a necessary or sufficient condition to the finding of a deprivation of the right of speedy trial. Rather, they are related factors and must be considered together with such other circumstances as may be relevant. [407 U.S. at 533]

In addition to possible prejudice, any court must thus carefully weigh the reasons for the delay in bringing an incarcerated defendant to trial. In the face of petitioner's repeated demands, did the State discharge its constitutional duty to make a diligent, good-faith effort to bring him to trial?

> Moreover, prejudice to a defendant caused by delay in bringing him to trial is not confined to the possible prejudice to his defense in those proceedings. Inordinate delay, wholly aside from possible prejudice to a defense on the merits, may seriously interfere with the defendant's liberty, whether he is free on bail or not, and may disrupt his employment, drain his financial resources, curtail his associations, subject him to public obloquy, and create anxiety in him, his family and his friends. These factors are more serious for some than for others, but they are inevitably present in every case to some extent, for every defendant will either be incarcerated pending trial or on bail subject to substantial restrictions on his liberty. [*Barker v. Wingo, supra*, at 537 (White, J., concurring)]

Some of these factors may carry quite different weight where a defendant is incarcerated after conviction in another State, but no court should overlook the possible impact pending charges might have on his prospects for parole and meaningful rehabilitation. *Strunk v. United States*, 412 U.S. 434 (1973).

The State of Arizona itself has conceded that this is a close case under *Barker v. Wingo* and that it is arguable whether the three-year delay was excusable. Because we agree and because "the right to a speedy trial is as fundamental as any of the rights secured by the Sixth Amendment," *Klopfer v. North Carolina*, 386 U.S. 213, 223 (1967), we grant the motion for leave to proceed *in forma pauperis* and the petition, vacate the judgment, and remand to the Arizona Supreme Court to reassess petitioner's case under the standards mandated by *Barker*.

Note from Warren:

Where, exactly, was the *prejudice* to Moore — given the fact that a speedy trial and acquittal on the Arizona charge would not have gotten him out of prison in California?

UNITED STATES v. LOVASCO
United States Supreme Court
431 U.S. 783 (1977)

Mr. Justice Marshall delivered the opinion of the Court.

We granted certiorari in this case to consider the circumstances in which the Constitution requires that an indictment be dismissed because of delay between the commission of an offense and the initiation of prosecution.

I

On March 6, 1975, respondent was indicted for possessing eight firearms stolen from the United States mails, and for dealing in firearms without a license. The offenses were alleged to have occurred between July 25 and August 31, 1973, more than 18 months before the indictment was filed. Respondent moved to dismiss the indictment due to the delay.

The District Court conducted a hearing on respondent's motion, at which the respondent sought to prove that the delay was unnecessary and that it had prejudiced his defense. In an effort to establish the former proposition, respondent presented a Postal Inspector's report on his investigation that was prepared one month after the crimes were committed, and a stipulation concerning the post-report progress of the probe. The report stated, in brief, that within the first month of the investigation, respondent had admitted to Government agents that he had possessed and then sold five of the stolen guns, and that the agents had developed strong evidence linking respondent to the remaining three weapons. * * * * The report also stated, however, that the agents had been unable to confirm or refute respondent's claim that he had found the guns in his car when he returned to it after visiting his son, a mail handler, at work. The stipulation into which the Assistant United States Attorney entered indicated that little additional information concerning the crimes was uncovered in the 17 months following the preparation of the

Inspector's report. * * * *

To establish prejudice to the defense, respondent testified that he had lost the testimony of two material witnesses due to the delay. The first witness, Tom Stewart, died more than a year after the alleged crimes occurred. At the hearing, respondent claimed that Stewart had been his source for two or three of the guns. The second witness, respondent's brother, died in April 1974, eight months after the crimes were completed. Respondent testified that his brother was present when respondent called Stewart to secure the guns, and witnessed all of respondent's sales. Respondent did not state how the witnesses would have aided the defense had they been willing to testify. * * * *

The Government made no systematic effort in the District Court to explain its long delay. The Assistant United States Attorney did expressly disagree, however, with defense counsel's suggestion that the investigation had ended after the Postal Inspector's report was prepared. The prosecutor also stated that it was the Government's theory that respondent's son, who had access to the mail at the railroad terminal from which the guns were "possibly stolen," was responsible for the thefts. * * * * Finally, the prosecutor elicited somewhat cryptic testimony from the Postal Inspector indicating that the case "as to these particular weapons involves other individuals"; that information had been presented to a grand jury "in regard to this case other than on the day of the indictment itself"; and that he had spoken to the prosecutors about the case on four or five occasions.

Following the hearing, the District Court found that by October 2, 1973, the date of the Postal Inspector's report, "the Government had all the information relating to defendant's alleged commission of the offenses charged against him," and that the 17-month delay before the case was presented to the grand jury "had not been explained or justified" and was "unnecessary and unreasonable." The court also found that "as a result of the delay defendant has been prejudiced by reason of the death of Tom Stewart, a material witness on his behalf." Accordingly, the court dismissed the indictment.

The Government appealed to the United States Court of Appeals for the Eighth Circuit. In its brief, the Government explained the months of inaction by stating:

> There was a legitimate Government interest in keeping the investigation open in the instant case. The defendant's son worked for the Terminal Railroad and had access to mail. It was the Government's position that the son was responsible for the theft and therefore further investigation to establish this fact was important. Although the investigation did not continue on a full time basis, there was contact between the United States Attorney's office and the Postal Inspector's office throughout and certain matters were brought before a Federal Grand Jury prior to the determination that the case should be presented for indictment.

The Court of Appeals accepted the Government's representation as to the motivation for the delay, but a majority of the court nevertheless affirmed the District Court's finding that the Government's actions were "unjustified, unnecessary, and unreasonable." The majority also found that respondent had established that his defense had been impaired by the loss of Stewart's testimony because it understood respondent to contend that "were Stewart's testimony available it would support respondent's claim that he did not know that the guns were stolen from the United States mails." The court therefore affirmed the District Court's dismissal of the three possession counts by a divided vote. * * * *

We granted certiorari and now reverse.

II

In *United States v. Marion*, 404 U.S. 307 (1971), this Court considered the significance, for constitutional purposes, of a lengthy preindictment delay. We held that, as far as the Speedy Trial Clause of the Sixth Amendment is concerned, such delay is wholly irrelevant, since our analysis of the language, history, and purposes of the Clause persuaded us that only "a formal indictment or information or else the actual restraints imposed by arrest and holding to answer a criminal charge engage the particular protections" of that provision. *Id.* at 320. * * * * We went on to note that statutes of limitations, which provide predictable, legislatively enacted limits on prosecutorial delay, provide "the primary guarantee, against bringing overly stale criminal charges." *Id.* at 322. But we did acknowledge that the "statute of limitations does not fully define defendants' rights with respect to the events occurring prior to indictment," *Id.* at 324, and that the Due Process Clause has a limited role to play in protecting against oppressive delay.

Respondent seems to argue that due process bars prosecution whenever a defendant suffers prejudice as a result of preindictment delay. To support that proposition, respondent relies on the concluding sentence of the Court's opinion in *Marion* where, in remanding the case, we stated that "events of the trial may demonstrate actual prejudice, but at the present time appellees' due process claims are speculative and premature." *Id.* at 326. But the quoted sentence establishes only that proof of actual prejudice makes a due process claim concrete and ripe for adjudication, not that it makes the claim automatically valid.

Thus *Marion* makes clear that proof of prejudice is generally a necessary but not sufficient element of a due process claim, and that the due process inquiry must consider the reasons for the delay as well as the prejudice to the accused.

The Court of Appeals found that the sole reason for the delay here was "a hope on the part of the Government that others might be discovered who may have participated in the theft." It concluded that this hope did not justify the delay, and therefore affirmed the dismissal of the indictment. But the Due Process Clause does not permit courts to abort criminal prosecutions simply because they disagree with a prosecutor's judgment as to when to seek an indictment. Judges are not free, in defining "due process," to impose on law enforcement officials our "personal and private notions" of fairness and to "disregard the limits that bind judges in their judicial function." *Rochin v. California*, 342 U.S. 165, 170 (1952). Our task is more circumscribed. We are to determine only whether the action complained of here, compelling respondent to stand trial after the Government delayed indictment to investigate further, violates those "fundamental conceptions of justice which lie at the base of our civil and political institutions," *Mooney v. Holohan*, 294 U.S. 103, 112 (1935), and which define "the community's sense of fair play and decency," *Rochin v. California, supra*, 342 U.S. at 173.

It requires no extended argument to establish that prosecutors do not deviate from "fundamental conceptions of justice" when they defer seeking indictments until they have probable cause to believe an accused is guilty; indeed it is unprofessional conduct for a prosecutor to recommend an indictment on less than probable cause. * * * * It should be equally obvious that prosecutors are under no duty to file charges as soon as probable cause exists but before they are satisfied they will be able to establish the suspect's guilt beyond a reasonable doubt. To impose such a duty "would have a deleterious effect both upon the rights of the accused and upon the ability of society to protect itself," *United States v. Ewell, supra*, 383 U.S. at 120. From the perspective of potential defendants, requiring prosecutions to commence when probable cause is established is undesirable, because it would increase the likelihood of unwarranted charges being filed, and would add to the time during which defendants stand accused but untried. * * * * These costs are by no means insubstantial since, as we recognized in *Marion*, a formal accusation may "interfere with the defendant's liberty, disrupt his employment, drain his financial resources, curtail his associations, subject him to public obloquy, and create anxiety in him, his family and his friends." 404 U.S. at 320. From the perspective of law enforcement officials, a requirement of immediate prosecution upon probable cause is equally unacceptable because it could make obtaining proof of guilt beyond a reasonable doubt impossible by causing potentially fruitful sources of information to evaporate before they are fully exploited. * * * * And from the standpoint of the courts, such a requirement is unwise because it would cause scarce resources to be consumed on cases that prove to be insubstantial, or that involve only some of the responsible parties or some of the criminal acts.[12] Thus, no one's interests would be well served by compelling prosecutors to initiate prosecutions as soon as they are legally entitled to do so.[13]

It might be argued that once the Government has assembled sufficient evidence to prove guilt beyond a reasonable doubt, it should be constitutionally required to file charges promptly, even if its investigation of the entire criminal transaction is not complete. Adopting such a rule, however, would have many of the same consequences as adopting a rule requiring immediate prosecution upon probable cause.

First, compelling a prosecutor to file public charges as soon as the requisite proof has been developed against one participant on one charge would cause numerous problems in those cases in which a criminal transaction involves more than one person or more than one illegal act. In some instances, an immediate arrest or indictment would impair the prosecutor's ability to continue his investigation, thereby preventing society from bringing lawbreakers to justice. In other cases, the prosecutor would be able to obtain additional indictments despite an early prosecution, but the necessary result would be multiple trials involving a single set of facts. Such trials place needless burdens on defendants, law enforcement officials, and courts.

---

[12] Defendants also would be adversely affected by trials involving less than all of the criminal acts for which they are responsible, since they likely would be subjected to multiple trials growing out of the same transaction or occurrence.

[13] See also *United States v. Marion*, 404 U.S. at 325: "There is no constitutional right to be arrested. The police are not required to guess at their peril the precise moment at which they have probable cause to arrest a suspect, risking a violation of the Fourth Amendment if they act too soon, and a violation of the Sixth Amendment if they wait too long. Law enforcement officers are under no constitutional duty to call a halt to a criminal investigation the moment they have the minimum evidence to establish probable cause, a quantum of evidence which may fall far short of the amount necessary to support a criminal conviction."

Second, insisting on immediate prosecution once sufficient evidence is developed to obtain a conviction would pressure prosecutors into resolving doubtful cases in favor of early and possibly unwarranted prosecutions. The determination of when the evidence available to the prosecution is sufficient to obtain a conviction is seldom clear-cut, and reasonable persons often will reach conflicting conclusions. In the instant case, for example, since respondent admitted possessing at least five of the firearms, the primary factual issue in dispute was whether respondent knew the guns were stolen, as required by 18 U.S.C. § 1708. Not surprisingly, the Postal Inspector's report contained no direct evidence bearing on this issue. The decision whether to prosecute, therefore, required a necessarily subjective evaluation of the strength of the circumstantial evidence available and the credibility of respondent's denial. Even if a prosecutor concluded that the case was weak and further investigation appropriate, he would have no assurance that a reviewing court would agree. To avoid the risk that a subsequent indictment would be dismissed for preindictment delay, the prosecutor might feel constrained to file premature charges, with all the disadvantages that would entail.[14]

Finally, requiring the Government to make charging decisions immediately upon assembling evidence sufficient to establish guilt would preclude the Government from giving full consideration to the desirability of not prosecuting in particular cases. The decision to file criminal charges, with the awesome consequences it entails, requires consideration of a wide range of factors in addition to the strength of the Government's case, in order to determine whether prosecution would be in the public interest.[15] Prosecutors often need more information than proof of a suspect's guilt, therefore, before deciding whether to seek an indictment. Again the instant case provides a useful illustration. Although proof of the identity of the mail thieves was not necessary to convict respondent of the possessory crimes with which he was charged, it might have been crucial in assessing respondent's culpability, as distinguished from his legal guilt. If, for example, further investigation were to show that respondent had no role in or advance knowledge of the theft and simply agreed, out of paternal loyalty, to help his son dispose of the guns once respondent discovered his son had stolen them, the United States Attorney might have decided not to prosecute, especially since at the time of the crime respondent was over 60 years old and had no prior criminal record.[16] Requiring prosecution once the

---

[14] In addition, if courts were required to decide in every case when the prosecution should have commenced, it would be necessary for them to trace the day-by-day progress of each investigation. Maintaining daily records would impose an administrative burden on prosecutors, and reviewing them would place an even greater burden on the courts.

[15] See, e.g., ABA Project on Standards for Criminal Justice, *The Prosecution Function*, § 3.9(b):

"The prosecutor is not obliged to present all charges which the evidence might support. The prosecutor may in some circumstances and for good cause consistent with the public interest decline to prosecute, notwithstanding that evidence may exist which would support a conviction. Illustrative of the factors which the prosecutor may properly consider in exercising his discretion are:

   (i)   the prosecutor's reasonable doubt that the accused is in fact guilty;

   (ii)   the extent of the harm caused by the offense;

   (iii) the disproportion of the authorized punishment in relation to the particular offense or the offender;

   (iv) possible improper motives of a complainant;

   (v)   reluctance of the victim to testify;

   (vi) cooperation of the accused in the apprehension or conviction of others;

   (vii) availability and likelihood of prosecution by another jurisdiction."

[16] Of course, in this case further investigation proved unavailing and the United States Attorney

evidence of guilt is clear, however, could prevent a prosecutor from awaiting the information necessary for such a decision.

We would be most reluctant to adopt a rule which would have these consequences absent a clear constitutional command to do so. We can find no such command in the Due Process Clause of the Fifth Amendment. In our view, investigative delay is fundamentally unlike delay undertaken by the Government solely "to gain tactical advantage over the accused," *United States v. Marion*, 404 U.S. at 324, precisely because investigative delay is not so one-sided.[17] Rather than deviating from elementary standards of "fair play and decency," a prosecutor abides by them if he refuses to seek indictments until he is completely satisfied that he should prosecute and will be able promptly to establish guilt beyond a reasonable doubt. Penalizing prosecutors who defer action for these reasons would subordinate the goal of "orderly expedition" to that of "mere speed," *Smith v. United States*, 360 U.S. 1, 10 (1959). This the Due Process Clause does not require. We therefore hold that to prosecute a defendant following investigative delay does not deprive him of due process, even if his defense might have been somewhat prejudiced by the lapse of time.

In the present case, the Court of Appeals stated that the only reason the Government postponed action was to await the results of additional investigation. Although there is, unfortunately, no evidence concerning the reasons for the delay in the record, the court's "finding" is supported by the prosecutor's implicit representation to the District Court, and explicit representation to the Court of Appeals, that the investigation continued during the time that the Government deferred taking action against respondent. The finding is, moreover, buttressed by the Government's repeated assertions in its petition for certiorari, its brief, and its oral argument in this Court, "that the delay was caused by the government's efforts to identify persons in addition to respondent who may have participated in the offenses." * * * * We must assume that these statements by counsel have been made in good faith. In light of this explanation, it follows that compelling respondent to stand trial would not be fundamentally unfair. The Court of Appeals therefore erred in affirming the District Court's decision dismissing the indictment.

III

In *Marion*, we conceded that we could not determine in the abstract the circumstances in which preaccusation delay would require dismissing prosecutions. More than five years later, that statement remains true. Indeed, in the intervening years so few defendants have established that they were prejudiced by delay that neither this Court nor any lower court has had a sustained opportunity to consider the constitutional significance of various reasons for delay.[19] We therefore leave to the lower courts, in the first instance, the task of applying the settled principles of

---

ultimately decided to prosecute based solely on the Inspector's report. But this fortuity cannot transform an otherwise permissible delay into an impermissible one.

[17] In *Marion*, we noted with approval that the Government conceded that a "tactical" delay would violate the Due Process Clause. The Government renews that concession here, and expands it somewhat by stating: "A due process violation might also be made out upon a showing of prosecutorial delay incurred in reckless disregard of circumstances, known to the prosecution, suggesting that there existed an appreciable risk that delay would impair the ability to mount an effective defense," *Id.* at 32–33. As the Government notes, however, there is no evidence of recklessness here.

[19] Professor Amsterdam has catalogued some of the noninvestigative reasons for delay:

due process that we have discussed to the particular circumstances of individual cases. We simply hold that in this case the lower courts erred in dismissing the indictment.

Reversed.

MR. JUSTICE STEVENS, dissenting.

* * * *

The findings of the District Court, as approved by the Court of Appeals, establish four relevant propositions: (1) this is a routine prosecution; (2) after the Government assembled all of the evidence on which it expects to establish respondent's guilt, it waited almost 18 months to seek an indictment; (3) the delay was prejudicial to respondent's defense; and (4) no reason whatsoever explains the delay. We may reasonably infer that the prosecutor was merely busy with other matters that he considered more important than this case.

The question presented by those facts is not an easy one. Nevertheless, unless we are to conclude that the Constitution imposes no constraints on the prosecutor's power to postpone the filing of formal charges to suit his own convenience, I believe we must affirm the judgment of the Court of Appeals. A contrary position "can be tenable only if one assumes that the constitutional right to a fair hearing includes no right whatsoever to a prompt hearing." *Moody v. Daggett*, 429 U.S. 78, 91 (Stevens, J., dissenting). The requirement of speedy justice has been part of the Anglo-American common-law tradition since the Magna Carta. It came to this country and was embodied in the early state constitutions, see the Massachusetts Constitution of 1780, Part I, Art. XI, and later in the Sixth Amendment to the United States Constitution. As applied to this case, in which respondent made numerous anxious inquiries of the Postal Inspectors concerning whether he would be indicted, in which the delay caused substantial prejudice to the respondent, and in which the Government has offered no justification for the delay, the right to speedy justice should be honored.

If that right is not honored in a case of this kind, the basic values which the Framers intended to protect by the Sixth Amendment's guarantee of a speedy trial, and which motivated Congress to enact the Speedy Trial Act of 1974, will become nothing more than managerial considerations for the prosecutor to manipulate.

Proof of the offense may depend upon the testimony of an undercover informer who maintains his "cover" for a period of time before surfacing to file charges against one or more persons with whom he has dealt while disguised. If there is more than one possible charge against a suspect, some of them may be held back pending the disposition of others, in order to avoid the burden upon the prosecutor's office of handling charges that may turn out to be unnecessary to obtain the degree of punishment that the prosecutor seeks. There are many other motives for delay, of course, including some sinister ones, such as a desire to postpone the beginning of defense investigation, or the wish to hold a "club" over the defendant.

Additional reasons for delay may be partly or completely beyond the control of the prosecuting authorities. Offenses may not be immediately reported; investigation may not immediately identify the offender; an identified offender may not be immediately apprehendable. An indictment may be delayed for weeks or even months until the impaneling of the next grand jury. It is customary to think of these delays as natural and inevitable, but various prosecutorial decisions such as the assignment of manpower and priorities among investigations of known offenses may also affect the length of such delays. [*Speedy Criminal Trial: Rights and Remedies*, 27 Stan.L.Rev. 525, 527–528 (1975).]

I respectfully dissent.

Notes from Warren:

1. Won't a delay in arrest almost *always* give the government a "tactical advantage over the accused"? If the government knows that it will later arrest and charge the defendant, the government can take steps to preserve evidence right after the crime was committed (e.g., by interviewing witnesses, writing reports, etc.), while if the defendant does not even know he will be charged, his memory of the events on the relevant day will tend to fade — as will the memories of his witnesses. Is this enough to come within the "due process" exception created by the Court in *Lovasco*? Why (not)?

2. *Commonwealth v. Scher*, 732 A.2d 1278 (Pa. Super. 1999), involved the following facts:

> This case arises from the June 2, 1976 shooting death of Martin Dillon, which occurred at "Gun Smoke," a hunting camp owned by the Dillon family. Dillon was killed as a result of being shot in the chest with Dr. Scher's sixteen-gauge shotgun. Dr. Scher and Dillon were the only persons present at Gun Smoke that day; the two friends had gone to the camp, as was their custom, to partake in skeet shooting.

The coroner determined that the death was accidental, and the District Attorney decided not to prosecute. In 1980, a new District Attorney did nothing with the case. In 1989, a new District Attorney asked the state to investigate, and two state investigators discovered a rumor that prior to Dillon's death, Scher was having an affair with Dillon's wife. (Scher subsequently married Dillon's widow.) The investigators had Dillon's body exhumed and a new autopsy performed. "On June 27, 1997, more than twenty years after the date of the alleged crime, Dr. Scher was arrested for Dillon's murder. A jury convicted Dr. Scher of first-degree murder." The court reversed, finding a violation of Due Process:

> In this Commonwealth, there is no statute of limitation for murder prosecutions. Statutes of limitation are not, however, the sole protection afforded to the accused with respect to the time within which charges must be filed. The constitutional right to due process also protects defendants from having to defend stale charges, and criminal charges should be dismissed if improper pre-arrest delay causes prejudice to the defendant's right to a fair trial * * * *

> Intentional delays for improper purposes will not be sanctioned. In addition, although weighted less heavily than deliberate delays, negligent conduct can also be considered, since the ultimate responsibility for such circumstances must rest with the government rather than the defendant. Where the defendant has established actual prejudice due to an unusually lengthy government-caused pre-indictment delay, it then becomes incumbent upon the government to provide the court with its reason for the delay.

> The standard to be used in a due process claim for pre-indictment delay has to do with where the fulcrum for the balancing test is to be placed. In *Marion*, the Court states that the presence of actual prejudice resulting from pre-indictment delays would not by itself warrant the dismissal of a

criminal prosecution. The greater the length of the delay and the more substantial the actual prejudice to the defendant becomes, the greater the reasonableness and the necessity for the delay will have to be to balance out the prejudice. However, despite the degree of actual prejudice, for a judgment in favor of dismissal, there must be some culpability on the government's part either in the form of intentional misconduct or negligence. * * * *

Where there has been an excessive and prejudicial pre-arrest delay, we will not only inquire as to whether there has been any intentional delay by the prosecution to gain a tactical advantage over the accused, but we will also consider whether the prosecution has been negligent by failing to pursue a reasonably diligent criminal investigation. * * * *

The court found that Scher had been prejudiced by the delay:

As to the first prong of the *Marion/Lovasco* test, Dr. Scher argues that he has suffered actual and concrete prejudice as a result of the pre-arrest delay. We agree.

We note that there were numerous instances at the preliminary hearings and at trial where witnesses were unable to remember many facts because their memories had waned over the preceding twenty years. Moreover, many key witnesses were deceased at the time of trial. * * * *

Whether or not the prolonged delay by the Commonwealth in prosecuting its case was intentional, it caused the Commonwealth to gain a remarkable advantage over Dr. Scher. Certain important witnesses were deceased and, therefore, unavailable to Dr. Scher in presenting his case. Moreover, numerous witnesses called by both the Commonwealth and Dr. Scher were unable to remember facts relevant to this case.

The court also found that the District Attorney's office had negligently caused the delay:

The shooting occurred in 1976, and at that time an investigation commenced to determine whether Dillon's death was accidental or the result of a homicide. The District Attorney's office, following an investigation, determined that there was insufficient evidence to proceed with an arrest. Thereafter, an eight-year lapse of activity ensued. In fact, the incumbent District Attorney from 1980 until 1988 had no knowledge that the Dillon file existed. It was not until 1989, following a personal request from the Dillon family, that the investigation was reopened. However, a comprehensive investigation was not commenced until 1994, nearly 18 years following Dillon's death.

Although we are convinced that the delay caused by former District Attorneys Little and Kelly was not due to intentional misconduct, we cannot find that their investigation was one of reasonable diligence. There was no ongoing criminal investigation; in fact, there was no activity whatsoever regarding the case for more than eight years. Even Deputy Attorney General Campolongo, the prosecuting attorney in this matter, criticized the Commonwealth's investigation, when he stated at a preliminary hearing that: "A proper autopsy was not conducted, and a proper investigation was not done until fairly recently when this matter was brought to the attention of the state police and to the attention of the Attorney General's office."

A divided Pennsylvania Supreme Court reinstated Sher's conviction. *Commonwealth v. Scher*, 569 Pa. 284, 803 A.2d 1204 (2002).

(3) In *People v. Nelson*, 142 Cal.App.4th 696 (2006), a woman was murdered in 1976. In 2002, Nelson was charged with her murder — based on DNA evidence. The court affirmed his conviction, rejecting his argument that the delay violated the Due Process Clause:

> It must be shown that the delay was deliberately undertaken to gain a tactical advantage over the defendant.

> In the trial court, defendant's counsel stated: "The defense makes no argument that the authorities somehow 'had it in' for defendant or that they delayed the investigation in order to gain some advantage over him." This concession is fatal to the claim of error based on the federal Constitution.

> In his reply brief, defendant acknowledges his concession but argues it was before an evidentiary hearing revealed that the prosecution delayed until the forensic use of DNA was developed to the point that defendant could be identified and tried for the murder. According to defendant, the development of sophisticated DNA techniques was the tactical advantage the prosecution gained through delay. We reject the contention. A prosecutor should not begin a prosecution until he or she is satisfied the defendant should be prosecuted and the evidence will establish guilt beyond a reasonable doubt. The development of forensic techniques that were not available at the time of an initial investigation provides justification for a delay in prosecution. And the development of forensic science to the point it was possible to identify and prosecute defendant is not prejudice within the meaning of due process principles.

UNITED STATES v. LOUD HAWK

United States Supreme Court
474 U.S. 302 (1986)

JUSTICE POWELL delivered the opinion of the Court.

In this case we must decide, first, whether the Speedy Trial Clause of the Sixth Amendment[1] applies to time during which respondents were neither under indictment nor subjected to any official restraint, and, second, whether certain delays occasioned by interlocutory appeals were properly weighed in assessing respondents' right to a speedy trial. A divided panel of the Court of Appeals for the Ninth Circuit weighed most of the 90 months from the time of respondents' arrests

---

[1] The Speedy Trial Clause of the Sixth Amendment reads: "In all criminal prosecutions, the accused shall enjoy the right to a speedy and public trial."

The more stringent provisions of the Speedy Trial Act, 18 U.S.C. § 3161 et seq., have mooted much litigation about the requirements of the Speedy Trial Clause as applied to federal prosecutions. The time devoted to pretrial appeals, however, is automatically excluded under the Act. § 3161(d)(2) and (h)(1)(E). These respondents must therefore seek any relief under the Speedy Trial Clause.

and initial indictment in November 1975 until the District Court's dismissal of the indictment in May 1983 towards respondents' claims under the Speedy Trial Clause. We conclude that the time that no indictment was outstanding against respondents should not weigh towards respondents' speedy trial claims. We also find that in this case the delay attributable to interlocutory appeals by the Government and respondents do not establish a violation of the Speedy Trial Clause. Accordingly, we reverse the holding of the Court of Appeals that respondents were denied their right to a speedy trial.

I

On November 14, 1975, pursuant to a tip from the Federal Bureau of Investigation, Oregon State Troopers stopped two vehicles in search of several federal fugitives.[2] After an exchange of gunfire and a motor chase, State Troopers captured all but one of the respondents, Dennis Banks. * * * Both vehicles were locked and impounded while federal and state authorities obtained search warrants.

A federal grand jury indicted respondents on November 25, 1975, on charges of possessing firearms and explosives. Trial in the United States District Court for the District of Oregon was set for the week of February 9, 1976. On December 22, 1975, a grand jury returned a five-count superseding indictment. This indictment charged all respondents with three counts relating to possession and transportation in commerce of an unregistered destructive device (the dynamite counts) and two counts relating to unlawful possession of firearms (the firearms counts).

Two days later, respondents filed a motion to suppress all evidence concerning the dynamite, arguing that federal and state officials had intentionally and negligently destroyed the dynamite before the defense had the opportunity to examine it. After initially denying respondents' motion, * * * and after two continuances at respondents' behest, * * * the District Court granted respondents' motion to suppress on March 31, 1976. Three weeks later, the Government appealed the suppression order, * * * and moved that trial on all counts be continued pending the outcome of the appeal. The District Court denied the Government's request for a continuance, and when the case was called for trial, the Government answered not ready. Pursuant to Federal Rule of Criminal Procedure 48(b), the District Judge dismissed the indictment with prejudice. Six months had passed since the original indictment.

The Government immediately appealed the dismissal, and the two appeals were consolidated. The Court of Appeals heard argument on October 15, 1976, and a divided panel affirmed in an unreported opinion on July 26, 1977. On the Government's motion, the court voted on October 17, 1977, to hear the case en banc. On March 6, 1978, the Court of Appeals en banc remanded for findings of fact on whether federal officials participated in the destruction of the dynamite and whether respondents were prejudiced by its destruction. The court retained jurisdiction over the appeal pending the District Court's findings. The District

---

[2] Dennis James Banks, one of the respondents in this action, was active in the American Indian Movement, and was a fugitive when these events occurred. The siege and occupation of Wounded Knee had taken place 60 months before, and the FBI was tracking Banks and his party as fugitives from that affair. For a description of the battle of Wounded Knee and the resultant violence and death, see *United States v. Banks*, 383 F.Supp. 389 (SD 1974).

Court issued its findings on August 23, 1978, and the case returned to the Court of Appeals.

On August 7, 1979, the Court of Appeals reversed the suppression order and directed that the dynamite counts be reinstated. The court also held that although the Government could have gone to trial on the firearms counts pending the appeal, the District Court erred in dismissing those counts with prejudice. The Court of Appeals denied respondents' petition for rehearing on October 1, 1979. Respondents petitioned for certiorari; we denied the petition on March 3, 1980. The mandate of the Court of Appeals issued on March 12, 1980, 46 months after the Government filed its notice of appeal from the dismissal of the indictment. Respondents were unconditionally released during that time.

Following remand, the District Court ordered the Government to reindict on the firearms charges. * * * * Respondents filed a number of motions during June and July of 1980 in response to the superseding indictment, * * * including a motion to dismiss for vindictive prosecution. On August 8, 1980, the District Court granted the vindictive prosecution motion as to KaMook Banks and denied it as to respondents Dennis Banks, Render, and Loud Hawk. Both sides appealed. Respondents remained free on their own recognizance during this appeal.

The appeals were consolidated, and the Court of Appeals ordered expedited consideration. The court heard argument on January 7, 1981, but did not issue its decision until July 29, 1982. The court sustained the Government's position on all issues. Respondents' petitions for rehearing were denied on October 5, 1982. Respondents again petitioned for certiorari, and we denied the petition on January 10, 1983. The Court of Appeals' mandate issued on January 31, 1983, almost 29 months after the appeals were filed.

The District Court scheduled trial to begin on April 11, 1983. The Government sought and received a continuance until May 3, 1983, because of alleged difficulties in locating witnesses more than seven years after the arrests. Subsequently, the court on its own motion continued the trial date until May 23, 1983, and then again rescheduled the trial for June 13. The record in this Court does not reveal the reasons for these latter two continuances. Defendants objected to each continuance.

On May 20, 1983, the District Court again dismissed the indictment, this time on the ground that respondents' Sixth Amendment right to a speedy trial had been violated. The Government appealed, and unsuccessfully urged the District Court to request that the Court of Appeals expedite the appeal. On its own motion the court treated the appeal as expedited, and heard argument on January 4, 1984. A divided panel affirmed on August 30, 1984. We granted certiorari, and now reverse.

II

The Government argues that under *United States v. MacDonald*, 456 U.S. 1 (1982), the time during which defendants are neither under indictment nor subject to any restraint on their liberty should be excluded — weighed not at all — when considering a speedy trial claim.[12] Respondents contend that even during the time the charges against them were dismissed, the Government was actively pursuing its

---

[12] In *MacDonald*, we held that where the Government has dismissed an indictment and the defendant is not subject to actual restraints on his liberty, the Speedy Trial Clause does not apply.

case and they continued to be subjected to the possibility that bail might be imposed. This possibility, according to respondents, is sufficient to warrant counting the time towards a speedy trial claim.

The Court has found that when no indictment is outstanding, only the " *actual* restraints imposed by arrest and holding to answer a criminal charge engage the particular protections of the speedy trial provision of the Sixth Amendment." *United States v. Marion*, 404 U.S. 307, 320 (1971) (emphasis added). As we stated in *MacDonald*: "The speedy trial guarantee is designed to minimize the possibility of lengthy incarceration prior to trial, to reduce the lesser, but nevertheless substantial, impairment of liberty imposed on an accused while released on bail, and to shorten the disruption of life caused by arrest and the presence of unresolved criminal charges." 456 U.S. at 8.

During much of the litigation, respondents were neither under indictment nor subject to bail.[13] Further judicial proceedings would have been necessary to subject the respondents to any actual restraints. As we stated in *MacDonald*: "with no charges outstanding, personal liberty is certainly not impaired to the same degree as it is after arrest while charges are pending. After the charges against him have been dismissed, a citizen suffers no restraints on his liberty and is no longer the subject of public accusation: his situation does not compare with that of a defendant who has been arrested and held to answer." 456 U.S. at 9.

Respondents argue that the speedy trial guarantee should apply to this period because the Government's desire to prosecute them was a matter of public record. Public suspicion, however, is not sufficient to justify the delay in favor of a defendant's speedy trial claim. We find that after the District Court dismissed the indictment against respondents and after respondents were freed without restraint, they were "in the same position as any other subject of a criminal investigation." *MacDonald*, supra, at 9. The Speedy Trial Clause does not purport to protect a defendant from all effects flowing from a delay before trial. The clause does not, for example, limit the length of a preindictment criminal investigation even though "the suspect's knowledge of an ongoing criminal investigation will cause stress, discomfort, and perhaps a certain disruption in normal life." *Id.* at 9.

Nor does the fact that respondents were ordered to appear at the evidentiary hearing held on remand in the District Court during the first appeal — an appearance they waived — constitute the sort of "actual restraint" required under our precedents as a basis for application of the Speedy Trial Clause. Finally, we are not persuaded that respondents' need for counsel while their case was technically dismissed supports their speedy trial claim. Although the retention of counsel is frequently an inconvenience and an expense, the Speedy Trial Clause's core concern is impairment of liberty; it does not shield a suspect or a defendant from every expense or inconvenience associated with criminal defense.

We therefore find that under the rule of *MacDonald*, when defendants are not incarcerated or subjected to other substantial restrictions on their liberty, a court should not weigh that time towards a claim under the Speedy Trial Clause.

---

[13] In those instances where the defendant is subject to incarceration or bail, the courts would have to engage in a balancing of the restrictions imposed and their effect on the defendant, the necessity for delay, and the length of delay, using the approach we have outlined below.

III

The remaining issue is how to weigh the delay occasioned by an interlocutory appeal when the defendant is subject to indictment or restraint. As we have recognized, the Sixth Amendment's guarantee of a speedy trial "is an important safeguard to prevent undue and oppressive incarceration prior to trial, to minimize anxiety and concern accompanying public accusation and to limit the possibilities that long delay will impair the ability of an accused to defend himself." *United States v. Ewell*, 383 U.S. 116, 120 (1966). These safeguards may be as important to the accused when the delay is occasioned by an unduly long appellate process as when the delay is caused by a lapse between the initial arrest and the drawing of a proper indictment, or by continuances in the date of trial, *Barker v. Wingo*, 407 U.S. 514, 517–518 (1972).

At the same time, there are important public interests in the process of appellate review. The assurance that motions to suppress evidence or to dismiss an indictment are correctly decided through orderly appellate review safeguards both the rights of defendants and the "rights of public justice." *Beavers v. Haubert*, 198 U.S. 77, 87 (1905). The legislative history of 18 U.S.C. § 3731 "makes it clear that Congress intended to remove all statutory barriers to Government appeals and to allow appeals whenever the Constitution would permit." *United States v. Wilson*, 420 U.S. 332, 337 (1975).

It is, of course, true that the interests served by appellate review may sometimes stand in opposition to the right to a speedy trial. But, as the Court observed in *United States v. Ewell, supra*, 383 U.S. at 121:

> It has long been the rule that when a defendant obtains a reversal of a prior, unsatisfied conviction, he may be retried in the normal course of events. This rule has been thought wise because it protects the societal interest in trying people accused of crime, rather than granting them immunization because of legal error at a previous trial, and because it enhances the probability that appellate courts will be vigilant to strike down previous convictions that are tainted with reversible error. These policies, so carefully preserved in this Court's interpretation given the Double Jeopardy Clause, would be seriously undercut by an interpretation of the Speedy Trial Clause that raised a Sixth Amendment obstacle to retrial following successful attack on conviction.

In *Barker*, we adopted a four-part balancing test to determine whether a series of continuances infringed upon the defendant's right to a speedy trial. That test assessed the "length of delay, the reason for the delay, the defendant's assertion of his right, and prejudice to the defendant." The *Barker* test furnishes the flexibility to take account of the competing concerns of orderly appellate review on the one hand, and a speedy trial on the other. We therefore adopt this functional test to determine the extent to which appellate time consumed in the review of pretrial motions should weigh towards a defendant's speedy trial claim. Under this test, we conclude that in this case the delays do not justify the "unsatisfactorily severe remedy of dismissal" in this case.

A

Barker's first, third, and fourth factors present no great difficulty in application. The first factor, the length of delay, defines a threshold in the inquiry: there must be a delay long enough to be "presumptively prejudicial." *Id.* at 530. Here, a 90-month delay in the trial of these serious charges is presumptively prejudicial and serves to trigger application of *Barker's* other factors.

The third factor — the extent to which respondents have asserted their speedy trial rights — does not support their position. Although the Court of Appeals found that respondents have repeatedly moved for dismissal on speedy trial grounds, that finding alone does not establish that respondents have appropriately asserted their rights. We held in *Barker* that such assertions from defendants are "entitled to strong evidentiary weight" in determining whether their rights to a speedy trial have been denied. These assertions, however, must be viewed in the light of respondents' other conduct.

Here, respondents' speedy trial claims are reminiscent of Penelope's tapestry.[14] At the same time respondents were making a record of claims in the District Court for speedy trial, they consumed six months by filing indisputably frivolous petitions for rehearing and for certiorari after this Court's decision in *United States v. Hollywood Motor Car Co.*, 458 U.S. 263 (1982) (federal courts without jurisdiction to hear defendant's interlocutory appeal from dismissal of indictment). They also filled the District Court's docket with repetitive and unsuccessful motions.

The Court of Appeals gave "little weight" to the fourth factor, prejudice to respondents. At most, the court recognized the possibility of "impairment of a fair trial that may well result from the absence or loss of memory of witnesses in this case." That possibility of prejudice is not sufficient to support respondents' position that their speedy trial rights were violated. In this case, moreover, delay is a two-edged sword. It is the Government that bears the burden of proving its case beyond a reasonable doubt. The passage of time may make it difficult or impossible for the Government to carry this burden.

B

The flag all litigants seek to capture is the second factor, the reason for delay. In *Barker*, we held that "different weights should be assigned to different reasons." *Id.* at 531. While a "deliberate attempt to delay the trial in order to hamper the defense," would be weighed heavily against the Government, a delay from "overcrowded courts" — as was the situation here — would be weighed "less heavily." *Ibid.* Given the important public interests in appellate review, it hardly need be said that an interlocutory appeal by the Government ordinarily is a valid reason that justifies delay. In assessing the purpose and reasonableness of such an appeal, courts may consider several factors. These include the strength of the Government's position on the appealed issue, the importance of the issue in the posture of the case, and — in some cases — the seriousness of the crime. *United States v. Herman*, 576 F.2d 1139, 1146 (CA5, 1978) (Wisdom, J.). For example, a delay resulting from an appeal would weigh heavily against the Government if the issue were clearly tangential or frivolous. Moreover, the charged offense usually must be sufficiently

---

[14] Homer, *The Oddessy*, Book II, lines 91–105 (R. Lattimore trans. 1965).

serious to justify restraints that may be imposed on the defendant pending the outcome of the appeal.

Under *Barker*, delays in bringing the case to trial caused by the Government's interlocutory appeal may be weighed in determining whether a defendant has suffered a violation of his rights to a speedy trial. It is clear in this case, however, that respondents have failed to show a reason for according these delays any effective weight towards their speedy trial claims. There is no showing of bad faith or dilatory purpose on the Government's part. The Government's position in each of the appeals was strong, and the reversals by the Court of Appeals are prima facie evidence of the reasonableness of the Government's action. Moreover, despite the seriousness of the charged offenses, the District Court chose not to subject respondents to any actual restraints pending the outcome of the appeals.

The only remaining question is the weight to be attributed to delays caused by respondents' interlocutory appeals. In that limited class of cases where a pretrial appeal by the defendant is appropriate, see, e.g., *Hollywood Motor Car Co.*, 458 U.S. at 265–266, delays from such an appeal ordinarily will not weigh in favor of a defendant's speedy trial claims. A defendant with a meritorious appeal would bear the heavy burden of showing an unreasonable delay caused by the prosecution in that appeal, or a wholly unjustifiable delay by the appellate court. A defendant who resorts to an interlocutory appeal normally should not be able upon return to the district court to reap the reward of dismissal for failure to receive a speedy trial. As one Court of Appeals has noted in the context of a District Court's consideration of pretrial motions:

> Having sought the aid of the judicial process and realizing the deliberateness that a court employs in reaching a decision, the defendants are not now able to criticize the very process which they so frequently called upon. [*United States v. Auerbach*, 420 F.2d 921, 924 (CA5, 1969)]

In the present case, respondents' appeal was allowable under the law of the Ninth Circuit before our decision in *Hollywood Motor Car, supra*. But we find that their position was so lacking in merit that the time consumed by this appeal should not weigh in support of respondents' speedy trial claim. Nor do we weigh the additional delay of six months resulting from respondents' frivolous action in seeking rehearing and certiorari toward respondents' speedy trial claim.

IV

We cannot hold, on the facts before us, that the delays asserted by respondents weigh sufficiently in support of their speedy trial claim to violate the Speedy Trial Clause. They do not justify the severe remedy of dismissing the indictment. Accordingly, the judgment of the Court of Appeals for the Ninth Circuit is reversed.

JUSTICE MARSHALL, with whom JUSTICE BRENNAN, JUSTICE BLACKMUN, and JUSTICE STEVENS join, dissenting.

The Court holds today that the Speedy Trial Clause of the Sixth Amendment does not apply to a Government appeal from a district court's dismissal of an indictment, unless the defendant is incarcerated or otherwise under restraint during that appeal. The majority supports this result by equating the present case to *United States v. MacDonald*, 456 U.S. 1 (1982). That analysis, however, both ignores the considerable differences between this case and *MacDonald* and gives short shrift to the interests protected by the Speedy Trial Clause. I further disagree with the majority's application of *Barker v. Wingo*, 407 U.S. 514 (1972), to the remaining appellate delays in this case.

I

The majority concludes that when an appeal arises out of the district court's dismissal of an indictment, the lack of an outstanding indictment absolves the Government of its responsibility to provide a speedy trial. However, we have never conditioned Sixth Amendment rights solely on the presence of an outstanding indictment. Those rights attach to anyone who is "accused," * * * and we have until now recognized that one may stand publicly accused without being under indictment. The majority offers two reasons for concluding that respondents did not enjoy the right to a speedy trial during the Government's appeals. First, respondents were suffering only "public suspicion," and not a formal accusation. Second, they were not subject to "actual restraints" on their liberty. Both of these rationales are seriously flawed.

A

In *United States v. Marion*, 404 U.S. 307 (1971), we held that the Speedy Trial Clause does not apply until the Government, either through arrest or indictment, asserts probable cause to believe that a suspect has committed a crime. Before that time the individual, while possibly aware of the Government's suspicion, is not "the subject of public accusation," and his only protection against delay comes from the Due Process Clause and the applicable statute of limitations. The Court applied the same rationale in *MacDonald*. In that case, military charges of murder against MacDonald, an Army officer, were dropped after an investigation. MacDonald was then given an honorable discharge, only to be indicted by a civilian grand jury nearly four years later for the same murders. The Court held that this delay did not implicate the speedy trial right because "the Speedy Trial Clause has no application after the Government, acting in good faith, formally drops charges." The Court reasoned that after the termination of the first formal prosecution, MacDonald was "in the same position as any other subject of a criminal investigation," and thus was no more an "accused" than was the defendant in *Marion* before his arrest.

The same cannot be said of respondents in the present case. * * * * Unlike one who has not been arrested, or one who has had the charges against him dropped, respondents did not enjoy the protection of the statute of limitations while the Government prosecuted its appeal. That protection was an important aspect of our holding in *Marion* that pre-arrest delay is not cognizable under the Speedy Trial Clause. More importantly, in contrast to *MacDonald*, the Government has not "dropped" anything in this case. * * * * There has been at all relevant times a case on a court docket captioned *United States v. Loud Hawk* — I can think of no more formal indication that respondents stand accused by the Government.

The majority argues that while "the Government's desire to prosecute respondents was a matter of public record," that desire constituted only "public suspicion" that is insufficient to call Sixth Amendment rights into play, citing *Marion* and *MacDonald*. The reason that the Government's desire to prosecute in both of those cases did not constitute an "accusation," however, is that the Government had not yet formalized its commitment. Indeed, in *MacDonald*, the Government dismissed the murder charges because it "concluded that they were untrue," 456 U.S. at 10, thus acknowledging that the first formal accusation had been a mistake and extinguishing the prior probable cause determination. In the present case, the Government has made no such confession of error and continues to align its full resources against respondents in judicial proceedings.

The most telling difference between this case and *MacDonald*, however, is the fact that respondents' liberty could have been taken from them at any time during the Government's appeal. One of the primary purposes of the speedy trial right, of course, is to prevent prolonged restraints on liberty, *Barker v. Wingo*, 407 U.S. at 532, and the absence of any possibility of such restraints was a vital part of our *MacDonald* holding. In contrast, Congress has declared explicitly, in 18 U.S.C. § 3731, that a person in respondents' position shall be subject to the same restraints as an arrested defendant awaiting trial.[4] Thus the District Court had the undoubted authority to condition respondents' release on the posting of bail, or indeed to keep them in jail throughout the appeal, see 18 U.S.C.A. § 3142(e). Respondents' release could have been accompanied by restrictions on travel, association, employment, abode, and firearms possession, or conditioned on their reporting regularly to law enforcement officers and/or keeping a curfew. See § 3142(c). Considering all the circumstances, therefore, I believe that respondents' position is most closely analogous to that of a defendant who has been arrested but not yet indicted.

B

As if acknowledging that the delay in this case is more analogous to post-arrest, pre-indictment delay than to pre-arrest delay, the majority concedes that had respondents been incarcerated or forced to post bond during the Government's appeal, the automatic exclusion rule of *MacDonald* would not apply. Yet, inexplicably, the majority then suggests that the Speedy Trial Clause applies to post-arrest, pre-indictment delay only when the defendant has been subjected to " *actual* restraints" (emphasis added by majority opinion). The majority completely misreads *Marion* while creating a rule that is flatly inconsistent with our prior holdings.

We held in *Marion* that pre-arrest delay is not cognizable under the Speedy Trial Clause, but we certainly did not disturb the settled rule that the Government's formal institution of criminal charges, whether through arrest or indictment, always calls the speedy trial right into play. Although it specified detention and bail as possible deleterious effects of a formal criminal charge, *Marion* nowhere suggested that it is the restraints themselves, rather than the assertion of probable cause, that constitute an accusation. Nor did we hold that a criminal charge has less constitutional significance when a defendant is released on recognizance rather than on bail. The majority identifies no logic or precedent supporting its novel conclusion that a defendant who is arrested and released on bail is "accused," while a defendant

---

[4] 18 U.S.C. § 3731 provides in pertinent part: "Pending the prosecution and determination of the appeal the defendant shall be released in accordance with chapter 207 of this title." Chapter 207, 18 U.S.C. §§ 3141–3156, contains the procedures for pretrial release, and permits the district courts to impose various restraints pending trial. The Government concedes that respondents could have been incarcerated or put under other restraints during the Government's appeals.

who is arrested and released without bail, on the same evidence, is not "accused."[5]

There can be no question that one who had been arrested and released under 18 U.S.C.A. § 3141(a) would be entitled, under *Marion*, to the protections of the Speedy Trial Clause. Because respondents were by statute subject to the same restraints as that hypothetical defendant, I am at a loss to understand why they should enjoy less protection.

II

The majority also declines to hold the Government accountable for delay attributable to appeals during which respondents were under indictment. In doing so the majority emphasizes the second *Barker* factor — the reason for the delay. Because it concludes that "there is no showing of bad faith or dilatory purpose on the Government's part," the majority declines to accord any "effective weight" to this factor in the speedy trial balance. In reaching this conclusion, it virtually ignores the most obvious "reason for the delay" in this case — the fact that the Court of Appeals was unable to decide these appeals in a reasonably prompt manner.

In *Barker*, we explained the application of the "reason for the delay" factor as follows:

> Different weights should be assigned to different reasons. A deliberate attempt to delay the trial in order to hamper the defense should be weighted heavily against the government. A more neutral reason such as negligence or overcrowded courts should be weighted less heavily but nevertheless should be considered since the ultimate responsibility for such circumstances must rest with the government rather than with the defendant.

The majority's application of this factor to the appellate delays in this case makes government misconduct or bad faith a virtual prerequisite to a finding of a speedy trial violation. * * * The majority analyzes the reason behind the appellate delay solely in terms of the reasonableness of the Government's behavior in taking and prosecuting the appeal. This approach is inconsistent with the policies behind the speedy trial right. We recognized in *Barker* that the right protects both the defendant's interest in fairness and society's interest in providing swift justice. Courts as well as prosecutors must necessarily work to promote those interests if they are to have any vitality. Because it is the Government as a whole — including the courts — that bears the responsibility to provide a speedy trial, the prosecutor's good faith cannot suffice to discharge that responsibility.[8]

---

[5] It is worth noting that the Speedy Trial Act puts time limits on the Government beginning with "the date on which the defendant was arrested or served with a summons," 18 U.S.C. § 3161, without regard to the terms of the defendant's release.

Moreover, Federal Rule of Criminal Procedure 48(b), which "provides for enforcement of the speedy trial right," *Pollard v. United States*, 352 U.S. 354, 361 (1957), states: "If there is unnecessary delay in presenting the charge to a grand jury or in filing an information against a defendant who has been held to answer to the district court, the court may dismiss the indictment, information or complaint." That language clearly confers the same rights on a defendant who is arrested and unconditionally released as one who is released on conditions.

[8] This assumes, of course, that the defendant wants a speedy trial and is not intentionally hindering the Government's attempt to provide one. That assumption may be open to question in this case. The

The Court of Appeals frankly admitted that "most of the delay must be attributed to the processes of this court," a conclusion that is difficult to escape. This case involves appeals from pretrial rulings. The Court of Appeals had every reason to know that these appeals should have been ruled upon as expeditiously as possible. Yet it took over five years for the Court of Appeals to decide two appeals, one of them "expedited." No complicated analysis is needed to identify the reason for the delay in this case.

I would hold, simply, that a nonfrivolous appeal by any party permits a *reasonable* delay in the proceedings. The number and complexity of the issues on appeal, or the number of parties, might permit a greater or lesser delay in a given case. The Government, not the defendant, must suffer the ultimate consequences of delays attributable to "overcrowded courts," even at the appellate level.[9] In the present case, the amount of time that the appeals consumed is patently unreasonable. I would therefore weigh the second *Barker* factor against the Government in this case.

III

The majority has seriously misapplied our precedents in concluding that delay resulting when the Government appeals the dismissal of an indictment is excludable for speedy trial purposes unless the defendant is subjected to actual restraints during that appeal. Its application of *Barker v. Wingo* to this case also undercuts the very purpose of the speedy trial right. I respectfully dissent.

Notes from Warren:

1. In *U.S. v. Simmons*, 536 F.2d 827 (9th Cir.1976), the court applied the four *Barker v. Wingo* factors to a defendant who had been released on his own recognizance, but held that the fact that the defendant was at liberty "constitute a showing of minimal prejudice of a type normally attending criminal prosecution. This showing, without more, did not deprive Simmons of his right to a speedy trial."

2. In *U.S. v. Smith*, 94 F.3d 204 (6th Cir.1996), the court held that, while the Speedy Trial Clause applies only to trial court proceedings, the Due Process Clause gives the defendant the right to speedy resolution of his *appeal* (or even the prosecution's appeal). This is so even though the Constitution provides no right to an appeal. The court noted that:

> An appeal that needlessly takes ten years to adjudicate is undoubtedly of little use to a defendant who has been wrongly incarcerated on a ten-year sentence. In our view, the factors set forth in *Barker* and subsequent

---

majority points out that respondents' strategically-timed demands for a speedy trial ring somewhat hollow in light of respondents' overall behavior during the litigation. Were that the basis for the Court's opinion, I might be able to accept a remand to the Court of Appeals for further consideration of that factor. I am unable, however, to agree with the majority's analysis of the second *Barker v. Wingo* factor.

[9] The majority's focus on the prosecution's, rather than the court's, contribution to the delay undoubtedly comes in part from a reluctance to permit district courts to tell a court of appeals, or possibly this Court, that it has taken too long to decide a case. However, appellate courts have no privilege to decline constitutional obligations. The appellate courts would be better advised to adopt procedures for the speedy resolution of interlocutory criminal appeals than to force district courts into the uncomfortable position of dismissing indictments because of appellate delay.

speedy-appeal cases provide the relevant considerations for investigating such unconstitutional delays.

DOGGETT v. UNITED STATES
United States Supreme Court
505 U.S. 647 (1992)

JUSTICE SOUTER delivered the opinion of the Court.

In this case we consider whether the delay of 8 1/2 years between petitioner's indictment and arrest violated his Sixth Amendment right to a speedy trial. We hold that it did.

I

On February 22, 1980, petitioner Marc Doggett was indicted for conspiring with several others to import and distribute cocaine. Douglas Driver, the Drug Enforcement Administration's principal agent investigating the conspiracy, told the United States Marshal's Service that the DEA would oversee the apprehension of Doggett and his confederates. On March 18, 1980, two police officers set out under Driver's orders to arrest Doggett at his parents' house in Raleigh, North Carolina, only to find that he was not there. His mother told the officers that he had left for Colombia four days earlier.

To catch Doggett on his return to the United States, Driver sent word of his outstanding arrest warrant to all United States Customs stations and to a number of law enforcement organizations. He also placed Doggett's name in the Treasury Enforcement Communication System (TECS), a computer network that helps Customs agents screen people entering the country, and in the National Crime Information Center computer system, which serves similar ends. The TECS entry expired that September, however, and Doggett's name vanished from the system.

In September 1981, Driver found out that Doggett was under arrest on drug charges in Panama and, thinking that a formal extradition request would be futile, simply asked Panama to "expel" Doggett to the United States. Although the Panamanian authorities promised to comply when their own proceedings had run their course, they freed Doggett the following July and let him go to Colombia, where he stayed with an aunt for several months. On September 25, 1982, he passed unhindered through Customs in New York City and settled down in Virginia. Since his return to the United States, he has married, earned a college degree, found a steady job as a computer operations manager, lived openly under his own name, and stayed within the law.

Doggett's travels abroad had not wholly escaped the Government's notice, however. In 1982, the American Embassy in Panama told the State Department of his departure to Colombia, but that information, for whatever reason, eluded the DEA, and Agent Driver assumed for several years that his quarry was still serving time in a Panamanian prison. Driver never asked DEA officials in Panama to check into Doggett's status, and only after his own fortuitous assignment to that country in 1985 did he discover Doggett's departure for Colombia. Driver then simply assumed Doggett had settled there, and he made no effort to find out for sure or to track Doggett down, either abroad or in the United States. Thus Doggett remained lost to the American criminal justice system until September 1988, when the Marshal's Service ran a simple credit check on several thousand people subject to outstanding arrest warrants and, within minutes, found out where Doggett lived and worked. On September 5, 1988, nearly 6 years after his return to the United States and 8 1/2 years after his indictment, Doggett was arrested.

He naturally moved to dismiss the indictment, arguing that the Government's failure to prosecute him earlier violated his Sixth Amendment right to a speedy trial. The Federal Magistrate hearing his motion applied the criteria for assessing speedy trial claims set out in *Barker v. Wingo*, 407 U.S. 514 (1972): "length of delay, the reason for the delay, the defendant's assertion of his right, and prejudice to the defendant." The Magistrate found that the delay between Doggett's indictment and arrest was long enough to be "presumptively prejudicial," that the delay "clearly was attributable to the negligence of the government," and that Doggett could not be faulted for any delay in asserting his right to a speedy trial, there being no evidence that he had known of the charges against him until his arrest. The Magistrate also found, however, that Doggett had made no affirmative showing that the delay had impaired his ability to mount a successful defense or had otherwise prejudiced him. In his recommendation to the District Court, the Magistrate contended that this failure to demonstrate particular prejudice sufficed to defeat Doggett's speedy trial claim. The District Court took the recommendation and denied Doggett's motion. Doggett then entered a conditional guilty plea under Federal Rule of Criminal Procedure 11(a)(2), expressly reserving the right to appeal his ensuing conviction on the speedy trial claim. A split panel of the Court of Appeals affirmed. * * * *

II

The Sixth Amendment guarantees that, "in all criminal prosecutions, the accused shall enjoy the right to a speedy trial." On its face, the Speedy Trial Clause is written with such breadth that, taken literally, it would forbid the government to delay the trial of an "accused" for any reason at all. Our cases, however, have qualified the literal sweep of the provision by specifically recognizing the relevance of four separate enquiries: whether delay before trial was uncommonly long, whether the government or the criminal defendant is more to blame for that delay, whether, in due course, the defendant asserted his right to a speedy trial, and whether he suffered prejudice as the delay's result. See *Barker, supra*, 407 U.S. at 530.

The first of these is actually a double enquiry. Simply to trigger a speedy trial analysis, an accused must allege that the interval between accusation and trial has crossed the threshold dividing ordinary from "presumptively prejudicial" delay, since, by definition, he cannot complain that the government has denied him a "speedy" trial if it has, in fact, prosecuted his case with customary promptness. If the accused makes this showing, the court must then consider, as one factor among several, the extent to which the delay stretches beyond the bare minimum needed to trigger judicial examination of the claim. This latter enquiry is significant to the speedy trial analysis because, as we discuss below, the presumption that pretrial delay has prejudiced the accused intensifies over time. In this case, the extraordinary 8 1/2 year lag between Doggett's indictment and arrest clearly suffices to trigger the speedy trial enquiry[1]; its further significance within that enquiry will be dealt with later.

As for *Barker's* second criterion, the Government claims to have sought Doggett with diligence. The findings of the courts below are to the contrary, however, and we review trial court determinations of negligence with considerable deference. The Government gives us nothing to gainsay the findings that have come up to us, and we see nothing fatal to them in the record. For six years, the Government's investigators made no serious effort to test their progressively more questionable assumption that Doggett was living abroad, and, had they done so, they could have found him within minutes. While the Government's lethargy may have reflected no more than Doggett's relative unimportance in the world of drug trafficking, it was still findable negligence, and the finding stands.

The Government goes against the record again in suggesting that Doggett knew of his indictment years before he was arrested. Were this true, *Barker's* third factor, concerning invocation of the right to a speedy trial, would be weighed heavily against him. But here again, the Government is trying to revisit the facts. At the hearing on Doggett's speedy trial motion, it introduced no evidence challenging the testimony of Doggett's wife, who said that she did not know of the charges until his arrest, and of his mother, who claimed not to have told him or anyone else that the police had come looking for him. From this the Magistrate implicitly concluded that Doggett had won the evidentiary battle on this point. * * * *

III

The Government is left, then, with its principal contention: that Doggett fails to make out a successful speedy trial claim because he has not shown precisely how he was prejudiced by the delay between his indictment and trial.

A

We have observed in prior cases that unreasonable delay between formal accusation and trial threatens to produce more than one sort of harm, including "oppressive pretrial incarceration," "anxiety and concern of the accused," and "the possibility that the accused's defense will be impaired" by dimming memories and loss of exculpatory evidence. *Barker*, 407 U.S. at 532. Of these forms of prejudice, "the most serious is the last, because the inability of a defendant adequately to prepare his case skews the fairness of the entire system." 407 U.S. at 532. Doggett claims this kind of prejudice, and there is probably no other kind that he can claim, since he was subjected neither to pretrial detention nor, he has successfully contended, to awareness of unresolved charges against him.

The Government answers Doggett's claim by citing language in three cases, *United States v. Marion*, 404 U.S. 307 (1971), *United States v. MacDonald*, 456 U.S. 1 (1982), and *United States v. Loud Hawk*, 474 U.S. 302 (1986), for the proposition

---

[1] Depending on the nature of the charges, the lower courts have generally found postaccusation delay "presumptively prejudicial" at least as it approaches one year. See 2 W. LaFave & J. Israel, *Criminal Procedure* § 18.2; Joseph, *Speedy Trial Rights in Application*, 48 Fordham L.Rev. 611, 623, n. 71 (1980) (citing cases). We note that, as the term is used in this threshold context, "presumptive prejudice" does not necessarily indicate a statistical probability of prejudice; it simply marks the point at which courts deem the delay unreasonable enough to trigger the *Barker* enquiry.

that the Speedy Trial Clause does not significantly protect a criminal defendant's interest in fair adjudication. In so arguing, the Government asks us, in effect, to read part of *Barker* right out of the law, and that we will not do. In context, the cited passages support nothing beyond the principle, which we have independently based on textual and historical grounds, that the Sixth Amendment right of the accused to a speedy trial has no application beyond the confines of a formal criminal prosecution. Once triggered by arrest, indictment, or other official accusation, however, the speedy trial enquiry must weigh the effect of delay on the accused's defense just as it has to weigh any other form of prejudice that *Barker* recognized.

As an alternative to limiting Barker, the Government claims Doggett has failed to make any affirmative showing that the delay weakened his ability to raise specific defenses, elicit specific testimony, or produce specific items of evidence. Though Doggett did indeed come up short in this respect, the Government's argument takes it only so far: consideration of prejudice is not limited to the specifically demonstrable, and, as it concedes, affirmative proof of particularized prejudice is not essential to every speedy trial claim. *Barker* explicitly recognized that impairment of one's defense is the most difficult form of speedy trial prejudice to prove because time's erosion of exculpatory evidence and testimony "can rarely be shown." 407 U.S. at 532. And though time can tilt the case against either side, one cannot generally be sure which of them it has prejudiced more severely. Thus, we generally have to recognize that excessive delay presumptively compromises the reliability of a trial in ways that neither party can prove or, for that matter, identify. While such presumptive prejudice cannot alone carry a Sixth Amendment claim without regard to the other *Barker* criteria, it is part of the mix of relevant facts, and its importance increases with the length of delay.

B

This brings us to an enquiry into the role that presumptive prejudice should play in the disposition of Doggett's speedy trial claim. We begin with hypothetical and somewhat easier cases and work our way to this one.

Our speedy trial standards recognize that pretrial delay is often both inevitable and wholly justifiable. The government may need time to collect witnesses against the accused, oppose his pretrial motions, or, if he goes into hiding, track him down. We attach great weight to such considerations when balancing them against the costs of going forward with a trial whose probative accuracy the passage of time has begun by degrees to throw into question. Thus, in this case, if the Government had pursued Doggett with reasonable diligence from his indictment to his arrest, his speedy trial claim would fail. Indeed, that conclusion would generally follow as a matter of course however great the delay, so long as Doggett could not show specific prejudice to his defense.

The Government concedes, on the other hand, that Doggett would prevail if he could show that the Government had intentionally held back in its prosecution of him to gain some impermissible advantage at trial. That we cannot doubt. *Barker* stressed that official bad faith in causing delay will be weighed heavily against the government, and a bad-faith delay the length of this negligent one would present an overwhelming case for dismissal.

Between diligent prosecution and bad-faith delay, official negligence in bringing an accused to trial occupies the middle ground. While not compelling relief in every case where bad-faith delay would make relief virtually automatic, neither is negligence automatically tolerable simply because the accused cannot demonstrate exactly how it has prejudiced him. It was on this point that the Court of Appeals erred, and on the facts before us, it was reversible error.

Barker made it clear that "different weights are to be assigned to different reasons" for delay. Although negligence is obviously to be weighed more lightly than a deliberate intent to harm the accused's defense, it still falls on the wrong side of the divide between acceptable and unacceptable reasons for delaying a criminal prosecution once it has begun. And such is the nature of the prejudice presumed that the weight we assign to official negligence compounds over time as the presumption of evidentiary prejudice grows. Thus, our toleration of such negligence varies inversely with its protractedness, *cf. Arizona v. Youngblood*, 488 U.S. 51 (1988), and its consequent threat to the fairness of the accused's trial. Condoning prolonged and unjustifiable delays in prosecution would both penalize many defendants for the state's fault and simply encourage the government to gamble with the interests of criminal suspects assigned a low prosecutorial priority. The Government, indeed, can hardly complain too loudly, for persistent neglect in concluding a criminal prosecution indicates an uncommonly feeble interest in bringing an accused to justice; the more weight the Government attaches to securing a conviction, the harder it will try to get it.

To be sure, to warrant granting relief, negligence unaccompanied by particularized trial prejudice must have lasted longer than negligence demonstrably causing such prejudice. But even so, the Government's egregious persistence in failing to prosecute Doggett is clearly sufficient. The lag between Doggett's indictment and arrest was 8 1/2 years, and he would have faced trial 6 years earlier than he did but for the Government's inexcusable oversights. The portion of the delay attributable to the Government's negligence far exceeds the threshold needed to state a speedy trial claim; indeed, we have called shorter delays "extraordinary." See *Barker, supra,* 407 U.S. at 533. When the Government's negligence thus causes delay six times as long as that generally sufficient to trigger judicial review, see n. 1, *supra,* and when the presumption of prejudice, albeit unspecified, is neither extenuated, as by the defendant's acquiescence, e.g., nor persuasively rebutted, the defendant is entitled to relief.

IV

We reverse the judgment of the Court of Appeals and remand the case for proceedings consistent with this opinion.

JUSTICE THOMAS, with whom THE CHIEF JUSTICE and JUSTICE SCALIA join, dissenting.

Just as "bad facts make bad law," so too odd facts make odd law. Doggett's 8 1/2 -year odyssey from youthful drug dealing in the tobacco country of North Carolina, through stints in a Panamanian jail and in Colombia, to life as a computer operations manager, homeowner, and registered voter in suburban Virginia, is extraordinary. But even more extraordinary is the Court's conclusion that the Government denied Doggett his Sixth Amendment right to a speedy trial despite the fact that he has suffered none of the harms that the right was designed to prevent. I respectfully dissent.

I

We have long identified the "major evils" against which the Speedy Trial Clause is directed as "undue and oppressive incarceration" and the "anxiety and concern accompanying public accusation." *United States v. Marion*, 404 U.S. 307, 320 (1971). The Court does not, and cannot, seriously dispute that those two concerns lie at the heart of the Clause, and that neither concern is implicated here. Doggett was neither in United States custody nor subject to bail during the entire 8 1/2 -year period at issue. Indeed, as this case comes to us, we must assume that he was blissfully unaware of his indictment all the while, and thus was not subject to the anxiety or humiliation that typically accompany a known criminal charge.

Thus, this unusual case presents the question whether, independent of these core concerns, the Speedy Trial Clause protects an accused from two additional harms: (1) prejudice to his ability to defend himself caused by the passage of time; and (2) disruption of his life years after the alleged commission of his crime. The Court today proclaims that the first of these additional harms is indeed an independent concern of the Clause, and on that basis compels reversal of Doggett's conviction and outright dismissal of the indictment against him. As to the second of these harms, the Court remains mum — despite the fact that we requested supplemental briefing on this very point.

I disagree with the Court's analysis. In my view, the Sixth Amendment's speedy trial guarantee does not provide independent protection against either prejudice to an accused's defense or the disruption of his life. I shall consider each in turn.

A

As we have explained, "the Speedy Trial Clause's core concern is impairment of *liberty*." *United States v. Loud Hawk*, 474 U.S. 302, 312 (1986) (emphasis added). Whenever a criminal trial takes place long after the events at issue, the defendant may be prejudiced in any number of ways. But "the Speedy Trial Clause does not purport to protect a defendant from all effects flowing from a delay before trial." *Id.* at 311. The Clause is directed not generally against delay-related prejudice, but against delay-related prejudice to a defendant's liberty. * * * *

A lengthy pretrial delay, of course, may prejudice an accused's ability to defend himself. But, we have explained, prejudice to the defense is not the sort of impairment of liberty against which the Clause is directed. "Passage of time, whether before or after arrest, may impair memories, cause evidence to be lost, deprive the defendant of witnesses, and otherwise interfere with his ability to defend himself. *But this possibility of prejudice at trial is not itself sufficient reason to wrench the Sixth Amendment from its proper context.*" *Marion, supra,* 404 U.S. at 321–322 (emphasis added). Even though a defendant may be prejudiced by a pretrial delay, and even though the government may be unable to provide a valid justification for that delay, the Clause does not come into play unless the delay impairs the defendant's liberty. "Inordinate delay may impair a defendant's ability to present an effective defense. But the major evils protected against by the speedy trial guarantee exist *quite apart* from actual or possible prejudice to an accused's defense." 404 U.S. at 320 (emphasis added).

These explanations notwithstanding, we have on occasion identified the prevention of prejudice to the defense as an independent and fundamental objective of the

Speedy Trial Clause. In particular, in *Barker v. Wingo*, 407 U.S. 514, 532 (1972), we asserted that the Clause was "designed to protect" three basic interests: "(i) to prevent oppressive pretrial incarceration; (ii) to minimize anxiety and concern of the accused; and (iii) to limit the possibility that the defense will be impaired." Indeed, the *Barker* Court went so far as to declare that of these three interests, "the most serious is the last, because the inability of a defendant adequately to prepare his case skews the fairness of the entire system." 407 U.S. at 532.

We are thus confronted with two conflicting lines of authority, the one declaring that "limiting the possibility that the defense will be impaired" is an independent and fundamental objective of the Speedy Trial Clause, e.g., *Barker*, and the other declaring that it is not, e.g., *Marion, MacDonald, Loud Hawk*. The Court refuses to acknowledge this conflict. Instead, it simply reiterates the relevant language from *Barker* and asserts that *Marion, MacDonald*, and *Loud Hawk* "support nothing beyond the principle that the Sixth Amendment right of the accused to a speedy trial has no application beyond the confines of a formal criminal prosecution." That attempt at reconciliation is eminently unpersuasive.

It is true, of course, that the Speedy Trial Clause by its terms applies only to an "accused"; the right does not attach before indictment or arrest. But that limitation on the Clause's protection only confirms that preventing prejudice to the defense is not one of its independent and fundamental objectives. For prejudice to the defense stems from the interval between *crime* and trial, which is quite distinct from the interval between *accusation* and trial. If the Clause were indeed aimed at safeguarding against prejudice to the defense, then it would presumably limit all prosecutions that occur long after the criminal events at issue. A defendant prosecuted 10 years after a crime is just as hampered in his ability to defend himself whether he was indicted the week after the crime or the week before the trial — but no one would suggest that the Clause protects him in the latter situation, where the delay did not substantially impair his liberty, either through oppressive incarceration or the anxiety of known criminal charges. Thus, while the Court is correct to observe that the defendants in *Marion, MacDonald*, and *Loud Hawk* were not subject to formal criminal prosecution during the lengthy period of delay prior to their trials, that observation misses the point of those cases. With respect to the relevant consideration — *the defendants' ability to defend themselves despite the passage of time* — they were in precisely the same situation as a defendant who had long since been indicted. The initiation of a formal criminal prosecution is simply irrelevant to whether the defense has been prejudiced by delay.

Although being an "accused" is necessary to trigger the Clause's protection, it is not sufficient to do so. The touchstone of the speedy trial right, after all, is the substantial deprivation of liberty that typically accompanies an "accusation," not the accusation itself. That explains why a person who has been arrested but not indicted is entitled to the protection of the Clause, even though technically he has not been "accused" at all. And it explains why the lower courts consistently have held that, with respect to sealed (and hence secret) indictments, the protections of the Speedy Trial Clause are triggered not when the indictment is *filed*, but when it is *unsealed*. See, e.g., *United States v. Watson*, 599 F.2d 1149 (CA2 1979).

It is misleading, then, for the Court to accuse the Government of "asking us, in effect, to read part of *Barker* right out of the law," a course the Court resolutely rejects. For the issue here is not simply whether the relevant language from *Barker* should be read out of the law, but whether that language trumps the contrary logic of *Marion, MacDonald*, and *Loud Hawk*. The Court's protestations notwithstanding, the two lines of authority cannot be reconciled; to reaffirm the one is to undercut the other.

In my view, the choice presented is not a hard one. *Barker's* suggestion that preventing prejudice to the defense is a fundamental and independent objective of the Clause is plainly dictum. Never, until today, have we confronted a case where a defendant subjected to a lengthy delay after indictment nonetheless failed to suffer any substantial impairment of his liberty. I think it fair to say that *Barker* simply did not contemplate such an unusual situation. Moreover, to the extent that the *Barker* dictum purports to elevate considerations of prejudice to the defense to fundamental and independent status under the Clause, it cannot be deemed to have survived our subsequent decisions in *MacDonald* and *Loud Hawk*.

Just because the Speedy Trial Clause does not independently protect against prejudice to the defense does not, of course, mean that a defendant is utterly unprotected in this regard. To the contrary, "the applicable statute of limitations is the primary guarantee against bringing overly stale criminal charges," *Marion*, 404 U.S. at 322. These statutes "represent legislative assessments of relative interests of the State and the defendant in administering and receiving justice; they are made for the repose of society and the protection of those who may during the limitation have lost their means of defence." 404 U.S., at 322. Because such statutes are fixed by the legislature and not decreed by courts on an ad hoc basis, they "provide predictability by specifying a limit beyond which there is an irrebuttable presumption that a defendant's right to a fair trial would be prejudiced." 404 U.S. at 322.

Furthermore, the Due Process Clause always protects defendants against fundamentally unfair treatment by the government in criminal proceedings. See *United States v. Lovasco*, 431 U.S. 783. As we explained in *Marion*, "the Due Process Clause would require dismissal of an indictment if it were shown at trial that a delay caused substantial prejudice to a defendant's rights to a fair trial and that the delay was an intentional device to gain tactical advantage over the accused." 404 U.S. at 324.

Therefore, I see no basis for the Court's conclusion that Doggett is entitled to relief under the Speedy Trial Clause simply because the Government was negligent in prosecuting him and because the resulting delay may have prejudiced his defense.

B

It remains to be considered, however, whether Doggett is entitled to relief under the Speedy Trial Clause because of the disruption of his life years after the criminal events at issue. In other words, does the Clause protect a right to repose, free from secret or unknown indictments? In my view, it does not, for much the same reasons set forth above.

The common law recognized no right of criminals to repose. "The maxim of our law has always been 'Nullum tempus occurrit regi,' ['time does not run against the king'], and as a criminal trial is regarded as an action by the king, it follows that it may be brought at any time." 2 J. Stephen, *A History of the Criminal Law of England* 1, 2 (1883) (noting examples of delays in prosecution ranging from 14 to 35 years).

That is not to deny that our legal system has long recognized the value of repose, both to the individual and to society. But that recognition finds expression not in the sweeping commands of the Constitution, or in the common law, but in any number of specific statutes of limitations enacted by the federal and state legislatures. Such statutes not only protect a defendant from prejudice to his defense (as discussed above), but also balance his interest in repose against society's interest in the apprehension and punishment of criminals. In general, the graver the offense, the longer the limitations period; indeed, many serious offenses, such as murder, typically carry no limitations period at all. These statutes refute the notion that our society ever has recognized any general right of criminals to repose.

Doggett, however, asks us to hold that a defendant's interest in repose is a value independently protected by the Speedy Trial Clause. He emphasizes that at the time of his arrest he was "leading a normal, productive and law-abiding life," and that his "arrest and prosecution at this late date interrupted his life as a productive member of society and forced him to answer for actions taken in the distant past." However uplifting this tale of personal redemption, our task is to illuminate the protections of the Speedy Trial Clause, not to take the measure of one man's life.

There is no basis for concluding that the disruption of an accused's life years after the commission of his alleged crime is an evil independently protected by the Speedy Trial Clause. Such disruption occurs regardless of whether the individual is under indictment during the period of delay. Thus, had Doggett been indicted shortly before his 1988 arrest rather than shortly after his 1980 crime, his repose would have been equally shattered — but he would not have even a colorable speedy-trial claim. To recognize a constitutional right to repose is to recognize a right to be tried speedily after the offense. That would, of course, convert the Speedy Trial Clause into a constitutional statute of limitations — a result with no basis in the text or history of the Clause or in our precedents.

II

* * * * The Court's error, in my view, lies not so much in its particular application of the *Barker* test to the facts of this case, but more fundamentally in its failure to recognize that the speedy trial guarantee cannot be violated — and thus *Barker* does not apply at all — when an accused is entirely unaware of a pending indictment against him. * * * *

Today's opinion, I fear, will transform the courts of the land into boards of law-enforcement supervision. For the Court compels dismissal of the charges against Doggett not because he was harmed in any way by the delay between his indictment and arrest,[6] but simply because the Government's efforts to catch him are found wanting. Indeed, the Court expressly concedes that "if the Government had pursued Doggett with reasonable diligence from his indictment to his arrest, his speedy trial claim would fail." Our function, however, is not to slap the Government on the wrist for sloppy work or misplaced priorities, but to protect the

---

[6] It is quite likely, in fact, that the delay benefited Doggett. At the time of his arrest, he had been living an apparently normal, law-abiding life for some five years — a point not lost on the District Court Judge, who, instead of imposing a prison term, sentenced him to three years' probation and a $1000 fine. Thus, the delay gave Doggett the opportunity to prove what most defendants can only promise: that he no longer posed a threat to society. There can be little doubt that, had he been tried immediately after his cocaine-importation activities, he would have received a harsher sentence.

legal rights of those individuals harmed thereby. By divorcing the Speedy Trial Clause from all considerations of prejudice to an accused, the Court positively invites the Nation's judges to indulge in ad hoc and result-driven second-guessing of the government's investigatory efforts. Our Constitution neither contemplates nor tolerates such a role. I respectfully dissent.

Notes from Warren:

1. An interesting case, but does it have any bearing on *our* case?

2. In *U.S. v. Hayes*, 40 F.3d 362 (11th Cir.1994), a grand jury indicted Hayes and Thom in 1987 for fraud. The government had the indictment "sealed" — so no one else, not even the defendants, knew of it — because Thom was not in custody and the government did not want him to know of the indictment and hide or flee. In 1992, the government gave up its efforts to arrest Thom, and unsealed the indictment and proceeded to trial against Hayes. The court rejected Hayes' claim that his right to speedy trial was violated. While the 5-year delay was sufficient to require a careful review of the other *Barker* factors, the "cause of the delay" did not cut against the government:

> The Government's reason for sealing the indictment and delaying trial against Hayes was a valid one. The Government was attempting to apprehend Hayes' co- defendant, Thom, who was living in Zimbabwe. The indictment was sealed because the Government feared that Thom would frustrate its attempts to secure his arrest and deportation if he were aware of it.

> During the subsequent five years, the Government exercised diligence in attempting to persuade the Government of Zimbabwe to arrest and deport Thom. In January of 1992, having determined that its efforts would not be successful (although we note that the Government ultimately did secure his arrest in and deportation from England), the Government moved to unseal the indictment and proceeded to trial against Hayes.

> This is not a case where the Government made no efforts to prosecute the defendant during the delay. Cf. *Doggett v. United States*, 505 U.S. 647, 112 S.Ct. 2686, 120 L.Ed.2d 520 (1992). On the contrary, during the period of delay, the Government made persistent and documented efforts to prosecute Thom. Between June 1987 and November 29, 1991, the Government filed seventeen reports describing, *inter alia*, its efforts to have the United Kingdom intercede on behalf of the United States; repeated requests to Zimbabwe through the American Embassy and the U.K. to effect Thom's arrest and extradition or deportation; the filing of notices on Interpol's computer system; inquiries to the Zimbabwean Embassy concerning Thom's whereabouts; discussions between the U.K. and the United States concerning a request for extradition if Thom were deported to Britain; the filing of a provisional arrest warrant in the U.K.; and attempts by the United States to locate Thom in several other foreign countries.

> Even though these efforts caused a lengthy delay in prosecuting Hayes, the Government's persistence in trying to locate Thom was not unreasonable. There always appeared a reasonable expectation of success in obtaining jurisdiction over Thom, and the Government was diligent in its

efforts to do so. Under these circumstances, the delay in prosecuting Hayes will not be held against the Government.

3. In *Wilson v. Mitchell*, 250 F.3d 388 (6th Cir. 2001), Wilson was brought to trial and convicted 22 years after he was charged with committing a murder. The evidence at habeas corpus hearing showed that during the 22 years, he evaded capture and the government was lax in its efforts to catch him. The court held that his constitutional right to speedy trial was not violated:

> Wilson has failed to produce any evidence that places in dispute the trial court's determination that he vigorously evaded apprehension and discovery by the police for 22 years. Instead, Wilson has produced evidence suggesting that the state did not pursue every avenue available to it in searching for him. None of Wilson's evidence calls into question the trial court's conclusion that Wilson was "a fugitive who repeatedly changed his identity, name, physical appearance, and whereabouts to avoid being brought to trial on the charges." Thus, because he did not adduce clear and convincing evidence that contradicted the trial court's factual determination, we must presume that the finding of Wilson's active evasion was correct.

> What we are presented with, then, is a case in which blame for the 22-year delay can be placed on both Wilson and the state. This inquiry, however, is not a search for a blameless party. We are instead concerned with who "is more to blame for that delay." *Doggett*, 505 U.S. at 651. In *Doggett*, the Supreme Court discussed the extent to which a defendant must prove prejudice from a delay in prosecution. The amount of proof required is directly related to the state's reasonableness in its pursuit of a defendant. When a defendant is pursued with reasonable diligence, the speedy-trial claim fails. If, however, the state's pursuit was intentionally dilatory, these bad-faith tactics weigh heavily in favor of the defendant's speedy-trial claim. In between these two extremes, the *Doggett* Court held that the government's negligence requires toleration by the courts that "varies inversely with its protractedness . . . and its consequent threat to the fairness of the accused's trial." *Id.* at 657. Thus, the success of a speedy-trial challenge typically turns on the state's conduct and the injury resulting from that conduct.

> What *Doggett* does not answer, however, is the extent to which a defendant's attempt to evade discovery affects the Sixth Amendment analysis. We believe that the Court's usage of tort-law terminology in *Doggett* and *Barker* is particularly apt, and invites another tort analogy from the doctrine involving indemnity between two tortfeasors. Under general tort-law principles, an active tortfeasor is not entitled to either indemnity or contribution from a passive tortfeasor. *See, e.g.*, 18 Am.Jur.2d. *Contribution* § 50 (1985).

> Assuming then, as we must, that Wilson actively evaded discovery by changing his identity and appearance, and assuming that Wilson is correct in his contention that the police did not exercise reasonable diligence in their pursuit of him, we are presented with an analogous situation. We have an active wrongdoer (Wilson) and a passive wrongdoer (the state), both of whom are at fault for a 22 year delay between Wilson's indictment and

arrest. Nevertheless, under our tort analogy, because Wilson actively evaded discovery, and the state was, at worst, passive in its pursuit of him, we cannot attribute the primary responsibility for the delay to the state. Indeed, even if the police made mistakes in their search for Wilson, he is not entitled to relief on this ground so long as his active evasion "is more to blame for that delay." *Doggett*, 505 U.S. at 651.

3. In Steven Phillips, *No Heroes No Villains: The Story of a Murder Trial* (Random House, 1997), pp. 60–61, the author states:

The Constitution of the United States specifically guarantees to every individual accused of a crime the right to a speedy trial. Today that guarantee is a farce. Justice demands that the oldest cases be tried first, and backlog of untried cases is immense. Since the courts' trial capacities are limited, the average wait, from arrest to trial, for a homicide case in Bronx County is roughly eighteen months. One and a half years is spent before anyone even gets around to determining guilt or innocence, and for most homicide defendants this time is spent in jail.

Who can calculate the injustice worked upon defendants by this delay? Apart from the anxiety and torment of pre-trial incarceration in general, the fact remains that a significant number of these defendants who do go to trial are ultimately vindicated by an acquittal. What does one say to a man who has spent eighteen months in jail waiting for an acquittal — "I'm sorry"? This is just not good enough, but it is precisely what happens again and again. * * * *

Ironically, delay is a double-edged sword that as often hurts the prosecution and helps the defendant as the other way around. Prosecutors hate delay, for it inevitably weakens and sometimes even destroys their cases. In time, memories fade, or disappear altogether. Often important witnesses vanish, lose interest or die. The passage of time has ruined many strong cases, and many a guilty man has been acquitted because of delay.

VERMONT v. BRILLON
U.S. Supreme Court, 2009
___ U.S.___, 129 S.Ct. 1283

JUSTICE GINSBURG delivered the opinion of the Court.

This case concerns the Sixth Amendment guarantee that "[i]n all criminal prosecutions, the accused shall enjoy the right to a speedy . . . trial." Michael Brillon, defendant below, respondent here, was arrested in July 2001 on felony domestic assault and habitual offender charges. Nearly three years later, in June 2004, he was tried by jury, found guilty as charged, and sentenced to 12 to 20 years in prison. The Vermont Supreme Court vacated Brillon's conviction and held that the charges against him must be dismissed because he had been denied his right to a speedy trial.

During the time between Brillon's arrest and his trial, at least six different attorneys were appointed to represent him. Brillon "fired" the first, who served from July 2001 to February 2002. His third lawyer, who served from March 2002 until June 2002, was allowed to withdraw when he reported that Brillon had threatened his life. The Vermont Supreme Court charged against Brillon the delays associated with those periods, but charged against the State periods in which assigned counsel failed "to move the case forward."

We hold that the Vermont Supreme Court erred in ranking assigned counsel essentially as state actors in the criminal justice system. Assigned counsel, just as retained counsel, act on behalf of their clients, and delays sought by counsel are ordinarily attributable to the defendants they represent. For a total of some six months of the time that elapsed between Brillon's arrest and his trial, Brillon lacked an attorney. The State may be charged with those months if the gaps resulted from the trial court's failure to appoint replacement counsel with dispatch. Similarly, the State may bear responsibility if there is "a breakdown in the public defender system." But, as the Vermont Supreme Court acknowledged, the record does not establish any such institutional breakdown.

I

On July 27, 2001, Michael Brillon was arrested after striking his girlfriend. Three days later he was arraigned in state court in Bennington County, Vermont and charged with felony domestic assault. His alleged status as a habitual offender exposed him to a potential life sentence. The court ordered him held without bail.

Richard Ammons, from the county public defender's office, was assigned on the day of arraignment as Brillon's first counsel.[1] In October, Ammons filed a motion to recuse the trial judge. It was denied the next month and trial was scheduled for February 2002. In mid-January, Ammons moved for a continuance, but the State objected, and the trial court denied the motion.

On February 22, four days before the jury draw, Ammons again moved for a continuance, citing his heavy workload and the need for further investigation.

---

[1] Vermont's Defender General has "the primary responsibility for providing needy persons with legal services." Vt. Stat. Ann., Tit. 13, § 5253(a). These services may be provided "personally, through public defenders," or through contract attorneys. *Ibid.*

Ammons acknowledged that any delay would not count (presumably against the State) for speedy-trial purposes. The State opposed the motion, and at the conclusion of a hearing, the trial court denied it. Brillon, participating in the proceedings through interactive television, then announced: "You're fired, Rick." Three days later, the trial court-over the State's objection-granted Ammons' motion to withdraw as counsel, citing Brillon's termination of Ammons and Ammons' statement that he could no longer zealously represent Brillon. The trial court warned Brillon that further delay would occur while a new attorney became familiar with the case. The same day, the trial court appointed a second attorney, but he immediately withdrew based on a conflict.

On March 1, 2002, Gerard Altieri was assigned as Brillon's third counsel. On May 20, Brillon filed a motion to dismiss Altieri for, among other reasons, failure to file motions, "virtually no communication whatsoever," and his lack of diligence "because of heavy case load." At a June 11 hearing, Altieri denied several of Brillon's allegations, noted his disagreement with Brillon's trial strategy[4] and insisted he had plenty of time to prepare. The State opposed Brillon's motion as well. Near the end of the hearing, however, Altieri moved to withdraw on the ground that Brillon had threatened his life during a break in the proceedings. The trial court granted Brillon's motion to dismiss Altieri, but warned Brillon that "this is somewhat of a dubious victory in your case because it simply prolongs the time that you will remain in jail until we can bring this matter to trial."

That same day, the trial court appointed Paul Donaldson as Brillon's fourth counsel. At an August 5 status conference, Donaldson requested additional time to conduct discovery in light of his caseload. A few weeks later, Brillon sent a letter to the court complaining about Donaldson's unresponsiveness and lack of competence. Two months later, Brillon filed a motion to dismiss Donaldson — similar to his motion to dismiss Altieri — for failure to file motions and "virtually no communication whatsoever." At a November 26 hearing, Donaldson reported that his contract with the Defender General's office had expired in June and that he had been in discussions to have Brillon's case reassigned. The trial court released Donaldson from the case "without making any findings regarding the adequacy of Donaldson's representation."

Brillon's fifth counsel, David Sleigh, was not assigned until January 15, 2003; Brillon was without counsel during the intervening two months. On February 25, Sleigh sought extensions of various discovery deadlines, noting that he had been in trial out of town. On April 10, however, Sleigh withdrew from the case, based on "modifications to his firm's contract with the Defender General."

Brillon was then without counsel for the next four months. On June 20, the Defender General's office notified the court that it had received "funding from the legislature" and would hire a new special felony unit defender for Brillon. On August 1, Kathleen Moore was appointed as Brillon's sixth counsel. The trial court set November 7 as the deadline for motions, but granted several extensions in accord with the parties' stipulation. On February 23, 2004, Moore filed a motion to dismiss for lack of a speedy trial. The trial court denied the motion on April 19.

---

[4] Specifically, Altieri appeared reluctant to follow Brillon's tactic that he "bring in a lot of people" at trial, "some of them young kids and relatives in an attempt by Mr. Brillon — this is his theory — I don't want to use the words trash, to impeach the victim."

The case finally went to trial on June 14, 2004. Brillon was found guilty and sentenced to 12 to 20 years in prison. The trial court denied a post-trial motion to dismiss for want of a speedy trial, concluding that the delay in Brillon's trial was "in large part the result of his own actions" and that Brillon had "failed to demonstrate prejudice as a result of the pre-trial delay."

On appeal, the Vermont Supreme Court held 3 to 2 that Brillon's conviction must be vacated and the charges dismissed for violation of his Sixth Amendment right to a speedy trial. Citing the balancing test of *Barker v. Wingo*, 407 U.S. 514 (1972), the majority concluded that all four of the factors described in *Barker* — "length of delay, the reason for the delay, the defendant's assertion of his right, and prejudice to the defendant" — weighed against the State.

The court first found that the three-year delay in bringing Brillon to trial was "extreme" and weighed heavily in his favor. In assessing the reasons for that delay, the Vermont Supreme Court separately considered the period of each counsel's representation. It acknowledged that the first year, when Brillon was represented by Ammons and Altieri, should not count against the State. But the court counted much of the remaining two years against the State for delays "caused, for the most part, by the failure of several of defendant's assigned counsel, over an inordinate period of time, to move his case forward." As for the third and fourth factors, the court found that Brillon "repeatedly and adamantly demanded to be tried," and that his "lengthy pretrial incarceration" was prejudicial, despite his insubstantial assertions of evidentiary prejudice.

The dissent strongly disputed the majority's characterization of the periods of delay. It concluded that "the lion's share of delay in this case is attributable to defendant, and not to the state." But for Brillon's "repeated maneuvers to dismiss his lawyers and avoid trial through the first eleven months following arraignment," the dissent explained, "the difficulty in finding additional counsel would not have arisen."

We granted certiorari, and now reverse the judgment of the Vermont Supreme Court.

II

The Sixth Amendment guarantees that "in all criminal prosecutions, the accused shall enjoy the right to a speedy . . . trial." The speedy-trial right is "amorphous," "slippery," and "necessarily relative." *Barker*, 407 U.S., at 522. It is "consistent with delays and dependent upon circumstances." 407 U.S. at 522. In *Barker*, the Court refused to "quantify" the right "into a specified number of days or months" or to hinge the right on a defendant's explicit request for a speedy trial. Rejecting such "inflexible approaches," *Barker* established a "balancing test, in which the conduct of both the prosecution and the defendant are weighed." *Id.* at 529. "Some of the factors" that courts should weigh include "length of delay, the reason for the delay, the defendant's assertion of his right, and prejudice to the defendant." *Ibid.*

Primarily at issue here is the reason for the delay in Brillon's trial. *Barker* instructs that "different weights should be assigned to different reasons," and in applying *Barker*, we have asked "whether the government or the criminal defendant is more to blame for the delay." *Doggett v. United States*, 505 U.S. 647, 651 (1992). Deliberate delay "to hamper the defense" weighs heavily against the prosecution. *Barker*, 407 U.S., at 531. "More neutral reasons such as negligence or overcrowded courts" weigh less heavily "but nevertheless should be considered since the ultimate responsibility for such circumstances must rest with the government rather than with the defendant." *Ibid.*

In contrast, delay caused by the defense weighs against the defendant: "If delay is attributable to the defendant, then his waiver may be given effect under standard waiver doctrine." *Id.* at 529. Cf. *United States v. Loud Hawk*, 474 U.S. 302, 316 (1986) (noting that a defendant whose trial was delayed by his interlocutory appeal "normally should not be able . . . to reap the reward of dismissal for failure to receive a speedy trial"). That rule accords with the reality that defendants may have incentives to employ delay as a "defense tactic": delay may "work to the accused's advantage" because "witnesses may become unavailable or their memories may fade" over time. *Barker*, 407 U.S. at 521.

Because "the attorney is the defendant's agent when acting, or failing to act, in furtherance of the litigation," delay caused by the defendant's counsel is also charged against the defendant. *Coleman v. Thompson*, 501 U.S. 722, 753 (1991). The same principle applies whether counsel is privately retained or publicly assigned, for "once a lawyer has undertaken the representation of an accused, the duties and obligations are the same whether the lawyer is privately retained, appointed, or serving in a legal aid or defender program." *Polk County v. Dodson*, 454 U.S. 312, 318 (1981). "Except for the source of payment," the relationship between a defendant and the public defender representing him is "identical to that existing between any other lawyer and client." *Ibid.* Unlike a prosecutor or the court, assigned counsel ordinarily is not considered a state actor.

III

Barker's formulation "necessarily compels courts to approach speedy trial cases on an *ad hoc* basis," 407 U.S. at 530, and the balance arrived at in close cases ordinarily would not prompt this Court's review. But the Vermont Supreme Court made a fundamental error in its application of *Barker* that calls for this Court's correction. The Vermont Supreme Court erred in attributing to the State delays caused by "the failure of several assigned counsel to move his case forward," and in failing adequately to take into account the role of Brillon's disruptive behavior in the overall balance.

A

The Vermont Supreme Court's opinion is driven by the notion that delay caused by assigned counsel's "inaction" or failure "to move the case forward" is chargeable to the State, not the defendant. In this case, that court concluded, "a significant portion of the delay in bringing defendant to trial must be attributed to the state, even though most of the delay was caused by the inability or unwillingness of assigned counsel to move the case forward."

We disagree. An assigned counsel's failure "to move the case forward" does not warrant attribution of delay to the State. Contrary to the Vermont Supreme Court's analysis, assigned counsel generally are not state actors for purposes of a speedy-trial claim. While the Vermont Defender General's office is indeed "part of the criminal justice system," the individual counsel here acted only on behalf of Brillon, not the State.

Most of the delay that the Vermont Supreme Court attributed to the State must therefore be attributed to Brillon as delays caused by his counsel. During those periods, Brillon was represented by Donaldson, Sleigh, and Moore, all of whom requested extensions and continuances. Their "inability or unwillingness to move the case forward," may not be attributed to the State simply because they are assigned counsel.

A contrary conclusion could encourage appointed counsel to delay proceedings by seeking unreasonable continuances, hoping thereby to obtain a dismissal of the indictment on speedy-trial grounds. Trial courts might well respond by viewing continuance requests made by appointed counsel with skepticism, concerned that even an apparently genuine need for more time is in reality a delay tactic. Yet the same considerations would not attend a privately retained counsel's requests for time extensions. We see no justification for treating defendants' speedy-trial claims differently based on whether their counsel is privately retained or publicly assigned.

B

In addition to making assigned counsel's "failure to move the case forward" the touchstone of its speedy-trial inquiry, the Vermont Supreme Court further erred by treating the period of each counsel's representation discretely. The factors identified in *Barker* "have no talismanic qualities; courts must still engage in a difficult and sensitive balancing process." 407 U.S. at 533. Yet the Vermont Supreme Court failed appropriately to take into account Brillon's role during the first year of delay in "the chain of events that started all this."

Brillon sought to dismiss Ammons on the eve of trial. His strident, aggressive behavior with regard to Altieri, whom he threatened, further impeded prompt trial and likely made it more difficult for the Defender General's office to find replacement counsel. Even after the trial court's warning regarding delay, Brillon sought dismissal of yet another attorney, Donaldson. Just as a State's "deliberate attempt to delay the trial in order to hamper the defense should be weighted heavily against the State," *Barker*, 407 U.S. at 531, so too should a defendant's deliberate attempt to disrupt proceedings be weighted heavily against the defendant. Absent Brillon's deliberate efforts to force the withdrawal of Ammons and Altieri, no speedy-trial issue would have arisen. The effect of these earlier events should have been factored into the court's analysis of subsequent delay.

C

The general rule attributing to the defendant delay caused by assigned counsel is not absolute. Delay resulting from a systemic "breakdown in the public defender system" could be charged to the State. But the Vermont Supreme Court made no determination, and nothing in the record suggests, that institutional problems caused any part of the delay in Brillon's case.

In sum, delays caused by defense counsel are properly attributed to the defendant, even where counsel is assigned. "Any inquiry into a speedy trial claim necessitates a functional analysis of the right in the particular context of the case," *Barker*, 407 U.S. at 522, and the record in this case does not show that Brillon was denied his constitutional right to a speedy trial.

* * *

For the reasons stated, the judgment of the Vermont Supreme Court is reversed, and the case is remanded for further proceedings not inconsistent with this opinion.

Chapter 7

PLEA BARGAINING

"A defendant who pleads guilty receives mercy; a defendant who is convicted after trial receives justice."

— Brooklyn, N.Y., JUDGE MILTON MOLLEN[1]

SOME BACKGROUND

The overwhelming majority of lawsuits in America are resolved not by litigation, but by settlement. This includes personal injury suits, business disputes, and every other area of civil practice. Litigation is expensive for all parties and for the court system, and the outcome is never assured. Each side usually prefers to avoid being exposed to the "whims" of an unpredictable jury (or judge) if the case should go to trial.

The same is true in criminal cases. Over 80% of all criminal cases do not go to trial, but are settled. These settlements are achieved by "plea bargaining", where the defendant agrees to plead guilty to certain charges in return for certain benefits.

By pleading guilty, the defendant gives up important rights, including the right to a jury trial, the right to confront his accusers, the right to testify on his own behalf and to subpoena witnesses to testify for him, and his right to have the case against him proved beyond a reasonable doubt.

In return, the prosecutor agrees to do something for the defendant: she might drop some charges or reduce them to lower charges, or she might agree to recommend that the court impose a certain sentence on the defendant or that the defendant serve his sentence in a particular institution.

Each side agrees to give something up because each side stands to gain something. In addition, each side stands to *lose* something if the parties fail to reach an agreement.

What will the prosecutor lose? If negotiations break down, the prosecutor will have to go to trial. In many jurisdictions, the court system has trouble handling just the 20% or so of criminal cases that go to trial — there are just not enough judges and courtrooms to handle the volume. If prosecutors fail to plea bargain at least 80% of their cases, the trial calendar can quickly become overloaded. (If *all* cases went to trial, we might need *5 times* as many criminal judges, prosecutors, defense attorneys, and courtrooms!) Keep in mind that each defendant has the right to a

---

[1] Quoted in D. Jones, Crime Without Punishment (1979), at p. 42.

speedy trial, so if a heavy calendar means that some defendants cannot be tried within a reasonable time, their cases will have to be dismissed. The prosecutor must also think about the workload of *her* office. There are not enough prosecutors to take all cases to trial, so some must be plea bargained.

Like any aggressive lawyer, the prosecutor also cares about winning. She does not like to go to trial and lose, and she does not want this "criminal" to walk away from the courtroom with *no* conviction on *any* charge. So before engaging in plea bargaining, the prosecutor will assess her chances of losing by examining the case for any strengths and weaknesses. Does the evidence show all the elements of the crimes charged? Will a motion to suppress any evidence be granted? How credible are the prosecution witnesses? The defense witnesses? What kind of a jury is likely to be selected? If the defendant is convicted, how is the judge likely to sentence this defendant (with his prior record) for this offense? If the case has weaknesses, the prosecutor might wish to settle for less than the full conviction and punishment on all the charges.

Finally, the prosecutor might want something from the defendant which a conviction will not give her — such as help in finding or convicting other criminals. The prosecutor might be willing to give up certain things in order to get the defendant's "cooperation".

Defense counsel's thinking is similar. He too does not like to lose trials, so he will prepare for plea bargaining by reviewing the case carefully for strengths and weaknesses. He may want to engage in discovery and send out his own investigator before even talking to the prosecutor. He has another worry: facts may come out at trial which make the defendant look much worse than what the record shows so far, and this could affect the sentence the judge chooses to impose. (For example, the defendant might testify, and the judge might perceive his testimony as perjury and consider this in sentencing.) If defense counsel is a public defender, he too might have a heavy caseload pressing on the time he has available for trials.[2]

In any event, defense counsel knows that the pressures on the prosecutors and the courts will probably cause the prosecutor to offer *something* worthwhile in order to induce the vast majority of defendants to accept plea bargains. Why not take advantage of that something, for the benefit of his client? (Defense counsel must present and explain any plea offer to his client, and may recommend that the client accept or decline the offer, but the final decision as to whether to plead guilty always rests with the client.)

With all these things in mind, the two lawyers get down to horse-trading.

But the notion that criminal justice may be horse-traded at all is distasteful to some people: "The defendant either committed the crime or he didn't. If he did, he deserves the full punishment prescribed by the law. If he didn't, he deserves no punishment at all. Plea bargaining leads to neither of these results, but to something in between, which is always the wrong result. Also, plea bargaining gives defendants the impression that their sentences depend on lawyers' bargaining tactics rather than the evidence against them, and this is not a good way to get them to accept responsibility for their crimes and get them on the road to rehabilitation."

---

[2] A good discussion of plea bargaining tactics appears in Rodney J. Uphoff, *The Criminal Defense Lawyer As Effective Negotiator: A Systemic Approach*, 2 Clinical L.Rev. 73 (1995), which cites several other articles and books on the topic.

Victims also tend to dislike plea-bargaining, as it results in lower charges and sentences.

Such criticisms have occasionally led some prosecutors to stop plea bargaining. "No more plea bargaining by my office! Plead guilty to what we charge or go to trial!" But if enough defense attorneys take the second option — going to trial in large numbers — the result will be a large number of dismissals, because in most jurisdictions, our system does not provide enough resources to give all defendants a speedy trial. So most prosecutors hold their noses and engage in plea bargaining.

Defense advocates have also criticized plea bargaining, claiming that it discourages defendants from exercising their constitutional rights to trial, and gives many defendants the impression that their lawyers "sold them out" in order to maintain good relations with prosecutors and judges.

For many years, these criticisms had their effect. Only a few decades ago, the courts refused to recognize plea bargaining, and in fact considered it "illegal", by the following reasoning. The end result of a plea bargain is the defendant's plea of guilty, in open court. As this plea admits that the defendant committed a crime, the guilty plea was treated as a type of *confession*. A confession, as you know, is admissible in evidence only if it is " *voluntary*." If a confession has been induced by a *promise* (e.g., "Confess to this crime and I will let you out of here"), then the confession is "involuntary" and may not be admitted into evidence. By this analysis, a plea of guilty that was the product of a plea bargain was *always* "involuntary," as it was the product of promises made by the prosecutor. Thus, no plea of guilty could be accepted by a judge who knew it was induced by a plea bargain.[3]

The solution, then, was not to let the judge know. Not being stupid, however, the judge knew. But as long as the *record* did not show that he knew, everything was fine. The usual charade went something like this. Defense counsel would tell the defendant, "When the judge asks you if any promises were made to you, say 'no'." The judge would ask the ritual question, the defendant would give the ritual answer, the plea of guilty would be accepted, the plea bargain would be carried out, and everyone would go away satisfied (if not happy).

But many people were troubled by the hypocrisy of this scenario, and some worried that the judicial denial of the *existence* of plea bargaining meant that the courts were unable to *regulate* plea bargaining.

In 1970, in *Santobello v. New York* (the third case in this Chapter), the Supreme Court finally brought plea bargaining out of the closet, recognized its benefits, and legitimized it.

---

[3] A dramatic example of this occurred in *U.S. v. Shelton*. Shelton was charged with interstate transportation of a stolen car. He bargained with the prosecutor to plead guilty in return for a one-year sentence and dismissal of a pending charge in Florida. The prosecutor agreed, Shelton pleaded guilty, and the prosecutor delivered on his promise. Shelton then sought to set aside his guilty plea. The Court of Appeals initially agreed that Shelton was right, because his plea was induced by a promise. 242 F.2d 101 (5th Cir. 1957). But then the Court reversed itself (two judges dissenting), with one judge noting "the sheer audacity, not to say effrontery of movant's attempt, under the undisputed facts in this case, while holding on to benefits obtained by him in pleading guilty, to repudiate in the name of due process his acts in doing so and the support accorded his contentions and views in the opinions of the dissenting minority constitute a massive assault upon the validity of countless thousands of sentences entered upon pleas of guilty taken as this one was and the integrity of the federal judicial system, indeed upon the judicial process itself." 246 F.2d 571, 573 (5th Cir. 1957). And then the Supreme Court reversed the Court of Appeals! 356 U.S. 26 (1958).

Problem 7A

To: My law clerk

From: Al Fresco, Esq.

Date: May 1

Moe Stooge, Larry Stooge, and Curly Stooge were indicted for bank robbery (18 U.S.C. § 2113) and first degree murder of an FBI agent (18 U.S.C. § 1114; which provides for the death penalty unless the jury recommends otherwise). I am representing Larry. The transcript of the grand jury hearing shows the following testimony of FBI agent Phil Brick:

> Agent Ness and I were at the First National Bank, checking some bank records, when two masked men came in and held up the bank. After a teller gave them about $25,000, Ness drew his gun and told them to drop their guns. One of the robbers fired at Ness and hit him in the chest, killing him instantly. They ran out the door and got in a car being driven by a third man, and they drove off. I got the license number of the car, which was registered to Larry Stooge.
>
> I went to Larry's home and arrested him. He resisted, so I forgot to tell him his *Miranda* rights, and I asked him who helped him rob the bank. He said that he had driven the getaway car, and the two robbers were his two older brothers, Moe and Curly. When I told Larry that the robbers killed an FBI agent, Larry seemed very surprised. He said that Moe was their leader and didn't tell him very much.
>
> I then arrested Moe and told him what Larry said. Moe got angry and said that he went into the bank with Larry, and Larry shot Ness. I then arrested Curly, who said that he and Moe went into the bank, Moe shot Ness, and Larry drove the getaway car.

All three have pleaded not guilty to the charges.

Under federal sentencing guidelines, Larry might be sentenced to between 10 years, one month, and 12 years, 7 months, on the bank robbery charge. He might be sentenced to an additional term of between 15 years, 8 months, and 19 years, 7 months, on the first degree murder charge. The statute also provides for a possible death penalty on the first degree murder charge. Larry insists that he is innocent — he drove the car, but Moe had told him that Moe and Curley were going into the bank just to cash a check.

Pearl E. Gates, the Assistant U.S. Attorney handling the case, has offered to dismiss the murder charge if Larry pleads guilty to the robbery charge, and if Moe and Curley plead guilty to second degree murder.

Should I advise Larry to accept the offer? If I need any additional information, please let me know what it is. You might find the following helpful:

AMERICAN BAR ASSOCIATION STANDARDS FOR CRIMINAL JUSTICE

STANDARD 3-4.1: AVAILABILITY FOR PLEA DISCUSSIONS

(a) The prosecutor should have and make known a general policy or willingness to consult with defense counsel concerning disposition of charges by plea.

(b) A prosecutor should not engage in plea discussions directly with an accused who is represented by defense counsel, except with defense counsel's approval. Where the defendant has properly waived counsel, the prosecuting attorney may engage in plea discussions with the defendant, although, where feasible, a record of such discussions should be made and preserved.

(c) A prosecutor should not knowingly make false statements or representations as to fact or law in the course of plea discussions with defense counsel or the accused.

STANDARD 4-6.1: DUTY TO EXPLORE DISPOSITION WITHOUT TRIAL

(a) Whenever the law, nature, and circumstances of the case permit, defense counsel should explore the possibility of an early diversion of the case from the criminal process through the use of other community agencies.

(b) Defense counsel may engage in plea discussions with the prosecutor. Under no circumstances should defense counsel recommend to a defendant acceptance of a plea unless appropriate investigation and study of the case has been completed, including an analysis of controlling law and the evidence likely to be introduced at trial.

STANDARD 14-3.2: RELATIONSHIP BETWEEN DEFENSE COUNSEL AND CLIENT

(a) Defense counsel should conclude a plea agreement only with the consent of the defendant, and should ensure that the decision whether to enter a plea of guilty or nolo contendere is ultimately made by the defendant.

(b) To aid the defendant in reaching a decision, defense counsel, after appropriate investigation, should advise the defendant of the alternatives available and of considerations deemed important by defense counsel or the defendant in reaching a decision.

Problem 7B

To: My law clerk

From: Assistant U.S. Attorney Pearl E. Gates

Larry Stooge pleaded guilty last June to bank robbery at the end of his trial. Larry is now serving his sentence in federal prison, but he filed a motion to withdraw his guilty plea. Here is the transcript of the hearing where Larry pleaded guilty:

The Court: Well, I just sent the jury out to start their deliberations. But I understand that these defendants now wish to change their pleas to guilty to some of the charges, is that correct?

Mr. Able: That's right, your honor. My client, Larry Stooge, would like to plead guilty to bank robbery.

Assistant U.S. Attorney Gates: And the Government would like to move to dismiss the murder charge, your honor.

The Court: Mr. Stooge, if you plead guilty to bank robbery, federal sentencing guidelines allow me to sentence you to between 10 years, 1 month, and 12 years, 7 months, in federal prison. Instead of pleading guilty, you have the right to plead not guilty. If you plead not guilty, you will have the right to tried by a jury, with the assistance of counsel, and the right to confront and cross-examine witnesses against you, and the right to testify or not testify, as you wish. If you plead guilty, you waive all these rights. Do you understand what I have just told you?

Larry Stooge: Yes, Sir.

The Court: Is there a plea agreement in this case, counsel?

Ms. Gates: Yes, your honor. The Government has agreed to dismiss the murder charge, and Larry Stooge has agreed to plead guilty to bank robbery. He also agreed to waive his right to appeal and his right to challenge his guilty plea by habeas corpus or motion. This agreement is contingent on defendants Moe and Curly Stooge pleading guilty to second degree murder.

Mr. Able: We agree to those terms, your honor.

The Court: Mr. Stooge, is your decision to plead guilty voluntary and not the product of force or threats or promises apart from a plea agreement?

Larry Stooge: Yes, Sir. I don't think I'm guilty at all. I drove the car because Moe said he'd beat me up if I didn't. But I don't want to deal with any death penalty, so I'll plead guilty.

The Court: Well, I've read the grand jury transcript, and I think the plea bargain is fair, and I will include it in the judgment. I will accept your plea and dismiss the murder charge. I hereby sentence you to 12 years in prison.

Moe and Curly then each pleaded guilty to second degree murder, in accordance with plea bargains which they had agreed to.

Attached to Larry's motion to withdraw his guilty plea was his affidavit, which states:

> I did not rob any bank. Moe told me that he and Curley were going into the bank to make a withdrawal. Then he bopped me on the nose and said that if I didn't wait in the car, he would beat me up. Later, my lawyer told me that the prosecutor wanted all three of us to plead guilty to something. I wanted to have a trial, because I wasn't guilty, but my mother told me that I should try to help out my brothers. My lawyer told me that if I pleaded guilty to bank robbery, I would not have to worry about a death penalty, and the prosecutor would recommend that I get probation. At the hearing on my plea, the prosecutor did not do this. I really needed to get out on probation, because my wife is sick and needs my help. Also, my lawyer said that even if the judge denied probation, I would not get a

sentence of more than 5 years. I didn't mention any of this at my sentencing hearing because I thought it had all been arranged. Also, after my jury was dismissed, my lawyer talked to some of them, and they were ready to acquit me because they thought the prosecution hadn't proved that I knew my brothers were going to rob the bank.

I argued that there is no need for the judge to hold an evidentiary hearing to determine the truth of Larry's allegations, because none of them are sufficient to justify setting aside the guilty plea. Based on the attached authorities, how will the judge rule on this issue?

Also, if the plea is withdrawn, I would like to seek a new indictment against Larry for first degree murder, bank robbery, and two other bank robberies I think Larry was involved in. Any problem with this?

Federal Rules of Criminal Procedure

Rule 11.   Pleas

(a)   Entering a Plea.

(1)   In General. A defendant may plead not guilty, guilty, or (with the court's consent) nolo contendere.

(2)   Conditional Plea. With the consent of the court and the government, a defendant may enter a conditional plea of guilty or nolo contendere, reserving in writing the right to have an appellate court review an adverse determination of a specified pretrial motion. A defendant who prevails on appeal may then withdraw the plea.

(3)   Nolo Contendere Plea. Before accepting a plea of nolo contendere, the court must consider the parties' views and the public interest in the effective administration of justice.

(4)   Failure to Enter a Plea. If a defendant refuses to enter a plea or if a defendant organization fails to appear, the court must enter a plea of not guilty.

(b)   Considering and Accepting a Guilty or Nolo Contendere Plea.

(1)   Advising and Questioning the Defendant. Before the court accepts a plea of guilty or nolo contendere, the defendant may be placed under oath, and the court must address the defendant personally in open court. During this address, the court must inform the defendant of, and determine that the defendant understands, the following:

(A) the government's right, in a prosecution for perjury or false statement, to use against the defendant any statement that the defendant gives under oath;

(B) the right to plead not guilty, or having already so pleaded, to persist in that plea;

(C) the right to a jury trial;

(D) the right to be represented by counsel — and if necessary have the court appoint counsel — at trial and at every other stage of the proceeding;

(E) the right at trial to confront and cross-examine adverse witnesses, to be protected from compelled self-incrimination, to testify and present evidence, and to compel the attendance of witnesses;

(F) the defendant's waiver of these trial rights if the court accepts a plea of guilty or nolo contendere;

(G) the nature of each charge to which the defendant is pleading;

(H) any maximum possible penalty, including imprisonment, fine, and term of supervised release;

(I) any mandatory minimum penalty;

(J) any applicable forfeiture;

(K) the court's authority to order restitution;

(L) the court's obligation to impose a special assessment;

(M) the court's obligation to apply the Sentencing Guidelines, and the court's discretion to depart from those guidelines under some circumstances; and

(N) the terms of any plea-agreement provision waiving the right to appeal or to collaterally attack the sentence.

(2) Ensuring That a Plea Is Voluntary. Before accepting a plea of guilty or nolo contendere, the court must address the defendant personally in open court and determine that the plea is voluntary and did not result from force, threats, or promises (other than promises in a plea agreement).

(3) Determining the Factual Basis for a Plea. Before entering judgment on a guilty plea, the court must determine that there is a factual basis for the plea.

(c) Plea Agreement Procedure.

(1) In General. An attorney for the government and the defendant's attorney, or the defendant when proceeding pro se, may discuss and reach a plea agreement. The court must not participate in these discussions. If the defendant pleads guilty or nolo contendere to either a charged offense or a lesser or related offense, the plea agreement may specify that an attorney for the government will:

(A) not bring, or will move to dismiss, other charges;

(B) recommend, or agree not to oppose the defendant's request, that a particular sentence or sentencing range is appropriate or that a particular provision of the Sentencing Guidelines, or policy statement, or sentencing factor does or does not apply (such a recommendation or request does not bind the court); or

(C) agree that a specific sentence or sentencing range is the appropriate disposition of the case, or that a particular provision of the Sentencing Guidelines, or policy statement, or sentencing factor does or does not apply (such a recommendation or request binds the court once the court accepts the plea agreement).

(2) Disclosing a Plea Agreement. The parties must disclose the plea agreement in open court when the plea is offered, unless the court for good cause allows the parties to disclose the plea agreement in camera.

(3) Judicial Consideration of a Plea Agreement.

(A) To the extent the plea agreement is of the type specified in Rule 11(c)(1)(A) or (C), the court may accept the agreement, reject it, or defer a decision until the court has reviewed the presentence report.

(B) To the extent the plea agreement is of the type specified in Rule 11(c)(1)(B), the court must advise the defendant that the defendant has no right to withdraw the plea if the court does not follow the recommendation or request.

(4) Accepting a Plea Agreement. If the court accepts the plea agreement, it must inform the defendant that to the extent the plea agreement is of the type specified in Rule 11(c)(1)(A) or (C), the agreed disposition will be included in the judgment.

(5) Rejecting a Plea Agreement. If the court rejects a plea agreement containing provisions of the type specified in Rule 11(c)(1)(A) or (C), the court must do the following on the record and in open court (or, for good cause, in camera):

(A) inform the parties that the court rejects the plea agreement;

(B) advise the defendant personally that the court is not required to follow the plea agreement and give the defendant an opportunity to withdraw the plea; and

(C) advise the defendant personally that if the plea is not withdrawn, the court may dispose of the case less favorably toward the defendant than the plea agreement contemplated.

(d) Withdrawing a Guilty or Nolo Contendere Plea. A defendant may withdraw a plea of guilty or nolo contendere:

(1) before the court accepts the plea, for any reason or no reason; or

(2) after the court accepts the plea, but before it imposes sentence if:

(A) the court rejects a plea agreement under Rule 11(c)(5); or

(B) the defendant can show a fair and just reason for requesting the withdrawal.

(e) Finality of a Guilty or Nolo Contendere Plea. After the court imposes sentence, the defendant may not withdraw a plea of guilty or nolo contendere, and the plea may be set aside only on direct appeal or collateral attack.

(f) Admissibility or Inadmissibility of a Plea, Plea Discussions, and Related Statements. The admissibility or inadmissibility of a plea, a plea discussion, and any related statement is governed by Federal Rule of Evidence 410.

(g) Recording the Proceedings. The proceedings during which the defendant enters a plea must be recorded by a court reporter or by a suitable recording device. If there is a guilty plea or a nolo contendere plea, the record must include the inquiries and advice to the defendant required under Rule 11(b) and (c).

(h) Harmless Error. A variance from the requirements of this rule is harmless error if it does not affect substantial rights.

Notes from Pearl:

1. May the *judge* participate in plea bargaining?

In *U.S. v. Bruce*, 976 F.2d 552 (9th Cir.1992), the court vacated a conviction based on a plea bargain, because the judge had encouraged the defendant to "think carefully" about the offer. The court noted 3 purposes which underlie the prohibition of Rule 11(e)(1): (1) judicial participation in plea bargain risks "coercing" the defendant, who might believe that he would not receive a fair trial before this judge if he declines the offer, (2) judges should be judges, not advocates, and (3) such participation might impair the judge's ability to impartially adjudge the voluntariness of the plea or, if the offer is declined, to impartially adjudge the subsequent trial. See also *U.S. v. Rodriguez*, 197 F.3d 156 (5th Cir. 1999).

In *People v. Weaver*, 12 Cal.Rptr.3d 742 (2004), the court considered whether a *state* court judge may participate in plea bargaining:

> In the states there is a spectrum of opinion concerning the involvement of judges in plea negotiations. Some follow the federal rule and prohibit any involvement. In some of those jurisdictions judicial involvement in plea negotiations is considered so serious that reversal is required even without a finding that the plea was involuntary. Other states, while expressing concern with judicial involvement in plea negotiations, treat the matter on a case by base basis. Since the matter is case specific there is no general rule describing when court involvement has resulted in a coerced plea. Important factors, however, include whether the court was the moving force in pressing for a guilty plea after the defendant indicated a desire to go to trial and when the court during negotiations indicated conviction was a foregone conclusion. There is no rule in California forbidding judicial involvement in plea negotiations. Nonetheless courts have expressed strong reservation about the practice. In *People v. Williams* (1969) 269 Cal.App.2d 879, 884, the court stated that "special problems are presented when the *judge* participates in plea negotiations. Experience suggests that such judicial activity risks more, in terms of unintentional coercion of defendants, than it gains in promoting understanding and voluntary pleas, and thus most authorities recommend that it be kept to a minimum."

> The California Judges Benchbook makes this observation: "The degree and manner of a judge's participation in plea negotiation, i.e., his or her role, varies among judges. Many judges prefer to stay out of the actual negotiating process and be brought into the matter once a bargain has been attained. Success depends entirely on the approach taken by the prosecution and defense representatives. Some judges feel that they should actively participate in the negotiations as a mediator, as one seeking to bring conflicting or antagonistic views together on a reasonable solution. Here a cautious approach may achieve more. The judge should maintain

total neutrality and at the same time probe continually for a common meeting ground. Patience, tact, and persistence pay off in an increased number of dispositions."

One district attorney in a large county has suggested that there is a great advantage to the court's active participation, but cautions that, because of the court's power and dignity, the defendant and counsel for both sides must not be made to feel that the judge will feel unkindly toward them if negotiations fall through." (*California Judges Benchbook, Criminal Pretrial Proceedings* (Cont.Ed.Bar 1991) § 2.11, pp. 87–88.)

No one, not even appellant, doubts that it was the trial judge's intention to encourage a plea bargain that was in everyone's best interest. The judge, however, went too far. The judicial change of "hats" in this case is head spinning. At any given time he seemed to fill the role of judge, jury, defense counsel, prosecutor, psychiatrist, social worker and victims' advocate. While in some objective sense it may be that the judge, a person of long experience, did know what was best for everyone, that is beside the point.

The judge not only concluded and expressed that appellant, save for some irrationality on the part of the jury, would be convicted, he also concluded the crimes were the result of a particular and dangerous mental disorder. The judge's histrionic monologues were not the stuff of mediation or facilitation. They were the stuff of advocacy. His understandable and often expressed concern that the victims not be victimized again could reasonably be taken by appellant and others viewing the proceeding as a comment that the judge would not look favorably on those who would, to no end, harm the children the defendant already harmed. The level and manner of the judge's interest and involvement in the negotiation process, particularly that of record and in appellant's presence, colored every aspect of the proceeding.

There is no doubt the trial judge meant to do justice. Certainly it was the judge's intention to assist everyone by expressing in the clearest terms his assessment of the case. But, as the cases and commentators cited above have repeatedly noted, there are great risks in the trial court involving itself in the plea negotiation process. As that involvement increases in intensity, the risks become greater.

In asking that he be allowed to withdraw his guilty plea, appellant stated that a major source of pressure that led to that plea came from the trial court's comments and its apparent attitude towards him. Appellant described the court's conduct as abusive and antagonistic. Appellant concluded the judge believed he was guilty and dangerous and that he would not get a fair trial.

With all due respect to the trial judge, we understand why appellant reached these conclusions. The trial court's conduct was highly inappropriate. Appellant established good cause for the withdrawal of his plea. Certainly not every instance of judicial involvement in plea negotiations results in duress. While some jurisdictions totally foreclose judicial participation in plea bargaining, California does not. Judges can, in appropriate cases and in a reserved manner, play a useful part in that process. However, when the trial court abandons its judicial role and thrusts itself to the center of the negotiation process and makes repeated comments that suggest a less than neutral attitude about the case or the defendant, then great pressure exists for the defendant to accede to the court's wishes. We conclude that is what occurred here. The actions of the trial court in the context of this case overcame appellant's free judgment. The trial court therefore abused its discretion in denying appellant's motion to withdraw his plea.

The judgment is reversed. The matter is remanded to the trial court for a hearing not to be held by Judge Brown, at which appellant will be allowed to withdraw his plea of guilty.

In *U.S. v. O'Neill*, 437 F.3d 654 (7th Cir. 2006), the court stated:

Judges, it is well-settled, may not participate in plea negotiations. Fed.R.Crim.P. 11(c)(1). This proscription against judicial intervention in plea negotiations is widely construed as categorical. However, it is also certainly well-established that judges are permitted to take an active role in evaluating the agreement in Rule 11(c) cases. Where to draw the line between "intervention" and "evaluating" is where the rubber meets the road in this case.

JUDGE POSNER added:

Sentencing judges are placed in a quandary by being authorized on the one hand to reject a plea that specifies a sentence that the judge considers too lenient and on the other hand being forbidden by Fed.R.Crim.P. 11(c)(1) "to participate in these discussions," that is, the discussions between the prosecutor and the defense lawyer or defendant that resulted in the plea agreement. If the judge gives no explanation for why he is rejecting the agreement, the defendant is left in the dark, but if he explains the grounds of his rejection he may be thought to have initiated and participated in a discussion looking to the negotiation of a new plea agreement. Reconciling these directives is the judicial equivalent of squaring the circle.

2. In *U.S. v. Mezzanatto*, 513 U.S. 196 (1995), defendant and his attorney asked to meet with the prosecutor to discuss the possibility of a plea bargain. As a condition to the discussion, the prosecutor said that defendant would have to agree that any statements he made during the meeting could be used to impeach any contradictory statement he might give at trial, if the case went to trial. Defendant agreed and the discussion took place, but no plea bargain was reached. At trial, defendant took the stand, and then the prosecutor called one of the government agents who had attended the meeting, to testify that defendant had there made certain inconsistent statements. He was convicted, but the Court of Appeals reversed, holding that the agreement was unenforceable because it was inconsistent with Federal Rules of Criminal Procedure, Rule 11(e)(6).

The Supreme Court reversed the Court of Appeals, holding that a defendant's knowing, voluntary waiver of his rights under Rule 11(e)(6) is valid and enforceable, unless induced by fraud or coercion.

BOYKIN v. ALABAMA
United States Supreme Court
395 U.S. 238 (1969)

Mr. Justice Douglas delivered the opinion of the Court.

In the spring of 1966, within the period of a fortnight, a series of armed robberies occurred in Mobile, Alabama. The victims, in each case, were local shopkeepers open at night who were forced by a gunman to hand over money. While robbing one grocery store, the assailant fired his gun once, sending a bullet through a door into the ceiling. A few days earlier in a drugstore, the robber had allowed his gun to discharge in such a way that the bullet, on ricochet from the floor, struck a customer in the leg. Shortly thereafter, a local grand jury returned five indictments against petitioner, a 27-year-old Negro, for common law robbery — an offense punishable in Alabama by death.

Before the matter came to trial, the court determined that petitioner was indigent and appointed counsel to represent him. Three days later, at his arraignment, petitioner pleaded guilty to all five indictments. So far as the record shows, the judge asked no questions of petitioner concerning his plea, and petitioner did not address the court.

Trial strategy may of course make a plea of guilty seem the desirable course. But the record is wholly silent on that point and throws no light on it.

Alabama provides that when a defendant pleads guilty, "the court must cause the punishment to be determined by a jury" (except where it is required to be fixed by the court) and may "cause witnesses to be examined, to ascertain the character of the offense." Ala.Code, Tit. 15, § 277 (1958). In the present case, a trial of that dimension was held, the prosecution presenting its case largely through eyewitness testimony. Although counsel for petitioner engaged in cursory cross-examination, petitioner neither testified himself nor presented testimony concerning his character and background. There was nothing to indicate that he had a prior criminal record.

In instructing the jury, the judge stressed that petitioner had pleaded guilty in five cases of robbery, defined as "the felonious taking of money from another against his will by violence or by putting him in fear, carrying from ten years minimum in the penitentiary to the supreme penalty of death by electrocution." The jury, upon deliberation, found petitioner guilty and sentenced him severally to die on each of the five indictments. * * * *

It was error, plain on the face of the record, for the trial judge to accept petitioner's guilty plea without an affirmative showing that it was intelligent and voluntary. That error, under Alabama procedure, was properly before the court below and considered explicitly by a majority of the justices and is properly before us on review.

A plea of guilty is more than a confession which admits that the accused did various acts; it is itself a conviction; nothing remains but to give judgment and determine punishment. Admissibility of a confession must be based on a "reliable determination on the voluntariness issue which satisfies the constitutional rights of the defendant." *Jackson v. Denno*, 378 U.S. 368, 387. The requirement that the prosecution spread on the record the prerequisites of a valid waiver is no constitutional innovation. In *Carnley v. Cochran*, 369 U.S. 506, 516, we dealt with a problem of waiver of the right to counsel, a Sixth Amendment right. We held: "Presuming waiver from a silent record is impermissible. The record must show, or there must be an allegation and evidence which show, that an accused was offered counsel but intelligently and understandingly rejected the offer. Anything less is not waiver."

We think that the same standard must be applied to determining whether a guilty plea is voluntarily made. For, as we have said, a plea of guilty is more than an admission of conduct; it is a conviction. Ignorance, incomprehension, coercion, terror, inducements, subtle or blatant threats might be a perfect cover-up of unconstitutionality. * * * *

Several federal constitutional rights are involved in a waiver that takes place when a plea of guilty is entered in a state criminal trial. First, is the privilege against compulsory self-incrimination guaranteed by the Fifth Amendment and applicable to the States by reason of the Fourteenth. Second, is the right to trial by jury. Third, is the right to confront one's accusers. We cannot presume a waiver of these three important federal rights from a silent record.[5]

What is at stake for an accused facing death or imprisonment demands the utmost solicitude of which courts are capable in canvassing the matter with the accused, to make sure he has a full understanding of what the plea connotes and of its consequence. When the judge discharges that function, he leaves a record adequate for any review that may be later sought * * * and forestalls the spin-off of collateral proceedings that seek to probe murky memories.[7]

The three dissenting justices in the Alabama Supreme Court stated the law accurately when they concluded that there was reversible error "because the record does not disclose that the defendant voluntarily and understandingly entered his pleas of guilty."

Reversed.

Notes from Pearl:

1. Must the judge advise the defendant of the risk of *deportation*?

In *People v. Ford*, 86 N.Y.2d 397 (1995), Ford (a legal alien from Jamaica) believed his gun was unloaded and, while showing it to his girlfriend, put it to her head and pulled the trigger, killing her. He pleaded guilty to manslaughter. After serving his prison term, the Immigration & Naturalization Service sought to deport him for committing a crime involving "moral turpitude." He then moved to withdraw his guilty plea, claiming that the judge who accepted his guilty plea had failed to advise him of the risk of deportation.

---

[5] In the federal regime we have Rule 11 of the Federal Rules of Criminal Procedure, which governs the duty of the trial judge before accepting a guilty plea.

[7] "A majority of criminal convictions are obtained after a plea of guilty. If these convictions are to be insulated from attack, the trial court is best advised to conduct an on the record examination of the defendant which should include, inter alia, an attempt to satisfy itself that the defendant understands the nature of the charges, his right to a jury trial, the acts sufficient to constitute the offenses for which he is charged and the permissible range of sentences." *Commonwealth ex rel. West v. Rundle*, 428 Pa. 102, 105–106 (1968).

The trial court granted the motion, holding that "where the facts surrounding the episode to which defendant pleads would not suggest to a reasonable person that the plea involves an admission of grossly immoral activity then, in those rare cases, the defendant should be told that even though what he describes to the court does not involve moral turpitude, he may nevertheless be deported, if he pleads guilty." The New York Court of Appeals reversed:

> A trial court has the constitutional duty to ensure that a defendant, before pleading guilty, has a full understanding of what the plea connotes and its consequences. *Boykin v. Alabama*, 395 U.S. 238, 244. The court is not required to engage in any particular litany when allocuting the defendant, but due process requires that the record must be clear that "the plea represents a voluntary and intelligent choice among the alternative courses of action open to the defendant" *North Carolina v. Alford*, 400 U.S. 25, 31, citing *Boykin v. Alabama*, supra.

> Manifestly, a criminal court is in no position to advise on all the ramifications of a guilty plea personal to a defendant. Accordingly, the courts have drawn a distinction between consequences of which the defendant must be advised, those which are "direct", and those of which the defendant need not be advised, "collateral consequences". A direct consequence is one which has a definite, immediate and largely automatic effect on defendant's punishment. Illustrations of collateral consequences are loss of the right to vote or travel abroad (*Meaton v. United States*, 328 F.2d 379 (5th Cir.1964)), loss of civil service employment (*United States v. Crowley*, 529 F.2d 1066 (3d Cir.1976), loss of a driver's license (*Moore v. Hinton*, 513 F.2d 781 (5th Cir.1975)), loss of the right to possess firearms (Penal Law § 400.00 [1][b]), or an undesirable discharge from the Armed Services (*Redwine v. Zuckert*, 317 F.2d 336 (D.C.Cir.1963)). The failure to warn of such collateral consequences will not warrant vacating a plea because they are peculiar to the individual and generally result from the actions taken by agencies the court does not control.

> Deportation is a collateral consequence of conviction because it is a result peculiar to the individual's personal circumstances and one not within the control of the court system. Therefore, our Appellate Division and the Federal courts have consistently held that the trial court need not, before accepting a plea of guilty, advise a defendant of the possibility of deportation. [Citations.] We adopt that rule and conclude that in this case the court properly allocuted defendant before taking his plea of guilty to manslaughter in the second degree.

Ford also argued that *his counsel* was ineffective by failing to tell him about the possibility of deportation. The court disagreed, holding that so long as counsel does not mislead a defendant about a "collateral consequence" like deportation, he is not ineffective.

2. How much detail must the judge tell the defendant about the *sentence*?

The sentence which the judge might impose on the defendant would seem to be a "direct" consequence of the guilty plea, rather than a "collateral" consequence. But is it always? How much *detail* must the judge tell the defendant about the sentence?

In *Parry v. Rosemeyer*, 64 F.3d 110 (3rd Cir.1995), a Pennsylvania state court judge told Parry that he could be sentenced to between 11 and 23 months imprisonment, followed by 2 years probation, but failed to tell Parry that if he then violated the terms of his probation, he could be sent back to prison for another 2 to 10 years. Parry served his term of imprisonment, but while on probation, violated his terms of probation. His probation was revoked, and he was sentenced to another 2 to 10 years imprisonment. He claimed that his guilty plea was "involuntary and unknowing." The court disagreed:

> Revocation of probation is not an immediate and automatic consequence of pleading guilty. Like a subsequent state court conviction, revocation of probation may or may not occur sometime in the future, and whether it occurs is dependent on the actions of the defendant. A sentence of imprisonment upon revocation of probation is not generated by the plea but by the defendant's own unwillingness or inability to conform to the restrictions imposed as part of probation. Therefore, a term of imprisonment imposed in place of a revoked term of probation would be a direct consequence of violating a condition of probation (here, the condition that Parry not be rearrested), but not of pleading guilty. * * * *

> While the provision of information concerning a collateral consequence like revocation of probation might be useful to defendants and our opinion today should not be read as discouraging sentencing judges from providing such information, we do not think that the result we reach in this case is a harsh one. The judge's actions in imposing a term of imprisonment in place of the revoked term of probation were foreseeable under Pennsylvania law.

Parry also argued that *his counsel* was ineffective in not telling him of the consequences of violating probation. The court was "skeptical" of this claim, as Parry's lawyer got him a pretty good plea bargain, in light of the evidence against Parry and his prior criminal record. The court found it unnecessary to decide this question, as it found that Parry was not prejudiced by any error by counsel, as it was unlikely that if counsel *had* told Parry the consequences of violating probation, Parry would have rejected the deal and gone to trial.

3. Must the judge advise the defendant about *registration as a sex offender?*

In *State v. Breiner*, 562 N.W.2d 565 (N.D.1997), Breiner pleaded guilty to "corrupting a minor." Later, he moved to withdraw his plea, on the ground that the judge had failed to advise him that the conviction would require him to register as a sex offender. The court agreed with him:

> Registration as a sexual offender is a collateral, not a direct, consequence of a conviction, many appellate courts have concluded, so that a sentencing court's failure to advise the defendant about it is not grounds for withdrawal of the guilty plea. [Citations.] This majority view reasons that laws requiring a sexual offender to register are largely remedial, not punitive, and are designed to facilitate law enforcement and to protect children.

> In contrast, California holds that sexual offender registration is a direct consequence of conviction and that the sentencing court must advise a defendant of the requirement before accepting the guilty plea. *People v.*

McClellan, 6 Cal.4th 367 (1993). We are persuaded by the California Supreme Court's rationale that the registration requirement imposes a grave, and even onerous, additional punishment, especially for a misdemeanor offense: "In view of the unusual and onerous nature of the sex registration requirement that follows inexorably from a conviction, the trial court's duty surely included an obligation to advise petitioner of this sanction prior to accepting his guilty plea."

BRADY v. UNITED STATES
United States Supreme Court
397 U.S. 742 (1970)

Mr. Justice White delivered the opinion of the Court.

In 1959, petitioner was charged with kidnaping in violation of 18 U.S.C. § 1201(a). * * * * Since the indictment charged that the victim of the kidnaping was not liberated unharmed, petitioner faced a maximum penalty of death if the verdict of the jury should so recommend. Petitioner, represented by competent counsel throughout, first elected to plead not guilty. Apparently because the trial judge was unwilling to try the case without a jury, petitioner made no serious attempt to reduce the possibility of a death penalty by waiving a jury trial. Upon learning that his codefendant, who had confessed to the authorities, would plead guilty and be available to testify against him, petitioner changed his plea to guilty. His plea was accepted after the trial judge twice questioned him as to the voluntariness of his plea. Petitioner was sentenced to 50 years' imprisonment, later reduced to 30.

In 1967, petitioner sought relief under 28 U.S.C. § 2255, claiming that his plea of guilty was not voluntarily given because § 1201(a) operated to coerce his plea, because his counsel exerted impermissible pressure upon him, and because his plea was induced by representations with respect to reduction of sentence and clemency.

After a hearing, the District Court for the District of New Mexico denied relief. According to the District Court's findings, petitioner's counsel did not put impermissible pressure on petitioner to plead guilty and no representations were made with respect to a reduced sentence or clemency. The court held that § 1201(a) was constitutional and found that petitioner decided to plead guilty when he learned that his codefendant was going to plead guilty: petitioner pleaded guilty "by reason of other matters and not by reason of the statute" or because of any acts of the trial judge. The court concluded that "the plea was voluntarily and knowingly made." * * * *

That a guilty plea is a grave and solemn act to be accepted only with care and discernment has long been recognized. Central to the plea and the foundation for entering judgment against the defendant is the defendant's admission in open court that he committed the acts charged in the indictment. He thus stands as a witness against himself and he is shielded by the Fifth Amendment from being compelled to do so — hence the minimum requirement that his plea be the voluntary expression of his own choice. But the plea is more than an admission of past conduct; it is the defendant's consent that judgment of conviction may be entered without a trial — a waiver of his right to trial before a jury or a judge. Waivers of constitutional rights not only must be voluntary but must be knowing, intelligent acts done with sufficient awareness of the relevant circumstances and likely consequences. On neither score was Brady's plea of guilty invalid.

The trial judge in 1959 found the plea voluntary before accepting it; the District Court in 1968, after an evidentiary hearing, found that the plea was voluntarily made; the Court of Appeals specifically approved the finding of voluntariness. We see no reason on this record to disturb the judgment of those courts. Petitioner, advised by competent counsel, tendered his plea after his codefendant, who had already given a confession, determined to plead guilty and became available to testify against petitioner. It was this development that the District Court found to have triggered Brady's guilty plea.

The voluntariness of Brady's plea can be determined only by considering all of the relevant circumstances surrounding it. One of these circumstances was the possibility of a heavier sentence following a guilty verdict after a trial. It may be that Brady, faced with a strong case against him and recognizing that his chances for acquittal were slight, preferred to plead guilty and thus limit the penalty to life imprisonment rather than to elect a jury trial which could result in a death penalty. But even if we assume that Brady would not have pleaded guilty except for the death penalty provision of § 1201(a), this assumption merely identifies the penalty provision as a "but for" cause of his plea. That the statute caused the plea in this sense does not necessarily prove that the plea was coerced and invalid as an involuntary act.

The State to some degree encourages pleas of guilty at every important step in the criminal process. For some people, their breach of a State's law is alone sufficient reason for surrendering themselves and accepting punishment. For others, apprehension and charge, both threatening acts by the Government, jar them into admitting their guilt. In still other cases, the post-indictment accumulation of evidence may convince the defendant and his counsel that a trial is not worth the agony and expense to the defendant and his family. All these pleas of guilty are valid in spite of the State's responsibility for some of the factors motivating the pleas; the pleas are no more improperly compelled than is the decision by a defendant at the close of the State's evidence at trial that he must take the stand or face certain conviction.

Of course, the agents of the State may not produce a plea by actual or threatened physical harm or by mental coercion overbearing the will of the defendant. But nothing of the sort is claimed in this case; nor is there evidence that Brady was so gripped by fear of the death penalty or hope of leniency that he did not or could not, with the help of counsel, rationally weigh the advantages of going to trial against the advantages of pleading guilty. Brady's claim is of a different sort: that it violates the Fifth Amendment to influence or encourage a guilty plea by opportunity or promise of leniency and that a guilty plea is coerced and invalid if influenced by the fear of a possibly higher penalty for the crime charged if a conviction is obtained after the State is put to its proof.

Insofar as the voluntariness of his plea is concerned, there is little to differentiate Brady from (1) the defendant, in a jurisdiction where the judge and jury have the same range of sentencing power, who pleads guilty because his lawyer advises him that the judge will very probably be more lenient than the jury; (2) the defendant, in a jurisdiction where the judge alone has sentencing power, who is advised by counsel that the judge is normally more lenient with defendants who plead guilty than with those who go to trial; (3) the defendant who is permitted by prosecutor and judge to plead guilty to a lesser offense included in the offense charged; and (4) the defendant who pleads guilty to certain counts with the understanding that other charges will be dropped. In each of these situations,[8] as in Brady's case, the defendant might never plead guilty absent the possibility or certainty that the plea will result in a lesser penalty than the sentence that could be imposed after a trial and a verdict of guilty. We decline to hold, however, that a guilty plea is compelled and invalid under the Fifth Amendment whenever motivated by the defendant's desire to accept the certainty or probability of a lesser penalty rather than face a wider range of possibilities extending from acquittal to conviction and a higher penalty authorized by law for the crime charged.

The issue we deal with is inherent in the criminal law and its administration because guilty pleas are not constitutionally forbidden, because the criminal law characteristically extends to judge or jury a range of choice in setting the sentence in individual cases, and because both the State and the defendant often find it advantageous to preclude the possibility of the maximum penalty authorized by law. For a defendant who sees slight possibility of acquittal, the advantages of pleading guilty and limiting the probable penalty are obvious — his exposure is reduced, the correctional processes can begin immediately, and the practical burdens of a trial are eliminated. For the State there are also advantages — the more promptly imposed punishment after an admission of guilt may more effectively attain the objectives of punishment; and with the avoidance of trial, scarce judicial and prosecutorial resources are conserved for those cases in which there is a substantial issue of the defendant's guilt or in which there is substantial doubt that the State can sustain its burden of proof. * * * * It is this mutuality of advantage that perhaps explains the fact that at present well over three-fourths of the criminal convictions in this country rest on pleas of guilty,[10] a great many of them no doubt motivated at least in part by the hope or assurance of a lesser penalty than might be imposed if there were a guilty verdict after a trial to judge or jury.

Of course, that the prevalence of guilty pleas is explainable does not necessarily validate those pleas or the system which produces them. But we cannot hold that it is unconstitutional for the State to extend a benefit to a defendant who in turn extends a substantial benefit to the State and who demonstrates by his plea that he is ready and willing to admit his crime and to enter the correctional system in a frame of mind that affords hope for success in rehabilitation over a shorter period of time than might otherwise be necessary.

A contrary holding would require the States and Federal Government to forbid guilty pleas altogether, to provide a single invariable penalty for each crime defined by the statutes, or to place the sentencing function in a separate authority having no knowledge of the manner in which the conviction in each case was obtained. In any event, it would be necessary to forbid prosecutors and judges to accept guilty

---

[8] We here make no reference to the situation where the prosecutor or judge, or both, deliberately employ their charging and sentencing powers to induce a particular defendant to tender a plea of guilty. In Brady's case, there is no claim that the prosecutor threatened prosecution on a charge not justified by the evidence or that the trial judge threatened Brady with a harsher sentence if convicted after trial in order to induce him to plead guilty.

[10] It has been estimated that about 90%, and perhaps 95%, of all criminal convictions are by pleas of guilty; between 70% and 85% of all felony convictions are estimated to be by guilty plea. Newman, *Conviction, The Determination of Guilt or Innocence Without Trial,* 3 and n. 1 (1966).

pleas to selected counts, to lesser included offenses, or to reduced charges. The Fifth Amendment does not reach so far.

Bram v. United States, 168 U.S. 532 (1897), held that the admissibility of a confession depended upon whether it was compelled within the meaning of the Fifth Amendment. To be admissible, a confession must be "free and voluntary: that is, must not be extracted by any sort of threats or violence, nor obtained by any direct or implied promises, however slight, nor by the exertion of any improper influence." 168 U.S. at 542–543. * * * *

Bram is not inconsistent with our holding that Brady's plea was not compelled even though the law promised him a lesser maximum penalty if he did not go to trial. *Bram* dealt with a confession given by a defendant in custody, alone and unrepresented by counsel. In such circumstances, even a mild promise of leniency was deemed sufficient to bar the confession, not because the promise was an illegal act as such, but because defendants at such times are too sensitive to inducement and the possible impact on them too great to ignore and too difficult to assess. But *Bram* and its progeny did not hold that the possibly coercive impact of a promise of leniency could not be dissipated by the presence and advice of counsel, any more than *Miranda v. Arizona*, 384 U.S. 436 (1966), held that the possibly coercive atmosphere of the police station could not be counteracted by the presence of counsel or other safeguards.

Brady's situation bears no resemblance to Bram's. Brady first pleaded not guilty; prior to changing his plea to guilty he was subjected to no threats or promises in face-to-face encounters with the authorities. He had competent counsel and full opportunity to assess the advantages and disadvantages of a trial as compared with those attending a plea of guilty; there was no hazard of an impulsive and improvident response to a seeming but unreal advantage. His plea of guilty was entered in open court and before a judge obviously sensitive to the requirements of the law with respect to guilty pleas. Brady's plea, unlike Bram's confession, was voluntary.

The standard as to the voluntariness of guilty pleas must be essentially that defined by Judge Tuttle of the Court of Appeals for the Fifth Circuit:

> A plea of guilty entered by one fully aware of the direct consequences, including the actual value of any commitments made to him by the court, prosecutor, or his own counsel, must stand unless induced by threats (or promises to discontinue improper harassment), misrepresentation (including unfulfilled or unfulfillable promises), or perhaps by promises that are by their nature improper as having no proper relationship to the prosecutor's business (e.g. bribes).[13]

Under this standard, a plea of guilty is not invalid merely because entered to avoid the possibility of a death penalty. * * * *

III

The record before us also supports the conclusion that Brady's plea was intelligently made. He was advised by competent counsel, he was made aware of the nature of the charge against him, and there was nothing to indicate that he was

---

[13] *Shelton v. United States*, 246 F.2d 571, 572 n. 2 (5th Cir. 1957).

incompetent or otherwise not in control of his mental faculties; once his confederate had pleaded guilty and became available to testify, he chose to plead guilty, perhaps to ensure that he would face no more than life imprisonment or a term of years. Brady was aware of precisely what he was doing when he admitted that he had kidnaped the victim and had not released her unharmed.

It is true that Brady's counsel advised him that § 1201(a) empowered the jury to impose the death penalty and that nine years later in *United States v. Jackson*, 390 U.S. 570 138 (1968), the Court held that the jury had no such power as long as the judge could impose only a lesser penalty if trial was to the court or there was a plea of guilty. But these facts do not require us to set aside Brady's conviction.

Often the decision to plead guilty is heavily influenced by the defendant's appraisal of the prosecution's case against him and by the apparent likelihood of securing leniency should a guilty plea be offered and accepted. Considerations like these frequently present imponderable questions for which there are no certain answers; judgments may be made that in the light of later events seem improvident, although they were perfectly sensible at the time. The rule that a plea must be intelligently made to be valid does not require that a plea be vulnerable to later attack if the defendant did not correctly assess every relevant factor entering into his decision. A defendant is not entitled to withdraw his plea merely because he discovers long after the plea has been accepted that his calculus misapprehended the quality of the State's case or the likely penalties attached to alternative courses of action. More particularly, absent misrepresentation or other impermissible conduct by state agents, a voluntary plea of guilty intelligently made in the light of the then applicable law does not become vulnerable because later judicial decisions indicate that the plea rested on a faulty premise. A plea of guilty triggered by the expectations of a competently counseled defendant that the State will have a strong case against him is not subject to later attack because the defendant's lawyer correctly advised him with respect to the then existing law as to possible penalties but later pronouncements of the courts, as in this case, hold that the maximum penalty for the crime in question was less than was reasonably assumed at the time the plea was entered.

The fact that Brady did not anticipate *United States v. Jackson, supra,* does not impugn the truth or reliability of his plea. We find no requirement in the Constitution that a defendant must be permitted to disown his solemn admissions in open court that he committed the act with which he is charged simply because it later develops that the State would have had a weaker case than the defendant had thought or that the maximum penalty then assumed applicable has been held inapplicable in subsequent judicial decisions.

This is not to say that guilty plea convictions hold no hazards for the innocent or that the methods of taking guilty pleas presently employed in this country are necessarily valid in all respects. This mode of conviction is no more foolproof than full trials to the court or to the jury. Accordingly, we take great precautions against unsound results, and we should continue to do so, whether conviction is by plea or by trial. We would have serious doubts about this case if the encouragement of guilty pleas by offers of leniency substantially increased the likelihood that defendants, advised by competent counsel, would falsely condemn themselves. But our view is to the contrary and is based on our expectations that courts will satisfy themselves that pleas of guilty are voluntarily and intelligently made by competent defendants with adequate advice of counsel and that there is nothing to question the accuracy and reliability of the defendants' admissions that they committed the crimes with which they are charged. In the case before us, nothing in the record impeaches Brady's plea or suggests that his admissions in open court were anything but the truth.

Although Brady's plea of guilty may well have been motivated in part by a desire to avoid a possible death penalty, we are convinced that his plea was voluntarily and intelligently made and we have no reason to doubt that his solemn admission of guilt was truthful.

Affirmed.

Notes from Pearl:

1. Suppose the guilty plea is the "fruit" of an illegal search or seizure.

In *Smith v. U.S.*, 876 F.2d 655 (8th Cir.1989), Smith filed a *habeas corpus* petition, challenging his guilty plea on the grounds that it was the fruit of evidence obtained through an unconstitutional search and seizure, it was the fruit of a coerced confession, and that the prosecution had failed to disclose exculpatory evidence. The court disagreed: "In pleading guilty, a defendant waives all challenges to the prosecution except those relating to jurisdiction. Thus, Smith has waived his claims on search and seizure, privilege against self-incrimination, and failure to disclose favorable evidence."

Is *Smith's* latter point *always* correct? Suppose the defendant pleads guilty *without knowing* that the prosecutor has withheld certain exculpatory evidence, even though the defendant has moved for discovery of such evidence. Is the plea "knowing and intelligent"? No, held the court in *U.S. v. Wright*, 43 F.3d 491 (10th Cir.1994)

> Without the clearly exculpatory evidence before it, the trial court which accepted the plea could not, in fact, satisfy itself in any meaningful sense that petitioner's guilty plea was voluntarily and intelligently made by an informed defendant with adequate advice of counsel, and that there was nothing to question the accuracy and reliability of this defendant's admission that he had committed the crime with which he had been charged.

2. In *U.S. v. Ruiz*, 536 U.S. 622 (2002), the Court held that, before entering into a plea agreement, a prosecutor need not disclose to the defendant evidence that might be used to *impeach* a prosecution witness:

> The prosecutors' proposed plea agreement contains a set of detailed terms. Among other things, it specifies that "any known information establishing the factual innocence of the defendant" "has been turned over to the defendant," and it acknowledges the Government's "continuing duty to provide such information." At the same time it requires that the defendant "waive the right" to receive "impeachment information relating to any informants or other witnesses" as well as the right to receive information supporting any affirmative defense the defendant raises if the case goes to trial. Because Ruiz would not agree to this last-mentioned waiver, the prosecutors withdrew their bargaining offer. The Government then indicted Ruiz for unlawful drug possession. And despite the absence of

any agreement, Ruiz ultimately pleaded guilty. * * * *

The Ninth Circuit vacated the District Court's sentencing determination. The Ninth Circuit pointed out that the Constitution requires prosecutors to make certain impeachment information available to a defendant before trial. It decided that this obligation entitles defendants to receive that same information before they enter into a plea agreement. The Ninth Circuit also decided that the Constitution prohibits defendants from waiving their right to that information. * * * *

The constitutional question concerns a federal criminal defendant's waiver of the right to receive from prosecutors exculpatory impeachment material — a right that the Constitution provides as part of its basic "fair trial" guarantee. See U.S. Const., Amdts. 5, 6. See also *Brady v. Maryland*, 373 U.S. 83, 87 (1963) (Due process requires prosecutors to "avoid an unfair trial" by making available "upon request" evidence "favorable to an accused where the evidence is material either to guilt or to punishment"); *United States v. Agurs*, 427 U.S. 97, 112–113 (1976) (defense request unnecessary); *Kyles v. Whitley*, 514 U.S. 419, 435 (1995) (exculpatory evidence is evidence the suppression of which would "undermine confidence in the verdict"); *Giglio v. United States*, 405 U.S. 150, 154 (1972) (exculpatory evidence includes "evidence affecting" witness "credibility," where the witness' "reliability" is likely "determinative of guilt or innocence").

When a defendant pleads guilty he or she, of course, forgoes not only a fair trial, but also other accompanying constitutional guarantees. *Boykin v. Alabama*, 395 U.S. 238, 243 (1969) (pleading guilty implicates the Fifth Amendment privilege against self-incrimination, the Sixth Amendment right to confront one's accusers, and the Sixth Amendment right to trial by jury). Given the seriousness of the matter, the Constitution insists, among other things, that the defendant enter a guilty plea that is "voluntary" and that the defendant must make related waivers "knowingly, intelligently, and with sufficient awareness of the relevant circumstances and likely consequences." *Brady v. United States*, 397 U.S. 742, 748 (1970).

In this case, the Ninth Circuit in effect held that a guilty plea is not "voluntary" (and that the defendant could not, by pleading guilty, waive his right to a fair trial) unless the prosecutors first made the same disclosure of material impeachment information that the prosecutors would have had to make had the defendant insisted upon a trial. We must decide whether the Constitution requires that preguilty plea disclosure of impeachment information. We conclude that it does not.

First, impeachment information is special in relation to the *fairness of a trial*, not in respect to whether a plea is *voluntary* ("knowing," "intelligent," and "sufficiently aware").

Of course, the more information the defendant has, the more aware he is of the likely consequences of a plea, waiver, or decision, and the wiser that decision will likely be. But the Constitution does not require the prosecutor to share all useful information with the defendant. *Weatherford v. Bursey*, 429 U.S. 545, 559 (1977) ("There is no general constitutional right to discovery in a criminal case"). And the law ordinarily considers a waiver knowing, intelligent, and sufficiently aware if the defendant fully understands the nature of the right and how it would likely apply *in general* in the circumstances — even though the defendant may not know the *specific detailed* consequences of invoking it. A defendant, for example, may waive his right to remain silent, his right to a jury trial, or his right to counsel even if the defendant does not know the specific questions the authorities intend to ask, who will likely serve on the jury, or the particular lawyer the State might otherwise provide.

It is particularly difficult to characterize impeachment information as critical information of which the defendant must always be aware prior to pleading guilty given the random way in which such information may, or may not, help a particular defendant. The degree of help that impeachment information can provide will depend upon the defendant's own independent knowledge of the prosecution's potential case — a matter that the Constitution does not require prosecutors to disclose.

The Constitution, in respect to a defendant's awareness of relevant circumstances, does not require complete knowledge of the relevant circumstances, but permits a court to accept a guilty plea, with its accompanying waiver of various constitutional rights, despite various forms of misapprehension under which a defendant might labor. See *Brady v. United States*, 397 U.S. at 757 (defendant "misapprehended the quality of the State's case"); *McMann v. Richardson*, 397 U.S. 759, 770 (1970) (counsel "misjudged the admissibility" of a "confession"); *United States v. Broce*, 488 U.S. 563, 573 (1989) (counsel failed to point out a potential defense); *Tollett v. Henderson*, 411 U.S. 258, 267 (1973) (counsel failed to find a potential constitutional infirmity in grand jury proceedings). It is difficult to distinguish, in terms of importance, (1) a defendant's ignorance of grounds for impeachment of potential witnesses at a possible future trial from (2) the varying forms of ignorance at issue in these cases. * * * *

At the same time, a constitutional obligation to provide impeachment information during plea bargaining, prior to entry of a guilty plea, could seriously interfere with the Government's interest in securing those guilty pleas that are factually justified, desired by defendants, and help to secure the efficient administration of justice. The Ninth Circuit's rule risks premature disclosure of Government witness information, which, the Government tells us, could "disrupt ongoing investigations" and expose prospective witnesses to serious harm. And the careful tailoring that characterizes most legal Government witness disclosure requirements suggests recognition by both Congress and the Federal Rules Committees that such concerns are valid. See, *e.g.*, 18 U.S.C. § 3432 (witness list disclosure required in capital cases three days before trial with exceptions); § 3500 (Government witness statements ordinarily subject to discovery only after testimony given).

Consequently, the Ninth Circuit's requirement could force the Government to abandon its "general practice" of not "disclosing to a defendant pleading guilty information that would reveal the identities of cooperating informants, undercover investigators, or other prospective witnesses." It could require the Government to devote substantially more resources to trial preparation prior to plea bargaining, thereby depriving the plea-bargaining process of its main resource-saving advantages. Or it could lead the Government instead to abandon its heavy reliance upon plea bargaining in a vast number — 90% or more — of federal criminal cases. We cannot say that the Constitution's due process requirement demands so radical a change in the criminal justice process in order to achieve so comparatively small a constitutional benefit.

These considerations, taken together, lead us to conclude that the Constitution does not require the Government to disclose material impeachment evidence prior to entering a plea agreement with a criminal defendant.

3. In *Bousley v. U.S.*, 523 U.S. 614 (1998), Bousley pleaded guilty in 1990 to "using" a firearm, in violation of 18 U.S.C. § 924(c)(1). Five years later, the U.S. Supreme Court held for the first time (in *Bailey v. U.S.*, 516 U.S. 137 (1995)) that to prove such "use," the Government must prove "active employment" of the firearm. The Court held that "active employment" does not include mere possession of a firearm — even if the defendant stores a weapon near drugs or drug proceeds. Bousley then filed a petition for habeas corpus, claiming that his guilty plea was "not knowing and intelligent," because the judge had failed to tell him that such "active employment" was one of the elements of the crime. The Supreme Court (per Rehnquist, C.J.) agreed:

> A plea of guilty is constitutionally valid only to the extent it is "voluntary" and "intelligent." *Brady v. United States*, 397 U.S. 742, 748 (1970). We have long held that a plea does not qualify as intelligent unless a criminal defendant first receives "real notice of the true nature of the charge against him, the first and most universally recognized requirement of due process." *Smith v. O'Grady*, 312 U.S. 329, 334 (1941).

> *Amicus* contends that petitioner's plea was intelligently made because, prior to pleading guilty, he was provided with a copy of his indictment, which charged him with "using" a firearm. Such circumstances, standing alone, give rise to a presumption that the defendant was informed of the nature of the charge against him. Petitioner nonetheless maintains that his guilty plea was unintelligent because the District Court subsequently misinformed him as to the elements of a § 924(c)(1) offense. In other words, petitioner contends that the record reveals that neither he, nor his counsel, nor the court correctly understood the essential elements of the crime with which he was charged. Were this contention proven, petitioner's plea would be constitutionally invalid.

> Our decisions in *Brady v. United States*, *McMann v. Richardson*, 397 U.S. 759 (1970), and *Parker v. North Carolina*, 397 U.S. 790 (1970), relied upon by *amicus*, are not to the contrary. Each of those cases involved a criminal defendant who pleaded guilty after being correctly informed as to the essential nature of the charge against him. Those defendants later attempted to challenge their guilty pleas when it became evident that they had misjudged the strength of the Government's case or the penalties to which they were subject.

> For example, Brady, who pleaded guilty to kidnapping, maintained that his plea was neither voluntary nor intelligent because it was induced by a death penalty provision later held unconstitutional. We rejected Brady's voluntariness argument, explaining that a "plea of guilty entered by one

fully aware of the direct consequences" of the plea is voluntary in a constitutional sense "unless induced by threats, misrepresentation, or perhaps by promises that are by their nature improper as having no proper relationship to the prosecutor's business." *Id.* at 755. We further held that Brady's plea was intelligent because, although later judicial decisions indicated that at the time of his plea he "did not correctly assess every relevant factor entering into his decision," he was advised by competent counsel, was in control of his mental faculties, and "was made aware of the nature of the charge against him," *id.* at 756. In this case, by contrast, petitioner asserts that he was misinformed as to the true nature of the charge against him.

SANTOBELLO v. NEW YORK
United States Supreme Court
404 U.S. 257 (1971)

MR. CHIEF JUSTICE BURGER delivered the opinion of the Court.

We granted certiorari in this case to determine whether the State's failure to keep a commitment concerning the sentence recommendation on a guilty plea required a new trial.

The facts are not in dispute. The State of New York indicted petitioner in 1969 on two felony counts, Promoting Gambling in the First Degree, and Possession of Gambling Records in the First Degree, N.Y. Penal Law, c. 40, §§ 225.10, 225.20. Petitioner first entered a plea of not guilty to both counts. After negotiations, the Assistant District Attorney in charge of the case agreed to permit petitioner to plead guilty to a lesser-included offense, Possession of Gambling Records in the Second Degree, N.Y. Penal Law § 225.15, conviction of which would carry a maximum prison sentence of one year. The prosecutor agreed to make no recommendation as to the sentence.

On June 16, 1969, petitioner accordingly withdrew his plea of not guilty and entered a plea of guilty to the lesser charge. Petitioner represented to the sentencing judge that the plea was voluntary and that the facts of the case, as described by the Assistant District Attorney, were true. The court accepted the plea and set a date for sentencing. A series of delays followed, owing primarily to the absence of a pre-sentence report, so that by September 23, 1969, petitioner had still not been sentenced. By that date petitioner acquired new defense counsel.

Petitioner's new counsel moved immediately to withdraw the guilty plea. In an accompanying affidavit, petitioner alleged that he did not know at the time of his plea that crucial evidence against him had been obtained as a result of an illegal search. The accuracy of this affidavit is subject to challenge since petitioner had filed and withdrawn a motion to suppress, before pleading guilty. In addition to his motion to withdraw his guilty plea, petitioner renewed the motion to suppress and filed a motion to inspect the grand jury minutes.

These three motions in turn caused further delay until November 26, 1969, when the court denied all three and set January 9, 1970, as the date for sentencing. On January 9 petitioner appeared before a different judge, the judge who had presided over the case to this juncture having retired. Petitioner renewed his motions, and the court again rejected them. The court then turned to consideration of the sentence.

At this appearance, another prosecutor had replaced the prosecutor who had negotiated the plea. The new prosecutor recommended the maximum one-year sentence. In making this recommendation, he cited petitioner's criminal record and alleged links with organized crime. Defense counsel immediately objected on the ground that the State had promised petitioner before the plea was entered that there would be no sentence recommendation by the prosecution. He sought to adjourn the sentence hearing in order to have time to prepare proof of the first prosecutor's promise. The second prosecutor, apparently ignorant of his colleague's commitment, argued that there was nothing in the record to support petitioner's claim of a promise, but the State, in subsequent proceedings, has not contested that such a promise was made.

The sentencing judge ended discussion, with the following statement, quoting extensively from the pre-sentence report:

> Mr. Aronstein [Defense Counsel], I am not at all influenced by what the District Attorney says, so that there is no need to adjourn the sentence, and there is no need to have any testimony. It doesn't make a particle of difference what the District Attorney says he will do, or what he doesn't do. I have here, Mr. Aronstein, a probation report. I have here a history of a long, long serious criminal record. I have here a picture of the life history of this man. "He is unamenable to supervision in the community. He is a professional criminal." This is in quotes. "And a recidivist. Institutionaliza-tion —"; that means, in plain language, just putting him away, "is the only means of halting his anti-social activities," and protecting you, your family, me, my family, protecting society. "Institutionalization." Plain language, put him behind bars. Under the plea, I can only send him to the New York City Correctional Institution for men for one year, which I am hereby doing.

The judge then imposed the maximum sentence of one year. * * * *

This record represents another example of an unfortunate lapse in orderly prosecutorial procedures, in part, no doubt, because of the enormous increase in the workload of the often understaffed prosecutor's offices. The heavy workload may well explain these episodes, but it does not excuse them. The disposition of criminal charges by agreement between the prosecutor and the accused, sometimes loosely called "plea bargaining", is an essential component of the administration of justice. Properly administered, it is to be encouraged. If every criminal charge were subjected to a full-scale trial, the States and the Federal Government would need to multiply by many times the number of judges and court facilities.

Disposition of charges after plea discussions is not only an essential part of the process, but a highly desirable part for many reasons. It leads to prompt and largely final disposition of most criminal cases; it avoids much of the corrosive impact of enforced idleness during pre-trial confinement for those who are denied release pending trial; it protects the public from those accused persons who are prone to continue criminal conduct even while on pretrial release; and, by shortening the time between charge and disposition, it enhances whatever may be the rehabilitative prospects of the guilty when they are ultimately imprisoned.

However, all of these considerations presuppose fairness in securing agreement between an accused and a prosecutor. It is now clear, for example, that the accused pleading guilty must be counseled, absent a waiver. *Moore v. Michigan*, 355 U.S. 155 (1957). Fed. Rule Crim.Proc. 11, governing pleas in federal courts, now makes clear that the sentencing judge must develop, *on the record*, the factual basis for the plea, as, for example, by having the accused describe the conduct that gave rise to the charge. The plea must, of course, be voluntary and knowing and if it was induced by promises, the essence of those promises must in some way be made known. There is, of course, no absolute right to have a guilty plea accepted. A court may reject a plea in exercise of sound judicial discretion.

This phase of the process of criminal justice, and the adjudicative element inherent in accepting a plea of guilty, must be attended by safeguards to insure the defendant what is reasonably due in the circumstances. Those circumstances will vary, but a constant factor is that when a plea rests in any significant degree on a promise or agreement of the prosecutor, so that it can be said to be part of the inducement or consideration, such promise must be fulfilled.

On this record, petitioner "bargained" and negotiated for a particular plea in order to secure dismissal of more serious charges, but also on condition that no sentence recommendation would be made by the prosecutor. It is now conceded that the promise to abstain from a recommendation was made, and at this stage the prosecution is not in a good position to argue that its inadvertent breach of agreement is immaterial. The staff lawyers in a prosecutor's office have the burden of "letting the left hand know what the right hand is doing" or has done. That the breach of agreement was inadvertent does not lessen its impact.

We need not reach the question whether the sentencing judge would or would not have been influenced had he known all the details of the negotiations for the plea. He stated that the prosecutor's recommendation did not influence him and we have no reason to doubt that. Nevertheless, we conclude that the interests of justice and appropriate recognition of the duties of the prosecution in relation to promises made in the negotiation of pleas of guilty will be best served by remanding the case to the state courts for further consideration. The ultimate relief to which petitioner is entitled we leave to the discretion of the state court, which is in a better position to decide whether the circumstances of this case require only that there be specific performance of the agreement on the plea, in which case petitioner should be resentenced by a different judge, or whether, in the view of the state court, the circumstances require granting the relief sought by petitioner, i.e., the opportunity to withdraw his plea of guilty.[2] We emphasize that this is in no sense to question the fairness of the sentencing judge; the fault here rests on the prosecutor, not on the sentencing judge.

The judgment is vacated and the case is remanded for reconsideration not inconsistent with this opinion.

---

[2] If the state court decides to allow withdrawal of the plea, the petitioner will, of course, plead anew to the original charge on two felony counts.

Mr. Justice Douglas, concurring.

* * * *

I join the opinion of the Court and favor a constitutional rule for this as well as for other pending or oncoming cases. Where the "plea bargain" is not kept by the prosecutor, the sentence must be vacated and the state court will decide in light of the circumstances of each case whether due process requires (a) that there be specific performance of the plea bargain or (b) that the defendant be given the option to go to trial on the original charges. One alternative may do justice in one case, and the other in a different case. In choosing a remedy, however, a court ought to accord a defendant's preference considerable, if not controlling, weight inasmuch as the fundamental rights flouted by a prosecutor's breach of a plea bargain are those of the defendant, not of the State.

Notes from Pearl:

1. Should a court treat a plea agreement as an ordinary *contract*?

In *U.S. v. Lovell*, 81 F.3d 58 (7th Cir.1996), the court stated: "For the most part, general contract principles apply to the interpretation of plea agreements. As with contracts, the terms of the agreement can create binding promises on the parties, including the government."

In *In re Grand Jury Witness Ralph Altro*, 180 F.3d 372 (2nd Cir. 1999), Altro signed a plea agreement in which he agreed to plead guilty to postal burglary. The agreement contained an "integration clause," stating: "No additional understandings, promises, or conditions have been entered into other than those set forth in this Agreement." Seven months after the court accepted Altro's guilty plea, the Government subpoenaed him to testify before a grand jury regarding other persons who had been involved in the postal burglary. Altro refused. While no language in the plea agreement provided that Altro would be exempt from so testifying, Altro claimed that he understood the agreement to end his involvement in litigation over the burglary, and therefore the agreement *implicitly* exempted him. The trial court held him in contempt, and the appellate court affirmed: "In light of the express integration clause quoted above, a strict application of the parol evidence rule would preclude us from considering evidence of such an implicit understanding."

However, in *U.S. v. Ready*, 82 F.3d 551 (2nd Cir.1996), the court narrowly construed a provision in a plea agreement waiving Ready's right to appeal:

> We construe a criminal defendant's waiver of appellate rights narrowly. Applying that rule to this case, we conclude that the waiver in Ready's Maryland plea agreement did not include his right to appeal an illegally imposed restitution penalty.

> Plea agreements are construed according to contract law principles. But of course, different types of contracts are subjected to different interpretive rules and background understandings. See, e.g., *Farnsworth on Contracts* § 4.26 at 313–15 (2d ed. 1990) (in interpreting "standardized agreements," courts use several "judicial techniques" which sometimes have the effect of relieving the non-drafting party of its contractual

obligations). Plea agreements are unique contracts in which special due process concerns for fairness and the adequacy of procedural safeguards obtain. See Frank H. Easterbrook, *Plea Bargaining as Compromise*, 101 Yale L.J. 1969, 1974–75 (1992) ("The analogy between plea bargains and contracts is far from perfect. Plea bargains are preferable to mandatory litigation — not because the analogy to contract is overpowering, but because compromise is better than conflict."); Robert E. Scott & William J. Stuntz, *Plea Bargaining as Contract*, 101 Yale L.J. 1909, 1930 (1992).

In interpreting plea agreements, courts have necessarily drawn on the most relevant body of developed rules and principles of private law, those pertaining to the formation and interpretation of commercial contracts. But the courts have recognized that those rules have to be applied to plea agreements with two things in mind which may require their tempering in particular cases. First, the defendant's underlying "contract" right is constitutionally based and therefore reflects concerns that differ fundamentally from and run wider than those of commercial contract law. Second, with respect to federal prosecutions, the courts' concerns run even wider than protection of the defendant's individual constitutional rights — to concerns for the honor of the government, public confidence in the fair administration of justice, and the effective administration of justice in a federal scheme of government.

Several rules of interpretation, consistent with general contract law principles, are suited to the delicate private and public interests that are implicated in plea agreements. First, courts construe plea agreements strictly against the Government. This is done for a variety of reasons, including the fact that the Government is usually the party that drafts the agreement, and the fact that the Government ordinarily has certain awesome advantages in bargaining power.

Second, we construe the agreement against a general background understanding of legality. That is, we presume that both parties to the plea agreements contemplated that all promises made were legal, and that the non-contracting "party" who implements the agreement (the district judge) will act legally in executing the agreement. Since a general rule of construction presumes the legality and enforceability of contracts, 6A A. Corbin, *Contracts* §§ 1499, 1533 (1962), ambiguously worded contracts should not be interpreted to render them illegal and unenforceable where the wording lends itself to a logically acceptable construction that renders them legal and enforceable.

Finally, courts may apply general fairness principles to invalidate particular terms of a plea agreement. Plea agreements are subject to the public policy constraints that bear upon the enforcement of other kinds of contracts. See Restatement (Second) of Contracts, § 178 (1981) ("A promise or other term of an agreement is unenforceable on grounds of public policy if legislation provides that it is unenforceable or the interest in its enforcement is clearly outweighed in the circumstances by a public policy against the enforcement of such terms.").

In *People v. Rhoden*, 75 Cal.App.4th 1346 (1999), after the parties entered into a plea agreement, but before the defendant entered her guilty plea, the court issued a ruling favorable to the prosecution on an evidence issue. The prosecutor then withdrew from the plea agreement, over defendant's objection. A jury convicted her, and the appellate court affirmed. The court noted that "the minority view" followed by some courts binds the parties to a plea bargain once it is made, but the court declined to follow those cases:

> Some courts have analogized plea bargains to contracts under civil law. In *State v. Collins* (1980) 300 N.C. 142, the court stated:
>
>> When viewed in light of the analogous law of contracts, it is clear that plea agreements normally arise in the form of unilateral contracts. The consideration given for the prosecutor's promise is not defendant's corresponding promise to plead guilty, but rather is defendant's actual performance by so pleading. Thus, the prosecutor agrees to perform if and when defendant performs but has no right to compel defendant's performance. Similarly, the prosecutor may rescind his offer of a proposed plea arrangement before defendant consummates the contract by pleading guilty or takes other action constituting detrimental reliance upon the agreement.
>
> In *Reed v. Becka* (1999) 333 S.C. 676, the court reasoned:
>
>> A plea agreement is only an "offer" until the defendant enters a court-approved guilty plea. A defendant accepts the 'offer' by pleading guilty. Thus, until formal acceptance of the plea by the court has occurred, the plea binds no one, not the defendant, the State, or the court.
>
> In *United States v. Ocanas* (5th Cir.1980) 628 F.2d 353, the court applied similar reasoning:
>
>> The realization of whatever expectations the prosecutor and defendant have as a result of their bargain depends entirely on the approval of the trial court. Surely neither party contemplates any benefit from the agreement unless and until the trial judge approves the bargain and accepts the guilty plea. Neither party is justified in relying substantially on the bargain until the trial court approves it. We are therefore reluctant to bind them to the agreement until that time. As a general rule, then we think that either party should be entitled to modify its position and even withdraw its consent to the bargain until the plea is tendered and the bargain as it then exists is accepted by the court."
>
> Although we do not believe that plea bargains in criminal cases can be governed by civil contract law principles, we find these cases persuasive and adopt the majority view that a prosecutor may withdraw from a plea bargain before a defendant pleads guilty or otherwise detrimentally relies on that bargain.

2. If a judge finds that *part* of a plea agreement is invalid (because it is against public policy), may he *strike that part and enforce the remainder* of the agreement, or is he confined to *rejecting the entire* agreement and sending the parties back to the bargaining table (or to trial)? In *U.S. v. Perez*, 46 F.Supp.2d 59 (D.Mass.1999), the court held that sometimes it may strike part of the agreement:

The government argues that I cannot pick and choose among provisions in the agreement. It points to Rule 11(e)(2), which gives courts the authority to accept or reject plea agreements under subdivision (e)(1)(A) or (C), but does not mention any such authority to accept or reject pleas under subdivision (e)(1)(B). It claims that it follows that I may not "interfere with such plea agreements" at all — either by striking a term or by rejecting the agreement as a whole.

While I accept that I do not have the general authority to alter the terms of the agreement, I hold that I do have the authority to strike specific terms that would make an otherwise acceptable agreement fundamentally unjust and contrary to public policy. I follow the court in *United States v. Ready*, 82 F.3d 551 (2d Cir.1996), which held that "courts may apply general fairness principles to invalidate particular terms of a plea agreement." *Id.* at 559.

The *Ready* court grounded its authority to strike or invalidate particular terms of a plea agreement on contract principles. It relied on both the Restatement (Second) of Contracts, § 178 (1981) ("A promise or other term of an agreement is unenforceable on grounds of public policy if the interest in its enforcement is clearly outweighed in the circumstances by a public policy against the enforcement of such terms.").

This use of contract law in interpreting plea bargains is clearly consistent with First Circuit practice. At the same time, it is clear that a plea agreement is a unique kind of contract.

While such agreements serve an important role in the efficient operation of the criminal justice system, they also effect a waiver of defendant's rights: "However important plea bargaining may be in the administration of criminal justice, our opinions have established that a guilty plea is a serious and sobering occasion inasmuch as it constitutes a waiver of the fundamental rights to a jury trial, to confront one's accusers, to present witnesses in one's defense, to remain silent, and to be convicted [only] by proof beyond all reasonable doubt." *Santobello v. New York*, 404 U.S. 257, 264 (1971) (Douglas, J., concurring).

Because of the serious nature of the rights being waived in a plea, courts must adopt "judicial safeguards to protect the integrity of a plea agreement." *Id.*

I hold that it is an appropriate use of contract law, in an effort to safeguard the integrity of a plea agreement, to strike a clause from the agreement on the ground that it is contrary to public policy. Indeed, in my judgment, my choice to strike just the single clause is more fair, and no more in conflict with Rule 11(e), than the decisions of the *Johnson* and *Raynor* courts to reject altogether plea bargains conditioned with appeals waivers. See also *United States v. Melancon*, 972 F.2d 566, 568 (5th Cir.1992) (holding that courts have discretion to accept appeal waivers, but also holding "that a district court's refusal to accept such a waiver [for policy reasons] likewise would be within its discretion.").

3. Suppose defense counsel *fails to tell* defendant about a plea offer made by the prosecutor? Ineffective assistance of counsel, held the court in *Ex Parte Lemke*, 13

S.W.3d 791 (Tex. 2000).

BLACKLEDGE v. ALLISON
United States Supreme Court
431 U.S. 63 (1977)

Mr. Justice Stewart delivered the opinion of the Court.

Allison was indicted by a North Carolina grand jury for breaking and entering, attempted safe robbery, and possession of burglary tools. At his arraignment, where he was represented by court-appointed counsel, he initially pleaded not guilty. But after learning that his codefendant planned to plead guilty, he entered a guilty plea to a single count of attempted safe robbery, for which the minimum prison sentence was 10 years and the maximum was life. N.C.Gen.Stat. § 14-89.1 (1969).

In accord with the procedure for taking guilty pleas then in effect in North Carolina, the judge in open court read from a printed form 13 questions, generally concerning the defendant's understanding of the charge, its consequences, and the voluntariness of his plea. Allison answered "yes" or "no" to each question, and the court clerk transcribed those responses on a copy of the form, which Allison signed. So far as the record shows, there was no questioning beyond this routine; no inquiry was made of either defense counsel or prosecutor. Two questions from the form are of particular relevance to the issues before us: Question No. 8 "Do you understand that upon your plea of guilty you could be imprisoned for as much as minimum of 10 years to life?" to which Allison answered "Yes"; and Question No. 11 "Has the Solicitor, or your lawyer, or any policeman, law officer or anyone else made any promises or threat to you to influence you to plead guilty in this case?" to which Allison answered "No."

The trial judge then accepted the plea by signing his name at the bottom of the form under a text entitled "Adjudication," which recited the three charges for which Allison had been indicted, that he had been fully advised of his rights, was in fact guilty, and pleaded guilty to attempted safe robbery "freely, understandingly and voluntarily," with full awareness of the consequences, and "without undue, compulsion, duress, or promise of leniency."[1] Three days later, at a sentencing hearing, of

---

[1] The only record of the proceeding consists, therefore, of the executed form which reads as follows:

"The Defendant, being first duly sworn, makes the following answers to the questions asked by the Presiding Judge:

1. Are you able to hear and understand my statements and questions? Answer: Yes
2. Are you now under the influence of any alcohol, drugs, narcotics, medicines, or other pills? Answer: No
3. Do you understand that you are charged with the felony of Attempted Safe Cracking? Answer: Yes
4. Has the charge been explained to you, and are you ready for trial? Answer: Yes
5. Do you understand that you have the right to plead not guilty and to be tried by a Jury? Answer: Yes
6. How do you plead to the charge of Attempted Safe Cracking Guilty, not Guilty, or nolo contendere? Answer: Guilty
7. Are you in fact guilty? Answer: Yes
8. Do you understand that upon your plea of guilty you could be imprisoned for as much as minimum of 10 years to life? Answer: Yes
9. Have you had time to subpoena witnesses wanted by you? Answer: Yes
10. Have you had time to talk and confer with and have you conferred with your lawyer about this

which there is no record whatsoever, Allison was sentenced to 17–21 years in prison.

After unsuccessfully exhausting a state collateral remedy, Allison filed a pro se petition in a Federal District Court seeking a writ of habeas corpus. The petition alleged:

> His guilty plea was induced by an unkept promise, and therefore was not the free and willing choice of the petitioner, and should be set aside by this Court. An unkept bargain which has induced a guilty plea is grounds for relief. *Santobello v. New York*, 404 U.S. 257 (1971).

The petition went on to explain and support this allegation as follows:

> The petitioner was led to believe and did believe, by Mr. Pickard (Allison's attorney), that he (Mr. N. Glenn Pickard) had talked the case over with the Solicitor and the Judge, and that if the petitioner would plead guilty, that he would only get a 10 year sentence of penal servitude. This conversation, where the petitioner was assured that if he pleaded guilty, he would only get ten years was witnessed by another party other than the petitioner and counsel. The petitioner believing that he was only going to get a ten year active sentence, allowed himself to be pled guilty to the charge of attempted safe robbery, and was shocked by the Court with a 17–21 year sentence. The petitioner was promised by his Attorney, who had consulted presumably with the Judge and Solicitor, that he was only going

---

case, and are you satisfied with his services? Answer: Yes
11. Has the Solicitor, or your lawyer, or any policeman, law officer or anyone else made any promises or threat to you to influence you to plead guilty in this case? Answer: No
12. Do you now freely, understandingly and voluntarily authorize and instruct your lawyer to enter on your behalf a plea of guilty? Answer: Yes
13. Do you have any questions or any statement to make about what I have just said to you? Answer: No

I have read or heard read all of the above questions and answers and understand them, and the answers shown are the ones I gave in open Court, and they are true and correct.

Gary Darrell Allison, Defendant."

"The undersigned Presiding Judge hereby finds and adjudges:

I. That the defendant, Gary Darrell Allison, was sworn in open Court and the questions were asked him as set forth in the Transcript of Plea by the undersigned Judge, and the answers given thereto by said defendant are as set forth therein.

II. That this defendant, was represented by attorney, N. Glenn Pickard, who was court appointed; and the defendant through his attorney, in open Court, pleaded guilty to Attempted Safe Cracking as charged in the bill of indictment, of Breaking & Entering, Safe Burglary & Possession of Burglary Tools and in open Court, under oath further informs the Court that:
1. He is and has been fully advised of his rights and the charges against him;
2. He is and has been fully advised of the maximum punishment for said offenses charged, and for the offenses to which he pleads guilty;
3. He is guilty of the offenses to which he pleads guilty;
4. He authorizes his attorney to enter a plea of guilty to said charges;
5. He has had ample time to confer with his attorney, and to subpoena witnesses desired by him;
6. He is ready for trial;
7. He is satisfied with the counsel and services of his attorney;

And after further examination by the Court, the Court ascertains, determines and adjudges, that the plea of guilty, by the defendant is freely, understandingly and voluntarily made, without undue influence, compulsion or duress, and without promise of leniency. It is, therefore, Ordered that his plea of guilty be entered in the record, and that the Transcript of Plea and Adjudication be filed and recorded. This 24th day of January, 1972. Marvin Blount, Jr., Judge Presiding."

to get a ten year sentence, and therefore because of this unkept bargain, he is entitled to relief in this Court. The petitioner is aware of the fact that he was questioned by the trial Judge prior to sentencing, but as he thought he was only going to get ten years, and had been instructed to answer the questions, so that the Court would accept the guilty plea, this fact does not preclude him from raising this matter especially since he was not given the promised sentence by the Court. The fact that the Judge said that he could get more, did not affect the belief of the petitioner, that he was only going to get a ten year sentence.

The petitioner here, Warden Blackledge, filed a motion to dismiss and attached to it the "transcript" of the plea hearing, consisting of nothing more than the printed form filled in by the clerk and signed by Allison and the state-court judge. The motion contended that the form conclusively showed that Allison had chosen to plead guilty knowingly, voluntarily, and with full awareness of the consequences. The Federal District Court agreed that the printed form "conclusively shows that Allison was carefully examined by the Court before the plea was accepted. Therefore, it must stand." Construing Allison's petition as alleging merely that his lawyer's prediction of the severity of the sentence turned out to be inaccurate, the District Court found no basis for relief and, accordingly, dismissed the petition. * * * *

The Court of Appeals for the Fourth Circuit reversed. It held that Allison's allegation of a broken promise, as amplified by the explanation that his lawyer instructed him to deny the existence of any promises, was not foreclosed by his responses to the form questions at the state guilty-plea proceeding. The appellate court reasoned that when a pro se, indigent prisoner makes allegations that, if proved, would entitle him to habeas corpus relief, he should not be required to prove his allegations in advance of an evidentiary hearing, at least in the absence of counter affidavits conclusively proving their falsity. The case was therefore remanded for an evidentiary hearing. * * * *

II

Whatever might be the situation in an ideal world, the fact is that the guilty plea and the often concomitant plea bargain are important components of this country's criminal justice system. Properly administered, they can benefit all concerned. The defendant avoids extended pretrial incarceration and the anxieties and uncertainties of a trial; he gains a speedy disposition of his case, the chance to acknowledge his guilt, and a prompt start in realizing whatever potential there may be for rehabilitation. Judges and prosecutors conserve vital and scarce resources. The public is protected from the risks posed by those charged with criminal offenses who are at large on bail while awaiting completion of criminal proceedings. * * * *

These advantages can be secured, however, only if dispositions by guilty plea are accorded a great measure of finality. To allow indiscriminate hearings in federal postconviction proceedings, whether for federal prisoners under 28 U.S.C. § 2255 or state prisoners under 28 U.S.C. §§ 2241–2254, would eliminate the chief virtues of the plea system speed, economy, and finality. And there is reason for concern about that prospect. More often than not, a prisoner has everything to gain and nothing to lose from filing a collateral attack upon his guilty plea. If he succeeds in vacating the judgment of conviction, retrial may be difficult. If he convinces a court that his plea was induced by an advantageous plea agreement that was violated, he may obtain the benefit of its terms. A collateral attack may also be inspired by "a mere desire to be freed temporarily from the confines of the prison." *Price v. Johnston*, 334 U.S. 266, 284–285.

Yet arrayed against the interest in finality is the very purpose of the writ of habeas corpus to safeguard a person's freedom from detention in violation of constitutional guarantees. "The writ of habeas corpus has played a great role in the history of human freedom. It has been the judicial method of lifting undue restraints upon personal liberty." *Price v. Johnston, supra,* 334 U.S. 266, at 269. And a prisoner in custody after pleading guilty, no less than one tried and convicted by a jury, is entitled to avail himself of the writ in challenging the constitutionality of his custody. * * * *

In administering the writ of habeas corpus and its § 2255 counterpart, the federal courts cannot fairly adopt a per se rule excluding all possibility that a defendant's representations at the time his guilty plea was accepted were so much the product of such factors as misunderstanding, duress, or misrepresentation by others as to make the guilty plea a constitutionally inadequate basis for imprisonment.[6]

III

The allegations in this case were not in themselves so vague or conclusory, as to warrant dismissal for that reason alone. Allison alleged as a ground for relief that his plea was induced by an unkept promise.[8] But he did not stop there. He proceeded to elaborate upon this claim with specific factual allegations. The petition indicated exactly what the terms of the promise were; when, where, and by whom the promise had been made; and the identity of one witness to its communication. The critical question is whether these allegations, when viewed against the record of the plea hearing, were so palpably incredible, so patently frivolous or false, as to warrant summary dismissal. In the light of the nature of the record of the proceeding at which the guilty plea was accepted, and of the ambiguous status of the process of plea bargaining at the time the guilty plea was made, we conclude that Allison's petition should not have been summarily dismissed.

Only recently has plea bargaining become a visible practice accepted as a legitimate component in the administration of criminal justice. For decades, it was a *sub rosa* process shrouded in secrecy and deliberately concealed by participating defendants, defense lawyers, prosecutors, and even judges. * * * * Indeed, it was not until our decision in *Santobello v. New York* that lingering doubts about the legitimacy of the practice were finally dispelled.

---

[6] An analogy is to be found in the law of contracts. The parol evidence rule has as its very purpose the exclusion of evidence designed to repudiate provisions in a written integration of contractual terms. Yet even a written contractual provision declaring that the contract contains the complete agreement of the parties, and that no antecedent or extrinsic representations exist, does not conclusively bar subsequent proof that such additional agreements exist and should be given force. The provision denying the existence of such agreements, of course, carries great weight, but it can be set aside by a court on the grounds of fraud, mistake, duress, "or on some ground that is sufficient for setting aside other contracts." 3 A. Corbin, *Contracts* § 578 (2d ed. 1960).

[8] Allison's petition stated that his lawyer, "who had consulted presumably with the Judge and Solicitor," had promised that the maximum sentence to be imposed was 10 years. This allegation, in light of the other circumstances of this case, raised the serious constitutional question whether his guilty plea was knowingly and voluntarily made.

Allison was arraigned a mere 37 days after the *Santobello* decision was announced, under a North Carolina procedure that had not been modified in light of *Santobello* or earlier decisions of this Court * * * recognizing the process of plea bargaining. That procedure itself reflected the atmosphere of secrecy which then characterized plea bargaining generally. No transcript of the proceeding was made. The only record was a standard printed form. There is no way of knowing whether the trial judge in any way deviated from or supplemented the text of the form. The record is silent as to what statements Allison, his lawyer, or the prosecutor might have made regarding promised sentencing concessions. And there is no record at all of the sentencing hearing three days later, at which one of the participants might well have made a statement shedding light upon the veracity of the allegations Allison later advanced.

The litany of form questions followed by the trial judge at arraignment nowhere indicated to Allison (or indeed to the lawyers involved) that plea bargaining was a legitimate practice that could be freely disclosed in open court. Neither lawyer was asked to disclose any agreement that had been reached, or sentencing recommendation that had been promised. The process thus did nothing to dispel a defendant's relief that any bargain struck must remain concealed, a belief here allegedly reinforced by the admonition of Allison's lawyer himself that disclosure could jeopardize the agreement. Rather than challenging respondent's counsel's contention at oral argument in this Court that "at that time in North Carolina plea bargains were never disclosed in response to such a question on such a form," counsel for the petitioners conceded at oral argument that "that form was a minimum inquiry."

Although logically the general inquiry should elicit information about plea bargaining, it seldom has in the past. Particularly if, as Allison alleged, he was advised by counsel to conceal any plea bargain, his denial that any promises had been made might have been a courtroom ritual more sham than real. We thus cannot conclude that the allegations in Allison's habeas corpus petition, when measured against the "record" of the arraignment, were so "patently false or frivolous" as to warrant summary dismissal. * * * *

North Carolina has recently undertaken major revisions of its plea-bargaining procedures in part to prevent the very kind of problem now before us.[17] Plea bargaining is expressly legitimate. N.C.Gen.Stat. § 15A- 1021 (1975). The judge is directed to advise the defendant that courts have approved plea bargaining and he may thus admit to any promises without fear of jeopardizing an advantageous agreement or prejudicing himself in the judge's eyes. Specific inquiry about whether a plea bargain has been struck is then made not only of the defendant, but also of his counsel and the prosecutor. Finally, the entire proceeding is to be transcribed verbatim.

Had these commendable procedures been followed in the present case, Allison's petition would have been cast in a very different light. The careful explication of the legitimacy of plea bargaining, the questioning of both lawyers, and the verbatim

---

[17] In 1973, the North Carolina Legislature enacted a comprehensive set of procedures governing disposition by guilty plea and plea arrangement, modeled after the ALI Model Code of Pre-Arraignment Procedure, Art. 350 (Tent. Draft No. 5, 1972). One of the stated purposes of the reform was to allow "defendants to tell the truth in plea proceedings. They should not be expected to go before judges after plea negotiations and lie by saying no promises or agreements were made."

record of their answers at the guilty-plea proceedings would almost surely have shown whether any bargain did exist and, if so, insured that it was not ignored.[19] But the salutary reforms recently implemented by North Carolina highlight even more sharply the deficiencies in the record before the District Court in the present case.[20]

It may turn out upon remand that a full evidentiary hearing is not required. But Allison is entitled to careful consideration and plenary processing of his claim, including full opportunity for presentation of the relevant facts. Upon that understanding, the judgment of the Court of Appeals is affirmed.

Notes from Pearl:

1. In *U.S. v. Mandujano* [in Chapter 5, "The Grand Jury"], the Court took a pretty tough stand against perjury. In *Blackledge v. Allison*, Allison *lied* in his answer to Question 11, but the Court ignored this. What is the difference?

2. In *U.S. v. Robertson*, 29 F.Supp.2d 567 (D.Minn. 1998), Robertson was indicted on firearms and robbery charges, along with four other defendants who were allegedly involved in several jewelry store robberies (led by defendant Vong). All defendants except Vong and Robertson entered into plea bargains with the government, agreeing to "cooperate" (i.e., to testify for the Government against other defendants) in return for reduced sentences of between 60 and 90 months imprisonment. Robertson rejected a similar plea offer. Robertson's counsel (Mr. Strauss) told the court:

> Well, I want the Eighth Circuit to know, and maybe even the United States Supreme Court to know, that any deal of a client of mine that includes working for the Government is not representing the people. My client has instructed me specifically to turn down all plea agreements. So, with respect to my client turning down a plea agreement, I quite frankly am philosophically opposed to working for the Government, and when I had practiced before your Honor even in the times when I worked as a young lawyer under your tutelage, Your Honor, my goal was to represent people and not to represent the Government.

At trial, the other three defendants testified for the government, and both Vong and Robertson were convicted by the jury. At Robertson's sentencing hearing, the court noted that, under Federal Sentencing Guidelines, it would have "no choice but to sentence Robertson to a term of imprisonment exceeding 90 years." But the court then — "on its own motion" — vacated the jury's verdict as to Robertson and

---

[19] A principal purpose of the North Carolina statutory reforms was to permit quick disposition of baseless collateral attacks. Indeed, a petitioner challenging a plea given pursuant to procedures like those now mandated in North Carolina will necessarily be asserting that not only his own transcribed responses, but those given by two lawyers, were untruthful. Especially as it becomes routine for prosecutors and defense lawyers to acknowledge that plea bargains have been made, such a contention will entitle a petitioner to an evidentiary hearing only in the most extraordinary circumstances.

[20] This is not to suggest that a plea of guilty entered pursuant to procedures like those in effect at Allison's arraignment is necessarily vulnerable to collateral attack. It is simply to say that procedures like those now in effect in North Carolina serve (1) to prevent the occurrence of constitutional errors in the arraignment process, and (2) to discourage the filing of baseless petitions for habeas corpus and facilitate speedy but fair disposition of those that are filed. * * * *

ordered a new trial, because Robertson's counsel was ineffective in refusing to bargain with the Government:

> Counsel's comments regarding cooperation agreements is cause for concern as it appears that Robertson was never counseled by Mr. Strauss to accept any agreement offered by the Government, the result of which would take approximately 80 years off of his potential sentence. Unfortunately, matters did not get any better for Robertson during trial. * * * *

> Given the overwhelming evidence presented against Robertson at trial, including his "confession" and the testimony of his co-defendants, and the potential penalties involved, Mr. Strauss provided his client ineffective assistance of counsel by not advising his client to accept any of the plea negotiations offered by the Government.

> While Mr. Strauss may be philosophically opposed to cooperation agreements, it is his absolute duty as a criminal defense attorney to put his client's interests before his own. Mr. Strauss is not facing 90 years in prison, his client is, and this Court is convinced beyond doubt that this is so because of the counsel he received prior, during and after trial from Mr. Strauss.

STATE v. SOLANO

Arizona Supreme Court
150 Ariz. 398, 724 P.2d 17 (1986)

CAMERON, JUSTICE.

This is a review of a decision and opinion of the court of appeals which vacated defendants' pleas of guilty and sentences and remanded the matters for a new trial.

The sole issue on review is whether "package deal" plea agreements, offered to multiple defendants, each contingent upon the acceptance of all co-defendant's plea agreements, violate either Rule 17.4 of the Arizona Rules of Criminal Procedure or public policy.

On 6 September 1983, a search warrant was executed on a Scottsdale home and 1382 grams of 80 to 95 percent pure cocaine plus two small bags of marijuana were seized. Three people, Richard Solano, Vickie Hurst and Guy Lindstrom, were present in the house and were arrested. Sometime after their arrest, Richard Solano and Vickie Hurst were married. By indictment, a grand jury charged Richard Solano, Vickie Hurst-Solano and Guy Lindstrom each with one count of possession of a narcotic drug for sale with a value over $250, a class 2 felony, and one count of possession of marijuana, a class 6 felony.

Prior to trial, each defendant negotiated a plea agreement. These plea agreements were "package deals" in that the state conditioned each defendant's plea on the court's acceptance of the pleas from the other two defendants. Richard Solano's plea agreement provided that he would plead guilty to possession of cocaine for sale, a class 2 felony (presumptive sentence of 7 years, minimum sentence of 5.25 years, maximum sentence 14 years with probation not available). A.R.S. §§ 13–701, 13–702. He was to receive the minimum sentence of five and one quarter years but was not to be eligible for parole for five years. The possession of marijuana count was to be dismissed. Both Vickie Hurst-Solano and Guy Lindstrom agreed to enter an *Alford* plea, *North Carolina v. Alford*, 400 U.S. 25 (1970),* to the lesser charge of possession of cocaine, a class 4 felony (presumptive sentence 4 years, minimum sentence 2 years, maximum sentence 5 years, probation available). A.R.S. §§ 13–701, 13–702. They were each to be sentenced to the maximum sentence of five years. The possession of marijuana count was to be dismissed.

This "package deal" was presented to the trial court at a change of plea hearing. The court expressed concern over the contingent nature of the pleas and therefore deferred acceptance until review of the presentence reports. At the later hearing, the following transpired:

The Court: Time for sentencing and acceptance of the plea in Vickie K. Hurst-Solano, Guy Shane Lindstrom and Richard James Solano, CR-139393.

Mr. Donofrio: Charles Donofrio appearing on behalf of the State, Your Honor.

Mr. Anderson: My name is Ross Anderson, I'm here for Richard Solano and Vickie Solano. I'm retained.

Mr. Karasek: David Karasek appearing for Guy Shane Lindstrom.

The Court: Have you all had a chance to review the presentence report and notice that the presentence officer disagrees rather substantially with the stipulated sentence in the lesser two cases?

Mr. Donofrio: Yes, Your Honor.

The Court: I will tell you that that concerns me because the investigator here seems to feel that the participation of these two defendants, Lindstrom and Mrs. Solano, is so minimal that five year prison time is not justified.

Mr. Donofrio: Your Honor, that's not the State's position.

The Court: Well, I understand.

Mr. Donofrio: The State's position is that the quantity of the drugs was so substantial to call for a mandatory prison term. If these individuals were to go to trial and were convicted by a jury, they would have to serve five years flat prison time. We have not only reduced this charge from a class 2 to a class 4, we have also given them the opportunity to have soft time and they would be eligible for work furlough as soon as they leave the Alhambra Center, and as far as Hurst is concerned, as soon as she is through screening at Perryville, they would be eligible immediately for work furlough release of all types that are available to the Department of

---

* Ed.: In *Alford*, defendant was charged with first degree murder, but wanted to plead guilty to second degree murder in order to avoid a possible death penalty. But at the hearing where defendant pleaded guilty, he insisted that he was innocent. The trial court heard 3 witnesses give evidence that implicated defendant, and then accepted his plea. The Supreme Court upheld the conviction: "In view of the strong factual basis for the plea demonstrated by the State and Alford's clearly expressed desire to enter it despite his professed belief in his innocence, we hold that the trial judge did not commit constitutional error in accepting it." 400 U.S. at 38.

In *U.S. v. Cox*, 923 F.2d 519 (7th Cir.1991), the court held that even if there is a factual basis for the plea, the trial court has the discretion to *reject* the guilty plea where the defendant refuses to admit guilt, because "the public might well not understand or accept the fact that a defendant who denied his guilt was nonetheless placed in a position of pleading guilty and going to jail."

Corrections. Mr. Solano is the only one that is going to come under the heavy hand of the Department of Corrections.

Mr. Donofrio: I believe that it's because of the amount of drugs, the amount that was given by the presentence report is $140,000 worth of cocaine, is a bare minimum of the value of that cocaine. Taking it just at a hundred dollars a gram, it's $138,000 that was 85 to 100 percent pure. There was 490 grams of 100 percent pure cocaine. There were 892 grams of 85 to 100 percent pure cocaine. Being cut just once, would double that, and I believe that the Court has knowledge that oftentimes is stepped on many times. We have an estimate that that was worth at least a half million dollars on the street. The State's position further being that all three of these individuals are living in a house in Scottsdale at a very nice neighborhood, all unemployed, not working, all sharing in the proceeds of that drug.

Mr. Anderson responded by admitting that "Mr. Donofrio has been most generous under the circumstances of the plea agreement" but that the court should "try to help us convince Mr. Donofrio and the County Attorney" that probation was better for Hurst-Solano and Lindstrom.

After discussing the mandatory nature of the sentencing process, the court declined to interfere with the plea bargain stating:

The Court: I'm powerless.

The court then asked Richard Solano if he had anything to say before sentencing.

Mr. Solano: Yes, sir. The one most important thing is that I was a friend of another culprit in this. The major culprit, Mr. Zuber, is not here. He's not present. He ran and I just want you to know that I'm not the one that was the main person. I admit my involvement and I'm ready to serve my time, do what I have to do, but I want you to know that I was not the main person and this is not from — I didn't start this thing. I was wrapped up in it. I got involved with it and I know that it's not the right thing at all.

The Court: How tragic you got your wife into it.

Mr. Solano: That's the most important thing I want to say.

The Court: In a matter of a few weeks time she goes from a clean record to a felon in prison. Thanks to you.

Mr. Solano: The thing I want to say about her is that she had absolutely nothing to do with it because she was there with me, for me, she had absolutely nothing to do with that. That's all I can tell you.

The Court: A fingerprint on a bag of cocaine?

Mr. Solano: I know, but she was not involved with it, but that's the reason why we're signing this and that's the reason why we can't fight it.

The Court: Okay.

The trial judge then sentenced the three defendants in conformity with the plea agreements.

The Solanos filed separate appeals that were consolidated in the court of appeals. The court of appeals vacated the Solanos' convictions and sentences, finding that such contingent plea agreements violated both Rule 17.4, Ariz.R.Crim.P., 17 A.R.S. and public policy. We granted the state's petition for review because we disagree with the majority decision of the court of appeals.

The Rules of Criminal Procedure recognize validly negotiated plea agreements as an essential part of the criminal justice system and specifically provide for their existence. Rule 17.4, Ariz.R.Crim.P., 17 A.R.S. Rule 17.4(a) provides:

> a. *Plea Negotiations.* The parties may negotiate concerning, and reach an agreement on, any aspect of the disposition of the case. The court shall not participate in any such negotiation.

The trial court, while not allowed to participate in these plea negotiations, must review any plea agreement reached to ensure that the public is protected and the ends of justice are being served. However, in reviewing a plea agreement, the trial court may only accept the terms in their entirety or reject them in their entirety.

The defendants argue that by making their plea agreements contingent on the acceptance of each co-defendant's plea agreement, the trial court was deprived of its ability to review each agreement individually for its acceptability. The court of appeals agreed, finding that such a contingent plea agreement "improperly places an impermissible burden on the exercise of the court's duties under rule 17.4 to review each plea agreement to see if the ends of justice and the protection of the public are being served, to reject any inappropriate sentence provision, to either accept or reject each plea individually, and to give each defendant an opportunity to withdraw his or her plea if the plea agreement or any provision of it is rejected by the court."

We agree with the court of appeals that Rule 17.4 requires that each defendant's plea agreement must be considered and accepted or rejected individually. It does not follow, however, that the court may not accept joint and contingent pleas. If the plea agreements are individually reviewed and found acceptable, the court may approve all of them. The court may also reject one or more of the plea agreements reached as part of the package deal. When the court rejects one of a series of contingent plea agreements, the rest must also fail. As Rule 17.4(a) provides, the state and defendant may negotiate on "any aspect of the disposition of the case." The power to negotiate under Rule 17.4(a) appears to us to be broad enough to allow such package or contingent plea agreements. We hold, therefore, that "package deal" plea agreements are not prohibited by Rule 17.4, Ariz.R.Crim.P., 17 A.R.S. or by U.S. and State Constitutions. *United States v. Nuckols*, 606 F.2d 566, 569 (5th Cir.1979). See also *United States v. Castello*, 724 F.2d 813, 815 (9th Cir.1984); *In re Ibarra*, 34 Cal.3d 277 (1983); *People v. Rodriguez*, 362 N.Y.S.2d 116 (1974); *State ex rel. White v. Gray*, 57 Wis.2d 17 (1973).

Defendants also contend that contingent or "package deal" plea agreements violate public policy. The court of appeals agreed, stating:

> We believe that "package-deal" plea bargains of the nature presently before us aggravate the disadvantages of the plea bargaining system to an unacceptable degree. Individual consideration and determination of a defendant's case is too greatly impeded. Furthermore, when family members or spouses are involved, the coercion of one in exchange for leniency

to another thwarts the required voluntariness of the plea.

The court of appeals then held that all "package deal" plea agreements are *per se* violative of public policy. We do not agree.

This type of plea agreement can be beneficial to both the state and to the defendant as well as to the public. The California Supreme Court has noted as to the state that:

> The "package-deal" may be a *valuable tool* to the prosecutor, who has a need for *all* defendants, or none, to plead guilty. The prosecutor may be properly interested in avoiding the time, delay and expense of trial of all the defendants. He is also placed in a difficult position should one defendant plead and another go to trial, because the defendant who pleads may become an adverse witness on behalf of his codefendant, free of jeopardy. Thus, the prosecutor's motivation for proposing a "package-deal" bargain may be strictly legitimate and free of extrinsic forces. [*In re Ibarra*, 34 Cal.3d 277, 289 n. 5 (1983), (emphasis in original).]

In the instant case, Richard Solano did not receive the maximum punishment provided for his crime and his wife was sentenced under a lesser charge. Vickie Hurst-Solano and Guy Lindstrom were allowed to plead guilty to a lesser offense — a "deal" that they both evidently believed was beneficial to them and to which their attorneys agreed. A defendant may find it beneficial to tie his plea to another. The defendant should have that option.

We note, however, that "package deal" plea agreements are fraught with danger and agree with the California Supreme Court that whenever a plea is taken pursuant to a "package deal" the trial court is required to conduct a careful inquiry into the totality of the circumstances surrounding the plea. In conducting this inquiry, we adopt the factors listed in *In re Ibarra*: (1) whether the inducement to plead was proper, in that the prosecutor acted in good faith and had a reasonable case against any third party to whom leniency is promised; (2) whether there is a factual basis for the plea, in terms of supportable evidence and proportionality of sentence; (3) whether the nature and degree of coercion and psychological pressure upon the defendant indicate the plea is involuntary; (4) whether the promise of leniency to another was a significant or insignificant concern to the defendant in his choice to plead guilty; and (5) whether any other relevant factor impermissibly influenced defendant's plea.

In the instant case, it appears that the trial court carefully reviewed the plea bargains of each defendant before accepting them all and that the factors listed in *In re Ibarra* were met. The record indicates that 1) the prosecutor acted in good faith; 2) there was a factual basis for the pleas; 3) the pleas were voluntary; 4) the promise of leniency was of significant concern to each of the defendants and 5) no other facts impermissibly influenced the defendants to plead guilty.

The opinion of the court of appeals is vacated and the sentences imposed by the trial court affirmed.

GORDON, VICE CHIEF JUSTICE, dissenting.

I respectfully dissent. It has long been established that pleas obtained through "coercion, terror, inducements, and subtle or blatant threats" are involuntary and violative of due process. *Boykin v. Alabama*, 395 U.S. 238 243 (1969). The constitutional status of guilty pleas induced by offers of adverse or lenient treatment to a person other than the accused presents a serious problem. *Bordenkircher v. Hayes*, 434 U.S. 357, 364, n. 8 (1978). These pleas pose a greater danger of coercion than purely bilateral plea bargaining, *U.S. v. Nuckols*, 606 F.2d 566, 569 (5th Cir.1979), and present a greater danger of inducing a false guilty plea by skewing the assessment of risks a defendant must consider. *Bordenkircher v. Hayes*, 434 U.S. at 364, n. 8. See also *Brady v. U.S.*, 397 U.S. 742, 750 (1970) (the agents of the state may not produce a plea by actual or threatened physical harm or by mental coercion overwhelming the will of the defendant).

While I realize that a criminal defendant has no right to a plea bargain, this does not mean the rules of the plea bargaining process should be further expanded to enhance the prosecutor's great discretionary power. Plea bargaining should not be reduced to a shameful imitation of a midday game show, where a deal is struck only when "the price is right" with no knowledge of what's behind door number three.

In the present case, the situation required the trial court to accept or reject *in toto* three plea agreements all contingent upon each other, two of which involved a husband and wife. These "package deals" make the job of the trial court geometrically more difficult than if it were simply reviewing three "non-package deals". Not only must the trial court determine that Rule 17 is satisfied and that the voluntariness requirement of *Boykin v. Alabama* is met, but it must then review the pleas in relation to each other for fear that the entire package may unravel. I believe this practice places too much pressure on the trial court to accept a package deal because of the possibility of a domino effect. The criminal justice system in the United States under our constitution is distinguished from all others in the world in that in this country each accused is accorded individual attention and treatment at all stages of the criminal prosecution. At no time does he become an average person or a member of a group. He is to be treated at all times as that distinct human being that he is. If we tie people together in a plea bargain package, however attractive the wrapping or the ribbon, we detract from the individuality of the persons involved, and force the trial judge to determine whether the end justifies the means. In these days of overcrowded calendars, it is unrealistic to believe that a harried trial judge would not be tempted to yield to a slightly unfair package in order to reduce his case load. This is simply not a desirable procedure and is designed solely to put undue leverage on the defendants and trial court.

The majority opinion illustrates that the trial court felt powerless in this situation, even after expressing concern that the sentences of two of the three defendants were possibly not justified. I agree with the majority of the court of appeals which would invalidate package deals. While such deals may not be so offensive to be declared unconstitutional per se, we should not be required to stretch our rules of criminal procedure to their absolute breaking point. As the majority points out, "package deal plea agreements are fraught with danger". If they are, why should we encourage parties to travel down this treacherous path and establish such an elaborate and subjective five factor test?

When large numbers of family members are involved in such pleas I seriously question whether an accurate assessment of voluntariness can be made and believe the pressure on the trial court to accept all of the contingent pleas will be overwhelming. To believe otherwise is to ignore human experience and the strength of family bonds.

Notes from Pearl:

1. In *Solano*, how — exactly — did the "package deal" affect what each defendant was willing to accept? Did any defendant accept a sentence *different* from what he or she would have accepted had he or she been the *only* defendant charged?

2. Other cases on "package deals"

In *U.S. v. Wright*, 43 F.3d 491 (10th Cir. 1994), the court held: "To lawfully threaten third parties with prosecution during the course of plea negotiations, the government must have probable cause that those third persons committed the crime that the government threatens to charge."

In *State v. Dahn*, 516 N.W.2d 539 (Minn. 1994), defendant was the eldest son of an immigrant from Southeast Asia who "was apparently expected to take care of the family after his father's death." He agreed to a package deal plea bargain, contingent on his younger brother also pleading guilty, but the trial court was not told of the package deal when it accepted defendant's guilty plea. The Minnesota Supreme Court held that under these circumstances, he must be given a post-conviction hearing on the voluntariness of his plea.

> "Package deal" agreements are generally dangerous because of the risk of coercion; this is particularly so in cases involving related third parties, where there is a risk that a defendant, who would otherwise exercise his or her right to a jury trial, will plead guilty out of a sense of family loyalty. *
> * * *

> The Model Code of Pre-Arraignment Procedure, as adopted by the Council of the American Law Institute, contains no provision forbidding the offer of lenient treatment to a third party as an inducement to plead guilty. However, the Advisory Committee to the Code recommended forbidding such inducements. As stated in the Commentary:

>> The Reporter believes such inducements present a special risk that an innocent defendant will plead guilty and that a guilty defendant will receive treatment that does not meet his correctional needs and that he does not deserve in terms of his own character and dangerousness. Furthermore, allowing such offers may create a risk that a prosecutor who would otherwise be willing to offer greater leniency to the defendant avoids that issue by making the offer with respect to another person. American Law Institute, *Model Code of Pre-Arraignment Procedure*, Commentary to § 350.3 at 615–16 (1975). * * * *

> We therefore hold that the state must fully inform the trial court of the details of these agreements at the time a defendant enters a "package deal" plea, and the trial court must then conduct further inquiries to determine whether the plea is voluntarily made. In future cases, a defendant must be allowed to withdraw his or her guilty plea if the state fails to fully inform the trial court of the nature of the plea, or if the trial court fails to adequately inquire into the voluntariness of the plea at the time of the guilty plea.

See also *State v. Bey*, 17 P.3d 322 (Kan. 2001).

In *U.S. v. Pollard*, 959 F.2d 1011 (D.C.Cir.1992), Pollard was a research specialist for the U.S. Navy who sold secrets to Israeli agents. He pleaded guilty to conspiracy to deliver national defense information to a foreign government. Three years later, he moved to withdraw his plea, arguing that the government had improperly "wired" his plea to his wife's guilty plea to related charges. Pollard's wife had been ill, and he wanted to minimize her incarceration by ensuring that her plea agreement was accepted.

Jonathan Pollard claims that by refusing to offer Anne Pollard a plea agreement unless he also entered into a plea agreement, the government overreached; it used improper, indeed unconstitutional, pressure to force him to plead guilty. We note, however, that Pollard does not contest his guilt. He does not ask for a new trial to establish his innocence. We are not faced with the prospect that an innocent man was involuntarily compelled to plead guilty. Still, that is not dispositive. Government coercion of a certain degree and kind would invalidate the plea agreement even though Pollard does not contest his guilt. * * * *

Pollard's more substantial involuntariness argument is that wired pleas are unconstitutional. The Supreme Court has specifically reserved judgment on "the constitutional implications of a prosecutor's offer during plea bargaining of adverse or lenient treatment for some person other than the accused." *Bordenkircher v. Hayes*, 434 U.S. 357, 364 n. 8 (1978).

The circuits that have considered the question, however, while occasionally expressing distaste for the practice, have uniformly agreed that it does not, per se, offend due process or the privilege against compulsory self-incrimination. See *U.S. v. Marquez*, 909 F.2d 738, 742 (2d Cir.1990) (citing cases from First, Fourth, Fifth, Sixth, Seventh, Eighth, Tenth, and Eleventh Circuits).

We agree with our sister circuits that plea wiring does not violate the Constitution. The question, of course, is whether the practice of plea wiring is so coercive as to risk inducing false guilty pleas. To say that a practice is "coercive" or renders a plea "involuntary" means only that it creates improper pressure that would be likely to overbear the will of some innocent persons and cause them to plead guilty. Only physical harm, threats of harassment, misrepresentation, or "promises that are by their nature improper as having no proper relationship to the prosecutor's business (e.g., bribes)' " render a guilty plea legally involuntary. *Brady v. U.S.*, 397 U.S. 742, 750 (1970). Almost anything lawfully within the power of a prosecutor acting in good faith can be offered in exchange for a guilty plea. No constitutionally impermissible compulsion arises, for instance, when a defendant is forced to choose between the possibility of a mandatory minimum sentence of ten years in prison if he goes to trial or a suspended sentence on a reduced charge if he pleads.

In *Brady*, the Supreme Court held that "a plea of guilty is not invalid merely because entered to avoid the possibility of a death penalty." *Id.* at 755. Even where the defendant continues to maintain his innocence, having to face the death penalty as the price of trial does not invalidate a guilty plea, as long as the record contains adequate evidence of actual guilt. See *North Carolina v. Alford*, 400 U.S. 25, 37–38 (1970).

We can understand how it might be thought that a threat of long imprisonment for a loved one, particularly a spouse, would constitute even greater pressure on a defendant than a direct threat to him. Whether one could generalize as to that proposition depends, we suppose, on one's view of human nature. But it does not seem to be the sort of widely-shared intuition upon which a constitutional rule should be based. We must be mindful, moreover, that if the judiciary were to declare wired pleas unconstitutional, the consequences would not be altogether foreseeable and perhaps would not be beneficial to defendants. Would Pollard, for instance, have been better off had he not been able to bargain to aid his wife? Would his wife have been better off? Would the bargaining take place in any event, but with winks and nods rather than in writing?

Nor do we believe that Mrs. Pollard's medical condition makes an otherwise acceptable linkage of their pleas unconstitutional. The appropriate dividing line between acceptable and unconstitutional plea wiring does not depend upon the physical condition or personal circumstances of the defendant; rather, it depends upon the conduct of the government. Where, as here, the government had probable cause to arrest and prosecute both defendants in a related crime, and there is no suggestion that the government conducted itself in bad faith in an effort to generate additional leverage over the defendant, we think a wired plea is constitutional. Once the government had probable cause to prosecute Mrs. Pollard and had obtained a valid indictment, it was entitled, despite her illness, to prosecute her fully — or to offer lenience for her in exchange for Pollard's plea. See *United States v. Clark*, 931 F.2d 292 (5th Cir.1991) (plea offered by man, who maintains his innocence, in order to help his "sick, pregnant and innocent" wife held not involuntary); *Bontkowski v. United States*, 850 F.2d 306 (7th Cir.1988) (threat to prosecute validly indicted pregnant woman does not constitute unconstitutional coercion of her husband).

At minimum, Pollard argues, wired pleas raise special dangers of coercion, so that a district court faced with such a plea must undertake a more searching inquiry into the voluntariness of the plea than would normally be required. Even if that were so, we are satisfied that the district court adequately discharged its obligations here. The colloquy between the court and Pollard was so extensive that there could be little doubt about Pollard's willingness to plead. Pollard had several opportunities to confess any misgivings to the judge, but he never gave the slightest hint that his plea was anything other than voluntary. In fact, Richard Hibey, who was Pollard's attorney at the time, brought to the court's attention at the end of the plea proceeding a document captioned "Waiver of Trial by Jury," which Pollard had executed. And when counsel did so, he specifically stated, "I think the Court has taken care of the waiver under Rule 11."

3. In *State v. Moen*, 76 P.3d 721 (Wash. 2003), Moen was arrested for sale of marijuana. The city of Spokane invoked civil proceedings to have a 2000 Ford Taurus Moen allegedly used in the sale forfeited to the city. When Moen invoked discovery to obtain the name of the confidential informant used by the police, the prosecutor notified Moen that if he insisted on learning the name of the informant, the prosecutor would not plea bargain with him. Moen sought and obtained the name, the prosecutor refused to plea bargain, Moen went to trial, and was convicted of 3 counts of selling marijuana. On appeal, Moen argued that the refusal to bargain

violated his right to due process of law, as it tended to chill his right to use discovery in a civil action. The court disagreed:

> Unquestionably, the State has a legitimate interest in protecting confidential informants. *Roviaro v. United States, 353 U.S. 53 (1957)* (acknowledging the importance of both criminal discovery and confidential informants and setting forth procedures for protecting both). * * * *

> We recognize that the prosecutor's policy requires the defendant to forgo his right to request disclosure of an informant's identity. However, a condition insisted on by the State that requires a defendant to give up a constitutional right does not, by itself, violate due process. Agreements to forgo seeking an exceptional sentence, to decline prosecuting all offenses, to pay restitution on uncharged crimes, and to waive the right to appeal are all permissible components of valid plea agreements. The theoretical basis for all plea bargaining is that defendants will agree to waive their constitutional rights.

> More aggressive exercises of prosecutorial authority have been upheld. For example, due process is not violated when a prosecutor carries out a threat made during plea bargaining to reindict a defendant on more serious charges if the defendant refuses to plead guilty to lesser charges. *Bordenkircher v. Hayes*, 434 U.S. 357, 358 (1978).

4. May the parties bargain for *sex*?

In *State v. Horning*, 158 Ariz. 106 (1988), the court upheld another package-deal involving a husband and wife, but set aside the husband's plea bargain, wherein the prosecutor had agreed to refrain from opposing his effort to obtain a conjugal jail visit from his wife. The court agreed with the husband's contention that "Allowing the state to leverage the strong, though short-term needs of a defendant for sex with his wife by manipulating conjugal visits in order to coerce a plea agreement is extremely inappropriate public policy." The Court said:

> We hold, however, that the state may never employ conjugal access as a factor of inducement to a guilty plea. While a defendant's short-term interest in such access may be powerful, it is a manifestly irrational basis for embracing the long-term consequences of a guilty plea. Its presence in a plea agreement demonstrates, *ipso facto*, a "degree of coercion and psychological pressure upon the defendant" that renders his plea involuntary.

Horning puzzles me. I am not sure I see the difference between the pressure on Vickie Solano (to help her husband get a lighter sentence) and the pressure on Horning (to have sex with his wife). Neither had anything to do with the crime each was accused of committing, and yet one makes the plea "involuntary" and the other doesn't. Is the court saying that one "urge" was more worthy than the other, in the eyes of the judges?

Questions:

a. *Brady* held that a defendant may "voluntarily" enter a guilty plea avoid a potential death penalty — i.e., to save his life. *Horning* holds that a defendant may not "voluntarily" enter a guilty plea to save his sex life. Is *Horning* consistent with *Brady*?

b. In *Brady*, the Court warned that it would have "serious doubts" about guilty pleas entered in circumstances which "substantially increased the likelihood that defendants, advised by competent counsel, would falsely condemn themselves." Was this likelihood increased in *Solano*? In *Horning*?

c. I don't understand how posing these questions in terms of whether a plea is "voluntary" can help me predict the outcome of a case. As *every* defendant is pressured by what the prosecutor offers, isn't *every* plea "involuntary" — in the sense that the defendant would not have pleaded guilty but for the prosecutor's offer? On the other hand, if this same defendant has had the opportunity to think over the offer and receive the advice of counsel before making an informed choice, didn't the defendant accept the offer "voluntarily"? When a court concludes that a plea was "involuntary", what is the court really saying?

UNITED STATES v. MELANCON
U.S. Court of Appeals, 5th Circuit
972 F.2d 566 (1992)

DUHE, CIRCUIT JUDGE

Defendant-Appellant Brian Melancon seeks review of his sentence to 108 months' imprisonment for conspiring to distribute methylenedioxymethamphetamine. Because Melancon waived his right to appeal as part of his plea agreement, we dismiss.

Appellant was indicted for conspiring to distribute methylenedioxymethamphetamine (MDMA or "ecstasy") in September 1990. Appellant reached a plea agreement with the Government by July 1991. Pursuant to that agreement, Appellant pleaded guilty to conspiracy to distribute MDMA and the parties stipulated that he had possessed 36,000 tablets of the drug. Also as part of the plea agreement, Appellant waived his right to appeal his sentence. The Government contends that in light of this waiver, we should dismiss Appellant's appeal. We agree.

The right to appeal is a statutory right, not a constitutional right. The Supreme Court has repeatedly recognized that a defendant may waive constitutional rights as part of a plea bargaining agreement. *Town of Newton v. Rumery*, 480 U.S. 386 (1987). It follows that a defendant may also waive statutory rights, including the right to appeal. We so held in *United States v. Sierra*, No. 91-4342 (5th Cir. Dec. 6, 1991), in which the defendant waived the right to appeal her sentence in exchange for a limitation on her maximum term of imprisonment. Several circuits similarly have enforced such waivers. *United States v. Rutan*, 956 F.2d 827 (8th Cir.1992); *United States v. Navarro-Botello*, 912 F.2d 318 (9th Cir.1990); *United States v. Wiggins*, 905 F.2d 51 (4th Cir.1990). But, as we recognized in *Sierra*, the waiver must be informed and voluntary.

Appellant does not assert that his waiver was anything less than voluntary and, after de novo review of the record, we are satisfied that it was informed. As directed by Rule 11 of the Federal Rules of Criminal Procedure, the district court held a hearing at which it reviewed the charges and plea agreement with Appellant and his counsel. The review of the plea agreement included the following colloquy concerning Appellant's waiver of the right to appeal:

The Court: You understand that paragraph six of this and this is very important that you knowingly, that means you know what you are doing, and by reasoning, have exercised the choice to intelligently and voluntarily would waive the right to appeal the sentence imposed in this case on any ground, including the right of appeal conferred by Title 18, United States Code, § 3742, in exchange for the concessions made by the United States of America in this agreement, do you understand that?

Defendant Melancon: Yes, sir.

The district court informed Appellant of the statutory maximum penalty of twenty years, the imposition of supervised release, and the use of the sentencing guidelines. The court also stated that it was not bound by any agreement between the parties regarding sentencing and explained its authority to depart from the guideline sentencing range.

Although Appellant's plea agreement differs from the one enforced in *Sierra* in that Appellant was not promised a specific sentence, the uncertainty of Appellant's sentence does not render his waiver uninformed. Appellant understood that the court had exclusive authority to set the sentence. He knew that the court would do so in accordance with the sentencing guidelines and that the court had the power to depart from the guideline recommendation. Appellant was also aware of the maximum terms of imprisonment and supervised release applicable to his crime.[3] Most important, he knew that he had a "right to appeal his sentence and that he was giving up that right." *Rutan*, 956 F.2d at 830. * * * *

We hold that a defendant may, as part of a valid plea agreement, waive his statutory right to appeal his sentence. Appellant voluntarily and knowingly entered such an agreement, waiving his right to appeal. His appeal is, therefore, dismissed.

Nothing in this opinion, however, should be interpreted as indicating that a district court is not free to determine whether plea waivers of the right to appeal are unacceptable. We recognize that there may be sound policy reasons for refusing to accept such waivers, and that district courts might disagree with the policy choice made by the court in this case to accept a plea agreement appeal waiver. Today, we simply decide that this district court operated within its discretion in accepting the plea agreement appeal waiver; and we note that a district court's refusal to accept such a waiver likewise would be within its discretion.

PARKER, DISTRICT JUDGE, concurring specially:

I concur specially because I cannot dissent. This panel is bound by the unpublished, per curiam opinion, *United States v. Sierra*. Unfortunately, the rule articulated in that decision compels me to find that Appellant Melancon's plea agreement waiver of his right to appeal was a knowing, intelligent and voluntary

---

[3] The district court ultimately imposed a sentence within the range described. We do not address, therefore, the question whether Appellant knowingly waived the right to appeal a sentence contrary to the district court's assurances.

act. I write separately to express why I think the rule embraced by this Circuit in *Sierra* is illogical and mischievous — and to urge the full Court to examine the " *Sierra* rule," and to reject it.

In *Sierra*, this Circuit adopted the rule previously promulgated in other circuits — that guilty plea provisions calling upon the defendant to waive his or her right to appeal are valid as long as this waiver is "informed and voluntary." The following syllogism, as reiterated in today's opinion, underlies this rule: "The right to appeal is a statutory right, not a constitutional right. The Supreme Court has repeatedly recognized that a defendant may waive constitutional rights as part of a plea bargaining agreement. It follows that a defendant may also waive statutory rights, including the right to appeal." * * * *

It matters not that this is a drug case. It matters not that this (attempted) appeal may well be without merit on its substantive points. It matters that we take care to see that the so called "war on drugs" not count among its casualties constitutional integrity.

I. Sierra's *Futuristic "Knowing and Intelligent" Waiver*

As an initial matter, I do not think that a defendant can ever knowingly and intelligently waive, as part of a plea agreement, the right to appeal a sentence that has yet to be imposed at the time he or she enters into the plea agreement; such a "waiver" is inherently uninformed and unintelligent. The *Sierra* Court followed the Fourth and Ninth Circuits in holding that a waiver of the right to appeal one's sentence is "knowing" and "informed" as long as the accused realizes that the effect of this waiver is that he or she will not be able to appeal. Accordingly, today's majority opinion states: "Appellant Melancon knew that he had a 'right to appeal his sentence and that he was giving up that right.' " But this roundabout conclusion — first articulated by the Fourth Circuit in *United States v. Wiggins*, and followed so far by the courts subsequently confronting the issue — misapprehends the nature of the requirement that waivers of important rights be knowing and intelligent.

In the typical waiver cases, the act of waiving the right occurs at the moment the waiver is executed. For example: one waives the right to silence, and then speaks; one waives the right to have a jury determine one's guilt, and then admits his or her guilt to the judge. In these cases, the defendant knows what he or she is about to say, or knows the nature of the crime to which he or she pleads guilty. While one cannot fully know the consequences of confessing or pleading guilty, one does know what is being yielded up at the time he or she yields it.

Like the Court in *Sierra*, today my colleagues cite a *typical* waiver case — *Newton v. Rumery*, 480 U.S. 386 (1987) — for the categorical proposition that one may waive a constitutional right as part of a plea bargaining agreement. But in *Newton*, the right waived was the right to sue under 42 U.S.C. § 1983. Thus, the waiver in *Newton*, too, was of a known quantity: a lawsuit — of which the one waiving had full knowledge, and over which the one waiving exercised control. * * * *

The situation is completely different when one waives the right to appeal a Guidelines-circumscribed sentence before the sentence has been imposed. What is really being waived is not some abstract right to appeal, but the right to correct an erroneous application of the Guidelines or an otherwise illegal sentence. *This right cannot come into existence until after the judge pronounces sentence*; it is only then that the defendant knows what errors the district court has made — i.e., what errors exist to be appealed, or waived. See Fed.R.Crim.P. 11, 1989 Amendment advisory committee's note (respecting the amendment's mandate that the district court inform the defendant that the court is required to consider any applicable guidelines but may depart from them under some circumstances, so as to assure that the existence of the Guidelines will be known to the defendant before a plea of guilty or *nolo contendere* is accepted: "Since it will be impracticable, if not impossible, to know which guidelines will be relevant prior to the formulation of a presentence report and resolution of disputed facts, the amendment does not require the court to specify which guidelines will be important or which grounds for departure might prove to be significant.").

In categorically citing cases concerning the waiver of the right to appeal known quantities, to support the proposition that the waiver of the right to appeal unknown errors may be likewise "informed," today's opinion simply perpetuates a fallacy embraced in *Sierra* — a strain of the *fallacy of accident*.[7] It is, then, a shaky foundation indeed that props up *Sierra*, and one unworthy of providing the underpinning for such a significant rule of this Circuit.[8] Yet even if I were convinced that the sort of futuristic waiver at issue in this case could be knowing and intelligent, I could not support it. Any systemic benefits that might inhere in this type waiver cannot overcome its extremely deleterious effects upon judicial and congressional integrity, and individual constitutional rights.

II. The Sierra *Rule Moves Sentencing Out of (Over)Sight*

The "*Sierra* rule" reiterated today has roots in still another *fallacy of Accident* — one embraced without question by a majority of the Fourth Circuit in *United States v. Clark*, 865 F.2d 1433 (4th Cir.1989), and readopted without hesitation in the Fourth Circuit case underlying *Sierra*: *Wiggins*. In *Clark*, a majority of the *en banc* Fourth Circuit made the following mistake: "if defendants can waive fundamental constitutional rights such as the right to counsel, or the right to a jury trial, *surely* they are not precluded from waiving procedural rights granted by statute." *Clark*, 865 F.2d at 1437 (emphasis added). However, even assuming *arguendo* that the right to appeal one's sentence is not a fundamental, but a "mere" statutory right, it does *not* necessarily follow that the statutory right to appeal is waivable because "lesser" than waivable constitutional rights. Individual rights are not all that are at issue here.

28 U.S.C. § 1291 and the provisions of 18 U.S.C. § 3742 cannot be understood as mere conferrals of individual rights to appeal a sentence under the Sentencing Guidelines. Rather, these statutory provisions, along with the Sentencing Guidelines themselves, speak directly to the power of the federal courts and should be read as imposing limitations upon individual and judicial authority. Such limitations cannot be "waived" by parties. * * * *

---

[7] *See generally* Irving M. Copi & Carl Cohen, *Introduction to Logic* 100–101 (8th ed. 1990) ("when we apply a generalization to individual cases that it does not properly govern, we commit the *fallacy of accident*.").

[8] *See id.* at 101 (regarding the *fallacy of Accident*: "there is no fallacy more insidious than that of treating a statement which in many connections is not misleading as if it were true always and without qualification.").

A sentencing court may depart upward or downward from the applicable guidelines, to impose a sentence outside the "guideline range," if the court finds that an aggravating or mitigating circumstance exists that was not adequately taken into consideration by the Sentencing Commission in formulating the Guidelines. 18 U.S.C. § 3553(b). But this Circuit has been quite inflexible in its demands: (1) that the sentencing court state its reasons for any such departure, and (2) that the sentence imposed pursuant to such a departure be *reasonable* in light of the sentencing court's articulated reasons. The *Sierra* rule obstructs this Circuit's orders respecting Sentencing Guidelines departures, by insulating violations of these orders from review. Also insulated from appellate review under the *Sierra* rule is the district court judge's adoption of the "guideline range" calculated under the Sentencing Guidelines by nonjudicial probation officers. Moreover, waivers of the sort at issue in this case insulate from review factual inadequacies in the presentence reports generated by nonjudicial probation officers in Sentencing Guidelines cases. Appellate review ensures that the record adequately support whatever factual findings the district court judge makes or adopts. The *Sierra* rule cancels this insurance.

In brief: every erroneous application of the Guidelines frustrates the complex policy goals that Congress and the United States Sentencing Commission intended for the Guidelines to further. The *Sierra* rule works a breach of the Judiciary's duty to ensure that the goals of Congress and the Sentencing Commission are met. And the fact that — as my colleagues emphasize — "the district court ultimately imposed a sentence within the applicable guideline range" affords no systemic shelter from *Sierra's* certain storm of judicial encroachment.

III. The Sierra Rule Neuters Federal Rule of Criminal Procedure 11.

While today's majority opinion addresses to some extent the district court's performance pursuant to Federal Rule of Criminal Procedure 11, such an analysis is not commanded by the majority opinion. And the *Sierra* rule actually appears to sanction district court disavowal of Rule 11.

District court satisfaction of the "core concerns" of Rule 11 is supposed to help guarantee that "a plea of guilty and the ensuing conviction comprehend all of the factual and legal elements necessary to sustain a binding, final judgment of guilt and a lawful sentence." *United States v. Broce*, 488 U.S. 563, 569 (1989). Rule 11's core concerns are: whether the plea was coerced; whether the accused understands the nature of the charges against him or her; and whether the accused understands the consequences of his or her plea. Adherence to Rule 11's core concerns is crucial, given the final consequences of pleading guilty. In pleading guilty the defendant may be foregoing a number of procedural and substantive rights, which rights might lead to acquittal or dismissal if the defendant's case proceeded toward trial.

Appellant Melancon's plea agreement says that he waived his "right to appeal the *sentence* imposed in his case on any ground, including any appeal right conferred by Title 18, United States Code, § 3742." And the circuit opinions upon which *Sierra* relies address only the plea agreement waiver of the right to appeal a forthcoming sentence. But *Sierra* itself states that a defendant may waive the right to appeal his or her conviction and sentence, as long as the waiver was "informed." Thus, *Sierra* appears to go so far as to insulate from direct review the district court judge's performance relative to Federal Rule of Criminal Procedure 11 — i.e., by crushing the tripartite "core concern" scrutiny called for by Rule 11 and its interpretive case law into a quick colloquy about one concern: Is the defendant's waiver of his or her right to appeal a sentence "knowing, intelligent and voluntary?" * * * *

V. What "Good" are These Waivers?

Even if I did not consider the sort of futuristic waiver at issue in this case to be inherently uninformed, unintelligent and involuntary, I would think it unacceptable because any benefits it might confer are too minuscule to overcome its deleterious consequences.

Most fundamentally: there is no reason to believe the waiver of appellate rights is an indispensable part of plea bargaining. Plenty of plea agreements were made prior to the reign of these appellate right waiver clauses.

Second: if the *Sierra* rule represents the collective opinion of the members of this Court that these waivers will stem the tide of appeals in this type case, the Court is engaging in wishful thinking at best and self-delusion at least. Such appeals will simply come equipped with additional arguments about whether one's right to appeal has been waived "intelligently, knowingly and voluntarily." And because the *Sierra* rule serves to force Rule 11 complaints into habeas corpus pleadings — see *United States v. Rutan*, 956 F.2d 827, 829 (8th Cir.1992) — this Court can surely expect to see an increase in habeas corpus cases. Thus, far from *decreasing* the Court's workload in this area of the criminal law, the *Sierra* rule appears certain to *increase* it.

Yet, assuming that Efficiency *can* be heard to advocate our adherence to the *Sierra* rule, her argument is, at best, weak. Any small "gain" in "speed," "economy", or "finality" derived from *Sierra's* continued sovereignty is overwhelmed by the rule's exorbitant, unacceptable cost to judicial and congressional integrity, and individual constitutional rights.

VI. Conclusion

For the reasons I have addressed, I concur merely in the panel's judgment, and only because *stare decisis* says I must. I strongly urge the Circuit, *en banc*, to examine the *Sierra* rule — and to disclaim it. The *Sierra* rule is a legal woods colt whose questionable ancestry will surely result in offspring of which this Circuit will not be proud.

Notes from Pearl:

1. In *U.S. v. Bushert*, 997 F.2d 1343 (11th Cir.1993), the court followed the majority in *Melancon*, noting that every other federal appeals court has done the same. But some other courts have agreed with Judge Parker's concurrence. See *U.S. v. Perez*, 46 F.Supp.2d 59 (D.Mass. 1999), and *U.S. v. Raynor*, 989 F.Supp. 43 (D.D.C. 1997) ("The one voice of reason is Judge Parker's concurring opinion in *U.S. v. Melancon*").

In *People v. Sherrick*, 19 Cal.App.4th 657 (1993), the court held invalid a portion of a plea bargain waiving the right to appeal a sentence, because a "general waiver of the right of appeal did not include error occurring after the waiver because it was not knowingly and intelligently made. Such a waiver of possible future error does not appear to be within defendant's contemplation and knowledge at the time the waiver was made."

But compare *U.S. v. Hahn*, 359 F.3d 1315 (10th Cir. 2004), where the court upheld such waivers, because "Although many waivers pertain to future events — a waiver of the right to trial by jury is a good example — their prospective nature has never been thought to place them off limits or to render the defendant's act 'unknowing.' " The court said, however, that:

> Appellate waivers are subject to certain exceptions, including [1] where the district court relied on an impermissible factor such as race, [2] where ineffective assistance of counsel in connection with the negotiation of the waiver renders the waiver invalid, [3] where the sentence exceeds the statutory maximum, or [4] where the waiver is otherwise unlawful.

The court also explained how it would handle claims that defendant had waived his right to appeal:

> To preserve the benefit of the government's bargain and employ our appellate waiver enforcement analysis, henceforth, when a defendant who has waived his appellate rights in a plea agreement files a notice of appeal and the government wishes to enforce this waiver, the government will file a "Motion for Enforcement of the Plea Agreement." This motion will address the three-prong enforcement analysis provided above, but not the underlying merits of the defendant's appeal. The defendant will then have the opportunity to respond. The Clerk of the Court will forward the government's motion, and any responding briefs, to the panel. The parties will not be directed to brief the underlying merits of the defendant's appeal.

> If the panel finds that the plea agreement is enforceable, it will summarily dismiss the appeal. If the panel finds the plea agreement unenforceable, it will issue a ruling consistent with this finding.

In *Spann v. State*, 704 N.W.2d 486 (Minn. 2005), the court held that a waiver of the right to appeal in exchange for a reduce sentence is invalid:

> We recognize that a majority of other jurisdictions have held that allowing a defendant to waive his right to appeal is not inherently illegal or unfair. Jurisdictions allowing a defendant to waive his or her right to appeal a conviction require that the waiver be made "intelligently, voluntarily and with an understanding of the consequences." [citations] These jurisdictions have justified the allowance of appeal waivers stating that, while the criminal defendant's right to appeal is important, it is no more fundamental than other rights a defendant is allowed to waive.

> There may also be some advantages to allowing a defendant to waive the right to appeal the waiver: (1) brings closure to the state, defendant, and victims; (2) increases judicial economy; (3) gives the defendant power with which to bargain; and (4) reduces frivolous appeals. *See, e.g., United States v. Andis, 333 F.3d 886, 889 (8th Cir.2003).* But we note that most of the jurisdictions upholding appeal waivers have decided the issue in the context of a pretrial plea agreement in which the defendant has pleaded guilty in exchange for a reduced sentence and not in the context of the waiver of the right to appeal after the defendant has been convicted and sentenced. [citations]

Other jurisdictions, while allowing a defendant to waive the right to appeal, have explicitly placed restrictions on the appeal waiver. *See, e.g.,* *Andis*, 333 F.3d at 889. The Eighth Circuit Court of Appeals stated that it "will not enforce a waiver where to do so would result in a miscarriage of justice" and concluded that claims involving an illegal sentence, a sentence in violation of the terms of the agreement, and claims asserting ineffective assistance of counsel are not waivable. Other courts have also included prosecutorial misconduct among the claims that the defendant cannot waive.

The Supreme Court of Arizona has determined, however, that inclusion of an appeal waiver in a plea or other agreement is inherently coercive and allowing the defendant to waive this right provides the defendant with little bargaining power. *State v. Ethington*, 121 Ariz. 572, 592 P.2d 768 (1979). Essentially, the court held that the right to appeal is so vital to the protection of the defendant's rights that it cannot be waived. The court stated that the public policy of ensuring that defendants are afforded their basic rights "forbids a prosecutor from insulating himself from review by bargaining away a defendant's appeal rights." The court further held that the right to appeal was not negotiable in plea bargaining and that a defendant, as a matter of public policy, would be allowed to bring a timely appeal from a conviction notwithstanding an agreement waiving an appeal.
* * * *

Due process guarantees in our state and federal constitutions include the right to a fair trial. The requirement that a defendant receives a fair trial makes the waiver of the right to appeal after being convicted at trial as a result of an agreement with the state fundamentally different from the defendant's waiver of personal rights or waiver by default. Therefore, we conclude, based on public policy and due process considerations, that a defendant may not, after conviction at trial and sentencing, waive the right to appeal.

The right to appeal implicates not only matters personal to the defendant, but broader issues as well. Once the defendant is convicted, institutional concerns that the conviction was fair and proper become paramount. "There is no legitimate State interest in preserving an unjust conviction for the sake of the conviction alone." Although the state argues that allowing a defendant to waive his right to appeal allows the defendant to obtain a concrete benefit, such as a reduced sentence, in exchange for waiving the right to appeal, the need to have trial proceedings reviewed for error outweighs a defendant's interest in accepting a particular benefit.

Moreover, requiring a defendant to waive his right to appeal after conviction in order to receive some benefit offered by the state is particularly coercive because the disparity in bargaining power between the defendant and the state increases significantly after the defendant has been convicted. Before trial, the defendant and the state face the same uncertainly as to what the outcome of the trial will be. A criminal defendant can therefore make a calculated decision as to what is in his best interest and may plead guilty if the plea is knowing, intelligent, and voluntary. After trial, a defendant has only his right of appeal with which to bargain. Requiring the defendant to give up the right to appeal in exchange for a reduced sentence forces the defendant to choose between a guaranteed reduced sentence and a fair trial. Allowing a defendant to waive his right to appeal after conviction and trial would foster a judicial system that discourages development of the law while encouraging the preservation of unfair trials.

Further, prosecutors have a duty to "seek justice, not merely to convict." *State v. Blasus*, 445 N.W.2d 535, 539 (Minn.1989) (quoting ABA Standards Relating to the Prosecution Function, Standard 1.1(c)). Offering a benefit to a defendant in return for the defendant waiving appeal rights as part of negotiating an agreement with the state runs afoul of that duty because it puts the state in a position to hide its own misconduct and errors. As some commentators have suggested, the state would be most likely to offer such benefits in return for waiver of the defendant's right to appeal in cases in which the defendant has meritorious issues to raise on appeal. *See* Robert K. Calhoun, *Waiver of the Right to Appeal*, 23 Hastings Const. L.Q. 127, 167 (1995). We agree with the Supreme Court of Arizona that the public policy requiring prosecutors to ensure that defendants are afforded their basic rights does not allow a prosecutor to insulate his or her actions from review by making a bargain with the defendant requiring the defendant to waive all rights to appeal. *Ethington*, 592 P.2d at 769. *Ethington* involved a waiver of the right to appeal in the plea agreement context. The concerns raised there are magnified in the context of a conviction after trial.

Public policy also requires that courts take an active role in ensuring the fairness of trials. Courts have a duty to be a "check against potential abuses of prosecutorial powers." Allowing the state to require a defendant to waive the right to appeal after conviction in order to obtain some benefit has the potential to frustrate that duty. Simply saying that the defendant is free to reject the state's offer does not eliminate the problem. Once conviction occurs, a waiver of the right to appeal seals trial errors. As noted earlier, due process requires that a criminal defendant receive a fair trial. Forcing the defendant to choose between a fair trial and a "known benefit" puts the defendant in an untenable situation and erodes the fairness of criminal trials. Further, as with our concern with prosecutors having an incentive to enter into plea agreements requiring a waiver of the right to appeal, so too are we concerned that courts may have an incentive to accept an appeal waiver agreement as it would also insulate the court from reversal for its errors.

We therefore conclude that allowing a defendant to waive his right to appeal after trial conviction and sentencing is inconsistent with the court's role as an objective supervisor whose purpose includes maintaining the integrity of the judicial system. * * * *

There is no integrity in allowing a defendant to waive appeal rights when he has been convicted and sentenced after a trial. The waiver of the right to appeal based on an agreement with the state after the defendant has been convicted and sentenced after a trial is of a fundamentally different nature than waiver of a defendant's rights before trial. Given that difference and the coercive nature of agreements requiring a defendant to waive the right to appeal after being convicted at trial in order to receive a reduced sentence, we also conclude that retention of the right to appeal after a conviction is necessary both for the protection of the defendant's rights and maintaining the fairness of the judicial process and cannot be waived. The broader interests we preserve in our holding today are to ensure uniformity, rationality, and fairness in criminal trials.

Allowing a defendant to waive his right to appeal creates a system that discourages the development of the law, permits the results of unfair trials to be preserved, and may encourage prosecutors and courts to hide their errors. Accordingly, we hold that Spann's waiver of his appeal rights under the stipulation agreement is invalid and unenforceable. Spann's right to appeal is reinstated.

JUSTICE ANDERSON dissented:

Among the policy reasons in support of plea-agreement appeal waivers is the need for finality in the process:

> The chief virtues of plea agreements are speed, economy, and finality. Waivers of appeal in plea agreements preserve the finality of judgments and sentences imposed pursuant to valid pleas of guilty. We also note that plea agreements are of value to the accused in order to gain concessions from the government. *United States v. Rutan*, 956 F.2d 827, 829 (8th Cir.1992).

The majority asserts that plea-agreement appeal waivers are fundamentally different from post-trial/post-sentence waivers, the latter implicating broader institutional concerns related to the integrity of the conviction. But the institutional concerns related to the integrity of a conviction obtained by plea agreement or by trial are equally important; and courts are required to conduct a Rule 15 inquiry to ensure that a plea is "accurate, voluntary, and intelligent (i.e., knowingly and understandingly made)."

I recognize that there is a trend in the circuits of instituting a greater level of scrutiny of plea-bargain appeal waivers. *See, e.g., Andis, 333* F.3d at 890–91 (excepting from appeal waivers claims of illegal sentences, breach of the plea agreement and ineffective assistance of counsel); *Teeter,* 257 F.3d at 25, nn. 9 & 10 (stating that appeal waivers would not preclude sentencing claims based on constitutionally impermissible factors or sentences in excess of the maximum penalty allowed by law); *Brown,* 232 F.3d at 405–06 (expressing concern about an inartfully drafted appeal waiver permitting appeals based on claims of ineffective assistance of counsel and prosecutorial misconduct but precluding appeals from a sentence in excess of the statutory maximum); *United States v. Rosa*, 123 F.3d 94, 101 (2d Cir.1997) (holding that appellate court oversight permits review of appeal waivers on a case-by-case basis).

I also understand that commentators have expressed much concern over plea-bargain appeal waivers. These concerns, however, have little application in a post-trial/post-sentence waiver of appellate rights following an appeal and submission of an appellate brief by legal counsel on a defendant's behalf. When a bargain is made for a specific sentence within the presumptive range of a guidelines system, the policies underlying the right to appeal have less force. But those rights that go to the very center of the validity of the appeal waiver, including effective assistance of counsel and the requirement that the waiver be voluntary and intelligent, are unwaivable. Because of our holding in *State v. Misquadace*, 644 N.W.2d 65, 71–72 (Minn.2002), a defendant should also not be able to waive claims of sentencing error. Additionally, I would except claims based on prosecutorial misconduct from any waiver.

2. Why do you think most appellate judges reject the arguments in the *Melancon* concurring opinion? Do these judges have any *stake* in seeing that the waivers are upheld?

3. Suppose defendant's plea agreement waives his right to "collaterally attack" the judgment (via a petition for writ of *habeas corpus*) — and later he collaterally attacks the judgment on the ground that his attorney was incompetent in negotiating the plea agreement or that defendant "involuntarily" agreed to the plea bargain. In *Jones v. U.S.*, 167 F.3d 1142 (7th Cir.1999), the court held:

> Justice dictates that a claim of ineffective assistance of counsel in connection with the negotiation of a cooperation agreement cannot be barred by the agreement itself — the very product of the alleged ineffectiveness. To hold otherwise would deprive a defendant of an opportunity to assert his Sixth Amendment right to counsel where he had accepted the waiver in reliance on delinquent representation. Similarly, where a waiver is not the product of the defendant's free will — for example, where it has been procured by government coercion or intimidation — the defendant cannot be said to have knowingly and voluntarily relinquished his rights. It is intuitive that in these circumstances the waiver is ineffective against a challenge based on involuntariness. Mindful of the limited reach of this holding, we reiterate that waivers are enforceable as a general rule; the right to mount a collateral attack pursuant to § 2255 survives only with respect to those discrete claims which relate directly to the negotiation of the waiver.

In *Allen v. Thomas*, 161 F.3d 667 (11th Cir. 1999), the court held that Allen did not waive his right to seek federal habeas corpus because his plea agreement did not say this clearly, neither the state court judge nor Allen's lawyers informed him that his plea agreement waived this right, and the state failed to prove that Allen otherwise knew that he was waiving this right.

4. For an extensive discussion of these issues, see Robert C. Calhoun, *Waiver of the Right to Appeal*, 23 Hast.Const.L.Q. 127 (1995).

BARNES v. STATE
Minnesota Court of Appeals
489 N.W.2d 273 (1992)

DAVIES, JUDGE

This appeal is from an order denying a postconviction petition seeking the withdrawal of appellant Barnes' plea of guilty to aggravated robbery. We reverse and remand.

Facts

Appellant Russell Barnes was charged with first degree burglary, aggravated robbery, and four counts of second degree assault. Barnes pleaded not guilty and the case went to trial.

On the second day of jury deliberations, one of the jurors became ill. The trial court gave Barnes a choice whether to have a mistrial declared, or to proceed with 11 jurors. Barnes decided to proceed with the 11 remaining jurors.

The jury was unable to reach a decision and the trial judge assembled the parties in chambers on the afternoon of the third day of deliberations. The court disclosed notes from the jury, one of which was from the previous evening, and reported the jury was deadlocked at an 8-3 vote. A more recent note, dated the same day, indicated the jury "continued to be split on all counts," and gave the votes that had been taken, without indicating whether majorities favored guilty or not guilty. The trial court indicated it was thinking of letting the jury deliberate through that evening, then declaring a mistrial. The prosecutor urged that a mistrial be declared, while defense counsel stated he would have to talk with Barnes. The trial court indicated its intent to keep the jury at the courthouse until 10 p.m.

Defense counsel testified that he was called to the courthouse at about 9:30 p.m. that evening, for the apparent purpose of discharging a hung jury. At the urging of the court, plea discussions were then renewed because a mistrial seemed certain. When the jury was called in, however, they reported that they were making progress and further deliberations would be useful. Jury deliberations and plea negotiations continued.

Barnes had rejected the prosecutor's first offer to dismiss the other charges if Barnes pleaded guilty to aggravated robbery, with no agreement as to sentence. After the jury reported progress, the prosecutor offered to add an agreement that the sentence would not exceed 64 months. Defense counsel took this offer to the county jail and talked to Barnes, who refused it.

When defense counsel called to inform the court of Barnes' refusal of the offer, the judge's court reporter informed counsel that the jury had reached a verdict. Defense counsel also learned, either through the court reporter or directly from the prosecutor, that the plea offer was still open. Defense counsel returned to Barnes and told him what he had learned, stating it was Barnes' decision whether to accept, but that he'd have to make the decision quickly. They then returned to the courthouse, where they discussed the votes reported by the jury earlier. When the trial judge entered the conference room, the judge was told no decision had been reached on a plea. Barnes testified that he had the impression the judge knew something which he (Barnes) did not, and that the judge was doing him a favor by delaying return of the jury's verdict so Barnes could consider the plea offer. Barnes reasoned that the judge would not have been holding up the verdict unless it was a guilty verdict. Defense counsel testified that neither he nor Barnes asked the trial judge anything while he was in the conference room, and that Barnes had still not made a decision when they re-entered the courtroom.

Barnes then agreed to enter a guilty plea to aggravated robbery. He denied committing the offenses charged, but admitted he was present at the time. The trial court accepted the guilty plea, ending the trial. Nonetheless, following acceptance of the plea, the jury verdict of not guilty was made known. Prior to sentencing,

Barnes moved to vacate the plea as involuntary and against the interests of justice. Barnes also moved for judgment of acquittal. The trial court denied both motions.

Barnes filed a postconviction petition, again seeking to withdraw his guilty plea. The trial court, although noting the unusual circumstances under which Barnes pleaded guilty, denied the petition, finding that Barnes was given a reasonable time to consider his plea and concluding that the plea was voluntarily entered.

Issue: Did the trial court abuse its discretion in denying the postconviction petition for withdrawal of the guilty plea?

Analysis

To be valid, a guilty plea must be voluntary, knowing, and intelligent. A guilty plea may be withdrawn before sentencing if it is "fair and just" to do so. Minn.R.Crim.P. 15.05, subd. 2. A plea may be withdrawn after sentencing "to correct a manifest injustice." Minn.R.Crim.P. 15.05, subd. 1. The trial court's decision whether to allow withdrawal of a guilty plea is reviewed under an abuse of discretion standard. * * * *

Barnes contends that the jury unexpectedly reaching a verdict after three days of deliberations created a stressful circumstance that made his plea involuntary. Although it is doubtful that time pressures by themselves could make a plea involuntary, we must consider Barnes' claim in the context of postverdict plea bargaining. We conclude that, under the circumstances of this case, no public policy justified placing Barnes under the stress of a plea negotiation which amounted to nothing more than a wager on the verdict the jury had already reached.[1]

In approving the practice of plea bargaining, the supreme court has spoken of "the right of a defendant to be protected from improvident plea bargaining." *State v. Johnson*, 279 Minn. 209, 214 (1968). The court has stated: "Plea bargaining between competent counsel and with the intelligent acquiescence of the defendant is not in conflict with public policy." Plea bargaining serves the important function of reducing the number of cases to be tried, thereby alleviating the burden on the courts. Postverdict plea bargaining does not serve this function, however, except as to appeals.

The trial court may accept a plea agreement "when the interest of the public in the effective administration of justice would thereby be served." Minn.R.Crim.P. 15.04, subd. 3(2). A number of factors are to be considered in determining whether a negotiated plea has such support. Minn.R.Crim.P. 15.04, subd. 3(2)(a)-(f). Those policies are not significantly served in this case. Because trial was substantially completed, the plea did not avoid trial or alleviate delay in the disposition of other cases. See Minn.R.Crim.P. 15.04, subd. 3(2)(d), 3(2)(f). From this record, it does not appear that the plea hastened sentencing, made alternative correctional measures possible, or resulted in Barnes' cooperation with police on other cases. See Minn.R.Crim.P. 15.04, subd. 3(2)(a), 3(2)(c), 3(2)(e).

---

[1] In his post-trial motion, Barnes claimed that representations made by the trial judge caused him to plead guilty. At the postconviction hearing he testified, however, only that he made an assumption based on the judge's action in holding up the jury verdict. Our decision here is not based on any assertion of misconduct by the trial judge.

Neither, in this case, did it serve any function that would justify foregoing the considered judgment of the fact-finder as to the guilt or innocence of the defendant. Barnes entered a guilty plea, denying his guilt of the charges against him, including the aggravated robbery charge to which he pleaded guilty. Thus, the plea did not serve the purpose of an acknowledgement of guilt. See Minn.R.Crim.P. 15.04, subd. 3(2)(b).

We acknowledge that in some circumstances a postverdict guilty plea may serve some of the purposes for which plea bargaining has traditionally been recognized. We pass no judgment on the situation of a defendant's freely acknowledging guilt and bypassing the jury's verdict. We recognize, however, that society has an interest in the accurate adjudication of criminal charges. What occurred here was an unadorned wager on the jury's decision.

We acknowledge that in any plea negotiation a defendant's estimation of the likely verdict of a jury is a principal factor in his decision. A defendant may plead guilty simply out of fear that a jury will find him guilty. However, in this case, Barnes had little time to adjust from the near-certain prospect of a mistrial to the necessity of speculating on what the jury's verdict was going to be. Barnes had steadfastly refused all plea offers and passed up an opportunity for a mistrial. By all indications, he was intent on seeing the trial through to its conclusion.

The trial court encouraged plea bargaining when a mistrial appeared inevitable and when a negotiated plea could have avoided the necessity of a new trial. Once a verdict had been reached, however, the parties continued plea negotiations without any apparent thought or direction from the court as to whether a plea was still appropriate or unduly stressful on Barnes. It cannot be said that Barnes "intelligently acquiesced," *Johnson*, 279 Minn. at 214, in the postverdict plea bargaining. We conclude that the plea was involuntary, improvident, and lacking the intelligent acquiescence of Barnes.

The trial court abused its discretion in denying appellant's motion to withdraw his guilty plea. Reversed and remanded.

Notes from Pearl:

1. Suppose that the prosecutor and Barnes's lawyer assumed the jury would *acquit*, and before the verdict they entered into a plea bargain calling for a very short jail sentence. After learning that the jury was ready to *convict*, should the court now grant the *prosecutor's* motion to set aside the plea bargain?

2. Suppose that Barnes's plea agreement had included a waiver of the right to appeal. Should this have affected the court's decision?

3. Suppose that, while the jury in a *civil* case is deliberating, the plaintiff and defendant come to a settlement agreement, whereby the defendant promises to pay the plaintiff $100,000. After the agreement is signed, they learn that the jury was just about to return a verdict for the defendant. May the defendant now rescind the agreement, citing *Barnes*?

4. After the Court of Appeals decision, what happens *now*? The jury *would* have found him not guilty, but they didn't return a verdict, so he is not not guilty. All the Court of Appeals decided was that Barnes should be allowed to withdraw his guilty plea, so this means that he now faces a *new trial* — where he might well be found

guilty.

In fact, here is what happened to Barnes. After the Court of Appeals remanded Barnes' case to the trial court, the prosecutor offered him a stipulation: if Barnes would consent to a court trial — based solely on the transcript of the prior jury trial — and the judge found him guilty, the prosecutor would recommend a sentence of no more than 27 months. As Barnes had already been in custody for 27 months and would receive credit for time served if convicted, he agreed. The judge then read the transcript, found him guilty, sentenced him to 27 months, gave him credit for time served, and sent him home. *State v. Barnes*, 1993 WL 515813 (Minn.Ct.App., 1993).

5. In *Commonwealth v. Stagner*, 3 S.W.3d 738 (Ky. 1999), Stagner was charged with theft and related charges. While the jury was deliberating, he bargained with the prosecutor, resulting in plea of guilty to theft of more than $300, a felony. The jury then returned with its verdict: guilty of misdemeanor theft. Stagner's motion to withdraw his plea was denied, and the Kentucky Supreme Court affirmed. The court distinguished *Barnes*, noting that Kentucky has no statute comparable to Minnesota's Rule 15.04 (which allows withdrawal of a guilty plea if it is "fair and just" to do so). The court also stated:

> While we agree with the proposition that a plea negotiation amounts to a "wager on the verdict," such is the case in virtually all criminal trials where a defendant chooses to plead guilty instead of risking an unfavorable jury verdict. The entry of a guilty plea during jury deliberations simply does not create a coercive environment that results in an involuntary plea.

Chapter 8

THE JURY VENIRE

In all criminal prosecutions, the accused shall enjoy the right to a speedy and public trial, by an impartial jury of the State and district wherein the crime shall have been committed.

6th Amendment, U.S. Constitution

Our civilisation has decided, and very justly decided, that determining the guilt or innocence of men is a thing too important to be trusted to trained men. When it wants a library catalogued, or the solar system discovered, or any trifle of that kind, it uses up its specialists. But when it wishes anything done which is really serious, it collects twelve of the ordinary men standing round.

G.K. Chesterton, "The Twelve Men", in <u>Tremendous Trifles</u> *80 (1922)*

WHY USE A JURY?

No country in the world uses the jury as much as the United States — not even England, the source of our jury system. Many countries follow the European "inquisitorial" model, which uses professional judges — sometimes serving on a "mixed panel" with lay people — instead of independent lay juries.[1] We have a different tradition, and every state and the federal government provides for some type of jury trial in most criminal (and most civil) cases.

Why? Are part-time jurors smarter or more knowledgable than full-time judges?[2] Is it more efficient to use 12 deciders instead of one? Is our system less likely than the European "inquisitorial" system to lead to the conviction of innocent people? Doubts about these questions have led some states to try to cut back on the availability of jury trials, or to cut down on the traditional 12-person unanimous verdict requirements. These efforts have often come from Louisiana, whose legal system draws heavily on its French heritage, with its European legal system, in which the jury does not play such an important role.

In *Duncan v. Louisiana*, 391 U.S. 145 (1968), the Supreme Court held that the Due Process Clause of the 14th Amendment incorporates the 6th Amendment right to jury trial and applies it to the states. Alluding to the European system, the Court indicated that the right to jury trial "is not necessarily fundamental to fairness in

---

[1] The "inquisitorial" system is described more fully in Chapter 17, *infra*.

[2] The ABA Journal, March, 1993, p. 43, reported the following incident: "The plaintiff's attorney in a personal injury trial getting under way in a Cairo, Ill., courtroom was conducting voir dire. He asked the jurors if they could give the plaintiff a large sum of money for his injuries if warranted by the evidence, even as much as several hundred thousand dollars. One woman answered with a simple, 'No'. When the lawyer pressed for a reason, she responded: 'I am a single mother, and I didn't even have enough money for a baby-sitter to come to court today. I don't care how bad he's hurt, I can't afford to give him anything.' "

every criminal system that might be imagined but is fundamental in the context of the criminal processes maintained by the American States." *Id.* at 150, fn. 14. The Court explained:

> A right to jury trial is granted to criminal defendants in order to prevent oppression by the Government. Those who wrote our constitutions knew from history and experience that it was necessary to protect against unfounded criminal charges brought to eliminate enemies and against judges too responsive to the voice of higher authority. The framers of the constitutions strove to create an independent judiciary but insisted upon further protection against arbitrary action. Providing an accused with the right to be tried by a jury of his peers gave him an inestimable safeguard against the corrupt or overzealous prosecutor and against the compliant, biased, or eccentric judge. If the defendant preferred the common-sense judgment of a jury to the more tutored but perhaps less sympathetic reaction of the single judge, he was to have it. Beyond this, the jury trial provisions in the Federal and State Constitutions reflect a fundamental decision about the exercise of official power — a reluctance to entrust plenary powers over the life and liberty of the citizen to one judge or to a group of judges. Fear of unchecked power, so typical of our State and Federal Governments in other respects, found expression in the criminal law in this insistence upon community participation in the determination of guilt or innocence. The deep commitment of the Nation to the right of jury trial in serious criminal cases as a defense against arbitrary law enforcement qualifies for protection under the Due Process Clause of the Fourteenth Amendment, and must therefore be respected by the States. [*Id.* at 155–156]

While recognizing "the long debate . . . as to the wisdom of permitting untrained laymen to determine the facts in civil and criminal proceedings," the Court felt that "juries do understand the evidence and come to sound conclusions in most of the cases presented to them." *Id.* at 157.

JUSTICE HARLAN dissented:

> It can hardly be gainsaid, however, that the principal original virtue of the jury trial — the limitations a jury imposes on a tyrannous judiciary — has largely disappeared. We no longer live in a medieval or colonial society. Judges enforce laws enacted by democratic decision, not by regal fiat. They are elected by the people or appointed by the people's elected officials, and are responsible not to a distant monarch alone but to reviewing courts, including this one.

> The jury system can also be said to have some inherent defects, which are multiplied by the emergence of the criminal law from the relative simplicity that existed when the jury system was devised. It is a cumbersome process, not only imposing great cost in time and money on both the State and the jurors themselves, but also contributing to delay in the machinery of justice. Untrained jurors are presumably less adept at reaching accurate conclusions of fact than judges, particularly if the issues are many or complex. And it is argued by some that trial by jury, far from increasing public respect for law, impairs it: the average man, it is said, reacts favorably neither to the notion that matters he knows to be complex

are being decided by other average men, nor to the way the jury system distorts the process of adjudication. [Id. at 188–189]

In *McKeiver v. Pennsylvania*, 403 U.S. 528 (1971), the Court noted that it had held that the Due Process Clause requires that *juvenile court* proceedings must include notice of charges, the right to counsel, the right to confront witnesses through cross-examination, and proof beyond a reasonable doubt. Nevertheless, the Court held that Due Process does *not* include the *right to a jury trial* in such proceedings:

> One cannot say that in our legal system the jury is a necessary component of accurate factfinding. There is much to be said for it, to be sure, but we have been content to pursue other ways for determining facts. Juries are not required, and have not been, for example, in equity cases, in workmen's compensation, in probate, or in deportation cases. Neither have they been generally used in military trials. * * * *

> The imposition of the jury trial on the juvenile court system would not strengthen greatly, if at all, the fact-finding function, and would, contrarily, provide an attrition of the juvenile court's assumed ability to function in a unique manner. * * * * If the jury trial were to be injected into the juvenile court system as a matter of right, it would bring with it into that system the traditional delay, the formality, and the clamor of the adversary system and, possibly, the public trial.

JUSTICE WHITE concurred:

> Although the function of the jury is to find facts, that body is not necessarily or even better at the job than the conscientious judge. Nevertheless, the consequences of criminal guilt are so severe that the Constitution mandates a jury to prevent abuses of official power by insuring, where demanded, community participation in imposing serious deprivations of liberty and to provide a hedge against corrupt, biased, or political justice. * * * *

> To the extent that the jury is a buffer to the corrupt or overzealous prosecutor in the criminal law system, the distinctive intake policies and procedures of the juvenile court system to a great extent obviate this important function of the jury. As for the necessity to guard against judicial bias, a system eschewing blameworthiness and punishment for evil choice is itself an operative force against prejudice and short-tempered justice.

WHAT IS A "JURY"?

In *Williams v. Florida*, 399 U.S. 78 (1970), the Court held that it is not constitutionally necessary for a "jury" to have 12 persons — a "jury" must be large enough to permit true group deliberation, and 6 persons are sufficient. In *Ballew v. Georgia*, 435 U.S. 223 (1978), the Court held that a group of less than 6 persons is not a proper "jury".

In *Apodaca v. Oregon*, 406 U.S. 404 (1972), a majority of the Court held that the 6th Amendment requires a federal "jury" to reach its decision *unanimously*, but a different majority held that the 14th Amendment imposes no such requirement on the states. In *Burch v. Louisiana*, 441 U.S. 130 (1979), the Court invalidated a statute that permitted a verdict by 5 out of 6 "jurors".

Most states require unanimous verdicts in criminal cases.

HOW IS A JURY SELECTED?

The 6th Amendment also requires an "impartial" jury. What does this mean, and what jury selection methods will ensure that an "impartial" jury is empaneled?

Typically, a jury is selected in the following manner. A jury commissioner gathers names of potential jurors from lists of registered voters, telephone subscribers, licensed drivers, and the like. When a jury is needed, the commissioner orders enough people to appear to constitute a *venire* — usually between 30 and 60 people. When the venire arrives, the court clerk puts each name into a box, and then draws out 13 or 14 names (in order to get 12 jurors plus one or two *alternate jurors*, who can replace jurors who get sick). These people are seated in the jury box, and they swear to tell the truth in response to questions posed by the judge and the lawyers. This questioning is called *voir dire* ("to speak the truth"). Some jurisdictions allow the lawyers to conduct *voir dire*, and others give the judge the discretion to conduct *voir dire*, asking written questions submitted by the lawyers and perhaps giving the lawyers a limited period of time to ask questions directly. If a juror's answers convince the judge that the juror cannot be fair to both sides, the judge will sustain a *challenge for cause* to that juror, and the juror will be excused. There is no limit on the number of challenges for cause that may be made or sustained. Each lawyer will also get a limited number of *peremptory challenges*, which need not be explained or justified and which must be sustained by the judge. When a challenge to a prospective juror is sustained, that person is excused. Then a new name is drawn from the box, and that person is seated, sworn, and subjected to *voir dire*, and may then be challenged. When each lawyer has exhausted his or her peremptories or has declared satisfaction with the jury, the jurors are then *empaneled* (sworn to follow the judge's instructions), and the trial begins in front of this jury *panel*.

Problem 8

To: My law clerk

From: Justin Tyme, Esq.

Date: March 21

I am representing Gregory Grunt, who was indicted two years ago by a federal grand jury for vehicular manslaughter (a serious felony) on an Indian reservation. Grunt is a private in the Army, stationed at a large Army base nearby. While on leave, he went on a fishing trip. He drove through a nearby Indian reservation, and he struck and killed an 14-year old Native American girl. A police officer tested him for intoxication, and a breath test allegedly showed a blood alcohol content of .15 (the legal limit is .10).

Soon after the accident, there was a lot of publicity. Newspapers and TV stations in the area reported that the girl was a straight-A student and a star athlete, and that Grunt's blood alcohol level was over the legal limit. One article said that Grunt had admitted to the police officer that he had drunk a six-pack of beer soon before the accident, and that he had driven through a stop sign right before the accident. When Grunt's trial began, the publicity continued ("Grunt Trial Begins", proclaimed one headline), detailing the evidence presented by the prosecution and the defendant (who had testified that he had only two beers and was not drunk). Two articles had photos of Grunt in them. Several articles reported Grunt's defenses: (1) that lab technicians screwed up the blood test, and Grunt's blood alcohol level was not over.10, and (2) that the victim ran out in the road so fast that not even a sober driver could have stopped in time.

When the jury brought in its guilty verdict, this got a lot of publicity, and one major newspaper had the story on page 2 with the headline "Grunt Guilty". The newspapers also reported that at Grunt's sentencing hearing, the courtroom was packed with members of PADD (Persons Against Drunk Driving), wearing PADD buttons. The judge sentenced Grunt to 4 years in prison, even though Grunt had no prior record.

I then filed an appeal, and last month the Court of Appeal reversed the conviction because of an error in the judge's instructions to the jury. Newspapers reported the reversal ("Court Throws Out Grunt Conviction"), and one included a comment of an assistant U.S. Attorney calling the decision "totally illogical and contrary to law".

The case has been set for retrial next month. I am very concerned about the kind of jury we will get to try Grunt. There is large Army base nearby (where Grunt is stationed) and also a fair-sized Air Force base, so quite a number of residents of the area are military personnel. Under federal law, however, they are all barred from serving on juries. This doesn't seem fair to me. Also, I feel that many people in the community already know a lot about this case, so I am not sure that Grunt can get a fair trial in this judicial district. On the other hand, there are a lot of relatives of military people in this district, and I'd like to have some of them as jurors.

I guess I can avoid all of these problems if I simply waive a jury and let the judge try the case. Some of the scientific evidence on the blood test is so technical that I'm not sure a bunch of jurors will understand it anyway.

Please read the attached authorities and give some ideas about what we might do on these issues. If we need any more information, tell me what we need and how to get it.

United States Code, Title 28

§ 1861. **Declaration of policy**

It is the policy of the United States that all litigants in Federal courts entitled to trial by jury shall have the right to grand and petit juries selected at random from a fair cross section of the community in the district or division wherein the court convenes. It is further the policy of the United States that all citizens shall have the opportunity to be considered for service on grand and petit juries in the district courts of the United States, and shall have an obligation to serve as jurors when summoned for that purpose.

§ 1862. Discrimination prohibited

No citizen shall be excluded from service as a grand or petit juror in the district courts of the United States or in the Court of International Trade on account of race, color, religion, sex, national origin, or economic status.

§ 1863. Plan for random jury selection

(a) Each United States district court shall devise and place into operation a written plan for random selection of grand and petit jurors that shall be designed to achieve the objectives of sections 1861 and 1862 of this title. * * * *

(b) Among other things, such plan shall

(1) either establish a jury commission, or authorize the clerk of the court, to manage the jury selection process * * * *

(2) specify whether the names of prospective jurors shall be selected from the voter registration lists or the lists of actual voters of the political subdivisions within the district or division. The plan shall prescribe some other source or sources of names in addition to voter lists where necessary to foster the policy and protect the rights secured by sections 1861 and 1862 of this title. * * * *

(3) specify detailed procedures to be followed by the jury commission or clerk in selecting names from the sources specified in paragraph (2) of this subsection. These procedures shall be designed to ensure the random selection of a fair cross section of the persons residing in the community in the district or division wherein the court convenes. * * * *

(4) provide for a master jury wheel (or a device similar in purpose and function) into which the names of those randomly selected shall be placed. * * * *

(5)(A) except as provided in subparagraph (B), specify those groups of persons or occupational classes whose members shall, on individual request therefor, be excused from jury service. Such groups or classes shall be excused only if the district court finds, and the plan states, that jury service by such class or group would entail undue hardship or extreme inconvenience to the members thereof, and excuse of members thereof would not be inconsistent with sections 1861 and 1862 of this title.

(B) specify that volunteer safety personnel, upon individual request, shall be excused from jury service. For purposes of this subparagraph, the term "volunteer safety personnel" means individuals serving a public agency in an official capacity, without compensation, as firefighters or members of a rescue squad or ambulance crew.

(6) specify that the following persons are barred from jury service on the ground that they are exempt: (A) members in active service in the Armed Forces of the United States; (B) members of the fire or police departments of any State, the District of Columbia, any territory or possession of the United States, or any subdivision of a State, the District of Columbia, or such territory or possession; (C) public officers in the executive, legislative, or judicial branches of the Government of the United States, or of any

State, the District of Columbia, any territory or possession of the United States, or any subdivision of a State, the District of Columbia, or such territory or possession, who are actively engaged in the performance of official duties. * * * *

(7) fix the time when the names drawn from the qualified jury wheel shall be disclosed to parties and to the public. * * *

§ 1864. Drawing of names from the master jury wheel; completion of juror qualification form

(a) From time to time as directed by the district court, the clerk or a district judge shall publicly draw at random from the master jury wheel the names of as many persons as may be required for jury service. * * * *

(b) Any person summoned pursuant to subsection (a) of this section who fails to appear as directed shall be ordered by the district court forthwith to appear and show cause for his failure to comply with the summons. * * * *

§ 1865. Qualifications for jury service

(a) The chief judge of the district court, or such other district court judge as the plan may provide, on his initiative or upon recommendation of the clerk or jury commission, shall determine solely on the basis of information provided on the juror qualification form and other competent evidence whether a person is unqualified for, or exempt, or to be excused from jury service. * * * *

(b) In making such determination the chief judge of the district court, or such other district court judge as the plan may provide, shall deem any person qualified to serve on grand and petit juries in the district court unless he

(1) is not a citizen of the United States eighteen years old who has resided for a period of one year within the judicial district;

(2) is unable to read, write, and understand the English language with a degree of proficiency sufficient to fill out satisfactorily the juror qualification form;

(3) is unable to speak the English language;

(4) is incapable, by reason of mental or physical infirmity, to render satisfactory jury service; or

(5) has a charge pending against him for the commission of, or has been convicted in a State or Federal court of record of, a crime punishable by imprisonment for more than one year and his civil rights have not been restored.

§ 1866. Selection and summoning of jury panels

(a) The jury commission, or in the absence thereof the clerk, shall maintain a qualified jury wheel and shall place in such wheel names of all persons drawn from the master jury wheel who are determined to be qualified as jurors and not exempt or excused pursuant to the district court plan. From time to time, the jury commission or the clerk shall publicly draw at random from the qualified jury wheel such number of names of persons as may be required for assignment to grand and petit jury panels. The jury commission or the clerk shall prepare a separate list of names of persons assigned to each grand and petit jury panel.

(b) When the court orders a grand or petit jury to be drawn, the clerk or jury commission or their duly designated deputies shall issue summonses for the required number of jurors. * * * *

(c) * * * * [A]ny person summoned for jury service may be (1) excused by the court * * * *, upon a showing of undue hardship or extreme inconvenience, for such period as the court deems necessary, * * * * or (2) excluded by the court on the ground that such person may be unable to render impartial jury service or that his service as a juror would be likely to disrupt the proceedings, or (3) excluded upon peremptory challenge as provided by law, or (4) excluded pursuant to the procedure specified by law upon a challenge by any party for good cause shown, or (5) excluded upon determination by the court that his service as a juror would be likely to threaten the secrecy of the proceedings, or otherwise adversely affect the integrity of jury deliberations. * * * *

§ 1867. Challenging compliance with selection procedures

(a) In criminal cases, before the voir dire examination begins, or within seven days after the defendant discovered or could have discovered, by the exercise of diligence, the grounds therefor, whichever is earlier, the defendant may move to dismiss the indictment or stay the proceedings against him on the ground of substantial failure to comply with the provisions of this title in selecting the grand or petit jury. * * * *

[Enacted in 1948, with subsequent amendments.]

Federal Rules of Criminal Procedure

Rule 18. Place of Prosecution and Trial

Unless a statute or these rules permit otherwise, the government must prosecute an offense in a district where the offense was committed. The court must set the place of trial within the district with due regard for the convenience of the defendant and the witnesses, and the prompt administration of justice.

Rule 21. Transfer for Trial

(a) **For Prejudice.** Upon the defendant's motion, the court must transfer the proceeding against that defendant to another district if the court is satisfied that so great a prejudice against the defendant exists in the transferring district that the defendant cannot obtain a fair and impartial trial there.

(b) **For Convenience.** Upon the defendant's motion, the court may transfer the proceeding, or one or more counts, against that defendant to another district for the convenience of the parties and witnesses and in the interest of justice.

(c) **Proceedings on Transfer.** When the court orders a transfer, the clerk must send to the transferee district the file, or a certified copy, and any bail taken. The prosecution will then continue in the transferee district.

(d) **Time to File a Motion to Transfer.** A motion to transfer may be made at or before arraignment or at any other time the court or these rules prescribe.

Rule 23. Jury or Nonjury Trial

(a) Jury Trial. If the defendant is entitled to a jury trial, the trial must be by jury unless:

(1) the defendant waives a jury trial in writing;

(2) the government consents; and

(3) the court approves.

(b) Jury Size.

(1) In General. A jury consists of 12 persons unless this rule provides otherwise.

(2) Stipulation for a Smaller Jury. At any time before the verdict, the parties may, with the court's approval, stipulate in writing that:

(A) the jury may consist of fewer than 12 persons; or

(B) a jury of fewer than 12 persons may return a verdict if the court finds it necessary to excuse a juror for good cause after the trial begins.

(3) Court Order for a Jury of 11. After the jury has retired to deliberate, the court may permit a jury of 11 persons to return a verdict, even without a stipulation by the parties, if the court finds good cause to excuse a juror.

(c) Nonjury Trial. In a case tried without a jury, the court must find the defendant guilty or not guilty. If a party requests before the finding of guilty or not guilty, the court must state its specific findings of fact in open court or in a written decision or opinion.

Rule 24. Trial Jurors

(a) Examination.

(1) In General. The court may examine prospective jurors or may permit the attorneys for the parties to do so.

(2) Court Examination. If the court examines the jurors, it must permit the attorneys for the parties to:

(A) ask further questions that the court considers proper; or

(B) submit further questions that the court may ask if it considers them proper.

(b) Peremptory Challenges. Each side is entitled to the number of peremptory challenges to prospective jurors specified below. The court may allow additional peremptory challenges to multiple defendants, and may allow the defendants to exercise those challenges separately or jointly.

(1) Capital Case. Each side has 20 peremptory challenges when the government seeks the death penalty.

(2) Other Felony Case. The government has 6 peremptory challenges and the defendant or defendants jointly have 10 peremptory challenges when the defendant is charged with a crime punishable by imprisonment of more than one year.

(3) Misdemeanor Case. Each side has 3 peremptory challenges when the defendant is charged with a crime punishable by fine, imprisonment of one year or less, or both.

(c) Alternate Jurors.

(1) In General. The court may impanel up to 6 alternate jurors to replace any jurors who are unable to perform or who are disqualified from performing their duties.

(2) Procedure.

(A) Alternate jurors must have the same qualifications and be selected and sworn in the same manner as any other juror.

(B) Alternate jurors replace jurors in the same sequence in which the alternates were selected. An alternate juror who replaces a juror has the same authority as the other jurors.

(3) Retaining Alternate Jurors. The court may retain alternate jurors after the jury retires to deliberate. The court must ensure that a retained alternate does not discuss the case with anyone until that alternate replaces a juror or is discharged. If an alternate replaces a juror after deliberations have begun, the court must instruct the jury to begin its deliberations anew.

(4) Peremptory Challenges. Each side is entitled to the number of additional peremptory challenges to prospective alternate jurors specified below. These additional challenges may be used only to remove alternate jurors.

(A) One or Two Alternates. One additional peremptory challenge is permitted when one or two alternates are impaneled.

(B) Three or Four Alternates. Two additional peremptory challenges are permitted when three or four alternates are impaneled.

(C) Five or Six Alternates. Three additional peremptory challenges are permitted when five or six alternates are impaneled.

Rule 31. Jury Verdict

(a) Return. The jury must return its verdict to a judge in open court. The verdict must be unanimous.

(b) Partial Verdicts, Mistrial, and Retrial.

(1) Multiple Defendants. If there are multiple defendants, the jury may return a verdict at any time during its deliberations as to any defendant about whom it has agreed.

(2) Multiple Counts. If the jury cannot agree on all counts as to any defendant, the jury may return a verdict on those counts on which it has agreed.

(3) Mistrial and Retrial. If the jury cannot agree on a verdict on one or more counts, the court may declare a mistrial on those counts. The government may retry any defendant on any count on which the jury could not agree.

(c)   Lesser Offense or Attempt. A defendant may be found guilty of any of the following:

> **(1)** an offense necessarily included in the offense charged;

> **(2)** an attempt to commit the offense charged; or

> **(3)** an attempt to commit an offense necessarily included in the offense charged, if the attempt is an offense in its own right.

(d)   Jury Poll. After a verdict is returned but before the jury is discharged, the court must on a party's request, or may on its own, poll the jurors individually. If the poll reveals a lack of unanimity, the court may direct the jury to deliberate further or may declare a mistrial and discharge the jury.

In *Witherspoon v. Illinois*, 391 U.S. 510 (1968), defendant was charged with murder. The jury would decide whether he was guilty, and (if so) would then go on to decide whether he should receive the death penalty. The trial court sustained the prosecutor's challenge for cause to every prospective juror who "expressed qualms" about capital punishment (in addition to those who said they "could never" vote for a death penalty), which eliminated about half of the venire. The resulting jury found defendant guilty and then fixed his penalty at death.

Defendant argued that the *guilty verdict* should be reversed, because a jury from which people with qualms about the death penalty have been excluded "must necessarily be biased in favor of conviction, for the kind of juror who would be unperturbed by the prospect of sending a man to his death, he contends, is the kind of juror who would too readily ignore the presumption of the defendant's innocence, accept the prosecution's verdict of the facts, and return a verdict of guilt." The Supreme Court rejected this argument, as the data furnished by defendant to prove this point "are too tentative and fragmentary to establish that jurors not opposed to the death penalty tend to favor the prosecution in the determination of guilt."

However, the Court did reverse the *death penalty*, as "this jury fell woefully short of that impartiality to which the petitioner was entitled under the Sixth and Fourteenth Amendments. Guided by neither rule nor standard, free to select or reject as it sees fit, a jury that must choose between life imprisonment and capital punishment can do little more — and must do nothing less — than express the conscience of the community on the ultimate question of life or death. Yet, in a nation less than half of whose people believe in the death penalty, a jury composed exclusively of such people cannot speak for the community."

1. Exclusions From the Venire

TAYLOR v. LOUISIANA
United States Supreme Court
419 U.S. 522 (1975)

MR. JUSTICE WHITE delivered the opinion of the Court.

When this case was tried, Art. VII, § 41, of the Louisiana Constitution, and Art. 402 of the Louisiana Code of Criminal Procedure provided that a woman should not be selected for jury service unless she had previously filed a written declaration of her desire to be subject to jury service. The constitutionality of these provisions is the issue in this case.

I

Appellant, Billy J. Taylor, was indicted by the grand jury of St. Tammany Parish, in the Twenty-second Judicial District of Louisiana, for aggravated kidnaping. On April 12, 1972, appellant moved the trial court to quash the petit jury venire drawn for the special criminal term beginning with his trial the following day. Appellant alleged that women were systematically excluded from the venire and that he would therefore be deprived of what he claimed to be his federal constitutional right to "a fair trial by jury of a representative segment of the community."

The Twenty-second Judicial District comprises the parishes of St. Tammany and Washington. The appellee has stipulated that 53% of the persons eligible for jury service in these parishes were female, and that no more than 10% of the persons on the jury wheel in St. Tammany Parish were women. During the period from December 8, 1971, to November 3, 1972, 12 females were among the 1,800 persons drawn to fill petit jury venires in St. Tammany Parish. It was also stipulated that the discrepancy between females eligible for jury service and those actually included in the venire was the result of the operation of La. Const., Art. VII, § 41, and La.Code Crim.Proc., Art. 402. In the present case, a venire totaling 175 persons was drawn for jury service beginning April 13, 1972. There were no females on the venire.

Appellant's motion to quash the venire was denied that same day. * * * *

II

The Louisiana jury-selection system does not disqualify women from jury service, but in operation its conceded systematic impact is that only a very few women, grossly disproportionate to the number of eligible women in the community, are called for jury service. In this case, no women were on the venire from which the petit jury was drawn. The issue we have, therefore, is whether a jury-selection system which operates to exclude from jury service an identifiable class of citizens constituting 53% of eligible jurors in the community comports with the Sixth and Fourteenth Amendments.

The State first insists that Taylor, a male, has no standing to object to the exclusion of women from his jury. But Taylor's claim is that he was constitutionally entitled to a jury drawn from a venire constituting a fair cross section of the community and that the jury that tried him was not such a jury by reason of the exclusion of women. Taylor was not a member of the excluded class; but there is no rule that claims such as Taylor presents may be made only by those defendants who are members of the group excluded from jury service. In *Peters v. Kiff*, 407 U.S. 493 (1972), the defendant, a white man, challenged his conviction on the ground that Negroes had been systematically excluded from jury service. Six Members of the Court agreed that petitioner was entitled to present the issue and concluded that he had been deprived of his federal rights. Taylor, in the case before us, was similarly entitled to tender and have adjudicated the claim that the exclusion of women from jury service deprived him of the kind of factfinder to which he was constitutionally entitled.

III

The background against which this case must be decided includes our holding in *Duncan v. Louisiana*, 391 U.S. 145 (1968), that the Sixth Amendment's provision for jury trial is made binding on the States by virtue of the Fourteenth Amendment. Our inquiry is whether the presence of a fair cross section of the community on venires, panels, of lists from which petit juries are drawn is essential to the fulfillment of the Sixth Amendment's guarantee of an impartial jury trial in criminal prosecutions.

The Court's prior cases are instructive. Both in the course of exercising its supervisory powers over trials in federal courts and in the constitutional context, the Court has unambiguously declared that the American concept of the jury trial contemplates a jury drawn from a fair cross section of the community. A unanimous Court stated in *Smith v. Texas*, 311 U.S. 128, 130 (1940), that "it is part of the established tradition in the use of juries as instruments of public justice that the jury be a body truly representative of the community." To exclude racial groups from jury service was said to be "at war with our basic concepts of a democratic society and a representative government." A state jury system that resulted in systematic exclusion of Negroes as jurors was therefore held to violate the Equal Protection Clause of the Fourteenth Amendment. *Glasser v. United States*, 315 U.S. 60, 85–86 (1942), in the context of a federal criminal case and the Sixth Amendment's jury trial requirement, stated that "our notions of what a proper jury is have developed in harmony with our basic concepts of a democratic system and representative government," and repeated the Court's understanding that the jury 'be a body truly representative of the community' and not the organ of any special group or class."

A federal conviction by a jury from which women had been excluded, although eligible for service under state law, was reviewed in *Ballard v. United States*, 329 U.S. 187 (1946). Noting the federal statutory "design to make the jury a cross-section of the community" and the fact that women had been excluded, the Court exercised its supervisory powers over the federal courts and reversed the conviction. * * * *

The unmistakable import of this Court's opinions, at least since 1940, *Smith v. Texas, supra*, and not repudiated by intervening decisions, is that the selection of a petit jury from a representative cross section of the community is an essential component of the Sixth Amendment right to a jury trial. Recent federal legislation governing jury selection within the federal court system has a similar thrust. Shortly prior to this Court's decision in *Duncan v. Louisiana*, the Federal Jury

Selection and Service Act of 1968, 28 U.S.C. §§ 1861 et. seq., was enacted. In that Act, Congress stated "the policy of the United States that all litigants in Federal courts entitled to trial by jury shall have the right to grand and petit juries selected at random from a fair cross section of the community in the district or division wherein the court convenes." 28 U.S.C. § 1861. In that Act, Congress also established the machinery by which the stated policy was to be implemented. 28 U.S.C. §§ 1862–1866. * * * *

We accept the fair-cross-section requirement as fundamental to the jury trial guaranteed by the Sixth Amendment and are convinced that the requirement has solid foundation. The purpose of a jury is to guard against the exercise of arbitrary power — to make available the commonsense judgment of the community as a hedge against the overzealous or mistaken prosecutor and in preference to the professional or perhaps overconditioned or biased response of a judge. *Duncan v. Louisiana*, 391 U.S. at 155–156. This prophylactic vehicle is not provided if the jury pool is made up of only special segments of the populace or if large, distinctive groups are excluded from the pool. Community participation in the administration of the criminal law, moreover, is not only consistent with our democratic heritage but is also critical to public confidence in the fairness of the criminal justice system. Restricting jury service to only special groups or excluding identifiable segments playing major roles in the community cannot be squared with the constitutional concept of jury trial. "Trial by jury presupposes a jury drawn from a pool broadly representative of the community as well as impartial in a specific case. The broad representative character of the jury should be maintained, partly as assurance of a diffused impartiality and partly because sharing in the administration of justice is a phase of civic responsibility." *Thiel v. Southern Pacific Co.*, 328 U.S. 217, 227 (1946) (Frankfurter, J., dissenting).

IV

We are also persuaded that the fair-cross-section requirement is violated by the systematic exclusion of women, who in the judicial district involved here amounted to 53% of the citizens eligible for jury service. This conclusion necessarily entails the judgment that women are sufficiently numerous and distinct from men and that if they are systematically eliminated from jury panels, the Sixth Amendment's fair-cross-section requirement cannot be satisfied. This very matter was debated in *Ballard v. United States, supra*. Positing the fair-cross-section rule — there said to be a statutory one — the Court concluded that the systematic exclusion of women was unacceptable. The dissenting view that an all-male panel drawn from various groups in the community would be as truly representative as if women were included, was firmly rejected:

> The thought is that the factors which tend to influence the action of women are the same as those which influence the action of men — personality, background, economic status — and not sex. Yet it is not enough to say that women when sitting as jurors neither act nor tend to act as a class. Men likewise do not act as a class. But, if the shoe were on the other foot, who would claim that a jury was truly representative of the community if all men were intentionally and systematically excluded from the panel? The truth is that the two sexes are not fungible; a community made up exclusively of one is different from a community composed of both; the subtle interplay of influence one on the other is among the

imponderables. To insulate the courtroom from either may not in a given case make an iota of difference. Yet a flavor, a distinct quality is lost if either sex is excluded. The exclusion of one may indeed make the jury less representative of the community than would be true if an economic or racial group were excluded. [329 U.S. at 193–194][12]

In this respect, we agree with the Court in *Ballard*: If the fair-cross-section rule is to govern the selection of juries, as we have concluded it must, women cannot be systematically excluded from jury panels from which petit juries are drawn. This conclusion is consistent with the current judgment of the country, now evidenced by legislative or constitutional provisions in every State and at the federal level qualifying women for jury service.[13]

V

There remains the argument that women as a class serve a distinctive role in society and that jury service would so substantially interfere with that function that the State has ample justification for excluding women from service unless they volunteer, even though the result is that almost all jurors are men. It is true that *Hoyt v. Florida*, 368 U.S. 57 (1961), held that such a system * * * did not deny due process of law or equal protection of the laws because there was a sufficiently rational basis for such an exemption.[15] But *Hoyt* did not involve a defendant's Sixth

---

[12] Compare *Peters v. Kiff*, 407 U.S. 493, 502–504 (1972) (opinion of Marshall, J.):

These principles compel the conclusion that a State cannot, consistent with due process, subject a defendant to indictment or trial by a jury that has been selected in an arbitrary and discriminatory manner, in violation of the Constitution and laws of the United States. Illegal and unconstitutional jury selection procedures cast doubt on the integrity of the whole judicial process. They create the appearance of bias in the decision of individual cases, and they increase the risk of actual bias as well.

But the exclusion from jury service of a substantial and identifiable class of citizens has a potential impact that is too subtle and too pervasive to admit of confinement to particular issues or particular cases.

Moreover, we are unwilling to make the assumption that the exclusion of Negroes has relevance only for issues involving race. When any large and identifiable segment of the community is excluded from jury service, the effect is to remove from the jury room qualities of human nature and varieties of human experience, the range of which is unknown and perhaps unknowable. It is not necessary to assume that the excluded group will consistently vote as a class in order to conclude, as we do, that its exclusion deprives the jury of a perspective on human events that may have unsuspected importance in any case that may be presented.

Controlled studies of the performance of women as jurors conducted subsequent to the Court's decision in *Ballard* have concluded that women bring to juries their own perspectives and values that influence both jury deliberation and result. See generally Rudolph, *Women on Juries — Voluntary or Compulsory?*, 44 J.Am.Jud.Soc. 206 (1961).

[13] This is a relatively modern development. Under the English common law, women, with the exception of the trial of a narrow class of cases, were not considered to be qualified for jury service by virtue of the doctrine of proper *defectum sexus*, a "defect of sex." 3 W. Blackstone, Commentaries. This common-law rule was made statutory by Parliament in 1870, and then rejected by Parliament in 1919. In this country, women were disqualified by state law to sit as jurors until the end of the 19th century. They were first deemed qualified for jury service by a State in 1898, Utah Rev.Stat.Ann., Tit. 35, § 1297. Today, women are qualified as jurors in all the States. * * * *

[15] The state interest, as articulated by the Court, was based on the assumption that "woman is still regarded as the center of home and family life." *Hoyt v. Florida, supra*, at 62. Louisiana makes a similar argument here, stating that its grant of an automatic exemption from jury service of females involves only the State's attempt "to regulate and provide stability to the state's own idea of family life."

Amendment right to a jury drawn from a fair cross section of the community and the prospect of depriving him of that right if women as a class are systematically excluded. The right to a proper jury cannot be overcome on merely rational grounds. * * * * There must be weightier reasons if a distinctive class representing 53% of the eligible jurors is for all practical purposes to be excluded from jury service. No such basis has been tendered here.

The States are free to grant exemptions from jury service to individuals in case of special hardship or incapacity and to those engaged in particular occupations the uninterrupted performance of which is critical to the community's welfare. It would not appear that such exemptions would pose substantial threats that the remaining pool of jurors would not be representative of the community. A system excluding all women, however, is a wholly different matter. It is untenable to suggest these days that it would be a special hardship for each and every woman to perform jury service or that society cannot spare any women from their present duties.[17] This may be the case with many, and it may be burdensome to sort out those who should be exempted from those who should serve. But that task is performed in the case of men, and the administrative convenience in dealing with women as a class is insufficient justification for diluting the quality of community judgment represented by the jury in criminal trials. * * * *

Accepting as we do, however, the view that the Sixth Amendment affords the defendant in a criminal trial the opportunity to have the jury drawn from venires representative of the community, we think it is no longer tenable to hold that women as a class may be excluded to given automatic exemptions based solely on sex if the consequence is that criminal jury venires are almost totally male. To this extent, we cannot follow the contrary implications of the prior cases, including *Hoyt v. Florida*. If it was ever the case that women were unqualified to sit on juries or were so situated that none of them should be required to perform jury service, that time has long since passed. If at one time it could be held that Sixth Amendment juries must be drawn from a fair cross section of the community but that this requirement permitted the almost total exclusion of women, this is not the case today. Communities differ at different times and places. What is a fair cross section at one time or place is not necessarily a fair cross section at another time or a different place. Nothing persuasive has been presented to us in this case suggesting that all-male venires in the parishes involved here are fairly representative of the local population otherwise eligible for jury service.

---

[17] In *Hoyt v. Florida, supra,* the Court placed some emphasis on the notion, advanced by the State there and by Louisiana here in support of the rationality of its statutory scheme, that "woman is still regarded as the center of home and family life." 368 U.S. at 62. Statistics compiled by the Department of Labor indicate that in October 1974, 54.2% of all women between 18 and 64 years of age were in the labor force. Additionally, in March 1974, 45.7% of women with children under the age of 18 were in the labor force; with respect to families containing children between the ages of six and 17, 67.3% of mothers who were widowed, divorced, or separated were in the work force, while 51.2% of the mothers whose husbands were present in the household were in the work force. Even in family units in which the husband was present and which contained a child under three years old, 31% of the mothers were in the work force. While these statistics perhaps speak more to the evolving nature of the structure of the family unit in American society than to the nature of the role played by women who happen to be members of a family unit, they certainly put to rest the suggestion that all women should be exempt from jury service based solely on their sex and the presumed role in the home.

VII

Our holding does not augur or authorize the fashioning of detailed jury selection codes by federal courts. The fair-cross-section principle must have much leeway in application. The States remain free to prescribe relevant qualifications for their jurors and to provide reasonable exemptions so long as it may be fairly said that the jury lists or panels are representative of the community. * * * * But, as we have said, Louisiana's special exemption for women operates to exclude them from petit juries, which in our view is contrary to the command of the Sixth and Fourteenth Amendments.

It should also be emphasized that in holding that petit juries must be drawn from a source fairly representative of the community we impose no requirement that petit juries actually chosen must mirror the community and reflect the various distinctive groups in the population. Defendants are not entitled to a jury of any particular composition; but the jury wheels, pools of names, panels, or venires from which juries are drawn must not systematically exclude distinctive groups in the community and thereby fail to be reasonably representative thereof.

The judgment of the Louisiana Supreme Court is reversed.

Mr. Justice Rehnquist, dissenting.

The Court's opinion reverses a conviction without a suggestion, much less a showing, that the appellant has been unfairly treated or prejudiced in any way by the manner in which his jury was selected. In so doing, the Court invalidates a jury-selection system which it approved by a substantial majority only 13 years ago. I disagree with the Court and would affirm the judgment of the Supreme Court of Louisiana.

The majority opinion canvasses various of our jury trial cases, beginning with *Smith v. Texas*, 311 U.S. 128 (1940). Relying on carefully chosen quotations, it concludes that the "unmistakable import" of our cases is that the fair-cross-section requirement "is an essential component of the Sixth Amendment right to a jury trial." I disagree. Fairly read, the only "unmistakable import" of those cases is that due process and equal protection prohibit jury-selection systems which are likely to result in biased or partial juries. *Smith v. Texas* concerned the equal protection claim of a Negro who was indicted by a grand jury from which Negroes had been systematically excluded. *Glasser v. United States*, 315 U.S. 60 (1942), dealt with allegations that the only women selected for jury service were members of a private organization which had conducted pro-prosecution classes for prospective jurors. * * * *

I cannot conceive that today's decision is necessary to guard against oppressive or arbitrary law enforcement, or to prevent miscarriages of justice and to assure fair trials. Especially is this so when the criminal defendant involved makes no claims of prejudice or bias. The Court does accord some slight attention to justifying its ruling in terms of the basis on which the right to jury trial was read into the Fourteenth Amendment. It concludes that the jury is not effective, as a prophylaxis against arbitrary prosecutorial and judicial power, if the "jury pool is made up of only special segments of the populace or if large, distinctive groups are excluded from the pool." It fails, however, to provide any satisfactory explanation of the mechanism by which the Louisiana system undermines the prophylactic role of the jury, either in general or in this case. The best it can do is to posit "a flavor, a distinct quality," which allegedly is lost if either sex is excluded." However, this "flavor" is not of such importance that the Constitution is offended if any given petit jury is not so enriched. This smacks more of mysticism than of law. The Court does not even purport to practice its mysticism in a consistent fashion — presumably doctors, lawyers, and other groups, whose frequent exemption from jury service is endorsed by the majority, also offer qualities as distinct and important as those at issue here.

Notes from Justin:

1. The 6th Amendment gives Taylor the right to an "impartial" jury. Were the 12 men who tried Taylor "partial" to the prosecution? Is this what the Court held?

In Andrew Leipold, *Constitutionalizing Jury Selection In Criminal Cases: A Critical Evaluation*, 86 Georgetown L.J. 945, 963 (1998), the author states:

> The absence of women from the jury pool does not by itself suggest that the men who serve will be biased against women, nor does it suggest that the male jurors will be missing any of the other qualities mentioned above. The male jurors may be partial for other reasons, or may in fact be prejudiced against women, but there is nothing about the identity of the excluded jurors that tells us when this will be true. So, in the abstract, depriving a defendant of a diverse jury does not deprive him of an impartial decision-maker.

2. Is *Taylor* consistent with *Witherspoon*? In *Witherspoon*, didn't the Court (at least on the *guilt* issue) examine the impartiality of the jurors by looking at the impartiality of the 12 jurors *actually seated* — regardless of who was *excluded*? Did *Taylor* take this approach?

3. I suppose that there are cases in which a male defendant might benefit from having women on his jury — for example, where the defendant claims he was trying to defend a woman from attack. Is *Taylor* such a case? How did the Court view the *facts* of *Taylor*? (What *were* the facts of *Taylor*?)

4. The Court says that Louisiana "excluded" women from juries. Is this a fair characterization of what Louisiana did? Didn't Louisiana give women a *choice* — to serve or not to serve? (Wouldn't Louisiana *men* have been delighted with such a choice?)

5. In Ann Poulin, *The Jury: The Criminal Justice System's Different Voice*, 62 U.Cinn.L.Rev. 1377, 1395–96 (1994), the author states:

> Comparing approaches of girls and boys to solving problems, Carol Gilligan (in *A Different Voice*) recognized that different subjects brought different voices to the exercise. She concluded that, when solving problems, boys tended to refer to abstract and rational concepts of fairness, whereas girls tended to refer to relationships and principles of affiliation and responsibility. Although Gilligan viewed the differences as gender related, she acknowledged that the difference in voice can be found in both genders.
>
> Thus, setting aside gender-based generalizations, Gilligan's observations concerning the different ways in which people approach a problem cast useful light on jury behavior. The law is framed in abstract, logical,

rational terms. The jury will generally be directed to approach its task in those terms. Some jurors naturally tend to use that analytical approach and will comfortably comply with the court's instructions. Of those jurors, some will engage in straight-forward application of the law to reach a verdict, while others may depart from the law given by the court. As Gilligan points out, a person who applies the logical, rational model will not always come to a decision governed by the law; rational analysis can lead to the decision that the law is wrong and should be disregarded. We can also expect that some jurors will take a different analytical path and will analyze the case in terms of relationship and responsibility. These jurors are likely to view the evidence differently, and their natural tendencies will be counter to the logical, rational analysis prescribed in the court's instructions. Consequently, these jurors' analysis will differ both from that of other jurors and from that contemplated by the expressed law, particularly if the trial court communicates its instructions ineffectively or if those instructions are somewhat general. Thus, Gilligan's insights suggest both that the jury's analysis may not follow rational abstract rules and that the analysis may vary with the composition of the jury. Both of these possibilities contribute to the difference of the jury's voice.

6. Supposedly in response to *Taylor; Peters v. Kiff*, and similar cases, officials in DeKalb County, Georgia decided to meet their "fair cross-section" obligations by the following method:

By an analysis of Census data, the entire voting-age population of the county is broken down into those groups treated as "cognizable". The relevant groups are black males, black females, white males, white females, "other" males, and "other" females, each subdivided into age groups 18 to 24, 25 to 34, 35 to 44, 45 to 54, 55 to 64, and 65 plus. Taken together, these categories yield a grid of 36 squares. Each square is assigned "requested quota totals" by percentage and, for a jury list of given magnitude, by head count. The computer fills the quotas by a random draw from the list of registered voters in the various categories. (Yes, Georgia records the race of registered voters. This longstanding practice, once arguably unconstitutional, is now welcomed by the Justice Department as a means of facilitating its review of the state's compliance with the Voting Rights Act.)

The computer selection is necessarily less random for some classes of voters than others. Any black male age 18 to 34, who registers to vote, is virtually guaranteed a spot on the jury list. By contrast, the chance that someone in my own group (middle-age white male voters) will find his name on the most recent list is just over one in eight.

The disparities are less pronounced for other sectors of the grid, but black voters overall are still nearly 40% more likely to be drawn than white voters. Jury duty is commonly thought to one of the burdens of citizenship, not one of its benefits, and its uneven incidence along racial lines appears to deny equal treatment to black voters — subjecting them, in effect, to a racially discriminatory tax on suffrage. [Andrew Kull, "The King Case's Wrong Lesson", Los Angeles Daily Journal, 12/24/92, p. 4.]

Do you think the DeKalb system is (a) constitutionally required, (b) constitutionally permissible, (c) good social policy? (Are these the same questions, or different?)

7. In *Duren v. Missouri*, 439 U.S. 357 (1979), the state automatically exempted from jury service all women requesting not to serve. The Court set out the following test:

> In order to establish a prima facie violation of the fair-cross-section requirement, the defendant must show (1) that the group alleged to be excluded is a "distinctive" group in the community; (2) that the representation of this group in venires from which juries are selected is not fair and reasonable in relation to the number of such persons in the community; and (3) that this underrepresentation is due to systematic exclusion of the group in the jury-selection process.

Applying this test, the Court found that: (1) as *Taylor* held, women are a distinctive group, (2) while 54% of the community was female, only 15% of the average venire was female, and (3) this discrepancy was "systematic" — i.e., "inherent" in the process used — as defendant showed that it occurred "not just occasionally, but in every weekly venire for a period of nearly a year.

After defendant shows a prima facie case, the burden shifts to the prosecution to show that a "significant state interest" justifies the state's policy. The Court recognized "that a State may have an important interest in assuring that those members of the family responsible for the care of children are available to do so," and "an exemption appropriately tailored to this interest would, we think, survive a fair-cross-section challenge." While permissible exemptions "may inevitably involve some degree of overinclusiveness or underinclusiveness," a policy "exempting all women because of the preclusive domestic responsibilities of some women is insufficient justification for their disproportionate exclusion of jury venires."

8. In *U.S. v. Odeneal*, 517 F.3d 406 (6th Cir. 2008), the court held:

> The jury administrator testified that individual names chosen to be placed on the "master wheel" were drawn exclusively from voter registration lists provided by the state. Defendants argue that by using voter registration lists instead of other methods, such as drivers license registrations, African-Americans are systematically excluded because African-Americans register to vote in lower proportions than other groups. Defendants' argument is not persuasive. Voter registration lists are the presumptive statutory source for potential jurors. 28 U.S.C. § 1863(b). The circuit courts are in complete agreement that neither the Act nor the Constitution require that a supplemental source of names be added to voter lists simply because an identifiable group votes in a proportion lower than the rest of the population.

BARBER v. PONTE
U.S. Court of Appeals, 1st Circuit
772 F.2d 996 (1985)

TORRUELLA, CIRCUIT JUDGE

This matter is before us for review *en banc* of our decision in *Barber v. Ponte*, 772 F.2d 982 (1st Cir.1985) wherein we reaffirmed the holding of this circuit, first espoused in *United States v. Butera*, 420 F.2d 564 (1st Cir.1970), to the effect that "young adults" (ages 18–34) constitute a sufficiently cohesive group to be cognizable in determining whether they are adequately represented within the jury venires for sixth amendment purposes. Upon further consideration, we reverse our prior ruling in this case and overrule our holding in *Butera* and its progeny.

At his trial before the Superior Court of Massachusetts, appellant challenged the composition of the venires from which was chosen the jury that tried and convicted him. As indicated, his challenge was based on his contention that persons between the ages of 18 to 34, his definition of "young adults," were under-represented in the venires. He supported this allegation by presenting in evidence a study that statistically establishes a substantial disparity in the traverse jurors in the 18 to 34 age group as compared with the general population encompassing this age group. Appellant presented no other evidence before the state trial court on this issue. This challenge was denied at all state court levels, as well as by the district court.

Apparently appellant was under the misapprehension, as he has been throughout this appeal, that the establishment of mere statistical disparity in the chosen age group is sufficient to establish a prima facie violation under the sixth amendment. It is beyond argument, however, that the first step in such a claim is the demarcation of a "distinctive" group. *Duren v. Missouri*, 439 U.S. 357 (1979); *Taylor v. Louisiana*, 419 U.S. 522, 530 (1975). This requires: (1) that the group be defined and limited by some clearly identifiable factor (for example, sex or race), (2) that a common thread or basic similarity in attitude, ideas, or experience run through the group, and (3) that there be a community of interest among the members of the group, such that the group's interests cannot be adequately represented if the group is excluded from the jury selection process. The reason for these require-ments is readily apparent. In choosing a jury we are looking not merely for a statistical mirror of arbitrary segments of the population's composition. The goal that we seek is that the jury generally represent the attitudes, values, ideas and experience of the eligible citizens that compose the community where the trial is taking place.

The Supreme Court has never gone so far as to hold that the constitution requires venires to be, statistically, a substantially true mirror of the community. While courts often speak in terms of "fair cross section," they have realized that practical reasons, as well as the sterility of such an endeavor, militate against total realization of this ideal. Some people are simply less available than others to serve as jurors, such as highly mobile people with few local contacts, like college students or traveling salesmen; people tied to jobs that are traditionally considered essential to the welfare of the community like firemen, police officers, physicians; and people with social or physical impairments like alcoholics, the hearing impaired, or individuals not versant in the English language. Because a true cross section is practically unobtainable, courts have tended to allow a fair degree of leeway in designating jurors so long as the state or community does not actively prevent people from serving or actively discriminate, and so long as the system is reasonably open to all. Strict statistical analysis has been used only in situations where special groups that have been discriminated against are involved. *Duren v. Missouri*, *supra*; *Taylor v. Louisiana*, *supra*.

Only if we test the goal of communal attitudinal representation against groups that can be identified through principled criteria can we adequately conclude whether the goal has been met. Furthermore, only if principled criteria are established can appropriate guidance be given to courts and administrators to allow them to determine, in the future, not only whether the goal has been achieved, but also the composition of other groups that litigants may wish to challenge.

In the present case, there is simply no evidence in the record for determining that people between the ages of 18 and 34 (as opposed to some other ages) belong to a particular group. The essence of a distinctive group is that its members share specific common characteristics. Yet, what can we identify as the common characteristics of people in an age group that spans a sixteen-year gap, covering such dynamic years in a person's life as those that are encompassed between the ages of 18 to 34? To be sure, they are all younger than people over 34. But what is the evidence that the attitudes and thinking of, say, 30 year olds have more in common with 18 year olds than they do with 40 year olds, or for that matter, going to the other end of the scale, that 18 year olds have more in common with 28 year olds than with 16 year olds? How do we know that there should not be two groups, 18 to 28 and 28 to 35, or three, or four groups encompassing other boundaries?

The only way to establish the present group, particularly in view of the absence of any scientific or expert evidence in this record, is by arbitrary fiat superimposed on intuition. Even assuming we can be flatly arbitrary, we cannot seriously say that a grouping whose contours are rationally unsupportable is "distinctive." Is not a "distinctive" group, by definition, one whose membership is reasonably set apart from others by clear lines of demarcation?

Without much effort we can point to various significant social indicators that would seem to punctuate clear differences in the attitudes, values, ideas and experiences of 18 year olds vis-a-vis 34 year olds, to pick only the outer boundaries of appellant's "young adults" classification. Taking judicial notice of official statistics, we can note meaningful contrasts in such social indicators as their marital and divorce rates, school enrollment and educational attainment, economic status, employment rate, criminality, experience in such matters as service in the armed forces in time of war or even in peacetime, mental health, attitude towards such important social issues as abortion, and participation in the political processes, and in the ownership of capital property. Such differences emphasize the inappropriateness of grouping potently dissimilar age categories, if we are to do other than pay mere lip service to the teachings of *Duren*.

Of course, we can say, "It does not matter what the precise contours are — disproportionality is bad whether the group is 18 to 28, 18 to 35, or 18 to 45." But if we establish this criteria without more, must we not also be prepared to let each complainant's attorney select his own age group, based solely upon the age boundaries that suit his purposes by showing the greatest statistical disparity, merely to gain tactical advantage rather than to meet constitutional standards? If we take this approach, then we are clearly doing something different from what the Supreme Court contemplated when it formulated the "distinctive group" concept in *Duren*. We are losing sight of the goal pursued, that of seeking attitudinal representativeness, and exchanging it for statistical bureaucracy. And as a corollary to all this, those charged with administering the day-to-day workings of the jury system would have great difficulty in determining whether they have complied with the Constitution if they have to contend with such a fluid mark. What guidelines or criteria will they use to determine whether all "groups" are properly represented in the venires?

Implying that any important deviation from a statistical cross section is suspect is torturing the words "distinctive group" into a very different concept. The *Duren* court used the concept of "distinctive group" in a case where women were subjected to discrimination. It is fair to assume that the court wanted to give heightened scrutiny to groups needing special protection, not to all groups generally. There is nothing to indicate that it meant to take the further step of requiring jury venires to reflect mathematically precise cross sections of the communities from which they are selected. Yet if the age classification is adopted, surely blue-collar workers, yuppies, Rotarians, Eagle Scouts, and an endless variety of other classifications will be entitled to similar treatment. These are not the groups that the court has traditionally sought to protect from under-representation on jury venires. See, e.g., *Hill v. Texas*, 316 U.S. 400 (1942) (blacks); *Duren v. Missouri, supra* (women); *United States v. Brady*, 579 F.2d 1121 (9th Cir.1978) (Indians).

That is not to say, however, that if a classification were *specifically* and *systematically excluded* from jury duty the same standard would be used as here, where defendant simply relies on a statistically disparity in the venires to challenge its constitutionality. If certain people are specifically and systematically excluded from jury duty, then the jury-administrating authority would have created its own group. Clearly, the state has no right to deliberately exclude specific classes or groups from juries without some very special reason. Thus, it may not forbid blue-collar workers, chess players, Masons, etc., from serving on juries. But if there are, as in the present case, mere statistical imbalances, unexplained, the problem is different. Statistical imbalances can be due to a host of factors — younger people may be away at school, serving in the armed forces, surfing in Hawaii, etc. Unless one is prepared to say that there is an affirmative constitutional duty to produce a true cross section on the venire for every imaginable group that exists in our complex society, something which no court has even come close to holding, we should avoid the overwhelming problems and sterile solutions that will result from attempting to subdivide a continuum of ages into "distinctive groups."

Although the Supreme Court has not ruled upon whether age groups are "distinctive" enough for sixth amendment purposes, every circuit that has considered this issue, except the First, until now, has ruled against appellant's contention. [Citations.] We are convinced not by the weight of their numbers but by that of the logic and policy they espouse. We thus join them.

Our earlier decision is vacated and the decision of the district court is affirmed.

BOWNES, CIRCUIT JUDGE (dissenting).

Young adults between 18 and 35 constitute both a large (37.82% of the population) and easily identifiable group (all that is needed are birthdates) in Norfolk County. It seems indisputable that an individual's response to nearly every facet of his or her life, including life goals and ambitions, health, personal relationships, family and death, evolve and change over the course of one's adult life. And, despite the fact that societal distinctions based on age are ubiquitous, affecting everything from insurance rates to availability for military service, eligibility for political office and media advertising campaigns, the majority believes this is inadequate justification for finding that adults 18–35 comprise a discernible group for jury selection purposes.

The majority decides that young adults between 18 and 35 are not a cognizable group for sixth amendment purposes because there are differences in attitudes, experiences, and ideas within the group and because petitioner has not shown that all young adults possess a community of interest different from persons 35 and older that would be inadequately represented if persons under 35 are excluded from the jury selection process. If this is a sound premise, it is unclear to me why the majority believes that young adults cannot be *"actively"* or *"systematically"* excluded. The holding that young adults are not a cognizable group and, therefore, need not be included in the jury pool to make it a reasonable cross section of the community, but cannot be overtly excluded is inherently contradictory. Indeed, if the conjunction of age information as to each potential venireman and the dramatic disproportionality of representation of young adults is not enough to prove systematic discrimination, at least as a *prima facie* matter, the majority's concession would seem to be reserved for the unlikely case in which there is smoking-gun evidence in the form of explicitly discriminatory statements.

I do not agree with the majority's attempt to distinguish this case from others in which the Supreme Court has taken judicial notice of cognizable groups. Diversity within a group and overlap of attitudes and experiences of group and nongroup members are as characteristic of groups the Supreme Court has repeatedly recognized to be cognizable as petitioner's young adult group. In *Ballard v. United States*, 329 U.S. 187 (1946), the Court found that women constituted a cognizable group despite the government's protestations that women do not act as a class or have common attitudes, experiences and ideas.

In addition to women and blacks, the Supreme Court has recognized the cognizability of Mexican-Americans (*Hernandez v. Texas*, 347 U.S. 475 (1954)), daily wage earners (*Thiel v. Southern Pacific Co.*, 328 U.S. 217 (1946)), and persons holding personal or religious scruples against capital punishment who are able to act impartially (*Witherspoon v. Illinois*, 391 U.S. 510 (1968)). Other circuit courts have recognized the cognizability of Indians (*United States v. Brady*, 579 F.2d 1121 (9th Cir.1978), and Jewish persons (*United States v. Siragusa*, 450 F.2d 596 (2d Cir.1971). All of these groups contain persons with a broad and diverse range of attitudes and experiences and many members of these cognizable groups undoubtedly share the attitudes and experiences of persons outside the group. To require a litigant to show that the members of a group are influenced by the same factors or cast their vote as a lot would make a mockery of the democratic values the jury system is designed to protect. It would require a litigant to stereotype and overgeneralize the attributes and experiences of a group in order for it to be recognized as one against which discrimination is unconstitutional.

The validity of a petitioner's challenge depends, of course, on his showing that a "substantial" group has been excluded. It may well be that narrow age spans would not constitute a large enough percentage of the population to be cognizable. Here, however, where petitioner has used an age span encompassing virtually all those who could be classified as young adults and a group comprising 38% of the population, it is clear that the group is substantial enough to require inclusion in the process. The majority finds that the contours of the group of persons identified as young adults between 18 and 35, is too amorphous to have constitutional significance. But amorphousness is not confined to age groups. In what generation does a Mexican-American or Puerto Rican become simply a Texas or New Yorker and cease to be part of a cognizable group? Very few groups can be descriptively circumscribed by legal definitions. In *Thiel*, the Supreme Court recognized what this court does not, that broad groups, even if not susceptible to precise definition, contribute to the fabric of our society and the vitality of our justice system and cannot be sifted out of the jury selection process.

The real basis of the court's opinion seems to be the majority's belief that adults between the ages of 18 and 35 do not constitute a "special group" worthy of heightened scrutiny. In their bright-line fever to confine cognizability, the majority compresses the sixth amendment cross-section requirement into the equal protection clause. This they do in face of the Supreme Court's long-standing and consistent position that the two are not congruent. See, e.g., *Peters v. Kiff*, 407 U.S. 493, 499–500 (1972) ("even in 1880 the Court recognized that other constitutional values [besides the equal protection clause] were implicated").

* * * *

While the Constitution does not require a defendant's *jury* to be a true mirror of the community, the Constitution does require that the venire reasonably reflect the composition of the community. *Taylor v. Louisiana*, 419 U.S. at 538. The position taken by the court that the cross-section requirement of the sixth amendment requires only that "special groups" such as women and blacks not be systematically excluded is contrary to the principles embodied in the sixth amendment and articulated in Supreme Court precedent. * * * *

By finding that only a few "special groups" can be assured a place in jury venires and that the "fair cross section" requirement is an impractical "ideal," the court emphasizes one of the distinctions between the young and old to which I would rather not ascribe: "Your old men shall dream dreams, your young men shall see visions." JOEL: 2:28.

Notes from Justin:

1. In *People v. McCoy*, 40 Cal.App.4th 778 (1995), the jury commissioner's staff erroneously excused many prospective jurors who were *70 years of age and older*. After McCoy was convicted, his attorney moved for a new trial — and put on expert testimony in an effort to show that this group was in fact "a cognizable and distinct class":

> Social psychologist and social science researcher Dr. Carol Huffine testified as an expert in longitudinal research. She was of the opinion that people born during a particular period of time ("age cohorts") share unique and distinct attitudes, perspectives, and beliefs because they have experienced historical events or social change at the same stage of their lives. To illustrate, she described a study that attempted to determine the long-term effects on different age cohorts of having experienced economic deprivation between 1929 and 1933. Personality tests administered to adolescent boys born in 1928 and 1929 indicated that as a group, they displayed feelings of "incompetence, hopelessness, a sense of victimization." The same tests administered to adolescent boys born in 1921 and 1922 indicated they felt competent, optimistic, and hopeful. Tested again at age 40, both groups were basically normal and healthy, but the older cohorts demonstrated "more robust" psychological health. In Dr. Huffine's opinion, because persons 70 and older experienced the depression, World War II, and the post war economic boom at the same stage of their lives, they have similar

attitudes and beliefs making them distinct from other groups, even those only a few years younger.

Psychologist Dr. Morton A. Lieberman testified as an expert in gerontology. He too was of the opinion that persons in a particular age group share a "common and distinct perspective," both because of the common personal and historical events they have experienced and because of the common attitudes and behaviors expressed by society toward particular groups. He distinguished between the "young old," who are 60 to 69, and the "old old," who are 70 and older. He was of the opinion that the latter group as a whole has more "acceptance, tolerance, and spirituality." They also have a "different kind of perspective and way of looking at information and processing it and judging it," described by some as "wisdom."

This valiant effort failed. The trial court denied the motion, and the appellate court affirmed:

> Clearly the County should not have routinely excused persons 70 and over who did not request excuses. See Code Civ.Proc. § 204 (eligible persons may be excused from jury service only for undue hardship upon themselves). Nevertheless, the trial court in this case was not persuaded by appellant's expert testimony that these individuals constituted a distinctive or cognizable group, and appellant has not established that the court acted unreasonably or arbitrarily. Although Dr. Huffine was of the opinion that persons 70 and over share unique attitudes and beliefs not common to other groups, even those only slightly younger, she did not specify what those shared attitudes might be, other than political conservatism. Dr. Lieberman was of the opinion that the "old old" have more "acceptance, tolerance, and spirituality" than the "young old" of 60 to 69. The trial court reasonably could have concluded that the age parameters of these groups were too arbitrary and the proposed shared characteristics too amorphous and ill-defined to satisfy the *Duren* standards.

2. In *U.S. v. Barry*, 71 F.3d 1269 (7th Cir.1995), defendant challenged the constitutionality of the portion of 28 U.S.C. § 1865(b)(5) that disqualifies from jury service any person who has *a felony charge pending* against him:

> The nub of the Barrys' argument is that excluding people charged with a felony from a jury pool works to keep African-Americans out of the mix at a rate out of proportion to their numbers in the general population. The disparity claimed is on the order of eight- to thirteen-fold. The alleged disparate racial effect is the basis for the claimed violation of the Equal Protection Clause of the Fifth Amendment to the Constitution. In addition, the Barrys contend that the exclusion of accused persons deprives a defendant of his right to a "fair cross-section" of the population in the array from which his jury is drawn and on the grand jury which indicts him, in violation of the Fifth and Sixth Amendments to the Constitution.

The court disagreed:

> Simply being charged with a crime says something about a person, something which is material to his ability to serve as a juror. After being charged, and before conviction, there will already have been a finding — by

a judge or a grand jury — of probable cause to believe that the person charged committed the crime. Based on that finding, it is rational to conclude that there is probable cause to believe that the person may not respect the law. It is rational to believe that such a person may not take seriously his obligation to follow the law as a juror is sworn to do.

The government argues also that possible juror bias justifies the exclusion. However, we think that there is no need to theorize about whether an accused felon is likely to be biased against the government or, on the other hand, whether he is likely to think, from some personal experience, that all persons charged will be likely to lie to avoid conviction and so be biased against the defendant. We cannot predict what he might do because he has been charged with a crime. The important point is that there will have been a finding of probable cause to believe that he has, in fact, disregarded the law. It is rational and not entirely theoretical to think he could do so again — in favor of one side or the other — if he were a juror.

Accordingly, we cannot find that the classification violates the Equal Protection Clause.

The court also rejected defendant's claim that the exclusion violated the 6th Amendment:

We are not convinced that alleged felons comprise a distinctive group. They have in common that they may have run afoul of the criminal justice system. However, there are many and varied ways to do that: dealing drugs, murder, extortion, rape, kidnapping, or tax evasion, embezzlement, and sometimes driving offenses. It is possible that an alleged tax evader may have something in common with a charged kidnapper, but the remote chance that he might, does not support a finding that the group is distinct.

Furthermore, looking to the purposes of the fair cross-section requirement, we note that in most cases, by running afoul of the law, accused persons have shown poor judgment, as the Barrys freely acknowledge. Theirs is hardly the common-sense judgment of the community.

3. In *State v. Ji*, 832 P.2d 1176 (Kan., 1992), the court upheld the constitutionality of a statute which excluded *illiterate* persons from serving as jurors: "Jurors must have a reasonable knowledge of the language in which the proceedings are conducted to enable them to perform their duties and to ensure the defendant receives a fair trial. We disagree with the defendant's assertion that a distinct class of persons in the community was constitutionally excluded from the jury panel."

4. In *U.S. v. Benmuhar*, 658 F.2d 14 (1st Cir. 1981), the court upheld a federal statute requiring that jurors sitting in federal court be able *to read and write the English language* — even in Puerto Rico, where many people speak only Spanish:

Federal district courts in part are designed to provide trial alternatives for litigants, resident and nonresident, who seek the uniformity, expertise, and familiarity that they believe they may find in a national rather than a local forum. Primary use of the national language is both symbolically and functionally significant in achieving this goal. Nonresident citizens who do not speak Spanish may use the Puerto Rican federal district court without unusual requirements. The Attorney General of the United States may appear personally or by representative without being limited by considerations of fluency in Spanish. Other judges may sit by designation as needed without regard to their ability in Spanish. Possible translation distortions in indictments and complaints based on statutes written in English are avoided, as they are again during appellate review.

5. In *State v. Spivey*, 700 S.W.2d 812 (Mo. 1985), the court upheld a state statute excluding *deaf* people from jury service:

> The profoundly deaf juror may comprehend oral communication only by lip reading, or through sign language. Sign language requires an interpreter, who would have to be present during jury deliberation. Whatever method is used, there is no assurance that the trial proceedings or jury discussion would be fully communicated to the deaf juror. Matters of inflection and intonation would be entirely lost. It might be argued that a trial in which one or more jurors cannot hear the proceedings is less than fair. We conclude that inclusion of deaf jurors is not a constitutional requirement.

6. In *State v. Chidester*, 570 N.W.2d 78 (Iowa 1997), a court attendant excused from jury duty all persons whose employers would not pay them while serving on a jury and all farmers who were about to plant or harvest their crops. The court held that neither group was "distinctive":

> *Persons whose employers will not compensate them* during jury service do not qualify as a distinctive group for purposes of the Sixth Amendment. First, these individuals were not excluded due to an "immutable characteristic." The next time these persons are called for jury duty, they may have a different job and be able to serve. These potential jurors were excluded for economic reasons that arguably affect their ability to serve.

> We also think the underlying purposes of the fair-cross-section requirement are not undermined by the exclusion of these individuals. The record shows the persons excused because their employers would not compensate them while they served as jurors are a diverse group. We cannot conclude that these individuals had similar ideas, attitudes, or experiences such that a defendant would be denied the benefit of this group's peculiar common sense if they were excluded from the venire. See *Anaya v. Hansen*, 781 F.2d 1, 5 (1st Cir.1986) (finding "blue collar workers" were not a distinctive group because there was a "lack of coherence" within this group); *State v. Boyd*, 867 S.W.2d 330, 335 (Tenn.Ct.App.1992) (rejecting Sixth Amendment challenge to selection system that excluded nonvoters because this group did not "have a cohesiveness of attitudes, ideas, or experiences which may not be represented by others in the community"). We also think the exclusion of this diverse group of people does not give rise to an appearance of unfairness. Finally, as we noted above, these individuals are not necessarily forever precluded from jury duty. * * * *

> The question whether *farmers* are a distinctive group is not as easily answered. Some courts have upheld the exemption from jury duty of occupational groups on the basis such groups have not been shown to share unique attitudes, ideas, or experiences, and therefore, do not constitute a "distinctive group." E.g., *State v. Puente*, 431 N.E.2d 987, 989 (Ohio 1982) (considering exemption of doctors, dentists, and lawyers from jury service); *Boyd*, 876 S.W.2d at 336 (considering systematic exclusion of doctors,

lawyers, and the clergy); *cf. Commonwealth v. Matthews*, 548 N.E.2d 843, 848 (Mass.1990) (considering exclusion of "suburban parents" and "caretakers of adolescent children"). Other courts have skipped the distinctive-group analysis and have simply held the government had a legitimate reason to exclude the occupational group under consideration. E.g., *U.S. v. Terry*, 60 F.3d 1541, 1544 (11th Cir.1995) (holding routine exclusion of members of fire and police departments did not violate the fair-cross-section requirement "because it is good for the community that these workers not be interrupted in their work"); *State v. Williams*, 659 S.W.2d 778, 781 (Mo.1983) (upholding statutory exemption of lawyers from jury duty for policy reasons).

This court has previously followed the latter approach in considering a statutory exemption from jury duty of all "acting professors and teachers." *State v. Williams*, 264 N.W.2d 779, 781 (Iowa 1978). We found no constitutional infirmity in the statute, noting a state has the authority "to grant exemptions from jury service to individuals in case of special hardship or incapacity and to those engaged in particular occupations the uninterrupted performance of which is critical to the community." (quoting *Taylor v. Louisiana*, 419 U.S. 522, 534 (1975)).

We find it unnecessary here, as well, to decide whether farmers are a distinctive group for Sixth Amendment purposes. We think the unique requirements of their occupation justify the limited exemption from jury service allowed by the Webster County court attendant. A farmer's livelihood depends upon timing. There is a narrow window of opportunity to plant crops under the right conditions and harvest them at the right time. Wet weather can arrive at any time and frustrate all attempts to plant those final acres or harvest the last few fields. Consequently, even one day lost to jury duty may mean a setback of several days or even weeks in accomplishing these tasks. Under these unique circumstances, we find ample basis for finding a special hardship to farmers in serving on a jury during planting or harvesting season. Accordingly, their exclusion from jury service during these periods is justified and does not violate the fair-cross-section requirement of the Sixth Amendment.

WALKER v. GOLDSMITH
U.S. Court of Appeals, 9th Circuit
902 F.2d 16 (1990)

Per Curium

Petitioner, an Arizona state prisoner, appeals the district court's summary denial of habeas relief. Walker argues that his sixth amendment right to a jury that represents a fair cross section of the community and his fourteenth amendment right to equal protection were violated because the venire pool from which his trial jury was selected did not include those whose surnames began with the letters "W," "X," "Y," and "Z". * * * *

Walker was tried before a jury in the Arizona Superior Court for Pima County. He was convicted of aggravated assault and leaving the scene of an accident on September 30, 1983. He was sentenced to 10 years imprisonment. On May 1, 1987,

Walker petitioned the Pima County Superior Court for post-conviction relief based on the failure to include those with surnames beginning with the letters W through Z in the venire from which his trial jury had been selected. Walker contended that this group constituted a recognizable and distinct class.[1] The Pima County Superior Court refused to recognize that those with surnames beginning with the letters W through Z constitute a cognizable class. * * * *

Walker must establish that those persons with surnames beginning with the letters W through Z are a "recognizable, distinct class, singled out for different treatment under the laws, as written or as applied," as a first step in establishing his claim that the Pima County venire system violated his right to equal protection. *Castaneda v. Partida*, 430 U.S. 482, 494 (1977). He fails to do so.

A recognizable and distinct class for the purposes of jury selection is one "which, in some objectively discernible and significant way, is distinct from the rest of society, and whose interests cannot be adequately represented by other members of the jury panel." *United States v. Potter*, 552 F.2d 901, 904 (9th Cir., 1977). Persons whose surnames begin with the letters W through Z do not constitute such a class in this case.

The district court's order is thus affirmed.

Notes from Justin:

1. At first blush, *Walker* seems clearly different from *Taylor*. But is it? *Taylor* held that when a large group is excluded, this can affect the outlook of the jury in "unknown and unknowable" ways, and therefore such exclusion is not permitted. "Ws through Zs" are certainly a large part of our population, and *who knows* how their exclusion might affect the makeup of the jury? Maybe their grade-school teachers always lined students up alphabetically, with the Ws through Zs always in the rear, thereby inflicting alphabet neurosis on these unfortunate people. They might show some sympathy for a fellow-W, like Walker! How, exactly, can *Walker* be reconciled with *Taylor*?

2. In *Walker*, the court took its test for "cognizable class" from *U.S. v. Potter*: the group must be "distinct from the rest of society" *and* have interests that "cannot be adequately represented by other member of the jury panel". Did *Taylor* mention this second requirement? Is it *consistent* with *Taylor*?

The California Supreme Court apparently thought so, in *Rubio v. Superior Court*, 24 Cal.3d 93 (1979). By statute, California barred ex-felons and resident aliens from serving on juries. The court held that to be a "cognizable class", a group must have a common experience which causes them to "share a common perspective", which no other members of the community are capable of representing. Ex-felons share a common perspective (due to their incarceration and stigma), but ex-misdemeanants and ex-juvenile offenders have had similar experiences and can represent that perspective. Resident aliens share a common perspective (due to exclusion from the political process and to discrimination), but naturalized citizens

---

[1] Walker's contention that this group is a recognizable and distinct class is based on a survey by Dr. Trevor Weston. See Autry & Barker, *Academic Correlates of Alphabetical Order of Surname*, 8 J. Sch. Psychology 22, 22 (1970). Weston claims that those whose surnames begin with the letters S through Z are 50% more likely to develop a condition called "alphabetic neurosis" than are those whose surnames begin with the letters A through R.

have had similar experiences and can represent that perspective. So *neither* ex-felons nor resident aliens qualify as "cognizable classes". Dissenting Justice Tobriner felt that the second requirement was inconsistent with cases holding that Chicanos and wage-earners are "cognizable classes", even though other groups might represent their perspectives.

3. *Walker* is not the only case involving a novel attempt to extend *Taylor*. In *Leibengood v. State*, 866 S.W.2d 732 (Tex.Ct.App.1993), defendant, a dwarf charged with murder, "filed a motion for a specific array of jurors to be assembled for his trial. He wanted some persons in the venire under five feet tall who would understand the prejudices of taller people against little people and the emotional and mental processes of little people. He wanted at least an opportunity for a jury of his peers. He argues that dwarf persons are a cognizable group. They have common needs and attitudes, as well as experiencing common frustrations and discriminations." The court rejected the claim:

> Even assuming that people under five feet tall are a "distinctive" group, Leibengood failed to meet prongs two and three of the *Duren* test. He did not provide any statistical evidence on the percentage of the community made up of little people or the statistical profile of venire panels, so that any underrepresentation of little people on jury venires could be demonstrated. Nor did Leibengood show that any underrepresentation was due to the systematic exclusion of little people from the jury-selection process.

2.   Pretrial Publicity

In all criminal prosecutions, the accused shall enjoy the right to a speedy and public trial, by an impartial jury of the State and district wherein the crime shall have been committed, which district shall have been previously ascertained by law. . . .

U.S. Constitution, 6th Amendment

MURPHY v. FLORIDA
United States Supreme Court
421 U.S. 794 (1975)

MR. JUSTICE MARSHALL delivered the opinion of the Court.

The question presented by this case is whether the petitioner was denied a fair trial because members of the jury had learned from news accounts about a prior felony conviction or certain facts about the crime with which he was charged. Under the circumstances of this case, we find that petitioner has not been denied due process, and we therefore affirm the judgment below.

I

Petitioner was convicted in the Dade County, Fla., Criminal Court in 1970 of breaking and entering a home, while armed, with intent to commit robbery and of assault with intent to commit robbery. The charges stemmed from the January 1968 robbery of a Miami Beach home and petitioner's apprehension, with three others, while fleeing from the scene.

The robbery and petitioner's arrest received extensive press coverage because petitioner had been much in the news before. He had first made himself notorious for his part in the 1964 theft of the Star of India sapphire from a museum in New York. His flamboyant lifestyle made him a continuing subject of press interest; he was generally referred to — at least in the media — as "Murph the Surf".

Before the date set for petitioner's trial on the instant charges, he was indicted on two counts of murder in Broward County, Fla. Thereafter the Dade County court declared petitioner mentally incompetent to stand trial; he was committed to a hospital and the prosecutor *nolle prossed* the robbery indictment. In August 1968, he was indicted by a federal grand jury for conspiring to transport stolen securities in interstate commerce. After petitioner was adjudged competent for trial, he was convicted on one count of murder in Broward County (March 1969) and pleaded guilty to one count of the federal indictment involving stolen securities (December 1969). The indictment for robbery was refiled in August 1969 and came to trial one year later.

The events of 1968 and 1969 drew extensive press coverage. Each new case against petitioner was considered newsworthy, not only in Dade County but elsewhere as well. The record in this case contains scores of articles reporting on petitioner's trials and tribulations during this period; many purportedly relate statements that petitioner or his attorney made to reporters.

Jury selection in the present case began in August 1970. Seventy-eight jurors were questioned. Of these, 30 were excused for miscellaneous personal reasons; 20 were excused peremptorily by the defense or prosecution; 20 were excused by the court as having prejudged petitioner; and the remaining eight served as the jury and two alternates. Petitioner's motions to dismiss the chosen jurors, on the ground that they were aware that he had previously been convicted of either the 1964 Star of India theft or the Broward County murder, were denied, as was his renewed motion for a change of venue based on allegedly prejudicial pretrial publicity.

At trial, petitioner did not testify or put in any evidence; assertedly in protest of the selected jury, he did not cross-examine any of the State's witnesses. He was convicted on both counts. * * * *

II

* * * *

Petitioner relies principally upon *Irvin v. Dowd*, 366 U.S. 717 (1961), *Rideau v. Louisiana*, 373 U.S. 723 (1963), *Estes v. Texas*, 381 U.S. 532 (1965), and *Sheppard v. Maxwell*, 384 U.S. 333 (1966). In each of these cases, this Court overturned a state-court conviction obtained in a trial atmosphere that had been utterly corrupted by press coverage.

In *Irvin v. Dowd*, the rural community in which the trial was held had been subjected to a barrage of inflammatory publicity immediately prior to trial, including information on the defendant's prior convictions, his confession to 24 burglaries and six murders including the one for which he was tried, and his unaccepted offer to plead guilty in order to avoid the death sentence. As a result, eight of the 12 jurors had formed an opinion that the defendant was guilty before the trial began; some went "so far as to say that it would take evidence to overcome their belief" in his guilt. 366 U.S. at 728. In these circumstances, the Court readily found actual prejudice against the petitioner to a degree that rendered a fair trial impossible.

Prejudice was presumed in the circumstances under which the trials in *Rideau, Estes,* and *Sheppard* were held. In those cases, the influence of the news media, either in the community at large or in the courtroom itself, pervaded the proceedings. In *Rideau,* the defendant had "confessed" under police interrogation to the murder of which he stood convicted. A 20-minute film of his confession was broadcast three times by a television station in the community where the crime and the trial took place. In reversing, the Court did not examine the *voir dire* for evidence of actual prejudice because it considered the trial under review "but a hollow formality" — the real trial had occurred when tens of thousands of people, in a community of 150,000, had seen and heard the defendant admit his guilt before the cameras.

The trial in *Estes* had been conducted in a circus atmosphere, due in large part to the intrusions of the press, which was allowed to sit within the bar of the court and to overrun it with television equipment. Similarly, *Sheppard* arose from a trial infected not only by a background of extremely inflammatory publicity but also by a courthouse given over to accommodate the public appetite for carnival. The proceedings in these cases were entirely lacking in the solemnity and sobriety to which a defendant is entitled in a system that subscribes to any notion of fairness and rejects the verdict of a mob. They cannot be made to stand for the proposition that juror exposure to information about a state defendant's prior convictions or to news accounts of the crime with which he is charged alone presumptively deprives the defendant of due process. To resolve this case, we must turn, therefore, to any indications in the totality of circumstances that petitioner's trial was not fundamentally fair.

III

The constitutional standard of fairness requires that a defendant have "a panel of impartial, indifferent jurors." *Irvin v. Dowd,* 366 U.S. at 722. Qualified jurors need not, however, be totally ignorant of the facts and issues involved.

To hold that the mere existence of any preconceived notion as to the guilt or innocence of an accused, without more, is sufficient to rebut the presumption of a prospective juror's impartiality would be to establish an impossible standard. It is sufficient if the juror can lay aside his impression or opinion and render a verdict based on the evidence presented in court. [*Id.* at 723.]

At the same time, the juror's assurances that he is equal to this task cannot be dispositive of the accused's rights, and it remains open to the defendant to demonstrate "the actual existence of such an opinion in the mind of the juror as will raise the presumption of partiality." *Ibid.*

The *voir dire* in this case indicates no such hostility to petitioner by the jurors who served in his trial as to suggest a partiality that could not be laid aside. Some of the jurors had a vague recollection of the robbery with which petitioner was charged and each had some knowledge of petitioner's past crimes,[3] but none betrayed any belief in the relevance of petitioner's past to the present case.[4] Indeed, four of the six jurors volunteered their views of its irrelevance, and one suggested that people who have been in trouble before are too often singled out for suspicion of each new crime — a predisposition that could only operate in petitioner's favor.

In the entire *voir dire* transcript furnished to us, there is only one colloquy on which petitioner can base even a colorable claim of partiality by a juror. In response to a leading and hypothetical question, presupposing a two- or three-week presentation of evidence against petitioner and his failure to put on any defense, one juror conceded that his prior impression of petitioner would dispose him to convict.[5] We cannot attach great significance to this statement, however, in light of the leading nature of counsel's questions and the juror's other testimony indicating that he had no deep impression of petitioner at all.

The juror testified that he did not keep up with current events and, in fact, had never heard of petitioner until he arrived in the room for prospective jurors where some veniremen were discussing him. He did not know that petitioner was "a convicted jewel thief" even then; it was petitioner's counsel who informed him of this fact. And he volunteered that petitioner's murder conviction, of which he had just

---

[3] One juror who did not know that petitioner had been previously convicted for the theft of the Star of India sapphire, one who did not know of the murder conviction, and one who had never heard about the securities case were informed about them by petitioner's counsel, who then asked whether that knowledge would not prejudice them against petitioner. We will not readily discount the assurances of a juror insofar as his exposure to a defendant's past crimes comes from the defendant or counsel. We note also, and disapprove, counsel's habitual references to his client, at *voir dire*, as "Murph the Surf" rather than by his name.

[4] We must distinguish between mere familiarity with petitioner or his past and an actual predisposition against him, just as we have in the past distinguished largely factual publicity from that which is invidious or inflammatory. To ignore the real differences in the potential for prejudice would not advance the cause of fundamental fairness, but only make impossible the timely prosecution of persons who are well known in the community, whether they be notorious or merely prominent.

[5] The entire exchange appears at App. 139:

"Q: Now, when you go into that jury room and you decide upon Murphy's guilt on innocence, you are going to take into account that fact that he is a convicted murderer; aren't you?

A: Not if we are listening to the case, I wouldn't.

Q: But you know about it?

A: How can you not know about it?

Q: Fine, thank you. When you go into the jury room, the fact that he is a convicted murderer, that is going to influence your verdict; is it not?

A: We are not trying him for murder.

Q: The fact that he is a convicted murderer and jewel thief, that would influence your verdict?

A: I didn't know he was a convicted jewel thief.

Q: Oh, I see. I am sorry I put words in your mouth. Now, sir, after two or three weeks of being locked up in a downtown hotel, as the Court determines, and after hearing the State's case, and after hearing no case on behalf of Murphy, and hearing no testimony from Murphy saying, 'I am innocent, Mr. [juror's name],' — when you go into the jury room, sir, all these facts are going to influence your verdict?

A: I imagine it would be.

Q: And in fact, you are saying if Murphy didn't testify, and if he doesn't offer evidence, 'My experience of him is such that right now I would find him guilty.'

A: I believe so."

heard, would not be relevant to his guilt or innocence in the present case, since "we are not trying him for murder."

Even these indicia of impartiality might be disregarded in a case where the general atmosphere in the community or courtroom is sufficiently inflammatory, but the circumstances surrounding petitioner's trial are not at all of that variety. Petitioner attempts to portray them as inflammatory by reference to the publicity to which the community was exposed. The District Court found, however, that the news articles concerning petitioner had appeared almost entirely during the period between December 1967 and January 1969, the latter date being seven months before the jury in this case was selected. They were, moreover, largely factual in nature.

The length to which the trial court must go in order to select jurors who appear to be impartial is another factor relevant in evaluating those jurors' assurances of impartiality. In a community where most veniremen will admit to a disqualifying prejudice, the reliability of the others' protestations may be drawn into question; for it is then more probable that they are part of a community deeply hostile to the accused, and more likely that they may unwittingly have been influenced by it. In *Irvin v. Dowd*, for example, the Court noted that 90% of those examined on the point were inclined to believe in the accused's guilt, and the court had excused for this cause 268 of the 430 veniremen. In the present case, by contrast, 20 of the 78 persons questioned were excused because they indicated an opinion as to petitioner's guilt. * * * * This may indeed be 20 more than would occur in the trial of a totally obscure person, but it by no means suggests a community with sentiment so poisoned against petitioner as to impeach the indifference of jurors who displayed no animus of their own.

In sum, we are unable to conclude, in the circumstances presented in this case, that petitioner did not receive a fair trial. Petitioner has failed to show that the setting of the trial was inherently prejudicial or that the jury-selection process of which he complains permits an inference of actual prejudice. The judgment of the Court of Appeals must therefore be affirmed.

Mr. JUSTICE BRENNAN, dissenting.

I dissent. *Irvin v. Dowd*, 366 U.S. 717 (1961), requires reversal of this conviction. As in that case, petitioner here was denied a fair trial. The risk that taint of widespread publicity regarding his criminal background, known to all members of the jury, infected the jury's deliberations is apparent, the trial court made no attempt to prevent discussion of the case or petitioner's previous criminal exploits among the prospective jurors, and one juror freely admitted that he was predisposed to convict petitioner. [This juror's *voir dire* appears at footnote 5 of the majority opinion.] * * * *

I cannot agree with the Court that the obvious bias of this juror may be overlooked simply because the juror's response was occasioned by a "leading and hypothetical question". Indeed, the hypothetical became reality when petitioner chose not to take the stand and offered no evidence. Thus petitioner was tried by a juror predisposed, because of his knowledge of petitioner's previous crimes, to find him guilty of this one.

Others who ultimately served as jurors revealed similar prejudice toward petitioner on *voir dire*. One juror conceded that it would be difficult, during deliberations, to put out of his mind that petitioner was a convicted criminal. He also admitted that he did not "hold a convicted felon in the same regard as another person who has never been convicted of a felony," and admitted further that he had termed petitioner a "menace".

A third juror testified that she knew from several sources that petitioner was a convicted murderer,[1] and was aware that the community regarded petitioner as a criminal who "should be put away". She disclaimed having a fixed opinion about the result she would reach, but acknowledged that the fact that petitioner was a convicted criminal would probably influence her verdict:

Q: Now, if you go into that jury room and deliberate with your fellow jurors, in your deliberations, will you consider the fact that Murphy is a convicted murderer and jewel thief?

A: Well, he has been convicted of murder. So, I guess that is what I would —

Q: You would consider that in your verdict, right?

A: Right.

Q: And that would influence your verdict; would it not?

A: If that is what you say, I guess it would.

Q: I am not concerned about what I say, because if I said it, they wouldn't print it. It would influence your verdict?

A: It probably would.

Q: When you go into that jury room, you cannot forget the fact that it is Murph the Surf; that he is a convicted murderer, and a jewel thief — you can't put that out of your mind, no matter what they tell you; can you, ma'am?

A: Probably not.

Q: And it would influence your verdict; right?

A: Probably.

Still another juror testified that the comments of venire members in discussing the case had made him "sick to [his] stomach." He testified that one venireman had said that petitioner was "thoroughly rotten", and that another had said: "Hang him, he's guilty."

Moreover, the Court ignores the crucial significance of the fact that at no time before or during this daily buildup of prejudice against Murphy did the trial judge instruct the prospective jurors not to discuss the case among themselves. Indeed, the trial judge took no steps to insulate the jurors from media coverage of the case or from the many news articles that discussed petitioner's last criminal exploits.

---

[1] The juror stated that she acquired a portion of her knowledge of petitioner's criminal background from an article in that week's Miami Herald entitled, "Defense Exhausts Jury Challenges in Murphy Trial," which included the sentence: "Jury selection will continue today in the trial of beach boy hoodlum serving a life sentence for murder in connection with the Whisky Creek slaying of two secretaries in 1968."

It is of no moment that several jurors ultimately testified that they would try to exclude from their deliberations their knowledge of petitioner's past misdeeds and of his community reputation. *Irvin* held in like circumstances that little weight could be attached to such selfserving protestations:

> No doubt each juror was sincere when he said that he would be fair and impartial to petitioner, but the psychological impact requiring such a declaration before one's fellows is often its father. Where so many, so many times, admitted prejudice, such a statement of impartiality can be given little weight. As one of the jurors put it, "You can't forget what you hear and see." [366 U.S. at 728]

On the record of this *voir dire*, therefore, the conclusion is to me inescapable that the attitude of the entire venire toward Murphy reflected the "then current community pattern of thought as indicated by the popular news media," *id.* at 725, and was infected with the taint of the view that he was a "criminal" guilty of notorious offenses, including that for which he was on trial. It is a plain case, from a review of the entire *voir dire*, where the extent and nature of the publicity has caused such a buildup of prejudice that excluding the preconception of guilt from the deliberations would be too difficult for the jury to be honestly found impartial. In my view, the denial of a change of venue was therefore prejudicial error, and I would reverse the conviction.

Note from Justin:

1. I don't understand what interests cut *against* a change of venue. If there is even the slightest chance that defendant might not get an impartial jury, *why not* change venue?

2. Does pretrial publicity require the trial judge to conduct a more intensive *voir dire*? In *Mu'min v. Virginia*, 500 U.S. 415 (1991), the Court held that the due process clause did not require a state court judge to ask prospective jurors specific questions about news coverage of the crime, even though 8 of the 12 jurors admitted that they had read about the crime, where the judge asked general questions about whether the jurors could be fair despite what they had read. The Court noted that many murders had been committed in the area covered by the newspapers, and the articles were more about the failures of law enforcement than the defendant's acts.

3. In *Johnson v. U.S.*, 307 F.Supp.2d 380 (D.Conn. 2003), a black defendant argued that he received ineffective assistance of counsel because his trial attorney "did not request that the Court question the white jurors as to their feelings about blacks following the O.J. Simpson trial. The verdict in the Simpson trial was announced on October 3, 1995, two days before the jury in Johnson's trial found him guilty. Petitioner asserts that the Simpson verdict created a high potential for 'unconscious racism' which would likely have an effect on the jury's deliberations. He argues that the publicity surrounding the O.J. Simpson trial was so prejudicial as to require a mistrial." The court disagreed:

> Johnson was convicted of possession with intent to sell narcotics, a charge completely unrelated to the murder charges in the O.J. Simpson trial. This Court is therefore satisfied that the jurors retained the requisite impartiality despite the verdict announced in the O.J. Simpson trial, and that there was no possibility for a mistrial.

POWELL v. SUPERIOR COURT
California Court of Appeal
232 Cal.App.3d 785 (1991)

THE COURT. (Before KLEIN, P. J., DANIELSON, J., CROSKEY, J., and HINZ, J.)

Petitioners Laurence Powell, Theodore J. Briseno, Stacey C. Koon, and Timothy E. Wind (collectively defendants) are police officers charged with specific charges of assault by force likely to produce great bodily injury and with a deadly weapon (Pen. Code, §§ 245, subd. (a)(1), 12022, subd. (a)(2), 1192.7, subd. (c)(8), 1203, subd. (e)(3)); and an officer unnecessarily assaulting or beating any person, (§§ 149, 1192.7, subd. (c)(8), 1203, subd. (e)(3)). In addition, Koon and Powell are charged with submission of a false police report by a peace officer (§ 118.1), and Koon is charged with the crime of accessory after the fact (§§ 32, 245, subd. (a)(1), 149).

All the charges arise from their conduct during the apprehension and arrest of Rodney King, a suspect.

Defendants seek a writ of mandate directing the trial court to vacate its order denying a motion to change venue and to order this case transferred to another county because of the pretrial publicity. For the many reasons discussed herein, we are compelled to direct a change of venue. We therefore grant the petition.

Summary Statement

Unbeknownst to the Los Angeles Police Department (LAPD) officers involved, the incident was videotaped by a nearby resident who sold it to a local TV station. The initial showing caused shock, revulsion, outrage and disbelief among viewers. A fire storm immediately developed in the Los Angeles area, so intense and pervasive was the reaction to the videotape.

The defendants were charged with the crimes enumerated above. Questions developed about the integrity of the LAPD and its chief. The mayor of Los Angeles called for the resignation of the chief of police. That action polarized the community. The police commission became vociferously involved, as did the city council. The mayor and the chief each appointed a committee of outstanding citizens to examine the LAPD and to make recommendations. These committees were subsequently succeeded by a single commission. Its final report called for, inter alia, significant changes in the management and training practices of the LAPD.

As might be expected, the incident and the resultant political turmoil received massive local media coverage, including newspapers, radio and TV which has impacted the residents. We emphasize, however, that were this simply a matter of extraordinary publicity we might have reached a different conclusion. What compels our decision in this case is the high level of political turmoil and controversy which this incident has generated, which continues to this day and appears likely to continue at least until the time when a trial of this matter can be had.

We have duly considered such political controversy along with the other relevant factors pertinent to a review of the trial court's denial of the venue change motion-the size of jury pool, the status of the victim and the accused, the nature of the offense-and conclude we must reverse the trial court and direct a change of venue. So extensive and pervasive has been the coverage, and so intense has become the political fallout, potential jurors have been infected to the extent there is a reasonable likelihood that a fair and impartial trial cannot be had in Los Angeles County.

Factual and Procedural Background

The incident occurred on March 3, 1991. Almost immediately, local TV news (KTLA, Channel 5) had obtained the rights to air the videotape. From its initial showing, the predictable reactions ranged from shock, outrage, revulsion, and fear to disbelief-all powerful human emotions to be capitalized on by the media. It was shown over and over and over again, mainly locally, but eventually, with Channel 5's release of the tape, everywhere in the world.

Locally, the question quickly arose as to how such an incident could be perpetrated by officers of the LAPD, a force with a reputation as one of the finest police departments in the world. Was this just isolated, aberrant, disgraceful conduct by a few rogue officers, or was the problem of greater significance? Was racial bias involved, given the arrestee was a Black and the defendants were all White? Was the LAPD command structure somehow at fault, and if so, did the fault include the chief, given a sergeant was on the scene? Was police training generally inadequate and, in particular, lacking in confrontational arrest procedures and sensitivity training?

Answers were sought by concerned citizens, politicians, the LAPD and investigative media. Abuse of the police car radio communication system soon came to light, disclosing numerous racist and sexist remarks. A review of the Los Angeles County District Attorney's files revealed a failure to prosecute claims of police violence on citizens, but ready prosecution of resisting arrest cases. Minority Black and Hispanic citizens came forward proclaiming the incident was not an isolated one, but conduct all too often occurring in their own communities.

Daryl F. Gates, the chief of police (Chief), defended the LAPD. Nevertheless, calls from many quarters came for him to resign, including from the mayor of Los Angeles, Tom Bradley (Mayor), himself a Black. The police commission, appointed by the Mayor, attempted to relieve the Chief of his duties by placing him on inactive status. However, the city council reinstated him on the authority of the Los Angeles City Charter provisions purporting to guarantee his independence and because of a threatened lawsuit.

Powerful factions began to develop in support of and in opposition to the Chief, which polarized politicians and ordinary residents alike. An impasse was created which checkmated a resolution of the many issues which had been raised.

During this time, the Chief endorsed and campaigned for a candidate in a vigorously contested city council race. Also, the Mayor and the Chief each designated members of what became a single blue ribbon commission to investigate the LAPD and to make recommendations. Further, the Mayor called for the resignation of certain members of the embattled police commission, and then replaced two of them. One replacement, a Black, was a former deputy chief with three decades of service, who gave testimony critical of the Chief before the Commission.

The Commission filed its report within the last several weeks, recommending a number of management changes for the LAPD, including a modification of the city charter with respect to the term of office and retention of the chief of police. An issue presented by the report was whether a citywide election was necessary to implement some of the recommendations.

Defendants were arraigned on March 26, 1991, and pled not guilty. Numerous discovery motions were filed. Defendants filed a motion for change of venue. The prosecution filed an opposition to which the defendants replied. Following a lengthy hearing, the trial court denied the motion.

On June 6, 1991, the defendants petitioned this court for a writ of mandate and requested a stay of the trial. On June 12, 1991, this court granted a stay of the trial and the jury selection process, but allowed other pretrial matters to proceed.

On June 17, 1991, the trial court wrote a letter to this court indicating it was willing, contrary to its repeatedly stated position that a change of venue was not legally justified, to "forthwith transfer the venue of this case." The trial court also requested this court to vacate the stay immediately so that such order could be made on or before June 19, the date set for trial. On June 18, 1991, this court issued an order indicating its prior order did not preclude a change of venue and that no further action was required by this court with respect to the trial court's letter.

On June 18, 1991, apparently in response to a negative reaction from the district attorney's office to the possibility of a venue change, the trial court engaged in an ex parte communication with members of that office by sending a law clerk to convey the trial court's assurances the venue issue would be handled properly. The next day, June 19, the trial court again reversed its position on the change of venue issue, indicating the trial would remain in Los Angeles County.

Thereafter, affidavits of prejudice for cause were filed by the defendants against the trial judge. In response, the trial judge indicated he would resist efforts to remove him from presiding over the trial. As of this date, the resolution of that issue is pending.

Discussion

* * * *

Appellate standard of review.

On a pretrial petition the appellate court must make an independent determination of the circumstances surrounding a defendant's request for change of venue to determine whether a fair trial is obtainable in the county of original venue. Section 1033, subdivision (a), requires a change of venue "when it appears that there is a reasonable likelihood that a fair and impartial trial cannot be had in the county." "Reasonable likelihood" has been interpreted as requiring something less than "more probable than not," and something more than merely possible. *People v. Bonin* (1988) 46 Cal.3d 659, 673.

A motion for change of venue shall be granted upon a determination that dissemination of potentially prejudicial material results in a reasonable likelihood a fair trial cannot be had in the county of original venue. A showing of actual prejudice is not required. *Martinez v. Superior Court* (1981) 29 Cal.3d 574, 578

Relevant factors to be considered on review.

The question is whether the potential jurors can view the case with the requisite impartiality. Material factors to be considered in resolving the question include the size of the potential jury pool, the nature and extent of the publicity, the status of the accused and the victim, the nature and gravity of the offense, and the existence of political turmoil arising from the incident.

a. Immense size of potential jury pool not controlling here.

Size of the potential jury pool is one of the factors considered on a motion for change of venue. The larger the local population, the more likely it is that preconceptions about the case have not become embedded in the public consciousness.

Los Angeles County covers 4,083 square miles. The source list used in the selection of potential jurors in Los Angeles Superior Court includes the list of persons who voted in recent elections and the records of the Department of Motor Vehicles. The potential jury pool in Los Angeles County is 6.526 million according to the Jury Services Division of the Los Angeles County Superior Court.

The People contend the potential jury pool in Los Angeles County is so large that other facts are rendered irrelevant. The trial court apparently based its ruling primarily upon the size of the population in Los Angeles County. That premise has been unacceptable in other cases: "Carried to its logical conclusion, the district attorney's argument, if valid, would require that all motions for a change of venue in Los Angeles County must be denied because of its population, regardless of the amount of pretrial publicity which surrounds a notorious criminal case. This contention is disposed of by the court in *Maine* in the following language: "We do not intend to suggest, however, that a large city may not also become so hostile to a defendant as to make a fair trial unlikely." *Maine v. Superior Court*, 68 Cal.2d at p. 387, fn. 13.

In support of the motion for change of venue, defendants rely, in part, on polls of residents of Los Angeles County as reported in the Los Angeles Times. On March 10, 1991, within a week of the incident, the Los Angeles Times reported 86 percent of those surveyed had seen the videotape of the offense and 92 percent believed excessive force had been used. On March 22, 1991, the Los Angeles Times reported 94 percent of all persons surveyed in another poll described themselves as "upset" by the incident and almost two-thirds believed the force used was racially motivated.

Defendants retained experts to conduct a public opinion survey in the community. In a random sample of 1,000 people, 97 percent were aware of the incident. That 97 percent was then broken down into a number of categories: 3 percent believed defendants were not guilty of any offense; 14 percent had formed no opinion; 81 percent felt defendants were guilty; 70 percent of the persons from the group who felt defendants were guilty had a "strong" view about the incident.

These figures, reflecting preconceived attitudes, are significantly higher than those in similar surveys made in *Williams v. Superior Court*, 34 Cal.3d at page 590, in which a writ of mandate was granted directing the trial court to grant a change of venue. Moreover, size of community, while an important factor, is not controlling. Each case must turn on its own facts. Here, questions peculiar to the county of original venue have rendered the seating of a jury panel without preconceived opinions as to some aspects of the case practically impossible. The factors discussed below lessen the significance of the fact that the case arises in an expansive metropolitan area with a large pool of potential jurors.

b. Nature and extent of the publicity.

As indicated, the publicity surrounding the incident itself has been unequaled in Los Angeles County. Of even greater importance is the impact upon the citizenry of the political uproar resulting from the incident.

(1) Print media coverage massive.

The largest newspaper in Los Angeles County is the Los Angeles Times with a daily circulation of 1,242,864 and an additional 300,000 on Sundays. The county also has many other newspapers of lesser circulation, including the Daily News of the San Fernando Valley, the Press Telegram (Long Beach), the Star News (Pasadena), The Outlook (Santa Monica), and newspapers covering other communities in the greater Los Angeles area. These newspapers have blanketed Los Angeles County with coverage of the incident and related issues.

Their coverage included front page pictures, feature stories, in-depth analyses, editorials, letters to the editors, results of numerous polls conducted by individual newspapers, pictures of key individuals, and biting political cartoons. Articles have appeared daily since the incident, sometimes with several related stories in the same edition. It is impossible to pick up a copy of the Los Angeles Times and not find at least one related story, including one recent article wherein it is charged that officers who publicly criticized the chief are suffering retaliation within the department. *797

(2) Radio coverage extensive.

Two major radio news outlets, KNX and KFWB, which cover Los Angeles County (with a combined listening audience of over 3 million), as well as many other radio stations, have given the incident and the resultant flurry of community and political activity extensive, daily coverage. Radio news is available around the clock to persons in their homes and offices and to the hundreds of thousands of commuters on the freeways. Again, it is impossible to listen to any station without hearing stories relating to the latest developments, including jokes, whether it be coverage of a news conference with the Chief, the Mayor, or an interview with the "person in the street."

(3) TV coverage, graphic and devastating.

Los Angeles's Channel 5 (KTLA) obtained copies of the now notorious videotape by buying the rights thereto from a citizen who witnessed and taped it. Its initial screening caused overwhelming reactions as viewers watched several officers land 56 baton blows and 6 kicks about the body of the downed man. It was an exposition of brutality and emotions ran high. It eventually was seen by viewers all over the world, and the world's reaction filtered back to a shocked community. Since the initial showings of the incident, local TV stations, like the other media, have provided daily coverage of all resultant events.

Channels 2 and 4 have featured local talk shows wherein interviews of the Chief, the Mayor and members of the Commission, the city council and the police commission have been conducted. The late night talk show hosts have invoked humor in criticizing all political personalities involved. Indeed, a resident of Los Angeles County cannot watch TV news without being subjected to the many ramifications of this volatile topic.

While it is true that in some cases the pervasive nature of modern communications media limits the effectiveness of change of venue the nature of the publicity in other notorious criminal cases, such as Manson, is totally unlike the publicity surrounding this case. The publicity in Manson arose from the nature of the crimes, the manner in which the murders had been committed, and the persons involved. Manson was not entangled in local politics, did not focus on local politicians, and did not involve issues unique to Los Angeles County.

c. Status of victim and accused.

Important and unusual factors in this case are the status of the defendants as White law enforcement officers and the arrestee as a Black, the widespread media usage of the videotape disclosing the nature of the arrest, and the publication of internal police department documents.

It cannot be disputed that difficulty in obtaining a fair trial in Los Angeles County is exacerbated by the fact the defendants are police officers, sworn to protect citizens, to uphold the law and to maintain peace in the community. Their status is the basis of the intense coverage and repeated showing of the videotape. The fact that the videotape depicts local officers in such conduct threatens the community's ability to rely on its police and has caused a high level of indignation, outrage, and anxiety.

d. Nature and gravity of the offense.

Simply stated, the charges here are assault and battery under color of law. While rendered more important in the public consciousness because of the dramatic videotape and the persons charged are law enforcement officers, the crime of assault and battery does not compare to the gruesome murders involved in other notorious cases tried in Los Angeles County, e.g., Charles Manson, the "Night Stalker," the "Hillside Strangler." Although Los Angeles County was able to seat a fair and impartial jury in cases with widespread publicity involving crimes even more heinous than the offenses charged here, those crimes did not involve defendants who were local police officers or the ensuing local political controversy.

e. Political factors.

As previously indicated, shortly after the incident, a political furor erupted which has been compressed into an intense four-month period. The Mayor called for the Chief either to resign or to retire. The police commission placed the Chief on inactive status; he responded with a lawsuit. The city council intervened reinstating the Chief. A power struggle ensued among the Chief, the Mayor, the city council and the police commission.

During this period, vigorously contested elections for city council positions were occurring throughout the city. All candidates took positions essentially in support of either the Mayor or the Chief. The Chief himself endorsed and campaigned for at least one candidate who was seeking another term to represent northwest valley residents. Such support was even reflected in bumper stickers.

In an effort to resolve the political crisis and address many of the issues which had been raised, the Commission was formed. All 10 members were high profile citizens of the greater Los Angeles area. The Commission's charge was to review the structure and operation of the LAPD. Confidential testimony was given and other evidence was received over a three-month period. A 228-page report was filed by the Commission on July 9, 1991, with many recommendations. With respect to the position of police chief, it recommended term limitations and additional power within the police commission to fire a chief. Such recommendations may require a citywide election to amend the city charter.

In addition, the Commission's report made a number of findings. For example, it found that: (1) excessive force was used by many officers; (2) racial and sexual bias was reflected in the conduct of many officers; (3) sexism existed within the LAPD; (4) there had been a failure of the LAPD command structure effectively to monitor, discipline and control officers accused of improper conduct; (5) there was frequent use of the Mobile Digital Terminal communication system to make scurrilous and offensive racist and sexist remarks without concern for possible reprimand from LAPD leaders; and (6) there had been a lack of accountability of the LAPD to civilian oversight authorities.

Following the issuance of the report, rumors abounded as to the Chief's plans, alternatively to remain at the helm indefinitely, or until a replacement was found, or until the voters spoke at an election, or to retire or to resign at a date of his choosing. Although as of this date his status is apparently resolved, it is still a matter of continuing and acrimonious debate.

There is a claim that officers who gave damaging testimony about the department and the Chief before the Commission suffered retaliation within the department. The same complaint was made by officers making critical public comments. On the other hand, officers who were publicly supportive of the Chief were expecting promotions within the department.

Also in the wake of the report, two police commission members resigned and were promptly replaced. One replacement had been, until his retirement, the highest ranking Black officer in the department, who had been publicly critical of the Chief and now calls for the Chief's resignation. The other replacement is a woman of long-standing public service to the Los Angeles community who also is demanding the Chief step down.

Such political factors have no place in a criminal proceeding, and when they are likely to appear, as here, they constitute an independent reason for a venue change.
* * * *

In addition, we note that this court has received a document which can be construed only as a threat of community violence if the case is transferred to another venue. The document was widely publicized in the Los Angeles Times and other local newspapers. The possibility of riots also has been mentioned on television news coverage. In dealing with the issue, under similar circumstances, a

Florida court recently held: "We simply cannot approve the result of a trial conducted, in an atmosphere in which the entire community was justifiably concerned with the dangers which would follow an acquittal, but which would be obviated if the defendant was convicted. Surely, the fear that one's own county would respond to a not guilty verdict by erupting into violence is as highly 'impermissible a factor,' as can be contemplated. Surely too, there was an over-whelmingly 'unacceptable risk,' " of an adverse effect upon the right of every citizen to a fair determination of guilt or innocence based solely upon evidence presented at trial. *Lozano v. State* (Fla.Dist.Ct.App. 1991) 584 So.2d 19, 22–23.

The threat of violence here does not yet arise from the ultimate determination of guilt or innocence but from this pretrial procedural matter dealing with venue. If the mere possibility an order directing that trial be conducted outside Los Angeles County gives rise to such threats, we must draw the inevitable inference about the possibility of threats which could surface during the trial itself. Such unacceptable attempts to influence the judicial proceedings at this early stage add another impermissible factor into the boiling cauldron surrounding this case, making it imperative to take every step possible to ensure that an impartial unbiased jury be seated.

"When a spectacular crime has aroused community attention and a suspect has been arrested, the possibility of an unfair trial may originate in widespread publicity describing facts, statements and circumstances which tend to create a belief in his guilt. Indispensable to any morally acceptable system of criminal justice is a verdict based upon evidence and argument received in open court, not from outside sources. When community attention is focused upon the suspect of a spectacular crime, the news media's dissemination of incriminatory circumstances sharply threatens the integrity of the coming trial. The goal of a fair trial in the locality of the crime is practically unattainable when the jury panel has been bathed in streams of circumstantial incrimination flowing from the news media. An honest juror may admit knowledge or tentative prejudgment and find himself excluded. Many will sincerely try to set aside their preconceptions and give assurance of impartiality, yet unconsciously bend to the influence of initial impressions gained from the news media." *Corona v. Superior Court* (1972) 24 Cal.App.3d 872, 877–879.

While we recognize that the incident and some of its ramifications have received widespread publicity elsewhere, the impact on residents of Los Angeles is unques-tionably much greater because of the unabated and acrimonious total involvement of city officials and local community leaders. There is no doubt that these political biases would invade the jury box if the case were tried in Los Angeles County.

Conclusion

Every person charged with a criminal offense is entitled to a trial free of the unacceptable risk of impermissible factors coming into play. "The potential of community bias mounts in direct ratio to the pervasiveness of publicity. In counties geographically removed from the locale of the crime, lack of a sense of community involvement will permit jurors a degree of objectivity unattainable" in the locale of the crime itself. *Corona v. Superior Court*, supra, 24 Cal.App.3d at p. 883. Most significantly, such jurors are far less likely to be involved in the prevailing political controversies which we have set out in some detail and which appear to be reasonably limited to the greater Los Angeles area.

The record presented before the trial court was sufficient to support defendants' contention they cannot receive a fair trial in Los Angeles County and their contention becomes increasingly more obvious as each day passes. The events of which we have taken judicial notice not only add further support to the defendants' contention but lead us inexorably to conclude there is more than the statutory "reasonable likelihood" standard present here. Under the totality of the circumstances, a change of venue is clearly necessary to assure that defendants have a fair and impartial trial.

We conclude there is a substantial probability Los Angeles County is so saturated with knowledge of the incident, so influenced by the political controversy surrounding the matter and so permeated with preconceived opinions that potential jurors cannot try the case solely upon the evidence presented in the courtroom. Accordingly, we grant the petition for writ of mandate.

We leave the ultimate selection of the site for a fair trial to the trial court with directions to weigh the various factors bearing upon the selesion of a forum free from the unacceptable risk that a fair trial cannot be conducted. In implementing the transfer, the trial court must follow the procedure set forth in California Rules of Court, rules 842 and 843.

Disposition

Let a peremptory writ of mandate issue directing the trial court to grant the motion for change of venue, to determine a site where a fair trial can be held, and to transfer the case to that site. Upon transfer to another county, the stay of the trial and related jury selection proceedings, heretofore issued by this court, is vacated.

Notes from Justin:

1. **If venue must be changed,** *where to?*

In *State v. Lozano* 616 So.2d 73 (Fla.Ct.App.1993), Lozano was a Miami police officer who shot and killed a motorcyclist who was fleeing a traffic stop. A passenger also died in the resulting crash. Lozano was Hispanic, and both victims were black. The incident triggered riots in Miami's black community. Lozano was charged in Dade County (where Miami is located) with two counts of manslaughter. He moved for a change of venue, arguing that Miami jurors would be reluctant to vote for acquittal for fear of causing further violence. The motion was denied and Lozano was convicted, but the Court of Appeal reversed, ruling that the motion should have been granted. The case was remanded to the trial court to determine where to send the case. The trial court heard testimony from witnesses who "described (1) the general feeling of alienation between the black community and the judicial system — a feeling that they are not an equal participant; and (2) a perception that the shootings of blacks by non-black policemen are handled differently than other shootings. Both concerns have been increased by the Rodney King verdict.* Neither

---

* While the Lozano case was pending, an amateur video-photographer filmed several white Los Angeles police officers in the act of beating black motorist Rodney King. The officers were tried in suburban Simi Valley for assault, under state law. After a jury of 10 whites, one Asian, and one Hispanic

concern should exist in a free society." The court tried to find a county with demographics similar to those of Dade County, which was about 20% black and 50% Hispanic. Though noting that "Dade County has no twin in this state," the court ordered the case transferred to one of the two large counties with a percentage of black voters equal to or greater than Dade's: Leon County (where Tallahassee is located), which has a black population of 20.6%. "This will ensure that blacks will be on the jury that tries this case to the extent that the law permits."

Both Lozano and the State appealed, making the same argument: the trial court erred by selecting a county on the basis of the race of the victims, rather than the race of the defendant. The Court of Appeals agreed. "The trial court deliberately acted so as to increase the number of Black jurors. In doing this, the trial court virtually guaranteed the absence of Hispanic jurors. 'Purposeful racial discrimination in the selection of the venire violates a defendant's right to equal protection because it denies him the protection that a trial by jury is intended to secure.' *Batson v. Kentucky*, 476 U.S. 79, 86 (1986)." The court ordered the case tried in Orange County (where Orlando is located) — which is mostly white.

Lozano was tried by an Orlando jury of 3 whites, 2 Hispanics, and one black. They acquitted him.

The problems raised by the *Lozano* and Rodney King cases are discussed in Levinson, *Change of Venue and the Role of the Criminal Jury*, 66 So.Calif.L.Rev. 1533 (1993) and Gilbert, *An Ounce of Prevention: A Constitutional Prescription for Choice of Venue In Racially Sensitive Cases*, 67 Tulane L.Rev. 1855 (1993).

These cases seem to raise this question: should the community in which the crime is (allegedly) committed have a "right" to have the case tried in that community, or at least in a community with a similar ethnic composition? If so, what happens when that "right" threatens to collide with the defendant's right to an "impartial jury"?

2. Instead of moving the trial, how about *bringing in* a jury from another county?

In *State v. Harris*, 660 A.2d 539 (N.J.Super.1995), a black man was charged with murdering a white woman in Trenton, Mercer County, which has a large black population. Due to pretrial publicity, the trial court ruled that defendant could not get a fair trial with a Mercer County jury. But instead of moving the trial to another county, the court kept the trial in Mercer County, but — because virtually all the trial witnesses lived in Mercer County — decided to bring in a "foreign jury" from another county. But from which county? The trial court selected Hunterdon County — which is mainly white — because it is contiguous to Mercer. The court rejected defendant's argument that the foreign jury should come from a county with a racial make-up similar to Mercer's. But the appellate court reversed:

> We conclude that the same state constitutional policies which underlie the limitations imposed upon a prosecutor's use of peremptory challenges to exclude members of a particular race from a jury also require a trial court to consider racial demographics in exercising its authority under Rule 3:14-2 to change the venue of a criminal trial or to impanel a foreign jury. * * * * If a trial court disregards racial demographics in selecting a county

---

acquitted the officers, riots broke out in black neighborhoods of Los Angeles. A subsequent federal trial on civil rights charges took place in Los Angeles before a mixed jury, resulting in convictions.

for a change of venue or as the source for impanelling a foreign jury, resulting in a jury pool with a significantly smaller percentage of a racial minority than would be generated in the county where the crime was committed, it will reduce the likelihood that the jurors ultimately selected will be members of different groups whose respective biases will tend to cancel each other out" in the course of jury deliberations. Such an exercise of judicial discretion also detracts from the legitimacy of the judicial process in the eyes of the public, especially members of the minority group who are underrepresented in the jury pool. * * * *

Furthermore, if it were permissible for a court to completely disregard racial demographics in selecting a county for a change of venue or impanelling a foreign jury, it would create a serious risk that a defendant would be inhibited from asserting one constitutional right — the right to a trial before a jury that is untainted by prejudicial publicity — out of fear that the assertion of that right could result in the sacrifice of another constitutional right — the right to a trial before a jury composed of a representative cross-section of the community where the crime was committed. * * * *

Therefore, we hold that to protect a defendant's right to a jury that is reasonably comparable to one drawn from a representative cross-section of the community in which the crime was committed and to promote that community's confidence in the fairness of the trial, a trial court should consider racial demographics together with other relevant factors in selecting a county for a change of venue or as the source of a foreign jury. Racial demographics should be a particularly weighty factor in selecting the source of a foreign jury when the victim and the defendant belong to different races. Since the trial court selected Hunterdon County as the source of the jury that will hear this case based in part on its view that racial demographics should be disregarded in impanelling a foreign jury, we reverse that part of its order.

Commentator Stuart Taylor was troubled by the *Harris* decision:

Was the New Jersey court just crafting a rule for those rare cases in which venue is changed or jurors are imported? After all, a black defendant might not feel much better about facing an all-white jury if the reason was that his alleged crimes had been committed in a 98% percent white county.

So there is reason to wonder whether the New Jersey ruling may be a first step down the road toward some kind of right to a jury of one's racial peers, enforced by racial quotas in jury selection. Such quotas have, in fact, been urged by a few scholars, including Cornell Law School professor Sheri Johnson, who has written that black defendants should have a right to juries that include at least three black members.

Whatever the rules should be, it's becoming increasingly clear that the jury system will be in grave peril if we cannot reverse our society's drive toward ever deeper racial polarization and tribalism. The staggering racial divisions over the O.J. Simpson case — with 78% of whites in one recent poll believing him to be guilty of double murder and 71% of blacks believing him to be innocent — do not bode well.

Such polls, and some scholarly studies, confirm what common experience suggests: Racial identification has a sufficiently large effect on the outlook of many jurors that — other things being equal — black and white defendants alike often fare better with jurors of their own race, at least in racially charged cases.

This represents a particular problem for black defendants. This is not necessarily to say that white people are less impartial than blacks when it comes to judging black defendants; indeed, in the case of Simpson, against whom there is a mountain of evidence, race-based partiality seems widespread in the black community. But a great many more black defendants are disadvantaged by the racial dynamics of the jury system.

Even when white jurors are meticulously fair to black defendants, that's not always the perception in the black community. Imagine if the venue of the Simpson case had been changed to, say, a white suburb, and he was convicted there by an all-white jury. No matter how overwhelming the evidence of guilt, the perception among black people that Simpson had been railroaded would be rampant and destructive. * * * *

How many black jurors should a black defendant be entitled? One — or three — or six? Why not all 12? And would the right to black jurors obtain only in cases of interracial crimes or in all criminal cases?

What about other racial minorities? How would we round up enough black (or Asian, or Hispanic, or Aleut) jurors — in, say, Maine — to fill the quota for every minority defendant? How would any mandate of racial representation on juries be administered? By cordoning off separate sections of the courtroom during jury selection — one for blacks, one for whites — and then taking one person from the black section for every three from the white section?

What kind of statement would the judicial system be making if it mandated such practices? That jurors are expected to judge defendants on the basis of racial solidarity and that minority jurors are being sought out not for their presumed impartiality, but for their presumed feelings of solidarity with minority defendants?

The bottom line is that racial quotas in jury selection are a terribly disturbing idea whose time — mercifully — has not come. Yet such proposals may be increasingly hard to resist if we lose our collective confidence in the ability of all jurors to be reasonably impartial regardless of the race of the parties. If that happens, will what is left of the jury system to worth saving?

The New Jersey court's decision in *Harris* nonetheless seems right. That's because, on the peculiar facts of the case, the perception of unfairness to the black defendant was especially powerful and easily avoided. * * * *

Would the appellate court come out the same way if, for example, a white defendant charged with raping and murdering a black woman in an overwhelmingly white county objected to having his jury imported from mostly black Newark? It should. While demographics suggest that few (if any) white defendants will be in a position to invoke the rule of the *Harris* case, there should be no racial double standard in applying the rule.

It is disconcerting to find myself endorsing the introduction of the potentially virulent germ of racialism into any aspect of jury selection. But it would be even more disconcerting to have to explain to a presumptively innocent black defendant in an interracial rape-murder case why the price of invoking his right to a jury untainted by pretrial publicity should be an all-white jury. [Stuart Taylor, Jr., *Should Differing Demographics and Perceptions Dictate Racial Awareness In Jury Selection?* San Francisco Recorder, 8/8/95.]

For further consideration of the use of "foreign juries," see *State v. Timmendequas*, 161 N.J. 515 (1999). (Timmendequas murdered Megan Kanka, which led to the enactment of "Megan's laws" in several states.)

3. Should black jurors be encouraged to "nullify" the law?

Professor Paul Butler, in *Racially Based Jury Nullification: Black Power in the Criminal Justice System*, 105 Yale L.J. 677 (1995) proposed that black jurors use their power of "nullification" (i.e., to "nullify" the judge's instructions on the law by disregarding them) by acquitting black defendants charged with non-violent crimes — including drug crimes. His proposal has drawn quite a bit of fire. See, e.g., Andrew. D Leipold, *The Dangers of Race-Based Jury Nullification: A Response to Professor Butler*, 44 UCLA L.Rev. 109 (1996). For an example of what might happen if jurors follow Professor Butler's proposal, see *U.S. v. Thomas*, 116 F.3d 606 (2nd Cir.1997).

Professor Butler's proposal was considered and rejected in *People v. Douglas*, 680 N.Y.S.2d 145 (1998):

Jury nullification is an assumption of power which the jury has no right to exercise. A jury has no more "right" to find a "guilty" defendant "not guilty" than it has to find a "not guilty" defendant "guilty," and the fact that the former cannot be corrected by a court, while the latter can be, does not create a right out of the power to misapply the law. Such verdicts are lawless, a denial of due process and constitute and exercise of erroneously seized power.

The idea of deciding cases on the basis of racial politics as opposed to reasonable doubt is not new; however, its modern day proponents advance the logic that if the system routinely fails, here, African-American defendants, then African Americans must abandon the system. This goes beyond the lofty premise of juror leniency in refusing to enforce unjust laws or laws that have been unjustly enforced. Race-based jury nullification was a repellant practice when white supremacists on Southern juries refused to convict those accused of violence against African Americans; it is no better practiced by black jurors, even if motivated by legitimate anger. There is an unfortunate yet increasing perception that African-American jurors vote to acquit defendants for racial reasons. It has a particular resonance in this venue.[14] Racial allegiance, white or black, has no place in a court of

---

[14] "The race factor seems particularly evident in such urban environments as Bronx County where juries are more than 80% black and Hispanic. There, black defendants are acquitted in felony cases

law; in the jury room, judgment and discretion are inseparable.

4. Can the trial be moved *out of the state*?

In *U.S. v. McVeigh*, 918 F.Supp. 1467 (W.D.Okla.1996), McVeigh was charged with using a truck bomb to blow up a federal building in Oklahoma City, killing 168 people. The grand jury indictment was issued in Oklahoma City, and that is where the case was set for trial. The trial court found that massive pretrial publicity precluded a fair trial in Oklahoma City, and granted a motion for change of venue. The prosecutor suggested transfer to the Northern District of Oklahoma (in Tulsa), but the court disagreed:

> The parties have submitted a large volume of evidence concerning news coverage of the explosion, the rescue effort, the investigations by law enforcement agencies and media sources, the arrests of the defendants, court proceedings and community activities. Extensive print news coverage in Oklahoma City, Tulsa and Lawton has been submitted. Videotapes of local and national telecasts from April 19, 1995, to the date of the motions hearing were admitted and have been reviewed.
>
> Initially, national media coverage of the explosion was extremely comprehensive. Dramatic pictures of the Murrah Federal Building were shown nationwide immediately after the explosion. There was intensive coverage of the rescue efforts. The immediate reactions of the President, the Attorney General, and an FBI spokesman were broadcast across the nation. There were extensive interviews with injured victims, members of the families of the dead and missing persons, rescue and relief workers, and residents of Oklahoma City. The Governor of the State of Oklahoma was a continual presence in the media coverage, providing strong leadership and articulating the needs and spirit of the entire state.
>
> The arrest of Timothy McVeigh on April 21 in Perry, Oklahoma as a bombing suspect produced film showing him in restraints and clad in bright orange jail clothing being led into a van while surrounded by a very vocal and angry crowd. Some bystanders could be heard shouting "murderer" and "baby killer." This footage was seen nationwide and was widely used in later television broadcasts about other developments in the government's investigation. There was widespread publicity about a search for another suspect described as John Doe # 2. The arrest of Terry Nichols and a search of his brother's farm in Michigan were other subjects of national publicity.
>
> As time passed, differences developed in both the volume and focus of the media coverage in Oklahoma compared with local coverage outside of Oklahoma and with national news coverage. These differences were discussed in the testimony of Russell Scott Armstrong, an expert in news media analysis. In the weeks following the explosion, there was less media coverage of the explosion outside of Oklahoma. Developments in the

---

47.6% of the time — nearly three times the national acquittal rate of 17% for all races. Hispanics are acquitted 37.6% of the time. This is so even though the majority of crime victims in the Bronx are black or Hispanic." Holden, et al., "Color Blinded? Race Seems to Play An Increasing Role In Many Jury Verdicts," Wall St. J., Oct. 4, 1995, at A1.

government investigation were reported, but such reports were primarily factual in nature. Oklahoma coverage, in contrast, remained focused on the explosion and its aftermath for a much longer period of time. Television stations conducted their own investigations, interviewing "eyewitnesses" and showing reconstructions and simulations of alleged events. Such "investigative journalism" continued for more than four months after the explosion. Perhaps most significant was the continuing coverage of the victims and their families. The Oklahoma coverage was more personal, providing individual stories of grief and recovery. As late as December 1995, television stations in Oklahoma City and Tulsa were broadcasting special series of individual interviews with family members and people involved in covering the explosion and its aftermath.

According to Armstrong, these differences in media coverage reflect the different needs of the Oklahoma media market compared to the nationwide media market. He observed that, as a national story of great importance, people across the country wanted to know the "who, what, where, why, and when" of this event. The nation was interested in the human story of suffering and renewal, but in a more general sense. In contrast, because this was a crime that occurred in their state, Oklahomans wanted to know every detail about the explosion, the investigation, the court proceedings and, in particular, the victims.

Armstrong opined that the greater informational needs of Oklahomans resulted from a perception that Oklahomans are united as a family with a spirit unique to the state. Indeed, the "Oklahoma family" has been a common theme in the Oklahoma media coverage, with numerous reports of how the explosion shook the entire state, and how the state has pulled together in response. The political leadership of the state has repeatedly and consistently emphasized the bonds tying all Oklahomans together as family and proclaiming to the nation and the world that the survival and recovery from this tragedy is "Oklahoma's story." * * * *

There is an evident and understandable pride of accomplishment in all that has been done to try to return to normalcy. Prominently displayed in the state capitol building is the artwork of survivors and families of the deceased done at a state sponsored gathering at Quartz Mountain under the heading "Celebration of the Spirit." Many Oklahomans view a trial of this case as an additional challenge and want the opportunity to demonstrate their ability to be fair in spite of this extraordinary provocation of their emotions of anger and vengeance. They seek participation in the trial to demonstrate an ability to overcome a tragedy with such powerful emotional impact that people have come to measure time by it.

Pride is defined as satisfaction in an achievement, and the people of Oklahoma are well deserving of it. But it is easy for those feeling pride to develop a prejudice, defined as "(a) an adverse judgment or opinion formed beforehand or without knowledge or examination of the facts and (b) a preconceived preference or idea." The American Heritage Dictionary of the English Language (3d ed.1992). The existence of such a prejudice is difficult to prove. Indeed it may go unrecognized in those who are affected by it. The prejudice that may deny a fair trial is not limited to a bias or discriminatory attitude. It includes an impairment of the deliberative process of deductive reasoning from evidentiary facts resulting from an attribution to something not included in the evidence. That something has its most powerful effect if it generates strong emotional responses and fits into a pattern of normative values.

In this case the repetition of emotionally intense stories of loss and grief and the valiant efforts to overcome the consequences of this event have developed a common belief that the citizens of Oklahoma can and must take what many believe to be the necessary last step on the road to recovery — participation in the trial of these accused men. The character of the crimes charged is so contrary to the public expectation of human behavior that there is a prevailing belief that some action must be taken to make things right again. That theme is dominant in the comments of people interviewed by television reporters asking about their reactions to court proceedings in this case. The common reference is to "seeing that justice is done." There is a fair inference that only a guilty verdict with a death sentence could be considered a just result in the minds of many.

The emotional burden of the explosion and its consequences has been intensified by the repeated and heavy emphasis on the innocence of the victims and the impact of their loss on their families. The tragic sense is heightened by the deaths of infants and very young children in the day care center. The horror of that fact has been powerfully portrayed by the symbols of teddy bears and angels displayed everywhere in Oklahoma. They were placed on a Christmas Tree at the State Capitol. The public sympathy for victims is so strong that it has been manifested in the very courthouse where these motions were heard, when on the first day of the hearing a T-shirt was sold bearing the following inscription: "Those Lost Will Never Leave Our Hearts Or be Forgotten April 19, 1995 United States Court Western District of Oklahoma." The shirt also exhibited the purple ribbon which is a ubiquitous symbol of empathy and unity throughout Oklahoma, even appearing on special license plates.

The intensity of the humanization of the victims in the public mind is in sharp contrast with the prevalent portrayals of the defendants. They have been demonized. The videotape footage and fixed photographs of Timothy McVeigh in Perry have been used regularly in almost all of the television news reports of developments in this case. All of the Oklahoma television markets have been saturated with stories suggesting the defendants are associated with "right wing militia groups." File film shows people in combat fatigues firing military style firearms to illustrate the suggested association. That theme has particularly been emphasized with Terry Nichols and his brother. These films have also been shown in Denver and on national news programs but not with the frequency of the use by broadcast outlets in Oklahoma.

New film showing the defendants in restraints and body armor was taken in the sally port of the jail in Oklahoma City when they were being brought to court for hearing these motions. It was shown nationally and locally in connection with reports of the court proceedings.

The possible prejudicial impact of this type of publicity is not something measurable by any objective standards. The parties have submitted data from opinion surveys done by qualified experts who have given their opinions about the results and their meaning. The government places heavy reliance on this evidence to support the position that a fair and impartial jury can be selected in the Northern District of Oklahoma for a trial in Tulsa. Such surveys are but crude measures of opinion at the time of the interviews. Human behavior is far less knowable and predictable than chemical reactions or other subjects of study by scientific methodology. There is no laboratory experiment that can come close to duplicating the trial of criminal charges. There are so many variables involved that no two trials can be compared regardless of apparent similarities. That is the very genius of the American jury trial.

The expert witnesses who have studied in this area have suggested that *voir dire* of the jury panel is the only technique available to minimize the effects of pre-trial publicity and that most jurors develop fixed opinions by the conclusion of lawyers' opening statements. While those opinions may be justified by the research done, consisting largely of simulated trials, this view is inconsistent with this court's long experience with jury trials both as lawyer and judge. That experience fortifies a faith that a properly conducted trial with competent counsel on both sides with adequate resources available to them will reveal the historical facts relevant to the charges and that jurors who have adequate protection from external influences will reach a just verdict according to the law and evidence.

Extensive publicity before trial does not, in itself, preclude fairness. In many respects media exposure presents problems not qualitatively different from that experienced in earlier times in small communities where gossip and jurors' personal acquaintances with lawyers, witnesses and even the accused were not uncommon. Properly motivated and carefully instructed jurors can and have exercised the discipline to disregard that kind of prior awareness. Trust in their ability to do so diminishes when the prior exposure is such that it evokes strong emotional responses or such an identification with those directly affected by the conduct at issue that the jurors feel a personal stake in the outcome. That is also true when there is such identification with a community point of view that jurors feel a sense of obligation to reach a result which will find general acceptance in the relevant audience. * * * *

If a defendant is found guilty on any of the present charges, the jury will then be required to determine whether death is justified for the offense of conviction after consideration of the mitigating and aggravating factors presented by evidence received at a further hearing. 18 U.S.C. §§ 3591–3593. * * * * There must be individualized consideration of the defendant and any mitigating evidence relevant to him. *Lockett v. Ohio,* 438 U.S. 586 (1978).

Because the penalty of death is by its very nature different from all other punishments in that it is final and irrevocable, the issue of prejudice raised by the present motions must include consideration of whether there is a showing of a predilection toward that penalty. Most interesting in this regard is the frequency of the opinions expressed in recent televised interviews of citizens of Oklahoma emphasizing the importance of assuring certainty in a verdict of guilty with an evident implication that upon such a verdict death is the appropriate punishment. It is significant that there is a citizens' movement in Oklahoma to support pending legislation which would sharply limit the reviewability of a death sentence.

Upon all of the evidence presented, this court finds and concludes that there is so great a prejudice against these two defendants in the State of Oklahoma that they cannot obtain a fair and impartial trial at any place fixed by law for holding court in that state. The court also finds and concludes that an appropriate alternative venue is in the District of Colorado.

Denver, Colorado meets all of the criteria that have been cited by past cases as relevant when selecting an alternative venue. Denver is a large metropolitan community with many community resources. It is readily accessible, being well-served by daily non-stop flights from all relevant cities. The court facilities in Denver are well-suited for accommodating the special needs of this trial. The United States Marshal for the District of Colorado is well equipped to provide adequate security services. A large jury pool is available.

In reaching this ruling, the court is acutely aware of the wishes of the victims of the Oklahoma City explosion to attend this trial and that it will be a hardship for those victims to travel to Denver. The attorneys for the government have earnestly argued that statutory provisions for victims must be considered by the court. * * * * The interests of the victims in being able to attend this trial in Oklahoma are outweighed by the court's obligation to assure that the trial be conducted with fundamental fairness and with due regard for all constitutional requirements.

Later, the court arranged for closed-circuit television of the McVeigh trial in Denver, to be viewed live in Oklahoma City by victims' families who could not go to Denver.

The Denver jury convicted McVeigh and sentenced him to death.

On appeal, McVeigh argued that the *Denver* jury had been contaminated by pretrial publicity — of a different type. The appellate court rejected this argument (and many others) and affirmed, in *U.S. v. McVeigh*, 153 F.3d 1166 (10th Cir. 1998):

As with the bombing itself, news of McVeigh's arrest received a great deal of attention in the media, and was ubiquitously reported on television, radio, and in print. The image of McVeigh being led, wearing orange jail clothing, through an angry crowd into a van by authorities appeared in print and electronic media nationwide. In its ruling granting McVeigh's motion for change of venue the district court noted that it had considered the alternative of moving the trial to Tulsa, Oklahoma, but because of the intensity of the emotional impact of the bombing, and its attendant publicity, on all Oklahomans, it would be impossible for McVeigh to receive a fair jury trial anywhere in the State of Oklahoma. The district court decided to move the trial to Denver, a large metropolitan area where a "large jury pool is available." In this ruling the district court implicitly found that the Denver jury pool was not as intensely affected by the bombing or the subsequent publicity as was the Oklahoma jury pool.

On February 14, 1997, the district court sent out jury summons to hundreds of people living in the Denver area, notifying them that they had been randomly selected as potential jurors for the McVeigh trial. The notification admonished its recipients to avoid publicity concerning the case that might interfere with their ability to remain impartial. The notification advised the potential jurors that "there have been many things written and said about the explosion in Oklahoma City. Much of it may be speculation, rumor and incorrect information." The notification further stressed the need for all potential jurors to be impartial and willing to base their decision solely on the law and the evidence. The notification concluded with a short, preliminary questionnaire which included a question asking if "there is any reason that would prevent you from serving on this jury."

Two weeks later, on February 28, the Dallas Morning News published an article on its Internet home page claiming that it was in possession of internal, confidential defense documents that revealed McVeigh had confessed to his own lawyers that he had indeed bombed the Murrah Building in Oklahoma City. See Pete Slover, "McVeigh Saw 'Body Count' As Best Way To Make Statement In Oklahoma City Bombing, Defense Reports State" (Feb. 28, 1997). This story was picked up and reported by both the national and Denver news media.

According to the reports, McVeigh had told his lawyers that he deliberately set off the bomb during the daytime in order to obtain a higher "body count"; that he had committed the bombing out of a desire to make a point to the federal government, presumably that the government mishandled the 1993 siege of the Branch Davidian compound near Waco, Texas; and that he was assisted in the bombing by Terry Nichols, with whom McVeigh had participated in a number of robberies in order to obtain money and supplies needed to create the bomb. See id.

On March 4, a chambers conference was held at which the court and parties discussed this development and whether the trial date, originally set for March 31, should be delayed. At this conference, McVeigh's counsel told the court that McVeigh did not want a continuance, but rather desired to go forward with voir dire and seating a jury.

On March 11, Playboy Magazine published on its Internet web site an article that claimed to contain information from documents "lawfully obtained" from McVeigh's counsel. See Ben Fenwick, The Road to Oklahoma City (visited March 11, 1997). This article differed from the Dallas Morning News article mainly in the scope of detail with which it describes McVeigh's alleged activities during the time leading up to the bombing and the alleged motivation for the crime. See id. As with the Dallas Morning News story, information contained within the Playboy article was widely disseminated in the national media, as well as in the Denver media. Soon after this, McVeigh filed a motion to dismiss the indictment or, in the alternative, to postpone the trial for a minimum of one year, due to the "presumed effects of recent publication of stories" that McVeigh had made incriminating statements. The district court dismissed this motion, holding that "fair-minded persons" would not be "so influenced by anything contained in this recent publicity" that they could not remain impartial.

On March 19, 352 prospective jurors were summoned to the Jefferson County Fairgrounds to fill out an extended questionnaire. Before filling out the questionnaire the court commented that news reports of events are often inaccurate, that most people remain skeptical about such reports, and admonished the potential jurors to set aside all publicity surrounding the case as well as any "impressions or opinions" that they may have formed based upon media reports. The court also observed that the constitutional right to a fair trial "depends on the willingness of citizens to decide the case based entirely on the evidence that they see and hear at the trial. That requires a commitment to set aside any preconceived impressions or opinions." After the potential jurors had completed the questionnaires, the court informed them that from that moment on they were required to follow "the same instructions that will be given to the jury selected in this case." The court ordered the prospective jurors "beginning right now to avoid any news reports of any kind or any communication or publication of any kind that concerns any issues related to the charges in this case."

McVeigh filed an interlocutory writ of prohibition with this court seeking an order "directing the district court to continue the trial for an indefinite period on grounds of prejudicial pretrial publicity." We denied his petition, holding that because *voir dire* had not yet taken place any ruling on pretrial publicity was premature, given the trial court's "broad discretion in gauging the effects of allegedly prejudicial publicity and in taking responsive measures to ensure a fair trial."

Voir dire commenced on March 31. Four of the seated jurors indicated either on the questionnaire or during *voir dire* that they had seen headlines or casually overheard reports of McVeigh's alleged confession, but in each case they indicated that their exposure was only superficial and that they were skeptical of the accuracy of the report. None of the rest of the seated jurors indicated that they had even heard about the alleged confession. Each of the seated jurors affirmed that he or she could remain impartial and decide the case based only on the facts presented in court.

As this court has held, the claim of presumed prejudice is rarely invoked and only in extreme situations. Moreover, the defendant bears the burden of establishing that prejudice should be presumed.

In order for the reviewing court to reach a presumption that inflammatory pretrial publicity so permeated the community as to render impossible the seating of an impartial jury, the court must find that the publicity in essence displaced the judicial process, thereby denying the defendant his constitutional right to a fair trial. See *Sheppard*, 384 U.S. at 342–45, 352–57 (noting that "bedlam reigned at the courthouse during the trial" due to media's intrusive and pervasive presence in the courtroom, inflammatory news reports, often broadcast live from the courtroom, and media hounding of jurors and the defendant); *Estes v. Texas*, 381 U.S. 532, 577–80 (1965) (Warren, C.J., concurring) (media invasion of courtroom pierced the constitutional shield normally provided to the defendant by destroying "the dignity and integrity of the trial process"); *Rideau v. Louisiana*, 373 U.S. 723, 725–27 (1963) (repeated broadcast in defendant's small community of defendant's video taped "confession" to local authorities resulted in a "kangaroo court" that derailed due process and quashed any hope of fair trial in that locale). In such cases, we simply cannot rely on jurors claims that they can be impartial and declare the publicity to be prejudicial as a matter of law.

However, the bar facing the defendant wishing to prove presumed prejudice from pretrial publicity is extremely high. Indeed, despite the proliferation of the news media and its technology, the Supreme Court has not found a single case of presumed prejudice in this country since the watershed case of *Sheppard*.

McVeigh's claim of presumed prejudice fails to clear this high hurdle. The circumstances that led the Court to presume prejudice in *Sheppard, Estes*, and *Rideau* simply do not exist in this case. First, McVeigh's attempt to show presumed prejudice is substantially weakened by the fact that, unlike the defendants in *Sheppard* and *Rideau*, he did receive a change in venue, removing his trial from the eye of the emotional storm in Oklahoma to the calmer metropolitan climate of Denver. Second, mere television images of the defendant in prison garb being led through an angry crowd do not come close to the type of inflammatory publicity required to reach the disruptive force seen in *Sheppard, Estes*, and *Rideau*. For this reason, we focus mainly on the prejudicial effect on the Denver jury pool of the publication of reports that McVeigh confessed the crime to his attorneys.

The disclosure and publication of information obtained from documents purporting to contain confidential communications between an individual and his attorneys indicates a lack of self-restraint and ethical compass on the part of those individuals responsible for doing so. However, the fact that McVeigh's attorneys denied the validity of the confessions gave rise to publicly aired doubts of the accuracy of the reports, a fact that somewhat lessened the reports' prejudicial impact on the public mind. Indeed, the Dallas Morning News Internet article includes in its headline the following words: "Suspect's attorney disputes reliability of documents." Unlike *Rideau*, here there was no video taped broadcast of an actual confession. Nor was there a reproduction of a printed confession signed by McVeigh. In short, the publicity here did not contain an actual confession but only the second-hand or perhaps even third-hand or more unattributed hearsay report of a confession. Such an indirect report of a confession will have far less impact than the situation where the actual confession is broadcast. The hearsay nature of the reports of McVeigh's confession, the publicized denial of the accuracy of those reports, the strong admonitions given by the court both before and after the publicity about the purported confession, the fact that a large number of the venirepersons summoned were not even aware of the reports of McVeigh's alleged confession, and the change of venue, all persuade us that the pretrial publicity of which McVeigh complains in this case did not manifest itself so as to corrupt due process. Thus, it does not warrant a presumption of prejudice.

In reviewing for actual prejudice, we examine the circumstances of the publicity and the voir dire, and merely determine whether the judge had a reasonable basis for concluding that the jurors selected could be impartial. Moreover: Impartiality does not mean jurors are totally ignorant of the case. Indeed, it is difficult to imagine how an intelligent venireman could be completely uninformed of significant events in his community. It is sufficient if the juror can lay aside his impression or opinion and render a verdict based on the evidence presented in court. What we must decide here is whether the district court abused its discretion in determining that the seated jury could disregard the adverse pretrial publicity and render an impartial verdict.

We do not believe that the district court abused its discretion. Here, the district court went to great lengths to admonish all potential jurors to ignore the publicity surrounding the issues of the case. In fact, McVeigh does not argue that the district court failed to take strong measures to ensure juror impartiality, but rather takes the position that the district court's admonitions had the unintended effect of increasing the jury pool's interest in publicity about the case and informed potential jurors of the answers that would be expected of them if they hoped to get on the jury. The assertion that the court's admonitions had the unintended effect of increasing the venirepersons' interest in publicity may be tested by asking if an abnormally large number of venirepersons indicated having knowledge of the alleged confession. To the contrary, a significant number of venirepersons indicated that they had not heard the news of McVeigh's alleged confession, suggesting that the court's earlier admonitions to avoid publicity associated with the case had the desired effect. McVeigh's claim that the court's admonitions served to instruct already prejudiced would-be jurors how to mask that prejudice in order to get onto the jury calls for pure speculation. We could equally speculate that the court's admonitions — that it is normal for people to be affected by publicity, and that a "good juror" is expected to put any conclusions based upon that publicity aside — might encourage those who had formed an opinion based upon pretrial publicity to disclose that fact without fear of shame and to encourage them to agree to set those opinions aside. McVeigh's claim fails.

Moreover, each of the seated jurors in this case was asked if he or she could put aside media reports and decide the case only on evidence presented in court. Each responded that he or she could. Voir dire was by no means a hurried affair; each seated juror's *voir dire* accounted for an average of forty-eight transcript pages, or a period of an hour or so. The members of the jury pool were subjected to two screening questionnaires, individual questioning by the court, and questioning by counsel for both the government and McVeigh. Questioning by the court and the parties goes a long way towards ensuring that any prejudice, no matter how well hidden, will be revealed.

Finally, each of the four seated jurors who mentioned having heard something about McVeigh confessing also unequivocally stated that he or she nonetheless could keep an open mind about the case and would adjudicate it on its merits. Granted, the fact that potential jurors declare that they can remain impartial in the face of negative pretrial publicity is not always dispositive of the question. However, we give due deference to jurors' declarations of impartiality and the trial court's credibility determination that those declarations are sincere. Unlike an appellate court, the trial court has the opportunity to make a first-hand evaluation of a juror's demeanor and responsiveness to *voir dire* questions in deciding impartiality issues.

5. Can pretrial publicity contaminate a *grand* jury?

In *In The Matter of The Grand Jury Investigation of The Death of Amadou Diallo*, 688 N.Y.S.2d 386 (1999), four white New York City police officers were charged with homicide of a black man they shot down with a fusillade of 41 bullets. (The officers claimed they believed the man had drawn a gun, but no gun was found on his body.) Black groups demonstrated outside the courthouse where the New York City grand jury sat deciding whether to indict the officers. Attorneys for the officers asked the court to move the grand jury to an undisclosed location, in order to insulate them from improper influences, or to stay the proceedings until the furor died down. The court agreed that "improper influences and exposure to bias can so undermine the Grand Jury's integrity as to require dismissal of the resulting indictment." Nevertheless, the court denied the motion:

> After an in-depth inquiry (on a sealed record) by this Court, the Grand Jury panel, without a single dissenting voice, unequivocally indicated that it could continue to exercise its solemn responsibility to fairly, impartially and objectively hear and decide the present matter free of outside "influences". Significantly, the Grand Jurors further revealed that they did not have any preconceived ideas or beliefs about the facts of the case or as to what results should ensue. The Court also ascertained that the Grand Jury has not been influenced by any outside pressures from any direction whatsoever, i.e., via print media, radio, television or public demonstrations. In this regard, the Grand Jury solemnly pledged to ascertain the facts and to render justice fairly and evenhandedly in accordance with the law, while giving each witness, whether civilian or police officer, fair consideration.

> Lastly, when asked if they could continue to deliberate fairly and honestly in this courthouse — as opposed to hearing this case elsewhere and insulated from any outside pressures or demonstrations — the Grand Jury emphatically answered in the affirmative.

> Consequently, in view of the Grand Jurors' answers to the Court's queries, it is readily apparent that there is absolutely no sound basis in the record to stay the proceedings or to move the Grand Jury to an undisclosed location. Thus, to rule otherwise, under these circumstances, would clearly constitute an unwarranted judicial intrusion upon the Grand Jury process.

The grand jury indicted the officers for murder. Because of extensive pretrial publicity, the trial court granted defendants' motion for change of venue and transferred the trial to Albany, where the officers were acquitted.

Chapter 9

THE JURY PANEL

Problem 9

To: My law clerk

From: Justin Tyme, Esq.

Re: *U.S. v. Grunt*

Date: April 20

During jury selection, the clerk pulled 12 names out of the box, and those 12 people were seated in the jury box.

The judge told the 12 people what the case was about, and asked them a number of questions, including "Is there any reason why you could not be fair to both sides in this case?" Juror Number 3, Ms. Helen F. Troy, answered as follows:

Ms. Troy: I just moved here from another state, where I was a member of PADD, Persons Against Drunk Driving. I don't know if that disqualifies me or not, your honor.

The Court: I am familiar with that organization. Its statement of principles says that the courts are too easy on drunk drivers and accept technical defenses instead of protecting the public. Do you subscribe to those principles?

Ms. Troy: Yes, I do.

The Court: Will you put aside your association with PADD during this trial and follow my instructions to the jury about the law in this case?

Ms. Troy: Yes, I will do the best I can.

Defense Counsel: The defense would like to challenge Ms. Troy for cause, your honor.

The Court: I will deny your challenge, counsel. I think Ms. Troy can be a fair juror. Also, if I disqualified everyone who was against drunk driving, we'd never get a jury in cases like this.

I then exercised a peremptory challenge against Troy. Troy was replaced by Mr. Larry Lush. The judge asked him if he could be fair to both sides, and he said:

Mr. Lush: I think so, your honor, but you should know that I have had some trouble with drinking and driving myself.

The Court: What sort of trouble?

Mr. Lush: I was convicted of drunk driving 5 years ago. I think I've cured the problem now. I haven't totally stopped drinking, but I stay away from cars when I drink.

The Court: Would your experience prevent you from following my instructions and being fair to the prosecution as well as the defense in this case?

Mr. Lush: No, I don't think so.

Assistant U.S. Attorney Frieda Fedd challenged Lush for cause, and the judge sustained the challenge, over my objection.

After the judge finished his *voir dire*, he gave each attorney a few minutes to engage in their own *voir dire*.

There was one Native American prospective juror, Ms. Millie Mills. We went into the judge's chambers with her, and the judge told her, "There will be testimony from a police officer that after the accident, the defendant said, 'I just hit some dumb Indian. Big deal.' The defendant denies making that statement. Will this have any effect on your ability to be a fair juror in this case?" Ms. Mills said, "Even if he said it, I've heard slurs against us all my life. I'm used to it." The judge said, "Is there anything else you think we should know about you?" Ms. Mills said, "Well, the girl was a member of my tribe, which has about 2,000 members. But I didn't know her or her family personally." The judge asked, "Would that prevent you from being fair to the defendant?" Ms. Mills said, "No. I try to be fair to everyone."

When we got back into the courtroom, I told Grunt what had happened, and then I exercised one of my peremptories against Ms. Mills. The judge asked me why, and I said, "In view of Ms. Mills' tribal affiliation with the alleged victim and some rather inflammatory testimony that will come out at trial, my client would feel more comfortable if Ms. Mills were not on the jury." The judge said, "I'm afraid that the Supreme Court no longer allows peremptory challenges in this situation. Denied."

In our community, quite a few people belong to a religious sect called the Born-Again Biblists — the "BB's". They are strongly against drinking alcohol, and all their literature says so. One of the prospective jurors, Ms. Goody, said that she was a BB. The judge asked her if she could be fair to a defendant who had been drinking beer, and she said, "I think so." I challenged her for cause, showing the judge some of the BB literature. He denied the challenge. I then tried to exercise a peremptory challenge against Ms. Goody, and the judge asked me, "Are you doing this because she is a BB?" I said yes, and he denied my peremptory challenge: "Same problem as before, counsel."

Three of the prospective jurors had some connection to the military. Mr. Major was a retired Marine captain. Ms. Dreadnaught was married to a Chief Petty Officer in the Navy. And Mr. Bird was in an Air Force ROTC program at a nearby college. The prosecutor exercised peremptory challenges against all three. I objected, arguing that he was bouncing them just because of their military connection. The judge said to Fedd, "I'm not sure that Mr. Tyme has made out a prima facie case of discriminatory intent, but assuming he has, would you like to explain the reasons for your challenges?" Fedd replied, "I'd rather not, but I suppose I'd better. The fact that those people were connected to the military in some way had nothing to do with my decisions. Mr. Major said that he had once contested a traffic ticket and lost. Ms. Dreadnaught spoke very loudly and seemed domineering, like she might control the jury. And Mr. Bird winked at me when he got in the jury box, which I took as kind of male chauvinist pig thing to do. A woman wouldn't do that." I pointed out that another juror — Mr. Pfister, who had no military connection — had once been convicted of a misdemeanor, but Fedd had not challenged him. The judge overruled my objection.

We ended up with a jury of 4 white men, 5 white women, 2 black women, and 1 Asian man. We also had 2 alternates, a Hispanic man and a white woman. None of these people had any connection to the military. I moved to dismiss the entire panel and start over, because of the judge's rulings. The judge denied my motion.

We went to trial, and Grunt was convicted. I have filed a notice of appeal. Please read the attached authorities, give me some good arguments to raise in the appeal, and advise me on how the Court of Appeal is likely to rule.

1.   The Challenge For Cause

UNITED STATES v. SALAMONE
U.S. Court of Appeals, 3rd Circuit
800 F.2d 1216 (1986)

HIGGENBOTHOM, CIRCUIT JUDGE.

This appeal arises from the conviction of appellant Salvatore Salamone pursuant to a multicount indictment charging him with various firearms offenses. Our opinion is restricted to one issue: whether potential jurors in an action involving charges brought under the gun control statutes may be dismissed for cause solely due to their affiliation with the National Rifle Association. For the reasons set forth below we will reverse the judgment of the district court.

Appellant was tried before a jury in the United States District Court for the Middle District of Pennsylvania on various firearms charges alleging the possession of and failure to register an illegally made machine gun, and conspiracy to falsify, and falsification of, firearms transaction records through the use of fictitious names for the purchase of handguns. Prior to trial, during *voir dire*, the district court excused for cause one potential juror and five potential alternates solely on the basis of their affiliation with the National Rifle Association ("NRA"). Of the jurors selected, ten had firearms in their homes. Of the six alternates selected, five had firearms in their homes. Two of the alternates ultimately served on the jury. Salamone was convicted on six of the seven counts with which he was charged. He was sentenced to a total of twenty years imprisonment and $35,000 in fines. This appeal followed. * * * *

During voir dire for the main jury panel, the court posed the following questions to the prospective jurors:

The Court: Are you now or have you ever been a member of or affiliated in any way with the National Rifle Association?

Mr. Laughlin: I've been a member of the NRA.

The Court: All right. Do you support the principles of that organization, Mr. Laughlin?

Mr. Laughlin: Yes, I do.

The Court: Okay. Mrs. Houtz.

Mrs. Houtz: My husband is a member of NRA. He does support it.

The Court: And he does support it?

Mrs. Houtz: Yes.

The Court: All right. Are you now or have you ever been a member of or affiliated in any way with a gun, marksmanship or sporting club/organization? Mr. Laughlin.

Mr. Laughlin: I belong to the Bucktail club and hunting club in Emporium.

The Court: Are you now or have you ever been a member of or affiliated in any way with a survivalist club or organization? The United States Constitution, as amended by the Bill of Rights, the first ten amendments, it states in one of those amendments, "The right of the people to keep and bear arms shall not be infringed." The United States has, in fact, laws restricting the possession and transfer of automatic weapons and machine guns; additionally, it has laws requiring, under most circumstances, buyers of firearms to supply certain information and to fill out documents at the time firearms are purchased. The Courts of the United States have consistently ruled that such laws are proper and are not in conflict with the provision of the Bill of Rights which I have just read to you about the right of the people to keep and bear arms not being infringed. Despite such Court rulings, is any juror opposed to such laws on constitutional grounds or other grounds? [No Response.]

The Court: The possession and transfer of an automatic weapon or machine gun is, in most cases, illegal. If I should instruct you along those lines at the conclusion of the trial, would any juror have any difficulty following any such instruction for any reason? Is any juror opposed to gun control? I would assume, Mr. Laughlin, you are opposed to it?

Mr. Laughlin: That's correct, yes.

The Court: And I would assume, Mrs. Houtz, you are opposed to it?

Mrs. Houtz: Yes.

The Court: Anybody else opposed to gun control? Mr. Hayes.

Mr. Hayes: Yes.

The Court: Are you opposed to all gun control or small arms control or what?

Mr. Hayes: I would just be opposed to shotguns and rifles.

The Court: Shotguns and rifles, but you would not be opposed to control with respect to, let's say, Saturday night specials, is that what you're saying?

Mr. Hayes: Yes.

The Court: All right. Anybody else with a yes answer? Notwithstanding your opposition to certain gun control, Mr. Hayes, do you feel you could serve fairly and impartially on this jury?

Mr. Hayes: Yes.

After completion of *voir dire*, the district court entertained challenges for cause. The following exchange took place:

Mr. Clark: Your Honor, the government would challenge for cause Mr. Laughlin.

The Court: On what ground?

Mr. Clark:	He stated he was a former member of the NRA and is —
The Court:	Well, why —
Mr. Clark:	He's a member and firm opponent —
The Court:	Wait.
Mr. Clark:	— of gun control.
The Court:	Well, why is that disqualification for cause? It may be, but I need some illumination on that.
Mr. Clark:	Your Honor, the government's position in respect to that would be that because the charges here deal with the regulation of the possession of automatic weapons, machine guns and because the charges also deal with the falsification of ATF Forms 4473, which are forms of gun control.
The Court:	Well, I have got enough on it now. What is your — do you oppose that challenge?
Mr. Casale:	Yes.
The Court:	What is the basis of the opposition?
Mr. Casale:	The basis of the opposition is that the defense doesn't feel that any member of the NRA automatically disqualifies unless he says, I can't sit on this jury fairly.
The Court:	Well, the NRA blocked a bill in the last Congress which would have prevented the importation and sale and, I believe, manufacture of armor piercing bullets. That legislation was supported by the police chiefs and police organizations throughout the nation. And I think that somebody who is a member of that organization may well not be able to sit on this case impartially. So I'll grant that one.

The government made no further challenges for cause.[6]

During *voir dire* for the selection of alternates, several jurors indicated some affiliation with the NRA. Mrs. Hart and Mrs. Shatford stated that their husbands were members of the NRA. Mr. Stavisky indicated that he supported the principles of the NRA. Mr. Brown represented that he was a life member of the NRA. And, finally, Mrs. Gemberling indicated that five of her relatives were members of the NRA. All were challenged and excluded for cause solely on the basis of their affiliation with the NRA.[7]

---

[6] Both Mrs. Houtz and Mr. Hayes were eliminated from the jury on peremptory challenges. It is unclear from the record which party exercised the challenges.

[7] During *voir dire* of the alternates, the court did not specifically repeat the questions that had been directed to the main panel members. Rather, each juror was instructed to inform the court if they would have answered any of the questions posed to the main panel in the affirmative. This procedure is considered within the trial court's discretion in conducting *voir dire*. The following excerpts reflect the responses of the excluded alternates with regard to their affiliation with the NRA.

  The Court: Would you have answered yes to any of the questions?
  Ms. Shatford: Yes.
  The Court: What ones?
  Ms. Shatford: My husband does own guns. He is a member of the NRA.
  The Court: Would you have answered yes to some of the questions?

Each of the alternates were summarily dismissed solely on the basis of their "close affiliation with the NRA," without further inquiry from the court or argument by counsel. * * * *

In *Rosales-Lopez v. United States*, 451 U.S. 182 (1981), the Supreme Court observed that " *voir dire* plays a critical function in assuring the criminal defendant that his Sixth Amendment right to an impartial jury will be honored. Without an adequate *voir dire*, the trial judge's responsibility to remove prospective jurors who will not be able impartially to follow the court's instructions and evaluate the evidence cannot be fulfilled. Similarly, lack of adequate *voir dire* impairs the defendant's right to exercise peremptory challenges." *Id.* at 188. Federal Rule of Criminal Procedure 24 commits to the trial judge the function of conducting an appropriate *voir dire*. "Because the obligation to impanel an impartial jury lies in the first instance with the trial judge, and because he must rely largely on his immediate perceptions, federal judges have been accorded ample discretion in determining how best to conduct the *voir dire.*" *Rosales-Lopez*, 451 U.S. at 189. This discretion extends to the determination of what questions should be asked to the potential jurors. "This 'testing' by *voir dire* remains a preferred and effective means of determining a juror's impartiality and assuring the accused of a fair trial." *United States v. Martin*, 746 F.2d 964, 973 (3d Cir.1984).

According full recognition to these general principles, however, it is nonetheless equally clear that the trial judge's broad discretion is not without limitation. "While impaneling a jury, the trial court has a serious duty to determine the question of actual bias. In exercising its discretion, the trial court must be zealous to protect the rights of an accused." *Dennis v. United States*, 339 U.S. 162, 168 (1950).

In the instant appeal, Salamone's challenge to the district court's *voir dire* does not allege a failure to uncover actual bias, thereby resulting in the paneling of partial jurors. Rather, Salamone's objection is to the presumed bias of potential jurors which occasioned the arbitrary exclusion of an entire class of otherwise qualified jurors from his panel. "In disqualifying all NRA-related jurors without particularized inquiry," Salamone argues, "the trial judge simply assumed that any person connected with that association was incapable of fairly applying existing

---

Mr. Stavisky: Yes.

The Court: What ones?

Mr. Stavisky: One is, I have firearms, hunting rifles, and I support the principles of the NRA; I'm not a member.

The Court: Would you have answered yes to any of the questions?

Mrs. Hart: Yes. My husband is a member of the NRA and we have — he has several rifles and shotguns and he has a handgun.

The Court: Would you have answered yes to any of the questions we put to the first jurors?

Mr. Brown: Yes.

The Court: What ones?

Mr. Brown: I'm a life member of the NRA. I own hunting guns.

The Court: Would you have answered yes to any of the questions we asked the first jurors in this case?

Mrs. Gemberling: Yes.

The Court: What ones?

Mrs. Gemberling: There's five of them in my family that are members of the NRA. My husband has hunting guns and pistols and I am opposed to gun control.

law."[10] Compare *King v. State*, 287 Md. 530 (Ct.App.1980) (in prosecution for distribution and for possession of marijuana, error to exclude two jurors for cause on basis that they favored change in law with regard to possession and distribution of marijuana without further inquiry into their ability to set aside their personal beliefs and apply the law to the facts).

The government contends that no abuse occurs in the exclusion of jurors whose views on gun control might affect their ability to serve impartially on a jury considering implementation of gun control statutes. The government conveniently ignores, however, the total absence on this record of any indication that the excluded jurors individually possessed such views which would rightfully justify their dismissal. Instead, the government relies on a theory of "implied bias,"[11] in suggesting that "where as here, the charges involve state and federal gun registration — a subject on which the NRA's opposition is well-known — a trial judge is well within his discretion in excluding those opponents from the jury for cause." Under such circumstances, the government maintains "if the judge believes, as he reasonably could, that bias against enforcing a particular statute would make it difficult for the juror to vote for conviction even if the evidence supported guilt, additional questioning would simply be superfluous."

We find the government's position untenable and potentially dangerous. To allow trial judges and prosecutors to determine juror eligibility based solely on their perceptions of the external associations of a juror threatens the heretofore guarded right of an accused to a fair trial by an impartial jury as well as the integrity of the judicial process as a whole. Taken to its illogical conclusion, the government's position would sanction, inter alia, the summary exclusion for cause of NAACP members from cases seeking the enforcement of civil rights statutes, Moral Majority activists from pornography cases, Catholics from cases involving abortion

---

[10] Salamone further suggests that: "this unfounded assumption — which would render the President of the United States, the Vice-President, their wives, and over 3 million other Americans unfit to serve as jurors in gun-law cases — is flatly inconsistent with our democratic traditions. Its effect is to invidiously exclude from appellant's jury all persons connected to a distinct group solely because that group had chosen to affiliate for a political purpose." More specifically, Amicus National Rifle Association argues that the conduct of the district court constitutes an encroachment on the excluded jurors' first amendment rights of freedom of association. Because we consider only the rights of the accused, we do not reach the first amendment issue.

[11] In *Smith v. Phillips*, 455 U.S. 209 (1982), the Supreme Court declined to impute bias to a properly seated juror who subsequently applied for employment with the District Attorney's Office prosecuting the case on which he sat. The Court held that a post-conviction hearing in which defendant is afforded the opportunity to prove actual bias was all that was constitutionally required. (In a separate concurrence, Justice O'Connor indicated her belief that the presumption of implied bias may be appropriate under certain circumstances: "Some examples might include a revelation that the juror is an actual employee of the prosecuting agency, that the juror is a close relative of one of the participants in the trial or the criminal transaction, or that the juror was a witness or somehow involved in the criminal transaction."). While we make no categorical rejection of the theory of "implied bias", we note that Justice O'Connor's hypotheticals bear no resemblance to this case.

Just recently, this court considered the propriety of the trial court's refusal to exclude a juror under the "implied bias" theory. See *United States v. Ferri*, 778 F.2d 985 (3d Cir.1985) (refusing to find error in the district court's refusal to disqualify a juror under the theory of implied bias); see also *Dennis v. United States*, 339 U.S. 162 (1950) (rejecting argument that employees of Federal Government were inherently biased in contempt action for failure to appear before the House Committee on UnAmerican Activities and therefore should have been excluded for cause on *voir dire*); *Richardson v. Communication Workers of America*, 530 F.2d 126 (8th Cir.1976) (finding no abuse of discretion by trial court in refusing to summarily disqualify from jury all union members without some indication of bias in wrongfully discharged employee's action against unions).

clinic protests, members of NOW from sex discrimination cases, and subscribers to Consumer Reports from cases involving products liability claims.[12]

Moreover, the government's position misconceives the grounds for juror disqualification. "Jury competence is an individual rather than a group or class matter." *Thiel v. Southern Pacific Co.*, 328 U.S. 217, 220 (1946). Challenges for cause "permit rejection of jurors on narrowly specified, provable and legally cognizable bases of partiality." *Swain v. Alabama*, 380 U.S. 202, 220 (1965). The central inquiry in the determination whether a juror should be excused for cause is whether the juror holds a particular belief or opinion that will "prevent or substantially impair the performance of his duties as a juror in accordance with his instructions and his oath." *Wainwright v. Witt*, 469 U.S. 412 (1985). See also *Patton v. Yount*, 467 U.S. 1025, 1036–37 (1984) (noting that the constitutional standard for juror impartiality rests on the determination whether "he can lay aside his opinion and render a verdict based on the evidence presented in court"). Juror bias need not be established with "unmistakable clarity". *Witt*, 105 S.Ct. at 852. Thus, the factual determination by the trial court whether a juror can in fact serve impartially is entitled to special deference by the reviewing court.

In the instant appeal, however, at no time were the excluded jurors questioned as to their ability to faithfully and impartially apply the law. Indeed, no inquiries whatsoever were directed to the excluded jurors to determine the nature and extent of their commitment to any principles that might have impaired their ability to serve impartially. While we recognize that the scope and content of *voir dire* is committed to the sound discretion of the trial court, that discretion will "include the decision as to what questions should be asked when the court itself decides to examine the prospective jurors so long as inquiries relevant to the discovery of actual bias are not omitted." *United States v. Dansker*, 537 F.2d 40, 56 (3d Cir.1976). Where the appropriate inquiries have been made and the district court has made a judgment on the basis of the jurors' responses, normally, that judgment will not be disturbed.[13] The usual factors cautioning restraint in appellate review, i.e., credibility and demeanor evidence, however, are simply absent from this record. Thus, the "factual determination" by the district court in the instant appeal, being totally devoid of any foundation, leaves us with the single conclusion that the *voir dire* was inadequate to preserve and protect the rights of the accused. Absent the requisite nexus — that the challenged affiliation will "prevent or substantially impair" a juror's impartiality — no juror may be excluded for cause on the basis of his or her membership in an organization that adheres to a particular view. Failure to make the necessary inquiry deprives the trial court of the benefit of the factual predicate that justifies an exclusion for cause. In the words of Mr. Justice Murphy in *Thiel v.*

---

[12] We recognize that the government's argument rests upon a theory of implied partiality of prospective jurors who belong to "anti-enforcement" organizations. However, we think that the distinction the government attempts to make is precarious at best. Members of an overzealous organization favoring expansive application of particular statutes may likewise be "presumed" to lack the requisite impartiality to faithfully apply the law to the facts adduced at trial. Arguments similar to the government's have been rejected in other contexts. See, e.g., *United States v. Alabama*, 582 F.Supp. 1197, 1203 (N.D.Ala.1984) ("Judge's color, sex or religion does not constitute bias in favor of that color, sex or religion."); *Pennsylvania v. Local Union 542*, 388 F.Supp. 155, 165 (E.D.Pa.1974) (Black judge is not *per se* disqualified from adjudicating claims of racial discrimination.).

[13] Nothing in this opinion is intended to upset settled practice in the district courts of excluding without further inquiry prospective jurors with well recognized characteristics warranting dismissal, such as blood relation to the parties or counsel.

Southern Pacific Co., 328 U.S. 217, the conduct of the trial judge and the position urged by the government today would "open the door to class distinctions and discriminations which are abhorrent to the democratic ideals of trial by jury."

We conclude that the cursory disqualification by the district judge of all jurors with NRA affiliations constitutes an abuse of discretion and is not in accord with the "essential demands of fairness" to which appellant was entitled.

C.

The question remains, however, whether Salamone is entitled to relief on this basis. In this Circuit we adhere to the rule that "the trial court's determination as to a juror's actual bias will be reversed only for a manifest abuse of discretion." *Government of Virgin Islands v. Gereau*, 502 F.2d 914, 934 (3d Cir.1974). As indicated above, we think that such a "manifest abuse" is evident on this record, and on this basis alone Salamone is entitled to a new trial. * * * *

At the outset, we note that were we faced with the inadequate questioning of a single excluded juror we might apply a different standard for determining the prejudicial effect of the erroneous exclusion. However, where such a "manifest abuse of discretion" results in the wholesale exclusion of a particular group, we do not deem it necessary for the defendant to affirmatively demonstrate the existence of actual prejudice in the resulting jury panel. Under such circumstances, prejudice may be presumed. * * * *

It is the nature of the practices here challenged that proof of actual harm, or lack of harm, is virtually impossible to adduce. For there is no way to determine what jury would have been selected under a constitutionally valid selection system, or how that jury would have decided the case. Consequently, it is necessary to decide on principle which side shall suffer the consequences of unavoidable uncertainty.

In the instant appeal, essential demands of fairness dictate that the errors of the prosecutor and trial judge not be visited upon appellant, Salamone. The government improperly "created its own group," *Barber v. Ponte*, 772 F.2d 982, 1000 (1st Cir.1985), and the trial court, without justification, excluded all members of that group from Salamone's jury. To require appellant to adduce proof of what could have happened puts the defendant in the predicament of providing proof that is virtually impossible to adduce. This leaves the defendant without an effective remedy for improper conduct in the selection process and provides incentive for such conduct to recur. Accordingly, we conclude that the wholesale, arbitrary and irrational exclusion of jurors with affiliations with the NRA from Salamone's jury is presumptively prejudicial. * * * *

Nor does application of the harmless error doctrine alter this result. From our review of the record, we cannot conclude that the error involved in the instant appeal was harmless. Salamone challenges the summary exclusion of seven prospective jurors solely on the basis of their affiliation — no matter how attenuated — with the NRA. While we recognize that appellant has no right to a jury of the proper number of Democrats and Republicans, young persons and old persons, white-collar executives and blue-collar laborers, and so on, he is entitled to a jury from which none of those, or any other group, has been summarily excluded without regard to their ability to serve as jurors in the particular case. "The consequent injury is not limited to the defendant — there is injury to the jury system, to the law as an institution, to the community at large, and to the democratic ideal reflected in the processes of our courts." *Ballard v. United States*, 329 U.S. 187, 195 (1946). Moreover, appellant suffered an even more tangible harm. As noted by Justice Rehnquist in *McDonough Power Equipment, Inc. v. Greenwood*, 464 U.S. 548 (1984), "Demonstrated bias in the responses to questions on *voir dire* may result in a juror being excused for cause; hints of bias not sufficient to warrant challenges for cause may assist parties in exercising their peremptory challenges." Freed of the burden of substantiating its challenges for cause, the government in the instant appeal was thereby afforded a broader exercise of its peremptory challenges. * * * * Unlike the situation in *Lockhart v. McMcree*, where the Court rejected the argument that the "absence of 'Witherspoon-excludables' slanted the jury in favor of conviction," 106 S.Ct. at 1767, we cannot conclude with confidence that the improper exclusion of the prospective jurors in this case, in conjunction with the expanded use of the peremptory challenges afforded to the government, produced an impartial jury.

Nor are we convinced that the representation of gun owners on Salamone's petit jury resolves the issue. *Cf. Turner v. Murray*, 106 S.Ct. 1683 (1986) (notwithstanding fact that jury impaneled consisted of eight whites and four blacks, rights of black capital defendant accused of murdering white man were violated where trial judge failed on *voir dire* to question prospective jurors on racial prejudice). Defensive possession of weapons by the average citizen is hardly a clear indication of neutrality on the issue of gun control.[8]

In sum, we find that the inadequate *voir dire* by the trial court set into motion a series of events, all of which had an incalculable, prejudicial effect on appellant's right to a fair trial by an impartial jury. Thus, we conclude that the erroneous exclusion of prospective jurors with NRA affiliations was not harmless and appellant's judgment of conviction cannot stand.

For the foregoing reasons, the judgment of the district court will be reversed, and the case remanded for proceedings consistent with this opinion.

Notes from Justin:

1. What questions did the trial judge fail to ask the NRA members that he should have asked?

2. Is the standard applied to challenges for cause *by defendant* the same as the standard applied to challenges *by the prosecutor*? *Should* the standard be the same?

3. Suppose that, instead of being charged with possession of *machine guns*, Salamone had been charged only with possession of an *unlicensed handgun*. In that case, could a challenge for cause be based solely on NRA membership?

4. In *U.S. v. Torres*, 128 F.3d 38 (2nd Cir. 1997), Torres and Devery were charged with money-laundering the proceeds of their heroin sales, based on evidence that they had "structured" deposits by dividing them into amounts less than $10,000, to avoid reporting them. Over defendants' objections, the trial court excused several

---

[8] We do not mean to suggest that any of the individual jurors impaneled in appellant's case were excusable for cause on the ground of actual bias. Rather, we find that the expanded use of prosecutorial peremptory challenge necessarily afforded the government a greater opportunity to impanel a jury biased in its favor.

prospective jurors for cause. After conviction, defendants claimed that this was error. The court of appeals disagreed:

> Traditionally, challenges for cause have been divided into two categories: (1) those based on actual bias, and (2) those grounded in implied bias. Today we explicitly recognize what courts have implicitly assumed to exist — a third category, that of "inferable bias."
>
> Actual bias is "bias in fact" — the existence of a state of mind that leads to an inference that the person will not act with entire impartiality. A juror is found by the judge to be partial either because the juror admits partiality or the judge finds actual partiality based upon the juror's *voir dire* answers. Actual bias cannot be found unless a prospective juror is adequately questioned on *voir dire* with respect to his or her ability to apply the law impartially. But once the proper questions have been asked at *voir dire*, the trial court, when impaneling a jury, has broad discretion in its rulings on challenges therefor.
>
> In the case before us, Juror No. 27 had engaged in prior structuring activity. Some seven years prior to his selection as a venireperson, he had deposited money into a partnership account for a real estate venture in two amounts of less than $10,000 in order to avoid having to file a Currency Transaction Report. When questioned by the court at *voir dire* as to whether the instructions on the law of structuring would affect his ability to be fair and impartial in this case, he was unequivocal in stating that he could not be impartial under the circumstances. When asked to explain, he stated: "Because I did it. I did it and you are telling me that I did something illegal, so I feel like you are accusing me of a criminal act."
>
> Similarly, Jurors Nos. 38 and replacement 38 stated in substance that, because of personal experiences with drug dealers, they would not believe a drug dealer's testimony. Juror No. 38's second cousin was murdered by a drug dealer. When asked whether this fact would affect his ability to be fair and impartial, he said: "I would have in-bred doubt in my mind about that person to begin with, just because of my experiences in the past with such individuals. I don't think I could remain unbiased towards that person's testimony." Replacement Juror No. 38 had a friend who was killed two years earlier by a drug addict. He stated: "If drug dealers were witnesses or something like that, I think they're the worst people on earth and I wouldn't believe them no matter what they said." When specifically asked whether he could make a fair judgment as to the credibility of such a witness, he responded: "I don't think I would be able to do that. I don't think they have any credibility."
>
> We find that the trial court properly questioned Jurors Nos. 27, 38, and replacement 38 with respect to their ability to be impartial and did not abuse its discretion in concluding that their responses to its questions evidenced actual bias. * * * *

The court next addressed the trial court's order excusing for cause Juror No. 7, who had once structured deposits for a company she worked for:

> Implied or presumed bias is "bias conclusively presumed as a matter of law." It is attributed to a prospective juror regardless of actual partiality.

In contrast to the inquiry for actual bias, which focuses on whether the record at *voir dire* supports a finding that the juror was in fact partial, the issue for implied bias is whether an average person in the position of the juror in controversy would be prejudiced. And in determining whether a prospective juror is impliedly biased, his statements upon voir dire about his ability to be impartial are totally irrelevant.

For this reason, a finding of implied bias does not rely on any questioning by the trial judge as to the prospective juror's assessment of his or her partiality. Accordingly, in the limited cases in which bias is properly presumed, the judge does not have to ask the juror if he or she could faithfully apply the law.

Moreover, disqualification on the basis of implied bias is mandatory. Such automatically presumed bias deals mainly with jurors who are related to the parties or who were victims of the alleged crime itself. * * * *

In presuming bias, the law has employed an "average man" test: "Every procedure which would offer a possible temptation to the average man to forget the burden of proof required to convict the defendant, or which might lead him not to hold the balance nice, clear and true between the State and the accused, denies the latter due process of law." This test, in a sense, derives from the statement of Chief Justice Marshall, that, even though a person "may declare that he feels no prejudice in the case, the law cautiously incapacitates him from serving on the jury because it suspects prejudice, because in general persons in a similar situation would feel prejudice."

In the case before us, Judge Preska found that, "even if actual bias was not expressly elicited, Juror No. 7 was impaired by implied bias."

Appellants contend, however, that the doctrine of implied bias is reserved for "exceptional situations" in which objective circumstances cast concrete doubt on the impartiality of a juror. We agree.

Our court has consistently refused to create a set of unreasonably constricting presumptions that jurors be excused for cause due to certain occupational or other special relationships which might bear directly or indirectly on the circumstances of a given case, where there is no showing of actual bias or prejudice. More specifically, we have held that, in cases where members of the venire are challenged on the basis of prior jury service at a trial involving similar but unrelated offenses, at which some of the same government witnesses testified, actual bias must be proved, and may not be conclusively presumed.

The excusal of Juror No. 7, thus, cannot be justified either by a finding of actual bias or by implied bias. Juror No. 7 was never asked during *voir dire* whether, notwithstanding her prior experience of structuring a cash transaction, she could faithfully follow the judge's instructions and impartially apply the law. And, as discussed above, such an inquiry must be made before the judge can find actual bias. Moreover, the case of Juror No. 7 does not fall into the narrow category of presumed bias, which is reserved for "exceptional situations." Just as we have refused to carve out an overly broad category of presumed bias based on occupational or status relationships, so we also decline to hold as a general matter that, where a juror has engaged in conduct similar to that of the defendant at trial, the trial judge must presume bias. Such cases are unlikely to present the "extreme situations" that call for mandatory removal. The exclusion of Juror No. 7 was, therefore, not compulsory.

But while the situations in which a trial judge must find implied bias are strictly limited and must be truly "exceptional," it does not follow that the trial judge is without discretion to infer bias outside of this narrow category of cases. On the contrary, there exist a few circumstances that involve no showing of actual bias, and that fall outside of the implied bias category, where a court may, nevertheless, properly decide to excuse a juror. We call this third category "inferable bias." * * * *

Bias may be inferred when a juror discloses a fact that bespeaks a risk of partiality sufficiently significant to warrant granting the trial judge discretion to excuse the juror for cause, but not so great as to make mandatory a presumption of bias. There is no actual bias because there is no finding of partiality based upon either the juror's own admission or the judge's evaluation of the juror's demeanor and credibility following *voir dire* questioning as to bias. And there is no implied bias because the disclosed fact does not establish the kind of relationship between the juror and the parties or issues in the case that mandates the juror's excusal for cause.

Nonetheless, inferable bias is closely linked to both of these traditional categories. Just as the trial court's finding of actual bias must derive from *voir dire* questioning, so the court is allowed to dismiss a juror on the ground of inferable bias only after having received responses from the juror that permit an inference that the juror in question would not be able to decide the matter objectively. In other words, the judge's determination must be grounded in facts developed at *voir dire*. And this is so even though the juror need not be asked the specific question of whether he or she could decide the case impartially. Moreover, once facts are elicited that permit a finding of inferable bias, then, just as in the situation of implied bias, the juror's statements as to his or her ability to be impartial become irrelevant.

We do not need to consider the precise scope of a trial judge's discretion to infer bias. It is enough for the present to note that cases in which a juror has engaged in activities that closely approximate those of the defendant on trial are particularly apt. The exercise of the trial judge's discretion to grant challenges for cause on the basis of inferred bias is especially appropriate in such situations. Because in such cases the bias of a juror will rarely be admitted by the juror himself, partly because the juror may have an interest in concealing his own bias and partly because the juror may be unaware of it, partiality necessarily must be inferred from surrounding facts and circumstances.

In the case at hand, bias was inferred only from particular facts disclosed during the *voir dire* examination of the prospective juror. Much of the government's evidence against Devery concerned his structuring of cash deposits. As a result of facts developed during *voir dire*, the district court found that Juror No. 7 had at one time been "involved in activity like that charged in the Indictment," and that her bias "was evident in the acts to which she admitted, which too closely resembled acts at the core of this trial." Under the circumstances, the court further elaborated that "the mental gymnastics required for her to separate her own experience with Currency Transaction Reports from the extensive testimony about CTRs brought out at trial would have been too precarious and too strenuous to have been expected of any juror."

Given the similarity of Juror No. 7's structuring activity to the conduct alleged against appellant Devery in this case, it was reasonable for Judge Preska to conclude that the average person in Juror No. 7's position might have felt personally threatened. The judge focused on an objective evaluation of the juror's past experience and its relation to the case being tried. The juror would have had to sit through weeks of testimony and other evidence relating to suspicious structuring activity that was — in at least one respect — similar to her own previous conduct. As Judge Preska summarized: "After she was instructed on the law, this juror may have felt that, in weighing on the defendant's guilt or innocence, she was confronting the legality of her own past acts as well."

We do not today hold that, even in such circumstances, the district court would have erred had it kept Juror No. 7 on the jury. But we do hold that the court acted within its discretion in excusing her from the jury. In other words, after a careful review of the record, we conclude that Judge Preska acted within her discretion in finding that "the inquiries made of Juror No. 7 revealed a sufficient factual basis" to allow the court to draw the inference — especially given the hypertechnical nature of the offense of structuring — that the juror would be unable to divorce her consideration of this case from her own structuring experience.

5. Is a *police officer* automatically disqualified from sitting on a jury hearing a criminal case by reason of "presumed bias"?

The Louisiana Supreme Court so held in *State v. Simmons*, 390 So.2d 1317 (La. 1980), but in *State v. Ballard*, 747 So.2d 1077 (La. 1999), the same court overruled *Simmons*:

> Applying *Simmons*, a trial court must disqualify a law enforcement officer even if the officer testifies under oath that he or she may render an impartial verdict according to the law and evidence.

> Law enforcement officers are sworn to uphold the laws of the state, which laws include the provision of a fair trial to each and every defendant. If a law enforcement officer testifies under oath during *voir dire* that he can be a fair and impartial juror, the trial judge has the discretion to determine whether that officer is speaking the truth. The disqualification of all law enforcement officers from service on a jury disregards whether or not the judge, whose rulings on challenges for cause are given great deference in all other instances, accepts the officer as a fair and impartial juror. We find that such a disqualification amounts to an irrebuttable presumption of untrustworthiness in law enforcement officers and is an affront to police officers in this state. When this court in *Simmons* held: "the guarantee of an impartial trial in Article 1, Section 16, of the Louisiana Constitution of

1974 is offended by the presence on a jury of a badge-wearing law enforcement officer," it failed to explain this connection, all the while implying that wearing a badge is somehow a mark of intrinsic bias, offending those who have been awarded a badge as a police officer in this state.

Chief Justice Calogero concurred, noting that "particular care should be taken in determining the ability of law enforcement agents to serve as fair and impartial jurors in a criminal trial."

6. In *Franklin v. Anderson*, 434 F.3d 412 (6th Cir. 2006), during voir dire, defense counsel asked prospective juror Arthur: "Do you feel [the defendant] should get on the stand to prove he's innocent?" Arthur replied, "To me, I do, you know. I do." The court held that Arthur "so completely misunderstood the presumption of innocence and burden of proof that she could not have made a fair assessment of the evidence of Franklin's guilt."

7. In *U.S. v. Polichemi*, 219 F.3d 698 (7th Cir. 2000), the trial court denied a challenge for cause to a prospective juror (Ms. Nape) who was a 15-year employee of the U.S. Attorney's office that was prosecuting the case. The appellate court held that the challenge should have been granted:

> In *U.S. v. Haynes*, 398 F.2d 980 (2nd Cir. 1968), the Second Circuit traced the implied bias doctrine back to Chief Justice John Marshall's opinion in *U.S. v. Burr* 25 F.Cas. 49 (C.C.D. Va. 1807), one of several opinions in the prosecution of Aaron Burr. There the Chief Justice addressed the ways in which the law strives to assure an impartial jury: "Why is it that the most distant relative of a party cannot serve upon his jury? Certainly the single circumstance of relationship, taken in itself, unconnected with its consequences, would furnish no objection. The real reason of the rule is, that the law suspects the relative of partiality; suspects his mind to be under a bias, which will prevent his fairly hearing and fairly deciding on the testimony which may be offered to him. The end to be obtained is an impartial jury; to secure this end, a man is prohibited from serving on it whose connexion with a party is such as to induce a suspicion of partiality." The Second Circuit later reviewed different grounds on which jurors were excusable for presumptive bias under the common law: kinship, interest, former jury service in the same cause, or because the prospective juror was a master, servant, counselor, steward, or of the same society or corporation.

> We agree with the United States that government employment alone is not, and should not be, enough to trigger the rule under which an employee is disqualified from serving as a juror in a case involving her employer. But one need not adopt such a broad rule to find a problem in this case. Here, Nape was a long-time employee of the very U.S. Attorney's Office that was conducting the prosecution.

8. **May the judge create a "representative" jury?**

In *U.S. v. Nelson*, 277 F.3d 164 (2nd Cir. 2002), Nelson was charged with killing a Chassidic Jew (Yankel Rosenbaum) when a crowd of black people were urged to attack Jews in the Crown Heights section of Brooklyn after a Jewish driver had driven his car into two black children. The court stated:

From the outset of the trial, the district court, no doubt responding to the politically charged nature of the case and to the controversial State court acquittal of Nelson, made clear his intention to empanel "a moral jury that renders a verdict that has moral integrity." The district court stated that "this trial is occurring for the same reason Rodney King's trial occurred, the second trial, because the first jury did not represent the community." The court relatedly and repeatedly expressed its desire to *empanel* a jury (and not merely *begin from a venire*) "that represents this community." Indeed, the district court made its intentions concerning jury selection absolutely plain to the parties, stating:

> I have an agenda here which I have made very clear from the very beginning, to end up with a jury that represents the community that will have moral validity; and if there is a hung jury, that itself will be a statement to both sides about both what is the process and the problems are with our society. To me, justice will be served.

Pursuant to this policy, the court denied Nelson's challenge for cause to a Jewish prospective juror who said on *voir dire* that he "honestly didn't know" if he could give Nelson a fair trial. The court also selected jurors out of order in order to help achieve a mix of blacks and Jews on the jury.

The district court took these unusual steps expressly to secure an empaneled jury containing both African Americans and Jews in a racial and religious balance that the district court believed would cause the public to "understand," so that "nobody could complain whatever the result." In response, defense counsel explicitly stated that this method of jury selection "would be agreeable to the defendants." Moreover, the defendants themselves consented to the proposal and did soon the record.

The court of appeals reversed Nelson's conviction, holding that the trial court's "jurymandering" was improper. "Although the motives behind the district court's race- and religion-based jury selection procedures were undoubtedly meant to be tolerant and inclusive rather than bigoted and exclusionary, that fact cannot justify the district court's race-conscious actions. The significance of a jury in our polity as a body chosen apart from racial and religious manipulations is too great to permit categorization by race or religion even from the best of intentions."

The court of appeals also held that this defect was not waivable by the defendant.

The government contends, however, that since in this case the parties agreed to the racial and religious reconstruction of the jury, as they undoubtedly did, whatever objections (either constitutional or otherwise) exist to the court's action have been waived and cannot now be raised. The difficulty with this argument is that, if it were to be countenanced, parties could always, with the court's consent, empanel a jury that was of precisely the racial and religious mix that they wished. If the court was of like mind, there would be nothing to stop civil litigants from agreeing, for example, that a contract or tort action between them should be heard by a jury composed only of members of their own racial or religious groups. And all Congress's and the Supreme Court's language about "race neutrality in jury selection" as a "measure of the judicial system's commitment to the commands of the Constitution," would be a dead letter. Of course, parties can, in appropriate situations, opt out of the judicial system-say by agreeing to arbitration. And if they do so, they can choose arbiters of whatever racial or religious sorts they wish. But that is totally different from bending the *judicial system* to their racial and religious preferences. For, unlike private institutions, the judicial system belongs not to the parties but to the nation.

STATE v. LOGAN
Minnesota Supreme Court
535 N.W.2d 320 (1995)

COYNE, JUSTICE.

Defendant, Benjamin Matthew Logan, appeals from judgment of conviction of two counts of first-degree murder in the killing of two clerks during an armed robbery of a Minneapolis gun store on the evening of June 23, 1992. The decisive issue on appeal is whether the trial court erred in denying a defense challenge for cause of one of the jurors, who candidly said he would be more inclined to believe the testimony of police officers than of other witnesses. If the trial court erred in allowing this juror to serve, then defendant was deprived of a fair trial by an impartial jury of 12 people and he is entitled to a new trial. Concluding that the trial court erred and that defendant was denied a fair trial by an impartial jury, we reverse the judgment of conviction and remand for a new trial.

In answering questions in the preliminary jury questionnaire, prospective juror K.G. said that he would favor the testimony of police officers over the testimony of other witnesses, that it was "their job to bring forth sound evidence." He also said that he believed that there had been an increase in violent crime that must be dealt with and that he was certain this feeling would carry "some weight" with him in deciding defendant's guilt, although he would "try" to put it aside.

Asked at *voir dire* by the judge to "expand on that a little bit," K.G. said that in his view police officers are "in the law and order business" and he had "never really had the situation where he had to feel they didn't do their job." He said that "their testimony — that's their day-in, day-out task. They should know what to do in the instances that are presented to them." Asked if they might be mistaken, K.G. said, "Sure." Asked if he would blindly accept their testimony, K.G. said, "No, I wouldn't accept blindly, but I certainly — I value them." Asked if he would apply the same standard for determining their credibility as he would apply to the testimony of "a lay person," K.G. said, "I probably would, yeah."

After asking K.G. about his concern over an increase in violent crime, the judge asked if he could sit on a jury and decide the case on the evidence and according to the trial court's instructions, notwithstanding his feelings about violent crime. K.G. replied, "I am sure it would have some weight. I just don't know how much." Asked if he would put that aside, he replied, "I would try to, yes." Asked again, he said, "I certainly could try, yes."

Defense counsel asked K.G. about his friendship with a Minneapolis police detective and how he would feel next time he saw the detective if in the interim he had sat as a juror and found defendant not guilty of a double homicide. K.G. replied, "I guess I would feel disappointment." But he said he did not think he would owe the detective an explanation. The following exchange then occurred concerning K.G.'s view of police officers and their credibility.

Q: Is it fair to say that you have got a rather positive view of law enforcement?

A: Yes. They have always treated me fairly.

Q: When do you think you first formulated that positive view?

A: It's probably a long time ago.

Q: Most of your life?

A: Most of my life. I have always felt good about it.

Q: Okay. On your questionnaire, you indicated you would favor the testimony of a police officer as opposed to a lay witness by virtue of — do you remember filling that out?

A: Mm hmm.

Q: That is by virtue of the fact that they're police officers, right?

A: Mm hmm.

Q: So is it fair to say that you would, because of this long-held feeling, positive feeling you have about police officers, you are more inclined to believe what they tell you from the witness stand than what other people tell you, right?

A: I think so, yes.

Q: Okay. And this is a feeling that you have had for a long time and strongly have it?

A: I guess I didn't know I had it, but —

Q: Okay. You told the Judge that you thought that police officers sometimes made mistakes, right?

A: Mm hmm, I'm sure everybody does.

Q: Do you think they make mistakes less often than other people?

A: I have no idea.

Q: Okay. Do you think they lie under oath?

A: I don't think so.

Q: That's inconsistent with, as you described, their job is to bring forth sound evidence?

A: Mm hmm.

Q: Right?

A: Mm hmm.

Q: So you would agree with me that police officers, unlike other witnesses, always testify truthfully?

A: You know, I don't know. I can't speak for them, but you know, I will hope so.

Q: You would be real hard-pressed during the course of this trial to make a conclusion in your mind that a police officer knowingly testified untruthfully?

A: Right, I just — I would not feel that he would or she would, whoever is involved with it.

Q: Is it —

A: It wouldn't be my understanding or — or concern that they would.

Q: Would it be fair to say it would be virtually impossible for you to conclude as a juror that a police officer had testified falsely in this case?

A: Yes. I think.

Defense counsel then approached the bench and sought to have K.G. removed for cause.

The prosecutor, Fred Karasov, asked for and obtained permission to try to rehabilitate K.G., getting K.G. to admit that it was not inconceivable that some police officer might lie. The prosecutor then asked K.G. a series of leading questions, the answers to which indicated that K.G. would follow the instructions of the court to the best of his ability — that he thought he could be fair.

The following exchange between defense counsel and K.G. then occurred:

Q: Perhaps you can alleviate some of the confusion I'm now suffering. Because as I understood you, first you said you would favor the testimony of police officers. And then you said — that you told me that due to your positive impression you have of police, it was virtually impossible for you to conclude that a police officer had lied about anything under oath. And then you told Mr. Karasov that you could — police officers lied just like anybody else and could lie under oath. And you would hold all witnesses to the same standard of judging credibility and wouldn't favor a police officer's testimony just because they're a police officer. Could you clear that up for me, please?

A: Well, I think it was in the series of the way the questions were asked. But, you know, I just, you know, my belief is that, you know, based on the question that was presented in the questionnaire, about police officers, if I hold them in high regard. I mean, I'm not to the point of saying that I would take their testimony or what they say as the number one priority, but I happen to respect their work and what they do. And, you know, I answered the question as best I could on that because I do feel that I'm going to favor in some way, shape or form what they do because that's how I feel. That's just how I feel. Although, when asked — I would certainly be objective, you know, as best I could.

When defense counsel asked K.G. if in this case he would be more likely to believe the testimony of a police officer over that of defendant, the prosecutor objected and the trial court sustained the objection. The trial court also sustained an objection by the prosecutor to a rephrased question which asked K.G. whether he would be prone to resolve any evidentiary conflict in the case in favor of the police. Asked which he considered the greater travesty of justice, convicting an innocent person or acquitting a guilty person, K.G. replied, "Probably acquitting a guilty one." The trial court then sustained a prosecutor's objection when defense counsel asked K.G. whether, if there was doubt in his mind as to guilt or innocence in this case, he would err on the side of guilt.

Defense counsel repeated his challenge for cause, and the trial court denied the challenge for cause. Defendant's attorney had already used all of the allowed peremptory challenges. With the illness of one juror and the failure of another to appear, K.G. became a member of the jury which evaluated the conflicting testimony of a Minneapolis police officer and of defendant as to what defendant said during an unrecorded interrogation.

The jury began deliberations late on the afternoon of November 9, 1993. Its deliberations continued on November 10, 11, 12 and 13 before it reached a verdict on the afternoon of November 13.

Minnesota Rule of Criminal Procedure 26.02, subdivision 5 provides, in relevant part, that a juror may be challenged for cause on a number of grounds, including: "1. The existence of a state of mind on the part of the juror, in reference to the case or to either party, which satisfies the court that the juror cannot try the case impartially and without prejudice to the substantial rights of the party challenging."

If a prospective juror during *voir dire* admits to this "state of mind" described in the rule, then the juror should be excused, unless, of course, the prospective juror is "rehabilitated." 2 Wayne R. LaFave & Jerold H. Israel, *Criminal Procedure* § 21.3(c) (1984). Typically rehabilitation takes the form of the prospective juror stating unequivocally that he/she will follow the trial court's instructions and will fairly evaluate the evidence. Moreover, most judges, when faced with such an unequivocal assertion, "will accept the statement at face value (as perhaps the judge must, if he or she is not to make judgments on the juror's personal integrity.)" *Id.* at 730 (quoting Jon VanDyke, *Jury Selection Procedures* 146 (1977)).

If the trial court accepts such an assertion and allows the juror to sit, then the question for a reviewing court on appeal is whether the trial court erred in accepting the juror's unequivocal assertion of fairness at face value. As the United States Supreme Court said in *Patton v. Yount*, 467 U.S. 1025, 1036 (1984), there are two typical questions of historical fact for a reviewing court in a case like this: "Did the juror swear that he could set aside any opinion he might hold and decide the case on the evidence, and should the juror's protestation of impartiality have been believed. As a general rule, the trial court's resolution of the question whether the prospective juror's protestation of impartiality is believable is entitled to 'special deference' because 'the determination is essentially one of credibility, and therefore largely one of demeanor.' " *Id.* at 1037–38.

Generally, the trial court is free to bear in mind that prospective jurors "may never have been subjected to the type of leading questions and cross-examination tactics that frequently are employed," and the trial court is free to believe "those statements that were the most fully articulated or that appeared to have been least influenced by leading." *Id.* at 1039.

In the instant case the prospective juror in question, K.G., candidly admitted he likely would give greater credence to the testimony of police officers than to the testimony of other witnesses. The prosecutor, in a series of leading questions, got the juror to state that he would "try" to be fair and that to the best of his ability he would follow the instructions given by the trial court. However, given the opportunity by defense counsel to again express himself in his own words, the juror reverted to saying, "I do feel that I'm going to favor in some way, shape or form what they do because that's how I feel. That's just how I feel. Although, when asked — I would certainly be objective, you know, as best I could."

On this record we believe that it would have been prudent for the prosecutor to join defense counsel in urging the trial court to excuse the juror for cause. Instead, the experienced prosecutor persisted in asking the trial court to reject the challenge for cause.

While we believe trial courts must have considerable discretion in ruling on such challenges, we conclude that the trial court erred in rejecting defense counsel's challenge in this case because the juror did not "swear that he could set aside any opinion he might hold and decide the case on the evidence," *id.* at 1036, but only that he would try.

If defendant had then had peremptory challenges available and had not exercised one of them to strike K.G., then the question would be whether defendant could complain about K.G.'s sitting on the jury. Here, however, that is not a problem because defense counsel had already used up all of defendant's peremptory challenges, and the juror in question sat in judgment of defendant.

This leaves the question whether defendant is entitled to a new trial automatically or whether the error is subject to harmless error analysis.

Our decision in *State v. Stufflebean*, 329 N.W.2d 314, 317–18 (Minn.1983), suggested that in an appeal based on juror bias, the appellant must show not only that the challenged juror was subject to challenge for cause but also that actual prejudice resulted from the failure to dismiss the juror in response to the defendant's objection. On the record before us we are satisfied that actual prejudice did result from seating K.G. as a juror and that the defendant is, therefore, entitled to a new trial. On the other hand, the United States Supreme Court has stated that when it has been shown that those charged with bringing a defendant to judgment lack objectivity, "a reviewing court can neither indulge a presumption of regularity nor evaluate the resulting harm." *Vasquez v. Hillery*, 474 U.S. 254, 263–64 (1986). Accordingly, we agree that if the members of a petit jury are selected on improper criteria or if a biased juror is improperly allowed to sit in judgment of a criminal defendant and the issue is properly raised and preserved, the error has undermined the basic "structural integrity of the criminal tribunal itself, and is not amenable to harmless-error review." *Id.* * * * *

ANDERSON, JUSTICE (dissenting).

I respectfully dissent from the majority's conclusion that the trial court erred in rejecting the request of defense counsel to remove juror K.G. for cause. * * * *

Because the trial judge is in the best position to observe and to evaluate the demeanor of the prospective juror, the judge should be given broad discretion in determining whether to remove a prospective juror for cause. This court will not lightly conclude the trial court abused its discretion if the juror indicates his or her "intention to set aside any preconceived notions, and demonstrates to the satisfaction of the trial judge that he or she is able to do so." *State v. Howard*, 324 N.W.2d 216, 220 (Minn.1982). * * * *

Other courts have held that a juror who harbors a bias or prejudice may nonetheless sit as an impartial juror if he or she expresses a willingness to try to be objective. For example, in *United States v. Jones*, the defendant was charged with conspiracy to distribute cocaine. 865 F.2d 188, 189 (8th Cir.1989). During *voir dire*, the trial court refused to strike a juror for cause who had expressed strong antidrug feelings. The defendant was convicted, and the Eighth Circuit Court of Appeals affirmed. The court of appeals held that the trial court did not abuse its broad discretion in refusing to strike the juror for cause because, although the juror was not sure if her strong antidrug feelings would influence the way in which she viewed the evidence, she indicated that she would do her best to base her decision on the evidence.

Under the facts of the present case, I cannot conclude that the trial court abused its broad discretion by refusing to remove juror K.G. for cause. At worst, some of K.G.'s answers to *voir dire* questions were vague. A close review of the record, however, reveals that, on the whole, K.G. indicated he would do his best to set aside his impressions and opinions. Although K.G. acknowledged that he in some way favors what the police do, he also clearly indicated during questioning by the trial judge, the prosecutor and defense counsel that he would be objective and would, to the best of his ability, follow the court's instructions. The trial judge was in the best position to view the demeanor of K.G. and to determine whether K.G. would set aside his impressions and opinions and follow the court's instructions. * * * *

Note from Justin:

1. *Gamble v. Commonwealth*, 68 S.W.3d 367 (Ky. 2002) also involved a trial judge's efforts to "rehabilitate" a prospective juror.

A black defendant challenged Juror #54 for cause, after Juror #54 expressed during *voir dire* his hostility to blacks. But after the judge asked Juror #54 if he could base his verdict on the evidence and receiving an affirmative answer, the judge denied the challenge. The appellate court reversed:

> While Juror # 54 was hesitant to label himself a bigot, and clearly embarrassed when voicing his views on race, he did state that: (1) he was racially biased; (2) he left his neighborhood because young black men were hanging around in the area; (3) when he walked into the courtroom he assumed that Appellant was the accused because of the color of his skin; (4) and he was opposed to, in fact, offended by, inter-racial relationships. Juror # 54 specifically stated that he felt that people who were involved in such relationships were low class, and that low class people were more likely to commit crimes. Juror # 54 stated that it was "hard to say" how the presence of an inter-racial relationship would affect his decision in this case. While Juror # 54 did eventually state that he could be fair and reach a decision on the evidence, every indication was that he holds racist ideas which affected his view of Appellant before the first piece of evidence was presented to him. In short, he had indicated a bias so strong that he could not be rehabilitated. Further questions do not provide a device to "rehabilitate" a juror who should be considered disqualified by his personal knowledge or his past experience, or his attitude as expressed on voir dire. "This juror had indicated a bias so strong that the prosecutor's questions did not serve to remove the disqualification." *Thomas v. Commonwealth*, Ky., 864 S.W.2d 252, 255 (1993). As this Court stated in *Montgomery v. Commonwealth*, 819 S.W.2d 713, 718 (1991):

One of the myths arising from the folklore surrounding jury selection is that a juror who has made answers which would otherwise disqualify him by reason of bias or prejudice may be rehabilitated by being asked whether he can put aside his personal knowledge, his views, or those sentiments and opinions he has already, and decide the case instead based solely on the evidence presented in court and the court's instruction. This has come to be referred to in the vernacular as the "magic question." But, as Chief Justice Hughes observed in *United States v. Wood*, 299 U.S. 123 (1936), "impartiality is not a technical conception. It is a state of mind." A trial court's decision whether a juror possessed "this mental attitude of appropriate indifference" must be reviewed in the totality of circumstances. It is not limited to the juror's response to a "magic question." In this case, the record is replete with circumstances establishing an inference of bias or prejudice on the part of jurors so pervasive that the jurors were beyond being rehabilitated as appropriate jurors by affirmative answer to such a question, however well intentioned.

2. If the trial judge erroneously overrules a challenge for cause, must the lawyer use a *peremptory* challenge to remove that prospective juror?

Suppose that, in *Logan*, defense counsel had a *peremptory* challenge left, and had used it to excuse K.G. — and this was defense counsel's *last* peremptory challenge, so he had none left to use against another prospective juror. If the trial court erred by sustaining the challenge for cause to K.G., should the conviction be reversed?

In *Ross v. Oklahoma*, 487 U.S. 81 (1988), prospective juror Huling said that if Ross were found guilty, he would vote for death automatically. Ross challenged Huling for cause, but the judge denied the challenge — erroneously, because *Witherspoon* had held that such a juror could not be unbiased in a capital case. Ross then used a *peremptory* challenge to excuse Huling. On appeal, Ross argued that forcing him to use his peremptory unnecessarily violated his 6th Amendment rights. The Court disagreed:

It is well settled that the Sixth and Fourteenth Amendments guarantee a defendant on trial for his life the right to an impartial jury. Had Huling sat on the jury that ultimately sentenced petitioner to death, and had petitioner properly preserved his right to challenge the trial court's failure to remove Huling for cause, the sentence would have to be overturned. But Huling did not sit. Petitioner exercised a peremptory challenge to remove him, and Huling was thereby removed from the jury as effectively as if the trial court had excused him for cause.

Any claim that the jury was not impartial, therefore, must focus not on Huling, but on the jurors who ultimately sat. None of those 12 jurors, however, was challenged for cause by petitioner, and he has never suggested that any of the 12 was not impartial. "The Constitution presupposes that a jury selected from a fair cross section of the community is impartial, regardless of the mix of individual viewpoints actually represented on the jury, so long as the jurors can conscientiously and properly carry out their sworn duty to apply the law to the facts of the particular case." *Lockhart v. McCree*, 476 U.S. 162, 184 (1986). * * * We conclude that petitioner has failed to establish that the jury was not impartial. * * * *

Petitioner points out that had he not used his sixth peremptory challenge to remove Huling, he could have removed another juror, including one who ultimately sat on the jury. Petitioner asserts, moreover, that had he used his sixth peremptory challenge differently, the prosecution may have exercised its remaining peremptory challenges differently in response, and consequently, the composition of the jury panel might have changed significantly.

Although we agree that the failure to remove Huling may have resulted in a jury panel different from that which would otherwise have decided the case, we do not accept the argument that this possibility mandates reversal. * * * *

Petitioner was undoubtedly required to exercise a peremptory challenge to cure the trial court's error. But we reject the notion that the loss of a peremptory challenge constitutes a violation of the constitutional right to an impartial jury. We have long recognized that peremptory challenges are not of constitutional dimension. *Swain v. Alabama*, 380 U.S. 202, 219 (1965). They are a means to achieve the end of an impartial jury. So long as the jury that sits is impartial, the fact that the defendant had to use a peremptory challenge to achieve that result does not mean the Sixth Amendment was violated. We conclude that no violation of petitioner's right to an impartial jury occurred.

Compare *State v. Baker*, 935 P.2d 503 (Utah 1997). Baker was charged with rape of a child, and Prospective Juror #19 said that his sister had been raped and he could not put this aside and give both sides a fair trial. When Juror #19 later said he changed his mind, the trial court denied Baker's challenge for cause — erroneously. Baker then used all of his four peremptories to remove *four other* jurors (four women — who had not been challenged for cause). This left Juror #19 on the jury, which ultimately convicted Baker. Baker sought to distinguish *Ross*, arguing that a biased juror *did* sit on the jury that convicted him. But the court affirmed the conviction, holding that while the Constitution gives a defendant a right to an impartial jury, it does not give him the right to a peremptory challenge to use against non-biased jurors. Therefore, as Baker could have used one of his "free" peremptory challenges to remove Juror #19, "his own inaction waived his objection to the empaneling of Juror #19."

Baker insists that the cure-or-waive rule invites "bizarre results." For example, he argues that the rule "would require the defendant and defense counsel to take affirmative action to ensure that any conviction obtained will stand up on appeal," thereby placing defense counsel in an ethical dilemma. According to Baker, the defense's duties are to seek an acquittal or, failing that, to preserve error so as to obtain a new trial. He suggests that it was the prosecution's responsibility to use a peremptory to remove the challenged juror when the defense failed to do so. Baker's argument ignores the fact that all parties, including the defense, have a duty not to sow error and that obtaining a jury most favorable to the defense is certainly no part of the prosecution's duty. Both parties and the court share a duty to help ensure a fair trial — a trial in which a jury impartially weighs the evidence. Here, the prosecution may well have been convinced, as the trial court apparently was, that juror 19 could act without bias, and Baker's own actions did nothing to dispel that notion. His failure to use a peremptory challenge to remove juror 19 was, in effect, a tactical withdrawal of his objection. In such a situation, we cannot expect the prosecution to be clairvoyant and somehow divine that it should use one of its own peremptories to remove the juror. Therefore, requiring the defendant in a criminal action to remove those jurors whom he perceives as biased against him is the most practical way to facilitate an impartial jury.

CHIEF JUSTICE ZIMMERMAN dissented:

I concede that the cure-or-waive rule would prevent the planting of error as a backstop against a guilty verdict. However, I do not find this justification for the rule particularly strong. I think it far more realistic to presume that defense counsel ordinarily will choose to strike a biased juror in the hope of avoiding a conviction rather than risking a conviction by calculatingly permitting a biased juror to sit and hoping for reversal on appeal. Defense counsel's primary duty is to seek an acquittal, not a reversible conviction. Therefore, I deem the benefits of the cure-or-waive rule to be rather speculative. * * * *

The majority's adoption of the cure-or-waive rule also tends to provide an additional incentive to trial judges not to strike jurors challenged for cause. The rule ensures not only that a conviction will not be reversed, but also that the trial court will not be held accountable for erroneously denying a for cause challenge, so long as the defendant has at least one peremptory challenge left. We should be loath to create a mechanism that could be seen as giving trial judges the ability to force defendants to use all their peremptories to cure trial court refusals to strike biased jurors. This is completely inconsistent with the fact that empaneling impartial jurors is primarily the responsibility of the trial judge.

In *U.S. v. Martinez-Salazar*, 528 U.S. 304 (2000), the court followed *Ross* and held that even in a federal prosecution, a defendant may not obtain a reversal because the trial court's erroneous denial of a challenge for cause "forced" defendant to use up a peremptory challenge. If the trial judge denies a challenge for cause, defendant has a choice: use a peremptory to excuse this juror, or let the juror sit and raise this issue later on appeal:

A hard choice is not the same as no choice. Martinez-Salazar received and exercised 11 peremptory challenges. That is all he is entitled to under the Rule. After objecting to the District Court's denial of his for-cause challenge, he had the option of letting Gilbert sit on the petit jury and, upon conviction, pursuing a Sixth Amendment challenge on appeal. Instead, he elected to use a challenge to remove Gilbert. In choosing to remove Gilbert rather than taking his chances on appeal, Martinez-Salazar did not lose a peremptory challenge. Rather, he used the challenge in line with a principal reason for peremptories: to help secure the constitutional guarantee of trial by an impartial jury.

2.   The Peremptory Challenge

How necessary it is that a prisoner should have a good opinion of his jury, the want of which might totally disconcert him. The law wills not that a litigant should be tried by any one man against whom he has conceived a prejudice, even without being able to assign a reason for such his dislike.

William Blackstone, *Commentaries*

a.   The Function of the Peremptory Challenge (as seen by the Courts)

In *State v. Davis*, 504 N.W.2d 767 (1993), the Minnesota Supreme Court summarized the role of the peremptory challenge:

> While jurors have their individual preconceived notions and prejudices, it is assumed that they can set them aside so as to be fair and impartial. The purpose of voir dire is to test that assumption. If it is made to appear that a prospective juror cannot be fair, the juror may be challenged for cause. The peremptory is needed, however, if the challenge for cause is denied by the court. It is needed also when there is legitimate concern for a juror's fairness but this concern is insufficient to be a challenge for cause. It happens often enough that a juror expresses doubt about being able to be fair, but then opposing counsel or the judge ostensibly "rehabilitates" the juror; in this problematic situation, the peremptory is useful. Also, without the peremptory, trial counsel may be deterred from asking probing questions on *voir dire* for concern that any hostility inadvertently raised could not be remedied by a peremptory strike.

> In other words, the peremptory gives added assurance of an accurate verdict by resolving doubts (up to a specified number) in favor of exclusion. The fact that some unbiased jurors may be excused in the process is an affordable price to pay for removing doubts about a particular juror's impartiality and competence, especially when the vote of one biased juror can make a critical difference.

> Then, too, the role of the litigants in determining the jury's composition provides one reason for wide acceptance of the jury system and of its verdicts. The randomness built into the jury pool to obtain a cross-section can seem, to the apprehensive litigant, to be arbitrary and unfair, leaving the litigant to the "luck of the draw." The peremptory alleviates this apprehensiveness by allowing the parties to exercise their own intuitive judgment with respect to perceived juror bias.

In *Swain v. Alabama*, 380 U.S. 202 (1965), the Court rejected a black defendant's claim that the prosecutor's exercise of peremptory challenges against black prospective jurors denied him equal protection of the laws (unless the defendant can show that the prosecutor does this as a matter of practice, to prevent blacks from serving on juries). The Court explained the importance of peremptory challenges.

> Alabama contends that its system of peremptory strikes — challenges without cause, without explanation and without judicial scrutiny — affords a suitable and necessary method of securing juries which in fact and in the

opinion of the parties are fair and impartial. This system, it is said, in and of itself, provides justification for striking any group of otherwise qualified jurors in any given case, whether they be Negroes, Catholics, accountants or those with blue eyes. Based on the history of this system and its actual use and operation in this country, we think there is merit in this position.
* * * *

In contrast to the course in England, where both peremptory challenge and challenge for cause have fallen into disuse, peremptories were and are freely used and relied upon in this country, perhaps because juries here are drawn from a greater cross-section of a heterogeneous society. The *voir dire* in American trials tends to be extensive and probing, operating as a predicate for the exercise of peremptories, and the process of selecting a jury protracted. The persistence of peremptories and their extensive use demonstrate the long and widely held belief that peremptory challenge is a necessary part of trial by jury. Although there is nothing in the Constitution of the United States which requires the Congress (or the States) to grant peremptory challenges, nonetheless the challenge is one of the most important of the rights secured to the accused. The denial or impairment of the right is reversible error without a showing of prejudice. For it is, as Blackstone says, an arbitrary and capricious right, and it must be exercised with full freedom, or it fails of its full purpose.

The function of the challenge is not only to eliminate extremes of partiality on both sides, but to assure the parties that the jurors before whom they try the case will decide on the basis of the evidence placed before them, and not otherwise. In this way the peremptory satisfies the rule that to perform its high function in the best way, justice must satisfy the appearance of justice. Indeed, the very availability of peremptories allows counsel to ascertain the possibility of bias through probing questions on the *voir dire* and facilitates the exercise of challenges for cause by removing the fear of incurring a juror's hostility through examination and challenge for cause. Although historically the incidence of the prosecutor's challenge has differed from that of the accused, the view in this country has been that the system should guarantee not only freedom from any bias against the accused, but also from any prejudice against his prosecution. Between him and the state, the scales are to be evenly held.

The essential nature of the peremptory challenge is that it is one exercised without a reason stated, without inquiry and without being subject to the court's control. While challenges for cause permit rejection of jurors on a narrowly specified, provable and legally cognizable basis of partiality, the peremptory permits rejection for a real or imagined partiality that is less easily designated or demonstrable. It is often exercised upon the sudden impressions and unaccountable prejudices we are apt to conceive upon the bare looks and gestures of another, upon a juror's habits and associations, or upon the feeling that the bare questioning a juror's indifference may sometimes provoke a resentment. It is no less frequently exercised on grounds normally thought irrelevant to legal proceedings or official action, namely, the race, religion, nationality, occupation or affiliations of people summoned for jury duty. For the question a prosecutor or defense counsel must decide is not whether a juror of a particular race or nationality is in fact partial, but whether one from a different group is less likely to be. It is well known that these factors are widely explored during the *voir dire*, by both prosecutor and accused. This Court has held that the fairness of trial by jury requires no less. Hence veniremen are not always judged solely as individuals for the purpose of exercising peremptory challenges. Rather they are challenged in light of the limited knowledge counsel has of them, which may include their group affiliations, in the context of the case to be tried.

With these considerations in mind, we cannot hold that the striking of Negroes in a particular case is a denial of equal protection of the laws. In the quest for an impartial and qualified jury, Negro and white, Protestant and Catholic, are alike subject to being challenged without cause. To subject the prosecutor's challenge in any particular case to the demands and traditional standards of the Equal Protection Clause would entail a radical change in the nature and operation of the challenge. The challenge, *pro tanto*, would no longer be peremptory, each and every challenge being open to examination, either at the time of the challenge or at a hearing afterwards. The prosecutor's judgment underlying each challenge would be subject to scrutiny for reasonableness and sincerity. And a great many uses of the challenge would be banned.

In the light of the purpose of the peremptory system and the function it serves in a pluralistic society in connection with the institution of jury trial, we cannot hold that the Constitution requires an examination of the prosecutor's reasons for the exercise of his challenges in any given case. The presumption in any particular case must be that the prosecutor is using the State's challenges to obtain a fair and impartial jury to try the case before the court. The presumption is not overcome and the prosecutor therefore subjected to examination by allegations that in the case at hand all Negroes were removed from the jury or that they were removed because they were Negroes. Any other result, we think, would establish a rule wholly at odds with the peremptory challenge system as we know it. Hence the motion to strike the trial jury was properly denied in this case.

b.   The Function of the Peremptory Challenge (as seen by *trial attorneys*)

1. In Bailey & Rothblatt, *Successful Techniques for Criminal Trials* (Bancroft-Whitney, 2nd ed., 1985) §§ 6:41–6:45, the authors give the following advice on how to use peremptory challenges to pick a "pro-defense" jury:

Physical Characteristics

Physical characteristics are particularly important to the lawyer defending a case in the federal courts where selection of jurors is made without personal interrogation, and only after the judge has asked all the questions. Generally speaking, the heavy, roundfaced, jovial-looking person is the most desirable. The undesirable juror is quite often the slight, underweight and delicate type. * * * * Of course, these generalizations and those that follow should be discarded if the questions you submit to the court or ask of jurors yourself uncover actual bias or prejudice.

Sex

Common sense will go a long way toward deciding the sexual composition of your jury. Depending on the issues to be tried, women jurors are desirable if the defendant happens to be a handsome young man. Similarly, an all-male jury is preferred where the defendant is a woman. Since the jury tends to try the attorney as well, it may be preferable to select a jury composed primarily of the sex opposite to your own. * * * *

Age and Marital Status

As a general rule, try to obtain jurors who are between 28 and 55 years of age. They will tend to be most alert and receptive to complex defenses. Younger persons may be favorable jurors if they have acquired a distrust of police officers. Married jurors are generally preferable to single ones, particularly if your client is a younger person.

Ethnic or Racial Background

It has often been said that persons of Italian, Irish, Jewish, Latin American and Southern European extraction are more desirable as jurors than people of British, Scandinavian, or German extraction. The latter are presumably more law-abiding, conservative and strict, with more rigid standards of conduct. Blind adherence to these over-generalized stereotypes can prove dangerous.

You must examine the background, nationality, and racial characteristics of the defendant and witnesses (both prosecution and defense). For example, if the witnesses that you seek to attack are of a particular origin, make certain that people of the same background do not dominate the jury. A vigorous cross-examination of a person of Jewish or Italian extraction, for example, might be resented by jurors of that same background.

Occupation and Skills

You want jurors whose minds can be molded. To that end, you do not want persons incapable of understanding the salient facts of your defense; nor do you desire persons of superior intelligence whose preconceived ideas will be difficult to dislodge. This latter type is also particularly dangerous because they will usually dominate the other jurors.

Generally, retired police officers, military men and their wives are undesirable. They have adhered to a strict line of conduct throughout their lives. They may believe that if a man is arrested, he is probably guilty. * * * *

Salesmen, actors, artists, and writers are highly desirable. They have enjoyed wide and varied experiences, have witnessed the good and bad in people and are prone to forgive an indiscretion in another. * * * *

Bankers, bank employees, members of management, and low-salaried white-collar workers are generally undesirable. They have been trained either to take or give orders, are forced to tow the line, and usually expect others to do the same.

2. Another perspective is offered by Acker, *Exercising Peremptory Challenges After Batson*, 24 Criminal Law Bulletin 203–204 (1988):

The effective use of *voir dire* and peremptory challenges is as much an art as a science. Volumes of literature surround these topics, with accompanying folklore . . . Clarence Darrow, for example, is on record as favoring the removal of women, the wealthy, Presbyterians, Baptists, and Scandinavian Lutherans from criminal juries.[1] Melvin Belli has offered that "women jurors are too brutal", and thus he reportedly prefers men to serve on juries. A prosecutor's training manual prepared by a Texas district attorney in the early 1970s strongly advised against selecting minority group members, "free thinkers and flower children," or women as jurors.

Attorneys generally attempt to push beyond crude group stereotypes by interrogating the individual members of the venire, but even if such questions are incisive, the responses must be received with caution. A courtroom is not a setting likely to inspire candid revelations from a person, especially if he will be perceived negatively as a result, or if his opinions are inconsistent with legal norms. Peremptory challenges accordingly must be exercised on some combination of the attorney's working assumptions about experience with human nature, and the limited information about a prospective juror that can be collected under the difficult and rather artificial circumstances of in-court questioning.

3. A practicing criminal defense attorney's view of the importance of the peremptory challenge appears in Herald Fahringer, *The Peremptory Challenge: An Endangered Species?*, 31 Criminal Law Bulletin 400 (1995):

> Challenges for cause will not solve the problem of jury prejudice because most jurors are reluctant to acknowledge their biases. No matter how hard lawyers strive to uncover prejudice, jurors will disavow it. This is because research in social psychology has established that the behavior and attitudes of jurors are influenced by the ceremonial flavor of the selection process. Under the circumstances of uncertainty and unfamiliarity that exist in the culture of the courtroom, jurors become very sensitive to "social comparison information," that is, signs from other people around them indicating the appropriateness of their behavior, attitudes, and feelings.
>
> Thus, during *voir dire*, jurors may attempt to answer in what they think is a socially appropriate manner instead of being honest. Opinions expressed in public often differ from opinions expressed in private. Even the most conscientious jurors' ability to express their feelings candidly, par-

---

[1] Ed.: Here is how Clarence Darrow put it, back in 1936:

You would be guilty of malpractice if you got rid of an Irishman, except for the strongest reasons. An Englishman is not so good as an Irishman, but still, he has come through a long tradition of individual rights, and is not afraid to stand alone; in fact, he is never sure that he is right unless the great majority is against him. The German is not so keen about individual rights except where they concern his own way of life. If he is a Catholic, then he loves music and art; he must be emotional, and will want to help you. If a Presbyterian enters the jury box and carefully rolls up his umbrella, and calmly and critically sits down, let him go. He is cold as the grave. Get rid of him with the fewest possible words before he contaminates the others. If possible, the Baptists are more hopeless than the Presbyterians. The Methodists are worth considering; they are nearer the soil. Beware of the Lutherans, especially the Scandinavians; they are almost always sure to convict. As to Unitarians, Universalists, Congregationalists, Jews and other agnostics, don't ask them too many questions; keep them anyhow, especially Jews and agnostics. Never take a wealthy man on a jury. He will convict, unless the defendant is accused of violating the anti-trust law.

[Darrow, *Attorney for the Defense*, Esquire Magazine, May 1936, pp. 36–37.]

ticularly on sensitive or controversial issues, is inhibited by a need to appear acceptable to other jurors. As the "right" or socially correct responses become clear during *voir dire*, answers from jurors become less and less reliable. In a word, jurors quickly acquire the paraphernalia of pretense and become eager to please. This psychology dooms them to a shameful conformity, which is at war with the candor required for the successful selection of a jury.

At a time when no one seems capable of answering a question directly, lawyers must find ways of detecting attitudes that may affect a juror's impartiality. Experienced trial lawyers can often recognize deep-seated prejudices that remain unspoken and are illegible to others. In the narrow social environment of a jury pool, every movement or expression seems to have its consequences. Human gestures sometimes have a way of speaking louder than words. The eyes of a trial lawyer skim over the faces of jurors the way a blind person's fingers glide over the Braille letters of some unfamiliar book, in search of signs that will help him or her make the right choice.

There is a litany of gestures that can tell a lawyer a lot. Is the juror's posture defiant? Are her arms folded across her chest? Does the juror appear intimidated, drawing his shoulders close together? A juror who leans forward and gestures while speaking shows attentiveness and a willingness to be involved. But a person who is slumped down in her chair may be bored. Once pronounced signals of hostility, disinterest, or distrust are identified and decoded, the juror should be excused. Without the power of a peremptory challenge, these strong antagonisms will remain on the jury and may ultimately taint the verdict.

4. Compare, however, Mitzi S. White, *The Nonverbal Behaviors in Jury Selection*, 31 Crim.L.Bulletin 414 (1995):

While researchers have not studied the effectiveness of specific folk wisdoms, they have examined whether lawyers using traditional jury selection methods are able to distinguish between favorable and unfavorable jurors. The results of these studies suggest that the average lawyer does a poor job of discriminating among jurors. In a study completed in the late 1950s, researchers extensively interviewed jurors participating in criminal and civil cases in a midwest federal district court. Those interviews revealed that lawyers often fail to identify unfavorable jurors. Many of the jurors seated by lawyers were found to have special biases that directly influenced their decisions in the cases. In addition, seated jurors often had not been entirely truthful when questioned during *voir dire*. Thus, contrary to the generally held belief among lawyers that they can discriminate among jurors, lawyers may not have a special window into the minds of jurors. * * * *

A more recent study also reported that the average lawyer is not adept at selecting favorable jurors. In this study, experienced lawyers and law students acted as defense lawyers in a manslaughter case. They selected jurors from written descriptions of individuals who had previously participated in a mock trial as jurors and judged the defendant as "probably guilty" or "probably innocent." The descriptions contained demographic information similar to that typically received by lawyers from the court prior to *voir dire*. Neither the lawyers or law students accurately distinguished between favorable and unfavorable jurors. Both groups chose more conviction prone jurors that acquittal prone jurors. Furthermore, when each group's acceptances and rejections were analyzed by whether jurors voted for acquittal or conviction, it was found that both lawyers and law students selected more jurors who voted for conviction than acquittal and rejected more jurors that voted for acquittal than conviction. * * * *

These studies are limited in scope and suffer from various methodological shortcomings. They do, however, show that the average lawyer is not particularly adept at selecting jurors. The previously mentioned finding that more skillful lawyers are able to select favorable jurors suggests that the lack luster showings of lawyers in the other studies may be due to a failure to control for differences in lawyer competence. Thus it may be that more talented trial lawyers are able to discern subtle differences among jurors that are unnoticed by less talented lawyers.

In recent years, social scientists have attempted to overcome the shortcomings of traditional methods of jury selection through the development of methods that make jury selection more scientific. Despite the serious substantive and methodological questions that have been raised in the scientific community concerning the efficacy of such methods, contemporary lawyers often rely on these methods in major trials.

A number of social science approaches to jury selection have been subsumed under the term "scientific jury selection." However, the primary method, to which this term applies and that also engendered the term, involves the construction of predictive models linking juror characteristics and attitudes to verdict preferences. In preparing these models, researchers randomly select individuals in the community from which the jury pool for the case will be drawn. These potential jurors are questioned about demographic characteristics, such as their age, education, They are also asked about their personal beliefs, verdict preference, and social attitudes with particular stress placed on obtaining information about social attitudes relevant to the case at hand. This information is then statistically analyzed to determine the relationships between potential jurors' demographic characteristics, personal beliefs, social attitudes, and verdict preferences. Based on the relationships that emerge from this analysis, a profile is constructed of the ideal juror. * * * *

While scientific jury selection has been used successfully in a number of well-publicized trials since the Harrisburg Seven, most support for it is anecdotal or based on claims by jury consultants. (Moreover, not all anecdotal support is positive, as the *McDonald* case illustrates. McDonald, a Green Beret doctor whose story has been recounted in the book *Fatal Vision* and a television movie based on the book, was accused of murdering his wife and two children. Based on a survey of 900 people in the community, a juror profile was developed that called for the selection of conservative whites over the age of 35. The final jury closely matched this profile. Yet the jurors unanimously convicted McDonald of first-degree murder.) * * * *

While a potpourri of studies, varying widely in methodology and variables, have examined relationships between jurors' characteristics and verdict preferences, only weak relationships have been found. Based on a review of the literature, for example, one study estimated that jurors' characteristics explain only 5% to 15% of the variance in jurors' verdict preferences.

Furthermore, even when weak relationships are found between jurors' characteristics and verdict preferences, they tend to be far too complex to be of utility in the courtroom. * * * * Another study found a similarly complex maze of relationships in a study of the relationship between juror's sex, race, education, and age and their verdict preferences in murder, rape, and robbery cases. No direct relationships between jurors' characteristics and verdict preferences were found. Relationships differed across sex, race, and type of case. For example, black females were more likely to convict than black males but no difference was found between white males and white females. Older people were more likely to convict in rape cases, whereas they were less likely to convict in murder cases.

As these studies indicate, researchers have not been able to identify simple sets of relationships that lawyers can readily use in the courtroom to select jurors. This lack of strong simple relationships between jurors' characteristics and verdict preferences is not surprising, given the innumerable situational factors that can influence a juror from the time he takes his seat until he casts his final vote. In particular, researchers have found that the strength of the evidence and the deliberative process are important determinants of how jurors vote. In a study based on post-trial interviews with jurors, one researcher found that evidence variables explained 34% of the variance in jurors' verdict preferences, whereas jurors' characteristics only accounted for 2% of the variance. Similarly, a study based on post-trial interviews with jurors primarily relied on the evidence in making their judgments. * * * *

Deliberations also exert a strong influence on how jurors vote. Research has shown that during deliberation, factions form. As factions become larger, members of the dominant faction speak more and consequently exert increased pressure on other jurors to change their position. As a result, group pressure may erode a juror's personal disposition towards a particular verdict if it is contrary to that advocated by the major faction.

c.   *Batson*

BATSON v. KENTUCKY
United States Supreme Court
476 U.S. 79 (1986)

JUSTICE POWELL **delivered the opinion of the Court.**

This case requires us to reexamine that portion of *Swain v. Alabama*, 380 U.S. 202 (1965), concerning the evidentiary burden placed on a criminal defendant who claims that he has been denied equal protection through the State's use of peremptory challenges to exclude members of his race from the petit jury. * * * *

I

Petitioner, a black man, was indicted in Kentucky on charges of second-degree burglary and receipt of stolen goods. On the first day of trial in Jefferson Circuit Court, the judge conducted *voir dire* examination of the venire, excused certain jurors for cause, and permitted the parties to exercise peremptory challenges.[2] The prosecutor used his peremptory challenges to strike all four black persons on the venire, and a jury composed only of white persons was selected. Defense counsel moved to discharge the jury before it was sworn on the ground that the prosecutor's removal of the black veniremen violated petitioner's rights under the Sixth and Fourteenth Amendments to a jury drawn from a cross-section of the community, and under the Fourteenth Amendment to equal protection of the laws. Counsel requested a hearing on his motion. Without expressly ruling on the request for a hearing, the trial judge observed that the parties were entitled to use their peremptory challenges to "strike anybody they want to." The judge then denied petitioner's motion, reasoning that the cross-section requirement applies only to selection of the venire and not to selection of the petit jury itself. The jury convicted petitioner on both counts. * * * *

II

In *Swain v. Alabama*, this Court recognized that a "State's purposeful or deliberate denial to Negroes on account of race of participation as jurors in the administration of justice violates the Equal Protection Clause." 380 U.S. at 203–204. This principle has been consistently and repeatedly reaffirmed in numerous decisions of this Court both preceding and following *Swain*.[3] We reaffirm the

---

[2]   The Kentucky Rules of Criminal Procedure authorize the trial court to permit counsel to conduct *voir dire* examination or to conduct the examination itself. Ky.Rule Crim.Proc. 9.38. After jurors have been excused for cause, the parties exercise their peremptory challenges simultaneously by striking names from a list of qualified jurors equal to the number to be seated plus the number of allowable peremptory challenges. Rule 9.36. Since the offense charged in this case was a felony, and an alternate juror was called, the prosecutor was entitled to six peremptory challenges, and defense counsel to nine. Rule 9.40.

[3]   * * * * The basic principles prohibiting exclusion of persons from participation in jury service on account of their race "are essentially the same for grand juries and for petit juries." *Alexander v. Louisiana*, 405 U.S. 625 (1972).

principle today.[4]

A

More than a century ago, the Court decided that the State denies a black defendant equal protection of the laws when it puts him on trial before a jury from which members of his race have been purposefully excluded. *Strauder v. West Virginia*, 100 U.S. 303 (1880). That decision laid the foundation for the Court's unceasing efforts to eradicate racial discrimination in the procedures used to select the venire from which individual jurors are drawn. In *Strauder*, the Court explained that the central concern of the recently ratified Fourteenth Amendment was to put an end to governmental discrimination on account of race. Exclusion of black citizens from service as jurors constitutes a primary example of the evil the Fourteenth Amendment was designed to cure.

In holding that racial discrimination in jury selection offends the Equal Protection Clause, the Court in *Strauder* recognized, however, that a defendant has no right to a "petit jury composed in whole or in part of persons of his own race." Id. at 305. * * * * "The number of our races and nationalities stands in the way of evolution of such a conception" of the demand of equal protection. *Akins v. Texas*, 325 U.S. 398, 403 (1945).[6] But the defendant does have the right to be tried by a jury whose members are selected pursuant to nondiscriminatory criteria. The Equal Protection Clause guarantees the defendant that the State will not exclude members of his race from the jury venire on account of race, * * * or on the false assumption that members of his race as a group are not qualified to serve as jurors.

Purposeful racial discrimination in selection of the venire violates a defendant's right to equal protection because it denies him the protection that a trial by jury is intended to secure. "The very idea of a jury is a body composed of the peers or equals of the person whose rights it is selected or summoned to determine; that is, of his neighbors, fellows, associates, persons having the same legal status in society as that which he holds." *Strauder*, supra, 100 U.S. at 308. The petit jury has occupied a central position in our system of justice by safeguarding a person accused of crime against the arbitrary exercise of power by prosecutor or judge. Those on the venire must be "indifferently chosen," to secure the defendant's right under the Fourteenth Amendment to "protection of life and liberty against race or color prejudice." *Strauder, supra*, 100 U.S. at 309.

---

[4] In this Court, petitioner has argued that the prosecutor's conduct violated his rights under the Sixth and Fourteenth Amendments to an impartial jury and to a jury drawn from a cross-section of the community. Petitioner has framed his argument in these terms in an apparent effort to avoid inviting the Court directly to reconsider one of its own precedents. On the other hand, the State has insisted that petitioner is claiming a denial of equal protection and that we must reconsider *Swain* to find a constitutional violation on this record. We agree with the State that resolution of petitioner's claim properly turns on application of equal protection principles and express no view on the merits of any of petitioner's Sixth Amendment arguments.

[6] Similarly, though the Sixth Amendment guarantees that the petit jury will be selected from a pool of names representing a cross-section of the community, *Taylor v. Louisiana*, 419 U.S. 522 (1975), we have never held that the Sixth Amendment requires that "petit juries actually chosen must mirror the community and reflect the various distinctive groups in the population," *id.* at 538. Indeed, it would be impossible to apply a concept of proportional representation to the petit jury in view of the heterogeneous nature of our society. Such impossibility is illustrated by the Court's holding that a jury of six persons is not unconstitutional. *Williams v. Florida*, 399 U.S. 78 (1970).

Racial discrimination in selection of jurors harms not only the accused whose life or liberty they are summoned to try. Competence to serve as a juror ultimately depends on an assessment of individual qualifications and ability impartially to consider evidence presented at a trial. A person's race simply is unrelated to his fitness as a juror. As long ago as *Strauder*, therefore, the Court recognized that by denying a person participation in jury service on account of his race, the State unconstitutionally discriminated against the excluded juror. The harm from discriminatory jury selection extends beyond that inflicted on the defendant and the excluded juror to touch the entire community. Selection procedures that purposefully exclude black persons from juries undermine public confidence in the fairness of our system of justice. Discrimination within the judicial system is most pernicious because it is "a stimulant to that race prejudice which is an impediment to securing to black citizens that equal justice which the law aims to secure to all others." *Strauder, supra*, 100 U.S. at 308.

B

In *Strauder*, the Court invalidated a state statute that provided that only white men could serve as jurors. We can be confident that no state now has such a law. The Constitution requires, however, that we look beyond the face of the statute defining juror qualifications and also consider challenged selection practices to afford "protection against action of the State through its administrative officers in effecting the prohibited discrimination." *Norris v. Alabama*, 294 U.S. at 589. Thus, the Court has found a denial of equal protection where the procedures implementing a neutral statute operated to exclude persons from the venire on racial grounds, * * * and has made clear that the Constitution prohibits all forms of purposeful racial discrimination in selection of jurors. While decisions of this Court have been concerned largely with discrimination during selection of the venire, the principles announced there also forbid discrimination on account of race in selection of the petit jury. Since the Fourteenth Amendment protects an accused throughout the proceedings bringing him to justice, the State may not draw up its jury lists pursuant to neutral procedures but then resort to discrimination at other stages in the selection process.

Accordingly, the component of the jury selection process at issue here, the State's privilege to strike individual jurors through peremptory challenges, is subject to the commands of the Equal Protection Clause.[12] Although a prosecutor ordinarily is entitled to exercise permitted peremptory challenges "for any reason at all, as long as that reason is related to his view concerning the outcome" of the case to be tried, *United States v. Robinson*, 421 F.Supp. 467, 473 (Conn.1976), the

---

[12] We express no views on whether the Constitution imposes any limit on the exercise of peremptory challenges by defense counsel. Nor do we express any views on the techniques used by lawyers who seek to obtain information about the community in which a case is to be tried, and about members of the venire from which the jury is likely to be drawn. Prior to *voir dire* examination, which serves as the basis for exercise of challenges, lawyers wish to know as much as possible about prospective jurors, including their age, education, employment, and economic status, so that they can ensure selection of jurors who at least have an open mind about the case. In some jurisdictions, where a pool of jurors serves for a substantial period of time, counsel also may seek to learn which members of the pool served on juries in other cases and the outcome of those cases. Counsel even may employ professional investigators to interview persons who have served on a particular petit jury. We have had no occasion to consider particularly this practice. Of course, counsel's effort to obtain possibly relevant information about prospective jurors is to be distinguished from the practice at issue here.

Equal Protection Clause forbids the prosecutor to challenge potential jurors solely on account of their race or on the assumption that black jurors as a group will be unable impartially to consider the State's case against a black defendant.

III

* * * *

A

Swain required the Court to decide, among other issues, whether a black defendant was denied equal protection by the State's exercise of peremptory challenges to exclude members of his race from the petit jury. 380 U.S. at 209–210. The record in *Swain* showed that the prosecutor had used the State's peremptory challenges to strike the six black persons included on the petit jury venire. *Id.* at 210. While rejecting the defendant's claim for failure to prove purposeful discrimination, the Court nonetheless indicated that the Equal Protection Clause placed some limits on the State's exercise of peremptory challenges. *Id.* at 222–224.

The Court sought to accommodate the prosecutor's historical privilege of peremptory challenge free of judicial control and the constitutional prohibition on exclusion of persons from jury service on account of race, *id.* at 222–224. While the Constitution does not confer a right to peremptory challenges, those challenges traditionally have been viewed as one means of assuring the selection of a qualified and unbiased jury, 380 U.S. at 219.[15] To preserve the peremptory nature of the prosecutor's challenge, the Court in *Swain* declined to scrutinize his actions in a particular case by relying on a presumption that he properly exercised the State's challenges. *Id.* at 221–222.

The Court went on to observe, however, that a state may not exercise its challenges in contravention of the Equal Protection Clause. It was impermissible for a prosecutor to use his challenges to exclude blacks from the jury "for reasons wholly unrelated to the outcome of the particular case on trial" or to deny to blacks "the same right and opportunity to participate in the administration of justice enjoyed by the white population." *Id.* at 224. Accordingly, a black defendant could make out a prima facie case of purposeful discrimination on proof that the peremptory challenge system was "being perverted" in that manner. *Ibid.* For example, an inference of purposeful discrimination would be raised on evidence that a prosecutor, "in case after case, whatever the circumstances, whatever the crime and whoever the defendant or the victim may be, is responsible for the removal of Negroes who have been selected as qualified jurors by the jury commissioners and who have survived challenges for cause, with the result that no Negroes ever serve on petit juries." *Id.* at 223. Evidence offered by the defendant in *Swain* did not meet that standard. While the defendant showed that prosecutors in the jurisdiction had exercised their strikes to exclude blacks from the jury, he offered no proof of the circumstances under which prosecutors were responsible for striking black jurors beyond the facts of his own case. *Id.* at 224–228.

---

[15] In *Swain*, the Court reviewed the "very old credentials" of the peremptory challenge system and noted the "long and widely held belief that peremptory challenge is a necessary part of trial by jury." 380 U.S. at 219.

A number of lower courts following the teaching of *Swain* reasoned that proof of repeated striking of blacks over a number of cases was necessary to establish a violation of the Equal Protection Clause. * * * * Since this interpretation of *Swain* has placed on defendants a crippling burden of proof,[17] prosecutors' peremptory challenges are now largely immune from constitutional scrutiny. For reasons that follow, we reject this evidentiary formulation as inconsistent with standards that have been developed since *Swain* for assessing a prima facie case under the Equal Protection Clause.

B

* * * *

Thus, since the decision in *Swain*, this Court has recognized that a defendant may make a prima facie showing of purposeful racial discrimination in selection of the venire by relying solely on the facts concerning its selection in his case. These decisions are in accordance with the proposition, articulated in *Arlington Heights v. Metropolitan Housing Corp.*, that "a consistent pattern of official racial discrimination" is not "a necessary predicate to a violation of the Equal Protection Clause. A single invidiously discriminatory governmental act" is not "immunized by the absence of such discrimination in the making of other comparable decisions." 429 U.S. at 266. For evidentiary requirements to dictate that several must suffer discrimination before one could object would be inconsistent with the promise of equal protection to all. * * * *

C

The standards for assessing a prima facie case in the context of discriminatory selection of the venire have been fully articulated since *Swain*. These principles support our conclusion that a defendant may establish a prima facie case of purposeful discrimination in selection of the petit jury solely on evidence concerning the prosecutor's exercise of peremptory challenges at the defendant's trial. To establish such a case, the defendant first must show that he is a member of a cognizable racial group, and that the prosecutor has exercised peremptory challenges to remove from the venire members of the defendant's race. Second, the defendant is entitled to rely on the fact, as to which there can be no dispute, that peremptory challenges constitute a jury selection practice that permits "those to discriminate who are of a mind to discriminate." *Avery v. Georgia, supra*, 345 U.S. at 562. Finally, the defendant must show that these facts and any other relevant circumstances raise an inference that the prosecutor used that practice to exclude the veniremen from the petit jury on account of their race. This combination of factors in the empanelling of the petit jury, as in the selection of the venire, raises

---

[17] The lower courts have noted the practical difficulties of proving that the State systematically has exercised peremptory challenges to exclude blacks from the jury on account of race. As the Court of Appeals for the Fifth Circuit observed, the defendant would have to investigate, over a number of cases, the race of persons tried in the particular jurisdiction, the racial composition of the venire and petit jury, and the manner in which both parties exercised their peremptory challenges. *United States v. Pearson*, 448 F.2d 1207, 1217 (CA5, 1971). The court believed this burden to be "most difficult" to meet. Ibid. In jurisdictions where court records do not reflect the jurors' race and where *voir dire* proceedings are not transcribed, the burden would be insurmountable.

the necessary inference of purposeful discrimination.

In deciding whether the defendant has made the requisite showing, the trial court should consider all relevant circumstances. For example, a "pattern" of strikes against black jurors included in the particular venire might give rise to an inference of discrimination. Similarly, the prosecutor's questions and statements during *voir dire* examination and in exercising his challenges may support or refute an inference of discriminatory purpose. These examples are merely illustrative. We have confidence that trial judges, experienced in supervising *voir dire*, will be able to decide if the circumstances concerning the prosecutor's use of peremptory challenges creates a prima facie case of discrimination against black jurors.

Once the defendant makes a prima facie showing, the burden shifts to the State to come forward with a neutral explanation for challenging black jurors. Though this requirement imposes a limitation in some cases on the full peremptory character of the historic challenge, we emphasize that the prosecutor's explanation need not rise to the level justifying exercise of a challenge for cause. But the prosecutor may not rebut the defendant's prima facie case of discrimination by stating merely that he challenged jurors of the defendant's race on the assumption — or his intuitive judgment — that they would be partial to the defendant because of their shared race. Just as the Equal Protection Clause forbids the States to exclude black persons from the venire on the assumption that blacks as a group are unqualified to serve as jurors, so it forbids the States to strike black veniremen on the assumption that they will be biased in a particular case simply because the defendant is black. The core guarantee of equal protection, ensuring citizens that their State will not discriminate on account of race, would be meaningless were we to approve the exclusion of jurors on the basis of such assumptions, which arise solely from the jurors' race. Nor may the prosecutor rebut the defendant's case merely by denying that he had a discriminatory motive or "affirming his good faith in individual selections." *Alexander v. Louisiana*, 405 U.S., at 632. If these general assertions were accepted as rebutting a defendant's prima facie case, the Equal Protection Clause "would be but a vain and illusory requirement." *Norris v. Alabama, supra*, 294 U.S. at 598. The prosecutor therefore must articulate a neutral explanation related to the particular case to be tried. * * * * The trial court then will have the duty to determine if the defendant has established purposeful discrimination.

IV

* * * *

Nor are we persuaded by the State's suggestion that our holding will create serious administrative difficulties. In those states applying a version of the evidentiary standard we recognize today, courts have not experienced serious administrative burdens, * * * and the peremptory challenge system has survived. We decline, however, to formulate particular procedures to be followed upon a defendant's timely objection to a prosecutor's challenges.[24]

---

[24] In light of the variety of jury selection practices followed in our state and federal trial courts, we make no attempt to instruct these courts how best to implement our holding today. For the same reason, we express no view on whether it is more appropriate in a particular case, upon a finding of

V

In this case, petitioner made a timely objection to the prosecutor's removal of all black persons on the venire. Because the trial court flatly rejected the objection without requiring the prosecutor to give an explanation for his action, we remand this case for further proceedings. If the trial court decides that the facts establish, prima facie, purposeful discrimination and the prosecutor does not come forward with a neutral explanation for his action, our precedents require that petitioner's conviction be reversed.[25]

JUSTICE MARSHALL, concurring.

The decision today will not end the racial discrimination that peremptories inject into the jury-selection process. That goal can be accomplished only by eliminating peremptory challenges entirely.

Misuse of the peremptory challenge to exclude black jurors has become both common and flagrant. Black defendants rarely have been able to compile statistics showing the extent of that practice, but the few cases setting out such figures are instructive. See *United States v. Carter*, 528 F.2d 844, 848 (CA8, 1975) (in 15 criminal cases in 1974 in the Western District of Missouri involving black defendants, prosecutors peremptorily challenged 81% of black jurors); *United States v. McDaniels*, 379 F.Supp. 1243 (ED La., 1974) (in 53 criminal cases in 1972–1974 in Eastern District of Louisiana involving black defendants, federal prosecutors used 68.9% of their peremptory challenges against black jurors, who made up less than one quarter of the venire); *McKinney v. Walker*, 394 F.Supp. 1015 (SC, 1974) (in 13 criminal trials in 1970–1971 in Spartansburg County, South Carolina, involving black defendants, prosecutors peremptorily challenged 82% of black jurors). Prosecutors have explained to courts that they routinely strike black jurors, see *State v. Washington*, 375 So.2d 1162 (La.1979). An instruction book used by the prosecutor's office in Dallas County, Texas, explicitly advised prosecutors that they conduct jury selection so as to eliminate "any member of a minority group."[3] In 100 felony trials in Dallas County in 1983–1984, prosecutors peremptorily struck 405 out of 467 eligible black jurors; the chance of a qualified black sitting on a jury was one-in-ten, compared to one-in-two for a white. * * * *

CHIEF JUSTICE BURGER, joined by Justice Rehnquist, dissenting.

* * * *

The Court's opinion, in addition to ignoring the teachings of history, also contrasts with *Swain* in its failure to even discuss the rationale of the peremptory challenge. *Swain* observed:

---

discrimination against black jurors, for the trial court to discharge the venire and select a new jury from a panel not previously associated with the case, or to disallow the discriminatory challenges and resume selection with the improperly challenged jurors reinstated on the venire.

[25] To the extent that anything in *Swain v. Alabama* is contrary to the principles we articulate today, that decision is overruled.

[3] An earlier jury-selection treatise circulated in the same county instructed prosecutors: "Do not take Jews, Negroes, Dagos, Mexicans or a member of any minority race on a jury, no matter how rich or how well educated." Quoted in Dallas Morning News, March 9, 1986.

The function of the challenge is not only to eliminate extremes of partiality on both sides, but to assure the parties that the jurors before whom they try the case will decide on the basis of the evidence placed for them, and not otherwise. In this way the peremptory satisfies the rule that "to perform its high function in the best way, justice must satisfy the appearance of justice." [*Id.* at 219]

Permitting unexplained peremptories has long been regarded as a means to strengthen our jury system in other ways as well. One commentator has recognized:

The peremptory, made without giving any reason, avoids trafficking in the core of truth in most common stereotypes. Common human experience, common sense, psychosociological studies, and public opinion polls tell us that it is likely that certain classes of people statistically have predispositions that would make them inappropriate jurors for particular kinds of cases. But to allow this knowledge to be expressed in the evaluative terms necessary for challenges for cause would undercut our desire for a society in which all people are judged as individuals and in which each is held reasonable and open to compromise. For example, although experience reveals that black males as a class can be biased against young alienated blacks who have not tried to join the middle class, to enunciate this in the concrete expression required of a challenge for cause is societally divisive. Instead we have evolved in the peremptory challenge a system that allows the covert expression of what we dare not say but know is true more often than not. [Babcock, *Voir Dire: Preserving "Its Wonderful Power,"* 27 Stan.L.Rev. 545, 553–554 (1975)]

For reasons such as these, this Court concluded in *Swain* that "the peremptory challenge is one of the most important of the rights in our justice system." 380 U.S. at 219. * * * *

An example will quickly demonstrate how today's holding, while purporting to "further the ends of justice," will not have that effect. Assume an Asian defendant, on trial for the capital murder of a white victim, asks prospective jury members, most of whom are white, whether they harbor racial prejudice against Asians. The basis for such a question is to flush out any juror who believes that Asians are violence-prone or morally inferior. Assume further that all white jurors deny harboring racial prejudice but that the defendant, on trial for his life, remains unconvinced by these protestations. Instead, he continues to harbor a hunch, an "assumption" or "intuitive judgment," that these white jurors will be prejudiced against him, presumably based in part on race. The time honored rule before today was that peremptory challenges could be exercised on such a basis. The Court explained in *Lewis v. United States,*

How necessary it is that a prisoner (when put to defend his life) should have good opinion of his jury, the want of which might totally disconcert him; the law wills not that he should be tried by any one man against whom he has conceived a prejudice even without being able to assign a reason for such his dislike. [146 U.S. at 376]

The effect of the Court's decision, however, will be to force the defendant to come forward and "articulate a neutral explanation," for his peremptory challenge, a burden he probably cannot meet. This example demonstrates that today's holding will produce juries that the parties do not believe are truly impartial. This will surely do more than "disconcert" litigants; it will diminish confidence in the jury system.

A further painful paradox of the Court's holding is that it is likely to interject racial matters back into the jury selection process, contrary to the general thrust of a long line of Court decisions and the notion of our country as a "melting pot."

Today we mark the return of racial differentiation, as the Court accepts a positive evil for a perceived one. Prosecutors and defense attorney's alike will build records in support of their claims that peremptory challenges have been exercised in a racially discriminatory fashion by asking jurors to state their racial background and national origin for the record, despite the fact that "such questions may be offensive to some jurors and thus are not ordinarily asked on *voir dire.*" *People v. Motton*, 39 Cal.3d 596, 604 (1985). 10/ This process is sure to tax even the most capable counsel and judges since determining whether a prima facie case has been established will "require a continued monitoring and recording of the 'group' composition of the panel present and prospective." *People v. Wheeler*, 22 Cal.3d 258, 294 (1978) (Richardson, J., dissenting). * * * *

JUSTICE REHNQUIST, with whom The Chief Justice joins, dissenting.

* * * *

I cannot subscribe to the Court's unprecedented use of the Equal Protection Clause to restrict the historic scope of the peremptory challenge, which has been described as "a necessary part of trial by jury." *Swain*, 380 U.S. at 219. In my view, there is simply nothing "unequal" about the State using its peremptory challenges to strike blacks from the jury in cases involving black defendants, so long as such challenges are also used to exclude whites in cases involving white defendants, Hispanics in cases involving Hispanic defendants, Asians in cases involving Asian defendants, and so on. This case-specific use of peremptory challenges by the State does not single out blacks, or members of any other race for that matter, for discriminatory treatment. Such use of peremptories is at best based upon seat-of-the-pants instincts, which are undoubtedly crudely stereotypical and may in many cases be hopelessly mistaken. But as long as they are applied across the board to jurors of all races and nationalities, I do not see — and the Court most certainly has not explained — how their use violates the Equal Protection Clause.

Notes from Justin:

1. Is *Batson* consistent with *Peters v. Kiff*?

In *Peters v. Kiff*, the Court seemed to say that blacks are a "cognizable class" because they are *different* from other racial groups, in some unknown and unknowable ways. See footnote 12 of *Taylor v. Louisiana*. In *Batson*, however, the Court seems to say that a prosecutor may *not* assume that blacks are different, when exercising peremptory challenges. Are these two cases consistent with each other?

In Andrew Leipold, *Constitutionalizing Jury Selection In Criminal Cases: A Critical Evaluation*, 86 Georgetown L.J. 945, 963 (1998), the author states:

Although the cross-section doctrine is premised on the notion that different races and genders often view the world differently, *Batson* has declared these differences legally irrelevant. In the context of peremptory challenges, the *Batson* doctrine prohibits the use of stereotypes, hunches, or experiences based on race or gender, whether they are true or false. Stated differently, since *Batson*, the Court has turned away from its assumption that the demographics of the jury might influence the outcome of cases, and decided that the Constitution requires the colorblind and gender-blind selection of jurors, regardless of the impact on the verdict.

A defendant is thus placed in a strange position: he is entitled to a jury drawn from a fair cross section specifically because it increases the odds that different groups and perspectives will be represented in the jury pool, which in turn helps ensure that the panel is impartial; when actually seating a jury, however, he may not take those same characteristics into account. He may not base his peremptory strikes on the very same proxy for viewpoints that the Court has already used to justify the cross-section requirement, even if his efforts are designed to bring about the exact benefit that the cross-section requirement provides. An attempt to support the cross-section requirement on impartiality grounds thus runs headlong into the rule that race or gender may not be used as a substitute for inclinations, biases, or possible votes.

2. In Kenneth J. Melilli, *Batson in Practice: What We Have Learned About Batson & Peremptory Challenges*, 71 Notre Dame L.Rev. 447, 452 (1996), the author states:

Reliance upon stereotypes is a virtually inherent aspect of a system of peremptory challenges. Was the *Batson* Court suggesting that the stereotypical assumption of same-race sympathy for the defendant is factually invalid? Although the evidence supporting such an assumption is controversial and questionable, there is certainly some support for the proposition that jurors are more sympathetic to defendants of their same race. Moreover, if the "same-race-as-the-defendant" theory is false, then how is the black defendant harmed when the prosecutor uses peremptory challenges to remove black venirepersons? To the extent that *Batson* is motivated by a desire to insure that black defendants do not suffer the consequences of verdicts by juries with inadequate black representation, that concern makes no sense if the racial identity of the defendant and the jurors is immaterial to such verdicts. If *Batson* is motivated by a concern for the criminal defendant, the irony is that such concern is premised upon the very same racial stereotype which *Batson* pronounces to be unconstitutional in the context of the peremptory challenge.

3. In *Holland v. Illinois*, 493 U.S. 474 (1990), a white defendant raised a *6th Amendment* challenge to the prosecutor's use of peremptory challenges to intentionally exclude all black potential jurors from his jury. The Court held that while he had standing to make this claim, the claim failed on the merits.

The Sixth Amendment requirement of a fair cross section on the venire is a means of assuring, not a representative jury (which the Constitution does not demand), but an impartial one (which it does). Without that requirement, the State could draw up jury lists in such manner as to produce a pool of prospective jurors disproportionately ill disposed towards one or all classes of defendants, and thus more likely to yield petit juries with similar disposition. The State would have, in effect, unlimited peremptory challenges to compose the pool in its favor. The fair-cross-section venire requirement assures, in other words, that in the process of selecting the petit jury the prosecution and defense will compete on an equal basis.

But to say that the Sixth Amendment deprives the State of the ability to "stack the deck" in its favor is not to say that each side may not, once a fair hand is dealt, use peremptory challenges to eliminate prospective jurors belonging to groups it believes would unduly favor the other side. Any theory of the Sixth Amendment leading to that result is implausible. * * * *

The rule that we announce today is not the only plausible reading of the text of the Sixth Amendment, but we think it best furthers the Amendment's central purpose as well. Although the constitutional guarantee runs only to the individual and not to the State, the goal it expresses is jury impartiality with respect to both contestants: neither the defendant nor the State should be favored. This goal, it seems to us, would positively be obstructed by a petit jury cross-section requirement which, as we have described, would cripple the device of peremptory challenges.

JUSTICE STEVENS dissented:

The fair-cross-section requirement mandates the use of a neutral selection mechanism to generate a jury representative of the community. It does not dictate that any particular group or race have representatives on a jury. The Constitution does not permit the easy assumption that a community would be fairly represented by a jury selected by proportional representation of different races any more than it does that a community would be represented by a jury composed of quotas of jurors of different classes. In fact, while a racially balanced jury would be representative of the racial groups in a community, the focus on race would likely distort the jury's reflection of other groups in society, characterized by age, sex, ethnicity, religion, education level or economic

4. In *Powers v. Ohio*, 499 U.S. 400 (1991), the Court held that a white defendant has standing under the *Equal Protection* clause to object to a prosecutor's exercise of peremptory challenges to exclude blacks, even though race was not implicated in the crime or the trial. The Court began by noting the harm that racial discrimination in jury selection does to the excluded group and the community at large, because jury service allows ordinary citizens to participate in democratic government.[2]

---

[2] The Court quoted De Toqueville's observations of 150 years ago:

The institution of the jury raises the people itself, or at least a class of citizens, to the bench of judicial authority and invests the people, or that class of citizens, with the direction of society.

The jury invests each citizen with a kind of magistry; it makes them all feel the duties which they are bound to discharge towards society; and the part which they take in the Government. By obliging men to turn their attention to affairs which are not exclusively their own, it rubs off that individual egotism which is the rust of society.

I do not know whether the jury is useful to those who are in litigation; but I am certain it

However, normally one does not have standing to assert someone else's rights. (For example, a defendant has no standing to move to suppress evidence on the ground that the police obtained it by violating someone else's 4th Amendment rights.) But there is an exception where 3 criteria are met: (1) the litigant has a "concrete interest" in asserting the right, (2) the litigant has a "close relation" to the third party, and (3) there is "some hindrance to the third party's ability to protect his own interests." The Court held that all 3 are met here. Regarding the first, the defendant has a concrete interest in "the integrity of the judicial process", and may become cynical about the jury's neutrality if he perceives that it has been selected in an unfair manner. Regarding the second, "the excluded juror and the criminal defendant have a common interest in eliminating racial discrimination from the courtroom," as the juror might suffer humiliation and lose confidence in the justice system, and the defendant "has much at stake in proving that his jury was improperly constituted due to an equal protection violation, for we have recognized that discrimination in the jury selection process may lead to the reversal of a conviction." Regarding the third, the Court said:

> The barriers to a suit by an excluded juror are daunting. Potential jurors are not parties to the jury selection process and have no opportunity to be heard at the time of their exclusion. Nor can excluded jurors easily obtain declaratory or injunctive relief when discrimination occurs through an individual prosecutor's exercise of peremptory challenges. Unlike a challenge to systematic practices of the jury clerk and commissioners . . . , it would be difficult for an individual juror to show a likelihood that discrimination against him at the *voir dire* stage will recur. And, there exist considerable practical barriers to suit by the excluded juror because of the small financial stake involved and the economic burdens of litigation. The reality is that a juror dismissed because of race probably will leave the courtroom possessing little incentive to set in motion the arduous process needed to vindicate his own rights.

The Court also rejected the views expressed in the last paragraph of Justice Rehnquist's dissent in *Batson:*

> The suggestion that racial classifications may survive when visited upon all persons is no more authoritative today than the case which advanced the theorem, *Plessy v. Ferguson,* 163 U.S. 537 (1896). This idea has no place in our modern equal protection jurisprudence. It is axiomatic that racial classifications do not become legitimate on the assumption that all persons suffer them in equal degree.

Justice Scalia dissented, arguing that the first criterion was not met. "The Court must, of course, speak in terms of the perception of unfairness rather than its reality, since only last term [in *Holland v. Illinois*] we held categorically that the exclusion of members of a particular race from a jury does not produce an unfair jury, and suggested that in some circumstances it may increase fairness."

In *Campbell v. Louisiana,* 523 U.S. 392 (1998), following *Powers,* the Court held that a white defendant has standing under the Equal Protection Clause to object to racial discrimination against blacks in selection of the *grand* jury which indicted him. Justice Thomas dissented: "I fail to understand how the rights of blacks

---

is highly beneficial to those who decide the litigation; and I look upon it as one of the most efficacious means for the education of the people which society can employ.

excluded from jury service can be vindicated by letting a white murderer go free."

5. **Does** *Batson* **apply to** *defense counsel***?** Yes, held the Court in *Georgia v. McCollum*, 505 U.S. 42 (1992):

> Be it at the hands of the State or the defense, if a court allows jurors to be excluded because of group bias, it is a willing participant in a scheme that could only undermine the very foundation of our system of justice — our citizens' confidence in it. Just as public confidence in criminal justice is undermined by a conviction in a trial where racial discrimination has occurred in jury selection, so is public confidence undermined where a defendant, assisted by racially discriminatory peremptory strikes, obtains an acquittal.

The Court found the requisite "state action" in the fact that the defendant was assisting the state in performing a governmental function: the selection of a jury. Justice O'Connor dissented from "the remarkable conclusion that the criminal defendants being prosecuted by the State act on behalf of their adversary when they exercise peremptory challenges".

Justice Thomas concurred: "I am certain that black criminal defendants will rue the day that this court ventured down this road that inexorably will lead to the elimination of peremptory strikes. * * * * Today's decision, while protecting jurors, leaves defendants with less means of protecting themselves. Unless jurors actually admit prejudice during *voir dire*, defendants generally must allow them to sit and run the risk that racial animus will affect the verdict."

Perhaps his fears have begun to materialize. In *State v. Knox*, 609 So.2d 803 (La. 1992), a black defendant was charged with "obscenity involving a white female victim". The Louisiana Supreme Court read *McCollum* to bar the defendant from exercising peremptory challenges against white jurors because of their race.

The NAACP Legal Defense and Educational Fund filed an *amicus* brief in *McCollum* urging that defense counsel be allowed to base peremptories on race:

> The ability to use peremptory challenges to exclude majority race jurors may be crucial to empanelling a fair jury. In many cases an African American, or other minority defendant, may be faced with a jury array in which his racial group is underrepresented to some degree, but not sufficiently to permit challenge under the Fourteenth Amendment. The only possible chance the defendant may have of having any minority jurors on the jury that actually tries him will be if he uses his peremptories to strike members of the majority race. [See Abbe Smith, *"Nice Work If You Can Get It": "Ethical" Jury Selection In Criminal Defense*, 67 Fordham L.Rev. 523, 545 (1998).]

d. What Is a "Cognizable Group"?

1. **Italian-Americans?** No, held *U.S. v. Bucci*, 839 F.2d 825 (1st Cir.1988):

> Whether Italian-Americans comprise a group needing "protection" from "community prejudices" is a "question of fact." Ethnic and racial definitions . . . change over time. The important consideration for equal protection purposes is not whether a number of people *see themselves* as forming a separate group, but whether others, by treating those people unequally,

put them in a distinct group. Because appellants did not even attempt to show that Italians-Americans either have been or are currently subjected to discriminatory treatment, their claim fails to meet the initial requirement under *Batson* that the defendant show his or her membership in a "cognizable" group.

2. Irish-Americans? Not a "cognizable group," held *Murchu (aka Murphy) v. U.S.*, 926 F.2d 50 (1st Cir.1991):

> We note the complete absence of any allegations or evidence that Americans of Irish ancestry — even if otherwise a cognizable group — were being subject to unequal treatment by their fellow Americans at the time of Murphy's trial, and hence needed protection from community prejudices. (We are hard pressed to conceive of how such a showing could have been made in Massachusetts, where the Irish ancestry of people in all walks of life, including leadership positions, is a well known fact — to mention but a few, the Mayor of Boston, the Senate President, and both U.S. Senators.)

3. White people? Cognizable, held *Gilchrist v. State*, 340 Md. 606 (Md.Ct.App.1995) — even though whites were not historically oppressed:

> The Supreme Court's opinion in *J.E.B. v. Alabama ex rel. T.B.* confirms that the *Batson* principle is not limited to the exclusion from juries of historically oppressed minorities. In *J.E.B.*, the Court considered whether the *Batson* principle could be invoked by a male defendant in a paternity and child support action, where the State had utilized its peremptory challenges to exclude all male prospective jurors. The basis for the Court's decision to apply the *Batson* principle to gender-based peremptory challenges was the heightened scrutiny of gender classifications under the Fourteenth Amendment's Equal Protection Clause.
>
> Consequently, it is clear that blacks are not the only cognizable racial group to which *Batson* applies. *Batson* held that equal protection guarantees forbid the State in a criminal prosecution to use peremptory challenges to exclude potential jurors solely on account of their race or on the assumption that because of their race they will be unable to be impartial. This protection applies equally to white persons and black persons. A peremptory challenge based on race cannot be squared with equal protection principles. Thus, under both Article 24 of the Maryland Declaration of Rights and the Equal Protection Clause of the Fourteenth Amendment, peremptory challenges may not be exercised on the basis of race.

See also *State v. Knox*, 609 So.2d 803 (La.S.Ct.1992); *State v. West*, 866 S.W.2d 150 (Mo.Ct.App.1993).

4. "Hispanics"? A harder question.

Not a cognizable group, held the court in *U.S. v. Duran de Amesquita*, 582 F.Supp. 1326 (S.D. Fla., 1984):

> For "Hispanics" to constitute a cognizable class, it must be shown that there exists a cohesiveness of attitudes, ideas or experience which distinguishes the class from the general social milieu; that a community of identifiable interests is present amongst "hispanics" which is not shared by

other segments of the populace.

If the proposed class were "Cuban-Americans," or "Spanish-Americans," or "Puerto Rican-Americans," the mental image of the "cognizable class" would be easy to discern. Mexican-Americans, for example, were held to be a cognizable class in *United States v. Test*, 550 F.2d 577 (10th Cir.1976). But to lump persons from so many countries (even continents) together as a distinct class requires the exercise of considerable philosophical imagination. I do not believe that persons of Nicaraguan or Salvadoran heritage and persons of Cuban heritage could comfortably equate their cultural backgrounds and attitudes one to another. Persons of Puerto Rican heritage could not comfortably equate their backgrounds and attitudes to those persons of Mexican heritage.

If persons with "hispanic" surnames could be established as a cognizable class in the Miami district, and such has not been established in this case (on this score, one should note that the identified population would include an unaccounted-for number of non-"hispanic" women who have married and adopted the "hispanic" surnames of their spouses), it would remain to be shown that the proportion of "hispanics" in the total population of the Miami division eligible to serve as jurors is significantly greater than the proportion called to serve as jurors over a significant period of time.

The Court finds that the statistical evidence presented in Defendants' Exhibit 4, Analysis Set C, may be relied upon by the Court. The independent survey conducted on behalf of the defendants is a reliable survey. However, defendants necessarily seek to make the use of Spanish surnames the bedrock of their challenge. The foundation is too porous. Because the Court cannot appraise the validity of the jury selection system by considering that all persons of Spanish surnames have a community of interests not shared by other segments of the populace, the defendants are unable to make out a case for "hispanics" as a cognizable group. There are just too many Jose Gonzalezes, Cardozos, Felixes and Ferres whose attitudes and experiences do not coalesce with those of other Jose Gonzalezes, Cardozos, Felixes and Ferres to allow the Court to consider them all to be members of one cognizable class for the purposes here discussed.

It is quite clear that there is in the Miami area a large number of the various kinds of people who are often referred to as "hispanics." It is equally clear under the law that a court cannot act upon only an assumption of disproportionate representation. The factual support for the "hispanic" attack is insufficient to establish the threshhold requirement of a cognizable class under either Fifth or Sixth Amendment analysis.

But in *State v. Alen*, 616 So.2d 452 (1993), the Florida Supreme Court thought otherwise:

Like many ethnic groups, there are a variety of distinctive variables that divide the Hispanic community into subgroups, just as there are a variety of variables that divide other cognizable classes such as African Americans. Notwithstanding these distinctions among Hispanics, the size and the external and internal cohesiveness of this ethnic group qualify Hispanics as a cognizable class. * * * *

When an identifying trait is a physically visible characteristic such as race or gender, the process of defining a class is comparably less arduous than defining a class of people in the same ethnic group. Although such salient characteristics as a person's native language and surname may represent ethnic commonality, we do not believe that these types of characteristics, standing alone, sufficiently describe Hispanics as a cognizable class. For example, a person who is born in Cuba, becomes a citizen of the United States at a young age, and is raised with English as her primary language, is no less Hispanic simply because she speaks English more frequently and fluently than she speaks Spanish. In the same vein, a person named Mary Smith who is born in the United States is no more Hispanic simply because she marries and adopts the surname of a man with a traditionally Hispanic name. Although a person's native language and surname may be used by a trial judge in determining whether a potential juror can be classified as a Hispanic, those characteristics are not strictly dispositive. We join the California Supreme Court in recognizing that

> Many ties bind Hispanics together as a cognizable group within the community. Hispanics often share an ethnic and cultural "community of interest," including language, history, music, and religion. In addition, Hispanics have made notable achievements in the professions, the arts, industry and public life. On a more somber note, Hispanics, in relation to other Americans, share a host of harsh realities, such as relatively high unemployment, poverty, relative lack of educational opportunity and, of import to the present case, discrimination directed at them precisely because they are Hispanic. [*People v. Trevino*, 39 Cal.3d 667 (1985)].

5. Assume that "Hispanics" *are* a "cognizable class." How does a trial lawyer *show* that a particular prospective juror *is* "Hispanic"?

In *Mejia v. State*, 599 A.2d 1207 (Md.Ct.Sp.App.1992), the prosecutor challenged a juror named Peter Estrada, and Mejia's counsel claimed that Mejia and Mr. Estrada were Hispanic. Maryland's intermediate appellate court held that neither Mejia's nor Mr. Estrada's name were enough:

Who or What Is Hispanic?

> In the absence of any guidance from the Supreme Court, we shall accept, at least tentatively, the appellant's definition of "Hispanic."[3] Webster's New World Dictionary (3d Col.Ed.1988) defines the noun "Hispanic" as: "A usually Spanish-speaking person of Latin American origin who lives in the United States." In the Statistical Abstract of the United States, 1990, U.S. Dept. of Commerce, Bureau of the Census, at 17, the category "Hispanic" is listed as one of five categories of "resident population." The other four are 1) "white," 2) "black," 3) "American Indians and Alaska natives," and 4) "Asian and Pacific Islanders." It is, of course, the Latin American aspect of what the term gropes to describe that transformed the term "Hispanic" into a category at least partially connoting race — a term more or less contrasted with "white" or "black" — rather than an ethnic or national

---

[3] Etymologically, "Hispanic" comes from "Hispania," the Latin name for the Roman province which was coterminous with what is essentially modern-day Spain. "Iberia," a geographic term, referred to the entire peninsula lying south and west of the Pyrenees. It embraced both "Hispania" and "Lusitania," modern-day Portugal.

category such as "Gallic," "Teutonic," or "Slavic." In Latin America, a thin layer of Spanish language, Spanish religion, and Spanish culture was overlaid upon a predominantly Indian base.

It is apparently, therefore, not a term used to describe Spaniards from Spain, not a term that is somehow equivalent to "French," "Italian," or "Norwegian." The Statistical Abstract of the United States, 1990, goes on at pp. 4–5 to state that "Hispanic persons," in the Current Population Survey, "were persons who reported themselves as Mexican-American, Chicano, Mexican, Puerto Rican, Cuban, Central or South American (Spanish countries), or other Hispanic origin." "Spanish" appears to be a term contrasted with "Hispanic" rather than being a sub-set included within it.

It appears, therefore, that the salient characteristics one should possess for qualifying as an Hispanic are 1) having Spanish as one's native language, 2) having a Spanish surname, and 3) being of Latin American origin. With this candidly amorphous and imprecise definition, we turn to the players in the jury selection process now under our scrutiny.

Was the Appellant, Ivan Antonio Mejia, Shown to be Hispanic?

It was clear that the appellant was a Spanish-language speaker who needed the benefit of an interpreter. We will assume that "Mejia" is a Spanish surname. (The Christian name "Ivan" might raise some eyebrows). These two characteristics do not alone establish, however, that one is necessarily an Hispanic. The majority of 39 million Spaniards have Spanish as their native language and have Spanish surnames and yet are apparently not Hispanic. So do a significant percentage of 58 million Filipinos, who are clearly not Hispanic. If Imelda Marcos and Corazon Aquino do not qualify as Hispanics, neither their native language nor their surnames would prove it.

If the appellant is, indeed, Hispanic, it would have been very easy for appellant's counsel to have established that fact. The burden of establishing it, however, is squarely upon the appellant and a part of that burden is the making of an adequate record. * * * * In terms of Hispanic status, how may we be reassured that the appellant was not actually from Barcelona instead of Mexicali? Or from Manila? And whose job was it to tell us?

Any failure to show that the appellant was Hispanic, however, would not be fatal to the appellant's cause. It is now clear that one does not have to be Hispanic to raise a *Batson* challenge to the striking of Hispanic jurors. *Powers v. Ohio*, 499 U.S. 400 (1991).

Was the Juror, Peter Estrada, Shown to be Hispanic?

The Hispanic credentials of the peremptorily challenged Peter Estrada are far less substantial than even those of the appellant. When Judge Hyatt asked the jurors whether any of them understood Spanish, none, including Estrada, responded affirmatively. The only evidence was that Estrada did not speak Spanish. Appellant's counsel nonetheless boldly proclaimed him to be Hispanic — on the basis of nothing but his surname. Appellant's counsel offered neither evidence nor casual observation in support of this assertion. Nor did he proffer any basis for his own expertise in such matters.

Even accepting, arguendo, that "Estrada" is a Spanish surname, Spanish surnames are enjoyed not only by Latin Americans but also by the vast majority of 39 million Spaniards, who are apparently not Hispanic, as well as by a significant percentage of 58 million Filipinos, who are definitely not Hispanic. Spanish surnames, furthermore, are enjoyed both by the vast majority of 10 million Portuguese, who are not Hispanic, and by 143 million Brazilians, who are also not Hispanic. In terms of Estrada's suspect status as a non-Hispanic, not only has the appellant failed to allay our fears that Estrada (or his father or his grandfather) might originally have hailed from Barcelona or from Manila, there are additional unallayed fears that he (or they) might have hailed from Lisbon or from Rio de Janeiro.

A Spanish surname alone is not simply a slender reed, it is an inadequate reed to support Hispanic status. If the President of Peru, Alberto Fujiwara — Peruvian born, Spanish-speaking but of Japanese ancestry — is, indeed, Hispanic, his surname will not prove it. If, on the other hand, Benjamin Nathan Cardozo, Benjamin Disraeli, and Baruch Spinoza were non-Hispanic, their surnames will not prove it. Appellant's counsel's bold assertion that Peter Estrada is Hispanic is nothing more than bold assertion. There was no adequate establishment of this as a fact.

Was the Rest of the Jury Panel Shown to be Non-Hispanic?

Once again, appellant's counsel boldly and broadly proclaims that except for Peter Estrada, the rest of the jury panel was non-Hispanic. His goal was to show that the State had struck the only Hispanic juror available to try the Hispanic appellant. Except for counsel's self-serving ipse dixit in this regard, however, there was no basis for such a conclusion with respect to the rest of the panel. From the jurors, including alternates, who were accepted or challenged, we can comb the record and come up with the surnames of 28 members of the 50-person panel. With respect to the other 22, however, there is nothing in the record to give us even the surnames, let alone any information beyond the names. For all we know, they may all have had Spanish surnames. Again, the burden of making a record was upon the appellant.

With respect to the 28 jurors whose surnames we can discover, moreover, that knowledge alone tells us little. Presumably, half of the jurors were women. How do we know that they were not all born Hispanic but are now using the names of their non-Hispanic husbands? Did Rita Cansini, for instance, cease to be Hispanic on the day she assumed the name "Rita Hayworth?" Did Lucille Ball, on the other hand, become Hispanic whenever she traveled as "Mrs. Desi Arnaz?"

In combing the record, moreover, we note that one of the jurors peremptorily struck by the appellant was Jean Porto. If "Porto" is not an Hispanic surname and it may not be, we are still not sure why we should so conclude.

Particularly in the melting pot of the United States and particularly when looking at second and third generation Americans, the foolishness of basing ethnic assumptions on surnames alone is self-evident. Posit the case of two Irish-American twins, Robert and Mary Martin, growing up as the next-door neighbors of two Mexican-American twins, Roberto and Maria Martinez. If Robert Martin marries Maria Martinez and his sister Mary Martin marries Roberto Martinez, are the Martinez children Hispanic and the ethnically indistinguishable Martin children non-Hispanic? On the day of their mutual wedding, did Mary Martin and Maria Martinez pass the mantilla, with Mary Martin Martinez becoming Hispanic even as Maria Martinez Martin became non-Hispanic? Or were they both thenceforth Hispanic? And what shall happen in terms of future ethnic status when their daughters move away to Minnesota to marry Swedish lumberjacks?

How many times may the "bloodline" be diluted before ethnic status evaporates? Or does ethnic status simply follow the male surname ad infinitum? There is something terribly arbitrary and imprecise about all of this; yet this is exactly the sort of unsubstantiated labeling the appellant sought to pawn off upon the court.

Unless tightly restrained, *Batson* could easily degenerate into an ethnic parlor game. While it may be an interesting diversion for the parlor, it is not, when breezily invoked, a sound basis for reversing judicial judgments. This is why procedural discipline must be maintained to make certain that the elaborate responses of *Batson* are not a knee-jerk reaction every time a charge of discrimination is laid.

But Maryland's highest court reversed this decision. *Mejia v. State*, 616 A.2d 356 (Md.Ct.App.1992). The court noted that, at trial, the prosecutor had not objected to defense counsel's claim that both Mejia and Estrada were Hispanic:

Because that issue has already been dispositively resolved, see *Hernandez v. N.Y.*, 500 U.S. 352 (1991), we are not concerned, in this case, with whether "Hispanics" is a cognizable group. Our concern is, rather, whether the petitioner presented a prima facie case that either he or Mr. Estrada, or both, is "Hispanic."

At no time, from the first mention of an "Hispanic problem" to the denial of the petitioner's objection to the State's striking of Mr. Estrada did the prosecutor make any comment, or observation contradicting the petitioner's express proffer. In fact, the *voir dire* proceedings, viewed as a whole, supports the petitioner's argument that the parties, and the trial judge, agreed that there was an "Hispanic problem." Just as what the prosecutor may say or ask during *voir dire* may be relevant, in the totality of the circumstances, to determining the prosecutor's motive in exercising peremptories, what the prosecutor does not say in the face of an assertion of fact is quite important on the question of the adequacy of the petitioner's *Batson* showing.

Accepting the State's position would mandate, whenever purposeful discrimination against a cognizable group is alleged, that a full-fledged adversary hearing be held to determine who is, or is not, a member of that cognizable racial group. That issue would have to be tried even though there is no apparent dispute as to a venireperson's membership in the cognizable group at issue. Lest it be said that he or she failed to make the requisite prima facie showing, the moving party would have to produce evidence to prove the composition of the venire and the race of each venireperson even when a person's membership in the cognizable racial group at issue, being dependent largely on visual observations, is more or less obvious. The trial process could become quite unwieldy.

The State's position also does not take account of the role that perception plays in the use of peremptories. It is the striking party's belief that a venireperson is a member of the cognizable group, not the proof of that fact, that prompts that party peremptorily to challenge that venireperson. The moving party's proffer tests that perception. When the striking party, in effect, accepts a proffer that an individual is a member of a cognizable group, against which it is alleged that peremptories are being used discriminatorily, he or she should be bound by it. * * * *

We conclude that, where, as here, neither the State nor the court expressed any disagreement with the petitioner's proffer of the preliminary fact that a venireperson was the only Hispanic in the venire, a prima facie showing of that fact was made. We also hold that, where the record reveals that but one person with an Hispanic background was in the venire and the State struck that person, it may be concluded that a prima facie case of purposeful discrimination has been proven.

The court concluded, however, that the prosecutor had not been given an adequate chance to give a "race neutral reason" as to why he had challenged Mr. Estrada, so the court remanded the case to the trial court to resolve that issue.

See also Lisette Simon, *Hispanics: Not A Cognizable Ethnic Group*, 63 U.Cin.L.Rev. 497 (1994).

6. In *Bridges v. State*, 695 A.2d 609 (Md.App. 1997), the court held that " *Batson* does not cover an age classification."

While the treatment of the aged in this Nation has not been wholly free of discrimination, such persons, unlike, say, those who have been discriminated on the basis of race or national origin, have not experienced a "history of purposeful unequal treatment" or been subjected to unique disabilities on the basis of stereotyped characteristics not truly indicative of their abilities.

Question: Does the next case cast any doubt on this reasoning?

J.E.B. v. ALABAMA
United States Supreme Court
511 U.S. 127 (1994)

JUSTICE BLACKMUN delivered the opinion of the Court.

In *Batson v. Kentucky*, 476 U. S. 79 (1986), this Court held that the Equal Protection Clause of the Fourteenth Amendment governs the exercise of peremptory challenges by a prosecutor in a criminal trial. The Court explained that although a defendant has "no right to a petit jury composed in whole or in part of persons of his own race," the "defendant does have the right to be tried by a jury whose members are selected pursuant to nondiscriminatory criteria." Since *Batson*, we have reaffirmed repeatedly our commitment to jury selection procedures that are fair and nondiscriminatory. We have recognized that whether the trial is criminal or civil, potential jurors, as well as litigants, have an equal protection right to jury selection procedures that are free from state-sponsored group stereotypes rooted in, and reflective of, historical prejudice. See *Powers v. Ohio*, 499 U. S. 400 (1991); *Edmonson v. Leesville Concrete Co.*, 500 U. S. 614 (1991); *Georgia v. McCollum*, 505 U. S. 42 (1992).

Although premised on equal protection principles that apply equally to gender discrimination, all our recent cases defining the scope of *Batson* involved alleged racial discrimination in the exercise of peremptory challenges. Today we are faced with the question whether the Equal Protection Clause forbids intentional discrimination on the basis of gender, just as it prohibits discrimination on the basis of race. We hold that gender, like race, is an unconstitutional proxy for juror competence and impartiality.

I

On behalf of relator T.B., the mother of a minor child, respondent State of Alabama filed a complaint for paternity and child support against petitioner J.E.B. in the District Court of Jackson County, Alabama. On October 21, 1991, the matter was called for trial and jury selection began. The trial court assembled a panel of 36 potential jurors, 12 males and 24 females. After the court excused three jurors for cause, only 10 of the remaining 33 jurors were male. The State then used 9 of its 10 peremptory strikes to remove male jurors; petitioner used all but one of his strikes to remove female jurors. As a result, all the selected jurors were female.

Before the jury was empaneled, petitioner objected to the State's peremptory challenges on the ground that they were exercised against male jurors solely on the basis of gender, in violation of the Equal Protection Clause of the Fourteenth Amendment. Petitioner argued that the logic and reasoning of *Batson* which prohibits peremptory strikes solely on the basis of race, similarly forbids intentional discrimination on the basis of gender. The court rejected petitioner's claim and empaneled the all-female jury. The jury found petitioner to be the father of the child and the court entered an order directing him to pay child support. On post-judgment motion, the court reaffirmed its ruling that *Batson* does not extend to gender-based peremptory challenges.

II

Discrimination on the basis of gender in the exercise of peremptory challenges is a relatively recent phenomenon. Gender-based peremptory strikes were hardly practicable for most of our country's existence, since, until the 19th century, women were completely excluded from jury service. So well-entrenched was this exclusion of women that in 1880 this Court, while finding that the exclusion of African-American men from juries violated the Fourteenth Amendment, expressed no doubt that a State "may confine the selection of jurors to males." *Strauder v. West Virginia*, 100 U. S. 303, 310.

Many States continued to exclude women from jury service well into the present century, despite the fact that women attained suffrage upon ratification of the Nineteenth Amendment in 1920. States that did permit women to serve on juries often erected other barriers, such as registration requirements and automatic exemptions, designed to deter women from exercising their right to jury service.

The prohibition of women on juries was derived from the English common law which, according to Blackstone, rightfully excluded women from juries under "the doctrine of *propter defectum sexus*, literally, the 'defect of sex.' " *United States v. DeGross*, 960 F. 2d 1433, 1438 (CA9 1992), quoting 2 W. Blackstone, Commentaries.[4] In this country, supporters of the exclusion of women from juries tended to couch their objections in terms of the ostensible need to protect women from the ugliness and depravity of trials. Women were thought to be too fragile and virginal to withstand the polluted courtroom atmosphere. See *Bailey v. State,*215 Ark. 53, 61 (1949) ("Criminal court trials often involve testimony of the foulest kind, and they sometimes require consideration of indecent conduct, the use of filthy and loathsome words, references to intimate sex relationships, and other elements that would prove humiliating, embarrassing and degrading to a lady"); *In re Goodell*, 39 Wis. 232, 245–246 (1875) (endorsing statutory ineligibility of women for admission to the bar because "reverence for all womanhood would suffer in the public spectacle of women so engaged"); *Bradwell v. State*, 16 Wall. 130, 141 (1872) ("The civil law, as well as nature herself, has always recognized a wide difference in the respective spheres and destinies of man and woman. Man is, or should be, woman's protector and defender. The natural and proper timidity and delicacy which belongs to the female sex evidently unfits it for many of the occupations of the paramount destiny and mission of woman are to fulfill the noble and benign offices of wife and mother. This is the law of the Creator"). *Cf. Frontiero v. Richardson*, 411 U. S. 677, 684 (1973) (This "attitude of 'romantic paternalism' put women, not on a pedestal, but in a cage"). * * * *

In *Taylor v. Louisiana*, 419 U. S. 522 (1975), we explained: "Restricting jury service to only special groups or excluding identifiable segments playing major roles in the community cannot be squared with the constitutional concept of jury trial." The diverse and representative character of the jury must be maintained "partly as assurance of a diffused impartiality and partly because sharing in the administration of justice is a phase of civic responsibility." *Id.* at 530–531.

III

Taylor relied on Sixth Amendment principles, but the opinion's approach is consistent with the heightened equal protection scrutiny afforded gender-based classifications. Since *Reed v. Reed*, 404 U. S. 71 (1971), this Court consistently has subjected gender-based classifications to heightened scrutiny in recognition of the real danger that government policies that professedly are based on reasonable considerations in fact may be reflective of "archaic and overbroad" generalizations about gender, or based on "outdated misconceptions concerning the role of females in the home rather than in the 'marketplace and world of ideas.' " *Craig v. Boren*, 429 U. S. 190, 198–199 (1976).

---

[4] In England there was at least one deviation from the general rule that only males could serve as jurors. If a woman was subject to capital punishment, or if a widow sought postponement of the disposition of her husband's estate until birth of a child, a writ *de ventre inspiciendo* permitted the use of a jury of matrons to examine the woman to determine whether she was pregnant. But even when a jury of matrons was used, the examination took place in the presence of 12 men, who also composed part of the jury in such cases. The jury of matrons was used in the United States during the Colonial period, but apparently fell into disuse when the medical profession began to perform that function.

Despite the heightened scrutiny afforded distinctions based on gender, respondent argues that gender discrimination in the selection of the petit jury should be permitted, though discrimination on the basis of race is not. Respondent suggests that "gender discrimination in this country has never reached the level of discrimination" against African-Americans, and therefore gender discrimination, unlike racial discrimination, is tolerable in the courtroom.

While the prejudicial attitudes toward women in this country have not been identical to those held toward racial minorities, the similarities between the experiences of racial minorities and women, in some contexts, "overpower those differences." As a plurality of this Court observed in *Frontiero v. Richardson*, 411 U.S. 677, 685 (1973): "Throughout much of the 19th century the position of women in our society was, in many respects, comparable to that of blacks under the pre-Civil War slave codes. Neither slaves nor women could hold office, serve on juries, or bring suit in their own names, and married women traditionally were denied the legal capacity to hold or convey property or to serve as legal guardians of their own children. And although blacks were guaranteed the right to vote in 1870, women were denied even that right — which is itself 'preservative of other basic civil and political rights' — until adoption of the Nineteenth Amendment half a century later." Certainly, with respect to jury service, African-Americans and women share a history of total exclusion, a history which came to an end for women many years after the embarrassing chapter in our history came to an end for African-Americans.

We need not determine, however, whether women or racial minorities have suffered more at the hands of discriminatory state actors during the decades of our Nation's history. It is necessary only to acknowledge that "our Nation has had a long and unfortunate history of sex discrimination," *id.* at 684, a history which warrants the heightened scrutiny we afford all gender-based classifications today. Under our equal protection jurisprudence, gender-based classifications require "an exceedingly persuasive justification" in order to survive constitutional scrutiny. Thus, the only question is whether discrimination on the basis of gender in jury selection substantially furthers the State's legitimate interest in achieving a fair and impartial trial.[6] In making this assessment, we do not weigh the value of peremptory challenges as an institution against our asserted commitment to eradicate invidious discrimination from the courtroom.[7] Instead, we consider whether peremptory challenges based on gender stereotypes provide substantial aid to a litigant's effort to secure a fair and impartial jury.[8]

---

[6] Because we conclude that gender-based peremptory challenges are not substantially related to an important government objective, we once again need not decide whether classifications based on gender are inherently suspect.

[7] Although peremptory challenges are valuable tools in jury trials, they "are not constitutionally protected fundamental rights; rather they are but one state-created means to the constitutional end of an impartial jury and a fair trial." *Georgia v. McCollum*, 505 U. S. 42 (1992).

[8] Respondent argues that we should recognize a special state interest in this case: the State's interest in establishing the paternity of a child born out of wedlock. Respondent contends that this interest justifies the use of gender-based peremptory challenges, since illegitimate children are themselves victims of historical discrimination and entitled to heightened scrutiny under the Equal Protection Clause. What respondent fails to recognize is that the only legitimate interest it could possibly have in the exercise of its peremptory challenges is securing a fair and impartial jury. This interest does not change with the parties or the causes. The State's interest in every trial is to see that the proceedings are carried out in a fair, impartial, and nondiscriminatory manner.

Far from proffering an exceptionally persuasive justification for its gender-based peremptory challenges, respondent maintains that its decision to strike virtually all the males from the jury in this case "may reasonably have been based upon the perception, supported by history, that men otherwise totally qualified to serve upon a jury might be more sympathetic and receptive to the arguments of a man alleged in a paternity action to be the father of an out-of-wedlock child, while women equally qualified to serve upon a jury might be more sympathetic and receptive to the arguments of the complaining witness who bore the child."[9]

We shall not accept as a defense to gender-based peremptory challenges "the very stereotype the law condemns." *Powers v. Ohio*, 499 U. S. 400, 410 (1991). Respondent's rationale, not unlike those regularly expressed for gender-based strikes, is reminiscent of the arguments advanced to justify the total exclusion of women from juries.[10] Respondent offers virtually no support for the conclusion that gender alone is an accurate predictor of juror's attitudes; yet it urges this Court to condone the same stereotypes that justified the wholesale exclusion of women from juries and the ballot box.[11] Respondent seems to assume that gross generalizations that would be deemed impermissible if made on the basis of race are somehow permissible when made on the basis of gender.

---

[9] Respondent cites one study in support of its quasi-empirical claim that women and men may have different attitudes about certain issues justifying the use of gender as a proxy for bias. See R. Hastie, S. Penrod & N. Pennington, *Inside the Jury* 140 (1983). The authors conclude: "Neither student nor citizen judgments for typical criminal case material have revealed differences between male and female verdict preferences. The picture differs only for rape cases, where female jurors appear to be somewhat more conviction-prone than male jurors". The majority of studies suggest that gender plays no identifiable role in jurors' attitudes. See, e.g., V. Hans & N. Vidmar, *Judging the Jury* 76 (1986) ("In the majority of studies there are no significant differences in the way men and women perceive and react to trials; yet a few studies find women more defense-oriented, while still others show women more favorable to the prosecutor"). Even in 1956, before women had a constitutional right to serve on juries, some commentators warned against using gender as a proxy for bias. See 1 F. Busch, *Law and Tactics in Jury Trials* § 143 (1949) ("In this age of general and specialized education, availed of generally by both men and women, it would appear unsound to base a peremptory challenge in any case upon the sole ground of sex.").

[10] A manual formerly used to instruct prosecutors in Dallas, Texas, provided the following advice: "I don't like women jurors because I can't trust them. They do, however, make the best jurors in cases involving crimes against children. It is possible that their 'women's intuition' can help you if you can't win your case with the facts." Alschuler, *The Supreme Court and the Jury: Voir Dire, Peremptory Challenges, and the Review of Jury Verdicts*, 56 U. Chi. L. Rev. 153, 210 (1989). Another widely circulated trial manual speculated: "If counsel is depending upon a clearly applicable rule of law and if he wants to avoid a verdict of 'intuition' or 'sympathy,' if his verdict in amount is to be proved by clearly demonstrated blackboard figures for example, generally he would want a male juror. But women are desired jurors when the plaintiff is a man. A woman juror may see a man impeached from the beginning of the case to the end, but there is at least the chance with the woman juror (particularly if the man happens to be handsome or appealing) that the plaintiff's derelictions in and out of court will be overlooked. A woman is inclined to forgive sin in the opposite sex; but definitely not her own." 3 M. Belli, *Modern Trials* §§ 51.67 and 51.68 (2d ed. 1982).

[11] Even if a measure of truth can be found in some of the gender stereotypes used to justify gender-based peremptory challenges, that fact alone cannot support discrimination on the basis of gender in jury selection. We have made abundantly clear in past cases that gender classifications that rest on impermissible stereotypes violate the Equal Protection Clause, even when some statistical support can be conjured up for the generalization. The Equal Protection Clause, as interpreted by decisions of this Court, acknowledges that a shred of truth may be contained in some stereotypes, but requires that state actors look beyond the surface before making judgments about people that are likely to stigmatize as well as to perpetuate historical patterns of discrimination.

Discrimination in jury selection, whether based on race or on gender, causes harm to the litigants, the community, and the individual jurors who are wrongfully excluded from participation in the judicial process. The litigants are harmed by the risk that the prejudice which motivated the discriminatory selection of the jury will infect the entire proceedings. The community is harmed by the State's participation in the perpetuation of invidious group stereotypes and the inevitable loss of confidence in our judicial system that state-sanctioned discrimination in the courtroom engenders.

When state actors exercise peremptory challenges in reliance on gender stereotypes, they ratify and reinforce prejudicial views of the relative abilities of men and women. Because these stereotypes have wreaked injustice in so many other spheres of our country's public life, active discrimination by litigants on the basis of gender during jury selection "invites cynicism respecting the jury's neutrality and its obligation to adhere to the law." *Powers v. Ohio*, 499 U. S. at 412. The potential for cynicism is particularly acute in cases where gender-related issues are prominent, such as cases involving rape, sexual harassment, or paternity. Discriminatory use of peremptory challenges may create the impression that the judicial system has acquiesced in suppressing full participation by one gender or that the "deck has been stacked" in favor of one side.

In recent cases we have emphasized that individual jurors themselves have a right to nondiscriminatory jury selection procedures. Contrary to respondent's suggestion, this right extends to both men and women. *Cf.* Brief for Respondent 9 (arguing that men deserve no protection from gender discrimination in jury selection because they are not victims of historical discrimination). All persons, when granted the opportunity to serve on a jury, have the right not to be excluded summarily because of discriminatory and stereotypical presumptions that reflect and reinforce patterns of historical discrimination.[13] Striking individual jurors on the assumption that they hold particular views simply because of their gender is "practically a brand upon them, affixed by law, an assertion of their inferiority." *Strauder v. West Virginia*, 100 U. S. 303, 308 (1880). It denigrates the dignity of the excluded juror, and, for a woman, reinvokes a history of exclusion from political participation.[14] The message it sends to all those in the courtroom, and all those who may later learn of the discriminatory act, is that certain individuals, for no reason other than gender, are presumed unqualified by state actors to decide important questions upon which reasonable persons could disagree.

---

[13] It is irrelevant that women, unlike African-Americans, are not a numerical minority and therefore are likely to remain on the jury if each side uses its peremptory challenges in an equally discriminatory fashion. Because the right to nondiscriminatory jury selection procedures belongs to the potential jurors, as well as to the litigants, the possibility that members of both genders will get on the jury despite the intentional discrimination is beside the point. The exclusion of even one juror for impermissible reasons harms that juror and undermines public confidence in the fairness of the system.

[14] The popular refrain is that *all* peremptory challenges are based on stereotypes of some kind, expressing various intuitive and frequently erroneous biases. But where peremptory challenges are made on the basis of group characteristics other than race or gender (like occupation, for example), they do not reinforce the same stereotypes about the group's competence or predispositions that have been used to prevent them from voting, participating on juries, pursuing their chosen professions, or otherwise contributing to civic life.

IV

Our conclusion that litigants may not strike potential jurors solely on the basis of gender does not imply the elimination of all peremptory challenges. Neither does it conflict with a State's legitimate interest in using such challenges in its effort to secure a fair and impartial jury. Parties still may remove jurors whom they feel might be less acceptable than others on the panel; gender simply may not serve as a proxy for bias. Parties may also exercise their peremptory challenges to remove from the venire any group or class of individuals normally subject to "rational basis" review. Even strikes based on characteristics that are disproportionately associated with one gender could be appropriate, absent a showing of pretext.[16]

If conducted properly, *voir dire* can inform litigants about potential jurors, making reliance upon stereotypical and pejorative notions about a particular gender or race both unnecessary and unwise. *Voir dire* provides a means of discovering actual or implied bias and a firmer basis upon which the parties may exercise their peremptory challenges intelligently.

The experience in the many jurisdictions that have barred gender-based challenges belies the claim that litigants and trial courts are incapable of complying with a rule barring strikes based on gender. As with race-based *Batson* claims, a party alleging gender discrimination must make a prima facie showing of intentional discrimination before the party exercising the challenge is required to explain the basis for the strike. When an explanation is required, it need not rise to the level of a "for cause" challenge; rather, it merely must be based on a juror characteristic other than gender, and the proffered explanation may not be pretextual.

Failing to provide jurors the same protection against gender discrimination as race discrimination could frustrate the purpose of *Batson* itself. Because gender and race are overlapping categories, gender can be used as a pretext for racial discrimination. Allowing parties to remove racial minorities from the jury not because of their race, but because of their gender, contravenes well-established equal protection principles and could insulate effectively racial discrimination from judicial scrutiny.

V

Equal opportunity to participate in the fair administration of justice is fundamental to our democratic system. It not only furthers the goals of the jury system. It reaffirms the promise of equality under the law — that all citizens, regardless of race, ethnicity, or gender, have the chance to take part directly in our democracy. When persons are excluded from participation in our democratic processes solely because of race or gender, this promise of equality dims, and the integrity of our judicial system is jeopardized.

In view of these concerns, the Equal Protection Clause prohibits discrimination in jury selection on the basis of gender, or on the assumption that an individual will be biased in a particular case for no reason other than the fact that the person happens to be a woman or happens to be a man. As with race, the "core guarantee

---

[16] For example, challenging all persons who have had military experience would disproportionately affect men at this time, while challenging all persons employed as nurses would disproportionately affect women. Without a showing of pretext, however, these challenges may well not be unconstitutional, since they are not gender- or race-based.

of equal protection, ensuring citizens that their State will not discriminate, would be meaningless were we to approve the exclusion of jurors on the basis of such assumptions, which arise solely from the jurors' gender." *Batson*, 476 U. S. at 97–98.

The judgment of the Court of Civil Appeals of Alabama is reversed and the case is remanded to that court for further proceedings not inconsistent with this opinion.

JUSTICE O'CONNOR, concurring.

I agree with the Court that the Equal Protection Clause prohibits the government from excluding a person from jury service on account of that person's gender. The State's proffered justifications for its gender-based peremptory challenges are far from the "exceedingly persuasive" showing required to sustain a gender-based classification. I therefore join the Court's opinion in this case. But today's important blow against gender discrimination is not costless. I write separately to discuss some of these costs, and to express my belief that today's holding should be limited to the government's use of gender-based peremptory strikes.

Batson itself was a significant intrusion into the jury selection process. *Batson* mini-hearings are now routine in state and federal trial courts, and *Batson* appeals have proliferated as well. Demographics indicate that today's holding may have an even greater impact than did *Batson* itself. In further constitutionalizing jury selection procedures, the Court increases the number of cases in which jury selection — once a sideshow — will become part of the main event.

For this same reason, today's decision further erodes the role of the peremptory challenge. The peremptory challenge is a practice of ancient origin and is part of our common law heritage. The principal value of the peremptory is that it helps produce fair and impartial juries. "Peremptory challenges, by enabling each side to exclude those jurors it believes will be most partial toward the other side, are a means of eliminating extremes of partiality on both sides, thereby assuring the selection of a qualified and unbiased jury." *Holland v. Illinois*, 493 U. S. 474, 484 (1990). The peremptory's importance is confirmed by its persistence: it was well established at the time of Blackstone and continues to endure in all the States.

Moreover, "the essential nature of the peremptory challenge is that it is one exercised without a reason stated, without inquiry and without being subject to the court's control." *Swain v Alabama*, 380 U. S. at 220. Indeed, often a reason for it cannot be stated, for a trial lawyer's judgments about a juror's sympathies are sometimes based on experienced hunches and educated guesses, derived from a juror's responses at *voir dire* or a juror's "bare looks and gestures." *Ibid*. That a trial lawyer's instinctive assessment of a juror's predisposition cannot meet the high standards of a challenge for cause does not mean that the lawyer's instinct is erroneous. Our belief that experienced lawyers will often correctly intuit which jurors are likely to be the least sympathetic, and our understanding that the lawyer will often be unable to explain the intuition, are the very reason we cherish the peremptory challenge. But, as we add, layer by layer, additional constitutional restraints on the use of the peremptory, we force lawyers to articulate what we know is often inarticulable.

In so doing we make the peremptory challenge less discretionary and more like a challenge for cause. We also increase the possibility that biased jurors will be allowed onto the jury, because sometimes a lawyer will be unable to provide an acceptable gender-neutral explanation even though the lawyer is in fact correct that the juror is unsympathetic. Similarly, in jurisdictions where lawyers exercise their strikes in open court, lawyers may be deterred from using their peremptories, out of the fear that if they are unable to justify the strike the court will seat a juror who knows that the striking party thought him unfit. Because I believe the peremptory remains an important litigator's tool and a fundamental part of the process of selecting impartial juries, our increasing limitation of it gives me pause.

Nor is the value of the peremptory challenge to the litigant diminished when the peremptory is exercised in a gender-based manner. We know that like race, gender matters. A plethora of studies make clear that in rape cases, for example, female jurors are somewhat more likely to vote to convict than male jurors. See R. Hastie, S. Penrod, & N. Pennington, *Inside the Jury*, 140–141 (1983) (collecting and summarizing empirical studies). Moreover, though there have been no similarly definitive studies regarding, for example, sexual harassment, child custody, or spousal or child abuse, one need not be a sexist to share the intuition that in certain cases a person's gender and resulting life experience will be relevant to his or her view of the case. "Jurors are not expected to come into the jury box and leave behind all that their human experience has taught them." *Beck v. Alabama*, 447 U. S. 625, 642 (1980). Individuals are not expected to ignore as jurors what they know as men — or women.

Today's decision severely limits a litigant's ability to act on this intuition, for the import of our holding is that any correlation between a juror's gender and attitudes is irrelevant as a matter of constitutional law. But to say that gender makes no difference as a matter of law is not to say that gender makes no difference as a matter of fact. I previously have said with regard to *Batson*: "That the Court will not tolerate prosecutors' racially discriminatory use of the peremptory challenge, in effect, is a special rule of relevance, a statement about what this Nation stands for, rather than a statement of fact." [Citation] Today's decision is a statement that, in an effort to eliminate the potential discriminatory use of the peremptory, gender is now governed by the special rule of relevance formerly reserved for race. Though we gain much from this statement, we cannot ignore what we lose. In extending *Batson* to gender we have added an additional burden to the state and federal trial process, taken a step closer to eliminating the peremptory challenge, and diminished the ability of litigants to act on sometimes accurate gender-based assumptions about juror attitudes.

These concerns reinforce my conviction that today's decision should be limited to a prohibition on the government's use of gender-based peremptory challenges. The Equal Protection Clause prohibits only discrimination by state actors. In *Edmonson*, we made the mistake of concluding that private civil litigants were state actors when they exercised peremptory challenges; in *Georgia v. McCollum*, 505 U. S. ___ (1992), we compounded the mistake by holding that criminal defendants were also state actors. Our commitment to eliminating discrimination from the legal process should not allow us to forget that not all that occurs in the courtroom is state action. Private civil litigants are just that — private litigants. The government erects the platform; it does not thereby become responsible for all that occurs upon it. * * * *

Accordingly, I adhere to my position that the Equal Protection Clause does not limit the exercise of peremptory challenges by private civil litigants and criminal defendants. This case itself presents no state action dilemma, for here the State of Alabama itself filed the paternity suit on behalf of petitioner. But what of the next case? Will we, in the name of fighting gender discrimination, hold that the battered wife — on trial for wounding her abusive husband — is a state actor? Will we preclude her from using her peremptory challenges to ensure that the jury of her peers contains as many women members as possible? I assume we will, but I hope we will not.

Justice Scalia, with whom The Chief Justice and Justice Thomas join, dissenting.

Today's opinion is an inspiring demonstration of how thoroughly up-to-date and right-thinking we Justices are in matters pertaining to the sexes (or as the Court would have it, the genders), and how sternly we disapprove the male chauvinist attitudes of our predecessors. The price to be paid for this display — a modest price, surely — is that most of the opinion is quite irrelevant to the case at hand. The hasty reader will be surprised to learn, for example, that this lawsuit involves a complaint about the use of peremptory challenges to exclude *men* from a petit jury. To be sure, petitioner, a man, used all but one of *his* peremptory strikes to remove *women* from the jury (he used his last challenge to strike the sole remaining male from the pool), but the validity of *his* strikes is not before us. Nonetheless, the Court treats itself to an extended discussion of the historic exclusion of women not only from jury service, but also from service at the bar (which is rather like jury service, in that it involves going to the courthouse a lot). All this, as I say, is irrelevant, since the case involves state action that allegedly discriminates against men. The parties do not contest that discrimination on the basis of sex[1] is subject to what our cases call "heightened scrutiny," and the citation of one of those cases (preferably one involving men rather than women) is all that was needed.

The Court also spends time establishing that the use of sex as a proxy for particular views or sympathies is unwise and perhaps irrational. The opinion stresses the lack of statistical evidence to support the widely held belief that, at least in certain types of cases, a juror's sex has some statistically significant predictive value as to how the juror will behave. This assertion seems to place the Court in opposition to its earlier Sixth Amendment "fair cross-section" cases. See, e.g., *Taylor v. Louisiana*, 419 U. S. 522, 532, n. 12 (1975) ("Controlled studies have concluded that women bring to juries their own perspectives and values that influence both jury deliberation and result"). But times and trends do change, and unisex is unquestionably in fashion. Personally, I am less inclined to demand statistics, and more inclined to credit the perceptions of experienced litigators who have had money on the line. But it does not matter. The Court's fervent defense of the proposition *il n'y a pas de différence entre les hommes et les femmes* (it stereotypes the opposite view as hateful "stereotyping") turns out to be, like its recounting of the history of sex discrimination against women, utterly irrelevant. Even if sex was a remarkably good predictor in certain cases, the Court would find its use in peremptories unconstitutional.

---

[1] Throughout this opinion, I shall refer to the issue as sex discrimination rather than (as the Court does) gender discrimination. The word "gender" has acquired the new and useful connotation of cultural or attitudinal characteristics (as opposed to physical characteristics) distinctive to the sexes. That is to say, gender is to sex as feminine is to female and masculine to male. The present case does not involve peremptory strikes exercised on the basis of femininity or masculinity (as far as it appears, effeminate men did not survive the prosecution's peremptories). The case involves, therefore, sex discrimination plain and simple.

Of course the relationship of sex to partiality *would have been* relevant if the Court had demanded in this case what it ordinarily demands: that the complaining party have suffered some injury. Leaving aside for the moment the reality that the defendant himself had the opportunity to strike women from the jury, the defendant would have some cause to complain about the prosecutor's striking male jurors if male jurors tend to be more favorable towards defendants in paternity suits. But if men and women jurors are (as the Court thinks) fungible, then the only arguable injury from the prosecutor's "impermissible" use of male sex as the basis for his peremptories is injury to the stricken juror, not to the defendant. Indeed, far from having suffered harm, petitioner, a state actor under our precedents, has himself actually inflicted harm on female jurors. The Court today presumably supplies petitioner with a cause of action by applying the uniquely expansive third-party standing analysis of *Powers v. Ohio*, 499 U. S. 400, 415 (1991), according petitioner a remedy because of the wrong done to male jurors. This case illustrates why making restitution to Paul when it is Peter who has been robbed is such a bad idea. Not only has petitioner, by implication of the Court's own reasoning, suffered no harm, but the scientific evidence presented at trial established petitioner's paternity with 99.92% accuracy. Insofar as petitioner is concerned, this is a case of harmless error if there ever was one; a retrial will do nothing but divert the State's judicial and prosecutorial resources, allowing either petitioner or some other malefactor to go free.

The core of the Court's reasoning is that peremptory challenges on the basis of any group characteristic subject to heightened scrutiny are inconsistent with the guarantee of the Equal Protection Clause. That conclusion can be reached only by focusing unrealistically upon individual exercises of the peremptory challenge, and ignoring the totality of the practice. Since all groups are subject to the peremptory challenge (and will be made the object of it, depending upon the nature of the particular case) it is hard to see how any group is denied equal protection. That explains why peremptory challenges coexisted with the Equal Protection Clause for 120 years. This case is a perfect example of how the system as a whole is even-handed. While the only claim before the Court is petitioner's complaint that the prosecutor struck male jurors, for every man struck by the government petitioner's own lawyer struck a woman. To say that men were singled out for discriminatory treatment in this process is preposterous. The situation would be different if both sides systematically struck individuals of one group, so that the strikes evinced group-based animus and served as a proxy for segregated venire lists. The pattern here, however, displays not a systemic sex-based animus but each side's desire to get a jury favorably disposed to its case. That is why the Court's characterization of respondent's argument as "reminiscent of the arguments advanced to justify the total exclusion of women from juries," is patently false. Women were categorically excluded from juries because of doubt that they were competent; women are stricken from juries by peremptory challenge because of doubt that they are well disposed to the striking party's case. There is discrimination and dishonor in the former, and not in the latter — which explains the 106-year interlude between our holding that exclusion from juries on the basis of race was unconstitutional, and our holding that peremptory challenges on the basis of race were unconstitutional.

Although the Court's legal reasoning in this case is largely obscured by anti-male-chauvinist oratory, to the extent such reasoning is discernible it invalidates much more than sex-based strikes. After identifying unequal treatment (by separating individual exercises of peremptory challenge from the process as a whole), the Court applies the "heightened scrutiny" mode of equal-protection analysis used for sex-based discrimination, and concludes that the strikes fail heightened scrutiny because they do not substantially further an important government interest. The Court says that the only important government interest that could be served by peremptory strikes is "securing a fair and impartial jury."[3] It refuses to accept respondent's argument that these strikes further that interest by eliminating a group (men) which may be partial to male defendants, because it will not accept any argument based on "the very stereotype the law condemns." This analysis, entirely eliminating the only allowable argument, implies that sex-based strikes do not even rationally further a legitimate government interest, let alone pass heightened scrutiny. That places *all* peremptory strikes based on *any* group characteristic at risk, since they can all be denominated "stereotypes." Perhaps, however (though I do not see why it should be so), only the stereotyping of groups entitled to heightened or strict scrutiny constitutes "the very stereotype the law condemns" — so that other stereotyping (e.g., wide-eyed blondes and football players are dumb) remains OK. Or perhaps when the Court refers to "impermissible stereotypes," it means the adjective to be limiting rather than descriptive — so that we can expect to learn from the Court's peremptory/ stereotyping jurisprudence in the future which stereotypes the Constitution frowns upon and which it does not.

Even if the line of our later cases guaranteed by today's decision limits the theoretically boundless *Batson* principle to race, sex, and perhaps other classifications subject to heightened scrutiny (which presumably would include religious belief), much damage has been done. It has been done, first and foremost, to the peremptory challenge system, which loses its whole character when (in order to defend against "impermissible stereotyping" claims) "reasons" for strikes must be given. The right of peremptory challenge is, as Blackstone says, "an arbitrary and capricious right; and it must be exercised with full freedom, or it fails of its full purpose." 4 W. Blackstone, Commentaries 353. The loss of the real peremptory will be felt most keenly by the criminal defendant, whom we have until recently thought "should not be held to accept a juror, apparently indifferent, whom he distrusted for any reason or for no reason." *Lamb v. State*, 36 Wis. 424, 426 (1874). And make no mistake about it: there really is no substitute for the peremptory. *Voir dire* (though it can be expected to expand as a consequence of today's decision) cannot fill the gap. The biases that go along with group characteristics tend to be biases that the juror himself does not perceive, so that it is no use asking about them. It is fruitless to inquire of a male juror whether he harbors any subliminal prejudice in favor of unwed fathers.

And damage has been done, secondarily, to the entire justice system, which will bear the burden of the expanded quest for "reasoned peremptories" that the Court demands. The extension of *Batson* to sex, and almost certainly beyond, will provide the basis for extensive collateral litigation, which especially the criminal defendant (who litigates full-time and cost-free) can be expected to pursue. While demographic reality places some limit on the number of cases in which race-based challenges will

---

[3] It does not seem to me that even this premise is correct. Wise observers have long understood that the appearance of justice is as important as its reality. If the system of peremptory strikes affects the actual impartiality of the jury not a bit, but gives litigants a greater belief in that impartiality, it serves a most important function. In point of fact, that may well be its greater value.

be an issue, every case contains a potential sex-based claim. Another consequence, as I have mentioned, is a lengthening of the *voir dire* process that already burdens trial courts.

The irrationality of today's strike-by-strike approach to equal protection is evident from the consequences of extending it to its logical conclusion. If a fair and impartial trial is a prosecutor's only legitimate goal; if adversarial trial stratagems must be tested against that goal in abstraction from their role within the system as a whole; and if, so tested, sex-based stratagems do not survive heightened scrutiny — then the prosecutor presumably violates the Constitution when he selects a male or female police officer to testify because he believes one or the other sex might be more convincing in the context of the particular case, or because he believes one or the other might be more appealing to a predominantly male or female jury. A decision to stress one line of argument or present certain witnesses before a mostly female jury — for example, to stress that the defendant victimized women — becomes, under the Court's reasoning, intentional discrimination by a state actor on the basis of gender.

In order, it seems to me, not to eliminate any real denial of equal protection, but simply to pay conspicuous obeisance to the equality of the sexes, the Court imperils a practice that has been considered an essential part of fair jury trial since the dawn of the common law. The Constitution of the United States neither requires nor permits this vandalizing of our people's traditions.

For these reasons, I dissent.

Notes from Justin:

1. At trial, *both* lawyers exercised peremptory challenges based on gender (or sex, as Justice Scalia would have it). Is the majority saying that both of these attorneys were *stupid*, unable to see that both men and women would see the case the same way? (If they were stupid, then they were wasting peremptories they might have put to better use. Won't *that* "penalty" discourage senseless use of peremptories based on gender? Lawyers who waste peremptories tend to lose cases — and clients!) Or is the majority saying that they were *malicious*, trying to deprive the challenged gender of their rights to participate in jury service? Or is the majority saying that even if these lawyers were both wise and well-intentioned, it doesn't matter, because there are interests at stake which are more important than those traditionally served by the peremptory challenge?

2. I am having some trouble reconciling this case with *Taylor v. Louisiana*. In *Taylor*, didn't the Court hold that women *are* different, in some "unknown and unknowable" ways, and therefore exclusion of women from juries deprives the defendant of a jury made up of a cross-section of the community? Doesn't *J.E.B.* hold (or imply) that women are *not* different, and therefore it is irrational for a trial attorney to exercise a peremptory challenge based on gender? Does *J.E.B.* silently overrule *Taylor*?

3. Take another look at my Note after *Batson*, summarizing some decisions re what is a "cognizable group". Does the reasoning of *J.E.B.* shed any light on whether those decisions are "correct"?

4. In *Riley v. Commonwealth*, 21 Va.App. 330 (1995), Riley was charged with rape and sodomy on a young woman who had been jogging in the early morning. The

prosecutor exercised peremptory challenges against 5 women ranging in age from 58 to 66 years old. The prosecutor explained:

> What I have done, by removing the people I struck, I have removed women who are most unlike the victim, in terms of age. I have left on those who share the victim's characteristics as much as I can, in terms of their sex and their age. There is not a discriminatory basis. This is a basis based on the facts that I have a rape victim who is, (A) She's a working female. I don't know what attitude other individuals who are older may take; and (B) I have a young lady who is out jogging, and I don't know what attitude older females may take, but I do know they're most unlike the victim, as far as I can determine from the scant evidence we have, their age and their lifestyle. I would point out to the Court that I have in the past, my experience, based on trying cases, and I am a veteran of seventeen years of trying cases, from Henrico County Circuit Court, is that in rape cases, feedback I have gotten from the jury afterwards, is that many times the elderly female jurors have difficulty accepting certain aspects of the cases, and they have a difficult time considering the evidence and reaching a verdict of guilt.

The trial court sustained the challenges, the trial proceeded, and the jury convicted Riley. But the appellate court reversed:

> The trial court determined that the Commonwealth's explanation was facially neutral, limiting its inquiry to the factor of age alone. The court correctly concluded that age is a permissible basis upon which to exercise a peremptory strike. See *Barksdale v. Commonwealth*, 17 Va.App. 456, 461 (1993). However, the court failed to address defense counsel's contention that the Commonwealth's strikes were gender-based.

> To survive challenge at step two, the strike must be based on a juror characteristic other than gender. *J.E.B.*, 114 S.Ct. at 1430. Here, however, the prosecutor's explanation clearly references his intention to strike only women — albeit older women — from the jury panel. The fact that the Commonwealth used age to identify which women to strike does not overcome the constitutional infirmity. The Commonwealth exercised its strikes based on the assumption that the women would hold particular views because of their gender. Such attempts to stereotype in the jury selection process are impermissible. Lying "at the very heart of the jury system" is the factual assumption that "jury competence is an individual rather than a group or class matter." *J.E.B.*, 114 S.Ct. at 1430 n. 19.

Questions:

a. Why is gender — but not age — a "stereotype"? Is the court saying that it is not fair to believe that all women think alike, but fair to believe that all elderly people think alike?

b. Suppose that, after the 5 peremptory challenges were sustained, the prosecutor had arranged to have the 5 challenged women sit in the audience and watch the trial — and then "vote". If all 5 (or 4 of the 5) had "voted" not guilty — while the jury convicted Riley — should this have convinced the appellate court that the prosecutor's explanation should be accepted?

Compare *State v. King*, 215 Wis.2d 295, 572 N.W.2d 530 (1997). King was a black man charged with sexually assaulting a white victim. The prosecutor used two of four peremptory strikes against the only 2 black prospective jurors, who were older women. The prosecutor (a female) denied that race was a factor in her decision, and she explained: "My experience in trying these cases is that older females are very judgmental of a sexual assault victim who is a female." The court held that this was not a proper justification:

> The State acknowledges that gender was a factor and that gender is not a valid reason for striking a juror. However, it argues that age is a valid reason and, since there were two reasons, we should adopt the "dual motivation test" to determine whether to allow these strikes. Under the dual motivation analysis, the party who exercised the strike must prove that the strike would have been exercised regardless of the discriminatory motivation. See *Wallace v. Morrison*, 87 F.3d 1271, 1275 (11th Cir.1996). Under this analysis, a prohibited factor, such as gender, does not automatically result in an equal protection violation. If there are other permissible motivating factors, the prohibited factor must be the decisive part of the motive. See *Howard v. Senkowski*, 986 F.2d 24, 27 (2nd Cir.1993). Although some federal circuits have adopted the dual motivation analysis, the Supreme Court has not ruled on this issue.

> We agree with King that in *State v. Jagodinsky*, 209 Wis.2d 577 (1997), this court rejected essentially the same argument, although it was not denominated "dual motivation." * * * * We stated: "In circumstances such as this, where the challenged party admits reliance on a prohibited discriminatory characteristic, we do not see how a response that other factors were also used is sufficient rebuttal under the second prong of *Batson*.

> We hold that the trial court clearly erred when it concluded that the prosecutor had not purposefully engaged in gender discrimination in striking jurors Moore and Thomas because gender was not the sole factor. Based on the prosecutor's statement that she struck these two jurors because they were older females and "older females are very judgmental of a sexual assault victim who is a female," the only correct conclusion on this record is that the prosecutor purposefully used gender as a basis for striking these two jurors.

In *Robinson v. U.S.*, 878 A.2d 1273 (D.C. 2005), the trial court allowed the prosecutor to exercise peremptory challenges to purposely exclude black women, because "race-and-gender combinations are not 'suspect categories' for equal protection purposes." The appellate court disagreed:

> When racial bias and gender bias unite to motivate discrimination against black female jurors, it makes no difference for *Batson* purposes that neither type of bias alone accounts for the strikes. If it is impermissible to exclude jurors because of their race *or* their gender, it is impermissible to exclude jurors because of their race *and* their gender. Two bad partial reasons for a peremptory strike do not add up to a good reason; they simply equate to a reason that is doubly bad. To prove a *Batson* violation, a defendant need not show that a prosecutor's strikes were motivated solely by racial or gender bias, to the exclusion of all other considerations. Such

a requirement would render *Batson* a virtual nullity and divorce it from the real world of jury selection, for the motivations behind peremptory strikes are seldom so crystallized and singular. Mixed motives are the norm. However, even if the prosecutor acted from mixed motives, some of which were non-discriminatory, his actions deny equal protection and violate *Batson* if race or gender influenced his decision. A peremptory challenge may not be based even partially on an unlawful discriminatory reason.

5. May a lawyer base a peremptory challenge on a prospective juror's *religion*?

In *State v. Davis*, 504 N.W.2d 767 (Minn. 1993), the prosecutor challenged a prospective juror because he was a member of the *Jehovah's Witnesses*, explaining that this "faith is of a mind that higher powers will take care of all things necessary. In my experience, Jehovah's Witnesses are reluctant to exercise authority over their fellow human beings in this courthouse." The court (over 3 dissents) held that, while *Batson* barred use of peremptories based on race because a history of use of such challenges against blacks, *religion* is different:

> The use of the peremptory strike to discriminate purposefully on the basis of religion does not, however, appear to be common and flagrant. We are not aware the peremptory is being so misused, nor does the defendant make any such claim. This is not to say that religious intolerance does not exist in our society, but only to say that there is no indication that irrational religious bias so pervades the peremptory challenge as to undermine the integrity of the jury system.

> Then, too, the nature of the bias sought to be eliminated by a *Batson* challenge is particularly illusive in the case of religion. Presumably, the bias sought to be eliminated in jury deliberations is intolerance for the doctrinal beliefs and practices of the adherents of a particular religious group. Yet when religious beliefs translate into judgments on the merits of the cause to be judged, it is difficult to distinguish, in challenging a juror, between an impermissible bias on the basis of religious affiliation and a permissible religion-neutral explanation. In the case before us, for example, would the explanation that the juror was "reluctant to exercise authority over their fellow human beings" be sufficient to overcome a prima facie case of religious bias? A juror's religious beliefs are inviolate, but when they are the basis for a person's moral values and produce societal views on such matters as the use of intoxicating liquor, cohabitation, necessity of medical treatment, civil disobedience, and the like, it would not seem that a peremptory strike based on these societal views should be attributed to a pernicious religious bias.

The U.S. Supreme Court denied *certiorari* in *Davis*. 511 U.S. 1115 (1994). But Justices Thomas dissented (with Justice Scalia) from the denial of *certiorari*:

> I find it difficult to understand how the Court concludes today that the judgment of the court below should not be vacated and the case remanded in light of our recent decision in *J.E.B. v. Alabama ex rel. T.B.*, 511 U.S. 127 (1994), which shatters the Supreme Court of Minnesota's understanding that *Batson's* equal protection analysis applies solely to racially based peremptory strikes. It is abundantly clear that the lower court was relying on just such a reading of *Batson*, for it reasoned that *Batson* embodies "a special rule of relevance" that operates only in the context of race, and

concluded that "outside the uniquely sensitive area of race the ordinary rule that a prosecutor may strike without giving any reason applies." In extending Equal Protection Clause analysis to prohibit strikes exercised on the basis of sex, *J.E.B.* explicitly disavowed that understanding of *Batson*.

Indeed, given the Court's rationale in *J.E.B.*, no principled reason immediately appears for declining to apply *Batson* to any strike based on a classification that is accorded heightened scrutiny under the Equal Protection Clause. The Court's decision in *J.E.B.* was explicitly grounded on a conclusion that peremptory strikes based on sex cannot survive "heightened scrutiny" under the Clause, because such strikes "are not substantially related to an important government objective." In breaking the barrier between classifications that merit strict equal protection scrutiny and those that receive what we have termed "heightened" or "intermediate" scrutiny, *J.E.B.* would seem to have extended *Batson's* equal protection analysis to all strikes based on the latter category of classifications — a category which presumably would include classifications based on religion. It is at least not obvious, given the reasoning in *J.E.B.*, why peremptory strikes based on religious affiliation would survive equal protection analysis. As Justice Scalia pointed out in dissent, *J.E.B.* itself provided no rationale for distinguishing between strikes exercised on the basis of various classifications that receive heightened scrutiny, and the Supreme Court of Minnesota certainly did not develop such a distinction. As described above, the court relied expressly on the understanding that *Batson* was confined to the context of race. Under these circumstances, this case should be remanded for the Supreme Court of Minnesota to consider explicitly whether a principled basis exists for confining the holding in *J.E.B.* to the context of sex.

I can only conclude that the Court's decision to deny certiorari stems from an unwillingness to confront forthrightly the ramifications of the decision in *J.E.B.* It has long been recognized by some members of the Court that subjecting the peremptory strike to the rigors of equal protection analysis may ultimately spell the doom of the strike altogether, because the peremptory challenge is by nature "an arbitrary and capricious right." Once the scope of the logic in *J.E.B.* is honestly acknowledged, it cannot be glibly asserted that the decision has no implications for peremptory strikes based on classifications other than sex, or that it does not imply further restrictions on the exercise of the peremptory strike outside the context of race and sex.

In my view, the petition should therefore be granted, the judgment below vacated, and the case remanded for reconsideration in light of *J.E.B.* I respectfully dissent.

The Connecticut Supreme Court agreed with Justice Thomas, in *State v. Hodge*, 248 Conn. 207 (1999). Justice McDonald disagreed:

The differences between race and gender and religious beliefs or affiliation are numerous and vital. A person's race and gender may be readily apparent, while "religious affiliation (or lack thereof) is not as self-evident." *Davis v. Minnesota*, 511 U.S. 1115, 1115 (1994) (Ginsberg, J., concurring). People generally do not wear their religions on their sleeves, and their beliefs are not readily apparent. Religious beliefs and affiliation also differ from race and gender in that people have control over the influence of their faith, belief or organized system of worship in their daily lives. Religion may be a chosen affiliation, and each person has free will to decide whether, and with what intensity, to practice a faith or adhere to a belief.

Furthermore, a showing of such an unconstitutional peremptory challenge would require counsel to question a venireperson about his or her religious convictions. Such questioning is quite properly disallowed under the first amendment to the United States constitution. "Ordinarily inquiry on *voir dire* into a venireperson's religious affiliation and beliefs is irrelevant and prejudicial, and to ask such questions is improper." *Davis v. Minnesota, supra,* 511 U.S. 1115 (Ginsberg, J., concurring). "Questions about religious beliefs are relevant only if pertinent to religious issues involved in the case, or if a religious organization is a party, or if the information is a necessary predicate for a *voir dire* challenge. The trial court, in the exercise of its discretion, controls the questions that can be asked to keep the *voir dire* within relevant bounds. Proper questioning for a challenge should be limited to asking jurors if they knew of any reason why they could not sit, if they would have any difficulty in following the law as given by the court, or if they would have any difficulty in sitting in judgment." *State v. Davis,* 504 N.W.2d 767, 772 (Minn.1993), *cert. denied,* 511 U.S. 1115 (1994). In the absence of a religious belief that may directly affect a venireperson's ability to serve on a jury in a particular case, religious beliefs are not relevant to the *voir dire* process and questions regarding religious beliefs should be disallowed.

Because of the thin line between one's religious beliefs and one's other beliefs and biases, other problems will arise. While challenges based upon race and gender often are obvious, challenges based upon a venireperson's religion will be more difficult to evaluate. The court may be required to separate religious beliefs from other beliefs, thus attempting to determine what constitutes "religion." This would force courts to make judgments concerning religious beliefs, a practice that is both difficult and constitutionally suspect.

The expansion of *Batson* to religious beliefs or affiliation would lead to its application to national origin, political affiliation and philosophy as well as other things that may distinguish potential jurors. While discrimination based on any of those differences, including religious beliefs or affiliation, is abhorrent, the continued expansion of *Batson* simply destroys the peremptory challenge. Trial lawyers have found these challenges necessary for centuries because peremptory challenges allow them to act on their intuition that a potential juror would not be sympathetic to their case. I see no reason to take from Connecticut trial lawyers that time-honored privilege.

In *U.S. v. Brown,* 352 F.3d 654 (2nd Cir. 2003), the court drew a distinction between religious *affiliation* and religious *beliefs.* A party may not base a peremptory challenge simply because a potential juror is *affiliated* with some religious group, but may base a peremptory on the particular religious beliefs of the person. "It would be improper and perhaps unconstitutional to strike a juror on the basis of his being a Catholic, a Jew, a Muslim, etc., but it would be proper to strike him on the basis of a belief that would prevent him from basing his decision on the evidence and instructions, even if the belief had a religious backing"

In *State v. Fuller*, 862 A.2d 1130, 1139–1140 (N.J. 2004), the court stated:

> Since *J.E.B.*, a number of state and federal courts have reviewed peremptory challenges based on religion and/or religious activities. [Citations.] That case law is instructive.

> We discern, in the absence of a definitive ruling from the United States Supreme Court, an emerging consensus to extend the equal protection analysis of *Batson* and *J.E.B.* to peremptory challenges based solely on religious affiliation and to find those challenges unconstitutional. Challenges based on religious beliefs or religious activities, however, are generally permitted. In respect of those challenges, the courts reason that the origin of a belief, religious, political or social, is irrelevant to the question whether the juror holding that belief will be able to carry out his or her duties in relation to the case at bar impartially and as instructed by the court.

6. Are *Jews* a religion, a race, a tribe. . . .?

Compare *Davis* with *Joseph v. State*, 636 So.2d 777 (Fla.Ct.App.1994), where the court held that *Jews* are a cognizable class in Dade County, Florida (where Miami is located). Such a class must be "objectively discernible" from the rest of the community, which requires that the group be (1) large enough to be recognized by the community as an identifiable class, and (2) distinguished from the rest of the community by "an internal cohesiveness of attitudes, ideas, or experiences that may not be adequately represented by other segments of society." Jews met the first requirement, as they constituted 10% of the population of Dade County. (Query: Does this suggest that they would *not* be a "cognizable class" in a county where their percentage is much smaller?) Jews also met the second requirement:

> Jews share a large core of attitudes and ideas which stem from their common religious beliefs. It is common knowledge that Jews celebrate their sabbath on Saturday, not Sunday, and do not celebrate Christmas. These two facts alone significantly distinguish Jews from other segments of society. Jews also share a common experience of persecution which distinguishes them from other segments of society, such as the attempted genocide of Jews, for reasons based solely upon their religion, at the hands of the Nazis.

The court also said that Jews are objectively discernible, by surname or by the wearing of a yarmulke, 6-pointed star, or Hassidic garb. (Compare, however, *U.S. v. Gelb*, 881 F.2d 1155 (2nd Cir. 1989): "Stereotypical ethnic or religious characterizations of surnames are unreliable and only tenuous indicia of a jury's makeup.")

Can *Joseph* be reconciled with *Davis*?

And compare *U.S. v. Somerstein*, 959 F.Supp. 592 (E.D.N.Y.1997), where officers and employees of a kosher caterer were charged with conspiracy to defraud union benefit funds. The prosecutor exercised 6 of its 9 peremptory challenges against prospective jurors who were Jewish or were related to Jews. While the court eventually found that none of these challenges were invoked for religious reasons, the court did hold that Jews were a "cognizable group" under *Batson*. First, the court agreed with Justice Thomas's dissent from the denial of *certiorari* in *Davis*: "The dissenting opinion in *Davis* best represents the state of the *Batson* doctrine at the present time." Alternatively, the court held that Jews are a *race*, not just a religion, so are directly covered by *Batson's* bar on racial use of the peremptory challenge.

7. What about *schoolteachers*?

In *U.S. v. Davis*, 40 F.3d 1069 (10th Cir.1994), the prosecutor exercised a peremptory challenge against an African-American woman, explaining that "it had a practice of striking all schoolteachers from juries." The court held that this was a "race neutral" explanation, so there was no violation of *Batson*. But defendant had a back-up argument:

> Defendant also argues, however, that by extending the *Batson* holding to women in *J.E.B. v. Alabama*, the Supreme Court has implicitly extended the Equal Protection Clause to protect prospective jurors who are teachers. Defendant asserts that women constitute a disproportionate share of teachers and therefore allowing the government to exclude teachers has a disparate impact on women. Although we question the wisdom of excluding any particular occupation from a jury panel, disparate impact is not a basis for a *Batson* challenge. Instead, defendant must show intent to discriminate. *J.E.B., supra*. Because defendant has not attempted to show that the government intended to exclude either African-Americans or women, we find no error.

8. Are *gays and lesbians* a "cognizable group"?

In *People v. Garcia*, 77 Cal.App.4th 1269 (2000), Garcia was charged with burglary. The prosecutor exercised peremptory challenges against two women who worked for a gay and lesbian foundation. Defense counsel objected, claiming that the challenge was based on sexual orientation. The trial court held that "sexual preference is not a cognizable group." The appellate court disagreed, basing its decision on *Rubio v. Superior Court*, 24 Cal.3d 93 (1979):

> The pivot of our analysis is the definition of the term, "cognizable group." In *Rubio*, our Supreme Court held that the right under the California Constitution to a jury drawn from a "representative cross-section of the community" is violated whenever a "cognizable group" within that community is systematically excluded from the jury venire. It explained that, "Two requirements must thus be met in order to qualify an asserted group as 'cognizable' for purposes of the representative cross-section rule. First, its members must share a common perspective arising from their life experience in the group, i.e., a perspective gained precisely because they are members of that group. It is not enough to find a characteristic possessed by some persons in the community but not by others; the characteristic must also impart to its possessors a common social or psychological outlook on human events. For example, in *Adams v. Superior Court* (1974) 12 Cal.3d 55, the claimed cognizable group was composed of all persons who had resided in the community for less than one year; at any given moment the members of that group could be identified with certainty and thereby distinguished from all other persons in the

community, but a majority of this court held that they had not acquired a true 'commonality of interest' merely by virtue of the brevity of their residence." *Id.* at 98.

Lesbians and gay men qualify under this standard. It cannot seriously be argued in this era of "don't ask; don't tell" that homosexuals do not have a common perspective — "a common social or psychological outlook on human events" — based upon their membership in that community. They share a history of persecution comparable to that of Blacks and women. While there is room to argue about degree, based upon their number and the relative indiscernibility of their membership in the group, it is just that: an argument about degree. It is a matter of quantity, not quality.

This is not to say that all homosexuals see the world alike. The Attorney General here derides the cognizability of this class with the rhetorical question, "What 'common perspective' is, or was, shared by Rep. Jim Kolbe (R-Ariz.), RuPaul, poet William Alexander Percy, Truman Capote, and Ellen DeGeneres?" He confuses "common perspective" with "common personality." Granted, the five persons he mentions are people of diverse backgrounds and life experiences. But they certainly share the common perspective of having spent their lives in a sexual minority, either exposed to or fearful of persecution and discrimination. That perspective deserves representation in the jury venire, and people who share that perspective deserve to bear their share of the burdens and benefits of citizenship, including jury service.

The Attorney General also insists "there is no evidence that gays or lesbians have a common social or psychological outlook on human events." But this misperceives the nature of the term "common perspective." Commonality of perspective does not result in identity of opinion. That is the whole reason exclusion based upon group bias is anathema. It stereotypes. It assumes all people with the same life experience will, given a set of facts, reach the same result.

A common perspective does no such thing. It affects how life experiences are seen, not how they are evaluated. And inclusion of a cognizable group in the jury venire does not assure any particular position; it assures only that the facts will be viewed from a variety of angles. It assures that as many different life views as possible will be represented in the important decisions of the judicial process. * * * *

There is a second prong to the *Rubio* test for cognizability — the one which fractured the majority in that case: "The party seeking to prove a violation of the representative cross-section rule must also show that no other members of the community are capable of adequately representing the perspective of the group assertedly excluded. This is so because the goal of the cross-section rule is to enhance the likelihood that the jury will be representative of significant community attitudes, not of groups per se. When a 'cognizable group' is defined too narrowly, it may duplicate another group in the community with a similar experience and viewpoint." *Rubio v. Superior Court, supra,* 24 Cal.3d at 98.

The question, then, is whether another group — or groups — in the community could adequately represent the views of homosexuals. We don't see how.

In *Rubio*, the issue was exclusion of felons and resident aliens. The court pointed out that to the extent felons have a different perspective on life, it is legally indistinguishable from that of misdemeanants who have served jail time, or citizens who have been committed to a facility like the California Youth Authority, or been involuntarily committed. The court dealt with the complaints of resident aliens in the same way, pointing out that all naturalized citizens were, for at least five years, resident aliens, and suffered the same disabilities and discrimination; their perspectives could therefore adequately represent those of resident aliens.

But we cannot think of anyone who shares the perspective of the homosexual community. Outside of racial and religious minorities, we can think of no group which has suffered such pernicious and sustained hostility, and such immediate and severe opprobrium as homosexuals. Certainly the Attorney General has suggested no one, and our search of case law and other literature has turned up no intimation of a group with their perspective. Both the defendant and the community are entitled to have that perspective represented in the jury venire. * * * *

The Attorney General complains that it is impractical to recognize gays and lesbians as a cognizable group. As he points out, sexual orientation is "not necessarily patent, nor a public matter a prospective juror should be required to declare." We acknowledge both those facts. But neither affects our decision. Race and ethnicity are not necessarily patent, either. While gross estimations of race can be made on the basis of physical appearances, such judgments are entirely subjective and often erroneous. And ethnicity has become virtually impossible to judge without inquiry. Our jury venires daily include Cubans named O'Rourke, Indonesians named Opdyke, and Anglos named Gomes. Every trial judge has encountered red-haired, freckle-faced Cardenases and Hispanic-looking Maguires. The country is a melting pot — and proud of it — and a large part of the great folly of stereotyping is that nowhere on earth have race and ethnicity become harder to determine than they are here. Yet the propriety of those criteria for cognizable groups is unassailable. Sexual orientation will present no greater difficulty.

Nor do we perceive a great problem lurking with regard to inquiring of jurors about their sexual orientation. It simply should not be done. The Attorney General is right in this regard: No one should be "outed" in order to take part in the civic enterprise which is jury duty. The whole point is that no one can be excluded because of sexual orientation. That being the case, no one should be allowed to inquire about it. If it comes out somehow, as it did here, the parties will doubtless factor it into their jury selection decisions, just as they factor in occupation, education, body-language, and whether the juror resembles their stupid Uncle Cletus. But there is no reason to allow inquiry about it.

We are also aware of the argument that gays and lesbians may not be a big enough group to be cognizable. * * * * Our record does not reflect the size of the homosexual community. Most reliable estimates seem to arrive at a number between 1–10 percent of the population. But the reference to a "large" group is one of relative numbers rather than absolute ones. * * * * We are confident the Attorney General would recoil from support of a prosecutor who excused prospective jurors on the sole basis they were Unitarian or Ainu. No one suggests either of these groups outnumbers gays and lesbians in California, but no one would question their cognizability.

In fine, gays and lesbians seem to meet the criteria for a cognizable group. We see no reason in the objections raised by the Attorney General not to acknowledge that status, and nothing in law or logic which would enable us to come to a different conclusion.

That group cannot be discriminated against in jury selection. For such discrimination would send an intolerable message, one which the United States Supreme Court has eloquently described: "The message it sends to all those in the courtroom, and all those who may later learn of the discriminatory act, is that certain individuals, for no reason other than [sexual orientation], are presumed unqualified by state actors to decide important questions upon which reasonable persons could disagree." *J. E. B. v. Alabama ex rel. T. B.*, 511 U.S. at 142. We will not send that message.

9. How about people who are *hard of hearing*?

In *U.S. v. Harris*, 197 F.3d 870 (7th Cir. 1999), the prosecutor exercised a peremptory challenge against a black woman who had multiple sclerosis, which rendered her hard of hearing. He explained that he exercised the challenge not because of her race, but because of her disability. Defendant argued that striking her because of her disability was improper. The court disagreed:

> Unlike race or gender, disability may legitimately affect a person's ability to serve as a juror. For example, disabled potential jurors who would be unable to understand testimony at trial or who would suffer pain or hardship from spending hours each day sitting in a courtroom are properly excused from service for cause. In addition, there are some disabilities, like Ms. Wilson's multiple sclerosis, that may not rise to the level of an exclusion for cause, but may, in a given case, provide a party legitimate concern about a potential juror's ability to serve. The narrow limitations on peremptory challenges provided by *Batson* and *J.E.B.* are a special rule of relevance, a statement about what this Nation stands for that is a product of the unique history of discrimination in this country. Unlike race or gender, the broad category of "disability" is not "unrelated to a person's fitness as a juror." *Batson*, 476 U.S. at 87.

10. And what about *blind* people?

In *U.S. v. Watson*, 483 F.3d 828 (D.C.Cir. 2007), the prosecutor planned to introduce photos and videos as evidence, and he exercised peremptory challenges against two blind prospective jurors. He explained: "These two blind jurors can cause the government a concern because a substantial amount of the government's evidence is either photographs or videos, the types of things, for the juror to understand the full impact, the juror must see." The court upheld the challenges, noting that the Supreme Court held in *City of Cleburne v. Cleburne Living Ctr., Inc.*, 473 U.S. 432 (1985) that classifications by disability do not receive heightened scrutiny under the Equal Protection Clause, held that "it is not necessarily irrational to think that a person is likely to acquire a more accurate understanding of a scene by seeing it rather than merely hearing about it."

UNITED STATES v. SANTIAGO-MARTINEZ
U.S. Court of Appeals, 9th Circuit
58 F.3d 422 (1995)

Per Curiam

We hold that the equal protection analysis in *Batson v. Kentucky*, 476 U.S. 79 (1986) does not apply to prohibit peremptory strikes on the basis of obesity.

The defendant in this case was convicted on felony drug charges and now seeks to use the striking of obese venire persons to overturn his conviction. A detailed recitation of the facts is not necessary. It suffices to say that the prosecutor struck three venire persons whom defendant's counsel claimed were obese. Defense counsel himself claimed to be obese, although he acknowledged that the defendant was not. The district court disagreed with defense counsel's claim of his own obesity, and also stated that it did not regard at least one of the struck venire persons to be obese. The district court denied defense counsel's challenge.

Batson held that the Equal Protection Clause of the Fourteenth Amendment governs the exercise of peremptory challenges by a prosecutor in a criminal trial. *Batson* involved a strike based on race, but the Supreme Court has applied its rationale to forbid strikes based solely on gender as well. *J.E.B. v. Alabama ex rel. T.B.*, 511 U.S. 127 (1994). The Court concluded in *J.E.B.* that peremptory strikes based solely on gender cannot survive "heightened scrutiny" under the Equal Protection Clause. The Court explained that "parties may exercise their peremptory challenges to remove from the venire any group or class of individuals normally subject to 'rational basis' review."

As the defendant candidly concedes, no court has yet held that discrimination on the basis of obesity is subject to "heightened scrutiny" under the Equal Protection Clause.[1] We are not surprised, and decline to be the first to so hold. The judgment is affirmed.

Note from Justin:

Now I'm totally confused. According to these decisions, lawyers *may* use peremptory challenges to exclude Italian-Americans, Irish-Americans, Jehovah's Witnesses, and fat people, but they *may not* use peremptories to exclude men, whites, Jews, or "non-blacks." Are there some underlying principles that reconcile these cases, or is the law (at least at present) a hopeless mess?

---

[1] Recognition of the class of obese persons for purposes of the Americans with Disabilities Act of 1990, 42 U.S.C. § 12101 et seq., does not subject the class to "heightened scrutiny" under the Equal Protection Clause.

e. Proving that a Challenge was Improper

In *Batson*, the Court indicated that where defense counsel claims that the prosecutor has exercised a peremptory challenge for racial reasons, the trial court should proceed as follows: *First*, determine whether defense counsel has made out a *prima facie* case that the prosecutor behaved improperly, *Second*, require the prosecutor to put forth a "neutral explanation for challenging black jurors," and *Third*, decide "if the defendant has established purposeful discrimination."

1. How much must counsel show to *raise an inference* of intentional discrimination?

The Court addressed this issue in *Johnson v. California*, 545 U.S. 162 (2005):

> Petitioner Jay Shawn Johnson, a black male, was convicted in a California trial court of second-degree murder and assault on a white 19-month-old child, resulting in death. During jury selection, a number of prospective jurors were removed for cause until 43 eligible jurors remained, 3 of whom were black. The prosecutor used 3 of his 12 peremptory challenges to remove the black prospective jurors. The resulting jury, including alternates, was all white.

> After the prosecutor exercised the second of his three peremptory challenges against the prospective black jurors, defense counsel objected on the ground that the challenge was unconstitutionally based on race under both the California and United States Constitutions. Defense counsel alleged that the prosecutor "had no apparent reason to challenge this prospective juror 'other than her racial identity.' " The trial judge did not ask the prosecutor to explain the rationale for his strikes. Instead, the judge simply found that petitioner had failed to establish a prima facie case under the governing state precedent, *People v. Wheeler*, 22 Cal.3d 258, 148 Cal.Rptr. 890, 583 P.2d 748 (1978), reasoning "that there's not been shown a *strong likelihood* that the exercise of the peremptory challenges were based upon a group rather than an individual basis," The judge did, however, warn the prosecutor that "we are very close."

> Defense counsel made an additional motion the next day when the prosecutor struck the final remaining prospective black juror. Counsel argued that the prosecutor's decision to challenge all of the prospective black jurors constituted a "systematic attempt to exclude African-Americans from the jury panel." The trial judge still did not seek an explanation from the prosecutor. Instead, he explained that his own examination of the record had convinced him that the prosecutor's strikes could be justified by race-neutral reasons. Specifically, the judge opined that the black venire members had offered equivocal or confused answers in their written questionnaires. Despite the fact that " 'the Court would not grant the challenges for cause, there were answers at least on the questionnaires themselves [such] that the Court felt that there was sufficient basis' " for the strikes. Therefore, even considering that all of the prospective black jurors had been stricken from the pool, the judge determined that petitioner had failed to establish a prima facie case. * * * *

In describing the burden-shifting framework, we assumed in *Batson* that the trial judge would have the benefit of all relevant circumstances, including the prosecutor's explanation, before deciding whether it was more likely than not that the challenge was improperly motivated. We did not intend the first step to be so onerous that a defendant would have to persuade the judge — on the basis of all the facts, some of which are impossible for the defendant to know with certainty — that the challenge was more likely than not the product of purposeful discrimination. Instead, a defendant satisfies the requirements of *Batson*'s first step by producing evidence sufficient to permit the trial judge to draw an inference that discrimination has occurred. * * * *

In this case the inference of discrimination was sufficient to invoke a comment by the trial judge "that 'we are very close,' " and on review, the California Supreme acknowledged that "it certainly looks suspicious that all three African-American prospective jurors were removed from the jury." Those inferences that discrimination may have occurred were sufficient to establish a prima facie case under *Batson*.

The facts of this case well illustrate that California's "more likely than not" standard is at odds with the prima facie inquiry mandated by *Batson*. The judgment of the California Supreme Court is therefore reversed, and the case is remanded for further proceedings not inconsistent with this opinion.

2. If the inference is raised, how does the prosecutor rebut it?

In *Hernandez v. N.Y.*, 500 U.S. 352 (1991), the prosecutor planned to use a translator at an attempted murder trial, to inform the jury in English of the testimony of certain Spanish-speaking witnesses. During *voir dire*, after the prosecutor exercised peremptory challenges against two "Hispanic" prospective jurors, defense counsel asserted that this violated *Batson*. The prosecutor then explained that he challenged those jurors because he was uncertain "as to whether they could accept the interpreter as the final arbiter of what was said by each of the witnesses." He explained that "They each looked away from me and said with some hesitancy that they would try, not that they could, but that they would try to follow the interpreter, and I feel that in a case where the interpreter will be for the main witnesses, they would have an undue impact upon the jury." The prosecutor also said that the alleged victims and his main witnesses were Hispanic, so he had no reason to want to exclude Hispanics from the jury. The trial court denied defendant's motion for a mistrial, and the Supreme Court affirmed, holding that — even *assuming* that the defendant had presented a *prima facie* showing that the prosecutor had based his challenges on race — the prosecutor's explanation was "race-neutral":

A neutral explanation in the context of our analysis here means an explanation based on something other than the race of the juror. At this step of the inquiry, the issue is the facial validity of the prosecutor's explanation. Unless a discriminatory intent is inherent in the prosecutor's explanation, the reason offered will be deemed race neutral.

Petitioner argues that Spanish-language ability bears a close relation to ethnicity, and that, as a consequence, it violates the Equal Protection Clause to exercise a peremptory challenge on the ground that a Latino potential juror speaks Spanish. He points to the high correlation between Spanish-language ability and ethnicity in New York, where the case was tried. We need not address that argument here, for the prosecutor did not rely on language ability without more, but explained that the specific responses and the demeanor of the two individuals during *voir dire* caused him to doubt their ability to defer to the official translation of Spanish-language testimony.

The prosecutor here offered a race-neutral basis for these peremptory strikes. As explained by the prosecutor, the challenges rested neither on the intention to exclude Latino or bilingual jurors, nor on stereotypical assumptions about Latinos or bilinguals. The prosecutor's articulated basis for these challenges divided potential jurors into two classes: those whose conduct during *voir dire* would persuade him they might have difficulty in accepting the translator's rendition of Spanish-language testimony and those potential jurors who gave no such reason for doubt. Each category would include both Latinos and non-Latinos. While the prosecutor's criterion might well result in the disproportionate removal of prospective Latino jurors, that disproportionate impact does not turn the prosecutor's actions into a per se violation of the Equal Protection Clause.

Petitioner contends that despite the prosecutor's focus on the individual responses of these jurors, his reason for the peremptory strikes has the effect of a pure, language-based reason because "any honest bilingual juror would have answered the prosecutor in the exact same way." Petitioner asserts that a bilingual juror would hesitate in answering questions like those asked by the judge and prosecutor due to the difficulty of ignoring the actual Spanish-language testimony. In his view, no more can be expected than a commitment by a prospective juror to try to follow the interpreter's translation.

But even if we knew that a high percentage of bilingual jurors would hesitate in answering questions like these and, as a consequence, would be excluded under the prosecutor's criterion, that fact alone would not cause the criterion to fail the race-neutrality test. Disparate impact should be given appropriate weight in determining whether the prosecutor acted with a forbidden intent, but it will not be conclusive in the preliminary race-neutrality step of the *Batson* inquiry. An argument relating to the impact of a classification does not alone show its purpose. Equal protection analysis turns on the intended consequences of government classifications. Unless the government actor adopted a criterion with the intent of causing the impact asserted, that impact itself does not violate the principle of race-neutrality. Nothing in the prosecutor's explanation shows that he chose to exclude jurors who hesitated in answering questions about following the interpreter because he wanted to prevent bilingual Latinos from serving on the jury. * * * *

Once the prosecutor offers a race-neutral basis for his exercise of peremptory challenges, "the trial court then has the duty to determine if the defendant has established purposeful discrimination." *Batson*, 476 U.S. at 98. While the disproportionate impact on Latinos resulting from the prosecutor's criterion for excluding these jurors does not answer the race-neutrality inquiry, it does have relevance to the trial court's decision on this question. "An invidious discriminatory purpose may often be inferred from the totality of the relevant facts, including the fact, if it is true, that the classification bears more heavily on one race than another." *Washington v. Davis*, 426 U.S. at 242. If a prosecutor articulates a basis for a peremptory challenge that results in the disproportionate exclusion of members of a certain race, the trial judge may consider that fact as evidence that the prosecutor's stated reason constitutes a pretext for racial discrimination.

In the context of this trial, the prosecutor's frank admission that his ground for excusing these jurors related to their ability to speak and understand Spanish raised a plausible, though not a necessary, inference that language might be a pretext for what in fact were race-based peremptory challenges. This was not a case where by some rare coincidence a juror happened to speak the same language as a key witness, in a community where few others spoke that tongue. If it were, the explanation that the juror could have undue influence on jury deliberations might be accepted without concern that a racial generalization had come into play. But this trial took place in a community with a substantial Latino population, and petitioner and other interested parties were members of that ethnic group. It would be common knowledge in the locality that a significant percentage of the Latino population speaks fluent Spanish, and that many consider it their preferred language, the one chosen for personal communication, the one selected for speaking with the most precision and power, the one used to define the self.

The trial judge can consider these and other factors when deciding whether a prosecutor intended to discriminate. For example, though petitioner did not suggest the alternative to the trial court here, Spanish-speaking jurors could be permitted to advise the judge in a discreet way of any concerns with the translation during the course of trial. A prosecutor's persistence in the desire to exclude Spanish-speaking jurors despite this measure could be taken into account in determining whether to accept a race-neutral explanation for the challenge.

The trial judge in this case chose to believe the prosecutor's race-neutral explanation for striking the two jurors in question, rejecting petitioner's assertion that the reasons were pretextual. In *Batson*, we explained that the trial court's decision on the ultimate question of discriminatory intent represents a finding of fact of the sort accorded great deference on appeal. * * * *

Deference to trial court findings on the issue of discriminatory intent makes particular sense in this context because, as we noted in *Batson*, the finding will "largely turn on evaluation of credibility." In the typical peremptory challenge inquiry, the decisive question will be whether counsel's race-neutral explanation for a peremptory challenge should be believed. There will seldom be much evidence bearing on that issue, and the best evidence often will be the demeanor of the attorney who exercises the challenge. As with the state of mind of a juror, evaluation of the prosecutor's state of mind based on demeanor and credibility lies peculiarly within a trial judge's province. * * * *

We discern no clear error in the state trial court's determination that the prosecutor did not discriminate on the basis of the ethnicity of Latino jurors.

In *U.S. v. Bishop*, 959 F.2d 820 (9th Cir.1992), a black defendant was charged with narcotics trafficking and assault on a federal officer. The prosecutor challenged a black juror on the ground that she lived in Compton — a predominantly low-income, black neighborhood — and was therefore "likely to take the side of those who are having a tough time" and likely to believe that the police "pick on" black people. Relying on *Hernandez*, the prosecutor argued that the high correlation between residence in that neighborhood and race was immaterial. The court disagreed:

> The prosecutor in *Hernandez* did not rely on Spanish proficiency alone. He justified his decision by pointing to the prospective jurors' avowed uncertainty as to whether they could set aside their own understanding of Spanish and listen only to the interpreter's version. Thus, there was a nexus between the jurors' characteristic — bilingualism — and their possible approach to the specific trial.

> No such nexus can be found here. For this case to be controlled by *Hernandez*, the government would have had to believe, based on Ms. Burr's conduct during *voir dire*, (1) that she had witnessed or heard incidents of violence or police behavior in Compton, and (2) that as a result, she would have found it difficult to assess the credibility of a particular witness fairly and impartially. For example, her responses to certain questions might have given rise to the prosecutor's impression.

> In contrast, the proffered reasons (that black people in Compton are likely to be hostile to the police because they have witnessed police activity and are inured to violence) are generic reasons, group-based presuppositions applicable in all criminal trials to residents of poor, predominantly black neighborhoods. They amounted to little more than the assumption that one who lives in an area heavily populated by poor black people could not fairly try a black defendant.

> To strike black jurors who reside in such communities on the assumption that they will sympathize with a black defendant rather than the police is akin to striking jurors who speak Spanish merely because the case involves Spanish-speaking witnesses. The Court in *Hernandez* strongly suggested that more was required — namely, the prosecutor's belief that the particular juror might not accept the proposed translation.

Is this a holding that the prosecutor's explanation was false — a mere disguise for racism? Or is it a holding that "black people who live in Compton" are a "cognizable class" — a subclass of black people that is protected? Or is it a holding that every peremptory challenge of a black person must now be justified by provable facts, not just by a party's intuition or "best guess"? If the latter, are most of Bailey & Rothblatt's recommendations (regarding selection of jurors based on sex, occupation, ethnicity, etc.) now illegal?

Compare *U.S. v. Uwaezhoke*, 995 F.2d 388 (3rd Cir.1993), where a black defendant was charged with importing heroin. The prosecutor exercised a peremptory challenge against a black juror, and explained that he did this because the juror was (1) a U.S. Post Office employee, and (2) because she was a single parent and a tenant living in Newark, New Jersey, and therefore may live in an area with drug problems. The trial court accepted these reasons.

On appeal, the government spelled out the first reason: while a postal employee has the same employer as the prosecutor, "it is also true that all crimes committed by postal employees at the work place are federal crimes that are prosecuted by the U.S. Attorney's Office. A prosecutor may prefer not to have postal employees on the jury because of a fear that some postal employees harbor an antipathy towards the U.S. Attorney's Office for prosecuting relatively minor, but job-related, theft and drug offenses, when similar crimes otherwise might be ignored by state and local prosecuting authorities."

The Court of Appeals accepted this, and moved on to the second reason:

> The government here claims that, because of Ms. Lucas' likely place of residence, she was more likely to have had direct exposure to a drug trafficking situation than other potential jurors as a class and that the government could legitimately prefer to assume the least risk of a juror having had such an exposure. Whether or not one accepts this explanation as an accurate description of the government's motivation in challenging Ms. Lucas, it is clearly race-neutral on its face.

> The prosecutors, at the time they exercised the peremptory challenge, knew that Ms. Lucas was a single parent of two children who was making the salary of a postal worker with four years of seniority and renting an apartment in Newark, New Jersey. It is, we believe, fair to infer that the prosecutors, in the absence of any more detailed information concerning Ms. Lucas, speculated that she might live in low income housing in Newark. Having so speculated, the prosecutors inferred that Ms. Lucas was more likely to have had direct exposure to drug trafficking than someone who did not live in low-income housing in Newark. While this conclusion may or may not be empirically correct, we cannot say that it exhibits racially discriminatory intent as a matter of law. Finally, the prosecutors concluded that if they had their preference (as they did so long as they retained a peremptory challenge), they would rather not have jurors who have had personal experience with drug trafficking. While neither the district court nor the defense attorney pressed the prosecutors to spell out their reasoning, it is possible that the prosecutors may have wanted to avoid jurors with direct drug experience for any number of legally legitimate reasons, the most likely of which is a concern that a personal experience may have left a strong impression on the juror, thus influencing her evaluation of the evidence in a way difficult for the prosecutors to predict.

> A prosecutor may rationally believe, for example, that a juror living in a neighborhood with a drug problem may fear retaliation from dealers there if she votes to convict an alleged drug trafficker or may have had an unpleasant contact with the police in the context of drug trafficking. We do not, of course, suggest that the information available to the government would support a finding that Ms. Lucas, more probably than not, would be an unqualified juror, or even an undesirable juror from the government's point of view. But that is not what peremptory challenges are all about. A primary reason for their existence is that it is not feasible for lawyers to

know much about individual jurors. Counsel must rely on educated guesses about probabilities based on their limited knowledge of a particular juror and their own life experiences. If a lawyer can show some specific conflict between information about a particular juror and the particular case to be tried, he or she is in a position to make a challenge for cause. Peremptory challenges are intended for those situations in which counsel cannot demonstrate such a specific conflict, but has some reason to believe a prospective juror may be less desirable from his or her perspective as contrasted with other jurors likely to be called in the event of a peremptory challenge. We can find nothing in the plurality opinion of *Hernandez* that suggests that the prosecutor must offer a nexus between a particular juror and the particular case that tends to demonstrate the juror would be unable to fairly evaluate the evidence; the opinion merely notes that the facts before it presented the question of how the absence of such a nexus would affect the determination of a *Batson* violation. We thus disagree with the Ninth Circuit's view that *Hernandez* "strongly suggests" that a nexus between particular juror and the facts of the case must exist in order for the prosecutor's explanation of a proposed challenge to be facially valid. *United States v. Bishop*, 959 F.2d 820, 825 (9th Cir.1992).

While it is certainly conceivable, as Mr. Uwaezhoke suggests, that the prosecutor took one look at Ms. Lucas' color and thought, "Blacks who live in poor neighborhoods cannot be trusted to fairly enforce drug laws against other blacks", it is equally possible that the prosecutor concluded that anyone, regardless of color, who lives in a poor neighborhood in Newark may have had personal experience with drug trafficking that would make their reaction to trial evidence unpredictable. We cannot find that discriminatory intent was inherent on the face of the government's explanation, and so we hold that the explanation is valid as a matter of law. If there was actual racial discrimination lurking behind this explanation, it can be found only as a matter of fact.

3. Does *Batson* mean that a lawyer may *never* exercise a peremptory challenge based on race?

Suppose the defendant is charged with the federal crime of "conspiring to violate civil rights." At trial, the prosecution will introduce evidence that the defendant burned a cross on a black family's lawn and left them a note containing racial epithets and threatening them with violence if they did not leave town. Isn't it reasonable for defense counsel to assume that almost *no* black person could view the evidence objectively and follow the judge's instruction to follow the law?

In *U.S. v. Pospisil*, 186 F.3d 1023 (8th Cir. 1999), the court held that, in such a case, defense counsel could not exercise a peremptory challenge against a black juror solely because of his race. See also *U.S. v. Mahan*, 190 F.3d 416 (6th Cir. 1999).

Questions:

(1) Does *Batson* bar such a challenge?

(2) *Should Batson* bar such a challenge?

(3) Suppose defense counsel had asserted a challenge *for cause.* Isn't this a case of "presumed bias" — i.e., no matter what answers a black juror gave on *voir dire*

(e.g., "I could set aside my feelings and be fair to the defendant"), "in general persons in a similar situation would feel prejudice" against the defendant? See *U.S. v. Torres*, in the Note after *U.S. v. Salamone, supra*. If a challenge for cause *might* be sustainable, should that mean that a *peremptory* challenge *must* be sustained?

4. **Does a lawyer violate *Batson* by *failing* to challenge a potential juror, because the lawyer wants a person of that race on the jury?** No, held the court in *U.S. v. Angel*, 355 F.3d 462 (6th Cir. 2004).

All of the Supreme Court's jury-discrimination cases to date prohibit both the government and the defense from *excluding* potential jurors because of their race. If we were to go beyond these rulings by holding that the Fifth Amendment can be violated whenever a lawyer decides to leave a member of a racial minority on the jury because of that person's race, we would be flying in the face of the general policy behind the Supreme Court's decisions, which is to allow members of racial minorities to serve on juries.

Adopting Angel's argument would also undermine a defendant's Sixth Amendment right to the effective assistance of counsel. In a case like the present one, where the defense attorney in good faith believes that the benefit of having a particular minority juror decide the client's case outweighs any negative aspects of that juror, the defense attorney would nevertheless be required to remove the juror with a peremptory challenge. The defense attorney, in other words, would be required to act contrary to what he or she perceives to be the best interests of the client. * * * *

Finally, Angel's argument conflicts with the fundamental principle that the law does not prohibit wrongful intent without an accompanying act. The criminal law, for example, has long recognized that "the mere harboring of an evil thought, such as the intent to engage in criminal conduct, does not constitute a crime; a crime is committed only if the evil thinker becomes an evil doer." 1 Wharton's Criminal Law § 25 (15th ed.2003). Here, Angel urges us to hold that the Constitution's equal protection guarantee requires the reversal of a conviction simply because trial counsel allegedly harbored the "evil thought" of leaving Chandler on the jury because she is African American. Neither precedent nor policy supports Angel's position, and we reject it.

JUDGE KEITH dissented:

The majority fixates on the need for a discriminatory *act* and finds that the *"failure to challenge* a juror, even if motivated by race" does not implicate the equal protection rights of either the juror or the defendant because the failure to challenge is not an *act*. It is at this point that the majority's reasoning squeezes the concept of use into the word "act," and in so doing strips the word use of its intended power. Yet, even the word act itself is inclusive enough to cover the conduct at issue is this case. According to Black's Law Dictionary: "In its most general sense, act signifies something done voluntarily by a person; the exercise of an individual's power; an effect produced in the external world by an exercise of the power of a person objectively, prompted by intention, and proximately caused by a motion of the will." Black's Law Dictionary 24 (6th ed.1991). * * * * The definition of a "criminal act" states that: "There can be no crime without some act, affirmative *or negative*. An omission or failure to act may constitute an act for purposes of criminal law."

PURKETT v. ELEM
United States Supreme Court
514 U.S. 765 (1995)

Per Curiam

Respondent was convicted of second-degree robbery in a Missouri court. During jury selection, he objected to the prosecutor's use of peremptory challenges to strike two black men from the jury panel, an objection arguably based on *Batson v. Kentucky*, 476 U.S. 79 (1986). The prosecutor explained his strikes:

> I struck juror number twenty-two because of his long hair. He had long curly hair. He had the longest hair of anybody on the panel by far. He appeared to not be a good juror for that fact, the fact that he had long hair hanging down shoulder length, curly, unkempt hair. Also, he had a mustache and a goatee type beard. And juror number twenty-four also has a mustache and goatee type beard. Those are the only two people on the jury with facial hair. And I don't like the way they looked, with the way the hair is cut, both of them. And the mustaches and the beards look suspicious to me.

The prosecutor further explained that he feared that juror number 24, who had had a sawed-off shotgun pointed at him during a supermarket robbery, would believe that "to have a robbery you have to have a gun, and there is no gun in this case."

The state trial court, without explanation, overruled respondent's objection and empaneled the jury. On direct appeal, respondent renewed his *Batson* claim. The Missouri Court of Appeals affirmed, finding that the "state's explanation constituted a legitimate 'hunch' " and that "the circumstances failed to raise the necessary inference of racial discrimination."

Respondent then filed a petition for habeas corpus under 28 U.S.C. § 2254, asserting this and other claims. Adopting the magistrate judge's report and recommendation, the District Court concluded that the Missouri courts' determination that there had been no purposeful discrimination was a factual finding entitled to a presumption of correctness under § 2254(d). Since the finding had support in the record, the District Court denied respondent's claim.

The Court of Appeals for the Eighth Circuit reversed and remanded with instructions to grant the writ of habeas corpus. It said: "Where the prosecution strikes a prospective juror who is a member of the defendant's racial group, solely on the basis of factors which are facially irrelevant to the question of whether that person is qualified to serve as a juror in the particular case, the prosecution must at least articulate some plausible race-neutral reason for believing that those factors will somehow affect the person's ability to perform his or her duties as a juror. In the present case, the prosecutor's comments, 'I don't like the way he looks, with the way the hair is cut. And the mustache and the beard look suspicious to me,' do not constitute such legitimate race-neutral reasons for striking juror 22." It concluded that the "prosecution's explanation for striking juror 22 was pretextual," and that the state trial court had "clearly erred" in finding that striking juror number 22 had not been intentional discrimination.

Under our *Batson* jurisprudence, once the opponent of a peremptory challenge has made out a prima facie case of racial discrimination (step 1), the burden of production shifts to the proponent of the strike to come forward with a race-neutral explanation (step 2). If a race-neutral explanation is tendered, the trial court must then decide (step 3) whether the opponent of the strike has proved purposeful racial discrimination. *Hernandez v. New York*, 500 U.S. 352, 358–359 (1991) (plurality opinion); *Batson*, supra, at 96–98. The second step of this process does not demand an explanation that is persuasive, or even plausible. "At this second step of the inquiry, the issue is the facial validity of the prosecutor's explanation. Unless a discriminatory intent is inherent in the prosecutor's explanation, the reason offered will be deemed race neutral." *Hernandez*, 500 U.S. at 360.

The Court of Appeals erred by combining *Batson's* second and third steps into one, requiring that the justification tendered at the second step be not just neutral but also at least minimally persuasive, i.e., a "plausible" basis for believing that "the person's ability to perform his or her duties as a juror" will be affected. It is not until the third step that the persuasiveness of the justification becomes relevant — the step in which the trial court determines whether the opponent of the strike has carried his burden of proving purposeful discrimination. *Batson*, supra, at 98; *Hernandez*, supra, at 359. At that stage, implausible or fantastic justifications may (and probably will) be found to be pretexts for purposeful discrimination. But to say that a trial judge may choose to disbelieve a silly or superstitious reason at step 3 is quite different from saying that a trial judge must terminate the inquiry at step 2 when the race-neutral reason is silly or superstitious. The latter violates the principle that the ultimate burden of persuasion regarding racial motivation rests with, and never shifts from, the opponent of the strike.

The Court of Appeals appears to have seized on our admonition in *Batson* that to rebut a prima facie case, the proponent of a strike "must give a 'clear and reasonably specific' explanation of his 'legitimate reasons' for exercising the challenges," *Batson*, 476 U.S. at 98, n. 20, and that the reason must be "related to the particular case to be tried," 476 U.S. at 98. This warning was meant to refute the notion that a prosecutor could satisfy his burden of production by merely denying that he had a discriminatory motive or by merely affirming his good faith. What it means by a "legitimate reason" is not a reason that makes sense, but a reason that does not deny equal protection. See *Hernandez*, supra, at 359.

The prosecutor's proffered explanation in this case — that he struck juror number 22 because he had long, unkempt hair, a mustache, and a beard — is race-neutral and satisfies the prosecution's step 2 burden of articulating a nondiscriminatory reason for the strike. "The wearing of beards is not a characteristic that is peculiar to any race." *EEOC v. Greyhound Lines, Inc.* 635 F.2d 188, 190, n. 3 (CA3 1980). And neither is the growing of long, unkempt hair. Thus, the inquiry properly proceeded to step 3, where the state court found that the prosecutor was not motivated by discriminatory intent.

In habeas proceedings in federal courts, the factual findings of state courts are presumed to be correct, and may be set aside, absent procedural error, only if they are "not fairly supported by the record." 28 U.S.C. § 2254(d)(8). Here the Court of Appeals did not conclude or even attempt to conclude that the state court's finding of no racial motive was not fairly supported by the record. For its whole focus was upon the reasonableness of the asserted nonracial motive (which it thought required by step 2) rather than the genuineness of the motive. It gave no proper basis for overturning the state court's finding of no racial motive, a finding which turned primarily on an assessment of credibility, see *Batson*, supra, at 98, n. 21.

Accordingly, respondent's motion for leave to proceed *in forma pauperis* and the petition for a writ of certiorari are granted. The judgment of the Court of Appeals is reversed, and the case is remanded for further proceedings consistent with this opinion.

JUSTICE STEVENS, with whom JUSTICE BREYER joins, dissenting.

* * * *

In *Hernandez*, this Court rejected a *Batson* claim stemming from a prosecutor's strikes of two Spanish-speaking Latino jurors. The prosecutor explained that he struck the jurors because he feared that they might not accept an interpreter's English translation of trial testimony given in Spanish. Because the prosecutor's explanation was directly related to the particular case to be tried, it satisfied the second prong of the *Batson* standard. Moreover, as the Court of Appeals noted, the plurality opinion in *Hernandez* expressly observed that striking all venirepersons who speak a given language, "without regard to the particular circumstances of the trial," might constitute a pretext for racial discrimination. 500 U.S. at 371–372 (opinion of Kennedy, J.). Based on our precedent, the Court of Appeals was entirely correct to conclude that the peremptory strike of juror 22 violated *Batson* because the reason given was unrelated to the circumstances of the trial.

Today, without argument, the Court replaces the *Batson* standard with the surprising announcement that any neutral explanation, no matter how "implausible or fantastic," even if it is "silly or superstitious," is sufficient to rebut a prima facie case of discrimination. A trial court must accept that neutral explanation unless a separate "step three" inquiry leads to the conclusion that the peremptory challenge was racially motivated. The Court does not attempt to explain why a statement that "the juror had a beard," or "the juror's last name began with the letter 'S' " should satisfy step two, though a statement that "I had a hunch" should not. It is not too much to ask that a prosecutor's explanation for his strikes be race neutral, reasonably specific, and trial related. Nothing less will serve to rebut the inference of race-based discrimination that arises when the defendant has made out a prima facie case. That, in any event, is what we decided in *Batson*. * * * *

Notes from Justin:

1. The Missouri Court of Appeals called the prosecutor's explanation for the challenges "a legitimate hunch." Why? Why might long hair, a mustache, and a goatee indicate that the person might not make a good juror for the prosecution?

2. The Court seems to say that, so long as the prosecutor gives *any* explanation which is — on its face — "race neutral", the prosecutor's challenges do not violate *Batson*. Is this a correct reading of *Purkett*, or is it too broad?

Suppose the prosecutor had said, "I struck Juror No. 22 because he is the only juror whose last name begins with the letter M." On its face, this explanation is "race neutral," isn't it? If Juror No. 22 is the only black prospective juror, the victim is white, and defendant is black, should the trial judge find that this prosecutor has not violated *Batson*? If the trial judge *does* find — on this record alone — that the prosecutor did not violate *Batson*, should an appellate court find that she erred?

3. Criminal defense attorneys reacted strongly to *Purkett*.

> Some charge that the opinion rips the heart out of *Batson*. *Purkett* "raises a burden that is relatively impossible to meet," charges Gary Guichard of Atlanta, a state public defender. "If the Court won't look at the plausibility of a race-neutral strike, then it sounds to me like I have to prove purposeful discrimination — what's in the prosecutor's mind. Unless you have a prosecutor who messes up badly, you're never going to get that kind of proof." * * * *
>
> While acknowledging criminal defense lawyers' concerns, Stanford Law Professor Barbara Babcock says they should embrace the opinion. "In these days of incredible prison sentences, it's important for a criminal defendant to have the chance to get rid of at least some potential jurors he even irrationally dislikes." * * * *
>
> Michael Stout, chair of the National Association of Criminal Defense Lawyers' peremptory challenge task force, said the U.S. Supreme Court may choose to revisit the issue. "My hope is that they did this quickly, and wanted to slow down the *Batson* train but didn't intend to go this far." [ABA Journal, February 1996, p. 20.]

4. But one criminal defense lawyer considers it *unethical for defense lawyers to comply* with *Georgia v. McCollum*. In Abbe Smith, *"Nice Work If You Can Get It": "Ethical" Jury Selection In Criminal Defense*, 67 Fordham L.Rev. 523, 530–531, 551–557, 565–566 (1998), the author described trials in which she exercised peremptory challenges in order to exclude jurors of a certain race, and tried to justify this:

> I recount these stories without shame. I am a client-centered criminal defense advocate, a partisan, and committed to representing my clients with devotion and zeal. In my view, I have no obligation as an attorney to fight cultural stereotypes unless they are being used against my client, or to serve the interests of the broader community, unless this somehow also serves my client.
>
> It is not that I believe that racial or demographic stereotypes are an accurate proxy for the attitudes and life experience of all prospective jurors. I do not. It is that, absent a meaningful exploration of the latter, I am stuck with the former, and it would be foolhardy or worse not to at least consider the generalizations on which the stereotypes are based. Indeed, in this article, I argue that it is unethical for a defense lawyer to disregard what is known about the influence of race and sex on juror attitudes in order to comply with *Batson v. Kentucky* and its progeny. I argue that although *Batson* (and *Georgia v. McCollum*, which extended the prohibition against race-based peremptory challenges to criminal defendants) has spawned an "ethics" of its own, this new ethics is at odds with other

long-standing and controlling ethical obligations of criminal defense lawyers. * * * *

There are two critical findings pertaining to race and ethnicity that ought to inform criminal defense lawyers in selecting a jury. One is that in assessing legal responsibility, we tend to favor the groups to which we belong. The other is that there is a strong correlation between race and attitudes about policing.

It is generally acknowledged that we tend to favor members of our own racial or ethnic group over those of other groups. Because an important part of identity is group membership, and because people like to feel good about themselves, we tend to perceive the groups to which we belong in positive terms. Consistent with the comparative nature of most evaluations, when we attribute an elevated stature to our own groups, we tend to attribute a lower one to other groups. Some researchers have found that "ingroup bias," favoring members of one's own group, is greatest in members of disadvantaged groups. This is especially so when the lower status is seen as undeserved. This would suggest that African Americans have a strong sense of empathy and connection with other African Americans — "same-race favoritism" — that might find expression on a jury.

With regard to attributions of guilt based on race, there seems to be a consensus that if the evidence is strong, the attitudes and biases of jurors are less important. When the evidence is not as compelling — that is, when it is a close case and the jury could go either way — juror bias may well influence verdicts.

There are many studies that suggest that white jurors attribute guilt to minority defendants more readily than to white defendants. * * * *

In some cities, when the number of African Americans on juries has been increased, there has been an accompanying decrease in conviction rates. That majority black juries tend to acquit criminal defendants more than majority white juries is certainly something defense lawyers should consider.

Because minorities are more often victims of police misconduct and discriminatory law enforcement, they may well be more skeptical of police testimony than whites. Black jurors may also have a different interpretation of certain evidence, based on their distinctive experience, than their white counterparts. For example, when a defendant flees the police, whites may assume (and may be instructed by the judge to legally infer) that this flight suggests consciousness of guilt. African American and other minority jurors might attribute that same conduct not to the guilty conscience of the defendant, but rather to the defendant's fear of mistreatment at the hands of the police. * * * *

No matter how personally distasteful or morally unsettling, zealous advocacy demands that criminal defense lawyers use whatever they can, including stereotypes, to defend their clients. Criminal lawyers are "not allowed to refrain from lawful advocacy simply because it offends" them.

This applies to jury selection as well as a range of other strategic decisions at trial. Although this is increasingly difficult in the face of *Batson, J.E.B.*, and *McCollum*, it must be done. The preeminent obligation of criminal defense lawyers is zealous advocacy, putting the government to its burden of proof and fighting for the individual accused above all others. Hence, in order to abide by this overriding professional obligation, criminal defense lawyers must do what they can to circumvent *McCollum*.

There are ways to do this. Much has been written about prosecutorial pretext in order to avoid the strictures of *Batson*. Defense lawyers can always cite occupation, neighborhood, lack of experience with the issues raised, and even failure to look the defendant in the eye as reasons for striking prospective jurors.

Questions: (1) Do you agree with Professor Smith's ethical stance? (2) Should her arguments re "ingroup bias" and the like justify a *prosecutor's* exercise of peremptory challenges based on race?

5. In *Minetos v. City University of New York*, 925 F.Supp. 177 (S.D.N.Y., 1996), the court considered the effect of *Purkett*:

Time has proven Mr. Justice Marshall's concurrence in *Batson* correct. Ten frustrating years have now passed since the Supreme Court's decision in *Batson*. *Purkett* promises to add more years of vexatious litigation over a right lacking constitutional statute in our jurisprudence. All peremptory challenges should now be banned as an unnecessary waste of time and an obvious corruption of the judicial process. Such a change would have the added benefit of putting an end to the awkward analyses set forth in *Batson* and its progeny which have proved over ten years to be uncertain in their application and which have caused great consternation in the courts. See e.g., *Purkett*, 115 S.Ct. at 1772–1774 (Stevens, J. dissenting).

A brief review of the case law shows that judicial interpretations of *Batson* are all over the map. This is particularly true of *Batson's* requirement that court's guess at what facially race-neutral reasons are, in fact, pretextual for discriminatory motives. See e.g. *Hernandez v. New York*, 500 U.S. 352 (1991) (striking all Spanish-speaking Latino venirepersons because they would not accept court interpretor's translation of Spanish-speaking witnesses was not pretextual); *United States v. Alvarado*, 951 F.2d 22 (2d Cir.1991) (striking African-American and Hispanic venirepersons for being young or for being social workers was not pretextual); *Polk v. Dixie Ins. Co.*, 972 F.2d 83 (5th Cir.1992) (striking African-American venireperson for lack of "eyeball contact" was not pretextual); *U.S. v. Clemons*, 843 F.2d 741 (3d Cir.1988) (striking all African-American venirepersons for being single and young was not pretextual); *United States v. Tucker*, 836 F.2d 334 (7th Cir.1988) (striking all African-American venirepersons for lack of education and business experience was not pretextual); but cf., *Garrett v. Morris*, 815 F.2d 509 (8th Cir.) (striking all African-American venirepersons for lack of education and knowledge was pretextual); *Splunge v. Clark*, 960 F.2d 705 (7th Cir.1992) (striking African American venireperson based on "feelings that she would not be a good juror" was pretextual); *United States v. Bishop*, 959 F.2d 820 (9th Cir.1992) (striking African-American venirepersons for living in low-income neighborhood was pretextual). * * * *

It is time to put an end to this charade. We have now had enough judicial experience with the *Batson* test to know that it does not truly unmask racial discrimination. In short, lawyers can easily generate facially neutral reasons for striking jurors and trial courts are hard pressed to second-guess them, rendering *Batson* and *Purkett's* protections illusory. After ten years, this court joins in Justice Marshall's call for an end to peremptory challenges and the racial discrimination they perpetuate.[9]

7. In *State v. Ross*, 154 Or.App. 121 (1998), the trial judge accepted the prosecutor's race-neutral explanation re why he exercised peremptory challenges against black jurors. The judge said: "I base that on the fact that, in part, I know [the prosecutor], and I know that he does not exclude jurors based on their race." The appellate court reversed:

It is apparent that the trial court did not confine its credibility fact finding role to the *voir dire* proceeding. Rather, it relied, in part, on its personal knowledge about the prosecutor. While we will give deference to a trial court's finding that a prosecutor actually intended to strike a prospective juror for race-neutral reasons and will presume that the court fulfilled its constitutional duty to ferret out purposeful discrimination, we cannot affirm a finding based on a court's personal, out-of-court, off-the-record knowledge about the prosecutor. To do so injects into the decision-making process an improper component because the trial court acted both as a character witness, vouching for the credibility of the prosecutor, and as the fact finder.

It could be that the prosecutor acted with race-neutral reasons for exercising the peremptory challenge, but the process of making the decision about that issue was tainted by the trial court's consideration of the contacts with the prosecutor outside the confines of the trial. The integrity of the process to prevent the challenge of jurors for other than race-neutral reasons is compromised if a trial court is permitted to consider its personal knowledge about the prosecutor. A trial court must confine its decision-making process to what occurred during *voir dire* and the evidence that is probative on that issue. Consequently, by including the subjective opinion about the prosecutor's character in its consideration of the issue, the trial court erred in making its assessment about whether defendant carried her burden of proof regarding purposeful discrimination. Under these circumstances, the only appropriate remedy is to reverse the trial court and remand for a new trial.

Questions:

1. If the prosecutor regularly appears before this judge, the judge will of course know something about this prosecutor. How is the judge to expunge

---

[9] Many commentators have likewise advocated the end of peremptory challenges, for example: David Zonana, *The Effect of Assumptions about Racial Bias on the Analysis of Batson's Three Harms and the Peremptory Challenge*, 1994 Ann.Surv.Am.L. 203 (1995); *The Supreme Court — Leading Cases: Equal Protection*, 105 Harv.L.Rev. 255 (1991); Robert L. Harris, Jr., *Redefining the Harm of Peremptory Challenges*, 32 Wm. & Mary L.Rev. 1027 (1991); Albert W. Altschuler, *The Supreme Court and the Jury: Voir Dire, Peremptory Challenges, and the Review of Jury Verdicts*, 56 U.Chi.L.Rev. 153 (1991).

this knowledge from his or her mind when making a *Purkett* determination
— which requires the judge to base his or her decision on the prosecutor's
subjective intent?

2. In *Ross*, was the judge's mistake simply one of being too open and honest
on the record?

3. After *Ross*, must Oregon judges recuse themselves from all cases in
which they know the prosecutor?

4. Is *Ross* (and the problems raised by *Ross*) the inevitable consequence of
Purkett (or perhaps of *Batson*)?

SNYDER v. LOUISIANA
United States Supreme Court, 2008
___ U.S. ___, 128 S.Ct. 1203

JUSTICE ALITO delivered the opinion of the Court.

Petitioner Allen Snyder was convicted of first-degree murder in a Louisiana
court and was sentenced to death. He asks us to review a decision of the Louisiana
Supreme Court rejecting his claim that the prosecution exercised some of its
peremptory jury challenges based on race, in violation of *Batson v. Kentucky*, 476
U.S. 79 (1986). We hold that the trial court committed clear error in its ruling on a
Batson objection, and we therefore reverse.

I

The crime for which petitioner was convicted occurred in August 1995. At that
time, petitioner and his wife, Mary, had separated. On August 15, they discussed the
possibility of reconciliation, and Mary agreed to meet with petitioner the next day.
That night, Mary went on a date with Howard Wilson. During the evening,
petitioner repeatedly attempted to page Mary, but she did not respond. At
approximately 1:30 a.m. on August 16, Wilson drove up to the home of Mary's
mother to drop Mary off. Petitioner was waiting at the scene armed with a knife. He
opened the driver's side door of Wilson's car and repeatedly stabbed the occupants,
killing Wilson and wounding Mary.

The State charged petitioner with first-degree murder and sought the death
penalty based on the aggravating circumstance that petitioner had knowingly
created a risk of death or great bodily harm to more than one person.

Voir dire began on Tuesday, August 27, 1996, and proceeded as follows. During
the first phase, the trial court screened the panel to identify jurors who did not meet
Louisiana's requirements for jury service or claimed that service on the jury or
sequestration for the duration of the trial would result in extreme hardship. More
than 50 prospective jurors reported that they had work, family, or other commitments that would interfere with jury service. In each of those instances, the nature
of the conflicting commitments was explored, and some of these jurors were
dismissed.

In the next phase, the court randomly selected panels of 13 potential jurors for
further questioning. The defense and prosecution addressed each panel and
questioned the jurors both as a group and individually. At the conclusion of this

questioning, the court ruled on challenges for cause. Then, the prosecution and the defense were given the opportunity to use peremptory challenges (each side had 12) to remove remaining jurors. The court continued this process of calling 13-person panels until the jury was filled. In accordance with Louisiana law, the parties were permitted to exercise "backstrikes." That is, they were allowed to use their peremptories up until the time when the final jury was sworn and thus were permitted to strike jurors whom they had initially accepted when the jurors' panels were called.

Eighty-five prospective jurors were questioned as members of a panel. Thirty-six of these survived challenges for cause; 5 of the 36 were black; and all 5 of the prospective black jurors were eliminated by the prosecution through the use of peremptory strikes. The jury found petitioner guilty of first-degree murder and determined that he should receive the death penalty. * * * *

II

Batson provides a three-step process for a trial court to use in adjudicating a claim that a peremptory challenge was based on race. First, a defendant must make a prima facie showing that a peremptory challenge has been exercised on the basis of race; second, if that showing has been made, the prosecution must offer a race-neutral basis for striking the juror in question; and third, in light of the parties' submissions, the trial court must determine whether the defendant has shown purposeful discrimination.

On appeal, a trial court's ruling on the issue of discriminatory intent must be sustained unless it is clearly erroneous. The trial court has a pivotal role in evaluating *Batson* claims. Step three of the *Batson* inquiry involves an evaluation of the prosecutor's credibility, and "the best evidence of discriminatory intent often will be the demeanor of the attorney who exercises the challenge," *Hernandez*, 500 U.S. at 365. In addition, race-neutral reasons for peremptory challenges often invoke a juror's demeanor (e.g., nervousness, inattention), making the trial court's first-hand observations of even greater importance. In this situation, the trial court must evaluate not only whether the prosecutor's demeanor belies a discriminatory intent, but also whether the juror's demeanor can credibly be said to have exhibited the basis for the strike attributed to the juror by the prosecutor. We have recognized that these determinations of credibility and demeanor lie peculiarly within a trial judge's province, and we have stated that "in the absence of exceptional circumstances, we would defer to the trial court." 500 U.S. at 366.

III

Petitioner centers his *Batson* claim on the prosecution's strikes of two black jurors, Jeffrey Brooks and Elaine Scott. Because we find that the trial court committed clear error in overruling petitioner's *Batson* objection with respect to Mr. Brooks, we have no need to consider petitioner's claim regarding Ms. Scott.

In *Miller-El v. Dretke*, the Court made it clear that in considering a *Batson* objection, or in reviewing a ruling claimed to be *Batson* error, all of the circumstances that bear upon the issue of racial animosity must be consulted. 545 U.S., at 239. Here, as just one example, if there were persisting doubts as to the outcome, a court would be required to consider the strike of Ms. Scott for the bearing it might have upon the strike of Mr. Brooks. In this case, however, the explanation given for the strike of Mr. Brooks is by itself unconvincing and suffices for the determination that there was *Batson* error.

When defense counsel made a *Batson* objection concerning the strike of Mr. Brooks, a college senior who was attempting to fulfill his student-teaching obligation, the prosecution offered two race-neutral reasons for the strike. The prosecutor explained:

> I thought about it last night. Number 1, the main reason is that he looked very nervous to me throughout the questioning. Number 2, he's one of the fellows that came up at the beginning of voir dire and said he was going to miss class. He's a student teacher. My main concern is for that reason, that being that he might, to go home quickly, come back with guilty of a lesser verdict so there wouldn't be a penalty phase. Those are my two reasons.

Defense counsel disputed both explanations, and the trial judge ruled as follows: "All right. I'm going to allow the challenge. I'm going to allow the challenge."

We discuss the prosecution's two proffered grounds for striking Mr. Brooks in turn.

A

With respect to the first reason, the Louisiana Supreme Court was correct that "nervousness cannot be shown from a cold transcript, which is why the trial judge's evaluation must be given much deference." As noted above, deference is especially appropriate where a trial judge has made a finding that an attorney credibly relied on demeanor in exercising a strike. Here, however, the record does not show that the trial judge actually made a determination concerning Mr. Brooks' demeanor. The trial judge was given two explanations for the strike. Rather than making a specific finding on the record concerning Mr. Brooks' demeanor, the trial judge simply allowed the challenge without explanation. It is possible that the judge did not have any impression one way or the other concerning Mr. Brooks' demeanor. Mr. Brooks was not challenged until the day after he was questioned, and by that time dozens of other jurors had been questioned. Thus, the trial judge may not have recalled Mr. Brooks' demeanor. Or, the trial judge may have found it unnecessary to consider Mr. Brooks' demeanor, instead basing his ruling completely on the second proffered justification for the strike. For these reasons, we cannot presume that the trial judge credited the prosecutor's assertion that Mr. Brooks was nervous.

B

The second reason proffered for the strike of Mr. Brooks — his student-teaching obligation — fails even under the highly deferential standard of review that is applicable here. At the beginning of voir dire, when the trial court asked the members of the venire whether jury service or sequestration would pose an extreme hardship, Mr. Brooks was 1 of more than 50 members of the venire who expressed concern that jury service or sequestration would interfere with work, school, family, or other obligations.

When Mr. Brooks came forward, the following exchange took place:

MR. JEFFREY BROOKS: I'm a student at Southern University, New Orleans. This is my last semester. My major requires me to student teach, and today I've already missed a half a day. That is part of my — it's required for me to graduate this semester.

[DEFENSE COUNSEL]:   Mr. Brooks, if you — how many days would you miss if you were sequestered on this jury? Do you teach every day?

MR. JEFFREY BROOKS: Five days a week.

[DEFENSE COUNSEL]:   Five days a week.

MR. JEFFREY BROOKS: And it's 8:30 through 3:00.

[DEFENSE COUNSEL]:   If you missed this week, is there any way that you could make it up this semester?

MR. JEFFREY BROOKS: Well, the first two weeks I observe, the remaining I begin teaching, so there is something I'm missing right now that will better me towards my teaching career.

[DEFENSE COUNSEL]:   Is there any way that you could make up the observed observation [sic] that you're missing today, at another time?

MR. JEFFREY BROOKS: It may be possible, I'm not sure.

[DEFENSE COUNSEL]:   Okay. So that —

THE COURT: Is there anyone we could call, like a Dean or anything, that we could speak to?

MR. JEFFREY BROOKS: Actually, I spoke to my Dean, Doctor Tillman, who's at the university probably right now.

THE COURT: All right.

MR. JEFFREY BROOKS: Would you like to speak to him?

THE COURT: Yeah.

MR. JEFFREY BROOKS: I don't have his card on me.

THE COURT: Why don't you give [a law clerk] his number, give [a law clerk] his name and we'll call him and we'll see what we can do.

(MR. JEFFREY BROOKS LEFT THE BENCH).

Shortly thereafter, the court again spoke with Mr. Brooks:

THE LAW CLERK: Jeffrey Brooks, the requirement for his teaching is a three hundred clock hour observation. Doctor Tillman at Southern University said that as long as it's just this week, he doesn't see that it would cause a problem with Mr. Brooks completing his observation time within this semester.

(MR. BROOKS APPROACHED THE BENCH)

THE COURT: We talked to Doctor Tillman and he says he doesn't see a problem as long as it's just this week, you know, he'll work with you on it. Okay?

MR. JEFFREY BROOKS: Okay.

(MR. JEFFREY BROOKS LEFT THE BENCH)."

Once Mr. Brooks heard the law clerk's report about the conversation with Doctor Tillman, Mr. Brooks did not express any further concern about serving on the jury, and the prosecution did not choose to question him more deeply about this matter.

The colloquy with Mr. Brooks and the law clerk's report took place on Tuesday, August 27; the prosecution struck Mr. Brooks the following day, Wednesday, August 28; the guilt phase of petitioner's trial ended the next day, Thursday, August 29; and the penalty phase was completed by the end of the week, on Friday, August 30.

The prosecutor's second proffered reason for striking Mr. Brooks must be evaluated in light of these circumstances. The prosecutor claimed to be apprehensive that Mr. Brooks, in order to minimize the student-teaching hours missed during jury service, might have been motivated to find petitioner guilty, not of first-degree murder, but of a lesser included offense because this would obviate the need for a penalty phase proceeding. But this scenario was highly speculative. Even if Mr. Brooks had favored a quick resolution, that would not have necessarily led him to reject a finding of first-degree murder. If the majority of jurors had initially favored a finding of first-degree murder, Mr. Brooks' purported inclination might have led him to agree in order to speed the deliberations. Only if all or most of the other jurors had favored the lesser verdict would Mr. Brooks have been in a position to shorten the trial by favoring such a verdict.

Perhaps most telling, the brevity of petitioner's trial — something that the prosecutor anticipated on the record during voir dire — meant that serving on the jury would not have seriously interfered with Mr. Brooks' ability to complete his required student teaching. As noted, petitioner's trial was completed by Friday, August 30. If Mr. Brooks, who reported to court and was peremptorily challenged on Wednesday, August 28, had been permitted to serve, he would have missed only two additional days of student teaching, Thursday, August 29, and Friday, August 30. Mr. Brooks' dean promised to "work with" Mr. Brooks to see that he was able to make up any student-teaching time that he missed due to jury service; the dean stated that he did not think that this would be a problem; and the record contains no suggestion that Mr. Brooks remained troubled after hearing the report of the dean's remarks. In addition, although the record does not include the academic calendar of Mr. Brooks' university, it is apparent that the trial occurred relatively early in the fall semester. With many weeks remaining in the term, Mr. Brooks would have needed to make up no more than an hour or two per week in order to compensate for the time that he would have lost due to jury service. When all of these considerations are taken into account, the prosecutor's second proffered justification for striking Mr. Brooks is suspicious.

The implausibility of this explanation is reinforced by the prosecutor's acceptance of white jurors who disclosed conflicting obligations that appear to have been at least as serious as Mr. Brooks'. We recognize that a retrospective comparison of jurors based on a cold appellate record may be very misleading when alleged similarities were not raised at trial. In that situation, an appellate court must be mindful that an exploration of the alleged similarities at the time of trial might have shown that the jurors in question were not really comparable. In this case, however, the shared characteristic, i.e., concern about serving on the jury due to conflicting obligations, was thoroughly explored by the trial court when the relevant jurors asked to be excused for cause.

A comparison between Mr. Brooks and Roland Laws, a white juror, is particularly striking. During the initial stage of voir dire, Mr. Laws approached the court and offered strong reasons why serving on the sequestered jury would cause him hardship. Mr. Laws stated that he was "a self-employed general contractor," with "two houses that are nearing completion, one with the occupants moving in this weekend." He explained that, if he served on the jury, "the people won't be able to move in." Mr. Laws also had demanding family obligations: "My wife just had a hysterectomy, so I'm running the kids back and forth to school, and we're not originally from here, so I have no family in the area, so between the two things, it's kind of bad timing for me."

Although these obligations seem substantially more pressing than Mr. Brooks', the prosecution questioned Mr. Laws and attempted to elicit assurances that he would be able to serve despite his work and family obligations. See *ibid* (prosecutor asking Mr. Laws "if you got stuck on jury duty anyway . . . would you try to make other arrangements as best you could?"). And the prosecution declined the opportunity to use a peremptory strike on Mr. Laws. If the prosecution had been sincerely concerned that Mr. Brooks would favor a lesser verdict than first-degree murder in order to shorten the trial, it is hard to see why the prosecution would not have had at least as much concern regarding Mr. Laws.

The situation regarding another white juror, John Donnes, although less fully developed, is also significant. At the end of the first day of voir dire, Mr. Donnes approached the court and raised the possibility that he would have an important work commitment later that week. Because Mr. Donnes stated that he would know the next morning whether he would actually have a problem, the court suggested that Mr. Donnes raise the matter again at that time. The next day, Mr. Donnes again expressed concern about serving, stating that, in order to serve, "I'd have to cancel too many things," including an urgent appointment at which his presence was essential. Despite Mr. Donnes' concern, the prosecution did not strike him.

As previously noted, the question presented at the third stage of the *Batson* inquiry is whether the defendant has shown purposeful discrimination. The prosecution's proffer of this pretextual explanation naturally gives rise to an inference of discriminatory intent. See *Purkett v. Elem*, 514 U.S. 765, 768 (1995) ("At the third stage, implausible or fantastic justifications may (and probably will) be found to be pretexts for purposeful discrimination").

In other circumstances, we have held that, once it is shown that a discriminatory intent was a substantial or motivating factor in an action taken by a state actor, the burden shifts to the party defending the action to show that this factor was not determinative. We have not previously applied this rule in a Batson case, and we need not decide here whether that standard governs in this context. For present purposes, it is enough to recognize that a peremptory strike shown to have been motivated in substantial part by discriminatory intent could not be sustained based on any lesser showing by the prosecution. And in light of the circumstances here — including absence of anything in the record showing that the trial judge credited the claim that Mr. Brooks was nervous, the prosecution's description of both of its proffered explanations as "main concerns," and the adverse inference noted above — the record does not show that the prosecution would have pre-emptively challenged Mr. Brooks based on his nervousness alone. Nor is there any realistic possibility that this subtle question of causation could be profitably explored further on remand at this late date, more than a decade after petitioner's trial.

We therefore reverse the judgment of the Louisiana Supreme Court and remand the case for further proceedings not inconsistent with this opinion.

JUSTICE THOMAS, with whom JUSTICE SCALIA joins, dissenting.

Petitioner essentially asks this Court to second-guess the fact-based determinations of the Louisiana courts as to the reasons for a prosecutor's decision to strike two jurors. The evaluation of a prosecutor's motives for striking a juror is at bottom a credibility judgment, which lies "peculiarly within a trial judge's province." *Hernandez v. New York*, 500 U.S. 352, 365 (1991) None of the evidence in the record as to jurors Jeffrey Brooks and Elaine Scott demonstrates that the trial court clearly erred in finding they were not stricken on the basis of race. Because the trial court's determination was a "permissible view of the evidence," I would affirm the judgment of the Louisiana Supreme Court. * * * *

The Court acknowledges two reasons why a trial court "has a pivotal role in evaluating *Batson* claims." First, the Court notes that the trial court is uniquely situated to judge the prosecutor's credibility because the best evidence of discriminatory intent "often will be the demeanor of the attorney who exercises the challenge." Second, it recognizes that the trial court's "first-hand observations" of the juror's demeanor are of "great importance" in determining whether the prosecutor's neutral basis for the strike is credible.

The Court's conclusion, however, reveals that it is only paying lipservice to the pivotal role of the trial court. The Court second-guesses the trial court's determinations in this case merely because the judge did not clarify which of the prosecutor's neutral bases for striking Mr. Brooks was dispositive. But we have never suggested that a reviewing court should defer to a trial court's resolution of a *Batson* challenge only if the trial court made specific findings with respect to each of the prosecutor's proffered race-neutral reasons. To the contrary, when the grounds for a trial court's decision are ambiguous, an appellate court should not presume that the lower court based its decision on an improper ground, particularly when applying a deferential standard of review.

The prosecution offered two neutral bases for striking Mr. Brooks: his nervous demeanor and his stated concern about missing class. The trial court, in rejecting defendant's Batson challenge, stated only "All right. I'm going to allow the challenge. I'm going to allow the challenge." The Court concedes that "the record does not show" whether the trial court made its determination based on Mr. Brooks' demeanor or his concern for missing class, but then speculates as to what the trial court might have thought about Mr. Brooks' demeanor. As a result of that speculation, the Court concludes that it "cannot presume that the trial court credited the prosecutor's assertion that Mr. Brooks was nervous." Inexplicably, however, the Court concludes that it can presume that the trial court impermissibly relied on the prosecutor's supposedly pretextual concern about Mr. Brooks' teaching schedule, even though nothing in the record supports that interpretation over the one the Court rejects.

Indeed, if the record suggests anything, it is that the judge was more influenced by Mr. Brooks' nervousness than by his concern for missing class. Following an exchange about whether his desire to get back to class would make Mr. Brooks more likely to support a verdict on a lesser included offense because it might avoid a penalty phase, defense counsel offered its primary rebuttal to the prosecutor's proffered neutral reasons. Immediately after argument on the nervousness point, the judge ruled on the Batson challenge, even interrupting the prosecutor to do so:

MR. VASQUEZ: His main problem yesterday was the fact that he didn't know if he would miss some teaching time as a student teacher. The clerk called the school and whoever it was and the Dean said that wouldn't be a problem. He was told that this would go through the weekend, and he expressed that that was his only concern, that he didn't have any other problems. As far as him looking nervous, hell, everybody out here looks nervous. I'm nervous.

MR. OLINDE: Judge, it's —

MR. VASQUEZ: Judge, that's — You know.

MR. OLINDE: — a question of this: It's a peremptory challenge. We need 12 out of 12 people. Mr. Brooks was very uncertain and very nervous looking and —

THE COURT: All right. I'm going to allow the challenge. I'm going to allow the challenge.

Although this exchange is certainly not hard-and-fast evidence of the trial court's reasoning, it undermines the Court's presumption that the trial judge relied solely on Mr. Brooks' concern for missing school.

The Court also concludes that the trial court's determination lacked support in the record because the prosecutor failed to strike two other jurors with similar concerns. Those jurors, however, were never mentioned in the argument before the trial court, nor were they discussed in the filings or opinions on any of the three occasions this case was considered by the Louisiana Supreme Court. Petitioner failed to suggest a comparison with those two jurors in his petition for certiorari, and apparently only discovered this "clear error" in the record when drafting his brief before this Court. We have no business overturning a conviction, years after the fact and after extensive intervening litigation, based on arguments not presented to the courts below. * * * *

Note from Justin:

In *People v. Johnson*, 47 Cal.3d 1194 (1989), the court considered how to deal with a peremptory challenge allegedly exercised because of a prospective juror's *demeanor*.

A black defendant, represented by a Jewish lawyer, was charged with murder of a white man. The prosecutor exercised peremptory challenges against prospective jurors who were black, Jewish, or Asian, and the resulting jury contained no persons in those groups. When the defense attorney complained, the prosecutor explained why he challenged the Jewish prospective jurors:

As to the Jewish jurors, the prosecutor stated that one was a "very nervous person," gave the defendants "a very noticeable smile," was opposed to the death penalty or leaned that way. The second person was 71 years old, looked tired, had a relative who was a lawyer, and felt the death penalty was not a deterrent. He seemed to have a great deal of rapport with defense counsel and appeared more friendly to the defendant than the average juror. The third person was 61 years old and was a "very tired appearing person." She was critical of a police department she had dealt with and she felt an officer had lied. She also gave defendants a very sympathetic look. The prosecutor thought the fourth person was "weird," that sympathy for the defendants might be a problem for him, and that he "didn't seem to be willing to commit to promises to make a decision based on the facts of the evidence." The prosecutor also stated he felt totally unable to relate to him.

The prosecutor gave similar explanations regarding his challenges to the blacks and Asians. The trial court rejected defense counsel's *Batson* claim, and the California Supreme Court affirmed the conviction.

Dissenting Justice Mosk was troubled by the prosecutor's reliance on his descriptions of prospective jurors as "nervous," "tired," "gave defendants a very sympathetic look," and the like. Referring to the court's decision in *People v. Wheeler* (1978) 22 Cal.3d 258, which foretold *Batson*, he stated:

It is true that in *Wheeler* we recognized that peremptory challenges have traditionally been triggered by evidence suggestive of bias ranging from the obviously serious to the apparently trivial, from the virtually certain to the highly speculative. By way of examples, we acknowledged that jurors have been struck "simply because their clothes or hair length suggest an unconventional lifestyle," or even — quoting from Blackstone — because of the juror's "bare looks and gestures," e.g., because "upon entering the box the juror may have smiled at the defendant". We explained that in the usual case these subjective reasons "are essentially neutral with respect to the various groups represented on the venire," and therefore "peremptory challenges predicated on such reasons do not significantly skew the population mix of the venire in one direction or another; rather, they promote the impartiality of the jury without destroying its representativeness."

This reasoning is undoubtedly valid as far as it goes, i.e., unless and until the trial court on motion finds the defendant has made a prima facie case that the prosecutor is using his peremptory challenges to deprive the defendant of his state constitutional right to a jury drawn from a representative cross-section of the community or his federal constitutional right to equal protection of the laws. That finding fundamentally alters the situation. After the finding, the prosecutor's peremptory challenges of the minority jurors are presumptively unconstitutional: "At this point the statutory provision that 'no reason need be given' for a peremptory challenge (Pen.Code § 1069) must give way to the constitutional imperative: the statute is not invalid on its face, but in these limited circumstances it would be invalid as applied if it were to insulate from inquiry a presumptive denial of the right to an impartial jury. That right is paramount because the peremptory challenge is not a constitutional necessity but a statutory privilege." *Wheeler*, 22 Cal.3d at 281, fn. 28. To overcome this presumptive unconstitutionality, the prosecutor must establish that the challenges in question were in fact exercised on grounds of specific bias rather than group bias; the trial court must then make a finding on the ultimate issue, i.e., whether the prosecutor has sustained his burden of justification; and if it finds that he has, the court will deny the *Wheeler* or *Batson* motion and the defendant will be tried by the jury thus chosen.

If the defendant is convicted, he will be entitled to appellate review of the *Wheeler* or *Batson* ruling in his appeal from the judgment. * * * * Meaningful appellate review of *Wheeler* or *Batson* rulings is obviously essential to protect that right. And it is all the more essential because the ruling in issue is largely discretionary. * * * * This is so, of course, because in making a discretionary ruling the trial court by definition finds less guidance in the law and hence may run a greater risk of error. It is true that appellate review of such rulings is often more difficult for the same reason. But the solution is to strengthen, not weaken, the process of appellate review. * * * *

The primary element of all appellate review is the record. Without a record sufficient for its needs, an appellate court cannot even begin to discharge its constitutional and statutory duties. In the present case, the record is adequate to enable us to determine whether there is factual and legal support for the prosecutor's objective reasons for striking the eight minority prospective jurors. But the record is wholly inadequate to allow us to make the same determination as to his subjective reasons. Thus there is no record whatever to support the prosecutor's claims that Mrs. Smalley was a "very nervous person" and gave the defendants a "very noticeable smile"; that Mr. Kirstel was a "very tired person" and "friendly-appearing" towards the defense; that Mrs. Sobel was a "very tired-appearing person" and gave the defendants a "very sympathetic look"; that Mr. Berliner was "weird" and dressed "out of the mainstream." * * * *

Indeed, the record was inadequate for this purpose even at the trial level. After the prosecutor gave his reasons, the court offered defense counsel the opportunity to respond. Counsel for codefendant replied that "obviously" he was unable to discuss the prosecutor's "feelings about this, that and the other," and that the "off-hand impressions" of the prosecutor "cannot be controverted at all." Counsel for defendant agreed that "much of the impressions, statements and reasons are not reflected by the record, and they concern jurors that have been passed for cause." Although the prosecutor insisted that most of his reasons were on the record, he conceded that "The ones obviously of the feelings against the parties are not necessarily on the record." Expressing his frustration, counsel for codefendant concluded by explaining,

> Your Honor, this is one of the problems, and I see it increasingly as we have played out this motion, is that the prosecutor now can use all kinds of out-of-the-record reasons for doing this, that and the other, which are totally unrebuttable. I think it's impossible for me to recall whether somebody smirked at the prosecutor or not or whether somebody gave a smile to one of the rest of us. Who knows? But this is the problem.

The court ignored the problem and proceeded to rule on the motion.

As an appellate court, however, we cannot ignore the problem. Just as the lack of a record prevented defense counsel from controverting the prosecutor's subjective reasons, so too it bars us from holding those reasons to be adequate. We cannot presume that one party's recollection of the facts is necessarily more accurate than the other's. * * * *

In the present context, it is the prosecutor who has the burden of making a showing that overcomes the prima facie case of discrimination found by the trial court. It is therefore also the prosecutor who must make a record of such showing that is adequate for appellate review. Indeed, he is the only party able to do so, because only he knows why he is challenging each particular juror. Having both the duty and the opportunity to make the necessary record, the prosecutor must be held responsible for its absence.

We adopted the *Wheeler* rule because we recognized our responsibility to insure that the constitutional right to a jury drawn from a representative cross-section of the community "not be reduced to a hollow form of words, but remain a vital and effective safeguard of the liberties of California citizens." 22 Cal.3d at 272. Applying that principle, both this court and the United States Supreme Court thereafter warned that the constitutional rights protected by the *Wheeler* and *Batson* rules would be defeated if the prosecutor were allowed to discharge his burden by giving vague reasons for his presumptively discriminatory challenges. * * * * In *Batson*, the United States Supreme Court cautioned that "If these general assertions were accepted as rebutting a defendant's prima facie case, the Equal Protection Clause would be but a vain and illusory requirement." 476 U.S. at 98.

A fortiori, these fundamental guaranties would also be nullified if a reviewing court were to hold sufficient the showing that the prosecutor offers us here — i.e., subjective reasons that are not only vague in content but are unsupported by any record whatever. Because a defendant can neither rebut such reasons at his *Wheeler* hearing nor challenge them on appeal, they would constitute a procedural barrier to redress as insuperable as the former rule of *Swain v. Alabama* (1965) 380 U.S. 202. And our condemnation of the *Swain* rule in *Wheeler* is equally applicable here: "It demeans the Constitution to declare a fundamental personal right under that charter and at the same time make it virtually impossible for an aggrieved citizen to exercise that right." 22 Cal.3d at 287.

But the majority disagreed. The court quoted a justice who had dissented from a decision which had adopted Justice Mosk's position:

I have my own hunch that what is really behind the majority's rejection of hunches, gut-feelings and body language is a fear that prosecutors will insincerely attempt to justify group bias with such reasons and that trial judges, some of whom are perceived as being unsympathetic toward the *Wheeler* rule, will rubber-stamp their explanations. I submit that if we cannot trust trial courts to do their job fairly, we might as well close up shop and that we, ourselves, were insincere when, in *Wheeler*, we professed our faith in the "good judgment" of the trial bench.

In *Dorsey v. State*, 868 So.2d 1192 (Fla. 2003), the court held that "a potential juror's nonverbal behavior, the existence of which is disputed by opposing counsel and neither observed by the trial court nor otherwise supported by the record, is not a proper basis to sustain a peremptory challenge as genuinely race neutral."

One more issue in *Johnson* caught my eye. Justice Mosk believed that he uncovered the true reason why the prosecutor wanted Jewish people off the jury:

> Although the objective reasons given by the prosecutor for challenging the Jewish jurors are thus unsupported by the record, the transcript does contain a line of questioning by the prosecutor that suggests another reason why he struck each member of this group of prospective jurors. In conducting his *voir dire* of Mr. Kirstel the prosecutor asked, "Do you think that as a juror you would maybe be a little bit more lenient towards a black person because he's a minority?" When Mr. Kirstel observed that, although he too was a minority because he was Jewish, he would not thus favor defendants, the prosecutor reiterated: "Okay. But especially if you think in terms of being a minority in maybe a religious sense, you would bend over backwards a little bit for a racial minority?" Again Mr. Kirstel replied that to the best of his ability he would not do so. But the prosecutor relentlessly pressed the point:

>> If it came up that you thought, well, gee, you know, Jews have been a minority for hundreds and hundreds of years — thousands of years — and they have been oppressed at many times and the black people have been oppressed in this country and I feel sorry for the defendants because they're black, if that started coming up for you do you think you'd be able to tell — at least recognize it and do your best to set it aside?

> The questions say more about the prosecutor than about Mr. Kirstel. They imply a belief that a Jew could be biased in favor of these defendants simply because of the history of oppression of the Jewish people. Such a belief, however, is precisely the kind of group bias that *Wheeler* condemns as an impermissible ground for striking the members of that group from the jury: to act on that ground is to violate the defendant's right to trial by a jury drawn from a representative cross-section of the community under article I, section 16, of the California Constitution.

Recall the advice given by Bailey & Rothblatt (in 1985) that "people of British, Scandinavian, or German extraction . . . are presumably more law-abiding, conservative and strict, with more rigid standards of conduct" than Italians, Irish, Jews, Latin Americans, and Southern Europeans. If a lawyer were to exercise peremptory challenges on this advice, should this be deemed a violation of *Batson*? Wouldn't Justice Mosk so hold?

f. Remedies

If the trial court finds that one of the attorneys has challenged a juror in violation of *Batson*, what *remedy* is appropriate — reseating the challenged juror, or striking the entire jury venire and starting over?

1. In *Jones v. State*, 105 Md.App. 257 (1995), after the trial court found that defense counsel had challenged several prospective jurors merely because they were white,

the trial court reseated those jurors. On appeal, the court rejected defendant's contention that this was improper:

> We next address appellant's contention that the trial court erred in reseating the five jurors after finding that defense counsel had violated *Batson*. Appellant claims that the court should have struck the entire venire instead and begun the jury selection process anew.
>
> The issue of what action should be taken by a trial court when a *Batson* violation has occurred is one of first impression in this State. The Supreme Court has provided us with no guidance in this regard. Indeed, the Court acknowledged in *Batson* that it was leaving this issue for another day. * * * * 476 U.S. at 99, n. 24).
>
> The appellate courts in other states appear to be genuinely split on this issue. Several states favor striking the entire panel upon a finding of purposeful discrimination. These states include: California (see *People v. Wheeler*, 22 Cal.3d 258; Florida (see *State v. Neil*, 457 So.2d 481 (Fla.1984)); Indiana (see *Minniefield v. State*, 539 N.E.2d 464, 466 (Ind.1989); and North Carolina (see *State v. McCollum*, 334 N.C. 208 (1993) (holding that the fairer approach is to dismiss the entire panel and begin jury selection anew because "to ask jurors who have been improperly excluded from a jury because of their race to then return to the jury to remain unaffected by that recent discrimination, and to render an impartial verdict without prejudice toward either the State or the defendant, would be to ask them to discharge a duty which would require near superhuman effort and which would be extremely difficult for a person possessed of any sensitivity whatsoever to carry out successfully")).
>
> Other states permit a trial judge to reseat the improperly stricken juror and continue jury selection. These states include: Georgia (see *Ellerbee v. State*, 215 Ga.App. 312 (1994)); Mississippi (see *Conerly v. State*, 544 So.2d 1370, 1372 (Miss.1989)); Missouri (see *State v. Grim*, 854 S.W.2d 403, 416 (Mo.)); and Wisconsin (see *State v. Walker*, 154 Wis.2d 158 (1990)). * * * *
>
> We agree that the proper approach is to permit the trial court to determine, in its discretion, whether a wrongfully excluded juror should be stricken altogether from the venire or should be reseated. The guiding factor in this determination should be the likelihood of the juror harboring any prejudice to the violating party as a result of being improperly excluded from the panel. For example, when a *Batson* challenge is made in the jury's presence and the violating party offers his non-discriminatory reason for striking the juror in front of that juror, there is the risk that the juror will bear animosity toward the party who exercised the strike. When, on the other hand, counsel explains his reasons for striking a particular juror at a bench conference, and the circumstances otherwise do not indicate to the juror that he was struck for improper reasons, the likelihood of prejudice is not present or is minimal. The potential for prejudice is important, of course, because at risk are the rights of the parties to a fair and impartial trial. * * * *
>
> Our holding, we believe, is consistent with the principles underlying *Batson*, and is grounded in both pragmatic and principled concerns. If, for instance, we were to require that an entirely new venire be called every

time there is a *Batson* violation, this would unfairly reward counsel for his improper conduct and give him exactly what he wanted, namely, a different jury panel. The party who has gone too far should not, as a matter of principle, be allowed to wipe the slate clean and start anew.[5] In addition, there is the practical realization that, if we were to require the trial court to strike the entire panel in every case of discrimination, then there might be those parties who would purposefully discriminate in exercising strikes for the sole purpose of getting a new panel.[6]

Also, it should not be forgotten that the exclusion of a juror on the basis of race is a violation of the juror's constitutional rights. While a prospective juror does not have a right to sit on a particular jury, he or she does have a constitutional right under the Equal Protection Clause not to be excluded from serving on a jury on the basis of his or her race. *Powers v. Ohio*, 499 U.S. 400, 409 (1991) (White, J., concurring); *Holland v. Illinois*, 493 U.S. 474, 488 (1990). Requiring discharge of the juror in every instance would not only reward the party who has violated the Constitution but would serve to punish the juror. * * * *

Lastly, we note that concerns for judicial economy support reseating the stricken juror. Starting the jury selection process over every time there is a *Batson* violation would be both burdensome and costly. The remedy of reseating the juror is a sensible, efficacious way of protecting both the rights of prospective jurors and the parties in the case.

2. In *U.S. v. Huey*, 76 F.3d 638 (5th Cir. 1996), Huey (a white) and Garcia (an Hispanic) were jointly tried on drug offenses. The government planned to introduce into evidence tapes and transcripts that showed Huey using "harsh and offensive racial epithets." For this reason, Huey's counsel exercised peremptory challenges against 5 black prospective jurors (each of whom had said that the tapes and transcripts would not influence their determination of guilt or innocence). Both the government and Garcia objected, but the trial court allowed the challenges. Both Huey and Garcia were convicted. The court of appeals reversed:

The only reason articulated in the record for why these jurors — as a class and not individually — should not serve is that they would be biased after hearing the derogatory language and racial slurs contained on the tapes. This reason was premised only on the race of these jurors; no mention was ever made of any nonracial characteristic of any individual juror. Thus, the explanation in the record for these strikes is nothing more than an assumption of partiality based on race and a form of racial stereotyping, both of which have been repeatedly condemned by the courts. The Supreme Court has firmly "rejected the view that assumptions of partiality based on race provide a legitimate basis for disqualifying a person as an impartial juror." We do so again today.

---

[5] We also recognize, however, that if the entire venire were struck, this might, under some circumstances, work to penalize the violating party, since the result might be that some of the jurors he did not strike, and very much wanted on the jury, would be dismissed.

[6] Any skepticism of the bar, however, does not go so far as to foresee that counsel might purposefully state the reasons for his or her objection to a particular juror, whether warranted or not, in the jury's presence so that entire panel could be stricken.

The court held that Garcia — a co-defendant — had standing to contest Huey's challenges on appeal. And so did Huey himself!

> We are not unaware that there is some irony in reversing Huey's conviction, given that it was his counsel who made the discriminatory strikes. We are convinced, however, that this result is consistent with the teachings of *Batson* and its progeny. In addition to harming individual defendants and prospective jurors, racial discrimination in the selection of jurors impugns the integrity of the judicial system and the community at large. * * * * Although we recognize that some might fear that this resolution could become a source of mischief in the hands of some co-defendants, we believe that not only is this resolution mandated by *Batson* and its progeny, but that such mischief can be avoided with relative ease by the exercise of diligent oversight and sound judgment on the part of trial judges, and through their proper application of the well-known three-step inquiry for ensuring race-neutral use of peremptory challenges.

The court in *U.S. v. Boyd*, 86 F.3d 719 (7th Cir.1996) was faced with a similar situation, but refused to follow *Huey*:

> Our conclusion that the exercise of a peremptory challenge by the defense, in violation of *Batson* and *McCollum*, does not entitle the defendant to a new trial unless the challenge amounts to ineffective assistance of counsel, places us in respectful disagreement with *United States v. Huey*, 76 F.3d 638 (5th Cir.1996). There were two defendants in *Huey*; one objected to the other's improper peremptory challenge, and the judge waved off the objection. The court of appeals held that not only the objecting defendant but also the defendant who exercised the improper challenge were entitled to new trials. The panel in *Huey* observed that *Batson* and *McCollum* set limits on peremptory challenges to protect the interests of jurors and the system of justice. Because the rule serves interests other than those of the accused, the court believed, a defendant can obtain a new trial by attacking his own decision. This is a non-sequitur. Important social interests allow a judge to block the defense from taking certain action; that is the holding of *McCollum*. It does not follow that by violating these important social interests a defendant can help himself to a new trial.
>
> Consider a few parallels. Perjury is forbidden — it is a felony; it may be the basis of an enhanced sentence, and a belief that the client is about to commit perjury permits counsel to expose the scheme and withdraw. Powerful social interests put perjury off limits. A judge will do what is possible to stop perjury before it occurs, and penalize perjury if these devices fail. Does it follow that a defendant who commits perjury only to find that the device backfires — perhaps because the jury concludes that the liar must be covering up guilt — is entitled to a new trial? No, it does not follow. Then there is the choice of counsel. Society has interests in preventing obstruction of justice by defendants, who may try to coordinate through their lawyers. *Wheat v. United States*, 486 U.S. 153 (1988), accordingly holds that a court may insist that each defendant be separately represented. Does it follow that when the judge permits joint representation, and the defendants waive any potential conflict of interest, they may nonetheless obtain a new trial by pointing to the social interests that could

have been invoked to prevent joint representation? No, it does not follow.

Huey did not discuss any of these parallel situations. And two of the three members of the panel in *Huey* filed a concurring opinion to remark that its outcome will undermine public trust in the criminal justice system. Indeed so. Giving a defendant a new trial because of his own violation of the Constitution would make a laughingstock of the judicial process. If a decision of the Supreme Court gave the accused the right to bootstrap his own violation of *Batson* into a new trial, we would be obliged to enforce that holding. But there is no such decision, and the principle that no one is entitled to profit from his own wrong governs the conduct of trials as well as the imposition of criminal sanctions.

3. How about a "self help" remedy: instead of objecting to opposing counsel's improper challenges to a group, simply use *your* challenges to remove *your opponent's* group, leaving behind a mixed jury? In *Miesner v. State*, 665 So.2d 978 (Ala.Ct.Crm.App., 1995), this is exactly what the prosecutor did, challenging blacks in response to defense counsel's challenges to whites. The prosecutor explained:

> There are 17 black people on the jury, in the venire; there are 13 white folks. I did not feel I wanted to strike any more white people, because the Defense struck black male, white male, white male, white male, white male, white female, and they're striking off all the white folks. I wanted a balanced jury. I wanted some white people on the jury. I think I've tried two or three cases where they've been all black, and I've had strange results, and I want a cross section. I want whites and blacks, males and females. So, since the Defense was striking all the white folks off, all the white males, all the strong white males, and a strong white female, I felt that I needed to strike from the black females. * * * * In other words, it's a catch-22. Of course, race came into consideration. But to be absolutely honest, race was a factor.

The court held that this was improper, as *Batson* absolutely forbids the prosecutor to base peremptory challenges on race.

g.   Reconsidering the Peremptory Challenge

Now that *Batson* and its progeny have created all these difficulties with the peremptory challenge, is the peremptory challenge worth the trouble of saving? If the peremptory challenge were eliminated — as Justice Marshall's concurrence in *Batson* urged — we might save a lot of court time taken up by the challenges and disputes over whether *Batson* or *McCollum* was violated. Why *not* just get rid of it?

Prior to trial by a *judge*, the attorneys may *not voir dire the judge* as to her attitudes and possible bias. A party may challenge a judge for cause only if there is independent evidence that a judge is biased in the case. While some states (such as California) allow a peremptory challenge to a judge (no more than one per case), this right is seldom exercised. Why treat a jury different from a judge?

The judge is pretty much a known quantity. He or she is a trained lawyer, has been selected (through election or appointment) by some process that has reviewed the candidate's qualifications, and has had experience hearing evidence and finding facts. And if you want to see how she operates, you may inspect her at any time:

just walk into her courtroom and see how she handles another case. She will also have a reputation in the legal community that you can check out. All these things give us confidence in the judge that we do not have in the jury.

By contrast, the jury is a bunch of amateurs the lawyers have never seen before or even heard of — "twelve strangers pulled in off the street". (Take another look at the quote from G.K Chesterton at the outset of this chapter). Entrusting your client's fate to such people can be a frightening experience, for both you and your client. Who are these people? Can they be fair to my side? Do they *respect* the law enough to follow the judge's instructions? Are they *intelligent* enough to understand my arguments and the judge's instructions? A lawyer must have some power to find out something about these people and remove those who do not seem qualified, if the parties and the public are to have any confidence a jury's verdict.

The challenge *for cause* helps, but it might not be enough. To prove bias well enough for a challenge for cause to be sustained, usually the lawyer must get the juror *to admit* facts or attitudes that show bias. Most people, however, do not like to admit such things — especially in a room full of other people. But even without admissions of bias, the lawyer (or his client) might "feel" that this juror will not give him a fair shake. This feeling might be based on all sorts of attitudes and preconceptions held by the lawyer or client — not all of them provable or even admirable. But shouldn't such feelings be considered if we want litigants and the public to have confidence in the jury's verdict and respect for the judicial system?

Also, the very *pursuit* of admissions of bias — through penetrating *voir dire* questions — might annoy, embarrass, and alienate the juror being questioned. If the lawyer fails to convince the judge to sustain a challenge for cause to this juror, the lawyer might be stuck with a juror who *now* has a reason to dislike the lawyer. Having the peremptory challenge as a back-up to the challenge for cause gives the lawyer some leeway in asking the questions he needs to ask to make proper challenges for cause.[3]

For all these reasons, the verdict of most trial lawyers (on all sides) is: *if we are to keep the jury*, we must also keep the peremptory challenge. Do you agree?

3.   Reconsidering the Jury

But this leads to the next question: why keep the jury? If you were designing a legal system, would you include juries?

We might approach the question this way: if you were designing a system of government, would you allow 12 unelected, untrained citizens chosen at random to decide whether to declare war? Whether to raise taxes? Whether to adopt a death penalty? Whether to *impose* a death penalty on an individual? Whether to decide

---

[3] In some jurisdictions, the right to voir dire has been restricted. Primary responsibity for voir dire has been moved from the lawyers to the judge, who knows less about the evidence to be presented in the case and is less able to ask jurors questions about what the evidence will show. Judges sometimes allow the lawyers to supplement the judge's voir dire with a few questions of their own, but judges often have their own agendas: to move the case along.

Where restrictions on voir dire prevent lawyers from finding out much about the juror as an individual, and where <u>Batson</u> and its progeny prevent the lawyer from basing peremptory challenges on "stereotypes", what is left? How can a trial lawyer intelligently use a peremptory challenge? Is it now safer just to waive a jury and submit to a bench trial?

an individual's guilt or innocence of a crime? Whether to impose liability for money damages on someone? Is there any difference between these activities? (If you think that deciding cases is "less important", consider the riots that occurred after the verdicts in the "Rodney King" and *Lozano* trials.)

How is your decision about whether juries are a good idea affected by *how we select* juries? Would you have less confidence in juries if (1) only the judge (not the lawyers) may ask questions during *voir dire* (presently the practice in federal and some state courts), (2) the right to peremptory challenge is limited by *Batson* and its progeny, or — as some have proposed — is totally eliminated (3) jury decisions need not be unanimous, and/or (4) juries become smaller? If *all* of these things happen — a distinct possibility — is the American jury worth saving?

Chapter 10

JOINDER & SEVERANCE

Suppose a bank is held up by three men: the stick-up man, a lookout, and the driver of the getaway car. Dan, Don, and Dale are charged with the crime. If each is tried separately, much of the evidence at each of the 3 trials will be the same: the teller will testify three times about the holdup, the security guard will testify three times that he saw the three drive off together, etc. And at least 36 innocent citizens will be dragged into court for jury duty. Wouldn't it be easier on the witnesses, cheaper for the government, and impinge on the jury time of only one-third as many citizens, if the three men could be tried in a single, joint trial?

But suppose things get a bit sticky. Suppose Dan confessed to the police, admitting that he and the other two committed the crime together. The confession is inadmissible hearsay as to Don and Dale, but admissible against Dan as an admission.

Or suppose Dan plans to testify at trial that he drove the getaway car for Don and Dale, but he had no idea that Don and Dale had gone into the bank to rob it. Should Don and Dale be forced to go to trial with a "rat" like Dan?

Which is more important — efficiency or "fairness"? Do we *have to* choose one or the other, or are there ways to have *both*? Maybe these difficulties call for a little creative thinking.

Problem 10

To: My law clerk

From: U.S. District Court Judge Ali Katz

Re: *U.S. v. Ames, et. al.*

The grand jury indicted ten defendants on one count of conspiracy to commit mail and wire fraud and 100 counts of mail and wire fraud. The ten are Al Ames, Bob Bones, Charles Charles, Donna Dipp, Ethyl Egan, Fred Ford, Gus Gains, Hillary Hill, Irma Irving, and Jim Johns. Testimony before the grand jury showed the following:

Ames and Bones are petroleum engineers. They leased land in Canyon County, Wyoming, where they planned to drill for oil. To get the funds needed for drilling, they formed Gorgeous Gusher Company, which would solicit funds from investors through "telemarketing" — getting lists of potential investors and phoning them with sales pitches. They hired Charles, an accountant, to set up the books and manage the office, and they gave him the title of "Chief Executive Officer". Then they hired Dipp as sales manager. She supervised the other six defendants, who did the phone soliciting. Ames and Bones phoned in information on oil development to Charles, who relayed it to Dipp and the sales force for use in soliciting investors. 100 investors put a total of $1 million into the Company. None of them ever got a nickel back.

The phone solicitors had told investors that Gorgeous Gusher had geologists' reports which said that Canyon County was "loaded with oil" and drilling at the site would "almost certainly" produce oil in such large quantities that the investors would probably get all their money back in less than a year, and after that it was "all gravy".

The U.S. Attorney put on evidence that tended to show that these statements were false. Three oil experts testified that the chance of finding oil in Canyon County was not high, and even if oil was found, it would not produce enough barrels to provide more than a modest return on investment.

Bones gave a written statement to Larry Letter, a U.S. Post Office Investigator assigned to the case. The statement reads:

> When Ames and I gave our daily briefings to Charles, we sometimes exaggerated the prospects of finding oil in substantial amounts. Once, Ames told him that we had already struck oil, which wasn't true. I told Charles that Ames had overstated it and we were about to find oil, but that wasn't exactly true either.

Letter then told the grand jury that:

> I also interviewed Charles. He admitted that the information that the phone solicitors gave to the investors came from him. He said that he got it from Ames and Bones, who phoned him every day with reports on developments in Wyoming. Charles then passed it on to the solicitors at daily sales meetings.

> I also interviewed Dipp. She admitted that she told the phone solicitors to exaggerate, but she says that Charles told her to do this.

Ames, Charles, and Hill have each moved for a severance. The other defense attorneys do not join or oppose the motion, but the U.S. Attorney opposes it.

Ames' lawyer says that Ames will testify that he told Charles the truth — that the chances of finding oil were good but not great, and there was a reasonable chance for a "big hit". He will put on oil experts to testify that these statements were true. He contends that if the statements to investors went beyond this, then someone else — Charles, Dipp, and/or the others — must have been doing the lying.

Charles' lawyer says that Charles will testify that he didn't know any of the information was false. He said he didn't know much about oil, and Ames and Bones were the experts, so he took their word for it. Charles says that Bones told him recently that Ames is lying and Charles is telling the truth, but Bones will not take the stand at trial.

Dipp will testify that she and the phone solicitors had no idea that any of the information was false. They told potential investors no more than what Charles told them to say. Hill will testify that she worked only part-time, about two days a week. She missed most of the sales meetings, and she raised only about $5,000 from just one investor.

The lawyers estimate that trial will take 100 court days. Please read the attached authorities and advise me what to do.

UNITED STATES CONSTITUTION, 6TH AMENDMENT

In all criminal prosecutions, the accused shall enjoy the right . . . to be confronted with the witnesses against him.

Federal Rules of Criminal Procedure

Rule 8.   Joinder of Offenses and of Defendants

(a) **Joinder of Offenses.** The indictment or information may charge a defendant in separate counts with 2 or more offenses if the offenses charged — whether felonies or misdemeanors or both — are of the same or similar character, or are based on the same act or transaction, or are connected with or constitute parts of a common scheme or plan.

(b) **Joinder of Defendants.** The indictment or information may charge 2 or more defendants if they are alleged to have participated in the same act or transaction, or in the same series of acts or transactions, constituting an offense or offenses. The defendants may be charged in one or more counts together or separately. All defendants need not be charged in each count.

Rule 13.   Joint Trial of Separate Cases

The court may order that separate cases be tried together as though brought in a single indictment or information if all offenses and all defendants could have been joined in a single indictment or information.

Rule 14.   Relief from Prejudicial Joinder

(a) **Relief.** If the joinder of offenses or defendants in an indictment, an information, or a consolidation for trial appears to prejudice a defendant or the government, the court may order separate trials of counts, sever the defendants' trials, or provide any other relief that justice requires.

(b) **Defendant's Statements.** Before ruling on a defendant's motion to sever, the court may order an attorney for the government to deliver to the court for in camera inspection any defendant's statement that the government intends to use as evidence.

BRUTON v. UNITED STATES
United States Supreme Court
391 U.S. 123 (1968)

Mr. Justice Brennan delivered the opinion of the Court.

This case presents the question, last considered in *Delli Paoli v. United States*, 352 U.S. 232, whether the conviction of a defendant at a joint trial should be set aside although the jury was instructed that a codefendant's confession inculpating the defendant had to be disregarded in determining his guilt or innocence.

A joint trial of petitioner and one Evans in the District Court for the Eastern District of Missouri resulted in the conviction of both by a jury on a federal charge of armed postal robbery. A postal inspector testified that Evans orally confessed to him that Evans and petitioner committed the armed robbery. The postal inspector obtained the oral confession, and another in which Evans admitted he had an accomplice whom he would not name, in the course of two interrogations of Evans at the city jail in St. Louis, Missouri, where Evans was held in custody on state criminal charges. Both petitioner and Evans appealed their convictions to the Court of Appeals. That court set aside Evans' conviction on the ground that his oral confessions to the postal inspector should not have been received in evidence against him. However, the court, relying upon *Delli Paoli*, affirmed petitioner's conviction, because the trial judge instructed the jury that, although Evans' confession was competent evidence against Evans, it was inadmissible hearsay against petitioner and therefore had to be disregarded in determining petitioner's guilt or innocence. * * * *

We hold that, because of the substantial risk that the jury, despite instructions to the contrary, looked to the incriminating extrajudicial statements in determining petitioner's guilt, admission of Evans' confession in this joint trial violated petitioner's right of cross-examination secured by the Confrontation Clause of the Sixth Amendment. We therefore overrule *Delli Paoli* and reverse.

The basic premise of *Delli Paoli* was that it is "reasonably possible for the jury to follow" sufficiently clear instructions to disregard the confessor's extrajudicial statement that his codefendant participated with him in committing the crime. If it were true that the jury disregarded the reference to the codefendant, no question would arise under the Confrontation Clause, because by hypothesis the case is treated as if the confessor made no statement inculpating the nonconfessor. But since *Delli Paoli* was decided, this Court has effectively repudiated its basic premise. Before discussing this, we pause to observe that in *Pointer v. Texas*, 380 U.S. 400, we confirmed "that the right of cross-examination is included in the right of an accused in a criminal case to confront the witnesses against him" secured by the Sixth Amendment; "a major reason underlying the constitutional confrontation rule is to give a defendant charged with crime an opportunity to cross-examine the witnesses against him." * * * *

Here Evans' oral confessions were in fact testified to, and were therefore actually in evidence. That testimony was legitimate evidence against Evans and to that extent was properly before the jury during its deliberations. Even greater, then, was the likelihood that the jury would believe Evans made the statements and that they were true — not just the self-incriminating portions, but those implicating petitioner as well. Plainly, the introduction of Evans' confession added substantial, perhaps even critical, weight to the Government's case in a form not subject to cross-examination, since Evans did not take the stand. Petitioner thus was denied his constitutional right of confrontation.

Delli Paoli assumed that this encroachment on the right to confrontation could be avoided by the instruction to the jury to disregard the inadmissible hearsay evidence. But, as we have said, that assumption has since been effectively repudiated. True, the repudiation was not in the context of the admission of a confession inculpating a codefendant, but in the context of a New York rule which submitted to the jury the question of the voluntariness of the confession itself. *Jackson v. Denno*, 378 U.S. 368. Nonetheless the message of *Jackson* for *Delli Paoli* was clear. We there held that a defendant is constitutionally entitled at least to have the trial judge first determine whether a confession was made voluntarily before submitting it to the jury for an assessment of its credibility. More specifically, we expressly rejected the proposition that a jury, when determining the confessor's guilt, could be relied on to ignore his confession of guilt should it find the confession involuntary. Significantly, we supported that conclusion in part by reliance upon the dissenting opinion of Mr. Justice Frankfurter for the four Justices who dissented in *Delli Paoli*.

That dissent challenged the basic premise of *Delli Paoli* that a properly instructed jury would ignore the confessor's inculpation of the nonconfessor in determining the latter's guilt. "The fact of the matter is that too often such admonition against misuse is intrinsically ineffective in that the effect of such a nonadmissible declaration cannot be wiped from the brains of the jurors. The admonition therefore becomes a futile collocation of words and fails of its purpose as a legal protection to defendants against whom such a declaration should not tell." The dissent went on to say, "The Government should not have the windfall of having the jury be influenced by evidence against a defendant which, as a matter of law, they should not consider but which they cannot put out of their minds." To the same effect is the statement of Mr. Justice Jackson in his concurring opinion in *Krulewitch v. United States*, 336 U.S. 440, 453: "The naive assumption that prejudicial effects can be overcome by instructions to the jury all practicing lawyers know to be unmitigated fiction." * * * *

In addition to *Jackson*, our action in 1966 in amending Rule 14 of the Federal Rules of Criminal Procedure also evidences our repudiation of *Delli Paoli's* basic premise. Rule 14 authorizes a severance where it appears that a defendant might be prejudiced by a joint trial.[6] The Rule was amended in 1966 to provide expressly that "in ruling on a motion by a defendant for severance the court may order the attorney for the government to deliver to the court for inspection in camera any statements or confessions made by the defendants which the government intends to introduce in evidence at the trial" The Advisory Committee on Rules said in explanation of the amendment:

> A defendant may be prejudiced by the admission in evidence against a co-defendant of a statement or confession made by that co-defendant. This prejudice cannot be dispelled by cross-examination if the co-defendant does not take the stand. Limiting instructions to the jury may not in fact erase the prejudice. The purpose of the amendment is to provide a procedure whereby the issue of possible prejudice can be resolved on the motion for severance. * * * *

Another reason cited in defense of *Delli Paoli* is the justification for joint trials in general, the argument being that the benefits of joint proceedings should not have to be sacrificed by requiring separate trials in order to use the confession against the declarant. Joint trials do conserve state funds, diminish inconvenience to witnesses and public authorities, and avoid delays in bringing those accused of crime to trial. But the answer to this argument was cogently stated by Judge Lehman of the New York Court of Appeals, dissenting in *People v. Fisher*, 249 N.Y. 419, 432: "We still adhere to the rule that an accused is entitled to confrontation of the witnesses against him and the right to cross-examine them. We destroy the

---

[6] Joinder of defendants is governed by Rules 8(b) and 14 of the Federal Rules of Criminal Procedure. "The rules are designed to promote economy and efficiency and to avoid a multiplicity of trials, where these objectives can be achieved without substantial prejudice to the right of the defendants to a fair trial." *Daley v. United States*, 231 F.2d 123, 125. An important element of a fair trial is that a jury consider only relevant and competent evidence bearing on the issue of guilt or innocence.

age-old rule which in the past has been regarded as a fundamental principle of our jurisprudence by a legalistic formula, required of the judge, that the jury may not consider any admissions against any party who did not join in them. We secure greater speed, economy and convenience in the administration of the law at the price of fundamental principles of constitutional liberty. That price is too high."

Finally, the reason advanced by the majority in *Delli Paoli* was to tie the result to maintenance of the jury system. "Unless we proceed on the basis that the jury will follow the court's instructions where those instructions are clear and the circumstances are such that the jury can reasonably be expected to follow them, the jury system makes little sense." 352 U.S., at 242. We agree that there are many circumstances in which this reliance is justified. Not every admission of inadmissible hearsay or other evidence can be considered to be reversible error unavoidable through limiting instructions; instances occur in almost every trial where inadmissible evidence creeps in, usually inadvertently. "A defendant is entitled to a fair trial but not a perfect one" *Lutwak v. United States*, 344 U.S. 604, 619. It is not unreasonable to conclude that in many such cases the jury can and will follow the trial judge's instructions to disregard such information. Nevertheless, as was recognized in *Jackson v. Denno*, there are some contexts in which the risk that the jury will not, or cannot, follow instructions is so great, and the consequences of failure so vital to the defendant, that the practical and human limitations of the jury system cannot be ignored. Such a context is presented here, where the powerfully incriminating extrajudicial statements of a codefendant, who stands accused side-by-side with the defendant, are deliberately spread before the jury in a joint trial. Not only are the incriminations devastating to the defendant but their credibility is inevitably suspect, a fact recognized when accomplices do take the stand and the jury is instructed to weigh their testimony carefully given the recognized motivation to shift blame onto others. The unreliability of such evidence is intolerably compounded when the alleged accomplice, as here, does not testify and cannot be tested by cross-examination. It was against such threats to a fair trial that the Confrontation Clause was directed.

We, of course, acknowledge the impossibility of determining whether in fact the jury did or did not ignore Evans' statement inculpating petitioner in determining petitioner's guilt. But that was also true in the analogous situation in *Jackson v. Denno*, and was not regarded as militating against striking down the New York procedure there involved. It was enough that that procedure posed "substantial threats to a defendant's constitutional rights to have an involuntary confession entirely disregarded and to have the coercion issue fairly and reliably determined. These hazards we cannot ignore." 378 U.S. at 389. Here the introduction of Evans' confession posed a substantial threat to petitioner's right to confront the witnesses against him, and this is a hazard we cannot ignore. Despite the concededly clear instructions to the jury to disregard Evans' inadmissible hearsay evidence inculpating petitioner, in the context of a joint trial we cannot accept limiting instructions as an adequate substitute for petitioner's constitutional right of cross-examination. The effect is the same as if there had been no instruction at all.

Reversed.

Mr. Justice White, dissenting.

* * * *

The defendant's own confession may not be used against him if coerced, not because it is untrue but to protect other constitutional values. The jury may have great difficulty understanding such a rule and following an instruction to disregard the confession. In contrast, the codefendant's admissions cannot enter into the determination of the defendant's guilt or innocence because they are unreliable. This the jury can be told and can understand. Just as the Court believes that juries can reasonably be expected to disregard ordinary hearsay or other inadmissible evidence when instructed to do so, I believe juries will disregard the portions of a codefendant's confession implicating the defendant when so instructed. Indeed, if we must pick and choose between hearsay as to which limiting instructions will be deemed effective and hearsay the admission of which cannot be cured by instructions, codefendants' admissions belong in the former category rather than the latter, for they are not only hearsay but hearsay which is doubly suspect. If the Court is right in believing that a jury can be counted on to ignore a wide range of hearsay statements which it is told to ignore, it seems very old to me to question its ability to put aside the codefendant's hearsay statements about what the defendant did.

It is a common experience of all men to be informed of ' "facts" relevant to an issue requiring their judgment, and yet to disregard those 'facts' because of sufficient grounds for discrediting their veracity or the reliability of their source. Responsible judgment would be impossible but for the ability of men to focus their attention wholly on reliable and credible evidence, and jurymen are no less capable of exercising this capacity than other men. Because I have no doubt that serious-minded and responsible men are able to shut their minds to unreliable information when exercising their judgment, I reject the assumption of the majority that giving instructions to a jury to disregard a codefendant's confession is an empty gesture.

The rule which the Court announces today will severely limit the circumstances in which defendants may be tried together for a crime which they are both charged with committing. Unquestionably, joint trials are more economical and minimize the burden on witnesses, prosecutors, and courts. They also avoid delays in bringing those accused of crime to trial. This much the Court concedes. It is also worth saying that separate trials are apt to have varying consequences for legally indistinguishable defendants. The unfairness of this is confirmed by the common prosecutorial experience of seeing codefendants who are tried separately strenuously jockeying for position with regard to who should be the first to be tried. * *
* *

Notes from Judge Katz:

1. What *should* the trial court have done here to protect Bruton's rights?

2. In Chapter 8, we saw cases (such as *Duncan v. Louisiana*) treating the American jury as the greatest thing since indoor plumbing. In *Bruton*, however, the Court doesn't trust the jury to follow a simple instruction from the judge. Any inconsistency here?

3. If *you* were sitting on the *Bruton* jury, could *you* have followed the judge's instructions? If so, do you have any reason to think that your fellow jurors couldn't do the same? If not, does this mean that you disagree with the *Bruton* Supreme Court opinion?

4. Suppose that the parties in *Bruton* had all waived a jury trial, and the case was tried by the *judge*. Would this have affected the Court's analysis? In *Cockrell v. Oberhauser*, 413 F.2d 256 (9th Cir.1969), the court held that "The *Bruton* rule does not apply to [defendant] because she was tried by the court and not by a jury. Nothing in *Bruton* suggests that a judge is incapable of applying the law of limited admissibility which he has himself announced." Is the court saying that judges are smarter than jurors? More "objective" than jurors?

5. **Suppose the co-defendant *testifies*.**

In *Nelson v. O'Neil*, 402 U.S. 622 (1970), O'Neil and Runnels were jointly charged with car theft, kidnapping, and robbery. After the victim testified and identified the two defendants as the criminals, a policeman testified that Runnels had admitted the crimes and implicated O'Neil as his confederate. Runnels then took the stand, claimed an alibi, and denied having confessed to the policeman. O'Neil's lawyer did not cross-examine Runnels. O'Neil then testified, telling the same alibi. The trial court instructed the jury not to consider Runnels' alleged confession against O'Neil. Both were convicted. The Court of Appeal reversed, holding that the right of confrontation meant a right to *effective* confrontation, and O'Neil could effectively cross-examine Runnels only if Runnels had "affirmed the statement as his".

The Supreme Court disagreed. It noted that constitutional problems arose in *Bruton* because D1 could not "confront" D2 about his out-of-court statement, as D2 had exercised his right not to take the stand. Here, however, D2 *did* take the stand, so D1 *could* "confront" (i.e., cross-examine) him. Therefore, O'Neil had not been denied his right of confrontation. In rejecting the Court of Appeals' reasoning, the Supreme Court stated:

> Had Runnels in this case "affirmed the statement as his," the respondent would certainly have been in far worse straits than those in which he found himself when Runnels testified as he did. For then counsel for the respondent could only have attempted to show through cross-examination that Runnels had confessed to a crime he had not committed, or, slightly more plausibly, that those parts of the confession implicating the respondent were fabricated. This would, moreover, have required an abandonment of the joint alibi defense, and the production of a new explanation for the respondent's presence with Runnels in the white Cadillac at the time of their arrest. To be sure, Runnels might have "affirmed the statement" but denied its truthfulness, claiming, for example, that it had been coerced, or made as part of a plea bargain. But cross-examination by the respondents' counsel would have been futile in that event as will. For once Runnels had testified that the statement was false, it could hardly have profited the respondent for his counsel through cross-examination to try to shake that testimony. If the jury were to believe that the statement was false as to Runnels, it could hardly conclude that it was not false as to the respondent as well.

The short of the matter is that, given a joint trial and a common defense, Runnels' testimony respecting his alleged out-of-court statement was more favorable to the respondent than any that cross-examination by counsel could possibly have produced, had Runnels "affirmed the statement as his." It would be unrealistic in the extreme in the circumstances here presented to hold that the respondent was denied either the opportunity or the benefit of full and effective cross-examination of Runnels.

We conclude that where a codefendant takes the stand in his own defense, denies making an alleged out-of-court statement implicating the defendant, and proceeds to testify favorably to the defendant concerning the underlying facts, the defendant has been denied no rights protected by the Sixth and Fourteenth Amendments.

6. In *Randolph v. Commonwealth*, 482 S.E.2d 101 (Va.Ct.App.1997), after Chambers was arrested for pickpocketing at an airport, she told Officer Hutton that she and several other people (including Randolph) had come to the airport to pick pockets. Because the prosecution planned to introduce this statement at trial, Randolph moved for a severance. The trial court denied Randolph's motion, Chambers's statement was allowed in at Randolph's trial, and Randolph was convicted. The appellate court affirmed.

The court noted that the Supreme Court had left open the possibility that a co-defendant's statement might be admissible against the defendant under some "firmly-rooted exception" to the hearsay rule. An admission of a co-conspirator is such an exception, *if* the admission is made in furtherance of the conspiracy. This does not apply here, because Chambers' statement was made *after* the conspiracy terminated. But Chambers' statement was a *declaration against penal interest* — another "firmly rooted" exception to the hearsay rule — where the declarant is "unavailable" to testify at trial (which Chambers was, as she refused to take the stand). Therefore, Chambers' statement *was admissible against Randolph*, so there was no reason to grant a severance.

But wasn't this also true in *Bruton*? Wouldn't *Randolph's* reasoning effectively overrule *Bruton*?

The Court appeared to answer this question in *Lilly v. Virginia*, 119 S.Ct. 1887 (1999). Lilly and his brother Mark were charged with murder, but tried separately. At Lilly's trial, the prosecutor called Mark to testify, but Mark refused, asserting his privilege against self-incrimination. The prosecutor then introduced Mark's confession, which implicated both Mark and Lilly. The Virginia Supreme Court held that this was proper, even though Mark's statement was hearsay, because Mark's confession was a statement against penal interest by an unavailable witness, and this was a "firmly rooted exception" to the rule against hearsay. The U.S. Supreme Court disagreed:

> The "against penal interest" exception to the hearsay rule — unlike other previously recognized firmly rooted exceptions — is not generally based on the maxim that statements made without a motive to reflect on the legal consequences of one's statement, and in situations that are exceptionally conducive to veracity, lack the dangers of inaccuracy that typically accompany hearsay. The exception, rather, is founded on the broad assumption that a person is unlikely to fabricate a statement against his own interest at the time it is made. * * * *

If Mark were a codefendant in a joint trial, however, even the use of his confession to prove his guilt might have an adverse impact on the rights of his accomplices. When dealing with admissions against penal interest, we have taken great care to separate using admissions against the declarant (the first category above) from using them against other criminal defendants (the third category). [The second category is introduction of the declarant's statement by the defendant, who claims that it shows that the declarant (not defendant) committed the crime.]* * * *

In the years since *Bruton* was decided, we have reviewed a number of cases in which one defendant's confession has been introduced into evidence in a joint trial pursuant to instructions that it could be used against him but not against his codefendant. Despite frequent disagreement over matters such as the adequacy of the trial judge's instructions, or the sufficiency of the redaction of ambiguous references to the declarant's accomplice, we have consistently either stated or assumed that the mere fact that one accomplice's confession qualified as a statement against his penal interest did not justify its use as evidence against another person. See *Gray v. Maryland*, 523 U.S. 185 (1998). * * * *

The third category includes cases, like the one before us today, in which the government seeks to introduce a confession by an accomplice which incriminates a criminal defendant. The practice of admitting statements in this category under an exception to the hearsay rule — to the extent that such a practice exists in certain jurisdictions — is, unlike the first category or even the second, of quite recent vintage. * * * *

Most important, this third category of hearsay encompasses statements that are inherently unreliable. Wigmore's treatise still expressly distinguishes accomplices' confessions that inculpate themselves and the accused as beyond a proper understanding of the against-penal-interest exception because an accomplice often has a considerable interest in "confessing and betraying his cocriminals" 5 Wigmore, *Evidence*, § 1477. Consistent with this scholarship and the assumption that underlies the analysis in our *Bruton* line of cases, we have over the years "spoken with one voice in declaring presumptively unreliable accomplices' confessions that incriminate defendants" *Bruton*, 391 U.S. at 136 (such statements are "inevitably suspect"). * * * *

It is clear that our cases consistently have viewed an accomplice's statements that shift or spread the blame to a criminal defendant as falling outside the realm of those hearsay exceptions that are so trustworthy that adversarial testing can be expected to add little to the statements' reliability. * * * *

The decisive fact, which we make explicit today, is that accomplices' confessions that inculpate a criminal defendant are not within a firmly rooted exception to the hearsay rule as that concept has been defined in our Confrontation Clause jurisprudence.

However, in *State v. Dennis*, 523 S.E.2d 173 (S.C. 1999), the court held that the "excited utterance" exception to the hearsay rule is "firmly rooted." Therefore, a bystander's testimony that he heard a co-defendant's "excited" statement that he had just seen the defendant shoot the victim was admissible at their joint trial.

In *Stevens v. People*, 29 P.3d 305 (Colo. 2001), the court held that an accomplice's confession to the police was admissible against Stevens, even though Stevens was unable to cross-examine the accomplice (who had exercised his 5th Amendment right not to testify). The court distinguished *Lilly*, holding that even though the statement-against-interest exception was not "firmly rooted", the confession nevertheless was reliable, because it was detailed and the accomplice made no effort to minimize his own responsibility and shift blame to Stevens. Justice Bender dissented.

RICHARDSON v. MARSH
United States Supreme Court
481 U.S. 200 (1987)

Justice Scalia delivered the opinion of the Court.

In *Bruton v. United States*, 391 U.S. 123 (1968), we held that a defendant is deprived of his rights under the Confrontation Clause when his nontestifying codefendant's confession naming him as a participant in the crime is introduced at their joint trial, even if the jury is instructed to consider that confession only against the codefendant. Today we consider whether *Bruton* requires the same result when the codefendant's confession is redacted to omit any reference to the defendant, but the defendant is nonetheless linked to the confession by evidence properly admitted against him at trial.

I

Respondent Clarissa Marsh, Benjamin Williams, and Kareem Martin were charged with assaulting Cynthia Knighton and murdering her 4-year-old son, Koran, and her aunt, Ollie Scott. Respondent and Williams were tried jointly, over her objection. (Martin was a fugitive at the time of trial.)

At the trial, Knighton testified as follows: On the evening of October 29, 1978, she and her son were at Scott's home when respondent and her boyfriend Martin visited. After a brief conversation in the living room, respondent announced that she had come to "pick up something" from Scott and rose from the couch. Martin then pulled out a gun, pointed it at Scott and the Knightons, and said that "someone had gotten killed and Scott knew something about it." Respondent immediately walked to the front door and peered out the peephole. The doorbell rang, respondent opened the door, and Williams walked in, carrying a gun. As Williams passed respondent, he asked, "Where's the money?" Martin forced Scott upstairs, and Williams went into the kitchen, leaving respondent alone with the Knightons. Knighton and her son attempted to flee, but respondent grabbed Knighton and held her until Williams returned. Williams ordered the Knightons to lie on the floor and then went upstairs to assist Martin. Respondent, again left alone with the Knightons, stood by the front door and occasionally peered out the peephole. A few minutes later, Martin, Williams, and Scott came down the stairs, and Martin handed a paper grocery bag to respondent. Martin and Williams then forced Scott and the Knightons into the basement, where Martin shot them. Only Cynthia Knighton survived.

In addition to Knighton's testimony, the State introduced (over respondent's objection) a confession given by Williams to the police shortly after his arrest. The confession was redacted to omit all reference to respondent — indeed, to omit all indication that *anyone* other than Martin and Williams participated in the crime.[1] The confession largely corroborated Knighton's account of the activities of persons other than respondent in the house. In addition, the confession described a conversation Williams had with Martin as they drove to the Scott home, during which, according to Williams, Martin said that he would have to kill the victims after the robbery. At the time the confession was admitted, the jury was admonished not to use it in any way against respondent. Williams did not testify.

After the State rested, respondent took the stand. She testified that on October 29, 1978, she had lost money that Martin intended to use to buy drugs. Martin was upset, and suggested to respondent that she borrow money from Scott, with whom she had worked in the past. Martin and respondent picked up Williams and drove to Scott's house. During the drive, respondent, who was sitting in the backseat, "knew that [Martin and Williams] were talking" but could not hear the conversation because "the radio was on and the speaker was right in her ear." Martin and respondent were admitted into the home, and respondent had a short conversation with Scott, during which she asked for a loan. Martin then pulled a gun, and respondent walked to the door to see where the car was. When she saw Williams, she opened the door for him. Respondent testified that during the robbery she did not feel free to leave and was too scared to flee. She said that she did not know why she prevented the Knightons from escaping. She admitted taking the bag from Martin, but said that after Martin and Williams took the victims into the basement, she left the house without the bag. Respondent insisted that she had possessed no prior knowledge that Martin and Williams were armed, had heard no conversation about anyone's being harmed, and had not intended to rob or kill anyone.

During his closing argument, the prosecutor admonished the jury not to use Williams' confession against respondent. Later in his argument, however, he linked

---

[1] The redacted confession in its entirety read: "On Sunday evening, October the 29th, 1978, at about 6:30 p.m., I was over to my girl friend's house at 237 Moss, Highland Park, when I received a phone call from a friend of mine named Kareem Martin. He said he had been looking for me and James Coleman, who I call Tom. He asked me if I wanted to go on a robbery with him. I said okay. Then he said he'd be by and pick me up. About 15 or 20 minutes later Kareem came by in his black Monte Carlo car. I got in the car and Kareem told me he was going to stick up this crib, told me the place was a numbers house. Kareem said there would be over $5,000 or $10,000 in the place. Kareem said he would have to take them out after the robbery. Kareem had a big silver gun. He gave me a long barrelled [sic].22 revolver. We then drove over to this house and parked the car across the big street near the house. The plan was that I would wait in the car in front of the house and then I would move the car down across the big street because he didn't want anybody to see the car. Okay, Kareem went up to the house and went inside. A couple of minutes later I moved the car and went up to the house. As I entered, Kareem and this older lady were in the dining room, a little boy and another younger woman were sitting on the couch in the front room. I pulled my pistol and told the younger woman and the little boy to lay on the floor. Kareem took the older lady upstairs. He had a pistol, also. I stayed downstairs with the two people on the floor. After Kareem took the lady upstairs I went upstairs and the lady was laying on the bed in the room to the left as you get up the stairs. The lady had already given us two bags full of money before we ever got upstairs. Kareem had thought she had more money and that's why we had went upstairs. Me and Kareem started searching the rooms but I didn't find any money. I came downstairs and then Kareem came down with the lady. I said, 'Let's go, let's go.' Kareem said no. Kareem then took the two ladies and little boy down the basement and that's when I left to go to the car. I went to the car and got in the back seat. A couple of minutes later Kareem came to the car and said he thinks the girl was still living because she was still moving and he didn't have any more bullets. He asked me how come I didn't go down the basement and I said I wasn't doing no shit like that. He then dropped me back off at my girl's house in Highland Park and I was supposed to get together with him today, get my share of the robbery after he had counted the money. That's all."

respondent to the portion of Williams' confession describing his conversation with Martin in the car.[2] (Respondent's attorney did not object to this.) After closing arguments, the judge again instructed the jury that Williams' confession was not to be considered against respondent.

The jury convicted respondent of two counts of felony murder in the perpetration of an armed robbery and one count of assault with intent to commit murder.

Respondent then filed a petition for a writ of habeas corpus pursuant to 28 U.S.C. § 2254. She alleged that her conviction was not supported by sufficient evidence and that introduction of Williams' confession at the joint trial had violated her rights under the Confrontation Clause. The District Court denied the petition. The Court of Appeals reversed. The Court of Appeals held that, in determining whether *Bruton* bars the admission of a nontestifying codefendant's confession, a court must assess the confession's "inculpatory value" by examining not only the face of the confession, but also all of the evidence introduced at trial. Here, Williams' account of the conversation in the car was the only direct evidence that respondent knew before entering Scott's house that the victims would be robbed and killed. Respondent's own testimony placed her in that car. In light of the "paucity" of other evidence of malice and the prosecutor's linkage of respondent and the statement in the car during closing argument, admission of Williams' confession "was powerfully incriminating to respondent with respect to the critical element of intent." Thus, the Court of Appeals concluded, the Confrontation Clause was violated. We granted certiorari.

II

The Confrontation Clause of the Sixth Amendment, extended against the States by the Fourteenth Amendment, guarantees the right of a criminal defendant "to be confronted with the witnesses against him." The right of confrontation includes the right to cross-examine witnesses. See *Pointer v. Texas*, 380 U.S. 400, 404 (1965). Therefore, where two defendants are tried jointly, the pretrial confession of one cannot be admitted against the other unless the confessing defendant takes the stand.

Ordinarily, a witness whose testimony is introduced at a joint trial is not considered to be a witness "against" a defendant if the jury is instructed to consider that testimony only against a codefendant. This accords with the almost invariable assumption of the law that jurors follow their instructions, which we have applied in many varying contexts. For example, in *Harris v. New York*, 401 U.S. 222 (1971), we held that statements elicited from a defendant in violation of *Miranda v. Arizona*, 384 U.S. 436 (1966), can be introduced to impeach that defendant's credibility, even though they are inadmissible as evidence of his guilt, so long as the jury is instructed accordingly. Similarly, in *Spencer v. Texas*, 385 U.S. 554 (1967), we held

---

[2] The prosecutor said: "It's important in light of [respondent's] testimony when she says Kareem drives over to Benjamin Williams' home and picks him up to go over. What's the thing that she says? 'Well, I'm sitting in the back seat of the car.' 'Did you hear any conversation that was going on in the front seat between Kareem and Mr. Williams?' 'No, couldn't hear any conversation. The radio was too loud.' I asked you whether that is reasonable. Why did she say that? Why did she say she couldn't hear any conversation? She said, 'I know they were having conversation but I couldn't hear it because of the radio.' Because if she admits that she heard the conversation and she admits to the plan, she's guilty of at least armed robbery. So she can't tell you that."

that evidence of the defendant's prior criminal convictions could be introduced for the purpose of sentence enhancement, so long as the jury was instructed it could not be used for purposes of determining guilt. See also *Tennessee v. Street*, 471 U.S. 409 (1985) (instruction to consider accomplice's incriminating confession only for purpose of assessing truthfulness of defendant's claim that his own confession was coerced); *Watkins v. Sowders*, 449 U.S. 341, 347 (1981) (instruction not to consider erroneously admitted eyewitness identification evidence); *Walder v. United States*, 347 U.S. 62 (1954) (instruction to consider unlawfully seized physical evidence only in assessing defendant's credibility). In *Bruton*, however, we recognized a narrow exception to this principle: We held that a defendant is deprived of his Sixth Amendment right of confrontation when the facially incriminating confession of a nontestifying codefendant is introduced at their joint trial, even if the jury is instructed to consider the confession only against the codefendant. We said: "There are some contexts in which the risk that the jury will not, or cannot, follow instructions is so great, and the consequences of failure so vital to the defendant, that the practical and human limitations of the jury system cannot be ignored. Such a context is presented here, where the powerfully incriminating extrajudicial statements of a codefendant, who stands accused side-by-side with the defendant, are deliberately spread before the jury in a joint trial."

There is an important distinction between this case and *Bruton*, which causes it to fall outside the narrow exception we have created. In *Bruton*, the codefendant's confession "expressly implicated" the defendant as his accomplice. Thus, at the time that confession was introduced there was not the slightest doubt that it would prove "powerfully incriminating." By contrast, in this case the confession was not incriminating on its face, and became so only when linked with evidence introduced later at trial (the defendant's own testimony).

Where the necessity of such linkage is involved, it is a less valid generalization that the jury will not likely obey the instruction to disregard the evidence. Specific testimony that "the defendant helped me commit the crime" is more vivid than inferential incrimination, and hence more difficult to thrust out of mind. Moreover, with regard to such an explicit statement the only issue is, plain and simply, whether the jury can possibly be expected to forget it in assessing the defendant's guilt; whereas with regard to inferential incrimination the judge's instruction may well be successful in dissuading the jury from entering onto the path of inference in the first place, so that there is no incrimination to forget. In short, while it may not always be simple for the members of a jury to obey the instruction that they disregard an incriminating inference, there does not exist the overwhelming probability of their inability to do so that is the foundation of *Bruton's* exception to the general rule.[3]

Even more significantly, evidence requiring linkage differs from evidence incriminating on its face in the practical effects which application of the *Bruton* exception would produce. If limited to facially incriminating confessions, *Bruton* can be complied with by redaction — a possibility suggested in that opinion itself. If extended to confessions incriminating by connection, not only is that not possible, but it is not even possible to predict the admissibility of a confession in advance of

---

[3] The dissent is mistaken in believing we "assume that Williams' confession did not incriminate respondent." To the contrary, the very premise of our discussion is that respondent would have been harmed by Williams' confession if the jury had disobeyed its instructions. Our disagreement pertains not to whether the confession incriminated respondent, but to whether the trial court could properly assume that the jury did not use it against her.

trial. The "contextual implication" doctrine articulated by the Court of Appeals would presumably require the trial judge to assess at the end of each trial whether, in light of all of the evidence, a nontestifying codefendant's confession has been so "powerfully incriminating" that a new, separate trial is required for the defendant. This obviously lends itself to manipulation by the defense — and even without manipulation will result in numerous mistrials and appeals.

It might be suggested that those consequences could be reduced by conducting a pretrial hearing at which prosecution and defense would reveal the evidence they plan to introduce, enabling the court to assess compliance with *Bruton ex ante* rather than ex post. If this approach is even feasible under the Federal Rules (which is doubtful — see, e.g., Fed.Rule Crim.Proc. 14), it would be time consuming and obviously far from foolproof.

One might say, of course, that a certain way of assuring compliance would be to try defendants separately whenever an incriminating statement of one of them is sought to be used. That is not as facile or as just a remedy as might seem. Joint trials play a vital role in the criminal justice system, accounting for almost one-third of federal criminal trials in the past five years. Memorandum from David L. Cook, Administrative Office of the United States Courts, to Supreme Court Library (1987). Many joint trials — for example, those involving large conspiracies to import and distribute illegal drugs — involve a dozen or more codefendants. Confessions by one or more of the defendants are commonplace — and indeed the probability of confession increases with the number of participants, since each has reduced assurance that he will be protected by his own silence. It would impair both the efficiency and the fairness of the criminal justice system to require, in all these cases of joint crimes where incriminating statements exist, that prosecutors bring separate proceedings, presenting the same evidence again and again, requiring victims and witnesses to repeat the inconvenience (and sometimes trauma) of testifying, and randomly favoring the last-tried defendants who have the advantage of knowing the prosecution's case beforehand. Joint trials generally serve the interests of justice by avoiding inconsistent verdicts and enabling more accurate assessment of relative culpability — advantages which sometimes operate to the defendant's benefit. Even apart from these tactical considerations, joint trials generally serve the interests of justice by avoiding the scandal and inequity of inconsistent verdicts. The other way of assuring compliance with an expansive *Bruton* rule would be to forgo use of codefendant confessions. That price also is too high, since confessions "are more than merely 'desirable'; they are essential to society's compelling interest in finding, convicting, and punishing those who violate the law." *Moran v. Burbine*, 475 U.S. 412, 426 (1986).

The rule that juries are presumed to follow their instructions is a pragmatic one, rooted less in the absolute certitude that the presumption is true than in the belief that it represents a reasonable practical accommodation of the interests of the state and the defendant in the criminal justice process. On the precise facts of *Bruton*, involving a facially incriminating confession, we found that accommodation inadequate. As our discussion above shows, the calculus changes when confessions that do not name the defendant are at issue. While we continue to apply *Bruton* where we have found that its rationale validly applies, we decline to extend it further. We hold that the Confrontation Clause is not violated by the admission of a nontestifying codefendant's confession with a proper limiting instruction when, as here, the confession is redacted to eliminate not only the defendant's name, but any reference to his or her existence.[5]

In the present case, however, the prosecutor sought to undo the effect of the limiting instruction by urging the jury to use Williams' confession in evaluating respondent's case. On remand, the court should consider whether, in light of respondent's failure to object to the prosecutor's comments, the error can serve as the basis for granting a writ of habeas corpus.

The judgment of the Court of Appeals is reversed, and the case is remanded for further proceedings consistent with this opinion.

JUSTICE STEVENS, with whom JUSTICE BRENNAN and JUSTICE MARSHALL join, dissenting.

The rationale of our decision in *Bruton* applies without exception to all inadmissible confessions that are "powerfully incriminating." Today, however, the Court draws a distinction of constitutional magnitude between those confessions that directly identify the defendant and those that rely for their inculpatory effect on the factual and legal relationships of their contents to other evidence before the jury. Even if the jury's indirect inference of the defendant's guilt based on an inadmissible confession is much more devastating to the defendant's case than its inference from a direct reference in the codefendant's confession, the Court requires the exclusion of only the latter statement. This illogical result demeans the values protected by the Confrontation Clause. Moreover, neither reason nor experience supports the Court's argument that a consistent application of the rationale of the *Bruton* case would impose unacceptable burdens on the administration of justice. * * * *

Instructing the jury that it was to consider Benjamin Williams' confession only against him, and not against Clarissa Marsh, failed to guarantee the level of certainty required by the Confrontation Clause. The uncertainty arose because the prosecution's case made it clear at the time Williams' statement was introduced that the statement would prove "powerfully incriminating" of the respondent as well as of Williams himself. There can be absolutely no doubt that spreading Williams' carefully edited confession before the jury intolerably interfered with the jury's solemn duty to treat the statement as nothing more than meaningless sounds in its consideration of Marsh's guilt or innocence.

At the time that Williams' confession was introduced, the evidence already had established that respondent and two men committed an armed robbery in the course of which the two men killed two persons and shot a third. There was a sharp dispute, however, on the question whether respondent herself intended to commit a robbery in which murder was a foreseeable result, or knew that the two men planned to do so. The quantum of evidence admissible against respondent was just sufficient to establish this intent and hence to support her conviction. * * * *

In the edited statement that the jury was instructed not to consider against Marsh, Williams described the conversation he had with Kareem Martin while they were in a car driving to their victims' residence. In that conversation, Martin stated

---

[5] We express no opinion on the admissibility of a confession in which the defendant's name has been replaced with a symbol or neutral pronoun.

that "he would have to take them out after the robbery." The State's principal witness had testified that Martin and Marsh arrived at the victims' house together. The jury was therefore certain to infer from the confession that respondent had been in the car and had overheard the statement by Martin. Viewed in the total context of the trial evidence, this confession was of critical importance because it was the only evidence directly linking respondent with the specific intent, expressed before the robbery, to kill the victims afterwards. If Williams had taken the witness stand and testified, respondent's lawyer could have cross-examined him to challenge his credibility and to establish or suggest that the car radio was playing so loudly that Marsh could not have overheard the conversation between the two men from the back seat. An acknowledgment of the possibility of such facts by Williams would have done much more to eliminate the certainty beyond a reasonable doubt that Marsh knew about the murder plan than could possibly have been achieved by the later testimony of respondent herself. Moreover, the price respondent had to pay in order to attempt to rebut the obvious inference that she had overheard Martin was to remind the jury once again of what he had said and to give the prosecutor a further opportunity to point to this most damaging evidence on the close question of her specific intent.

The facts in this case are, admittedly, different from those in *Bruton* because Williams' statement did not directly mention respondent. Thus, instead of being "incriminating on its face," it became so only when considered in connection with the other evidence presented to the jury. The difference between the facts of *Bruton* and the facts of this case does not eliminate their common, substantial, and constitutionally unacceptable risk that the jury, when resolving a critical issue against respondent, may have relied on impermissible evidence.

II

The facts that joint trials conserve prosecutorial resources, diminish inconvenience to witnesses, and avoid delays in the administration of criminal justice have been well known for a long time. It is equally well known that joint trials create special risks of prejudice to one of the defendants, and that such risks often make it necessary to grant severances. See *Bruton*, 391 U.S. at 131; Fed.Rule Crim.Proc. 14 (Relief from Prejudicial Joinder). The Government argues that the costs of requiring the prosecution to choose between severance and not offering the codefendant's confession at a joint trial outweigh the benefits to the defendant. On the scales of justice, however, considerations of fairness normally outweigh administrative concerns. * * * *

The concern about the cost of joint trials, even if valid, does not prevail over the interests of justice. Moreover, the Court's effort to revive this concern in a state criminal case rests on the use of irrelevant statistics. The Court makes the startling discovery that joint trials account for "almost one-third of federal criminal trials in the past five years." In the interest of greater precision, the Court might have stated that there were 10,904 federal criminal trials involving more than one defendant during that 5-year period. The Court might have added that the data base from which that figure was obtained does not contain any information at all to show the number of times that confessions were offered in evidence in those 10,904 federal cases. The relevance of this data is also difficult to discern because all of the cases in this Court that involved joint trials conducted after *Bruton* was decided, in which compliance with the rule of that case was at issue, appear to have originated in a state court. Federal prosecutors seem to have had little difficulty, in conducting the literally thousands of joint trials to which the Court points, in maintaining "both the efficiency and the fairness of the criminal justice system" that the Court speculates will occur if *Bruton's* reasoning is applied to this case. Presumably the options of granting immunity, making plea bargains, or simply waiting until after a confessing defendant has been tried separately before trying to use his admissions against an accomplice have enabled the Federal Government to enforce the criminal law without sacrificing the basic premise of the Confrontation Clause.[7]

The Court also expresses concern that trial judges will be unable to determine whether a codefendant's confession that does not directly mention the defendant and is inadmissible against him will create a substantial risk of unfair prejudice. In most such cases the trial judge can comply with the dictates of *Bruton* by postponing his or her decision on the admissibility of the confession until the prosecution rests, at which time its potentially inculpatory effect can be evaluated in the light of the government's entire case. The Court expresses concern that such a rule would enable "manipulation by the defense," by which the Court presumably means the defense might tailor its evidence to make sure that a confession which does not directly mention the defendant is deemed powerfully incriminating when viewed in light of the prosecution's entire case. As a practical matter, I cannot believe that there are many defense lawyers who would deliberately pursue this high-risk strategy of "manipulating" their evidence in order to enhance the prejudicial impact of a codefendant's confession. Moreover, a great many experienced and competent trial judges throughout the Nation are fully capable of managing cases and supervising counsel in order to avoid the problems that seem insurmountable to appellate judges who are sometimes distracted by illogical distinctions and irrelevant statistics.

I respectfully dissent.

Notes from Judge Katz:

1. *How* does a court redact a confession?

In *People v. Fletcher*, 13 Cal.4th 451 (1996), the court addressed this problem:

Following *Richardson v. Marsh*, 481 U.S. 200, many federal and state courts have addressed the issue reserved by the high court: whether redacting a nontestifying codefendant's confession to replace references to

---

[7] The Court expresses an apparently deep-seated fear that an even-handed application of *Bruton* would jeopardize the use of joint trials. This proposition rests on the unsupported assumption that the number of powerfully incriminating confessions that do not name the defendant is too large to be evaluated on a case-by-case basis. The Court then proceeds to the ostensible administrative outrages of the separate trials that would be necessary, contending that it would be unwise to compel prosecutors to "bring separate proceedings, presenting the same evidence again and again, requiring victims and witnesses to repeat the inconvenience (and sometimes trauma) of testifying, and randomly favoring the last-tried defendants who have the advantage of knowing the prosecution's case beforehand." This speculation also floats unattached to any anchor of reality. Since the likelihood that more than one of the defendants in a joint trial will have confessed is fairly remote, the prospect of "presenting the same evidence again and again" is nothing but a rhetorical flourish. At worst, in the typical case, two trials may be required, one for the confessing defendant and another for the nonconfessing defendant or defendants. And even in that category, presumably most confessing defendants are likely candidates for plea bargaining.

the defendant's name with a "symbol or neutral pronoun" avoids violation of a defendant's rights under the Confrontation Clause. The result has been a split in authority, with one group taking the position that such redaction is always or almost always sufficient (e.g., *U.S. v. Strickland* (7th Cir.1991) 935 F.2d 822, 826; *U.S. v. Vogt* (4th Cir.1990) 910 F.2d 1184, 1192; *State v. Craney* (Me.1995) 662 A.2d 899, 903), and another group expressing the view that whether such redaction is sufficient must be determined on a case-by-case basis (e.g., *U.S. v. Van Hemelryck* (11th Cir.1991) 945 F.2d 1493, 1502–1503; *U.S. v. Hoac* (9th Cir.1993) 990 F.2d 1099, 1107; *U.S. v. Long* (8th Cir.1990) 900 F.2d 1270, 1280). * * * *

Whether instructing the jury to disregard a nontestifying codefendant's confession in determining a defendant's guilt adequately protects the defendant's Sixth Amendment right of confrontation depends upon whether the jurors can reasonably be expected to obey the instruction. See *Richardson v. Marsh*, supra, 481 U.S. 200, 206–208. In turn, the jurors' ability to obey the instructions depends upon how directly and how forcefully the codefendant's confession incriminates the nondeclarant defendant.

Substituting a pronoun or other neutral term for the defendant's name will make the confession less directly incriminating, but it does not invariably provide sufficient assurance that the average reasonable juror will be able to obey an instruction to disregard the confession when considering the guilt of the nondeclarant. A confession redacted with neutral pronouns may still prove impossible to "thrust out of mind" *Richardson v. Marsh*, supra, 481 U.S. 200, 208), if, for example, it contains references to distinctive clothing, mannerisms, place of residence, or other information that readily and unmistakably identifies the person referred to as the nondeclarant defendant. This point is illustrated by the facts of *People v. Terry* (1970) 2 Cal.3d 362.

In *Terry*, two defendants, Harold Terry and Juanelda Allen, were jointly charged with two murders. At their joint trial, the prosecution introduced a confession by Allen that implicated Terry. The confession was redacted by substituting the word "deleted" for the name "Harold." But, as this court remarked, "the result was somewhat ridiculous" and "it must have been obvious to everyone that 'deleted' and Terry were one and the same." The identity of "deleted" was obvious because the confession indicated that "deleted" was a male African-American who lived with Allen, while the jury could see that Terry was a male African-American and it knew, from other evidence introduced at the trial, that Terry and Allen had been living together during the events described in Allen's confession. Thus, "the jury was bound to know that 'deleted' must have been Terry" and Allen's confession "clearly implicated Terry and accused him of both homicides." We concluded that the trial court had erred in allowing the redacted confession to be admitted in evidence, although we also concluded that Terry had not been prejudiced by the error.

In such cases, where any reasonable juror must inevitably perceive that the defendant on trial is the person designated by pronoun or neutral term in the codefendant's confession, an assumption that a limiting instruction could "be successful in dissuading the jury from entering onto the path of inference" (*Richardson v. Marsh*, supra, 481 U.S. 200, 208) would be little short of absurd. On the other hand, there are instances in which replacing a nondeclarant defendant's name with a symbol or neutral pronoun will be effective in protecting the nondeclarant's rights under the Confrontation Clause. For example, a confession that is redacted to substitute pronouns or similar neutral and nonidentifying terms for the name of a codefendant will be sufficient if the codefendant was just one of a large group of individuals any one of whom could equally well have been the coparticipant mentioned in the confession.

Although this case-by-case approach requires consideration of evidence other than the confession itself, we are persuaded that the "practical effects" mentioned by the high court in *Richardson v. Marsh* present no insurmountable problems in this context.

2. Let's be creative. Instead of redaction or severance, *how about one trial with two juries?* Both juries would hear all the testimony, with one exception: the non-confessing defendant's jury would be excused when the confessing defendant's confession is read to his jury. What do you think about this as a general policy? Would it have worked in *Richardson*? The trial court employed such a procedure in *State v. Lambright*, 138 Ariz. 63 (1983):

> In the pre-trial stages, it appeared to the trial judge that this case could present problems under *Bruton*, [which] prohibits the introduction of a defendant's statements to incriminate a codefendant in a joint trial, where the declarant is unavailable for cross-examination due to the assertion of his fifth amendment right to silence. In the instant case, the state intended to use statements of both Smith and Lambright at trial, and each of these statements incriminated both the declarant and the codefendant. * * *

> After considering the confessions, and finding it impractical to attempt to edit out the portions incriminating the other defendant, the trial judge decided to sever the two cases. However, because most of the evidence was admissible against both defendants, and because the trial was expected to last over a week and included several out-of-state witnesses, rather than hold separate trials the judge decided to conduct a single trial using two juries.

> Under this "dual jury" procedure, two juries were chosen from separate venires, each to decide the guilt or innocence of only one defendant. The trial was held in a courtroom in the federal courthouse in Tucson which was large enough to accommodate both juries. The two juries were kept physically separated, and were carefully instructed not to speak with persons on the other jury. When information relevant to both defendants was being presented, both juries remained in the courtroom. When evidence admissible against only one defendant was being presented, the jury for the other defendant was excused. When both juries were present, one sat in the jury box and the other sat in designated rows of chairs on the other side of the courtroom. The positions of the respective juries were alternated daily. Separate opening and closing arguments were made, each in front of one jury only. The juries were given separate instructions, and then sent to deliberate separately. When the first jury reached a verdict, it was not made public until the deliberations of the other jury had concluded.

In the instant case both defendants were convicted on all counts, and each defendant assigns as error the use of the dual jury procedure.

It appears that a number of courts have approved the dual jury procedure. See, e.g. *United States v. Hayes*, 676 F.2d 1359 (11th Cir.1982); *United States v. Rimar*, 558 F.2d 1271 (6th Cir.1978); *United States v. Rowan*, 518 F.2d 685 (6th Cir.1975); *People v. Wardlow*, 118 Cal.App.3d 375 (1981); *People v. Brooks*, 92 Mich.App. 393 (1979). These cases generally find that this procedure satisfies the defendants' constitutional rights as well as the end of judicial economy. See also *United States v. Sidman*, 470 F.2d 1158 (9th Cir.1972) (1973) (holds procedure satisfies each of defendant's constitutional rights, including rights to impartial jury and due process). In addition to complying with the formal confrontational requirements of *Bruton*, the procedure may effectively avoid the "spectacle" of antagonistic defenses.

Besides the courts which generally approve the dual jury procedure, there are courts which have given limited approval to the procedure, suggesting that appropriate guidelines be developed before the procedure is put into common use. See, e.g. *United States v. Sidman*, 470 F.2d 1158 (9th Cir.1972); *State v. Watson*, 397 So.2d 1337 (La.1981).

Some other courts have discouraged or disapproved of future use of the procedure, finding the risks of error inherent in the procedure too great. See, e.g., *Scarborough v. State*, 50 Md.App. 276 (1981); *State v. Corsi*, 86 N.J. 172 (1981). The principal risk of this procedure appears to be that while both juries are present, there may be some unintentional disclosure or reference to information admissible against only one defendant which may constitute reversible error. "It is the possibility that inadvertent revelations will disclose to the separate juries the inadmissible evidence which concerns us." *People v. Rainge*, 112 Ill.App.3d 396, 419 (1983). This risk is demonstrated by *United States v. Sidman, supra*, in which such an error actually occurred. During trial, an inadvertent *Bruton* problem arose when in the presence of both juries the prosecutor was allowed to question a witness regarding a statement of defendant Sidman which incriminated both himself and his co-defendant. Although Sidman's conviction was affirmed, the co-defendant had to be retried. * * * *

The main thrust of defendant's argument is that the dual jury procedure is inherently prejudicial, breeding confusion and speculation in the minds of the jury. We join the overwhelming authority to the contrary, however, and find that the procedure is not inherently prejudicial. * * * *

We note that although courts have utilized the dual jury procedure in other murder cases,* * * * we feel that death penalty cases are inappropriate vehicles for experimentation with new procedures, and the practice should be avoided in the future.

In *People v. Fletcher*, 13 Cal.4th 451, 468, fn. 5 (1996), the court considered a similar idea — while using only a single jury:

Another alternative that has been suggested, but apparently never used in this state, is a joint but bifurcated trial in which the jury first determines the guilt of the nondeclarant defendant, then receive evidence of the nontestifying codefendant's extrajudicial confession, and finally proceeds to determine the guilt or innocence of that defendant. See Dickett, *Sixth Amendment — Limiting the Scope of Bruton* (1988) 78 J.Crim L. & Criminology 984, 1010 [suggesting this alternative procedure]. We note, however, that federal appellate courts have reversed convictions of defendants whose guilt has been determined in a bifurcated trial, concluding that it may be practically impossible for a jury to determine one defendant's guilt without impermissibly prejudging the guilt of another defendant jointly tried. See, e.g., *United States v. McIver* (11th Cir.1982) 688 F.2d 726, 729–730.

ZAFIRO v. UNITED STATES
United States Supreme Court
506 U.S. 534 (1993)

Justice O'Connor delivered the opinion of the Court.

Rule 8(b) of the Federal Rules of Criminal Procedure provides that defendants may be charged together "if they are alleged to have participated in the same act or transaction or in the same series of acts or transactions constituting an offense or offenses." Rule 14 of the Rules, in turn, permits a district court to grant a severance of defendants if "it appears that a defendant or the government is prejudiced by a joinder." In this case, we consider whether Rule 14 requires severance as a matter of law when codefendants present "mutually antagonistic defenses."

I

Gloria Zafiro, Jose Martinez, Salvador Garcia, and Alfonso Soto were accused of distributing illegal drugs in the Chicago area, operating primarily out of Soto's bungalow in Chicago and Zafiro's apartment in Cicero, a nearby suburb. One day, government agents observed Garcia and Soto place a large box in Soto's car and drive from Soto's bungalow to Zafiro's apartment. The agents followed the two as they carried the box up the stairs. When the agents identified themselves, Garcia and Soto dropped the box and ran into the apartment. The agents entered the apartment in pursuit and found the four petitioners in the living room. The dropped box contained 55 pounds of cocaine. After obtaining a search warrant for the apartment, agents found approximately 16 pounds of cocaine, 25 grams of heroin, and 4 pounds of marijuana inside a suitcase in a closet. Next to the suitcase was a sack containing $22,960 in cash. Police officers also discovered 7 pounds of cocaine in a car parked in Soto's garage.

The four petitioners were indicted and brought to trial together. At various points during the proceeding, Garcia and Soto moved for severance, arguing that their defenses were mutually antagonistic. Soto testified that he knew nothing about the drug conspiracy. He claimed that Garcia had asked him for a box, which he gave Garcia, and that he (Soto) did not know its contents until they were arrested. Garcia did not testify, but his lawyer argued that Garcia was innocent: The box belonged to Soto and Garcia was ignorant of its contents.

Zafiro and Martinez also repeatedly moved for severance on the ground that their defenses were mutually antagonistic. Zafiro testified that she was merely

Martinez's girlfriend and knew nothing of the conspiracy. She claimed that Martinez stayed in her apartment occasionally, kept some clothes there, and gave her small amounts of money. Although she allowed Martinez to store a suitcase in her closet, she testified, she had no idea that the suitcase contained illegal drugs. Like Garcia, Martinez did not testify. But his lawyer argued that Martinez was only visiting his girlfriend and had no idea that she was involved in distributing drugs.

The District Court denied the motions for severance. The jury convicted all four petitioners of conspiring to possess cocaine, heroin, and marijuana with the intent to distribute. In addition, Garcia and Soto were convicted of possessing cocaine with the intent to distribute, and Martinez was convicted of possessing cocaine, heroin, and marijuana with the intent to distribute.

Petitioners appealed their convictions. Garcia, Soto, and Martinez claimed that the District Court abused its discretion in denying their motions to sever. (Zafiro did not appeal the denial of her severance motion, and thus, her claim is not properly before this Court.) The Court of Appeals acknowledged that "a vast number of cases say that a defendant is entitled to a severance when the 'defendants present mutually antagonistic defenses' in the sense that 'the acceptance of one party's defense precludes the acquittal of the other defendant.' " Noting that "mutual antagonism and other characterizations of the effort of one defendant to shift the blame from himself to a codefendant neither control nor illuminate the question of severance," the Court of Appeals found that the defendants had not suffered prejudice and affirmed the District Court's denial of severance. We granted the petition for certiorari, and now affirm the judgment of the Court of Appeals.

II

Rule 8(b) states that "two or more defendants may be charged in the same indictment or information if they are alleged to have participated in the same act or transaction or in the same series of acts or transactions constituting an offense or offenses." There is a preference in the federal system for joint trials of defendants who are indicted together. Joint trials "play a vital role in the criminal justice system." *Richardson v. Marsh*, 481 U.S. 200, 209 (1987). They promote efficiency and "serve the interests of justice by avoiding the scandal and inequity of inconsistent verdicts." *Id.* at 210. For these reasons, we repeatedly have approved of joint trials. But Rule 14 recognizes that joinder, even when proper under Rule 8(b), may prejudice either a defendant or the Government. Thus, the Rule provides, "if it appears that a defendant or the government is prejudiced by a joinder of . . . defendants . . . for trial together, the court may order an election or separate trials of counts, grant a severance of defendants or provide whatever other relief justice requires."

In interpreting Rule 14, the Courts of Appeals frequently have expressed the view that "mutually antagonistic" or "irreconcilable" defenses may be so prejudicial in some circumstances as to mandate severance. Notwithstanding such assertions, the courts have reversed relatively few convictions for failure to grant a severance on grounds of mutually antagonistic or irreconcilable defenses. The low rate of reversal may reflect the inability of defendants to prove a risk of prejudice in most cases involving conflicting defenses.

Nevertheless, petitioners urge us to adopt a bright-line rule, mandating severance whenever codefendants have conflicting defenses. We decline to do so.

Mutually antagonistic defenses are not prejudicial *per se*. Moreover, Rule 14 does not require severance even if prejudice is shown; rather, it leaves the tailoring of the relief to be granted, if any, to the district court's sound discretion.

We believe that, when defendants properly have been joined under Rule 8(b), a district court should grant a severance under Rule 14 only if there is a serious risk that a joint trial would compromise a specific trial right of one of the defendants, or prevent the jury from making a reliable judgment about guilt or innocence. Such a risk might occur when evidence that the jury should not consider against a defendant and that would not be admissible if a defendant were tried alone is admitted against a codefendant. For example, evidence of a codefendant's wrong-doing in some circumstances erroneously could lead a jury to conclude that a defendant was guilty. When many defendants are tried together in a complex case and they have markedly different degrees of culpability, this risk of prejudice is heightened. Evidence that is probative of a defendant's guilt but technically admissible only against a codefendant also might present a risk of prejudice. Conversely, a defendant might suffer prejudice if essential exculpatory evidence that would be available to a defendant tried alone were unavailable in a joint trial. The risk of prejudice will vary with the facts in each case, and district courts may find prejudice in situations not discussed here. When the risk of prejudice is high, a district court is more likely to determine that separate trials are necessary, but, as we indicated in *Richardson v. Marsh*, less drastic measures, such as limiting instructions, often will suffice to cure any risk of prejudice.

Turning to the facts of this case, we note that petitioners do not articulate any specific instances of prejudice. Instead they contend that the very nature of their defenses, without more, prejudiced them. Their theory is that when two defendants both claim they are innocent and each accuses the other of the crime, a jury will conclude (1) that both defendants are lying and convict them both on that basis, or (2) that at least one of the two must be guilty without regard to whether the Government has proved its case beyond a reasonable doubt.

As to the first contention, it is well settled that defendants are not entitled to severance merely because they may have a better chance of acquittal in separate trials. Rules 8(b) and 14 are designed "to promote economy and efficiency and to avoid a multiplicity of trials, so long as these objectives can be achieved without substantial prejudice to the right of the defendants to a fair trial." *Bruton*, 391 U.S., at 131, n. 6. While "an important element of a fair trial is that a jury consider *only* relevant and competent evidence bearing on the issue of guilt or innocence," a fair trial does not include the right to exclude relevant and competent evidence. A defendant normally would not be entitled to exclude the testimony of a former codefendant if the district court did sever their trials, and we see no reason why relevant and competent testimony would be prejudicial merely because the witness is also a codefendant.

As to the second contention, the short answer is that petitioners' scenario simply did not occur here. The Government argued that all four petitioners were guilty and offered sufficient evidence as to all four petitioners; the jury in turn found all four petitioners guilty of various offenses. Moreover, even if there were some risk of prejudice, here it is of the type that can be cured with proper instructions, and "juries are presumed to follow their instructions." *Richardson, supra*, 481 U.S., at 211. The District Court properly instructed the jury that the Government had "the burden of proving beyond a reasonable doubt" that each defendant committed the crimes with which he or she was charged. The court then instructed the jury that it must "give separate consideration to each individual defendant and to each separate charge against him. Each defendant is entitled to have his or her case determined from his or her own conduct and from the evidence that may be applicable to him or to her." In addition, the District Court admonished the jury that opening and closing arguments are not evidence and that it should draw no inferences from a defendant's exercise of the right to silence. These instructions sufficed to cure any possibility of prejudice.

Rule 14 leaves the determination of risk of prejudice and any remedy that may be necessary to the sound discretion of the district courts. Because petitioners have not shown that their joint trial subjected them to any legally cognizable prejudice, we conclude that the District Court did not abuse its discretion in denying petitioners' motions to sever. The judgment of the Court of Appeals is affirmed.

JUSTICE STEVENS, concurring in the judgment.

When two people are apprehended in possession of a container filled with narcotics, it is probable that they both know what is inside. The inference of knowledge is heightened when, as in this case, both people flee when confronted by police officers, or both people occupy the premises in which the container is found. At the same time, however, it remains entirely possible that one person did not have such knowledge. That, of course, is the argument made by each of the defendants in this case: that he or she did not know what was in the crucial box or suitcase.

Most important here, it is also possible that *both* persons lacked knowledge of the contents of the relevant container. Moreover, that hypothesis is compatible with individual defenses of lack of knowledge. There is no logical inconsistency between a version of events in which one person is ignorant, and a version in which the other is ignorant; unlikely as it may seem, it is at least theoretically possible that both versions are true, in that both persons are ignorant. In other words, dual ignorance defenses do not necessarily translate into "mutually antagonistic" defenses, as that term is used in reviewing severance motions, because acceptance of one defense does not necessarily preclude acceptance of the other and acquittal of the codefendant.

In my view, the defenses presented in this case did not rise to the level of mutual antagonism. First, as to Garcia and Martinez, neither of whom testified, the only defense presented was that the Government had failed to carry its burden of proving guilt beyond a reasonable doubt. Nothing in the testimony presented by their codefendants, Soto and Zafiro, supplemented the Government's proof of their guilt in any way. Soto's testimony that he did not know the contents of the box he delivered with Garcia, as discussed above, could have been accepted *in toto* without precluding acquittal of his codefendant. Similarly, the jury could have accepted Zafiro's testimony that she did not know the contents of the suitcase found in her apartment, and also acquitted Martinez.

It is true, of course, that the jury was unlikely to believe that none of the defendants knew what was in the box or suitcase. Accordingly, it must be acknowledged that if the jury had believed that Soto and Zafiro were ignorant, then it would have been more likely to believe that Garcia and Martinez were not. That, however, is not the standard for mutually antagonistic defenses. And in any event, the jury in this case obviously did not believe Soto and Zafiro, as it convicted both of them. Accordingly, there is no basis, in law or fact, for concluding that the testimony of Soto and Zafiro prejudiced their codefendants.

There is even less merit to the suggestion that Soto or Zafiro was prejudiced by the denial of their severance motions. Neither Garcia nor Martinez testified at all, of course, and the District Court explicitly cautioned the jury that the arguments made by their attorneys were not to be considered as evidence. Moreover, the assertion by his counsel that Garcia did not know the contents of the box is not inconsistent with Soto's ignorance or innocence; nor is the similar assertion by counsel for Martinez inconsistent with Zafiro's possible innocence. In my opinion, the District Court correctly determined that the defenses presented in this case were not "mutually antagonistic".

I would save for another day evaluation of the prejudice that may arise when the evidence or testimony offered by one defendant is truly irreconcilable with the innocence of a codefendant. Because the facts here do not present the issue squarely, I hesitate in this case to develop a rule that would govern the very different situation faced in cases like *People v. Braune*, 363 Ill. 551 (1936), in which mutually exclusive defenses transform a trial into "more of a contest between the defendants than between the people and the defendants." Under such circumstances, joinder may well be highly prejudicial, particularly when the prosecutor's own case-in-chief is marginal and the decisive evidence of guilt is left to be provided by a codefendant.

The burden of overcoming any individual defendant's presumption of innocence, by proving guilt beyond a reasonable doubt, rests solely on the shoulders of the prosecutor. Joinder is problematic in cases involving mutually antagonistic defenses because it may operate to reduce the burden on the prosecutor, in two general ways. First, joinder may introduce what is in effect a second prosecutor into a case, by turning each codefendant into the other's most forceful adversary.[3] Second, joinder may invite a jury confronted with two defendants, at least one of whom is almost certainly guilty, to convict the defendant who appears the more guilty of the two regardless of whether the prosecutor has proven guilt beyond a reasonable doubt as to that particular defendant.[4] Though the Court is surely correct that this second risk may be minimized by careful instructions insisting on separate consideration of the evidence as to each codefendant, the danger will remain relevant to the prejudice inquiry in some cases.

Given these concerns, I cannot share the Court's enthusiastic and unqualified "preference" for the joint trial of defendants indicted together. The Court correctly notes that a similar preference was announced a few years ago in *Richardson v. Marsh*, and that the Court had sustained the permissibility of joint trials on at least two prior occasions. There will, however, almost certainly be multidefendant cases

---

[3] "Defendants who accuse each other bring the effect of a second prosecutor into the case with respect to their codefendant. In order to zealously represent his client, each codefendant's counsel must do everything possible to convict the other defendant. The existence of this extra prosecutor is particularly troublesome because the defense counsel are not always held to the limitations and standards imposed on the government prosecutor." *U.S. v. Tootick*, 952 F.2d 1078, 1082 (CA9 1991).

[4] See *State v. Vinal*, 198 Conn. 644, 652 (1986) (in joint trial with mutually antagonistic defenses, "where one defendant is found not guilty, it becomes likely under these circumstances that the conviction of the losing defendant is more a result of his codefendant's success in defending himself than it is a product of the state's satisfaction of its constitutional duty to prove the accused guilty beyond a reasonable doubt").

in which a series of separate trials would be not only more reliable, but also more efficient and manageable than some of the mammoth conspiracy cases which the Government often elects to prosecute. And in all cases, the Court should be mindful of the serious risks of prejudice and overreaching that are characteristic of joint trials, particularly when a conspiracy count is included in the indictment. Justice Jackson's eloquent description of these concerns in his separate opinion in *Krulewitch v. United States*, 336 U.S. 440, 454 (1949), explains why there is much more at stake here than administrative convenience.

I agree with the Court that a "bright-line rule, mandating severance whenever codefendants have conflicting defenses" is unwarranted. For the reasons discussed above, however, I think district courts must retain their traditional discretion to consider severance whenever mutually antagonistic defenses are presented. Accordingly, I would refrain from announcing a preference for joint trials, or any general rule that might be construed as a limit on that discretion.

Because I believe the District Court correctly decided the severance motions in this case, I concur in the Court's judgment of affirmance.

Notes from Judge Katz:

1. In his concurring opinion, Justice Stevens alluded to "the very different situation faced in cases like *People v. Braune*, 363 Ill. 551 (1936)." In *Braune*, Dr. Dale assisted Dr. Braune in performing an abortion on Ms. Dwyer. Her intestine was inadvertently severed, causing her death. Both doctors were jointly charged with manslaughter. Dr. Braune moved for a severance, submitting his affidavit stating that Dr. Dale had impregnated Ms. Dwyer and then botched an earlier abortion attempt, causing the uterus to rupture and fall into the intestine, unbeknownst to Dr. Braune. Braune alleged that Dale would testify at trial and blame Braune for the death. Dr. Dale also filed a severance motion, denying Braune's assertions, and claiming that Braune would testify at trial, but Dale could not effectively cross-examine Braune because of their antagonistic defenses. The trial court denied both motions. At trial, each defense counsel tore into the other's witnesses. (For example, when Dale put on a medical professor as a character witness, Braune's attorney brought out that the professor knew Dale in college as "Udelsky".) Both doctors were convicted. The Illinois Supreme Court reversed:

> The trial was in many respects more of a contest between the defendants than between the people and the defendants. It produced a spectacle where the people frequently stood by and witnessed a combat in which the defendants attempted to destroy each other. Any set of circumstances which is sufficient to deprive a defendant of a fair trial if tried jointly with another is sufficient to require a separate trial.

How, exactly, is this "very different" from the situation in *Zafiro*? Would the *Zafiro* majority have reversed the convictions in *Braune*?

2. In *U.S. v. Breinig*, 70 F.3d 850 (6th Cir.1995), Breinig and his former wife (Moore) were indicted for evading income taxes by underreporting income from their family lawn-mowing and snowplowing business. Both moved for a severance: Breinig claimed that his defense was "violently antagonistic" to Moore's, and Moore claimed that she could not endure sitting through a joint trial with Breinig "without breaking down." The trial court denied both motions. The case went to trial —

Moore was acquitted, but Breinig was convicted.

The trial took place against a backdrop of severe antagonism between the defendants; their relationship was hostile since before their divorce. At trial, each defendant denied responsibility for evading tax obligations and cast blame on the other. Moore claimed that she lacked the capacity to form the requisite *mens rea* to have evaded taxes "willfully" because she was dominated and controlled by Breinig, and Breinig claimed that because Moore kept all the books and an accounting firm prepared their taxes, he had no knowledge of the underreporting.

Moore's defense of diminished capacity was based largely on the testimony of a psychiatrist and a psychologist who had treated her in 1990. Over Breinig's objections, the expert witnesses testified to Moore's mental instability; to her extreme insecurities; to her suicidal tendencies; to Breinig's infidelities; and to Moore's low self-esteem. The evidence presented to the jury showed that Breinig committed adultery during the course of his marriage to Moore, and that he alienated the couple's children, which caused Moore to feel abandoned by them. Additional testimony revealed that the defendant "abandoned" Moore, and that he "manipulated" her throughout the course of a twenty-four-year marriage resulting in Moore's extreme dependence on Breinig. All of this evidence was admitted only in support of Moore's defenses, but amounted, nevertheless, to dramatic evidence of Breinig's bad character. * * * *

Breinig argues that the denial of severance and separate trials rendered his trial unfair by denying him due process of law under the Fifth Amendment. Because of the inherently antagonistic defenses the parties presented, evidence that was admitted to support Moore's theory of the case, and which the jury was properly permitted to consider, was at the same time highly prejudicial evidence of Breinig's bad character. This evidence would have been inadmissible against Breinig had he been tried alone.

The Court of Appeal reversed Breinig's conviction:

Breinig argues that because his defense was sharply antagonistic to Moore's defense, he should have been granted severance. However, this is not the appropriate standard after *Zafiro*. A mutually antagonistic defense is not prejudicial per se, and Rule 14 does not mandate severance on that ground as a matter of law. Rather, the appropriate standard to be used for evaluating a motion for severance once defendants have been properly joined under Rule 8(b), is that of "a serious risk that a joint trial would compromise a specific trial right of one of the defendants, or prevent the jury from making a reliable judgment about guilt or innocence."

Breinig's claim of prejudice meets this standard. The unfairness in Breinig's trial resulted not from a mutually antagonistic defense, but from evidence the jury was permitted to hear and evaluate and which was, as to Breinig, impermissible and highly inflammatory evidence of his bad character. The jury was told, by well-credentialed experts, that Breinig was an adulterous, mentally abusive, and manipulating spouse. Such testimony, of course, would have been inadmissible against him under any theory of the Federal Rules of Evidence on a trial for tax evasion. Because Breinig's credibility was in issue, the jury's consideration of categorically inadmissible evidence was manifestly prejudicial, and unfairly so. It provided the government with an unfair windfall that the rules of evidence and elemental notions of fairness would otherwise not allow, and that Rule 8(b) does not envision. We find, therefore, that Breinig has carried the heavy burden of showing that the prejudice he suffered was compelling and unfair.

3. In *U.S. v. Johnson*, 219 F.3d 349 (4th Cir. 2000), co-defendants Shaheem Johnson and Raheem Johnson were *identical twins* tried together for conspiracy to sell narcotics. The court affirmed their convictions:

> The Johnsons also argue that because they are identical twins, the jury could easily have been confused, and they should have been tried separately. However, they cite nothing in the record to indicate that witnesses confused them or that they were not separately identified. Thus, we are not convinced that they were prejudiced by being tried together merely because they are twins.

4. After reading these pronouncements on joinder and severance from the lofty perch of the Supreme Court, let's get down in the pits and listen to a trial judge for a moment.

UNITES STATES v. ANDREWS, et. al.
U.S. District Court, Northern District of Illinois
754 F. Supp. 1197 (1990)

ASPEN, DISTRICT JUDGE:

The labyrinthine 305-page, 175-count indictment in this case, nearly two inches thick and weighing almost four pounds, names thirty-eight defendants, thirty-seven of whom are alleged to have been members or associates of the El Rukns, an infamous Chicago street gang. It details a maze of well over 250 factually separate criminal acts committed from 1966 to 1989 in many different locations and, for each act, alleges the participation of varying combinations of defendants and countless unindicted co-conspirators. The government's justification for including many of these otherwise unconnected criminal events in one indictment and one trial is that each was allegedly committed to attain power, control, and wealth for the street gang.

Defendants Jackie Clay, Harry Evans, Henry Leon Harris, Earl Hawkins, Eugene Hunter, Derrick Kees, Anthony Sumner, Freddie Elwood Sweeney, and Ricky Dean Williams have all pleaded guilty. Further guilty pleas are not anticipated. Defendants Roger Bowman, Floyd Davis, Eddie Franklin, Bernard Green, Melvin Mayes, Walter Pollard, and Edward Williams are presently fugitives and may not be apprehended in time for trial. This means that at least twenty-two defendants, but as many as twenty-nine, will be going to trial.

Several defendants have filed motions to sever this indictment pursuant to Rule 8(b) or, in the alternative, Rule 14 of the Federal Rules of Criminal Procedure, and the issue before the Court is whether we should permit these 175 diverse charges to be tried in a single mega-trial of unprecedented projected duration. We believe that we should not. Therefore, for the reasons discussed below, although we deny the Rule 8(b) motions, the Rule 14 motions are granted.

I. Indictment

A. Count One-RICO Conspiracy

Count One of the indictment charges all but one of the defendants with conspiracy to violate the Racketeering Influenced and Corrupt Organizations Act ("RICO"), 18 U.S.C. § 1962(d), and alleges that the El Rukn organization is a racketeering "enterprise" as defined by 18 U.S.C. § 1961(4). It describes a cohesive organization with tightly controlled operations and a formal chain of command. As alleged, unindicted co-conspirator Jeff Fort masterminded the activities of the El Rukns and wielded ultimate and unquestioned authority. He was assisted by thirty-five defendants whom the government contends were El Rukn "generals" or "officers," the organization's second and third levels of command, respectively. The government contends that the remaining two defendants named in Count One, although not El Rukn members, were otherwise intimately associated with the organization.

Under the direction and control of Fort, the named defendants and other unindicted co-conspirators are alleged to have conducted El Rukn affairs through the commission of an astonishing number of racketeering acts, including at least twenty murders, twelve attempted murders, eleven conspiracies to murder, one act of kidnapping, wide-scale drug trafficking, and numerous acts of obstruction of justice, including one attempt to bribe a judge and several acts of witness intimidation, retaliation, and tampering. As alleged, all of these wide-ranging and diverse offenses are connected, although at times somewhat loosely, to the affairs of the El Rukn street gang.

B. Count Two-Substantive RICO

Count Two charges thirty-six defendants with substantive violations of RICO under 18 U.S.C. § 1962(c) and recounts 128 separate acts of racketeering, many of which are also alleged in Count One. The number of racketeering acts that each defendant is alleged to have committed ranges from as many as seventy for Melvin Mayes to only two for Isiah Kitchen. The nature of acts charged also varies. Some defendants are charged with numerous violent racketeering acts and only one or two narcotics-related acts, while other defendants are charged solely with narcotics-related acts.

1. Violent Racketeering Acts

According to the allegations in Count Two, the long string of violent racketeering acts began in May 1974, when several defendants murdered Gilbert Connors, the brother of a rival drug dealer, to prevent encroachment on the El Rukn drug trade. To facilitate a cover-up of this crime, the same defendants subsequently killed Gregory Freeman on May 22, 1974, and blamed this murder on a witness to the Connors homicide. As a result, El Rukn members were able to persuade the witness to refuse to testify and the charges in both the Connors and Freeman murder cases were subsequently dropped.

Other murders were committed to enforce and enhance Jeff Fort's control over the El Rukns. Fort ordered El Rukn members, including several defendants, to kill disloyal members and former El Rukn leaders, including Willie McLilly, Roy Love, and Mickey Cogwell. McLilly and Love were killed on November 29, 1974, and Cogwell was killed on February 25, 1977.

The El Rukns also went to extreme lengths to protect its members from criminal prosecution. In August 1977, eighteen defendants conspired to kill Audrina Thomas to prevent her from testifying against two El Rukn generals charged with murder. Then, in a case of mistaken identity, Thomas' sister, Rowena James, was shot and killed on September 1, 1977. In January of 1987, four defendants and other El Rukn members kidnapped Patricia McKinley in an attempt to prevent her from testifying against an El Rukn general charged with the murder of Maurice Coleman.

The El Rukns committed a slew of other murders and attempted murders related to narcotics activity. On March 12, 1980, pursuant to Fort's order, two defendants killed Douglas Ellison because of a dispute involving a narcotics debt. Three months later, eight defendants conspired to murder Lemont Timberlake because he failed to accede to demands to stop dealing narcotics in El Rukn-controlled territory. This plan was carried out on June 17, 1980, when Timberlake was shot and killed in a vacant lot on the south side of Chicago.

From about April 1981 to January 1983, as a result of a drug territorial dispute, twenty-three defendants conspired to kill the top leaders and members of the Titanic Stones, a rival gang, including Eugene Hairston, George Thomas, Barnett Hall, Ray East, Robert East, and Willie Bibbs. During that same time period, Willie Bibbs and Barnett Hall were killed and George Thomas was the target of an attempted murder. In the course of the Thomas attempt, on January 23, 1983, five defendants and other gang members killed Charmaine Nathan and shot and attempted to kill Sheila Jackson.

In April 1985, as a result of another drug territorial dispute with a rival gang, twenty-three defendants conspired to kill various members of the King Cobra street gang. In furtherance of this conspiracy, during the last week of April, teams of El Rukns cruised the streets of Chicago in efforts to locate and murder King Cobra members. During this time, several defendants and other El Rukn members murdered Robert Jackson, Rico Chalmers, Glendon McKinley, and Vicki Nolden and attempted to murder Theotis Clark and Andre Chalmers. McKinley and Nolden were innocent bystanders swept up in the wave of violence.

The El Rukns committed other murders and attempted murders as a result of separate drug territorial disputes. * * * *

2. Non-Violent Racketeering Acts

Count Two alleges ninety-seven additional racketeering acts which, with one exception, are narcotics-related offenses. * * *

C. Count Three: Narcotics Conspiracy

Racketeering Act 31 is repeated as a separate "substantive" offense in Count Three. This Count describes a conspiracy to possess with intent to distribute, and to distribute, multi-kilogram quantities of heroin and cocaine, hundreds of pounds of marijuana, thousands of amphetamine pills, thousands of Talwin and Triplenamin pills, multi-liter quantities of codeine syrup, and large quantities of Phencyclidine (PCP). * * * *

II. Severance Discussion

Numerous defendants have filed motions to sever this indictment claiming that they are improperly joined pursuant to Rule 8(b), or, in the alternative, that joinder is unduly prejudicial pursuant to Rule 14. We will discuss these motions in turn.

A. Rule 8(b)

Rule 8(b) permits joinder of an unlimited number of defendants "if they are alleged to have participated in the same act or transaction or in the same series of acts or transactions constituting an offense or offenses." In determining whether joinder is proper under this Rule, a court must look to the face of the indictment. If the indictment alleges a conspiracy, it is well established that all members of that conspiracy are properly joined.

Although the defendants agree with this settled principle, they nonetheless argue that they are improperly joined. Relying on *Kotteakos v. United States*, 328 U.S. 750 (1946), they argue that the indictment fails to satisfy Rule 8(b) because it alleges multiple distinct conspiracies, including separate conspiracies to murder, obstruct justice, and distribute narcotics. In *Kotteakos*, the Supreme Court reversed the convictions of the petitioners where the evidence established at least eight separate conspiracies connected only by a common participant. The Court stated that a defendant has a right "not to be tried en masse for the conglomeration of distinct and separate offenses committed by others." *Id.* at 775. Thus, according to the defendants here, *Kotteakos* requires a finding that they are improperly joined.

While their characterization of the indictment is correct, the defendants are wrong that the allegation of separate conspiracies renders joinder improper under Rule 8(b). With the advent of RICO, Congress significantly broadened the scope of the government's authority to bring defendants together in one indictment. It conferred this broad authority without eviscerating the principals set forth in *Kotteakos* or "radically altering traditional conspiracy doctrine." *United States v. Riccobene*, 709 F.2d 214, 224 (3d Cir.1983). Instead, Congress simply outlawed a particular conspiratorial agreement, the object of which could include the commission of a wide array of separate and distinct offenses.

Section 1962(d) of the RICO statute proscribes agreements "to conduct or participate in the affairs of an enterprise through a pattern of racketeering activity." A single "pattern of racketeering activity" can include numerous distinct conspiracies.

Consequently, a series of agreements that under pre-RICO law would constitute multiple conspiracies could under RICO be tried as a single "enterprise" conspiracy in violation of § 1962(d). Therefore, consistent with the rationale of *Kotteakos*, the defendants in this case are properly joined because they are each alleged members of a single and unifying RICO conspiracy. The separate and distinct underlying conspiracies are simply part of the "same series of acts or transactions constituting this offense." Fed.R.Crim.P. 8(b). * * * *

We conclude that these defendants are properly joined. Accordingly, their motions to sever pursuant to Rule 8(b) are denied.

B. Rule 14

Having decided that the requirements of Rule 8(b) are met by the allegations in the indictment, we turn to Rule 14. As indicated above, although joinder is technically proper under Rule 8(b), Rule 14 authorizes severance if such joinder is prejudicial to the defendants. * * * *

The District Court is given wide latitude in determining whether a Rule 14 severance is appropriate. The decision is within its "sound discretion" and "will not be overturned absent a clear showing of an abuse of that discretion." *United States v. Caliendo*, 910 F.2d 429, 437 (7th Cir.1990). To determine if severance is appropriate in the present case, we must weigh the public interest in a joint trial of the twenty-two to twenty-nine defendants against the possibility of undue prejudice or confusion arising from such a trial.

1. Public Interest

a. Advantages of Joint Trial

To strike the appropriate balance, we recognize, as we must, the oft-cited "strong public interest in having persons jointly indicted tried together, especially where the evidence against the defendants arose out of the same acts or series of acts." *United States v. Turk*, 870 F.2d 1304, 1306 (7th Cir.1989). Joint trials generally "reduce the expenditure of judicial and prosecutorial time and the claims the criminal justice system makes on witnesses, who need not return to court for additional trials." *United States v. Buljubasic*, 808 F.2d 1260, 1263 (7th Cir.1987). For this reason, joint trials are considered "an essential element of the quick administration of justice." *United States v. Walters*, 913 F.2d 388, 393 (7th Cir.1990). Certainly, "if every defendant who wanted a severance was given one, the slow pace of our court system would go from a crawl to paralysis." *Id.*

Joint trials are also favored because of their purported effect on the accurate determination of culpability. Joint trials reduce the chance that each defendant will try to create a reasonable doubt by blaming an absent colleague, even though one or the other (or both) undoubtedly committed a crime. The joint trial gives the jury the best perspective on all of the evidence and therefore increases the likelihood of a correct outcome.

b. Special Concerns Raised by Prospect of Joint Mega-Trial

It has long been assumed that the advantages referred to above adequately support a strong presumption in favor of joint trials and against severance. See *Bruton v. United States*, 391 U.S. 123, 143 (1968) (White, J., dissenting). Thus, to prevail in a motion for severance, a defendant ordinarily "must show that she could not possibly have a fair trial without a severance." *Caliendo*, 910 F.2d at 437. However, the recent proliferation of complex, multi-defendant trials in this district and others, prompted in large part by RICO, has raised doubts about the foundations of this onerous burden. See generally Federal Bar Council Committee on Second Circuit Courts, *A Proposal Concerning Problems Created by Extremely Long Criminal Trials* (1989) (hereinafter *Extremely Long Criminal Trials*). Some courts, when faced with a multitude of defendants indicted together under the expansive RICO umbrella, have questioned the wisdom of blindly embracing the purported advantages of a joint trial while, at the same time, disregarding the manifest difficulties presented by what is commonly called a "mega-trial." See, e.g., *United States v. Mancuso*, 130 F.R.D. 128, 131 (D.Nev.1990); *United States v. Gallo*, 668 F.Supp. 736, 754 (E.D.N.Y.1987).

A careful review of these difficulties reveals a point of diminishing returns with respect to the net benefits of a joint trial as the number of defendants and complexity of the indictment increases. Accordingly, at some point, the oft-cited advantages of a joint trial are outweighed by the manifest disadvantages of a large and protracted trial. Based on this abstract supposition, the Second Circuit, in *United States v. Casamento*, 887 F.2d 1141, 1152 (2d Cir.1989), adopted a presumption against a joint trial and for severance when faced with the prospect of a mega-trial. It counseled that in the event the estimated length of the government's case is more than four months, the prosecutor should "present a reasoned basis to support a conclusion that a joint trial of all the defendants is more consistent with the fair administration of justice than some manageable division of the case into separate trials for groups of defendants." *Id.* If, in addition to an estimated length of more than four months, the case involves more than ten defendants, "the prosecutor should make an especially compelling justification for a joint trial." *Id.*

Although the approach of the Second Circuit is necessarily arbitrary, it is well-taken. It correctly recognizes that the broad societal disadvantages of large and protracted joint trials, some of which are referred to below, may outweigh their arguable advantages. Accordingly, a strong presumption in favor of joint trials is not justified in the context of an inordinately complex mega-trial like the one proposed here, where the principal nexus between the charges is that the defendants allegedly were associated with the same criminally-oriented gang.

c. Disadvantages of Joint Mega-Trial

One disadvantage, which is particularly relevant in this case, is the significant exacerbation of the public cost of providing defense counsel to each defendant. All but one of the defense attorneys currently representing a defendant in this case are being federally funded. Testimony directly implicating most of their clients is projected to last not more than a few weeks, and, for many, not more than a few days. Thus, in a single trial, most of these twenty-one to twenty-eight appointed attorneys would be compelled to sit idly for the duration of a lengthy trial where the vast majority of evidence deals solely with the criminal activities of other attorneys' clients. See *United States v. Phillips*, 664 F.2d 971, 1017 n. 68 (5th Cir.1981) (defendant complains that only 120 pages of 12,000 page transcript concerned his activities); *United States v. Morrow*, 537 F.2d 120, 137 (1982) (only twenty-five pages of transcript devoted to testimony concerning defendant's activities out of a total record of "over fifty volumes"); *United States v. Kelly*, 349 F.2d 720, 759 (2d Cir.1965) (defendant's name first mentioned three months into a nine-month trial and then only sporadically thereafter); see also *Extremely Long Criminal Trials*, at 2 (discussing unidentified case where a defendant's name was not mentioned until after six months of trial). The added expense of this idle attorney time would needlessly escalate the total public cost of providing these attorneys. Indeed, if this proposed joint trial were to last as long as projected (two years by defense counsel, one year by the Court, and five to six months by the prosecution), this added expense would be exorbitant. According to the estimates of defendant Derrick Porter and based on the current hourly rate for court-appointed counsel of $40 out-of-court and $60 in-court, the cost of twenty-one court-appointed attorneys for a one-year trial is at least $1.6 million. Here, a significant majority of this total would be wasted as compensation to defense counsel for idle time.

Another significant disadvantage is the havoc this case would wreak upon this Court's already burdened docket. A trial of the length proposed by the government would obviously prevent this Court from fulfilling its obligations to litigants in other pending cases, both civil and criminal. We would be required to preside over just one case for an indefinite and prolonged period of time, which, in turn, would result in unconscionable delays in many of our other cases.[12] Moreover, the trial management tasks presented by such a case promise to be unwieldy. A case of this nature would require the prompt attendance of dozens of persons, any one of whose absence would bring the proceedings to an abrupt halt. No day in court would be free from the ominous specter of yet another delay caused by the lateness or absence of any of the more than one hundred witnesses, eighteen jurors and alternates, twenty-two to twenty-nine defendants, twenty-two to twenty-nine defense counsel and tens of court, security, and government personnel. Additionally, the myriad of inevitable motions, objections, and sidebar discussions would in all likelihood result in further lengthy and unpredictable delays.

A trial of the mammoth proportions advocated by the government would also place enormous personal burdens on the jurors, the defendants, defense counsel and the Court. Sitting as a juror in a case of this nature increases the normal inconvenience of jury duty to almost unacceptable proportions. To be taken away from personal and occupational endeavors for a year or more to "sit stoically and silently for hours every day, day after day," is an unconscionable disruption of a

---

[12] The requisite expenditure of judicial time for a trial of the scope requested by the government also does violence to the mandate of Congress that all litigation before the District Court proceed promptly and without undue delay. See Speedy Trial Act, 18 U.S.C. § 3161 (1988). Not only will litigants be unable to go to trial on other pending criminal and civil cases in this court during the pendency of the mega-trial, but the off-the-bench time this court would normally devote to other traditional judicial responsibilities will be significantly decreased. These responsibilities are not limited to presiding over jury trials. The judge must preside as well at motion and status calls and at sentencing hearings. He conducts emergency hearings for temporary restraining orders and preliminary injunctions. He decides motions and writes opinions, resolves discovery disputes, and negotiates settlements in civil cases. To fulfill these obligations, the judge requires non-courtroom time to read cases, statutes, pre-sentence reports, motions, briefs and other pleadings, magistrate reports, and law clerk memoranda and draft opinions. The judge is also expected to have a passing familiarity with the hundreds of pages of slip sheet opinions he receives from the Clerks of the United States Supreme Court and Seventh Circuit each month. He must additionally reserve time to read and answer mail, return telephone calls, confer with his staff and, yes, simply to contemplate the many legal questions he must resolve. There is a finite amount of hours in the day to meet these demands. So the impact of a mega-trial on judicial routine can be disastrous. During a mega-trial involving a multitude of defendants and more than 250 criminal acts, all the judge's non-jury hours would be consumed with managing the mega-trial. Off-the-bench time would be used primarily to resolve the inevitable motions *in limine*, discovery disputes, and "housekeeping" problems generated by the approximately two dozen trial lawyers, all of whom, unlike the judge, will have put aside all other legal commitments and will be spending every professional hour in single-minded activity involving only the mega-trial. For the judge, there would be little time or energy left for his other responsibilities. Thus, lawyers and parties in the other three hundred criminal and civil cases pending on the judge's calendar would suffer the immediate fall-out from decreased judicial activity and the inevitable impaired judicial performance resulting from an all consuming mega-trial. But the long term damage to our justice system, although more subtle, would be just as debilitating. Failed efforts to succeed in the impossible task of managing a mega-trial and a full caseload at the same time can only lead to judicial "burnout", which in turn will result in impaired judicial performance lasting long after the mega-trial's conclusion.

person's personal and employment life. This disruption would be magnified exponentially if, as is a possibility in this case, it became necessary to sequester the jury. In a lengthy, multi-defendant trial, this entire process is draining, disorienting, exhausting, and often demoralizing. These are uniquely inordinate burdens to place upon citizens assuming the civic responsibility of jury duty. Moreover, it is unrealistic to expect that this onerous and unfair hardship will not impact adversely on the jury's proper functioning. It should be self-apparent that a juror frustrated[14] or hostile[15] because of an unduly prolonged trial will not be a fair and conscientious juror. See *Extremely Long Criminal Trials*, at 2 (speculating that jury's verdict acquitting each of the two dozen defendants in *United States v. Accetturo*, 842 F.2d 1408 (3rd Cir.1988), after a fifteen-month trial, represented "either an angry attack on the prosecution for the length of the trial or an abdication of the jurors' responsibilities occasioned by their inability or refusal to deliberate over the enormous volume of evidence").

The defendants themselves would also be unnecessarily burdened. At least seventeen of the twenty-two defendants currently in custody are being detained solely as a result of this indictment. The time spent in jail prior to trial has already been prolonged by the expansive discovery required and the large number and excessive complexity of pretrial motions. These defendants, presumed innocent, are entitled to as swift a rendering of justice as the circumstances allow. Prolonged pretrial incarceration and a trial of undue length strains this right to its breaking point.

The more than twenty court-appointed defense attorneys would also be deleteriously affected by a lengthy trial. It is one thing to expect urban defense attorneys with heavy overhead expenses to work at the reduced hourly rates mandated by the Criminal Justice Act when the case's duration can be measured in weeks. It is quite another matter, however, to expect these attorneys to survive economically on these comparatively Spartan hourly fees in a case anticipated to last as long as a year or two. Not only would their present earnings be diminished, but there would be long-range adverse effects on their practices due to such a lengthy full-time commitment. These severe repercussions to their professional careers would be particularly damaging in this case where most of the attorneys are sole practitioners.

The judge's ability to rule objectively and dispassionately would also be unduly compromised. The grinding tension of such a long, complex case, particularly where the judge is making rulings which are continuously on the borderline of probative force and prejudice, is debilitating. Moreover, after the case has been under way for some time, the judge is increasingly concerned about the possibility of a mistrial, which would require yet another extended period in tying up the court. Thus, as the trial develops, it becomes increasingly difficult for the court to view objectively the

---

[14] The frustrations in dealing with legal terminology in a prolonged criminal jury case is described by a former juror: "Being a juror was a terrible thing. I'm not smart and I'm not educated, and I don't know if its right to put a person like me in that position of being a judge. It was awful. I had to think like I've never thought before. I had to try to understand words like justice and truth and . . ." Villasenor, *Jury: The People v. Juan Corona*.

[15] Juror hostility as a result of boredom is tersely exemplified by a poem found in the jury room after the conclusion of a five week trial: "Oh, give me a break, just a ten minute break, When I don't have to sit and listen to this shit, Oh, give me chance to get up and dance, For it's such a bore, I long for the door." *Jury Comprehension*, at 24.

case and its evidentiary decisions without the added tension of avoiding errors that might result in a mistrial or reversal.

Thus, it is clear that a "monster" trial such as the one proposed here presents uniquely significant inefficiencies and hardships. These disadvantages far outweigh any arguable advantages of a joint trial, including the potential reduction in aggregate trial time, which in this case in any event is doubtful. Accordingly, a strong presumption in favor of a joint trial is not justified in the context of a mega-trial. Indeed, since several separate and shorter trials involving smaller groups of defendants would largely eliminate the disadvantages of such a trial, the public interest supports a strong presumption against a joint mega-trial and in favor of severance.

2. Prejudice to Defendants

A Rule 14 analysis also requires us to assess the potential prejudice of a joint trial to the defendants. Every joint trial involves some inherent degree of prejudice. Ordinarily, we would consider whether the defendants have demonstrated that this prejudice outweighs the presumption in favor of a joint trial. But this is not an ordinary case. Since we have concluded the public interest weighs against a joint trial in this case, the defendants have no presumption to overcome. Indeed, in the context of this mega-trial, the scales are tipped decidedly in favor of severance.

The Seventh Circuit has provided some guidance in assessing the degree of prejudice presented by the prospect of a joint trial. It has identified four situations in which this prejudice may require severance under Rule 14: (1) antagonistic defenses conflicting to the point of being irreconcilable and mutually exclusive; (2) massive and complex evidence making it almost impossible for the jury to separate evidence as it relates to each defendant when determining each defendant's innocence or guilt; (3) a co-defendant's statement inculpating the moving defendant; and (4) gross disparity in the weight of the evidence against defendants. *United States v. Garner*, 837 F.2d at 1413. Satisfaction of any one of these criteria may mandate severance.

a. "Massive and Complex Evidence"

We will begin our discussion of possible prejudice with the *Garner* court's second specified concern, "massive and complex evidence," because this concern most compellingly requires severance in this instance. The necessity of severance in this context reflects the precept that we use "every safeguard to individualize each defendant in his relation to the mass." *Kotteakos*, 328 U.S. at 773. The critical question then is whether it is within the jury's capacity to follow admonitory instructions and to keep separate, collate and appraise evidence relevant only to each defendant. In other words, is it reasonable to conclude that as a practical matter the jury will give each defendant the individual justice that the law demands? We find that it is not reasonable to so conclude.

It is fanciful to believe that any jury would be able, or even willing, to intelligently and thoroughly deliberate over the enormous volume of evidence expected at a single trial of this action. In its present form, the trial would involve twenty-two to twenty-nine defendants accused of over 150 factually separate criminal acts spanning a period of over twenty years and involving at least twenty-five different provisions of the state and federal penal codes. The government concedes that the volume of evidence at such a trial would be "massive," and we find that solely by virtue of its volume the evidence would be equally "complex".[20] After this long and arduous trial, the jury would be required to sift through a virtual warehouse of evidence to determine what items were presented against which defendant and as to which criminal act. It would then be obliged to resolve a plethora of difficult factual issues and to strictly apply the detailed and complex law as provided by hundreds of pages of jury instructions. The inevitable length of such a trial dramatically increases the difficulty of this Herculean task. Both common sense and scientific study dictate that as the volume of evidence and corresponding length of trial increases, the degree and quality of jury comprehension decreases proportionately. To expect any jury to accurately recall and appraise the vast amount of detailed testimonial and documentary evidence it heard many months or even a year earlier is unrealistically optimistic.

The difficulty of this task would be increased further by the inevitable admission of large amounts of evidence on a limited basis. While much of the anticipated evidence would be technically relevant to the RICO charges under Federal Rule of Evidence 401 as to all of the defendants, a large part of it would surely be excluded under Evidence Rule 403 against most of the defendants because it would be cumulative or prejudicial. Other evidentiary rules would also compel the surgical admission of evidence against only selected defendants. With respect to co-conspirator's statements under Evidence Rule 801(d)(2)(E), for example, the evidence would be admitted on an especially complicated basis due to the multitude of conspiracies charged as subparts to the over-arching RICO conspiracy. These conspiracies, as factually convoluted as any ever charged in this district, involve varying combinations of defendants, exist for differing periods of times, and involve defendants who allegedly join and leave the conspiracies at various times.

All of this would require the jury to understand and apply a web of hundreds of complicated and intricate limiting instructions to evidence that it may barely recall in the first place. The task, akin to solving a hideously complicated puzzle, would be overwhelming. Although in most cases "it is within the jury's capacity to follow the trial court's limiting instruction requiring separate consideration for each defendant and the evidence admitted against him," *United States v. Diaz*, 876 F.2d 1344, 1358 (7th Cir.1989), there are some cases "in which the risk that the jury will not, or cannot, follow instructions is so great, and the consequences of failure so vital to the defendant, that the practical and human limitations of the jury system cannot be ignored." *Bruton*, 391 U.S. at 135. This is such a case. The sheer volume and complexity of the anticipated instructions make it impossible to ignore the limitations of the jury system. The real danger, of course, is that the jury would, in spite of all precautions, consider evidence admissible only as to some defendants in determining the culpability of others and in the process convict some defendants because of their association with the mass. Another equally unacceptable probability is that the jurors may convict or acquit some defendants as a result of their confusion in sorting out the mass of evidence, charges, and jury instructions.

Notwithstanding the immense difficulties facing the jury that we have just charted, the government argues that the jury would not be overwhelmed by its task.

---

[20] In arguing that this case is not "complex" in its brief, the government engages in a complicated discussion about how simple this case is. The complexity of this argument itself exemplifies the problems the jury would have in rendering thoughtful verdicts at a single trial.

The government contends that with its proposed organized presentation of the evidence and the use of various visual aids, the jury, after a trial projected to last a year or more, would be able to a make a thoughtful and considered determination of the culpability of each of the twenty-two or more defendants and be able to intelligently apply the more than twenty-five distinct provisions of the various relevant penal codes to the more than 150 separate criminal acts committed over the course of more than twenty years. This proposition strikes us as a great deal of make-believe. Unquestionably, the human mind is limited in its ability to accept, synthesize, and recall information accurately. To try this case in its present form would, at the very least, push these abilities to their uncertain limits. This places in jeopardy the most important objective of a criminal trial: accurate fact-finding. We cannot place the liberty of twenty-two or more individuals at stake under such circumstances. Thus, because there is likely to be "massive and complex evidence making it almost impossible for the jury to separate evidence as it relates to each defendant when determining each defendant's innocence or guilt," we find that severance is appropriate under Rule 14.

b. Disparity of Evidence

Severance is also independently appropriate in this case because of the gross disparity in the weight of the evidence against the defendants. A "gross disparity" in the evidence presents a danger that some defendants will suffer "spillover prejudice" due to the accumulation of evidence against other defendants. When that occurs, a defendant may suffer a transference of guilt merely due to his association with a more culpable defendant. Thus, we again must consider whether it is within the jury's capacity to adhere to instructions requiring separate consideration of the evidence admitted against each defendant.[22] Generally, unless the disparity of evidence is unquestionably severe, courts presume that the jury will faithfully observe such instructions. In this case, however, the evidentiary disparity is unquestionably severe and, consequently, we will not presume the jury has the necessary capacity.

At one end of the spectrum, three defendants have been charged with the commission of less than five racketeering acts under RICO. This group includes Isiah Kitchen, who is charged with only two narcotics-related acts and a separate weapons possession offense. Four other defendants are charged with only five racketeering acts. Moving along the spectrum, several other defendants are charged with twelve or more racketeering acts. Among this group is James Speights, who is accused of nineteen racketeering acts, including participation in seven murder conspiracies and one witness kidnapping. At the far end of the spectrum, Alan Knox is charged with thirty-nine racketeering acts. These acts include two murders, participation in ten murder conspiracies, and the illegal purchase of a LAW rocket with the intent to perform terrorist acts against the United States on behalf of the Libyan government. If fugitive Melvin Mayes is apprehended, the apparent disparity will be increased further because he is charged with seventy racketeering acts. Thus, it is evident from the vastly

---

[22] In considering the appropriateness of severance due to either "massive and complex evidence" or a "gross disparity" of evidence, the principal concern is that a defendant may suffer "spillover prejudice" However, as to "massive and complex evidence," the concern does not result from a defendant's association with a more culpable defendant, but rather from the sheer volume of evidence of wrong doing and the potential consequent inability or unwillingness of the jury to compartmentalize evidence.

disproportionate number of criminal acts charged against these defendants that there is likely to be a "gross disparity" in the weight of the evidence presented. If the Seventh Circuit's directive to sever where there is a "gross disparity" of the evidence is to have any meaning at all, it must apply to this case.

The government argues that even if the evidence is sufficiently disparate to warrant severance, the danger of "spillover prejudice" is mitigated in this case because in any event most of the evidence would be admissible at each of the separately severed trials. It contends that it would be entitled to offer evidence of all of the charged racketeering activity at each separate trial to prove the entire pattern of racketeering activity and the full scope of the enterprise. This argument is unpersuasive simply because all the evidence would not be admissible at the separate trials. A great deal of evidence technically admissible under Evidence Rule 401 would certainly be excluded at each severed trial because of its lack of connection to the active criminal deeds of any of the defendants at those particular trials. This exclusion is dictated by Evidence Rule 403 which mandates the exclusion of evidence whose probative value is substantially outweighed by the "danger of unfair prejudice" and by "considerations of undue delay, waste of time, or needless presentation of cumulative evidence" Fed.R.Evid. 403. Thus, because of its functional inadmissibility, the technical admissibility of the evidence at separate trials does not militate against severance here.

Therefore, due to extreme evidentiary disparity, a trial in its present form unquestionably raises the specter of "spillover prejudice" and the resulting danger of "guilt by association" such that each defendant's fundamental right to an independent determination of his guilt or innocence is jeopardized. Severance is appropriate here on this ground alone.

c. Antagonistic Defenses

The potential for "antagonistic defenses conflicting to the point of being irreconcilable and mutually exclusive" is also an important concern in this case. *Garner*, 837 F.2d at 1413.

Generally, severance is not required where there is a mere hostility between defenses and some finger-pointing between defendants. *United States v. Turk*, 870 F.2d 1304, 1306 (7th Cir.1989); see also *Buljubasic*, 808 F.2d at 1263 ("finger-pointing is an acceptable cost of the joint trial and at times is even beneficial because it helps complete the picture before the trier of fact"). Severance is only required where the hostile defenses are irreconcilable and mutually exclusive such that the acceptance of one defendant's defense will preclude the acquittal of the other defendant. See *United States v. Pacheco*, 794 F.2d 7, 9 (1st Cir.1986) (to require severance, antagonism must go "beyond mere fingerpointing into the realm of fundamental disagreement over core and basic facts"). While it is true, as the government points out, that no defendant has done more than speculate about the potential for this type of antagonism, we think that it is nonetheless appropriate to consider this factor.

The sheer number of defendants to be tried makes conflicting trial strategies and a significant degree of finger-pointing a virtual certainty. This potential prejudice is compounded here because the jury may not comprehend the individual defense theories due to the mass confusion caused by twenty-two or more attorneys vigorously pursuing his or her own course while seeking his or her own client's acquittal. Moreover, if any of these separate courses became too antagonistic during the trial so as to then mandate severance, a great waste of time and judicial resources would result. Although this potential prejudice may not require severance at this initial stage, we believe that the real possibility of it eventually occurring weighs heavily in favor of severing this trial.

C. Balance Struck in Favor of Severance

In summary, the potential prejudice against the defendants in this case and the administrative and fiscal advantages of separate trials outweigh any of the possible advantages of conducting a joint trial. Indeed, a trial of this magnitude would be appropriate in only the rarest circumstances. Nonetheless, in spite of its inherent prejudice and affront to the public interest, the mega-trial too often has been improperly tolerated and even endorsed by some participants in our judicial system.

In the first instance, of course, the decision to bring a multitude of defendants and charges within the scope of a single indictment is within the province of the prosecutor. Some courts and commentators have urged prosecutorial restraint with regard to the use of this discretion. See, e.g., *United States v. Agueci*, 310 F.2d 817, 840 (2d Cir.1962) (solution to problem of mass trials "is largely in the hand of the United States Attorney," who has initial charging discretion). Indeed, a prosecutor has an obligation to use some measure of restraint and to consider the effect of a sizable indictment on the integrity of the resulting trial. As stated by Justice Sutherland in *Berger v. United States*: "The United States Attorney is the representative not of an ordinary party to a controversy, but of a sovereignty whose obligation to govern impartially is as compelling as its obligation to govern at all; and whose interest, therefore, in a criminal prosecution is not that it shall win a case, but that justice shall be done." 295 U.S. 78, 88 (1935). In this case, the government demonstrated little or no concern for any such obligation when it charged thirty-eight defendants in this convoluted 175-count, 305-page indictment.

Unfortunately, prosecutors have long been willing to bring cases of this nature despite the violence they do to the notion of a fair trial.[23] Indeed, prosecutors generally have demonstrated an increasing "penchant for drawing together ever-more complex and extensive conspiracies into a single indictment." *U.S. v. Kopituk*, 690 F.2d at 1320. This phenomenon can be explained by the fact that prosecutors have significant incentives to bring mass indictments, not the least of which is the consequent ability to procure a large number of convictions in what they perceive to be the shortest amount of time. The regrettable truth, however, is that these incentives[24] carry far greater weight in the charging decision than any concern for a fair and manageable trial. It seems unlikely, then, that the recent increase in mega-trials will soon be curbed at the initiative of the prosecution.

---

[23] See, e.g., *U.S. v. Casamento*, 887 F.2d at 1149 (21-defendant, 17-month trial involved 275 witnesses and thousands of exhibits and produced over 40,000 pages of transcript); *United States v. Accetturo*, 842 F.2d 1408, 1410 (3d Cir.1988) (24-defendant trial lasted 15 months); *United States v. Kopituk*, 690 F.2d 1289, 1320 (11th Cir.1982) (12-defendant, 70-count trial that lasted seven months produced 22,000 pages of transcript and involved 130 witnesses); *United States v. Braasch*, 505 F.2d 139, 144–45 (7th Cir.1974) (trial of 24 conspirators included 48 witnesses and produced a 6,836 page record).

[24] It has also been argued by some that the media "splash" coincident to the announcement of a mass indictment is a disincentive to rational charging policies.

It is also unlikely that appellate courts will be able to offer a great deal of assistance in this regard. After a lengthy trial resulting in conviction, the denial of severance is, understandably, rarely overturned. In the Seventh Circuit, the matter is judged by an "abuse of discretion" standard and "will be disturbed on appeal only if it results in manifest and substantial prejudice" *U.S. v. Brunn*, 809 F.2d at 407. As a practical matter, this onerous burden is to some degree more difficult to meet in the context of a mega-trial where there is a natural reluctance to render moot such a massive commitment of time and money. Simply put, appellate courts, by virtue of their role in the judicial system, are not in a position to effectively deter the mega-trial. The resulting and almost invariably silent tolerance of such trials at the appellate level perpetuates their continued existence.

Thus, it seems that the trial court is the place where the tide of mega-trials must be stemmed.[26] It certainly has the authority to do so given its virtually unbounded discretion to grant severance in such cases. Indeed, the trial court is compelled to use this discretion to "secure simplicity in procedure, and fairness in administration" and, consequently, should never tolerate a trial that involves a multitude of charges against a throng of defendants. Fed.R.Crim.P. 2. The defendants' motions for severance are granted under Rule 14.

III. Severance Plan Overview

Having determined that severance is appropriate, we next turn to the specifics of the severance plan. Because at this stage of the proceedings the government is the only party with complete knowledge of the evidence that it will present in this case, it is in the best position to suggest an efficient and effective severance plan. However, unfortunately, it has declined our previous requests to participate in the formulation of such a plan.

Therefore, without input from the government, we adopt a severance plan that attempts to address the considerations discussed above and to strike a balance between other practical and competing concerns. To begin, we have sought to drastically reduce the volume of evidence against each defendant unrelated to his active participation in El Rukn affairs and his alleged crimes. At the same time, we have sought to ensure that the introduction of evidence is not so restricted as to unduly impair the government's case against any defendant or its opportunity to secure a conviction carrying significant penalties. Additionally, it is important to limit the duplication of evidence at the separate trials and, accordingly, minimize aggregate trial time and the corresponding expenditure of both public and judicial resources.

With these considerations in mind, the defendants will be divided into five non-overlapping groups to be tried at five separate trials. While the government will be permitted to go forward at all five trials with Counts One and Two, the RICO

---

[26] United States Judge for the Fifth Circuit Patrick E. Higginbotham counsels: "I see little justification for multiple indictments with counts numbering in the hundreds. Of course, the decision to prosecute, as well as much of the composition of the charges themselves, is within the constitutionally fenced preserve of the Executive Branch of government. Once the indictments are signed and filed, however, I take the view that the matter of prosecution becomes a shared responsibility between the Article II and III branches of the government. As a trial judge, I have had some success in severing out and sequencing trials to overcome the problems of the unduly lengthened indictment." Judges' Manual for the Management of Complex Criminal Jury Cases § 2.7 (1982).

conspiracy and substantive RICO counts respectively, it will not be permitted to try all of the racketeering acts charged in these counts at every trial. Instead, some acts will not be tried at all and the remaining acts will be divided between the five trials and, for the most part, tried only once. Of course, non-RICO substantive counts will be tried along with their corresponding RICO racketeering acts. Likewise, substantive counts that correspond to racketeering acts that are not tried will be held in abeyance, to be tried at a subsequent phase of trials if it becomes necessary. * * * *

GRAY v. MARYLAND
United States Supreme Court
523 U.S. 185 (1998)

JUSTICE BREYER delivered the opinion of the Court.

The issue in this case concerns the application of *Bruton v. United States*, 391 U.S. 123 (1968). *Bruton* involved two defendants accused of participating in the same crime and tried jointly before the same jury. One of the defendants had confessed. His confession named and incriminated the other defendant. The trial judge issued a limiting instruction, telling the jury that it should consider the confession as evidence only against the codefendant who had confessed and not against the defendant named in the confession. *Bruton* held that, despite the limiting instruction, the Constitution forbids the use of such a confession in the joint trial.

The case before us differs from *Bruton* in that the prosecution here redacted the codefendant's confession by substituting for the defendant's name in the confession a blank space or the word "deleted." We must decide whether these substitutions make a significant legal difference. We hold that they do not and that *Bruton's* protective rule applies.

I

In 1993, Stacy Williams died after a severe beating. Anthony Bell gave a confession, to the Baltimore City police, in which he said that he (Bell), Kevin Gray, and Jacquin "Tank" Vanlandingham had participated in the beating that resulted in Williams' death. Vanlandingham later died. A Maryland grand jury indicted Bell and Gray for murder. The State of Maryland tried them jointly.

The trial judge, after denying Gray's motion for a separate trial, permitted the State to introduce Bell's confession into evidence at trial. But the judge ordered the confession redacted. Consequently, the police detective who read the confession into evidence said the word "deleted" or "deletion" whenever Gray's name or Vanlandingham's name appeared. Immediately after the police detective read the redacted confession to the jury, the prosecutor asked, "after he gave you that information, you subsequently were able to arrest Mr. Kevin Gray; is that correct?" The officer responded, "That's correct." The State also introduced into evidence a written copy of the confession with those two names omitted, leaving in their place blank white spaces separated by commas. The State produced other witnesses, who said that six persons (including Bell, Gray, and Vanlandingham) participated in the beating. Gray testified and denied his participation. Bell did not testify.

When instructing the jury, the trial judge specified that the confession was evidence only against Bell; the instructions said that the jury should not use the confession as evidence against Gray. The jury convicted both Bell and Gray. Gray appealed.

Maryland's intermediate appellate court accepted Gray's argument that *Bruton* prohibited use of the confession and set aside his conviction. Maryland's highest court disagreed and reinstated the conviction. We granted certiorari in order to consider *Bruton's* application to a redaction that replaces a name with an obvious blank space or symbol or word such as "deleted."

II

In deciding whether *Bruton's* protective rule applies to the redacted confession before us, we must consider both *Bruton*, and a later case, *Richardson v. Marsh*, 481 U.S. 200 (1987), which limited *Bruton's* scope. * * * *

III

Originally, the codefendant's confession in the case before us, like that in *Bruton*, referred to, and directly implicated another defendant. The State, however, redacted that confession by removing the nonconfessing defendant's name. Nonetheless, unlike Richardson's redacted confession, this confession refers directly to the "existence" of the nonconfessing defendant. The State has simply replaced the nonconfessing defendant's name with a kind of symbol, namely the word "deleted" or a blank space set off by commas. The redacted confession, for example, responded to the question "Who was in the group that beat Stacey," with the phrase, "Me, and a few other guys." And when the police witness read the confession in court, he said the word "deleted" or "deletion" where the blank spaces appear. We therefore must decide a question that *Richardson* left open, namely whether redaction that replaces a defendant's name with an obvious indication of deletion, such as a blank space, the word "deleted," or a similar symbol, still falls within *Bruton's* protective rule. We hold that it does.

Bruton, as interpreted by *Richardson*, holds that certain "powerfully incriminating extrajudicial statements of a codefendant" — those naming another defendant-considered as a class, are so prejudicial that limiting instructions cannot work. Unless the prosecutor wishes to hold separate trials or to use separate juries or to abandon use of the confession, he must redact the confession to reduce significantly or to eliminate the special prejudice that the *Bruton* Court found. Redactions that simply replace a name with an obvious blank space or a word such as "deleted" or a symbol or other similarly obvious indications of alteration, however, leave statements that, considered as a class, so closely resemble *Bruton's* unredacted statements that, in our view, the law must require the same result.

For one thing, a jury will often react similarly to an unredacted confession and a confession redacted in this way, for the jury will often realize that the confession refers specifically to the defendant. This is true even when the State does not blatantly link the defendant to the deleted name, as it did in this case by asking whether Gray was arrested on the basis of information in Bell's confession as soon as the officer had finished reading the redacted statement. Consider a simplified but typical example, a confession that reads "I, Bob Smith, along with Sam Jones, robbed the bank." To replace the words "Sam Jones" with an obvious blank will not likely fool anyone. A juror somewhat familiar with criminal law would know immediately that the blank, in the phrase "I, Bob Smith, along with, robbed the bank," refers to defendant Jones. A juror who does not know the law and who therefore wonders to whom the blank might refer need only lift his eyes to Jones, sitting at counsel table, to find what will seem the obvious answer, at least if the juror hears the judge's instruction not to consider the confession as evidence against Jones, for that instruction will provide an obvious reason for the blank. A more sophisticated juror, wondering if the blank refers to someone else, might also wonder how, if it did, the prosecutor could argue the confession is reliable, for the prosecutor, after all, has been arguing that Jones, not someone else, helped Smith commit the crime.

For another thing, the obvious deletion may well call the jurors' attention specially to the removed name. By encouraging the jury to speculate about the reference, the redaction may overemphasize the importance of the confession's accusation-once the jurors work out the reference. That is why Judge Learned Hand, many years ago, wrote in a similar instance that blacking out the name of a codefendant not only "would have been futile. There could not have been the slightest doubt as to whose names had been blacked out," but "even if there had been, that blacking out itself would have not only laid the doubt, but underscored the answer." *United States v. Delli Paoli*, 229 F.2d 319, 321 (C.A.2 1956), overruled by *Bruton v. United States*, 391 U.S. 123 (1968). See also *Malinski v. New York*, 324 U.S. 401, 430 (1945) (Rutledge, J., dissenting) (describing substitution of names in confession with "X" or "Y" and other similar redactions as "devices so obvious as perhaps to emphasize the identity of those they purported to conceal").

Finally, *Bruton's* protected statements and statements redacted to leave a blank or some other similarly obvious alteration, function the same way grammatically. They are directly accusatory. Evans' statement in *Bruton* used a proper name to point explicitly to an accused defendant. And *Bruton* held that the "powerfully incriminating" effect of what Justice Stewart called "an out-of-court accusation," 391 U.S. at 138 (Stewart, J., concurring), creat‍ a special, and vital, need for cross-examination — a need that would be immediately obvious had the codefendant pointed directly to the defendant in the courtroom itself. The blank space in an obviously redacted confession also points directly to the defendant, and it accuses the defendant in a manner similar to Evans' use of Bruton's name or to a testifying codefendant's accusatory finger. By way of contrast, the factual statement at issue in *Richardson* — a statement about what others said in the front seat of a car — differs from directly accusatory evidence in this respect, for it does not point directly to a defendant at all.

We concede certain differences between *Bruton* and this case. A confession that uses a blank or the word "delete" (or, for that matter, a first name or a nickname) less obviously refers to the defendant than a confession that uses the defendant's full and proper name. Moreover, in some instances the person to whom the blank refers may not be clear: Although the follow-up question asked by the State in this case eliminated all doubt, the reference might not be transparent in other cases in which a confession, like the present confession, uses two (or more) blanks, even though only one other defendant appears at trial, and in which the trial indicates that there are more participants than the confession has named. Nonetheless, as we have said, we believe that, considered as a class, redactions that replace a proper name with an obvious blank, the word "delete," a symbol, or similarly notify the jury that a name has been deleted are similar enough to Bruton's unredacted confessions as to warrant the same legal results.

IV

The State, in arguing for a contrary conclusion, relies heavily upon *Richardson*. But we do not believe *Richardson* controls the result here. We concede that *Richardson* placed outside the scope of *Bruton's* rule those statements that incriminate inferentially. We also concede that the jury must use inference to connect the statement in this redacted confession with the defendant. But inference pure and simple cannot make the critical difference, for if it did, then *Richardson* would also place outside *Bruton's* scope confessions that use shortened first names, nicknames, descriptions as unique as the "red-haired, bearded, one-eyed man-with-a-limp," *United States v. Grinnell Corp.*, 384 U.S. 563, 591 (1966) (Fortas, J., dissenting), and perhaps even full names of defendants who are always known by a nickname. This Court has assumed, however, that nicknames and specific descriptions fall inside, not outside, *Bruton's* protection. See *Harrington v. California*, 395 U.S. 250, 253 (1969) (assuming *Bruton* violation where confessions describe codefendant as the "white guy" and gives a description of his age, height, weight, and hair color). The Solicitor General, although supporting Maryland in this case, concedes that this is appropriate.

That being so, *Richardson* must depend in significant part upon *the kind of, not the simple fact of, inference*. *Richardson's* inferences involved statements that did not refer directly to the defendant himself and which became incriminating "only when linked with evidence introduced later at trial." The inferences at issue here involve statements that, despite redaction, obviously refer directly to someone, often obviously the defendant, and which involve inferences that a jury ordinarily could make immediately, even were the confession the very first item introduced at trial. Moreover, the redacted confession with the blank prominent on its face, in *Richardson's* words, "facially incriminates" the codefendant. Like the confession in *Bruton* itself, the accusation that the redacted confession makes "is more vivid than inferential incrimination, and hence more difficult to thrust out of mind." 481 U.S., at 208.

Nor are the policy reasons that *Richardson* provided in support of its conclusion applicable here. *Richardson* expressed concern lest application of *Bruton's* rule apply where "redaction" of confessions, particularly "confessions incriminating by connection," would often "not be possible," thereby forcing prosecutors too often to abandon use either of the confession or of a joint trial. Additional redaction of a confession that uses a blank space, the word "delete," or a symbol, however, normally is possible. Consider as an example a portion of the confession before us: The witness who read the confession told the jury that the confession (among other things) said, "Question: Who was in the group that beat Stacey? "Answer: Me, deleted, deleted, and a few other guys." Why could the witness not, instead, have said: "Question: Who was in the group that beat Stacey? "Answer: Me and a few other guys." *Richardson* itself provides a similar example of this kind of redaction. The confession there at issue had been "redacted to omit all reference to respondent-indeed, to omit all indication that anyone other than Martin and Williams participated in the crime," and it did not indicate that it had been redacted. But cf. post, at 4, (Scalia, J., dissenting) (suggesting that the Court has "never before endorsed . . . the redaction of a statement by some means other than the deletion of certain words, with the fact of the deletion shown").

The *Richardson* Court also feared that the inclusion, within *Bruton's* protective rule, of confessions that incriminated "by connection" too often would provoke mistrials, or would unnecessarily lead prosecutors to abandon the confession or joint trial, because neither the prosecutors nor the judge could easily predict, until after the introduction of all the evidence, whether or not *Bruton* had barred use of the confession. To include the use of blanks, the word "delete," symbols, or other indications of redaction, within *Bruton's* protections, however, runs no such risk. Their use is easily identified prior to trial and does not depend, in any special way, upon the other evidence introduced in the case. * * * *

For these reasons, we hold that the confession here at issue, which substituted blanks and the word "delete" for the respondent's proper name, falls within the class of statements to which *Bruton's* protections apply.

The judgment of the Court of Appeals is vacated, and the case is remanded for further proceedings not inconsistent with this opinion.

APPENDIX TO OPINION OF THE COURT

[Typewritten Version of Handwritten Redacted Statement, State's Exhibit 5B]

This is a statement of Anthony Bell, taken on 1-4-94 at 0925 hrs in the small interview room. Statement taken by Det. Pennington and Det. Ritz.

(Q)   Is your name Anthony Bell?

(A)   Yes.

(Q)   Are 19 years old and your date of Birth is 6-17-74?

(A)   Yes.

(Q)   Can you read and write?

(A)   Yes.

(Q)   Are you under the influence of alcohol or drugs?

(A)   No.

(Q)   You were explained your Explanation of Rights, do you fully understand them?

(A)   Yes.

(Q)   Are you willing to answer questions without an attorney present at this time?

(A)   Yes.

Anthony Bell. [Page -2-]

(Q)   Has anyone promised you anything if you answer questions?

(A)   No.

(Q)   What can you tell me about the beating of Stacey Williams that occurred on 10 November 1993?

(A)   An argument broke out between and Stacey in the 500 blk of Louden Ave Stacey got smacked and then ran into Wildwood Parkway. Me, and a few other guys ran after Stacey. We caught up to him on Wildwood Parkway. We beat Stacey up. After we beat Stacey up, we walked him back to Louden Ave I then walked over and used the phone. Stacey and the others walked down Louden.

(Q)   When Stacey was beaten on Wildwood Parkway, how was he beaten?

Anthony Bell [Page -3-]

(A)   Hit, kicked.

(Q)   Who hit and kicked Stacey?

(A)   I hit Stacey, he was kicked but I don't know who kicked him.

(Q)   Who was in the group that beat Stacey?

(A)   Me, and a few other guys.

(Q)   Do you have the other guys' names?

    (A), and me, I don't remember who was out there.

(Q)   Did anyone pick Stacey up and drop him to the ground?

(A)   No when I was there.

(Q)   What was the argument over between Stacey and

Anthony Bell [Page -4-]

(A)   Some money that Stacey owed.

(Q)   How many guys were hitting on Stacey?

(A)   About six guys.

(Q)   Do you have a black jacket with Park Heights written on the back?

(A)   Yeh.

(Q)   Who else has these jacket?

    (A)

(Q)   After reading this statement would you sign it?

(A)   Yes

Anthony Bell

Det. William F. Ritz Det. Homer Pennington

Justice Scalia, with whom the Chief Justice, Justice Kennedy, and Justice Thomas join, dissenting.

In *Richardson v. Marsh*, we declined to extend the "narrow exception" of *Bruton* beyond confessions that facially incriminate a defendant. Today the Court "concedes that *Richardson* placed outside the scope of *Bruton's* rule those statements that incriminate inferentially," "concedes that the jury must use inference to connect the statement in this redacted confession with the defendant," but nonetheless extends *Bruton* to confessions that have been redacted to delete the defendant's name. Because I believe the line drawn in *Richardson* should not be changed, I respectfully dissent.

The almost invariable assumption of the law is that jurors follow their instructions. This rule "is a pragmatic one, rooted less in the absolute certitude that the presumption is true than in the belief that it represents a reasonable practical accommodation of the interests of the state and the defendant in the criminal justice process." *Richardson*, 481 U.S., at 211. We have held, for example, that the state may introduce evidence of a defendant's prior convictions for the purpose of sentencing enhancement, or statements elicited from a defendant in violation of *Miranda v. Arizona*, 384 U.S. 436 (1966), for the purpose of impeachment, so long as the jury is instructed that such evidence may not be considered for the purpose of determining guilt. *Harris v. New York*, 401 U.S. 222 (1971). The same applies to codefendant confessions: "a witness whose testimony is introduced at a joint trial is not considered to be a witness 'against' a defendant if the jury is instructed to consider that testimony only against a codefendant." *Richardson*, supra, at 206. In *Bruton*, we recognized a "narrow exception" to this rule: "We held that a defendant is deprived of his Sixth Amendment right of confrontation when the facially incriminating confession of a nontestifying codefendant is introduced at their joint trial, even if the jury is instructed to consider the confession only against the codefendant."

We declined in *Richardson*, however, to extend *Bruton* to confessions that incriminate only by inference from other evidence. When incrimination is inferential, "it is a less valid generalization that the jury will not likely obey the instruction to disregard the evidence." Today the Court struggles to decide whether a confession redacted to omit the defendant's name is incriminating on its face or by inference. On the one hand, the Court "concedes that the jury must use inference to connect the statement in this redacted confession with the defendant," but later asserts, on the other hand, that "the redacted confession with the blank prominent on its face 'facially incriminates'" him. The Court should have stopped with its concession: the statement "Me, deleted, deleted, and a few other guys" does not facially incriminate anyone but the speaker. The Court's analogizing of "deleted" to a physical description that clearly identifies the defendant (which we have assumed *Bruton* covers) does not survive scrutiny. By "facially incriminating," we have meant incriminating independent of other evidence introduced at trial. *Richardson*, supra, at 208–209. Since the defendant's appearance at counsel table is not evidence, the description "red-haired, bearded, one-eyed man-with-a-limp," would be facially incriminating — unless, of course, the defendant had dyed his hair black and shaved his beard before trial, and the prosecution introduced evidence concerning his former appearance. Similarly, the statement "Me, Kevin Gray, and a few other guys" would be facially incriminating, unless the defendant's name set forth in the indictment was not Kevin Gray, and evidence was introduced to the effect that he sometimes used "Kevin Gray" as an alias. By contrast, the person to whom "deleted" refers in "Me, deleted, deleted, and a few other guys" is not apparent from anything the jury knows independent of the evidence at trial. Though the jury may speculate, the statement expressly implicates no one but the speaker.

Of course the Court is correct that confessions redacted to omit the defendant's name are more likely to incriminate than confessions redacted to omit any reference to his existence. But it is also true — and more relevant here — that confessions redacted to omit the defendant's name are less likely to incriminate than confessions that expressly state it. The latter are "powerfully incriminating" as a class, *Bruton*, supra, at 124, n. 1; the former are not so. Here, for instance, there were two names deleted, five or more participants in the crime, and only one other defendant on trial. The jury no doubt may "speculate about the reference," as it speculates when evidence connects a defendant to a confession that does not refer to his existence. The issue, however, is not whether the confession incriminated petitioner, but whether the incrimination is so "powerful" that we must depart from the normal presumption that the jury follows its instructions. I think it is not — and I am certain that drawing the line for departing from the ordinary rule at the facial identification of the defendant makes more sense than drawing it anywhere else.

The Court's extension of *Bruton* to name-redacted confessions "as a class" will seriously compromise "society's compelling interest in finding, convicting, and punishing those who violate the law." *Moran v. Burbine*, 475 U.S. 412, 426 (1986). We explained in *Richardson* that forgoing use of codefendant confessions or joint trials was "too high" a price to insure that juries never disregard their instructions. 481 U.S. at 209–210. The Court minimizes the damage that it does by suggesting that "additional redaction of a confession that uses a blank space, the word 'delete,' or a symbol normally is possible." In the present case, it asks, why could the police officer not have testified that Bell's answer was "Me and a few other guys"? The answer, it seems obvious to me, is because that is not what Bell said. Bell's answer was "Me, Tank, Kevin and a few other guys." Introducing the statement with full disclosure of deletions is one thing; introducing as the complete statement what was in fact only a part is something else. And of course even concealed deletions from the text will often not do the job that the Court demands. For inchoate offenses — conspiracy in particular — redaction to delete all reference to a confederate would often render the confession nonsensical. If the question was "Who agreed to beat Stacey?", and the answer was "Me and Kevin," we might redact the answer to "Me and [deleted]," or perhaps to "Me and somebody else," but surely not to just "Me" — for that would no longer be a confession to the conspiracy charge, but rather the foundation for an insanity defense. To my knowledge we have never before endorsed — and to my strong belief we ought not endorse — the redaction of a statement by some means other than the deletion of certain words, with the fact of the deletion shown. The risk to the integrity of our system (not to mention the increase in its complexity) posed by the approval of such free-lance editing seems to me infinitely greater than the risk posed by the entirely honest reproduction that the Court disapproves.

The United States Constitution guarantees, not a perfect system of criminal justice (as to which there can be considerable disagreement), but a minimum standard of fairness. Lest we lose sight of the forest for the trees, it should be borne in mind that federal and state rules of criminal procedure — which can afford to seek perfection because they can be more readily changed — exclude nontestifying-codefendant confessions even where the Sixth Amendment does not. Under the Federal Rules of Criminal Procedure (and Maryland's), a trial court may order separate trials if joinder will prejudice a defendant. See Fed. Rule Crim. Proc. 14; Md.Crim. Rule 4-253. Maryland courts have described the term "prejudice" as a "term of art," which "refers only to prejudice resulting to the defendant from the reception of evidence that would have been inadmissible against that defendant had there been no joinder." *Ogonowski v. State*, 87 Md.App. 173 (1991). The federal rule expressly contemplates that in ruling on a severance motion the court will inspect "in camera any statements or confessions made by the defendants which the government intends to introduce in evidence at the trial." Fed. Rule Crim. Proc. 14. Federal and most state trial courts (including Maryland's) also have the discretion to exclude unfairly prejudicial (albeit probative) evidence. Fed. Rule Evid. 403; Md. Rule Evid. 5-403 (1998). Here, petitioner moved for a severance on the ground that the admission of Bell's confession would be unfairly prejudicial. The trial court denied the motion, explaining that where a confession names two others, and the evidence is that five or six others participated, redaction of petitioner's name would not leave the jury with the "unavoidable inference" that Bell implicated Gray.

I do not understand the Court to disagree that the redaction itself left unclear to whom the blank referred.[2] That being so, the rule set forth in *Richardson* applies, and the statement could constitutionally be admitted with limiting instruction. This remains, insofar as the Sixth Amendment is concerned, the most "reasonable practical accommodation of the interests of the state and the defendant in the criminal justice process." *Richardson*, 481 U.S., at 211. For these reasons, I would affirm the judgment of the Court of Appeals of Maryland.

Note from Judge Katz:

So far, we've been considering problems arising from joinder of *defendants*. Problems might also arise from joinder of *offenses*.

In *State v. Taylor*, 347 Md. 363 (1997), Taylor was charged in 5 separate indictments with 5 separate incidents of child abuse on his 14-year old stepson. The indictments were consolidated for trial, despite Taylor's motion to sever the charges. At trial, Taylor's attorney argued that Taylor's acts were within the range

---

[2] The Court does believe, however, that the answer to a "follow-up question" — "All right, now, officer, after he gave you that information, you subsequently were able to arrest Mr. Kevin Gray; is that correct?" ("That's correct") — "eliminated all doubt" as to the subject of the redaction. That is probably not so, and is certainly far from clear. Testimony that preceded the introduction of Bell's confession had already established that Gray had become a suspect in the case, and that a warrant had been issued for his arrest, before Bell confessed. Respondent contends that, given this trial background, and in its context, the prosecutor's question did not imply any connection between Bell's confession and Gray's arrest, and was simply a means of making the transition from Bell's statement to the next piece of evidence, Gray's statement. That is at least arguable, and an appellate court is in a poor position to resolve such a contextual question de novo. That is why objections to trial testimony are supposed to be made at the time — so that trial judges, who hear the testimony in full, live context, can make such determinations in the first instance. But if the question did bring the redaction home to the defendant, surely that shows the impropriety of the question rather than of the redaction — and the question was not objected to. The failure to object deprives petitioner of the right to complain of some incremental identifiability added to the redacted statement by the question and answer. Of course the Court's reliance upon this testimony belies its contention that name — redacted confessions are powerfully incriminating "as a class."

of "permissible parental discipline." The jury convicted him of two counts of child abuse. The appellate court held that the motion to sever was properly denied:

> Taylor complains that the defense was prejudiced by the joinder and, thus, by the admission of the other crimes evidence, which under the circumstances, showed nothing more than propensity, allowing the jury to conclude that he was a "bad person" and should therefore be convicted, or deserves punishment for other bad conduct and so may be convicted even though the evidence is lacking.

> [The test for joinder of offenses is] a two part test. First, is the evidence concerning each of the charged offenses mutually admissible; and second, does the interest in judicial economy outweigh the arguments favoring separate trials. The second part of the test should not be in dispute in the instant case. A paramount interest of our criminal justice system should be avoiding unnecessary trials and the accompanying trauma to young victims of multiple acts of child abuse. These children should not have to testify at multiple trials if the evidence would be the same at each trial and all of the acts of alleged abuse would be mutually admissible at each trial.

As for the first part of the test, the court held that "even if Taylor were tried separately for each child abuse charge, all of the other alleged acts of child abuse would be admissible in each trial to prove Taylor's intent, malice, and absence of mistake."

> Where a parent uses severe corporal punishment, often the only way to determine whether the punishment is a non-criminal act of discipline that was unintentionally harsh or whether it constitutes the felony of child abuse is to look at the parent's history of disciplining the child. The probative value of recent corporal punishment used on a child in order to determine the parental disciplinarian's malice and intent far exceeds its potential for unfair prejudice. In the instant case, the fact that Taylor was only convicted of acts of violence that left physical evidence of their severity and was acquitted on three other charges of child abuse gives some indication that the jury was not inflamed or prejudiced by the testimony about prior acts of corporal punishment. Victims of child abuse often cannot speak for themselves or are very reluctant to testify unfavorably about a parent, even an abusive parent. A parent's other disciplinary acts can be the most probative evidence of whether his or her disciplinary corporal punishment is imposed maliciously, with an intent to injure, or with a sincere desire to use appropriate corrective measures.

> Since each of Taylor's acts of violence against Keith would be admissible in each prosecution for child abuse, there was no reason to require five separate trials and the trial judge did not abuse his discretion in consolidating all cases for trial.

In *Morales v. State*, 143 P.3d 463 (Nev. 2006), Morales was charged with two crimes: robbery, and possession of a gun by an ex-felon. The charges arose out of the same event, because the prosecution planned to prove that the gun possession occurred during the charged robbery. But there was a problem: the prosecution would also have to prove that Morales was an ex-felon, and this might unduly prejudice the jury to convict him. So the trial court *bifurcated* the trial: first the jury would try the robbery charge, and after they reached a verdict on robbery, they would hear the evidence that Morales was an ex-felon and then return a verdict on the gun charge. He was convicted of both charges. He appealed, arguing that the trial court should have severed the case into two complete trials. Nevada Supreme Court affirmed, holding that bifurcation protected Morales's rights while promoting judicial economy.

Chapter 11

DOUBLE JEOPARDY

". . . nor shall any person be subject for the same offence to be twice put in jeopardy of life or limb. . . ."

5th Amendment, U.S. Constitution

In *Benton v. Maryland*, 395 U.S. 784 (1969), the Court held that "the double jeopardy prohibition of the Fifth Amendment represents a fundamental ideal in our constitutional heritage", and therefore it should be applied to the states through the Due Process Clause of the 14th Amendment. The Court explained:

> The fundamental nature of the guarantee against double jeopardy can hardly be doubted. Its origins can be traced to Greek and Roman times, and it became established in the common law of England long before this Nation's independence. As with many other elements of the common law, it was carried into the jurisprudence of this Country through the medium of Blackstone, who codified the doctrine in his Commentaries: "The plea of autrefoits acquit, or a former acquittal, is grounded on this universal maxim of the common law of England, that no man is to be brought into jeopardy of his life more than once for the same offence." Today, every State incorporates some form of the prohibition in its constitution or common law. As this Court put it in *Green v. United States*, 355 U.S. 184, 187–188 (1957):

> > The underlying idea, one that is deeply ingrained in at least the Anglo-American system of jurisprudence, is that the State with all its resources and power should not be allowed to make repeated attempts to convict an individual for an alleged offense, thereby subjecting him to embarrassment, expense and ordeal and compelling him to live in a continuing state of anxiety and insecurity, as well as enhancing the possibility that even though innocent he may be found guilty.

Double jeopardy issues arise in several different contexts and give rise to several different rules. This is because the courts have held that there are several different *purposes* to the handful of words in the Double Jeopardy clause of the 5th Amendment. As you read the cases in this chapter, see if you can discern these purposes.

Problem 11

To: My law clerk

From: Carmelita Closer, Esq.

My client, Moe DeLawn, was initially charged with robbery[1] and forcible rape[2] of 17-year-old Patty Cake on April 1. Before trial, the court granted my motion to suppress a statement Moe gave to the police. At trial, Ms. Cake testified that she was at a party, got a bit drunk, and went into the backyard with a man she didn't know. She testified that the man forced her to have sex with him and then took her watch, which was worth about $300. She identified Moe as the man who did it. During my cross-examination, however, she testified as follows:

Q: How did he force you to have sex?

A: He just got on top of me and did it, without asking or anything.

Q: Did you make it clear to him that you did not want to have sex with him?

A: I didn't want to have sex, but I don't remember if I told him that.

Q: Did he take the watch, or did you give it to him in the hope that he would leave?

A: I don't remember, exactly. I think he took it.

Moe then took the witness stand, and he testified that he was at home watching television when the alleged crimes occurred. The jury acquitted Moe of both charges.

A month later, the D.A. filed new charges against Moe: larceny[3] and statutory rape[4] of Ms. Cake on April 1. I moved to dismiss the charges, claiming double jeopardy. I introduced a copy of the transcript of the first trial. The judge denied my motion.

We began to *voir dire* the prospective jurors. I exercised a couple of peremptory challenges, and then told the judge that I was quite pleased with the remaining jurors. When questioning the next prospective juror, however, the prosecutor asked: "Did you read anything in the newspaper about Mr. DeLawn's confession in this case?" I objected, and the judge said: "That question was wholly improper. I am dismissing this jury and the entire venire. We will start again tomorrow with a new venire."

Next morning, I made a second motion to dismiss on the ground of double jeopardy, but the judge denied my motion.

A jury was selected and sworn, and the trial proceeded. The testimony took three

---

[1] Penal Code § 211 provides that "Robbery is the trespassory taking of personal property from the possession of another, from his person or immediate presence, and against his will, accomplished by means of force or fear, with the intent to steal."

[2] Penal Code § 261 provides that "Rape is an act of sexual intercourse accomplished against a person's will by means of force or fear."

[3] Penal Code § 210 provides that "Larceny is the trespassory taking of the personal property of another with the intent to steal."

[4] Penal Code § 261.5 provides that "Statutory rape is an act of sexual intercourse accomplished with a female not the wife of the perpetrator, where the female is under the age of 18 years."

days. On Friday afternoon, after final argument and jury instructions, the jury retired to the jury room to deliberate. Two hours later, the jury foreman sent a note to the judge which said, "We are divided 10 to 2, and the 2 are hanging very tough. I don't think anyone is going to change. What should we do?"

The judge read the note to the lawyers. Then he said, "I have a big murder trial scheduled to begin here Monday morning. I don't see much point in putting that case over just so this jury can spend more time getting nowhere. I am declaring a mistrial."

Two months later, the murder trial ended, and the court set Moe's trial to begin again. I filed a third motion to dismiss on the ground of double jeopardy, but the judge again denied it.

The trial began. Ms. Cake testified as before, and so did Moe. Despite my best efforts, the jury convicted Moe on both counts: larceny and statutory rape.

I am now appealing these convictions. Please read the attached cases and advise me of the best arguments I can make in the appeal, and how the court is likely to rule on them.

ASHE v. SWENSON
United States Supreme Court
397 U.S. 436 (1969)

MR. JUSTICE STEWART delivered the opinion of the Court.

In *Benton v. Maryland*, 395 U.S. 784, the Court held that the Fifth Amendment guarantee against double jeopardy is enforceable against the States through the Fourteenth Amendment. The question in this case is whether the State of Missouri violated that guarantee when it prosecuted the petitioner a second time for armed robbery in the circumstances here presented. * * * *

Sometime in the early hours of the morning of January 10, 1960, six men were engaged in a poker game in the basement of the home of John Gladson at Lee's Summit, Missouri. Suddenly three or four masked men, armed with a shotgun and pistols, broke into the basement and robbed each of the poker players of money and various articles of personal property. The robbers — and it has never been clear whether there were three or four of them — then fled in a car belonging to one of the victims of the robbery. Shortly thereafter, the stolen car was discovered in a field, and later that morning three men were arrested by a state trooper while they were walking on a highway not far from where the abandoned car had been found. The petitioner was arrested by another officer some distance away.

The four were subsequently charged with seven separate offenses — the armed robbery of each of the six poker players and the theft of the car. In May 1960, the petitioner went to trial on the charge of robbing Donald Knight, one of the participants in the poker game. At the trial the State called Knight and three witnesses. Each of them described the circumstances of the holdup and itemized his own individual losses. The proof that an armed robbery had occurred and that personal property had been taken from Knight as well as from each of the others was unassailable. The testimony of the four victims in this regard was consistent both internally and with that of the others. But the State's evidence that the petitioner had been one of the robbers was weak. Two of the witnesses thought that there had been only three robbers altogether, and could not identify the petitioner as one of them. Another of the victims, who was the petitioner's uncle by marriage, said that at the "patrol station" he had positively identified each of the other three men accused of the holdup, but could say only that the petitioner's voice "sounded very much like" that of one of the robbers. The fourth participant in the poker game did identify the petitioner, but only by his "size and height, and his actions."

The cross-examination of these witnesses was brief, and it was aimed primarily at exposing the weakness of their identification testimony. Defense counsel made no attempt to question their testimony regarding the holdup itself or their claims as to their losses. Knight testified without contradiction that the robbers had stolen from him his watch, $250 in cash, and about $500 in checks. His billfold, which had been found by the police in the possession of one of the three other men accused of the robbery, was admitted in evidence. The defense offered no testimony and waived final argument.

The trial judge instructed the jury that if it found that the petitioner was one of the participants in the armed robbery, the theft of "any money" from Knight would sustain a conviction. * * * * He also instructed the jury that if the petitioner was one of the robbers, he was guilty under the law even if he had not personally robbed Knight. * * * * The jury — though not instructed to elaborate upon its verdict — found the petitioner "not guilty due to insufficient evidence."

Six weeks, later the petitioner was brought to trial again, this time for the robbery of another participant in the poker game, a man named Roberts. The petitioner filed a motion to dismiss, based on his previous acquittal. The motion was overruled, and the second trial began. The witnesses were for the most part the same, though this time their testimony was substantially stronger on the issue of the petitioner's identity. For example, two witnesses who at the first trial had been wholly unable to identify the petitioner as one of the robbers, now testified that his features, size, and mannerisms matched those of one of their assailants. Another witness who before had identified the petitioner only by his size and actions now also remembered him by the unusual sound of his voice. The State further refined its case at the second trial by declining to call one of the participants in the poker game whose identification testimony at the first trial had been conspicuously negative. The case went to the jury on instructions virtually identical to those given at the first trial. This time the jury found the petitioner guilty, and he was sentenced to a 35-year term in the state penitentiary.

The Supreme Court of Missouri affirmed the conviction, holding that the "plea of former jeopardy must be denied." The petitioner then brought the present habeas corpus proceeding in the United States District Court, claiming that the second prosecution had violated his right not to be twice put in jeopardy. Considering itself bound by this court's decision in *Hoag v. New Jersey*, 356 U.S. 464, the District Court denied the writ, although apparently finding merit in the petitioner's claim. * * * * The Court of Appeals for the Eighth Circuit affirmed.

As the District Court and the Court of Appeals correctly noted, the operative facts here are virtually identical to those of *Hoag v. New Jersey, supra*. In that case the defendant was tried for the armed robbery of three men who, along with others, had been held up in a tavern. The proof of the robbery was clear, but the evidence identifying the defendant as one of the robbers was weak, and the defendant interposed an alibi defense. The jury brought in a verdict of not guilty. The defendant was then brought to trial again, on an indictment charging the robbery of a fourth victim of the tavern holdup. This time the jury found him guilty. After appeals in the state courts proved unsuccessful, Hoag brought his case here.

Viewing the question presented solely in terms of Fourteenth Amendment due process — whether the course that New Jersey had pursued had "led to fundamental unfairness," this Court declined to reverse the judgment of conviction, because "in the circumstances shown by this record, we cannot say that petitioner's later prosecution and conviction violated due process." * * * * The Court found it unnecessary to decide whether "collateral estoppel" — the principle that bars relitigation between the same parties of issues actually determined at a previous trial — is a due process requirement in a state criminal trial, since it accepted New Jersey's determination that the petitioner's previous acquittal did not in any event give rise to such an estoppel. And in the view the Court took of the issues presented, it did not, of course, even approach consideration of whether collateral estoppel is an ingredient of the Fifth Amendment guarantee against double jeopardy.

The doctrine of *Benton v. Maryland*, 395 U.S. 784, puts the issues in the present case in a perspective quite different from that in which the issues were perceived in *Hoag v. New Jersey, supra*. The question is no longer whether collateral estoppel is a requirement of due process, but whether it is a part of the Fifth Amendment's guarantee against double jeopardy. And if collateral estoppel is embodied in that guarantee, then its applicability in a particular case is no longer a matter to be left for state court determination within the broad bounds of "fundamental fairness," but a matter of constitutional fact we must decide through an examination of the entire record.

"Collateral estoppel" is an awkward phrase, but it stands for an extremely important principle in our adversary system of justice. It means simply that when an issue of ultimate fact has once been determined by a valid and final judgment, that issue cannot again be litigated between the same parties in any future lawsuit. Although first developed in civil litigation, collateral estoppel has been an established rule of federal criminal law.

The federal decisions have made clear that the rule of collateral estoppel in criminal cases is not to be applied with the hypertechnical and archaic approach of a 19th century pleading book, but with realism and rationality. Where a previous judgment of acquittal was based upon a general verdict, as is usually the case, this approach requires a court to "examine that record of a prior proceeding, taking into account the pleadings, evidence, charge, and other relevant matter, and conclude whether a rational jury could have grounded its verdict upon an issue other than that which the defendant seeks to foreclose from consideration." * * * * The inquiry "must be set in a practical frame and viewed with an eye to all the circumstances of the proceedings." *Sealfon v. United States*, 332 U.S. 575, 579. Any test more technically restrictive would, of course, simply amount to a rejection of the rule of collateral estoppel in criminal proceedings, at least in every case where the first judgment was based upon a general verdict of acquittal.[9]

---

[9] "If a later court is permitted to state that the jury may have disbelieved substantial and uncontradicted evidence of the prosecution on a point the defendant did not contest, the possible multiplicity of prosecutions is staggering. In fact, such a restrictive definition of 'determined' amounts simply to a rejection of collateral estoppel, since it is impossible to imagine a statutory offense in which the government has to prove only one element or issue to sustain a conviction." Mayers & Yarbrough,

Straightforward application of the federal rule to the present case can lead to but one conclusion. For the record is utterly devoid of any indication that the first jury could rationally have found that an armed robbery had not occurred, or that Knight had not been a victim of that robbery. The single rationally conceivable issue in dispute before the jury was whether the petitioner had been one of the robbers. And the jury by its verdict found that he had not. The federal rule of law, therefore, would make a second prosecution for the robbery of Roberts wholly impermissible.

The ultimate question to be determined, then, in the light of *Benton v. Maryland, supra,* is whether this established rule of federal law is embodied in the Fifth Amendment guarantee against double jeopardy. We do not hesitate to hold that it is.[10] For whatever else that constitutional guarantee may embrace, it surely protects a man who has been acquitted from having to "run the gantlet" a second time. *Green v. United States,* 355 U.S. 184, 190.

The question is not whether Missouri could validly charge the petitioner with six separate offenses for the robbery of the six poker players. It is not whether he could have received a total of six punishments if he had been convicted in a single trial of robbing the six victims. It is simply whether, after a jury determined by its verdict that the petitioner was not one of the robbers, the State could constitutionally hale him before a new jury to litigate that issue again.

After the first jury had acquitted the petitioner of robbing Knight, Missouri could certainly not have brought him to trial again upon that charge. Once a jury had determined upon conflicting testimony that there was at least a reasonable doubt that the petitioner was one of the robbers, the State could not present the same or different identification evidence in a second prosecution for the robbery of Knight in the hope that a different jury might find that evidence more convincing. The situation is constitutionally no different here, even though the second trial related to another victim of the same robbery. For the name of the victim, in the circumstances of this case, had no bearing whatever upon the issue of whether the petitioner was one of the robbers.

In this case, the State in its brief has frankly conceded that following the petitioner's acquittal, it treated the first trial as no more than a dry run for the second prosecution: "No doubt the prosecutor felt the state had a provable case on the first charge and, when he lost, he did what every good attorney would do — he refined his presentation in light of the turn of events at the first trial." But this is precisely what the constitutional guarantee forbids.

The judgment is reversed.

Bis Vexari: New Trials and Successive Prosecutions, 74 Harv. L.Rev. 1, 38.

[10] It is true that we have never squarely held collateral estoppel to be a constitutional requirement. Until perhaps a century ago, few situations arose calling for its application. For at common law, and under early federal criminal statutes, offense categories were relatively few and distinct. A single course of criminal conduct was likely to yield but a single offense. In more recent times, with the advent of specificity in draftsmanship and the extraordinary proliferation of overlapping and related statutory offenses, it became possible for prosecutors to spin out a startlingly numerous series of offenses from a single alleged criminal transaction. As the number of statutory offenses multiplied, the potential for unfair and abusive reprosecutions became far more pronounced. The federal courts soon recognized the need to prevent such abuses through the doctrine of collateral estoppel, and it became a safeguard firmly embedded in federal law. Whether its basis was a constitutional one was a question of no more than academic concern until this Court's decision in *Benton v. Maryland, supra.*

Mr. Justice Brennan, whom Mr. Justice Douglas and Mr. Justice Marshall join, concurring.

I agree that the Double Jeopardy Clause incorporates collateral estoppel as a constitutional requirement and therefore join the Court's opinion. However, even if the rule of collateral estoppel had been inapplicable to the facts of this case, it is my view that the Double Jeopardy Clause nevertheless bars the prosecution of petitioner a second time for armed robbery. The two prosecutions, the first for the robbery of Knight and the second for the robbery of Roberts, grew out of one criminal episode, and therefore I think it clear on the facts of this case that the Double Jeopardy Clause prohibited Missouri from prosecuting petitioner for each robbery at a different trial. * * * *

In my view, the Double Jeopardy Clause requires the prosecution, except in most limited circumstances,[7] to join at one trial all the charges against a defendant that grow out of a single criminal act, occurrence, episode, or transaction. This "same transaction" test of "same offence" not only enforces the ancient prohibition against vexatious multiple prosecutions embodied in the Double Jeopardy Clause, but responds as well to the increasingly widespread recognition that the consolidation in one lawsuit of all issues arising out of a single transaction or occurrence best promotes justice, economy, and convenience. * * * * Modern rules of criminal and civil procedure reflect this recognition. * * * * The Federal Rules of Criminal Procedure liberally encourage the joining of parties and charges in a single trial. Rule 8(a) provides for joinder of charges that are similar in character, or arise from the same transaction or from connected transactions or form part of a common scheme or plan. Rule 8(b) provides for joinder of defendants. Rule 13 provides for joinder of separate indictments or informations in a single trial where the offenses alleged could have been included in one indictment or information.[11] These rules represent considered modern thought concerning the proper structuring of criminal litigation. * * * *

Fortunately for petitioner, the conviction at the second trial can be reversed under the doctrine or collateral estoppel, since the jury at the first trial clearly resolved in his favor the only contested issue at that trial, which was the identification of him as one of the robbers. There is at least doubt whether collateral estoppel would have aided him had the jury been required to resolve additional contested issues on conflicting evidence.[13] But correction of the abuse of criminal process should not in any event be made to depend on the availability of collateral estoppel. Abuse of the criminal process is foremost among the feared evils that led

---

[7] For example, where a crime is not completed or not discovered, despite diligence on the part of the police, until after the commencement of a prosecution for other crimes arising from the same transaction, an exception to the "same transaction" rule should be made to permit a separate prosecution. Another exception would be necessary if no single court had jurisdiction of all the alleged crimes.

[11] Rule 14 provides for separate trials under court order where joinder would be prejudicial to either the prosecution or the defense. Cf. Fed.Rule Civ.Proc. 42. Even where separate trials are permitted to avoid prejudicial joinder, the "same transaction" rule can serve a useful purpose since the defendant is at least informed at one time of all the charges on which he will actually be tried, and can prepare his defense accordingly. Moreover, the decision on whether charges are to be tried jointly or separately will rest with the judge rather than the prosecutor. And separate trials may not be ordered, of course, where the proofs will be repetitious, or the multiplicity of trials vexatious, or where the multiplicity will enable the prosecution to use the experience of the first trial to strengthen its case in a subsequent trial.

[13] And, of course, collateral estoppel would not prevent multiple prosecutions when the first trial ends in a verdict of guilty.

to the inclusion of the Double Jeopardy Clause in the Bill of Rights. That evil will be most effectively avoided, and the Clause can thus best serve its worthy ends, if "same offence" is construed to embody the "same transaction" standard. Then both federal and state prosecutors will be prohibited from mounting successive prosecutions for offenses growing out of the same criminal episode, at least in the absence of a showing of unavoidable necessity for successive prosecutions in the particular case.[14]

MR. CHIEF JUSTICE BURGER, dissenting.

The Court's opinion omits some relevant facts. The other victims' testimony at the second trial corroborated that of Mrs. Gladson that four robbers were present during the time in which the robbery took place. Gladson identified three robbers — Brown, Larson, and Ashe — as having been in the basement for the first minutes of the robbery; also he stated that one or more of the robbers had left the basement after 20 or 25 minutes. Roberts identified Brown, Larson, and Ashe as the men who formed the original group who entered the basement and testified that after the robbery, two of the three men, including Ashe, left the room. Two men returned in a short time with car keys, but Johnson had replaced Ashe as one of the two. There can be no doubt that the record shows four persons in the robbery band. The jury found Ashe guilty of robbing Roberts — the only charge before it.

The concept of double jeopardy and our firm constitutional commitment is against repeated trials "for the *same offence*." This Court, like most American jurisdictions, has expanded that part of the Constitution into a "same evidence" test. * * * * For example, in *Blockburger v. United States*, 284 U.S. 299, 304 (1932), it was stated, so far as here relevant, that

> [T]he test to be applied to determine whether there are two offenses or only one is whether each provision (i.e., each charge) requires *proof of a fact which the other does not*. [Emphasis added]

Clearly and beyond dispute the charge against Ashe in the second trial required proof of a fact — robbery of Roberts — which the charge involving Knight did not. The Court, therefore, has had to reach out far beyond the accepted offense-defining rule to reach its decision in this case. What it has done is to superimpose on the same-evidence test a new and novel collateral-estoppel gloss.

The collateral-estoppel concept — originally a product only of civil litigation — is a strange mutant as it is transformed to control this criminal case. In civil cases, the doctrine was justified as conserving judicial resources as well as those of the parties to the actions and additionally as providing the finality needed to plan for the future. It ordinarily applies to parties on each side of the litigation who have the

---

[14] The question of separate trials for different crimes committed during a single criminal transaction is entirely distinct from and independent of the question of prosecutorial discretion to select the charges on which a defendant shall be prosecuted; and it is also distinct from and independent of the question of the imposition of separate punishments for different crimes committed during a single transaction. The Double Jeopardy Clause does not limit the power the Congress and the States to split a single transaction into separate crimes so as to give the prosecution a choice of charges. Moreover, the clause does not, as a general matter, prohibit the imposition at one trial of cumulative penalties for different crimes committed during one transaction. Thus no crime need go unpunished. However, the clause does provide an outer limit on the power of federal and state courts to impose cumulative punishments for a single criminal transaction.

same interest as or who are identical with the parties in the initial litigation. Here the complainant in the second trial is not the same as in the first, even though the State is a party in both cases. Very properly, in criminal cases, finality and conservation of private, public and judicial resources are lesser values than in civil litigation. Also, courts that have applied the collateral-estoppel concept to criminal actions would certainly not apply it to both parties, as is true in civil cases, i.e., here, if Ashe had been convicted at the first trial, presumably no court would then hold that he was thereby by foreclosed from litigating the identification issue at the second trial.

Perhaps, then, it comes as no surprise to find that the only expressed rationale for the majority's decision is that Ashe has "run the gauntlet" once before. This is not a doctrine of the law or legal reasoning but a colorful and graphic phrase, which, as used originally in an opinion of the Court written by Mr. Justice Black, was intended to mean something entirely different. The full phrase is "run the gauntlet once *on that charge*" (emphasis added); it is to be found in *Green v. United States*, 355 U.S. 184, 190 (1957), where no question of multiple crimes against multiple victims was involved. Green, having been found guilty of second degree murder on a charge of first degree, secured a new trial. This Court held nothing more than that Green, once put in jeopardy — once having "run the gauntlet on that charge" — of first degree murder, could not be compelled to defend against that charge again on retrial.

Today's step in this area of constitutional law ought not be taken on no more basis than casual reliance on the "gauntlet" phrase lifted out of the context in which it was originally used. This is decision by slogan. Some commentators have concluded that the harassment inherent in standing trial a second time is a sufficient reason for use of collateral estoppel in criminal trials. * * * * If the Court is today relying on a harassment concept to superimpose a new brand of collateral-estoppel gloss on the "same evidence" test, there is a short answer; this case does not remotely suggest harassment of an accused who robbed six victims and the harassment aspect does not rise to constitutional levels. * * * *

Finally, the majority's opinion tells us "that the rule of collateral estoppel in criminal cases is not to be applied with the hypertechnical and archaic approach of a 19th century pleading book, but with realism and rationality."

With deference I am bound to pose the question: what is reasonable and rational about holding that an acquittal of Ashe for robbing Knight bars a trial for robbing Roberts? To borrow a phrase from the Court's opinion, what could conceivably be more "hypertechnical and archaic" and more like the stilted formalisms of 17th and 18th century common-law England, than to stretch jeopardy for robbing Knight into jeopardy for robbing Roberts?

After examining the facts of this case, the Court concludes that the first jury must have concluded that Ashe was not one of the robbers — that he was not present at the time. Also, since the second jury necessarily reached its decision by finding he was present, the collateral-estoppel doctrine applies. But the majority's analysis of the facts completely disregards the confusion injected into the case by the robbery of Mrs. Gladson. To me, if we are to psychoanalyze the jury, the evidence adduced at the first trial could more reasonably be construed as indicating that Ashe had been at the Gladson home with the other three men but was not one of those involved in the basement robbery. Certainly, the evidence at the first trial was equivocal as to whether there were three or four robbers, whether the man who robbed Mrs. Gladson was one of the three who robbed the six male victims, and whether a man other than the three had robbed Mrs. Gladson. Then, since the jury could have thought that the "acting together" instruction given by the trial court in both trials only applied to the actual taking from the six card players, and not to Mrs. Gladson, the jury could well have acquitted Ashe but yet believed that he was present in the Gladson home. On the other hand, the evidence adduced at the second trial resolved issues other than identity that may have troubled the first jury. If believed, that evidence indicated that a fourth robber, Johnson, not Ashe, was with Mrs. Gladson when Ashe, Larson, and Brown were robbing the male victims. Johnson did go to the basement where the male victims were located, but only after the other three had already taken the stolen items and when the robbers were preparing for their departure in a car to be stolen from Roberts.

Accordingly, even the facts in this case, which the Court's opinion considers to "lead to but one conclusion," are susceptible of an interpretation that the first jury did not base its acquittal on the identity ground which the Court finds so compelling. The Court bases its holding on sheer "guesswork," which should have no place particularly in our review of state convictions by way of habeas corpus.

The essence of Mr. Justice Brennan's concurrence is that this was all one transaction, one episode, or, if I may so characterize it, one frolic, and, hence, only one crime. His approach, like that taken by the Court, totally overlooks the significance of there being six entirely separate charges of robbery against six individuals.

This "single frolic" concept is not a novel notion; it has been urged in various courts including this Court. One of the theses underlying the "single frolic" notion is that the criminal episode is "indivisible." The short answer to that is that to the victims, the criminal conduct is readily divisible and intensely personal; each offense is an offense against a person. For me, it demeans the dignity of the human personality and individuality to talk of "a single transaction" in the context or six separate assaults on six individuals.

No court that elevates the individual rights and human dignity of the accused to a high place — as we should — ought to be so casual as to treat the victims as a single homogenized lump of human clay. I would grant the dignity of individual status to the victims as much as to those accused, not more but surely no less.

Notes from Carmelita:

1. In his concurring opinion, Justice Brennan construes the words "same offence" in the 5th Amendment to mean all crimes committed in the "same transaction." Therefore, he concludes, Ashe should have had one trial for robbing all 6 victims. Yet, in his footnote 14, Justice Brennan says that — if Ashe were convicted — he could be *punished* separately for each robbery, even though the 5th Amendment deals with multiple *punishment* as well as multiple *trials*. Isn't Justice Brennan using the same words in the 5th Amendment ("same offence") to reach two contradictory results?

2. **May collateral estoppel be applied *against* the defendant?**

In *People v. Majado*, 22 Cal.App.2d 323 (1937), defendant had been charged with failing to support an illegitimate child. He denied paternity, but he was found guilty.

He again failed to support the child, and he was once again charged with failure to support. The court held that he was collaterally estopped from again denying paternity. Otherwise, he could "put the People to the expense of many trials before this two-year-old child reaches its majority, in each of which the fact of parentage must again be established. Eventually, he might secure a jury which would find that he was not the father of the child and, since that judgment could not be set aside, we would then have the same fact judicially determined both ways."

In *Gutierrez v. Superior Court*, 24 Cal.App.4th 153 (1994), someone shot Zarate, who was seriously wounded. Defendant was charged with attempted murder of Zarate. He claimed at trial that he had been mistakenly identified as the shooter, but he was convicted. After the trial, Zarate died, and defendant was charged with murder. The prosecutor moved that defendant be barred from relitigating the issue of whether he shot Zarate, and that the jury be instructed that the only issue to be decided was whether defendant's shot caused her death. The trial court granted the motion, but the appellate court reversed, holding that even though the issue of identity was the same in both cases and defendant had a fair opportunity to litigate the issue in the first case, defendant's due process right to a jury trial on all issues "far outweighs" any interest in judicial economy. While collateral estoppel also furthers consistency of verdicts, consistency "is not the sole measure of the integrity of judicial decisions", and denial of defendant's right to a jury trial would undermine public confidence in the courts. The court distinguished *Majado*, noting that the issue there was defendant's continuing *status*, and that allowing him to keep relitigating his paternity would provide "an incentive for repeat violations of the law".

Justice Woods dissented, calling the jury trial an "expensive, time consuming, sometimes ineffectual" device, which "perseveres only so long as it enjoys public confidence. That confidence is undermined by the specter of a system which would allow one fair jury to find Mr. Gutierrez did shoot Sandra Zarate and another fair jury to find he did not. To permit such a specter is to encourage erosion of jury trial as we know it and to aid proposals for non-unanimous verdicts, for 10 or 8- or 6-person juries, and for further elimination of the jury trial for 'minor' offenses. Jury trial is the cornerstone of our justice system. I would preserve it, not degrade it."

For a similar dispute, see *People v. Goss*, 446 Mich. 587, 521 N.W.2d 312 (1994).

In *U.S. v. Gallardo-Mendez*, 150 F.3d 1240 (10th Cir.1998), defendant pleaded guilty in 1991 to illegally reentering the United States after being deported. In 1996, he was indicted for "illegal reentry by a deported alien." At the prosecutor's request, the trial judge instructed the jury: "There has been a judicial determination in litigation, to which the defendant was a party, that on and prior to July 26, 1991, defendant was an alien and not a citizen of the United States. The defendant is bound by that determination." The jury convicted defendant, but the Court of Appeal reversed:

> We are not convinced according preclusive effect to guilty pleas would, in fact, serve the interests of "wise public policy and common sense judicial administration." The prospect of being collaterally estopped at some future date may discourage criminal defendants from settling criminal charges by pleading guilty. The judicial burdens of ensuring guilty pleas are entered "knowingly," given the prospect of potential complex collateral estoppel applications, arguably would be enhanced. Additionally, the process of

determining whether or not collateral estoppel is appropriate in a subsequent criminal proceeding can itself be cumbersome.

Moreover, while "wise public policy and judicial efficiency" may be sufficient reasons to apply collateral estoppel in civil cases, they do not have the same weight and value in criminal cases. In a criminal prosecution, the defendant has at stake an "interest of transcending value," his liberty. * * * * We note also that the Supreme Court did not make the doctrine of collateral estoppel available to criminal defendants as a matter of judicial efficiency; the Court found a constitutional mandate for use of the doctrine by the defendant in the Fifth Amendment guarantee against double jeopardy. *Ashe v. Swenson*, 397 U.S. at 445. Therefore, the liberty interest of a criminal defendant takes priority over the usual concerns for efficient judicial administration so often found in civil proceedings.

In *U.S. v. Arnett*, 327 F.3d 845 (9th Cir. 2003), Arnett was charged with using a firearm during a bank robbery in Oregon. "Antique" guns (made before 1898) do not qualify as "firearms", and Arnett presented expert testimony that his gun was an antique. The jury convicted him. He was then charged with using a firearm to commit several more bank robberies in California. He admitted that he used the same weapon during these robberies, but wanted to once again present evidence that the gun was an antique. The court recognized that *U.S. v. Pelullo*, 14 F.3d 881 (3rd Cir. 1994) held that "a defendant's right to a jury trial necessitates that every jury empaneled for a prosecution consider evidence of guilt afresh and without the judicial direction attending collateral estoppel." Nevertheless, the court in *Arnett* held:

> The district court did not err in applying collateral estoppel to bar Arnett from relitigating the Oregon jury's determination that the shotgun he used in all of his robberies was not an antique. On the facts of this case, we see nothing unfair in applying the doctrine to bar Arnett's defense. This is a classic example of the proper application of collateral estoppel. * * * *

> Common-sense judicial administration supports the application of collateral estoppel in criminal cases. In the Oregon trial, Arnett was accorded his constitutional right to trial by jury, including the right to cross-examine all witnesses against him regarding the facts essential to his conviction. The Oregon jury heard Arnett's evidence, including Wood's expert testimony, and the jury determined that his defense had no merit. The application of collateral estoppel is proper in the California case as to those facts pertaining to the identical defense rejected by the Oregon jury. Allowing Arnett to relitigate his antiquity defense after a full and fair opportunity to do so in Oregon would result in a needless waste of scarce judicial resources and would threaten the integrity of the judicial process by increasing the chance of an inconsistent verdict. No constitutional provision requires such a result.

See also *State v. Scarborough*, 181 S.W.3d 650 (Tenn. 2005), and Kennelly, *Precluding the Accused: Offensive Collateral Estoppel in Criminal Cases*, 80 Va.L.Rev. 1379 (1994).

3. Should collateral estoppel apply against the prosecution where the defendant in the second case was *not one of the defendants in the first case*?

In *Woodford v. Municipal Court*, 37 Cal.App.3d 874 (1974), Woodford was charged with violating California's obscenity statute by showing a film, "Mona, The Virgin Nymph", at the Guild Theater in San Diego. Woodford moved to bar the prosecution, claiming collateral estoppel, because another film exhibitor (Borelli) had been prosecuted for showing the same film in Palo Alto; Borelli's sole defense had been that the film was not obscene, and a Palo Alto jury acquitted Borelli. The court rejected Woodford's claim:

> In the enforcement of laws against obscenity, multiple and successive prosecutions of different defendants based upon the sale or exhibition of the same book or film will naturally occur. If the People are successful in one or a dozen or more of such prosecutions, they cannot use those convictions against other defendants who sell or exhibit the same material. If one defendant succeeds in obtaining an adjudication of nonobscenity, the public policy of this state should not be to preclude the People from prosecuting other defendants. Application of the defense of collateral estoppel in such situations would produce anomalous results, would not serve the objective of preventing a defendant from being harassed or twice vexed by litigation, and would not accord sufficient consideration to the public interest in the enforcement of laws against obscenity.

Compare *People v. Taylor*, 12 Cal.3d 686 (1974), where Taylor drove a getaway car for Daniels and Smith while they robbed a liquor store, and Smith was shot and killed by the owner of the store. Daniels was charged with robbery and murder, and was convicted of robbery but acquitted of murder, based on his claim that he lacked "malice". Then Taylor was tried for robbery and murder. The court held that the murder charge was barred by collateral estoppel, because Taylor could be guilty of murder only as an aider and abettor to the robbery, i.e., only "vicariously" for the crimes of Daniels. The court acknowledged that had Daniels been convicted, this would not estop Taylor from asserting his innocence, as he was not a party to the Daniels case. But this lack of "mutuality" was no bar to Taylor's claim, because of the "need for judicial economy" and the need "to prevent the compromising of the integrity of the judicial system caused by the rendering of inconsistent verdicts".

However, in *Standefer v. U.S.*, 447 U.S. 10 (1980), IRS Agent Niederberger had been charged with receiving several bribes from Standefer. He was convicted on some charges and acquitted on others. Then Standefer was charged with "aiding and abetting" Niederberger with accepting the bribes — by giving him the bribes. Standefer claimed that the Government was collaterally estopped as to the charges for which Niederberger had been acquitted. The Court disagreed, distinguishing civil cases that had rejected a "mutuality" requirement.

> First, in a criminal case, the Government is often without the kind of "full and fair opportunity to litigate" that is a prerequisite of estoppel. Several aspects of our criminal law make this so: the prosecution's discovery rights in criminal cases are limited, both by rules of court and constitutional privileges; it is prohibited from being granted a directed verdict or from obtaining a judgment notwithstanding the verdict no matter how clear the evidence in support of guilt; it cannot secure a new trial on the ground that an acquittal was plainly contrary to the weight of the evidence; and it cannot secure appellate review where a defendant has been acquitted.

The absence of these remedial procedures in criminal cases permits juries to acquit out of compassion or compromise or because of their assumption of a power which they had no right to exercise, but to which they were disposed through lenity. It is of course true that verdicts induced by passion and prejudice are not unknown in civil suits. But in civil cases, post-trial motions and appellate review provide an aggrieved litigant a remedy; in a criminal case the Government has no similar avenue to correct errors. Under contemporary principles of collateral estoppel, this factor strongly militates against giving an acquittal preclusive effect.

The application of nonmutual estoppel in criminal cases is also complicated by the existence of rules of evidence and exclusion unique to our criminal law. It is frequently true in criminal cases that evidence inadmissible against one defendant is admissible against another. The exclusionary rule, for example, may bar the Government from introducing evidence against one defendant because that evidence was obtained in violation of his constitutional rights. And the suppression of that evidence may result in an acquittal. The same evidence, however, may be admissible against other parties to the crime "whose rights were not violated." *Alderman v. United States*, 394 U.S. 165, 171–172 (1969). In such circumstances, where evidentiary rules prevent the Government from presenting all its proof in the first case, application of nonmutual estoppel would be plainly unwarranted. * * * *

Finally, this case involves an ingredient not present in [the civil cases]: the important federal interest in the enforcement of the criminal law. [The civil cases] were disputes over private rights between private litigants. In such cases, no significant harm flows from enforcing a rule that affords a litigant only one full and fair opportunity to litigate an issue, and there is no sound reason for burdening the courts with repetitive litigation.

That is not so here. The purpose of a criminal court is not to provide a forum for the ascertainment of private rights. Rather it is to vindicate the public interest in the enforcement of the criminal law while at the same time safeguarding the rights of the individual defendant. The public interest in the accuracy and justice of criminal results is greater than the concern for judicial economy professed in civil cases and we are thus inclined to reject, at least as a general matter, a rule that would spread the effect of an erroneous acquittal to all those who participated in a particular criminal transaction. To plead crowded dockets as an excuse for not trying criminal defendants is in our view neither in the best interests of the courts, nor the public. In short, this criminal case involves competing policy considerations that outweigh the economy concerns that undergird the estoppel doctrine.

4. If defendant's testimony persuades the jury to acquit, may the prosecutor nevertheless charge the defendant with *perjury*?

In *U.S. v. Nash*, 447 F.2d 1382 (4th Cir. 1971), Nash had been charged with stealing mail, testified that she did not steal mail, and was *acquitted*. The government then charged her with *perjury*, claiming that she lied when she testified that she did not steal mail. The court held that the perjury charge was barred by collateral estoppel:

We conclude that the jury in the first case undoubtedly passed upon the believability of Estelle Nash's statements made under oath. The jury may have been in error, but certainly it appraised the defendant's credibility. It is inconceivable that there would have been an acquittal if the jury had not accorded truth to her testimony.

Compare, however, *U.S. v. Ruhbayan*, 325 F.3d 197 (4th Cir. 2003).

In *U.S. v. Castillo-Basa* 483 F.3d 890 (9th Cir. 2007), defendant was charged with illegal entry into the U.S. after being deported. At trial, the only issue was whether he had been brought afforded a deportation hearing before his deportation. Defendant testified that he had not been present at a deportation hearing. The jury acquitted him. The Government then charged him with perjury, based on a later-discovered tape indicating that he was at the hearing. The court held that the perjury prosecution was barred by the Double Jeopardy Clause:

> This case presents an important question that cuts to the heart of the Double Jeopardy Clause. It involves the right of a defendant to be free from repeated prosecutions in which the government retries him until it obtains a guilty verdict. The government was unable to convict Castillo-Basa the first time it tried him, for illegal reentry, in large part because its counsel failed to locate and present a crucial tape recording that was within its possession. To its surprise, the jury acquitted him. Now, having "found" the tape, the government seeks to prosecute Castillo-Basa again, this time for perjury committed in connection with the illegal reentry trial. The central issue at the second trial would be the same as it was at the first: was Castillo-Basa afforded a deportation hearing at which he was present?
>
> The Double Jeopardy Clause requires the government to put on its strongest case the first time; it forbids it to conduct a series of prosecutions, involving the same fundamental issues, in which it presents additional arguments and evidence at each iteration. Here, the government has already had its chance to prove that Castillo-Basa had a deportation hearing and that his testimony to the contrary was false. It failed, largely because it didn't introduce the evidence that it had in its possession. Under the Double Jeopardy Clause, the government may not take a mulligan.
>
> The outcome in this case follows directly from basic principles of collateral estoppel that are inherent in the Double Jeopardy Clause. See *Ashe v. Swenson*, 397 U.S. 436 (1970). The only issue in dispute during Castillo-Basa's trial for illegal reentry was whether he had been brought before an immigration judge and afforded a deportation hearing prior to his deportation. The ultimate question at issue in the second prosecution — for perjury — would be whether he testified falsely at the previous trial that he had not been present at a deportation hearing. When the jury acquitted Castillo-Basa of the illegal reentry offense, it decided, as the government acknowledged below, that a deportation hearing had not been held and, thus, that he had not been brought before an immigration judge for such a hearing. Accordingly, in rendering its verdict, the jury necessarily decided that Castillo-Basa's testimony on the critical question of the deportation hearing was not false. The Double Jeopardy Clause bars the government from trying a second time to attempt to show that Castillo-

Basa was afforded the hearing in question and that his testimony to the contrary was untruthful. * * * *

The issue before us is not whether Castillo-Basa committed perjury. Indeed, it would appear that he likely did. The question, however, is whether the government is barred from trying him for that wrongful conduct a second time, after a jury has once decided that the testimony at issue was not false. We recognize that the Double Jeopardy Clause, like some of our other constitutional protections, may on occasion result in a guilty individual's escaping punishment. That is a price, however, that we are willing to pay in order to preserve the basic liberties guaranteed by our Constitution. Were we to permit the government to try individuals repeatedly for the same offense, not only the guilty would ultimately be convicted. Rather, the innocent too would, sooner or later, encounter a jury that would be persuaded by the prosecutor's arguments, especially as the cost-physical, emotional, and financial — of successive trials would frequently break the will and the spirit of the unjustly accused and leave them without the strength or ability to conduct a successful defense. In many cases the practical result would be that innocent persons, being without the resources to counter the unlimited force brought against them by the power of the state, would plead guilty, sometimes to lesser offenses, sometimes to a lesser number of serious charges. Such a system of justice would be intolerable in our society. Instead, we have wisely opted for a process in which an individual who has been adjudged not guilty may not be charged again for the same offense or held to answer more than once for conduct that the jury has decided he did not commit. Under our constitutional rule, once an issue, such as whether Castillo-Basa told the truth, has been determined in his favor, rightly or wrongly, by a jury, he may not again be compelled to defend himself on that issue.

5. Should collateral estoppel apply where the *plaintiff* in the second case was *not* the plaintiff in the first case? See the next case.

STEPHENS v. ATTORNEY GENERAL of CALIFORNIA
U.S. Court of Appeals, 9th Circuit
23 F.3d 248 (1994)

Per Curiam.

Gill A.C. Stephens filed a petition for writ of habeas corpus in the district court pursuant to 28 U.S.C. § 2254. The district court denied the petition. We affirm.

A detective from the Los Angeles Police Department approached Stephens while he was standing in line to board a Greyhound bus. After talking to Stephens for a few moments, the detective and his partner searched Stephens' bags and found cocaine. Stephens was arrested and charged in United States District Court for a violation of 21 U.S.C. § 841(a)(1), possession with intent to distribute cocaine.

Stephens maintains that he never consented to the search of his bags. At an evidentiary hearing, the district court found that Stephens had not given his consent, held that the search violated the Fourth Amendment, and granted Stephens' motion to suppress the cocaine. Rather than appealing the order, the United States Attorney dismissed the indictment.

The detectives brought the case to the Los Angeles District Attorney, who prosecuted Stephens under state law in California Superior Court. Stephens again moved to suppress the cocaine. This time, the state judge credited the detectives' testimony that Stephens had given them permission to search his bags and ruled that the cocaine was admissible. Stephens pled guilty and then appealed. * * * *

Stephens . . . argues that the doctrine of collateral estoppel barred the state court from relitigating the issue of the legality of the search. * * * *

"Under collateral estoppel, once a court has decided an issue of fact or law necessary to its judgment, that decision may preclude relitigation of the issue in a suit on a different cause of action involving a party to the first case." *Allen v. McCurry*, 449 U.S. 90, 94 (1980). However, collateral estoppel cannot be applied to a litigant who was not a party or in privity with a party to the earlier proceeding, and who therefore never had an opportunity to be heard. *Id.* at 95.

The state was not a party to the initial evidentiary hearing in federal court and was not in privity with the federal prosecutors. The state would be bound by the prior determination only if state prosecutors had participated actively in the federal prosecution. *People v. Meredith*, 11 Cal.App.4th 1548 (1992). Although the same Los Angeles police detectives testified at both the federal and state hearings, this did not create privity between the state and federal prosecutors. At the federal hearing, the detectives did not have the authority to act in the state's name or to decide how the prosecution would proceed.

Affirmed.

BROWN v. OHIO
United States Supreme Court
432 U.S. 161 (1977)

Mr. Justice Powell delivered the opinion of the Court.

The question in this case is whether the Double Jeopardy Clause of the Fifth Amendment bars prosecution and punishment for the crime of stealing an automobile following prosecution and punishment for the lesser included offense of operating the same vehicle without the owner's consent.

I

On November 29, 1973, the petitioner, Nathaniel Brown, stole a 1965 Chevrolet from a parking lot in East Cleveland, Ohio. Nine days later, on December 8, 1973, Brown was caught driving the car in Wickliffe, Ohio. The Wickliffe police charged him with "joyriding", taking or operating the car without the owner's consent, in violation of Ohio Rev.Code Ann. § 4549.04(D).[1] The complaint charged that

> On or about December 8, 1973, Nathaniel H. Brown did unlawfully and purposely take, drive or operate a certain motor vehicle to wit, a 1965 Chevrolet, without the consent of the owner, one Gloria Ingram.

---

[1] § 4549.04(D) provided at the time: "No person shall purposely take, operate, or keep any motor vehicle without the consent of its owner." A violation was punishable as a misdemeanor.

Brown pleaded guilty to this charge and was sentenced to 30 days in jail and a $100 fine.

Upon his release from jail on January 8, 1974, Brown was returned to East Cleveland to face further charges, and on February 5 he was indicted by the Cuyahoga County grand jury. The indictment was in two counts, the first charging the theft of the car "on or about the 29th day of November, 1973," in violation of Ohio Rev.Code Ann. § 4549.04(A)[2], and the second charging joyriding on the same date in violation of § 4549.04(D). A bill of particulars filed by the prosecuting attorney specified that:

> On or about the 29th day of November, 1973, Nathaniel Brown unlawfully did steal a Chevrolet motor vehicle, and take, drive or operate such vehicle without the consent of the owner, Gloria Ingram.

Brown objected to both counts of the indictment on the basis of former jeopardy.

On March 18, 1974, at a pretrial hearing in the Cuyahoga County Court of Common Pleas, Brown pleaded guilty to the auto theft charge on the understanding that the court would consider his claim of former jeopardy on a motion to withdraw the plea.[3] Upon submission of the motion, the court overruled Brown's double jeopardy objections. The court sentenced Brown to six months in jail but suspended the sentence and placed Brown on probation for one year.

The Ohio Court of Appeals affirmed. It held that under Ohio law the misdemeanor of joyriding was included in the felony of auto theft:

> Every element of the crime of operating a motor vehicle without the consent of the owner is also an element of the crime of auto theft. The difference between the crime of stealing a motor vehicle and operating a motor vehicle without the consent of the owner is that conviction for stealing requires proof of an intent on the part of the thief to *permanently* deprive the owner of possession. The crime of operating a motor vehicle without the consent of the owner is a lesser included offense of auto theft.

Although this analysis led the court to agree with Brown that "for purposes of double jeopardy the two prosecutions involve the same statutory offense,"[4] it nonetheless held the second prosecution permissible:

> The two prosecutions are based on two separate acts of the appellant, one which occurred on November 29th and one which occurred on December 8th. Since appellant has not shown that both prosecutions are based on the same act or transaction, the second prosecution is not barred by the double jeopardy clause.

The Ohio Supreme Court denied leave to appeal. We granted certiorari to consider Brown's double jeopardy claim, and we now reverse.

---

[2] § 4549.04(A) provided: "No person shall steal any motor vehicle." A violation was punishable as a felony.

[3] The joyriding count of the indictment was *nol prossed*.

[4] As the Ohio Court of Appeals recognized, the Wickliffe and Cuyahoga County prosecutions must be viewed as the acts of a single sovereign under the Double Jeopardy Clause. *Waller v. Florida*, 397 U.S. 387 (1970).

II

The Double Jeopardy Clause of the Fifth Amendment, applicable to the States through the Fourteenth, provides that no person shall "be subject for the same offence to be twice put in jeopardy of life or limb." It has long been understood that separate statutory crimes need not be identical either in constituent elements or in actual proof in order to be the same within the meaning of the constitutional prohibition. The principal question in this case is whether auto theft and joyriding, a greater and lesser included offense under Ohio law, constitute the "same offence" under the Double Jeopardy Clause.

Because it was designed originally to embody the protection of the common-law pleas of former jeopardy, the Fifth Amendment double jeopardy guarantee serves principally as a restraint on courts and prosecutors. The legislature remains free under the Double Jeopardy Clause to define crimes and fix punishments; but once the legislature has acted courts may not impose more than one punishment for the same offense and prosecutors ordinarily may not attempt to secure that punishment in more than one trial. * * * *

The Double Jeopardy Clause "protects against a second prosecution for the same offense after acquittal. It protects against a second prosecution for the same offense after conviction.

And it protects against multiple punishments for the same offense." *North Carolina v. Pearce*, 395 U.S. 711, 717. Where consecutive sentences are imposed at a single criminal trial, the role of the constitutional guarantee is limited to assuring that the court does not exceed its legislative authorization by imposing multiple punishments for the same offense. Where successive prosecutions are at stake, the guarantee serves "a constitutional policy of finality for the defendant's benefit." *United States v. Jorn*, 400 U.S. 470, 479 (1971). That policy protects the accused from attempts to relitigate the facts underlying a prior acquittal, see *Ashe v. Swenson*, 397 U.S. 436 (1970), and from attempts to secure additional punishment after a prior conviction and sentence, see *Green v. United States*, 355 U.S. 184, 187–188 (1957).

The established test for determining whether two offenses are sufficiently distinguishable to permit the imposition of cumulative punishment was stated in *Blockburger v. United States*, 284 U.S. 299, 304 (1932):

> The applicable rule is that where the same act or transaction constitutes a violation of two distinct statutory provisions, the test to be applied to determine whether there are two offenses or only one, is whether each provision requires proof of an additional fact which the other does not.

This test emphasizes the elements of the two crimes. "If each requires proof of a fact that the other does not, the *Blockburger* test is satisfied, notwithstanding a substantial overlap in the proof offered to establish the crimes." *Iannelli v. United States*, 420 U.S. 770, 785 (1975).

If two offenses are the same under this test for purposes of barring consecutive sentences at a single trial, they necessarily will be the same for purposes of barring successive prosecutions. Where the judge is forbidden to impose cumulative punishment for two crimes at the end of a single proceeding, the prosecutor is forbidden to strive for the same result in successive proceedings. Unless "each statute requires proof of an additional fact which the other does not," *Morey v.*

Commonwealth, 108 Mass. 433, 434 (1871), the Double Jeopardy Clause prohibits successive prosecutions as well as cumulative punishment.[6]

We are mindful that the Ohio courts have the final authority to interpret that State's legislation. Here the Ohio Court of Appeals has authoritatively defined the elements of the two Ohio crimes: joyriding consists of taking or operating a vehicle without the owner's consent, and auto theft consists of joyriding with the intent permanently to deprive the owner of possession. Joyriding is the lesser included offense. The prosecutor who has established joyriding need only prove the requisite intent in order to establish auto theft; the prosecutor who has established auto theft necessarily has established joyriding as well.

Applying the *Blockburger* test, we agree with the Ohio Court of Appeals that joyriding and auto theft, as defined by the court, constitute "the same statutory offense" within the meaning of the Double Jeopardy Clause. For it is clearly not the case that "each statute requires proof of a fact which the other does not." 284 U.S. at 304. As is invariably true of a greater and lesser included offense, the lesser offense joyriding requires no proof beyond that which is required for conviction of the greater auto theft. The greater offense is therefore by definition the "same" for purposes of double jeopardy as any lesser offense included in it.

This conclusion merely restates what has been this Court's understanding of the Double Jeopardy Clause at least since *In re Nielsen* was decided in 1889. In that case, the Court endorsed the rule that "where a person has been tried and convicted for a crime which has various incidents included in it, he cannot be a second time tried for one of those incidents without being twice put in jeopardy for the same offense." 131 U.S. at 188.

Although in this formulation the conviction of the greater precedes the conviction of the lesser, the opinion makes it clear that the sequence is immaterial. Thus, the Court treated the formulation as just one application of the rule that two offenses are the same unless each requires proof that the other does not. And as another application of the same rule, the Court cited with approval the decision of *State v. Cooper*, 13 N.J.L. 361 (1833), where the New Jersey Supreme Court held that a

---

[6] The *Blockburger* test is not the only standard for determining whether successive prosecutions impermissibly involve the same offense. Even if two offenses are sufficiently different to permit the imposition of consecutive sentences, successive prosecutions will be barred in some circumstances where the second prosecution requires the relitigation of factual issues already resolved by the first. Thus in *Ashe v. Swenson*, 397 U.S. 436 (1970), where an acquittal on a charge of robbing one of several participants in a poker game established that the accused was not present at the robbery, the Court held that principles of collateral estoppel embodied in the Double Jeopardy Clause barred prosecutions of the accused for robbing the other victims. And in *In re Nielsen*, 131 U.S. 176 (1889), the Court held that a conviction of a Mormon on a charge of cohabiting with his two wives over a 2 1/2-year period barred a subsequent prosecution for adultery with one of them on the day following the end of that period.

In both cases, strict application of the *Blockburger* test would have permitted imposition of consecutive sentences had the charges been consolidated in a single proceeding. In *Ashe*, separate convictions of the robbery of each victim would have required proof in each case that a different individual had been robbed. In *Nielsen*, conviction for adultery required proof that the defendant had sexual intercourse with one woman while married to another; conviction for cohabitation required proof that the defendant lived with more than one woman at the same time. Nonetheless, the Court in both cases held the separate offenses to be the "same" for purposes of protecting the accused from having to "run the gauntlet a second time." *Ashe*, supra, 397 U.S. at 446 (1957).

Because we conclude today that a lesser included and a greater offense are the same under *Blockburger*, we need not decide whether the repetition of proof required by the successive prosecutions against Brown would otherwise entitle him to the additional protection offered by *Ashe* and *Nielsen*.

conviction for arson barred a subsequent felony-murder indictment based on the death of a man killed in the fire. Whatever the sequence may be, the Fifth Amendment forbids successive prosecution and cumulative punishment for a greater and lesser included offense.[7]

III

After correctly holding that joyriding and auto theft are the same offense under the Double Jeopardy Clause, the Ohio Court of Appeals nevertheless concluded that Nathaniel Brown could be convicted of both crimes because the charges against him focused on different parts of his 9-day joyride. We hold a different view. The Double Jeopardy Clause is not such a fragile guarantee that prosecutors can avoid its limitations by the simple expedient of dividing a single crime into a series of temporal or spatial units. The applicable Ohio statutes, as written and as construed in this case, make the theft and operation of a single car a single offense. Although the Wickliffe and East Cleveland authorities may have had different perspectives on Brown's offense, it was still only one offense under Ohio law.[8] Accordingly, the specification of different dates in the two charges on which Brown was convicted cannot alter the fact that he was placed twice in jeopardy for the same offense in violation of the Fifth and Fourteenth Amendments.

Reversed.

MR. JUSTICE BLACKMUN, with whom THE CHIEF JUSTICE and MR. JUSTICE REHNQUIST join, dissenting.

I, of course, have no quarrel with the Court's general double jeopardy analysis. I am unable to ignore as easily as the Court does, however, the specific finding of the Ohio Court of Appeals that the two prosecutions at issue here were based on petitioner's separate and distinct acts committed, respectively, on November 29 and on December 8, 1973.

Petitioner was convicted of operating a motor vehicle on December 8 without the owner's consent. He subsequently was convicted of taking and operating the same motor vehicle on November 29 without the owner's consent and with the intent permanently to deprive the owner of possession. It is possible, of course, that at some point the two acts would be so closely connected in time that the Double Jeopardy Clause would require treating them as one offense. This surely would be so with respect to the theft and any simultaneous unlawful operation. Furthermore, as a matter of statutory construction, the allowable unit of prosecution may be a course of conduct rather than the separate segments of such a course. I feel that neither of these approaches justifies the Court's result in the present case. Nine

---

[7] An exception may exist where the State is unable to proceed on the more serious charge at the outset because the additional facts necessary to sustain that charge have not occurred or have not been discovered despite the exercise of due diligence. See *Ashe v. Swenson, supra,* 397 U.S. at 453, n. 7 (Brennan, J., concurring).

[8] We would have a different case if the Ohio Legislature had provided that joyriding is a separate offense for each day in which a motor vehicle is operated without the owner's consent. We also would have a different case if in sustaining Brown's second conviction the Ohio courts had construed the joyriding statute to have that effect. We then would have to decide whether the state courts' construction, applied retroactively in this case, was such "an unforeseeable judicial enlargement of a criminal statute" as to violate due process.

days elapsed between the two incidents that are the basis of petitioner's convictions. During that time, the automobile moved from East Cleveland to Wickliffe. It strains credulity to believe that petitioner was operating the vehicle every minute of those nine days. A time must have come when he stopped driving the car. When he operated it again nine days later in a different community, the Ohio courts could properly find, consistently with the Double Jeopardy Clause, that the acts were sufficiently distinct to justify a second prosecution. Only if the Clause requires the Ohio courts to hold that the allowable unit of prosecution is the course of conduct would the Court's result here be correct. On the facts of this case, no such requirement should be inferred, and the state courts should be free to construe Ohio's statute as they did.

This Court, I fear, gives undeserved emphasis, to the Ohio Court of Appeals' passing observation that the Ohio misdemeanor of joyriding is an element of the Ohio felony of auto theft. That observation was merely a preliminary statement, indicating that the theft and any simultaneous unlawful operation were one and the same. But the Ohio Court of Appeals then went on flatly to hold that such simultaneity was not present here. Thus, it seems to me, the Ohio courts did precisely what this Court, at professes to say they did not do.

In my view, we should not so willingly circumvent an authoritative Ohio holding as to Ohio law. I would affirm the judgment of the Court of Appeals.

Notes from Carmelita:

1. Is an apple the "same" as an apple pie? Did the Court really hold that a lesser-included offence is the "same" as the greater offence? Does this make any sense, in light of (1) what the word "same" usually means and (2) the purpose(s) of the Double Jeopardy clause? (These questions are discussed in Akhil Amar, *Double Jeopardy Law Made Simple*, 106 Yale L.J. 1807 (1997).)

2. What *purpose* of the Double Jeopardy clause was the Court trying to further in *Brown*? Was the Court concerned that the defendant was facing *trial* more than once? (This was the concern of the Court in *Ashe*.) Or was the Court concerned that the defendant was facing *punishment* more than once? Put another way, would the Court's concerns have vanished if Brown had faced both charges in *one* trial instead of two?

3. In *Grady v. Corbin* 495 U.S. 508 (1990), the Court stated that "the *Blockburger* test is simply a rule of statutory construction, a guide to determining whether the legislature intended multiple punishments."

4. In *People v. Scott*, 15 Cal.4th 1188 (1997), Scott pleaded guilty to *attempted murder* of Jensen — and then Jensen died. Scott was then charged with *murder* of Jensen. Scott claimed double jeopardy, but the court disagreed:

> Defendant argues that, at the time he pleaded guilty to attempted murder, the prosecution knew or should have known that the victim's death was inevitable. If this be so, it is irrelevant. What is pertinent is that the fact necessary to the murder charge — the victim's death — had not yet occurred, not that it might, or even inevitably would, occur sometime in the future. A person cannot be prosecuted, and hence cannot be placed in jeopardy, for a crime not yet complete no matter how likely its future completion might be.

Is this consistent with footnote 7 of *Brown*?

5. How does the "same offense" apply where defendant commits *one act* that violates *more than one statute*?

In *Harmon v. State*, 11 P.3d 393 (Alaska Ct.App. 2000), Harmon had sex with his sister when she was drunk. He was convicted of sexual assault ("sexual penetration with a person who the offender knows is incapacitated") and incest ("sexual penetration with another who is related, either legitimately or illegitimately, as a brother or sister of the whole"). The court affirmed both convictions, rejecting Harmon's claim of double jeopardy:

> The two statutes require proof of different conduct. For the subsection of second-degree sexual assault that was charged in this case, the State was obliged to prove that Harmon engaged in sexual penetration with a person Harmon knew was incapacitated. To prove incest in this case, the State was obliged to prove that Harmon engaged in sexual penetration with his sister. Harmon's conviction for second-degree sexual assault did not require proof that Harmon's victim was his blood relative. Harmon's conviction for incest did not require proof that Harmon knew that his victim was incapacitated.

> Furthermore, the social interests to be vindicated or protected by each statute are different. The trial judge recognized society's interest in preventing any sexual penetration between closely related people. He also recognized the different social interest protected by the subsection of second-degree sexual assault that was charged here, protecting incapacitated persons from sexual penetration.

In *U.S. v. Barrett*, 933 F.2d 355 (6th Cir.1991), defendant was sentenced for both attempted distribution of marijuana and conspiracy to distribute the same marijuana, based on evidence that he had acted as a middleman in trying to procure marijuana for the buyers. The court upheld the sentences and held that these are not the "same offence".

> The attempted distribution charge does not require multiple persons for its commission; a single individual could do this. A conspiracy to distribute charge is an agreement between or among individuals to distribute controlled substances in violation of § 846. No overt act is required [and such an overt act is required for attempt].

But compare *Thurman v. State*, 602 N.E.2d 548 (Indiana Ct.App.1992), where the defendant was convicted and sentenced for possession of cocaine and "dealing" the same cocaine. The court held that possession was a lesser-included offense in "dealing", and therefore they are the "same offense," and imposing sentences for both violates defendant's right against double jeopardy.

In *U.S. v. Freyre-Lazaro*, 3 F.3d 1496 (11th Cir.1993), the court held that possession with intent to distribute cocaine is a lesser included offense of possession with intent to distribute the same cocaine within 1,000 feet of an elementary school. The court stated: "While the government may charge a defendant with both a greater and a lesser included offense and may prosecute those offenses at a single trial, the court may not enter separate convictions or impose cumulative punishments for both offenses unless the legislature has authorized such punishment."

In *People v. Murphy*, 134 Cal.App.4th 1504 (2005), Murphy gave an undercover officer a rock of cocaine for $20. Based on this single act, she was convicted of both sale of cocaine and possession of cocaine for sale. The court upheld both convictions:

> A conviction for the greater offense of selling the cocaine (count one) does not require, as one of its statutory elements, the lesser offense of possessing the cocaine for sale (count two); possession is not an essential element of the sale offense. For example, one can broker a sale of a controlled substance that is within the exclusive possession of another.

In *U.S. v. Davenport*, 519 F.3d 940 (9th Cir. 2008), defendant argued that that *possessing* child pornography is a lesser included offense of *receiving* child pornography, because "It is impossible to 'receive' something without, at least at the very instant of 'receipt,' also 'possessing' it." A majority of the court agreed.

In *State v. Hazelton*, 181 Vt. 118 (2006), defendant forced a 10-year-old girl to have sex with him — one time. He was convicted of violating two crimes: (1) § 3252(a)(1)(A): "compelling another person to participate in a sexual act without consent," and (2) § 3252(a)(3): having sex with a person under the age of 16. The court held that double jeopardy permitted only one conviction:

> Despite some surface difference, the two offenses charged against defendant are essentially the same. The substantive elements of criminal sexual contact with an unmarried minor under the age of sixteen under § 3252(a)(3) are the same as the substantive elements of sexual assault compelled "without consent" under § 3252(a)(1)(A).
>
> On cursory review, the two charges against defendant do seem facially different. While both sexual-assault crimes require proof that defendant engaged in a sexual act with another person, each offense appears to include additional elements that the other does not. Compelled sexual assault, punishable under § 3252(a)(1)(A), (B) or (C), addresses an offender who "compels" a victim to engage in a sexual act, either without consent, by threat or force, or by putting the victim in fear of immediate injury to any person. Strict liability sexual assault, or so-called statutory rape, criminalized by § 3252(a)(3), turns on whether the person engaged by an offender in a sexual act was not married to the offender and was under the age of sixteen at the time. Neither compulsion nor consent are elements of, or even relevant to, the § 3252(a)(3) offense of statutory rape, so that, typically, nothing more than a calendar and the person's birth certificate are required to determine the statute's applicability.
>
> While differences between the two crimes may be apparent, they are not real. Despite the language in § 3252(a)(1) (A) outlawing one who "compels the other person to participate in a sexual act without the consent of the other person," no actual force or compulsion is necessary to commit the offense. No greater degree of compulsion is actually required for a violation of subsection (a)(1)(A) than is included as a matter of law in the offense of statutory rape under subsection (a)(3). The victim is "compelled" to engage in a sexual act in violation of § 3252 (a)(1)(A) as the result of an offender's conduct to unilaterally engage another in a sexual act "without consent," that is, without any indication that the victim is freely willing to participate. See 13 V.S.A. § 3251(3) ("Consent' means words or actions by a person indicating a voluntary agreement to engage in a sexual act."). The element

of compulsion is satisfied by lack of consent alone. That any compulsion beyond lack of consent is not an element of § 3252(a)(1)(A) is confirmed by the statute's explicit coverage of sexual assault compelled by actual threat, force, or intimidation in subsequent subsections 3252(a)(1)(B) and (C), as well as our holding in *State v. Nash* that subsections (A), (B) and (C) of § 3252(a)(1) "are separate ways by which the single offense of 'compelling' may be committed." 144 Vt. 427, 433 (1984).

At the time of this offense, it was long settled under Vermont law that it was legally impossible for an unmarried child under the age of sixteen to consent to sexual acts. *State v. Thompson*, 150 Vt. 640, 644 (1989). Because sexual acts with a single child under sixteen years old were nonconsensual as a matter of law, such acts with such a child were necessarily "compelled" merely by the child's incapacity to consent. "The legislature, among others, would certainly be surprised to find that sexual assault on a minor does not involve force or aggression and is consensual, even though consent by a minor is not legally possible." *Id.*

JUSTICE DOOLEY dissented:

I am reminded of the well-worn maxim that when a decision uses the word "clearly," it is a certain signal that the opposite is true. * * * *

Aggravated sexual assault is a life imprisonment crime, essentially the maximum penalty under our law. This penalty applies to the most heinous of crimes, like murder. To hold that it applies to consensual sexual activity of a male of nineteen years or older and a female under fifteen years is wholly disproportionate to other offenses for which the penalty is reserved. I don't think it is an answer to the extreme nature of the punishment that sexual conduct must occur twice or that conduct that is consensual in fact is deemed nonconsensual by the law. While I recognize that the Legislature, and not this Court, determines the range of permissible punishment for an offense, the obvious mismatch between the punishment and the offense should give us pause in determining the scope of the crime. * * * *

The obvious plain meaning of the statutory scheme is that the two subsections define separate crimes because consent in § 3252(a)(1)(A) means consent in fact as defined in § 3251(3). Thus, if an adult defendant commits a consented-to sexual act with another person of age fifteen or less, the defendant is guilty of statutory rape in violation of § 3252(a)(3). If the other person does not consent to the sexual act, and is compelled to participate, defendant is also guilty of sexual assault under § 3252(a)(1)(A). For purposes of this crime, consent is determined by the definition in § 3251(3) and not the age of the other person. In this case, the *Blockburger* presumption is consistent with the plain meaning of the language. Even if it were not, any ambiguity in the meaning of the statutes should be resolved under the *Blockburger* presumption.

This construction is consistent with the likely intent of the Legislature. Rather than intending to criminalize the exact same conduct twice, the Legislature drew a distinction between a circumstance where a minor consents to sexual activity without coercion and a situation where a minor is coerced into having sex. The latter is a separate and additional crime because of the presence of the coercion. This interpretation is supported by the presence of the word "compels" in § 3252(a)(1). The majority has read that word out of the statute, holding that each of the alternative elements in § 3252(a)(1)(A), (B) and (C) are alternative methods of compulsion. That may be a fair construction of (B) and (C) because each of these elements involve an element of compulsion. It is not a fair construction of (A), however, if the language means only that the victim is under sixteen years of age, because the majority has read compulsion out of the element. As the majority emphasizes, this is a strict liability crime provable only by a calendar and the person's birth certificate. Thus, the Legislature's intent to criminalize only compelled behavior is violated by the majority's construction of § 3252(a)(1)(A).

6. How does the "same offense" apply where defendant is charged with felony murder *and the underlying felony?*

In *Whalen v. U.S.*, 445 U.S. 684 (1980), Whalen was convicted of rape and felony murder (based on the felony of rape), and sentenced to consecutive terms of 20 years to life for murder and 15 years to life for rape. The Court held that this violated the Double Jeopardy Clause.

> In this case, resort to the *Blockburger* rule leads to the conclusion that Congress did not authorize consecutive sentences for rape and for a killing committed in the course of the rape, since it is plainly not the case that "each provision requires proof of a fact which the other does not." A conviction for killing in the course of a rape cannot be had without proving all the elements of the offense of rape.

> The Government contends that felony murder and rape are not the "same" offense under *Blockburger*, since the former offense does *not in all cases* require proof of a rape; that is, D.C.Code § 22-2401 proscribes the killing of another person in the course of committing rape or robbery or kidnapping or arson, etc. Where the offense to be proved does not include proof of a rape — for example, where the offense is a killing in the perpetration of a robbery — the offense is of course different from the offense of rape, and the Government is correct in believing that cumulative punishments for the felony murder and for a rape would be permitted under *Blockburger*. In the present case, however, proof of rape is a necessary element of proof of the felony murder, and we are unpersuaded that this case should be treated differently from other cases in which one criminal offense requires proof of every element of another offense. There would be no question in this regard if Congress, instead of listing the six lesser included offenses in the alternative, had separately proscribed the six different species of felony murder under six statutory provisions. It is doubtful that Congress could have imagined that so formal a difference in drafting had any practical significance, and we ascribe none to it.

JUSTICE REHNQUIST dissented:

> I believe it clear that a legislature could, if it so desired, provide for separate punishments under two statutory provisions, even though those provisions define the "same offense" within the meaning of *Blockburger*. To take a simple example, a legislature might set the penalty for assault at two

years' imprisonment while setting the penalty for assault with a deadly weapon as "two years for assault and an additional two years for assault with a deadly weapon." Even though the former crime is obviously a lesser included offense of the latter crime — or, in the rubric of *Blockburger*, the first offense does not require proof of any fact that the second does not — neither *Blockburger* nor the Double Jeopardy Clause would preclude the imposition of the "cumulative" sentence of two years.

See also *State v. Contreras*, 903 P.2d 228 (N.Mex.1995), where defendant killed a cab driver during an armed robbery. Based on the armed robbery, he was convicted of felony murder. The trial court imposed consecutive sentences for both murder and armed robbery. The New Mexico Supreme Court held that Double Jeopardy barred sentencing for both crimes, as this would impose punishment greater than what the legislature intended. The court cited cases from several other states that held likewise.

7. How does the "same offense" apply *where defendant commits two or more related acts in a short space of time?*

In *Greer v. State*, 539 S.W.2d 855 (Tenn.1976), Greer was charged with burglary and rape, based on evidence that he had broken into a woman's home and raped her. He was convicted and sentenced on both charges. He appealed, claiming that punishing him for both crimes violated the double jeopardy clause. The court disagreed:

> The crime of burglary is considered completed when the entry is executed with a concomitant intent to commit a felony inside the building entered. It follows that a second crime committed after the burglarious act is completed constitutes a separate crime, susceptible of a separate conviction and punishment. Thus the trial judge in this case was not precluded as a matter of law from the imposition of consecutive sentences based on the verdict of the jury.

In *State v. Rambert*, 459 S.E.2d 510 (N.C.1995), Rambert fired three shots at Dillahunt, who was sitting in a car. The first shot hit the windshield. Dillahunt drove forward, and a second bullet struck the passenger door. Rembert pursued Dillahunt and fired a third shot into the rear bumper. Rembert was convicted and sentenced on three counts of discharging a firearm into occupied property. On appeal, he argued that conviction and sentence on more than one count violated Double Jeopardy, because "evidence that he fired three shots from one gun into occupied property within a short period of time would support a conviction and sentence on only one count, not three counts," i.e., this was a single "offense." The court disagreed:

> Defendant's actions were three distinct and, therefore, separate events. Each shot, fired from a pistol, as opposed to a machine gun or other automatic weapon, required that defendant employ his thought processes each time he fired the weapon. Each act was distinct in time, and each bullet hit the vehicle in a different place.

In *State v. Ingram*, 687 A.2d 1279 (Conn.App.Ct.1996), Ingram entered the Bank of New Haven, pointed a gun at teller Holland, and demanded money, which Holland gave him. Ingram then went to teller Alsever and did the same, and then he went to teller Vigliotto and did it again. He was convicted of three counts of robbery. On appeal, he argued that double jeopardy precluded a conviction on more than one count, as the three incidents were part of the "same course of conduct" and involved the same victim: the Bank of New Haven.

The court disagreed, noting: "The proper double jeopardy inquiry when a defendant is convicted of multiple violations of the same statutory provision is whether the legislature intended to punish the individual acts separately or to punish only the course of action which they constitute. That issue, though essentially constitutional, becomes one of statutory construction." The court then found that robbery is not merely theft of property: "Robbery is an offense against the person, the distinguishing characteristic of which is the intimidation of the victim." As Ingram intimidated three separate victims, he is guilty of three separate "offenses." See also *People v. Bonner*, 80 Cal.App.4th 759 (2000) (defendant who tries to rob two victims in same incident may be convicted of two counts of *attempted* robbery).

But compare *People v. Marquez*, 78 Cal.App.4th 1302 (2000), where Marquez went into a restaurant and robbed a waitress of $70 of her tip money and $600 in the cash drawer. The court held that this was one robbery, not two:

> In one seamless ill-conceived effort, defendant walked up to the counter at Lyon's Restaurant, threatened waitress Julie Feldt with a handgun, thereby convincing her to hand over her tips lying on the counter and Lyon's operating money from the cash drawer. This was an indivisible transaction involving a single victim who was forced to relinquish possession of two separately owned amounts of money at the same place and at the same time. * * * *

> Since the central element of robbery is force or fear, a defendant may be convicted of a separate robbery for each victim of such force or fear, even if the victims are in joint possession of the property taken. Here in contrast, the defendant committed only one larceny against a single victim of one threatened application of force occurring at the same place and time. In these circumstances the single larceny can only support a single count of robbery.

And compare the above cases with *State v. Adel*, 136 Wash.2d 629 (1998). Narcotics officers searched Adel's store and his car, which was parked outside. They found 3 marijuana cigarette butts in the car's ashtray and a small amount of marijuana near the store's cash register. The total from both places was less than 0.3 gram — "approximately the weight of three large paper clips." Adel was charged and convicted of two counts of possession of marijuana — one for the marijuana in the car and one for the marijuana in the store. The Washington Supreme Court reversed, holding that double jeopardy barred prosecution for two counts:

> If Adel's possession of marijuana in two places constitutes just one criminal act, or one "unit of prosecution," then Adel's two convictions violate double jeopardy by punishing him twice for the same offense. Double jeopardy is implicated whether or not Adel's sentences are served concurrently or consecutively. A defendant's having two convictions creates other adverse consequences besides jail time. Adel's is a unique situation where the adverse consequences of having two convictions are far greater than had there been one conviction. As a legal alien, Adel is subject to

deportation if convicted of two drug charges. See 8 U.S.C. § 1227(a)(2)(B)(i).

To determine if a defendant has been punished multiple times for the same offense, this court has traditionally applied the "same evidence" test. Under the same evidence test, double jeopardy is violated if a defendant is convicted of offenses which are the same in law and in fact. The same evidence test mirrors the federal "same elements" standard adopted in *Blockburger v. United States*, 284 U.S. 299, 304 (1932).

A Court of Appeals commissioner dismissed Adel's double jeopardy argument by relying upon the same evidence test. The commissioner found the two marijuana convictions were not the same in fact, each being based upon separate evidence, so the commissioner held the two convictions withstood the double jeopardy attack. The commissioner's reliance upon the same evidence test in this case is misplaced.

Both the same evidence test and *Blockburger's* same elements test are inapplicable to Adel's situation because both tests apply only to a situation where a defendant has multiple convictions for violating several statutory provisions. When a defendant is convicted for violating one statute multiple times, the same evidence test will never be satisfied. As previously mentioned, the same evidence test asks whether the convicted offenses are the same in law and the same in fact. Two convictions for violating the same statute will always be the same in law, but they will never be the same in fact. In charging two violations of the same statute, the prosecutor will always attempt to distinguish the two charges by dividing the evidence supporting each charge into distinct segments.

The proper inquiry in this case is what "unit of prosecution" has the Legislature intended as the punishable act under the specific criminal statute. The Legislature has the power, limited by the Eighth Amendment, to define criminal conduct and set out the appropriate punishment for that conduct. The proper question for this case is what act or course of conduct has the Legislature defined as the punishable act for simple possession of a controlled substance? When the Legislature defines the scope of a criminal act (the unit of prosecution), double jeopardy protects a defendant from being convicted twice under the same statute for committing just one unit of the crime. See *Bell v. U.S.*, 349 U.S. 81 (double jeopardy violated when defendant convicted on two counts of transporting women across state lines when two women were transported at the same time); *In re Snow*, 120 U.S. 274 (1887) (double jeopardy violated when defendant convicted on multiple counts of plural cohabitation when the cohabitation was continuous and ongoing). The unit of prosecution issue is unique in this aspect: While the issue is one of constitutional magnitude on double jeopardy grounds, the issue ultimately revolves around a question of statutory interpretation and legislative intent.

If the Legislature has failed to denote the unit of prosecution in a criminal statute, the United States Supreme Court has declared the ambiguity should be construed in favor of lenity. *Bell*, 349 U.S. at 84 ("If Congress does not fix the punishment for a federal offense clearly and without ambiguity, doubt will be resolved against turning a single transaction into multiple offenses"). The United States Supreme Court has been especially vigilant of overzealous prosecutors seeking multiple convictions based upon spurious distinctions between the charges. *Brown v. Ohio*, 432 U.S. 161, 169 (1977) ("The Double Jeopardy Clause is not such a fragile guarantee that prosecutors can avoid its limitations by the simple expedient of dividing a single crime into a series of temporal or spatial units."); *Snow*, 120 U.S. at 282 (if prosecutors were allowed arbitrarily to divide up ongoing criminal conduct into separate time periods to support separate charges, such division could be done ad infinitum, resulting in hundreds of charges).

We now turn to the facts of this case. The first step in the unit of prosecution inquiry is to analyze the criminal statute. The relevant portion of the possession statute states, "any person found guilty of possession of forty grams or less of marihuana shall be guilty of a misdemeanor." RCW 69.50.401(e). Possession has been defined as personal custody or dominion and control. If the State establishes the nature of the substance and the defendant's possession of it, then the elements of unlawful possession have been met. RCW 69.50.401(e) fails to indicate whether the Legislature intended to punish a person multiple times for simple possession based upon the drug being stashed in multiple places. This lack of statutory clarity favors applying the rule of lenity and finding Adel guilty on only one count of simple possession. Further analysis supports this finding.

The Legislature's intent is obviously relevant when construing an ambiguous statute. One way of construing legislative intent regarding the unit of prosecution for a simple possession crime is to refer to the 40 gram cutoff between a misdemeanor and a felony. See RCW 69.50.401(e). The Legislature has indicated the desire to punish possession of over 40 grams of marijuana as a more serious crime. In doing so, the Legislature focused solely on the quantity of the drug, and did not reference the spatial or temporal aspects of possession. Indeed, if officers had found 21 grams in Adel's store, and 21 grams in his car, prosecutors most certainly would have attempted to aggregate the two stashes and charge Adel with felony possession. *Cf. State v. Lopez*, 79 Wash.App. 755, 762, (1995) ("If the source of the drug or the manner in which it was possessed was a determining factor, a careful defendant could avoid the heightened penalty simply by making sure he acquired them in or divided them into amounts of less than two kilograms.").

The State's argument that Adel violated the possession statute multiple times simply because he constructively possessed the drug in two different places rests on a slippery slope of prosecutorial discretion to multiply charges. How far apart do drugs have to be kept to constitute "separate" stashes? Under the State's theory it seems a defendant could be convicted of three counts of possession if the drug was found in the defendant's sock, pant pocket, and purse — each "location" being a "separate" place. A reasonable person would respond that all the drugs found were on the defendant's person, and the drugs could not be segregated by the different locations on the defendant's person to justify separate convictions. The same reasonable response can be made in Adel's situation: All of the drugs found in this case were within Adel's dominion and control at the same time. The possession statute does not authorize multiple convictions based upon a drug being stashed in multiple places within a defendant's actual or constructive possession.

In *State v. Mason*, 31 Wash.App. 680 (1982), the proprietor of a steam bath and massage parlor was convicted on three counts of promoting prostitution for her employment of three different women who committed acts of prostitution at the business. The Court of Appeals analyzed the statute criminalizing the promotion of prostitution and then reasoned:

> The apparent evils the legislature sought to attack were "advancing prostitution" and "profiting from prostitution." A person is equally guilty of either of those evils whether he has only one prostitute working for him or several. We find this case substantially indistinguishable from the plural cohabitation in *Snow* and the interstate transportation of two women in *Bell*.

This analysis is particularly insightful as applied to Adel's situation. The Legislature declared it a misdemeanor to possess 40 grams or less of marijuana. A person is equally guilty of possession whether that person has the drug stashed in one place, or hidden in several places under the person's dominion and control. There is no statutory indication the Legislature intended to punish a person multiple times merely because the person separates and keeps small amounts of marijuana in different locations. We find the unit of prosecution in RCW 69.50.401(e) is possessing 40 grams of marijuana or less, regardless of where or in how many locations the drug is kept. Adel's conduct constitutes only one violation of the statute, so we reverse one of his two convictions, and we remand for resentencing on the remaining conviction.

8. How does the "same offense" apply where a single act allegedly violates the statutes of *two jurisdictions?*

In *Gillis v. State*, 633 A.2d 888 (Md.Ct.App.1993), Gillis was charged in Delaware Superior Court with the murder of Byron Parker. After he was acquitted, Parker's body was found in Maryland, so Maryland authorities charged him in Maryland with murder of Parker. Gillis claimed double jeopardy, but the court rejected his argument:

> Under the "dual sovereignty" doctrine, separate sovereigns deriving their power from different sources are each entitled to punish an individual for the same conduct if that conduct violates each sovereignty's laws. This well-established principle was reaffirmed in a pair of cases decided by the United States Supreme Court in 1959. See *Abbate v. United States*, 359 U.S. 187 (1959) (concluding Double Jeopardy Clause did not bar federal prosecutions based upon the same acts for which the defendants were previously convicted in an Illinois state court); *Bartkus v. Illinois*, 359 U.S. 121 (1959) (determining that due process was not violated when a defendant was acquitted of federal charges and then convicted in a state prosecution based upon substantially identical facts). In justifying the dual sovereignty doctrine, the Supreme Court stated: "If the States are free to prosecute criminal acts violating their laws, and the resultant state prosecutions bar federal prosecutions based on the same acts, federal law enforcement shall necessarily be hindered." *Abbate*, 359 U.S. at 195. Likewise, if a federal

acquittal prohibited a subsequent state prosecution, that would conflict with the states' obligation "to maintain peace and order within their confines." *Bartkus*, 359 U.S. at 137.

Most recently, in *Heath v. Alabama*, 474 U.S. 82 (1985), the United States Supreme Court reached the "inescapable" conclusion that the dual sovereignty doctrine permitted separate prosecutions for the same murder by both the states of Georgia and Alabama. The Court noted:

> The dual sovereignty doctrine is founded on the common-law conception of crime as an offense against the sovereignty of the government. When a defendant in a single act violates the 'peace and dignity' of two sovereigns by breaking the laws of each, he has committed two distinct 'offences.' As the Court explained in *Moore v. Illinois*, 14 L.Ed. 306 (1852), "an offence, in its legal signification, means the transgression of a law." Consequently, when the same act transgresses the laws of two sovereigns, it cannot be truly averred that the offender has been twice punished for the same offence; but only that by one act he has committed two offences, for each of which he is justly punishable.

Recognizing that "the States are no less sovereign with respect to each other than they are with respect to the Federal Government," *Heath*, 474 U.S. at 89, and acknowledging the importance of allowing each state to create and enforce its criminal code, the Court observed that "to deny a State its power to enforce its criminal laws because another State has won the race to the courthouse 'would be a shocking and untoward deprivation of the historic right and obligation of the States to maintain peace and order within their confines."

In *U.S. v. Koon*, 34 F.3d 1416 (9th Cir.1994), a videotape captured Koon and other Los Angeles police officers beating a black man, Rodney King. The officers were charged in California state court with assault with a deadly weapon and excessive use of force by a police officer, but they were acquitted. A federal grand jury then indicted them for violating King's civil rights, in violation of 18 U.S.C. § 242. They were convicted, and appealed, claiming that Double Jeopardy barred the second case. The court disagreed:

> The Double Jeopardy Clause of the Fifth Amendment provides "nor shall any person be subject for the same offense to be twice put in jeopardy of life or limb." Nevertheless, under the doctrine of dual sovereignty, successive prosecutions based on the same underlying conduct do not violate the Fifth Amendment's Double Jeopardy Clause if the prosecutions are brought by separate sovereigns. *Heath v. Alabama*, 474 U.S. 82, 93 (1985).
>
> Our circuit has recognized a narrow exception to this general rule: if the second prosecution, otherwise permissible under the dual sovereignty rule, is not pursued to vindicate the separate interests of the second sovereign, but is merely pursued as a sham on behalf of the sovereign first to prosecute, it may be subject to a successful double jeopardy challenge. This exception is referred to as the " *Bartkus* exception" in reference to the Supreme Court case from which it was derived. See *Bartkus v. Illinois*, 359 U.S. 121 (1959).

To establish double jeopardy, it is not sufficient for the defendant to show that there was cooperation between federal and state authorities; rather, the defendant must prove that the subsequent prosecuting entity is a "tool" for the first, or the proceeding is a "sham," done at the behest of the prior authority.[19] * * * *

Appellants point to several factors which, they contend, warrant a hearing in this case: (1) the federal investigation began when the crime occurred and remained active during the state investigation and prosecution; (2) federal and state authorities cooperated with each other, and the state delivered evidence and investigative reports to federal authorities after the state prosecution; (3) witnesses who testified in the federal trial were interviewed by the federal authorities soon after the incident; and (4) the Briseno videotape was admitted into evidence in the federal trial.

Despite these factors, appellants point to nothing that suggests the federal prosecution was merely a sham. These factors at most show cooperation between federal and state authorities. The fact that the federal government has conducted its own investigation weakens appellants' argument, as it indicates that the federal government was not a "tool" of the state authorities. Moreover, the fact that evidence developed from the state trial was used in the federal trial does not create a double jeopardy problem.

In sum, there is no evidence that the federal prosecution was a "sham" or a "cover" for the state prosecution.

9. When does jeopardy "attach"?

In *Crist v. Bretz*, 437 U.S. 28 (1978), defendants were charged by information with larceny. After a jury was empaneled and sworn, but before the first witness was sworn, the prosecutor dismissed the information — in order to file a new information correcting one of the counts. Defendants claimed that the new information was barred by Double Jeopardy. The Supreme Court agreed:

The reason for holding that jeopardy attaches when the jury is empaneled and sworn lies in the need to protect the interest of an accused in retaining a chosen jury. That interest was described in *Wade v. Hunter* as a defendant's "valued right to have his trial completed by a particular tribunal." 336 U.S. at 689. It is an interest with roots deep in the historic development of trial by jury in the Anglo-American system of criminal justice. Throughout that history there ran a strong tradition that once banded together a jury should not be discharged until it had completed its solemn task of announcing a verdict.

---

[19] The *Bartkus* exception is narrow, and seldom successfully pursued. Our decision in *U.S. v. Figueroa-Soto*, 938 F.2d 1015 (9th Cir.1991) demonstrates the narrowness of the exception. There we concluded that the *Bartkus* exception did not apply, even though the state prosecuted at the request of federal authorities; federal agents assisted the state prosecution, sat at the state prosecutor's table, and testified as witnesses; evidence collected by federal authorities was given to state authorities for use in the state trial; the sentence of one prosecution witness was postponed until he had testified at the state trial; a federal forfeiture proceeding was delayed so as not to prejudice the state prosecution; FBI agents prepared state trial witnesses; and the state prosecutor was appointed as special assistant to the U.S. Attorney and paid by the state for the subsequent federal prosecution.

In *People v. Aleman*, 281 Ill.App. 991 (1996), in 1977 Aleman was charged with murder of Billy Logan. Aleman waived a jury, and was acquitted by Judge Wilson. 17 years later, however, the prosecutor recharged him with *the same murder*. Aleman claimed double jeopardy, but the prosecutor argued that Aleman was never in much "jeopardy," because he had bribed Judge Wilson by paying him $10,000 for the acquittal! The appellate court agreed with the prosecutor:

> Of particular importance here is that "jeopardy denotes risk. In the constitutional sense, jeopardy describes the risk that is traditionally associated with a criminal prosecution." *Breed v. Jones*, 421 U.S. 519, 528 (1975). The word "acquittal" invokes no talismanic protection; courts are duty-bound to examine the substance of the claim. A court may not apply rigid or mechanical rules in interpreting the double jeopardy clause.

> Aleman's argument for dismissal of the instant indictments is based essentially upon double jeopardy's emphasis on finality, urging that "an acquittal is an acquittal," citing cases to establish this "absolute" constitutional hypothesis. Several cases do state broadly that a verdict of acquittal cannot be reviewed without putting a defendant twice in jeopardy; however, none of them involve any fraud on behalf of defendants or the lower courts.

> Fairness and finality to both parties are integral components of double jeopardy. The State also must be provided with at least "one fair opportunity to offer whatever proof" it can assemble. See *Burks v. U.S.*, 437 U.S. 1, 16 (1978).

> The protections afforded by double jeopardy are not as absolute and conclusive as Aleman suggests; exceptions are recognized and applied when appropriate. Two such exceptions are relevant to the present case: first, a sham trial, which results in an acquittal because the State does not submit evidence, cannot be considered jeopardy. *People v. Deems*, 81 Ill.2d 384 (1980). In *Deems*, the circuit court denied the State's motion to dismiss and held trial. The State presented no evidence at trial and even admitted that defendant did not commit the pending charge but sought to indict defendant for a different crime. Although the circuit court acquitted defendant, the *Deems* court held that jeopardy had not attached to defendant's case although the trial ended in an "acquittal," because the proceeding bore none of those characteristics except the label. The *Deems* court, therefore, found that the first "trial" was a sham because "defendant was at no time in danger of being found guilty of any offense."

> The second relevant exception to the absolutism of double jeopardy is fraud or collusion. The circuit court's interim ruling in the case *sub judice* correctly noted that "a judgment of acquittal procured by a defendant through fraud is a nullity and does not put him in jeopardy." That jeopardy cannot attach to proceedings infected with fraud or collusion is ineluctable.
> * * * *

> Similarly, the common law supports the State's contention that a defendant who was acquitted due to fraud or collusion was never placed in jeopardy and, therefore, could be reprosecuted. Fraudulent actions by defendants have been recognized historically as exceptions to the consti-

tutional protections afforded by double jeopardy principles.[5] See *State v. Brown*, 16 Conn. 54 (1843); *State v. Jones*, 7 Ga. 422 (1849); *State v. Bell*, 81 N.C. 551 (1879); *State v. Howell*, 220 S.C. 178, 66 S.E.2d 701 (1951); *State v. Johnson*, 248 S.C. 153 (1966).

Did Aleman's actions in the case *sub judice* rise to the level of fraud or collusion such that he was not subjected to "the risk that is traditionally associated with a criminal prosecution"? The answer must be in the affirmative, considering analogous circumstances. * * * *

Given his involvement in the bribery of Judge Wilson in order to procure an acquittal in his 1977 murder trial, we conclude that Aleman clearly was not subject to the risk normally associated with a criminal prosecution. The principles of double jeopardy do not bar the instant reindictment and reprosecution.

By bribing the judge, Aleman prevented a fair "resolution" of the first proceeding.

The full story of Harry Aleman's escapades is told in Maurice Possley & Rick Kogan, *Everybody Pays: Two Men, One Murder and the Price of Truth* (Penguin Putnam, 2001). See also Rudstein, *Double Jeopardy and the Fraudulently Obtained Acquittal*, 60 Mo.L.Rev. 607 (1995).

10. A defense attorney launched a valiant (but vain) double jeopardy challenge in *U.S. v. Asher*, 96 F.3d 270 (7th Cir.1996). Tommy Asher participated in a large car theft ring. He was indicted for conspiracy, pleaded guilty, and went to prison. On his release, he rejoined *the same ring*, and was *again* indicted for conspiracy. His lawyer moved to dismiss the indictment, claiming double jeopardy, and arguing that Asher had *already* been convicted for *that* conspiracy:

To support his claim of double jeopardy, Asher relies almost exclusively on the test first set forth in *Blockburger v. United States*, 284 U.S. 299, 304 (1932). The *Blockburger* or "same elements" test "inquires whether each offense contains an element not contained in the other; if not, they are the 'same offense' and double jeopardy bars additional punishment and successive prosecution." *United States v. Dixon*, 509 U.S. 688, 696 (1993). Asher has failed to recognize, however, that by its very terms the *Blockburger* test applies only where "the same act or transaction constitutes a violation of two distinct statutory provisions." 284 U.S. at 304. In this situation, the test is used as a rule of statutory construction to determine "whether Congress intended to impose multiple punishment for a single act which violates several statutory provisions." *Albernaz v. United States*, 450 U.S. 333, 338 (1981).

At issue in this case, however, is not whether different statutory provisions should be considered the same offense. Asher was convicted in 1990 for violating the conspiracy statute, and the current indictment charges him under the same statute. Yet to succeed on a double jeopardy claim, a defendant must demonstrate that the prosecutions are for the same offense both "in law" and "in fact." Thus the relevant question in this

---

[5] The State correctly maintains that the fraud in the instant case is unlike perjury. A perjurer is subject to cross-examination and impeachment; fraud is far more pernicious because the outcome is predetermined, regardless of the evidence presented at trial. * * * *

case is whether the two conspiracy charges are the same "in fact," i.e., whether Asher is being prosecuted twice for the same conduct. * * * *

Because the essence of a conspiracy is an agreement to commit a crime, "a determination of whether the Government can prosecute on more than one conspiracy rests on whether there exists more than one agreement." *United States v. Chiattello*, 804 F.2d 415, 418 (7th Cir.1986). We have therefore held that the Double Jeopardy Clause prohibits the government from arbitrarily subdividing a conspiracy and instituting multiple prosecutions for a single illegal agreement. Yet the government in the current case has not arbitrarily subdivided a single conspiracy. Rather, Asher entered into a new agreement to commit a crime when he decided to rejoin the stolen vehicle ring following his release from prison. Undoubtedly, Congress could have chosen to punish rejoining a conspiracy in addition to punishing the original conspiracy without running afoul of the Double Jeopardy Clause. Asher's reentry into the conspiracy was a distinct act that could, consistently with the Double Jeopardy Clause, expose him to a new prosecution despite his prior conviction for participating in the same conspiracy.

As aptly expressed by the Supreme Court, "one who insists that the music stop and the piper be paid at a particular point must at least have stopped dancing himself before he may seek such an accounting." *Garrett v U.S.*, 471 U.S. 773, 790 (1985). Asher's return to his criminal behavior after his original conviction therefore leads us to conclude that the conspiracy charge in the instant case does not offend the Double Jeopardy Clause.

COMMONWEALTH v. BALOG
Pennsylvania Superior Court
576 A.2d 1092 (1990)

DEL SOLE, JUDGE:

In this case, we are asked to decide whether the trial court abused its discretion when it ordered a mistrial, over defense counsel's objections, as a result of Appellant/Defendant's statement that his co-conspirator had been found not guilty in an earlier trial. Because we find that there was no "manifest necessity" to order a mistrial, we reverse the trial court's denial of Appellant's motion to dismiss, and order the instant action dismissed on the basis that Appellant's re-prosecution would violate the Double Jeopardy provisions of the United States and Pennsylvania Constitutions.

Appellant, James Edward Balog, was charged with rape, corruption of minors, involuntary deviate sexual intercourse, indecent assault, and criminal conspiracy to commit these crimes. An alleged accomplice, Charles Belch, was charged with the same offenses. At his earlier, separate trial, a jury convicted Mr. Belch of corruption of minors and acquitted him of the other offenses.

Mr. Balog testified at trial that he had just briefly met the alleged victim, Marlene Hackney, at Charles Belch's house during a New Year's Eve party. He also stated that he had attended several other parties that evening where he had been drinking heavily, and then returned to Mr. Belch's house where he fell asleep on the couch. On cross-examination he was asked about certain inconsistencies between this account of his activities and a prior statement he made to State Trooper Fuller. Assistant District Attorney Heneks asked:

Q: Now, Mr. Balog, again I will ask you the question, did Trooper Fuller ask you anything in regard to Marlene Hackney?

A: I don't believe he did. He just said that she made some allegations.

Q: And in response to that, did you tell him that you don't recall messing with the girl?

A: I told him I don't recall.

Q: That's right.

A: That's what I told him.

Q: Well, isn't that, in fact, a different statement than I don't recall messing with the girl?

A: I can't tell you exactly what I told him on that day.

Q: But you're not quarreling with Trooper Fuller putting that information down that you don't recall messing with the girl?

A: He could have put down anything that he wanted.

Q: And are you saying that you said that?

A: I don't recall what I said. It has been 15 or 16 months ago.

Q: But if I understand, you are not really denying that either?

A: Of course, I am denying it. I didn't say I did anything with her. Charlie was not guilty; why should I be found guilty?

At this point the Commonwealth moved for a mistrial, and the defense objected stating that to a declare a mistrial at this time would be highly prejudicial to the defendant, and that the statement was just a spontaneous response from a layman who was not familiar with trial procedure. Nevertheless, the court ruled that the statement that Charles Belch was not guilty was highly prejudicial to the Commonwealth and granted a mistrial.

Following the discharge of the jury, Appellant moved for dismissal of the information claiming that the trial judge abused his discretion in granting a mistrial, and alternatively, that the conspiracy charges against the Appellant should be dismissed because of the acquittal of the alleged co-conspirator on the same charges. The trial court denied this motion holding that there was manifest necessity to grant the mistrial. It stated, "for defendant to blurt out that since Belch was not guilty why should he be found guilty was certainly prejudicial to the Commonwealth".

Pennsylvania Rule of Criminal Procedure 1118(b) provides that: "When an event prejudicial to the defendant occurs during trial only the defendant may move for a mistrial; the motion shall be made when the event is disclosed. Otherwise, the trial judge may declare a mistrial only for reasons of manifest necessity."

Since Justice Story's 1824 opinion in *United States v. Perez*, 6 L.Ed. 165, 9 Wheat. 579, 580, it has been well settled that the question whether under the Double Jeopardy Clause there can be a new trial after a mistrial has been declared without the defendant's request or consent depends on where there is a manifest necessity for the mistrial, or the ends of public justice would otherwise be defeated. *Commonwealth v. Bartolomucci*, 468 Pa. 338 (1976). "Where the judge, acting without the defendant's consent aborts the proceeding, the defendant has been deprived of his valued right to have his trial completed by a particular tribunal." *United States v. Jorn*, 400 U.S. 470, 484 (1971).

Reprosecution and the subjection of an individual to the hazard of trial and possible conviction more than once for an alleged offense, is only "grudgingly allowed." *United States v. Wilson*, 420 U.S. 332, 343 (1975), cited in *Commonwealth v. Williams*, 373 Pa.Super. 270 (1988). "The underlying idea, one that is deeply ingrained in at least the Anglo-American system of jurisprudence, is that the state with all its resources and power should not be allowed to make repeated attempts to convict an individual for an alleged offense." *Id.* at 273.[*] In determining whether the circumstances surrounding the declaration of a mistrial constitute manifest necessity, we apply the standards established by both Pennsylvania and federal decisions.

The *Perez* doctrine of manifest necessity stands as a command to trial judges not to declare a mistrial without the defendant's consent until a scrupulous exercise of judicial discretion leads to the conclusion that a termination of the trial is manifestly necessary. Failure to consider if there are less drastic alternatives to a mistrial creates doubt about the propriety of the exercise of the trial judge's discretion and is grounds for barring retrial because it indicates that the court failed to properly consider the defendant's significant interest in whether or not to take the case from the jury.

It is well established that any doubt relative to the existence of manifest necessity should be resolved in favor of the defendant. Therefore, the failure of the court to consider less drastic alternatives before declaring a mistrial, which we have said creates doubt about the propriety of the exercise of the trial judge's discretion, may bar retrial because of double jeopardy protections.

---

[*] Ed. — In *Arizona v. Washington*, 434 U.S. 497 (1978), the Supreme Court elaborated on this point:

Because jeopardy attaches before the judgment becomes final, the constitutional protection also embraces the defendant's "valued right to have his trial completed by a particular tribunal." * * * * The reasons why this "valued right" merits constitutional protection are worthy of repetition. Even if the first trial is not completed, a second prosecution may be grossly unfair. It increases the financial and emotional burden on the accused, prolongs the period in which he is stigmatized by an unresolved accusation of wrongdoing, * * * and may even enhance the risk that an innocent defendant may be convicted. The danger of such unfairness to the defendant exists whenever a trial is aborted before it is completed. * * * * Consequently, as a general rule, the prosecutor is entitled to one, and only one, opportunity to require an accused to stand trial.

Unlike the situation in which the trial has ended in an acquittal or conviction, retrial is not automatically barred when a criminal proceeding is terminated without finally resolving the merits of the charges against the accused. Because of the variety of circumstances that may make it necessary to discharge a jury before a trial is concluded, and because those circumstances do not invariably create unfairness to the accused, his valued right to have the trial concluded by a particular tribunal is sometimes subordinate to the public interest in affording the prosecutor one full and fair opportunity to present his evidence to an impartial jury. Yet in view of the importance of the right, and the fact that it is frustrated by any mistrial, the prosecutor must shoulder the burden of justifying the mistrial if he is to avoid the double jeopardy bar. His burden is a heavy one. The prosecutor must demonstrate "manifest necessity" for any mistrial declared over the objection of the defendant.

Our supreme court has intentionally avoided establishing a catalog of situations in which a mistrial is dictated by manifest necessity, and has instead stated that each case must "turn on the particular facts". *Commonwealth v. Bolden*, 472 Pa. 602, 638 (1977). However, there are certain circumstances in which the courts commonly grant a mistrial for manifest necessity. The illness of the presiding judge which is expected to delay trial for a significant period (two weeks or more), is one of those circumstances, *Commonwealth v. Robson*, 461 Pa. 615 (1975). However, the most frequently encountered circumstance constituting manifest necessity, and thus justifying discharging a jury without placing the defendant twice in jeopardy, is the inability of the jury to agree on a verdict such that the jury is hopelessly deadlocked. *Commonwealth v. Kivlin*, 267 Pa.Super. 270. In such cases a mistrial is the natural result of the practical inability of the original tribunal to complete the trial.

Nevertheless, if there is any doubt that a deadlocked jury exists, then manifest necessity for a mistrial is not present. Thus, in *Bartolomucci*, where the trial court failed to inquire directly of the jury, either individually or through the foreman, about its inability to agree, our supreme court held that the declaration of a mistrial was an improper exercise of discretion. Such an inquiry would have provided greater certainty about the hopelessness of breaking that deadlock, or the possibility of overcoming the impasse by further deliberations, and therefore the necessity for the mistrial was open to doubt.

In other cases where findings of manifest necessity were predicated upon an uncorroborated and therefore doubtful assertion that a Commonwealth witness was ill, our courts have ruled that the trial court did not have the facts to justify subjecting appellants to the continuing ordeal of a pending trial. *Commonwealth v. Ferguson*, 446 Pa. 24 (1971).

Similarly, the existence of doubts about whether it was necessary to terminate a trial when a juror was released from sequestration, resulted in a holding that the declaration of a mistrial was not manifestly necessary. *Walton v. Aytch*, 466 Pa. 172, 182 (1976). In this case, during the course of the trial, the trial judge decided that the jury had to be sequestered because of the surrounding publicity. Two of the jurors asked to be excused because of the hardship this would cause, with the result that there were no alternate jurors available. Subsequently, the judge was informed that one of the twelve remaining jurors was very distressed because she had been unable to find a baby-sitter for her children. As a result, without consulting either counsel, the trial judge allowed the juror to go home without requesting her to return the next day, and the trial was aborted.

Our Supreme Court ruled in *Aytch* that the propriety of the declaration of a mistrial was not free from doubt. The trial court could have at least attempted to contact counsel, particularly the defense counsel, to see if they had any suggestions about what to do in this situation. This would have indicated that the decision to terminate the trial was tempered by a consideration of the defendant's interest in having his trial concluded by the tribunal in which it was initiated. Furthermore, the court failed to consider the less drastic alternatives of sending a court officer with the juror to maintain the sequestration, or lifting the sequestration order.

When a trial court acts too hastily and fails to consider reasonable alternatives to a mistrial, the United States Supreme Court and the Pennsylvania Appellate Courts have reached the same conclusion, that retrial would violate Double

Jeopardy Rights. In *Commonwealth v. Bradley*, 311 Pa.Super. 330 (1983), we ruled that the trial court's hasty decision to grant a mistrial based on evidence that a private conversation had taken place between defense counsel and a Commonwealth witness during lunch recess, which interrupted the witness' direct testimony, constituted an abuse of discretion. The trial court failed to consider the less drastic alternative of allowing defense counsel to cross-examine the witness about the substance of the conversation, and the context in which certain ambiguous statements were made.

In *Jorn*, supra, the Supreme Court ruled that the trial judge abused his discretion in discharging the jury when, despite assurances by both the first witness and prosecuting attorney that the five taxpayers involved in the litigation had all been warned of their constitutional rights, the judge refused to permit them to testify. The judge was unwilling to listen to the prosecutor's explanation, cutting him off in midstream, and acted so abruptly in discharging the jury, that had counsel been disposed to suggest a reasonable alternative, such as a granting a continuance, there would have been no opportunity to do so. The trial court's failure to scrupulously exercise its discretion when ordering a mistrial, led the Court to conclude that reprosecution would subject the defendant to double jeopardy.

Finally, in *Commonwealth v. Hatten*, 344 Pa.Super. 362 (1985), we held that a prosecutor's disclosure in a joint trial of defendant and her co-defendant, that co-defendant had threatened the complaining witness, did not justify a declaration of a mistrial, when the mistrial was requested only by the co-defendant and the defendant requested a severance of the two cases in order to proceed with the trial. Apart from failing to consider the alternatives to declaring a mistrial, this court noted that disclosure of the defendant's threat would not have necessarily required reversal on appeal had appellant been convicted. Therefore, it was held that a mistrial was not manifestly necessary, and the trial court should have severed the two cases.

Applying the principles derived from the preceding cases to the facts in this case, we must conclude that the trial judge abused his discretion in declaring a mistrial and discharging the jury. The trial court admits that the defendant "blurted out" that his co-conspirator was found not guilty under the pressure of cross-examination, and therefore, although it was Appellant's conduct which caused the court's actions, it was not intentional conduct designed to provoke a mistrial and then a dismissal for reasons of double jeopardy.

We believe that our focus on intentional conduct designed to provoke a mistrial is justified by reference to the case law concerning mistrials granted on the motion of the defendant. When a defendant moves for a mistrial, the request ordinarily is assumed to remove any barrier to reprosecution, even when the defendant's motion results from prosecutorial or judicial error. *Commonwealth v. Bolden*, 472 Pa. 602, 638 (1977). However, when the conduct giving rise to the successful motion for a mistrial was intended to provoke the defendant into moving for a mistrial, then retrial is barred. *Commonwealth v. Simons*, 514 Pa.10 (1987). Thus, if the defendant moves for a mistrial because of intentional prosecutorial misconduct designed to provoke a mistrial in order to secure a more favorable opportunity to convict, then retrial is barred.

Similarly, if the conduct of a defense witness is intentionally designed to provoke a successful mistrial request by the Commonwealth in order to secure a more favorable outcome, then retrial is not barred.

Here, there is no evidence of intentional conduct. Mr. Balog was under pressure, and blurted out his statement. As a layperson, he did not know the rules of evidence, and did not know he was not allowed to refer to the outcome of different, though related, trial.

Furthermore, we cannot agree with the trial court's holding that Mr. Balog's statement was certainly prejudicial. Although, there are no cases discussing the prejudicial effect of a defense witness revealing that a co-conspirator had been acquitted, (all such appeals by the Commonwealth would be barred by double jeopardy), there is some case law discussing the prejudicial effect of revealing that a co-conspirator had been convicted. In *Commonwealth v. Howard*, 375 Pa.Super. 43 (1988), this court held that repeated references by the prosecution during closing argument to the fact that a co-conspirator had been convicted on the same evidence by another jury, did not warrant a new trial. Therefore, since this more egregious and intentional series of references to a co-conspirator's prior conviction is not per se reversible error, requiring a new trial, it would seem logical that reference to a co-conspirator's prior acquittal does not per se require a mistrial. As in *Hatten, supra*, the fact that the defendant's error would not necessarily warrant reversal upon appeal, is further evidence that the declaration of a mistrial was not manifestly necessary.

Most importantly, however, the trial court's failure to consider the less drastic alternative of curative instructions shows that the court did not adequately consider the importance to the defendant of being able, once and for all, to have his trial completed by a particular tribunal. *Jorn, supra*, 400 U.S. at 484. This court has stated that a court should not presume the likelihood of prejudice and dismiss a prospective juror for cause, when that juror is aware, through pre-trial publicity, of a previous mistrial. *Commonwealth v. Hashem*, 363 Pa.Super. 111 (1987). Analogously, a trial court may not presume that a jury will disregard judicial instructions admonishing them to disregard improper evidence of a previous acquittal of a co-conspirator.

Failure to consider alternatives before declaring a mistrial raises doubt as to the existence of manifest necessity to terminate the trial. This doubt must be resolved in favor of Appellant who opposed such a declaration. Therefore we hold that the trial court abused its discretion in declaring a mistrial, and we grant Appellant's motion to dismiss this case.

This action is dismissed, as retrial would be violative of Appellant's rights under the Double Jeopardy Clause of the United States and Pennsylvania Constitutions.

HUDOCK, JUDGE, dissenting.

Respectfully, I must dissent. While I share the majority's reverence for the Double Jeopardy Clause and fully understand its historical basis, I do not believe that when a defendant himself frustrates the quest for truth, which is what a trial is supposed to be, he should be rewarded by discharge. I believe that appellant's conduct here, whether designed to do so or not, so skewed the truth seeking process that manifest necessity for a mistrial existed.

In *Arizona v. Washington*, 434 U.S. 497 (1978) the U.S. Supreme Court held that where defense counsel made improper and prejudicial comments during his opening statement, a mistrial was properly declared and retrial not barred. The Court stated:

> Unlike the situation in which the trial has ended in an acquittal or conviction, retrial is not automatically barred when a criminal proceeding is terminated without resolving the merits of the charges against the accused. Because of the variety of circumstances that may make it necessary to discharge a jury before a trial is concluded, and because those circumstances do not invariably create unfairness to the accused, his valued right to have the trial concluded by a particular tribunal is sometimes subordinate to the public interest in affording the prosecutor one full and fair opportunity to present his evidence to an impartial jury, the prosecutor must demonstrate "manifest necessity" for the mistrial declared over the objection of the defendant. [*Id.* at 505.]

The Court went on to state that the words "manifest necessity" do not describe a standard that can be applied mechanically or without attention to the particular problem confronting the trial judge, and that the word "necessity" cannot be interpreted literally. Rather, a "high degree" of necessity is required before a mistrial could be appropriate over defendant's objection. The Court further noted that the difficulty which led to the mistrial in that case "falls in an area where the trial judge's determination is entitled to special respect". *Id.* at 510.

The majority points out that there were other alternatives open to the trial judge, such as a curative instruction. The Supreme Court in *Arizona v. Washington* recognized that some trial judges may have proceeded with the trial after giving the jury appropriate cautionary instructions, but the court refused to hold that the availability of such an alternative precluded a mistrial being declared on the grounds of "manifest necessity". The court reiterated that in a literal sense the mistrial was not "necessary" but that "the overriding interest in the evenhanded administration of justice requires that we accord the highest degree of respect to the trial judge's evaluation of the likelihood that the impartiality of one or more jurors may have been affected by the improper comment of defense counsel". *Id.* at 511.

In the case *sub judice*, the entire record must be read to appreciate the seriousness of defendant's unsolicited comment that ". . . Charlie was not guilty. Why should I be found guilty?" The trial court's opinion and the majority opinion here set forth only twenty or so lines of the transcript of trial testimony preceding the challenged remarks. In that context, I agree that the remark is ambiguous, if not meaningless, for the identity of "Charlie" and his connection to the case is not made known. However, after reading the entire record, it becomes abundantly clear who "Charlie" is — he is the conspirator about whom the victim testifies at great length and in graphic detail. She tells how "Charlie" held her while appellant raped and sodomized her and how appellant held her while "Charlie" did the same. No juror could have heard this, and testimony about "Charlie" from other witnesses, without knowing that appellant was advising them of the fact that "Charlie" had been acquitted of these charges. This is especially prejudicial since "Charlie" testified he had consensual sex with the victim on the evening in question. Under these circumstances, I would give great deference to the trial judge who "saw and heard the jurors during their *voir dire* examination", who is "most familiar" with the evidence and background of the case", who has "listened to the tone of the argument" and has "observed the apparent reaction of the jurors", and who is far more "conversant with the factors relevant to the determination than any reviewing court can possibly be". *Id.* at 513–514.

Of course, as *Arizona v. Washington* instructs, paying great deference to a trial court's decision to grant a mistrial does not mean that his decision is beyond being questioned. He still must exercise "sound discretion" in declaring a mistrial, recognizing "the importance to the defendant of being able, once and for all, to conclude his confrontation with society through the verdict of a tribunal he might believe to be favorably disposed to his fate." *Id.* at 514.

Here the court considered arguments from both counsel before making its decision. In its opinion in support of the order denying defendant's motion to dismiss, the court set forth the reasons for its decision. It believed that the prosecutor had not provoked or in any way suggested the making of the statement by defendant, and that the statement was highly prejudicial to the Commonwealth. The court further noted that "even with curative instructions from the court, the fact than an alleged accomplice/co-conspirator was found not guilty could not be erased from the jurors' minds". Thus it is clear that the court did consider and reject the only alternative to a mistrial under the facts presented, a curative instruction. While the court did not take an evening to ponder and research the matter as the trial court did in *Arizona v. Washington*, it did not need that amount of time to consider the only realistic option available. * * * *

I would hold that since appellant himself poisoned the waters of truth, he should not benefit from his wrongdoing. Neither party has a right to have his case decided by a jury which may be tainted by bias; in these circumstances, "the public's interest in fair trials designed to end in just judgments" must prevail over the defendant's "valued right" to have his trial concluded before the first jury impaneled. *Arizona v. Washington*, 434 U.S. at 516.

The trial court here properly declared a mistrial for reasons of manifest necessity, and, accordingly, I dissent.

Notes from Carmelita:

1. *What constitutes "manifest necessity"?*

In *Collins v. Commonwealth*, 589 N.E.2d 287 (Mass.1992), the prosecutor's father-in-law died during the trial, making the prosecutor unavailable for a week, and the District Attorney moved for a mistrial. Defense counsel opposed the motion, requesting the court to ask the jurors if they were willing to come back in a week and resume the trial. He argued: "We have already gone through a fair amount of painstaking care picking the jury yesterday, and I believe it's a good cross section that we have chosen, and so I would ask that. I think that that would be an alternative least restrictive on Mr. Collins' rights to a jury that has already been picked and impaneled and sworn." The judge granted the motion, as a week is "just too long to keep a jury of 14 people who may have other plans", and some may not show up after the week off. Before a retrial could occur, defendant moved to dismiss, claiming double jeopardy. The Massachusetts Supreme Judicial Court held that double jeopardy barred the retrial, because the record failed to show any "manifest necessity" for granting the mistrial. "The judge should have inquired into the feasibility of the juror's returning one week later."

In *U.S. v. Pavloyianis*, 996 F.2d 1467 (2nd Cir.1993), defendant was charged with conspiracy to distribute heroin. After his trial and conviction, the prosecutor revealed that one of the key prosecution witnesses had committed perjury. The prosecutor consented to a new trial, but defendant demanded dismissal, arguing that a new trial would be barred by double jeopardy. After noting that the Supreme Court had held that double jeopardy should apply where the prosecutor engages in misconduct with the purpose of "goading" defendant into moving for a mistrial, the court held that this should be extended to a situation where the prosecutor engages in misconduct "with the intention of denying the defendant an opportunity to win an acquittal" that the prosecutor believed was likely. Here, it was not clear that the prosecutor knew that the testimony was perjured at the time it was given, and in any event, there was no evidence that the prosecutor believed that an acquittal was likely when he offered the testimony. Therefore, defendant was entitled to a new trial, but not a dismissal.

In *U.S. v. Allen*, 755 A.2d 402 (D.C. 2000), Allen was charged with possession of cocaine with intent to distribute. The judge instructed the jury on this charge and on the lesser-included offense of possession of cocaine. The jury convicted Allen of the lesser charge and told the judge that it was unable to reach a unanimous verdict on the greater charge. The trial judge ruled that a retrial on the greater charge was barred by the prohibition against Double Jeopardy, but the appellate court reversed:

> Early in its double jeopardy jurisprudence, the Supreme Court concluded that if a jury convicts on some counts but is silent as to the others, the discharge of the jury is tantamount to an acquittal, but if the jury formally disagrees on the verdict for an offense, retrial is not precluded. *
> * * *
>
> Although the Supreme Court has not squarely ruled on the issue before us, involving retrial after the jury has expressed an inability to agree on the greater charge but has convicted on the lesser included charge, our review of the hung jury and implicit acquittal Supreme Court cases set forth above leads us to the conclusion * * * that Allen's case is controlled by the hung jury principles rather than those governing an implicit acquittal. In the implicit acquittal cases, the jury is completely silent as to its verdict on the particular charge at issue — that is, there is no record of the jury's inability to agree on that charge. In the hung jury cases, the jury's inability to agree expressly appears on the record. Here, the jury was not silent; it reported its inability to agree twice.

In *State v. Witsell*, 53 P.2d 1248 (Kan.App. 2002), the trial court issued a pretrial ruling barring the mention of a polygraph test taken by the defendant, but at trial Detective Shackelford mentioned the polygraph while being cross-examined by defense counsel. The trial court on its own declared a mistrial, finding that the error could not be cured by a jury instruction, because the jury would assume that defendant flunked the polygraph test (if he had passed, the prosecutor would not have proceeded with the prosecution). The court held that a new trial would violate the prohibition against double jeopardy:

> When a mistrial is granted without the consent of the defendant, there must have been a "manifest necessity" for the mistrial in order for a retrial to be permissible under double jeopardy concepts.

In the present case, defendant and the State agree the trial court, under the test announced above, properly declared a mistrial. We need not address this question further.

But for the manifest necessity doctrine to apply to allow retrial, the fault for the mistrial cannot lie at the feet of the prosecution or the judge. There simply can be no "manifest necessity" for prosecutorial or judicial misconduct.

In the present case, the trial court found, as a matter of fact, Detective Shackelford was "so connected with the prosecution of the case that it made a finding that *as an agent of the prosecutor*, that is the goading of the defendant into a mistrial." The trial court found the detective to be an agent of the State/prosecution. This is a finding of fact to which we give the trial court great deference.

So far as we can determine, whether police misconduct precipitating a mistrial should be imputed to a prosecutor is a question of first impression in this state.

Here, the trial court made a finding of fact that Detective Shackelford was an agent of the State. That finding is supported by adequate, though conflicting, evidence. The trial court understood the detective's personal, vested interest in the outcome of the case and her pride in obtaining a conviction. She conducted the investigation, interviewed witnesses, marshaled the evidence, and presented her case to the prosecutor.

Further, the trial court found Detective Shackelford, as the lead case detective, was uncomfortable with cross-examination and wished to terminate it and found factually she intentionally violated the order in limine and caused the mistrial.

In the context of an allegation the State violated *Brady v. Maryland*, 373 U.S. 83 (1963), our Supreme Court held the mere fact a prosecutor may not have had actual knowledge of evidence in the possession of law enforcement officials does not prevent imputation of that knowledge to the prosecutor in the interest of justice.

The reasoning of those cases applies to the present case. To allow a retrial would have the unfortunate effect of providing a mechanism whereby the State could get a second chance at the defendant when the first trial starts to "go bad" for the State or its witnesses.

Additionally, it would be fundamentally unfair to subject defendant to a second trial when the factually found intentional conduct of the lead investigator and one of the State's primary witnesses sabotages the proceedings. After all, the Double Jeopardy Clause protects a defendant against governmental actions intended to provoke a mistrial.

2. In *Burks v. U.S.*, 437 U.S. 1 (1978), Burks was convicted of bank robbery, but the appellate court reversed, holding that the evidence was insufficient to support the verdict. The appellate court remanded the case for possible retrial, but the Supreme Court held that double jeopardy would bar a retrial. While a retrial *is* permitted when the reversal is for "trial error," it is *not* permitted when the reversal is for *insufficiency of the evidence*:

Various rationales have been advanced to support the policy of allowing retrial to correct trial error, but in our view the most reasonable justification is this. It would be a high price indeed for society to pay were every accused granted immunity from punishment because of any defect sufficient to constitute reversible error in the proceedings leading to conviction. In short, reversal for trial error, as distinguished from evidentiary insufficiency, does not constitute a decision to the effect that the government has failed to prove its case. As such, it implies nothing with respect to the guilt or innocence of the defendant. Rather, it is a determination that a defendant has been convicted through a judicial process which is defective in some fundamental respect, e. g., incorrect receipt or rejection of evidence, incorrect instructions, or prosecutorial misconduct. When this occurs, the accused has a strong interest in obtaining a fair readjudication of his guilt free from error, just as society maintains a valid concern for insuring that the guilty are punished.

The same cannot be said when a defendant's conviction has been overturned due to a failure of proof at trial, in which case the prosecution cannot complain of prejudice, for it has been given one fair opportunity to offer whatever proof it could assemble. Moreover, such an appellate reversal means that the government's case was so lacking that it should not have even been submitted to the jury. Since we necessarily afford absolute finality to a jury's verdict of acquittal — no matter how erroneous its decision — it is difficult to conceive how society has any greater interest in retrying a defendant when, on review, it is decided as a matter of law that the jury could not properly have returned a verdict of guilty. * * * *

While this is not the appropriate occasion to re-examine in detail the standards for appellate reversal on grounds of insufficient evidence, it is apparent that such a decision will be confined to cases where the prosecution's failure is clear. Given the requirements for entry of a judgment of acquittal, the purposes of the Clause would be negated were we to afford the government an opportunity for the proverbial "second bite at the apple."

3. For more on double jeopardy, see George C. Thomas III, *Double Jeopardy: The History, The Law* (NYU Press, 1998); reviewed by Susan R. Klein, *Double Jeopardy's Demise*, 88 California Law Review 1001 (2000).

Chapter 12

SENTENCING

THE JUDGE'S ROLE IN SENTENCING

Suppose Dan is convicted of robbery. We have seen the many difficult legal issues that got us to the point of conviction. Now he must be sentenced, and this raises more issues.

The length and nature of Dan's sentence will affect his prospects for rehabilitation, how well society will be protected against his penchant for crime, how good an example we set which might deter others from committing crimes, and how his victims and other "court-watchers" will respect the criminal justice system.

But are these "legal" questions — or are they sociological, psychological, and political questions? Put another way, are judges really suited to decide them — and are lawyers really suited to argue them? One federal judge did not think so:

> Viewed as a group, the people who enter upon service as trial judges are somewhat elderly, more experienced than most lawyers in litigation, almost totally unencumbered by learning or experience relevant to sentencing, and inclined by temperament and circumstance toward the major orthodoxies. Nothing they had studied in law school touched our subject more than remotely. Probably a large majority had no contact, or trivial contact, with criminal proceedings of any kind during their years of practice. Those who had such exposure worked preponderantly on the prosecution side. Whether or not this produces a troublesome bias, the best that can be said is that prosecutors tend generally either to refrain altogether from taking positions on sentencing or to deal with the subject at a bargaining level somewhat removed from the plane of penological ideals.

> Thus qualified, the new judge may be discovered within days or weeks fashioning judgments of imprisonment for long years. No training, formal or informal, precedes the first of these awesome pronouncements. Such formal and intentional education, other than from the job itself, as may happen along the way is likely to be fleeting, random, anecdotal, and essentially trivial. Shop talk with fellow judges — at least in my experience on a court where the judges are numerous, convivial, and likely to talk shop in the court lunchroom and other gathering places — rarely lights on problems of sentencing. Because the sentence is not appealable except on rare and extraordinary grounds, there is little occasion for the kind of relatively organized reflection instigated by the reading of advance sheets. The experienced trial judge, then, is one who has imposed many sentences, improving, we would hope, from a course of solitary brooding and conversations with probation officers, consulting in the end himself as the final authority, and perhaps sinking deeper each year the footings of

premises that have never been tested by detached scrutiny or by open debate.

Given the sure combination of substantially unbounded discretion and decision-makers unrestrained by shared professional standards, it is not astonishing that the commonplace worry in any discussion of sentencing concerns "disparity." The factual basis for the worry is clear and huge; nobody doubts that essentially similar people in large numbers receive widely divergent sentences for essentially similar or identical crimes. The causes of the problem are equally clear: judges vary widely in their explicit views and "principles" affecting sentencing; they vary, too, in the accidents of birth and biography generating the guilts, the fears, and the rages that affect almost all of us at times and in ways we often cannot know. The judge who reports there is no surge of emotion when he imposes a stiff sentence is likely to be mistaken, unperceptive, or a person of alarmingly flat affect. It is unnecessary, though not irrelevant, to frighten ourselves with the statistical probability and direct personal knowledge that some percentage of judges may be psychotic. It is disturbing enough that a charged encounter like the sentencing proceeding, while it is the gravest of legal matters, should turn so arbitrarily upon the variegated passions and prejudices of individual judges. [Frankel, *Lawlessness in Sentencing*, 41 Cin.L.Rev. 1, 6–8 (1972)]

Judge Frankel then quoted Barnes, *The Story of Punishment — A Record of Man's Inhumanity To Man*, 265–266 (1930):

The diagnosis and treatment of the criminal is a highly technical medical and sociological problem for which the lawyer is rarely any better fitted than a real estate agent or a plumber. We shall ultimately come to admit that society has been as unfortunate in handing over criminals to lawyers and judges in the past as it once was in entrusting medicine to shamans and astrologers, and surgery to barbers. A hundred years ago we allowed lawyers and judges to have the same control of the insane classes as they still exert over the criminal groups, but we now recognize that insanity is a highly diversity and complex medical problem which we entrust to properly trained experts in the field of neurology and psychiatry. We may hope that in another hundred years the treatment of the criminal will be equally thoroughly and willingly submitted to medical and sociological experts.

"DETERMINATE" AND "INDETERMINATE" SENTENCING SYSTEMS

Consider two possible sentencing statutes. First, "The judge shall sentence a person convicted of armed robbery to whatever sentence the judge deems appropriate." Second, "The sentence for armed robbery shall in all cases be exactly 5 years."

The first is an extreme "indeterminate" sentencing statute: from reading the statute, you have no idea what sentence Dan will receive. The second is an extreme "determinate" sentencing statute: from reading the statute, you can determine exactly what sentence every armed robber will receive.

The first statute has the virtue of enabling the judge to tailor Dan's sentence to Dan. If Dan has no prior record, committed the robbery because he was desperate for money to support his family, and did not hurt anyone, the judge will not want to sentence him as harshly as a career robber who routinely bops his victims on the head. The statute lets him do this.

The second statute doesn't. But it has another virtue: uniformity. Under the first statute, a person in Dan's situation might receive probation from Judge X, 10 years in prison from Judge Y, and anything else from Judge Z. The apparent unfairness of this "disparity" will draw complaints from both convicts and the public about the haphazardness of the system.

Over the years, various jurisdictions have flipped back and forth between indeterminate and determinate sentencing systems. Seldom, however, have the statutes been as extreme as the above examples. A typical indeterminate statute will allow the judge to select a sentence within a range, e.g., "1 to 5 years", and a typical determinate statute will limit the judge to "2, 3, or 4 years, depending on consideration of the following list of factors:. . . ."

Often, the contest between determinate and indeterminate systems reflects a contest between branches of government. Under an indeterminate system, the judiciary controls sentencing. (Sometimes, however, *an administrative agency* will share or control the sentencing decision.) And then — usually after some judge imposes a sentence perceived by the public as "too light" in a notorious case — the legislature takes over, imposing its own "determinate" sentences and depriving "soft-hearted" judges of discretion. This often has the practical effect of transferring sentencing power to the *prosecutor*, who has almost total discretion to select the *charge*, which in turn will determine the *sentence* (if the defendant is convicted of that charge). A prosecutor who has enough evidence to convict a defendant of robbery might choose (perhaps via a plea bargain) to charge him instead with larceny, possession of stolen property, or some other related lesser charge — thereby controlling the sentence under a determinate sentencing system.

THE FEDERAL SENTENCING GUIDELINES

Federal sentencing was formerly done under indeterminate statutes, giving federal judges broad powers. This resulted in a "lawless" sentencing system: federal judges used broad discretion that was virtually unreviewable by appellate courts, and there were wide disparities in sentences different judges would give to similarly-situated defendants. The public knew little of this system, but several law professors found it quite disturbing — they were used to a legal system with reasoned opinions, reported cases, and consistency. After campaigning for reform, they got it — but they also got something they didn't expect. Once sentencing was placed on the political agenda of Congress, politicians (reflecting the desires of their constituents) substantially increased the *length* of federal sentences. The reformers said, "It's unfair to give one person one year and another ten years for the same crime," and the politicos responded, "You're right — they should both get 20!"

In 1984, Congress revamped the system, changed to determinate sentencing, and instructed the U.S. Sentencing Commission to promulgate Sentencing Guidelines. 18 U.S.C. §§ 3551 et.seq.; 28 U.S.C. §§ 991–998. The resulting Guidelines were held to be constitutional in *Mistretta v. U.S.*, 488 U.S. 361 (1989). The Supreme Court explained how the Guidelines came about:

For almost a century, the Federal Government employed in criminal cases a system of indeterminate sentencing. Statutes specified the penalties for crimes but nearly always gave the sentencing judge wide discretion to decide whether the offender should be incarcerated and for how long, whether he should be fined and how much, and whether some lesser restraint, such as probation, should be imposed instead of imprisonment or fine. This indeterminate-sentencing system was supplemented by the utilization of parole, by which an offender was returned to society under the "guidance and control" of a parole officer.

Both indeterminate sentencing and parole were based on concepts of the offender's possible, indeed probable, rehabilitation, a view that it was realistic to attempt to rehabilitate the inmate and thereby to minimize the risk that he would resume criminal activity upon his return to society. It obviously required the judge and the parole officer to make their respective sentencing and release decisions upon their own assessments of the offender's amenability to rehabilitation. As a result, the court and the officer were in positions to exercise, and usually did exercise, very broad discretion. This led almost inevitably to the conclusion on the part of a reviewing court that the sentencing judge "sees more and senses more" than the appellate court; thus, the judge enjoyed the "superiority of his nether position," for that court's determination as to what sentence was appropriate met with virtually unconditional deference on appeal. The decision whether to parole was also predictive and discretionary. The correction official possessed almost absolute discretion over the parole decision.

Historically, federal sentencing — the function of determining the scope and extent of punishment — never has been thought to be assigned by the Constitution to the exclusive jurisdiction of any one of the three Branches of government. Congress, of course, has the power to fix the sentence for a federal crime, and the scope of judicial discretion with respect to a sentence is subject to congressional control. Congress early abandoned fixed-sentence rigidity, however, and put in place a system of ranges within which the sentencer could choose the precise punishment. Congress delegated almost unfettered discretion to the sentencing judge to determine what the sentence should be within the customarily wide range so selected. This broad discretion was further enhanced by the power later granted the judge to suspend the sentence and by the resulting growth of an elaborate probation system. Also, with the advent of parole, Congress moved toward a "three-way sharing" of sentencing responsibility by granting correction personnel in the Executive Branch the discretion to release a prisoner before the expiration of the sentence imposed by the judge. Thus, under the indeterminate-sentence system, Congress defined the maximum, the judge imposed a sentence within the statutory range (which it usually could replace with probation), and the Executive Branch's parole official eventually determined the actual duration of imprisonment. Serious disparities in sentences, however, were common. Rehabilitation as a sound penological theory came to be questioned and, in any event, was regarded by some as an unattainable goal for most cases. In 1958, Congress authorized the creation of judicial sentencing institutes and joint councils, to formulate standards and criteria for sentencing. In 1973, the United

States Parole Board adopted guidelines that established a "customary range" of confinement. Congress in 1976 endorsed this initiative through the Parole Commission and Reorganization Act, 18 U.S.C. §§ 4201–4218, an attempt to envision for the Parole Commission a role, at least in part, to moderate the disparities in the sentencing practices of individual judges. That Act, however, did not disturb the division of sentencing responsibility among the three Branches. The judge continued to exercise discretion and to set the sentence within the statutory range fixed by Congress, while the prisoner's actual release date generally was set by the Parole Commission.

This proved to be no more than a way station. Fundamental and widespread dissatisfaction with the uncertainties and the disparities continued to be expressed. Congress had wrestled with the problem for more than a decade when, in 1984, it enacted the sweeping reforms that are at issue here. [Citations omitted.]

Many federal judges have been quite upset at this removal of their ability to tailor the sentence to the individual defendant — along with the substantially increased length of mandated sentences for many crimes. A few judges have been quite vocal on this matter.

UNITED STATES v. PATILLO
U.S. District Court, Central District of California
817 F.Supp. 839 (1993)

J. Spencer Letts, District Judge.

On April 14, 1992, the defendant Johnny Patillo pled guilty to a single count indictment that charged him with possession with intent to distribute approximately 680.7 grams of crack cocaine. 21 U.S.C. § 841(a)(1). On December 18, 1992, the court sentenced defendant, after orally making findings that it was compelled to impose a mandatory minimum sentence of ten years under 21 U.S.C. § 841(b)(1)(A). The Sentencing Guidelines called for a sentence of between 151 and 188 months (twelve years seven months to fifteen years), a range from which the court found departure appropriate. The court indicated that written findings would follow, which are set forth below.

I. Minimum Sentence

At least at the outset, this sentencing appeared to place me in the position of making the most difficult choice I have yet faced, between my judicial oath of office, which requires me to uphold the law as I understand it, and my conscience, which requires me to avoid intentional injustice. When I took defendant's plea of guilty in this case, he seemed to me to be the clearest possible example of everything that is wrong with guideline sentencing and statutorily imposed mandatory minimum sentences.

On January 16, 1992, defendant, a twenty-seven year old African-American man, brought a package containing approximately 681 grams of crack cocaine to a Federal Express office in Los Angeles and attempted to send the package to Dallas, Texas. According to defendant, he had never previously been involved in trafficking drugs, but had accepted a neighbor's offer of $500 to put the package in the mail. At the time, he was subject to extraordinary financial pressures, due to an accumulation of debt for student loans, credit cards, phone bills and rent. Defendant admits knowing that the package contained illegal drugs, but has steadfastly denied prior knowledge of the type of drug, or the amount of the drug the package contained. As far as the court can determine, defendant had never before been involved in any criminal activity. He had obtained a college education and held a steady job up until the time he was incarcerated.

The government's position is that the court cannot legally impose a sentence of less than ten years in this case, and it is correct. The ten year minimum is specifically mandated by a statute, 21 U.S.C. § 841(b)(1)(A), which has been upheld as constitutional by the Ninth Circuit Court of Appeals in decisions that bind this court. The court postponed sentencing several times in the hope of finding some reasoned basis for holding that precedent does not bind the court. This, however, has proved impossible. Defendant has argued that the mandatory minimum is unconstitutionally vague, that it is racially discriminatory, and that it violates due process and the Eighth Amendment. Ninth Circuit precedent rejects these arguments, and instead compels this court to apply the mandatory minimum. See *United States v. Shaw*, 936 F.2d 412, 416 (9th Cir.1991) (Section 841(b) is not unconstitutionally vague for failing to define "cocaine base"); *United States v. Harding*, 971 F.2d 410, 413 (9th Cir.1992) (Section 841(b)'s distinction between cocaine base and cocaine does not violate equal protection) (1993); *United States v. Hoyt*, 879 F.2d 505, 512–14 (9th Cir.1989) (ten year mandatory minimum for first time offenders required by 21 U.S.C. § 841(b)(1)(A) does not violate the Eighth Amendment's protection against cruel and unusual punishment or the Fifth Amendment's equal protection and due process guarantees).

I, however, will no longer apply this law without protest, and with no hope for change.

Statutory mandatory minimum sentences create injustice because the sentence is determined without looking at the particular defendant.[2] Under 21 U.S.C. § 841(b)(1)(A), the mandatory minimum sentence is triggered by two factors only: (1) the type of drug and (2) the amount of drug. In this case, it is the fact that the package defendant brought to Federal Express contained 681 grams of crack cocaine which raises this offense to one in which the minimum sentence is ten years, without possibility of parole. If the package contained a different narcotic, or a lesser quantity of the same substance, defendant might have been sentenced to straight probation.

By agreement with the government, defendant's plea of guilty in this case rested upon his admission that he delivered a package to Federal Express which contained approximately 681 grams of cocaine base, and that at the time he made the delivery, he knew that the package contained an illegal substance. That is all his plea of guilty entailed. Defendant did not admit to knowing that the substance in the envelope was cocaine base, or to knowing that the package contained 681 grams of crack. In fact,

---

[2] Other sentencing judges have similarly criticized the injustice they are forced to mete out in sentencing through the imposition of mandatory minimum sentences. The Honorable Jack Weinstein, for example, recently stated, "Injustice sometimes results from the rigid operation of the high mandatory minimum sentences contained in the federal drug laws. Until Congress reconsiders its minimum sentence policy — or the United States Attorney exercises a compassionate judgment — the court has no power to consider the injustice of minimum terms in individual cases." *United States v. Gaviria*, 804 F.Supp. 476, 480 (E.D.N.Y.1992).

he expressly denied any such knowledge.

Admittedly, the pre-sentence report ("PSR") filed by the Probation Office contains information which might cause one to speculate that defendant may have had a somewhat greater involvement in the business of drug trafficking than he has admitted. Any such information, however, is purely circumstantial. This court cannot form a reasoned conclusion based upon this information, and the government has made no effort to develop it. It has not been developed further because defendant's role in the business of drug trafficking is almost entirely irrelevant for sentencing purposes. The court considered information regarding the defendant's role in drug trafficking, but as explained below, only as a basis for departure.

The minimum ten year sentence to be served by defendant was determined by Congress before he ever committed a criminal act. Congress decided to hit the problem of drugs, as they saw it, with a sledgehammer, making no allowance for the circumstances of any particular case. Under this sledgehammer approach, it can make no difference whether defendant actually owned the drugs with which he was caught, or whether, at a time when he had an immediate need for cash, he was slickered into taking the risk of being caught with someone else's drugs. Under the statutory minimum, it can make no difference whether he is a life time criminal or a first time offender. Indeed, under this sledgehammer approach, it could make no difference if the day before making this one slip in an otherwise unblemished life, defendant had rescued fifteen children from a burning building, or had won the Congressional Medal Of Honor while defending his country.

I do not advocate giving up the attempt to rid our society from the evils of drug use. Drug crimes are not "victimless crimes," and it would be naive to suggest otherwise. Drug users use more than their share of many social benefits, and therefore victimize everyone who must pay for them. The need for money with which to buy drugs is the most frequent reason for committing crimes given by defendants convicted in this court. These crimes have victims. Drug users also have children, who suffer the effects of their parents' drug use.

I have no great difficulty imposing lengthy prison sentences upon proven high-volume drug merchants, and others proven to be high in the chain of drug distribution.[3] In some cases I would have imposed the same sentence in the exercise of pure discretion, not governed by any guideline. If, for example, defendant had admitted that he knew what was in the package he delivered to Federal Express, or if the government had been required to prove it, this court could sentence him as the government recommends, with a clear conscience, although still not without misgivings.

Since the days when amputation of the offending hand was routinely used as the punishment for stealing a loaf of bread, however, one of the basic precepts of criminal justice has been that the punishment fit the crime. This is the principle which, as a matter of law, I must violate in this case.[4]

---

[3] Unfortunately, in this court's experience, those high in the chain of drug distribution are seldom caught, and seldom prosecuted.

[4] The Eighth Amendment contains a constitutional requirement that sentences be proportionate to a defendant's crime. The Supreme Court, however, has interpreted this requirement narrowly; therefore defendant's sentence does not violate the Eighth Amendment's proportionality requirement. In *Harmelin v. Michigan*, 111 S.Ct. 2680, 2705 (1991), the plurality held that the Eighth Amendment forbids sentences which are "grossly disproportionate" to the crime. Under this standard, it found

Defendant could have been prosecuted for this offense by the state, rather than the federal government. A review of the relevant California state criminal statute suggests that had that occurred most likely he would have been incarcerated for a period of between one and two years. See Cal.Health & Safety Code § 11351.5 (possession of cocaine base for sale punishable by a term of imprisonment of three, four or five years, with eligibility for parole after half-time served). Surely there are those who would say that this would be too short a period for the owner of drugs for distribution. I cannot imagine, however, those who would argue that such a sentence would be inadequate for a first time offender who merely delivered a package to a Federal Express office, knowing that it contained illegal drugs, but not knowing what drugs or the quantity.

I, for one, do not understand how it came to be that the courts of this nation, which stood for centuries as the defenders of the rights of minorities against abuse at the hands of the majority, have so far abdicated their function that this defendant must serve a ten year sentence.[6]

No doubt there are civilized nations in which the penalty for crimes against the state, such as assassination and treason, are set in advance without reference to who does them and in what circumstances. There may even be some civilized nations in which the penalties for historic biblical offenses such as first degree murder are set in advance. It is hard to imagine, however, that there is any other country in western civilization in which a crime such as this one — simply picking up an unknown quantity of an unknown illegal substance — is treated as the legal equivalent of the conscious commission of a capital offense. It is hard to imagine that there is any other nation in which a convicted rapist with a long and unsavory history of prior misconduct can be sentenced by the judge who presides over his

---

however that a sentence of life imprisonment without parole for possessing more than 650 grams of cocaine did not violate the Eighth Amendment.

[6] In upholding mandatory minimum sentences, the courts have instituted racial disparity in sentencing. Defendant was convicted on a crack cocaine charge, rather than a powder cocaine charge. A study of all drug offenders sentenced in federal court from April 1, 1992 to July 31, 1992 revealed that 92.6% of those sentenced for possession of crack cocaine were black, while 45% of those sentenced for powder cocaine were white. The Federal Public Defender in Los Angeles concluded twenty-three crack cases in 1991. All the defendants were black. Jim Newton, "Harsher Crack Sentences Criticized as Racial Inequity," Los Angeles Times, November 23, 1992, at A20. Under the Guidelines, every gram of crack is considered the equivalent of one hundred grams of powder cocaine. A defendant convicted of selling fifty grams of crack must be sentenced to at least ten years in prison; to trigger the same minimum ten year sentence for a defendant convicted on powder cocaine charges, the defendant would have to have tried to sell five kilograms of cocaine. As the courts have noted in upholding mandatory sentences under 21 U.S.C. § 841(b)(1), sound reasons exist for treating crack more severely than powder cocaine. See e.g., *United States v. Harding*, 971 F.2d 410, 413 (9th Cir.1992) (Congress' decision to treat crack more severely than cocaine is based on its more profound physiological and psychological effects, including addictiveness, and the manner in which it is distributed). However treating crack one hundred times more severely than cocaine, seems arbitrary at best, and disproportionately affects black defendants. The arbitrary nature of the one hundred fold difference in the treatment of crack and cocaine may be seen in comparison to the treatment of methamphetamine and ice under the Guidelines. Methamphetamine, a powerful stimulant, can be converted into a smokable version called ice; smoking ice is more addictive and more dangerous than snorting methamphetamine for the same reason that smoking crack is more dangerous to users than snorting cocaine. However under the Guidelines, one gram of ice is treated as ten grams of methamphetamine, rather than one hundred grams. Ice dealers and methamphetamine dealers are almost exclusively white. The court can surmise no reason for treating crack one hundred times more seriously than powder cocaine, and treating ice only ten times more seriously than methamphetamine.

trial to a sentence which will make him eligible for parole in a less than three years,[7] while defendant, a first time offender with a spotless prior record, stands to be sentenced by a Congress who has never seen him and never judged him to a minimum sentence of ten years, without the possibility of parole.

In my view a criminal justice system that does not require not only those who accuse a criminal, but also those who sentence him, to confront him and publicly acknowledge their acts as their own, to his face, is worse than uncivilized. It is barbaric.

II. Departure From The Sentencing Guidelines

Having reluctantly determined that the mandatory minimum applies, the court departs down to the mandatory minimum sentence of ten years. * * * * Title 18 U.S.C. § 3553(b) allows a court to depart from the applicable guideline range where the court finds that "there exists an aggravating or mitigating circumstance of a kind, or to a degree, not adequately taken into consideration by the Sentencing Commission in formulating the guidelines." The court finds that defendant's crime presents several circumstances not adequately considered by the Commission.

[The court went on to find that (1) Defendant was "a minor player in the drug trade, (2) his crime was "aberrant behavior", and that (3) "Defendant assisted his Probation Officer during the Los Angeles riots, in a way which speaks to his tremendous character".]

Whether this court is right that there are adequate grounds for departure from the Guidelines will be judged, as a matter of law, by judges of the Ninth Circuit. They will neither see defendant nor hear him, but they will decide his sentence. This is not to say or suggest, in any way, that any of the judges of the Ninth Circuit are unconscientious people, or are less sensitive to the problems of the "drug war" than the district court judges. The truth is to the contrary. But they are bound by their own decisions and those of the Supreme Court.

Note:

Another judicial protest against the federal sentencing guidelines was voiced in *U.S. v. Harris*, 154 F.3d 1082 (9th Cir.1998) — but this time the protest did not go uncontested. Harris and Steward were convicted of committing five armed robberies (with firearms) of restaurants and hotels ("interference with interstate commerce by robbery," which violates 18 U.S.C. § 1951(a)), while both were college students. Harris was sentenced to the statutory minimum: 95 years in prison without the possibility of parole. Steward's sentence was about half that. The Court of Appeals reluctantly affirmed:

> As a federal court of appeals bound to follow precedent, we find that we are unable to alter what are essentially life sentences for Defendants. Congress mandated their sentences. We recognize the threat to society represented by armed robberies. We also recognize the need to deal harshly with repeat offenders. We do not, however, believe that the identification of a defendant as a repeat offender should complete the analysis of the appropriate sentence for that defendant.

---

[7] See Cal.Penal Code § 264 (rape is punishable by imprisonment for three, six or eight years).

By mandating such high minimum sentences in 18 U.S.C. § 924(c)(1), Congress has removed the carefully circumscribed discretion granted to district courts in the Sentencing Guidelines to consider possible mitigating circumstances. We feel a just system of punishment demands that some level of discretion be vested in sentencing judges to consider mitigating circumstances. See, e.g., Karen Lutjen, Note, *Culpability and Sentencing Under Mandatory Minimums and the Federal Sentencing Guidelines: The Punishment No Longer Fits the Criminal*, 10 Notre Dame J.L. Ethics & Pub. Pol'y 389, 389 (1996) ("If the proportional link between culpability and the punishment imposed is severed, then the foundations upon which the criminal justice system are based are rendered morally suspect."); Henry Scott Wallace, *Mandatory Minimums and the Betrayal of Sentencing Reform: A Legislative Dr. Jekyll and Mr. Hyde*, 40 Fed. B. News & J. 158, 159 (1993) (noting the failings of mandatory minimum schemes and questioning their "election-eve" wisdom). We urge Congress to reconsider its harsh scheme of mandatory minimum sentences without the possibility for parole.

We do not believe that Harris needs to be in prison when he is 100, or Steward when he is 70, without the possibility for reconsideration of their sentences. The district court judge stated that, given the discretion, he would have sentenced Harris to 36.4 years and Steward to 29.75 years. Although, as already noted, we cannot say that Defendants' sentences are "grossly disproportionate" to their crimes, we feel these lower sentences would have appropriately punished them, would have deterred others, and would have left Defendants with the possibility of rehabilitation, a possibility denied by their current sentences. Harris' sentence, and possibly Steward's as well, constitutes a life sentence. Thus, he will never regain his freedom. Because such a sentence does not even purport to serve a rehabilitative function, the sentence must rest on a rational determination that the punished criminal conduct is so atrocious that society's interest in deterrence and retribution wholly outweighs any considerations of reform or rehabilitation of the perpetrator. We cannot in good conscience say that Defendants' crimes rise to that level.

We urge Congress to reconsider mandatory minimum sentences. Given the political expediency of such sentencing schemes and the resulting improbability of their repeal, we likewise urge the President to examine overlong sentences such as these. The President should scrutinize cases in which the inmate has already been incarcerated for many years and consider clemency after an appropriate length of time in worthy cases. In such cases, the public interest will be well served by the release of the defendant.

The full 9th Circuit Court of Appeals refused to rehear the case *en banc*, but Judge Kozinski (joined by 4 other judges) dissented from this refusal:

Contrary to the panel's insulting suggestion, Congress has not adopted mandatory minimum sentences as a matter of "political expediency." Rather, Congress carefully and over many years considered the views of a wide variety of law enforcement experts and concluded that giving sentencing judges discretion in setting the punishment for certain violent crimes does not serve the interests of our society. By contrast, the judges on the panel offer nothing but their gut feelings that the sentences here are too harsh.

The panel delivers its sermon to Congress as if it were dispensing received wisdom. The gospel according to the Ninth Circuit is that any rational, moral sentencing scheme must allow for the possibility of reform or rehabilitation of the offender, except in the most atrocious cases. This is one view of the matter, but not the only view. A rational legislator could surely decide that the criminal laws should serve a single purpose: to protect law-abiding citizens from those who commit violent crimes-particularly repeat offenders — and that rehabilitation of the perpetrator should be given no consideration. Beyond that, a legislator might consider a wealth of data showing quite convincingly that rehabilitation simply does not work for violent criminals-and that those who purport to determine when such criminals have been "rehabilitated" are frequently and tragically wrong.

A widely-reported study by the United States Department of Justice shows that in 1991, criminals out on parole or probation committed over 90,000 violent crimes in this country: over 13,000 murders; almost 13,000 rapes; almost 40,000 robberies; almost 20,000 assaults. Of the 2,716 inmates on death row in 1993, almost two-thirds had prior felony convictions, and 28% (some 700) were on parole, probation or pre-trial release at the time of their capital offense.

None of these people were released with the expectation that they would commit mayhem; somebody — a judge, a parole board, a probation officer or some other "expert" — determined that these folks were safe. But the experts were wrong, disastrously wrong, and more than 90,000 innocent people a year pay, often with their lives and bodies, for such mistakes. Of course, these figures represent only those who got caught, so we can infer that parole and probation violators were responsible for many more violent crimes than even these staggering figures suggest.

Rehabilitation and reform are worthy goals; we all want to believe that no one is beyond redemption. But that is very far from saying — as the panel does — that a sentencing scheme which does not leave room for rehabilitation, or which gives rehabilitation a very low priority, is irrational and immoral. It might be different if rehabilitation could be determined with precision. But our bitter national experience with revolving-door justice shows that rehabilitation is both hard to achieve and extremely difficult to detect. Rational, moral lawmakers could well conclude that people who commit violent crimes are so unlikely to be rehabilitated — and so likely to victimize innocent people — that locking them up for a very long time, perhaps for good, is the only way to secure our safety.

A fair amount of scholarly research supports this view. Noted criminologist John J. DiIulio points out that most violent crimes are committed by a tiny percentage of the population who are habitual offenders and have no realistic prospect of reform. See John J. DiIulio, Jr., *Help Wanted: Economists, Crime and Public Policy*, 10 J. Econ. Persp. 3, 8 (1996).

Nor can the panel justify its view on the ground that these crimes were relatively mild — they were not. Harris, Steward and their cohorts committed a series of vicious robberies, sticking guns in their victims' faces while promising to murder them if they didn't do as they were told. One victim described his ordeal as he was forced to open a cabinet containing money:

> I started to turn to see what was going on and that's when I got hit the first time with the gun up side the head. The impact knocked my glasses off and the glasses landed about 12 feet away. I told him that I couldn't see the right key to open the cabinet because I didn't have my glasses. Unfortunately, I have really bad vision without my glasses, and that prompted being hit with the gun several more times and kicked in the head and about the body almost two dozen times. At the time I was thinking, "My God, one of these times, he's just going to cave in my skull." * * * *

Both scholarly research and anecdotal evidence suggest that people who are willing to use physical violence against other people often start out small and work their way to more serious stuff. Not all violent criminals may be repeat offenders, but those who have committed violent crimes on more than one occasion are likely to commit even more violent crimes in the future, if given a chance to do so. Is it irrational, is it immoral for a conscientious legislator to refuse to take that chance with the lives and safety of the public he is sworn to serve by insisting that repeat violent offenders be locked up for a very long time? I should think not.

Contrary to the panel's disrespectful insinuation of "election-eve" wisdom, Congress has been thoughtful and deliberate in its efforts to tighten up sentences for violent crimes, considering evidence of experts on both sides of the issue, and gauging the effects of one piece of legislation before enacting another. * * * *

Before passing the Armed Career Criminal Act of 1984, Pub.L. No. 98–473, ch. 18, 98 Stat. 2185, the first major federal statute providing mandatory minimum sentences for repeat armed robbers, Congress had the benefit of extensive testimony from law enforcement officers and other experts on the feasibility and proper role of mandatory minimum sentences. Senator Specter subsequently sought an expansion of the Act based on its initial effectiveness and popularity among law enforcement officials:

> The career criminal statute has worked precisely as planned and deserves to be expanded. Local prosecutors use the law in two ways. First, district attorneys refer the toughest criminals to the U.S. Attorney for prosecution in Federal courts, which can provide more swift and certain trial and sentencing. Second, district attorneys use the mere prospect of such referral and the extremely stiff penalties to get a favorable guilty plea at the local level. I believe that this "leveraging" effect is one of the most important aspects of the statute. We have seen major cases in which local prosecutors have obtained guilty pleas and stiff sentences simply by raising the possibility of referring the case to Federal authorities for prosecution under the armed career criminal statute. As a member of the Senate Judiciary Committee, I have held hearings in many of the country's largest cities in order to encourage

prosecution of career criminals. Based on the testimony presented at these Senate hearings by victims, sheriffs, U.S. attorneys, police, local prosecutors, and other criminal justice officials, and in light of the initial success of the statute, I am convinced that we must expand the law.

The success of Justice Department initiatives such as Project Triggerlock, which subjected thousands of repeat armed offenders to federal mandatory minimums by allowing state prosecutors to transfer cases involving repeat offenders to federal court, firmed up Congress's commitment to mandatory minimum sentences. See, e.g., 141 Cong. Rec. S6487-01 (daily ed. May 11, 1995) (statement of Sen. DeWine) (reporting that Project Triggerlock took 15,000 career criminals off the street in only 18 months). No less influential have been the opinions of federal and state law enforcement officials. Testimony of officials from the Justice Department and the Bureau of Alcohol, Tobacco and Firearms (BATF), as well as a BATF study, served as a basis for adding more mandatory minimum sentences to the Omnibus Crime Control Act of 1991. Another BATF report to Congress found that as of May 25, 1994, minimum mandatory sentences had prevented over 4 million violent offenses, representing nearly $11 billion in savings to intended victims. * * * *

While cause and effect are always difficult to determine, there is reason to believe that the policy of stiff, determinate sentences adopted both by the federal government and many states is working: Violent crime has declined 7 years in a row, with robbery down 32% and murder 31% since 1991. See Fox Butterfield, *Decline of Violent Crimes is Linked to Crack Market*, N.Y. Times, Dec. 28, 1998, at A18. Other factors may also have contributed to this trend, but "there is no question that the almost quadrupling of the number of people incarcerated since 1970, to 1.8 million, has incapacitated many criminals and prevented many crimes." *Id.*; see also William J. Bennett, John J. DiIulio, Jr., & John P. Walters, *Body Count* 115 (1996) (arguing that longer incarceration reduces crime); *Developments in the Law — Alternatives to Incarceration*, 111 Harv. L.Rev. 1863, 1880–84 (1998) (reporting that much of the increase in incarceration levels over the last two decades is attributable to mandatory minimum sentences and that statistical data on crime rates since 1960 support an inference that increased incarceration has helped control crime by "incapacitating dangerous people, who otherwise would do a great deal of harm to the general public").

Against this background, the panel's assertion that "a just system of punishment demands that some level of discretion be vested in sentencing judges to consider mitigating circumstances," is more of a polemic than an indisputable truth. As Judge Kleinfeld points out, judges are not very good at figuring out whether a convicted criminal has been rehabilitated: "We have no professional competence and obtain no useful evidence for looking into offenders' hearts to evaluate their remorse or for judging whether they have truly repented and will in the future maintain law-abiding lives." Andrew J. Kleinfeld, *The Sentencing Guidelines Promote Truth and Justice*, Fed. Probation, Dec. 1991, at 16, 17. The simple truth is that every time a violent criminal — and in particular a repeat offender — is released into society, law-abiding citizens are put at risk. Rational lawmakers could surely conclude that justice consists, not in a highly uncertain and enormously costly effort to rehabilitate those who have violated the rights of others again and again, but in protecting citizens from the predation of remorseless criminals.

Unlike some other sentencing schemes, where later offenses are punished more severely than earlier ones, the scheme here merely ensures that defendants don't get a wholesale discount when they commit a series of violent acts. Why the panel believes that a second, third, fourth and fifth armed robbery ought to be punished less severely than each of the earlier ones, is beyond me. After all, robberies conducted at the point of a gun are extremely dangerous; they can, and often do, result in shootings and hostage-takings. Every new robbery carries more or less the same risks as each of the previous ones, putting the lives of a new group of innocent people in danger. How can it be immoral or unjust to require the defendants to pay exactly the same penalty for each of the crimes they committed? And since when does justice and morality require us to reduce the punishment for each successive crime because defendants chose to commit several violent crimes one after another? Many rational, moral people believe that those who commit five robberies ought to be punished more than five times as severely as people who commit only one.

As I said at the outset, these are legislative decisions. They call for the kind of judgment we are neither equipped nor empowered to make, and it strikes me as unseemly for our court to take sides on this policy issue. Were I a legislator, I'm not sure how I would vote as to mandatory minimum sentences. But I'm a judge, so I need only determine whether Congress acted rationally enough to pass constitutional muster. For the reasons explained above, it clearly did and that ends the matter for me. If my colleagues feel they have something useful to add to the debate, they can do so as individuals and not on behalf of the court. But since they have chosen to deliver their homily from the bench we share, I write to explain that they do not speak for us. [165 F.3d 1277 (1999)]

For another defense of the Federal Sentencing Guidelines and the notion that judges' discretion should be limited, see Frank O. Bowman III, *Fear of Law: Thoughts on* Fear of Judging *And The State of the Federal Sentencing Guidelines*, 44 Saint Louis U.L.J. 299 (2000). The article appears in the Spring 2000 issue of the journal, which contains several articles by judges and law professors who appeared at a symposium on sentencing.

SENTENCING IN CALIFORNIA

The Federal Sentencing Guidelines are quite long (over 700 pages) and complicated, and to learn about them properly would take a separate book — not just a chapter in this book. For this reason, we will examine sentencing in a jurisdiction that has a similar history, and now has a system which is a bit simpler than the Federal Guidelines.

For many years, California had an indeterminate system, though very little power resided with the judge. The statute would authorize the judge to sentence Dan to a range, e.g., "1 to 5 years". However, the choice of sentence within this range was made not by the judge, but by an administrative agency called the Adult

Authority, after this agency had a few months to evaluate Dan in prison.

In 1976, California switched, resulting in the statutes and rules we will examine in this chapter. It has been called a "presumptive sentence" system — a certain sentence is presumed to be the correct one, unless the judges finds facts which justify "mitigating" or "aggravating" the sentence. The California Supreme Court described the purpose behind the new law in *People v. Martin* 42 Cal.3d 437 (1986):

> The determinate sentencing law expresses a rather definitive legislative effort to diminish inequitable disparities in punishment to the extent practicable. The effort was motivated in part by judicial decisions disapproving administration of the Indeterminate Sentence Law in certain particulars, but it was at least equally the result of an accumulation of evidence that under the indeterminate sentencing system there were wide disparities in terms of both who went to prison and their lengths of stay for similar offenses. The evidence was punctuated by the developing national consensus that significant disparities in the punishment imposed upon like individuals committing like offenses was a pernicious evil endangering the very integrity of the criminal justice system. Numerous empirical studies revealed that the chief explanation for sentencing disparity was not the differences in defendants but the differences in judges. Thus the movement to promote uniformity in sentencing was in no small part a movement to diminish judicial discretion. [Citations omitted.]

THE LAWYER'S ROLE IN SENTENCING

American Bar Association, Standards For Criminal Justice

Standard 18-6.3: Duties of Counsel

(a) The duties of the prosecution and defense attorneys do not cease upon conviction of the defendant. While it should be recognized that sentencing is the function of the court, the attorneys nevertheless have a duty of assisting the court in as helpful a manner as possible.

(b) The prosecutor should recognize that the severity of the sentence is not necessarily an indication of the effectiveness or the efficiency of his or her office. In addition, the prosecutor, no less than the judge, has the duty to resist public clamor or improper outside pressure of any sort.

(c) The prosecutor should have an opportunity to address the court at sentencing and to offer a sentencing recommendation, and, when requested by the sentencing court, should have the obligation to do so.

(d) The duties of the prosecutor with respect to each specific sentence should include the following steps: (i) The prosecutor should satisfy himself or herself that the factual basis for the sentence will be both adequate and accurate, and that the record of the sentencing proceeding will accurately reflect circumstances of the offense and characteristics of the defendant which were not disclosed during the guilt phase of the case: (A) If the prosecutor has access to the presentence report, the prosecutor should measure it against information at his or her disposal in order to be able to amplify parts which do not sufficiently reveal matters which are relevant to a proper sentence. The prosecutor should also take proper steps to controvert any inaccuracies in the report in accordance with the procedures specified in standard 18-5.5(b). The first such step should normally involve an attempt to avoid the formal production of evidence in open court by reaching an informal agreement with the defense attorney and the probation officer; or (B) If the prosecutor does not have access to the presentence report, the prosecutor should present at the sentencing proceeding those facts at his or her disposal which are relevant to a proper sentence. Such presentation should also be preceded by the notice contemplated by standard 18-5.5(b) in order that new allegations may be verified by the probation officer; (ii) Reasonably prior to the sentencing proceeding, the prosecutor should disclose to the defense and to the court through the probation officer all information in the prosecutor's files which is favorable to the defendant on the sentencing issue; (iii) If a plea was the result of plea discussion or an agreement which included a position on the sentence, the prosecutor should disclose its terms to the court; (iv) The prosecutor should determine whether there are grounds for the imposition of a special term based on particular characteristics of the defendant (standards 18-2.5(b) and 18-4.4). If the prosecutor finds such grounds, he or she should cause the notice contemplated by standard 18-6.5(b)(i) to be served on the defendant and defense attorney. The prosecutor may then prepare a factual case for presentation at the sentencing proceeding.

(e) The defense attorney should recognize that the sentencing stage is the time at which for many defendants the most important service of the entire proceeding can be performed.

(f) The duties of the defense attorney with respect to each specific sentence should include the following steps:

(i) The attorney should familiarize himself or herself with all of the sentencing alternatives that are available for the offense of which the client has been convicted and with community and other facilities which may be of assistance in a plan for meeting the needs of the defendant. Such preparation should also include familiarization with the practical consequences of different sentences and with the normal pattern of sentences for the offense involved, including any guidelines applicable at either the sentencing or parole states;

(ii) The attorney should satisfy himself or herself that the factual basis for the sentence will be adequate both for the purposes of the sentencing court and, to the extent ascertainable, for the purposes of subsequent dispositional authorities. The attorney should take particular care to make certain that the record of the sentencing proceedings will accurately reflect all relevant mitigating circumstances relating either to the offense or to the characteristics of the defendant which were not disclosed during the guilt phrase of the case and to ensure that such record will be adequately preserved:

(A) If the attorney has access to the presentence report, this duty should at a minimum involve verification of the essential bases of the report and amplification at the sentencing proceeding of parts which seem to be inadequate. The attorney should also take proper steps to controvert any inaccuracies in the report which are adverse to the client's interests. The first such step should normally involve an attempt to avoid the formal production of evidence in open court by reaching an informal agreement as provided in standard 18-5.5(b); or

(B) If the attorney does not have access to the presentence report, this duty should at a minimum involve the attorney's best attempt using the means at his or her disposal to ascertain the relevant facts. The attorney should also have the obligation to present at the sentencing proceeding all facts which are not known by the attorney to be before the court and which in the interest of the client ought to be considered in reaching a sentence;

(C) In either case, the attorney should also satisfy himself or herself that the defendant understands the nature of the presentence investigation process, and in particular the significance of statements made by the defendant to probation officers and related personnel. In some circumstances, it may be appropriate for the attorney to attend the probation officer's interview with the defendant, and on such occasions the attorney should seek to accommodate his or her schedule to that of the probation department;

(iii) If a plea was the result of plea discussion or an agreement which included a position of the prosecution on the sentence, the attorney should disclose its terms to the court;

(iv) In appropriate cases, the attorney should make special efforts to investigate the desirability of a disposition which would particularly meet the needs of the defendant, such as probation accompanied by employment of community facilities or commitment to an institution for special treatment. If such a disposition is available and seems appropriate, the attorney, with the consent of the defendant, should make a recommendation at the sentencing proceeding that it be utilized.

(g) Neither the prosecution nor defense counsel should seek to re-try an individual sentence in the media of public communication.

Problem 12

To: My Law Clerk

From: Shelly Shmendrick, Esq.

My client, Dan Dingle, has been charged with a violation of California Penal Code § 212.5(a) — first degree robbery. The complaint also alleges that Dingle used a gun. Here is a copy of the police report:

Police Report

At 9 p.m. this evening, I received a phone call from Mr. Fred Fogey, who said that he had just been robbed at the Ritz Hotel. I went to the hotel and interviewed Mr. Fogey and his wife, Frieda. They said that they had just left their room on the 12th floor, when they were confronted by a white male, wearing a parka zipped up to the lower part of his face and a S.F. Giants cap pulled down over his forehead. The man pointed a gun at Mr. Fogey and said "Give me your wallet, man, or I'll kill you." Mr. Fogey gave him the wallet, and the man ran off. Mr. Fogey saw some other people waiting for an elevator, and he yelled at them to stop the man, but the man ran past them and down the stairway. Both Mr. **and Mrs. Fogey are** in their late 50's, and they were very frightened and shaken **up. Mr. Fogey had** about $150 in cash and several credit cards in his wallet.

I looked around the hall where the robbery occurred, and I found a toy pistol near the stairway. I took the Fogeys to the station and showed them a mug book of photos of local low-life. They both picked out Dan Dingle.

I went to Dingle's apartment and arrested him. He said that he had been in the apartment all night watching TV with his girlfriend, Bonnie Berry. Bonnie said the same thing.

Sgt. Joe Thursday

The Deputy D.A. handling the case is Winnie Whitehat, who suggested a plea bargain. She says that if we go to trial and lose, she will ask the judge to sentence Dan to the upper term for first degree robbery, plus an enhancement for the gun use. But if Dan pleads guilty to second degree robbery, she will drop the first degree charge and the gun enhancement, and recommend the middle term for second degree robbery.

I have talked to Dan and Bonnie, and the alibi seems pretty good, if the jury believes them. I think both will make OK witnesses, so our chances of getting an acquittal are maybe 50-50. If we lose, I would like to get Dan the lowest sentence possible, maybe even probation.

There are a few facts about Dan you should know. He says that he was convicted of felony drunk driving about 3 years ago, and he has been arrested a couple of times for shoplifting and house-breaking. He has used cocaine quite a bit in the past, but he says that he is now trying to get off the stuff.

Should I advise Dan to accept Winnie's offer? What alternatives should I consider? If you need any more information, let me know what it is and I will try to get it. You might find the attached authorities helpful.

CALIFORNIA PENAL CODE

§ 211. Robbery Defined

Robbery is the felonious taking of personal property in the possession of another, from his person or immediate presence, and against his will, accomplished by means of force or fear.

§ 212. Fear Defined

The fear mentioned in § 211 may be either:

1. The fear of an unlawful injury to the person or property of the person robbed, or of any relative of his or member of his family; or,

2. The fear of an immediate and unlawful injury to the person or property of anyone in the company of the person robbed at the time of the robbery.

§ 212.5. Robbery; Degrees

(a) Every robbery of any person who is performing his or her duties as an operator of any bus, taxicab, cable car, streetcar, trackless trolley, or other vehicle, including a vehicle operated on stationary rails or on a track or rail suspended in the air, and used for the transportation of persons for hire, every robbery of any passenger which is perpetrated on any of these vehicles, and every robbery which is perpetrated in an inhabited dwelling house, a vessel, as defined in § 21 of the Harbors and Navigation Code, which is inhabited and designed for habitation, or a trailer coach, as defined in the Vehicle Code, which is inhabited, or the inhabited portion of any other building, is robbery of the first degree.

(b) All kinds of robbery other than those listed in subdivision (a) are of the second degree.

§ 213. Robbery; Punishment

(a) Robbery is punishable as follows:

(1) Robbery of the first degree: by imprisonment in the state prison for three, four, or six years.

(2) Robbery of the second degree: by imprisonment in the state prison for two, three, or five years.

(b) Notwithstanding § 664, attempted robbery is punishable by imprisonment in the state prison.

§ 667: *Habitual criminals; enhancement of sentence*

(a)

(1) [A]ny person convicted of a serious felony who previously has been convicted of a serious felony in this state or of any offense committed in another jurisdiction which includes all of the elements of any serious felony, shall receive, in addition to the sentence imposed by the court for the present offense, a five-year enhancement for each such prior conviction on charges brought and tried separately. The terms of the present offense and each enhancement shall run consecutively.

(2) This subdivision shall not be applied when the punishment imposed under other provisions of law would result in a longer term of imprisonment. There is no requirement of prior incarceration or commitment for this subdivision to apply.

(3) The Legislature may increase the length of the enhancement of sentence provided in this subdivision by a statute passed by majority vote of each house thereof.

(4) As used in this subdivision, "serious felony" means a serious felony listed in subdivision (c) of § 1192.7.[1] * * * *

---

[1] § 1192.7 defines "serious felony" to include murder, voluntary manslaughter, mayhem, rape, lewd act on a child, any felony in which defendant inflicted great bodily injury or used a firearm, attempted murder, assault with intent to commit rape or robbery, assault with a deadly weapon on a police officer, burglary of an inhabited dwelling house, robbery, kidnapping, sale of heroin, cocaine, or methamphetamine, carjacking — and some less common felonies.

(b) It is the intent of the Legislature in enacting subdivisions (b) to (i), inclusive, to ensure longer prison sentences and greater punishment for those who commit a felony and have been previously convicted of serious and/or violent felony offenses.

(c) Notwithstanding any other law, if a defendant has been convicted of a felony and it has been pled and proved that the defendant has one or more prior [serious felony] convictions[2] . . . , the court shall adhere to each of the following:

(1) There shall not be an aggregate term limitation for purposes of consecutive sentencing for any subsequent felony conviction.

(2) Probation for the current offense shall not be granted, nor shall execution or imposition of the sentence be suspended for any prior offense.

(3) The length of time between the prior felony conviction and the current felony conviction shall not affect the imposition of sentence.

(4) There shall not be a commitment to any other facility other than the state prison. * * * *

(5) The total amount of credits awarded pursuant to Article 2.5 (commencing with § 2930) of Chapter 7 of Title 1 of Part 3 shall not exceed one-fifth of the total term of imprisonment imposed and shall not accrue until the defendant is physically placed in the state prison. * * * *

(e) For purposes of subdivisions (b) to (i), inclusive, and in addition to any other enhancement or punishment provisions which may apply, the following shall apply where a defendant has a prior felony conviction:

(1) If a defendant has one prior felony conviction that has been pled and proved, the determinate term or minimum term for an indeterminate term shall be twice the term otherwise provided as punishment for the current felony conviction.

(2)

(A) If a defendant has two or more prior felony convictions as defined in subdivision (d) that have been pled and proved, the term for the current felony conviction shall be an indeterminate term of life imprisonment with a minimum term of the indeterminate sentence calculated as the greater of:

(i) Three times the term otherwise provided as punishment for each current felony conviction subsequent to the two or more prior felony convictions.

(ii) Imprisonment in the state prison for 25 years.

(iii) The term determined by the court pursuant to § 1170 for the underlying conviction, including any enhancement applicable under Chapter 4.5 (commencing with § 1170) of Title 7 of Part 2, or any period prescribed by § 190 or § 3046.

(B) The indeterminate term described in subparagraph (A) shall be served consecutive to any other term of imprisonment for which a consecutive term may be imposed by law. Any other term imposed

---

[2] *See* footnote 1.

subsequent to any indeterminate term described in subparagraph (A) shall not be merged therein but shall commence at the time the person would otherwise have been released from prison.[3]

(f)

(1) Notwithstanding any other law, subdivisions (b) to (i), inclusive, shall be applied in every case in which a defendant has a prior felony conviction as defined in subdivision (d). The prosecuting attorney shall plead and prove each prior felony conviction except as provided in paragraph (2).

(2) The prosecuting attorney may move to dismiss or strike a prior felony conviction allegation in the furtherance of justice pursuant to § 1385, or if there is insufficient evidence to prove the prior conviction. If upon the satisfaction of the court that there is insufficient evidence to prove the prior felony conviction, the court may dismiss or strike the allegation.[4]

(g) Prior felony convictions shall not be used in plea bargaining as defined in subdivision (b) of § 1192.7. The prosecution shall plead and prove all known prior felony convictions and shall not enter into any agreement to strike or seek the dismissal of any prior felony conviction allegation except as provided in paragraph (2) of subdivision (f). * * * *

(j) The provisions of this section shall not be amended by the Legislature except by statute passed in each house by rollcall vote entered in the journal, two-thirds of the membership concurring, or by a statute that becomes effective only when approved by the electors.

---

[3] This subsection was enacted by the initiative process in 1994. Known as California's "Three Strikes and You're Out" law, it has been called "an extreme example of populist preemption of criminal justice policy making." Franklin Zimring, *Populism, Democratic Government, and the Decline of Expert Authority: Some Reflections on "Three Strikes" in California*, 28 Pacific L.J. 243 (1996).

Has California's "3 Strikes" approach deterred crime? See Franklin Zimring, et. al., Punishment and Democracy: Three Strikes and You're Out in California (Oxford University Press 2001). This study was criticized in Brian P. Janiskee and Edward J. Erler, Crime Punishment, and Romero: An Analysis of the Case Against California's Three Strikes Law, 39 Duq. L. Rev. 43 (2000), and defended in Franklin Zimring & Sam Kamin, *Facts, Fallacies, & California's Three Strikes*, 40 Duquesne L.Rev. 605 (2002), where the authors conclude that "the Three Strikes law reduced California crime by only six-tenths of one percent. This contradicts the claim by California's Attorney General that the drop in crime during the 'Three Strikes Era' was over 30%. In fact, our final estimate of the deterrent effect in the monograph under review was between zero and 2% of California crime."

[4] This subsection raised the hackles of many trial judges, who felt that they should have the right to strike prior felony allegations even if the prosecutor decided not to move to have the priors stricken. Finally, in *People v. Superior Court (Romero)*, 13 Cal.4th 497 (1996), the court held:

Penal Code § 1385, subdivision (a), authorizes a trial court to dismiss a criminal action "in furtherance of justice" on its own motion. We have held that the power to dismiss an action includes the lesser power to strike factual allegations relevant to sentencing, such as the allegation that a defendant has prior felony convictions. This case raises the question whether a court may, on its own motion, strike prior felony conviction allegations in cases arising under the law known as "Three Strikes and You're Out." § 667, subds.(b)-(i), added by Stats.1994, ch. 12, § 1, effective Mar. 7, 1994; see also § 1170.12, added by initiative, Gen. Election Nov. 8, 1994 [Proposition 184].)

Although the Legislature may withdraw the statutory power to dismiss in furtherance of justice, we conclude it has not done so in the Three Strikes law. Accordingly, in cases charged under that law, a court may exercise the power to dismiss granted in § 1385, either on the court's own motion or on that of the prosecuting attorney, subject, however, to strict compliance with the provisions of § 1385 and to review for abuse of discretion.

§ 1170. *Legislative findings; determinate sentencing; imposition; preimprisonment credit; resentence; reasons for sentence; informing of parole period; review by board of prison terms; sentences for similar crimes.*

(a)(1) The Legislature finds and declares that the purpose of imprisonment for crime is punishment. This purpose is best served by terms proportionate to the seriousness of the offense with provision for uniformity in the sentences of offenders committing the same offense under similar circumstances. The Legislature further finds and declares that the elimination of disparity and the provision of uniformity of sentences can best be achieved by determinate sentences fixed by statute in proportion to the seriousness of the offense as determined by the Legislature to be imposed by the court with specified discretion.

(2) In any case in which the punishment prescribed by statute for a person convicted of a public offense is a term of imprisonment in the state prison of 16 months, two or three years; two, three, or four years; two, three, or five years; three, four, or five years; two, four, or six years; three, four, or six years; three, five, or seven years; three, six, or eight years; five, seven, or nine years; five, seven, or 11 years, or any other specification of three time periods, the court shall sentence the defendant to one of the terms of imprisonment specified unless such convicted person is given any other disposition provided by law, including a fine, jail, probation, or the suspension of imposition or execution of sentence. . . . In sentencing the convicted person, the court shall apply the sentencing rules of the Judicial Council. The court, unless it determines that there are circumstances in mitigation of the punishment prescribed, shall also impose any other term which it is required by law to impose as an additional term. * * * *

(b) When a judgment of imprisonment is to be imposed and the statute specifies three possible terms, the court shall order imposition of the middle term, unless there are circumstances in aggravation or mitigation of the crime. At least four days prior to the time set for imposition of judgment, either party or the victim, or the family of the victim if the victim is deceased, may submit a statement in aggravation or mitigation to dispute facts in the record or the probation officer's report, or to present additional facts. In determining whether there are circumstances that justify imposition of the upper or lower term, the court may consider the record in the case, the probation officer's report, other reports including reports received pursuant to § 1203.03 and statements in aggravation or mitigation submitted by the prosecution, the defendant, or the victim, or the family of the victim if the victim is deceased, and any further evidence introduced at the sentencing hearing. The court shall set forth on the record the facts and reasons for imposing the upper or lower term. * * * *

(c) The court shall state the reasons for its sentence choice on the record at the time of sentencing. The court shall also inform the defendant that as part of the sentence after expiration of the term he or she may be on parole for a period as provided in § 3000.

****

(f)

(1) Within one year after the commencement of the term of imprisonment, the Board of Prison Terms shall review the sentence to determine whether the sentence is disparate in comparison with the sentences imposed in

similar cases. If the Board of Prison Terms determines that the sentence is disparate, the board shall notify the judge, the district attorney, the defense attorney, the defendant, and the Judicial Council. The notification shall include a statement of the reasons for finding the sentence disparate. Within 120 days of receipt of this information, the sentencing court shall schedule a hearing and may recall the sentence and commitment previously ordered and resentence the defendant in the same manner as if the defendant had not been sentenced previously, provided the new sentence is no greater than the initial sentence. In resentencing under this subdivision the court shall apply the sentencing rules of the Judicial Council and shall consider the information provided by the Board of Prison Terms.

(2) The review under this section shall concern the decision to deny probation and the sentencing decisions enumerated in paragraphs (2), (3), and (4) of subdivision (a) of Section 1170.3 and apply the sentencing rules of the Judicial Council and the information regarding the sentences in this state of other persons convicted of similar crimes so as to eliminate disparity of sentences and to promote uniformity of sentencing.

(g) Prior to sentencing pursuant to this chapter, the court may request information from the Board of Prison Terms concerning the sentences in this state of other persons convicted of similar crimes under similar circumstances.

§ 1170.1 * * * *Enhancements* * * *

(e) All enhancements shall be alleged in the accusatory pleading and either admitted by the defendant in open court or found to be true by the trier of fact.

§ 1202.7. *Probation; legislative findings and declarations; primary considerations in granting.*

The Legislature finds and declares that the provision of probation services is an essential element in the administration of criminal justice. The safety of the public, which shall be a primary goal through the enforcement of court-ordered conditions of probation; the nature of the offense; the interests of justice, including punishment, reintegration of the offender into the community, and enforcement of conditions of probation; the loss to the victim; and the needs of the defendant shall be the primary considerations in the granting of probation.

§ 1203. *Probation; conditional sentence; probation officer investigation, report, and recommendations; restitution fine; court determination; misdemeanor conviction; persons ineligible for probation; release to another state; financial evaluation regarding restitution.*

(a) As used in this code, "probation" shall mean the suspension of the imposition or execution of a sentence and the order of conditional and revocable release in the community under the supervision of the probation officer. As used in this code, "conditional sentence" shall mean the suspension of the imposition or execution of a sentence and the order of revocable release in the community subject to the conditions established by the court without the supervision of the probation officer. It is the intent of the Legislature that both conditional sentence and probation are authorized whenever probation is authorized in any code as a sentencing option for infractions or misdemeanors.

(b) Except as provided in subdivision (j), in every case in which a person is convicted of a felony and is eligible for probation, before judgment is pronounced, the court shall immediately refer the matter to the probation officer to investigate and report to the court, at a specified time, upon the circumstances surrounding the crime and the prior history and record of the person, which may be considered either in aggravation or mitigation of the punishment. The probation officer shall immediately investigate and make a written report to the court of his or her findings and recommendations, including his or her recommendations as to the granting or denying of probation and the conditions of probation, if granted. Pursuant to § 828 of the Welfare and Institutions Code, the probation officer shall include in his or her report any information gathered by a law enforcement agency relating to the taking of the defendant into custody as a minor, which shall be considered for purposes of determining whether adjudications of commissions of crimes as a juvenile warrant a finding that there are circumstances in aggravation pursuant to § 1170 or to deny probation. The probation officer shall also include in the report his or her recommendation of the amount the defendant should be required to pay as a restitution fine pursuant to § 13967 of the Government Code. The probation officer shall also include in his or her report a recommendation as to whether the court shall require, as a condition of probation, restitution to the victim or to the Restitution Fund. The report shall be made available to the court and the prosecuting and defense attorneys at least five days, or upon request of the defendant or prosecuting attorney, nine days prior to the time fixed by the court for the hearing and determination of the report, and shall be filed with the clerk of the court as a record in the case at the time of the hearing. The time within which the report shall be made available and filed may be waived by written stipulation of the prosecuting and defense attorneys which is filed with the court or an oral stipulation in open court which is made and entered upon the minutes of the court. At a time fixed by the court, the court shall hear and determine the application, if one has been made, or, in any case, the suitability of probation in the particular case. At the hearing, the court shall consider any report of the probation officer and shall make a statement that it has considered such report which shall be filed with the clerk of the court as a record in the case. If the court determines that there are circumstances in mitigation of the punishment prescribed by law or that the ends of justice would be served by granting probation to the person, it may place the person on probation. If probation is denied, the clerk of the court shall immediately send a copy of the report to the Department of Corrections at the prison or other institution to which the person is delivered.

(c) If a defendant is not represented by an attorney, the court shall order the probation officer who makes the probation report to discuss its contents with the defendant.

(d) In every case in which a person is convicted of a misdemeanor, the court may either refer the matter to the probation officer for an investigation and a report or summarily pronounce a conditional sentence. If such a case is not referred to the probation officer, in sentencing the person, the court may consider any information concerning the person which could have been included in a probation report. The court shall inform the person of the information to be considered and permit him or her to answer or controvert such information. For this purpose, upon the request of the person, the court shall grant a continuance before the judgment is pronounced.

(e) Except in unusual cases where the interests of justice would best be served if the person is granted probation, probation shall not be granted to any of the following persons:

(1) Unless the person had a lawful right to carry a deadly weapon, other than a firearm, at the time of the perpetration of the crime or his or her arrest, any person who has been convicted of arson, robbery, burglary, burglary with explosives, rape with force or violence, murder, attempt to commit murder, trainwrecking, kidnapping, escape from the state prison, or a conspiracy to commit one or more of those crimes and was armed with such a weapon at either of those times.

(2) Any person who used or attempted to use a deadly weapon upon a human being in connection with the perpetration of the crime of which he or she has been convicted.

(3) Any person who willfully inflicted great bodily injury or torture in the perpetration of the crime of which he or she has been convicted.

(4) Any person who has been previously convicted twice in this state of a felony or in any other place of a public offense which, if committed in this state, would have been punishable as a felony. * * * *

§ 2931: *Reduction of Term for Good Behavior*

(a) In any case in which a prisoner was sentenced to the state prison pursuant to § 1170 . . . , the Department of Corrections shall have the authority to reduce the term prescribed under such section by one-third for good behavior and participation. . . .

§ 2933: *Worktime Credits on Sentences*

(a) It is the intent of the Legislature that persons convicted of a crime and sentenced to the state prison under § 1170 serve the entire sentence imposed by the court, except for a reduction in the time served in the custody of the Director of Corrections for performance in work, training or education programs established by the Director of Corrections. Worktime credits shall apply for performance in work assignments and performance in elementary, high school, or vocational education programs. Enrollment in a two- or four-year college program leading to a degree shall result in the application of time credits equal to that provided in § 2931. For every six months of full-time performance in a credit qualifying program, as designated by the director, a prisoner shall be awarded worktime credit reductions from his or her term of confinement of six months. A lesser amount of credit based on this ratio shall be awarded for any lesser period of continuous performance. * * * * Under no circumstances shall any prisoner receive more than six months' credit reduction for any six-month period under this section.

(b) Worktime credit is a privilege, not a right. Worktime credit must be earned and may be forfeited pursuant to the provisions of § 2932. Except as provided in subdivision (a) of § 2932, every prisoner shall have a reasonable opportunity to participate in a full-time credit qualifying assignment in a manner consistent with institutional security and available resources. * * * *

§ 3000: *Parole*

(a)(1) The Legislature finds and declares that the period immediately following incarceration is critical to successful reintegration of the offender into society and to positive citizenship. It is in the interest of public safety for the state to provide for the supervision of and surveillance of parolees, including the judicious use of revocation actions, and to provide educational, vocational, family and personal counseling necessary to assist parolees in the transition between imprisonment and discharge. A sentence pursuant to § 1168 or § 1170 shall include a period of parole, unless waived, as provided in this section. * * * *

(3) The Legislature finds and declares that diligent effort must be made to ensure that parolees are held accountable for their criminal behavior, including, but not limited to, the satisfaction of restitution fines and orders.

(b) Notwithstanding any provision to the contrary in Article 3 (commencing with § 3040) of this chapter, the following shall apply:

   (1) At the expiration of a term of imprisonment of one year and one day, or a term of imprisonment imposed pursuant to § 1170 or at the expiration of a term reduced pursuant to § 2931, if applicable, the inmate shall be released on parole for a period not exceeding three years, unless the parole authority for good cause waives parole and discharges the inmate from custody of the department.

   (2) In the case of any inmate sentenced under § 1168, the period of parole shall not exceed five years in the case of an inmate imprisoned for any offense other than first or second degree murder for which the inmate has received a life sentence, and shall not exceed three years in the case of any other inmate, unless in either case the parole authority for good cause waives parole and discharges the inmate from custody of the department. * * * *

   (3) The parole authority shall consider the request of any inmate regarding the length of his or her parole and the conditions thereof.

   (4) Upon successful completion of parole, or at the end of the maximum statutory period of parole specified for the inmate under paragraph (1) or (2), as the case may be, whichever is earlier, the inmate shall be discharged from custody. * * * * Time during which parole is suspended because the prisoner has absconded or has been returned to custody as a parole violator shall not be credited toward any period of parole unless the prisoner is found not guilty of the parole violation.[5] * * * *

   (5) The Department of Corrections shall meet with each inmate at least 30 days prior to his or her good time release date and shall provide, under guidelines specified by the parole authority, the conditions of parole and the length of parole up to the maximum period of time provided by law. The

---

[5] In *Morrissey v. Brewer*, 408 U.S. 471 (1972), the Court held that parole may not be *revoked* unless certain minimal due process rights are accorded to the parolee. These include the right to written notice of the claimed violations of parole, the right to be heard and to present evidence, the right to a "neutral and detached" hearing body, and the right to a written statement of reasons. The rules of evidence which apply at trial do not apply to parole revocation hearings; hearsay is admissible.

inmate has the right to reconsideration of the length of parole and conditions thereof by the parole authority. * * * *

§ 12022. *Felony; Commission or Attempt With Firearm or Use of Deadly or Dangerous Weapon; Controlled Substance Violations; Additional Punishment; Disposal of Weapon.*

(a) (1) Except as provided in subdivisions (c) and (d), any person who is armed with a firearm in the commission or attempted commission of a felony shall, upon conviction of such felony or attempted felony, in addition and consecutive to the punishment prescribed for the felony or attempted felony of which he or she has been convicted, be punished by an additional term of one year, unless such arming is an element of the offense of which he or she was convicted. This additional term shall apply to any person who is a principal in the commission or attempted commission of a felony if one or more of the principals is armed with a firearm, whether or not such person is personally armed with a firearm. * * * *

(b) Any person who personally uses a deadly or dangerous weapon in the commission or attempted commission of a felony shall, upon conviction of such felony or attempted felony, in addition and consecutive to the punishment prescribed for the felony or attempted felony of which he or she has been convicted, be punished by an additional term of one year, unless use of a deadly or dangerous weapon is an element of the offense of which he or she was convicted. * * * *

California Rules of Court

Rule 406: Reasons

(a) *How given.* If the sentencing judge is required to give reasons for a sentence choice, the judge shall state in simple language the primary factor or factors that support the exercise of discretion or, if applicable, state that the judge has no discretion. The statement need not be in the language of these rules. It shall be delivered orally on the record.

(b) *When reasons required.* Sentence choices that generally require a statement of a reason include: (1) granting probation; (2) imposing a prison sentence and thereby denying probation; (3) declining to commit to the Youth Authority an eligible juvenile found amenable for treatment; (4) selecting a term other than the middle statutory term for either an offense or an enhancement; (5) imposing consecutive sentences; (6) imposing full consecutive sentences under § 667.6(c) rather than consecutive terms under § 1170.1(a), when the court has that choice; (7) striking or staying the punishment for an enhancement; (8) imposing both weapons and injury enhancements on a single count under § 1170.1(e); (9) waiving a restitution fine; (10) not committing an eligible defendant to the California Rehabilitation Center.

Rule 408: Criteria Not Exclusive

(a) The enumeration in these rules of some criteria for the making of discretionary sentencing decisions does not prohibit the application of additional criteria reasonably related to the decision being made. Any such additional criteria shall be stated on the record by the sentencing judge.

(b) The order in which criteria are listed does not indicate their relative weight or importance.

Rule 409: Consideration of Criteria

Relevant criteria enumerated in these rules shall be considered by the sentencing judge, and shall be deemed to have been considered unless the record affirmatively reflects otherwise.

Rule 410: General Objectives In Sentencing

General objectives of sentencing include:

(a) Protecting society.

(b) Punishing the defendant.

(c) Encouraging the defendant to lead a law abiding life in the future and deterring him from future offenses.

(d) Deterring others from criminal conduct by demonstrating its consequences.

(e) Preventing the defendant from committing new crimes by isolating him for the period of incarceration.

(f) Securing restitution for the victims of crime.

(g) Achieving uniformity in sentencing.

Because in some instances these objectives may suggest inconsistent dispositions, the sentencing judge shall consider which objectives are of primary importance in the particular case.

The sentencing judge should be guided by statutory statements of policy, the criteria in these rules, and the facts and circumstances of the case.

Rule 411: Presentence Investigations & Reports

(a) *Eligible defendant.* If the defendant is eligible for probation, the court shall refer the matter to the probation officer for a presentence investigation and report. Waivers of the presentence report should not be accepted except in unusual circumstances.

(b) *Ineligible defendant.* Even if the defendant is not eligible for probation, the court should refer the matter to the probation officer for a presentence investigation and report.

(c) *Supplemental reports.* The court shall order a supplemental probation officer's report in preparation for sentencing proceedings that occur a significant period of time after the original report was prepared.

(d) *Purpose of presentence investigation report.* Probation officers' reports are used by judges in determining the appropriate length of a prison sentence and by the Department of Corrections in deciding upon the type of facility and program in which to place a defendant, and are also used in deciding whether probation is appropriate. Section 1203c requires a probation officer's report on every person sentenced to prison; ordering the report before sentencing in probation-ineligible cases will help ensure a well-prepared report.

Rule 411.5: Probation Officer's Presentence Investigation Report

(a) *Contents.* A probation officer's presentence investigation report in a felony case shall include at least the following:

(1) A face sheet showing at least: (i) the defendant's name and other identifying data; (ii) the case number; (iii) the crime of which the defendant was convicted; (iv) the date of commission of the crime, the date of conviction, and any other dates relevant to sentencing; (v) the defendant's custody status; and (vi) the terms of any agreement upon which a plea of guilty was based.

(2) The facts and circumstances of the crime and the defendant's arrest, including information concerning any co-defendants and the status or disposition of their cases. The source of all such information shall be stated.

(3) A summary of the defendant's record of prior criminal conduct, including convictions as an adult and sustained petitions in juvenile delinquency proceedings. Records of an arrest or charge not leading to a conviction or the sustaining of a petition shall not be included unless supported by facts concerning the arrest or charge.

(4) Any statement made by the defendant to the probation officer, or a summary thereof, including the defendant's account of the circumstances of the crime.

(5) Information concerning the victim of the crime, including:

(i) the victim's statement or a summary thereof, if available;

(ii) the amount of the victim's loss, and whether or not it is covered by insurance; and

(iii) any information required by law.

(6) Any relevant facts concerning the defendant's social history, including but not limited to those categories enumerated in Penal Code § 1203.10, organized under appropriate subheadings, including, whenever applicable, "Family," "Education," "Employment and income," "Military," "Medical/psychological," "Record of substance abuse or lack thereof," and any other relevant subheadings.

(7) Collateral information, including written statements from:

(i) official sources such as defense and prosecuting attorneys, police (subsequent to any police reports used to summarize the crime), probation and parole officers who have had prior experience with the defendant, and correctional personnel who observed the defendant's behavior during any period of presentence incarceration; and

(ii) interested persons, including family members and others who have written letters concerning the defendant.

(8) An evaluation of factors relating to disposition. This section shall include:

(i) a reasoned discussion of the defendant's suitability and eligibility for probation, and if probation is recommended, a proposed plan including recommendation for the conditions of probation and any special need for supervision;

(ii) if a prison sentence is recommended or is likely to be imposed, a reasoned discussion of aggravating and mitigating factors affecting the sentence length; and

(iii) a discussion of the defendant's ability to make restitution, pay any fine or penalty which may be recommended, or satisfy any special conditions of probation which are proposed. Discussions of factors affecting suitability for probation and affecting the sentence length shall refer to any sentencing rule directly relevant to the facts of the case, but no rule shall be cited without a reasoned discussion of its relevance and relative importance.

(9) The probation officer's recommendation. When requested by the sentencing judge or by standing instructions to the probation department, the report shall include recommendations concerning the length of any prison term that may be imposed, including the base term, the imposition of concurrent or consecutive sentences, and the imposition or striking of the additional terms for enhancements charged and found.

(10) Detailed information on presentence time spent by the defendant in custody, including the beginning and ending dates of the period(s) of custody; the existence of any other sentences imposed on the defendant during the period of custody; the amount of good behavior, work, or participation credit to which the defendant is entitled; and whether the sheriff or other officer holding custody, the prosecution, or the defense wishes a hearing be held for the purposes of denying good behavior, work, or participation credit.

(11) A statement of mandatory and recommended restitution, restitution fines, other fines, and costs to be assessed against the defendant, including chargeable probation services and attorney fees under § 987.8 when appropriate, findings concerning the defendant's ability to pay, and a recommendation whether any restitution order shall become a judgment under § 1203(j) if unpaid.

(b) *Format.* The report shall be on paper 8 1/2 by 11 inches in size and shall follow the sequence set out in subdivision (a) to the extent possible.

(c) *Sources.* The source of all information shall be stated. Any person who has furnished information included in the report shall be identified by name or official capacity unless a reason is given for not disclosing the person's identity.

Rule 412: Reasons

(a) *Defendant's agreement as reason.* It is an adequate reason for a sentence or other disposition that the defendant, personally and by counsel, has expressed agreement that it be imposed and the prosecuting attorney has not expressed an objection to it. The agreement and lack of objection shall be recited on the record.

(b) *Agreement to sentence abandons 654 claim.* By agreeing to a specified prison term personally and by counsel, a defendant who is sentenced to that term or a shorter one abandons any claim that a component of the sentence violates § 654's prohibition of double punishment, unless that claim is asserted at the time the agreement is recited on the record.

Rule 414: Criteria Affecting Probation

Criteria affecting the decision to grant or deny probation include:

(a) Facts relating to the crime, including:

(1) The nature, seriousness, and circumstances of the crime as compared to other instances of the same crime.

(2) Whether the defendant was armed with or used a weapon.

(3) The vulnerability of the victim.

(4) Whether the defendant inflicted physical or emotional injury.

(5) The degree of monetary loss to the victim.

(6) Whether the defendant was an active or passive participant.

(7) Whether the crime was committed because of an unusual circumstance, such as great provocation, which is unlikely to recur.

(8) Whether the manner in which the crime was carried out demonstrated criminal sophistication or professionalism on the part of the defendant.

(9) Whether the defendant took advantage of a position of trust or confidence to commit the crime.

(b) Facts relating to the defendant, including:

(1) Prior record of criminal conduct; whether as an adult or a juvenile, including the recency and frequency of prior crimes; and whether the prior record indicates a pattern of regular or increasingly serious criminal conduct.

(2) Prior performance on probation or parole and present probation or parole status.

(3) Willingness to comply with the terms of probation.

(4) Ability to comply with reasonable terms of probation as indicated by the defendant's age, education, health, mental faculties, history of alcohol or other substance abuse, family background and ties, employment and military service history, and other relevant factors.

(5) The likely effect of imprisonment on the defendant and his or her dependents.

(6) The adverse collateral consequences on the defendant's life resulting from the felony conviction.

(7) Whether the defendant is remorseful.

(8) The likelihood that if not imprisoned the defendant will be a danger to others.

Rule 420: Selection Of Base Term Of Imprisonment

(a) When a sentence of imprisonment is imposed, or the execution of a sentence of imprisonment is ordered suspended, the sentencing judge shall select the upper, middle, or lower term on each count for which the defendant has been convicted, as provided in § 1170(b) and these rules. The middle term shall be selected unless imposition of the upper or lower term is justified by circumstances in aggravation or mitigation.

(b) Circumstances in aggravation and mitigation shall be established by a preponderance of the evidence. Selection of the upper term is justified only if, after a consideration of all the relevant facts, the circumstances in aggravation outweigh the circumstances in mitigation. The relevant facts are included in the case record, the probation officer's report, other reports and statements properly received, statements in aggravation or mitigation, and any further evidence introduced at the sentencing hearing. Selection of the lower term is justified only if, considering the same facts, the circumstances in mitigation outweigh the circumstances in aggravation.

(c) To comply with § 1170(b), a fact charged and found as an enhancement may be used as a reason for imposing the upper term only if the court has discretion to strike the punishment for the enhancement and does so. The use of a fact of an enhancement to impose the upper term of imprisonment is an adequate reason for striking the additional term of imprisonment, regardless of the effect on the total term.

(d) A fact that is an element of the crime shall not be used to impose the upper term.

(e) The reasons for selecting the upper or lower term shall be stated orally on the record, and shall include a concise statement of the ultimate facts which the court deemed to constitute circumstances in aggravation or mitigation justifying the term selected.

Rule 421: Circumstances In Aggravation

Circumstances in aggravation include:

(a) Facts relating to the crime, whether or not charged or chargeable as enhancements, including the fact that:

(1) The crime involved great violence, great bodily harm, threat of great bodily harm, or other acts disclosing a high degree of cruelty, viciousness, or callousness.

(2) The defendant was armed with or used a weapon at the time of the commission of the crime.

(3) The victim was particularly vulnerable.

(4) The defendant induced others to participate in the commission of the crime or occupied a position of leadership or dominance of other participants in its commission.

(5) The defendant induced a minor to commit or assist in the commission of the crime.

(6) The defendant threatened witnesses, unlawfully prevented or dissuaded witnesses from testifying, suborned perjury, or in any other way illegally interfered with the judicial process.

(7) The defendant was convicted of other crimes for which consecutive sentences could have been imposed but for which concurrent sentences are being imposed.

(8) The manner in which the crime was carried out indicates planning, sophistication, or professionalism.

(9) The crime involved an attempted or actual taking or damage of great monetary value.

(10) The crime involved a large quantity of contraband.

(11) The defendant took advantage of a position of trust or confidence to commit the offense.

(b) Facts relating to the defendant, including the fact that:

(1) The defendant has engaged in violent conduct which indicates a serious danger to society.

(2) The defendant's prior convictions as an adult or sustained petitions in juvenile delinquency proceedings are numerous or of increasing seriousness.

(3) The defendant has served a prior prison term.

(4) The defendant was on probation or parole when the crime was committed.

(5) The defendant's prior performance on probation or parole was unsatisfactory.

(c) Any other facts statutorily declared to be circumstances in aggravation.

Rule 423: Circumstances In Mitigation

Circumstances in mitigation include:

(a) Facts relating to the crime, including the fact that:

(1) The defendant was a passive participant or played a minor role in the crime.

(2) The victim was an initiator of, willing participant in, or aggressor or provoker of the incident.

(3) The crime was committed because of an unusual circumstance, such as great provocation, which is unlikely to recur.

(4) The defendant participated in the crime under circumstances of coercion or duress, or the criminal conduct was partially excusable for some other reason not amounting to a defense.

(5) The defendant, with no apparent predisposition to do so, was induced by others to participate in the crime.

(6) The defendant exercised caution to avoid harm to persons or damage to property, or the amounts of money or property taken were deliberately small, or no harm was done or threatened against the victim.

(7) The defendant believed that he or she had a claim or right to the

property taken, or for other reasons mistakenly believed that the conduct was legal.

(8) The defendant was motivated by a desire to provide necessities for his or her family or self.

(b) Facts relating to the defendant, including the fact that:

(1) The defendant has no prior record, or an insignificant record of criminal conduct, considering the recency and frequency of prior crimes.

(2) The defendant was suffering from a mental or physical condition that significantly reduced culpability for the crime.

(3) The defendant voluntarily acknowledged wrongdoing prior to arrest or at an early stage of the criminal process.

(4) The defendant is ineligible for probation and but for that ineligibility would have been granted probation.

(5) The defendant made restitution to the victim.

(6) The defendant's prior performance on probation or parole was satisfactory.

Rule 425:   Criteria Affecting Concurrent or Consecutive Sentences

Criteria affecting the decision to impose consecutive rather than concurrent sentences include:

(a) *Criteria relating to crimes.* Facts relating to the crimes, including whether or not:

(1) The crimes and their objectives were predominantly independent of each other.

(2) The crimes involved separate acts of violence or threats of violence.

(3) The crimes were committed at different times or separate places, rather than being committed so closely in time and place as to indicate a single period of aberrant behavior.

(b) *Other criteria and limitations.* Any circumstances in aggravation or mitigation may be considered in deciding whether to impose consecutive rather than concurrent sentences, except (i) a fact used to impose the upper term, (ii) a fact used to otherwise enhance the defendant's prison sentence, and (iii) a fact that is an element of the crime shall not be used to impose consecutive sentences.

Rule 428:   Criteria Affecting Imposition of Enhancements

(a) *Imposing or not imposing enhancement.* No reason need be given for imposing a term for an enhancement that was charged and found true.

If the judge has statutory discretion to strike the additional term for an enhancement, the court may consider and apply any of the circumstances in mitigation enumerated in these rules or, pursuant to rule 408, any other reasonable circumstances in mitigation that are present.

The judge should not strike the allegation of the enhancement.

* * * *

Rule 433: *Matters To Be Considered At Time Set For Sentencing*

(a) In every case, at the time set for sentencing pursuant to § 1191, the sentencing judge shall hold a hearing at which the judge shall:

(1) Hear and determine any matters raised by the defendant pursuant to § 1201.

(2) Determine whether a defendant who is eligible for probation should be granted or denied probation, unless consideration of probation is expressly waived by the defendant personally and by counsel.

(b) If the imposition of sentence is to be suspended during a period of probation after a conviction by trial, the trial judge shall make factual findings as to circumstances which would justify imposition of the upper or lower term if probation is later revoked, based upon evidence admitted at the trial.

(c) If a sentence of imprisonment is to be imposed, or if the execution of a sentence of imprisonment is to be suspended during a period of probation, the sentencing judge shall:

(1) Hear evidence in aggravation and mitigation, and determine, pursuant to § 1170(b), whether to impose the upper, middle or lower term; and set forth on the record the facts and reasons for imposing the upper or lower term.

(2) Determine whether any additional term of imprisonment provided for an enhancement charged and found shall be stricken.

(3) Determine whether the sentences shall be consecutive or concurrent if the defendant has been convicted of multiple crimes.

(4) Determine any issues raised by statutory prohibitions on the dual use of facts and statutory limitations on enhancements, as required in rules 441 and 447.

(5) Pronounce the court's judgment and sentence, stating the terms thereof and giving reasons for those matters for which reasons are required by law.

(d) All these matters shall be heard and determined at a single hearing unless the sentencing judge otherwise orders in the interests of justice.

(e) When a sentence of imprisonment is imposed under subdivision (c) or under rule 435, the sentencing judge shall inform the defendant, pursuant to § 1170(c), of the parole period provided by § 3000 to be served after expiration of the sentence in addition to any period of incarceration for parole violation.

Rule 437: *Statements In Aggravation & Mitigation*

(a) Statements in aggravation and mitigation referred to in § 1170(b) shall be filed and served at least four days prior to the time set for sentencing pursuant to § 1191 or the time set for pronouncing judgment upon revocation of probation pursuant to § 1203.2(c) if imposition of sentence was previously suspended.

(b) A party seeking consideration of circumstances in aggravation or mitigation may file and serve a statement pursuant to § 1170(b) and this rule.

(c) A statement in aggravation or mitigation shall include:

(1)   A summary of facts which the party relies upon as circumstances in aggravation or mitigation justifying imposition of the upper or lower term.

(2) Notice of intention to dispute facts or offer evidence in aggravation or mitigation at the sentencing hearing. The statement shall generally describe the evidence to be offered, including a description of any documents and the names and expected substance of the testimony of any witnesses. No evidence in aggravation or mitigation may be introduced at the sentencing hearing unless it was described in the statement, or unless its admission is permitted by the sentencing judge in the interests of justice.

(d)   Assertions of fact in a statement in aggravation or mitigation shall be disregarded unless they are supported by the record in the case, the probation officer's report or other reports properly filed in the case, or other competent evidence.

(e) In the event the parties dispute the facts upon which the conviction rested, the court shall conduct a presentence hearing and make appropriate corrections, additions, or deletions in the presentence probation report or order a revised report.

UNITED STATES v. GRAYSON
United States Supreme Court
438 U.S. 41 (1978)

Mr. Chief Justice Burger delivered the opinion of the Court.

We granted certiorari to review a holding of the Court of Appeals that it was improper for a sentencing judge, in fixing the sentence within the statutory limits, to give consideration to the defendant's false testimony observed by the judge during the trial.

I

In August 1975, respondent Grayson was confined in a federal prison camp under a conviction for distributing a controlled substance. In October, he escaped but was apprehended two days later by FBI agents in New York City. He was indicted for prison escape in violation of 18 U.S.C. § 751(a).

During its case in chief, the United States proved the essential elements of the crime, including his lawful confinement and the unlawful escape. In addition, it presented the testimony of the arresting FBI agents that Grayson, upon being apprehended, denied his true identity.

Grayson testified in his own defense. He admitted leaving the camp but asserted that he did so out of fear: "I had just been threatened with a large stick with a nail protruding through it by an inmate that was serving time at Allenwood, and I was scared, and I just ran." He testified that the threat was made in the presence of many inmates by prisoner Barnes who sought to enforce collection of a gambling debt and followed other threats and physical assaults made for the same purpose. Grayson called one inmate, who testified: "I heard Barnes talk to Grayson in a loud voice one day, but that's all. I never seen no harm, no hands or no shuffling whatsoever."

Grayson's version of the facts was contradicted by the Government's rebuttal evidence and by cross-examination on crucial aspects of his story. For example, Grayson stated that after crossing the prison fence he left his prison jacket by the side of the road. On recross, he stated that he also left his prison shirt but not his trousers. Government testimony showed that on the morning after the escape, a shirt marked with Grayson's number, a jacket, and a pair of prison trousers were found outside a hole in the prison fence.[1] Grayson also testified on cross-examination: "I do believe that I phrased the rhetorical question to Captain Kurd, who was in charge of the prison, and I think I said something if an inmate was being threatened by somebody, what would he do? First of all he said he would want to know who it was." On further cross-examination, however, Grayson modified his description of the conversation. Captain Kurd testified that Grayson had never mentioned in any fashion threats from other inmates. Finally, the alleged assailant, Barnes, by then no longer an inmate, testified that Grayson had never owed him any money and that he had never threatened or physically assaulted Grayson.

The jury returned a guilty verdict, whereupon the District Judge ordered the United States Probation Office to prepare a presentence report. At the sentencing hearing, the judge stated:

> I'm going to give my reasons for sentencing in this case with clarity, because one of the reasons may well be considered by a Court of Appeals to be impermissible; and although I could come into this Court Room and sentence this Defendant to a five-year prison term without any explanation at all, I think it is fair that I give the reasons so that if the Court of Appeals feels that one of the reasons which I am about to enunciate is an improper consideration for a trial judge, then the Court will be in a position to reverse this Court and send the case back for re-sentencing.

> In my view a prison sentence is indicated, and the sentence that the Court is going to impose is to deter you, Mr. Grayson, and others who are similarly situated. Secondly, *it is my view that your defense was a complete fabrication without the slightest merit whatsoever. I feel it is proper for me to consider that fact in the sentencing, and I will do so.*" (Emphasis added.)

He then sentenced Grayson to a term of two years' imprisonment, consecutive to his unexpired sentence.[2]

On appeal, a divided panel of the Court of Appeals for the Third Circuit directed that Grayson's sentence be vacated and that he be resentenced by the District

---

[1] The testimony regarding the prison clothing was important for reasons in addition to the light it shed on quality of recollection. Grayson stated that after unpremeditatedly fleeing the prison with no possessions and crossing the fence, he hitchhiked to New York City — a difficult task for a man with no trousers. The United States suggested that by prearrangement Grayson met someone, possibly a woman friend, on the highway near the break in the fence and that this accomplice provided civilian clothes. It introduced evidence that the friend visited Grayson often at prison, including each of the three days immediately prior to his penultimate day in the camp.

[2] The District Court in this case could have sentenced Grayson for any period up to five years. 18 U.S.C. § 751(a).

Court without consideration of false testimony. * * * *

II

In *Williams v. New York*, 337 U.S. 241 (1949), Mr. Justice Black observed that the "prevalent modern philosophy of penology is that the punishment should fit the offender and not merely the crime," and that, accordingly, sentences should be determined with an eye toward the "reformation and rehabilitation of offenders." But it has not always been so. In the early days of the Republic, when imprisonment had only recently emerged as an alternative to the death penalty, confinement in public stocks, or whipping in the town square, the period of incarceration was generally prescribed with specificity by the legislature. Each crime had its defined punishment. The "excessive rigidity of the mandatory or fixed sentence system" soon gave way in some jurisdictions, however, to a scheme permitting the sentencing judge — or jury — to consider aggravating and mitigating circumstances surrounding an offense, and, on that basis, to select a sentence within a range defined by the legislature. Nevertheless, the focus remained on the crime: Each particular offense was to be punished in proportion to the social harm caused by it and according to the offender's culpability. The purpose of incarceration remained, primarily, retribution and punishment.

Approximately a century ago, a reform movement asserting that the purpose of incarceration, and therefore the guiding consideration in sentencing, should be rehabilitation of the offender, dramatically altered the approach to sentencing. A fundamental proposal of this movement was a flexible sentencing system permitting judges and correctional personnel, particularly the latter, to set the release date of prisoners according to informed judgments concerning their potential for, or actual, rehabilitation and their likely recidivism. Indeed, the most extreme formulations of the emerging rehabilitation model, with its "reformatory sentence," posited that "convicts regardless of the nature of their crime can never be rightfully imprisoned except upon proof that it is unsafe for themselves and for society to leave them free, and when confined can never be rightfully released until they show themselves fit for membership in a free community." Lewis, *The Indeterminate Sentence*, 9 Yale L.J. 17, 27 (1899).

This extreme formulation, although influential, was not adopted unmodified by any jurisdiction. "The influences of legalism and realism were powerful enough to prevent the enactment of this form of indeterminate sentencing. Concern for personal liberty, skepticism concerning administrative decisions about prisoner reformation and readiness for release, insistence upon the preservation of some measure of deterrent emphasis, and other such factors, undoubtedly, led, instead, to a system — indeed, a complex of systems — in which maximum terms were generally employed." Tappan, *Sentencing Under the Model Penal Code*, 23 law & Contemp. Prob. 528, 530 (1958). Thus it is that today* the extent of a federal prisoner's confinement is initially determined by the sentencing judge, who selects a term within an often broad, congressionally prescribed range; release on parole is then available on review by the United States Parole Commission, which, as a general rule, may conditionally release a prisoner any time after he serves one-third of the judicially fixed term. To an unspecified degree, the sentencing judge is

---

* Ed. — Note that "today" was in 1978, several years before the Federal Sentencing Guidelines were enacted.

obligated to make his decision on the basis, among others, of predictions regarding the convicted defendant's potential, or lack of potential, for rehabilitation.

Indeterminate sentencing under the rehabilitation model presented sentencing judges with a serious practical problem: how rationally to make the required predictions so as to avoid capricious and arbitrary sentences, which the newly conferred and broad discretion placed within the realm of possibility. An obvious, although only partial, solution was to provide the judge with as much information as reasonably practical concerning the defendant's "character and propensities, his present purposes and tendencies," *Pennsylvania ex rel. Sullivan v. Ashe*, 302 U.S. 51, 55 (1937), and, indeed, "every aspect of his life." *Williams v. New York*, 337 U.S. at 250. Thus, most jurisdictions provided trained probation officers to conduct presentence investigations of the defendant's life and, on that basis, prepare a presentence report for the sentencing judge.

Constitutional challenges were leveled at judicial reliance on such information, however. In *Williams v. New York*, a jury convicted the defendant of murder but recommended a life sentence. The sentencing judge, partly on the basis of information not known to the jury but contained in a presentence report, imposed the death penalty. The defendant argued that this procedure deprived him of his federal constitutional right to confront and cross-examine those supplying information to the probation officer and, through him, to the sentencing judge. The Court rejected this argument. It noted that traditionally "a sentencing judge could exercise a wide discretion in the sources and types of evidence used to assist him in determining the kind and extent of punishment to be imposed within limits fixed by law." *Id.* at 246. "And modern concepts individualizing punishment have made it all the more necessary that a sentencing judge not be denied an opportunity to obtain pertinent information," *id.* at 247; indeed, "to deprive sentencing judges of this kind of information would undermine modern penological procedural policies that have been cautiously adopted throughout the nation after careful consideration and experimentation." *Id.* at 249–250. Accordingly, the sentencing judge was held not to have acted unconstitutionally in considering either the defendant's participation in criminal conduct for which he had not been convicted or information secured by the probation investigator that the defendant was a "menace to society." See *id.* at 244.

Of course, a sentencing judge is not limited to the often far-ranging material compiled in a presentence report. "Before making the sentencing determination, a judge may appropriately conduct an inquiry broad in scope, largely unlimited either as to the kind of information he may consider, or the source from which it may come." *United States v. Tucker*, 404 U.S. 443, 446 (1972). Congress recently reaffirmed this fundamental sentencing principle by enacting 18 U.S.C. § 3577:

> No limitation shall be placed on the information concerning the background, character, and conduct of a person convicted of an offense which a court of the United States may receive and consider for the purpose of imposing an appropriate sentence.

Thus, we have acknowledged that a sentencing authority may legitimately consider the evidence heard during trial, as well as the demeanor of the accused. *Chaffin v. Stynchcombe*, 412 U.S. 17, 32 (1973). More to the point presented in this case, one serious study has concluded that the trial judge's "opportunity to observe the defendant, particularly if he chose to take the stand in his defense, can often provide useful insights into an appropriate disposition." ABA Project on Standards for Criminal Justice, Sentencing Alternatives and Procedures § 5.1 (App. Draft 1968).

A defendant's truthfulness or mendacity while testifying on his own behalf, almost without exception, has been deemed probative of his attitudes toward society and prospects for rehabilitation and hence relevant to sentencing. Soon after *Williams* was decided, the Tenth Circuit concluded that "the attitude of a convicted defendant with respect to his willingness to commit a serious crime — perjury — is a proper matter to consider in determining what sentence shall be imposed within the limitations fixed by statute." *Humes v. United States*, 186 F.2d 875, 878 (1951). The Second, Fourth, Fifth, Sixth, Seventh, Eighth, and Ninth Circuits have since agreed. Judge Marvin Frankel's analysis for the Second Circuit is persuasive:

> The effort to appraise "character" is, to be sure, a parlous one, and not necessarily an enterprise for which judges are notably equipped by prior training. Yet it is in our existing scheme of sentencing one clue to the rational exercise of discretion. If the notion of "repentance" is out of fashion today, the fact remains that a manipulative defiance of the law is not a cheerful datum for the prognosis a sentencing judge undertakes. Impressions about the individual being sentenced — the likelihood that he will transgress no more, the hope that he may respond to rehabilitative efforts to assist with a lawful future career, the degree to which he does or does not deem himself at war with his society — are, for better or worse, central factors to be appraised under our theory of "individualized" sentencing. The theory has its critics. While it lasts, however, a fact like the defendant's readiness to lie under oath before the judge who will sentence him would seem to be among the more precise and concrete of the available indicia. [*United States v. Hendrix*, 505 F.2d 1233, 1236 (1974).]

Only one Circuit has directly rejected the probative value of the defendant's false testimony in his own defense. In *Scott v. United States*, 419 F.2d 264, 269 (1969), the court argued that:

> The peculiar pressures placed upon a defendant threatened with jail and the stigma of conviction make his willingness to deny the crime an unpromising test of his prospects for rehabilitation if guilty. It is indeed unlikely that many men who commit serious offenses would balk on principle from lying in their own defense. The guilty man may quite sincerely repent his crime but yet, driven by the urge to remain free, may protest his innocence in a court of law.

The *Scott* rationale rests not only on the realism of the psychological pressures on a defendant in the dock — which we can grant — but also on a deterministic view of human conduct that is inconsistent with the underlying precepts of our criminal justice system. A "universal and persistent" foundation stone in our system of law, and particularly in our approach to punishment, sentencing, and incarceration, is the "belief in freedom of the human will and a consequent ability and duty of the normal individual to choose between good and evil." *Morissette v. United States*, 342 U.S. 246, 250 (1952). Given that long-accepted view of the "ability and duty of the normal individual to choose," we must conclude that the defendant's readiness to lie under oath — especially when, as here, the trial court finds the lie to be flagrant — may be deemed probative of his prospects for rehabilitation.

III

Against this background, we evaluate Grayson's constitutional argument that the District Court's sentence constitutes punishment for the crime of perjury for which he has not been indicted, tried, or convicted by due process. A second argument is that permitting consideration of perjury will "chill" defendants from exercising their right to testify on their own behalf.

A

In his due process argument, Grayson does not contend directly that the District Court had an impermissible purpose in considering his perjury and selecting the sentence. Rather, he argues that this Court, in order to preserve due process rights, not only must prohibit the impermissible sentencing practice of incarcerating for the purpose of saving the Government the burden of bringing a separate and subsequent perjury prosecution, but also must prohibit the otherwise permissible practice of considering a defendant's untruthfulness for the purpose of illuminating his need for rehabilitation and society's need for protection. He presents two interrelated reasons. The effect of both permissible and impermissible sentencing practices may be the same: additional time in prison. Further, it is virtually impossible, he contends, to identify and establish the impermissible practice. We find these reasons insufficient justification for prohibiting what the Court and the Congress have declared appropriate judicial conduct.

First, the evolutionary history of sentencing, set out in Part II, demonstrates that it is proper — indeed, even necessary for the rational exercise of discretion — to consider the defendant's whole person and personality, as manifested by his conduct at trial and his testimony under oath, for whatever light those may shed on the sentencing decision. The "parlous" effort to appraise "character," degenerates into a game of chance to the extent that a sentencing judge is deprived of relevant information concerning "every aspect of a defendant's life." *Williams v. New York*, 337 U.S. at 250. The Government's interest, as well as the offender's, in avoiding irrationality is of the highest order. That interest more than justifies the risk that Grayson asserts is present when a sentencing judge considers a defendant's untruthfulness under oath.

Second, in our view, *Williams* fully supports consideration of such conduct in sentencing. There the Court permitted the sentencing judge to consider the offender's history of prior antisocial conduct, including burglaries for which he had not been duly convicted. This it did despite the risk that the judge might use his knowledge of the offender's prior crimes for an improper purpose.

Third, the efficacy of Grayson's suggested "exclusionary rule" is open to serious doubt. No rule of law, even one garbed in constitutional terms, can prevent improper use of firsthand observations of perjury. The integrity of the judges, and their fidelity to their oaths of office, necessarily provide the only, and in our view adequate, assurance against that.

B

Grayson's argument that judicial consideration of his conduct at trial impermissibly "chills" a defendant's statutory right, 18 U.S.C. § 3481, and perhaps a constitutional right to testify on his own behalf is without basis. The right guaranteed by law to a defendant is narrowly the right to testify truthfully in accordance with the oath — unless we are to say that the oath is mere ritual without meaning. This view of the right involved is confirmed by the unquestioned constitutionality of perjury statutes, which punish those who willfully give false testimony. Further support for this is found in an important limitation on a defendant's right to the assistance of counsel: Counsel ethically cannot assist his client in presenting what the attorney has reason to believe is false testimony. See *Holloway v. Arkansas*, 435 U.S. 475, 480 (1978). Assuming, arguendo, that the sentencing judge's consideration of defendants' untruthfulness in testifying has any chilling effect on a defendant's decision to testify falsely, that effect is entirely permissible. There is no protected right to commit perjury.

Grayson's further argument that the sentencing practice challenged here will inhibit exercise of the right to testify truthfully is entirely frivolous. That argument misapprehends the nature and scope of the practice we find permissible. Nothing we say today requires a sentencing judge to enhance, in some wooden or reflex fashion, the sentences of all defendants whose testimony is deemed false. Rather, we are reaffirming the authority of a sentencing judge to evaluate carefully a defendant's testimony on the stand, determine — with a consciousness of the frailty of human judgment — whether that testimony contained willful and material falsehoods, and, if so, assess in light of all the other knowledge gained about the defendant the meaning of that conduct with respect to his prospects for rehabilitation and restoration to a useful place in society. Awareness of such a process realistically cannot be deemed to affect the decision of an accused but unconvicted defendant to testify truthfully in his own behalf.

Accordingly, we reverse the judgment of the Court of Appeals and remand for reinstatement of the sentence of the District Court.

Mr. Justice Stewart, with whom Mr. Justice Brennan and Mr. Justice Marshall join, dissenting.

The Court begins its consideration of this case, with the assumption that the respondent gave false testimony at his trial. But there has been no determination that his testimony was false. This respondent was given a greater sentence than he would otherwise have received — how much greater we have no way of knowing — solely because a single judge thought that he had not testified truthfully. In essence, the Court holds today that whenever a defendant testifies in his own behalf and is found guilty, he opens himself to the possibility of an enhanced sentence. Such a sentence is nothing more or less than a penalty imposed on the defendant's exercise of his constitutional and statutory rights to plead not guilty and to testify in his own behalf.

It does not change matters to say that the enhanced sentence merely reflects the defendant's "prospects for rehabilitation" rather than an additional punishment for testifying falsely.[3] The fact remains that all defendants who choose to testify, and

---

[3] Indeed, without doubting the sincerity of trial judges one may doubt whether the single incident of a defendant's trial testimony could ever alter the assessment of rehabilitative prospects so drastically as to justify a perceptibly greater sentence. A sentencing judge has before him a presentence report, compiled by trained personnel, that is designed to paint as complete a picture of the defendant's life and character as is possible. If the defendant's suspected perjury is consistent with the evaluation of the report, its impact on the rehabilitative assessment must be minimal. If, on the other hand, it suggests

only those who do so, face the very real prospect of a greater sentence based upon the trial judge's unreviewable perception that the testimony was untruthful. The Court prescribes no limitations or safeguards to minimize a defendant's rational fear that his truthful testimony will be perceived as false.[4] Indeed, encumbrance of the sentencing process with the collateral inquiries necessary to provide such assurance would be both pragmatically unworkable and theoretically inconsistent with the assumption that the trial judge is merely considering one more piece of information in his overall evaluation of the defendant's prospects for rehabilitation. But without such safeguards I fail to see how the Court can dismiss as "frivolous" the argument that this sentencing practice will "inhibit exercise of the right to testify truthfully."

A defendant's decision to testify may be inhibited by a number of considerations, such as the possibility that damaging evidence not otherwise admissible will be admitted to impeach his credibility. These constraints arise solely from the fact that the defendant is quite properly treated like any other witness who testifies at trial. But the practice that the Court approves today actually places the defendant at a disadvantage, as compared with any other witness at trial, simply because he is the defendant. Other witnesses risk punishment for perjury only upon indictment and conviction in accord with the full protections of the Constitution. Only the defendant himself, whose testimony is likely to be of critical importance to his defense[5], faces the additional risk that the disbelief of a single listener will itself result in time in prison.

The minimal contribution that the defendant's possibly untruthful testimony might make to an overall assessment of his potential for rehabilitation cannot justify imposing this additional burden on his right to testify in his own behalf. I do not believe that a sentencing judge's discretion to consider a wide range of information in arriving at an appropriate sentence (*Williams v. New York*, 337 U.S. 241) allows him to mete out additional punishment to the defendant simply because of his personal belief that the defendant did not testify truthfully at the trial.

Accordingly, I would affirm the judgment of the Court of Appeals.

Notes from Shelly:

1. In *People v. Redmond*, 29 Cal.3d 904 (1981), the court upheld an upper term sentence, citing *Grayson*. "A trial court's conclusion that a defendant has committed

---

such a markedly different character that different sentencing treatment seems appropriate, the defendant is *effectively* being punished for perjury without even the barest rudiments of due process.

[4] For example, the dissenting judge in the Court of Appeals in this case suggested that a sentencing judge "should consider his independent evaluation of the testimony and behavior of the defendant only when he is convinced beyond a reasonable doubt that the defendant intentionally lied on material issues of fact and the falsity of the defendant's testimony is necessarily established by the finding of guilt." 550 F.2d 103, 114 (Rosenn, J., dissenting). Contrary to Judge Rosenn, I do not believe that the latter requirement was met in this case. The jury could have believed Grayson's entire story but concluded, in the words of the trial judge's instructions on the defense of duress, that "an ordinary man" would not "have felt it necessary to leave the Allenwood Prison Camp when faced with the same degree of compulsion, coercion or duress as the Defendant was faced with in this case."

[5] Notwithstanding the standard instruction that the jury is not to draw any adverse inference from the defendant's failure to testify, "a defendant who does not take the stand will probably fatally prejudice his chances of acquittal." Note, *The Influence of the Defendant's Plea on Judicial Determination of Sentence*, 66 Yale L.J. 204, 212 n.36 (1956).

perjury may be considered as one fact to be considered in fixing punishment, as it bears on defendant's character and prospects for rehabilitation."

2. In *United States v. Dunnigan*, 507 U.S. 87 (1993), the Court applied *Grayson's* reasoning to the new Federal Sentencing Guidelines, allowing the judge to consider defendant's perjury at trial when sentencing her under the Guidelines.

PEOPLE v. SMITH
California Court of Appeal, 4th District
94 Cal.App.3d 433 (1979)

The Court:

Michael S. Smith appeals his conviction of two counts of robbery (Pen.Code § 211), one of which carried the allegation he used a knife (Pen.Code § 12022(b)). Smith pleaded guilty and urges sentencing error on appeal.

The court imposed the aggravated term of four years for robbery, enhanced it by one year for use of a knife and ordered a concurrent sentence on the other robbery conviction. In choosing the aggravated term, the court cited the circumstances that there were multiple victims, the victims were particularly vulnerable and there was a threat of great bodily harm to the victims.

Smith contends the term "particularly vulnerable" appearing in California Rules of Court, rule 421(a)(3), is vague and the finding of particular vulnerability in this case is unjustified.

Smith and Dale Booth, both members of the Marine Corps and absent without official leave from duty, having suffered a mechanical failure in the car they were riding to freedom, were seeking ways of obtaining money to get the car rolling again. They joined with Kerry Buschmann and decided to "roll" someone. They selected an elderly man at a fast-food establishment in Pacific Beach. When they failed in an attempt to have the elderly man invite them to his apartment, they followed him to his apartment house. Smith and Booth decided to break into the old man's apartment. Buschmann demurred.

Smith and Booth broke into an apartment. It apparently was not the old man's because the burglars found two women asleep in a bedroom. Smith and Booth climbed on the bed atop the women. Booth brandished a knife, cutting the hand of one victim. Smith and Booth demanded all their money. One victim gave them $18 from both victims' purses.

Having procured some money, Smith and Booth decided to have some fun. They sexually harassed and abused the two victims and a third woman resident of the apartment who arrived on the scene later. This went on for some four hours. Smith used a knife in the course of the robberies and assaults. We need not further detail the events of the evening, since only the issue of vulnerability is raised.

Smith professes great difficulty in discerning what the term "particularly vulnerable" means. His and Booth's involvement with the victims in this case provides an excellent illustration of the term. Having demonstrated their proclivity for victimizing the susceptible when they first determined to roll an old man, then to burgle him, these two armed marines climbed on top of two sleeping women in the middle of the night without any warning. Smith and his confederate exploited the very vulnerability Smith finds difficult to discern.

We find no vagueness in the term "particularly vulnerable" and no difficulty in applying it here. "Particularly", as used here, means in a special or unusual degree, to an extent greater than in other cases. "Vulnerability" means defenseless, unguarded, unprotected, accessible, assailable, one who is susceptible to the defendant's criminal act. An attack upon a vulnerable victim takes something less than intestinal fortitude. In the jargon of football players, it is a cheap shot.

The victims in this case were particularly vulnerable. Smith admitted he, at one point, increased their vulnerability by making them take off their underpants so they would not run out of the apartment.

Judgment affirmed.

PEOPLE v. TAKENCAREOF
California Court of Appeal, 5th District
119 Cal.App.3d 492 (1981)

ANDREEN, Associate Justice.

Defendants Kenny Wayne Takencareof and Jeffrey Don Blomdahl appeal from judgments sentencing them to prison for second degree burglary.

The burglary for which they were sentenced was the first of three crimes perpetrated on the same evening against the St. Clair office building in Bakersfield. Two separate entries were made with the intent to commit larceny; finally the building was entered a third time and burned to destroy fingerprints. Several people were involved other than defendants. The burglaries caused minimal loss; the items taken were of little value. The arson, however, caused approximately $200,000 in damage to the structure, $50,000 to $75,000 loss to the contents and great inconvenience to the tenants, with considerable disruption of business. * * * *

The two defendants were charged with two counts of burglary and one of arson, all of the same office building.

During trial, Takencareof withdrew his plea of not guilty to the first count of burglary and entered of plea of guilty. The jury acquitted him of the other two counts. Blomdahl was found guilty of the same count of burglary; the jury was unable to arrive at a verdict as to the other two counts. A mistrial was declared as to these two counts, followed by a dismissal in the interest of justice. * * * *

Although Takencareof was acquitted of the arson charge, the court clearly considered damage caused by the arson at the sentencing hearing. The court sentenced Takencareof as follows: "Probation will be denied, because the offense involved multiple victims, substantial loss to a large law firm, Mr. Siegel's business was destroyed, lives disrupted."[3]

Since neither of the two burglaries caused substantial damage, the reasons given by the judge for the sentencing (substantial loss to a law firm, destruction of a

---

[3] It should be noted that the trial court did not state its reasons for imprisonment as its sentencing choice as mandated under California Rules of Court, rule 439(d). Although error was committed, the articulation of the reasons for denial of probation cured the failure, providing that the reasons were sufficient. Meaningful appellate review is possible in this case by examining the factors used in denying probation.

business and lives disrupted) must mean that the court was relying on the *sequelae* of the arson when making its sentencing choice. The court did not state why it did not feel bound by the jury's verdict of not guilty of the arson charge. We assume it was because the court believed that it should apply a different standard of proof to the sentencing determination. Whether this is appropriate is a matter of first impression. We address the issue of the proper standard preponderance of the evidence or proof beyond a reasonable doubt to be used in such a circumstance.

California Rules of Court, rule 439(b), provides that the preponderance of evidence standard should be used when determining whether circumstances in aggravation or mitigation have been established in order to determine whether the upper or lower term of imprisonment should be selected.[4] This is constitutionally permissible. *People v. Nelson* (1978) 85 Cal.App.3d 99, 103–104. By analogy, it would appear that the same standard should be used in determining whether to sentence to prison. Proof by a preponderance of the evidence is the standard in the absence of a statute or decisional law to the contrary. Evid.Code § 115. * * * *

We believe that in those cases where the defendant has not previously been restrained of his freedom by state action, and the trier of fact has found him not guilty of a count in a multiple count prosecution, the same standard of proof of beyond a reasonable doubt should apply to both conviction and sentencing. It would be anomalous to hold that if the jury finds the defendant not guilty of a count utilizing the constitutionally exacting standard of proof beyond a reasonable doubt, he should face the same alleged crime at sentencing under a preponderance of evidence standard.

We are unprepared to hold that two standards operate simultaneously in a case where a defendant is acquitted. Such a holding would be ludicrous. A defendant who won a victory at the hands of the jury could nevertheless be subjected to a more harsh sentence if he was contemporaneously found guilty of another crime in the same case.

This reasoning is consistent with the holding in *People v. Richards* (1976) 17 Cal.3d 614, which disapproved of a restitution order to a victim in a purported crime of which the defendant was acquitted. The words of the court are appropriate here: "In the course of convincing a jury to doubt his guilt on one charge, a defendant should not have the additional task of persuading the judge regarding the subsequent sentencing disposition on other charges." *Id.* at 624.

The above reasoning is unaffected by the holdings in *In re Coughlin* (1976) 16 Cal.3d 52, and *In re Dunham* (1976) 16 Cal.3d 63. In *Coughlin* the defendant was acquitted of burglary in the municipal court. Later, there was a hearing in superior court to determine whether his probation should be revoked. He was on probation following convictions of burglary and receipt of stolen property. It was held that evidence tending to prove that the defendant was guilty of the burglary could be admitted at the probation revocation hearing without violating due process principles or the proscription against double jeopardy. The reasoning of the court was that Penal Code § 1203.2(a) authorizes revocation of probation when the court has *reason to believe* that he has violated any of the conditions of his probation.

----

[4] The rule leaves unstated the test to be used during the balancing process. We need not address that issue here.

As said in *In re Coughlin:* "It is unquestionable that the probation decision necessarily involves an element of risk and consequent potential danger to a society that may be victimized. Premature release from imprisonment may soon result in a repetition of criminal conduct. Thus, decisions involving probation require the exercise of an *informed* discretion, following a careful balancing of the respective interests of the offender and the public generally. Such a delicate balance cannot be achieved by foreclosing the courts from consideration of evidence bearing directly upon the offender's willingness and ability to complete a successful period of probation. As stated in *People v. Andre*, 37 Cal.App.3d 516 at 520–521: "Probation and parole are granted in the hope and expectation that the conditional release, under supervision, will better serve to rehabilitate a defendant than would supervised incarceration. The court, or the paroling authority, need not wait until the defendant proves, by new acts of criminality, that the hope and expectation were unfounded. *Acts short of criminality, or evidence which leaves a criminal violation still uncertain, may well, in the judgment of the court of authority, indicate that the hoped for rehabilitation is on the road to complete failure* and that a more restrictive process is required both to protect society and to assist the defendant toward ultimate rehabilitation."

In *Dunham* the court made a similar holding in reference to proceedings before the Adult Authority. Reliance was placed on the authority's "delicate duty to decide when a convicted offender can be safely allowed to return to and remain in society, the authority is in a different posture than the court which decides his original guilt. To blind the authority to relevant facts in this special context is to incur a risk of danger to the public which, at least as of this date, outweighs the competing considerations of a problematical gain in deterrence." *In re Dunham, supra*, 16 Cal.3d at 68.

We recognize that the jury's finding on Counts Two and Three in the instant case did not conclusively establish Takencareof's innocence, but merely found that the charges were not proven beyond a reasonable doubt. But he is in quite a different position than one who is on probation or parole. The violation of the probationer's or parolee's status subjects him to commitment or return to prison on the original charge if the decisionmaking body determines that his continued freedom is inimical to society's safety. Although the order of commitment in the instant case was on the basis of the burglary contained in the first count, Takencareof, a first offender whose liberty was not restricted by probation or parole, was in reality sent to prison on a charge of which he was acquitted. This was error. * * * *

In reference to Takencareof, the judgment is affirmed, but the matter is remanded to the trial court for resentencing in accordance with the views expressed herein.

Notes from Shelly:

1. How should a judge find facts at a sentencing hearing?

In *U.S. v. Rodriguez*, 67 F.3d 1312 (7th Cir.1995), defendant was sentenced to life imprisonment (without possibility of parole) for conspiracy to sell marijuana. While the jury was never asked to find the *quantity* of marijuana involved, and the evidence suggested that it might have been as low as 10 ounces, the judge at the sentencing hearing found that defendant had sold 1,000 kilograms. A panel of the Court of Appeals affirmed, and Rodriguez the asked for an *en banc* rehearing before the entire Court. This petition was denied, but Judge Posner felt that a full hearing should have been granted:

> The defendant was sentenced to life in prison without possibility of parole. He had been charged with conspiracy to sell marijuana, and the judge instructed the jury that all it had to find in order to convict was that the defendant had conspired to sell a "measurable" amount of marijuana. The prosecutor invited the jury to convict on the basis of evidence that the defendant had delivered ten ounces. At the sentencing hearing following the defendant's conviction, the judge found by a preponderance of the evidence that the defendant had actually sold more than 1,000 kilograms of marijuana, and this amount, together with the defendant's criminal history, triggered a mandatory sentence of life imprisonment. 21 U.S.C. § 841(b). Although there is no doubt that the evidence satisfied the preponderance standard, the government does not claim to have established the defendant's responsibility for the sale of 1,000 kilograms by clear and convincing evidence or beyond a reasonable doubt. The jurors were actually rather troubled by the issue of guilt — enough so that the judge had to give an *Allen*-type charge to blast a verdict out of them.

> The question on which rehearing en banc is sought is whether a heightened standard of proof, either clear and convincing evidence or proof beyond a reasonable doubt, is required in a case in which the real trial occurs at the sentencing hearing rather than at the trial of guilt. * * * *

> The extraordinary severity of the punishments prescribed by Congress for sellers of marijuana, and Congress's increasing tendency to specify mandatory minimum prison terms, thereby curtailing the sentencing discretion of judges and the Sentencing Commission, are controversial. But I accept absolutely the power of Congress to adopt these policies and I have no desire to attempt an end run around them.

> Yet even if their legitimacy, if not necessarily their wisdom, is wholeheartedly accepted, as I think it my duty as a judge to do, there is a serious question whether it is permissible to sentence a person to life in prison, without possibility of parole, at the end of a brief and casual sentencing hearing in which there is no jury, in which the rules of evidence are not enforced, in which the standard of proof is no higher than in an ordinary civil case, and in which the judge's decision will make the difference between a light punishment and a punishment that is the maximum that our system allows short of death. Had the defendant been sentenced on the basis of a sale of 10 ounces of marijuana, his sentence might have been as short as 18 months. The difference between 18 months and life is, obviously, enormous. Given the defendant's criminal history, his sentence would have been longer than 18 months, perhaps twice or even three times longer, but, for a man of Rodriguez's age (49), still far short of life in prison.

> The general formula for deciding what procedural safeguards due process requires was set forth in *Mathews v. Eldridge*, 424 U.S. 319 (1976). It requires weighing the magnitude and likelihood of error if the safeguard is not adopted against the cost of the safeguard. Given that evidence presented at a sentencing hearing is often unreliable, both because the rules of evidence are not enforced in such hearings and because evidence of

quantity of drugs sold is ordinarily given by criminals, the defendants' former associates, the risk of error cannot be reckoned trivial; and the magnitude of the potential error is enormous in a case in which quantity will determine whether the defendant gets a light sentence (even four and a half years is light by contemporary federal standards) or the heaviest possible short of death. The burden or cost of requiring a heightened standard of proof is limited to the possibility and consequences of occasionally giving a defendant a sentence lighter than he really deserves. This is not a trivial cost. But it should be tolerable if only clear and convincing evidence, and not proof beyond a reasonable doubt, is required.

Conceivably the intermediate standard of proof would reduce the number of errors both in favor of and against defendants, for it would induce the government to conduct a more thorough investigation in preparation for the sentencing hearing, thus putting before the judge a more complete and accurate picture of the facts. More thorough investigation implies, I acknowledge, a cost to the government, a cost that might in turn reduce the government's ability to prosecute the guilty or obtain adequate sentences in every case. Few benefits come without a cost. But to imprison for life a person who sells 10 ounces of marijuana is a miscarriage of justice of sufficient magnitude to warrant some expenditure of resources to prevent. I do not say that Rodriguez in fact sold only 10 ounces. I claim only that the risk of error concerning the quantity is unjustifiably enhanced if the government need only prove the larger quantity by a preponderance of the evidence.

It might be argued that the difference between the preponderance standard and the standard of clear and convincing evidence is too gossamer to change the outcome in any actual case. I doubt that. I agree that fine distinctions between standards of proof or of appellate review have little significance in practice. But the difference between the standard of proof by a preponderance of the evidence, a standard that in this case permitted the judge to send the defendant away for life if he thought the odds 51-49 in favor of the defendant's having sold the 1,000 kilograms, and proof beyond a reasonable doubt, is so large that there is room for an intermediate standard that can be practically, not merely conceptually, distinguished from the extremes.

This analysis suggests that due process may require a heightened standard of proof at least in cases where the issue is life imprisonment versus a much shorter term. There is an even better argument, however, that the heightened standard should be required in such cases simply as an intelligent rule of the federal common law of criminal procedure, without reference to the Constitution. Neither the Sentencing Reform Act nor the guidelines specifies a burden of persuasion, so courts must devise their own. We are free to modify this standard as wisdom gained from experience suggests. The present case is not a guidelines case, but the principle is the same. The statute under which Rodriguez was sentenced does not specify the burden of proof at the sentencing hearing. That issue has been left to the federal courts to resolve. * * * *

I do not go so far as to say that I would vote to adopt the higher standard of proof if rehearing en banc were granted. That is a difficult question, in part because of the difficulty of defining the scope of such a rule. I say only that the question is sufficiently important, the stakes in personal liberty sufficiently great, that the full court should examine it.

2. At a sentencing hearing, may a judge find facts inconsistent with those "found" by the jury?

In *U.S. v. Watts*, 519 U.S. 148 (1997), a jury convicted Watts of possession of cocaine base, but acquitted him of using a firearm in connection with a drug offense. But during a sentencing hearing, the trial court found that Watts had used the firearm during the drug offense, and added "two points" to his "base offense level," resulting in an increased sentence. The Court of Appeals reversed, but the Supreme Court held that the trial court had acted properly under the federal Sentencing Guidelines:

> The Court of Appeals' position to the contrary not only conflicts with the implications of the Guidelines, but it also seems to be based on erroneous views of our double jeopardy jurisprudence. The Court of Appeals asserted that, when a sentencing court considers facts underlying a charge on which the jury returned a verdict of not guilty, the defendant "suffers punishment for a criminal charge for which he or she was acquitted." However, sentencing enhancements do not punish a defendant for crimes of which he was not convicted, but rather increase his sentence because of the manner in which he committed the crime of conviction. * * * *

> The Court of Appeals likewise misunderstood the preclusive effect of an acquittal, when it asserted that a jury "rejects" some facts when it returns a general verdict of not guilty. The Court of Appeals failed to appreciate the significance of the different standards of proof that govern at trial and sentencing. We have explained that "acquittal on criminal charges does not prove that the defendant is innocent; it merely proves the existence of a reasonable doubt as to his guilt." *United States v. One Assortment of 89 Firearms*, 465 U.S. 354, 361 (1984). It is impossible to know exactly why a jury found a defendant not guilty on a certain charge. An acquittal is not a finding of any fact. An acquittal can only be an acknowledgment that the government failed to prove an essential element of the offense beyond a reasonable doubt. Without specific jury findings, no one can logically or realistically draw any factual finding inferences. Thus, the jury cannot be said to have "necessarily rejected" any facts when it returns a general verdict of not guilty.

> For these reasons, an acquittal in a criminal case does not preclude the Government from relitigating an issue when it is presented in a subsequent action governed by a lower standard of proof. * * * * We acknowledge a divergence of opinion among the Circuits as to whether, in extreme circumstances, relevant conduct that would dramatically increase the sentence must be based on clear and convincing evidence. The cases before us today do not present such exceptional circumstances, and we therefore do not address that issue. We therefore hold that a jury's verdict of acquittal does not prevent the sentencing court from considering conduct underlying the acquitted charge, so long as that conduct has been proved by a preponderance of the evidence.

In *U.S. v. Putra*, 110 F.3d 705 (9th Cir.1997), the court followed *Watts* and upheld Putra's sentence — even though the trial judge had considered charges on which the jury had acquitted Putra. Chief Judge Hug concurred:

I read the majority opinion of the Supreme Court in *United States v. Watts* to be based upon an interpretation of the Sentencing Guidelines. As Justice Breyer notes in concurring, "I join the Court's *per curiam* opinion while noting that it poses no obstacle to the Commission itself deciding whether or not to enhance a sentence on the basis of conduct that a sentencing judge concludes did take place, but in respect to which a jury acquitted the defendant." I hope that the Sentencing Commission will give special consideration to the jurisprudential wisdom of basing a sentence on alleged conduct of which a defendant has been acquitted by a jury.

The prosecution has elected to charge the defendant with two offenses. The defendant has mounted a defense to both charges. The judicial processes have been utilized to determine guilt or innocence. The jury has been asked to devote the time and energy to hear the evidence presented at trial, to consider that evidence in light of the instructions, and to render a verdict. It is difficult for me to see how the jury's effort is not seriously undercut, and in fact nullified, when the sentence of a defendant, after an acquittal on a charge, is the same as if the defendant had been convicted.

I can envision the difficulty of a defense counsel explaining to his client, "The jury convicted you of one count, but acquitted you of the other, however, under the Sentencing Guidelines the judge has sentenced you as though you were convicted of both." A likely reply, "But doesn't the judge have to respect the jury's determination?" The attorney explains, "Oh no, you see the judge views the facts under a different burden of proof." The defendant: "Then for all practical purposes the jury's acquittal had no effect at all; I thought I had the right to a jury finding me guilty of the crime before I got sentenced for committing it." Attorney: "No, you don't seem to understand; the judge doesn't have to pay any attention to what the jury did, because he operates under a different burden of proof. We lawyers and judges understand that sort of thing, even though it may not make common sense to you."

One wonders what the reaction of the jury would be if the jurors were told at the outset, "If you convict the defendant on one charge, but acquit her on the other, the judge, utilizing a different burden of proof, can sentence the defendant as though you had convicted her on both." Would this resonate with the jury as being fair to the defendant, worthwhile of their time and effort, and instill respect and admiration for our system of justice? I seriously doubt it.

The man on the street would be quite surprised to learn that our present guideline approach to sentencing permits a person to be charged with two offenses, convicted of one, acquitted of the other, and yet be sentenced as though he had been convicted of both. Sentencing on the basis of acquitted conduct gives the impression of a judge being able to second-guess a jury that has acquitted a defendant, despite our explanations about burdens of proof. For this reason, I believe consideration of this issue by the Sentencing Commission is most advisable.

3. Does the defendant have a right to remain silent at a sentencing hearing?

A criminal defendant may not be forced to testify at trial — the 5th Amendment privilege against self-incrimination guarantees this right. But does the defendant retain this right *at his sentencing hearing*?

In *Mitchell v. U.S.*, 526 U.S. 314 (1999), Mitchell pleaded guilty to selling cocaine. Her sentence would depend on whether she sold more than 5 kilograms. There was conflicting evidence before the sentencing judge regarding whether she sold more than this, but the judge found that she did sell more than 5 kilograms — in part because Mitchell did not testify to the contrary. The appellate court affirmed, but the Supreme Court reversed, holding that Mitchell retained her privilege against self-incrimination at the sentencing hearing and that the judge could not draw adverse inferences from her exercise of this right to remain silent:

> Treating a guilty plea as a waiver of the privilege at sentencing would be a grave encroachment on the rights of defendants. * * * * Over 90% of federal criminal defendants whose cases are not dismissed enter pleas of guilty or *nolo contendere*. Were we to accept the Government's position, prosecutors could indict without specifying the quantity of drugs involved, obtain a guilty plea, and then put the defendant on the stand at sentencing to fill in the drug quantity. The result would be to enlist the defendant as an instrument in his or her own condemnation, undermining the long tradition and vital principle that criminal proceedings rely on accusations proved by the Government, not on inquisitions conducted to enhance its own prosecutorial power.

> We reject the position that either petitioner's guilty plea or her statements at the plea colloquy functioned as a waiver of her right to remain silent at sentencing.

> The centerpiece of the Third Circuit's opinion is the idea that the entry of the guilty plea completes the incrimination of the defendant, thus extinguishing the privilege. Where a sentence has yet to be imposed, however, this Court has already rejected the proposition that "incrimination is complete once guilt has been adjudicated," *Estelle v. Smith*, 451 U.S. 454, 462 (1981), and we reject it again today. * * * *

> It is true, as a general rule, that where there can be no further incrimination, there is no basis for the assertion of the privilege. We conclude that principle applies to cases in which the sentence has been fixed and the judgment of conviction has become final. If no adverse consequences can be visited upon the convicted person by reason of further testimony, then there is no further incrimination to be feared.

> Where the sentence has not yet been imposed, a defendant may have a legitimate fear of adverse consequences from further testimony. As the Court stated in *Estelle*: "Any effort by the State to compel the defendant to testify against his will at the sentencing hearing clearly would contravene the Fifth Amendment." 451 U.S. at 463. * * * *

> The Fifth Amendment by its terms prevents a person from being "compelled in any criminal case to be a witness against himself." To maintain that sentencing proceedings are not part of "any criminal case" is contrary to the law and to common sense. As to the law, under the Federal

Rules of Criminal Procedure, a court must impose sentence before a judgment of conviction can issue. See Rule 32(d)(1). As to common sense, it appears that in this case, as is often true in the criminal justice system, the defendant was less concerned with the proof of her guilt or innocence than with the severity of her punishment. Petitioner faced imprisonment from one year upwards to life, depending on the circumstances of the crime. To say that she had no right to remain silent but instead could be compelled to cooperate in the deprivation of her liberty would ignore the Fifth Amendment privilege at the precise stage where, from her point of view, it was most important.

In *State v. Burgess*, 943 A.2d 727 (N.H. 2008), the court discussed the difference between defendant's *silence about his guilt* and defendant's *failure to show remorse*:

Even though a court may not constitutionally consider a defendant's refusal to admit guilt as a factor in sentencing, some courts hold that a defendant's silence after trial may be considered as a failure to accept responsibility or failure to express remorse, and thus indicate that an individual has a reduced potential for rehabilitation, without violating the defendant's right to remain silent. See, e.g., United States v. Johnson, 903 F.2d 1084, 1090 (7th Cir.1990); Barnes, 637 A.2d at 402–03. These courts draw a "distinction between imposing a harsher sentence upon a defendant based on his or her lack of remorse, and punishing a defendant for his or her refusal to admit guilt, the latter being a violation, inter alia, of a criminal defendant's right to due process, to remain silent and to appeal." State v. Kamana'o, 103 Hawai'i 315, 82 P.3d 401, 407 (2003). In these jurisdictions, unless the sentencing court suggests that the defendant's admission of guilt would reduce his sentence, no constitutional right is violated when the court considers the defendant's silence as a failure to accept responsibility or express remorse for the limited purpose of determining whether rehabilitation efforts would be fruitful.

Other courts have rejected this distinction and hold that a sentencing court may not consider a defendant's silence at sentencing as indicating a lack of remorse without violating his privilege against self-incrimination. See State v. Hardwick, 183 Ariz. 649 (Ct.App.1995) ("A convicted defendant's decision not to publicly admit guilt [by expressing remorse] is irrelevant to a sentencing determination, and the trial court's use of this decision to aggravate a defendant's sentence offends the Fifth Amendment privilege against self-incrimination."). Noting that "even courts which permit consideration of a lack of remorse note that there is a fine line between punishing a defendant for remaining silent and proper consideration of his failure to show remorse," Jackson, 643 A.2d at 1380, the courts generally reason that, because the terms contrition and remorse connote an acknowledgement of guilt on the part of a defendant, a defendant's lack of contrition is, for legal purposes, tantamount to a refusal to admit guilt. Accordingly, since contrition or remorse necessarily imply guilt, it would be irrational or disingenuous to expect or require one who maintains his innocence to express contrition or remorse.

While these courts recognize that rehabilitation is an important factor to consider at sentencing and that lack of remorse can be considered as a factor in sentencing, they reason that allowing a court to draw an adverse inference from a defendant's silence at sentencing when he has maintained his innocence throughout the proceedings would force upon the defendant the Hobson's choice which is condemned by the Fifth Amendment specifically, that the defendant must either incriminate himself at the sentencing hearing and show remorse (with respect to a crime he claims he did not commit) or, in the alternative, stand on his right to remain silent and suffer the imposition of a greater sentence.

We agree with the courts rejecting the distinction between using a defendant's silence to infer a failure to express remorse and using it to punish a defendant for refusing to admit guilt. "Remorse" is defined as "a gnawing distress arising from a sense of guilt for past wrongs," Webster's Third New International Dictionary 1921 (unabridged ed.2002), or "deep and painful regret for wrongdoing," Random House Dictionary of the English Language 1214 (1966). Thus, for a defendant to truthfully express remorse, he must to some degree acknowledge wrongdoing or guilt. In this respect, we see no practical difference between a defendant's failure to express remorse and his refusal to admit guilt.

In either case, the defendant must admit wrongdoing and jeopardize his post-trial remedies, testify falsely and risk a perjury conviction, or remain silent and risk obtaining a greater sentence. The privilege against self-incrimination prevents the state from forcing the choice of this 'cruel trilemma' on the defendant. Accordingly, because the only affirmative way for a defendant who maintains his innocence throughout the criminal process to express remorse at sentencing is to forego his right to remain silent, a court may not constitutionally draw an adverse inference of lack of remorse from the defendant's silence at sentencing.

(4) In *U.S. v. Nichols*, 438 F.3d 437 (4th Cir. 2006), the court held that statements obtained during interrogation conducted after defendant had requested an attorney were admissible at a *sentencing* hearing:

We agree with the Seventh Circuit that statements obtained in violation of *Miranda*, if they are otherwise voluntary, may generally be considered at sentencing. The Supreme Court has repeatedly held that although statements obtained in violation of *Miranda* are inadmissible in the government's case-in-chief at trial, such statements, if reliable, may be used for other purposes and in other ways. For example, the Court has held that in the absence of actual coercion, statements obtained without warning a defendant of his right to counsel under *Miranda* may be used to impeach the defendant's testimony at trial. *See Harris v. New York, 401 U.S. 222 (1971)*. The Court has similarly upheld the introduction, for impeachment purposes, of otherwise voluntary statements obtained after a suspect had invoked his *Miranda* right to counsel but before counsel was provided. *See Oregon v. Hass, 420 U.S. 714 (1975)*. Further, the Court has held that the Fifth Amendment does not bar the admission at trial of the testimony of witnesses discovered through a defendant's unwarned but otherwise voluntary statements, *see Michigan v. Tucker, 417 U.S. 433 (1974)*, nor does it bar the introduction of physical evidence discovered as a result of such statements, *see United States v. Patane, 542 U.S. 630 (2004)*. Moreover, the Court has held that when a defendant makes unwarned but otherwise voluntary statements, the Fifth Amendment normally does not require suppression of subsequent statements made after *Miranda* warnings are given. *See Elstad, 470 U.S. at 318.*

These decisions have relied on the same rationale as cases permitting the consideration of illegally seized evidence at sentencing-namely, a balancing of the deterrent effect expected to be achieved by extending the *Miranda* exclusionary rule against the harm resulting from the exclusion of reliable evidence from the truth-finding process.

Applying these principles here, we conclude that the policies underlying the *Miranda* exclusionary rule normally will not justify the exclusion of illegally obtained but reliable evidence from a sentencing proceeding. We believe that in most cases, the exclusion of evidence obtained in violation of *Miranda* from the government's case-in-chief at trial will provide ample deterrence against police misconduct.

PEOPLE v. BENNETT
California Court of Appeal, 5th District
128 Cal.App.3d 354 (1981)

The Court:

Appellant was convicted after jury trial of two counts of robbery (Pen.Code § 211) with the use of a firearm (Pen.Code § 12022.5). The trial court sentenced appellant to concurrent five-year upper base terms on both counts and imposed the two-year gun use enhancement on count one.

Appellant contends that resentencing is required because the trial court based two aggravating factors on the fact of the gun use and because the record failed to support another factor, the victim's particular vulnerability.

For discussion purposes, we adopt respondent's factual summary: "At approximately 8:15 p.m. on June 7, 1980, appellant Troy Thomas Bennett, Susan Bennett, and William Harris entered the Foodland Market on Marks and Bullard in the City of Fresno. Appellant and Bennett approached head clerk Duke Reed, and appellant told Reed he had been shortchanged when he was in the market earlier that day. Reed told appellant there was nothing he could do about it tonight. Appellant then turned around, produced a sawed-off shotgun, and ordered Reed to open the safe. Bennett accompanied Reed to the safe. After the safe was opened, Bennett ordered Reed to put the money in the Foodland shopping bag held in her hand. Meanwhile, appellant pointed the shotgun at Melinda Mastores, a checker in the store, and told her to get the money out of the cash register drawer. Appellant also waved the shotgun about, ordering people in the store to take the money out of their purses. After the appellant and Bennett took the money from Melinda, Duke, and the people in line at the checkstand, they ran out the door, with Harris walking out very casually behind them. The three then drove away. After a high-speed chase by law enforcement officials, the appellant, Susan Bennett, and William Harris were apprehended. Appellant admitted to helping rob the Foodland Market and testified that he was armed at the time. Appellant also testified that prior to entering the market, he had been drinking and was under the influence of Phencyclidine (PCP or angel dust)."

The sentencing hearing occurred October 9, 1980. The judge had read a probation officer's report (RPO) dated October 2, 1980. The RPO noted, in mitigation, that appellant had admitted culpability shortly after his arrest. The RPO cited these aggravating factors:

> These offenses involved the threat of great bodily harm. The defendant obviously occupied a position of leadership and was personally armed with an illegal weapon during the commission of this offense. Also, it appears the defendant and co-defendant Susan Burris (also known as Susan Bennett) planned this crime (Rule 421, Section 1, Subsections, 1, 2, 5 and 8). The defendant has engaged in a pattern of violent conduct which indicates he is a serious danger to society. His prior convictions for crimes as a juvenile and adult are significant and are becoming increasingly serious. The defendant has served a prior prison term for Rape and had felony warrants outstanding for his arrest for an alleged robbery, two counts of aggravated assault and escape when he committed the instant offense. It also appears the defendant's prior performance on probation as a juvenile was less than satisfactory (Rule 421, Section b, Subsections 1, 2, 3 and 5).

After hearing argument on the base term, the judge imposed the upper term and stated:

> The reasons I have chosen the upper term is, one, that the crime involved the threat of great bodily harm. Two, that the victims were particularly vulnerable, being clerks in the market. That the Defendant was convicted of two counts of robbery, for which consecutive sentences could be imposed, but which the Court intends to impose concurrent sentences. That the crime involved the taking of property by violence, and that the Defendant has engaged in a previous pattern of violent conduct, which indicates he's a serious menace to the society.

The judge went on to impose the gun use enhancement, "the Court not using that as a ground for selection of the upper term."

Vulnerability

Rule 421(a)(3), California Rules of Court, cites as an aggravating factor relating to the crime that "The victim was particularly vulnerable." This phrase has generated substantial litigation. In *People v. Ramos* (1980) 106 Cal.App.3d 591, 606–608, this court upheld the trial court's finding of particular vulnerability where the defendant and two others assaulted and robbed the victim in his own home. The victim was isolated and not subject to help from passers-by. We observed: "Rather than merely focus on the victim's physical traits, it was quite proper to consider the total milieu in which the commission of the crime occurred." *Id.* at p. 607.

In the instant case, appellant argues that neither the victim's personal characteristics nor the setting of the crime supports a finding of particular vulnerability. Respondent counters that the finding rests on evidence that three persons were trying to rob the market, that appellant, while under the influence of alcohol and drugs, was screaming and brandishing a sawed-off shotgun.

We agree with appellant. Preliminarily, we note that the sentencing judge did not undertake a detailed exegesis of the issue. Rather, he appeared to reason that the victims were particularly vulnerable simply because they were market clerks. A market clerk might be statistically more likely to suffer a robbery than would a homeowner, for example, because there are more commercial than residential robberies. However, this fact alone does not establish particular vulnerability within the meaning of the rule.

We can picture situations where a market clerk is particularly vulnerable, for example, where he is alone, in the wee hours of the morning, at an isolated convenience market when the robbery occurs. In the instant case, the robbery occurred at a supermarket, located in a shopping center, at 8:15 p.m., in June, with five store employees and 40 or 50 customers present. The total milieu rebutted a finding of particular vulnerability.[1]

Threat of Great Bodily Injury

Rule 421(a)(1), California Rules of Court, cites as an aggravating factor that: "The crime involved great violence, great bodily harm, threat of great bodily harm, or other acts disclosing a high degree of cruelty, viciousness or callousness, whether or not charged or chargeable as an enhancement under § 12022.7." The judge found that the crime involved a threat of great bodily harm.

Appellant argues that since there were no direct verbal threats or other evidence of a threat of great bodily harm apart from the gun use itself, an improper dual use of facts occurred. Respondent counters that appellant grabbed the box boy and a customer who were trying to leave the store and pointed the gun at the victims. The former fact does not comprise a threat of great bodily harm and the latter fact was part and parcel of the gun use itself. *People v. Smith* (1980) 101 Cal.App.3d 964.

We agree with appellant that an improper dual use occurred.

Taking By Violence

The judge found that "the crime involved the taking of property by violence." Appellant argues again that this finding could only be based on the gun use, that "there was no surplusage whatsoever in this case of violence." We agree. The taking of property from the victims was effected through the gun use. The technical batteries which occurred when appellant grabbed the box boy and a female customer to prevent them from leaving did not show a violent taking of property.

Disposition

The judge was aware of the dual use prohibition and recited that he had not relied on the gun use to impose the upper term. But the record suggests that the judge construed the dual use rule too narrowly because two of the five aggravating factors could only have been based factually on the gun use. Also, while supermarkets may be statistically popular targets, this alone does not show particular vulnerability.

Appellant has not challenged the remaining two aggravating factors cited by the judge, which are supported by the record. Nevertheless, when three of the five

---

[1] This is not to minimize an extremely dangerous, terrifying situation produced by a robbery by an agitated person brandishing a sawed-off shotgun. However, the fact of the gun use could not be used to show vulnerability because a gun use enhancement was imposed.

factors have fallen by the wayside, remand for resentencing is appropriate because we cannot say that the result is a foregone conclusion.

The matter is remanded for resentencing in accordance with the principles expressed herein. In all other respects, it is affirmed.

Note from Shelly:

I'm not sure I understand what "particularly vulnerable" means. Isn't *anyone* faced with a sawed-off shotgun "particularly vulnerable"? Does a young, healthy supermarket clerk working in the daytime have a better ability to ward off shotgun pellets than an old, unhealthy clerk working alone late at night?

PEOPLE v. McNALLY
California Court of Appeal, 5th District
181 Cal.App.3d 1048 (1986)

HANSON, ACTING PRESIDING JUSTICE.

An information charged appellant with vehicular manslaughter with gross negligence in count I (Pen.Code § 192(c)(3)), driving under the influence of alcohol with injury in count II (Veh.Code § 23153(a)), and driving with a blood alcohol level of .10 or above causing injury in count III (Veh.Code § 23153(b)). After a seven-day trial, the jury returned a verdict of guilty on all counts.

Appellant was sentenced to a six-year term on count I and an eight-month consecutive term on count II. The sentence on count III was stayed pursuant to § 654.

Facts

On January 21, 1984, appellant, the owner and president of California Gun Specialties, hosted an annual sales meeting at the Lamp Liter Inn in Visalia. A cocktail party and dinner were held. Testimony is conflicting as to the amount of alcohol consumed by appellant. Various people testified that appellant did not appear to be intoxicated.

At approximately 11:30 p.m., appellant left the Lamp Liter Inn; around midnight, appellant traveled on Country Center Drive toward the Caldwell Avenue intersection. The speed limit on Country Center Drive is 30 mph; the speed limit on Caldwell Avenue is 45 mph. The traffic on Caldwell Avenue has the right of way; a stop sign is at the Caldwell intersection. Experts for the prosecution and eyewitnesses testified appellant was traveling at a speed of about 50 to 55 mph; he failed to slow down or stop at the stop sign. When he entered the intersection, appellant, driving a Ford Bronco vehicle, struck a Volkswagen automobile traveling on Caldwell Avenue carrying Karen Wonacott and Russell Bitney. Bitney was seriously injured in the accident; Wonacott was killed.

When Officer Jeff Goodwin of the Visalia Police Department arrived, he saw Bitney and Wonacott lying on the ground away from the vehicle. Although he felt no pulse, Goodwin administered CPR to Wonacott until an ambulance arrived. When Goodwin turned his attention to appellant, he noticed the smell of alcohol and that appellant was unstable in his coordination. Appellant's conduct during a field sobriety test administered by another officer led Goodwin to believe appellant was under the influence of alcohol. A blood test taken about an hour later showed appellant's blood alcohol level to be.155.

Discussion

I

[The Court reversed the conviction on Count 1 because of improper jury instructions.]

II

A trial court has broad discretion to grant or deny probation, unless there is a statutory limitation. For purposes of sentencing on remand, we share our concern with the method used. The granting of probation is not a matter of right, but a discretionary choice. However, an erroneous understanding by the trial court of its discretionary power does not result in a true exercise of discretion.

Here, the trial court ignored factors favoring the grant of probation, and considered only criteria in support of a denial of probation. Furthermore, the criteria relied upon do not apply to these facts.

A trial court must state the factors which support the denial of probation and the sentencing of a defendant to state prison. California Rules of Court, rule 414, lists criteria to be considered in granting or denying probation. The criteria address facts relevant to the crime and to the defendant. The trial court relied on only two factors in rule 414 to deny probation: (1) the nature, seriousness and circumstances of the crime (rule 414(c)(1)); and (2) the vulnerability of the victim and the degree of harm or loss to the victim (rule 414(c)(2)).

The court in *People v. Bloom* (1983) 142 Cal.App.3d 310, in considering aggravation in sentencing, expressed concern for reliance on the criterion of vulnerability of a victim and the degree of harm or loss suffered in cases involving vehicular manslaughter caused by a driver under the influence of alcohol. In *Bloom*, the defendant struck the victim's car head-on as he swerved in and out of traffic. He was traveling at a higher rate of speed than the cars he was trying to avoid hitting. The court noted that all victims of drunk drivers are vulnerable victims. The court concluded that precisely for this reason drunk-driving victims should not be considered vulnerable to an extent greater than in other cases. The court reasoned the element of vulnerability is inherent in the very crime of vehicular manslaughter caused by a driver under the influence of alcohol, and to use that factor to aggravate the term is improper. "Felony drunk driving presupposes an entirely innocent and unsuspecting victim." *People v. Levitt* (1984) 156 Cal.App.3d 500, 515. The drunk driver does not seek to take deliberate advantage of the vulnerability of victims, unlike the situation in other criminal cases. The *Bloom* court did not, however, completely foreclose the use of this criterion in future cases: "While we can visualize extraordinary situations in which a drunk driving victim might be considered to be 'particularly vulnerable,' such a situation is not present here, and therefore the court erred in applying rule 421(a)(3) to this case." 167 Cal.App.3d at 322.

The trial judge below expressed his knowledge of the <u>Bloom</u> case, but only attempted to distinguish it on its facts. The judge noted that visibility at the intersection of Caldwell Avenue and Country Center Drive was severely limited because of structures and trees and the speed at which appellant was traveling gave Bitney little opportunity for evasive action to avoid a collision.

The judge addressed the other aspect of rule 414(c)(2) — the degree of harm or loss: "The degree of harm or loss to the victim under 414(c)(2) is an additional consideration which goes without saying. It was enormous. Death and serious bodily injury occurred." The degree of harm or loss to the victim of course was "enormous"; however, felony vehicular manslaughter is based on the death of a victim. We note that rule 421(a)(3), addressing circumstances in aggravation, has been upheld in criminal cases involving violent felonies where the circumstances of the crime "make the defendant's act 'especially contemptible.' " There is no evidence here other than the crime itself to support such a conclusion.

The trial court found other factors to uphold the sentencing in <u>Bloom</u>, such as an extremely high blood alcohol reading of the defendant and a lack of remorse.

We find insufficient facts to remove the case from the holding and discussion in the *Bloom* case. We cannot say the victims were particularly vulnerable under the statute (Cal.Rules of Court, rule 414(c)(2)) so as to support a denial of probation. It was error here, as in *Bloom*, to rely upon the vulnerability subsection to support denial. Nor can we rely upon the tragic death and bodily injury to uphold the denial of probation under the seriousness of the crime criterion under these facts.

The probation officer addressed the relevant rule 414 factors in his report. The judge mentioned the two factors discussed, then concluded: "I would say that taking those two factors, 414(c)(1) and 414(c)(2), outweigh the other factors concerning the granting or denying of probation that have come before the court, and that is my reason for in the first sentence choice denying probation and imposing a prison sentence."

Appellant's act of driving his truck while under the influence of alcohol resulted in the death of one person and injury to another; no one disputed this. The seriousness of the crime is not diminished because appellant has no prior criminal record and apparently is an upstanding member of the community. However, the reasons as stated are insufficient to deny probation under California Rules of Court.

Reliance solely on rule 414(c)(1) and (c)(2) on the state of this record and under the reasoning found in *Bloom*, is insufficient to support the denial of probation. To hold otherwise would indicate the statute itself prevents the granting of probation under all such similar circumstances. We must consider the statute in its perspective; we note that even though the Legislature recently increased the punishment for the crime itself (§ 193), the Legislature did not see fit to impose a statutory prohibition preventing the granting of probation. Under the wording of the Rules of Court, we reverse for the court's consideration of all pertinent factors to grant or deny probation in resentencing.

III

We also question other sentencing choices. Ordinarily, if a court states adequate reasons for rejecting probation, it need not explain its choice of imposing the middle term of punishment. Statutory presumption favors the middle term unless there are circumstances in aggravation or mitigation. § 1170, subd.(b).

Although it would have been acceptable to select the middle term without giving any basis, the judge explained his choice as follows:

> Under circumstances in aggravation, this is under Rule 421 of the California Rules of Court, and Rule 423, the circumstances in mitigation are to be weighed. Again, I am thoroughly familiar with those. I have compared circumstances in mitigation against circumstances in aggravation, and it is the court's opinion that neither one really outweighs the other that much. In other words, I cannot see a justification here under the mitigating circumstances when comparing them to the circumstances in aggravation to grant a mitigated — or impose a mitigated sentence.

> Also, in considering the numerous circumstances in mitigation against the at least three or more circumstances in aggravation, and I will mention them after awhile, I do not see the justification for a maximum or aggravated sentence of eight years. My choice would be after looking at the circumstances in aggravation and comparing them with those in mitigation to impose the middle sentence of six years.

The court did not specify what mitigating factors were involved. In imposing a consecutive term, the judge listed the following aggravating factors: (1) the crime involved multiple victims, (2) the crime involved great bodily injury, and (3) the victim was particularly vulnerable.

The first aggravating factor involves the allegation that multiple victims were involved. Cal.Rules of Court, rule 421(a)(4). Case law has dealt with the exact same language in rule 425, which specifies factors justifying a consecutive sentence. In *People v. Humphrey* (1982) 138 Cal.App.3d 881, 882, the court stated: "The trial court improperly relied on the multiple-victim factor under California Rules of Court, rule 425(a)(4). We find the rule applies only to a situation where a defendant is convicted of two or more counts or crimes and at least one of those counts involves multiple victims." The count alleging vehicular manslaughter involves only one victim — Karen Wonacott. It was improper to use this reason as a possible aggravating factor for the sentence on the vehicular manslaughter count.[*]

The second possible aggravating factor concerns whether the crime involved great bodily injury. Cal.Rules of Court, rule 421(c)(1). This aggravating factor requires more than the basic fact of bodily harm. To be an aggravating factor, appellant must have committed cruel, vicious, and callous acts beyond the basic crime of vehicular manslaughter. "The essence of 'aggravation' relates to the effect of a particular fact in making the offense distinctively worse than the ordinary." *People v. Moreno* (1982) 128 Cal.App.3d 103, 110.

Bodily harm resulting in death is an element of felony vehicular manslaughter. Reliance upon that fact alone is improper when trying to aggravate a term of imprisonment. Although Wonacott's death was most tragic, cruelty, viciousness, or callousness on appellant's part beyond the occurrence of the accident was not shown. It was not established that this crime was distinctively worse than the usual

---

[*] Ed. — In 1991, the "multiple victims" provision in Rule 421 was deleted. The Advisory Committee commented: "Former subdivision (a)(4), concerning multiple victims, was deleted to avoid confusion; cases in which that possible circumstance in aggravation was relied on were frequently reversed on appeal because there was only a single victim in a particular count."

and tragic felony vehicular manslaughter.

The final aggravating factor mentioned by the trial judge considered the vulnerability of the victims. The problems surrounding this factor were discussed in terms of the denial of probation. The same basic analysis applies. If Bitney and Wonacott were not vulnerable victims under *Bloom* for purposes of probation, they cannot be considered vulnerable victims for purposes of aggravating the sentence.

Because all three stated aggravating factors do not apply, only the mitigating factors remain. Weighing the trial judge's statement regarding the balancing of factors, had the judge ignored inapplicable aggravating factors, he could and might have mitigated the sentence to the lower term of four years.

IV

Appellant urges the six-year base term he received for felony vehicular manslaughter with gross negligence constitutes cruel and unusual punishment as it applies to him and the facts of his case. Appellant points to the fact his behavior (a blood alcohol level of only .155) did not demonstrate a high degree of culpability. Furthermore, he has no prior criminal record, no history of alcohol abuse, and "an impeccable record of service to his family and community." "A punishment may violate article I, § 6, of the Constitution if, although not cruel or unusual in its method, it is so disproportionate to the crime for which it is inflicted that it shocks the conscience and offends fundamental notions of human dignity." *In re Lynch* (1972) 8 Cal.3d 410, 424. Three techniques are used to determine whether a particular punishment constitutes cruel and unusual punishment. First, the nature of the offense and/or the offender, with regard to the degree of danger both present to society is considered. *Id.* at 425. Second, the challenged penalty is compared with other penalties in the same jurisdiction for different offenses which are deemed more serious. *Id.* at p. 426. Finally, the challenged penalty is compared with penalties in other jurisdictions for the same offense. *Id.* at 427.

In most cases, even if the latter two tests demonstrate disproportionality, if the first test shows otherwise, the determination on the first test is controlling. *People v. Gayther* (1980) 110 Cal.App.3d 79, 90. The Legislature is given a broad discretion in enacting penal statutes specifying punishment for crime. A mechanical application of the three tests is not warranted.

Appellant argues vigorously that his culpability was of a lesser degree than in cases involving felony vehicular manslaughter with gross negligence. Appellant points to other cases where the defendants had higher blood alcohol levels and were traveling at faster speeds when the accidents occurred. However, appellant tested above the designated legal level of intoxication; he was driving his truck with a .155 blood alcohol level. Although he was not traveling at an excessive speed, appellant proceeded down a road and through a stop sign without slowing at an intersection with somewhat limited visibility. On these facts, culpability was no less than that of others given the same punishment.

Appellant has no prior criminal record, no prior record of alcohol abuse, and is reputed to be a valuable member of the community. Even so, this was not "a crime of ordinary gravity committed under ordinary circumstances," nor was it a nonviolent crime. See *In re Lynch, supra*, 8 Cal.3d at 425–426 (the court seemed to look at the crime in the abstract, the punishment imposed, then to the background of the particular defendant.) Appellant was the cause of the accident that resulted in a death. Great deference is given to legislative determinations on punishment. A statute will not be overturned unless its constitutionality "clearly, positively and unmistakably appears." *People v. Main*, 152 Cal.App.3d at 692. Given the terms prescribed for manslaughter in general, and for murder, we cannot conclude that a six-year prison sentence for felony vehicular manslaughter with gross negligence is cruel and unusual punishment.[3] The term is not so disproportionate to the crime as to shock the conscience and offend fundamental notions of human dignity. * * * *

The judgment as to counts II and III is affirmed. The judgment as to count I is reversed. The matter is remanded for retrial and/or resentencing in accord with the opinions expressed herein.

Notes from Shelly:

1. Regarding the "cruel and unusual punishment" argument, here is an excerpt from the Appellant's brief in *McNally*:

> The court may examine "the penological purposes of the prescribed punishment" when considering the question of cruel or unusual punishment. *In re Foss* (1974) 10 Cal.3d 910, 919–920. In the case at bench, those purposes, to the extent that they are discernable, do not justify a punishment of 6 years in state prison.

> If Appellant had engaged in the identical conduct he engaged in here, but — for any of a variety of reasons — had not caused any death or injury, he would have been guilty of violating Vehicle Code § 23152(a) (driving under the influence) or § 23152(b) (driving with .10 or more blood alcohol). Vehicle Code § 23160(a) provides that one convicted of a first violation of § 23152 shall be imprisoned not less than 96 hours nor more than 6 months, although § 23161 permits probation on certain conditions.

> To our knowledge, the only study of sentencing practices under these statutes [shows that in 97% of the cases, first offenders received no more than 48 hours in jail, a fine, and 3 years probation, and in 3%, the sentence was 96 hours in jail, a fine, and a 6-months license suspension.]

> Appellant was charged with speeding and running a stop sign, as well as driving under the influence. Therefore, let us assume that, because of these alleged infractions, he would have received the harshest penalty: the 96 hour jail term meted out to only 3% of the first offenders.

> The 6-year sentence imposed on Appellant is *over 540 times* the 96 hour sentence he would have received had Karen Wonacott not been killed. If he receives good behavior and work credits and serves only 3 years, he will have served over 270 times the 96 hours.

> This, we contend, is cruel punishment, as it is arbitrary, imposing an extraordinary additional sentence which is based on a fortuity not under

---

[3] Appellant contends his term is statistically out of proportion with the term he would have received had he been stopped only for driving under the influence and suggests a more statistically proportionate term for his crime is one year of imprisonment. It is the Legislature's function to designate terms of imprisonment — not the court's. The comparison based purely on statistical proportions fails to consider that more weight is given to a death rather than to a simple statutory violation.

Appellant's control and which has no bearing on his culpability.

This, we contend, is unusual punishment, for no other California crime carries such a disparity in punishment between conduct which causes harm and identical conduct which causes no harm.

The leading article on this issue in American legal literature is by Professor Schulhofer, *Harm or Punishment: A Critique of Emphasis on the Results of Conduct in the Criminal Law*, 122 U.Penna.L.Rev. 1497 (1974). In this article, the author considers whether the imposition of a harsher penalty solely because harm results serves any of the fundamental purposes of the criminal law — giving particular attention to vehicular homicide statutes, as there the disparity in penalty is usually the greatest. He concludes that the purpose of deterrence is not served, as one who is not deterred by the penalty for driving under the influence *and* the risk of injury or death to himself from this particular crime is unlikely to be deterred by the very slight risk (under 5%, studies show) that he will cause another's death and thereby be punished for vehicular manslaughter.

Schulhofer also says that "selection of those who cause harm [for a stiffer punishment] is a kind of lottery, just as selection of those born on certain days, determined at random, would be a kind of lottery." While retaliation seems to loom as the dominant motive for a punishment based on results — an eye for an eye — "most American jurisdictions exclude retaliation from the legitimate goals of the criminal law." Regarding vehicular homicide, he states that "emphasis on results seems devoid of support in the arguments considered", and he concludes that "The crime of vehicle homicide or involuntary manslaughter should for practical purposes disappear from the statute books."

We are not asking this court to invalidate California's manslaughter statute, as Schulhofer might. We are willing to assume that it is permissible — for whatever reason — to impose a higher penalty on wrongful conduct because it happens to cause an injury or death. The question then becomes: how much higher? In California, for almost every crime, the answer to this question is <u>twice</u> as high — not 270 or 540 times as high.

Under Penal Code § 664, one who *attempts* a crime but fails in its accomplishment — i.e., fails to cause harm — receives one-half the punishment for the completed crime. Thus, while one who murders is no more culpable than one who attempts murder, the "successful" murderer receives only twice the punishment that the attempted murderer receives. The robber receives only twice what the attempted robber receives. The rapist receives only twice what the attempted rapist receives. And the same is true of arson, burglary, sale of heroin, and a host of other serious crimes.

Note that all of these crimes are *intentional* crimes, involving much higher culpability than an unintentional crime such as involuntary manslaughter. What possible valid penological purpose can there be in telling one who *plans* a killing, "If you succeed, your penalty will be *doubled*" and telling a drunk driver who does *not* intend to kill, "If you 'succeed' in causing a death, your penalty will be increased *540-fold*"?

We do not deny that high penalties on drunk driving may deter drunk driving and decrease traffic fatalities. If the Legislature chooses to *increase* the penalties for *all* such culpable conduct which might lead to such fatalities — i.e., *drunk driving itself* — we see no problem with this, as it will apply to *all* defendants who have the same culpability. When, however, the Legislature selects a small handful of these defendants — no more culpable than the others — and increases their penalty 540 times, this is cruel and unusual. It is not necessary to do this in order to add to the deterrent effect of the law, as the Legislature could accomplish this purpose simply be increasing the penalty for drunk driving. * * * *

If this court agrees with our contention that 6 years in prison is cruel or unusual punishment in this case, we propose the following remedy. We do not ask that the vehicular manslaughter statute be invalidated. We do not ask that Appellant go unpunished. The most appropriate remedy is to grant probation to Appellant on the conditions that his trial counsel proposed, including one year in jail ("only" 90 times the 96 hours imposed on no-injury drunk drivers). This would be in addition to a fine, community service work, and probation, as well as the effects that the conviction would have on his life — including the disgrace of being stigmatized as a felon, a drunk driver, a manslaughterer.

2. As the *McNally* court noted, *In re Lynch*, 8 Cal.3d 410 (1972), held that a sentence might be so disproportionate to the offense that it imposes cruel and unusual punishment. Is this still good law?

In *Harmelin v. Michigan*, 501 U.S. 957 (1991), defendant was given a mandatory sentence of life imprisonment (without possibility of parole) for possession of 672 grams of cocaine. A majority of the Court rejected defendant's argument that because the penalty was disproportionate to the offense, the sentence constituted cruel and unusual punishment, in violation of the Eighth Amendment. Justices Scalia and Rehnquist felt that the Eighth Amendment restricted only certain *types* of punishment (such as branding), but did not restrict the *length* of imprisonment in *any* situation. Justices Kennedy, O'Connor, and Souter would not go this far, but felt that this defendant's offense was not minor and the sentence was within the range permitted by the Eighth Amendment. Justices White, Blackmun, and Stevens dissented, arguing that defendant's offense should not always *mandate* life imprisonment, particularly because Michigan punishes first degree murder by the same penalty, and defendant's offense is not as serious as that crime.

3. In *State v. Bartlett*, 171 Ariz. 302 (1992), the Arizona Supreme Court counted the votes in *Harmelin* and decided that a majority of the justices did not intend to bar all 8th Amendment review of "disproportionate sentences," and held that a 40-year sentence without possibility of early release was grossly disproportionate to defendant's crimes (consensual sexual intercourse with two 14 year old girls), and thus violated the 8th Amendment.

4. In *Ewing v. California*, 123 S.Ct. 1179 (2003), the Court rejected an Eighth Amendment challenge to California's application of its "three strikes" law to a man whose third strike was grand larceny: theft of three golf clubs priced at $399 each. The Court applied *Harmelin*, but held that "The Eighth Amendment does not require strict proportionality between crime and sentence. Rather, it forbids only

extreme sentences that are grossly disproportionate to the crime." Applying this to Ewing, the Court held:

> In weighing the gravity of Ewing's offense, we must place on the scales not only his current felony, but also his long history of felony recidivism. Any other approach would fail to accord proper deference to the policy judgments that find expression in the legislature's choice of sanctions. In imposing a three strikes sentence, the State's interest is not merely punishing the offense of conviction, or the "triggering" offense: It is in addition the interest in dealing in a harsher manner with those who by repeated criminal acts have shown that they are simply incapable of conforming to the norms of society as established by its criminal law. To give full effect to the State's choice of this legitimate penological goal, our proportionality review of Ewing's sentence must take that goal into account.

> Ewing's sentence is justified by the State's public-safety interest in incapacitating and deterring recidivist felons, and amply supported by his own long, serious criminal record. Ewing has been convicted of numerous misdemeanor and felony offenses, served nine separate terms of incarceration, and committed most of his crimes while on probation or parole. His prior "strikes" were serious felonies including robbery and three residential burglaries. To be sure, Ewing's sentence is a long one. But it reflects a rational legislative judgment, entitled to deference, that offenders who have committed serious or violent felonies and who continue to commit felonies must be incapacitated. The State of California was entitled to place upon Ewing the onus of one who is simply unable to bring his conduct within the social norms prescribed by the criminal law of the State. Ewing's is not the rare case in which a threshold comparison of the crime committed and the sentence imposed leads to an inference of gross disproportionality.

> We hold that Ewing's sentence of 25 years to life in prison, imposed for the offense of felony grand theft under the three strikes law, is not grossly disproportionate and therefore does not violate the Eighth Amendment's prohibition on cruel and unusual punishments.

PEOPLE v. REYES
California Court of Appeal, 3rd District
195 Cal.App.3d 957 (1987)

HARVEY, ASSOCIATE JUSTICE.

After a jury trial, defendant was convicted of one count of robbery (Pen.Code § 211) but acquitted of the special allegation that during the robbery he inflicted great bodily injury on a person who was 60 years of age or older. § 1203.09(a). Defendant was sentenced to the upper term of five years. Defendant appeals, contending that the court erred in failing to consider defendant's alcoholism as a circumstance in mitigation, by imposing the upper term for inflicting great bodily injury when he was acquitted of that charge by the jury, by instructing the jury with CALJIC No. 2.21, and by imposing a restitution fine of $300. We affirm.

So far as it is pertinent to this appeal, the evidence showed that defendant hit the 74-year-old victim, Wilfred Marsden, on the head as Marsden bent down to put his key into the lock of his apartment house. The blow knocked Marsden down, and defendant then alternately beat Marsden and rummaged through his pockets, taking Marsden's change purse and wallet containing $330. Marsden sustained bruises on his head, his nose was cut and required three stitches, he had a cut running back from his lip towards his right ear that required ten stitches to close, and he spent about five hours in the hospital while his wounds were treated.

A neighbor, Dow Patten, interrupted defendant's attack on Marsden, whereupon defendant ran, only to be caught by Patten after a substantial chase. The police arrived and took defendant into custody. When taken into custody, defendant had a strong odor of alcohol on his person, and appeared to be intoxicated; nevertheless, he had control over his arms and legs, spoke sensibly, was able to get in and out of the patrol car, and responded appropriately to questions. A blood test showed defendant's blood alcohol content at .11 percent.

The probation report noted that "defendant admits to a problem with alcohol abuse. He described binges, maintains that he experiences blackouts, and drinks anything and everything." It also reported that defendant had three convictions for driving under the influence of alcohol. Defendant complains that the trial court failed to consider alcoholism as a mitigating circumstance, citing *People v. Simpson* (1979) 90 Cal.App.3d 919, 927.

The Simpson case does not hold that alcoholism must always be considered as a mitigating factor. The court said, "The trial court must consider the possibility that his alcoholism is a circumstance in mitigation within the meaning of rule 423, and must then weigh this factor along with other relevant circumstances." *Id.* at 928. In *People v. Regalado* (1980) 108 Cal.App.3d 531, 540, the same court that decided *Simpson* explained its decision as follows:

> The peculiar and somewhat pathetic facts of *People v. Simpson* demonstrate, by way of contrast to the facts in *Regalado*, a situation in which a sentencing court must give the influence of an individual's addictive need its full mitigating weight. In *Simpson*, defendant was an alcoholic who, after having shared approximately 10 quarts of beer and a fifth of rum with his companion, broke the window of a liquor store in order to obtain more alcohol. Police followed a trail of broken bottles leading from the store and found the defendant hiding in the identical place where he had hidden before when he had previously burglarized the same liquor store. Without question and as a matter of law, the defendant in *Simpson* "was suffering from a mental or physical condition that significantly reduced his culpability for the crime." Rule 423(b)(2). Therefore, "his conduct was partially excusable for some other reason not amounting to a defense." Rule 423(a)(4).

In *Regalado*, the defendant was on probation, and as a condition of probation was on an in-patient drug rehabilitation program. He left without permission and within a few hours committed the burglary for which he was convicted. The trial court imposed the upper term for the offense. One of the arresting officers believed the defendant was under the influence of a drug at the time of his arrest, and the other reached the opposite conclusion. But they agreed that the defendant did not require assistance to stand, did not appear disoriented or confused, was able to converse with the officers, and was cooperative. His possession of burglary equipment when arrested showed that he was capable of premeditating and planning the commission of the crime. In the light of these circumstances, the same court that decided *Simpson* decided that the upper term was properly imposed in *Regalado*.

Here, too, the record shows that the court at least considered the possibility that alcoholism might partially excuse defendant's behavior. That is, the record shows that the court read and considered the probation report. Defense counsel specifically argued the defendant's alcoholism was a mitigating factor. But, as in *Regalado*, the court rejected the possibility that defendant's behavior was partially excusable. The record supports that determination. Defendant had only a .11 blood alcohol level. Like the defendant in *Regalado*, defendant here did not require assistance to stand, did not appear disoriented or confused, and was able to converse intelligently with the arresting officers. As in *Regalado*, the record here does not compel a conclusion that defendant was suffering from a mental or physical condition that significantly reduced his culpability for the crime.

We thus join a growing number of courts that have cited *Simpson* only for the purpose of distinguishing it. Some of these cases are indistinguishable substantively from *Simpson*.

In *Simpson*, the defendant burglarized a liquor store, stealing liquor and cigarettes. He was placed on three years probation, sentenced to a county jail disciplinary term, and required to participate in alcoholic counseling programs. Within two months, he escaped from the sheriff's rehabilitation facility and ten weeks later burglarized the same liquor store, again stealing a quantity of liquor and cigarettes.

Similarly, in *People v. Regalado*, the defendant was on probation for burglary, one condition of the probation being his placement in a drug-rehabilitation program. Simpson escaped from the sheriff's rehabilitation facility; Regalado left the drug-rehabilitation facility in violation of the court's probation order, and the same night he committed a burglary. One of the arresting officers believed him to be under the influence of drugs at the time of the offense. Yet the court rejected the *Simpson* holding and found that Regalado's repeated failure to deal with his addiction, despite the opportunity provided through probation supervision, justified the court in treating the probation violation and repeated criminal conduct as aggravating circumstances.

In *People v. Reid*, 133 Cal.App.3d at 371, the court referred to *People v. Regalado* and said, "Similarly, the probation report here indicated the longstanding nature of appellant's drug addiction and his failure to deal with the problem." The trial court imposed the upper term and the appellate court affirmed. In *People v. Lambeth*, 112 Cal.App.3d 495, the defendant committed a pharmacy robbery to steal narcotics and syringes. (In *Simpson*, the defendant burgled a liquor store to obtain liquor.) Similar to the defendants in *Simpson* and *Regalado*, the *Lambeth* defendant had also escaped from a Kansas half-way house. The *Lambeth* court affirmed a sentence to the upper term for robbery, citing *Regalado* and stating: "The probation report abundantly established that appellant was a long-time career criminal with little desire to change." *Id.* at 501.

In *Simpson*, despite the defendant's youth (approximately 23 years of age), the court was dealing with a defendant with juvenile and adult convictions for petty theft, joyriding, drunkenness, car theft, grand theft from the person (purse snatch), burglaries, and escape. As in *Regalado, Reid*, and *Lambeth*, he had demonstrated a total lack of interest in changing his life style and in rehabilitation. Like the others, *Simpson* had escaped from a rehabilitation facility, and was continuing a pattern of criminal conduct to support his substance abuse.

Those cases that have distinguished *Simpson* hold that where the defendant has a pattern of substance abuse and addiction or alcoholism, where the defendant has failed to deal with the problem despite opportunities to do so, where he continues in criminal conduct to support his pattern of substance abuse, an aggravated or upper term is appropriate. *Simpson* held that, as a matter of law, the defendant's alcoholism was a factor in mitigation. That holding is plainly contrary to the holdings of the other cases cited above.

As a policy matter, when a defendant has a drug-addiction or substance abuse problem, where the defendant has failed to deal with the problem despite repeated opportunities, where the defendant shows little or no motivation to change his life style, and where the substance abuse problem is a substantial factor in the commission of crimes, the need to protect the public from further crimes by that individual suggests that a longer sentence should be imposed, not a shorter sentence. For example, the felony drunk-driver who is suffering from an uncontrolled alcoholism should be sentenced to a longer term, not a shorter one, in order to prevent him from driving under the influence again. The robber or burglar who is taking either drugs or money to buy drugs to support his addiction, and who shows little incentive or ability to deal with his drug abuse problem, should be prevented from committing further burglaries or robberies for a longer time, not a shorter time. That was precisely the analysis that the trial judge went through in *People v. Simpson*, which analysis was held erroneous. The holding in *Simpson* that the need to support the alcoholism by repeated burglaries is a mitigating factor in those burglaries is plainly wrong. The holdings in *Regalado, Reid,* and *Lambeth* are plainly correct.

The error in the *Simpson* decision is that it concluded that if the defendant's mental or physical condition of alcoholism was a substantial factor in the commission of the crime, then it necessarily "significantly reduced his culpability for the crime" or made the crime "partially excusable." *Lambeth, Regalado,* and *Reid* reject this analysis. Alcoholism or drug addiction may be regarded as a "mental or physical condition"; but a separate finding that the condition significantly reduced culpability or partially excused the conduct must be made. Where those or any other substance abuse problems are out of control, the defendant either engages in crime to support his substance abuse habit, or uses that habit as an excuse or explanation for continued criminal conduct,[3] and the defendant shows little incentive or ability to change, the substance abuse habit does not "significantly reduce" his culpability for the crime, nor does it make the criminal conduct "partially excusable."

Indeed, where, as in *Simpson, Reid, Regalado,* and *Lambeth,* the substance abuse problem has led to behavior described as aggravating factors in rule 421, such as a pattern of criminal conduct dangerous to society, violations of parole or probation, and unsatisfactory performance on probation or parole, the addiction or alcoholism is properly considered as a part of those aggravating factors because it suggests a high probability of further depredations on the public whenever the defendant is again out of custody.

---

[3] This might be termed the "Flip Wilson defense": "The devil [drugs or alcohol] made me do it."

For these reasons, we conclude that *People v. Simpson* was wrongly decided, and we decline to follow it.

This does not mean that alcoholism or drug-addiction can never be considered as a mitigating factor under rule 423a(4) or 423b(2). We can readily conceive of defendants who have made a serious effort to cope with their substance abuse problems but who, having committed a crime during a time of relapse, might well be considered for a lower term under those rules. A drug dependency growing out of medical treatment might be considered to reduce culpability under some circumstances. There may be other circumstances where the defendant's alcohol or drug addiction might be considered in mitigation. But, where that addiction has simply provided the defendant with a continuing incentive or excuse to commit crimes, we see no reason why that addiction should be considered as a circumstance in mitigation.

Defendant next contends that, inasmuch as the jury found that he was not guilty of inflicting great bodily injury upon the victim, the court improperly considered the injury to the victim as an aggravating factor. In *People v. Takencareof* (1981) 119 Cal.App.3d 492, the defendant was charged with two counts of burglary and one count of arson. He pleaded guilty to one count of burglary, but he was acquitted of the other charges after a jury trial. When sentencing the defendant for the burglary, the trial court referred to the great harm caused by the arson as a circumstance that warranted denial of probation. The appellate court held that, inasmuch as the defendant was acquitted of the arson, the trial court could not base its burglary sentence upon the conclusion that the defendant actually committed arson.

Defendant argues that the jury's finding here should also preclude the trial court's use of the victim's injury as an aggravating circumstance in sentencing. The situation here, however, is quite different from that considered in *People v. Takencareof*. Here, the jury's verdict is not inconsistent with the trial court's finding that the victim was elderly and fragile and defendant used gratuitous violence, force, and cruelty upon the victim. Here, there is no question that defendant kicked the victim and beat the victim after the victim was knocked down. All the jury found was that these acts did not inflict "great bodily injury" within the meaning of § 1203.09. The jury did not find that the victim suffered no injury at all or that the defendant did not inflict any injury. The trial court's finding in aggravation is supported by the evidence, and it is not contrary to the jury's finding. * * * *

The judgment is affirmed.

APPRENDI v. NEW JERSEY
United States Supreme Court
530 U.S. 466 (2000)

JUSTICE STEVENS delivered the opinion of the Court.

A New Jersey statute classifies the possession of a firearm for an unlawful purpose as a "second-degree" offense. N.J. Stat. Ann. § 2C:39-4(a). Such an offense is punishable by imprisonment for "between five years and 10 years." § 2C:43-6(a)(2). A separate statute, described by that State's Supreme Court as a "hate crime" law, provides for an "extended term" of imprisonment if the trial judge finds, by a preponderance of the evidence, that "the defendant in committing the crime acted with a purpose to intimidate an individual or group of individuals because of race, color, gender, handicap, religion, sexual orientation or ethnicity." N.J. Stat. Ann. § 2C:44-3(e). The extended term authorized by the hate crime law for second-degree offenses is imprisonment for "between 10 and 20 years." § 2C:43-7(a)(3).

The question presented is whether the Due Process Clause of the Fourteenth Amendment requires that a factual determination authorizing an increase in the maximum prison sentence for an offense from 10 to 20 years be made by a jury on the basis of proof beyond a reasonable doubt.

I

At 2:04 a.m. on December 22, 1994, petitioner Charles C. Apprendi, Jr., fired several.22-caliber bullets into the home of an African-American family that had recently moved into a previously all-white neighborhood in Vineland, New Jersey. Apprendi was promptly arrested and, at 3:05 a.m., admitted that he was the shooter. After further questioning, at 6:04 a.m., he made a statement — which he later retracted — that even though he did not know the occupants of the house personally, "because they are black in color he does not want them in the neighborhood."

A New Jersey grand jury returned a 23-count indictment charging Apprendi with four first-degree, eight second-degree, six third-degree, and five fourth-degree offenses. The charges alleged shootings on four different dates, as well as the unlawful possession of various weapons. None of the counts referred to the hate crime statute, and none alleged that Apprendi acted with a racially biased purpose.

The parties entered into a plea agreement, pursuant to which Apprendi pleaded guilty to two counts (3 and 18) of second-degree possession of a firearm for an unlawful purpose, N.J. Stat. Ann. § 2C:39-4a, and one count (22) of the third-degree offense of unlawful possession of an antipersonnel bomb, § 2C:39-3a; the prosecutor dismissed the other 20 counts. Under state law, a second-degree offense carries a penalty range of 5 to 10 years, § 2C:43-6(a)(2); a third-degree offense carries a penalty range of between 3 and 5 years, § 2C:43-6(a)(3). As part of the plea agreement, however, the State reserved the right to request the court to impose a higher "enhanced" sentence on count 18 (which was based on the December 22 shooting) on the ground that that offense was committed with a biased purpose, as described in § 2C:44-3(e). Apprendi, correspondingly, reserved the right to challenge the hate crime sentence enhancement on the ground that it violates the United States Constitution.

At the plea hearing, the trial judge heard sufficient evidence to establish Apprendi's guilt on counts 3, 18, and 22; the judge then confirmed that Apprendi understood the maximum sentences that could be imposed on those counts. Because the plea agreement provided that the sentence on the sole third-degree offense (count 22) would run concurrently with the other sentences, the potential sentences on the two second-degree counts were critical. If the judge found no basis for the biased purpose enhancement, the maximum consecutive sentences on those counts would amount to 20 years in aggregate; if, however, the judge enhanced the sentence on count 18, the maximum on that count alone would be 20 years and the maximum for the two counts in aggregate would be 30 years, with a 15-year period of parole ineligibility.

After the trial judge accepted the three guilty pleas, the prosecutor filed a formal motion for an extended term. The trial judge thereafter held an evidentiary hearing on the issue of Apprendi's "purpose" for the shooting on December 22. Apprendi adduced evidence from a psychologist and from seven character witnesses who testified that he did not have a reputation for racial bias. He also took the stand himself, explaining that the incident was an unintended consequence of overindulgence in alcohol, denying that he was in any way biased against African-Americans, and denying that his statement to the police had been accurately described. The judge, however, found the police officer's testimony credible, and concluded that the evidence supported a finding "that the crime was motivated by racial bias." Having found "by a preponderance of the evidence" that Apprendi's actions were taken "with a purpose to intimidate" as provided by the statute, the trial judge held that the hate crime enhancement applied. Rejecting Apprendi's constitutional challenge to the statute, the judge sentenced him to a 12-year term of imprisonment on count 18, and to shorter concurrent sentences on the other two counts.

Apprendi appealed, arguing, *inter alia*, that the Due Process Clause of the United States Constitution requires that the finding of bias upon which his hate crime sentence was based must be proved to a jury beyond a reasonable doubt, *In re Winship*, 397 U.S. 358 (1970). Over dissent, the Appellate Division of the Superior Court of New Jersey upheld the enhanced sentence. Relying on our decision in *McMillan v. Pennsylvania*, 477 U.S. 79 (1986), the appeals court found that the state legislature decided to make the hate crime enhancement a "sentencing factor," rather than an element of an underlying offense — and that decision was within the State's established power to define the elements of its crimes. The hate crime statute did not create a presumption of guilt, the court determined, and did not appear "tailored to permit the finding to be a tail which wags the dog of the substantive offense." Characterizing the required finding as one of "motive," the court described it as a traditional "sentencing factor," one not considered an "essential element" of any crime unless the legislature so provides. While recognizing that the hate crime law did expose defendants to "greater and additional punishment," the court held that that "one factor standing alone" was not sufficient to render the statute unconstitutional. * * * *

We granted certiorari and now reverse. * * * *

III

In his 1881 lecture on the criminal law, Oliver Wendell Holmes, Jr., observed: "The law threatens certain pains if you do certain things, intending thereby to give you a new motive for not doing them. If you persist in doing them, it has to inflict the pains in order that its threats may continue to be believed." New Jersey threatened Apprendi with certain pains if he unlawfully possessed a weapon and with additional pains if he selected his victims with a purpose to intimidate them because of their race. As a matter of simple justice, it seems obvious that the procedural safeguards designed to protect Apprendi from unwarranted pains should apply equally to the two acts that New Jersey has singled out for punishment. Merely using the label "sentence enhancement" to describe the latter surely does not provide a principled basis for treating them differently.

At stake in this case are constitutional protections of surpassing importance: the proscription of any deprivation of liberty without "due process of law," Amdt. 14, and the guarantee that "in all criminal prosecutions, the accused shall enjoy the right to a speedy and public trial, by an impartial jury," Amdt. 6. Taken together, these rights indisputably entitle a criminal defendant to a jury determination that he is guilty of every element of the crime with which he is charged, beyond a reasonable doubt.

The historical foundation for our recognition of these principles extends down centuries into the common law. "To guard against a spirit of oppression and tyranny on the part of rulers," and "as the great bulwark of our civil and political liberties," 2 J. Story, Commentaries on the Constitution of the United States 540–541 (4th ed. 1873), trial by jury has been understood to require that "the truth of every accusation, whether preferred in the shape of indictment, information, or appeal, should afterwards be confirmed by the unanimous suffrage of twelve of the defendant's equals and neighbours." 4 W. Blackstone, Commentaries on the Laws of England 343 (1769) (hereinafter Blackstone). See also *Duncan v. Louisiana*, 391 U.S. 145, 151–154 (1968).

Equally well founded is the companion right to have the jury verdict based on proof beyond a reasonable doubt. "The demand for a higher degree of persuasion in criminal cases was recurrently expressed from ancient times, though its crystallization into the formula 'beyond a reasonable doubt' seems to have occurred as late as 1798. It is now accepted in common law jurisdictions as the measure of persuasion by which the prosecution must convince the trier of all the essential elements of guilt." *Winship*, 397 U.S. at 361. We went on to explain that the reliance on the "reasonable doubt" standard among common-law jurisdictions "reflects a profound judgment about the way in which law should be enforced and justice administered." *Id.* at 361–362.

Any possible distinction between an "element" of a felony offense and a "sentencing factor" was unknown to the practice of criminal indictment, trial by jury, and judgment by court as it existed during the years surrounding our Nation's founding. As a general rule, criminal proceedings were submitted to a jury after being initiated by an indictment containing "all the facts and circumstances which constitute the offence, stated with such certainty and precision, that the defendant may be enabled to determine the species of offence they constitute, in order that he may prepare his defence accordingly and that there may be no doubt as to the judgment which should be given, if the defendant be convicted." J. Archbold, *Pleading and Evidence in Criminal Cases* 44 (15th ed. 1862). The defendant's ability to predict with certainty the judgment from the face of the felony indictment flowed from the invariable linkage of punishment with crime.

Thus, with respect to the criminal law of felonious conduct, "the English trial judge of the later eighteenth century had very little explicit discretion in sentencing. The substantive criminal law tended to be sanction- specific; it prescribed a particular sentence for each offense. The judge was meant simply to impose that sentence (unless he thought in the circumstances that the sentence was so inappropriate that he should invoke the pardon process to commute it)." Langbein, *The English Criminal Trial Jury on the Eve of the French Revolution, in The Trial Jury in England, France, Germany* 1700–1900, pp. 36–37 (1987). As Blackstone, among many others, has made clear, "the judgment, though pronounced or awarded by the judges, is not their determination or sentence, but the determination and sentence of the law." 3 Blackstone 396.

This practice at common law held true when indictments were issued pursuant to statute. Just as the circumstances of the crime and the intent of the defendant at the time of commission were often essential elements to be alleged in the indictment, so too were the circumstances mandating a particular punishment. "Where a statute annexes a higher degree of punishment to a common-law felony, if committed under particular circumstances, an indictment for the offence, in order to bring the defendant within that higher degree of punishment, must expressly charge it to have been committed under those circumstances, and must state the circumstances with certainty and precision." Archbold, *Pleading and Evidence in Criminal Cases*, at 51. If, then, "upon an indictment under the statute, the prosecutor prove the felony to have been committed, but fail in proving it to have been committed under the circumstances specified in the statute, the defendant shall be convicted of the common-law felony only." *Id.* at 188.

We should be clear that nothing in this history suggests that it is impermissible for judges to exercise discretion — taking into consideration various factors relating both to offense and offender — in imposing a judgment within the range prescribed by statute. We have often noted that judges in this country have long exercised discretion of this nature in imposing sentence within statutory limits in the individual case. See, e.g., *Williams v. New York*, 337 U.S. 241, 246 (1949) ("Both before and since the American colonies became a nation, courts in this country and in England practiced a policy under which a sentencing judge could exercise a wide discretion in the sources and types of evidence used to assist him in determining the kind and extent of punishment to be imposed within limits fixed by law.") * * * *

The historic link between verdict and judgment and the consistent limitation on judges' discretion to operate within the limits of the legal penalties provided highlight the novelty of a legislative scheme that removes the jury from the determination of a fact that, if found, exposes the criminal defendant to a penalty exceeding the maximum he would receive if punished according to the facts reflected in the jury verdict alone.

We do not suggest that trial practices cannot change in the course of centuries and still remain true to the principles that emerged from the Framers' fears "that the jury right could be lost not only by gross denial, but by erosion." *Jones v. United States*, 526 U.S. 227, 247–248 (1999). But practice must at least adhere to the basic principles undergirding the requirements of trying to a jury all facts necessary to constitute a statutory offense, and proving those facts beyond reasonable doubt. As we made clear in *Winship*, the "reasonable doubt" requirement "has a vital role in our criminal procedure for cogent reasons." 397 U.S. at 363. Prosecution subjects the criminal defendant both to "the possibility that he may lose his liberty upon conviction and the certainty that he would be stigmatized by the conviction." *Ibid.* We thus require this, among other, procedural protections in order to "provide concrete substance for the presumption of innocence," and to reduce the risk of imposing such deprivations erroneously. *Ibid.* If a defendant faces punishment beyond that provided by statute when an offense is committed under certain circumstances but not others, it is obvious that both the loss of liberty and the stigma attaching to the offense are heightened; it necessarily follows that the defendant should not — at the moment the State is put to proof of those circumstances — be deprived of protections that have, until that point, unquestionably attached. * * * *

IV

In sum, our reexamination of our cases in this area, and of the history upon which they rely, confirms the opinion that we expressed in *Jones*. Other than the fact of a prior conviction, any fact that increases the penalty for a crime beyond the prescribed statutory maximum must be submitted to a jury, and proved beyond a reasonable doubt. With that exception, we endorse the statement of the rule set forth in the concurring opinions in that case: "It is unconstitutional for a legislature to remove from the jury the assessment of facts that increase the prescribed range of penalties to which a criminal defendant is exposed. It is equally clear that such facts must be established by proof beyond a reasonable doubt." 526 U.S., at 252–253 (opinion of Stevens, J.).[16]

V

The New Jersey statutory scheme that Apprendi asks us to invalidate allows a jury to convict a defendant of a second-degree offense based on its finding beyond a reasonable doubt that he unlawfully possessed a prohibited weapon; after a subsequent and separate proceeding, it then allows a judge to impose punishment identical to that New Jersey provides for crimes of the first degree, N.J. Stat.Ann. § 2C:43-6(a)(1), based upon the judge's finding, by a preponderance of the evidence, that the defendant's "purpose" for unlawfully possessing the weapon was "to intimidate" his victim on the basis of a particular characteristic the victim possessed. In light of the constitutional rule explained above, and all of the cases supporting it, this practice cannot stand. * * * *

---

[16] The principal dissent would reject the Court's rule as a "meaningless formalism," because it can conceive of hypothetical statutes that would comply with the rule and achieve the same result as the New Jersey statute. While a State could, hypothetically, undertake to revise its entire criminal code in the manner the dissent suggests — extending all statutory maximum sentences to, for example, 50 years and giving judges guided discretion as to a few specially selected factors within that range — this possibility seems remote. Among other reasons, structural democratic constraints exist to discourage legislatures from enacting penal statutes that expose every defendant convicted of, for example, weapons possession, to a maximum sentence exceeding that which is, in the legislature's judgment, generally proportional to the crime. This is as it should be. Our rule ensures that a State is obliged "to make its choices concerning the substantive content of its criminal laws with full awareness of the consequence, unable to mask substantive policy choices" of exposing all who are convicted to the maximum sentence it provides. *Patterson v. New York*, 432 U.S., at 228–229, n. 13 (Powell, J., dissenting). So exposed, "the political check on potentially harsh legislative action is then more likely to operate." *Ibid.*

In all events, if such an extensive revision of the State's entire criminal code were enacted for the purpose the dissent suggests, or if New Jersey simply reversed the burden of the hate crime finding (effectively assuming a crime was performed with a purpose to intimidate and then requiring a defendant to prove that it was not), we would be required to question whether the revision was constitutional under this Court's prior decisions.

Finally, the principal dissent ignores the distinction the Court has often recognized, see, e.g., *Martin v. Ohio*, 480 U.S. 228 (1987), between facts in aggravation of punishment and facts in mitigation. If facts found by a jury support a guilty verdict of murder, the judge is authorized by that jury verdict to sentence the defendant to the maximum sentence provided by the murder statute. If the defendant can escape the statutory maximum by showing, for example, that he is a war veteran, then a judge that finds the fact of veteran status is neither exposing the defendant to a deprivation of liberty greater than that authorized by the verdict according to statute, nor is the Judge imposing upon the defendant a greater stigma than that accompanying the jury verdict alone. Core concerns animating the jury and burden-of-proof requirements are thus absent from such a scheme.

The effect of New Jersey's sentencing "enhancement" here is unquestionably to turn a second-degree offense into a first degree offense, under the State's own criminal code. The law thus runs directly into our warning in *Mullaney* that *Winship* is concerned as much with the category of substantive offense as "with the degree of criminal culpability" assessed. This concern flows not only from the historical pedigree of the jury and burden rights, but also from the powerful interests those rights serve. The degree of criminal culpability the legislature chooses to associate with particular, factually distinct conduct has significant implications both for a defendant's very liberty, and for the heightened stigma associated with an offense the legislature has selected as worthy of greater punishment. * * * *

New Jersey would also point to the fact that the State did not, in placing the required biased purpose finding in a sentencing enhancement provision, create a "separate offense calling for a separate penalty." Merely because the state legislature placed its hate crime sentence "enhancer" "within the sentencing provisions" of the criminal code "does not mean that the finding of a biased purpose to intimidate is not an essential element of the offense." Indeed, the fact that New Jersey, along with numerous other States, has also made precisely the same conduct the subject of an independent substantive offense makes it clear that the mere presence of this "enhancement" in a sentencing statute does not define its character. * * * *

Finally, this Court has previously considered and rejected the argument that the principles guiding our decision today render invalid state capital sentencing schemes requiring judges, after a jury verdict holding a defendant guilty of a capital crime, to find specific aggravating factors before imposing a sentence of death. *Walton v. Arizona*, 497 U.S. 639, 647–649 (1990). For reasons we have explained, the capital cases are not controlling:

> Neither the cases cited, nor any other case, permits a judge to determine the existence of a factor which makes a crime a capital offense. What the cited cases hold is that, once a jury has found the defendant guilty of all the elements of an offense which carries as its maximum penalty the sentence of death, it may be left to the judge to decide whether that maximum penalty, rather than a lesser one, ought to be imposed. The person who is charged with actions that expose him to the death penalty has an absolute entitlement to jury trial on all the elements of the charge. [*Almendarez-Torres*, 523 U.S. at 257, n. 2 (Scalia, J., dissenting)][21]

The New Jersey procedure challenged in this case is an unacceptable departure from the jury tradition that is an indispensable part of our criminal justice system. Accordingly, the judgment of the Supreme Court of New Jersey is reversed, and the case is remanded for further proceedings not inconsistent with this opinion.

---

[21] The principal dissent, in addition, treats us to a lengthy disquisition on the benefits of determinate sentencing schemes, and the effect of today's decision on the federal Sentencing Guidelines. The Guidelines are, of course, not before the Court. We therefore express no view on the subject beyond what this Court has already held.

JUSTICE THOMAS, with whom JUSTICE SCALIA joins as to Parts I and II, concurring.

This case turns on the seemingly simple question of what constitutes a "crime." Under the Federal Constitution, "the accused" has the right (1) "to be informed of the nature and cause of the accusation" (that is, the basis on which he is accused of a crime), (2) to be "held to answer for a capital, or otherwise infamous crime" only on an indictment or presentment of a grand jury, and (3) to be tried by "an impartial jury of the State and district wherein the crime shall have been committed." Amdts. 5 and 6. See also Art. III, § 2, cl. 3 ("The Trial of all Crimes . . . shall be by Jury"). With the exception of the Grand Jury Clause, see *Hurtado v. California*, 110 U.S. 516, 538 (1884), the Court has held that these protections apply in state prosecutions, *Herring v. New York*, 422 U.S. 853, 857 (1975). Further, the Court has held that due process requires that the jury find beyond a reasonable doubt every fact necessary to constitute the crime. *In re Winship*, 397 U.S. 358, 364 (1970).

All of these constitutional protections turn on determining which facts constitute the "crime" — that is, which facts are the "elements" or "ingredients" of a crime. In order for an accusation of a crime (whether by indictment or some other form) to be proper under the common law, and thus proper under the codification of the common-law rights in the Fifth and Sixth Amendments, it must allege all elements of that crime; likewise, in order for a jury trial of a crime to be proper, all elements of the crime must be proved to the jury (and, under *Winship*, proved beyond a reasonable doubt).

Thus, it is critical to know which facts are elements. This question became more complicated following the Court's decision in *McMillan v. Pennsylvania*, 477 U.S. 79 (1986), which spawned a special sort of fact known as a sentencing enhancement. Such a fact increases a defendant's punishment but is not subject to the constitutional protections to which elements are subject. Justice O'Connor's dissent, in agreement with *McMillan* and *Almendarez-Torres v. United States*, 523 U.S. 224 (1998), takes the view that a legislature is free (within unspecified outer limits) to decree which facts are elements and which are sentencing enhancements.

Sentencing enhancements may be new creatures, but the question that they create for courts is not. Courts have long had to consider which facts are elements in order to determine the sufficiency of an accusation (usually an indictment). The answer that courts have provided regarding the accusation tells us what an element is, and it is then a simple matter to apply that answer to whatever constitutional right may be at issue in a case — here, *Winship* and the right to trial by jury. A long line of essentially uniform authority addressing accusations, and stretching from the earliest reported cases after the founding until well into the 20th century, establishes that the original understanding of which facts are elements was even broader than the rule that the Court adopts today.

This authority establishes that a "crime" includes every fact that is by law a basis for imposing or increasing punishment (in contrast with a fact that mitigates punishment). Thus, if the legislature defines some core crime and then provides for increasing the punishment of that crime upon a finding of some aggravating fact — of whatever sort, including the fact of a prior conviction — the core crime and the aggravating fact together constitute an aggravated crime, just as much as grand larceny is an aggravated form of petit larceny. The aggravating fact is an element of the aggravated crime. Similarly, if the legislature, rather than creating grades of crimes, has provided for setting the punishment of a crime based on some fact —

such as a fine that is proportional to the value of stolen goods — that fact is also an element. No multi-factor parsing of statutes, of the sort that we have attempted since *McMillan*, is necessary. One need only look to the kind, degree, or range of punishment to which the prosecution is by law entitled for a given set of facts. Each fact necessary for that entitlement is an element. * * * *

Finally, I need not in this case address the implications of the rule that I have stated for the Court's decision in *Walton v. Arizona*, 497 U.S. 639 (1990). *Walton* did approve a scheme by which a judge, rather than a jury, determines an aggravating fact that makes a convict eligible for the death penalty, and thus eligible for a greater punishment. In this sense, that fact is an element. But that scheme exists in a unique context, for in the area of capital punishment, unlike any other area, we have imposed special constraints on a legislature's ability to determine what facts shall lead to what punishment — we have restricted the legislature's ability to define crimes. Under our recent capital-punishment jurisprudence, neither Arizona nor any other jurisdiction could provide — as, previously, it freely could and did — that a person shall be death eligible automatically upon conviction for certain crimes. We have interposed a barrier between a jury finding of a capital crime and a court's ability to impose capital punishment. Whether this distinction between capital crimes and all others, or some other distinction, is sufficient to put the former outside the rule that I have stated is a question for another day.[11]

For the foregoing reasons, as well as those given in the Court's opinion, I agree that the New Jersey procedure at issue is unconstitutional.

JUSTICE O'CONNOR, with whom THE CHIEF JUSTICE, JUSTICE KENNEDY, and JUSTICE BREYER join, dissenting.

I

Our Court has long recognized that not every fact that bears on a defendant's punishment need be charged in an indictment, submitted to a jury, and proved by the government beyond a reasonable doubt. Rather, we have held that the "legislature's definition of the elements of the offense is usually dispositive." *McMillan v. Pennsylvania*, 477 U.S. 79, 85 (1986). Although we have recognized that there are obviously constitutional limits beyond which the States may not go in this regard, and that in certain limited circumstances *Winship's* reasonable-doubt requirement applies to facts not formally identified as elements of the offense charged, we have proceeded with caution before deciding that a certain fact must be treated as an offense element despite the legislature's choice not to characterize it as such. We have therefore declined to establish any bright-line rule for making such judgments and have instead approached each case individually, sifting through the considerations most relevant to determining whether the legislature has acted properly within its broad power to define crimes and their punishments or instead has sought to evade the constitutional requirements associated with the characterization of a fact as an offense element.

---

[11] It is likewise unnecessary to consider whether (and, if so, how) the rule regarding elements applies to the Sentencing Guidelines, given the unique status that they have under *Mistretta v. United States*, 488 U.S. 361 (1989). But it may be that this special status is irrelevant, because the Guidelines have the force and effect of laws.

In one bold stroke the Court today casts aside our traditional cautious approach and instead embraces a universal and seemingly bright-line rule limiting the power of Congress and state legislatures to define criminal offenses and the sentences that follow from convictions thereunder. * * * *

II

That the Court's rule is unsupported by the history and case law it cites is reason enough to reject such a substantial departure from our settled jurisprudence. Significantly, the Court also fails to explain adequately why the Due Process Clauses of the Fifth and Fourteenth Amendments and the jury trial guarantee of the Sixth Amendment require application of its rule. Upon closer examination, it is possible that the Court's "increase in the maximum penalty" rule rests on a meaningless formalism that accords, at best, marginal protection for the constitutional rights that it seeks to effectuate.

Any discussion of either the constitutional necessity or the likely effect of the Court's rule must begin, of course, with an understanding of what exactly that rule is. However, that discussion is complicated here by the Court's failure to clarify the contours of the constitutional principle underlying its decision. In fact, there appear to be several plausible interpretations of the constitutional principle on which the Court's decision rests.

For example, under one reading, the Court appears to hold that the Constitution requires that a fact be submitted to a jury and proved beyond a reasonable doubt only if that fact, as a formal matter, extends the range of punishment beyond the prescribed statutory maximum. A State could, however, remove from the jury (and subject to a standard of proof below "beyond a reasonable doubt") the assessment of those facts that define narrower ranges of punishment, within the overall statutory range, to which the defendant may be sentenced.

Thus, apparently New Jersey could cure its sentencing scheme, and achieve virtually the same results, by drafting its weapons possession statute in the following manner: First, New Jersey could prescribe, in the weapons possession statute itself, a range of 5 to 20 years' imprisonment for one who commits that criminal offense. Second, New Jersey could provide that only those defendants convicted under the statute who are found by a judge, by a preponderance of the evidence, to have acted with a purpose to intimidate an individual on the basis of race may receive a sentence greater than 10 years' imprisonment. * * * *

Under another reading of the Court's decision, it may mean only that the Constitution requires that a fact be submitted to a jury and proved beyond a reasonable doubt if it, as a formal matter, increases the range of punishment beyond that which could legally be imposed absent that fact. A State could, however, remove from the jury (and subject to a standard of proof below "beyond a reasonable doubt") the assessment of those facts that, as a formal matter, decrease the range of punishment below that which could legally be imposed absent that fact. Thus, New Jersey could cure its sentencing scheme, and achieve virtually the same results, by drafting its weapons possession statute in the following manner: First, New Jersey could prescribe, in the weapons possession statute itself, a range of 5 to 20 years' imprisonment for one who commits that criminal offense. Second, New Jersey could provide that a defendant convicted under the statute whom a judge finds, by a preponderance of the evidence, not to have acted with a purpose to intimidate an individual on the basis of race may receive a sentence no greater than 10 years' imprisonment. * * * *

If either of the above readings is all that the Court's decision means, the Court's principle amounts to nothing more than chastising the New Jersey Legislature for failing to use the approved phrasing in expressing its intent as to how unlawful weapons possession should be punished. If New Jersey can, consistent with the Constitution, make precisely the same differences in punishment turn on precisely the same facts, and can remove the assessment of those facts from the jury and subject them to a standard of proof below "beyond a reasonable doubt," it is impossible to say that the Fifth, Sixth, and Fourteenth Amendments require the Court's rule. For the same reason, the "structural democratic constraints" that might discourage a legislature from enacting either of the above hypothetical statutes would be no more significant than those that would discourage the enactment of New Jersey's present sentence-enhancement statute. In all three cases, the legislature is able to calibrate punishment perfectly, and subject to a maximum penalty only those defendants whose cases satisfy the sentence-enhancement criterion. No constitutional values are served by so formalistic an approach, while its constitutional costs in statutes struck down are real.

Given the pure formalism of the above readings of the Court's opinion, one suspects that the constitutional principle underlying its decision is more far reaching. The actual principle underlying the Court's decision may be that any fact (other than prior conviction) that has the effect, in real terms, of increasing the maximum punishment beyond an otherwise applicable range must be submitted to a jury and proved beyond a reasonable doubt. The principle thus would apply not only to schemes like New Jersey's, under which a factual determination exposes the defendant to a sentence beyond the prescribed statutory maximum, but also to all determinate-sentencing schemes in which the length of a defendant's sentence within the statutory range turns on specific factual determinations (e.g., the federal Sentencing Guidelines). Justice Thomas essentially concedes that the rule outlined in his concurring opinion would require the invalidation of the Sentencing Guidelines.

I would reject any such principle. Given our approval of — and the significant history in this country of — discretionary sentencing by judges, it is difficult to understand how the Fifth, Sixth, and Fourteenth Amendments could possibly require the Court's or Justice Thomas' rule. Finally, in light of the adoption of determinate-sentencing schemes by many States and the Federal Government, the consequences of the Court's and Justice Thomas' rules in terms of sentencing schemes invalidated by today's decision will likely be severe. * * * *

Under the discretionary-sentencing schemes, a factual determination made by a judge on a standard of proof below "beyond a reasonable doubt" often made the difference between a lesser and a greater punishment.

For example, in *Williams v. New York*, a jury found the defendant guilty of first-degree murder and recommended life imprisonment. The judge, however, rejected the jury's recommendation and sentenced Williams to death on the basis of additional facts that he learned through a pre-sentence investigation report and that had neither been charged in an indictment nor presented to the jury. In rejecting Williams' due process challenge to his death sentence, we explained that there was a long history of sentencing judges exercising "wide discretion in the sources and types of evidence used to assist them in determining the kind and extent of punishment to be imposed within limits fixed by law." Specifically, we held that the Constitution does not restrict a judge's sentencing decision to information that is charged in an indictment and subject to cross-examination in open court. "The due process clause should not be treated as a device for freezing the evidential procedure of sentencing in the mold of trial procedure."

Under our precedent, then, a State may leave the determination of a defendant's sentence to a judge's discretionary decision within a prescribed range of penalties. When a judge, pursuant to that sentencing scheme, decides to increase a defendant's sentence on the basis of certain contested facts, those facts need not be proved to a jury beyond a reasonable doubt. The judge's findings, whether by proof beyond a reasonable doubt or less, suffice for purposes of the Constitution. Under the Court's decision today, however, it appears that once a legislature constrains judges' sentencing discretion by prescribing certain sentences that may only be imposed (or must be imposed) in connection with the same determinations of the same contested facts, the Constitution requires that the facts instead be proved to a jury beyond a reasonable doubt. I see no reason to treat the two schemes differently. In this respect, I agree with the Solicitor General that "a sentence that is constitutionally permissible when selected by a court on the basis of whatever factors it deems appropriate does not become impermissible simply because the court is permitted to select that sentence only after making a finding prescribed by the legislature." Although the Court acknowledges the legitimacy of discretionary sentencing by judges, it never provides a sound reason for treating judicial factfinding under determinate-sentencing schemes differently under the Constitution. * * * *

Consideration of the purposes underlying the Sixth Amendment's jury trial guarantee further demonstrates why our acceptance of judge-made findings in the context of discretionary sentencing suggests the approval of the same judge-made findings in the context of determinate sentencing as well. One important purpose of the Sixth Amendment's jury trial guarantee is to protect the criminal defendant against potentially arbitrary judges. It effectuates this promise by preserving, as a constitutional matter, certain fundamental decisions for a jury of one's peers, as opposed to a judge. For example, the Court has recognized that the Sixth Amendment's guarantee was motivated by the English experience of "competition between judge and jury over the real significance of their respective roles," *Jones*, 526 U.S. at 245, and "measures that were taken to diminish the juries' power," ibid. We have also explained that the jury trial guarantee was understood to provide "an inestimable safeguard against the corrupt or overzealous prosecutor and against the compliant, biased, or eccentric judge. If the defendant preferred the common-sense judgment of a jury to the more tutored but perhaps less sympathetic reaction of the single judge, he was to have it." *Duncan v. Louisiana*, 391 U.S. 145, 156 (1968). Blackstone explained that the right to trial by jury was critically important in criminal cases because of "the violence and partiality of judges appointed by the crown, who might then, as in France or Turkey, imprison, dispatch, or exile any man that was obnoxious to the government, by an instant declaration, that such is their will and pleasure." 4 Blackstone, Commentaries, at 343.

Clearly, the concerns animating the Sixth Amendment's jury trial guarantee, if they were to extend to the sentencing context at all, would apply with greater strength to a discretionary-sentencing scheme than to determinate sentencing. In the former scheme, the potential for mischief by an arbitrary judge is much greater, given that the judge's decision of where to set the defendant's sentence within the prescribed statutory range is left almost entirely to discretion. In contrast, under a determinate-sentencing system, the discretion the judge wields within the statutory range is tightly constrained. Accordingly, our approval of discretionary-sentencing schemes, in which a defendant is not entitled to have a jury make factual findings relevant to sentencing despite the effect those findings have on the severity of the defendant's sentence, demonstrates that the defendant should have no right to demand that a jury make the equivalent factual determinations under a determinate-sentencing scheme.

The Court appears to hold today, however, that a defendant is entitled to have a jury decide, by proof beyond a reasonable doubt, every fact relevant to the determination of sentence under a determinate-sentencing scheme. If this is an accurate description of the constitutional principle underlying the Court's opinion, its decision will have the effect of invalidating significant sentencing reform accomplished at the federal and state levels over the past three decades. Justice Thomas' rule, as he essentially concedes, would have the same effect.

Prior to the most recent wave of sentencing reform, the Federal Government and the States employed indeterminate-sentencing schemes in which judges and executive branch officials (e.g., parole board officials) had substantial discretion to determine the actual length of a defendant's sentence. Studies of indeterminate-sentencing schemes found that similarly situated defendants often received widely disparate sentences. Although indeterminate sentencing was intended to soften the harsh and uniform sentences formerly imposed under mandatory-sentencing systems, some studies revealed that indeterminate sentencing actually had the opposite effect.

In response, Congress and the state legislatures shifted to determinate-sentencing schemes that aimed to limit judges' sentencing discretion and, thereby, afford similarly situated offenders equivalent treatment. See, e.g., Cal.Penal Code Ann. § 1170. The most well known of these reforms was the federal Sentencing Reform Act of 1984, 18 U.S.C. § 3551 et seq. In the Act, Congress created the United States Sentencing Commission, which in turn promulgated the Sentencing Guidelines that now govern sentencing by federal judges. Whether one believes the determinate-sentencing reforms have proved successful or not — and the subject is one of extensive debate among commentators — the apparent effect of the Court's opinion today is to halt the current debate on sentencing reform in its tracks and to invalidate with the stroke of a pen three decades' worth of nationwide reform, all in the name of a principle with a questionable constitutional pedigree. Indeed, it is ironic that the Court, in the name of constitutional rights meant to protect criminal defendants from the potentially arbitrary exercise of power by prosecutors and judges, appears to rest its decision on a principle that would render unconstitutional efforts by Congress and the state legislatures to place constraints on that very power in the sentencing context.

Finally, perhaps the most significant impact of the Court's decision will be a practical one — its unsettling effect on sentencing conducted under current federal and state determinate-sentencing schemes. As I have explained, the Court does not say whether these schemes are constitutional, but its reasoning strongly suggests that they are not. Thus, with respect to past sentences handed down by judges under determinate-sentencing schemes, the Court's decision threatens to unleash a flood of petitions by convicted defendants seeking to invalidate their sentences in whole or in part on the authority of the Court's decision today. Statistics compiled by the United States Sentencing Commission reveal that almost a half-million cases have been sentenced under the Sentencing Guidelines since 1989. Federal cases constitute only the tip of the iceberg. In 1998, for example, federal criminal prosecutions represented only about 0.4% of the total number of criminal prosecutions in federal and state courts. Because many States, like New Jersey, have determinate-sentencing schemes, the number of individual sentences drawn into question by the Court's decision could be colossal.

The decision will likely have an even more damaging effect on sentencing conducted in the immediate future under current determinate-sentencing schemes. Because the Court fails to clarify the precise contours of the constitutional principle underlying its decision, federal and state judges are left in a state of limbo. Should they continue to assume the constitutionality of the determinate-sentencing schemes under which they have operated for so long, and proceed to sentence convicted defendants in accord with those governing statutes and guidelines? The Court provides no answer, yet its reasoning suggests that each new sentence will rest on shaky ground. The most unfortunate aspect of today's decision is that our precedents did not foreordain this disruption in the world of sentencing. Rather, our cases traditionally took a cautious approach to questions like the one presented in this case. The Court throws that caution to the wind and, in the process, threatens to cast sentencing in the United States into what will likely prove to be a lengthy period of considerable confusion.

III

Because I do not believe that the Court's "increase in the maximum penalty" rule is required by the Constitution, I would evaluate New Jersey's sentence-enhancement statute, N.J. Stat. Ann. § 2C:44-3, by analyzing the factors we have examined in past cases. First, the New Jersey statute does not shift the burden of proof on an essential ingredient of the offense by presuming that ingredient upon proof of other elements of the offense. Second, the magnitude of the New Jersey sentence enhancement, as applied in petitioner's case, is constitutionally permissible. Under New Jersey law, the weapons possession offense to which petitioner pleaded guilty carries a sentence range of 5 to 10 years' imprisonment. N.J. Stat. Ann. §§ 2C:39-4(a), 2C:43-6(a)(2). The fact that petitioner, in committing that offense, acted with a purpose to intimidate because of race exposed him to a higher sentence range of 10 to 20 years' imprisonment. § 2C:43-7(a)(3). The 10-year increase in the maximum penalty to which petitioner was exposed falls well within the range we have found permissible. See *Almendarez-Torres* (approving 18-year enhancement). Third, the New Jersey statute gives no impression of having been enacted to evade the constitutional requirements that attach when a State makes a fact an element of the charged offense. For example, New Jersey did not take what had previously been an element of the weapons possession offense and transform it into a sentencing factor.

In sum, New Jersey "simply took one factor that has always been considered by sentencing courts to bear on punishment" — a defendant's motive for committing the criminal offense — "and dictated the precise weight to be given that factor" when the motive is to intimidate a person because of race. The Court claims that a purpose to intimidate on account of race is a traditional *mens rea* element, and not a motive. To make this claim, the Court finds it necessary once again to ignore our settled precedent. In *Wisconsin v. Mitchell*, 508 U.S. 476 (1993), we considered a statute similar to the one at issue here. The Wisconsin statute provided for an increase in a convicted defendant's punishment if the defendant intentionally selected the victim of the crime because of that victim's race. In a unanimous decision upholding the statute, we specifically characterized it as providing a sentence enhancement based on the "motive" of the defendant. That same characterization applies in the case of the New Jersey statute. The motive for committing an offense has traditionally been an important factor in determining a defendant's sentence. New Jersey, therefore, has done no more than what we held permissible in *McMillan*; it has taken a traditional sentencing factor and dictated the precise weight judges should attach to that factor when the specific motive is to intimidate on the basis of race. * * * *

On the basis of our prior precedent, then, I would hold that the New Jersey sentence-enhancement statute is constitutional, and affirm the judgment of the Supreme Court of New Jersey.

JUSTICE BREYER, with whom CHIEF JUSTICE REHNQUIST joins, dissenting.

The majority holds that the Constitution contains the following requirement: "any fact [other than recidivism] that increases the penalty for a crime beyond the prescribed statutory maximum must be submitted to a jury, and proved beyond a reasonable doubt." This rule would seem to promote a procedural ideal — that of juries, not judges, determining the existence of those facts upon which increased punishment turns. But the real world of criminal justice cannot hope to meet any such ideal. It can function only with the help of procedural compromises, particularly in respect to sentencing. And those compromises, which are themselves necessary for the fair functioning of the criminal justice system, preclude implementation of the procedural model that today's decision reflects. At the very least, the impractical nature of the requirement that the majority now recognizes supports the proposition that the Constitution was not intended to embody it.

I

In modern times the law has left it to the sentencing judge to find those facts which (within broad sentencing limits set by the legislature) determine the sentence of a convicted offender. The judge's factfinding role is not inevitable. One could imagine, for example, a pure "charge offense" sentencing system in which the degree of punishment depended only upon the crime charged (e.g., eight mandatory years for robbery, six for arson, three for assault). But such a system would ignore many harms and risks of harm that the offender caused or created, and it would ignore many relevant offender characteristics. Hence, that imaginary "charge offense" system would not be a fair system, for it would lack proportionality, i.e., it would treat different offenders similarly despite major differences in the manner in which each committed the same crime.

There are many such manner-related differences in respect to criminal behavior. Empirical data collected by the Sentencing Commission makes clear that, before the Guidelines, judges who exercised discretion within broad legislatively determined sentencing limits (say, a range of 0 to 20 years) would impose very different sentences upon offenders engaged in the same basic criminal conduct, depending, for example, upon the amount of drugs distributed (in respect to drug crimes), the amount of money taken (in respect to robbery, theft, or fraud), the presence or use of a weapon, injury to a victim, the vulnerability of a victim, the offender's role in the offense, recidivism, and many other offense-related or offender-related factors. The majority does not deny that judges have exercised, and, constitutionally speaking, may exercise sentencing discretion in this way.

Nonetheless, it is important for present purposes to understand why judges, rather than juries, traditionally have determined the presence or absence of such sentence-affecting facts in any given case. And it is important to realize that the reason is not a theoretical one, but a practical one. It does not reflect (Justice Scalia's opinion to the contrary notwithstanding) an ideal of procedural "fairness," but rather an administrative need for procedural compromise. There are, to put it simply, far too many potentially relevant sentencing factors to permit submission of all (or even many) of them to a jury. As the Sentencing Guidelines state the matter,

> a bank robber with (or without) a gun, which the robber kept hidden (or brandished), might have frightened (or merely warned), injured seriously (or less seriously), tied up (or simply pushed) a guard, a teller or a customer, at night (or at noon), for a bad (or arguably less bad) motive, in an effort to obtain money for other crimes (or for other purposes), in the company of a few (or many) other robbers, for the first (or fourth) time that day, while sober (or under the influence of drugs or alcohol), and so forth. [Sentencing Guidelines, Part A, at 1.2.]

The Guidelines note that "a sentencing system tailored to fit every conceivable wrinkle of each case can become unworkable and seriously compromise the certainty of punishment and its deterrent effect." To ask a jury to consider all, or many, such matters would do the same.

At the same time, to require jury consideration of all such factors — say, during trial where the issue is guilt or innocence — could easily place the defendant in the awkward (and conceivably unfair) position of having to deny he committed the crime yet offer proof about how he committed it, e.g., "I did not sell drugs, but I sold no more than 500 grams." And while special postverdict sentencing juries could cure this problem, they have seemed (but for capital cases) not worth their administrative costs. Hence, before the Guidelines, federal sentencing judges typically would obtain relevant factual sentencing information from probation officers' presentence reports, while permitting a convicted offender to challenge the information's accuracy at a hearing before the judge without benefit of trial-type evidentiary rules.

It is also important to understand how a judge traditionally determined which factors should be taken into account for sentencing purposes. In principle, the number of potentially relevant behavioral characteristics is endless. A judge might ask, for example, whether an unlawfully possessed knife was "a switchblade, drawn or concealed, opened or closed, large or small, used in connection with a car theft (where victim confrontation is rare), a burglary (where confrontation is unintended) or a robbery (where confrontation is intentional)." United States Sentencing Commission, Preliminary Observations of the Commission on Commissioner Robinson's Dissent 3, n. 3 (May 1, 1987). Again, the method reflects practical, rather than theoretical, considerations. Prior to the Sentencing Guidelines, federal law left the individual sentencing judge free to determine which factors were relevant. That freedom meant that each judge, in an effort to tailor punishment to the individual offense and offender, was guided primarily by experience, relevance, and a sense of proportional fairness.

Finally, it is important to understand how a legislature decides which factual circumstances among all those potentially related to generally harmful behavior it should transform into elements of a statutorily defined crime (where they would become relevant to the guilt or innocence of an accused), and which factual circumstances it should leave to the sentencing process (where, as sentencing factors, they would help to determine the sentence imposed upon one who has been found guilty). Again, theory does not provide an answer. Legislatures, in defining crimes in terms of elements, have looked for guidance to common-law tradition, to history, and to current social need. And, traditionally, the Court has left legislatures considerable freedom to make the element determination.

By placing today's constitutional question in a broader context, this brief survey may help to clarify the nature of today's decision. It also may explain why, in respect to sentencing systems, proportionality, uniformity, and administrability are all aspects of that basic "fairness" that the Constitution demands. And it suggests my basic problem with the Court's rule: A sentencing system in which judges have discretion to find sentencing-related factors is a workable system and one that has long been thought consistent with the Constitution; why, then, would the Constitution treat sentencing statutes any differently?

                                    II

As Justice Thomas suggests, until fairly recent times many legislatures rarely focused upon sentencing factors. Rather, it appears they simply identified typical forms of antisocial conduct, defined basic "crimes," and attached a broad sentencing range to each definition — leaving judges free to decide how to sentence within those ranges in light of such factors as they found relevant. But the Constitution does not freeze 19th-century sentencing practices into permanent law. And dissatisfaction with the traditional sentencing system (reflecting its tendency to treat similar cases differently) has led modern legislatures to write new laws that refer specifically to sentencing factors.

Legislatures have tended to address the problem of too much judicial sentencing discretion in two ways. First, legislatures sometimes have created sentencing commissions armed with delegated authority to make more uniform judicial exercise of that discretion. Congress, for example, has created a federal Sentencing Commission, giving it the power to create Guidelines that (within the sentencing range set by individual statutes) reflect the host of factors that might be used to determine the actual sentence imposed for each individual crime. Federal judges must apply those Guidelines in typical cases (those that lie in the "heartland" of the crime as the statute defines it) while retaining freedom to depart in atypical cases.

Second, legislatures sometimes have directly limited the use (by judges or by a commission) of particular factors in sentencing, either by specifying statutorily how a particular factor will affect the sentence imposed or by specifying how a commission should use a particular factor when writing a guideline. Such a statute might state explicitly, for example, that a particular factor, say, use of a weapon, recidivism, injury to a victim, or bad motive, "shall" increase, or "may" increase, a particular sentence in a particular way.

The issue the Court decides today involves this second kind of legislation. The Court holds that a legislature cannot enact such legislation (where an increase in the maximum is involved) unless the factor at issue has been charged, tried to a jury, and found to exist beyond a reasonable doubt. My question in respect to this holding is, simply, "why would the Constitution contain such a requirement"?

III

In light of the sentencing background described in Parts I and II, I do not see how the majority can find in the Constitution a requirement that "any fact" (other than recidivism) that increases the maximum penalty for a crime "must be submitted to a jury." As Justice O'Connor demonstrates, this Court has previously failed to view the Constitution as embodying any such principle, while sometimes finding to the contrary. The majority raises no objection to traditional pre-Guidelines sentencing procedures under which judges, not juries, made the factual findings that would lead to an increase in an individual offender's sentence. How does a legislative determination differ in any significant way? For example, if a judge may on his or her own decide that victim injury or bad motive should increase a bank robber's sentence from 5 years to 10, why does it matter that a legislature instead enacts a statute that increases a bank robber's sentence from 5 years to 10 based on this same judicial finding?

With the possible exception of the last line of Justice Scalia's concurring opinion, the majority also makes no constitutional objection to a legislative delegation to a commission of the authority to create guidelines that determine how a judge is to exercise sentencing discretion. But if the Constitution permits Guidelines, why does it not permit Congress similarly to guide the exercise of a judge's sentencing discretion? That is, if the Constitution permits a delegatee (the commission) to exercise sentencing-related rulemaking power, how can it deny the delegator (the legislature) what is, in effect, the same rulemaking power?

The majority appears to offer two responses. First, it argues for a limiting principle that would prevent a legislature with broad authority from transforming (jury-determined) facts that constitute elements of a crime into (judge-determined) sentencing factors, thereby removing procedural protections that the Constitution would otherwise require. The majority's cure, however, is not aimed at the disease.

The same "transformational" problem exists under traditional sentencing law, where legislation, silent as to sentencing factors, grants the judge virtually unchecked discretion to sentence within a broad range. Under such a system, judges or prosecutors can similarly "transform" crimes, punishing an offender convicted of one crime as if he had committed another. A prosecutor, for example, might charge an offender with five counts of embezzlement (each subject to a 10-year maximum penalty), while asking the judge to impose maximum and consecutive sentences because the embezzler murdered his employer. And, as part of the traditional sentencing discretion that the majority concedes judges retain, the judge, not a jury, would determine the last-mentioned relevant fact, i.e., that the murder actually occurred.

This egregious example shows the problem's complexity. The source of the problem lies not in a legislature's power to enact sentencing factors, but in the traditional legislative power to select elements defining a crime, the traditional legislative power to set broad sentencing ranges, and the traditional judicial power to choose a sentence within that range on the basis of relevant offender conduct. Conversely, the solution to the problem lies, not in prohibiting legislatures from enacting sentencing factors, but in sentencing rules that determine punishments on the basis of properly defined relevant conduct, with sensitivity to the need for procedural protections where sentencing factors are determined by a judge (for example, use of a "reasonable doubt" standard), and invocation of the Due Process Clause where the history of the crime at issue, together with the nature of the facts to be proved, reveals unusual and serious procedural unfairness.

Second, the majority, in support of its constitutional rule, emphasizes the concept of a statutory "maximum." The Court points out that a sentencing judge (or a commission) traditionally has determined, and now still determines, sentences within a legislated range capped by a maximum (a range that the legislature itself sets). I concede the truth of the majority's statement, but I do not understand its relevance.

From a defendant's perspective, the legislature's decision to cap the possible range of punishment at a statutorily prescribed "maximum" would affect the actual sentence imposed no differently than a sentencing commission's (or a sentencing judge's) similar determination. Indeed, as a practical matter, a legislated mandatory "minimum" is far more important to an actual defendant. A judge and a commission, after all, are legally free to select any sentence below a statute's maximum, but they are not free to subvert a statutory minimum. And, as Justice Thomas indicates, all the considerations of fairness that might support submission to a jury of a factual matter that increases a statutory maximum, apply a fortiori to any matter that would increase a statutory minimum. To repeat, I do not understand why, when a legislature authorizes a judge to impose a higher penalty for bank robbery (based, say, on the court's finding that a victim was injured or the defendant's motive was bad), a new crime is born; but where a legislature requires a judge to impose a higher penalty than he otherwise would (within a pre-existing statutory range) based on similar criteria, it is not.

IV

I certainly do not believe that the present sentencing system is one of "perfect equity," (Scalia, J., concurring), and I am willing, consequently, to assume that the majority's rule would provide a degree of increased procedural protection in respect to those particular sentencing factors currently embodied in statutes. I nonetheless believe that any such increased protection provides little practical help and comes at too high a price. For one thing, by leaving mandatory minimum sentences untouched, the majority's rule simply encourages any legislature interested in asserting control over the sentencing process to do so by creating those minimums. That result would mean significantly less procedural fairness, not more.

For another thing, this Court's case law, prior to *Jones v. United States*, 526 U.S. 227 (1999), led legislatures to believe that they were permitted to increase a statutory maximum sentence on the basis of a sentencing factor. And legislatures may well have relied upon that belief. See, e.g., 21 U.S.C. § 841(b) (providing penalties for, among other things, possessing a "controlled substance" with intent to distribute it, which sentences vary dramatically depending upon the amount of the drug possessed, without requiring jury determination of the amount); N.J. Stat. Ann. §§ 2C:43-6, 2C:43-7, 2C:44-1a-f, 2C:44-3 (setting sentencing ranges for crimes, while providing for lesser or greater punishments depending upon judicial findings regarding certain "aggravating" or "mitigating" factors); Cal.Penal Code Ann. § 1170 (similar); see also Cal. Court Rule 420(b) (providing that "circumstances in aggravation and mitigation" are to be established by the sentencing judge based on "the case record, the probation officer's report, and other reports and statements properly received").

As Justice O'Connor points out, the majority's rule creates serious uncertainty about the constitutionality of such statutes and about the constitutionality of the confinement of those punished under them. The few amicus briefs that the Court received in this case do not discuss the impact of the Court's new rule on, for example, drug crime statutes or state criminal justice systems. This fact, I concede, may suggest that my concerns about disruption are overstated; yet it may also suggest that so absolute a constitutional prohibition is unexpected. Moreover, the rationale that underlies the Court's rule suggests a principle — jury determination of all sentencing-related facts — that, unless restricted, threatens the workability of every criminal justice system (if applied to judges) or threatens efforts to make those systems more uniform, hence more fair (if applied to commissions).

Finally, the Court's new rule will likely impede legislative attempts to provide authoritative guidance as to how courts should respond to the presence of traditional sentencing factors. The factor at issue here — motive — is such a factor. Whether a robber takes money to finance other crimes or to feed a starving family can matter, and long has mattered, when the length of a sentence is at issue. The State of New Jersey has determined that one motive — racial hatred — is particularly bad and ought to make a difference in respect to punishment for a crime. That determination is reasonable. The procedures mandated are consistent with traditional sentencing practice. Though additional procedural protections might well be desirable, for the reasons Justice O'Connor discusses and those I have discussed, I do not believe the Constitution requires them where ordinary sentencing factors are at issue. Consequently, in my view, New Jersey's statute is constitutional.

I respectfully dissent.

Note from Shelly:

1. Justice Scalia concurred, writing this response to Justice Breyer's dissent:

> I feel the need to say a few words in response to Justice Breyer's dissent. It sketches an admirably fair and efficient scheme of criminal justice designed for a society that is prepared to leave criminal justice to the State. (Judges, it is sometimes necessary to remind ourselves, are part of the State — and an increasingly bureaucratic part of it, at that.) The founders of the American Republic were not prepared to leave it to the State, which is why the jury-trial guarantee was one of the least controversial provisions of the Bill of Rights. It has never been efficient; but it has always been free.
>
> As for fairness, which Justice Breyer believes "in modern times," the jury cannot provide: I think it not unfair to tell a prospective felon that if he commits his contemplated crime he is exposing himself to a jail sentence of 30 years — and that if, upon conviction, he gets anything less than that he may thank the mercy of a tenderhearted judge (just as he may thank the

mercy of a tenderhearted parole commission if he is let out inordinately early, or the mercy of a tenderhearted governor if his sentence is commuted). Will there be disparities? Of course. But the criminal will never get more punishment than he bargained for when he did the crime, and his guilt of the crime (and hence the length of the sentence to which he is exposed) will be determined beyond a reasonable doubt by the unanimous vote of 12 of his fellow citizens.

In Justice Breyer's bureaucratic realm of perfect equity, by contrast, the facts that determine the length of sentence to which the defendant is exposed will be determined to exist (on a more-likely-than-not basis) by a single employee of the State. It is certainly arguable (Justice Breyer argues it) that this sacrifice of prior protections is worth it. But it is not arguable that, just because one thinks it is a better system, it must be, or is even more likely to be, the system envisioned by a Constitution that guarantees trial by jury. What ultimately demolishes the case for the dissenters is that they are unable to say what the right to trial by jury does guarantee if, as they assert, it does not guarantee — what it has been assumed to guarantee throughout our history — the right to have a jury determine those facts that determine the maximum sentence the law allows. They provide no coherent alternative.

Justice Breyer proceeds on the erroneous and all-too-common assumption that the Constitution means what we think it ought to mean. It does not; it means what it says. And the guarantee that "in all criminal prosecutions, the accused shall enjoy the right to trial, by an impartial jury" has no intelligible content unless it means that all the facts which must exist in order to subject the defendant to a legally prescribed punishment must be found by the jury.

2. What effect (if any) does this recent decision have on the California statutes and rules of court set out at the beginning of this Chapter? What effect (if any) does it have on your analysis of Problem 11?

3. In *Ring v. Arizona*, 536 U.S. 584 (2002), Ring was convicted by a jury of murder, and then the judge sentenced him to death.

Under Arizona law, Ring could not be sentenced to death, the statutory maximum penalty for first-degree murder, unless further findings were made. The State's first-degree murder statute prescribes that the offense "is punishable by death or life imprisonment as provided by § 13-703." Ariz.Rev.Stat. Ann. § 13- 1105(C). The cross-referenced section, § 13-703, directs the judge who presided at trial to "conduct a separate sentencing hearing to determine the existence or nonexistence of certain enumerated circumstances for the purpose of determining the sentence to be imposed." § 13-703(C). The statute further instructs: "The hearing shall be conducted before the court alone. The court alone shall make all factual determinations required by this section or the constitution of the United States or this state."

At the conclusion of the sentencing hearing, the judge is to determine the presence or absence of the enumerated "aggravating circumstances" and any "mitigating circumstances." The State's law authorizes the judge to sentence the defendant to death only if there is at least one aggravating circumstance and "there are no mitigating circumstances sufficiently substantial to call for leniency." § 13-703(F).

The Arizona Supreme Court held that this procedure did not violate *Apprendi*, but the U.S. Supreme Court disagreed:

> Arizona suggests that judicial authority over the finding of aggravating factors may be a better way to guarantee against the arbitrary imposition of the death penalty. The Sixth Amendment jury trial right, however, does not turn on the relative rationality, fairness, or efficiency of potential factfinders. Entrusting to a judge the finding of facts necessary to support a death sentence might be an admirably fair and efficient scheme of criminal justice designed for a society that is prepared to leave criminal justice to the State. The founders of the American Republic were not prepared to leave it to the State, which is why the jury-trial guarantee was one of the least controversial provisions of the Bill of Rights. It has never been efficient; but it has always been free.

> In any event, the superiority of judicial factfinding in capital cases is far from evident. Unlike Arizona, the great majority of States responded to this Court's Eighth Amendment decisions requiring the presence of aggravating circumstances in capital cases by entrusting those determinations to the jury. * * * *

> The right to trial by jury guaranteed by the Sixth Amendment would be senselessly diminished if it encompassed the factfinding necessary to increase a defendant's sentence by two years, but not the factfinding necessary to put him to death. We hold that the Sixth Amendment applies to both.

4. In *Blakely v. Washington*, 542 U.S. 296 (2004), Blakely pleaded guilty in state court to kidnapping, admitting facts that would support a maximum sentence of 53 months. The judge found an additional fact — he had acted with "deliberate cruelty" — and raised the sentence to 90 months. The Supreme Court (pr Justice Scalia) reversed:

> The facts supporting that finding were neither admitted by petitioner nor found by a jury. The State nevertheless contends that there was no *Apprendi* violation because the relevant "statutory maximum" is not 53 months, but the 10-year maximum for class B felonies in § 9A.20.021(1)(b). It observes that no exceptional sentence may exceed that limit.

> Our precedents make clear, however, that the "statutory maximum" for *Apprendi* purposes is the maximum sentence a judge may impose *solely on the basis of the facts reflected in the jury verdict or admitted by the defendant.* See *Ring, supra,* at 602 ("the maximum he would receive if punished according to the facts reflected in the jury verdict alone"). In other words, the relevant "statutory maximum" is not the maximum sentence a judge may impose after finding additional facts, but the maximum he may impose *without* any additional findings. When a judge inflicts punishment that the jury's verdict alone does not allow, the jury has not found all the facts which the law makes essential to the punishment, and the judge exceeds his proper authority.

The judge in this case could not have imposed the exceptional 90-month sentence solely on the basis of the facts admitted in the guilty plea. Those facts alone were insufficient because, as the Washington Supreme Court has explained, "a reason offered to justify an exceptional sentence can be considered only if it takes into account factors other than those which are used in computing the standard range sentence for the offense," which in this case included the elements of second-degree kidnaping and the use of a firearm. Had the judge imposed the 90-month sentence solely on the basis of the plea, he would have been reversed. The "maximum sentence" is no more 10 years here than it was 20 years in *Apprendi* (because that is what the judge could have imposed upon finding a hate crime) or death in *Ring* (because that is what the judge could have imposed upon finding an aggravator).

* * * *

Our commitment to *Apprendi* in this context reflects not just respect for longstanding precedent, but the need to give intelligible content to the right of jury trial. That right is no mere procedural formality, but a fundamental reservation of power in our constitutional structure. Just as suffrage ensures the people's ultimate control in the legislative and executive branches, jury trial is meant to ensure their control in the judiciary. * * * *

Apprendi carries out this design by ensuring that the judge's authority to sentence derives wholly from the jury's verdict. Without that restriction, the jury would not exercise the control that the Framers intended.

JUSTICE O'CONNOR dissented, noting that:

The consequences of today's decision will be as far reaching as they are disturbing. Washington's sentencing system is by no means unique. Numerous other States have enacted guidelines systems, as has the Federal Government. See, *e.g.*, Alaska Stat. § 12.55.155; Ark.Code Ann. § 16-90-804; Fla. Stat. § 921.0016; Kan. Stat. Ann. § 21-4701 *et seq.*; Mich. Comp. Laws Ann. § 769.34; Minn.Stat. § 244.10; N.C. Gen.Stat. § 15A-1340.16; Ore. Admin. Rule § 213-008-0001; 204 Pa.Code § 303 *et seq.*; 18 U.S.C. § 3553; 28 U.S.C. § 991 *et seq.* Today's decision casts constitutional doubt over them all and, in so doing, threatens an untold number of criminal judgments.

Question: Under *Blakely*, is California's sentencing scheme constitutional?

CUNNINGHAM v. CALIFORNIA
United States Supreme Court, 2007
549 U.S. 270

JUSTICE GINSBURG delivered the opinion of the Court.

California's determinate sentencing law (DSL) assigns to the trial judge, not to the jury, authority to find the facts that expose a defendant to an elevated "upper term" sentence. The facts so found are neither inherent in the jury's verdict nor embraced by the defendant's plea, and they need only be established by a preponderance of the evidence, not beyond a reasonable doubt. The question presented is whether the DSL, by placing sentence-elevating factfinding within the judge's province, violates a defendant's right to trial by jury safeguarded by the Sixth and Fourteenth Amendments. We hold that it does.

As this Court's decisions instruct, the Federal Constitution's jury-trial guarantee proscribes a sentencing scheme that allows a judge to impose a sentence above the statutory maximum based on a fact, other than a prior conviction, not found by a jury or admitted by the defendant. Apprendi v. New Jersey, 530 U.S. 466 (2000); Ring v. Arizona, 536 U.S. 584 (2002); Blakely v. Washington, 542 U.S. 296 (2004); United States v. Booker, 543 U.S. 220 (2005). "The relevant 'statutory maximum,'" this Court has clarified, "is not the maximum sentence a judge may impose after finding additional facts, but the maximum he may impose without any additional findings." Blakely, 542 U.S. at 303–304. In petitioner's case, the jury's verdict alone limited the permissible sentence to 12 years. Additional factfinding by the trial judge, however, yielded an upper term sentence of 16 years. The California Court of Appeal affirmed the harsher sentence. We reverse that disposition because the four-year elevation based on judicial factfinding denied petitioner his right to a jury trial.

I

A

Petitioner John Cunningham was tried and convicted of continuous sexual abuse of a child under the age of 14. Under the DSL, that offense is punishable by imprisonment for a lower term sentence of 6 years, a middle term sentence of 12 years, or an upper term sentence of 16 years. Cal.Penal Code Ann. § 288.5(a). As further explained below, the DSL obliged the trial judge to sentence Cunningham to the 12-year middle term unless the judge found one or more additional facts in aggravation. Based on a post-trial sentencing hearing, the trial judge found by a preponderance of the evidence six aggravating circumstances, among them, the particular vulnerability of Cunningham's victim, and Cunningham's violent conduct, which indicated a serious danger to the community. In mitigation, the judge found one fact: Cunningham had no record of prior criminal conduct. Concluding that the aggravators outweighed the sole mitigator, the judge sentenced Cunningham to the upper term of 16 years. * * * *

B

Enacted in 1977, the DSL replaced an indeterminate sentencing regime in force in California for some 60 years. Under the prior regime, courts imposed open-ended prison terms (often one year to life), and the parole board — the Adult Authority — determined the amount of time a felon would ultimately spend in prison. In contrast, the DSL fixed the terms of imprisonment for most offenses, and eliminated the possibility of early release on parole. Through the DSL, California's lawmakers aimed to promote uniform and proportionate punishment. Penal Code § 1170(a)(1). (Murder and certain other grave offenses still carry lengthy indeterminate terms with the possibility of early release on parole.)

For most offenses, including Cunningham's, the DSL regime is implemented in the following manner. The statute defining the offense prescribes three precise terms of imprisonment — a lower, middle, and upper term sentence. E.g., Penal Code § 288.5(a) (a person convicted of continuous sexual abuse of a child "shall be punished by imprisonment in the state prison for a term of 6, 12, or 16 years"). Penal Code § 1170(b) controls the trial judge's choice; it provides that "the court shall order imposition of the middle term, unless there are circumstances in aggravation or mitigation of the crime." "Circumstances in aggravation or mitigation" are to be determined by the court after consideration of several items: the trial record; the probation officer's report; statements in aggravation or mitigation submitted by the parties, the victim, or the victim's family; "and any further evidence introduced at the sentencing hearing."

The DSL directed the State's Judicial Council to adopt Rules guiding the sentencing judge's decision whether to "impose the lower or upper prison term." Penal Code § 1170.3(a)(2). Restating § 1170(b), the Council's Rules provide that "the middle term shall be selected unless imposition of the upper or lower term is justified by circumstances in aggravation or mitigation." Rule 4.420(a). "Circumstances in aggravation," as crisply defined by the Judicial Council, means "facts which justify the imposition of the upper prison term." Rule 4.405(d). Facts aggravating an offense, the Rules instruct, "shall be established by a preponderance of the evidence," Rule 4.420(b), and must be "stated orally on the record." Rule 4.420(e).

The Rules provide a nonexhaustive list of aggravating circumstances, including "facts relating to the crime," Rule 4.421(a), "facts relating to the defendant," Rule 4.421(b), and "any other facts statutorily declared to be circumstances in aggravation," Rule 4.421(c). Beyond the enumerated circumstances, "the judge is free to consider any 'additional criteria reasonably related to the decision being made.'" Rule 4.408(a). "A fact that is an element of the crime," however, "shall not be used to impose the upper term." Rule 4.420(d).

In sum, California's DSL, and the rules governing its application, direct the sentencing court to start with the middle term, and to move from that term only when the court itself finds and places on the record facts — whether related to the offense or the offender — beyond the elements of the charged offense.

Justice ALITO maintains, however, that a circumstance in aggravation need not be a fact at all. In his view, a policy judgment, or even a judge's "subjective belief" regarding the appropriate sentence, qualifies as an aggravating circumstance. California's Rules, however, constantly refer to "facts." As just noted, the Rules define "circumstances in aggravation" as "facts which justify the imposition of the upper prison term." Rule 4.405(d). And "circumstances in aggravation," the Rules unambiguously declare, "shall be established by a preponderance of the evidence," Rule 4.420(b), a clear factfinding directive to which there is no exception. * * * *

Notably, the Penal Code permits elevation of a sentence above the upper term based on specified statutory enhancements relating to the defendant's criminal history or circumstances of the crime. See, e.g., Penal Code § 667 et seq.; § 12022 et seq. Unlike aggravating circumstances, statutory enhancements must be charged in the indictment, and the underlying facts must be proved to the jury beyond a reasonable doubt. Penal Code § 1170.1(e). A fact underlying an enhancement cannot do double duty; it cannot be used to impose an upper term sentence and, on top of that, an enhanced term. Penal Code § 1170(b). Where permitted by statute, however, a judge may use a fact qualifying as an enhancer to impose an upper term rather than an enhanced sentence. Ibid.; Rule 4.420(c).

II

This Court has repeatedly held that, under the Sixth Amendment, any fact that exposes a defendant to a greater potential sentence must be found by a jury, not a judge, and established beyond a reasonable doubt, not merely by a preponderance of the evidence. While this rule is rooted in longstanding common-law practice, its explicit statement in our decisions is recent. In Jones v. United States, 526 U.S. 227 (1999), we examined the Sixth Amendment's historical and doctrinal foundations, and recognized that judicial factfinding operating to increase a defendant's otherwise maximum punishment posed a grave constitutional question. While the Court construed the statute at issue to avoid the question, the Jones opinion presaged our decision, some 15 months later, in Apprendi v. New Jersey, 530 U.S. 466 (2000).

Charles Apprendi was convicted of possession of a firearm for an unlawful purpose, a second-degree offense under New Jersey law punishable by five to ten years' imprisonment. A separate "hate crime" statute authorized an "extended term" of imprisonment: Ten to twenty years could be imposed if the trial judge found, by a preponderance of the evidence, that "the defendant in committing the crime acted with a purpose to intimidate an individual or group of individuals because of race, color, gender, handicap, religion, sexual orientation or ethnicity." The judge in Apprendi's case so found, and therefore sentenced the defendant to 12 years' imprisonment. This Court held that the Sixth Amendment proscribed the enhanced sentence. Other than a prior conviction, we held in *Apprendi*, "any fact that increases the penalty for a crime beyond the prescribed statutory maximum must be submitted to a jury, and proved beyond a reasonable doubt."

We have since reaffirmed the rule of *Apprendi*, applying it to facts subjecting a defendant to the death penalty, Ring v. Arizona, 536 U.S. 584 (2002), facts permitting a sentence in excess of the "standard range" under Washington's Sentencing Reform Act, Blakely v. Washington, 542 U.S. 296 (2004), and facts triggering a sentence range elevation under the then-mandatory Federal Sentencing Guidelines, United States v. Booker, 543 U.S. 220 (2005). *Blakely* and *Booker* bear most closely on the question presented in this case.

Ralph Howard Blakely was convicted of second-degree kidnapping with a firearm, a class B felony under Washington law. While the overall statutory maximum for a class B felony was ten years, the State's Sentencing Reform Act added an important qualification: If no facts beyond those reflected in the jury's verdict were found by the trial judge, a defendant could not receive a sentence above a "standard range" of 49 to 53 months. The Reform Act permitted but did not require a judge to exceed that standard range if she found "substantial and compelling reasons justifying an exceptional sentence." The Reform Act set out a nonexhaustive list of aggravating facts on which such a sentence elevation could be based. It also clarified that a fact taken into account in fixing the standard range — i.e., any fact found by the jury — could under no circumstances count in the determination whether to impose an exceptional sentence. Blakely was sentenced to 90 months' imprisonment, more than three years above the standard range, based on the trial judge's finding that he had acted with deliberate cruelty.

Applying the rule of *Apprendi*, this Court held Blakely's sentence unconstitutional. The State in Blakely had endeavored to distinguish *Apprendi* on the ground that "under the Washington guidelines, an exceptional sentence is within the court's discretion as a result of a guilty verdict." We rejected that argument. The judge could not have sentenced Blakely above the standard range without finding the additional fact of deliberate cruelty. Consequently, that fact was subject to the Sixth Amendment's jury-trial guarantee. It did not matter, we explained, that Blakely's sentence, though outside the standard range, was within the 10-year maximum for class B felonies:

> Our precedents make clear that the 'statutory maximum' for *Apprendi* purposes is the maximum sentence a judge may impose solely on the basis of the facts reflected in the jury verdict or admitted by the defendant. In other words, the relevant 'statutory maximum' is not the maximum sentence a judge may impose after finding additional facts, but the maximum he may impose without any additional findings. When a judge inflicts punishment that the jury's verdict alone does not allow, the jury has not found all the facts 'which the law makes essential to the punishment,' and the judge exceeds his proper authority.

Because the judge in Blakely's case could not have imposed a sentence outside the standard range without finding an additional fact, the top of that range — 53 months, and not 10 years — was the relevant statutory maximum.

The State had additionally argued in Blakely that *Apprendi's* rule was satisfied because Washington's Reform Act did not specify an exclusive catalog of potential facts on which a judge might base a departure from the standard range. This Court rejected that argument as well. "Whether the judge's authority to impose an enhanced sentence depends on finding a specified fact one of several specified facts or any aggravating fact (as here)," we observed, "it remains the case that the jury's verdict alone does not authorize the sentence." Further, we held it irrelevant that the Reform Act ultimately left the decision whether or not to depart to the judge's discretion: "Whether the judicially determined facts require a sentence enhancement or merely allow it," we noted, "the verdict alone does not authorize the sentence."

Freddie Booker was convicted of possession with intent to distribute crack cocaine and was sentenced under the Federal Sentencing Guidelines. The facts found by Booker's jury yielded a base Guidelines range of 210 to 262 months' imprisonment, a range the judge could not exceed without undertaking additional factfinding. The judge did so, finding by a preponderance of the evidence that Booker possessed an amount of drugs in excess of the amount determined by the jury's verdict. That finding boosted Booker into a higher Guidelines range. Booker was sentenced at the bottom of the higher range, to 360 months in prison.

In an opinion written by Justice STEVENS for a five-Member majority, the Court held Booker's sentence impermissible under the Sixth Amendment. In the majority's judgment, there was "no distinction of constitutional significance between the Federal Sentencing Guidelines and the Washington procedures at issue in *Blakely*." Both systems were "mandatory and imposed binding requirements on all sentencing judges." Justice STEVENS' opinion for the Court, it bears emphasis, next expressed a view on which there was no disagreement among the Justices. He acknowledged that the Federal Guidelines would not implicate the Sixth Amendment were they advisory:

> If the Guidelines as currently written could be read as merely advisory provisions that recommended, rather than required, the selection of particular sentences in response to differing sets of facts, their use would not implicate the Sixth Amendment. We have never doubted the authority of a judge to exercise broad discretion in imposing a sentence within a statutory range. Indeed, everyone agrees that the constitutional issues presented by this case would have been avoided entirely if Congress had omitted from the federal Sentencing Reform Act the provisions that make the Guidelines binding on district judges. For when a trial judge exercises his discretion to select a specific sentence within a defined range, the defendant has no right to a jury determination of the facts that the judge deems relevant.

> The Guidelines as written, however, are not advisory; they are mandatory and binding on all judges.

In an opinion written by Justice BREYER, also garnering a five-Member majority, the Court faced the remedial question, which turned on an assessment of legislative intent: What alteration would Congress have intended had it known that the Guidelines were vulnerable to a Sixth Amendment challenge? Three choices were apparent: the Court could invalidate in its entirety the Sentencing Reform Act of 1984(SRA), the law comprehensively delineating the federal sentencing system; or it could preserve the SRA, and the mandatory Guidelines regime the SRA established, by attaching a jury-trial requirement to any fact increasing a defendant's base Guidelines range; finally, the Court could render the Guidelines advisory by severing two provisions of the SRA, 18 U.S.C. § 3553(b)(1) and 3742(e). Recognizing that "reasonable minds can, and do, differ" on the remedial question, the majority concluded that the advisory Guidelines solution came closest to the congressional mark.

Under the system described in Justice BREYER's opinion for the Court in *Booker*, judges would no longer be tied to the sentencing range indicated in the Guidelines. But they would be obliged to "take account of" that range along with the sentencing goals Congress enumerated in the SRA at 18 U.S.C. § 3553(a). Having severed § 3742(e), the provision of the SRA governing appellate review of sentences under the mandatory Guidelines scheme, the Court installed, as consistent with the Act and the sound administration of justice, a "reasonableness" standard of review. Without attempting an elaborate discussion of that standard, Justice BREYER's remedial opinion for the Court observed: "Section 3553(a) remains in effect, and sets forth numerous factors that guide sentencing. Those factors in turn will guide appellate courts, as they have in the past, in determining whether a sentence is reasonable." The Court emphasized the provisional character of the *Booker* remedy. Recognizing that authority to speak "the last word" resides in Congress, the Court said:

> The ball now lies in Congress' court. The National Legislature is equipped to devise and install, long term, the sentencing system, compatible with the Constitution, that Congress judges best for the federal system of justice.

We turn now to the instant case in light of both parts of the Court's *Booker* opinion, and our earlier decisions in point.

III

Under California's DSL, an upper term sentence may be imposed only when the trial judge finds an aggravating circumstance. An element of the charged offense, essential to a jury's determination of guilt, or admitted in a defendant's guilty plea, does not qualify as such a circumstance. Instead, aggravating circumstances depend on facts found discretely and solely by the judge. In accord with *Blakely*, therefore, the middle term prescribed in California's statutes, not the upper term, is the relevant statutory maximum.

Because circumstances in aggravation are found by the judge, not the jury, and need only be established by a preponderance of the evidence, not beyond a reasonable doubt, the DSL violates *Apprendi's* bright-line rule: Except for a prior conviction, "any fact that increases the penalty for a crime beyond the prescribed statutory maximum must be submitted to a jury, and proved beyond a reasonable doubt."

While that should be the end of the matter, in *People v. Black*, the California Supreme Court held otherwise. In that court's view, the DSL survived examination under our precedent intact. See 35 Cal.4th 1238, 1254–1261. The *Black* court acknowledged that California's system appears on surface inspection to be in tension with the rule of Apprendi. But in "operation and effect," the court said, the DSL "simply authorizes a sentencing court to engage in the type of factfinding that traditionally has been incident to the judge's selection of an appropriate sentence within a statutorily prescribed sentencing range." Therefore, the court concluded, "the upper term is the 'statutory maximum' and a trial court's imposition of an upper term sentence does not violate a defendant's right to a jury trial under the principles set forth in *Apprendi, Blakely*, and *Booker*."

The *Black* court's conclusion that the upper term, and not the middle term, qualifies as the relevant statutory maximum, rested on several considerations. First, the court reasoned that, given the ample discretion afforded trial judges to identify aggravating facts warranting an upper term sentence, the DSL "does not represent a legislative effort to shift the proof of particular facts from elements of a crime (to be proved to a jury) to sentencing factors (to be decided by a judge). Instead, it afforded the sentencing judge the discretion to decide, with the guidance of rules and statutes, whether the facts of the case and the history of the defendant justify the higher sentence. Such a system does not diminish the traditional power of the jury."

We cautioned in *Blakely*, however, that broad discretion to decide what facts may support an enhanced sentence, or to determine whether an enhanced sentence is warranted in any particular case, does not shield a sentencing system from the force of our decisions. If the jury's verdict alone does not authorize the sentence, if, instead, the judge must find an additional fact to impose the longer term, the Sixth Amendment requirement is not satisfied.

The *Black* court also urged that the DSL is not cause for concern because it reduced the penalties for most crimes over the prior indeterminate sentencing regime. Furthermore, California's system is not unfair to defendants, for they "cannot reasonably expect a guarantee that the upper term will not be imposed" given judges' broad discretion to impose an upper term sentence or to keep their punishment at the middle term. The *Black* court additionally noted that the DSL requires statutory enhancements (as distinguished from aggravators) — e.g., the use of a firearm or other dangerous weapon, infliction of great bodily injury, Penal Code §§ 12022, 12022.7–.8 — to be charged in the indictment and proved to a jury beyond a reasonable doubt.

The *Black* court's examination of the DSL, in short, satisfied it that California's sentencing system does not implicate significantly the concerns underlying the Sixth Amendment's jury-trial guarantee. Our decisions, however, leave no room for such an examination. Asking whether a defendant's basic jury-trial right is preserved, though some facts essential to punishment are reserved for determination by the judge, we have said, is the very inquiry *Apprendi's* "bright-line rule" was designed to exclude.

Ultimately, the Black court relied on an equation of California's DSL system to the post- Booker federal system. "The level of discretion available to a California judge in selecting which of the three available terms to impose," the court said, "appears comparable to the level of discretion that the high court has chosen to permit federal judges in post- *Booker* sentencing." The same equation drives Justice ALITO's dissent.

The attempted comparison is unavailing. This Court in *Booker* held the Federal Sentencing Guidelines incompatible with the Sixth Amendment because the Guidelines were "mandatory and imposed binding requirements on all sentencing judges." "Merely advisory provisions," recommending but not requiring "the selection of particular sentences in response to differing sets of facts," all Members of the Court agreed, "would not implicate the Sixth Amendment." To remedy the constitutional infirmity found in *Booker*, the Court's majority excised provisions that rendered the system mandatory, leaving the Guidelines in place as advisory only.

California's DSL does not resemble the advisory system the *Booker* Court had in view. Under California's system, judges are not free to exercise their "discretion to select a specific sentence within a defined range." California's Legislature has adopted sentencing triads, three fixed sentences with no ranges between them. Cunningham's sentencing judge had no discretion to select a sentence within a range of 6 to 16 years. His instruction was to select 12 years, nothing less and nothing more, unless he found facts allowing the imposition of a sentence of 6 or 16 years. Factfinding to elevate a sentence from 12 to 16 years, our decisions make plain, falls within the province of the jury employing a beyond-a-reasonable-doubt standard, not the bailiwick of a judge determining where the preponderance of the evidence lies.

Nevertheless, the *Black* court attempted to rescue the DSL's judicial factfinding authority by typing it simply a reasonableness constraint, equivalent to the constraint operative in the federal system post- *Booker.* Reasonableness, however, is not, as the *Black* court would have it, the touchstone of Sixth Amendment analysis. The reasonableness requirement *Booker* anticipated for the federal system operates within the Sixth Amendment constraints delineated in our precedent, not as a substitute for those constraints. Because the DSL allocates to judges sole authority to find facts permitting the imposition of an upper term sentence, the system violates the Sixth Amendment. It is comforting, but beside the point, that California's system requires judge-determined DSL sentences to be reasonable. *Booker's* remedy for the Federal Guidelines, in short, is not a recipe for rendering our Sixth Amendment case law toothless.

To summarize: Contrary to the *Black* court's holding, our decisions from Apprendi to Booker point to the middle term specified in California's statutes, not the upper term, as the relevant statutory maximum. Because the DSL authorizes the judge, not the jury, to find the facts permitting an upper term sentence, the system cannot withstand measurement against our Sixth Amendment precedent.

IV

As to the adjustment of California's sentencing system in light of our decision, the ball lies in California's court. We note that several States have modified their systems in the wake of *Apprendi* and *Blakely* to retain determinate sentencing. They have done so by calling upon the jury — either at trial or in a separate sentencing proceeding — to find any fact necessary to the imposition of an elevated sentence.[17]

As earlier noted, California already employs juries in this manner to determine statutory sentencing enhancements. Other States have chosen to permit judges genuinely "to exercise broad discretion within a statutory range,"[18] which, "everyone agrees," encounters no Sixth Amendment shoal. California may follow the paths taken by its sister States or otherwise alter its system, so long as the State observes Sixth Amendment limitations declared in this Court's decisions.

For the reasons stated, the judgment of the California Court of Appeal is reversed in part, and the case is remanded for further proceedings not inconsistent with this opinion.

JUSTICE ALITO, with whom JUSTICE KENNEDY and JUSTICE BREYER join, dissenting.

The California sentencing law that the Court strikes down today is indistinguishable in any constitutionally significant respect from the advisory Guidelines scheme that the Court approved in United States v. Booker, 543 U.S. 220 (2005). Both sentencing schemes grant trial judges considerable discretion in sentencing; both subject the exercise of that discretion to appellate review for "reasonableness"; and both — the California law explicitly, and the federal scheme implicitly — require a sentencing judge to find some factor to justify a sentence above the minimum that could be imposed based solely on the jury's verdict. Because this Court has held unequivocally that the post- Booker federal sentencing system satisfies the requirements of the Sixth Amendment, the same should be true with regard to the

---

[17] States that have so altered their systems are Alaska, Arizona, Kansas, Minnesota, North Carolina, Oregon, and Washington. Alaska Stat. §§ 12.55.155(f), 12.55.125(c) (2004); Ariz.Rev.Stat. Ann. § 13-702.01; Kan. Stat. Ann. §§ 21-4716(b), 21-4718(b); Minn.Stat. § 244.10, subd. 5; N.C. Gen.Stat. Ann. § 15A-1340.16(a1); 2005 Ore. Sess. Laws, ch. 463, §§ 3(1), 4(1); Wash. Rev.Code §§ 9.94A.535, 9.94A.537. The Colorado Supreme Court has adopted this approach as an interim solution. Lopez v. People, 113 P.3d 713, 716 (Colo.2005). See also Stemen & Wilhelm, Finding the Jury: State Legislative Responses to Blakely v. Washington, 18 Fed. Sentencing Rptr. 7 (Oct.2005) (majority of affected States have retained determinate sentencing systems).

[18] See Ind.Code Ann. § 35-50-2-1.3(a); Tenn.Code Ann. § 40-35-210(c).

California system. I therefore respectfully dissent.

I

In Apprendi v. New Jersey, 530 U.S. 466 (2000), and the cases that have followed in its wake, the Court has held that under certain circumstances a criminal defendant possesses the Sixth Amendment right to have a jury find facts that result in an increased sentence. The Court, however, has never suggested that all factual findings that affect a defendant's sentence must be made by a jury. On the contrary, in *Apprendi* and later cases, the Court has consistently stated that when a trial court makes a fully discretionary sentencing decision (such as a sentencing decision under the pre-Sentencing Reform Act of 1984 federal sentencing system), the Sixth Amendment permits the court to base the sentence on its own factual findings.

Applying this rule, the *Booker* Court unanimously agreed that judicial factfinding under a purely advisory guidelines system would likewise comport with the Sixth Amendment. * * * *

Under the post- *Booker* system, if a defendant believes that his or her sentence was based on an erroneous factual determination, it seems clear that the defendant may challenge that finding on appeal. The post- *Booker* system permits a defendant to obtain appellate review of the reasonableness of a sentence, and a sentence that the sentencing court justifies solely on the basis of an erroneous finding of fact can hardly be regarded as reasonable. Thus, under the post — *Booker* system, there will be cases — and, in all likelihood, a good many cases - in which the question whether a defendant will be required to serve a greater or lesser sentence depends on whether a court of appeals sustains a finding of fact made by the sentencing judge.

A simple example illustrates this point. Suppose that a defendant is found guilty of 10 counts of mail fraud in that the defendant made 10 mailings in furtherance of a scheme to defraud. Under the mail fraud statute, the district court would have discretion to sentence the defendant to any sentence ranging from probation up to 50 years of imprisonment (5 years on each count). Suppose that the sentencing judge imposes the maximum sentence allowed by statute — 50 years of imprisonment — without identifying a single fact about the offense or the offender as a justification for this lengthy sentence. Surely that would be an unreasonable sentence that could not be sustained on appeal.

Suppose, alternatively, that the sentencing court finds that the mail fraud scheme caused a loss of $1 million and that the victims were elderly people of limited means, and suppose that the court, based on these findings, imposes a sentence of 10 years of imprisonment. If the defendant challenges the sentence on appeal on the ground that these findings are erroneous, the question whether the defendant will be required to serve 10 years or some lesser sentence may well depend on the validity of the district court's findings of fact.

Booker, then, approved a sentencing system that (1) requires a sentencing judge to "consult" and "take into account" legislatively defined sentencing factors and guidelines; (2) subjects a sentencing judge's exercise of sentencing discretion to appellate review for "reasonableness"; and (3) requires sentencing judges to make factual findings in order to support the exercise of this discretion.

II

The California sentencing law that the Court strikes down today is not meaningfully different from the federal scheme upheld in *Booker*.

As an initial matter, the California law gives a judge at least as much sentencing discretion as does the post- *Booker* federal scheme. California's system of sentencing triads and separate "enhancements" was enacted to achieve sentences "in proportion to the seriousness of the offense as determined by the Legislature to be imposed by the court with specified discretion." Cal.Penal Code Ann. § 1170(a)(1). This "specified discretion" is quite broad. Under the statute, a sentencing court "shall order imposition of the middle term" of the base-term triad, "unless there are circumstances in aggravation or mitigation of the crime." § 1170(b). While the court may not rely on any fact that is an essential element of the crime or of a proven enhancement, the "sentencing judge retains considerable discretion to identify aggravating factors." People v. Black, 35 Cal.4th 1238, 1247 (2005).

In exercising its sentencing discretion, a California court can look to any of the 16 specific aggravating circumstances, see Cal. Rule of Court 4.421, or 15 specific mitigating circumstances, see Rule 4.423, itemized in the California Rules of Court. A California trial court can also consider the "general objectives of sentencing," including protecting society, punishing the defendant, encouraging the defendant to lead a law-abiding life and deterring the defendant from committing future offenses, deterring others from criminal conduct by demonstrating its consequences, preventing the defendant from committing new crimes by means of incarceration, securing restitution for crime victims, and achieving uniformity in sentencing. Rule 4.410(a). And if a California trial court finds that its sentencing authority is unduly restricted by these factors, which the California Supreme Court has recognized "are largely the articulation of considerations sentencing judges have always used in making these decisions," People v. Hernandez, 46 Cal.3d 194, 205 (1988).

In short, under California law, the " 'circumstances' the sentencing judge may look to in aggravation or in mitigation of the crime include 'practically everything which has a legitimate bearing' on the matter in issue." People v. Guevara, 88 Cal.App.3d 86, 93 (1979); see also Rule 4.410(b) ("The sentencing judge should be guided by statutory statements of policy, the criteria in these rules, and the facts and circumstances of the case").

The California scheme — like the federal "advisory Guidelines" — does require that this discretion be exercised reasonably. Indeed, the California Supreme Court, authoritatively construing the California statute, has explained that § 1170(b)'s "requirement that an aggravating factor exist is merely a requirement that the decision to impose the upper term be reasonable." Even when a court imposes the "presumptive" middle term, its decision is reviewable for abuse of discretion — that is, its decision to sentence at the "standard" term must be reasonable.

Moreover, the California system, like the post-*Booker* federal regime, recognizes that a sentencing judge must have the ability to look at all the relevant facts — even those outside the trial record and jury verdict — in exercising his or her discretion.
* * * *

Notes from Shelly:

Note: After *Cunningham* was decided, the California Legislature amended California Penal Code section 1170 as follows. Does it cure the defect found by the Supreme Court in *Cunningham?*

§ 1170. Determinate sentencing

(a)

(1) The Legislature finds and declares that the purpose of imprisonment for crime is punishment. This purpose is best served by terms proportionate to the seriousness of the offense with provision for uniformity in the sentences of offenders committing the same offense under similar circumstances. The Legislature further finds and declares that the elimination of disparity and the provision of uniformity of sentences can best be achieved by determinate sentences fixed by statute in proportion to the seriousness of the offense as determined by the Legislature to be imposed by the court with specified discretion.

(2) Notwithstanding paragraph (1), the Legislature further finds and declares that programs should be available for inmates, including, but not limited to, educational programs, that are designed to prepare nonviolent felony offenders for successful reentry into the community. The Legislature encourages the development of policies and programs designed to educate and rehabilitate nonviolent felony offenders. In implementing this section, the Department of Corrections and Rehabilitation is encouraged to give priority enrollment in programs to promote successful return to the community to an inmate with a short remaining term of commitment and a release date that would allow him or her adequate time to complete the program.

(3) In any case in which the punishment prescribed by statute for a person convicted of a public offense is a term of imprisonment in the state prison of any specification of three time periods, the court shall sentence the defendant to one of the terms of imprisonment specified unless the convicted person is given any other disposition provided by law, including a fine, jail, probation, or the suspension of imposition or execution of sentence or is sentenced pursuant to subdivision (b) of Section 1168 because he or she had committed his or her crime prior to July 1, 1977. In sentencing the convicted person, the court shall apply the sentencing rules of the Judicial Council. The court, unless it determines that there are circumstances in mitigation of the punishment prescribed, shall also impose any other term that it is required by law to impose as an additional term. Nothing in this article shall affect any provision of law that imposes the death penalty, that authorizes or restricts the granting of probation or suspending the execution or imposition of sentence, or expressly provides for imprisonment in the state prison for life. In any case in which the amount of preimprisonment credit under Section 2900.5 or any other provision of law is equal to or exceeds any sentence imposed pursuant to this chapter, the entire sentence shall be deemed to have been served and the defendant shall not be actually delivered to the custody of the secretary. The court shall

advise the defendant that he or she shall serve a period of parole and order the defendant to report to the parole office closest to the defendant's last legal residence, unless the in-custody credits equal the total sentence, including both confinement time and the period of parole. The sentence shall be deemed a separate prior prison term under Section 667.5, and a copy of the judgment and other necessary documentation shall be forwarded to the secretary.

(b) When a judgment of imprisonment is to be imposed and the statute specifies three possible terms, the court shall order imposition of the middle term, unless there are circumstances in aggravation or mitigation of the crime. At least four days prior to the time set for imposition of judgment, either party or the victim, or the family of the victim if the victim is deceased, may submit a statement in aggravation or mitigation to dispute facts in the record or the probation officer's report, or to present additional facts. In determining whether there are circumstances that justify imposition of the upper or lower term, the court may consider the record in the case, the probation officer's report, other reports including reports received pursuant to Section 1203.03 and statements in aggravation or mitigation submitted by the prosecution, the defendant, or the victim, or the family of the victim if the victim is deceased, and any further evidence introduced at the sentencing hearing. The court shall set forth on the record the facts and reasons for imposing the upper or lower term. The court may not impose an upper term by using the fact of any enhancement upon which sentence is imposed under any provision of law. A term of imprisonment shall not be specified if imposition of sentence is suspended.

(c) The court shall state the reasons for its sentence choice on the record at the time of sentencing. The court shall also inform the defendant that as part of the sentence after expiration of the term he or she may be on parole for a period as provided in Section 3000.

(d) When a defendant subject to this section or subdivision (b) of Section 1168 has been sentenced to be imprisoned in the state prison and has been committed to the custody of the secretary, the court may, within 120 days of the date of commitment on its own motion, or at any time upon the recommendation of the secretary or the Board of Parole Hearings, recall the sentence and commitment previously ordered and resentence the defendant in the same manner as if he or she had not previously been sentenced, provided the new sentence, if any, is no greater than the initial sentence. The resentence under this subdivision shall apply the sentencing rules of the Judicial Council so as to eliminate disparity of sentences and to promote uniformity of sentencing. Credit shall be given for time served.

(e)

(1) Notwithstanding any other law and consistent with paragraph (1) of subdivision (a), if the secretary or the Board of Parole Hearings or both determine that a prisoner satisfies the criteria set forth in paragraph (2), the secretary or the board may recommend to the court that the prisoner's sentence be recalled.

(2) The court shall have the discretion to resentence or recall if the court finds that the facts described in subparagraphs (A) and (B) or subparagraphs (B) and (C) exist:

(A) The prisoner is terminally ill with an incurable condition caused by an illness or disease that would produce death within six months, as determined by a physician employed by the department.

(B) The conditions under which the prisoner would be released or receive treatment do not pose a threat to public safety.

(C) The prisoner is permanently medically incapacitated with a medical condition that renders him or her permanently unable to perform activities of basic daily living, and results in the prisoner requiring 24-hour total care, including, but not limited to, coma, persistent vegetative state, brain death, ventilator-dependency, loss of control of muscular or neurological function, and that incapacitation did not exist at the time of the original sentencing.

The Board of Parole Hearings shall make findings pursuant to this subdivision before making a recommendation for resentence or recall to the court. This subdivision does not apply to a prisoner sentenced to death or a term of life without the possibility of parole.

(3) Within 10 days of receipt of a positive recommendation by the secretary or the board, the court shall hold a hearing to consider whether the prisoner's sentence should be recalled.

(4) Any physician employed by the department who determines that a prisoner has six months or less to live shall notify the chief medical officer of the prognosis. If the chief medical officer concurs with the prognosis, he or she shall notify the warden. Within 48 hours of receiving notification, the warden or the warden's representative shall notify the prisoner of the recall and resentencing procedures, and shall arrange for the prisoner to designate a family member or other outside agent to be notified as to the prisoner's medical condition and prognosis, and as to the recall and resentencing procedures. If the inmate is deemed mentally unfit, the warden or the warden's representative shall contact the inmate's emergency contact and provide the information described in paragraph (2).

(5) The warden or the warden's representative shall provide the prisoner and his or her family member, agent, or emergency contact, as described in paragraph (4), updated information throughout the recall and resentencing process with regard to the prisoner's medical condition and the status of the prisoner's recall and resentencing proceedings.

(6) Notwithstanding any other provisions of this section, the prisoner or his or her family member or designee may independently request consideration for recall and resentencing by contacting the chief medical officer at the prison or the secretary. Upon receipt of the request, the chief medical officer and the warden or the warden's representative shall follow the procedures described in paragraph (4). If the secretary determines that the prisoner satisfies the criteria set forth in paragraph (2), the secretary or board may recommend to the court that the

prisoner's sentence be recalled. The secretary shall submit a recommendation for release within 30 days in the case of inmates sentenced to determinate terms and, in the case of inmates sentenced to indeterminate terms, the secretary shall make a recommendation to the Board of Parole Hearings with respect to the inmates who have applied under this section. The board shall consider this information and make an independent judgment pursuant to paragraph (2) and make findings related thereto before rejecting the request or making a recommendation to the court. This action shall be taken at the next lawfully noticed board meeting.

(7) Any recommendation for recall submitted to the court by the secretary or the Board of Parole Hearings shall include one or more medical evaluations, a postrelease plan, and findings pursuant to paragraph (2).

(8) If possible, the matter shall be heard before the same judge of the court who sentenced the prisoner.

(9) If the court grants the recall and resentencing application, the prisoner shall be released by the department within 48 hours of receipt of the court's order, unless a longer time period is agreed to by the inmate. At the time of release, the warden or the warden's representative shall ensure that the prisoner has each of the following in his or her possession: a discharge medical summary, full medical records, state identification, parole medications, and all property belonging to the prisoner. After discharge, any additional records shall be sent to the prisoner's forwarding address.

(10) The secretary shall issue a directive to medical and correctional staff employed by the department that details the guidelines and procedures for initiating a recall and resentencing procedure. The directive shall clearly state that any prisoner who is given a prognosis of six months or less to live is eligible for recall and resentencing consideration, and that recall and resentencing procedures shall be initiated upon that prognosis.

(f) Any sentence imposed under this article shall be subject to the provisions of Sections 3000 and 3057 and any other applicable provisions of law.

(g) A sentence to state prison for a determinate term for which only one term is specified, is a sentence to state prison under this section.

2. In *Oregon v. Ice*, 129 S.Ct. 711 (2009), the Court held that the Sixth Amendment does not prevent a state from allowing a judge (rather than a jury) to find the facts necessary to impose *consecutive* (rather than concurrent) sentences on the defendant, because of "the historical practice and the authority of States over the administration of their criminal justice systems." Four justices dissented.

Chapter 13

APPEALS

Fragmentary evidence suggesting that reversal rates in criminal appeals range from just under 5% to close to 14% in various state systems or federal circuits, and that rates of "modification" of judgment short of reversal are higher still, highlights the practical importance to defendants of appellate review.

Meltzer, *Harmless Error and Constitutional Remedies*, 61 U.Chicago L.Rev. 1, 8 (1994).

Telegram, lawyer to client: "The jury brought in its verdict. Justice has prevailed."

Telegram, client to lawyer: "Appeal immediately!"

Anonymous

Criminal cases are appealed more often than civil cases. This might be because the stakes are seen as higher, but there is another reason. In *Douglas v. California* (1963) 372 U.S. 353, the Court held that if a state allows a criminal appeal to those who can afford to pay for it (as all states do), it must also give the same right to an indigent defendant — and the state must pay for the defendant's appellate lawyer. Most criminal defendants (probably over 90%) are indigent. While litigants in civil cases might be deterred from appealing by the substantial costs involved, no such deterrent faces the indigent criminal appeal. So in most jurisdictions, the number or percentage of criminal appeals exceeds the number of civil appeals by a wide margin.

This means a lot of work for lawyers — especially young lawyers setting up their own practices. These novices often sign up with appellate courts for appointment in criminal appeals. Such appointments won't make you rich — as the hourly rates and flat fees paid by courts are not high — but they will help pay the rent and give you valuable experience.

This isn't the place to teach you how to handle appeals[1], and it's not the place to review all the possible trial court errors that might be grounds for reversal. There are, however, some problems peculiar to criminal appellate practice that tend to arise with some frequency. These will be addressed in this chapter.

---

[1] For some practical advice, see Moskovitz, *Winning An Appeal* (Lexis).

Problem 13

To: My law clerk

From: Paula Peel, Esq.

I have been appointed to represent Hans Stempel and Franco Bollo in appealing their convictions for robbing a United States Post Office branch office. Here are some excerpts from the reporter's transcript of the trial:

Prosecution Witness: Postal Employee Lotta Letters

LL: I was working at the post office window when two men came up. One of them pointed a gun at me and said, "Give me all your money and stamps." I gave him about $500 from my cash drawer and about 50 sheets of first class stamps. All were a new issue, with pictures of various cowboys on them. Then they both walked away, out of the post office, and got into a beige Toyota.

Assistant U.S. Attorney: Ms. Letters, do you see either of the men in the courtroom?

LL: Yes. The one who pointed the gun at me is the tall one sitting over there, Mr. Bollo. The man who was with him was the other defendant, Mr. Stempel.

AUSA: Are you sure?

LL: Well, I'm sure about Mr. Bollo. I'm less sure about Mr. Stempel, because the man in the post office with Mr. Bollo was wearing a hat pretty low down. But I think it was him. He was the same height and build, and I saw his face for a moment.

Prosecution Witness: Postal Inspector Penny Postcard

PP: Right after the robbery, Letters called me and told me what happened. I drove over to her branch office, and on the way I saw two men driving along in a beige Toyota. I pulled them over, got them out of the car, and searched them. I found 50 sheets of cowboy stamps in Bollo's jacket pocket, and I found $600 in cash in Stempel's wallet.

The U.S. Attorney then introduced the stamps and money that Postcard had found on the defendants. Attorneys for both men had moved before trial to suppress this evidence (and Postcard's testimony). At the hearing on the motion, Postcard had testified pretty much as she did later at trial. The judge denied the motion.

Prosecution Witness: Fred Fink

FF: I was in jail serving 30 days for drunk driving. After Bollo was arrested, he was put in my cell. Bollo told me that he had held up the post office and gotten a bunch of cowboy stamps and some money.

Defense Witness: Defendant Hans Stempel

HS: I didn't rob any post office. I was walking down the street when I saw Bollo driving along. I waved to him. He stopped, and some guy in the car got out and walked away. Bollo told me to get in. I did, and he drove off. Then the postal cop stopped us. I had $600 in my wallet because I had won it the night before in a poker game.

Defense Witness: Defendant Franco Bollo

FB:

I did not rob the post office. I had been in the post office earlier that day and bought some sheets of stamps, so maybe Letters remembered me from then and later got me mixed up with the robber. What Stempel said is true. I dropped off a friend of mine and then gave Stempel a lift.

After the verdict came in, Stempel filed a motion for new trial. At the hearing on the motion, Stempel's lawyer (Esther Queen) called Juror Melba Toast to the stand:

EQ:

Ms. Toast, do you remember during voir dire my asking each juror whether he or she knew anything about the defendants?

MT:

Yes, I do.

EQ:

And do you remember Juror Minny Mall's answer to my question?

MT:

She said she didn't know anything about them.

EQ:

Did she tell you anything different later?

MT:

Yes. While we were deliberating, she said that she went to the same high school as Stempel. She said that she didn't know him personally, but he had a reputation as being pretty sleazy.

The judge denied Stempel's motion.

I spoke to Bollo and Stempel. Both insist that they are innocent and that the prosecution witnesses were lying or mistaken. They are both adamant about appealing their convictions. Bollo says if I won't write a brief for him, he will write his own. The court we are appealing to has a Local Rule 4, which says:

a. Counsel wishing to withdraw from a criminal appeal must first file a brief identifying any potential issues in the appeal and explaining why each lacks merit.

b. In addition, counsel must discuss the case with the appellant and inform him or her that appellant may file his or her own brief. If appellant files such a brief, counsel must file a brief explaining why each of appellant's points lacks merit.

c, The Court will review all briefs and the record before deciding whether to allow counsel to withdraw.

Please read the attached authorities and advise me what to do in the appeals. I have the complete transcripts of the trial, so if there is anything else we should look at, let me know what it is.

Federal Rules of Criminal Procedure

Rule 52. Harmless and Plain Error

(a) Harmless Error. Any error, defect, irregularity, or variance that does not affect substantial rights must be disregarded.

(b) Plain Error. A plain error that affects substantial rights may be considered even though it was not brought to the [trial] court's attention.

CHAPMAN v. CALIFORNIA
United States Supreme Court
386 U.S. 18 (1967)

MR. JUSTICE BLACK delivered the opinion of the Court.

Petitioners, Ruth Elizabeth Chapman and Thomas LeRoy Teale, were convicted in a California state court upon a charge that they robbed, kidnaped, and murdered a bartender. She was sentenced to life imprisonment and he to death. At the time of the trial, Art I, § 13, of the State's Constitution provided that "in any criminal case, whether the defendant testifies or not, his failure to explain or to deny by his testimony any evidence or facts in the case against him may be commented upon by the court and by counsel, and may be considered by the court or the jury." Both petitioners in this case chose not to testify at their trial, and the State's attorney prosecuting them took full advantage of his right under the State Constitution to comment upon their failure to testify, filling his argument to the jury from beginning to end with numerous references to their silence and inferences of their guilt resulting therefrom. The trial court also charged the jury that it could draw adverse inferences from petitioners' failure to testify. Shortly after the trial, but before petitioners' cases had been considered on appeal by the California Supreme Court, this Court decided *Griffin v. California*, 380 U.S. 609, in which we held California's constitutional provision and practice invalid on the ground that they put a penalty on the exercise of a person's right not to be compelled to be a witness against himself, guaranteed by the Fifth Amendment to the United States Constitution and made applicable to California and the other States by the Fourteenth Amendment. On appeal, the State Supreme Court, admitting that petitioners had been denied a federal constitutional right by the comments on their silence, nevertheless affirmed, applying the State Constitution's harmless-error provision, which forbids reversal unless "the court shall be of the opinion that the error complained of has resulted in a miscarriage of justice." We granted certiorari limited to these questions:

> Where there is a violation of the rule of *Griffin v. California*, (1) can the error be held to be harmless, and (2) if so, was the error harmless in this case?

In this Court, petitioners contend that both these questions are federal ones to be decided under federal law; that under federal law we should hold that denial of a federal constitutional right, no matter how unimportant, should automatically result in reversal of a conviction, without regard to whether the error is considered harmless; and that, if wrong in this, the various comments on petitioners' silence cannot, applying a federal standard, be considered harmless here. * * * *

II.

We are urged by petitioners to hold that all federal constitutional errors, regardless of the facts and circumstances, must always be deemed harmful. Such a holding, as petitioners correctly point out, would require an automatic reversal of their convictions and make further discussion unnecessary. We decline to adopt any such rule. All 50 States have harmless-error statutes or rules, and the United States long ago through its Congress established for its courts the rule that judgments shall not be reversed for "errors or defects which do not affect the substantial rights of the parties." 28 U.S.C. § 2111. None of these rules on its face distinguishes between federal constitutional errors and errors of state law or federal statutes and rules. All of these rules, state or federal, serve a very useful purpose insofar as they block setting aside convictions for small errors or defects that have little, if any, likelihood of having changed the result of the trial. We conclude that there may be some constitutional errors which in the setting of a particular case are so unimportant and insignificant that they may, consistent with the Federal Constitution, be deemed harmless, not requiring the automatic reversal of the conviction.

III.

In fashioning a harmless-constitutional-error rule, we must recognize that harmless-error rules can work very unfair and mischievous results when, for example, highly important and persuasive evidence, or argument, though legally forbidden, finds its way into a trial in which the question of guilt or innocence is a close one. What harmless-error rules all aim at is a rule that will save the good in harmless-error practices while avoiding the bad, so far as possible.

The federal rule emphasizes "substantial rights", as do most others. The California constitutional rule emphasizes "a miscarriage of justice," but the California courts have neutralized this to some extent by emphasis, and perhaps overemphasis, upon the court's view of "overwhelming evidence." We prefer the approach of this Court in deciding what was harmless error in our recent case of *Fahy v. Connecticut*, 375 U.S. 85. There we said: "The question is whether there is a reasonable possibility that the evidence complained of might have contributed to the conviction." *Id.* at 86–87. Although our prior cases have indicated that there are some constitutional rights so basic to a fair trial that their infraction can never be treated as harmless error,[8] this statement in *Fahy* itself belies any belief that all trial errors which violate the Constitution automatically call for reversal. At the same time, however, like the federal harmless-error statute, it emphasizes an intention not to treat as harmless those constitutional errors that "affect substantial rights" of a party.

An error in admitting plainly relevant evidence which possibly influenced the jury adversely to a litigant cannot, under *Fahy*, be conceived of as harmless. Certainly error, constitutional error, in illegally admitting highly prejudicial evidence or comments, casts on someone other than the person prejudiced by it a burden to show that it was harmless. It is for that reason that the original common-law harmless-error rule put the burden on the beneficiary of the error either to prove that there was no injury or to suffer a reversal of his erroneously

---

[8] See, e.g., *Payne v. Arkansas*, 356 U.S. 560 (coerced confession); *Gideon v. Wainwright*, 372 U.S. 335 (right to counsel); *Tumey v. Ohio*, 273 U.S. 510 (impartial judge).

obtained judgment. There is little, if any, difference between our statement in *Fahy* about "whether there is a reasonable possibility that the evidence complained of might have contributed to the conviction" and requiring the beneficiary of a constitutional error to prove beyond a reasonable doubt that the error complained of did not contribute to the verdict obtained.

We, therefore, do no more than adhere to the meaning of our *Fahy* case when we hold, as we now do, that before a federal constitutional error can be held harmless, the court must be able to declare a belief that it was harmless beyond a reasonable doubt. While appellate courts do not ordinarily have the original task of applying such a test, it is a familiar standard to all courts, and we believe its adoption will provide a more workable standard, although achieving the same result as that aimed at in our *Fahy* case.

IV.

Applying the foregoing standard, we have no doubt that the error in these cases was not harmless to petitioners. To reach this conclusion one need only glance at the prosecutorial comments. The California Supreme Court fairly summarized the extent of these comments as follows:

> Such comments went to the motives for the procurement and handling of guns purchased by Mrs. Chapman, funds or the lack thereof in Mr. Teale's possession immediately prior to the killing, the amount of intoxicating liquors consumed by defendants at the Spot Club and other taverns, the circumstances of the shooting in the automobile and the removal of the victim's body therefrom, who fired the fatal shots, why defendants used a false registration at a motel shortly after the killing, the meaning of a letter written by Mrs. Chapman several days after the killing, why Teale had a loaded weapon in his possession when apprehended, the meaning of statements made by Teale after his apprehension, why certain clothing and articles of personal property were shipped by defendants to Missouri, what clothing Mrs. Chapman wore at the time of the killing, conflicting statements as to Mrs. Chapman's whereabouts immediately preceding the killing and, generally, the overall commission of the crime.

Thus, the state prosecutor's argument and the trial judge's instruction to the jury continuously and repeatedly impressed the jury that from the failure of petitioners to testify, to all intents and purposes, the inferences from the facts in evidence had to be drawn in favor of the State — in short, that by their silence petitioners had served as irrefutable witnesses against themselves. And though the case in which this occurred presented a reasonably strong "circumstantial web of evidence" against petitioners, it was also a case in which, absent the constitutionally forbidden comments, honest, fair-minded jurors might very well have brought in not-guilty verdicts. Under these circumstances, it is completely impossible for us to say that the State has demonstrated, beyond a reasonable doubt, that the prosecutor's comments and the trial judge's instruction did not contribute to petitioners' convictions. Such a machine-gun repetition of a denial of constitutional rights, designed and calculated to make petitioners' version of the evidence worthless, can no more be considered harmless than the introduction against a defendant of a coerced confession. See, e.g., *Payne v. Arkansas*, 356 U.S. 560. Petitioners are entitled to a trial free from the pressure of unconstitutional inferences.

Reversed and remanded.

MR. JUSTICE STEWART, concurring in the result.

In devising a harmless-error rule for violations of federal constitutional rights, both the Court and the dissent proceed as if the question were one of first impression. But in a long line of cases, involving a variety of constitutional claims in both state and federal prosecutions, this Court has steadfastly rejected any notion that constitutional violations might be disregarded on the ground that they were "harmless". Illustrations of the principle are legion.

When involuntary confessions have been introduced at trial, the Court has always reversed convictions regardless of other evidence of guilt. As we stated in *Lynumn v. Illinois*, 372 U.S. 528, 537, the argument that the error in admitting such a confession "was a harmless one is an impermissible doctrine". Even when the confession is completely "unnecessary" to the conviction, the defendant is entitled to "a new trial free of constitutional infirmity." *Haynes v. Washington*, 373 U.S. at 518–519.

When a defendant has been denied counsel at trial, we have refused to consider claims that this constitutional error might have been harmless. "The right to have the assistance of counsel is too fundamental and absolute to allow courts to indulge in nice calculations as to the amount of prejudice arising from its denial." *Glasser v. United States*, 315 U.S. 60, 76. That, indeed, was the whole point of *Gideon v. Wainwright*, 372 U.S. 335. Even before trial, when counsel has not been provided at a critical stage, "we do not stop to determine whether prejudice resulted." *Hamilton v. Alabama*, 368 U.S. 52, 55.

A conviction must be reversed if the trial judge's remuneration is based on a scheme giving him a financial interest in the result, even if no particular prejudice is shown and even if the defendant was clearly guilty. *Tumey v. Ohio*, 273 U.S. 510. To try a defendant in a community that has been exposed to publicity highly adverse to the defendant is per se ground for reversal of his conviction; no showing need be made that the jurors were in fact prejudiced against him. *Sheppard v. Maxwell*, 384 U.S. 333.

When a jury is instructed in an unconstitutional presumption, the conviction must be overturned, though there was ample evidence apart from the presumption to sustain the verdict. *Bollenbach v. United States*, 326 U.S. 607. Reversal is required when a conviction may have been rested on a constitutionally impermissible ground, despite the fact that there was a valid alternative ground on which the conviction could have been sustained. *Stromberg v. California*, 283 U.S. 359. In a long line of cases leading up to and including *Whitus v. Georgia*, 385 U.S. 545, it has never been suggested that reversal of convictions because of purposeful discrimination in the selection of grand and petit jurors turns on any showing of prejudice to the defendant.

To be sure, constitutional rights are not fungible goods. The differing values which they represent and protect may make a harmless-error rule appropriate for one type of constitutional error and not for another. I would not foreclose the possibility that a harmless-error rule might appropriately be applied to some constitutional violations.[2] Indeed, one source of my disagreement with the court's opinion is its implicit assumption that the same harmless-error rule should apply indiscriminately to all constitutional violations.

But I see no reason to break with settled precedent in this case, and promulgate a novel rule of harmless error applicable to clear violations of *Griffin v. California*, 380 U.S. 609. * * * *

Notes from Paula:

1. "Errors are the insects in the world of law, traveling through it in swarms, often unnoticed in their endless procession. Many are plainly harmless; some appear ominously harmful. Some, for all the benign appearance of their spindly traces, mark the way for a plague of followers that deplete trials of fairness."

Thus spake Roger Traynor, then Chief Justice of the California Supreme Court, in *The Riddle of Harmless Error* (1970) (Foreword). He went on to note that "There was a time in the law, extending into our own century, when no error was lightly forgiven". He gave as an example an earlier decision from his own court that reversed a conviction because the indictment charged the defendant with entering a building with intent to commit "larcey". *Id.* at 3–4. Though defendant clearly had larceny in his heart, the court refused to dip into its supply of n's and repair the indictment — or to hold the error harmless. *People v. St.Clair*, 56 Cal. 406 (1888).

An appellate judge assesses "harmlessness" by guessing what the jury would have done if the error had not been committed. This is usually done by examining the weight of the admissible evidence. Justice Traynor has some doubts as to how feasible this is:

> The appellate court is limited to the mute record made below. Many factors may affect the probative value of testimony, such as age, sex, intelligence, experience, occupation, demeanor, or temperament of the witness. A trial court or jury before whom witnesses appear is at least in a position to take note of such factors. An appellate court has no way of doing so. It cannot know whether a witness answered some questions forthrightly be evaded others. It may find an answer convincing and truthful in written form that may have sounded unreliable at the time it was given. A well-phrased sentence in the record may have seemed rehearsed at the trial. A clumsy sentence in the record may not convey the ring of truth that attended it when the witness groped his way to its articulation. What clues are there in the cold print to indicate where the truth lies. What clues are there to indicate where the half-truth lies? [*Id.* at 20–21.]

> How can anyone determine what went on in the mind of another or of twelve others who serve as triers of fact? The only source of direct evidence would be their own testimony. If the facts had been tried by a jury, such testimony would be precluded by the rule forbidding affidavits or evidence of any sort that tends to contradict, impeach, or defeat the jury's verdict.

---

[2] For example, quite different considerations are involved when evidence is introduced which was obtained in violation of the Fourth and Fourteenth Amendments. The exclusionary rule in that context balances the desirability of deterring objectionable police conduct against the undesirability of excluding relevant and reliable evidence. The resolution of these values with interests of judicial economy might well dictate a harmless-error rule for such violations.

Thus, there is no possibility of tapping the only source of direct evidence on the effect, if any, of an error upon the jury's verdict. [*Id.* at 23.]

2. It has been noted that "there is a widespread perception that in the Supreme Court, as well as in state and lower federal courts, errors of some substance are nonetheless found harmless so as to permit the affirmance of convictions." Meltzer, *Harmless Error and Constitutional Remedies*, 61 U.Chicago L.Rev. 1, 4 (1994).

ANDERS v. CALIFORNIA
United States Supreme Court
386 U.S. 738 (1967)

MR. JUSTICE CLARK delivered the opinion of the Court.

We are here concerned with the extent of the duty of a court-appointed appellate counsel to prosecute a first appeal from a criminal conviction, after that attorney has conscientiously determined that there is no merit to the indigent's appeal.

After he was convicted of the felony of possession of marijuana, petitioner sought to appeal and moved that the California District Court of Appeal appoint counsel for him. Such motion was granted; however, after a study of the record and consultation with petitioner, the appointed counsel concluded that there was no merit to the appeal. He so advised the court by letter and, at the same time, informed the court that petitioner wished to file a brief in his own behalf. At this juncture, petitioner requested the appointment of another attorney. This request was denied and petitioner proceeded to file his own brief pro se. The State responded and petitioner filed a reply brief. On January 9, 1959, the District Court of Appeal unanimously affirmed the conviction.

On January 21, 1965, petitioner filed an application for a writ of habeas corpus in the District Court of Appeal in which he sought to have his case reopened. In that application he raised the issue of deprivation of the right to counsel in his original appeal because of the court's refusal to appoint counsel at the appellate stage of the proceedings. The court denied the application on the same day, in a brief unreported memorandum opinion. The court stated that it "had again reviewed the record and had determined the appeal to be without merit." The court also stated that "the procedure prescribed by *In re Nash* was followed in this case."[2] On June 25, 1965, petitioner submitted a petition for a writ of habeas corpus to the Supreme Court of California, and the petition was denied without opinion by that court on July 14, 1965. Among other trial errors, petitioner claimed that both the judge and the prosecutor had commented on his failure to testify contrary to the holding of this Court in *Griffin v. California*, 380 U.S. 609 (1965). We have concluded that California's action does not comport with fair procedure and lacks that equality that is required by the Fourteenth Amendment.

---

[2] *In re Nash*, 61 Cal.2d 491 (1964), held that the requirements of *Douglas v. California*, 372 U.S. 353 (1963), are met in the event appointed counsel thoroughly studies the record, consults with the defendant and trial counsel and conscientiously concludes, and so advises the appellate court, that there are no meritorious grounds of appeal; and provided that the appellate court is satisfied from its own review of the record, in light of any points personally raised by the defendant, that appointed counsel's conclusion is correct. The appeal then proceeds without the appointment of other counsel and decision is reached without argument.

I.

For a decade or more, a continuing line of cases has reached this Court concerning discrimination against the indigent defendant on his first appeal. Beginning with *Griffin v. Illinois*, 351 U.S. 12 (1956) where it was held that equal justice was not afforded an indigent appellant where the nature of the review "depends on the amount of money he has," and continuing through *Douglas v. California*, 372 U.S. 353 (1963), this Court has consistently held invalid those procedures "where the rich man, who appeals as of right, enjoys the benefit of counsel's examination into the record, research of the law, and marshalling of arguments on his behalf, while the indigent, already burdened by a preliminary determination that his case is without merit, is forced to shift for himself." * * * *

II.

In petitioner's case, his appointed counsel wrote the District Court of Appeal, stating: "I will not file a brief on appeal as I am of the opinion that there is no merit to the appeal. I have visited and communicated with Mr. Anders and have explained my views and opinions to him. He wishes to file a brief in this matter on his own behalf." The District Court of Appeal, after having examined the record, affirmed the conviction. We believe that counsel's bare conclusion, as evidenced by his letter, was not enough. It smacks of the treatment that Eskridge received, which this Court condemned, that permitted a trial judge to withhold a transcript if he found that a defendant "has been accorded a fair and impartial trial, and in the Court's opinion no grave or prejudicial errors occurred therein." *Eskridge v. Washington State Board*, 357 U.S. 214, 215 (1958). Such a procedure, this Court said, "cannot be an adequate substitute for the right to full appellate review available to all defendants" who may not be able to afford such an expense. * * * *

Here, the court-appointed counsel had the transcript, but refused to proceed with the appeal because he found no merit in it. He filed a no-merit letter with the District Court of Appeal, whereupon the court examined the record itself and affirmed the judgment. On a petition for a writ of habeas corpus, some six years later, it found the appeal had no merit. It failed, however, to say whether it was frivolous or not, but, after consideration, simply found the petition to be "without merit". The Supreme Court, in dismissing this habeas corpus application, gave no reason at all for its decision and so we do not know the basis for its action. We cannot say that there was a finding of frivolity by either of the California courts or that counsel acted in any greater capacity than merely as *amicus curiae*. Hence, California's procedure did not furnish petitioner with counsel acting in the role of an advocate nor did it provide that full consideration and resolution of the matter as is obtained when counsel is acting in that capacity. The necessity for counsel so acting is highlighted by the possible disadvantage the petitioner suffered here. In his pro se brief, which was filed in 1959, he urged several trial errors, but failed to raise the point that both the judge and the prosecutor had commented to the jury regarding petitioner's failure to testify. In 1965, this Court in *Griffin v. California*, outlawed California's comment rule, as embodied in Art. I, § 13, of the California Constitution.

III.

The constitutional requirement of substantial equality and fair process can only be attained where counsel acts in the role of an active advocate in behalf of his client, as opposed to that of *amicus curiae*. The no-merit letter and the procedure it triggers do not reach that dignity. Counsel should, and can with honor and without conflict, be of more assistance to his client and to the court. His role as advocate requires that he support his client's appeal to the best of his ability. Of course, if counsel finds his case to be wholly frivolous, after a conscientious examination of it, he should so advise the court and request permission to withdraw. That request must, however, be accompanied by a brief referring to anything in the record that might arguably support the appeal. A copy of counsel's brief should be furnished the indigent and time allowed him to raise any points that he chooses; the court — not counsel — then proceeds, after a full examination of all the proceedings, to decide whether the case is wholly frivolous. If it so finds, it may grant counsel's request to withdraw and dismiss the appeal insofar as federal requirements are concerned, or proceed to a decision on the merits, if state law so requires. On the other hand, if it finds any of the legal points arguable on their merits (and therefore not frivolous) it must, prior to decision, afford the indigent the assistance of counsel to argue the appeal.

This requirement would not force appointed counsel to brief his case against his client but would merely afford the latter that advocacy which a nonindigent defendant is able to obtain. It would also induce the court to pursue all the more vigorously its own review because of the ready references not only to the record, but also to the legal authorities as furnished it by counsel. The no-merit letter, on the other hand, affords neither the client nor the court any aid. The former must shift entirely for himself, while the court has only the cold record, which it must review without the help of an advocate. Moreover, such handling would tend to protect counsel from the constantly increasing charge that he was ineffective and had not handled the case with that diligence to which an indigent defendant is entitled. This procedure will assure penniless defendants the same rights and opportunities on appeal — as nearly as is practicable — as are enjoyed by those persons who are in a similar situation but who are able to afford the retention of private counsel.

The judgment is reversed and the case is remanded for further proceedings not inconsistent with this opinion.

MR. JUSTICE STEWART, whom MR. JUSTICE BLACK and MR. JUSTICE HARLAN join, dissenting.

The system used by California for handling indigent appeals was described by the California Supreme Court in *In re Nash*, 61 Cal.2d 491, 495: "We believe that the requirement of the *Douglas* case is met when, as in this case, counsel is appointed to represent the defendant on appeal, thoroughly studies the record, consults with the defendant and trial counsel, and conscientiously concludes that there are no meritorious grounds of appeal. If thereafter the appellate court is satisfied from its own review of the record in the light of any points raised by the defendant personally that counsel's assessment of the record is correct, it need not appoint another counsel to represent the defendant on appeal and may properly decide the appeal without oral argument."

The Court today holds this procedure unconstitutional, and imposes upon appointed counsel who wishes to withdraw from a case he deems "wholly frivolous" the requirement of filing "a brief referring to anything in the record that might arguably support the appeal." But if the record did present any such "arguable" issues, the appeal would not be frivolous and counsel would not have filed a 'no-merit' letter in the first place.

The quixotic requirement imposed by the Court can be explained, I think, only upon the cynical assumption that an appointed lawyer's professional representation to an appellate court in a "no-merit" letter is not to be trusted. That is an assumption to which I cannot subscribe. I cannot believe that lawyers appointed to represent indigents are so likely to be lacking in diligence, competence, or professional honesty. Certainly there was no suggestion in the present case that the petitioner's counsel was either incompetent or unethical.

But even if I could join in this degrading appraisal of the *in forma pauperis* bar, it escapes me how the procedure that the Court commands is constitutionally superior to the system now followed in California. The fundamental error in the Court's opinion, it seems to me, is its implicit assertion that there can be but a single inflexible answer to the difficult problem of how to accord equal protection to indigent appellants in each of the 50 States.

Believing that the procedure under which Anders' appeal was considered was free of constitutional error, I would affirm the judgment.

Notes from Paula:

1. According to the majority, what — exactly — was wrong with the California procedure?

2. The majority says that it is trying to afford the indigent appellant the same rights as those of the non-indigent appellant. Isn't this ultimately a futile effort? A non-indigent appellant may hire an experienced appellate attorney who charges several hundred dollars an hour, while an indigent appellant must accept a young novice who is willing to work for the much smaller fees doled out by the state. While *Anders* allows the state to permit the indigent's attorney to withdraw in some situations (even over the indigent's objection, presumably) the non-indigent defendant may pay his attorney to stay in the case and argue *anything*. Or may he?

3. An appellate attorney will find it difficult to argue that the trial court erred without a *transcript* of the trial that shows such error. But transcripts cost money. A free appellate lawyer isn't much use unless the state also provides a free transcript. In *Griffin v. Illinois*, 351 U.S. 73 (1956), the Court held that indigent defendants must be provided with a free transcript.

4. In *Chandler v. State*, 988 S.W.2d 827 (Texas Ct.App. 1999), the court refused to accept an "*Anders* brief" (moving to withdraw on the ground that the appeal was frivolous) from an attorney who had represented the appellant *at trial*:

> One of the issues that must be researched and analyzed in an *Anders* brief is the effectiveness of trial counsel. The trial attorney may be appointed on appeal, but given the bias and prejudice appellate counsel may have in evaluating his own performance at trial, as well as the reality that counsel who does not understand the law during trial may not recognize the same error on appeal, we conclude that it is not appropriate for appointed appellate counsel to file an *Anders* brief in a case in which counsel also served as trial counsel.

If appellate counsel, who also served as trial counsel, reaches a point in the appeal where he or she believes the appeal is frivolous and that an *Anders* brief is appropriate, then counsel should file a motion to withdraw with this Court, explaining the conflict. This Court may then abate the appeal to the trial court for appointment of new appellate counsel, who will be in an unconflicted position and better able to analyze whether an *Anders* brief is appropriate. Clearly, the trial court may avoid this conflict altogether by not appointing trial counsel to handle the appeal.

5. In Moskovitz, *Indigent Criminal Defendants Should Pay For Their Appeals*, California Lawyer, May, 1982, page 8, the author suggests establishing an "inmate appeal fund". Each convicted defendant would be given about $200 by the state and — after receiving advice from an appellate attorney — decide whether to spend the money on an appeal or keep the money and drop the appeal. The author believes that such an effort to place the criminal defendant in the same decision-making position as the civil litigant could cut down on the number of losing appeals and save the court system a substantial amount of money. (A similar approach was used in *George v. State*, 944 P.2d 1181 (Alaska Ct.App. 1997), to justify a state law requiring prisoners to pay filing fees equal to 20% of their prison accounts when suing the state.) In addition, by filtering out the most hopeless of the appeals, this might change the current atmosphere, in which many an appellate judge begins her review of a criminal appeal with the assumption that it is just another loser.

6. In *State v. Cigic*, 639 A.2d 251 (N.H.1994), the New Hampshire Supreme Court held that the *Anders* procedure did not provide *enough* protection for the defendant, and instead adopted "a modified Idaho rule".

Both the State and the defendant acknowledge that an independent judicial review of the record, as guaranteed by *Anders*, benefits a defendant because it protects him or her from inadequate representation by appellate counsel. As the defendant argues, however, such a review may be prejudiced by the fact that appellate counsel has already determined, after a "conscientious examination" of the record, that the appeal is wholly frivolous. See *State v. McKenney*, 98 Idaho 551 (1977). In addition, the *Anders* approach puts counsel at odds with the client, forcing counsel into the awkward position of arguing against the client before the reviewing court, and leading the defendant to conclude that his or her interests have been compromised. See *State v. Gates*, 466 S.W.2d 681, 684 (Mo.1971). Finally, the *Anders* procedure places the appellate court in the inappropriate role of defense counsel, forcing the court to devise and recommend viable legal arguments for subsequent appellate counsel. In making such recommendations, the appellate court may appear to have lost its impartiality, displaying a potential bias in favor of any arguments it recommends.

Although most States follow the *Anders* procedure, the ABA Standards and several state courts have declined to conform with its guidelines. See ABA Standards for Criminal Justice, The Defense Function, Standard 4-8.3; see also *Commonwealth v. Moffett*, 383 Mass. 201 (1981); *Gates*, 466 S.W.2d at 683–84; *Sanchez v. State*, 85 Nev. 95 (1969). * * * *

The Idaho Supreme Court, in *McKenney*, noted that during the years it adhered to the procedure set forth in *Anders*, it never granted an attorney's motion to withdraw on the basis that the client's appeal was frivolous and without merit. The Idaho court held that "once counsel is appointed to represent an indigent client during appeal on a criminal case, no withdrawal will thereafter be permitted on the basis that the appeal is frivolous or lacks merit."

In another case, a District of Columbia Court of Appeals judge argued strenuously that the court should not have granted appellate counsel's motion to withdraw in a typical *Anders* situation, identifying at least two nonfrivolous issues that could have been raised on appeal. *Gale v. United States*, 429 A.2d 177, 178–81 (D.C.App.1981) (Ferren, J., dissenting). Interpreting *McKenney*, Judge Ferren stated a preference for the "Idaho rule," which would require counsel to choose the appellant's strongest argument, however weak, and argue it to the court as forcefully as possible. In doing so, according to Judge Ferren, appellate counsel would be compelled to investigate and brief an issue that "may be less frivolous than it initially appears." The State would then respond to the argument, and the appellate court, rather than undertaking an independent review of the entire record, would decide the case on the merits of the issue or issues raised. Judge Ferren observed that the Idaho rule thus preserves the adversarial nature of criminal appeals, which "is much to be preferred over the *Anders* process in which the appellate judge feels obliged to act as a lawyer and the appellate lawyer feels constrained to rule as a judge." * * * *

The State insists that adoption of the Idaho rule in New Hampshire would lead appellate advocates to compromise their ethical duty "not to bring or defend a proceeding, or assert or controvert an issue therein, unless there is a basis for doing so that is not frivolous." N.H.R.Prof.Conduct 3.1. We agree with the State that, on occasion, adherence to the Idaho rule may require appellate counsel to bring a frivolous appeal. Such instances, however, would be extremely rare, especially in light of the fact that it is not considered frivolous to make "a good faith argument for an extension, modification or reversal of existing law." N.H.R.Prof.Conduct 3.1. In addition, the ABA Model Code Comments to Rule 3.1 state that "an action is not frivolous even though the lawyer believes that the client's position ultimately will not prevail." An action cannot be considered frivolous, therefore, if the lawyer is able "either to make a good faith argument on the merits of the action taken or to support the action taken by a good faith argument for an extension, modification or reversal of existing law." * * * *

We hold that the Idaho rule preserves the integrity of the attorney-client relationship better than a strict adherence to *Anders* does. In addition, the appellate process is better served by prohibiting the withdrawal of appellate counsel because the court will spend "less time and energy directly reviewing the case on the merits" and, assuming a nonfrivolous argument exists, "refusing to permit withdrawal would also obviate any need to substitute counsel to argue the appeal." *Commonwealth v. Moffett*, 383 Mass. at 206–07.

We therefore adopt the following procedure, drawn largely from the ABA Standards. See ABA Standards for Criminal Justice, The Defense Function, supra, Standard 4-8.3. Counsel first must discuss with the defendant whether to appeal. If, in counsel's estimation, the appeal lacks merit or is frivolous, counsel should so inform the defendant and seek to persuade the defendant to abandon the appeal. If the defendant chooses, notwithstanding counsel's advice, to proceed with the appeal, counsel must prepare and file the notice of appeal, including all arguable issues. For cases in which a transcript is required, a transcript shall be prepared and provided to the defendant. After appellate counsel is ordered to file a statement of reasons why the appeal should be accepted, or a brief, counsel must thoroughly examine the record and again determine whether any nonfrivolous arguments exist. If counsel concludes that the appeal is frivolous, counsel should again advise the defendant to withdraw the appeal. If the defendant decides not to withdraw the appeal, counsel must file a statement of reasons or a brief that argues the defendant's case as well as possible. Counsel cannot concede that the appeal is frivolous. If an appeal is truly frivolous, counsel's accurate summary of the facts and law will make that obvious. Thereafter, the appeal will proceed in the normal course.

See also *Ramos v. State*, 944 P.2d 856 (Nev.1997), where the court followed *Cigic* and called *Anders* "schizophrenic," "impractical," and "illogical." The court held:

Attorneys must argue for their clients without conceding an appeal is without merit. An action is not frivolous even though the lawyer believes that the client's position will ultimately not prevail. Indeed, appeals are few which do not have at least one issue that is not wholly frivolous. Such instances are sparse because counsel can present any good faith argument on the merits, a good faith challenge to the sufficiency of the evidence, or argue in good faith for an extension, modification or reversal of existing law.

As the *Cigic* court recognized, this procedure may, on rare occasions, force counsel to assert frivolous issues before the court. In those rare cases, we create an exception to the rules of professional conduct to allow the pursuit of a frivolous appeal.

Question: How can New Hampshire and Nevada courts refuse to follow a ruling of the U.S. Supreme Court?

7. In *Smith v. Commonwealth*, 524 Pa. 500 (1990), Smith appealed from a Parole Board decision revoking his parole, and he requested appointed counsel. The court appointed the public defender, who duly proceeded with the appeal, filing a brief for Smith arguing that the Board's decision to "recommit" Smith was invalid. The court determined the appeal to be *frivolous*, because Pennsylvania courts had repeatedly held that they would not review the discretionary recommitment when the recommitment period is within the "presumptive range" of the original sentence. The court ordered the public defender to pay the state's attorneys fees in defending against the appeal!

The public defender appealed this order to the Pennsylvania Supreme Court, arguing that what he did (arguing a weak point) was not much different from what the U.S. Supreme Court had already required in *Anders*: presenting the weak point but acknowledging that it was without merit. The court disagreed.

The concept of frivolity should not be construed as disfavoring legitimate attempts to change existing law. Even where long-standing case law on a particular point is contrary to an appellant's point of view, there may be a reasonable basis for arguing for the re-evaluation of that law. In this context, a distinction must be made as to situations where the repetitive appeal is being sought to perpetuate a concededly discredited position.

Here, appellant insists that his appeal to the Commonwealth Court was not frivolous because this Court has never considered the merits of the issue raised herein. Certainly, where an issue has not been addressed in this Court, its introduction in a lower court for the purpose of bringing it before this Court is not necessarily frivolous, even though the lower tribunal may have established a firm policy to the contrary. However, where such an approach is followed, it must be supported by a reasonable belief that this Court will be persuaded to change that existing policy. In view of the statutory and policy reasons for the Commonwealth Court's standard of review in this area, appellant's counsel could not legitimately argue that he held such a belief.

Turning now to the question of attorney's fees, we reject appellant's contention that the assessment of attorney's fees in this case was a violation of his constitutional right to appeal and his right to appointed counsel to assist in that appeal. Appellant argues that, if he had followed the position prescribed under *Anders v. California*, there would be no material difference from offering an advocate's brief setting forth the issues urged by the client. However, this argument fails to recognize the significant distinction between counsel's urging a position to a court and counsel's candid statement to the court of his assessment of the lack of merit in claims raised by the client. An argument presented to an appellate court is presumed by the court to be advocated by counsel, and in counsel's judgment to possess merit. In the *Anders* situation, counsel forth-rightly advises the tribunal of his or her assessment of the claim or claims being advanced by his clients. * * * *

We now hold that despite the constitutional right to counsel in an appeal from a criminal conviction, costs and attorney's fees may be assessed against court-appointed appellate counsel for the filing of a frivolous appeal.

Both the federal and state constitutions guarantee an indigent the right to have counsel appointed for the purpose of appealing a criminal conviction. This right guarantees the opportunity to assert a legitimate basis for challenging the ruling of a lower court. The right does not justify the assertion of patently frivolous claims, or give counsel license to engage in dilatory, obdurate, or vexatious conduct. As stated in *McCoy*: A lawyer, after all, has no duty, indeed no right, to pester a court with frivolous arguments, which is to say arguments that cannot conceivably persuade the court, so if he believes in good faith that there are no other arguments that he can make on his client's behalf he is honor bound to so advise the court and seek leave to withdraw as counsel. An appropriate sense of fairness has fostered the view that one should not be deprived of the full exercise of constitutional rights merely because of an impecunious situation. Yet this concern does not require that a special standard of behavior be designed for those who may be subject to an unfortunate financial situation. Criminal law is designed to protect all citizens and special exemptions cannot be made in the determination of guilt of alleged criminal behavior. This Court has concluded that the proper procedure, once counsel has determined that no basis exists for the assertion of a legitimate claim has been set forth in *Anders*: Counsel should, and can with honor and without conflict, be of more assistance to his client and to the court by filing a brief rather than a no-merit letter. His role as advocate requires that he support his client's appeal to the best of his ability. Of course, if counsel finds his case to be wholly frivolous, after a conscientious examination of it, he should so advise the court and request permission to withdraw. That request must, however, be accompanied by a brief referring to anything in the record that might arguably support the appeal. A copy of counsel's brief should be furnished the indigent and time allowed him to raise any points that he chooses; the court — not counsel — then proceeds, after a full examination of all the proceedings, to decide whether the case is wholly frivolous. If it so finds it may grant counsel's request to withdraw and dismiss the appeal insofar as federal requirements are concerned, or proceed to a decision on the merits, if state law so requires. On the other hand, if it finds any of the legal points arguable on their merits (and therefore not frivolous) it must, prior to decision, afford the indigent the assistance of counsel to argue the appeal.

The Board correctly highlights the distinction between offering an argument presented with an acknowledgement of its frivolousness and the same argument endorsed by counsel as being worthy of review. By filing an *Anders* brief, a lawyer does not advocate arguments he believes are "wholly frivolous"; rather, he presents them for the court's confirmation of his belief. Counsel serves the interests of both the client and the court by diligently investigating the possible grounds for appeal and advising the court of his decision that no legitimate grounds exist. *McCoy, supra,* at 436. Pursuing a concededly frivolous argument engages the attorney in conduct which is deliberately designed to mislead the tribunal.

JUSTICE ZAPPALA dissented:

I would not impose costs and fees against court appointed counsel for the filing of an appeal, even if it is found to be frivolous, because it is counsel's function to represent the defendant for the purposes of pursuing the appeal and it is done at the direction of the court. * * * * While I agree with the majority that counsel should advise the court of those instances in which his conscientious examination of his client's case discloses that the case is wholly frivolous, I do not agree that the filing of the appeal itself is a basis for the imposition of costs and fees. Counsel should not be penalized for his role in assisting his client's pursuit of constitutional rights.

There is merit to the Appellant's argument that there is no material difference between offering an advocate's brief setting forth the arguments advanced by the client and the procedure prescribed by the United States Supreme Court in *Anders v. California*. The majority perceives this argument as reflecting a fundamental misconception of our judicial process, but I perceive it as a practical reflection. No less effort is required of counsel in preparing an *Anders* brief than in preparing a brief in support of his client's position. The majority is intent then on penalizing counsel for failing to disclaim the validity of his client's position.

I do not see what is to be gained by penalizing counsel for what he is directed by the court to do — pursue the appeal. The appeal itself is not abandoned by counsel or his client even when an Anders brief is filed, but Rule 2744 [authorizing sanctions for frivolous appeals] was clearly intended to penalize the filing of a frivolous appeal and not counsel's failure to disclaim the merit of his client's position. The impact of Rule 2744 is in the disincentive to file a frivolous appeal, not to invite counsel's statement of its relative merits. Penalizing appellate counsel in cases in which the appeals will nevertheless be taken does nothing to accomplish the purpose of the rule.

See also *U.S. v. Cooper*, 170 F.3d 691 (7th Cir. 1999), where the court imposed sanctions on a defendant who represented himself in the appeal and filed a frivolous brief. The court noted that frivolous criminal appeals "clog the court system and, worse, they hurt meritorious criminal appeals by inviting sweeping rulings and by engendering judicial impatience with the entire class of criminal defendants."

HARRINGTON v. CALIFORNIA
United States Supreme Court
395 U.S. 250 (1969)

Mr. Justice Douglas delivered the opinion of the Court.

We held in *Chapman v. California*, 386 U.S. 18, that "before a federal constitutional error can be held harmless, the court must be able to declare a belief that it was harmless beyond a reasonable doubt." We said that, although "there are some constitutional rights so basic to a fair trial that their infraction can never be treated as harmless error", not all trial errors which violate the Constitution automatically call for reversal.

The question whether the alleged error in the present case was "harmless" under the rule of *Chapman* arose in a state trial for attempted robbery and first-degree murder. Four men were tried together — Harrington, a Caucasian, and Bosby, Rhone, and Cooper, Negroes — over an objection by Harrington that his trial should be severed. Each of his three codefendants confessed and their confessions were introduced at the trial with limiting instructions that the jury was to consider each confession only against the confessor. Rhone took the stand and Harrington's counsel cross-examined him. The other two did not take the stand.[1]

In *Bruton v. United States*, 391 U.S. 123, a confession of a codefendant who did not take the stand was used against Bruton in a federal prosecution. We held that Bruton had been denied his rights under the Confrontation Clause of the Sixth Amendment. Since the Confrontation Clause is applicable as well in state trials by reason of the Due Process Clause of the Fourteenth Amendment (*Pointer v. Texas*, 380 U.S. 400), the rule of *Bruton* applies here.

---

[1] All four were found to have participated in an attempted robbery, in the course of which a store employee was killed. Each was found guilty of felony murder and sentenced to life imprisonment.

The California Court of Appeal affirmed the convictions, and the Supreme Court denied a petition for a hearing. We granted the petition for certiorari to consider whether the violation of *Bruton* was on these special facts harmless error under *Chapman*.

Petitioner made statements which fell short of a confession but which placed him at the scene of the crime. He admitted that Bosby was the trigger man; that he fled with the other three; and that after the murder he dyed his hair black and shaved off his moustache. Several eyewitnesses placed petitioner at the scene of the crime. But two of them had previously told the police that four Negroes committed the crime. Rhone's confession, however, placed Harrington inside the store with a gun at the time of the attempted robbery and murder.

Cooper's confession did not refer to Harrington by name. He referred to the fourth man as "the white boy" or "this white guy". And he described him by age, height, and weight.

Bosby's confession likewise did not mention Harrington by name but referred to him as a blond-headed fellow or "the white guy" or "the Patty".

Both Cooper and Bosby said in their confessions that they did not see "the white guy" with a gun, which is at variance with the testimony of the prosecution witnesses.

Petitioner argues that it is irrelevant that he was not named in Cooper's and Bosby's confessions, that reference to "the white guy" made it as clear as pointing and shouting that the person referred to was the white man in the dock with the three Negroes. We make the same assumption. But we conclude that on these special facts the lack of opportunity to cross-examine Cooper and Bosby constituted harmless error under the rule of *Chapman*.

Rhone, whom Harrington's counsel cross-examined, placed him in the store with a gun at the time of the murder. Harrington himself agreed he was there. Others testified he had a gun and was an active participant. Cooper and Bosby did not put a gun in his hands when he denied it.[2] They did place him at the scene of the crime. But others, including Harrington himself, did the same. Their evidence, supplied through their confessions, was of course cumulative. But apart from them, the case against Harrington was so overwhelming that we conclude that this violation of *Bruton* was harmless beyond a reasonable doubt, unless we adopt the minority view in *Chapman* that a departure from constitutional procedures should result in an automatic reversal, regardless of the weight of the evidence.

It is argued that we must reverse if we can imagine a single juror whose mind might have been made up because of Cooper's and Bosby's confessions and who otherwise would have remained in doubt and unconvinced. We of course do not know the jurors who sat. Our judgment must be based on our own reading of the record and on what seems to us to have been the probable impact of the two confessions on the minds of an average jury. We admonished in *Chapman* against giving too much emphasis to "overwhelming evidence" of guilt, stating that constitutional errors affecting the substantial rights of the aggrieved party could not be considered to be harmless. By that test we cannot impute reversible weight to the two confessions.

---

[2] "All persons aiding and abetting the commission of a robbery are guilty of first degree murder when one of them kills while acting in furtherance of the common design." *People v. Washington*, 62 Cal.2d 777, 782 (1966).

We do not depart from *Chapman*; nor do we dilute it by inference. We reaffirm it. We do not suggest that, if evidence bearing on all the ingredients of the crime is tendered, the use of cumulative evidence, though tainted, is harmless error. Our decision is based on the evidence in this record. The case against Harrington was not woven from circumstantial evidence. It is so overwhelming that unless we say that no violation of *Bruton* can constitute harmless error, we must leave this state conviction undisturbed.

Affirmed.

Mr. Justice Brennan, with whom The Chief Justice and Mr. Justice Marshall join, dissenting.

The Court today overrules *Chapman v. California*, the very case it purports to apply. Far more fundamentally, it severely undermines many of the Court's most significant decisions in the area of criminal procedure.

In *Chapman*, we recognized that "harmless-error rules can work very unfair and mischievous results" unless they are narrowly circumscribed. We emphasized that "an error in admitting plainly relevant evidence which possibly influenced the jury adversely to a litigant cannot be conceived of as harmless." Thus, placing the burden of proof on the beneficiary of the error, we held that "before a federal constitutional error can be held harmless, the court must be able to declare a belief that it was harmless beyond a reasonable doubt." And, we left no doubt that for an error to be "harmless", it must have made no contribution to a criminal conviction.

Chapman, then, meant no compromise with the proposition that a conviction cannot constitutionally be based to any extent on constitutional error. The Court today by shifting the inquiry from whether the constitutional error contributed to the conviction to whether the untainted evidence provided "overwhelming" support for the conviction puts aside the firm resolve of *Chapman* and makes that compromise. As a result, the deterrent effect of such cases as *Mapp v. Ohio*, 367 U.S. 643 (1961); *Griffin v. California*, 380 U.S. 609 (1965); *Miranda v. Arizona*, 384 U.S. 436 (1966); *United States v. Wade*, 388 U.S. 218 (1967); and *Bruton v. United States*, 391 U.S. 123 (1968), on the actions of both police and prosecutors, not to speak of trial courts, will be significantly undermined.

The Court holds that constitutional error in the trial of a criminal offense may be held harmless if there is "overwhelming" untainted evidence to support the conviction. This approach, however, was expressly rejected in *Chapman*, and with good reason. For, where the inquiry concerns the extent of accumulation of untainted evidence rather than the impact of tainted evidence on the jury's decision, convictions resulting from constitutional error may be insulated from attack. By its nature, the issue of substantiality of evidence admits of only the most limited kind of appellate review. Thus, the Court's rule will often effectively leave the vindication of constitutional rights solely in the hands of trial judges. If, instead, the task of appellate courts is to appraise the impact of tainted evidence on a jury's decision, as *Chapman* required, these courts will be better able to protect against deprivations of constitutional rights of criminal defendants. The focus of appellate inquiry should be on the character and quality of the tainted evidence as it relates to the untainted evidence and not just on the amount of untainted evidence.

The instant case illustrates well the difference in application between the approach adopted by the Court today and the approach set down in *Chapman*. At issue is the evidence going to Harrington's participation in the crime of attempted robbery, not the evidence going to his presence at the scene of the crime. Without the admittedly unconstitutional evidence against Harrington provided by the confessions of codefendants Bosby and Cooper, the prosecutor's proof of Harrington's participation in the crime consisted of the testimony of two victims of the attempted robbery and of codefendant Rhone. The testimony of the victims was weakened by the fact that they had earlier told the police that all the participants in the attempted robbery were Negroes. Rhone's testimony against Harrington was self-serving in certain aspects. At the time of his arrest, Rhone was found in possession of a gun. On the stand, he explained that he was given the gun by Harrington after the attempted robbery, and that Harrington had carried the gun during the commission of the robbery. Thus, although there was more than ample evidence to establish Harrington's participation in the attempted robbery, a jury might still have concluded that the case was not proved beyond a reasonable doubt. The confessions of the other two codefendants implicating Harrington in the crime were less self-serving and might well have tipped the balance in the jurors' minds in favor of conviction. Certainly, the State has not carried its burden of demonstrating beyond a reasonable doubt that these two confessions did not contribute to Harrington's conviction.

There should be no need to remind this Court that the appellate role in applying standards of sufficiency or substantiality of evidence is extremely limited. To apply such standards as threshold requirements to the raising of constitutional challenges to criminal convictions is to shield from attack errors of a most fundamental nature and thus to deprive many defendants of basic constitutional rights. I respectfully dissent.

Note from Paula:

The *harmless error* rule should not be confused with another very important principle of appellate review: the *substantial evidence* rule. Where the appellant claims that the *admissible* evidence was insufficient to support a finding of guilt beyond a reasonable doubt, the appellate court looks to see if the verdict is supported by "substantial evidence". In doing this, the appellate court does *not* ask itself whether *it* believes that the evidence at trial showed guilty beyond a reasonable doubt. "Instead, the relevant question is whether, after viewing the evidence in the light most favorable to the prosecution, *any* rational trier of fact could have found the essential elements of the crime beyond a reasonable doubt." *Jackson v. Virginia* (1979) 443 U.S. 307, 319.

What is "substantial" evidence? Evidence which is "of ponderable legal significance, reasonable in nature, credible, and of solid value" (*People v. Johnson* (1980) 26 Cal.3d 557, 576) — whatever that means!

Under the substantial evidence rule, the appellate court "must view the evidence in a light most favorable to respondent and presume in support of the judgment the existence of every fact the trier could reasonably deduce from the evidence." *People v. Johnson, supra*, 26 Cal.3d at 576. This "cardinal rule of appellate review" is often overlooked by novice appellate lawyers — much to the annoyance of appellate judges, who grow tired of rejecting arguments that one side's evidence was more believable than the other's.

How does the "substantial evidence" rule differ from the "harmless error" rule? If Harrington had argued that substantial evidence did not support his conviction, how would the Court have analyzed this issue, and how would it have come out? How about *our* case?

ARIZONA v. FULMINANTE
United States Supreme Court
499 U.S. 279 (1991)

JUSTICE WHITE delivered the opinion of the Court.

The Arizona Supreme Court ruled in this case that respondent Oreste Fulminante's confession, received in evidence at his trial for murder, had been coerced and that its use against him was barred by the Fifth and Fourteenth Amendments to the United States Constitution. The court also held that the harmless-error rule could not be used to save the conviction. We affirm the judgment of the Arizona court, although for different reasons than those upon which that court relied.

I

Early in the morning of September 14, 1982, Fulminante called the Mesa, Arizona, Police Department to report that his 11-year-old stepdaughter, Jeneane Michelle Hunt, was missing. He had been caring for Jeneane while his wife, Jeneane's mother, was in the hospital. Two days later, Jeneane's body was found in the desert east of Mesa. She had been shot twice in the head at close range with a large caliber weapon, and a ligature was around her neck. Because of the decomposed condition of the body, it was impossible to tell whether she had been sexually assaulted.

Fulminante's statements to police concerning Jeneane's disappearance and his relationship with her contained a number of inconsistencies, and he became a suspect in her killing. When no charges were filed against him, Fulminante left Arizona for New Jersey. Fulminante was later convicted in New Jersey on federal charges of possession of a firearm by a felon.

Fulminante was incarcerated in the Ray Brook Federal Correctional Institution in New York. There he became friends with another inmate, Anthony Sarivola, then serving a 60-day sentence for extortion. The two men came to spend several hours a day together. Sarivola, a former police officer, had been involved in loansharking for organized crime but then became a paid informant for the Federal Bureau of Investigation. While at Ray Brook, he masqueraded as an organized crime figure. After becoming friends with Fulminante, Sarivola heard a rumor that Fulminante was suspected of killing a child in Arizona. Sarivola then raised the subject with Fulminante in several conversations, but Fulminante repeatedly denied any involvement in Jeneane's death. During one conversation, he told Sarivola that Jeneane had been killed by bikers looking for drugs; on another occasion, he said he did not know what had happened. Sarivola passed this information on to an agent of the Federal Bureau of Investigation, who instructed Sarivola to find out more.

Sarivola learned more one evening in October 1983, as he and Fulminante walked together around the prison track. Sarivola said that he knew Fulminante was "starting to get some tough treatment and whatnot" from other inmates because of the rumor. Sarivola offered to protect Fulminante from his fellow inmates, but told him, " 'You have to tell me about it,' you know. I mean, in other words, 'For me to give you any help.' " Fulminante then admitted to Sarivola that he had driven Jeneane to the desert on his motorcycle, where he choked her, sexually assaulted her, and made her beg for her life, before shooting her twice in the head.

Sarivola was released from prison in November 1983. Fulminante was released the following May, only to be arrested the next month for another weapons violation. On September 4, 1984, Fulminante was indicted in Arizona for the first-degree murder of Jeneane.

Prior to trial, Fulminante moved to suppress the statement he had given Sarivola in prison, as well as a second confession he had given to Donna Sarivola, then Anthony Sarivola's fiancee and later his wife, following his May 1984 release from prison. He asserted that the confession to Sarivola was coerced, and that the second confession was the "fruit" of the first. Following the hearing, the trial court denied the motion to suppress, specifically finding that, based on the stipulated facts, the confessions were voluntary. The State introduced both confessions as evidence at trial, and on December 19, 1985, Fulminante was convicted of Jeneane's murder. He was subsequently sentenced to death.

Fulminante appealed, arguing, among other things, that his confession to Sarivola was the product of coercion and that its admission at trial violated his rights to due process under the Fifth and Fourteenth Amendments of the United States Constitution. After considering the evidence at trial as well as the stipulated facts before the trial court on the motion to suppress, the Arizona Supreme Court held that the confession was coerced, but initially determined that the admission of the confession at trial was harmless error, because of the overwhelming nature of the evidence against Fulminante. Upon Fulminante's motion for reconsideration, however, the court ruled that this Court's precedent precluded the use of the harmless-error analysis in the case of a coerced confession. The court therefore reversed the conviction and ordered that Fulminante be retried without the use of the confession to Sarivola.[1] Because of differing views in the state and federal courts over whether the admission at trial of a coerced confession is subject to a harmless-error analysis, we granted the State's petition for certiorari. Although a majority of this Court finds that such a confession is subject to a harmless-error analysis, for the reasons set forth below, we affirm the judgment of the Arizona court.

II

We deal first with the State's contention that the court below erred in holding Fulminante's confession to have been coerced. * * * *

---

[1] In its initial opinion, the Arizona Supreme Court had determined that the second confession, to Donna Sarivola was not the "fruit of the poisonous tree," because it was made six months after the confession to Sarivola; it occurred after Fulminante's need for protection from Sarivola presumably had ended; and it took place in the course of a casual conversation with someone who was not an agent of the State. The court adhered to this determination in its supplemental opinion. This aspect of the Arizona Supreme Court's decision is not challenged here.

In applying the totality of the circumstances test to determine that the confession to Sarivola was coerced, the Arizona Supreme Court focused on a number of relevant facts. First, the court noted that "because Fulminante was an alleged child murderer, he was in danger of physical harm at the hands of other inmates." In addition, Sarivola was aware that Fulminante had been receiving "rough treatment from the guys." Using his knowledge of these threats, Sarivola offered to protect Fulminante in exchange for a confession to Jeneane's murder, and "in response to Sarivola's offer of protection, Fulminante confessed." Agreeing with Fulminante that "Sarivola's promise was 'extremely coercive,' " the Arizona Court declared: "The confession was obtained as a direct result of extreme coercion and was tendered in the belief that the defendant's life was in jeopardy if he did not confess. This is a true coerced confession in every sense of the word."[2]

We normally give great deference to the factual findings of the state court. Nevertheless, "the ultimate issue of 'voluntariness' is a legal question requiring independent federal determination." *Miller v. Fenton*, 474 U.S. 104, 110 (1985).

Although the question is a close one, we agree with the Arizona Supreme Court's conclusion that Fulminante's confession was coerced. The Arizona Supreme Court found a credible threat of physical violence unless Fulminante confessed. Our cases have made clear that a finding of coercion need not depend upon actual violence by a government agent;[4] a credible threat is sufficient. As we have said, "coercion can be mental as well as physical, and the blood of the accused is not the only hallmark of an unconstitutional inquisition." *Blackburn v. Alabama*, 361 U.S. 199, 206 (1960). * * * * Accepting the Arizona court's finding, permissible on this record, that there was a credible threat of physical violence, we agree with its conclusion that Fulminante's will was overborne in such a way as to render his confession the product of coercion.

III

Four of us, Justices Marshall, Blackmun, Stevens, and myself, would affirm the judgment of the Arizona Supreme Court on the ground that the harmless-error rule is inapplicable to erroneously admitted coerced confessions. We thus disagree with the Justices who have a contrary view.

The majority today abandons what until now the Court has regarded as the "axiomatic proposition that a defendant in a criminal case is deprived of due process of law if his conviction is founded, in whole or in part, upon an involuntary confession, without regard for the truth or falsity of the confession, and even though there is ample evidence aside from the confession to support the conviction." *Jackson v. Denno*, 378 U.S. 368, 376 (1964). The Court has repeatedly stressed that

---

[2] There are additional facts in the record, not relied upon by the Arizona Supreme Court, which also support a finding of coercion. Fulminante possesses low average to average intelligence; he dropped out of school in the fourth grade. He is short in stature and slight in build. Although he had been in prison before, he had not always adapted well to the stress of prison life. While incarcerated at the age of 26, he had "felt threatened by the prison population," and he therefore requested that he be placed in protective custody. Once there, however, he was unable to cope with the isolation and was admitted to a psychiatric hospital. * * * * In addition, we note that Sarivola's position as Fulminante's friend might well have made the latter particularly susceptible to the former's entreaties.

[4] The parties agree that Sarivola acted as an agent of the Government when he questioned Fulminante about the murder and elicited the confession.

the view that the admission of a coerced confession can be harmless error because of the other evidence to support the verdict is "an impermissible doctrine," for "the admission in evidence, over objection, of the coerced confession vitiates the judgment because it violates the Due Process Clause of the Fourteenth Amendment." *Payne v. Arkansas*, 356 U.S. 560. The rule was the same even when another confession of the defendant had been properly admitted into evidence. Today, a majority of the Court, without any justification, overrules this vast body of precedent without a word and in so doing dislodges one of the fundamental tenets of our criminal justice system.

In extending to coerced confessions the harmless error rule of *Chapman v. California*, 386 U.S. 18 (1967), the majority declares that because the Court has applied that analysis to numerous other "trial errors," there is no reason that it should not apply to an error of this nature as well. The four of us remain convinced, however, that we should abide by our cases that have refused to apply the harmless error rule to coerced confessions, for a coerced confession is fundamentally different from other types of erroneously admitted evidence to which the rule has been applied. Indeed, as the majority concedes, *Chapman* itself recognized that prior cases "have indicated that there are some constitutional rights so basic to a fair trial that their infraction can *never* be treated as harmless error," and it placed in that category the constitutional rule against using a defendant's coerced confession against him at his criminal trial. 386 U.S. at 23, and n. 8 (emphasis added). * * * *

Chapman specifically noted three constitutional errors that could not be categorized as harmless error: using a coerced confession against a defendant in a criminal trial, depriving a defendant of counsel, and trying a defendant before a biased judge. The majority attempts to distinguish the use of a coerced confession from the other two errors listed in *Chapman* first by distorting the decision in *Payne*, and then by drawing a meaningless dichotomy between "trial errors" and "structural defects" in the trial process. * * * *

The majority also attempts to distinguish "trial errors" which occur "during the presentation of the case to the jury," and which it deems susceptible to harmless error analysis, from "structural defects in the constitution of the trial mechanism," which the majority concedes cannot be so analyzed. This effort fails, for our jurisprudence on harmless error has not classified so neatly the errors at issue. For example, we have held susceptible to harmless error analysis the failure to instruct the jury on the presumption of innocence, *Kentucky v. Whorton*, 441 U.S. 786 (1979), while finding it impossible to analyze in terms of harmless error the failure to instruct a jury on the reasonable doubt standard, *Jackson v. Virginia*, 443 U.S. 307 (1979). These cases cannot be reconciled by labeling the former "trial error" and the latter not, for both concern the exact same stage in the trial proceedings. Rather, these cases can be reconciled only by considering the nature of the right at issue and the effect of an error upon the trial. A jury instruction on the presumption of innocence is not constitutionally required in every case to satisfy due process, because such an instruction merely offers an additional safeguard beyond that provided by the constitutionally required instruction on reasonable doubt. While it may be possible to analyze as harmless the omission of a presumption of innocence instruction when the required reasonable doubt instruction has been given, it is impossible to assess the effect on the jury of the omission of the more fundamental instruction on reasonable doubt. In addition, omission of a reasonable doubt instruction, though a "trial error," distorts the very structure of the trial because it creates the risk that the jury will convict the defendant even if the State has not met its required burden of proof.

These same concerns counsel against applying harmless error analysis to the admission of a coerced confession. A defendant's confession is probably the most probative and damaging evidence that can be admitted against him, so damaging that a jury should not be expected to ignore it even if told to do so, and because in any event it is impossible to know what credit and weight the jury gave to the confession. Concededly, this reason is insufficient to justify a per se bar to the use of any confession. Thus, *Milton v. Wainwright*, 407 U.S. 371 (1972), applied harmless-error analysis to a confession obtained and introduced in circumstances that violated the defendant's Sixth Amendment right to counsel. Similarly, the Courts of Appeals have held that the introduction of incriminating statements taken from defendants in violation of *Miranda v. Arizona*, 384 U.S. 436 (1966), is subject to treatment as harmless error.

Nevertheless, in declaring that it is "impossible to create a meaningful distinction between confessions elicited in violation of the Sixth Amendment and those in violation of the Fourteenth Amendment," the majority overlooks the obvious. Neither *Milton v. Wainwright* nor any of the other cases upon which the majority relies involved a defendant's coerced confession, nor were there present in these cases the distinctive reasons underlying the exclusion of coerced incriminating statements of the defendant.[7]

First, some coerced confessions may be untrustworthy. Consequently, admission of coerced confessions may distort the truth-seeking function of the trial upon which the majority focuses. More importantly, however, the use of coerced confessions, "whether true or false," is forbidden "because the methods used to extract them offend an underlying principle in the enforcement of our criminal law: that ours is an accusatorial and not an inquisitorial system — a system in which the State must establish guilt by evidence independently and freely secured and may not by coercion prove its charge against an accused out of his own mouth," *Rogers v. Richmond*, 365 U.S. at 540–541. This reflects the "strongly felt attitude of our society that important human values are sacrificed where an agency of the government, in the course of securing a conviction, wrings a confession out of an accused against his will," *Blackburn v. Alabama*, 361 U.S. at 206–207, as well as "the deep-rooted feeling that the police must obey the law while enforcing the law; that in the end life and liberty can be as much endangered from illegal methods used to convict those thought to be criminals as from the actual criminals themselves," *Spano v. N.Y.*, 360 U.S. at 320–321. Thus, permitting a coerced confession to be part of the evidence on which a jury is free to base its verdict of guilty is inconsistent with the thesis that ours is not an inquisitorial system of criminal justice.

As the majority concedes, there are other constitutional errors that invalidate a conviction even though there may be no reasonable doubt that the defendant is guilty and would be convicted absent the trial error. For example, a judge in a criminal trial "is prohibited from entering a judgment of conviction or directing the

---

[7] The same can be said of the *Miranda* cases. As the Court has recognized, a *Miranda* violation "does not mean that the statements received have actually been coerced, but only that the courts will presume the privilege against compulsory self-incrimination has not been intelligently exercised." *Oregon v. Elstad*, 470 U.S. 298, 310 (1985).

jury to come forward with such a verdict, regardless of how overwhelmingly the evidence may point in that direction." *United States v. Martin Linen Supply Co.*, 430 U.S. 564, 572–573 (1977). A defendant is entitled to counsel at trial, *Gideon v. Wainwright*, 372 U.S. 335 (1963), and as *Chapman* recognized, violating this right can never be harmless error. 386 U.S. at 23, and n. 8. In *Vasquez v. Hillery*, 474 U.S. 254 (1986), a defendant was found guilty beyond reasonable doubt, but the conviction had been set aside because of the unlawful exclusion of members of the defendant's race from the grand jury that indicted him, despite overwhelming evidence of his guilt. The error at the grand jury stage struck at fundamental values of our society, and "undermined the structural integrity of the criminal tribunal itself, and was not amenable to harmless-error review." *Id.* at 263–264. *Vasquez*, like *Chapman*, also noted that rule of automatic reversal when a defendant is tried before a judge with a financial interest in the outcome, *Tumey v. Ohio*, 273 U.S. 510, 535 (1927), despite a lack of any indication that bias influenced the decision. *Waller v. Georgia*, 467 U.S. 39, 49 (1984), recognized that violation of the guarantee of a public trial required reversal without any showing of prejudice and even though the values of a public trial may be intangible and unprovable in any particular case.

The search for truth is indeed central to our system of justice, but certain constitutional rights are not, and should not be, subject to harmless-error analysis because those rights protect important values that are unrelated to the truth-seeking function of the trial. The right of a defendant not to have his coerced confession used against him is among those rights, for using a coerced confession aborts the basic trial process and renders a trial fundamentally unfair.

For the foregoing reasons, the four of us would adhere to the consistent line of authority that has recognized as a basic tenet of our criminal justice system, before and after both *Miranda* and *Chapman*, the prohibition against using a defendant's coerced confession against him at his criminal trial. Stare decisis is "of fundamental importance to the rule of law," *Welch v. Texas Highways and Public Transp. Dept.*, 483 U.S. 468, 494 (1987); the majority offers no convincing reason for overturning our long line of decisions requiring the exclusion of coerced confessions.

IV

Since five Justices have determined that harmless error analysis applies to coerced confessions, it becomes necessary to evaluate under that ruling the admissibility of Fulminante's confession to Sarivola. *Chapman v. California*, 386 U.S. at 24, made clear that "before a federal constitutional error can be held harmless, the court must be able to declare a belief that it was harmless beyond a reasonable doubt." The Court has the power to review the record de novo in order to determine an error's harmlessness. In so doing, it must be determined whether the State has met its burden of demonstrating that the admission of the confession to Sarivola did not contribute to Fulminante's conviction. *Chapman, supra*, 386 U.S. at 26. Five of us are of the view that the State has not carried its burden and accordingly affirm the judgment of the court below reversing petitioner's conviction.

A confession is like no other evidence. Indeed, "the defendant's own confession is probably the most probative and damaging evidence that can be admitted against him. The admissions of a defendant come from the actor himself, the most knowledgeable and unimpeachable source of information about his past conduct. Certainly, confessions have profound impact on the jury, so much so that we may justifiably doubt its ability to put them out of mind even if told to do so." *Bruton v. United States*, 391 U.S. at 139–140 (White, J., dissenting). While some statements by a defendant may concern isolated aspects of the crime or may be incriminating only when linked to other evidence, a full confession in which the defendant discloses the motive for and means of the crime may tempt the jury to rely upon that evidence alone in reaching its decision. In the case of a coerced confession such as that given by Fulminante to Sarivola, the risk that the confession is unreliable, coupled with the profound impact that the confession has upon the jury, requires a reviewing court to exercise extreme caution before determining that the admission of the confession at trial was harmless.

In the Arizona Supreme Court's initial opinion, in which it determined that harmless-error analysis could be applied to the confession, the court found that the admissible second confession to Donna Sarivola rendered the first confession to Anthony Sarivola cumulative. The court also noted that circumstantial physical evidence concerning the wounds, the ligature around Jeneane's neck, the location of the body, and the presence of motorcycle tracks at the scene corroborated the second confession. The court concluded that "due to the overwhelming evidence adduced from the second confession, if there had not been a first confession, the jury would still have had the same basic evidence to convict" Fulminante.

We have a quite different evaluation of the evidence. Our review of the record leads us to conclude that the State has failed to meet its burden of establishing, beyond a reasonable doubt, that the admission of Fulminante's confession to Anthony Sarivola was harmless error. Three considerations compel this result.

First, the transcript discloses that both the trial court and the State recognized that a successful prosecution depended on the jury believing the two confessions. Absent the confessions, it is unlikely that Fulminante would have been prosecuted at all, because the physical evidence from the scene and other circumstantial evidence would have been insufficient to convict. Indeed, no indictment was filed until nearly two years after the murder.[8]

Although the police had suspected Fulminante from the beginning, as the prosecutor acknowledged in his opening statement to the jury, "What brings us to Court, what makes this case fileable, and prosecutable and triable is that later, Mr. Fulminante confesses this crime to Anthony Sarivola and later, to Donna Sarivola, his wife." After trial began, during a renewed hearing on Fulminante's motion to suppress, the trial court opined, "You know, I think from what little I know about this trial, the character of this man Sarivola for truthfulness or untruthfulness and his credibility is the centerpiece of this case, is it not?," to which the prosecutor responded, "It's very important, there's no doubt." Finally, in his closing argument, the prosecutor prefaced his discussion of the two confessions by conceding, "We have a lot of circumstantial evidence that indicates that this is our suspect, this is the fellow that did it, but it's a little short as far as saying that it's proof that he actually put the gun to the girl's head and killed her. So it's a little short of that. We recognize that."

---

[8] Although Fulminante had allegedly confessed to Donna Sarivola several months previously, police did not yet know of this confession, which Anthony Sarivola did not mention to them until June 1985. They did, however, know of the first confession, which Fulminante had given to Anthony Sarivola nearly a year before.

Second, the jury's assessment of the confession to Donna Sarivola could easily have depended in large part on the presence of the confession to Anthony Sarivola. Absent the admission at trial of the first confession, the jurors might have found Donna Sarivola's story unbelievable. Fulminante's confession to Donna Sarivola allegedly occurred in May 1984, on the day he was released from Ray Brook, as she and Anthony Sarivola drove Fulminante from New York to Pennsylvania. Donna Sarivola testified that Fulminante, whom she had never before met, confessed in detail about Jeneane's brutal murder in response to her casual question concerning why he was going to visit friends in Pennsylvania instead of returning to his family in Arizona. Although she testified that she was "disgusted" by Fulminante's disclosures, she stated that she took no steps to notify authorities of what she had learned. In fact, she claimed that she barely discussed the matter with Anthony Sarivola, who was in the car and overheard Fulminante's entire conversation with Donna. Despite her disgust for Fulminante, Donna Sarivola later went on a second trip with him. Although Sarivola informed authorities that he had driven Fulminante to Pennsylvania, he did not mention Donna's presence in the car or her conversation with Fulminante. Only when questioned by authorities in June 1985 did Anthony Sarivola belatedly recall the confession to Donna more than a year before, and only then did he ask if she would be willing to discuss the matter with authorities.

Although some of the details in the confession to Donna Sarivola were corroborated by circumstantial evidence, many, including details that Jeneane was choked and sexually assaulted, were not. As to other aspects of the second confession, including Fulminante's motive and state of mind, the only corroborating evidence was the first confession to Anthony Sarivola. Thus, contrary to what the Arizona Supreme Court found, it is clear that the jury might have believed that the two confessions reinforced and corroborated each other. For this reason, one confession was not merely cumulative of the other. While in some cases two confessions, delivered on different occasions to different listeners, might be viewed as being independent of each other, it strains credulity to think that the jury so viewed the two confessions in this case, especially given the close relationship between Donna and Anthony Sarivola.

The jurors could also have believed that Donna Sarivola had a motive to lie about the confession in order to assist her husband. Anthony Sarivola received significant benefits from federal authorities, including payment for information, immunity from prosecution, and eventual placement in the federal Witness Protection Program. In addition, the jury might have found Donna motivated by her own desire for favorable treatment, for she, too, was ultimately placed in the Witness Protection Program.

Third, the admission of the first confession led to the admission of other evidence prejudicial to Fulminante. For example, the State introduced evidence that Fulminante knew of Sarivola's connections with organized crime in an attempt to explain why Fulminante would have been motivated to confess to Sarivola in seeking protection. Absent the confession, this evidence would have had no relevance and would have been inadmissible at trial. The Arizona Supreme Court found that the evidence of Sarivola's connections with organized crime reflected on Sarivola's character, not Fulminante's, and noted that the evidence could have been used to impeach Sarivola. This analysis overlooks the fact that had the confession not been admitted, there would have been no reason for Sarivola to testify and thus no need to impeach his testimony. Moreover, we cannot agree that the evidence did not reflect on Fulminante's character as well, for it depicted him as someone who willingly sought out the company of criminals. It is quite possible that this evidence led the jury to view Fulminante as capable of murder. * * * *

Because a majority of the Court has determined that Fulminante's confession to Anthony Sarivola was coerced and because a majority has determined that admitting this confession was not harmless beyond a reasonable doubt, we agree with the Arizona Supreme Court's conclusion that Fulminante is entitled to a new trial at which the confession is not admitted. Accordingly the judgment of the Arizona Supreme Court is affirmed.

CHIEF JUSTICE REHNQUIST, with whom JUSTICE O'CONNOR joins, JUSTICE KENNEDY and JUSTICE SOUTER join as to Parts I and II, and JUSTICE SCALIA joins as to Parts II and III, delivering the opinion of the Court as to Part II, and dissenting as to Parts I and III.

The Court today properly concludes that the admission of an "involuntary" confession at trial is subject to harmless error analysis. Nonetheless, the independent review of the record which we are required to make shows that respondent Fulminante's confession was not in fact involuntary. And even if the confession were deemed to be involuntary, the evidence offered at trial, including a second, untainted confession by Fulminante, supports the conclusion that any error here was certainly harmless.

I

The question of whether respondent Fulminante's confession was voluntary is one of federal law. "Without exception, the Court's confession cases hold that the ultimate issue of 'voluntariness' is a legal question requiring independent federal determination." *Miller v. Fenton*, 474 U.S. 104, 110 (1985). * * * *

The admissibility of a confession such as that made by respondent Fulminante depends upon whether it was voluntarily made. "The ultimate test remains that which has been the only clearly established test in Anglo-American courts for two hundred years: the test of voluntariness. Is the confession the product of an essentially free and unconstrained choice by its maker? If it is, if he has willed to confess, it may be used against him. If it is not, if his will has been overborne and his capacity for self-determination critically impaired, the use of his confession offends due process." *Culombe v. Connecticut*, 367 U.S. 568, 602 (1961).

In this case the parties stipulated to the basic facts at the hearing in the Arizona trial court on respondent's motion to suppress the confession. Anthony Sarivola, an inmate at the Ray Brook Prison, was a paid confidential informant for the FBI. While at Ray Brook, various rumors reached Sarivola that Oreste Fulminante, a fellow inmate who had befriended Sarivola, had killed his step-daughter in Arizona. Sarivola passed these rumors on to his FBI contact, who told him "to find out more about it."

Sarivola, having already discussed the rumors with the defendant on several occasions, asked him whether the rumors were true, adding that he might be in a position to protect Fulminante from physical recriminations in prison, but that "he must tell him the truth." Fulminante then confessed to Sarivola that he had in fact killed his step-daughter in Arizona, and provided Sarivola with substantial details about the manner in which he killed the child. At the suppression hearing, Fulminante stipulated to the fact that "at no time did the defendant indicate he was in fear of other inmates nor did he ever seek Mr. Sarivola's 'protection.' " The trial court was also aware, through an excerpt from Sarivola's interview testimony which the defendant appended to his reply memorandum, that Sarivola believed Fulminante's time was "running short" and that he would "have went out of the prison horizontally." The trial court found that respondent's confession was voluntary.

The Supreme Court of Arizona stated that the trial court committed no error in finding the confession voluntary based on the record before it. But it overturned the trial court's finding of voluntariness based on the more comprehensive trial record before it, which included, in addition to the facts stipulated at the suppression hearing, a statement made by Sarivola at the trial that "the defendant had been receiving 'rough treatment from the guys, and if the defendant would tell the truth, he could be protected.' " It also had before it the presentence report, which showed that Fulminante was no stranger to the criminal justice system: he had six prior felony convictions, and had been imprisoned on three prior occasions.

On the basis of the record before it, the Supreme Court stated: "Defendant contends that because he was an alleged child murderer, he was in danger of physical harm at the hands of other inmates. Sarivola was aware that defendant faced the possibility of retribution from other inmates, and that in return for the confession with respect to the victim's murder, Sarivola would protect him. Moreover, the defendant maintains that Sarivola's promise was 'extremely coercive' because the 'obvious' inference from the promise was that his life would be in jeopardy if he did not confess. We agree."

Exercising our responsibility to make the independent examination of the record necessary to decide this federal question, I am at a loss to see how the Supreme Court of Arizona reached the conclusion that it did. Fulminante offered no evidence that he believed that his life was in danger or that he in fact confessed to Sarivola in order to obtain the proffered protection. Indeed, he had stipulated that "at no time did the defendant indicate he was in fear of other inmates nor did he ever seek Mr. Sarivola's 'protection.' " Sarivola's testimony that he told Fulminante that "if he would tell the truth, he could be protected," adds little if anything to the substance of the parties' stipulation. The decision of the Supreme Court of Arizona rests on an assumption that is squarely contrary to this stipulation, and one that is not supported by any testimony of Fulminante.

The facts of record in the present case are quite different from those present in cases where we have found confessions to be coerced and involuntary. Since Fulminante was unaware that Sarivola was an FBI informant, there existed none of "the danger of coercion resulting from the interaction of custody and official interrogation." *Illinois v. Perkins*, 496 U.S. ___ (1990). The fact that Sarivola was a government informant does not by itself render Fulminante's confession involuntary, since we have consistently accepted the use of informants in the discovery of evidence of a crime as a legitimate investigatory procedure consistent with the Constitution. See, e.g., *Kuhlmann v. Wilson*, 477 U.S. 436 (1986). The conversations between Sarivola and Fulminante were not lengthy, and the defendant was free at all times to leave Sarivola's company. Sarivola at no time threatened him or demanded that he confess; he simply requested that he speak the truth about the matter. Fulminante was an experienced habitue of prisons, and presumably able to fend for himself. In concluding on these facts that Fulminante's confession was involuntary, the Court today embraces a more expansive definition of that term than is warranted by any of our decided cases.

II

Since this Court's landmark decision in *Chapman*, in which we adopted the general rule that a constitutional error does not automatically require reversal of a conviction, the Court has applied harmless error analysis to a wide range of errors and has recognized that most constitutional errors can be harmless. See, e.g., *Clemons v. Mississippi*, 494 U.S. ___ (1990) (unconstitutionally overbroad jury instructions at the sentencing stage of a capital case); *Satterwhite v. Texas*, 486 U.S. 249 (1988) (admission of evidence at the sentencing stage of a capital case in violation of the Sixth Amendment Counsel Clause); *Carella v. California*, 491 U.S. 263 (1989) (jury instruction containing an erroneous conclusive presumption); *Pope v. Illinois*, 481 U.S. 497 (1987) (jury instruction misstating an element of the offense); *Rose v. Clark*, 478 U.S. 570 (1986) (jury instruction containing an erroneous rebuttable presumption); *Crane v. Kentucky*, 476 U.S. 683 (1986) (erroneous exclusion of defendant's testimony regarding the circumstances of his confession); *Delaware v. Van Arsdall*, 475 U.S. 673 (1986) (restriction on a defendant's right to cross examine a witness for bias in violation of the Sixth Amendment Confrontation Clause); *Rushen v. Spain*, 464 U.S. 114 (1983) (denial of a defendant's right to be present at trial); *United States v. Hasting*, 461 U.S. 499 (1983) (improper comment on defendant's silence at trial, in violation of the Fifth Amendment Self-Incrimination Clause); *Hopper v. Evans*, 456 U.S. 605 (1982) (statute improperly forbidding trial court's giving a jury instruction on a lesser-included offense in a capital case in violation of the Due Process Clause); *Kentucky v. Whorton*, 441 U.S. 786 (1979) (failure to instruct the jury on the presumption of innocence); *Moore v. Illinois*, 434 U.S. 220 (1977) (admission of identification evidence in violation of the Sixth Amendment Counsel Clause); *Brown v. United States*, 411 U.S. 223 (1973) (admission of the out-of-court statement of a nontestifying codefendant in violation of the Sixth Amendment Counsel Clause); *Milton v. Wainwright*, 407 U.S. 371 (1972) (confession obtained in violation of *Massiah v. United States*, 377 U.S. 201 (1964)); *Chambers v. Maroney*, 399 U.S. 42 (1970) (admission of evidence obtained in violation of the Fourth Amendment); *Coleman v. Alabama*, 399 U.S. 1 (1970) (denial of counsel at a preliminary hearing in violation of the Sixth Amendment Counsel Clause).

The common thread connecting these cases is that each involved "trial error" — error which occurred during the presentation of the case to the jury, and which may therefore be quantitatively assessed in the context of other evidence presented in order to determine whether its admission was harmless beyond a reasonable doubt. In applying harmless-error analysis to these many different constitutional violations, the Court has been faithful to the belief that the harmless-error doctrine is essential to preserve the "principle that the central purpose of a criminal trial is to decide the factual question of the defendant's guilt or innocence, and promotes public respect for the criminal process by focusing on the underlying fairness of the trial rather than on the virtually inevitable presence of immaterial error." *Van Arsdall, supra*, 475 U.S. at 681.

In *Chapman*, the Court stated that:

Although our prior cases have indicated that there are some constitutional rights so basic to a fair trial that their infraction can never be treated as harmless error,[8] this statement in *Fahy* itself belies any belief that all trial errors which violate the Constitution automatically call for reversal.

It is on the basis of this language in *Chapman* that Justice White in dissent concludes that the principle of *stare decisis* requires us to hold that an involuntary confession is not subject to harmless error analysis. I believe that there are several reasons which lead to a contrary conclusion. In the first place, the quoted language from *Chapman* does not by its terms adopt any such rule in that case. The language that "although our prior cases have indicated," coupled with the relegation of the cases themselves to a footnote, is more appropriately regarded as a historical reference to the holdings of these cases. * * * *

The admission of an involuntary confession — a classic "trial error" — is markedly different from the other two constitutional violations referred to in the *Chapman* footnote as not being subject to harmless-error analysis. One of those cases, *Gideon v. Wainwright*, 372 U.S. 335 (1963), involved the total deprivation of the right to counsel at trial. The other, *Tumey v. Ohio*, 273 U.S. 510 (1927), involved a judge who was not impartial. These are structural defects in the constitution of the trial mechanism, which defy analysis by "harmless-error" standards. The entire conduct of the trial from beginning to end is obviously affected by the absence of counsel for a criminal defendant, just as it is by the presence on the bench of a judge who is not impartial. Since our decision in *Chapman*, other cases have added to the category of constitutional errors which are not subject to harmless error the following: unlawful exclusion of members of the defendant's race from a grand jury, *Vasquez v. Hillery*, 474 U.S. 254 (1986); the right to self-representation at trial, *McKaskle v. Wiggins*, 465 U.S. 168 (1984); and the right to public trial, *Waller v. Georgia*, 467 U.S. 39 (1984). Each of these constitutional deprivations is a similar structural defect affecting the framework within which the trial proceeds, rather than simply an error in the trial process itself. "Without these basic protections, a criminal trial cannot reliably serve its function as a vehicle for determination of guilt or innocence, and no criminal punishment may be regarded as fundamentally fair." *Rose v. Clark*, 478 U.S. at 577–578.

It is evident from a comparison of the constitutional violations which we have held subject to harmless error, and those which we have held not, that involuntary statements or confessions belong in the former category. The admission of an involuntary confession is a "trial error," similar in both degree and kind to the erroneous admission of other types of evidence. The evidentiary impact of an involuntary confession, and its effect upon the composition of the record, is indistinguishable from that of a confession obtained in violation of the Sixth Amendment — of evidence seized in violation of the Fourth Amendment — or of a prosecutor's improper comment on a defendant's silence at trial in violation of the Fifth Amendment. When reviewing the erroneous admission of an involuntary confession, the appellate court, as it does with the admission of other forms of improperly admitted evidence, simply reviews the remainder of the evidence against the defendant to determine whether the admission of the confession was harmless beyond a reasonable doubt.

---

[8] See, e.g., *Payne v. Arkansas*, 356 U.S. 560 (coerced confession); *Gideon v. Wainwright*, 372 U.S. 335 (right to counsel); *Tumey v. Ohio*, 273 U.S. 510 (impartial judge).

Nor can it be said that the admission of an involuntary confession is the type of error which "transcends the criminal process." This Court has applied harmless-error analysis to the violation of other constitutional rights similar in magnitude and importance and involving the same level of police misconduct. For instance, we have previously held that the admission of a defendant's statements obtained in violation of the Sixth Amendment is subject to harmless-error analysis. In *Milton v. Wainwright*, 407 U.S. 371 (1972), the Court held the admission of a confession obtained in violation of *Massiah v. United States*, 377 U.S. 201 (1964), to be harmless beyond a reasonable doubt. We have also held that the admission of an out-of-court statement by a nontestifying codefendant is subject to harmless-error analysis. *Harrington v. California*, 395 U.S. 250 (1969). The inconsistent treatment of statements elicited in violation of the Sixth and Fourteenth Amendments, respectively, can be supported neither by evidentiary or deterrence concerns nor by a belief that there is something more "fundamental" about involuntary confessions. This is especially true in a case such as this one where there are no allegations of physical violence on behalf of the police. The impact of a confession obtained in violation of the Sixth Amendment has the same evidentiary impact as does a confession obtained in violation of a defendant's due process rights. Government misconduct that results in violations of the Fourth and Sixth Amendments may be at least as reprehensible as conduct that results in an involuntary confession. For instance, the prisoner's confession to an inmate-informer at issue in *Milton*, which the Court characterized as implicating the Sixth Amendment right to counsel, is similar on its facts to the one we face today. Indeed, experience shows that law enforcement violations of these constitutional guarantees can involve conduct as egregious as police conduct used to elicit statements in violation of the Fourteenth Amendment. It is thus impossible to create a meaningful distinction between confessions elicited in violation of the Sixth Amendment and those in violation of the Fourteenth Amendment.

Of course an involuntary confession may have a more dramatic effect on the course of a trial than do other trial errors — in particular cases it may be devastating to a defendant — but this simply means that a reviewing court will conclude in such a case that its admission was not harmless error; it is not a reason for eschewing the harmless error test entirely. The Supreme Court of Arizona, in its first opinion in the present case, concluded that the admission of Fulminante's confession was harmless error. That court concluded that a second and more explicit confession of the crime made by Fulminante after he was released from prison was not tainted by the first confession, and that the second confession, together with physical evidence from the wounds (the victim had been shot twice in the head with a large calibre weapon at close range and a ligature was found around her neck) and other evidence introduced at trial rendered the admission of the first confession harmless beyond a reasonable doubt.

III

I would agree with the finding of the Supreme Court of Arizona in its initial opinion — in which it believed harmless-error analysis was applicable to the admission of involuntary confessions — that the admission of Fulminante's confession was harmless. Indeed, this seems to me to be a classic case of harmless error: a second confession giving more details of the crime than the first was admitted in evidence and found to be free of any constitutional objection. Accordingly, I would affirm the holding of the Supreme Court of Arizona in its initial opinion, and reverse the judgment which it ultimately rendered in this case.

JUSTICE KENNEDY, concurring in the judgment.

For the reasons stated by The Chief Justice, I agree that Fulminante's confession to Anthony Sarivola was not coerced. In my view, the trial court did not err in admitting this testimony. A majority of the Court, however, finds the confession coerced and proceeds to consider whether harmless-error analysis may be used when a coerced confession has been admitted at trial. With the case in this posture, it is appropriate for me to address the harmless-error issue.

Again for the reasons stated by The Chief Justice, I agree that harmless-error analysis should apply in the case of a coerced confession. That said, the court conducting a harmless-error inquiry must appreciate the indelible impact a full confession may have on the trier of fact, as distinguished, for instance, from the impact of an isolated statement that incriminates the defendant only when connected with other evidence. If the jury believes that a defendant has admitted the crime, it doubtless will be tempted to rest its decision on that evidence alone, without careful consideration of the other evidence in the case. Apart, perhaps, from a videotape of the crime, one would have difficulty finding evidence more damaging to a criminal defendant's plea of innocence. For the reasons given by Justice White in Part IV of his opinion, I cannot with confidence find admission of Fulminante's confession to Anthony Sarivola to be harmless error.

The same majority of the Court does not agree on the three issues presented by the trial court's determination to admit Fulminante's first confession: whether the confession was inadmissible because coerced; whether harmless error analysis is appropriate; and if so whether any error was harmless here. My own view that the confession was not coerced does not command a majority.

In the interests of providing a clear mandate to the Arizona Supreme Court in this capital case, I deem it proper to accept in the case now before us the holding of five Justices that the confession was coerced and inadmissible. I agree with a majority of the Court that admission of the confession could not be harmless error when viewed in light of all the other evidence; and so I concur in the judgment to affirm the ruling of the Arizona Supreme Court.

Notes from Paula:

1. Chief Justice Rehnquist drew a distinction between "structural" errors and other errors. What's the difference? Consider LaFave & Israel, *Criminal Procedure* (West, 2nd ed.), § 27.6:

> Perhaps the two most significant factors governing the distinction among violations drawn there is the capacity of the appellate court to measure the error's impact on the outcome of the trial and the relationship of the right violated to interests that stand apart from ensuring that the trial verdict is not improperly influenced. Undoubtedly the characteristic of "structural" defects most frequently mentioned in Supreme Court opinions is their "inherently indeterminate" impact upon the outcome of the trial. Unlike trial errors, they do not relate to the introduction of particular items of evidence. * * * * Very often, the impact of violations in the structural

category could not be measured by reference to the evidence produced because the violation might well have had a bearing on the failure to produce other evidence, or take other actions, that would have been influential. The Court's treatment of the various constitutional violations relating to the right to counsel reflect this focus on the indeterminate impact of the error. The absence of counsel at trial obviously has an inherently indeterminate impact.

2. In *Sullivan v. Louisiana*, 508 U.S. 275 (1993), the Court held that an erroneous jury instruction on "reasonable doubt" required automatic reversal and was not subject to the harmless error rule:

> In *Fulminante*, we distinguished between, on the one hand, "structural defects in the constitution of the trial mechanism, which defy analysis by 'harmless-error' standards," and, on the other hand, trial errors which occur "during the presentation of the case to the jury, and which may therefore be quantitatively assessed in the context of other evidence presented." Denial of the right to a jury verdict of guilt beyond a reasonable doubt is certainly an error of the former sort, the jury guarantee being a "basic protection" whose precise effects are unmeasurable, but without which a criminal trial cannot reliably serve its function. The right to trial by jury reflects, we have said, "a profound judgment about the way in which law should be enforced and justice administered." *Duncan v. Louisiana*, 391 U.S. at 155. The deprivation of that right, with consequences that are necessarily unquantifiable and indeterminate, unquestionably qualifies as "structural error."

3. In *Rivera v. Illinois*, 129 S.Ct. 1446 (2009), the trial court erroneously denied defendant's peremptory challenge to a prospective juror. The Supreme Court held that this was not structural error:

> The Due Process Clause of the Fourteenth Amendment, Rivera maintains, requires reversal whenever a criminal defendant's peremptory challenge is erroneously denied. Rivera recalls the ancient lineage of the peremptory challenge and observes that the challenge has long been lauded as a means to guard against latent bias and to secure "the constitutional end of an impartial jury and a fair trial." *McCollum*, 505 U.S. at 57. When a trial court fails to dismiss a lawfully challenged juror, Rivera asserts, it commits structural error: the jury becomes an illegally constituted tribunal, and any verdict it renders is *per se* invalid. According to Rivera, this holds true even if the Constitution does not itself mandate peremptory challenges, because criminal defendants have a constitutionally protected liberty interest in their state-provided peremptory challenge rights. Cf. *Evitts v. Lucey*, 469 U.S. 387, 393 (1985) (although "the Constitution does not require States to grant appeals as of right to criminal defendants," States that provide such appeals "must comport with the demands of the Due Process and Equal Protection Clauses").

> The improper seating of a juror, Rivera insists, is not amenable to harmless-error analysis because it is impossible to ascertain how a properly constituted jury — here, one without juror Gomez — would have decided his case. Thus, he urges, whatever the constitutional status of peremptory challenges, automatic reversal must be the rule as a matter of federal law.

Rivera's arguments do not withstand scrutiny. If a defendant is tried before a qualified jury composed of individuals not challengeable for cause, the loss of a peremptory challenge due to a state court's good-faith error is not a matter of federal constitutional concern. Rather, it is a matter for the State to address under its own laws.

As Rivera acknowledges, this Court has consistently held that there is no freestanding constitutional right to peremptory challenges. See, *e.g.*, *Martinez-Salazar*, 528 U.S. at 311. We have characterized peremptory challenges as "a creature of statute," *Ross v. Oklahoma*, 487 U.S. 81, 89 (1988), and have made clear that a State may decline to offer them at all. *McCollum*, 505 U.S. at 57. When States provide peremptory challenges (as all do in some form), they confer a benefit beyond the minimum requirements of fair jury selection, and thus retain discretion to design and implement their own systems.

Because peremptory challenges are within the States' province to grant or withhold, the mistaken denial of a state-provided peremptory challenge does not, without more, violate the Federal Constitution. "A mere error of state law," we have noted, "is not a denial of due process." *Engle v. Isaac*, 456 U.S. 107, 121, n. 21 (1982). The Due Process Clause, our decisions instruct, safeguards not the meticulous observance of state procedural prescriptions, but the fundamental elements of fairness in a criminal trial.

The trial judge's refusal to excuse juror Gomez did not deprive Rivera of his constitutional right to a fair trial before an impartial jury. * * * *

We reject the notion that a juror is constitutionally disqualified whenever she is aware that a party has challenged her. Were the rule otherwise, a party could circumvent *Batson* by insisting in open court that a trial court dismiss a juror even though the party's peremptory challenge was discriminatory. Or a party could obtain a juror's dismissal simply by making in her presence a baseless for-cause challenge. Due process does not require such counterintuitive results.

4. In *Hedgpeth v. Pulida*, 129 S.Ct. 530 (2008), the Supreme Court held that while "a conviction based on a general verdict is subject to challenge if the jury was instructed on alternative theories of guilt and may have relied on an invalid one," the error is not structural, and is subject to harmless error review on appeal.

SMITH v. ROBBINS
United States Supreme Court
528 U.S. 259 (2000)

Not infrequently, an attorney appointed to represent an indigent defendant on appeal concludes that an appeal would be frivolous and requests that the appellate court allow him to withdraw or that the court dispose of the case without the filing of merits briefs. In *Anders v. California*, 386 U.S. 738 (1967), we held that, in order to protect indigent defendants' constitutional right to appellate counsel, courts must safeguard against the risk of granting such requests in cases where the appeal is not actually frivolous. We found inadequate California's procedure — which permitted appellate counsel to withdraw upon filing a conclusory letter stating that the appeal had "no merit" and permitted the appellate court to affirm the conviction upon reaching the same conclusion following a review of the record. We went on to set forth an acceptable procedure. California has since adopted a new procedure, which departs in some respects from the one that we delineated in *Anders*. The question is whether that departure is fatal. We hold that it is not. The procedure we sketched in *Anders* is a prophylactic one; the States are free to adopt different procedures, so long as those procedures adequately safeguard a defendant's right to appellate counsel.

I

A

Under California's new procedure, established in *People v. Wende*, 25 Cal.3d 436 (1979), counsel, upon concluding that an appeal would be frivolous, files a brief with the appellate court that summarizes the procedural and factual history of the case, with citations of the record. He also attests that he has reviewed the record, explained his evaluation of the case to his client, provided the client with a copy of the brief, and informed the client of his right to file a *pro se* supplemental brief. He further requests that the court independently examine the record for arguable issues. Unlike under the *Anders* procedure, counsel following *Wende* neither explicitly states that his review has led him to conclude that an appeal would be frivolous (although that is considered implicit), nor requests leave to withdraw. Instead, he is silent on the merits of the case and expresses his availability to brief any issues on which the court might desire briefing.

The appellate court, upon receiving a " *Wende* brief," must "conduct a review of the entire record," regardless of whether the defendant has filed a *pro se* brief. *Id.* at 441–442. * * * * If, however, it finds an arguable (i.e., nonfrivolous) issue, it orders briefing on that issue. *Id.* at 442, n. 3.[1]

B

In 1990, a California state-court jury convicted respondent Lee Robbins of second-degree murder (for fatally shooting his former roommate) and of grand theft of an automobile (for stealing a truck that he used to flee the State after committing the murder). Robbins was sentenced to 17 years to life. He elected to represent himself at trial, but on appeal he received appointed counsel. His appointed counsel, concluding that an appeal would be frivolous, filed with the California Court of Appeal a brief that complied with the *Wende* procedure. Robbins also availed himself of his right under *Wende* to file a *pro se* supplemental brief, filing a brief in which he contended that there was insufficient evidence to support his conviction and that the prosecutor violated *Brady v. Maryland*, 373 U.S. 83 (1963), by failing to disclose exculpatory evidence.

---

[1] In addition to this double review and double determination of frivolity, California affords a third layer of review, through the California Appellate Projects. The appellate projects are under contract to the court; their contractual duties include review of the records to assist court-appointed counsel in identifying issues to brief. If the court-appointed counsel can find no meritorious issues to raise and decides to file a *Wende* brief, an appellate project staff attorney reviews the record again to determine whether a *Wende* brief is appropriate. Thus, by the time the *Wende* brief is filed in the Court of Appeal, the record in the case has been reviewed both by the court-appointed counsel (who is presumably well qualified to handle the case) and by an experienced attorney on the staff of the appellate project.

The California Court of Appeal, agreeing with counsel's assessment of the case, affirmed. The court explained that it had "examined the entire record" and had, as a result, concluded both that counsel had fully complied with his responsibilities under *Wende* and that "no arguable issues exist." The court added that the two issues that Robbins raised in his supplemental brief had no support in the record. The California Supreme Court denied Robbins's petition for review.

After exhausting state postconviction remedies, Robbins filed in the United States District Court for the Central District of California the instant petition for a writ of habeas corpus pursuant to 28 U.S.C. § 2254. Robbins renewed his *Brady* claim, argued that the state trial court had erred by not allowing him to withdraw his waiver of his right to trial counsel, and added nine other claims of trial error. In addition, and most importantly for present purposes, he claimed that he had been denied effective assistance of appellate counsel because his appellate counsel's *Wende* brief failed to comply with *Anders*. *Anders* set forth a procedure for an appellate counsel to follow in seeking permission to withdraw from the representation when he concludes that an appeal would be frivolous; that procedure includes the requirement that counsel file a brief "referring to anything in the record that might arguably support the appeal."

The District Court agreed with Robbins's last claim, concluding that there were at least two issues that, pursuant to *Anders*, counsel should have raised in his brief (in a *Wende* brief, as noted above, counsel is not required to raise issues): first, whether the prison law library was adequate for Robbins's needs in preparing his defense after he elected to dismiss his appointed counsel and proceed pro se at trial, and, second, whether the trial court erred in refusing to allow him to withdraw his waiver of counsel. The District Court did not attempt to determine the likelihood that either of these two issues would have prevailed in an appeal. Rather, it simply concluded that, in the language of the *Anders* procedure, these issues "might arguably" have "supported the appeal," and thus that Robbins's appellate counsel, by not including them in his brief, deviated from the procedure set forth in *Anders*. The court concluded that such a deviation amounted to deficient performance by counsel. In addition, rather than requiring Robbins to show that he suffered prejudice from this deficient performance, the District Court applied a presumption of prejudice. Thus, based simply on a finding that appellate counsel's brief was inadequate under *Anders*, the District Court ordered California to grant respondent a new appeal within 30 days or else release him from custody.

The United States Court of Appeals for the Ninth Circuit agreed with the District Court on the *Anders* issue. * * * *

II

A

In *Anders*, we reviewed an earlier California procedure for handling appeals by convicted indigents. Pursuant to that procedure, Anders's appointed appellate counsel had filed a letter stating that he had concluded that there was "no merit to the appeal." * * * *

We held that "California's action does not comport with fair procedure and lacks that equality that is required by the Fourteenth Amendment." * * * *

Having rejected the California procedure, we proceeded, in a final, separate section (§ III), to set out what would be an acceptable procedure for treating frivolous appeals:

> If counsel finds his case to be wholly frivolous, after a conscientious examination of it, he should so advise the court and request permission to withdraw. That request must, however, be accompanied by a brief referring to anything in the record that might arguably support the appeal. A copy of counsel's brief should be furnished the indigent and time allowed him to raise any points that he chooses; the court — not counsel — then proceeds, after a full examination of all the proceedings, to decide whether the case is wholly frivolous. If it so finds it may grant counsel's request to withdraw and dismiss the appeal insofar as federal requirements are concerned, or proceed to a decision on the merits, if state law so requires. On the other hand, it if finds any of the legal points arguable on their merits (and therefore not frivolous) it must, prior to decision, afford the indigent the assistance of counsel to argue the appeal.

We then concluded by explaining how this procedure would be better than the California one that we had found deficient. Among other things, we thought that it would "induce the court to pursue all the more vigorously its own review because of the ready references not only to the record but also to the legal authorities as furnished it by counsel."

B

The Ninth Circuit ruled that this final section of *Anders*, even though unnecessary to our holding in that case, was obligatory upon the States. We disagree. We have never so held; we read our precedents to suggest otherwise; and the Ninth Circuit's view runs contrary to our established practice of permitting the States, within the broad bounds of the Constitution, to experiment with solutions to difficult questions of policy.

In *McCoy v. Court of Appeals of Wis., Dist. 1*, 486 U.S. 429 (1988), we rejected a challenge to Wisconsin's variation on the *Anders* procedure. Wisconsin had departed from *Anders* by requiring *Anders* briefs to discuss why each issue raised lacked merit. The defendant argued that this rule was contrary to *Anders* and forced counsel to violate his ethical obligations to his client. We, however, emphasized that the right to appellate representation does not include a right to present frivolous arguments to the court, and, similarly, that an attorney is "under an ethical obligation to refuse to prosecute a frivolous appeal." *Anders*, we explained, merely aims to "assure the court that the indigent defendant's constitutional rights have not been violated." Because the Wisconsin procedure adequately provided such assurance, we found no constitutional violation, notwithstanding its variance from *Anders*. We did, in *McCoy*, describe the procedure at issue as going "one step further" than *Anders*, thus suggesting that *Anders* might set a mandatory minimum, but we think this description of the Wisconsin procedure questionable, since it provided less effective advocacy for an indigent — in at least one respect — than does the *Anders* procedure. The Wisconsin procedure, by providing for one-sided briefing by counsel against his own client's best claims, probably made a court more likely to rule against the indigent than if the court had simply received an *Anders* brief. * * * *

Any view of the procedure we described in the last section of *Anders* that converted it from a suggestion into a straitjacket would contravene our established practice, rooted in federalism, of allowing the States wide discretion, subject to the minimum requirements of the Fourteenth Amendment, to experiment with solutions to difficult problems of policy. * * * *

In short, it is more in keeping with our status as a court, and particularly with our status as a court in a federal system, to avoid imposing a single solution on the States from the top down. We should, and do, evaluate state procedures one at a time, as they come before us, while leaving the more challenging task of crafting appropriate procedures to the laboratory of the States in the first instance. We will not cavalierly impede the States' ability to serve as laboratories for testing solutions to novel legal problems. Accordingly, we hold that the *Anders* procedure is merely one method of satisfying the requirements of the Constitution for indigent criminal appeals. States may — and, we are confident, will — craft procedures that, in terms of policy, are superior to, or at least as good as, that in *Anders*. The Constitution erects no barrier to their doing so.

III

Having determined that California's *Wende* procedure is not unconstitutional merely because it diverges from the *Anders* procedure, we turn to consider the *Wende* procedure on its own merits. We think it clear that California's system does not violate the Fourteenth Amendment, for it provides a criminal appellant pursuing a first appeal as of right the minimum safeguards necessary to make that appeal adequate and effective.

A

The precise rationale for the *Griffin* and *Douglas* lines of cases has never been explicitly stated, some support being derived from the Equal Protection Clause of the Fourteenth Amendment and some from the Due Process Clause of that Amendment. But our case law reveals that, as a practical matter, the two clauses largely converge to require that a State's procedure "afford adequate and effective appellate review to indigent defendants," *Griffin*, 351 U.S. at 20. A State's procedure provides such review so long as it reasonably ensures that an indigent's appeal will be resolved in a way that is related to the merit of that appeal.

In determining whether a particular state procedure satisfies this standard, it is important to focus on the underlying goals that the procedure should serve — to ensure that those indigents whose appeals are not frivolous receive the counsel and merits brief required by *Douglas*, and also to enable the State to protect itself so that frivolous appeals are not subsidized and public moneys not needlessly spent. For although, under *Douglas*, indigents generally have a right to counsel on a first appeal as of right, it is equally true that this right does not include the right to bring a frivolous appeal and, concomitantly, does not include the right to counsel for bringing a frivolous appeal.[10] To put the point differently, an indigent defendant who

---

[10] This distinction gives meaning to our previous emphasis on an indigent appellant's right to "advocacy." Although an indigent whose appeal is frivolous has no right to have an advocate make his case to the appellate court, such an indigent does, in all cases, have the right to have an attorney, zealous for the indigent's interests, evaluate his case and attempt to discern nonfrivolous arguments.

has his appeal dismissed because it is frivolous has not been deprived of "a fair opportunity" to bring his appeal, for fairness does not require either counsel or a full appeal once it is properly determined that an appeal is frivolous. The obvious goal of *Anders* was to prevent this limitation on the right to appellate counsel from swallowing the right itself, and we do not retreat from that goal today.

B

We think the *Wende* procedure reasonably ensures that an indigent's appeal will be resolved in a way that is related to the merit of that appeal. Whatever its strengths or weaknesses as a matter of policy, we cannot say that it fails to afford indigents the adequate and effective appellate review that the Fourteenth Amendment requires. A comparison of the *Wende* procedure to the procedures evaluated in our chief cases in this area makes this evident.

The *Wende* procedure is undoubtedly far better than those procedures we have found inadequate. Although we did not, in *Anders*, explain in detail why the California procedure was inadequate under each of these precedents, a significant factor was that the old California procedure did not require either counsel or the court to determine that the appeal was frivolous; instead, the procedure required only that they determine that the defendant was unlikely to prevail on appeal. * * * *

An additional problem with the old California procedure was that it apparently permitted an appellate court to allow counsel to withdraw and thereafter to decide the appeal without appointing new counsel. * * * * Under *Wende*, by contrast, *Douglas* violations do not occur, both because counsel does not move to withdraw and because the court orders briefing if it finds arguable issues.

In *Anders*, we also disapproved the old California procedure because we thought that a one paragraph letter from counsel stating only his "bare conclusion" that the appeal had no merit was insufficient. It is unclear from our opinion in *Anders* how much our objection on this point was severable from our objection to the lack of a finding of frivolity. In any event, the *Wende* brief provides more than a one-paragraph "bare conclusion." Counsel's summary of the case's procedural and factual history, with citations of the record, both ensures that a trained legal eye has searched the record for arguable issues and assists the reviewing court in its own evaluation of the case.

Finally, an additional flaw with the procedures in [prior cases] was that there was only one tier of review. The *Wende* procedure, of course, does not suffer from this flaw, for it provides at least two tiers of review.

Not only does the *Wende* procedure far exceed those procedures that we have found invalid, but it is also at least comparable to those procedures that we have approved. Turning first to the procedure we set out in the final section of *Anders*, we note that it has, from the beginning, faced consistent and severe criticism. One of the most consistent criticisms is that *Anders* is in some tension both with counsel's ethical duty as an officer of the court (which requires him not to present frivolous arguments) and also with his duty to further his client's interests (which might not permit counsel to characterize his client's claims as frivolous).[11] Califor-

---

[11] As one former public defender has explained, "an attorney confronted with the *Anders* situation

nia, through the *Wende* procedure, has made a good-faith effort to mitigate this problem by not requiring the *Wende* brief to raise legal issues and by not requiring counsel to explicitly describe the case as frivolous.

Another criticism of the *Anders* procedure has been that it is incoherent and thus impossible to follow. Those making this criticism point to our language in *Anders* suggesting that an appeal could be both "wholly frivolous" and at the same time contain arguable issues, even though we also said that an issue that was arguable was "therefore not frivolous." In other words, the *Anders* procedure appears to adopt gradations of frivolity and to use two different meanings for the phrase "arguable issue." The *Wende* procedure attempts to resolve this problem as well, by drawing the line at frivolity and by defining arguable issues as those that are not frivolous.[13]

Finally, the *Wende* procedure appears to be, in some ways, better than the one we approved in *McCoy* and, in other ways, worse. On balance, we cannot say that the latter, assuming *arguendo* that they outweigh the former, do so sufficiently to make the *Wende* procedure unconstitutional. The Wisconsin procedure we evaluated in *McCoy*, which required counsel filing an *Anders* brief to explain why the issues he raised in his brief lacked merit, arguably exacerbated the ethical problem already present in the *Anders* procedure. The *Wende* procedure, as we have explained, attempts to mitigate that problem. Further, it appears that in the *McCoy* scheme counsel discussed — and the appellate court reviewed — only the parts of the record cited by counsel in support of the "arguable" issues he raised. The *Wende* procedure, by contrast, requires a more thorough treatment of the record by both counsel and court. On the other hand, the *McCoy* procedure, unlike the *Wende* procedure, does assist the reviewing court by directing it to particular legal issues; as to those issues, this is presumably a good thing. But it is also possible that bad judgment by the attorney in selecting the issues to raise might divert the court's attention from more meritorious, unmentioned, issues. This criticism is, of course, equally applicable to the *Anders* procedure. Moreover, as to the issues that counsel does raise in a *McCoy* brief, the one-sided briefing on why those issues are frivolous may predispose the court to reach the same conclusion. The *Wende* procedure reduces these risks, by omitting from the brief signals that may subtly undermine the independence and thoroughness of the second review of an indigent's case.

---

has to do something that the Code of Professional Responsibility describes as unethical; the only choice is as to which canon he or she prefers to violate." Pengilly, *Never Cry Anders: The Ethical Dilemma of Counsel Appointed to Pursue a Frivolous Criminal Appeal*, 9 Crim. Justice J. 45, 64 (1986).

[13] A further criticism of *Anders* has been that it is unjust. More particularly, critics have claimed that, in setting out the *Anders* procedure, we were oblivious to the problem of scarce resources (with regard to both counsel and courts) and, as a result, crafted a rule that diverts attention from meritorious appeals of indigents and ensures poor representation for all indigents. See, e.g., Pritchard, *Auctioning Justice: Legal and Market Mechanisms for Allocating Criminal Appellate Counsel*, 34 Am.Crim. L.Rev. 1161, 1167–1168 (1997) (*Anders* has created a "tragedy of the commons" that, "far from guaranteeing adequate appellate representation for all criminal defendants, instead ensures that indigent criminal defendants will receive mediocre appellate representation, whether their claims are good or bad"); Doherty, *Wolf! Wolf! — The Ramifications of Frivolous Appeals*, 59 J.Crim. L., C. & P.S. 1, 2 (1968) ("The people who will suffer the most are the indigent prisoners who have been unjustly convicted; they will languish in prison while lawyers devote time and energy to hopeless causes on a first come-first served basis.") We cannot say whether the *Wende* procedure is better or worse than the *Anders* procedure in this regard (although we are aware of policy-based arguments that it is worse as to appellate courts — Brief for Retired Justice Armand Arabian *et al.* as *amici curiae*), but it is clear that, to the extent this criticism has merit, our holding today that the *Anders* procedure is not exclusive will enable States to continue to experiment with solutions to this problem.

Our purpose is not to resolve any of these arguments. The Constitution does not resolve them, nor does it require us to do so. We address not what is prudent or appropriate, but only what is constitutionally compelled. It is enough to say that the *Wende* procedure, like the *Anders* and *McCoy* procedures, and unlike the ones in *Douglas* and [other prior cases], affords adequate and effective appellate review for criminal indigents. Thus, there was no constitutional violation in this case simply because the *Wende* procedure was used. * * * *

JUSTICE STEVENS, with whom JUSTICE GINSBURG joins, dissenting.

While I join Justice Souter's cogent dissent without qualification, I write separately to emphasize two points that are obscured by the Court's somewhat meandering explanation of its sharp departure from settled law.

First, despite its failure to say so directly, the Court has effectively overruled *Anders*. Second, its unexplained rejection of the reasoning underlying our decision in *McCoy* illustrates the extent of today's majority's disregard for accepted precedent.

To make my first point it is only necessary to quote the Court's new standard for determining whether a State's appellate procedure affords adequate review for indigent defendants: "A State's procedure provides such review so long as it reasonably ensures that an indigent's appeal will be resolved in a way that is related to the merit of that appeal."

The California procedure reviewed in *Anders* would easily have satisfied that standard. Yet the Court today accepts California's current procedure because it "requires both counsel and the court to find the appeal to be lacking in arguable issues." But in defense of its position in *Anders*, California relied heavily on those very same requirements, i.e., "the additional feature of the State's system where the court also reads the full record." Brief for Respondent in *Anders v. California*, pp. 30–31. Our *Anders* decision held, however, that this "additional feature" was insufficient to safeguard the indigent appellant's rights.

To make my second point I shall draw on my own experience as a practicing lawyer and as a judge. On a good many occasions I have found that the task of writing out the reasons that support an initial opinion on a question of law — whether for the purpose of giving advice to my client or for the purpose of explaining my vote as an appellate judge — leads to a conclusion that was not previously apparent. * * * *

In short, simply putting pen to paper can often shed new light on what may at first appear to be an open-and-shut issue. For this reason, the Court is quite wrong to say that requiring counsel to articulate reasons for its conclusion results in "less effective advocacy."

An appellate court that employed a law clerk to review the trial transcripts in all indigent appeals in search of arguable error could be reasonably sure that it had resolved all of those appeals "in a way that is related" to their merits. It would not, however, provide the indigent appellant with anything approaching representation by a paid attorney. Like California's so-called *Wende* procedure, it would violate the "principle of substantial equality" that was described in *Anders* and *McCoy* and has been a part of our law for decades.

Justice Souter, with whom Justices Stevens, Ginsburg, & Breyer join, dissenting:

A defendant's right to representation on appeal is limited by the prohibition against frivolous litigation, and I realize that when a lawyer's corresponding obligations are at odds with each other, there is no perfect place to draw the line between them. But because I believe the procedure adopted in *People v. Wende* fails to assure representation by counsel with the adversarial character demanded by the Constitution, I respectfully dissent.

I

Although the Sixth Amendment guarantees trial counsel to a felony defendant (see *Gideon v. Wainwright*, 372 U.S. 335 (1963)), the Constitution contains no similarly freestanding, unconditional right to counsel on appeal, there being no obligation to provide appellate review at all (see *Ross v. Moffitt*, 417 U.S. 600 (1974)). When a State elects to provide appellate review, however, the terms on which it does so are subject to constitutional notice. See, e.g., *Griffin v. Illinois*, 351 U.S. 12, 18 (1956). * * * *

Two services of appellate counsel are on point here. Appellate counsel examines the trial record with an advocate's eye, identifying and weighing potential issues for appeal. This is review not by a dispassionate legal mind but by a committed representative, pledged to his client's interests, primed to attack the conviction on any ground the record may reveal. If counsel's review reveals arguable trial error, he prepares and submits a brief on the merits and argues the appeal.

The right to the first of these services, a partisan scrutiny of the record and assessment of potential issues, goes to the irreducible core of the lawyer's obligation to a litigant in an adversary system, and we have consistently held it essential to substantial equality of representation by assigned counsel. The paramount importance of vigorous representation follows from the nature of our adversarial system of justice. The right is unqualified when a defendant has retained counsel, and I can imagine no reason that it should not be so when counsel has been appointed.

Because the right to the second service, merits briefing, is not similarly unqualified, however, the issue we address today arises. The limitation on the right to a merits brief is that no one has a right to a wholly frivolous appeal, against which the judicial system's first line of defense is its lawyers. Being officers of the court, members of the bar are bound not to clog the courts with frivolous motions or appeals, and this is of course true regardless of a lawyer's retained or appointed status in a given case. The problem to which *Anders* responds arises when counsel views his client's appeal as frivolous, leaving him duty barred from pressing it upon a court.

The rub is that although counsel may properly refuse to brief a frivolous issue and a court may just as properly deny leave to take a frivolous appeal, there needs to be some reasonable assurance that the lawyer has not relaxed his partisan instinct prior to refusing, in which case the court's review could never compensate for the lawyer's failure of advocacy. A simple statement by counsel that an appeal has no merit, coupled with an appellate court's endorsement of counsel's conclusion, gives no affirmative indication that anyone has sought out the appellant's best arguments or championed his cause to the degree contemplated by the adversary system. Nor do such conclusions acquire any implicit persuasiveness through exposure to an interested opponent's readiness to mount a challenge. The government is unlikely to dispute or even test counsel's evaluation; one does not berate an opponent for giving up. To guard against the possibility, then, that counsel has not done the advocate's work of looking hard for potential issues, there must be some prod to find any reclusive merit in an ostensibly unpromising case and some process to assess the lawyer's efforts after the fact. A judicial process that renders constitutional error invisible is, after all, itself an affront to the Constitution.

In *Anders*, we devised such a mechanism to ensure respect for an appellant's rights. A lawyer's request to withdraw on the ground that an appeal is frivolous "must be accompanied by a brief referring to anything in the record that might arguably support the appeal." This simply means that counsel must do his partisan best, short of calling black white, to flag the points that come closest to being appealable; the lawyer's job is to state the issues that give the defendant his best chances to prevail, even if the best comes up short under the rule against trifling with the court. "The court — not counsel —," we continued, "then proceeds, after a full examination of all the proceedings, to decide whether the case is wholly frivolous."

Anders thus contemplates two reviews of the record, each of a markedly different character. First comes review by the advocate, the defendant's interested representative. His job is to identify the best issues the partisan eye can spot. Then comes judicial review from a disinterested judge, who asks two questions: whether the lawyer really did function as a committed advocate, and whether he misjudged the legitimate appealability of any issue. In reviewing the advocate's work, the court is responsible for assuring that counsel has gone as far as advocacy will take him with the best issues undiscounted. We have repeatedly described the task of an appellate court in terms of this dual responsibility. "First, the court must satisfy itself that the attorney has provided the client with a diligent and thorough search of the record for any arguable claim that might support the client's appeal. Second, it must determine whether counsel has correctly concluded that the appeal is frivolous." *McCoy*, 486 U.S., at 442.

Griffin and *Anders* thus require significantly more than the abstract evaluation of the merits of conceivably appealable points. Without the assurance that assigned counsel has done his best as a partisan, his substantial equality to a lawyer retained at a defendant's expense cannot be assumed. And without the benefit of the lawyer's statement of strongest claims, the appellate panel cannot act as a reviewing court, but is relegated to an inquisitorial role.

It is owing to the importance of assuring that an adversarial, not an inquisitorial, system is at work that I disagree with the Court's statement today that our cases approve of any state procedure that "reasonably ensures that an indigent's appeal will be resolved in a way that is related to the merit of that appeal." A purely inquisitorial system could satisfy that criterion, and so could one that appoints counsel only if the appellate court deems it useful. But we have rejected the former and have explicitly held the latter unconstitutional (see *Douglas*, 372 U.S. at 355), the reason in each case being that the Constitution looks to the means as well as to the ends.

II

We have not held the details of *Anders* to be exclusive, but it does make sense to read the case as exemplifying what substantial equality requires on behalf of indigent appellants entitled to an advocate's review and to reasonable certainty that arguable issues will be briefed on their merits. With *Anders* thus as a benchmark, California's *Wende* procedure fails to measure up. Its primary failing is in permitting counsel to refrain as a matter of course from mentioning possibly arguable issues in a no-merit brief; its second deficiency is a correlative of the first, in obliging an appellate court to search the record for arguable issues without benefit of an issue-spotting, no-merit brief to review.

Although *Wende* assumes that counsel will act as an advocate, it fails to assure, or even promote, the partisan attention that the Constitution requires. While the lawyer must summarize the procedural and factual history of the case with citations to the record, nothing in the *Wende* scheme requires counsel to show affirmatively, subject to evaluation, that he has made the committed search for issues and the advocate's assessment of their merits that go to the heart of appellate representation in our adversary system. It begs the question to say that "counsel's inability to find any arguable issues may readily be inferred from his failure to raise any," and it misses the point to argue that the indigent appellant is adequately protected because the lawyer assigned to a case under California's assigned counsel scheme may not file a *Wende* brief without the approval of a supervisor. The point is the need for some affirmative and express indicator that an advocate has been at work, in the form of a product that an appellate court can specifically review. Thus *Anders* requires counsel to flag the best issues for the sake of keeping counsel on his toes and giving focus to judicial review of his judgment. *Wende* on the other hand requires no indication of conceivable issues and hence nothing specifically reviewable by a court bound to preserve the system's adversary character. *Wende* does no more to protect the indigent's right to advocacy than the no-merit letter condemned in *Anders*.

On like reasoning, *Wende* is deficient in relying on a judge's nonpartisan review to assure that a defendant suffers no prejudice at the hands of a lawyer who has failed to document his best effort at partisan review. Exactly because our system assumes that a lawyer committed to a client is the most dependable guardian of the client's interest, we have consistently rejected procedures leaving the determination of frivolousness to the court in the first instance, or to the court following a conclusory declaration by counsel, or to the court assisted by counsel in the role of *amicus curiae*. The defect in these procedures is their entire reliance on review by a detached magistrate who does not apply the partisan scrutiny in the first instance that defendants with paid lawyers get as a matter of course.

It goes without saying, too, that *Wende's* reliance on judges to start from scratch in seeking arguable issues adds substantially to the burden on the judicial shoulders. While I have no need to decide whether this drawback of the *Wende* scheme is of constitutional significance, it raises questions that certainly underscore the constitutional failing of relying on judicial scrutiny uninformed by counsel's partisan analysis. In an *amicus* brief filed in this case, 13 retired Justices of the Supreme Court or Courts of Appeal of California have pointed out the "risk that the review of the cold record under the *Wende* scheme will be more perfunctory without the issue-spotting guidance, and associated record citations, of counsel." Brief for Retired Justice Armand Arabian et al. as *amici curiae* 5. The *amici* have candidly represented that "when a California appellate court receives a *Wende* brief, it assigns the case to a staff attorney who prepares a memorandum analyzing all possible legal issues in the case. Typically, the staff attorney then makes an oral presentation to the appellate panel." When the responsibility of counsel is thrown onto the court, the court gives way to a staff attorney; it could not be clearer that *Wende* is seriously at odds with the respective obligations of counsel and the courts as contemplated by the Constitution.

Notes from Paula:

1. In *Turner v. State*, 818 So.2d 1186 (Miss. 2001), the court held that where appointed appellate counsel believes that the appeal has no merit, appellate counsel must: (1) determine that the defendant is "unlikely to prevail on appeal." *Robbins*, 528 U.S. at 279, (2) file a brief indicating that he scoured the record thoroughly and "referring to anything in the record that might arguably support the appeal." *Anders*, 386 U.S. at 744, and (3) advise client of his right to file a pro se supplemental brief. At this point, the appellate court shall then make its own independent review of the record, in the manner followed in all other cases.

2. In *State v. Korth*, 650 N.W.2d 528 (S.D. 2002), the court held:

> The Oregon Supreme Court, after doing a thorough review of *Anders* and its progeny, held that appointed counsel representing an indigent defendant need not motion to withdraw from a case, even if the requested appeal is entirely frivolous. *State v. Balfour*, 311 Or. 434 (1991). Subsequently, Oregon adopted appellate procedural rules providing direction for the representation of indigent defendants.

> For future appeals where appointed counsel is presented with an *Anders*-type case, we find that the Oregon procedure of including a "Section A" (issues the attorney believes are meritorious) and "Section B" (issues the attorney believes are frivolous, but briefed at the client's request) successfully strikes a balance between protecting a defendant's Sixth Amendment right to appellate counsel, protecting Fourteenth Amendment due process and equal protection rights and upholding the ethical rules by which attorneys must abide. This procedure reaches the main goal of ensuring the case is decided on the merits.

> Furthermore, the defendant is afforded: notice of appeal; a state-paid transcript; appointed counsel charged with conducting a good faith, professional, thorough review of the case as the client's advocate; appointed counsel raising all issues for review according to counsel's exercise of professional and ethical judgment in the client's best interest; an opportunity for the client to raise any issue, with legal advice from counsel, notwithstanding the professional and ethical judgment made by the counsel that defendant's arguments are frivolous; and a Court of Appeals decision made on the same basis as in any appeal.

> Therefore, we find the appropriate and effective way to process this issue involving an absolute right to appeal and the right to appointed counsel for the indigent is for the filing of the "Section A" and "Section B" appellate brief. The former should be designated by the attorney as attorney issues, and the latter should be designated as issues that the client

requested be submitted.

This process avoids the unnecessary step of deciding appointed defense counsel's motions to withdraw, and offers a procedure where defendants are provided an effective means for presenting their arguments. Furthermore, we are providing a means by which appointed defense counsel can assist their clients with their arguments without violating ethical rule 3.1, which prohibits the presentation of wholly frivolous arguments. By following the above procedure, the potential for role reversal between appointed counsel and judges is avoided, and we ensure that appeals will be considered on the merits.

Chapter 14

THE RIGHT TO EFFECTIVE ASSISTANCE OF COUNSEL

> In all criminal prosecutions, the accused shall enjoy the right . . . to have the Assistance of Counsel for his defence.
>
> *6th Amendment, U.S. Constitution*

In *Rothgery v. Gillespie County*, 128 S.Ct. 2578 (2008), the Supreme Court held that "a criminal defendant's initial appearance before a judicial officer, where he learns the charge against him and his liberty is subject to restriction, marks the start of adversary judicial proceedings that trigger attachment of the Sixth Amendment right to counsel."

But more than 90% of criminal defendants are indigent — they have no money to pay for a lawyer. The right to counsel granted to them by the 6th Amendment is meaningless unless some way is found to pay lawyers to represent them. In *Gideon v. Wainwright*, 372 U.S. 335 (1963), the Court held that the 6th Amendment Right-to-Counsel clause applies to the states through the Due Process clause of the 14th Amendment and that *the state* must provide an indigent felony defendant with a lawyer at trial.[1] After *Gideon*, the Court applied the right to counsel to any "critical stage" of a criminal case, which was deemed to include certain pre-trial proceedings (such as arraignments and preliminary hearings) and post-trial proceedings (such as appeals). The court also held that that this right to appointed counsel applies even to misdemeanor cases, where the defendant is sentenced to some jail time. *Argersinger v. Hamlin*, 407 U.S. 25 (1972); *Scott v. Illinois*, 440 U.S. 367 (1979).

Suppose the defendant doesn't want a lawyer, but prefers to represent himself. Most defendants don't know enough to do it well and are too emotionally involved to do it with the detachment a good lawyers need. (This is why even a lawyer who represents himself is said "to have a fool for a client".) Not only may the self-representing defendant hurt himself, but he will make the trial take longer and might even turn it into somewhat of a circus. For all these reasons, may the judge *force* him to take a lawyer? No, held the Supreme Court in *Faretta v. California*, 422 U.S. 806 (1975) — the 6th Amendment right to counsel includes the right of *self*-representation.

> To force a lawyer on a defendant can only lead him to believe that the law contrives against him. Moreover, it is not inconceivable that in some rare instances, the defendant might in fact present his case more effectively by conducting his own defense. Personal liberties are not rooted in the law of averages. The defendant, and not his lawyer or the State, will

---

[1] For the fascinating story behind this case, read Anthony Lewis, Gideon's Trumpet (1964).

bear the personal consequences of a conviction. It is the defendant, therefore, who must be free personally to decide whether in his particular case counsel is to his advantage.

The Court noted that a trial court may appoint "advisory counsel" for a defendant who insisted on representing himself — even over the defendant's objection. 422 U.S. at 834, fn. 46.

Most defendants, of course, do accept the State's offer of free lawyering services. But *what kind* of lawyering? This chapter will explore that question.

Problem 14

To: My law clerk

From: Fern Grotto, Esq.

Re: *State v. Fresco*

I am handling an appeal for Al Fresco. I'd like to argue that his conviction should be reversed because Fresco did not receive effective assistance of counsel.

Fresco and his co-defendant, Minnie Stroni, were charged with sale of cocaine. Since both were indigent, Judge Lockemup appointed lawyer Howard Howe to represent both of them.

Howe is a partner in Dewey, Suem, and Howe, a local law firm which mainly represents plaintiffs in personal injury suits, and also does some criminal defense work. The county pays appointed counsel an hourly rate which is about half of Howe's usual hourly rate in civil cases. Appointed counsel must submit time sheets to the county indicating hours worked on the case, and the county then pays counsel for a "reasonable" number of hours — which does not always include all hours on the time sheets.

Howe read the police report, written by Police Officer Peter Penn. Penn said that, while working undercover, he heard that cocaine was being sold at 456 Easy Street. At about 4:00 p.m. on a Friday afternoon, he went to 456 Easy Street and knocked on the door. Stroni opened the door, and Penn said he wanted to buy some cocaine. Stroni said, "Just a minute," and went inside. Then Fresco came to the door and sold Penn some cocaine for $50. Penn then arrested both Fresco and Stroni.

Howe interviewed Stroni, who said that she had no idea that Fresco was selling cocaine. She said that Penn did not tell her that he wanted to buy cocaine, but merely that he wanted to speak to Fresco. Stroni simply went and told Fresco that someone at the door wanted to see him.

Howe then interviewed Fresco, who said that he had been at a birthday party for his mother (Frieda) at his mother's house that day, with about 20 other people. When he returned home to 456 Easy Street, he saw Penn on the porch putting handcuffs on Stroni. Penn then arrested Fresco too. Fresco says he did not sell cocaine to Penn, and he has no idea what happened before he arrived, because he wasn't there.

At trial, Officer Penn testified to the events described in his police report. Howe cross-examined him, but failed to shake any of his testimony: Penn was sure as to the events described. Fresco and Stroni then testified as described above. Howe asked each of them questions on direct examination, of course. Both were cross-examined by the prosecutor, but not by Howe.

After they testified, Howe spoke to Fresco privately. Howe said he had spoken to about 5 people who were at the birthday party. All remembered seeing Fresco there, but none could remember seeing him leave. Howe believed that Fresco's mother would be the best witness, as she remembered talking to him at about 4:00, so Howe planned to call her as a witness. Fresco said, "Leave my mother out of this. She doesn't know about this case, and I don't want her to know. It will upset her, and she might think the charges about me are true. Besides, she doesn't like to talk in public, and I think she will be so nervous that the jury won't believe her." Howe said, "I talked to her about that, and I think she will be fine. My job is to get you off, if I can. I'm going to call her." Howe then called Frieda as a witness. She testified that Fresco was at her house until about 4:00 p.m. on the day of the arrests. On cross-examination by the prosecutor, however, she admitted that she didn't look at a clock when Fresco left, and he might have left as early as 3:30.

Howe did not call any other witnesses. Fresco tells me that his sister Felicia was at his mother's birthday party, and she definitely recalls seeing him leave at 4:30. Howe did not interview Felicia.

The jury deliberated for about an hour, and them came back with guilty verdicts against both Fresco and Stroni.

Fresco faced a possible sentence of one to five years. Howe asked for probation, as Fresco had no prior criminal record. At the sentencing hearing, Judge Lockemup said to Fresco:

> I have a policy I have followed for years. If a defendant chooses to take the stand and lie, I tend to give him a stiffer sentence. If you had simply pleaded not guilty and let the jury decide the case on the police officer's testimony, and you been found guilty, I might have granted you probation. But when you take the stand and tell a story totally different from the police officer's story and the jury finds you guilty, the jury has basically said you have lied under oath. I don't like perjury in my court. I think every criminal defense lawyer in this community knows my policy. Probation denied. The sentence is five years.

Fresco tells me that Howe never told him about Judge Lockemup's "policy." He also said that he works as an electrician, and he just got a notice from the State that is electrician's license has been revoked because he was convicted of a felony. He said that he didn't know this could happen, and Howe never told him.

Please read the attached cases and advise me as to what arguments I might make on appeal, and what chance of success I have.

HOLLOWAY v. ARKANSAS

United States Supreme Court
435 U.S. 475 (1978)

MR. CHIEF JUSTICE BURGER delivered the opinion of the Court.

Petitioners, codefendants at trial, made timely motions for appointment of separate counsel, based on the representations of their appointed counsel that, because of confidential information received from the codefendants, he was confronted with the risk of representing conflicting interests and could not, therefore, provide effective assistance for each client. We granted certiorari to decide whether petitioners were deprived of the effective assistance of counsel by the denial of those motions.

I

Early in the morning of June 1, 1975, three men entered a Little Rock, Ark., restaurant and robbed and terrorized the five employees of the restaurant. During the course of the robbery, one of the two female employees was raped once; the other, twice. The ensuing police investigation led to the arrests of the petitioners.

On July 29, 1975, the three defendants were each charged with one count of robbery and two counts of rape. On August 5, the trial court appointed Harold Hall, a public defender, to represent all three defendants. Petitioners were then arraigned and pleaded not guilty. Two days later, their cases were set for a consolidated trial to commence September 4.

On August 13, Hall moved the court to appoint separate counsel for each petitioner because "the defendants had stated to him that there is a possibility of a conflict of interest in each of their cases." After conducting a hearing on this motion, and on petitioners' motions for a severance, the court declined to appoint separate counsel. * * * *

Before trial, the same judge who later presided at petitioners' trial conducted a hearing to determine the admissibility of a confession purportedly made by petitioner Campbell to two police officers at the time of his arrest. The essence of the confession was that Campbell had entered the restaurant with his codefendants and had remained, armed with a rifle, one flight of stairs above the site of the robbery and rapes (apparently serving as a lookout), but had not taken part in the rapes. The trial judge ruled the confession admissible, but ordered deletion of the references to Campbell's codefendants. At trial one of the arresting officers testified to Campbell's confession.

On September 4, before the jury was empaneled, Hall renewed the motion for appointment of separate counsel "on the grounds that one or two of the defendants may testify and if they do, then I will not be able to cross-examine them because I have received confidential information from them." The court responded, "I don't know why you wouldn't," and again denied the motion. * * * *

The prosecution then proceeded to present its case. The manager of the restaurant identified petitioners Holloway and Campbell as two of the robbers. Another male employee identified Holloway and petitioner Welch. A third identified only Holloway. The victim of the single rape identified Holloway and Welch as two of the robbers, but was unable to identify the man who raped her. The victim of the double rape identified Holloway as the first rapist. She was unable to identify the second rapist, but identified Campbell as one of the robbers.

On the second day of trial, after the prosecution had rested its case, Hall advised the court that, against his recommendation, all three defendants had decided to testify. He then stated:

MR. HALL: Now, since I have been appointed, I had previously filed a motion asking the Court to appoint a separate attorney for each defendant because of a possible conflict of interest. This conflict will probably be now coming up since each one of them wants to testify.

THE COURT: That's all right; let them testify. There is no conflict of interest. Every time I try more than one person in this court, each one blames it on the other one.

MR. HALL: I have talked to each one of these defendants, and I have talked to them individually, not collectively.

THE COURT: Now talk to them collectively.

The court then indicated satisfaction that each petitioner understood the nature and consequences of his right to testify on his own behalf, whereupon Hall observed:

I am in a position now where I am more or less muzzled as to any cross-examination.

THE COURT: You have no right to cross-examine your own witness.

MR. HALL: Or to examine them.

THE COURT: You have a right to examine them, but have no right to cross-examine them. The prosecuting attorney does that.

MR. HALL: If one defendant takes the stand, somebody needs to protect the other two's interest while that one is testifying, and I can't do that since I have talked to each one individually.

THE COURT: Well, you have talked to them, I assume, individually and collectively, too. They all say they want to testify. I think it's perfectly alright for them to testify if they want to, or not. It's their business. Each defendant said he wants to testify, and there will be no cross-examination of these witnesses, just a direct examination by you.

MR. HALL: Your Honor, I can't even put them on direct examination because if I ask them —

THE COURT: You can just put them on the stand and tell the Court that you have advised them of their rights and they want to testify; then you tell the man to go ahead and relate what he wants to. That's all you need to do.[4]

---

[4] The record reveals that both the trial court and defense counsel were alert to defense counsel's obligation to avoid assisting in the presentation of what counsel had reason to believe was false testimony, or, at least, testimony contrary to the version of facts given to him earlier and in confidence.

Holloway then took the stand on his own behalf, testifying that during the time described as the time of the robbery he was at his brother's home. His brother had previously given similar testimony. When Welch took the witness stand, the record shows Hall advised him, as he had Holloway, that "I cannot ask you any questions that might tend to incriminate any one of the three of you. Now, the only thing I can say is tell these ladies and gentlemen of the jury what you know about this case." Welch responded that he did not "have any kind of speech ready for the jury or anything. I thought I was going to be questioned." When Welch denied, from the witness stand, that he was at the restaurant the night of the robbery, Holloway interrupted, asking:

Your Honor, are we allowed to make an objection?

THE COURT: No, sir. Your counsel will take care of any objections.

MR. HALL: Your Honor, that is what I am trying to say. I can't cross-examine them.

THE COURT: You proceed like I tell you to, Mr. Hall. You have no right to cross-examine your own witnesses anyhow.

Welch proceeded with his unguided direct testimony, denying any involvement in the crime and stating that he was at his home at the time it occurred. Campbell gave similar testimony when he took the stand. He also denied making any confession to the arresting officers.

The jury rejected the versions of events presented by the three defendants and the alibi witness, and returned guilty verdicts on all counts. On appeal to the Arkansas Supreme Court, petitioners raised the claim that their representation by a single appointed attorney, over their objection, violated federal constitutional guarantees of effective assistance of counsel. In resolving this issue, the court relied on what it characterized as the majority rule: "The record must show some material basis for an alleged conflict of interest, before reversible error occurs in single representation of co-defendants." Turning to the record in the case, the court observed that Hall had failed to outline to the trial court both the nature of the confidential information received from his clients and the manner in which knowledge of that information created conflicting loyalties. Because none of the petitioners had incriminated codefendants while testifying, the court concluded that the record demonstrated no actual conflict of interests or prejudice to the petitioners, and therefore affirmed.

II

More than 35 years ago, in *Glasser v. United States*, 315 U.S. 60 (1942), this Court held that, by requiring an attorney to represent two codefendants whose interests were in conflict, the District Court had denied one of the defendants his Sixth Amendment right to the effective assistance of counsel. In that case, the Government tried five codefendants in a joint trial for conspiracy to defraud the United States. Two of the defendants, Glasser and Kretske, were represented initially by separate counsel. On the second day of trial, however, Kretske became dissatisfied with his attorney and dismissed him. The District Judge thereupon asked Glasser's attorney, Stewart, if he would also represent Kretske. Stewart responded by noting a possible conflict of interests: his representation of both Glasser and Kretske might lead the jury to link the two men together. Glasser also made known that he objected to the proposal. The District Court nevertheless appointed Stewart, who continued as Glasser's retained counsel, to represent Kretske. Both men were convicted.

Glasser contended in this Court that Stewart's representation at trial was ineffective because of a conflict between the interests of his two clients. This Court held that "the 'Assistance of Counsel' guaranteed by the Sixth Amendment contemplates that such assistance be untrammeled and unimpaired by a court order requiring that one lawyer should simultaneously represent conflicting interests." *Id.* at 70. The record disclosed that Stewart failed to cross-examine a Government witness whose testimony linked Glasser with the conspiracy and failed to object to the admission of arguably inadmissible evidence. This failure was viewed by the Court as a result of Stewart's desire to protect Kretske's interests, and was thus "indicative of Stewart's struggle to serve two masters." *Id.* at 75. After identifying this conflict of interests, the Court declined to inquire whether the prejudice flowing from it was harmless and instead ordered Glasser's conviction reversed. Kretske's conviction, however, was affirmed.

One principle applicable here emerges from *Glasser* without ambiguity. Requiring or permitting a single attorney to represent codefendants, often referred to as joint representation, is not per se violative of constitutional guarantees of effective assistance of counsel. This principle recognizes that in some cases multiple defendants can appropriately be represented by one attorney; indeed, in some cases, certain advantages might accrue from joint representation. In Mr. Justice Frankfurter's view: "Joint representation is a means of insuring against reciprocal recrimination. A common defense often gives strength against a common attack." *Glasser v. United States, supra,* at 92 (dissenting opinion).[5]

Since *Glasser* was decided, however, the courts have taken divergent approaches to two issues commonly raised in challenges to joint representation where — unlike this case — trial counsel did nothing to advise the trial court of the actuality or possibility of a conflict between his several clients' interests. First, appellate courts have differed on how strong a showing of conflict must be made, or how certain the reviewing court must be that the asserted conflict existed, before it will conclude that the defendants were deprived of their right to the effective assistance of counsel. Second, courts have differed with respect to the scope and nature of the affirmative duty of the trial judge to assure that criminal defendants are not deprived of their right to the effective assistance of counsel by joint representation of conflicting interests.[6]

We need not resolve these two issues in this case, however. Here trial counsel, by the pretrial motions of August 13 and September 4 and by his accompanying representations, made as an officer of the court, focused explicitly on the probable risk of a conflict of interests. The judge then failed either to appoint separate counsel or to take adequate steps to ascertain whether the risk was too remote to

---

[5] By inquiring in *Glasser* whether there had been a waiver, the Court also confirmed that a defendant may waive his right to the assistance of an attorney unhindered by a conflict of interests. In this case, however, Arkansas does not contend that petitioners waived that right.

[6] See ABA Project on Standards Relating to the Administration of Criminal Justice, *The Function of the Trial Judge* § 3.4(b) (1974): "Whenever two or more defendants who have been jointly charged, or whose cases have been consolidated, are represented by the same attorney, the trial judge should inquire into potential conflicts which may jeopardize the right of each defendant to the fidelity of his counsel."

warrant separate counsel. * * * * We hold that the failure, in the face of the representations made by counsel weeks before trial and again before the jury was empaneled, deprived petitioners of the guarantee of "assistance of counsel." This conclusion is supported by the Court's reasoning in *Glasser*:

> Upon the trial judge rests the duty of seeing that the trial is conducted with solicitude for the essential rights of the accused. The trial court should protect the right of an accused to have the assistance of counsel. Of equal importance with the duty of the court to see that an accused has the assistance of counsel is its duty to refrain from embarrassing counsel in the defense of an accused by *insisting, or indeed, even suggesting, that counsel undertake to concurrently represent interests which might diverge from those of his first client, when the possibility of that divergence is brought home to the court.* [315 U.S. at 71 (emphasis added)]

This reasoning has direct applicability in this case where the "possibility of (petitioners') inconsistent interests" was "brought home to the court" by formal objections, motions, and defense counsel's representations. It is arguable, perhaps, that defense counsel might have presented the requests for appointment of separate counsel more vigorously and in greater detail. As to the former, however, the trial court's responses hardly encouraged pursuit of the separate-counsel claim; and as to presenting the basis for that claim in more detail, defense counsel was confronted with a risk of violating, by more disclosure, his duty of confidentiality to his clients.

Additionally, since the decision in *Glasser*, most courts have held that an attorney's request for the appointment of separate counsel, based on his representations as an officer of the court regarding a conflict of interests, should be granted. See, e. g., *Shuttle v. Smith*, 296 F.Supp. 1315 (Vt.1969). In so holding, the courts have acknowledged and given effect to several interrelated considerations. An attorney representing two defendants in a criminal matter is in the best position professionally and ethically to determine when a conflict of interest exists or will probably develop in the course of a trial. Second, defense attorneys have the obligation, upon discovering a conflict of interests, to advise the court at once of the problem.[8] Finally, attorneys are officers of the court, and when they address the judge solemnly upon a matter before the court, their declarations are virtually made under oath. * * * * We find these considerations persuasive.

The State argues, however, that to credit Hall's representations to the trial court would be tantamount to transferring to defense counsel the authority of the trial judge to rule on the existence or risk of a conflict and to appoint separate counsel. In the State's view, the ultimate decision on those matters must remain with the trial judge; otherwise unscrupulous defense attorneys might abuse their "author-

---

[8] The American Bar Association in its Standards Relating to the Administration of Criminal Justice, *The Defense Function* § 3.5(b) (1974) cautions:

> Except for preliminary matters such as initial hearings or applications for bail, a lawyer or lawyers who are associated in practice should not undertake to defend more than one defendant in the same criminal case if the duty to one of the defendants may conflict with the duty to another. The potential for conflict of interest in representing multiple defendants is so grave that ordinarily a lawyer should decline to act for more than one of several co-defendants except in unusual situations when, after careful investigation, it is clear that no conflict is likely to develop and when the several defendants give an informed consent to such multiple representation.

ity," presumably for purposes of delay or obstruction of the orderly conduct of the trial.[10]

The State has an obvious interest in avoiding such abuses. But our holding does not undermine that interest. When an untimely motion for separate counsel is made for dilatory purposes, our holding does not impair the trial court's ability to deal with counsel who resort to such tactics. Nor does our holding preclude a trial court from exploring the adequacy of the basis of defense counsel's representations regarding a conflict of interests without improperly requiring disclosure of the confidential communications of the client.[11] In this case the trial court simply failed to take adequate steps in response to the repeated motions, objections, and representations made to it, and no prospect of dilatory practices was present to justify that failure.

III

The issue remains whether the error committed at petitioners' trial requires reversal of their convictions. It has generally been assumed that *Glasser* requires reversal, even in the absence of a showing of specific prejudice to the complaining codefendant, whenever a trial court improperly permits or requires joint representation. Some courts and commentators have argued, however, that appellate courts should not reverse automatically in such cases, but rather should affirm unless the defendant can demonstrate prejudice. See, e.g., *United States v. Woods*, 544 F.2d 242 (CA6 1976).

This Court has concluded that the assistance of counsel is among those "constitutional rights so basic to a fair trial that their infraction can never be treated as harmless error." *Chapman v. California*, 386 U.S. 18, 23. Accordingly, when a defendant is deprived of the presence and assistance of his attorney, either throughout the prosecution or during a critical stage in, at least, the prosecution of a capital offense, reversal is automatic. *Gideon v. Wainwright*, 372 U.S. 335 (1963).

That an attorney representing multiple defendants with conflicting interests is physically present at pretrial proceedings, during trial, and at sentencing does not warrant departure from this general rule. Joint representation of conflicting interests is suspect because of what it tends to prevent the attorney from doing. For example, in this case it may well have precluded defense counsel for Campbell from exploring possible plea negotiations and the possibility of an agreement to testify for the prosecution, provided a lesser charge or a favorable sentencing recommendation would be acceptable. Generally speaking, a conflict may also prevent an attorney from challenging the admission of evidence prejudicial to one client but perhaps favorable to another, or from arguing at the sentencing hearing the relative involvement and culpability of his clients in order to minimize the culpability of one by emphasizing that of another. Examples can be readily multiplied. The mere physical presence of an attorney does not fulfill the Sixth Amendment guarantee

---

[10] Such risks are undoubtedly present; they are inherent in the adversary system. But courts have abundant power to deal with attorneys who misrepresent facts.

[11] This case does not require an inquiry into the extent of a court's power to compel an attorney to disclose confidential communications that he concludes would be damaging to his client. *Cf.* ABA Code of Professional Responsibility, DR 4-101(C)(2) (1969). Such compelled disclosure creates significant risks of unfair prejudice, especially when the disclosure is to a judge who may be called upon later to impose sentences on the attorney's clients.

when the advocate's conflicting obligations have effectively sealed his lips on crucial matters.

Finally, a rule requiring a defendant to show that a conflict of interests — which he and his counsel tried to avoid by timely objections to the joint representation — prejudiced him in some specific fashion would not be susceptible of intelligent, evenhanded application. In the normal case where a harmless-error rule is applied, the error occurs at trial and its scope is readily identifiable. Accordingly, the reviewing court can undertake with some confidence its relatively narrow task of assessing the likelihood that the error materially affected the deliberations of the jury. But in a case of joint representation of conflicting interests the evil — it bears repeating — is in what the advocate finds himself compelled to refrain from doing, not only at trial but also as to possible pretrial plea negotiations and in the sentencing process. It may be possible in some cases to identify from the record the prejudice resulting from an attorney's failure to undertake certain trial tasks, but even with a record of the sentencing hearing available it would be difficult to judge intelligently the impact of a conflict on the attorney's representation of a client. And to assess the impact of a conflict of interests on the attorney's options, tactics, and decisions in plea negotiations would be virtually impossible. Thus, an inquiry into a claim of harmless error here would require, unlike most cases, unguided speculation.

Accordingly, we reverse and remand for further proceedings not inconsistent with this opinion.

Mr. Justice Powell with whom Mr. Justice Blackmun and Mr. Justice Rehnquist join, dissenting.

* * * *

Recognition of the limits of this Court's role in adding protective layers to the requirements of the Constitution does not detract from the Sixth Amendment obligation to provide separate counsel upon a showing of reasonable probability of need. In my view, a proper accommodation of the interests of defendants in securing effective assistance of counsel and that of the State in avoiding the delay, potential for disruption, and costs inherent in the appointment of multiple counsel,[2] can be achieved by means which sweep less broadly than the approach taken by the Court. I would follow the lead of the several Courts of Appeals that have recognized the trial court's duty of inquiry in joint representation cases without minimizing the constitutional predicate of "conflicting interests."* * * *

Ordinarily defense counsel has the obligation to raise objections to joint representation as early as possible before the commencement of the trial. * * * * When such a motion is made, supported by a satisfactory proffer, the trial court is under a duty to conduct "the most careful inquiry to satisfy itself that no conflict of interest would be likely to result and that the parties involved had no valid

---

[2] Each addition of a lawyer in the trial of multiple defendants presents increased opportunities for delay in setting the trial date, in disposing of pretrial motions, in selecting the jury, and in the conduct of the trial itself. Additional lawyers also may tend to enhance the possibility of trial errors. Moreover, in light of professional canons of ethics (cf. ABA Code of Professional Responsibility, DR 5-105(D) (1969)), a rule requiring separate counsel virtually upon demand may disrupt the operation of public defender offices.

objection." *United States v. DeBerry*, 487 F.2d 448, 453 (CA2 1973). At that hearing, the burden is on defense counsel, because his clients are in possession of the relevant facts, to make a showing of a reasonable likelihood of conflict or prejudice. Upon such a showing, separate counsel should be appointed. * * * *

Since the trial judge in this case failed to inquire into the substantiality of defense counsel's representations of September 4, 1975, the burden shifted to the State to establish the improbability of conflict or prejudice. I agree that the State's burden is not met simply by the assertion that the defenses of petitioners were not mutually inconsistent, for that is not an infrequent consequence of improper joint representation. Nevertheless, the record must offer some basis for a reasonable inference that "conflicting interests" hampered a potentially effective defense. Because the State has demonstrated that such a basis cannot be found in the record of this case,[5] I would affirm the judgment of the Supreme Court of Arkansas.

Notes from Fern:

1. What exactly *was* the conflict here? Why did lawyer Hall *need* to cross-examine Welch, and why *couldn't* he do so effectively?

2. In footnote 5 of Justice Powell's dissent, he presents some interesting speculation regarding the merits of the various defenses. Who probably knows more about this: Justice Powell or lawyer Hall?

3. The Court holds that the trial court failed "to take adequate steps to ascertain whether the risk was too remote to warrant separate counsel." What "steps" *could* the trial court have taken to ascertain this risk — without intruding on the confidentiality of the attorney-client privilege?

4. Normally, an appellate court will reverse a trial court judgment only if the trial court's error was *prejudicial* to the outcome of the case. Why did the Court in *Holloway* create an exception to this rule?

5. **Might a defense lawyer have a conflict with another client who is *not* being prosecuted?**

In *Lettley v. State*, 746 A.2d 392 (Md.Ct.App. 2000), Lettley was charged with attempted murder of Smith. His attorney moved to withdraw, telling the court that she represented another client (whom she did not name) who had admitted to her

---

[5] It is unlikely that separate counsel would have been able to develop an independent defense in this case, because of the degree of overlap in the identification testimony by the State's witnesses and because of the consistency of the alibis advanced by petitioners. Campbell and Welch, who are half brothers, both used the same alibi. Since Campbell was not identified as an actual participant in the rapes, it might be argued that separate counsel would have encouraged him to endorse his earlier confession in an effort to show that he was less culpable than his two codefendants. But, given his common alibi with Welch, Campbell would have found it difficult to extricate himself from his half brother's cause. In any event, such an argument would have been an appeal to jury nullification because, as the court below noted, Campbell's denial of direct involvement in the rapes "had no effect on his guilt as a principal." Conceivably Holloway, who gave an independent alibi, might have wished to argue that while the State had apprehended two of the real culprits, his arrest was due to a mistaken identification. It is most unlikely that separate counsel would have succeeded on such a tack because each witness who identified Holloway also identified one of the other two codefendants. Moreover, petitioners do not argue in this Court that joint representation impeded effective cross-examination of the State's witnesses. In sum, this is not a case where an inquiry into the possibility of "conflicting interests" reasonably might have revealed a basis for separate representation.

that he — and not Lettley — had shot Smith.

> In response to the court's questions, counsel told the court that the confessing client did not look like Appellant, although they had features in common. She noted that, but for the conflict, there were various things she could have done in Lettley's defense, but as a result of the conflict, she was unable to do so. As examples, she noted that she could have presented the information to the State's Attorney's Office and requested they investigate the other person; or she could have encouraged Lettley to go to the police and have the other person investigated. At trial, during cross-examination of the witnesses, she might present the witnesses with a photograph of the other person and ask them to identify that person as the shooter.

The trial court denied the motion to withdraw, because (1) as counsel was ethically barred from using the other client's admission and no other attorney would have access to that information, Lettley would be no worse off by keeping present counsel, (2) the judge had no reason to believe that the other client was telling the truth, and (3) allowing withdrawal would be an "open invitation" to defendants to delay trials by having someone contact their lawyers and say he did it. But the appellate court reversed:

> We believe that the trial court's decision to require counsel's continued representation was improper. The record is clear that there was indeed an actual conflict of interest which endangered Appellant's right to undivided loyalty and assistance. In order to properly defend Appellant counsel had, by implication, to incriminate her other client.

> Although dual representation in a criminal case is not *per se* an actual conflict of interest, defense counsel represented two clients with adverse interests. Counsel had privileged information from one client that was certainly relevant to cross examination of witnesses in Lettley's case, but she could not use that information because to use it would breach her ethical obligation to maintain the confidence of another client. If counsel does not use the information in cross-examining witnesses at Lettley's trial, she violates her duty to represent her client zealously. The interests of the confessing client and Lettley are in conflict. An actual conflict is evidenced by a tie with either a person or entity which would benefit from an unfavorable verdict for the defendant.

> The State argues, and the trial judge ruled, that because counsel was ethically forbidden to use the confessing client's confidential information in defense of Appellant, and because no other lawyer would have had access to that confidential information, there was no conflict of interest. We disagree. The conflict is inherent in the divided loyalties. It mattered little that new counsel would not be privy to the confidential information known to Appellant's counsel; a conflict nonetheless existed.

See also *Daniels v. State*, 17 P.3d 75 (Alaska Ct.App. 2001).

6. Suppose the defense counsel *does not raise the issue* of conflict.

In *Holloway*, the defense attorney raised the issue of conflict. Suppose he doesn't. How is the judge supposed to know whether a conflict exists, given the fact that the judge knows much less than the lawyer does about whether the defenses conflict? In *Cuyler v. Sullivan*, 446 U.S. 335 (1980), the Court held: "Unless the trial court knows or should know that a particular conflict exists, the court need not initiate an inquiry." But even if the trial judge does not commit error, what about the defense attorney? Is there some question about the *competence* of a defense lawyer who fails to raise the question of conflict when it should be raised?

Does the *prosecutor* have standing to move to disqualify defense counsel due to a conflict? Yes, held the court in *State ex rel. Blake v. Hatcher*, 624 S.E.2d 844 (W.Va. 2005), because of the government's "interest in the fairness and integrity of criminal trials."

7. Might a conflict of interest arise where counsel *plea bargains*?

In *Mosier v. Murphy*, 790 F.2d 62 (10th Cir.1986), Mosier, his wife Denise, and his mother-in-law Wanda were all charged with first degree murder. All three retained attorney Farrar to represent them. During Mosier's trial, the judge indicated that a death penalty was very unlikely. Mosier then agreed to a plea bargain whereby he would receive a life sentence and the charges against Denise and Wanda would be dismissed. Mosier later sought habeas corpus relief, arguing ineffective assistance of counsel, in that Farrar had a conflict of interest: under the plea bargain, Denise and Wanda would benefit from Mosier's plea of guilty. The court disagreed, noting that Farrar went to great lengths to protect Mosier's rights:

> John Mosier was tried separately from his putative co-defendants, Denise Mosier and Wanda Cable. There is no indication that attorney Farrar presented a defense which was inconsistent with the innocence of his wife and mother-in-law. And, just as the Supreme Court in *Cuyler v. Sullivan*, 446 U.S. 335, was impressed with the apparent willingness of Sullivan's attorney to call witnesses who might later be called in the co-defendants' trials, Wanda Cable was called by attorney Farrar as a witness for John Mosier. Indeed, the trial court judge was impressed enough with the defense that when taking Mr. Mosier's plea he commented that Mr. Farrar's representation at trial was not only adequate but very effective. Lastly, as in *Cuyler v. Sullivan*, there was no objection by anyone at trial to the multiple representation. This is particularly probative in light of the Court's acknowledgment in *Cuyler v. Sullivan* that the trial court must necessarily rely in large measure upon the good faith and good judgment of defense counsel.

8. In *Winkler v. Keane*, 7 F.3d 304 (2nd Cir.1993), Winkler was charged with murder. He agreed to pay his lawyer $25,000 if he was acquitted or found not guilty by reason of insanity. After trial and conviction, he petitioned for habeas corpus. The court held that the contingency fee agreement created an actual conflict of interest, because "trial counsel had a disincentive to seek a plea agreement, or to put forth mitigating defenses that would result in conviction of a lesser included offense." The court nevertheless held that the habeas petition was properly denied, because Winkler failed to show prejudice, having refused to plea bargain or submit evidence of lesser included offenses.

9. Suppose defense counsel is paid by someone other than the defendant.

In *Quintero v. U.S.*, 33 F.3d 1133 (9th Cir.1994), Quintero was convicted of possession with intent to distribute cocaine. He petitioned for a writ of *habeas corpus*, alleging that his trial lawyer "was paid by an unknown third party," and "neither he nor his family retained his counsel and that the attorney herself would not, or could not, identify the person who retained her." The court held that Quintero's allegations, if true, would entitle him to the writ:

> In *Wood v. Georgia*, 450 U.S. 261 (1981), the Supreme Court noted that there are inherent dangers that arise when a criminal defendant is represented by a lawyer hired and paid by a third party, particularly when the third party is the operator of the alleged criminal enterprise. One risk is that the lawyer will prevent his client from obtaining leniency by preventing the client from offering testimony against his former employer or from taking other actions contrary to the employer's interest. * * * *
>
> A drug conspiracy case involving large quantities of cocaine, fees paid by unknown third parties, and the potential for unindicted co-conspirators may be sufficient to demonstrate active representation of conflicting interests. * * * *
>
> Quintero contends that counsel's urging Quintero to reject the plea agreement evidenced that the conflict of interest affected counsel's performance. This contention has sufficient merit to warrant an evidentiary hearing.
>
> "In a case of joint representation of conflicting interests the evil is in what the advocate finds himself compelled to refrain from doing, not only at trial but also as to pretrial plea negotiations." *Holloway v. Arkansas*, 435 U.S. 475, 490 (1978). "One risk is that the lawyer will prevent his client from obtaining leniency by preventing the client from offering testimony against his former employer or from taking other actions contrary to the employer's interests." *Wood*, 450 U.S. at 269.
>
> In this case, the plea bargain may have been in Quintero's best interest. He claims that the government offered to recommend a 10 year sentence in exchange for a guilty plea. However, if the third party paying for Quintero's attorney was involved in the narcotics transaction, Quintero's guilty plea and cooperation with the government could have implicated that person. If that is the case, counsel's advice to reject a plea agreement could have been motivated by a desire to keep Quintero from implicating the fee payer. Quintero claims that the attorney stated, "I've never worked, and will not work, for a 'snitch.' Am I working for one now?" Such a comment, if true, suggests that Quintero did not in fact have the undivided loyalty of counsel which is "perhaps the most basic of counsel's duties.

10. *Appellate* lawyers' conflicts of interest.

Suppose the lawyer who represented defendant at trial also represents him on appeal, and his client urges him to argue on appeal that he had ineffective assistance of counsel at trial. If the lawyer believes that the issue has no merit, should he (1) make the argument anyway, (2) not make the argument, or (3) seek to withdraw?

In *People v. Bailey*, 9 Cal.App.4th 1252 (1992), Bailey was convicted of sale of cocaine. He appealed, claiming that his trial counsel was ineffective in failing to object to certain evidence. His trial counsel was appointed to represent him in the appeal. The court held that this was improper:

> We believe that there is an inherent conflict when appointed trial counsel in a criminal case is also appointed to act as counsel on appeal. We

therefore discourage the practice of allowing such appointments even when, as here, the client signs a declaration under penalty of perjury that he does not believe "there is any reason for another lawyer to review the records of my case regarding potential issues of ineffective assistance of counsel. I do not believe that such issues exist and I make no such request." We know, of course, that defendant later specifically requested his counsel raise such issues on appeal. In fact, defendant may now be estopped from raising such issues because of his declaration. Such manipulation by a defendant who, from the moment the trial began, attempted to use the issue of the adequacy of counsel as a ploy to stall proceedings will undoubtedly result in further proceedings on appeal to keep the "game" going.

The American Bar Association's Model Rules of Professional Conduct, rule 1.7(b) provides: "A lawyer shall not represent a client if the representation of that client may be materially limited by the lawyer's responsibility to another client or to a third person, or by the lawyer's own interests." And, as the comment points out, "The critical questions are the likelihood that a conflict will eventuate and, if it does, whether it will materially interfere with the lawyer's independent professional judgment in considering alternatives or foreclose courses of action that reasonably should be pursued on behalf of the client."

The result is often that which is evidenced here; namely, bogus issues are raised without much analysis of whether representation was deficient. Counsel is in the untenable position of urging his own incompetency. The issue of effective assistance of counsel is thus left open to further attack without a final resolution. We therefore disapprove appointed trial counsel being appointed to represent a defendant on appeal.

Similarly, in *U.S. v. Del Muro*, 87 F.3d 1078 (9th Cir.1996), Del Muro was convicted of immigration violations. He moved for a new trial, claiming that his trial counsel was ineffective, in failing to interview certain witnesses. The trial court refused to appoint new counsel to argue the motion for new trial. The Court of Appeal reversed:

When Del Muro's allegedly incompetent trial attorney was compelled to produce new evidence and examine witnesses to prove his services to the defendant were ineffective, he was burdened with a strong disincentive to engage in vigorous argument and examination, or to communicate candidly with his client. The conflict was not only actual, but likely to affect counsel's performance.

In *Williams v. State*, 805 A.2d 880 (Del. 2002), Williams's appellate attorney (O'Donnell) had recently represented another client (Garden) on appeal, arguing that the trial court had erred in failing to give great weight to a jury's recommendation *against* imposition of the death penalty. In Williams's appeal, the lawyer wanted to argue that the trial court erred in concluding that it must give great weight to the jury's recommendation *for* imposition of the death penalty.

O'Donnell is concerned that his representation of both clients on this issue will create the risk that an unfavorable precedent will be created for one client or the other. O'Donnell also is concerned that it may invite questions about his credibility with this Court and his clients' perception of his loyalty to each of them. The State agrees that O'Donnell has a conflict of interest that disqualifies him from representing Williams in this appeal.

The potential conflict identified by O'Donnell is termed a "positional" conflict of interest. It arises when two or more clients have opposing interests in unrelated matters. Positional conflicts of interests are addressed indirectly in Delaware Lawyers' Rules of Professional Conduct Rule 1.7. Rule 1.7(b) provides in part that a "lawyer shall not represent a client if the representation of that client may be materially limited by the lawyer's responsibility to another client." The Comment to Rule 1.7 states that:

> A lawyer may represent parties having antagonistic positions on a legal question that has arisen in different cases, unless representation of either client would be adversely affected. Thus it is ordinarily not improper to assert such positions in cases pending in different trial courts, *but it may be improper to do so in cases pending at the same time in an appellate court.*

The distinction between presenting conflicting positions to different trial courts, as opposed to the same appellate court, "appears to be based on the assumptions that a trial court's legal rulings are of significance only in the instant case, whereas appellate decisions make law of general application." The ABA Standing Committee on Ethics and Professional Responsibility, however, has repudiated the distinction made in the Comment to Rule 1.7 between trial and appellate courts. The Committee stated that in cases pending in different trial courts, and even in different jurisdictions, lawyers must carefully consider whether there is a positional conflict of interest between two or more clients.

In determining whether a positional conflict requires a lawyer's disqualification, the question is whether the lawyer can effectively argue both sides of the same legal question without compromising the interests of one client or the other. The lawyer must attempt to strike a balance between the duty to advocate any viable interpretation of the law for one client's benefit versus the other client's right to insist on counsel's fidelity to their legal position.

Under the circumstances presented in Williams' case, we find that O'Donnell has identified and demonstrated the existence of a disqualifying positional conflict. It would be a violation of the Delaware Rules of Professional Conduct for O'Donnell to advocate conflicting legal positions in two capital murder appeals that are pending simultaneously in this Court. Both the United States Constitution and the Delaware Constitution guarantee each of O'Donnell's clients a right to the effective assistance of counsel in a direct appeal following a capital murder conviction. Given his clients' disparate legal arguments, O'Donnell's independent obligations to his clients may compromise the effectiveness of his assistance as appellate counsel for one or both clients, unless his motion to withdraw is granted.

Accordingly, O'Donnell's motion to withdraw must be granted and substitute counsel will be appointed. O'Donnell and the State are both commended for their recognition of and adherence to the highest standards of professional conduct.

11. Suppose defense counsel later takes a job with the prosecutor.

In *Lux v. Commonwealth*, 24 Va.App. 561 (1977), a deputy public defender assisted Lux at his larceny trial, where Lux was convicted. The deputy then changed jobs: he went to work for the prosecutor. Later, the prosecutor moved to revoke Lux's suspended sentence. Lux moved to disqualify the entire prosecutor's office. The court held that the motion should be granted:

> Courts in other jurisdictions are divided as to whether the presence of a criminal defendant's former counsel in a prosecutor's office automatically precludes the entire office from proceeding against the defendant in a related matter. The majority of jurisdictions do not per se disqualify the entire prosecutor's office solely because one member of the staff had represented the defendant in a related matter. Instead, these jurisdictions permit another prosecutor to handle the case if the defendant's former counsel has been effectively screened from participating in the prosecution. [Citations] These courts hold that a prosecutor's public duty to seek justice rather than profits in combination with an effective "chinese wall" provides an adequate safeguard against the improper disclosure of a defendant's confidences. These courts also hold that a *per se* rule results in the unnecessary disqualification of prosecutors in cases where the risk of a breach of confidentiality is slight and inhibits the ability of prosecuting attorney's offices to hire the best possible employees.

> Jurisdictions that follow the minority rule prohibit screening to remedy imputed conflicts and per se disqualify the entire prosecutor's office, regardless of the good faith intent and motivation of the prosecutors involved. [Citations.] Courts in these jurisdictions hold that a per se rule is required to preserve public confidence in the criminal justice system by eliminating any appearance of impropriety.

> We hold that the employment of a criminal defendant's former counsel in a Commonwealth's Attorney's office does not per se disqualify the entire office from handling the prosecution of the defendant's case in a related matter. Instead, whether the apparent conflict of interest created when a criminal defendant's former counsel joins a Commonwealth's Attorney's office justifies the disqualification of other members of the office is a matter committed to the exercise of discretion by the trial court. We believe that a more flexible, case-by-case approach enables a trial court to protect a criminal defendant from the due process concern at issue — the disclosure of confidences revealed to his attorney during the attorney-client relationship — while avoiding unnecessary disqualifications and other disruptive effects that a *per se* rule would have on Commonwealth's Attorney's offices.

Here, the prosecutor failed to present evidence showing that Lux's former counsel "had been effectively screened from contact with the Commonwealth's attorney handling the revocation proceeding."

12. Standard 4-3.5 of the American Bar Association Standards for Criminal Justice (as amended in 1986) provides as follows:

Standard 4-3.5: Conflict of Interest

(a) At the earliest feasible opportunity defense counsel should disclose to the defendant any interest in or connection with the case or any other matter that might be relevant to the defendant's selection of a lawyer to represent him or her.

(b) Except for preliminary matters such as initial hearings or applications for bail, a lawyer or lawyers who are associated in practice should not undertake to defend more than one defendant in the same criminal case if the duty to one of the defendants may conflict with the duty to another. The potential for conflict of interest in representing multiple defendants is so grave that ordinarily a lawyer should decline to act for more than one of several codefendants except in unusual situations when, after careful investigation, it is clear that: (i) no conflict is likely to develop; (ii) the several defendants give an informed consent to such multiple representation; and (iii) the consent of the defendants is made a matter of judicial record. In determining the presence of consent by the defendants, the trial judge should make appropriate inquiries respecting actual or potential conflicts of interest of counsel and whether the defendants fully comprehend the difficulties that an attorney sometimes encounters in defending multiple clients. In some instances, accepting or continuing employment by more than one defendant in the same criminal case is unprofessional conduct.

(c) In accepting payment of fees by one person for the defense of another, a lawyer should be careful to determine that he or she will not be confronted with a conflict of loyalty since the lawyer's entire loyalty is due the accused. It is unprofessional conduct for the lawyer to accept such compensation except with the consent of the accused after full disclosure. It is unprofessional conduct for a lawyer to permit a person who recommends, employs, or pays the lawyer to render legal services for another to direct or regulate the lawyer's professional judgment in rendering such legal services.

(d) It is unprofessional conduct for a lawyer to defend a criminal case in which the lawyer's partner or other professional associate is or has been the prosecutor.

13. What if defense counsel has a "relationship" with the prosecutor?

In *People v. Jackson*, 167 Cal.App.3d 829 (1985), defense counsel engaged in a "dating" relationship with the prosecutor during defendant's trial — without telling defendant. The court held that this created a conflict of interest that prejudiced defendant's right to the effective assistance of counsel:

> We conclude that appointed counsel's failure to inform defendant of his relationship with the prosecutor requires reversal. As distinct from parties to casual social contacts, those who are involved in a sustained dating relationship over a period of months are normally perceived, if not in fact, as sharing a strong emotional or romantic bond. Such an apparently close relationship between counsel directly opposing each other in a criminal prosecution naturally and reasonably gives rise to speculation that the professional judgment of counsel as well as the zealous representation to

which an accused is entitled has been compromised. No matter how well intentioned defense counsel is in carrying out his responsibilities to the accused, he may be subject to subtle influences manifested, for example, in a reluctance to engage in abrasive confrontation with opposing counsel during settlement negotiations and trial advocacy.

A criminal defendant's right to decide for himself who best can conduct the case must be respected wherever feasible. Accordingly, counsel involved in a potential conflict situation such as that disclosed by this record may not proceed with the defense without first explaining fully to the accused the nature of his relationship with opposing counsel and affording the accused the opportunity, if he so desires, to secure counsel unencumbered by potential divided loyalties.

14. Suppose defense counsel has a "relationship" with *defendant's spouse*.

In *People v. Singer*, 226 Cal.App.3d 23 (1990), defense counsel engaged in a sexual relationship with *defendant's wife* (!) during defendant's trial — without telling defendant. Here too the court found a conflict of interest:

> Just as with the sexual-romantic relationship in *Jackson* between defense counsel and the prosecutor, the relationship here between defense counsel and defendant's wife deprived defendant of his constitutional right to the undivided loyalty and effort of his attorney. The validity of our adversarial system depends upon the guaranty of this "undivided loyalty and effort" for every criminal defendant. Given the instant facts, a defense attorney, in the extreme, might be influenced to see his client convicted and imprisoned so that the affair can continue or remain undiscovered. More subtle influences could arise where the wife is a potential witness in the case, as was true here. Reluctance to call or engage in abrasive confrontation with a witness could jeopardize a case as easily as reluctance to vigorously oppose counsel on the other side. The attorney could be tempted to avoid calling a witness who might impugn his lover's integrity or implicate him or her in the case. Also, it is logical to speculate, from the facts present here, that a defense attorney might forego trial strategies that would impose a costly burden on his lover. In other words, defense counsel might "pull his punches." Any of these considerations could jeopardize the duty of undivided loyalty owed the client. At the very minimum these informed speculations, based upon the record, indicate the existence of a potential, prejudicial conflict. * * * *

> Here, unlike *Jackson*, the conflict is all on the defense side. The state is not involved at all. However, erosion of public confidence in the criminal justice system is one of the main rationales of the *Jackson* case; and such public confidence suffers equally when conflicts of the kind present here exist. Given an undisclosed affair between the defendant's wife and his attorney, the professional attorney-client relationship becomes tainted and interwoven with a romantic relationship. Strategic case decisions may have been made by defense counsel to favor the interests of the wife over those of defendant, or to conceal the existence of the affair at defendant's expense. Either way a defendant is prejudiced by failing to have counsel unencumbered by potential divided loyalties. "It is important not only that there is in fact fairness in the judicial system but that the appearance of

fairness to the accused be maintained in order to sustain public confidence in the system.

In *Hernandez v. State*, 1999 WL 492587 (Fla.Ct.App. 1999), an appellate panel followed *Singer* in holding that defense counsel's sexual relationship with defendant's wife during trial warranted reversal of defendant's conviction:

> Holding a significant place in our conclusion that prejudice or actual harm need not be proven is practical reasoning: it would be virtually impossible in most cases, as here, to prove concrete facts that demonstrate that the defense attorney's efforts were less than those demanded by the case. Just as a dishonest basketball player "shaves" points so that the point spread is such as to win a placed bet for him or his associates, an attorney can shave his efforts, seeking to assure at least a partial loss for his client in order to continue his affair with his client's wife. It is difficult to prove point shaving. It is even more difficult, if not generally impossible, to demonstrate the legal equivalent.

> We also note that reduced efforts by defense counsel may not be deliberate. They may be unintended results. Sitting next to his client, day after day at trial, knowing he has betrayed his client, knowing he is going to do so again, surely would be a psychological burden, difficult to carry, particularly throughout a hotly contested trial. The impact of this conscious or unconscious "point shaving" could go unnoticed, or dismissed as a choice of trial tactics. But the attorney's efforts would be far less than the tirelessness mandated by the attorney-client relationship.

> We cannot reach into the mind of Hernandez' defense counsel in order to determine what he did or did not think and do, but we know that if the illicit bond between defense counsel and defendant's wife is strong enough, there is a likelihood, so extremely difficult to prove, that his powers of persuasion, his ability as a legal logician, and his demeanor as an advocate, all declined. How much and how meaningfully we do not know.

> We cannot justify leaving defendants in Hernandez' position with no remedy, which we effectively do if we require evidence of concrete acts of betrayal (other than the sexual betrayal itself). In order to be certain that we are providing justice it must be presumed that Hernandez has been prejudiced because of the sexual relationship between his attorney and Esther Hernandez.

The panel noted, however, some dangers in its ruling:

> The State argues that the sexual relationship may have been a "set up"; that is, that Esther Hernandez, alone or with her husband's consent, seduced attorney Quinon for the very purpose of creating a defense in the event of a conviction. The State also argues that the Hernandez marriage was not in fact a real one, but rather one of political convenience. On remand for the evidentiary hearing the State will have the opportunity to explore and present evidence as to these contentions as well as any other like possibility.

> Finally, we wish to assuage the concern that we are creating an escape route whereby a defendant and his or her spouse can, by the spouse's seduction of defense counsel, create an apparent basis for reversal. We

believe that most attorneys would not be interested or, out of simple moral force, would not succumb to such offerings. As for those who would consider doing so, the weight of punishment by The Florida Bar and of social disapproval should be sufficient deterrence. We also note that this case is only the second or third time that this situation has arisen on appeal nationwide.

But on *en banc* rehearing (*Hernandez v. State*, 750 So.2d 50 (Fla.Ct.App.1999)), the full appellate court set aside the panel's opinion:

> The existence of a "possible" or "potential" personal conflict of interest between counsel and his client does not justify or permit vacating a previous conviction in the absence of a showing that the asserted conflict had an adverse effect upon the lawyer's performance. *Cuyler v. Sullivan*, 446 U.S. 335 (1980). Not only has the defendant specifically acknowledged that there is no thus-required evidence of a lapse in the conduct of the defense, the circumstances, including that the trial below resulted in a guilty verdict only as to a simple misdemeanor charge but an acquittal as to the only felony and another misdemeanor of which he was accused and Hernandez's unqualified endorsement of the results achieved by the same lawyer in a concurrent Federal prosecution, affirmatively show directly to the contrary.

JUSTICE FLETCHER dissented:

> I remain unpersuaded that there was no actual conflict of interest brought about by attorney Quinon's utmost betrayal of his client Humberto Hernandez, and thus I believe prejudice must be presumed because of the nature of the betrayal, as set forth in the original panel opinion. As a consequence I have no choice but to dissent from the en banc opinion, which attempts to classify Quinon's cuckolding of Hernandez as a "possible" or "potential" (rather than an "actual") conflict of interest, thus requiring Hernandez to show, in addition to the conflict, that there was an "actual lapse" in Quinon's representation of Hernandez. * * * *

> Sex is at the top of the list of compelling emotional forces. It propelled Quinon into a conflict of interest with Hernandez with the precise effect on his representation being unknown and unknowable. Would Quinon, whose character may otherwise be sterling, hold back a bit at trial, or change his strategy, in order to assure Hernandez' unavailability to his wife — leaving Quinon a clear field? Those who know Quinon may not think it likely or even possible, but countless examples exist of betrayals of duty for sexual favors to the surprise of the betrayer's friends and family. I would point out only one, known to all of us: King David's betrayal of his loyal officer, Uriah, the Hittite, who was slain on King David's orders so that King David could possess Bathsheba. 2 Samuel 11. The difference between King David's deadly action and a trial counsel's deliberate weakening of the client's case lies not only in degree, but most important here, also in the likelihood of discovery. Obviously King David's action became supremely public. A trial counsel's surreptitious actions done in order to continue his sexual betrayal are not readily hunted down, as discussed in the original panel opinion. Requiring proof by a defendant that his attorney not only cuckolded him,

but reduced his trial performance, leaves that defendant with an impossible task, and thus no remedy.

15. In *Ward v. State*, 753 So.2d 705 (Florida Ct. App. 2000), Ward was charged with trespassing on the property of a local judge. A deputy public defender was assigned to represent Ward. The lawyer claimed a conflict of interest, because "defense counsel would have to make a vigorous attack on the victim's credibility and powers of observation, 'in essence calling him a liar,' to present a zealous and competent defense" — which might hurt the lawyer's ability to represent other clients in front in this judge. The trial court granted the motion to withdraw and assigned another lawyer from the public defender's office. The appellate court held this was error, as the conflict applied to the entire office.

16. In *Locasio v. U.S.*, 395 F.3d 51 (2nd Cir. 2005), co-defendant Gotti allegedly threatened to kill Locasio's lawyer if, at trial, he "individualized the interest of LoCascio at Gotti's expense." Gotti supposedly insisted that Locasio's lawyer limit his cross-examination of government witnesses and praise Gotti in his closing argument. The court held that "a credible death threat from a co-defendant ordering a lawyer to sacrifice a client's interests constitutes an actual conflict of interest." Locasio's conviction would have to be set aside if the allegations are true and they caused his lawyer to "pull his punches" while representing Locasio at trial.

17. Suppose the trial judge knows of that defense counsel has a potential conflict, but the judge fails to inquire further. After conviction, must the appellate court *automatically* reverse (i.e., is this "structural" error)? No, held the Court in *Mickens v. Taylor*, 122 S.Ct. 1237 (2002):

> The Sixth Amendment provides that a criminal defendant shall have the right to "the assistance of counsel for his defence." This right has been accorded, not for its own sake, but because of the effect it has on the ability of the accused to receive a fair trial. It follows from this that assistance which is ineffective in preserving fairness does not meet the constitutional mandate, see *Strickland v. Washington*, 466 U.S. 668, 685–686 (1984); and it also follows that defects in assistance that have no probable effect upon the trial's outcome do not establish a constitutional violation. As a general matter, a defendant alleging a Sixth Amendment violation must demonstrate "a reasonable probability that, but for counsel's unprofessional errors, the result of the proceeding would have been different." *Id.* at 694.
>
> There is an exception to this general rule. We have spared the defendant the need of showing probable effect upon the outcome, and have simply presumed such effect, where assistance of counsel has been denied entirely or during a critical stage of the proceeding. When that has occurred, the likelihood that the verdict is unreliable is so high that a case-by-case inquiry is unnecessary. But only in circumstances of that magnitude do we forgo individual inquiry into whether counsel's inadequate performance undermined the reliability of the verdict.
>
> We have held in several cases that "circumstances of that magnitude" may also arise when the defendant's attorney actively represented conflicting interests. The nub of the question before us is whether the principle established by these cases provides an exception to the general rule of *Strickland* under the circumstances of the present case. * * * *

The *Sullivan* standard [*Cuyler v. Sullivan*, 446 U.S. 335 (1980)] is not properly read as requiring inquiry into actual conflict as something separate and apart from adverse effect. An "actual conflict," for Sixth Amendment purposes, is a conflict of interest that adversely affects counsel's performance.

Petitioner's proposed rule of automatic reversal when there existed a conflict that did not affect counsel's performance, but the trial judge failed to make the *Sullivan*-mandated inquiry, makes little policy sense. As discussed, the rule applied when the trial judge is not aware of the conflict (and thus not obligated to inquire) is that prejudice will be presumed only if the conflict has significantly affected counsel's performance — thereby rendering the verdict unreliable, even though *Strickland* prejudice cannot be shown. The trial court's awareness of a potential conflict neither renders it more likely that counsel's performance was significantly affected nor in any other way renders the verdict unreliable. Nor does the trial judge's failure to make the *Sullivan*-mandated inquiry often make it harder for reviewing courts to determine conflict and effect, particularly since those courts may rely on evidence and testimony whose importance only becomes established at the trial.

STRICKLAND v. WASHINGTON
United States Supreme Court
466 U.S. 668 (1984)

JUSTICE O'CONNOR delivered the opinion of the Court.

This case requires us to consider the proper standards for judging a criminal defendant's contention that the Constitution requires a conviction or death sentence to be set aside because counsel's assistance at the trial or sentencing was ineffective.

I

During a ten-day period in September 1976, respondent planned and committed three groups of crimes, which included three brutal stabbing murders, torture, kidnapping, severe assaults, attempted murders, attempted extortion, and theft. After his two accomplices were arrested, respondent surrendered to police and voluntarily gave a lengthy statement confessing to the third of the criminal episodes. The State of Florida indicted respondent for kidnapping and murder and appointed an experienced criminal lawyer to represent him. Counsel actively pursued pretrial motions and discovery. He cut his efforts short, however, and he experienced a sense of hopelessness about the case, when he learned that, against his specific advice, respondent had also confessed to the first two murders. By the date set for trial, respondent was subject to indictment for three counts of first degree murder and multiple counts of robbery, kidnapping for ransom, breaking and entering and assault, attempted murder, and conspiracy to commit robbery. Respondent waived his right to a jury trial, again acting against counsel's advice, and pleaded guilty to all charges, including the three capital murder charges.

In the plea colloquy, respondent told the trial judge that, although he had committed a string of burglaries, he had no significant prior criminal record and that at the time of his criminal spree he was under extreme stress caused by his inability to support his family. He also stated, however, that he accepted responsibility for the crimes. The trial judge told respondent that he had "a great deal of respect for people who are willing to step forward and admit their responsibility," but that he was making no statement at all about his likely sentencing decision. Counsel advised respondent to invoke his right under Florida law to an advisory jury at his capital sentencing hearing. Respondent rejected the advice and waived the right. He chose instead to be sentenced by the trial judge without a jury recommendation.

In preparing for the sentencing hearing, counsel spoke with respondent about his background. He also spoke on the telephone with respondent's wife and mother, though he did not follow up on the one unsuccessful effort to meet with them. He did not otherwise seek out character witnesses for respondent. Nor did he request a psychiatric examination, since his conversations with his client gave no indication that respondent had psychological problems.

Counsel decided not to present and hence not to look further for evidence concerning respondent's character and emotional state. That decision reflected trial counsel's sense of hopelessness about overcoming the evidentiary effect of respondent's confessions to the gruesome crimes. It also reflected the judgment that it was advisable to rely on the plea colloquy for evidence about respondent's background and about his claim of emotional stress: the plea colloquy communicated sufficient information about these subjects, and by foregoing the opportunity to present new evidence on these subjects, counsel prevented the State from cross-examining respondent on his claim and from putting on psychiatric evidence of its own.

Counsel also excluded from the sentencing hearing other evidence he thought was potentially damaging. He successfully moved to exclude respondent's "rap sheet." Because he judged that a presentence report might prove more detrimental than helpful, as it would have included respondent's criminal history and thereby undermined the claim of no significant history of criminal activity, he did not request that one be prepared.

At the sentencing hearing, counsel's strategy was based primarily on the trial judge's remarks at the plea colloquy as well as on his reputation as a sentencing judge who thought it important for a convicted defendant to own up to his crime. Counsel argued that respondent's remorse and acceptance of responsibility justified sparing him from the death penalty. Counsel also argued that respondent had no history of criminal activity and that respondent committed the crimes under extreme mental or emotional disturbance, thus coming within the statutory list of mitigating circumstances. He further argued that respondent should be spared death because he had surrendered, confessed, and offered to testify against a co-defendant and because respondent was fundamentally a good person who had briefly gone badly wrong in extremely stressful circumstances. The State put on evidence and witnesses largely for the purpose of describing the details of the crimes. Counsel did not cross-examine the medical experts who testified about the manner of death of respondent's victims.

The trial judge found several aggravating circumstances with respect to each of the three murders. He found that all three murders were especially heinous, atrocious, and cruel, all involving repeated stabbings. All three murders were committed in the course of at least one other dangerous and violent felony, and since all involved robbery, the murders were for pecuniary gain. All three murders were committed to avoid arrest for the accompanying crimes and to hinder law enforcement. In the course of one of the murders, respondent knowingly subjected numerous persons to a grave risk of death by deliberately stabbing and shooting the murder victim's sisters-in-law, who sustained severe — in one case, ultimately fatal — injuries.

With respect to mitigating circumstances, the trial judge made the same findings for all three capital murders. First, although there was no admitted evidence of prior convictions, respondent had stated that he had engaged in a course of stealing. In any case, even if respondent had no significant history of criminal activity, the aggravating circumstances "would still clearly far outweigh" that mitigating factor. Second, the judge found that, during all three crimes, respondent was not suffering from extreme mental or emotional disturbance and could appreciate the criminality of his acts. Third, none of the victims was a participant in, or consented to, respondent's conduct. Fourth, respondent's participation in the crimes was neither minor nor the result of duress or domination by an accomplice. Finally, respondent's age (26) could not be considered a factor in mitigation, especially when viewed in light of respondent's planning of the crimes and disposition of the proceeds of the various accompanying thefts.

In short, the trial judge found numerous aggravating circumstances and no (or a single comparatively insignificant) mitigating circumstance. With respect to each of the three convictions for capital murder, the trial judge concluded: "A careful consideration of all matters presented to the court impels the conclusion that there are insufficient mitigating circumstances to outweigh the aggravating circumstances." He therefore sentenced respondent to death on each of the three counts of murder and to prison terms for the other crimes. The Florida Supreme Court upheld the convictions and sentences on direct appeal.

Respondent subsequently sought collateral relief in state court on numerous grounds, among them that counsel had rendered ineffective assistance at the sentencing proceeding. Respondent challenged counsel's assistance in six respects. He asserted that counsel was ineffective because he failed to move for a continuance to prepare for sentencing, to request a psychiatric report, to investigate and present character witnesses, to seek a presentence investigation report, to present meaningful arguments to the sentencing judge, and to investigate the medical examiner's reports or cross-examine the medical experts. In support of the claim, respondent submitted fourteen affidavits from friends, neighbors, and relatives stating that they would have testified if asked to do so. He also submitted one psychiatric report and one psychological report stating that respondent, though not under the influence of extreme mental or emotional disturbance, was "chronically frustrated and depressed because of his economic dilemma" at the time of his crimes.

The trial court denied relief, finding that the record evidence conclusively showed that the ineffectiveness claim was meritless. * * * * The trial court concluded that respondent had not shown that counsel's assistance reflected any substantial and serious deficiency measurably below that of competent counsel that was likely to have affected the outcome of the sentencing proceeding. The court specifically found that, "as a matter of law, the record affirmatively demonstrates beyond any doubt that even if counsel had done each of the things that respondent alleged counsel had failed to do at the time of sentencing, there is not even the remotest chance that the outcome would have been any different. The plain fact is that the aggravating circumstances proved in this case were completely overwhelming." The Florida

Supreme Court affirmed the denial of relief.

Respondent next filed a petition for a writ of habeas corpus in the United States District Court. * * * * On the legal issue of ineffectiveness, the District Court concluded that, although trial counsel made errors in judgment in failing to investigate nonstatutory mitigating evidence further than he did, no prejudice to respondent's sentence resulted from any such error in judgment.

On appeal, the Court of Appeals stated that the Sixth Amendment right to assistance of counsel accorded criminal defendants a right to "counsel reasonably likely to render and rendering reasonably effective assistance given the totality of the circumstances."* * * *

If there is only one plausible line of defense, the court concluded, counsel must conduct a "reasonably substantial investigation" into that line of defense, since there can be no strategic choice that renders such an investigation unnecessary. The same duty exists if counsel relies at trial on only one line of defense, although others are available. In either case, the investigation need not be exhaustive. It must include "an independent examination of the facts, circumstances, pleadings and laws involved." The scope of the duty, however, depends on such facts as the strength of the government's case and the likelihood that pursuing certain leads may prove more harmful than helpful. If there is more than one plausible line of defense, the court held, counsel should ideally investigate each line substantially before making a strategic choice about which lines to rely on at trial. If counsel conducts such substantial investigations, the strategic choices made as a result "will seldom if ever" be found wanting. Because advocacy is an art and not a science, and because the adversary system requires deference to counsel's informed decisions, strategic choices must be respected in these circumstances if they are based on professional judgment.

If counsel does not conduct a substantial investigation into each of several plausible lines of defense, assistance may nonetheless be effective. Counsel may not exclude certain lines of defense for other than strategic reasons. Limitations of time and money, however, may force early strategic choices, often based solely on conversations with the defendant and a review of the prosecution's evidence. Those strategic choices about which lines of defense to pursue are owed deference commensurate with the reasonableness of the professional judgments on which they are based. Thus, "when counsel's assumptions are reasonable given the totality of the circumstances and when counsel's strategy represents a reasonable choice based upon those assumptions, counsel need not investigate lines of defense that he has chosen not to employ at trial." Among the factors relevant to deciding whether particular strategic choices are reasonable are the experience of the attorney, the inconsistency of unpursued and pursued lines of defense, and the potential for prejudice from taking an unpursued line of defense. * * * *

The Court of Appeals thus laid down the tests to be applied in the Eleventh Circuit in challenges to convictions on the ground of ineffectiveness of counsel. A majority of the judges agreed that the case should be remanded for application of the newly announced standards.

Petitioners, who are officials of the State of Florida, filed a petition for a writ of certiorari seeking review of the decision of the Court of Appeals. The petition presents a type of Sixth Amendment claim that this Court has not previously considered in any generality. The Court has considered Sixth Amendment claims based on actual or constructive denial of the assistance of counsel altogether, as well as claims based on state interference with the ability of counsel to render effective assistance to the accused. E.g., *United States v. Cronic*, 466 U.S. 648 (1984). With the exception of *Cuyler v. Sullivan*, 446 U.S. 335 (1980), however, which involved a claim that counsel's assistance was rendered ineffective by a conflict of interest, the Court has never directly and fully addressed a claim of "actual ineffectiveness" of counsel's assistance in a case going to trial.

II

In a long line of cases that includes *Powell v. Alabama*, 287 U.S. 45, and *Gideon v. Wainwright*, 372 U.S. 335 (1963), this Court has recognized that the Sixth Amendment right to counsel exists, and is needed, in order to protect the fundamental right to a fair trial. The Constitution guarantees a fair trial through the Due Process Clauses, but it defines the basic elements of a fair trial largely through the several provisions of the Sixth Amendment, including the Counsel Clause:

> In all criminal prosecutions, the accused shall enjoy the right to a speedy and public trial, by an impartial jury of the State and district wherein the crime shall have been committed, which district shall have been previously ascertained by law, and to be informed of the nature and cause of the accusation; to be confronted with the witnesses against him; to have compulsory process for obtaining Witnesses in his favor, and to have the Assistance of Counsel for his defence.

Thus, a fair trial is one in which evidence subject to adversarial testing is presented to an impartial tribunal for resolution of issues defined in advance of the proceeding. The right to counsel plays a crucial role in the adversarial system embodied in the Sixth Amendment, since access to counsel's skill and knowledge is necessary to accord defendants the "ample opportunity to meet the case of the prosecution" to which they are entitled. Because of the vital importance of counsel's assistance, this Court has held that, with certain exceptions, a person accused of a federal or state crime has the right to have counsel appointed if retained counsel cannot be obtained. See *Argersinger v. Hamlin*, 407 U.S. 25 (1972). That a person who happens to be a lawyer is present at trial alongside the accused, however, is not enough to satisfy the constitutional command. The Sixth Amendment recognizes the right to the assistance of counsel because it envisions counsel's playing a role that is critical to the ability of the adversarial system to produce just results. An accused is entitled to be assisted by an attorney, whether retained or appointed, who plays the role necessary to ensure that the trial is fair.

For that reason, the Court has recognized that "the right to counsel is the right to the effective assistance of counsel." *McMann v. Richardson*, 397 U.S. 759, 771 (1970). Government violates the right to effective assistance when it interferes in certain ways with the ability of counsel to make independent decisions about how to conduct the defense. See, e.g., *Geders v. United States*, 425 U.S. 80 (1976) (bar on attorney-client consultation during overnight recess); *Herring v. New York*, 422 U.S. 853 (1975) (bar on summation at bench trial); *Brooks v. Tennessee*, 406 U.S. 605, 612–613 (1972) (requirement that defendant be first defense witness); *Ferguson v. Georgia*, 365 U.S. 570, 593–596 (1961) (bar on direct examination of defendant). Counsel, however, can also deprive a defendant of the right to effective assistance, simply by failing to render "adequate legal assistance," *Cuyler v. Sullivan, supra,* 446 U.S. at 344 (actual conflict of interest adversely affecting lawyer's performance renders assistance ineffective).

The Court has not elaborated on the meaning of the constitutional requirement of effective assistance in the latter class of cases — that is, those presenting claims of "actual ineffectiveness." In giving meaning to the requirement, however, we must take its purpose — to ensure a fair trial — as the guide. The benchmark for judging any claim of ineffectiveness must be whether counsel's conduct so undermined the proper functioning of the adversarial process that the trial cannot be relied on as having produced a just result.

The same principle applies to a capital sentencing proceeding such as that provided by Florida law. We need not consider the role of counsel in an ordinary sentencing, which may involve informal proceedings and standardless discretion in the sentencer, and hence may require a different approach to the definition of constitutionally effective assistance. A capital sentencing proceeding like the one involved in this case, however, is sufficiently like a trial in its adversarial format and in the existence of standards for decision, that counsel's role in the proceeding is comparable to counsel's role at trial — to ensure that the adversarial testing process works to produce a just result under the standards governing decision. For purposes of describing counsel's duties, therefore, Florida's capital sentencing proceeding need not be distinguished from an ordinary trial.

III

A convicted defendant's claim that counsel's assistance was so defective as to require reversal of a conviction or death sentence has two components. First, the defendant must show that counsel's performance was deficient. This requires showing that counsel made errors so serious that counsel was not functioning as the "counsel" guaranteed the defendant by the Sixth Amendment.

Second, the defendant must show that the deficient performance prejudiced the defense. This requires showing that counsel's errors were so serious as to deprive the defendant of a fair trial, a trial whose result is reliable. Unless a defendant makes both showings, it cannot be said that the conviction or death sentence resulted from a breakdown in the adversary process that renders the result unreliable.

A

As all the Federal Courts of Appeals have now held, the proper standard for attorney performance is that of reasonably effective assistance. The Court indirectly recognized as much when it stated in *McMann v. Richardson, supra,* 397 U.S. at 770, that a guilty plea cannot be attacked as based on inadequate legal advice unless counsel was not "a reasonably competent attorney" and the advice was not "within the range of competence demanded of attorneys in criminal cases." When a convicted defendant complains of the ineffectiveness of counsel's assistance, the defendant must show that counsel's representation fell below an objective standard of reasonableness. More specific guidelines are not appropriate. The Sixth Amendment refers simply to "counsel," not specifying particular requirements of effective assistance. It relies instead on the legal profession's maintenance of standards sufficient to justify the law's presumption that counsel will fulfill the role in the adversary process that the Amendment envisions. The proper measure of attorney performance remains simply reasonableness under prevailing professional norms.

Representation of a criminal defendant entails certain basic duties. Counsel's function is to assist the defendant, and hence counsel owes the client a duty of loyalty, a duty to avoid conflicts of interest. From counsel's function as assistant to the defendant derive the overarching duty to advocate the defendant's cause and the more particular duties to consult with the defendant on important decisions and to keep the defendant informed of important developments in the course of the prosecution. Counsel also has a duty to bring to bear such skill and knowledge as will render the trial a reliable adversarial testing process.

These basic duties neither exhaustively define the obligations of counsel nor form a checklist for judicial evaluation of attorney performance. In any case presenting an ineffectiveness claim, the performance inquiry must be whether counsel's assistance was reasonable considering all the circumstances. Prevailing norms of practice as reflected in American Bar Association standards and the like, e.g., ABA Standards for Criminal Justice 4-1.1 to 4-8.6 (2d ed. 1980) ("The Defense Function"), are guides to determining what is reasonable, but they are only guides. No particular set of detailed rules for counsel's conduct can satisfactorily take account of the variety of circumstances faced by defense counsel or the range of legitimate decisions regarding how best to represent a criminal defendant. Any such set of rules would interfere with the constitutionally protected independence of counsel and restrict the wide latitude counsel must have in making tactical decisions. Indeed, the existence of detailed guidelines for representation could distract counsel from the overriding mission of vigorous advocacy of the defendant's cause. Moreover, the purpose of the effective assistance guarantee of the Sixth Amendment is not to improve the quality of legal representation, although that is a goal of considerable importance to the legal system. The purpose is simply to ensure that criminal defendants receive a fair trial.

Judicial scrutiny of counsel's performance must be highly deferential. It is all too tempting for a defendant to second-guess counsel's assistance after conviction or adverse sentence, and it is all too easy for a court, examining counsel's defense after it has proved unsuccessful, to conclude that a particular act or omission of counsel was unreasonable. A fair assessment of attorney performance requires that every effort be made to eliminate the distorting effects of hindsight, to reconstruct the circumstances of counsel's challenged conduct, and to evaluate the conduct from counsel's perspective at the time. Because of the difficulties inherent in making the evaluation, a court must indulge a strong presumption that counsel's conduct falls within the wide range of reasonable professional assistance; that is, the defendant must overcome the presumption that, under the circumstances, the challenged action might be considered sound trial strategy. There are countless ways to provide effective assistance in any given case. Even the best criminal defense attorneys would not defend a particular client in the same way.

The availability of intrusive post-trial inquiry into attorney performance or of detailed guidelines for its evaluation would encourage the proliferation of ineffectiveness challenges. Criminal trials resolved unfavorably to the defendant would increasingly come to be followed by a second trial, this one of counsel's unsuccessful defense. Counsel's performance and even willingness to serve could be adversely affected. Intensive scrutiny of counsel and rigid requirements for acceptable assistance could dampen the ardor and impair the independence of defense counsel, discourage the acceptance of assigned cases, and undermine the trust between attorney and client.

Thus, a court deciding an actual ineffectiveness claim must judge the reasonableness of counsel's challenged conduct on the facts of the particular case, viewed as of the time of counsel's conduct. A convicted defendant making a claim of ineffective assistance must identify the acts or omissions of counsel that are alleged not to have been the result of reasonable professional judgment. The court must then determine whether, in light of all the circumstances, the identified acts or omissions were outside the wide range of professionally competent assistance. In making that determination, the court should keep in mind that counsel's function, as elaborated in prevailing professional norms, is to make the adversarial testing process work in the particular case. At the same time, the court should recognize that counsel is strongly presumed to have rendered adequate assistance and made all significant decisions in the exercise of reasonable professional judgment.

These standards require no special amplification in order to define counsel's duty to investigate, the duty at issue in this case. Strategic choices made after thorough investigation of law and facts relevant to plausible options are virtually unchallengeable; and strategic choices made after less than complete investigation are reasonable precisely to the extent that reasonable professional judgments support the limitations on investigation. In other words, counsel has a duty to make reasonable investigations or to make a reasonable decision that makes particular investigations unnecessary. In any ineffectiveness case, a particular decision not to investigate must be directly assessed for reasonableness in all the circumstances, applying a heavy measure of deference to counsel's judgments.

The reasonableness of counsel's actions may be determined or substantially influenced by the defendant's own statements or actions. Counsel's actions are usually based, quite properly, on informed strategic choices made by the defendant and on information supplied by the defendant. In particular, what investigation decisions are reasonable depends critically on such information. For example, when the facts that support a certain potential line of defense are generally known to counsel because of what the defendant has said, the need for further investigation may be considerably diminished or eliminated altogether. And when a defendant has given counsel reason to believe that pursuing certain investigations would be fruitless or even harmful, counsel's failure to pursue those investigations may not later be challenged as unreasonable. In short, inquiry into counsel's conversations with the defendant may be critical to a proper assessment of counsel's investigation decisions, just as it may be critical to a proper assessment of counsel's other litigation decisions.

B

An error by counsel, even if professionally unreasonable, does not warrant setting aside the judgment of a criminal proceeding if the error had no effect on the judgment. The purpose of the Sixth Amendment guarantee of counsel is to ensure that a defendant has the assistance necessary to justify reliance on the outcome of the proceeding. Accordingly, any deficiencies in counsel's performance must be prejudicial to the defense in order to constitute ineffective assistance under the Constitution.

In certain Sixth Amendment contexts, prejudice is presumed. Actual or constructive denial of the assistance of counsel altogether is legally presumed to result in prejudice. So are various kinds of state interference with counsel's assistance. Prejudice in these circumstances is so likely that case by case inquiry into prejudice is not worth the cost. Moreover, such circumstances involve impairments of the Sixth Amendment right that are easy to identify and, for that reason and because the prosecution is directly responsible, easy for the government to prevent.

One type of actual ineffectiveness claim warrants a similar, though more limited, presumption of prejudice. In *Cuyler v. Sullivan*, 446 U.S. at 345–350, the Court held that prejudice is presumed when counsel is burdened by an actual conflict of interest. In those circumstances, counsel breaches the duty of loyalty, perhaps the most basic of counsel's duties. Moreover, it is difficult to measure the precise effect on the defense of representation corrupted by conflicting interests. Given the obligation of counsel to avoid conflicts of interest and the ability of trial courts to make early inquiry in certain situations likely to give rise to conflicts, see, e.g., Fed.Rule Crim.Proc. 44(c), it is reasonable for the criminal justice system to maintain a fairly rigid rule of presumed prejudice for conflicts of interest. Even so, the rule is not quite the per se rule of prejudice that exists for the Sixth Amendment claims mentioned above. Prejudice is presumed only if the defendant demonstrates that counsel "actively represented conflicting interests" and "that an actual conflict of interest adversely affected his lawyer's performance." *Cuyler v. Sullivan, supra*, 446 U.S. at 350, 348.

Conflict of interest claims aside, actual ineffectiveness claims alleging a deficiency in attorney performance are subject to a general requirement that the defendant affirmatively prove prejudice. The government is not responsible for, and hence not able to prevent, attorney errors that will result in reversal of a conviction or sentence. Attorney errors come in an infinite variety and are as likely to be utterly harmless in a particular case as they are to be prejudicial. They cannot be classified according to likelihood of causing prejudice. Nor can they be defined with sufficient precision to inform defense attorneys correctly just what conduct to avoid. Representation is an art, and an act or omission that is unprofessional in one case may be sound or even brilliant in another. Even if a defendant shows that particular errors of counsel were unreasonable, therefore, the defendant must show that they actually had an adverse effect on the defense.

It is not enough for the defendant to show that the errors had some conceivable effect on the outcome of the proceeding. Virtually every act or omission of counsel would meet that test, and not every error that conceivably could have influenced the outcome undermines the reliability of the result of the proceeding. Respondent suggests requiring a showing that the errors "impaired the presentation of the defense." That standard, however, provides no workable principle. Since any error, if it is indeed an error, "impairs" the presentation of the defense, the proposed standard is inadequate because it provides no way of deciding what impairments are sufficiently serious to warrant setting aside the outcome of the proceeding.

On the other hand, we believe that a defendant need not show that counsel's deficient conduct more likely than not altered the outcome in the case. This outcome-determinative standard has several strengths. It defines the relevant inquiry in a way familiar to courts, though the inquiry, as is inevitable, is anything but precise. The standard also reflects the profound importance of finality in criminal proceedings. Moreover, it comports with the widely used standard for assessing motions for new trial based on newly discovered evidence. Nevertheless, the standard is not quite appropriate. The defendant must show that there is a reasonable probability that, but for counsel's unprofessional errors, the result of the proceeding would have been different. A reasonable probability is a probability sufficient to undermine confidence in the outcome.

* * * *

V

Having articulated general standards for judging ineffectiveness claims, we think it useful to apply those standards to the facts of this case in order to illustrate the meaning of the general principles. The record makes it possible to do so.

Application of the governing principles is not difficult in this case. The facts as described above, make clear that the conduct of respondent's counsel at and before respondent's sentencing proceeding cannot be found unreasonable. They also make clear that, even assuming the challenged conduct of counsel was unreasonable, respondent suffered insufficient prejudice to warrant setting aside his death sentence.

With respect to the performance component, the record shows that respondent's counsel made a strategic choice to argue for the extreme emotional distress mitigating circumstance and to rely as fully as possible on respondent's acceptance of responsibility for his crimes. Although counsel understandably felt hopeless about respondent's prospects, nothing in the record indicates, as one possible reading of the District Court's opinion suggests, that counsel's sense of hopelessness distorted his professional judgment. Counsel's strategy choice was well within the range of professionally reasonable judgments, and the decision not to seek more character or psychological evidence than was already in hand was likewise reasonable. The trial judge's views on the importance of owning up to one's crimes were well known to counsel. The aggravating circumstances were utterly overwhelming. Trial counsel could reasonably surmise from his conversations with respondent that character and psychological evidence would be of little help. Respondent had already been able to mention at the plea colloquy the substance of what there was to know about his financial and emotional troubles. Restricting testimony on respondent's character to what had come in at the plea colloquy ensured that contrary character and psychological evidence and respondent's criminal history, which counsel had successfully moved to exclude, would not come in. On these facts, there can be little question, even without application of the presumption of adequate performance, that trial counsel's defense, though unsuccessful, was the result of reasonable professional judgment.

With respect to the prejudice component, the lack of merit of respondent's claim is even more stark. The evidence that respondent says his trial counsel should have offered at the sentencing hearing would barely have altered the sentencing profile presented to the sentencing judge. As the state courts and District Court found, at most this evidence shows that numerous people who knew respondent thought he was generally a good person and that a psychiatrist and a psychologist believed he was under considerable emotional stress that did not rise to the level of extreme disturbance. Given the overwhelming aggravating factors, there is no reasonable probability that the omitted evidence would have changed the conclusion that the aggravating circumstances outweighed the mitigating circumstances and, hence, the sentence imposed. Indeed, admission of the evidence respondent now offers might even have been harmful to his case: his "rap sheet" would probably have been admitted into evidence, and the psychological reports would have directly contradicted respondent's claim that the mitigating circumstance of extreme emotional disturbance applied to his case.

Failure to make the required showing of either deficient performance or sufficient prejudice defeats the ineffectiveness claim. Here there is a double failure. More generally, respondent has made no showing that the justice of his sentence was rendered unreliable by a breakdown in the adversary process caused by deficiencies in counsel's assistance. Respondent's sentencing proceeding was not fundamentally unfair.

We conclude, therefore, that the District Court properly declined to issue a writ of habeas corpus. The judgment of the Court of Appeals is accordingly reversed.

JUSTICE MARSHALL, dissenting.

I

The opinion of the Court revolves around two holdings. First, the majority ties the constitutional minima of attorney performance to a simple "standard of reasonableness." Second, the majority holds that only an error of counsel that has sufficient impact on a trial to "undermine confidence in the outcome" is grounds for overturning a conviction. I disagree with both of these rulings.

A

My objection to the performance standard adopted by the Court is that it is so malleable that, in practice, it will either have no grip at all or will yield excessive variation in the manner in which the Sixth Amendment is interpreted and applied by different courts. To tell lawyers and the lower courts that counsel for a criminal defendant must behave "reasonably" and must act like "a reasonably competent attorney," is to tell them almost nothing. In essence, the majority has instructed judges called upon to assess claims of ineffective assistance of counsel to advert to their own intuitions regarding what constitutes "professional" representation, and has discouraged them from trying to develop more detailed standards governing the performance of defense counsel. In my view, the Court has thereby not only abdicated its own responsibility to interpret the Constitution, but also impaired the ability of the lower courts to exercise theirs. The debilitating ambiguity of an "objective standard of reasonableness" in this context is illustrated by the majority's failure to address important issues concerning the quality of representation mandated by the Constitution. It is an unfortunate but undeniable fact that a person of means, by selecting a lawyer and paying him enough to ensure he prepares thoroughly, usually can obtain better representation than that available to an indigent defendant, who must rely on appointed counsel, who, in turn, has limited time and resources to devote to a given case. Is a "reasonably competent attorney" a reasonably competent adequately paid retained lawyer or a reasonably competent appointed attorney? It is also a fact that the quality of representation available to ordinary defendants in different parts of the country varies significantly. Should the standard of performance mandated by the Sixth Amendment vary by locale? * * * * The majority offers no clues as to the proper responses to these questions.

The majority defends its refusal to adopt more specific standards primarily on the ground that "no particular set of detailed rules for counsel's conduct can satisfactorily take account of the variety of circumstances faced by defense counsel or the range of legitimate decisions regarding how best to represent a criminal defendant." I agree that counsel must be afforded "wide latitude" when making "tactical decisions" regarding trial strategy, but many aspects of the job of a criminal defense attorney are more amenable to judicial oversight. For example, much of the work involved in preparing for a trial, applying for bail, conferring with one's client, making timely objections to significant, arguably erroneous rulings of the trial judge, and filing a notice of appeal if there are colorable grounds therefore could profitably be made the subject of uniform standards.

B

I object to the prejudice standard adopted by the Court for two independent reasons. First, it is often very difficult to tell whether a defendant convicted after a trial in which he was ineffectively represented would have fared better if his lawyer had been competent. Seemingly impregnable cases can sometimes be dismantled by good defense counsel. On the basis of a cold record, it may be impossible for a reviewing court confidently to ascertain how the government's evidence and arguments would have stood up against rebuttal and cross-examination by a shrewd, well prepared lawyer. The difficulties of estimating prejudice after the fact are exacerbated by the possibility that evidence of injury to the defendant may be missing from the record precisely because of the incompetence of defense counsel. In view of all these impediments to a fair evaluation of the probability that the outcome of a trial was affected by ineffectiveness of counsel, it seems to me senseless to impose on a defendant whose lawyer has been shown to have been incompetent the burden of demonstrating prejudice.

Second and more fundamentally, the assumption on which the Court's holding rests is that the only purpose of the constitutional guarantee of effective assistance of counsel is to reduce the chance that innocent persons will be convicted. In my view, the guarantee also functions to ensure that convictions are obtained only through fundamentally fair procedures. * * * * The majority contends that the Sixth Amendment is not violated when a manifestly guilty defendant is convicted after a trial in which he was represented by a manifestly ineffective attorney. I cannot agree. Every defendant is entitled to a trial in which his interests are vigorously and conscientiously advocated by an able lawyer. A proceeding in which the defendant does not receive meaningful assistance in meeting the forces of the state does not, in my opinion, constitute due process.

In *Chapman v. California*, 386 U.S. 18, 23 (1967), we acknowledged that certain constitutional rights are "so basic to a fair trial that their infraction can never be treated as harmless error." Among these rights is "the right to the assistance of counsel at trial." *Id.* at 23. In my view, the right to effective assistance of counsel is entailed by the right to counsel, and abridgment of the former is equivalent to abridgment of the latter. * * * * I would thus hold that a showing that the performance of a defendant's lawyer departed from constitutionally prescribed standards requires a new trial regardless of whether the defendant suffered demonstrable prejudice thereby. * * * *

III

The majority suggests that, "for purposes of describing counsel's duties," a capital sentencing proceeding "need not be distinguished from an ordinary trial." I cannot agree.

The Court has repeatedly acknowledged that the Constitution requires stricter adherence to procedural safeguards in a capital case than in other cases.

> The penalty of death is qualitatively different from a sentence of imprisonment, however long. Death, in its finality, differs more from life imprisonment than a 100-year prison term differs from one of only a year or two. Because of that qualitative difference, there is a corresponding difference in the need for reliability in the determination that death is the appropriate punishment in a specific case. [*Woodson v. North Carolina,* 428 U.S. 280, 305 (1976)]

* * * *

In my view, a person on death row, whose counsel's performance fell below constitutionally acceptable levels, should not be compelled to demonstrate a "reasonable probability" that he would have been given a life sentence if his lawyer had been competent; if the defendant can establish a significant chance that the outcome would have been different, he surely should be entitled to a redetermination of his fate.

IV

The views expressed in the preceding section oblige me to dissent from the majority's disposition of the case before us. It is undisputed that respondent's trial counsel made virtually no investigation of the possibility of obtaining testimony from respondent's relatives, friends, or former employers pertaining to respondent's character or background. Had counsel done so, he would have found several persons willing and able to testify that, in their experience, respondent was a responsible, nonviolent man, devoted to his family, and active in the affairs of his church. Respondent contends that his lawyer could have and should have used that testimony to "humanize" respondent, to counteract the impression conveyed by the trial that he was little more than a cold-blooded killer. Had this evidence been admitted, respondent argues, his chances of obtaining a life sentence would have been significantly better. * * * *

If counsel had investigated the availability of mitigating evidence, he might well have decided to present some such material at the hearing. If he had done so, there is a significant chance that respondent would have been given a life sentence. In my view, those possibilities, conjoined with the unreasonableness of counsel's failure to investigate, are more than sufficient to establish a violation of the Sixth Amendment and to entitle respondent to a new sentencing proceeding.

I respectfully dissent.

Notes from Fern:

1. In *Strickland*, the Court held that, to warrant reversal, ineffective assistance of counsel must have been *prejudicial* to the defendant. In *Holloway*, the Court held that no such showing need be made. Can these two holdings be reconciled?

2. **Does *Strickland* apply where a lawyer does incomplete *legal research*?**

In *U.S. v. McNamara*, 867 F.Supp. 369 (E.D.Va.1994), defense counsel Donnelly did not object to a jury instruction which had been approved by a Court of Appeal decision (*U.S. v. Rogers*). Unbeknownst to defense counsel, however, the U.S. Supreme Court had granted *certiorari* in a case which questioned the validity of that instruction (*U.S. v. Ratzlaff*). Defendant was convicted, but was unable to raise on appeal the validity of the instruction, because his counsel had failed to object to it. The court held that he had been denied the effective assistance of counsel:

> In the modern environment of law practice, the law changes rapidly and develops in significant ways as a matter of course. One consequence of this modern environment, and of dramatic advancements in technology, is the advent of extensive resources for staying abreast of developments in the law. Numerous legal newspapers, periodicals such as United States Law Week, and on-line services serve this important purpose.
>
> The first question then is whether, in this environment, it is outside the wide range of reasonable conduct for a lawyer to fail to utilize some method of keeping up with changes in the law. The court concludes that it is. There are numerous issues that could be material to the representation of a client that might be affected by a recent court decision. The "counsel" guaranteed by the Sixth Amendment must at a minimum know the law that controls the cases on his or her docket particularly as those cases move toward trial. It is not possible to have that knowledge without some mechanism to make oneself aware of recent developments in the law.
>
> Given a general responsibility to keep abreast of recent developments in the law, the next issue is how far this responsibility extends. McNamara contends that, at a minimum, it is constitutionally deficient conduct for counsel to be completely unaware that the Supreme Court has granted certiorari to consider the meaning of an element of the offense with which his client is charged and, consequently, to neglect to preserve the point for appeal.
>
> The Government responds that failure to anticipate possible favorable developments in the law and to preserve assignments of error on the basis of those future developments does not constitute ineffective assistance of counsel. Thus, says the Government, because *Rogers* was the law of the Fourth Circuit at the time of McNamara's trial, it was not unreasonable for counsel to have failed to anticipate a change in it.
>
> This argument is appealing in its simplicity for it posits the bright-line rule that, if the law has been changed, a lawyer has to know it. If it has not, he does not. However, the argument misses what is the most compelling aspect of McNamara's argument: that counsel's conduct precluded Mc-

Namara from appealing based upon an issue which the Supreme Court had decided to review and which, if decided favorably to McNamara's position, would necessitate a remand for a new trial in the event of conviction on the controlling law in the circuit.

Contrary to the Government's suggestion, McNamara does not contend that Donnelly should have been clairvoyant or that he should have anticipated future favorable developments in the law. Rather, McNamara argues that Donnelly should have made himself aware of a significant legal event that already had occurred and had been reported, the granting of certiorari in *Ratzlaf*. A reasonable lawyer armed with this knowledge would have passed it on to his client as a potential and promising basis on which to challenge a conviction.

If Donnelly had discovered the Supreme Court's action before McNamara's trial, he could have objected to Instruction No. 29, preserving the issue for appeal and assuring his client a virtually certain reversal should the Supreme Court change the *Rogers* standard. If Donnelly had learned of the Supreme Court's action between the date of conviction and ten days after sentencing, he could have informed his client that it provided a basis for appeal. But, because counsel did not discover the Supreme Court's action, he was unable to make an informed decision how best to protect McNamara's rights.

On the facts of this case, the failure to discover the pendency of *Ratzlaf* was deficient conduct under *Strickland*. It was not sufficient to rely solely on the annotations to the United States Code in interpreting the elements of the offense charged. This insufficiency is illustrated by the fact that now, even after the Supreme Court has decided *Ratzlaf* in direct contradiction of *Rogers*, the annotations relied on by Donnelly still reflect *Rogers* as the law in the Fourth Circuit. The wide range of reasonableness requires that counsel take some action to update and verify the state of the law respecting the elements of the offense with which the client is charged. The failure to do that in this case prevented the discovery of *Ratzlaf* and the making of an informed decision on behalf of the client. This, in turn, deprived McNamara of the " 'counsel' guaranteed the defendant by the Sixth Amendment." *Strickland*, 466 U.S. at 687.

Of course, courts may not use ineffective assistance of counsel claims to second guess a strategic decision of counsel, even if that decision turns out to have harmed the client's position. See *Strickland v. Washington*, 466 U.S. 668, 689 (conduct not ineffective if it may be considered sound trial strategy). That, however, is not the issue presented by these facts because the undisputed record is that counsel was unaware that the Supreme Court had agreed to review the willfulness issue. Deficient performance by counsel may in fact deprive a lawyer of the ability to make a strategic or tactical decision. That is what happened in this case. Because counsel did not keep up with developments in the law then pending resolution before the Supreme Court, he never reached the point of deciding whether raising *Ratzlaf* would further or hinder his client's case.

The court concludes that a lawyer must be aware of the fact that an element of an offense he must defend at trial is under examination by the

Supreme Court, particularly where the decision on that issue has the potential to alter the controlling rule in the circuit and likely will be issued while his client's case is on direct appeal if an appeal is taken. At least at the confluence of these factors, it is beyond the wide range of acceptable professional conduct to be unaware of developments in the law.

3. In *Yarborough v. Gentry*, 124 S.Ct. 1 (2003), the Court held that a defense attorney's closing argument was not so weak as to constitute ineffective assistance of counsel. The Court said:

> Counsel has wide latitude in deciding how best to represent a client, and deference to counsel's tactical decisions in his closing presentation is particularly important because of the broad range of legitimate defense strategy at that stage. Closing arguments should sharpen and clarify the issues for resolution by the trier of fact, but which issues to sharpen and how best to clarify them are questions with many reasonable answers. Indeed, it might sometimes make sense to forgo closing argument altogether. Judicial review of a defense attorney's summation is therefore highly deferential — and doubly deferential when it is conducted through the lens of federal habeas.

4. In *People v. Day*, 2 Cal.App.4th 405 (1992), Day was charged with killing her boyfriend, and she claimed self-defense. There was evidence that the boyfriend had abused her. Defense counsel was not aware of the "battered woman syndrome", and presented no expert testimony explaining this syndrome to the jury, which convicted Day of involuntary manslaughter. The court held that the defense lawyer's failure to present this defense was ineffective assistance of counsel. (It seems notable, however, that while the court cited cases allowing similar evidence — such as rape trauma syndrome — it cited no California case squarely holding that evidence of battered woman syndrome is admissible!)

5. In *Javor v. U.S.*, 724 F.2d 831 (9th Cir.1984), the court held that "when an attorney for a criminal defendant sleeps through a substantial portion of the trial, such conduct is inherently prejudicial and thus no separate showing of prejudice is necessary. * * * * Prejudice is inherent in this case because unconscious or sleeping counsel is equivalent to no counsel at all. The mere physical presence of an attorney does not fulfill the Sixth Amendment entitlement to the assistance of counsel."

6. In *Ouber v. Guarino*, 293 F.3d 19 (1st Cir. 2002), defense counsel delivered his opening statement to the jury right after the prosecutor delivered his opening statement. Defense counsel told the jury that defendant would testify. But defendant did not testify. The court held that defense counsel was ineffective:

> At the heart of this appeal lies a broken promise (or, more precisely put, a series of broken promises): defense counsel's repeated vow that the jurors would hear what happened from the petitioner herself. Thus, the error attributed to counsel consists of two inextricably intertwined events: the attorney's initial decision to present the petitioner's testimony as the centerpiece of the defense (and his serial announcement of that fact to the jury in his opening statement) in conjunction with his subsequent decision to advise the petitioner against testifying. Taken alone, each of these decisions may have fallen within the broad universe of acceptable professional judgments. Taken together, however, they are indefensible. Neither the state court nor the Commonwealth has managed to identify any benefit

to be derived from such a decisional sequence, and we are unable to see the combination as part and parcel of a reasoned strategy. We therefore conclude that, in the absence of unforeseeable events forcing a change in strategy, the sequence constituted an error in professional judgment.

This assessment does not end our inquiry. The complex dynamics of trial engender numerous missteps, but only the most inexcusable will support a finding that counsel's performance was so substandard as to compromise a defendant's Sixth Amendment right to proficient legal representation. *Strickland*, 466 U.S. at 687.

To separate wheat from chaff — lapses of constitutional dimension from garden-variety bevues — we must assess the gravity of the error and then consider potential justifications for the attorney's actions, given what he knew or should have known at each relevant moment in time. * * * *

It is apodictic that a defendant cannot be compelled to testify in a criminal case, and criminal juries routinely are admonished — as was the jury here — not to draw an adverse inference from a defendant's failure to testify. But the defendant has the right to testify in her own defense, and, when such testimony is proffered, the impact on the jury can hardly be overestimated. When a jury is promised that it will hear the defendant's story from the defendant's own lips, and the defendant then reneges, common sense suggests that the course of trial may be profoundly altered. A broken promise of this magnitude taints both the lawyer who vouchsafed it and the client on whose behalf it was made.

The Commonwealth argues that a defendant's decision about whether to invoke the right to remain silent is a strategic choice, requiring a balancing of risks and benefits. Under ordinary circumstances, that is true. It is easy to imagine that, on the eve of trial, a thoughtful lawyer may remain unsure as to whether to call the defendant as a witness. If such uncertainty exists, however, it is an abecedarian principle that the lawyer must exercise some degree of circumspection. Had the petitioner's counsel temporized — he was under no obligation to make an opening statement at all, much less to open before the prosecution presented its case, and, even if he chose to open, he most assuredly did not have to commit to calling his client as a witness — this would be a different case.

Here, however, the circumstances were far from ordinary. The petitioner's counsel elected to make his opening statement at the earliest possible time. He did not hedge his bets, but, rather, acted as if he had no doubt about whether his client should testify. In the course of his opening statement, he promised, over and over, that the petitioner would testify and exhorted the jurors to draw their ultimate conclusions based on her credibility. In fine, the lawyer structured the entire defense around the prospect of the petitioner's testimony.

In the end, however, the petitioner's testimony was not forthcoming. Despite the fact that the lawyer had called the petitioner to the stand in both prior trials, he did a complete about-face. The lawyer states in his affidavit that he only realized that keeping his client off the witness stand was an option after the first day of trial. This realization came much too late.

The Commonwealth argues that defense counsel's mid-trial decision should be excused as a justified reaction to unfolding events. The theoretical underpinnings for this argument are sound: unexpected developments sometimes may warrant changes in previously announced trial strategies.

But although we cannot fault counsel for not guarding against the unforeseeable, the case at hand does not fit that description. Here, everything went according to schedule; nothing occurred during the third trial that could have blindsided a reasonably competent attorney or justified a retreat from a promise previously made. After all, the petitioner's lawyer had represented her during two previous trials for the same offense; the prosecution's case in chief did not differ significantly at the third trial; and the situation that confronted the attorney when he changed his mind about the desirability of presenting the petitioner's testimony was no different from the situation that existed at a comparable stage of the earlier trials. * * * *

The Commonwealth has another arrow in its quiver: it asserts that, had the petitioner testified, she would have been heavily impeached (and, thus, the decision not to testify was a legitimate one). Because of the damaging evidence that was available for impeachment had the petitioner testified — the drugs and cash found in the search — this argument has a patina of plausibility. The difficulty, however, is that counsel knew of this sword of Damocles — the threat that the impeaching evidence would be introduced — when he made his opening statement. Indeed, that evidence was used to cross-examine the petitioner during the two prior trials, and counsel appeared ready, willing, and able to handle that contingency.

The short of it is that, without exception, the events that occurred at the third trial should have been easily foreseeable to competent counsel at the time he made his opening statement. There were no surprises — and, thus, the lawyer's tergiversation could not be excused by changed circumstances. * * * *

To sum up, counsel committed an obvious error, without any semblance of a colorable excuse. There is simply no record support for the state court's finding that the attorney's conduct constituted a reasonable strategic choice. To the contrary, the only sensible conclusion that can be drawn from this record is that the attorney's performance was constitutionally deficient under *Strickland* — and severely so. We hold, therefore, that the state-court finding on this point constituted an unreasonable application of the *Strickland* performance prong.

7. In *Goodspeed v. State*, 120 S.W.3d 408 (Tex.App. 2003), the court held that a defense attorney's failure to ask any questions to prospective jurors during *voir dire* was ineffective assistance of counsel, noting that Texas law has jurors determine not only guilt or innocence, but also the defendant's sentence:

Counsel's waiver of Goodspeed's right to solicit information from prospective jurors (when such information could only help assist in intelligently exercising peremptory strikes) falls well below the objective standard of reasonableness. Given the need for fair and impartial jurors, careful and precise voir dire questioning by defense counsel usually tends to elicit answers that form the basis of a challenge for cause or, alternatively, provide a gender or race-neutral reason for the exercise of a peremptory challenge.

Moreover, by failing to examine the panel, the defense never had an opportunity to determine if any of the members of the venire should have been disqualified for not being able to consider the full range of punishment.

8. In our case, did lawyer Howe fail to provide "reasonably effective assistance" of counsel in his investigation of the case? In *Strickland*, the Court indicated that the American Bar Association's Standards for Criminal Justice "are guides to determining what is reasonable, but they are only guides". Here are a couple of Standards that you might find helpful:

AMERICAN BAR ASSOCIATION STANDARDS FOR CRIMINAL JUSTICE
(as amended in 1986)

Standard 4-4.1: Duty To Investigate

It is the duty of the lawyer to conduct a prompt investigation of the circumstances of the case and to explore all avenues leading to facts relevant to the merits of the case and the penalty in the event of conviction. The investigation should always include efforts to secure information in the possession of the prosecution and law enforcement authorities. The duty to investigate exists regardless of the accused's admissions or statements to the lawyer of facts constituting guilt or the accused's stated desire to plead guilty.

Commentary

Facts form the basis of effective representation. Effective representation consists of much more than the advocate's courtroom function per se. Adequate investigation may avert the need for courtroom confrontation. Considerable ingenuity may be required to locate persons who observed the criminal act charged or who have information concerning it. After they are located, their cooperation must be secured. It may be necessary to approach a witness several times to raise new questions stemming from facts learned from others. The resources of scientific laboratories may be required to evaluate certain kinds of evidence: analyses of fingerprints or handwriting, clothing, hair, or blood samples, or ballistics tests may be necessary. Neglect of any of these steps may preclude the presentation of an effective defense. * * * *

Standard 4-4.2: Illegal Investigation

It is unprofessional conduct for a lawyer knowingly to use illegal means to obtain evidence or information or to employ, instruct, or encourage others to do so.

Standard 4-8.6: Challenges To The Effectiveness Of Counsel

(a) If a lawyer, after investigation, is satisfied that another lawyer who served in an earlier phase of the case did not provide effective assistance, he or she should not hesitate to seek relief for the defendant on that ground.

(b) If a lawyer, after investigation, is satisfied that another lawyer who served in an earlier phase of the case provided effective assistance, he or she should so advise the client and may decline to proceed further.

(c) A lawyer whose conduct of a criminal case is drawn into question is entitled to testify concerning the matters charged and is not precluded from disclosing the truth concerning the accusation, even though this involves revealing matters which were given in confidence.

(8) If a defendant's lawyer violates a state or bar association rule of professional conduct, is that in itself ineffective assistance of counsel? No, held the court in *U.S. v. Nickerson*, 556 F.3d 1014 (9th Cir. 2009). What if a *disbarred* lawyer represents the defendant at trial? Not even this is automatically ineffective assistance, according to *U.S. v. Bosch*, 914 F.2d 1239 (9th Cir. 1990).

PEOPLE v. POZO
Colorado Supreme Court
746 P.2d 523 (1987)

KIRSHBAUM, JUSTICE.

I

Pozo, an alien legally residing in the United States, came to this country from Cuba in April 1980. In October 1982, pursuant to a plea agreement, Pozo entered pleas of guilty to second degree sexual assault and to escape. Pozo received a sentence to the Department of Corrections of two years for the escape conviction and a consecutive sentence of two years and six months for the sexual assault conviction. In May 1983, after a detainer was filed against him by the Immigration and Naturalization Service,[2] Pozo filed motions to vacate the judgments of conviction under Crim.P. 35(c). He asserted: (1) that he was not adequately advised of, nor did he understand the elements of the charges against him when he entered the pleas; and (2) that he did not receive effective assistance of counsel because his trial counsel did not advise him of the possible deportation consequences of his guilty pleas.

A hearing on these motions was held in June 1983. Pozo testified through an interpreter that in October 1982 he had not been aware of any possible deportation consequences of his guilty pleas and that he would not have entered such pleas had he been aware of those consequences. An affidavit signed by Pozo's trial counsel, stating that he had not discussed the possible deportation consequences of the guilty pleas with Pozo, was introduced into evidence. The trial court found that prior

---

[2] Pursuant to 8 U.S.C. § 1251(a)(4) (1982) an alien who is convicted of a crime of moral turpitude within five years of entry into this country may be deported.

to entering the guilty pleas Pozo had not discussed deportation consequences with his trial counsel or any other counsel and was not aware of such consequences. However, the trial court concluded that Pozo had been represented by competent and effective counsel. The Court of Appeals concluded that Pozo had been denied effective assistance of counsel, reversed the trial court's ruling and remanded the case to the trial court with directions to reinstate the original charges and allow Pozo to plead anew.

II

A plea of guilty effects a waiver of fundamental rights and, therefore, must be knowingly, intelligently and voluntarily made to be valid. *Hill v. Lockhart*, 474 U.S. 52 (1985); *Brady v. United States*, 397 U.S. 742 (1970). Under the sixth amendment to the United States Constitution and article II, section 16 of the Colorado Constitution, the voluntariness of a guilty plea entered by a defendant represented by counsel depends in part upon whether counsel's advice "was within the range of competence demanded of attorneys in criminal cases." *McMann v. Richardson*, 397 U.S. 759, 771. A defendant who enters a guilty plea cannot later claim the plea was involuntary merely because counsel's advice was wrong, so long as such advice is within general bounds of reasonable competence. *Id.*

In *Hill v. Lockhart*, the Supreme Court applied the two-part test of *Strickland v. Washington*, 466 U.S. 668 (1984), to a sixth amendment claim of ineffective assistance of counsel in connection with the entry of a guilty plea. Under *Strickland*, a defendant claiming a violation of the constitutional right to representation by competent counsel must show that his attorney's performance fell below an objective standard of reasonableness and that the deficient performance resulted in prejudice to the defendant. * * * *

It is well settled that a trial court is not required to advise a defendant *sua sponte* of potential federal deportation consequences of a plea of guilty to a felony charge when accepting such plea.[4] E.g., *Downs-Morgan v. United States*, 765 F.2d 1534 (11th Cir.1985); *United States v. Russell*, 686 F.2d 35, 39 (D.C.Cir.1982). This rule is grounded in the notion that in accepting a plea of guilty a trial court is not required to ascertain the defendant's knowledge or understanding of collateral consequences of the conviction. The trial court is required to advise the defendant only of the direct consequences of the conviction to satisfy the due process concerns that a plea be made knowingly and with full understanding of the consequences thereof.

Sixth amendment constitutional standards requiring effective assistance of counsel involve examination of quite different considerations, however. One who relies on the advice of a legally trained representative when answering criminal charges is entitled to assume that the attorney will provide sufficiently accurate advice to enable the defendant to fully understand and assess the serious legal proceedings in which he is involved. While justice does not demand errorless representation, attorneys must satisfy minimal standards of competency to render effective and, therefore, constitutionally acceptable representation. As noted in *Strickland, Lockhart* and *Hutchinson*, the conduct of attorneys must by necessity

---

[4] Six states have enacted statutes which require trial courts to inform alien defendants of possible deportation consequences of guilty pleas. Cal. Penal Code § 1016.5; Conn.Gen.Stat.Ann. § 54-1j; Mass.Gen.Laws Ann. ch. 278, § 29D; Or.Rev.Stat. § 135.385(2)(d); Tex.Code Crim.Proc.Ann. art. 26.13(a)(4); Wash.Rev.Code Ann. § 10.40.200.

THE RIGHT TO EFFECTIVE ASSISTANCE OF COUNSEL   CH. 14

be considered on a case-by-case basis in light of objective standards of minimally acceptable levels of professional performance prevailing at the time of the challenged conduct. The duty of counsel is, in essence, the duty to act as any reasonable attorney would act in the same circumstances. Thus, questions regarding the type of conduct or communication required of an attorney representing a client can rarely be answered by abstract concepts. From this perspective, it is not surprising that courts considering the issue of whether defense counsel has a duty to advise alien clients of potential deportation consequences have reached conflicting results.[5] Compare *People v. Padilla*, 151 Ill.App.3d 297 (1986) (failure to advise of deportation consequences constitutes ineffective assistance of counsel), and *Commonwealth v. Wellington*, 305 Pa.Super. 24 (1982) (counsel has a duty to inquire into and advise alien defendant of possible deportation consequences), with *Tafoya v. State*, 500 P.2d 247, 251 (Alaska 1972) (alien defendant received effective assistance of counsel despite counsel's failure to advise of deportation consequences), and *State v. Ginebra*, 511 So.2d 960 (1987) (counsel's failure to advise client of the collateral consequence of deportation does not constitute ineffective assistance of counsel), and *Mott v. State*, 407 N.W.2d 581 (Iowa 1987) (failure to advise alien defendant of collateral consequences cannot provide basis for a claim of ineffective assistance of counsel).

We are not prepared to state in absolute terms, as did the Court of Appeals, that an attorney has a duty to advise an alien client of the possible deportation consequences of a guilty plea. Nor can we conclude, as the trial court did, that an attorney has no such duty. The general issue framed by Pozo's Crim.P. 35(c) motions was whether he was denied effective assistance of counsel. Whether counsel adequately represented Pozo in view of the lack of advice concerning possible deportation consequences depends initially on whether counsel had a duty to apprise himself of this aspect of immigration law. If no such duty existed, counsel of course had no responsibility to discuss deportation consequences with Pozo. In essence, then, this case presents the question of whether an attorney's failure to research and investigate a particular body of law while representing a client rendered the attorney's assistance constitutionally ineffective. In cases alleging ineffective assistance of counsel, the trial court must judge the reasonableness of the attorney's conduct on the basis of all of the factual circumstances of the particular case, viewed in light of the prevailing standards of minimally acceptable professional conduct as of the time of the challenged conduct. Such inquiry must include an initial determination of whether the body of law was relevant to the circumstances of the client and the matters for which the attorney was retained. The inquiry must also include a determination of whether the attorney had reason to believe that the area of law in question was relevant to the client and the client's legal problems.

The California Court of Appeals recently had occasion to consider the duty of counsel to research and investigate immigration consequences in *People v. Soriano*, 194 Cal.App.3d 1470 (1987). In *Soriano*, defense counsel advised her client regarding immigration consequences despite counsel's admission that she had not

---

[5] It is generally recognized that when an alien defendant enters a guilty plea based on erroneous representations as to deportation consequences, he or she will in most cases be permitted to withdraw the plea. E.g., *United States v. Briscoe*, 432 F.2d 1351 (D.C.Cir.1970) (guilty plea may be subject to attack where defendant misled by prosecutor as to deportation consequences); *People v. Correa*, 108 Ill.2d 541 (1984) (counsel's assurance that plea would not change immigration status constitutes ineffective assistance).

fully researched the pertinent immigration law. Noting that counsel was aware that her client was an alien, and that she did not adequately investigate federal immigration law, the court concluded that defendant had been deprived of effective assistance of counsel.

Although *Soriano* is factually distinguishable from this case insofar as it involved erroneous representations by counsel, we find the court's underlying concern over counsel's failure to engage in rudimentary legal investigation compelling. In *People v. White*, 182 Colo. 417 (1973), this court addressed a similar problem. In *White*, the attorney in question neglected to investigate material factual circumstances of his client's case and failed to research the law concerning the crime with which his client had been charged. We concluded that the failure to perform such basic duties rendered counsel's assistance constitutionally ineffective.

In determining whether the performance of Pozo's counsel fell below an objective standard of reasonable conduct, an examination of the relevant statutes and governing law is necessary. An alien who pleads guilty to a crime involving moral turpitude is subject to deportation under 8 U.S.C. § 1251(a) (1982) which provides in part as follows: "Any alien in the United States shall, upon the order of the Attorney General, be deported who — * * * (4) is convicted of a crime involving moral turpitude committed within five years after entry and either sentenced to confinement or confined in a prison or corrective institution, for a year or more, or who at any time after entry is convicted of two crimes involving moral turpitude, not arising out of a single scheme of criminal misconduct, regardless of whether confined therefore and regardless of whether the convictions were in a single trial." Pozo, although a legal resident of the United States, is deemed an "alien" because he is neither a citizen nor a national of the United States. Therefore, he is subject to deportation under § 1251(a)(4) because he pled guilty to second degree sexual assault within five years of entering the country.

The harsh consequences of deportation may be averted, however, if the trial court having jurisdiction over the alien defendant recommends to the Attorney General, at the time of first imposing judgment or passing sentence or within thirty days thereafter, that the defendant not be deported. 8 U.S.C. § 1251(b). Although Congress intended that aliens would be deported routinely for convictions of serious crimes under 8 U.S.C. § 1251(a)(4), the recommendation of the sentencing judge, properly made in accordance with 8 U.S.C. § 1251(b), is binding upon the Attorney General. *Janvier v. U.S.*, 793 F.2d 449, 452–53 (2d Cir.1986). In practice, then, a sentencing judge can prevent the deportation of a convicted alien.

In view of these factors, we conclude that the potential deportation consequences of guilty pleas in criminal proceedings brought against alien defendants are material to critical phases of such proceedings. The determination of whether the failure to investigate those consequences constitutes ineffective assistance of counsel turns to a significant degree upon whether the attorney had sufficient information to form a reasonable belief that the client was in fact an alien. When defense counsel in a criminal case is aware that his client is an alien, he may reasonably be required to investigate relevant immigration law. This duty stems not from a duty to advise specifically of deportation consequences, but rather from the more fundamental principle that attorneys must inform themselves of material legal principles that may significantly impact the particular circumstances of their clients. In cases involving alien criminal defendants, for example, thorough knowledge of fundamental principles of deportation law may have significant impact on a client's decisions concerning plea negotiations and defense strategies.

The record in this case does not establish whether Pozo's counsel had reason to know before the plea was entered that Pozo was an alien. At the hearing on Pozo's Crim.P. 35(c) motion, the trial court concluded that Pozo's attorney's failure to advise his client of deportation consequences did not render the attorney's assistance ineffective; thus, the trial court did not address the questions of whether the attorney had reason to know that Pozo was an alien and what the standards of minimally acceptable professional conduct were at the time. These determinations may best be performed by the trial court upon an adequate record. Furthermore, as *Strickland* indicates, a finding that defense counsel had reason to know of Pozo's alien status and failed to conduct appropriate research would not render the attorney's performance inadequate in the absence of a finding that such conduct resulted in prejudice to Pozo. The trial court made no specific findings concerning the question of prejudice — and again, the trial court is in the best position to evaluate the evidence and the credibility of witnesses with regard to this portion of the *Strickland* test.[8]

Because critical determinations remain to be made before a conclusion concerning Pozo's claim of ineffective assistance of counsel can be made, the judgment of the Court of Appeals must be reversed and the case must be returned to the trial court for further proceedings.

ROVIRA, JUSTICE, dissenting:

* * * *

There is no contention by Pozo that he did not understand the direct consequences of his plea or that his plea was invalid because of any threat, misrepresentation, or other impropriety. Therefore, he is left with his "but/for argument," i.e., but/for the failure of my lawyer in not advising me that I might be deported if I pleaded guilty, I would not have pleaded guilty.

An ineffectiveness of counsel argument is immaterial with respect to a guilty plea except to the extent that it relates to the issues of voluntariness and understanding. *Lee v. Hopper*, 499 F.2d 456, 462 (5th Cir. 1974). A plea is considered knowing and voluntary when the defendant has been advised of all consequences which have a "definite, immediate, and largely automatic effect on the range of a defendant's

---

[8] In considering whether a defendant who challenges a previously entered guilty plea on the basis of ineffective assistance of counsel has suffered prejudice, trial courts must focus upon whether counsel's conduct affected the outcome of the plea process. *Hill v. Lockhart*, 474 U.S. 52 (1985). In *Hill*, the Supreme Court observed that, "in order to satisfy the *Strickland* prejudice requirement, the defendant must show that there is some reasonable probability that but for counsel's errors, he would not have pleaded guilty and would have insisted on going to trial." 474 U.S. at 59. Of course, the particular posture of a given case can affect the focus of inquiry into a claim of prejudice resulting from conduct that fell below an objectively reasonable minimal level of representation. For example, the court observed in *Strickland* that a trial court considering a post-conviction challenge to a guilty verdict must determine whether there is a reasonable probability that, absent counsel's errors, the factfinder would have entertained a reasonable doubt about the defendant's guilt, while a court considering a challenged death sentence must determine whether a reasonable probability exists that, absent counsel's errors, the sentencer would have declined to impose that penalty. 466 U.S. 668, 695. Whatever direction the inquiry into prejudice might take, determination of that issue will invariably involve questions of credibility for resolution by the trial court.

punishment." *People v. Heinz*, 197 Colo. 102, 106 (1979).

Our inquiry should be directed, then, solely to determine whether he understood the direct consequences of his plea. Clearly, as the majority acknowledges, deportation is a collateral consequence of conviction and not a direct consequence.

I agree with the substantial majority of courts that have utilized the collateral/direct consequence distinction to reject the claim that a defendant's ignorance of deportation consequences reflects ineffective assistance of counsel and renders his plea involuntary. See, e.g., *United States v. Campbell*, 778 F.2d 764 (11th Cir.1985); *United States v. Gavilan*, 761 F.2d 226 (5th Cir.1985). * * * *

The collateral/direct consequence distinction reflects the nature of the rights a defendant has in pleading guilty. The Supreme Court identified the bases for those rights in the following words: A defendant who enters such a guilty plea simultaneously waives several constitutional rights, including his privilege against compulsory self-incrimination, his right to trial by jury, and his right to confront his accusers. For this waiver to be valid under the Due Process Clause, it must be "an intentional relinquishment of a known right or privilege." *Johnson v. Zerbst*, 304 U.S. 458 (1938). Consequently, if a defendant's guilty plea is not equally voluntary and knowing, it has been obtained in violation of due process and is therefore void. Moreover, because a guilty plea is an admission of all the elements of a formal criminal charge, it cannot be truly voluntary unless the defendant possesses an understanding of the law in relation to the facts. *McCarthy v. United States*, 394 U.S. 459, 466 (1969).

In addition, a defendant must understand the penalty the legislature has fixed for the criminal conduct to which he is pleading guilty. Absent such an understanding, the defendant may plead guilty under a misguided expectation — however induced — that his plea will result in some measure of sentencing leniency.

None of those reasons supports the rule the majority adopts today. It cannot be disputed that a defendant may attach substantial importance to some collateral consequences of a guilty plea. We have never before held, however, that the potential importance of a particular collateral consequence may give rise to a constitutional right to be apprised of that consequence by defense counsel. The loss of one's right to vote, exclusion from military service, or other disabilities attached to a felony conviction may be just as harsh a consequence to a citizen defendant as deportation may be to an alien, yet courts have consistently denied that defendants have a constitutional right to be informed of the former collateral consequences.[1]

---

[1] Although deportation has an undeniable impact on a defendant's life, so do other collateral consequences which often flow from a guilty plea. Failure to inform the defendant of the following consequences of his guilty plea has been held not to render the plea invalid. *Wright v. United States*, 624 F.2d 557, 561 (5th Cir.1980) (a plea's possible enhancing effects on a subsequent sentence); *Moore v. Hinton*, 513 F.2d 781 (5th Cir.1975) (suspension of auto license); *United States v. Crowley*, 529 F.2d 1066, 1072 (3d Cir.) (loss of civil service job as result of felony conviction); *Cuthrell v. Director*, 475 F.2d 1364, 1366 (4th Cir.) (institution of separate civil proceedings against defendant for commitment to a mental health facility); *Hutchison v. United States*, 450 F.2d 930, 931 (10th Cir.1971) (loss of good time credit); *Waddy v. Davis*, 445 F.2d 1 (5th Cir.1971) (disenfranchisement); *United States v. Vermeulen*, 436 F.2d 72, 75 (2d Cir.1970) (possibility of imposition of consecutive sentences); *Meaton v. United States*, 328 F.2d 379 (5th Cir.1964) (deprivation of rights to vote and to travel abroad); *United States v. Cariola*, 323 F.2d 180 (3d Cir.1963) (deprivation of right to vote in some jurisdictions); *Redwine v. Zuckert*, 317 F.2d 336 (D.C.Cir.1963) (possibility of undesirable discharge from the armed forces); *State v. Riggins*, 466 A.2d 981 (N.J.Super.Ct.App.Div.1983) (loss of employment).

The majority opinion focuses on the potential deportation consequences of guilty pleas in criminal proceedings, and thereby opens the door to innumerable challenges to pleas based on the defendant's ignorance of other serious collateral consequences.

In *United States v. Timmreck*, 441 U.S. 780 (1978), the defendant sought habeas corpus relief and alleged that his guilty plea was involuntary because he was unaware of the mandatory parole term that would result from his conviction. A unanimous Supreme Court denied relief, and concluded with a caution that bears repeating here: "Every inroad on the concept of finality undermines confidence in the integrity of our procedures; and, by increasing the volume of judicial work, inevitably delays and impairs the orderly administration of justice. The impact is greatest when new grounds for setting aside guilty pleas are approved because the vast majority of criminal convictions result from such pleas. Moreover, the concern that unfair procedures may have resulted in the conviction of an innocent defendant is only rarely raised by a petition to set aside a guilty plea." 441 U.S. at 784.

The defendant has never claimed that he did not commit the crimes that he pleaded guilty to. Nothing has been brought to my attention which gives me reason to question the reliability of defendant's guilty plea as establishing his actual commission of the crimes charged.

An additional problem with the majority opinion is the burden it places on the trial courts to determine whether an attorney whose client is an alien has reasonably investigated relevant immigration law. The majority opinion states that "an examination of the relevant statutes and governing law" is necessary to determine "whether the performance of Pozo's counsel fell below an objective standard of reasonable conduct." It then considers 8 U.S.C. § 1251(a) and (b), and concludes that a sentencing judge can prevent the deportation of a convicted alien.

A cursory review of the United States immigration law and the applicable regulations suggests that the trial court will be required to hold an extensive evidentiary hearing in order to determine whether an attorney's performance was "reasonable." United States immigration law is complex and the regulations and judicial decisions interpreting the law represent a body of knowledge to which some attorneys devote their full time and attention. A public defender or attorney in private practice who represents defendants in criminal cases should not be found to be "ineffective" for failing to advise his client about a body of civil law which is not directly related to the issues involved in a Crim.P. 11 hearing. The majority, by opening the Pandora's box of collateral consequences, has further burdened an overtaxed judicial system. It has also provided defendants who have knowingly, intelligently, and voluntarily entered pleas of guilty an opportunity to withdraw those pleas, sometimes years after witnesses and evidence have been lost, on the ground that "but/for" their attorney's failure to advise of collateral consequences they would not have entered such a plea.

Notes from Fern:

1. As both the majority and dissent acknowledge, immigration law is pretty complex — some lawyers make a specialty of it. Is it reasonable to expect a criminal defense lawyer to study an entirely new field just to advise one of his many clients?

2. In *Berkow v. State*, 573 N.W.2d 91, affirmed at 583 N.W.2d 562 (Minnesota1998), the court stated:

> Federal and state court decisions vary widely as to whether an attorney's failure to inform a defendant of immigration consequences of a guilty plea constitutes ineffective assistance of counsel. See, e.g., *Williams v. State*, 641 N.E.2d 44, 49 (Ind.Ct.App.1995) (holding that failure to inform defendant is ineffective assistance of counsel); *Commonwealth v. Frometa*, 520 Pa. 552 (1989) (holding that failure to inform defendant is not ineffective assistance of counsel); *In re Amendments to Florida Rules of Criminal Procedure*, 536 So.2d 992, 992 (Fla.1988) (requiring court to inform defendant of immigration consequences, superseding *State v. Ginebra*, 511 So.2d 960, 960 (Fla.1987) (holding that counsel's assistance not ineffective)); *People v. Pozo*, 746 P.2d 523, 529 (Colo.1987) (stating that counsel's assistance is ineffective if counsel knew or had reason to know client was not citizen); *People v. Huante*, 143 Ill.2d 61 (1991) (ineffective assistance only if counsel actively misrepresented deportation consequences).

See also *People v. Sandoval*, 73 Cal.App.4th 404 (1999).

3. Rule 1.1 of the Model Rules of Professional Conduct Rule (1983) provides as follows:

Rule 1.1. Competence

A lawyer shall provide competent representation to a client. Competent representation requires the legal knowledge, skill, thoroughness and preparation reasonably necessary for the representation.

Comment

In determining whether a lawyer employs the requisite knowledge and skill in a particular matter, relevant factors include the relative complexity and specificalized nature of the matter, the lawyer's general experience, the lawyer's training and experience in the field in question, the preparation and study the lawyer is able to give the matter and whether it is feasible to refer the matter to, or associate or consult with, a lawyer of established competence in the field in question. In many instances, the required proficiency is that of a general practitioner. Expertise in a particular field of law may be required in some circumstances.

A lawyer need not necessarily have special training or prior experience to handle legal problems of a type with which the lawyer is unfamiliar. A newly admitted lawyer can be as competent as a practitioner with long experience. Some important legal skills, such as the analysis of precedent, the evaluation of evidence and legal drafting, are required in all legal problems. Perhaps the most fundamental legal skill consists of determining what kind of legal problems a situation may involve, a skill that necessarily transcends any particular specialized knowledge. A lawyer can provide adequate representation in a wholly novel field through necessary study. Competent representation can also be provided through the association of a lawyer of established competence in the field in question. * * * *

4. In *In re Alvernaz*, 2 Cal.4th 924 (1992), defendant was charged with robbery, burglary, and kidnapping. The prosecutor offered him a plea bargain that would result in a maximum sentence of 5 years. Defendant's lawyer told him that if he rejected the offer and went to trial, he had a "70%-80%" chance of acquittal, and if he was convicted, faced a maximum term of 8 years. Defendant rejected the offer, went to trial, was convicted, and was sentenced to 16 years. He then sought habeas corpus, claiming ineffective assistance of counsel. The court of appeal affirmed the denial of the petition, holding that a defendant suffers no prejudice from ineffective assistance of counsel at plea bargaining, where he thereafter receives a fair trial.

The California Supreme Court rejected this reasoning, holding that where defendant shows ineffective assistance in plea bargaining, he is entitled either to have the plea bargain carried out, or to a new trial. He must, however, also show prejudice: that had he received effective assistance, he would have accepted the plea bargain. To determine this, the court should consider whether counsel actually and accurately communicated the offer to defendant, the advice given by counsel, the disparity between the offer and the probable consequences of going to trial, and whether defendant indicated that he was receptive to the offer. (Defendant's "self-serving" statement that he would have accepted the offer is insufficient, as "a contrary holding would lead to an unchecked flow of easily fabricated claims".) Alvernaz had failed to show that he would have accepted the offer, as the evidence showed that he felt strongly that he would be acquitted at trial.

JOHNSON v. STATE
Georgia Court of Appeals
430 S.E.2d 821 (1993)

Imogene L. Walker, Atlanta, for appellant.

Lewis R. Slaton, Dist. Atty., Carla E. Young, Vivian D. Hoard, Asst. Dist. Attys., for appellee.

McMurray, Presiding Judge.

Defendant Johnson appeals his conviction of the offenses of rape and kidnapping.

The evidence construed in the light most favorable to the verdict shows that the victim was walking home from a friend's house at approximately 2:30 a.m. when the defendant sneaked up behind her, grabbed her, and pulled her over to the grounds of a nearby school. At the school grounds, defendant threw the victim down, tore off her clothes, and forcibly had sexual intercourse with the victim. This evidence was sufficient to enable a rational trier of fact to find defendant guilty beyond a reasonable doubt of rape and kidnapping.

Before and at trial, defendant expressed his concern as to whether, in view of the nature of the crimes with which he was charged, he would receive a fair trial in a courtroom where the judge, prosecuting attorney, and defense attorney were all women. Defendant sought the recusal of the trial judge and district attorney, as well as the appointment of male defense counsel.

Defendant enumerates as error the denial of his request that appointed counsel be relieved and other counsel be appointed, and argues that he "was prevented from fully participating in his defense because he was denied counsel of his preference." However, defendant has a "right to the effective assistance of counsel, not the right to the assistance of counsel satisfactory to the defendant." *Bailey v. State*, 240 Ga. 112. There is no showing that defendant was not provided with reasonably effective assistance of counsel, therefore we find no error in the denial of defendant's motion requesting a change of defense counsel. * * *

Next, defendant contends that the trial court erred in admitting evidence of his 1982 conviction of rape based on a plea of guilty. However, no objection to this evidence was presented at trial. This issue cannot be raised for the first time on appeal. *Weaver v. State*, 200 Ga.App. 82. * * * *

Judgment affirmed.

GOVERNMENT OF THE VIRGIN ISLANDS v. WEATHERWAX

U.S. Court of Appeals, 3rd Circuit
77 F.3d 1425 (1996)

STAPLETON, CIRCUIT JUDGE:

This is the second time that this habeas corpus proceeding has been before us. In the previous appeal, we reversed the district court's dismissal of Weatherwax's petition for a writ of habeas corpus and remanded for an evidentiary hearing on Weatherwax's claim of ineffective assistance of counsel. After holding the evidentiary hearing, the district court granted Weatherwax's petition for habeas relief. We will reverse.

William Weatherwax was indicted for the shooting death of St. Clair Hazel. A jury acquitted him of first degree murder but convicted him of second degree murder and unlawful possession of a weapon. We affirmed on direct appeal.

Weatherwax thereafter filed a petition for a writ of habeas corpus, raising several arguments. Only one of those arguments is relevant to this appeal. Weatherwax alleged that during his trial a juror was observed with a newspaper containing an article about the trial. The article allegedly reported an inaccurate and unfavorable account of Weatherwax's testimony. Both Weatherwax and members of his family informed defense counsel of this fact but the lawyer failed to bring the matter to the trial court's attention. Weatherwax claimed that his attorney's failure to bring this matter to the court's attention constituted ineffective assistance of counsel.

The district court rejected that argument, reasoning that the newspaper article was "a verbatim and dispassionate account of the testimony adduced at trial" which accordingly could not be prejudicial. We came to a different conclusion, however, finding that the actual trial testimony varied from the newspaper account in several significant respects. We found that the difference between the article version and the official transcript, "although subtle," could have been unfairly prejudicial because Weatherwax's testimony (but not the newspaper account) "argued against second degree murder and supported Weatherwax's self-defense testimony."[1]

We further found that "if the jurors read the damaging article with its distorted reporting of Weatherwax's testimony, the likelihood of resulting taint to the fairness

---

[1] The article reported only on the testimony the jury had heard the preceding day; it included no extra-record information about Weatherwax or the crime.

of the trial would be apparent and *Strickland's* second prong would also be met." We, therefore, instructed that if the district court found on remand (1) that a juror in fact had brought the newspaper into the jury room and (2) that Weatherwax's lawyer had been informed of this, then Weatherwax would have "made out a prima facie case of ineffective assistance of counsel under the *Strickland* standard." If such a "prima facie" case were established on remand, we instructed that, "the government must then be afforded the opportunity to question Weatherwax's counsel relative to his failure to request the *voir dire* in order to show, if applicable, that counsel proceeded on the basis of 'sound trial strategy.'"

On remand, the government did not contest Weatherwax's claims (1) that a juror in fact had had possession of a newspaper in the jury room and (2) that Weatherwax's lawyer had been informed of this. Thus, Weatherwax made out a prima facie case of ineffective assistance of counsel under *Strickland*, and the burden shifted to the government to show that Weatherwax's counsel had proceeded on the basis of "sound trial strategy."

To meet its burden, the government called Weatherwax's trial attorney, Michael Joseph. In response, Weatherwax called his sister and his brother-in-law, who were present during the trial, and gave his own account of the relevant events. With the sole exception noted below, the testimony of these witnesses was not in conflict.

Joseph, an experienced criminal defense lawyer and a lifelong resident of the Virgin Islands, was privately retained by Weatherwax. Weatherwax stayed with Joseph in his home during the last few days of pretrial preparation and throughout the trial. Joseph considered it "a very difficult case." Among other things, he explained to Weatherwax the strategy he intended to use in selecting a jury. That strategy was based in part on the fact that Weatherwax's case had created a racially charged atmosphere in the Virgin Islands because Weatherwax was white, a so-called "Continental," and the victim was black. It was also based on the facts surrounding the victim's death and Weatherwax's anticipated defense.

Joseph testified: "Q. Did you have a strategy, sir, with regard to selecting a jury? A. Of course. Q. And what was that strategy? A. I saw this case as a case in which the facts really were not too much in dispute as compared to the jury that would hear the facts and interpret the facts. For instance, it would be undenied that an unlicensed firearm was involved. It would be undenied that Mr. Weatherwax possessed an unlicensed firearm. It would be undenied that Mr. Weatherwax discharged an unlicensed firearm. It would be undenied that the person who was shot did not have a firearm. And it would be undenied that there would be witnesses who would have conflicting stories as to what danger he presented to Mr. Weatherwax. Therefore, I thought Mr. Weatherwax's perception as to what was happening to him, which is the gist of a self defense case, not what's really happening but whether the person reasonably perceived themselves to be in danger was the gist of this case and we needed jurors who would identify with that situation. Q. What were you striving to achieve in the composition of the Weatherwax jury? A. Sympathy. Q. And were you doing that based upon the profile of certain venire persons? A. Absolutely. Q. What were you looking for specifically? A. I was looking for as many Continentals on the jury as possible. Q. And for what reason did you do that? A. Sympathy. Q. Is that another way of saying you would assume that they identified with the defendant? A. Absolutely."

Joseph further testified that a second objective of his trial strategy was to persuade the jury to convict only on a lesser included offense in the event the evidence of self defense did not produce an acquittal on all counts.

The jury ultimately selected to hear Weatherwax's case consisted of three white and nine black jurors. It was the largest number of Continentals Joseph had ever seen on a Virgin Islands jury and he was "ecstatic."

On numerous occasions during the trial, the trial judge admonished the jury to avoid reading articles about the trial in the newspaper. He did not, however, instruct them not to read a newspaper.

On the morning of the last day of the trial, after Weatherwax had finished his testimony and just as the prosecution was about to call its rebuttal witnesses, Weatherwax's sister, Sally Lay, and his brother-in-law, William Lay, observed a juror walk from the jury room into the court room with a local newspaper under his arm. They did not observe him reading the newspaper and, accordingly, did not know what portion of the paper the juror had been exposed to. Mr. and Mrs. Lay advised Weatherwax and a bailiff of their observation. The bailiff took no action but advised them to speak to their lawyer.

The Lays, Weatherwax, and several other members of his family took the bailiff's advice and informed Joseph about the newspaper as he was entering the door of the courtroom. A conversation ensued. Weatherwax expressed the view that it was "not right" for the juror to have a newspaper and he as well as his relatives asked Joseph to do something about it. Mrs. Lay described the conversation and Joseph's response in the following terms: "Q. You didn't ask anything — all I'm asking you, ma'am, is you didn't ask him to do anything specific. You just asked him to do something about it? A. We asked him to do something about it, file a motion or something and he said he would file a motion for a mistrial tomorrow. Q. And that's not all he said, did he? He said something else didn't he? A. In this conversation? Q. Yes. A. Yes, he did. Q. What did he say? A. He said that he — well, he said a lot of things during the course of the conversation. Q. As specifically as you can recall, Mrs. Lay, I would like for you to tell the Court everything that Mr. Joseph said. A. He said that the juror with the newspaper is a white man. He would help Billy's case. He was on our side. Leave it alone. He would file a motion for a mistrial tomorrow. Q. So he told you essentially not to worry about it, didn't he? Ms. Lamont: Objection. The Court: It's cross examination. Ask her that question before you go on to something else. By Mr. Humphreys: Q. You may answer the question. Attorney Joseph told you not to worry about the situation, didn't he? A. No, he did not use those words. Q. But he did tell you, as a matter of fact, that he believed that the juror that you had identified was 'on your side,' didn't he? A. Yes. Q. And he also told you not to bring any attention to it, didn't he? A. Yes."

Neither Weatherwax nor his family thereafter brought the newspaper to the attention of the court.

Joseph testified that he had monitored the newspapers daily for inflammatory material and that he had read the article in that morning's paper before coming to court. He described in the following terms his reaction upon being advised of the Lays' observation: "A So telling me a juror has a newspaper and walks into court tells me — my impression was that's a pretty honest man. Q. Why was he an honest man? A. Because if he wanted assistance from the newspaper as to what is happening in court, he would have read it clandestinely. He wouldn't have just walked to court like that. Many people in this community **love the sports** page. Many people love to do crossword puzzles. If they don't do **their crossword** puzzle, they don't have a good day. Q. Do you believe that the possession of a newspaper, the possession, in and of itself, was a valid basis for a mistrial? A. Absolutely not. Q. Was it a valid basis for polling the jury? A. Not that jury. Q. Because you wanted that jury? A. Absolutely. On another jury I might have used it as an excuse. Q. So you did not request that the jury be polled? A. No. Q. Was that a strategic decision on your part, sir? A. Of course it was. That's what I'm trying to tell you, sir, that if anybody, including Judge Almeric Christian, had come and told me, 'Michael Joseph, it is my opinion that you should poll the jury,' I would have said, 'Your Honor, leave my jury alone.' "

The sole conflict in the testimony relates to whether Joseph committed himself during this conversation to the filing of a motion for a mistrial. Mrs. Lay insisted that he did: "Q. To your knowledge, what was done? A. Mr. Joseph said that he would take care of it and he would file a motion for a mistrial tomorrow."

Joseph testified that he said he would think about the matter but insisted that he did not commit to seeking a mistrial. "Q. Do you recall ever telling anyone that you might consider a motion for a mistrial? A. Not only do I not recall not telling anyone that. I would call any lawyer that would have moved for a mistrial on those grounds a fool because of the composition of the jury. It was a rare jury. Probably the odds of such a jury being selected again was nil. And if someone mentioned that to me, I probably would have laughed at them. I recall telling Billy that it was my opinion that this is the best shot he's getting right here, Mr. Weatherwax, that this jury was about the best jury he would ever get. Q. Well, let's get inside your thought process. You told the defendant that you would think about it. Did you, in fact, think about it? A. Of course. Q. Did you come to a conclusion about whether or not it would be important for you to either request a mistrial or request a polling of the jury? A. Again, it's important that you understand that this had been a jury that left me very happy, with a very happy feeling."

No motion for a mistrial was filed by Joseph and the newspaper incident was not pursued prior to the filing of this habeas proceeding.

The district court credited Joseph's testimony that he made a deliberate and strategic decision not to pursue the newspaper issue. It concluded, however, that during his conversation with the Weatherwax family he had led them to believe that the issue would be pursued in some way. Specifically, the district court found that "despite giving some assurances that he would 'file a motion,' Attorney Joseph determined that the incident did not warrant interfering with the composition of the jury."

Despite its conclusion that Joseph's decision had been deliberate and strategic, the district court nevertheless ruled that Joseph's failure to call the court's attention to the incident of alleged juror misconduct was unreasonable under the *Strickland* standard for measuring an attorney's performance. It explained:

> Counsel's decision not to notify the court of the juror's misconduct, was in the first instance a breach of a fundamental duty to his client, and in the second, a breach of his duty as an officer of this court. Accepting trial counsel's claim as to a strategy, this court finds that the decision denied the trial judge, and therefore counsel and client, the opportunity to conduct the searching inquiry that was required to determine the extent of the jury's

exposure to the extra-judicial evidence. As such, the decision cannot be said to have been reasonable exercise of professional judgment.

The court then addressed the second prong of the *Strickland* test and determined that the facts warranted relief under the doctrine of that case. It found that "because of trial counsel's disregard of his client's wishes and his duty to this court, there are no objective criteria upon which this court can determine prejudice, if any, as a result of the juror's misconduct. To the extent that a *voir dire* was not conducted, proof of prejudice is excused. Since finality concerns are weaker when one of the assurances that the result of the proceeding is reliable is absent, a new trial is warranted."

The district court reasoned that Joseph breached a duty to his client because he (a) failed to take steps necessary to secure a *voir dire* inquiry directed to the issue of whether the newspaper in fact had prejudiced the jury and (b) failed to consult with or follow directions from his client about strategic matters. Our de novo review leads us to a contrary conclusion. * * * *

In a sense, Joseph made his strategic choice not to move for a mistrial "after less than complete investigation"; he decided that it would be better to keep the jury intact without first inquiring into whether the jurors read or were influenced by the newspaper article. Still, Joseph's decision not to investigate the possibility of juror prejudice was itself a strategic decision. Unlike the usual case where a lawyer fails to fully investigate a matter, Joseph could not conduct an investigation without first bringing the newspaper incident to the court's attention. Once he brought the matter to the court's attention, however, he would relinquish to the court at least some control over whether this particular jury would decide his client's fate.

Given the limited information that Joseph had in front of him — that a juror had been seen with a newspaper, and that the newspaper contained a potentially damaging article — and given Joseph's view that this jury was the best that could be expected from Weatherwax's point of view, we think that the decision not to inform the court was reasonable "under prevailing professional norms." *Strickland*, 466 U.S. at 688. Joseph acted in what he believed to be his client's best interests. He believed that he had the best jury possible under the circumstances, and he made a judgment that many competent litigators would make under the same circumstances. Bringing the newspaper incident to the court's attention would have created a possibility that the court would either declare a mistrial or otherwise alter a jury which Joseph felt favored the defense.[3] Given the Supreme Court's statement that "there are countless ways to provide effective assistance in any given case," and the "strong presumption that counsel's conduct falls within the wide range of reasonable professional assistance," we cannot, without more, rule that Joseph's decision not to investigate further was unreasonable as a matter of strategy.[4]

---

[3] We do not agree with the dissent that Joseph could have satisfied his client's request without substantial risk of losing what he believed to be a favorable jury. "In every case where the trial court learns that a member or members of the jury may have received extra-record information with a potential for substantial prejudice, the trial court must determine whether the members of the jury have been prejudiced." *Government of the Virgin Islands v. Dowling*, 814 F.2d 134, 139 (3d Cir.1987). Thus, had Joseph brought the newspaper incident to the trial court's attention, the court would have had an affirmative obligation to conduct *voir dire* and would have had discretion, if it found exposure to the article, to excuse one or more jurors or to declare a mistrial.

[4] Unlike our dissenting colleague, we do not view as inherently unreasonable Joseph's judgment that it was in Weatherwax's interest to have a jury including three white jurors rather than one having fewer

The district court also found that Joseph's representation was ineffective because he failed to follow direction from or fully consult with his client when he decided not to bring the newspaper incident to the court's attention.

There is general agreement in the case law and the rules of professional responsibility that the authority to make decisions regarding the conduct of the defense in a criminal case is split between criminal defendants and their attorneys. See *Jones v. Barnes*, 463 U.S. 745, 751 (1983); 1 American Bar Association Standards for Criminal Justice § 4-5.2 [hereinafter "ABA Standards"]. While this general proposition is more clear than precisely where to draw the dividing line, the Supreme Court has provided some guidance that helps to narrow the issue.

In *Jones*, the Supreme Court held that although a criminal defendant has an equal access right to an appeal under the Due Process and Equal Protection Clauses, he has no constitutional right to insist that appellate counsel advance every non-frivolous argument the defendant wants raised. The Court's review of its prior jurisprudence in Jones reflected a recognition that "the accused has the ultimate authority to make certain fundamental decisions regarding the case." As examples of those "fundamental decisions," the Court pointed to the decisions concerning whether to plead guilty, to waive the right to trial by jury, to testify in one's own behalf, to take an appeal, or to waive the right to counsel.

In support of its analysis, the *Jones* Court referred to ABA Model Rule of Professional Conduct 1.2(a), which reserves decisions on fundamental matters to

---

or no white jurors. Lawyers necessarily make trial strategy judgments based on probabilities. While they occasionally have hard empirical data to rely upon, the probabilities they utilize are more frequently based on an assessment of human nature rooted in the lawyer's own personal experience. Weatherwax had testified that the victim started coming at him with a rock and that he feared for his life. Joseph believed that, as a matter of probability, jurors of Weatherwax's own racial background would be more likely to identify with Weatherwax and believe his fear to be genuine than would jurors of the victim/assailant's racial background. There is no way to determine whether Joseph's belief is empirically accurate. It has not been shown to be empirically inaccurate, however, and we are unwilling to say that it is a view that a reasonable attorney could not hold. The Supreme Court has held that neither the prosecution nor the defense may, consistent with the Equal Protection Clause, utilize state-created peremptory challenges to exclude jurors from service on a jury because of their race. *Batson v. Kentucky*, 476 U.S. 79 (1986); *Georgia v. McCollum*, 505 U.S. 42, 59 (1992). The Supreme Court has never concluded, however, that aversions and affinities arising from the attitudes and experiences of different racial groups do not exist or that they do not affect jury verdicts. There is some empirical evidence to the contrary. E.g., *McCleskey v. Kemp*, 481 U.S. 279, 287 (1987) (discussing a study indicating that black defendants who kill white victims have the greatest likelihood of receiving the death penalty); Jeffrey S. Brand, *The Supreme Court, Equal Protection, and Jury Selection: Denying That Race Still Matters*, 1994 Wis. L.Rev. 511, 628 n.584 (noting that studies have found that the likelihood of a decision to acquit is correlated to the race of the juror and of the defendant); *id.* at 619, 630 (arguing that, because of the way racism operates in the courtroom, a minority defendant ought to be able to use race-based peremptory challenges to increase minority participation on the jury); Nancy J. King, *Postconviction Review of Jury Discrimination: Measuring the Effects of Juror Race on Jury Decisions*, 92 Mich. L.Rev. 63, 80–99 (1993) (reviewing studies reporting that juror race influences jury decisions); Sheri Lynn Johnson, *Black Innocence and the White Jury*, 83 Mich. L.Rev. 1611, 1616–43 (1985) (discussing research reporting influence of juror racial bias on the determination of guilt); see also *McCollum*, 505 U.S. at 61 (Thomas, J., concurring) (recognizing the broad perception, confirmed by "common experience and common sense," that "conscious and unconscious prejudice persists in our society and that it may influence some juries"); *id.* at 68 (O'Connor, J., dissenting) ("It is by now clear that conscious and unconscious racism can affect the way white jurors perceive minority defendants and the facts presented at their trials, perhaps determining the verdict of guilt or innocence."). Nor has the Supreme Court ever held that ineffective assistance of counsel occurs whenever an attorney exercises his or her professional judgment based on the belief that such aversions and affinities may influence a jury's verdict. We do not believe it would so hold if presented with this case.

the client, and then expressly recognized the complementary proposition that non-fundamental decisions are to be made by counsel on the basis of his or her professional judgment exercised after consultation with the client: "A lawyer shall abide by a client's decisions concerning the objectives of representation and shall consult with the client as to the means by which they are to be pursued. In a criminal case, the lawyer shall abide by the client's decision, as to a plea to be entered, whether to waive jury trial and whether the client will testify." Model Rules of Professional Conduct, Proposed Rule 1.2(a). With the exception of these specified fundamental decisions, an attorney's duty is to take professional responsibility for the conduct of the case, after consulting with his client.

The ABA Standards for Criminal Justice recognize as being among the non-fundamental issues reserved for counsel's judgment "whether and how to conduct cross-examinations, what jurors to accept or strike, and what trial motions should be made." ABA Standards § 4-5.2(b). Several courts have also recognized *witness selection* as being among the non-fundamental decisions that counsel is entitled to make at trial. [Citations.] The Sixth Circuit Court of Appeals has concluded that *issue selection* similarly falls in this category. *Meeks v. Bergen*, 749 F.2d 322, 328 (6th Cir.1984) (criminal defense counsel may make strategic decision to assert self-defense rather than battered wife syndrome as defense at client's murder trial). The Eleventh Circuit Court of Appeals has concluded that counsel has the ultimate authority to decide issues concerning "what evidence should be introduced, what stipulations should be made, what objections should be raised, and what pre- trial motions should be filed." *U.S. v. Teague*, 953 F.2d 1525, 1531 (11th Cir., 1992). * * * *

The district court in this proceeding concluded that Joseph was required to follow Weatherwax's direct instruction to "do something," such as "file a motion." We disagree. Whether to file a motion in this context was not a "fundamental decision regarding the case." *Jones*, 463 U.S. at 751. Wherever the precise line between client and counsel decision- making should be drawn, this decision fell squarely within the realm of strategy and tactics and thus was a decision for Joseph to make.

Some of the decisions deemed "fundamental" — such as a decision whether to plead guilty or to take an appeal — relate directly to the objectives of the representation. Cf. Model Rules of Professional Conduct Rule 1.2(a) (1994) (stating that a lawyer must abide by a client's decisions concerning the objectives of representation). While the accused should receive the full and careful advice of her lawyer before entering a guilty plea or taking an appeal, these decisions ultimately must be made by the defendant herself. The lawyer can inform the client of the likely consequences of those decisions, but only the defendant knows whether she prefers to bear those consequences or prefers to accept the costs and consequences of going to trial or filing an appeal.

Other fundamental decisions, such as whether to forego assistance of counsel, to waive a jury trial, or to testify in one's own behalf, in a sense may be viewed as strategic decisions because they relate to the means employed by the defense to obtain the primary object of the representation — ordinarily, a favorable end result. Nevertheless, these decisions are so personal and crucial to the accused's fate that they take on an importance equivalent to that of deciding the objectives of the representation. As the Court explained in *Faretta*, for example, "although he may conduct his own defense ultimately to his own detriment, his choice must be honored out of 'that respect for the individual which is the lifeblood of the law." 422 U.S. at 834.

Joseph's decision not to bring the newspaper incident to the court's attention cannot be regarded as fundamental. First, Joseph's decision did not relate directly to the objectives of his representation at that point — acquittal of first degree murder and the lesser charges. Instead, Joseph's decision concerned only the means employed by the defense to reach that agreed-upon goal. As the commentary to Model Rule of Professional Conduct 1.2(a) states, while a lawyer must abide by a client's decisions concerning the objectives of her representation, a lawyer "is not required to employ means simply because a client may wish that the lawyer do so."

Nor did Joseph usurp Weatherwax's authority to make a fundamental personal decision comparable to decisions on whether to forego assistance of counsel, to waive a jury trial, or to testify in one's own behalf. Instead, Joseph's decision concerned whether he should object once he learned that a distorted newspaper account of the trial testimony may have made its way to the jury. It was clearly an important decision, but it was not one where respect for the individual's autonomy requires us to disregard the desirability of having professional judgment exercised in the client's best interest.

We believe Joseph's decision not to object was analogous to a strategic choice not to object to the admission of inadmissible hearsay evidence tendered by the prosecution. In both situations, the consequence of a failure to object is that the jury will (or in Weatherwax's case might) learn information untested by the adversarial process that it would not otherwise have learned. In both instances, defense counsel has the power to prevent that from happening, but decides that it is strategically advantageous not to make the objection. Contrary to the district court's suggestion, in neither instance is the defendant's right to a jury trial implicated. In both instances the decision is "the exclusive province of the lawyer," ABA Standards § 4-5.2(b), and if, as here, that decision has a rational basis, a court is without authority to second-guess counsel's judgment call.

That Joseph's decision was not a fundamental one and thus fell into "the exclusive province of the lawyer" does not end our inquiry, however. Important strategic and tactical decisions should be made only after a lawyer consults with his client. ABA Standards § 4-5.2(b); *Strickland*, 466 U.S. at 688 (noting counsel's "duties to consult with the defendant on important decisions and to keep the defendant informed of important developments in the course of the prosecution").

The interchange between Joseph and his client in the courthouse on the last morning of the trial cannot fairly, in our judgment, be described as a failure to consult. Considering the fact that the newspaper incident arose suddenly when counsel was entering the courtroom on the last morning of the trial, this interchange, while brief, was far from perfunctory. Mrs. Lay indicated that it lasted long enough for each of the family members to speak and for Joseph to say "a lot of things during the course of the conversation." Joseph listened to what the client's family had to report and to their views about what should be done. He evaluated that information and expressed his own view of what was in Weatherwax's best interests. Moreover, he explained the reasons behind his view — that this was the best jury Weatherwax could hope for. Neither Weatherwax nor his family complained at the hearing about Joseph not listening or cutting them off short. Their complaint was that they wanted him to "file a motion" and he did not file one. While this is true, it does not mean that Joseph failed to consult with his client about the decision to be made.

The requirement that counsel consult with his or her client concerning issues on which counsel has the final word serves a number of important purposes. First, it assures that the client will have the opportunity to assist with his own defense. As one court has noted, "while an attorney's education and experience give him superior knowledge of generalized technical information, the client possesses superior knowledge of another sort — knowledge of the facts and circumstances of his case." *Stano v. Dugger*, 921 F.2d 1125, 1146 n. 33 (11th Cir.). Second, the client's views and desires concerning the best course to be followed are relevant considerations that must be evaluated and taken into account by counsel. Without consultation, the views and desires of the client may not be known to counsel. Third, consultation serves to promote and maintain a cooperative client-counsel relationship. We have carefully reviewed the record in this case and we perceive no threat to the accomplishment of any of these objectives. Weatherwax had an ample opportunity to convey the information available to him and to share his own appraisal of the situation, and nothing about the length or character of the conference would appear to have strained the attorney-client relationship between Joseph and Weatherwax.

Consultation between counsel and client may in some circumstances serve a fourth purpose. If the client learns from a consultation that counsel is going to pursue a strategy contrary to the client's wish and the matter is important enough to the client to forego the benefits of his current representation, the consultation may afford the client an opportunity to seek different representation. Given that Joseph was found to have given some assurance that he would "file a motion" and not to have communicated his final decision to Weatherwax, this fourth purpose requires further discussion.

The constitutional duty to consult regarding issues on which counsel has the last word requires only that counsel act reasonably in light of the circumstances and what is likely to be accomplished by a consultation. When decisions must be made in the heat of battle at trial, for example, it will often be unreasonable to expect any consultation before the decision is made and implemented, either because the opportunity for meaningful consultation does not exist or because there is little if anything to be gained by consultation.

Even where there is an opportunity for consultation, counsel may reasonably elect not to communicate his final decision when counsel and client have previously exchanged their views on the issue and the alternative of changing representation is not a realistic one. In many trial situations, the nature or importance of the issue over which a client-counsel disagreement occurs cannot be expected to cause the client seriously to consider foregoing the advantages of the current representation. In other situations, consideration of a change in representation would be pointless because the court would not permit it at that stage in the proceedings.

Here, Weatherwax did not contend, and the district court did not find, that Weatherwax would have sought to change representation had he been advised of Joseph's final decision on the newspaper issue. Nor did Weatherwax contend, or the district court find, that Joseph should have anticipated that the district court might permit a continuance and change of representation on the last day of Weatherwax's jury trial. Indeed, Weatherwax did not argue, and the district court did not find, that there was an opportunity for meaningful consultation with Weatherwax after Joseph made his decision not to pursue the newspaper issue.

We cannot say on the basis of this record that Joseph acted unreasonably under all the circumstances in failing to tell Weatherwax, prior to the jury's verdict,[5] of his ultimate decision on the newspaper issue.[6] Joseph had rebuttal witnesses to cross-examine, a jury instruction conference to attend, and a summation to deliver. Even assuming there was a fair opportunity to consult further with Weatherwax, however, we do not believe Joseph could reasonably be expected to have anticipated that anything would be accomplished by taking that course. On the contrary, given the circumstances disclosed in the record, we believe that reasonable counsel in Joseph's position would not have believed either that Weatherwax would seriously consider a change in representation or that, if he did, the court would have permitted a change in representation at that stage of the proceedings. Not only would an extended continuance have been a burden on the jury, the trial court would have no assurance that new counsel would not insist on the same strategy upon which Joseph was insisting.

In short, after discussing the pros and cons of a tactical decision with his client, Joseph made a reasonable choice that was his to make. His failure to advise his client of that decision cannot be said to be unreasonable, and Weatherwax has thus failed to carry his burden of overcoming the presumption of constitutionally acceptable performance.

The district court also reasoned that Joseph's decision not to bring the newspaper incident to the court's attention was a "breach of his duty as an officer of the court." Joseph's duty to the trial court, in the district court's view, followed both from counsel's "duty to bring to bear such skill and knowledge as will render the trial a reliable adversarial testing process," *Strickland*, 466 U.S. at 688, and from the trial judge's repeated admonitions that the jury should avoid reading articles about the trial.

We express no opinion on whether *Strickland* or the trial court's repeated admonitions support the district court's theory that Joseph's duty as an officer of the court required him to bring the matter to the court's attention. As we have explained, Joseph acted as he did solely for the purpose of serving what he believed to be the best interests of his client and in a manner consistent with his other obligations to his client. Given this fact, even if Joseph had some duty to the court to inform it of the possibility of jury misconduct, we perceive no reason why the

---

[5] Nothing, of course, foreclosed Weatherwax from pursuing the newspaper issue after the verdict, by himself or through other counsel, as he ultimately did in this proceeding.

[6] The district court did not find that Joseph made his final decision on the newspaper issue during the courtroom conference and thus that Joseph was deliberately misleading his client when he said he would "do something." Accordingly, we decline to assume that this was the case. If such deception had occurred, however, there would appear to be no causal nexus between that deception and the alleged problem here — the resolution of Weatherwax's case by a jury that may have been exposed to a distorted newspaper account of the trial testimony. Whether Joseph made his final decision before or after the conclusion of the conference, the district court was not at liberty to overturn Weatherwax's conviction without making a finding, based on record evidence, that without Joseph's assurances about filing a motion, an objection would have been raised and the course of events altered. This is not to say that Weatherwax had the burden of showing that the newspaper article adversely affected the jury. We do say, however, that habeas corpus relief on the basis of Joseph's assurances would have been inappropriate where there was no reason to believe a different jury would have decided Weatherwax's case in the absence of those assurances.

breach of that duty should require the reversal of Weatherwax's conviction. If counsel breaches a duty to the court, this does not necessarily mean that the representation of his client was ineffective. Assuming that Joseph did violate some ethical duty to the court that would warrant disciplinary sanctions against him, that breach would provide no justification for a remedy that would, in effect, impose a sanction upon the government. Indeed, we believe that overturning a conviction in a situation of this kind on the basis of counsel's breach of an ethical duty to the court would create a perverse incentive for defense counsel to "build in" reversible error for their clients by violating their duties as officers of the court.

We accordingly hold that any breach of Joseph's duty to the court would not support the judgment of the district court.

For the foregoing reasons, the district court's judgment directing Weatherwax's retrial or release will be reversed and this case will be remanded with instructions that his petition for habeas relief be denied.

LEWIS, CIRCUIT JUDGE, dissenting.

A naive assumption about race served as the sole basis for Joseph's "strategic decision" to ignore the wishes of his client regarding the newspaper incident. I not only believe that the decision was unreasonable under prevailing professional norms; I also believe that it was based upon an underlying assumption that was explicitly rejected as unreasonable by the Supreme Court in *Batson v. Kentucky*, 476 U.S. 79 (1986) (rejecting the notion that it is reasonable to assume that black jurors will be partial to black defendants solely on account of their shared race). Accordingly, I dissent.[8]

Although the majority acknowledges the "racially charged" nature of this case, I do not believe it adequately pursues the extent to which race influenced Joseph's decision not to inform the court about the juror seen carrying a newspaper into the jury room, which included an inaccurate and unfavorable article about his client's testimony. In my view, in order to assess fairly whether Joseph's strategic choice was reasonable, we must candidly address the assumptions that influenced his decision.

In determining whether Joseph's actions constituted a sound trial strategy, the majority places great emphasis upon the fact that his decision stemmed from a belief that the "jury was the best that could be expected from Weatherwax's point of view." In light of this, the majority concludes, "the strategic decision not to inform the court was reasonable 'under prevailing professional norms.'"[9] In other words,

---

[8] This case does not require us to decide the broader and admittedly more difficult question of the reasonableness or legitimacy of trial strategies that are designed to appeal to the particular racial make-up of a jury. Rather, the views I express relate specifically to the issue of whether a strategic decision, grounded exclusively upon a lawyer's assumptions about the proclivities of jurors based solely upon their race, can be considered professionally reasonable when that decision runs counter to the express wishes of his or her client and increases the likelihood that that client's constitutional right to an impartial jury will be violated.

[9] According to the majority, "bringing the newspaper incident to the court's attention would have created a likelihood that the court would either declare a mistrial or excuse a juror whom Joseph felt favored the defense." A mistrial or the dismissal of a juror, however, would necessarily have required a finding that: (1) the newspaper article was read by one or more jurors; (2) that its contents were prejudicial to Weatherwax; and (3) that a juror who read the article was actually influenced by its

Joseph thought that "he had the best jury possible under the circumstances and he made a judgment that many competent litigators would make under the same circumstances." Respectfully, I believe my colleagues' focus is both legally and logically misplaced.

Arguably, most if not all decisions by counsel before, during and after a trial can be considered strategic. As a result, a finding that a particular decision was strategic, in and of itself, cannot answer the question whether that decision falls within the "wide range of competent assistance." See *Strickland v. Washington*, 466 U.S. 668, 694 (1984). Put differently, not all strategic decisions are by definition professionally reasonable. In order to determine whether a particular strategic decision constituted "competent assistance," we must assess the underlying basis for that decision — an inquiry that, in my view, is not sufficiently pursued by the majority. Moreover, because the majority does not fully confront why Joseph felt that this was the best possible jury from Weatherwax's perspective, its conclusion that Joseph's inaction was "reasonable 'under prevailing professional norms' " strikes me as quite a leap, to say the least.

The following hypothetical, I think, will help to illustrate my point.

Suppose that John Doe, a black man, is charged with first degree murder for shooting a white man, but claims that the killing was in self-defense. Furthermore, suppose that Doe's jury is all white. During the course of the trial Doe's attorney decides not to call to the stand a black man, who was a witness to the crime, despite Doe's request that the testimony be heard.

On appeal, Doe brings an ineffective assistance of counsel claim in which he alleges that his lawyer was incompetent based upon his decision not to introduce the eyewitness testimony of the black man, whom Doe felt potentially could have aided in his defense. In response to this charge, Doe's lawyer claims that he chose not to call this individual as a witness because he made a professional judgment and concluded that the witness's testimony would have had no impact upon the jury.

Under the majority's logic, the lawyer's explanation that the witness was not called because the testimony would have been ineffectual would, standing alone, constitute a sufficient basis upon which to conclude that Doe's counsel acted "reasonably 'under prevailing professional norms.' " In other words, the majority would not find it necessary to question why Doe's counsel felt that the eyewitness's testimony was not worth introducing.

Suppose, however, that the answer to the question the majority does not ask was that Doe's attorney made his decision not because he believed that the witness or his story would be incredible, but because he felt strongly that the testimony of a black person would simply carry no weight in the minds of an all-white jury because the victim was white. Surely, the majority would not conclude that Doe's counsel employed a reasonable strategy by allowing this type of outmoded racial stereotyping to influence a decision whether or not to call the witness. To countenance such an approach, under the guise of "strategic decisionmaking," would be to place a judicial imprimatur upon the type of evil that *Batson* and its progeny sought to

---

prejudicial nature. See *Government of the Virgin Islands v. Weatherwax*, 20 F.3d 572 (3d Cir.1994). If the court were to have found that a particular juror — presumably the white member of the jury seen carrying the newspaper — should be dismissed (i.e., that he was actually prejudiced by reading the article), then it is totally illogical to argue that Weatherwax would still have benefitted from the presence of that juror simply because the juror was white.

bury. I have no doubt that under such circumstances, we would not permit either a criminal defendant or our system of justice to risk being sacrificed to an odious form of racial reasoning disguised as a legitimate strategic judgment.

And yet, a close examination of the record in this case reveals that the logic underlying why Joseph decided not to bring the newspaper incident to the court's attention is very similar to that of Doe's attorney. * * * *

Simply put, Joseph disregarded his client's request that he "do something" about the newspaper incident because he felt that the three white jurors, solely because they were white, would sympathize with Weatherwax. In fact, Joseph's judgment was entirely motivated by race. For example, he stated that "Continentals [i.e. white people] are often retirees who are viewed as conservative and anti-crime." This admission reveals that there was no reason whatsoever for Joseph to conclude that the three white jurors would identify with Weatherwax other than their shared race. Why else would persons who are "conservative and anti-crime" identify with an individual charged with first degree murder and illegal possession of a firearm?

Joseph's troubling assumptions about the racial partisanship of the white jurors were so deep-seated that he was willing to risk allowing a white juror, who could have been prejudiced by an unfavorable article written about his client's testimony, to remain on the jury.[11] In Joseph's testimony before the district court, he went so far as to say "even if I were told that the jury was reading the paper, it would not have made much difference to me." In my opinion, to the extent such unfortunate assumptions might ever be considered reasonable, they simply cannot form the basis of a professionally reasonable strategic decision in light of the interests that weighed in favor of bringing the matter to the court's attention.

On one side of the scale was Joseph's assumption that the white jurors would sympathize with Weatherwax based only on their shared race, an approach which, predictably, backfired and which the Supreme Court explicitly rejected as unreasonable in *Batson*. On the merits, this assumption is undeserving of any weight, but if one were to pretend that it should carry any, one might conclude that it weighed in favor of not informing the court about the newspaper incident.[12] But on the other side of the scale were two legitimate and important considerations: (1) Weatherwax's explicit request that Joseph "do something" about the newspaper incident; and (2) the potential that a failure to do so could jeopardize Weatherwax's constitutional right to an impartial jury. When balanced against one another the

---

[11] During the hearing before the district court, Mrs. Lay testified that Joseph "said that the juror with the newspaper is a white man."

[12] As stated earlier, the unreasonableness of Joseph's assumption is demonstrated by the fact that he was willing to risk allowing white jurors, who may have been prejudiced against his client by reading an unfavorable article about his client's testimony, to remain on the jury simply based upon their race. In my opinion, such a judgment is professionally indefensible. In the majority's view, however, the underlying basis for Joseph's decision finds support in a variety of social science research, which tends to show that jurors are in fact partial to defendants of the same race. I do not dispute the legitimacy or accuracy of these studies or theories. Rather, I simply believe that it is unreasonable to assume that these "affinities" are so deep-seated that they would justify the risk of allowing a potentially biased or prejudiced juror to remain on the jury solely due to his or her race. For example, if Joseph had discovered that one of the white jurors was married to a relative of the crime victim, I am confident that the majority would not consider it reasonable for Joseph to want to keep that white juror on the case simply because of his or her race. Thus, it seems clear to me that concerns over juror prejudice — particularly when raised by a client — must trump assumptions about the racial partisanship of jurors.

only professionally responsible and reasonable choice for Joseph was to inform the trial court of what had occurred.[13]

Because Joseph's decision was motivated by improper, illegitimate, indefensible, outmoded stereotypical assumptions about the proclivities of whites and blacks when they are called upon to sit in judgment of their fellow citizens, and because his decision fell far outside "the wide range of professionally competent assistance," to which Weatherwax was entitled, I would affirm the district court's order. Accordingly, I dissent.

Notes from Fern:

1. In *Nichols v. Butler*, 953 F.2d 1550 (11th Cir. 1992), Nichols wanted to testify in his own defense. His attorney disagreed. In a heated argument, the attorney told Nichols that the trial was going well without Nichols testifying, and that if Nichols testified his prior felony record would come out and damage his case. Nichols continued to insist on testifying, and his lawyer said that if Nichols intended to testify, the lawyer would withdraw from the case. Nichols did not testify, and he was convicted.

The court held that Nichols was denied both the effective assistance of counsel and the right to testify. While a defense attorney should advise a defendant "in the strongest terms possible" when he believe it would be unwise for him to testify, he cannot "coerce" the defendant into not testifying by a threat to withdraw, because the constitutional right to testify "is personal to the defendant and cannot be waived either by the trial court or by defense counsel".

Judge Edmondson dissented, arguing that the constitutional right to testify is no more than a constitutional right to be free of governmental interference with the right to testify. Here there was no governmental interference. "When a criminal defendant attempts to overrule his lawyer's tactical decisions, he runs some risk that the lawyer will seek to withdraw. * * * * Counsel's decision not to call defendant was a reasonable one. I cannot say that defense counsel was ineffective in a constitutional sense."

2. Rule 1.2 (a) of the Model Rules of Professional Conduct provides as follows:

Rule 1.2: *Scope of Representation*

(a) A lawyer shall abide by a client's decisions concerning the objectives of representation, subject to paragraphs (c), (d) and (e), and shall consult with the

---

[13] Even if I could conceive of a convincing argument that Joseph's decision constituted a reasonable strategy, which I cannot, I would still conclude that his actions fell below professional norms. Rather than completely ignore his client's wishes, the more appropriate action for Joseph would have been to bring the matter to the attention of the court, and then to ask the court not to poll the jury because of its "favorable" make-up. The majority contends that "had Joseph brought the newspaper incident to the trial court's attention, the court would have had an affirmative obligation to conduct voir dire." See Government of the Virgin Islands v. Dowling, 814 F.2d 134, 139 (3d Cir.1987). I disagree. As the majority itself notes, "the newspaper article included no extra-record information about Weatherwax or the crime." Accordingly, I believe that by bringing the matter to the court's attention, Joseph would have accommodated the request of his client, while simultaneously protecting his trial strategy. Moreover, although less desirable, once Weatherwax was found guilty of second-degree murder, this course of action would have enabled Joseph to file a motion for a new trial based on the newspaper incident.

client as to the means by which they are to be pursued. A lawyer shall abide by a client's decision whether to accept an offer of settlement of a matter. In a criminal case, the lawyer shall abide by the client's decision, after consultation with the lawyer, as to a plea to be entered, whether to waive jury trial and whether the client will testify.

The Comment to this Rule states (in part):

> Both the lawyer and client have authority and responsibility in the objectives and means of representation. The client has ultimate authority to determine the purposes to be served by legal representation, within the limits imposed by law and the lawyer's professional obligations. Within those limits, a client also has a right to consult with the lawyer about the means to be used in pursuing those objectives. At the same time, a lawyer is not required to pursue objectives or employ means simply because a client may wish that the lawyer do so. A clear distinction between objectives and means sometimes cannot be drawn, and in many cases the client-lawyer relationship partakes of a joint undertaking. In questions of means, the lawyer should assume responsibility for technical and legal tactical issues, but should defer to the client regarding such questions as the expense to be incurred and concern for third persons who might be adversely affected. * * * *

3. The American Bar Association Standards of Criminal Justice (as amended in 1986) provides:

Standard 4-5.2: *Control & Direction of the Case*

(a) Certain decisions relating to the conduct of the case are ultimately for the accused and others are ultimately for defense counsel. The decisions which are to be made by the accused after full consultation with counsel are: (i) what plea to enter; (ii) whether to waive jury trial; and (iii) whether to testify in his or her own behalf.

(b) The decisions on what witnesses to call, whether and how to conduct cross-examination, what jurors to accept or strike, what trial motions should be made, and all other strategic and tactical decisions are the exclusive province of the lawyer after consultation with the client.

(c) If a disagreement on significant matters of tactics or strategy arises between the lawyer and the client, the lawyer should make a record of the circumstances, the lawyer's advice and reasons, and the conclusion reached. The record should be made in a manner which protects the confidentiality of the lawyer-client relationship.

Commentary

Allocation of Decision-making Power

As established by the history of the criminal justice process and the rights vested in an accused under the Constitution, certain basic decisions have come to belong to the client while others fall within the province of the lawyer. The requirement that the defendant personally enter a guilty plea and that it be voluntary and informed carries the implication that it is the defendant who must make the choice. Similarly, the decision whether to waive a jury trial has been considered as belonging to the defendant. With respect to the decision whether the defendant should testify, the lawyer "should give his client the benefit of his advice and experience, but the ultimate decision must be made by the defendant, and the defendant alone." In making each of these decisions — whether to plead guilty, whether to waive jury trial, and whether to testify — the accused should have the full and careful advice of counsel. Although counsel should not demand that the defendant follow what counsel perceives as the desirable course, counsel is free to engage in fair persuasion and to urge the client to follow the proffered professional advice. Ultimately, however, because of the fundamental nature of these three decisions, so crucial to the accused's fate, the accused must make the decisions. * * * *

Strategy and Tactics

In general, however, it may be said that the power of decision in matters of trial strategy and tactics rests with the lawyer. The lawyer must be allowed to determine which witnesses should be called on behalf of the defendant. Similarly, the lawyer must be allowed to decide whether to object to the admission of evidence, whether and how a witness should be cross-examined, and whether to stipulate to certain facts. Cases that have reversed convictions for failure of counsel to call certain witnesses, cross-examine, object to evidence, and the like, have been decided not on the ground that counsel should have heeded the client's wishes on such matters, but on a determination that these actions of counsel in these cases were not strategic or tactical decisions but, rather, revealed ineptitude, inexperience, lack of preparation, or unfamiliarity with basic legal principles amounting to ineffective assistance of counsel.

Many of the rights of an accused, including constitutional rights, are such that only trained experts can comprehend their full significance, and an explanation to any but the most sophisticated client would be futile. Numerous strategic and tactical decisions must be made in the course of a criminal trial, many of which are made in circumstances that do not allow extended, if any, consultation. Every experienced advocate can recall the disconcerting experience of trying to conduct the examination of a witness or follow opposing arguments or the judge's charge while the client "plucks at the attorney's sleeve" offering gratuitous suggestions. Some decisions, especially those involving which witnesses to call and in what sequence and what should be said in argument to the jury, can be anticipated sufficiently so that counsel can ordinarily consult with the client concerning them. Because these decisions require the skill, training, and experience of the advocate, the power of decision on them must rest with the lawyer, but that does not mean that the lawyer should completely ignore the client in making them. The lawyer should seek to maintain a cooperative relationship at all stages while maintaining the ultimate choice and responsibility for the strategic and tactical decisions in the case.

It is also important in a jury trial for the defense lawyer to consult fully with the accused about any lesser included offenses the trial court may be willing to submit to the jury. Indeed, because this decision is so important as well as so similar to the defendant's decision about the charges to which to plead, the defendant should be the one to decide whether to seek submission to the jury of lesser included offenses. For instance, in a murder prosecution, the defendant, rather than the defense attorney, should determine whether the court should be asked to submit to the jury the lesser included offense of manslaughter. * * * *

Chapter 15

ETHICAL OBLIGATIONS OF CRIMINAL DEFENSE LAWYERS

In several chapters, we have examined some ethical problems involving prosecutors (e.g., whether to prosecute, whether evidence must be disclosed to the defense, and how to use or misuse the grand jury). In this chapter, we will look at defense counsel.

Ethical problems arise in every area of law practice, including criminal law.[1] Occasionally, these problems surface in reported cases and disciplinary proceedings, such as those appearing in this chapter. Most often, however, only the affected lawyer (and sometimes his opponents or colleagues) knows the issue even exists. Usually, the lawyer can "get away with" unethical conduct (especially if it seems to help the client), as no one who knows of it is likely to complain.

But this is no way to practice law. Such conduct can easily become habitual, and the lawyer will quickly become known among judges and other lawyers as a "sharpie" or "shyster" who deserves neither respect nor trust. Even worse is the effect such practices can have on the *self*-respect of the lawyer. Competitive litigation can be fun, just as athletic competition can be fun. But what joy is there in winning by cheating? Can the athlete who wins the race by using illegal drugs really take pride in his "victory"? Can the lawyer who coaches his witness to shade the truth really take pride in his verdict?

Most lawyers want to follow the rules — *if* they know what they are. Figuring out the proper rule is not always easy, however, particularly where the situation requires the lawyer to tread the line between two potentially *conflicting* obligations: zealous representation of the client versus candor to the court.

This chapter explores some of these difficult issues.

Problem 15A

To: My Law Clerk

From: Mary Goround, Esq.

Date: March 10

As you know, our firm practices mostly tax and estate planning law. Last week, however, one of our wealthiest clients — Sunny Flower — asked us to represent

---

[1] Professor Monroe Freedman notes that lawyers might attempt to minimize ethical problems by avoiding areas of practice:

> Lawyers can and do avoid certain general areas of practice altogether because of the nature of the representation or the associations it requires. You will find, for example, that clients will cheat, steal, and even kill other people simply to enrich themselves. If you do not want to be associated with such clients, you can choose not to enter corporate practice. [Freedman, Understanding Lawyers' Ethics, p. 68, n. 16 (Matthew Bender, 1990)]

her son, Wally, who's in a spot of trouble. Sunny will pay Wally's legal expenses, and she would prefer that we try to work out a favorable plea bargain for Wally, to avoid the adverse publicity that a trial would bring.

Wally and Billy Clubb have been charged with rape of June Bugg. Wally has been released on $10,000 bail. Here is a transcript of my first interview with him:

Goround:	Wally, you and Billy have been charged with rape of June Bugg. I obtained a copy of the police report. It says that Ms. Bugg told the police that last Saturday night, she met the two of you in a bar, that you took her to Clubb's apartment, and that you held her down while Clubb raped her. She was very upset. She was supposed to get married on Sunday, but had to postpone the wedding. Your mother asked me to represent you. Could you please tell me what happened?
Flower:	The bitch probably wanted to screw, but she was so damn drunk she forgot about it.
Goround:	Mr. Flower, if you testify in this case, I'd like to clean up your language. Don't use words like "bitch" and "screw" and "damn" in front of the jury. Also, get rid of those old clothes and put on a suit and tie.
Flower:	Look, I'm a truck driver, so I talk rough and I don't even have a suit and tie. But I'll borrow one and clean up my act at trial, if you say so.
Goround:	So you were at Clubb's apartment?
Flower:	I didn't say that. Maybe I have an alibi. I was playing poker at my house, with my friends, Louie and Hughey. They'll both testify to that. Would that work?
Goround:	Is that what really happened?
Flower:	My mother knows you, but I don't. I don't know how much I should be telling you.
Goround:	Mr. Flower, I'm now acting as your lawyer, not your mother's. My job is to do everything I can to help you, and I have an ethical obligation to keep everything you tell me confidential. I promise not to reveal what you tell me about this case. I can lose my license to practice law if I do.
Flower:	Okay, counsellor, I have a legal question for you. If June doesn't show up at the trial, can they convict me?
Goround:	I don't see how.
Flower:	I think we're going to do all right. There's one more thing you can help me with. I have some friends living on Moose Island, off the coast of British Columbia. Suppose I was in Canada right now. Could I be extradited and brought back on this rape charge?
Goround:	Uh, I want to check out a few things. Please come back to see me tomorrow morning at 10 o'clock.

I don't believe Wally's alibi, and I am afraid that he might intimidate June or jump bail and run off to Canada. I went to the local bar association's monthly luncheon today, and I discussed my concerns with some lawyers I happened to be sitting with.

Ann is a senior partner with Wright, Wills, and Yawn, a very traditional law firm. She said, "Lean on him. Tell him straight out that it is immoral and illegal to lie in court, to intimidate a witness, or to jump bail. Mirandize him — tell him that if you think he will lie on the witness stand, you will let the court know about it. Don't tell him anything about extradition law. He would just abuse it."

Bob is a junior partner with Takeda, Munney, and Wrunn, which represents plaintiffs in personal injury cases. He said, "I read this book, *Anatomy of a Murder*.[2] In it, the client told the lawyer that he had killed someone. The lawyer said, 'If that's what happened, you'll probably be convicted and executed. But if you acted in a blind rage, I might be able to save you. Come back tomorrow and tell me what happened.' Why not just tell your client the truth about whether his alibi is convincing and the law of extradition and let him decide what to do? You were appointed to act as his lawyer, not his conscience. He has the right to decide what to do with his life."

Carla is general counsel for Avaricious Oil Co. She said, "Dump the bum. I don't understand why you would want to represent a lying rapist. Ask the court for permission to withdraw from the case."

Wally is coming in to see me tomorrow morning. Please read the attached authorities and advise me what to do.

Problem 15B

To: My Law Clerk

From: Mary Goround

Date: March 11

Wally came in this morning. Here is what happened:

Flower: I wasn't at any poker game. I was afraid you wouldn't believe the truth. I was at Clubb's apartment. June and Clubb had sex together, but nobody used any force on her. She was drunk as a skunk. Clubb can testify about how many drinks she had, and so can I. Look, she was so drunk that she probably doesn't really remember that I was there. You should argue to the jury that I wasn't there.

Goround: Let me think about that. Why would June lie about being raped?

Flower: I heard that she used to pick up guys at the bar and sleep with them, and then she decided to marry this guy Harry, who doesn't know much about her. I think Harry must have found out about her and Clubb, so she made up this story. I can get some guys to testify that they slept with her.

---

[2] Robert Traver, *Anatomy Of A Murder* (1958). The so-called "lecture scene" in this book (and movie) are discussed in Richard Wydick, *The Ethics of Witness Coaching*, 17 Cardozo L.Rev. 1 (1995), and in several books cited in Wydick's article at footnote 75.

Goround: Assuming such evidence would be admissible, it would be pretty embarrassing for her if we did that. It might mean that Harry won't marry her. I don't think I want to do that to her.

Flower: Look, your job is to help me, not her. She'll have to testify at the preliminary hearing. If you ask her about her sleeping with other guys, I think she'll fold — maybe even if the judge says she doesn't have to answer. She'll be so scared she won't even show up for the trial.

Goround: You seem to know a lot about criminal procedure.

Flower: I've been around.

Goround: Let me get back to you on how I'll handle the prelim. I have another question for you. Will June be able to identify you at trial?

Flower: I don't know. I'd seen her around the bar once or twice before, but I hadn't ever spoken to her before that night, and that night she was really drunk. Besides, I had a knit cap on my head all night, and I was wearing sunglasses.

What should I do now?

AMERICAN BAR ASSOCIATION MODEL CODE OF PROFESSIONAL RESPONSIBILITY

CANON 7. A LAWYER SHOULD REPRESENT A CLIENT ZEALOUSLY WITHIN THE BOUNDS OF THE LAW.

Ethical Consideration 7-1:

The duty of a lawyer, both to his client and to the legal system, is to represent his client zealously within the bounds of the law, which includes Disciplinary Rules and enforceable professional regulations. The professional responsibility of a lawyer derives from his membership in a profession which has the duty of assisting members of the public to secure and protect available legal rights and benefits. In our government of laws and not of men, each member of our society is entitled to have his conduct judged and regulated in accordance with the law, to seek any lawful objective through legally permissible means, and to present for adjudication any lawful claim, issue, or defense.

Model Rules of Professional Conduct
(enacted in 1983)[3]

Rule 1.2: Scope of Representation

* * * *

(d) A lawyer shall not counsel a client to engage, or assist a client, in conduct that the lawyer knows is criminal or fraudulent, but a lawyer may discuss the legal consequences of any proposed course of conduct with a

---

[3] Most states have adopted or adapted the Model Rules in some form.

client and may counsel or assist a client to make a good faith effort to determine the validity, scope, meaning or application of the law.

Rule 1.4:   Communication

(a) A lawyer shall:

(1) promptly inform the client of any decision or circumstance with respect to which the client's informed consent, as defined in Rule 1.0(e), is required by these Rules;

(2) reasonably consult with the client about the means by which the client's objectives are to be accomplished;

(3) keep the client reasonably informed about the status of the matter;

(4) promptly comply with reasonable requests for information; and

(5) consult with the client about any relevant limitation on the lawyer's conduct when the lawyer knows that the client expects assistance not permitted by the Rules of Professional Conduct or other law.

(b) A lawyer shall explain a matter to the extent reasonably necessary to permit the client to make informed decisions regarding the representation.

Rule 1.6:   Confidentiality of Information

(a) A lawyer shall not reveal information relating to the representation of a client unless the client gives informed consent, the disclosure is impliedly authorized in order to carry out the representation or the disclosure is permitted by paragraph (b).

(b) A lawyer may reveal information relating to the representation of a client to the extent the lawyer reasonably believes necessary:

(1) to prevent reasonably certain death or substantial bodily harm;

(2) to secure legal advice about the lawyer's compliance with these Rules;

(3) to establish a claim or defense on behalf of the lawyer in a controversy between the lawyer and the client, to establish a defense to a criminal charge or civil claim against the lawyer based upon conduct in which the client was involved, or to respond to allegations in any proceeding concerning the lawyer's representation of the client; or

(4) to comply with other law or a court order.

Rule 1.16:   Declining or Terminating Representation

(a) Except as stated in paragraph (c), a lawyer shall not represent a client or, where representation has commenced, shall withdraw from the representation of a client if:

(1) the representation will result in violation of the rules of professional conduct or other law;

(2) the lawyer's physical or mental condition materially impairs the lawyer's ability to represent the client; or

(3) the lawyer is discharged.

(b) Except as stated in paragraph (c), a lawyer may withdraw from representing a client if:

(1) withdrawal can be accomplished without material adverse effect on the interests of the client;

(2) the client persists in a course of action involving the lawyer's services that the lawyer reasonably believes is criminal or fraudulent;

(3) the client has used the lawyer's services to perpetrate a crime or fraud;

(4) the client insists upon taking action that the lawyer considers repugnant or with which the lawyer has a fundamental disagreement;

(5) the client fails substantially to fulfill an obligation to the lawyer regarding the lawyer's services and has been given reasonable warning that the lawyer will withdraw unless the obligation is fulfilled;

(6) the representation will result in an unreasonable financial burden on the lawyer or has been rendered unreasonably difficult by the client; or

(7) other good cause for withdrawal exists.

(c) A lawyer must comply with applicable law requiring notice to or permission of a tribunal when terminating a representation. When ordered to do so by a tribunal, a lawyer shall continue representation notwithstanding good cause for terminating the representation.

(d) Upon termination of representation, a lawyer shall take steps to the extent reasonably practicable to protect a client's interests, such as giving reasonable notice to the client, allowing time for employment of other counsel, surrendering papers and property to which the client is entitled and refunding any advance payment of fee or expense that has not been earned or incurred. The lawyer may retain papers relating to the client to the extent permitted by other law.

Rule 2.1:   Advisor

In representing a client, a lawyer shall exercise independent professional judgment and render candid advice. In rendering advice, a lawyer may refer not only to law but to other considerations such as moral, economic, social and political factors, that may be relevant to the client's situation.

Rule 3.1:   Meritorious Claims & Contentions

A lawyer shall not bring or defend a proceeding, or assert or controvert an issue therein, unless there is a basis in law and fact for doing so that is not frivolous, which includes a good faith argument for an extension, modification or reversal of existing law. A lawyer for the defendant in a criminal proceeding, or the respondent in a proceeding that could result in incarceration, may nevertheless so defend the proceeding as to require that every element of the case be established.

Rule 3.3:   Candor Toward the Tribunal

(a) A lawyer shall not knowingly:

(1) make a false statement of fact or law to a tribunal or fail to correct a false statement of material fact or law previously made to the tribunal by the lawyer;

(2) fail to disclose to the tribunal legal authority in the controlling jurisdiction known to the lawyer to be directly adverse to the position of the client and not disclosed by opposing counsel; or

(3) offer evidence that the lawyer knows to be false. If a lawyer, the lawyer's client, or a witness called by the lawyer, has offered material evidence and the lawyer comes to know of its falsity, the lawyer shall take reasonable remedial measures, including, if necessary, disclosure to the tribunal. A lawyer may refuse to offer evidence, other than the testimony of a defendant in a criminal matter, that the lawyer reasonably believes is false.

(b) A lawyer who represents a client in an adjudicative proceeding and who knows that a person intends to engage, is engaging or has engaged in criminal or fraudulent conduct related to the proceeding shall take reasonable remedial measures, including, if necessary, disclosure to the tribunal.

(c) The duties stated in paragraphs (a) and (b) continue to the conclusion of the proceeding, and apply even if compliance requires disclosure of information otherwise protected by Rule 1.6.

(d) In an ex parte proceeding, a lawyer shall inform the tribunal of all material facts known to the lawyer that will enable the tribunal to make an informed decision, whether or not the facts are adverse.

Rule 3.4:   Fairness to Opposing Party & Counsel

A lawyer shall not:

(a) unlawfully obstruct another party's access to evidence or unlawfully alter, destroy or conceal a document or other material having potential evidentiary value. A lawyer shall not counsel or assist another person to do any such act;

(b) falsify evidence, counsel or assist a witness to testify falsely, or offer an inducement to a witness that is prohibited by law;

(c) knowingly disobey an obligation under the rules of a tribunal, except for an open refusal based on an assertion that no valid obligation exists;

(d) in pretrial procedure, make a frivolous discovery request or fail to make reasonably diligent effort to comply with a legally proper discovery request by an opposing party;

(e) in trial, allude to any matter that the lawyer does not reasonably believe is relevant or that will not be supported by admissible evidence, assert personal knowledge of facts in issue except when testifying as a witness, or state a personal opinion as to the justness of a cause, the credibility of a witness, the culpability of a civil litigant or the guilt or innocence of an accused; or

(f) request a person other than a client to refrain from voluntarily giving relevant information to another party unless:

(1) the person is a relative or an employee or other agent of a client; and

(2) the lawyer reasonably believes that the person's interests will not be adversely affected by refraining from giving such information.

* * * *

Rule 4.1:   Truthfulness in Statements to Others

In the course of representing a client a lawyer shall not knowingly:

(a) make a false statement of material fact or law to a third person; or

(b) fail to disclose a material fact when disclosure is necessary to avoid assisting a criminal or fraudulent act by a client, unless disclosure is prohibited by Rule 1.6.

Rule 4.2:   Communication With Person Represented by Counsel

In representing a client, a lawyer shall not communicate about the subject of the representation with a person the lawyer knows to be represented by another lawyer in the matter, unless the lawyer has the consent of the other lawyer or is authorized to do so by law or a court order.

Rule 6.2:   Accepting Appointments

A lawyer shall not seek to avoid appointment by a tribunal to represent a person except for good cause, such as:

(a) representing the client is likely to result in violation of the Rules of Professional Conduct or other law;

(b) representing the client is likely to result in an unreasonable financial burden on the lawyer; or

(c) the client or the cause is so repugnant to the lawyer as to be likely to impair the client-lawyer relationship or the lawyer's ability to represent the client.

AMERICAN BAR ASSOCIATION, STANDARDS FOR CRIMINAL JUSTICE

STANDARD 4-3.1: ESTABLISHMENT OF RELATIONSHIP

(a) Defense counsel should seek to establish a relationship of trust and confidence with the accused and should discuss the objectives of the representation and whether defense counsel will continue to represent the accused if there is an appeal. Defense counsel should explain the necessity of full disclosure of all facts known to the client for an effective defense, and defense counsel should explain the extent to which counsel's obligation of confidentiality makes privileged the accused's disclosures. * * * *

STANDARD 4-3.2: INTERVIEWING THE CLIENT

(a) As soon as practicable, defense counsel should seek to determine all relevant facts known to the accused. In so doing, defense counsel should probe for all legally relevant information without seeking to influence the direction of the client's responses.

(b) Defense counsel should not instruct the client or intimate to the client in any way that the client should not be candid in revealing facts so as to afford defense counsel free rein to take action which would be precluded by counsel's knowing of such facts.

STANDARD 4-3.7: ADVICE AND SERVICE ON ANTICIPATED UNLAWFUL CONDUCT

(a) It is defense counsel's duty to advise a client to comply with the law, but counsel may advise concerning the meaning, scope, and validity of a law.

(b) Defense counsel should not counsel a client in or knowingly assist a client to engage in conduct which defense counsel knows to be illegal or fraudulent but defense counsel may discuss the legal consequences of any proposed course of conduct with a client.

(c) Defense counsel should not agree in advance of the commission of a crime that he or she will serve as counsel for the defendant, except as part of a bona fide effort to determine the validity, scope, meaning, or application of the law, or where the defense is incident to a general retainer for legal services to a person or enterprise engaged in legitimate activity.

(d) Defense counsel should not reveal information relating to representation of a client unless the client consents after consultation, except for disclosures that are impliedly authorized in order to carry out the representation and except that defense counsel may reveal such information to the extent he or she reasonably believes necessary to prevent the client from committing a criminal act that defense counsel believes is likely to result in imminent death or substantial bodily harm.

Commentary

Advising Compliance with Law

Since the system of justice cannot function if the professional participants — the advocates — do not comply with standards of honesty and integrity, the bar is firmly committed to the proposition that the lawyer's function must at every stage be performed within the law. Each of the contending advocates is assigned a different role or function, but each is an indispensable component of the system of justice and bound by its rules. While the justice system demands that defense counsel protect the confidences of the client, it also demands that counsel's duties be performed pursuant to the traditions and standards of professional conduct and in accordance with the law. When defense counsel realizes that a client expects assistance in violation of these requirements, he or she should consult with the client regarding the relevant limitations on counsel's conduct.

Defense counsel is entitled to seek withdrawal from a case at any stage if the client states an intent to violate the law.

Advising Unlawful Conduct

It is fundamental that the lawyer's function be performed within the law. The lawyer's professional capacity does not immunize him or her from responsibility if the lawyer aids and abets the commission of a crime. Of course, clients are nonetheless entitled to advice concerning the legality of prospective conduct. Defense counsel properly may give a candid opinion on the interpretation that may be given to any provision of law, for example, as well as an opinion on its validity. Thus, a lawyer consulted by a person or organization contemplating a test of the constitutionality of a law, as in a civil rights case, is not obliged to counsel against conduct that would provoke prosecution. Similarly, a corporation seeking to determine whether its proposed course of action would violate the antitrust laws can properly be advised by counsel of the applicability of those laws to the proposed conduct.

The lawyer is part of a judicial system charged with upholding the law. One of the lawyer's functions is to advise clients so that they avoid any violation of the law in the proper exercise of their rights. Hence, a lawyer is required to give an honest and candid opinion about the actual consequences that appear likely to result from a client's conduct. The fact that a client uses advice in a course of action that is criminal or fraudulent does not, of itself, make a lawyer a party to the course of action. However, a lawyer may not knowingly assist a client in such criminal or fraudulent conduct. There is a critical distinction between presenting an analysis of legal aspects of questionable conduct and recommending the means by which a crime or fraud might be committed with impunity.

Representation in Future Criminal Cases

An agreement, whether express or implied, to defend criminal prosecutions arising out of contemplated criminal acts is an incentive to the commission of crime. Thus, it is improper for a lawyer to knowingly enter into an arrangement with those engaged in organized crime to provide representation on a regular basis to the participants. The lawyer who agrees to represent a person against future charges of prostitution, gambling, narcotics violations, and the like, in violation of state or federal laws, is similarly encouraging illegal activity by his or her willingness to defend.

These situations should be distinguished from that of the lawyer who is under a general retainer for legal services to a lawful enterprise or who regularly represents a client engaged in legitimate activity and who is expected to defend criminal charges should they ever be brought against the client. Persons engaged in legitimate business activity may be exposed to possible violation of criminal laws, such as those regulating safety or business economics. The scope of the law may be uncertain and the managers of such enterprises are entitled to counsel. Regular employment or a retainer that contemplates the defense of a criminal charge, if one is brought in these circumstances, does not operate as an encouragement of law violation, provided that the lawyer fulfills the duty to advise compliance with the law.

A lawyer may properly agree in advance to defend a client who has stated an intention to violate a criminal statute when the violation is for the express purpose of testing in good faith the validity or scope of the law and the lawyer had advised the client that the law is open to question on such grounds.

Limits on Reporting of Threatened Crime

A fundamental principle in the client-lawyer relationship is that the lawyer maintain confidentiality of information relating to the representation. The client is thereby encouraged to communicate fully and frankly with the lawyer even as to embarrassing or legally damaging subject matter.

Furthermore, the observance of the ethical obligation of a lawyer to hold inviolate confidential information of the client not only facilitates the full development of facts essential to proper representation of the client; it also encourages people to seek early legal assistance. Almost without exception, clients come to lawyers in order to determine what their rights are and what is, in the maze of laws and regulations, deemed to be legal and correct. The common law recognizes that the client's confidences must be protected from disclosure. Based upon experience, lawyers know that almost all clients follow the advice given, and the law is thereby upheld.

The confidentiality rule is subject, however, to limited exceptions. In becoming privy to information about a client, a lawyer may foresee that the client intends serious harm to another person. To the extent a lawyer is required or permitted to disclose a client's purposes even in such circumstances the client will be inhibited from revealing facts that would enable the lawyer to counsel against a wrongful course of action. In general, the public is better protected if full and open communication by the client is encouraged than if it is inhibited.

Nonetheless, where defense counsel reasonably believes that a client intends prospective conduct that is criminal and likely to result in imminent death or substantial bodily harm, it is in the public interest that counsel have professional discretion to reveal information necessary to prevent such consequences. Section (d), following the ABA Model Rules of Professional Conduct, takes this position. A lawyer may make a disclosure in order to prevent homicide or serious bodily injury which the lawyer "reasonably believes" is intended by a client. The lawyer need not "know" such a result is intended. It is very difficult for a lawyer to "know" when such a heinous purpose will actually be carried out, for the client may have a change of mind.

Defense counsel's exercise of discretion in this regard requires consideration of such factors as the nature of the lawyer's relationship with the client and with those who might be injured by the client, the lawyer's own involvement in the transaction and factors that may extenuate the conduct in question. Where practical, the lawyer should seek to persuade the client to take suitable action. In any case, a disclosure adverse to the client's interest should be no greater than the lawyer reasonably believes necessary to the purpose. Defense counsel's decision not to take preventive action permitted by section (d) does not violate this Standard.

STANDARD 4-3.9: OBLIGATIONS OF HYBRID AND STANDBY COUNSEL

(a) Defense counsel whose duty is to actively assist a pro se accused should permit the accused to make the final decisions on all matters, including strategic and tactical matters relating to the conduct of the case.

(b) Defense counsel whose duty is to assist a pro se accused only when the accused requests assistance may bring to the attention of the accused matters beneficial to him or her, but should not actively participate in the conduct of the defense unless requested by the accused or insofar as directed to do so by the court.

STANDARD 4-4.3: RELATIONS WITH PROSPECTIVE WITNESSES

* * * *

(d) Defense counsel should not discourage or obstruct communication between prospective witnesses and the prosecutor. It is unprofessional conduct to advise any person other than a client, or cause such person to be advised, to decline to give to the prosecutor or defense counsel for codefendants information which such person has a right to give.

STANDARD 4-5.1: ADVISING THE ACCUSED

(a) After informing himself or herself fully on the facts and the law, defense counsel should advise the accused with complete candor concerning all aspects of the case, including a candid estimate of the probable outcome.

(b) Defense counsel should not intentionally understate or overstate the risks, hazards, or prospects of the case to exert undue influence on the accused's decision as to his or her plea.

(c) Defense counsel should caution the client to avoid communication about the case with witnesses, except with the approval of counsel, to avoid any contact with jurors or prospective jurors, and to avoid either the reality or the appearance of any other improper activity.

STANDARD 11-4.1: TIMELY PERFORMANCE OF DISCLOSURE

(a) Each jurisdiction should develop time limits within which discovery should be performed. The time limits should be such that discovery is initiated as early as practicable in the process. The time limit for completion of discovery should be sufficiently early in the process that each party has sufficient time to use the disclosed information adequately to prepare for trial.

(b) The time limits adopted by each jurisdiction should provide that, in the general discovery sequence, disclosure should first be made by the prosecution to the defense. The defense should then be required to make its correlative disclosure within a specified time after prosecution disclosure has been made.

(c) Each party should be under a continuing obligation to produce discoverable material to the other side. If, subsequent to compliance with these standards or orders pursuant thereto, a party discovers additional material or information which is subject to disclosure, the other party should promptly be notified of the existence of such additional material. If the additional material or information is discovered during or after trial, the court should also be notified.

NIX v. WHITESIDE
United States Supreme Court
475 U.S. 157 (1986)

CHIEF JUSTICE BURGER delivered the opinion of the Court.

We granted certiorari to decide whether the Sixth Amendment right of a criminal defendant to assistance of counsel is violated when an attorney refuses to cooperate with the defendant in presenting perjured testimony at his trial. * * * *

I

A

Whiteside was convicted of second degree murder by a jury verdict which was affirmed by the Iowa courts. The killing took place on February 8, 1977 in Cedar Rapids, Iowa. Whiteside and two others went to one Calvin Love's apartment late that night, seeking marihuana. Love was in bed when Whiteside and his companions arrived; an argument between Whiteside and Love over the marihuana ensued. At one point, Love directed his girlfriend to get his "piece," and at another point got up, then returned to his bed. According to Whiteside's testimony, Love then started to reach under his pillow and moved toward Whiteside. Whiteside stabbed Love in the chest, inflicting a fatal wound.

Whiteside was charged with murder, and when counsel was appointed, he objected to the lawyer initially appointed, claiming that he felt uncomfortable with a lawyer who had formerly been a prosecutor. Gary L. Robinson was then appointed and immediately began investigation. Whiteside gave him a statement that he had stabbed Love as the latter "was pulling a pistol from underneath the pillow on the bed." Upon questioning by Robinson, however, Whiteside indicated that he had not actually seen a gun, but that he was convinced that Love had a gun. No pistol was found on the premises; shortly after the police search following the stabbing, which had revealed no weapon, the victim's family had removed all of the victim's possessions from the apartment. Robinson interviewed Whiteside's companions who were present during the stabbing and none had seen a gun during the incident. Robinson advised Whiteside that the existence of a gun was not necessary to establish the claim of self defense, and that only a reasonable belief that the victim had a gun nearby was necessary even though no gun was actually present.

Until shortly before trial, Whiteside consistently stated to Robinson that he had not actually seen a gun, but that he was convinced that Love had a gun in his hand. About a week before trial, during preparation for direct examination, Whiteside for the first time told Robinson and his associate Donna Paulsen that he had seen something "metallic" in Love's hand. When asked about this, Whiteside responded that "in Howard Cook's case there was a gun. If I don't say I saw a gun, I'm dead."

Robinson told Whiteside that such testimony would be perjury and repeated that it was not necessary to prove that a gun was available but only that Whiteside reasonably believed that he was in danger. On Whiteside's insisting that he would testify that he saw "something metallic" Robinson told him, according to Robinson's testimony,

We could not allow him to testify falsely because that would be perjury, and as officers of the court we would be suborning perjury if we allowed him to do it; I advised him that if he did do that it would be my duty to advise the Court of what he was doing and that I felt he was committing perjury; also, that I probably would be allowed to attempt to impeach that particular testimony.

Robinson also indicated he would seek to withdraw from the representation if Whiteside insisted on committing perjury.[2]

Whiteside testified in his own defense at trial and stated that he "knew" that Love had a gun and that he believed Love was reaching for a gun and he had acted swiftly in self defense. On cross examination, he admitted that he had not actually seen a gun in Love's hand. Robinson presented evidence that Love had been seen with a sawed-off shotgun on other occasions, that the police search of the apartment may have been careless, and that the victim's family had removed everything from the apartment shortly after the crime. Robinson presented this evidence to show a basis for Whiteside's asserted fear that Love had a gun.

The jury returned a verdict of second-degree murder and Whiteside moved for a new trial, claiming that he had been deprived of a fair trial by Robinson's admonitions not to state that he saw a gun or "something metallic." The trial court held a hearing, heard testimony by Whiteside and Robinson, and denied the motion. The trial court made specific findings that the facts were as related by Robinson.

The Supreme Court of Iowa affirmed respondent's conviction. That court held that the right to have counsel present all appropriate defenses does not extend to using perjury, and that an attorney's duty to a client does not extend to assisting a client in committing perjury. Relying on DR 7-102(A)(4) of the Iowa Code of Professional Responsibility for Lawyers, which expressly prohibits an attorney from using perjured testimony, and Iowa Code § 720.3, which criminalizes subornation of perjury, the Iowa court concluded that not only were Robinson's actions permissible, but were required. The court commended "both Mr. Robinson and Ms. Paulsen for the high ethical manner in which this matter was handled."

B

Whiteside then petitioned for a writ of habeas corpus in the United States District Court for the Southern District of Iowa. In that petition, Whiteside alleged that he had been denied effective assistance of counsel and of his right to present a defense by Robinson's refusal to allow him to testify as he had proposed. The District Court denied the writ. Accepting the State trial court's factual finding that Whiteside's intended testimony would have been perjurious, it concluded that there could be no grounds for habeas relief since there is no constitutional right to present a perjured defense.

---

[2] Whiteside's version of the events at this pretrial meeting is considerably more cryptic:

Q: And as you went over the questions, did the two of you come into conflict with regard to whether or not there was a weapon?

A: I couldn't — I couldn't say a conflict. But I got the impression at one time that maybe if I didn't go along with — with what was happening, that it was no gun being involved, maybe that he will pull out of my trial.

The United States Court of Appeals for the Eighth Circuit reversed and directed that the writ of habeas corpus be granted. The Court of Appeals accepted the findings of the trial judge, affirmed by the Iowa Supreme Court, that trial counsel believed with good cause that Whiteside would testify falsely and acknowledged that under *Harris v. New York*, 401 U.S. 222 (1971), a criminal defendant's privilege to testify in his own behalf does not include a right to commit perjury. Nevertheless, the court reasoned that an intent to commit perjury, communicated to counsel, does not alter a defendant's right to effective assistance of counsel and that Robinson's admonition to Whiteside that he would inform the court of Whiteside's perjury constituted a threat to violate the attorney's duty to preserve client confidences. According to the Court of Appeals, this threatened violation of client confidences breached the standards of effective representation set down in *Strickland v. Washington*, 466 U.S. 668 (1984). The court also concluded that *Strickland's* prejudice requirement was satisfied by an implication of prejudice from the conflict between Robinson's duty of loyalty to his client and his ethical duties. We granted *certiorari*, and we reverse.

II

A

The right of an accused to testify in his defense is of relatively recent origin. Until the latter part of the preceding century, criminal defendants in this country, as at common law, were considered to be disqualified from giving sworn testimony at their own trial by reason of their interest as a party to the case.

By the end of the nineteenth century, however, the disqualification was finally abolished by statute in most states and in the federal courts. Although this Court has never explicitly held that a criminal defendant has a due process right to testify in his own behalf, cases in several Circuits have so held and the right has long been assumed. See, e.g., *United States v. Curtis*, 742 F.2d 1070, 1076 (CA7, 1984); *United States v. Bifield*, 702 F.2d 342, 349 (CA2, 1983). We have also suggested that such a right exists as a corollary to the Fifth Amendment privilege against compelled testimony, see *Harris v. New York*, supra, 401 U.S. at 225.

B

In *Strickland v. Washington*, we held that to obtain relief by way of federal habeas corpus on a claim of a deprivation of effective assistance of counsel under the Sixth Amendment, the movant must establish both serious attorney error and prejudice. To show such error, it must be established that the assistance rendered by counsel was constitutionally deficient in that "counsel made errors so serious that counsel was not functioning as 'counsel' guaranteed the defendant by the Sixth Amendment." *Strickland*, 466 U.S. at 687. To show prejudice, it must be established that the claimed lapses in counsel's performance rendered the trial unfair so as to "undermine confidence in the outcome" of the trial. *Id.* at 694.

In *Strickland*, we acknowledged that the Sixth Amendment does not require any particular response by counsel to a problem that may arise. Rather, the Sixth Amendment inquiry is into whether the attorney's conduct was "reasonably effective." To counteract the natural tendency to fault an unsuccessful defense, a court reviewing a claim of ineffective assistance must "indulge a strong presumption that counsel's conduct falls within the wide range of reasonable professional assistance." *Id.* at 689. In giving shape to the perimeters of this range of reasonable professional assistance, *Strickland* mandates that

> Prevailing norms of practice as reflected in American Bar Association Standards and the like, are guides to determining what is reasonable, but they are only guides. [*Id.* at 688]

Under the *Strickland* standard, breach of an ethical standard does not necessarily make out a denial of the Sixth Amendment guarantee of assistance of counsel. When examining attorney conduct, a court must be careful not to narrow the wide range of conduct acceptable under the Sixth Amendment so restrictively as to constitutionalize particular standards of professional conduct and thereby intrude into the State's proper authority to define and apply the standards of professional conduct applicable to those it admits to practice in its courts. In some future case challenging attorney conduct in the course of a state court trial, we may need to define with greater precision the weight to be given to recognized canons of ethics, the standards established by the State in statutes or professional codes, and the Sixth Amendment, in defining the proper scope and limits on that conduct. Here we need not face that question, since virtually all of the sources speak with one voice.

C

We turn next to the question presented: the definition of the range of "reasonable professional" responses to a criminal defendant client who informs counsel that he will perjure himself on the stand. We must determine whether, in this setting, Robinson's conduct fell within the wide range of professional responses to threatened client perjury acceptable under the Sixth Amendment.

In *Strickland*, we recognized counsel's duty of loyalty and his "overarching duty to advocate the defendant's cause." Plainly, that duty is limited to legitimate, lawful conduct compatible with the very nature of a trial as a search for truth. Although counsel must take all reasonable lawful means to attain the objectives of the client, counsel is precluded from taking steps or in any way assisting the client in presenting false evidence or otherwise violating the law. This principle has consistently been recognized in most unequivocal terms by expositors of the norms of professional conduct since the first Canons of Professional Ethics were adopted by the American Bar Association in 1908. The 1908 Canon 32 provided that:

> No client, corporate or individual, however powerful, nor any cause, civil or political, however important, is entitled to receive nor should any lawyer render any service or advice involving disloyalty to the law whose ministers we are, or disrespect of the judicial office, which we are bound to uphold, or corruption of any person or persons exercising a public office or private trust, or deception or betrayal of the public. He must observe and advise his client to observe the statute law.

Of course, this Canon did no more than articulate centuries of accepted standards of conduct. Similarly, Canon 37, adopted in 1928, explicitly acknowledges as an exception to the attorney's duty of confidentiality a client's announced attention to commit a crime: "The announced intention of a client to commit a crime is not included within the confidences which the attorney is bound to respect."

These principles have been carried through to contemporary codifications[4] of an attorney's professional responsibility. Disciplinary Rule 7-102 of the Model Code of Professional Responsibility (1980), entitled "Representing a Client Within the Bounds of the Law," provides that:

(A) In his representation of a client, a lawyer shall not:

* * * *

(4) Knowingly use perjured testimony or false evidence.

* * * *

(7) Counsel or assist his client in conduct that the lawyer knows to be illegal or fraudulent.

This provision has been adopted by Iowa, and is binding on all lawyers who appear in its courts. See Iowa Code of Professional Responsibility for Lawyers (1985). The more recent Model Rules of Professional Conduct (1983) similarly admonish attorneys to obey all laws in the course of representing a client:

Rule 1.2. *Scope of Representation*

* * * *

(d) A lawyer shall not counsel a client to engage, or assist a client, in conduct that the lawyer knows is criminal or fraudulent.

Both the Model Code of Professional Conduct and the Model Rules of Professional Conduct also adopt the specific exception from the attorney-client privilege for disclosure of perjury that his client intends to commit or has committed. DR 4-101(C)(3) (intention of client to commit a crime); Rule 3.3 (lawyer has duty to disclose falsity of evidence even if disclosure compromises client confidences). Indeed, both the Model Code and the Model Rules do not merely authorize disclosure by counsel of client perjury; they require such disclosure. See Rule 3.3(a)(4); DR 7-102(B)(1).

These standards confirm that the legal profession has accepted that an attorney's ethical duty to advance the interests of his client is limited by an equally solemn duty to comply with the law and standards of professional conduct; it specifically ensures that the client may not use false evidence. * * * * This special duty of an attorney to prevent and disclose frauds upon the court derives from the recognition that perjury is as much a crime as tampering with witnesses or jurors by way of promises and threats, and undermines the administration of justice.

---

[4] There currently exist two different codifications of uniform standards of professional conduct. The Model Code of Professional Responsibility was originally adopted by the American Bar Association in 1969, and was subsequently adopted (in many cases with modification) by nearly every state. The more recent Model Rules of Professional Conduct were adopted by the American Bar Association in 1983. Since their promulgation by the American Bar Association, the Model Rules have been adopted by 11 States: Arizona, Arkansas, Delaware, Minnesota, Missouri, Montana, Nevada, New Hampshire, New Jersey, North Carolina, and Washington. Iowa is one of the States that adopted a form of the Model Code of Professional Responsibility, but has yet to adopt the Model Rules.

The offense of perjury was a crime recognized at common law, and has been made a felony in most states by statute, including Iowa. Iowa Code § 720.2. An attorney who aids false testimony by questioning a witness, when perjurious responses can be anticipated, risks prosecution for subornation of perjury under Iowa Code § 720.3.

It is universally agreed that at a minimum the attorney's first duty when confronted with a proposal for perjurious testimony is to attempt to dissuade the client from the unlawful course of conduct. Model Rules of Professional Conduct, Rule 3.3. A statement directly in point is found in the Commentary to the Model Rules of Professional Conduct under the heading "False Evidence":

> When false evidence is offered by the client, however, a conflict may arise between the lawyer's duty to keep the client's revelations confidential and the duty of candor to the court. Upon ascertaining that material evidence is false, the lawyer *should seek to persuade the client that the evidence should not be offered* or, if it has been offered, that its false character should immediately be disclosed. [Model Rules of Professional Conduct, Rule 3.3, Comment (1983) (emphasis added)]

The Commentary thus also suggests that an attorney's revelation of his client's perjury to the court is a professionally responsible and acceptable response to the conduct of a client who has actually given perjured testimony. Similarly, the Model Rules and the commentary, as well as the Code of Professional Responsibility adopted in Iowa, expressly permit withdrawal from representation as an appropriate response of an attorney when the client threatens to commit perjury. Model Rules of Professional Conduct, Rule 1.16(a)(1), Rule 1.6, Comment (1983); Code of Professional Responsibility, DR 2-110(B),(C) (1980). Withdrawal of counsel when this situation arises at trial gives rise to many difficult questions including possible mistrial and claims of double jeopardy. * * *

The essence of the brief *amicus* of the American Bar Association, reviewing practices long accepted by ethical lawyers, is that under no circumstance may a lawyer either advocate or passively tolerate a client's giving false testimony. This, of course, is consistent with the governance of trial conduct in what we have long called "a search for truth." The suggestion sometimes made that "a lawyer must believe his client not judge him" in no sense means a lawyer can honorably be a party to or in any way give aid to presenting known perjury.

D

Considering Robinson's representation of respondent in light of these accepted norms of professional conduct, we discern no failure to adhere to reasonable professional standards that would in any sense make out a deprivation of the Sixth Amendment right to counsel. Whether Robinson's conduct is seen as a successful attempt to dissuade his client from committing the crime of perjury, or whether seen as a "threat" to withdraw from representation and disclose the illegal scheme, Robinson's representation of Whiteside falls well within accepted standards of professional conduct and the range of reasonable professional conduct acceptable under *Strickland*.

The Court of Appeals assumed for the purpose of the decision that Whiteside would have given false testimony had counsel not intervened; its opinion states,

We presume that appellant would have testified falsely. Counsel's actions prevented Whiteside from testifying falsely. We hold that counsel's action deprived appellant of due process and effective assistance of counsel. Counsel's actions also impermissibly compromised appellant's right to testify in his own defense by conditioning continued representation by counsel and confidentiality upon appellant's restricted testimony.

While purporting to follow the Iowa's highest court "on all questions of state law," the Court of Appeals reached its conclusions on the basis of federal constitutional due process and right to counsel.

The Court of Appeals' holding that Robinson's "action deprived Whiteside of due process and effective assistance of counsel" is not supported by the record since Robinson's action, at most, deprived Whiteside of his contemplated perjury. Nothing counsel did in any way undermined Whiteside's claim that he believed the victim was reaching for a gun. Similarly, the record gives no support for holding that Robinson's action "also impermissibly compromised Whiteside's right to testify in his own defense by conditioning continued representation and confidentiality upon Whiteside's restricted testimony." The record in fact shows the contrary: (a) that Whiteside did testify, and (b) he was "restricted" or restrained only from testifying falsely and was aided by Robinson in developing the basis for the fear that Love was reaching for a gun. Robinson divulged no client communications until he was compelled to do so in response to Whiteside's post-trial challenge to the quality of his performance. We see this as a case in which the attorney successfully dissuaded the client from committing the crime of perjury. Paradoxically, even while accepting the conclusion of the Iowa trial court that Whiteside's proposed testimony would have been a criminal act, the Court of Appeals held that Robinson's efforts to persuade Whiteside not to commit that crime were improper, first, as forcing an impermissible choice between the right to counsel and the right to testify; and second, as compromising client confidences because of Robinson's threat to disclose the contemplated perjury.[7]

Whatever the scope of a constitutional right to testify, it is elementary that such a right does not extend to testifying *falsely*.

* * * *

Whiteside's attorney treated Whiteside's proposed perjury in accord with professional standards, and since Whiteside's truthful testimony could not have prejudiced the result of his trial, the Court of Appeals was in error to direct the issuance of a writ of habeas corpus and must be reversed. Reversed.

JUSTICE BRENNAN, concurring in the judgment.

This Court has no constitutional authority to establish rules of ethical conduct for lawyers practicing in the state courts. Nor does the Court enjoy any statutory grant

---

[7] The Court of Appeals also determined that Robinson's efforts to persuade Whiteside to testify truthfully constituted an impermissible threat to testify against his own client. We find no support for a threat to testify against Whiteside while he was acting as counsel. The record reflects testimony by Robinson that he had admonished Whiteside that if he withdrew he "probably would be allowed to attempt to impeach that particular testimony," if Whiteside testified falsely. The trial court accepted this version of the conversation as true.

of jurisdiction over legal ethics.

Accordingly, it is not surprising that the Court emphasizes that it "must be careful not to narrow the wide range of professional conduct acceptable under the Sixth Amendment so restrictively as to constitutionalize particular standards of professional conduct and thereby intrude into the State's proper authority to define and apply the standards of professional conduct applicable to those it admits to practice in its courts." I read this as saying in another way that the Court *cannot* tell the states or the lawyers in the states how to behave in their courts, unless and until federal rights are violated.

Unfortunately, the Court seems unable to resist the temptation of sharing with the legal community its vision of ethical conduct. But let there be no mistake: the Court's essay regarding what constitutes the correct response to a criminal client's suggestion that he will perjure himself is pure discourse without force of law. As Justice Blackmun observes, *that* issue is a thorny one, but it is not an issue presented by this case. Lawyers, judges, bar associations, students and others should understand that the problem has not now been "decided."

I join Justice Blackmun's concurrence because I agree that respondent has failed to prove the kind of prejudice necessary to make out a claim under *Strickland v. Washington*, 466 U.S. 668 (1984).

JUSTICE BLACKMUN, with whom JUSTICE BRENNAN, JUSTICE MARSHALL, and JUSTICE STEVENS join, concurring in the judgment.

How a defense attorney ought to act when faced with a client who intends to commit perjury at trial has long been a controversial issue. But I do not believe that a federal habeas corpus case challenging a state criminal conviction is an appropriate vehicle for attempting to resolve this thorny problem. When a defendant argues that he was denied effective assistance of counsel because his lawyer dissuaded him from committing perjury, the only question properly presented to this Court is whether the lawyer's actions deprived the defendant of the fair trial which the Sixth Amendment is meant to guarantee. Since I believe that the respondent in this case suffered no injury justifying federal habeas relief, I concur in the Court's judgment.
* * * *

JUSTICE STEVENS, concurring in the judgment.

Justice Holmes taught us that a word is but the skin of a living thought. A "fact" may also have a life of its own. From the perspective of an appellate judge, after a case has been tried and the evidence has been sifted by another judge, a particular fact may be as clear and certain as a piece of crystal or a small diamond. A trial lawyer, however, must often deal with mixtures of sand and clay. Even a pebble that seems clear enough at first glance may take on a different hue in a handful of gravel.

As we view this case, it appears perfectly clear that respondent intended to commit perjury, that his lawyer knew it, and that the lawyer had a duty — both to the court and to his client, for perjured testimony can ruin an otherwise meritorious case — to take extreme measures to prevent the perjury from occurring. The lawyer was successful and, from our unanimous and remote perspective, it is now pellucidly clear that the client suffered no "legally cognizable prejudice."

Nevertheless, beneath the surface of this case there are areas of uncertainty that cannot be resolved today. A lawyer's certainty that a change in his client's recollection is a harbinger of intended perjury — as well as judicial review of such apparent certainty — should be tempered by the realization that, after reflection, the most honest witness may recall (or sincerely believe he recalls) details that he previously overlooked. Similarly, the post-trial review of a lawyer's pre-trial threat to expose perjury that had not yet been committed — and, indeed, may have been prevented by the threat — is by no means the same as review of the way in which such a threat may actually have been carried out. Thus, one can be convinced — as I am that this lawyer's actions were a proper way to provide his client with effective representation, without confronting the much more difficult questions of what a lawyer must, should, or may do after his client has given testimony that the lawyer does not believe. The answer to such questions may well be colored by the particular circumstances attending the actual event and its aftermath.

Because Justice Blackmun has preserved such questions for another day, and because I do not understand him to imply any adverse criticism of this lawyer's representation of his client, I join his opinion concurring in the judgment.

Notes from Mary:

1. **When does a defense lawyer "know" that his client intends to testify falsely?**

In *State v. McDowell*, 669 N.W.2d 204 (Wis.App. 2003), the court discussed this issue:

> On what basis can counsel determine whether a defendant intends to testify falsely? Must counsel "know" the intended testimony is false, or just "reasonably believe" it to be so? *Must* counsel then refrain from presenting the testimony, under the former, or *may* counsel present it, under the latter? And finally, how do these rules comport with the defendant's constitutional right to effective assistance of counsel?

> While Wisconsin courts have not answered these questions under our rules, some commentators and courts have addressed them in comparable contexts. Most recently, for example, the Supreme Judicial Court of Massachusetts, in the course of determining the standard by which counsel would "know" of a client's intended perjury, acknowledged the myriad approaches in the case law, including: "good cause to believe" a client intends to testify falsely; "compelling support" for such a conclusion; "knowledge beyond a reasonable doubt"; "firm factual basis"; "good-faith determination"; and "actual knowledge." *Commonwealth v. Mitchell*, 781 N.E.2d 1237, 1246–47 (Mass.2003).

> The Remington Center of the University of Wisconsin Law School (which provides legal assistance to prison inmates) "urges that this court adopt the most stringent standard, because anything less jeopardizes the defendant's right to have a jury decide the facts, undermines the relationship and role of defense counsel as zealous and loyal advocate, and is practically unworkable." Thus, the Remington Center recommends that we hold that "before defense attorneys can refuse to assist a client in testifying, they must know that the client will testify falsely based upon the client's affirmative statement of intent to lie." Subject to certain qualifica-

tion and elaboration, we agree.

We begin by explaining why we deem any lesser standard unsatisfactory. We base our analysis not only on the authorities and the standards they recommend, but also on our years of trial court experience presiding over hundreds of jury trials in criminal cases. In the trial courts, we gained understanding of the dynamics of defense representation and, in particular, of the forces that frequently motivate defense counsel to offer far less than zealous advocacy. To retreat from question-answer in presenting a defendant's testimony, when the defendant has *not* admitted any intent to testify falsely, would be a defining step in a sad parade — the pathetic parade that so often features the travesty of defense counsel marching defendants to negotiated guilty pleas and *Alford* pleas when defendants maintain their innocence.[15]

Any lesser standard — not requiring a client's admission to counsel of the intent to testify falsely — would eclipse the bright-line guidance that, the parties and the Remington Center agree, is needed. With a lesser standard, on what would counsel base a "reasonable belief"? How, really, would counsel "know," absent an admission from the defendant? And then, what would be counsel's corresponding duty? In trial preparation, would counsel investigate the facts in order to advocate zealously, or to determine the veracity of a client's account? Should counsel refrain from looking too carefully at the facts for fear of concluding that a client's account is false? Without a client's admission of intent to testify falsely, counsel sails swirling seas, changeable from one moment to the next, without a single star by which to chart a course.

Far better for counsel to remember that "except in the rarest of cases, attorneys who adopt 'the role of the judge or jury to determine the facts,' pose a danger of depriving their clients of the zealous and loyal advocacy required by the Sixth Amendment." *Nix*, 475 U.S. at 189. And far more realistic for counsel to maintain the unique humility of "not knowing," absent an admission by the client. * * * *

---

[15] *See North Carolina v. Alford, 400 U.S. 25 (1970).* An *Alford* plea is a guilty plea in which the defendant pleads guilty while either maintaining his innocence or not admitting having committed the crime. Although no *Alford* plea is involved in this appeal, *Alford* pleas highlight concerns about defense advocacy that are central to our discussion. Perhaps more than any other defense technique, *Alford* pleas expose the most alarming abandonment of advocacy. Simply stated, every *Alford* plea, in effect, presents a client telling counsel, "I'm innocent," and counsel advising, "Plead guilty anyway." The frequently heard explanation for *Alford* pleas is that, without them, defendants would not plead guilty and cases would go to trial. So? When defendants deny guilt, trials may follow and defendants (who just hours or days before were being counseled to plead guilty) sometimes are acquitted. Moreover, when a court declines to accept an *Alford* plea, a trial may *not* follow. Instead, in some cases, the prosecution re-evaluates the evidence and either moves for dismissal or for a proper amendment of the charges based on the evidence. In other cases, defendants, not allowed to enter *Alford* pleas, become more candid and admit guilt. That, in turn, leads to more meaningful sentencings, uncompromised by lingering protests of innocence. Thus, although *Alford* pleas are sanctioned by the decisions, they are incompatible with truth and justice. The fact that in Wisconsin a trial court *can* accept an *Alford* plea does not mean that a trial court should do so. Similarly, just as a client's declaration of innocence must control counsel's advice regarding a plea (regardless of what may be counsel's suspicions of the client's guilt), a client's declaration of intent to testify truthfully must control counsel's presentation of that testimony (regardless of what may be counsel's suspicions about the client's account).

Thus, we accept that counsel cannot be omniscient and, accordingly, we embrace the mandate, under SCR 20:3.3(a)(4), that counsel "shall not offer evidence that the lawyer *knows* to be false." Therefore, we conclude, absent the most extraordinary circumstances, criminal defense counsel, as a matter of law, cannot *know* that a client is going to testify falsely absent the client's admission of the intent to do so. Accordingly, we interpret SCR 20:3.3(c)'s suggestion that counsel "may refuse to offer evidence that the lawyer reasonably believes is false" to apply to circumstances beyond the borders surrounding the questions involving a criminal defendant's stated intention to testify falsely. Any other interpretation would, in our estimation, produce an irreconcilable conflict between the two rules.

And with our "absent extraordinary circumstances" qualification, we do not mean to obscure the bright line or invite endless litigation over what such circumstances might be. We simply recognize that, in the never-ending succession of factual scenarios confronting counsel and the courts, to *never* allow for the possibility that, absent the client's admission, counsel could "know" would be to ignore the truly exceptional case — one that, even absent a client's direct admission to counsel, might present virtually the same dilemma.[16]

Similarly, we do not obscure the bright line by holding, as one of the proposals at oral argument would have, that counsel can only "know" when the client's admission is corroborated. To do so would re-submerge counsel and the courts in the swamp of uncertainty over whether certain evidence was sufficient to corroborate that a client's intended false testimony is indeed false.

More pointedly, we emphasize the singular significance of the client's admission to counsel. *Despite* confessions *to others*, and despite what may seem to be overwhelming corroborative evidence, counsel must not presume to *know* whether a client's account is true. As the Remington Center reminds us, its Wisconsin Innocence Project has had direct experience with a case in which the evidence, including a confession, led defense counsel to be certain of his client's guilt of rape and murder. The defendant, after claiming innocence for several months, finally admitted his guilt to both counsel and the court. Years later, however, DNA evidence established his innocence.

The standard we set is consistent with the underlying principles in *Nix*. Although the Supreme Court did not address the precise questions we now answer, it is noteworthy that the Court announced what we deem to be its five unassailable standards *not* in the context of a case where counsel had mere misgivings about a client's account, but rather, in the course of defining "the range of 'reasonable professional' responses to a criminal defendant client who *informs counsel that he will perjure himself on the stand.*" *Nix*, 475 U.S. at 166.

---

[16] Consider, for example, the modern-day Bonnie and Clyde, caught full-faced on video and apprehended at the scene of the crime, who inform counsel of their intent to testify (*truthfully*, they say) that they were never even in the bank. The *absolutely conclusive* evidence of their presence, beyond all doubt, would present counsel's dilemma no less than if they had stated their intent to testify falsely.

Thus, we conclude that, with the rarest of exceptions, absent a criminal defendant's admission of an intent to testify falsely, defense counsel must protect the defendant's right to testify and, when the defendant decides to testify, assist the defendant with effective questioning to facilitate the presentation of the defendant's account. Short of "knowing" that one's client intends to testify falsely, counsel must proceed as a zealous advocate. Regardless of suspicions about a defendant's account, counsel must assist the defendant in presenting it if the defendant desires to do so and maintains that the account is true.

If, however, a defendant informs counsel of the intention to testify falsely, counsel's first duty is to attempt to dissuade the client from the unlawful course of conduct. Cynics aside, we do not dismiss the persuasive power of counsel to do so on ethical, legal, and moral grounds. Additionally, counsel may be persuasive on pragmatic grounds. By explaining what may be the evidentiary weakness of the false account, counsel can describe the likely consequences that, obviously, the defendant does not desire. Such consequences may include a greater likelihood of conviction brought about by a defendant's incredible account, a longer sentence, and the potential for a perjury prosecution. Thus, as the Supreme Court has emphasized, defense counsel's effort to dissuade a defendant from testifying falsely is wholly consistent with counsel's representation of a defendant's interests.

But some defendants will not be dissuaded. How, then, must defense counsel question the defendant who intends to testify falsely? A lawyer with a perjurious client must contend with competing considerations — duties of zealous advocacy, confidentiality and loyalty to the client on the one hand, and a responsibility to the courts and our truth-seeking system of justice on the other. To contend with these considerations, courts have considered many approaches arguably available to defense counsel — from fully facilitating the presentation of perjurious testimony with customary question-answer questioning, to refusing to allow a defendant to testify or withdrawing from representation. Under such circumstances, we conclude, only narrative questioning fairly accounts for both counsel's allegiance to the client and duty to the court. Only full disclosure to the court, followed by narrative questioning, provides the appropriate "method of effectuating both the right of the accused to testify and the duty of a defense lawyer not to assist in presenting known perjured testimony." Restatement (Third) of the Law Governing Lawyers § 120 (2000). * * * *

Therefore, if the attempt to turn the defendant away from perjury is unsuccessful, counsel must inform the defendant that: (1) he or she may move to withdraw; (2) future counsel will have to operate under the same legal standards, thus bringing about the likely repetition of the current circumstance; and (3) if continuing as counsel, he or she will not be allowed to suborn perjury and, therefore, will only be able to question the defendant by asking the usual formal, introductory questions, followed by a question or two eliciting a narrative response. Counsel must explain what that would entail and advise the defendant of the need to provide the full, intended account without added assistance of question-answer or re-direct questioning to further the perjurious account.

If unable to dissuade a defendant from testifying falsely, counsel, outside the presence of the jury of course, must advise opposing counsel and the trial court before the defendant testifies. The court, in turn, must examine counsel and the defendant to ensure a clear and full record of: (1) the basis for counsel's conclusion that the defendant intends to testify falsely; (2) the defendant's understanding of the right to testify, notwithstanding the intent to testify falsely; and (3) the defendant's, and counsel's, understanding of the nature and limitations of the narrative questioning that will result.

In *United States v. Long*, 857 F.2d 436 (8th Cir.1988), the court held that the lawyer must have a "firm factual basis" that the client will lie before acting on such a belief:

An attorney who acts on a belief of possible client perjury takes on the role of the fact finder, a role which perverts the structure of our adversary system. A lawyer who judges a client's truthfulness does so without the many safeguards inherent in our adversary system. He likely makes his decision alone, without the assistance of fellow fact finders. He may consider too much evidence, including that which is untrustworthy. Moreover, a jury's determination on credibility is always tempered by the requirement of proof beyond a reasonable doubt. A lawyer, finding facts on his own, is not necessarily guided by such a high standard. Finally, by taking a position contrary to his client's interest, the lawyer may irrevocably destroy the trust the attorney-client relationship is designed to foster. That lack of trust cannot easily be confined to the area of intended perjury. It may well carry over into other aspects of the lawyer's representation, including areas where the client needs and deserves zealous and loyal representation. For these reasons and others, it is absolutely essential that a lawyer have a firm factual basis before adopting a belief of impending perjury. [*Id.* at 445–446]

2. What is "narrative" testimony?

The court in *State v. McDowell*, above, and several other courts have said that a lawyer who is convinced that his client will perjure himself should present the client's testimony in a "narrative" form.

Former Chief Justice Burger described narrative testimony as the defendant's lawyer calling defendant to the witness stand and saying: "I understand you have a story to tell. You will now tell it." Freedman, *Understanding Lawyers' Ethics*, p. 117, n. 26 (Matthew Bender, 1990).

Professor Freedman has some qualms about the "narrative" solution to the problem of client perjury:

Beyond any question, [the narrative procedure] divulges the client's confidences. The judge is certain to understand what is going on, and it is generally agreed that the jury usually will as well. Even if the jury does not realize the significance of the unusual manner in which the defendant is testifying, the jury is sure to catch on when the defense lawyer in closing argument makes no reference to the defendant's exculpatory testimony. [*Id.* at 118]

In *People v. Johnson*, 62 Cal.App.4th 608 (1998), the court discussed several possible "solutions" to the problem of client perjury — and concluded that the "narrative" solution is the best:

> None of the approaches to a client's stated intention to commit perjury is perfect. Of the various approaches, we believe the narrative approach represents the best accommodation of the competing interests of the defendant's right to testify and the attorney's obligation not to participate in the presentation of perjured testimony since it allows the defendant to tell the jury, in his own words, his version of what occurred, a right which has been described as fundamental, and allows the attorney to play a passive role.

> In contrast, the two extremes — fully cooperating with the defendant's testimony and refusing to present the defendant's testimony — involve no accommodation of the conflicting interests; the first gives no consideration to the attorney's ethical obligations, the second gives none to the defendant's right to testify. The other intermediate solutions — persuasion, withdrawal and disclosure — often result in no solution, i.e., the defendant is not persuaded, the withdrawal leads to an endless chain of withdrawals and disclosure compromises client confidentiality and typically requires further action.

> We disagree with those commentators who have found the narrative approach necessarily communicates to the jury that defense counsel believes the defendant is lying. The jury may surmise the defendant desired to testify unhampered by the traditional question and answer format. Because the defendant in a criminal trial is not situated the same as other witnesses, it would not be illogical for a jury to assume that special rules apply to his testimony, including a right to testify in a narrative fashion. We do not believe the possibility of a negative inference the defendant is lying should preclude the use of the narrative approach since the alternative would be worse, i.e., the attorney's active participation in presenting the perjured testimony or exclusion of the defendant's testimony, neither of which strikes a balance between the competing interests involved.

> The danger that the defendant may testify falsely is mitigated by the fact that the defendant is subject to impeachment and can be cross-examined just like any other witness. The jury is no less capable of assessing the defendant's credibility than it is of any other witness. Further, to preclude the defendant's testimony entirely based on a possibility that defendant may lie, deprives the jury of making that assessment and may deprive the jury of hearing other, nonperjurious evidence to which the defendant would have testified about had he been given the opportunity. In utilizing the narrative approach, the jury has the benefit of hearing the defendant's version.

> The narrative approach also avoids having a pre-perjury hearing, a mini-trial on whether the defendant might commit perjury if called to the stand; a hearing which could result in the attorney testifying against the client and which would require the court to be able to see into the future and determine that an individual who has stated only an intention to testify

falsely (at least as according to his attorney) will actually testify falsely once on the witness stand.

In *People v. DePallo*, 729 N.Y.S.2d 649 (2001), the court approved having defendant testify in narrative form.

3. Suppose counsel believes that *a non-client* witness will lie.

In *People v. Gadson*, 19 Cal.App.4th 1700 (1993), defendant wanted to testify, and also wanted two other men to testify for him. His counsel apparently believed that all three would lie, and asked the court to allow all three to give narrative testimony. After warning defendant of the danger that the jury might infer that defense counsel did not believe the three, the court allowed it. After conviction, the appellate court approved this procedure.

Question: Should the court have made any distinction between the defendant and the other two men?

4. Should a lawyer who believes his client will lie on the stand *withdraw* from the case?

Professor Freedman points out some difficulties with *withdrawal* as a remedy:

> The lawyer should be forbidden to withdraw . . . if doing so would prejudice the client in any way. Prejudice cannot ordinarily be avoided if the case is near to trial or the trial has begun. Replacing the lawyer in those circumstances will delay the calendar, which is a major concern of all judges and the overriding concern of too many. The court will therefore require the lawyer to give extraordinary reasons for withdrawal, which would require the lawyer to reveal to the judge that the client intends to commit perjury. In addition, the new lawyer might well face the problem. Indeed, the client might force disqualification of a series of lawyers in the same way, ultimately forcing the judge to try the case without a defense lawyer, which can be a difficult and unsatisfactory procedure.
>
> In most cases, therefore, the attorney can withdraw only by revealing the client's confidences to the judge — that is by telling the judge that the client has admitted incriminating evidence to the lawyer but intends to try to lie his way out of it. Since the judge will be imposing sentence on the client in the event of a conviction, the prejudice to the client would be severe. The same kind of prejudice might also affect the defendant's appeal. [*Id.* at 116–117]

In *U.S. v. Midgett*, 342 F.3d 321 (4th Cir. 2003), Midgett's lawyer did not believe his story that he was not involved in a bank robbery, mainly because the lawyer could find no evidence corroborating Midgett's story, which was contradicted by other evidence. The lawyer so advised the judge and asked permission to withdraw as counsel, but "Rather than permitting his lawyer to withdraw, the court offered Midgett the choice of either acceding to defense counsel's refusal to put him on the stand or representing himself without further assistance of counsel." Midgett did not feel qualified to represent himself, so he kept the lawyer and did not testify. His conviction was reversed:

> Defense counsel's responsibility to his client was not dependent on whether he personally believed Midgett, nor did it depend on the amount of proof supporting or contradicting Midgett's anticipated testimony

regarding how the incident happened. In this situation, Midgett never indicated to his attorney that his testimony would be perjurious. Thus, his lawyer had a duty to assist Midgett in putting his testimony before the jury, which would necessarily include his help in Midgett's direct examination.

Defense counsel's mere belief, albeit a strong one supported by other evidence, was not a sufficient basis to refuse Midgett's need for assistance in presenting his own testimony.

5. If a lawyer seeks to withdraw, *what should he tell the judge?*

In *State v. Hischke*, 639 N.W.2d 6 (Iowa 2002), the court held that a defense attorney should be permitted to withdraw when he is "convinced with good cause" to believe that defendant will perjure himself. He is not required to conduct an independent investigation of the facts before coming to this conclusion. The court rejected defendant's contention that the lawyer must have "actual knowledge" that the client will lie on the stand:

> Such a standard would be virtually impossible to satisfy unless the lawyer had a direct confession from his or her client or personally witnessed the event in question. Consequently, the standard of actual knowledge would eviscerate the rules of professional responsibility forbidding a lawyer from presenting perjured testimony.

Concurring Justice Carter did not disagree, but felt that a lawyer who becomes "convinced with good cause" that his client will commit perjury may not do what Hughes's lawyer did — tell the trial judge that this is the reason he wants to withdraw:

> My disagreement with defense counsel's action flows from a belief that it is never proper for counsel to advise the court that counsel believes a client will testify falsely. Such conduct will inevitably damage the client's case beyond repair.

> Counsel who reach the conclusion that a client is about to testify falsely should first attempt to dissuade the client from giving the offending testimony. If unsuccessful, counsel should attempt a quiet withdrawal from the representation. The reasons set forth in the application to withdraw should only identify the existence of an unspecified attorney-client disagreement that might compromise the attorney's ethical responsibilities. At no time should the matter of impending perjury be disclosed. If the attempt to withdraw fails, then counsel should proceed with the case and conduct any questioning of the witness so as not to invite the suspected perjury. If the suspected perjury nonetheless occurs, counsel should make no reference of it in arguing the case to the trier of fact. I believe that if a lawyer proceeds in this manner, he or she may fully satisfy the lawyer's ethical obligation to prevent perjury without the necessity of advising the court as to the client's intent to testify falsely.

6. In *Scott v. State*, ___ So.2d ___, 2008 WL 5089815 (2008), Scott was charged with murder. Before trial,

> Scott's counsel attempted to withdraw from the case, which the trial court did not allow. Then, Scott's counsel, without initially revealing the

content of the conflict, explained to the judge in an ex parte hearing that he found himself in an ethical dilemma that could cost him his license to practice law. The trial judge inquired further in order to make her ruling. At that time, Scott's counsel revealed to the trial judge that Scott had confessed to him that he had committed the crime and was intent on falsely testifying. Scott's attorney explained he had not been able to dissuade Scott from offering perjured testimony.

The judge denied the motion to withdraw, but "held that Scott would be allowed to provide narrative testimony and would be subject to cross-examination." A jury convicted Scott. On appeal, his lawyer argued that because the judge had been told by Scott's lawyer that Scott had confessed to the murder, the judge should have recused himself. The appellate court agreed, but the state supreme court did not agree:

> [There was no] showing that the judge in any way treated Scott in a prejudicial manner. Scott took the stand on his own behalf, and the jury had an opportunity to determine for itself whether or not Scott's written confession and testimony were genuine and credible. *The jury never heard about the verbal confession to Scott's attorney.*
>
> Our trial judges are confronted daily with evidence that would tend to make defendants appear more culpable than not. We presume that our trial judges are aptly equipped to handle these issues and apply the law without fear of undue prejudice. * * * *
>
> Had the trial judge recused herself, any judge who would have presided over the case would have read the record, discovered the ex parte hearing proceedings, and thus would have been placed in exactly the same position as the original trial judge.

7. In *Commonwealth v. Mitchell*, 781 N.E.2d 1237 (Mass. 2003), the court upheld the constitutionality of Rule 3.3(e) of the Massachusetts Rules of Professional Conduct, which provides:

> In a criminal case, defense counsel who knows that the defendant, the client, intends to testify falsely may not aid the client in constructing false testimony, and has a duty strongly to discourage the client from testifying falsely, advising that such a course is unlawful, will have substantial adverse consequences, and should not be followed. If a criminal trial has commenced and the lawyer discovers that the client intends to testify falsely at trial, the lawyer need not file a motion to withdraw from the case if the lawyer reasonably believes that seeking to withdraw will prejudice the client. If, during the client's testimony or after the client has testified, the lawyer knows that the client has testified falsely, the lawyer shall call upon the client to rectify the false testimony and, if the client refuses or is unable to do so, the lawyer shall not reveal the false testimony to the tribunal. In no event may the lawyer examine the client in such a manner as to elicit any testimony from the client the lawyer knows to be false, and the lawyer shall not argue the probative value of the false testimony in closing argument or in any other proceedings, including appeals.

The court held:

The question what a criminal defense attorney should do when confronted with client perjury at trial has been a subject of considerable debate. The problem raises both ethical and constitutional concerns. Defense counsel must furnish zealous advocacy and preserve client confidences, but, at the same time, defense counsel has a duty under rule 3.3(e) to the court. In addition, the problem has constitutional implications by reason of its potential to deprive a defendant of his right to effective assistance of counsel, and his rights to due process and a fair trial, which include his right to testify in his own defense.

Not unexpectedly, courts have adopted differing standards to determine what an attorney must "know" before concluding that his client's testimony will be perjurious. The standards include the following: "good cause to believe the defendant's proposed testimony would be deliberately untruthful," *State v. Hischke*, 639 N.W.2d 6, 10 (Iowa 2002); "compelling support," *Sanborn v. State*, 474 So.2d 309, 313 n. 2 (Fla.Dist.Ct.App.1985); "knowledge beyond a reasonable doubt," *Shockley v. State*, 565 A.2d 1373, 1379 (Del.1989); a "firm factual basis," *United States ex rel. Wilcox v. Johnson*, 555 F.2d 115, 122 (3d Cir.1977); a "good-faith determination," *People v. Bartee*, 208 Ill.App.3d 105, 108; and "actual knowledge," *United States v. Del Carpio-Cotrina*, 733 F.Supp. 95, 99 (S.D.Fla.1990).

The trial judge properly rejected standards that were too lenient (good cause to believe) or too rigid, particularly the standard sought by the defendant, knowledge beyond a reasonable doubt. The knowledge beyond a reasonable doubt standard essentially would eviscerate rule 3.3(e). That standard is virtually impossible to satisfy unless the lawyer had a direct confession from his client or personally witnessed the event in question. The standard would also tend to compel defense attorneys to remain silent in the face of likely perjury that a sharp private warning could nip in the bud.

The judge correctly settled on the "firm basis in fact" standard. This standard satisfies constitutional concerns because it requires more than mere suspicion or conjecture on the part of counsel, more than a belief and more information than inconsistencies in statements by the defendant or in the evidence. Instead, the standard mandates that a lawyer act in good faith based on objective circumstances firmly rooted in fact. The lawyer may act on the information he or she possesses, and we decline to impose an independent duty on the part of counsel to investigate because such a duty would be incompatible with the fiduciary nature of the attorney-client relationship and is unnecessary when an attorney relies, in significant part, on incriminating admissions made by the client. * * * *

The narrative form of testimony was properly directed. This approach was adopted by the ABA in 1971. See ABA Standards for Criminal Justice 4-7.7 (Approved Draft 1971). Although the ABA later rejected this approach and currently suggests that the lawyer may examine as to truthful testimony, and although the approach has been criticized, the narrative approach continues to be a commonly accepted method of dealing with client perjury.

The defendant suggests that his trial counsel should have conducted a direct examination with respect to the "non-suspect" portions of his testimony and should also have argued the truthful portions of the defendant's testimony in his closing argument. The former suggestion has been justifiably criticized by the Criminal Justice Section of the ABA: "This is the worst approach of all. . . . This approach would be far worse for the client than saying nothing, not to mention it would be virtually impossible to control once the client takes the stand. And what about cross? How can you possibly prepare your clients for that? Tell them not to answer any questions that they do not like?" ABA Criminal Justice Section, Ethical Problems Facing the Criminal Defense Lawyer at 162 (1995). The latter suggestion is impractical, as it may call attention to testimony of the defendant that is not argued by trial counsel, and would likely lead to counsel's making an incoherent final argument. We shall not impose these requirements on counsel. Further, to permit the defendant to make an unsworn statement or his own closing argument would allow him to do what rule 3.3(e) prohibits his counsel from doing, arguing perjured testimony to the jury. * * * *

A summary of our disposition of this issue is now in order. The duties imposed on a criminal defense lawyer (zealous advocacy, preservation of client confidences, avoidance of a conflict of interest) and the constitutional rights granted a defendant (effective legal representation, opportunity to testify in his own defense, right to a fair trial) are circumscribed by what we demand of honorable lawyers and the core principle of our judicial system that seeks to make a trial a search for truth. The rights of a defendant are not so exclusive that justice can be subrogated to the defendant's perceived interests thereby dismissing or ignoring the interests of victims and the Commonwealth. Perjury, a most serious common-law felony, is antithetical to these values. In Massachusetts it is punishable in a noncapital case by up to twenty years' imprisonment, and in a capital case by possible life imprisonment.

The standard set forth in rule 3.3(e) "confirms that the legal profession has accepted that an attorney's ethical duty to advance the interests of his client is limited by an equally solemn duty to comply with the law and standards of professional conduct; it specifically ensures that the client may not use false evidence. This special duty of an attorney to prevent and disclose frauds upon the court derives from the recognition that perjury is as much a crime as tampering with witnesses or jurors by way of promises and threats, and undermines the administration of justice." Nix v. Whiteside, supra at 168–169.

The standard in no way abridges constitutional rights of a defendant. There is no constitutional or permissible right of a defendant to testify falsely. When defense counsel attempts to persuade a defendant to testify truthfully, counsel is not depriving the defendant of his right to counsel nor the right to testify truthfully. "In short, the responsibility of an ethical lawyer, as an officer of the court and a key component of a system of justice, dedicated to a search for truth, is essentially the same whether the client announces an intention to bribe or threaten witnesses or jurors or to commit or procure perjury. No system of justice worthy of the name can tolerate a lesser standard." *Id.* at 174.

To implement the obligations imposed by rule 3.3(e), when the question of perjured testimony by a defendant arises, we require, as the rule's knowledge element, that the lawyer, before invoking the rule, act in good faith and have a firm basis in objective fact. Conjecture or speculation that the defendant intends to testify falsely are not enough. Inconsistencies in the evidence or in the defendant's version of events are also not enough to trigger the rule, even though the inconsistencies, considered in light of the Commonwealth's proof, raise concerns in counsel's mind that the defendant is equivocating and is not an honest person. Similarly, the existence of strong physical and forensic evidence implicating the defendant would not be sufficient. Counsel can rely on facts made known to him, and is under no duty to conduct an independent investigation.

Once the matter is called to the court's attention, the judge should instruct the lawyer on how to proceed. (In evaluating the situation, the judge will have to rely on the representations of counsel, which of necessity will be cryptic, because counsel is the one who must make the disclosure while maintaining client confidences and allowing for continued zealous advocacy at trial.) Before giving instruction, the judge is not required to hold an evidentiary hearing, to appoint an independent lawyer for the defendant, or to conduct a colloquy, although the latter may be appropriate if it appears that the defendant does not clearly understand the situation he has created. It is acceptable for the defendant to testify by means of an open narrative. If the defendant, now informed, moves for appointment of new counsel (and, concomitantly, a mistrial), the judge should deny the motions unless the defendant can demonstrate that such motion must be allowed to prevent a miscarriage of justice. No comprehensive canon can be written on all aspects of practical implementation because each case will have its own idiosyncrasies, and the judge cannot then be informed of the details underlying counsel's invocation of rule 3.3(e). The judge possesses considerable discretion to vary any of the procedures discussed, if the interests of justice, or effective management of the trial so requires. As here, full exploration of the ramifications of counsel's invocation of rule 3.3(e) must be postponed until a motion for a new trial, at which time full details may permissibly be revealed.

8. May a lawyer advise a client to *change his appearance*?

It is clearly unethical for a lawyer to advise his client to lie on the witness stand, largely because this interferes with the jury's ability to perform its job — determining the truth. Is it also unethical for a lawyer to advise the client to change his or her *appearance*, in order to convey a certain misimpression to the jury?

In 1990, millionaire real estate developer Mike Blatt was tried for murder in an Oakland, California courtroom. The prosecutor alleged that Blatt had hired two men to kill his business partner with a crossbow. At trial, Blatt wore a gray suit and aviator glasses — "intended to project sober propriety, [but which] only seemed to corroborate testimony that portrayed him as a cutthroat." The case ended in a mistrial, the jury voting 9 to 3 for conviction.

Blatt fired his two male lawyers and hired two women lawyers and a "jury consultant" for the retrial. These people "concluded that they needed to recast Blatt's image. The sharpie suits were replaced by pastel sweaters. Blatt's hair was styled to make him look more dignified, less *Dating Game*, and the aviator glasses were banned, giving him a slightly befuddled look. [His lawyer] blew up one day at the sight of his cheesy-looking gray shoes. 'I want him in penny loafers from now on,' she decreed. Blatt, a man used to running his own businesses and controlling everything, gave complete control of his case and his life to [his lawyers]. 'He hated penny loafers,' [one of them] says."

The second jury also hung, this time 11 to 1 for acquittal. The prosecutor decided not to try the case a third time. "Mike Blatt walked into the sunlight for the first time in three years. He thanked the women who helped set him free. He was wearing a sweater and a pair of penny loafers." Nina Martin, "Culture Clash", *California Lawyer*, Aug., 1992, p. 77.

Did Blatt's lawyers in the second trial behave *unethically*? If not, did Blatt's lawyers in the first trial behave *incompetently*?

9. May a lawyer *try to impeach a witness he knows is telling the truth*?

In Steven Phillips, *No Heroes No Villians: The Story of a Murder Trial* (Random House, 1997), pp. 114–115, the author states:

> Imagine an old man with weak eyesight and a failing memory who was a victim of a robbery. He identifies the defendant, who has just privately confessed to his attorney. It is a relatively easy matter for a skilled defense attorney to rip the old man's testimony to shreds, casting grave doubts upon his credibility. He must do this even though he knows that the old man is telling the truth, for he is an advocate and his role is to obtain an acquittal for his client, not to search for the truth. To be sure, a defense lawyer may not mount a dishonest defense; he should not call defense witnesses who he knows will lie. Aside from that, his only obligation is to his client.

10. If a lawyer knows an adverse witness has mistakenly testified *in favor* of his client, should he correct the mistake?

Yes, held the court in *Torres v. Donnelly*, 554 F.3d 322 (2nd 2009). After a confused prosecution witness mistakenly testified about a photo identification, defense counsel entered into a stipulation correcting the mistake. The court held that he acted properly, as "an attorney's ethical duty to advance the interests of his client is limited by an equally solemn duty to comply with the law and standards of professional conduct; it specifically ensures that the client may not use false evidence."

MATTER OF NACKSON
New Jersey Supreme Court
555 A.2d 1101 (1989)

O'HERN, J.

We are asked to consider whether the attorney involved in this case properly declined to disclose to a grand jury the whereabouts of a client who had consulted the attorney about a fugitive warrant. We find that the balance between the public's right to every person's evidence and the need for confidentiality in the attorney-client relationship has been properly drawn, and affirm the Appellate Division's judgment holding that, in the circumstances of this case, the attorney properly declined to disclose the information.

I

For purposes of this appeal, we accept the facts recited in the State's brief. On November 13, 1978, the New Jersey State Police arrested Mark Meltzer in Hunterdon County on charges of criminal possession of narcotics. At the time of the arrest, Meltzer gave a Hialeah, Florida address. Bail was set by the municipal court in the amount of $10,000, ten percent cash. Shortly thereafter, the defendant posted bail and was released.

On April 29, 1979, a Warren County Grand Jury indicted Meltzer on charges of possession of and possession with an intent to distribute marijuana. On January 25, 1979, a letter appearance was entered on behalf of Meltzer by his attorney, Joseph Nackson. Thereafter, Nackson requested and received several adjournments of arraignment until September 14, 1979.

At that time, Nackson informed the Warren County Prosecutor's Office that Meltzer was in jail in Iowa and as a result could not appear. Consequently, Meltzer's bail was revoked and a bench warrant was issued for his arrest by the Superior Court. A search of the CDS Registry Act records indicated an address for Mark H. Meltzer at 1820 W. 46th Street, Apartment 605, Hialeah Avenue, Chicago, Illinois. Correspondence sent to addresses in both Florida and Chicago was returned "addressee unknown."

Although Nackson had never met with his client, he had spoken with him by telephone and had attempted to arrange a plea agreement for him with the Warren County Prosecutor's Office. Meltzer, aware that he was a fugitive, told his attorney that he would return to New Jersey to answer the pending indictment only if a plea agreement could be worked out. On June 25, 1987, Nackson telephoned the Warren County Prosecutor informing him that Meltzer had "reformed" and was a "legitimate businessman" somewhere in the Chicago area. The prosecutor demanded that Nackson reveal his client's exact whereabouts, but Nackson refused to disclose any further information, claiming an attorney-client privilege.

Nackson was then subpoenaed by the State to appear before the grand jury on July 2, 1987, to obtain information about Meltzer's whereabouts. That day, Nackson moved unsuccessfully before the Law Division to quash the subpoena. The court did rule, however, that Nackson could refuse to answer any questions protected by the attorney-client privilege.

Nackson told the grand jury that he had no knowledge of the whereabouts of his client, but that he recently had telephoned Meltzer somewhere in the Chicago area. Nackson refused to answer five questions, asserting the attorney-client privilege:

(1) What number did you call when you called him back (during the week of June 29, 1987)?

(2) Did you advise your client that in the opinion of the Warren County Prosecutor's Office, he was a fugitive from justice?

(3) Have you advised him that he should comply with the law? (4) Can you tell the Grand Jury what his occupation is?

(5) Can you tell the Grand Jury by whom he is employed at the present time?

The prosecutor then filed an order to show cause why Nackson should not be held in contempt. The Law Division found that the responses to questions two and three were indeed protected by the attorney-client privilege. However, the court required Nackson to answer the remaining questions concerning his client's telephone number, occupation, and employer. In the Law Division's view, the client's whereabouts and employer were not confidential information protected by the attorney-client privilege because such nondisclosure would "obstruct justice." The Appellate Division granted Nackson's motion for leave to appeal and a stay of the proceedings.[1] Reversing the judgment of the trial court, the Appellate Division held that if there were "less intrusive means for obtaining information necessary to return an indictment against the client of an attorney, those means must be pursued to avoid any infringement on the cherished Sixth Amendment and state constitutional right to counsel."

II

The right to counsel in criminal proceedings is enshrined in the federal and state constitutions. U.S. Const., Amend. VI; N.J. Const. of 1947, art. I, ¶ 10. The attendant privilege protecting the confidentiality of information furnished by a client to his attorney is similarly well-established in our law, *In re Kozlov*, 79 N.J. 232 (1979), and is now embodied in Rule 26 of the New Jersey Rules of Evidence and N.J.S.A. 2A:84A-20. The relationship between attorney and client is deeply rooted in the necessity that the public, for many of whom the law is but a collection of complexities, seek the recourse and trust of lawyers.

The privilege is codified not only in our statutes and rules of evidence, but also in our rules of ethical conduct. Rule 1:14. For example, Disciplinary Rule 4-101 of the Disciplinary Rules of the Code of Professional Responsibility in certain circumstances protected "information gained in the professional relationship that the client has requested be held inviolate or the disclosure of which would be embarrassing or would be likely to be detrimental to the client." Those disciplinary rules now have been replaced by the Rules of Professional Conduct, but the principles remain substantially the same.

---

[1] Meltzer was indicted later for bail-jumping by the grand jury notwithstanding Nackson's unanswered questions.

Viewing attorneys as ministers of justice, we have imposed on lawyers the disciplinary obligation of maintaining the confidences of their clients:

> The ethical obligation of every attorney to preserve the confidences and secrets of a client is basic to the legitimate practice of law. Such an obligation is necessary for several reasons. Persons who seek legal advice must be assured that the secrets and confidences they repose with their attorney will remain with their attorney, and their attorney alone. Preserving the sanctity of confidentiality of a client's disclosures to his attorney will encourage an open atmosphere of trust, thus enabling the attorney to do the best job he can for the client. [*Reardon v. Marlayne, Inc.*, 83 N.J. 460, 470 (1980).]

So grave is the necessity for full and open disclosure in the case of criminal representation that the court has equated it "with an intimacy equal to that of the confessional." *State v. Sugar*, 84 N.J. 1, 13 (1980).

"None of this is to say that the privilege, while exceedingly important, is sacrosanct." *In re Kozlov, supra*, 79 N.J. at 242. There may be circumstances so grave that the privilege must yield to the most fundamental values of our justice system. *Id.* at 243. In the current case, we need to address three questions: first, whether an address is to be regarded as a confidence by a client or as a communication related to the representation; second, whether the so-called "crime or fraud" exception to the privilege requires disclosure of the address; and finally, whether the circumstances are such that the privilege must yield to other fundamental values of our justice system. We will treat the client's telephone number and employer as a form of address.

III

A

Our Court has previously held that in some circumstances the whereabouts of a client may be protected by the attorney-client privilege. *Fellerman v. Bradley*, 99 N.J. 493 (1985). In *Fellerman* we held:

> We perceive no sound reason why the communication that consists of, or includes, a client's address should not, at least in a case such as this, be governed by the same considerations that obtain as to other communications that are accorded the privilege. We therefore decide the issues involved not on the basis of whether an address is, or may ever be, the subject of a protected confidential communication between a client and attorney, but on the basis of the purposes for which the privilege exists and the reasons for its assertion in the context of the particular case.

Thus, whether a client's address may be considered a confidence protected by the attorney-client privilege necessarily depends on the surrounding circumstances in which the address was given.

In *Fellerman*, we noted the familiar exceptions to the privilege based on the "crime or fraud" exception, N.J.S.A. 2A:84A-20(2)(a), Evid.R. 26(2)(a), or the requirements of DR 4-101(C)(2)-(3) that an attorney disclose confidences when required by law, court order, or when necessary to prevent the client from committing a crime. Considering the balance of factors involved and in light of the surrounding circumstances, we found disclosure of the client's address necessary to prevent injustice. Particularly important was the fact that there was a continuing relationship between client and counsel, and the court sought the address to effectuate the terms of an agreement made by the client to pay for an expert's expenses. Within the circumstances of *Fellerman*, withholding the address of the client would indeed be directly assisting a client in perpetrating a fraud on the court and "would permit a party 'to mock justice' by ignoring both a judgment and a separate enforcement order of the Superior Court" that he pay an expert's fee. *Id.* at 509.

B

The question whether the "crime or fraud exception" requires disclosure in the circumstances of this case is a close call. The "crime or fraud" exception is not limited, of course, to the actual perpetration of an offense. See *In re Yaccarino*, 101 N.J. 342, 383–84 (1985) ("The concept of fraud is sufficiently broad to encompass deceitful and deceptive acts that might not otherwise warrant criminal or civil sanctions."). The client here was under an affirmative duty to keep the court informed of his whereabouts. The terms of his bail release specifically required him to do so. Hence, the State argues that the client had no right to ask the attorney to do that which the client could not do — conceal his whereabouts and in effect "mock justice."

The argument is compelling. Lawyers are not tools of injustice. We agree that it would be wrong for an attorney to "blackmail" the Prosecutor's Office by withholding a fugitive client's phone number, unless an amenable plea bargain is arranged. See *In re Doe*, 456 N.Y.S.2d 312, 314–15 (Co.Ct.1982) (bail-jumper's counsel, who moved for a dismissal, was required to reveal his client's whereabouts to a grand jury). Our conceptual resistance to recognizing the privilege here stems from the near certainty that the client is a wrong-doer. Unlike a suspect accused of crime, who must be presumed to be innocent, we are virtually positive that this client has done something wrong by jumping bail. It is almost a contempt in the face of the court. However, the essential question facing this Court is whether such a client by his actions forfeits the right to seek counsel.

We are unable to agree that the continuing nature of the crime of bail-jumping warrants a different substantive treatment of the privilege. Justice Kennedy, while sitting on the Ninth Circuit Court of Appeals, noted that "the privilege encourages persons to seek advice as to future conduct. But so important is full disclosure that the law recognizes the privilege even if the advice is sought by one who has already committed a bad act." *United States v. Hodge and Zweig*, 548 F.2d 1347, 1355 (9th Cir., 1977). But, as Justice Kennedy pointed out, "a quid pro quo is exacted for the attorney-client confidence: the client must not abuse the confidential relation by using it to further a fraudulent or criminal scheme." *Id.* at 1355.

Courts that have addressed the question of disclosure have uniformly held that a determination of whether a client's whereabouts must be disclosed will depend on an analysis of the facts of the case and the nature of the communication involved. *In re Stolar*, 397 F.Supp. 520, 524 (S.D.N.Y.1975). In deciding whether the "crime or fraud" exception applies, the relevant factor to consider is whether the client consulted with the attorney in order (1) to aid the client "in the commission of any crime"; (2) to enable the client "to avoid any criminal investigation or proceeding pending at the time the advice was given"; or (3) to assist the client to "avoid lawful process in any proceeding pending at the time the advice was given." *In re Grand Jury Subpoenas Served Upon Field*, 408 F.Supp. 1169, 1173–74 (S.D.N.Y., 1976). Undoubtedly, it can be often a close question whether "the legal service was sought or obtained to aid the client in the planning or perpetration of a crime or a tort." *In re Selser*, 15 N.J. 393, 416 (1954) (Heher, J., dissenting).

An example of instances in which the whereabouts of a client may need protection is the matrimonial field. See *Taylor v. Taylor*, 45 Ill.App.3d 352 (1977) (attorney need not disclose whereabouts of wife who feared injury from husband). In the delicate and explosive situations that often occur in marital litigation, the ability of attorneys to handle their clients' affairs otherwise could be "seriously undermined." *Id.* at 358. Of course, the privilege is not a warrant to play games with courts. In *In re Jacqueline F.*, 47 N.Y.2d 215 (1979), the New York Court of Appeals held that the lawyer's client "cannot have her cake and eat it too" by appealing a custody decision while requiring her lawyer to conceal her whereabouts.

The argument can be made here, too, that Meltzer wants to "have his cake and eat it too," and that the attorney's advice promoted the continuing criminal violation of the defendant. But in this case advice and communication arguably were given for the purpose of ending that criminal violation. Unlike *Fellerman, supra*, the client had not induced the court to enter an order in disposing of an issue in the case to the client's benefit. Every defendant has a right to bail.

The case is similar to the troubling case in Florida in which a person consulted an attorney and told the attorney that "my name is 'so-and-so' and I think I may have been involved in the accident described in the paper." *Baltes v. Doe I*, 57 U.S.L.W. 2268 (Fla. Cir.Ct. Oct. 13, 1988). The client asked the attorney to communicate with the authorities in an effort to negotiate a plea to resolve the matter, but instructed the attorney not to reveal his identity. The prosecution there, as here, argued that the client is involved in a continuing crime, and that the attorney had "a duty not to participate in allowing it to continue" (the continuing crime being a failure to comply with the Florida statute requiring disclosure of information concerning an accident). The Florida court held that the attorney-client privilege protects an attorney from disclosing information that would lead to identifying the client, and that the "crime or fraud" exception did not apply because the substantive violation occurred only when the driver was at the scene of the accident and ended when he left the scene. Similarly, commentators have stated that "while the question is not free from doubt, it appears that the appropriate and prevailing view is that the attorney need not and should not disclose information received from his client which concerns continuing aspects or effects of past criminal conduct." Callan & David, *Professional Responsibility and the Duty of Confidentiality: Disclosure of Client Misconduct in an Adversary System*, 29 Rutgers L.R. 332, 365 (1976).

Meltzer broke the law when he failed to appear in court for the required appearance. As noted, he was indicted by the grand jury for this bail-jumping offense, a violation of N.J.S.A. 2C:29-7. Although Meltzer may be the most undeserving of clients, innocent people are sometimes suspected of crime. They should be able to consult counsel.

We are satisfied, then, that in the circumstances of this case the "crime or fraud" exception did not remove the communication of the client's address from the scope of privilege. However, we must address whether other principles applicable to the privilege may require disclosure.

C.

As we noted in our discussion of *Fellerman v. Bradley, supra,* 99 N.J. 493, the privilege is not absolute. Like other privileges, it must in some circumstances yield to the higher demands of order. See, e.g., *United States v. Nixon,* 418 U.S. 683, 710 (1974) (claim of executive privilege must yield to defendant's interest in fair trial because "whatever their origins, these exceptions to the demand for every man's evidence are not lightly created nor expansively construed, for they are in derogation of the search for the truth.") Our law is set forth in *In re Farber,* 78 N.J. 259 (1978), where we held that a newspaper reporter's privilege to keep an informant's confidence must yield to a defendant's right to a fair trial. *Cf. In re Richardson,* 31 N.J. 391, 401 (1960) (noting that the "matter is truly one of balance," and requiring an attorney to disclose identity of fee-payer). In addition to the requirement that a need to pierce the privilege be established, it must be shown "to the satisfaction of the trial judge, by a fair preponderance of the evidence including all reasonable inferences, that the information could not be secured from any less intrusive source." *In re Farber, supra,* 78 N.J. at 276–77).

The difficulty with this record is that the Law Division perceived the client's whereabouts to be outside the scope of the attorney-client privilege because of the "crime or fraud" exception. Consequently, no record was made to "the satisfaction of the trial judge" that would have enabled the court to resolve the balance of interests. Mr. Nackson's attorney proffered that the State could have obtained the telephone numbers by an interstate warrant served on the Chicago-area telephone utility. We agree with the prosecutor that this is an unsatisfactory suggestion. In both instances, the client's privacy interests are equally implicated.

Rather, the question might be asked concerning what efforts had been made through the F.B.I. or state law-enforcement authorities to update information on Meltzer. In such situations, the prosecution can first follow other means for pursuing a fugitive, such as searching F.B.I. computer files and conducting license searches and other investigative techniques. Outside references indicate that the prosecutor actually did make such efforts to locate Meltzer, but that information was not included in the record of appeal. The grand jury also was prepared to take additional testimony from a Chicago attorney (allegedly a blood relative of Meltzer who knew of his whereabouts), and to seek further information about a detainer on a motor vehicle violation presumably from the Chicago area.

If all reasonable efforts appeared futile, then a court would have first to balance the gravity of the public's interest in obtaining information against the client's legitimate expectations of confidentiality in imparting his whereabouts to his counsel who sought trial continuances for him. If the public's interest tips the balance against the client's expectation of confidentiality, then a court must determine if this need outweighs a right to seek the assistance of counsel. See *Commonwealth v. Maguigan,* 511 Pa. 112 (1986) (an attorney was compelled to disclose a client's whereabouts who violated bail on charges of rape, statutory rape, corrupting the morals of a minor, indecent assault, and indecent exposure).

In this case, such a balancing was not done because the Law Division regarded the information as non-privileged. Nevertheless, no further purpose will be served by a remand. Meltzer has since been arrested in Florida and taken to the Warren County Prosecutor's Office. There is also no doubt that Nackson was sincere and well intentioned in his actions. It takes no small measure of courage to stand alone before a grand jury and insist on upholding the requirements of the profession in the face of a contempt charge. Nackson was not obstructive, but in fact furnished the grand jury with relevant information about his client, the nature of his contacts, and his representation. He drew the line between the public's need for every person's evidence and the protection of his client's confidences where he believed his ethical obligation required it to be drawn. Nackson's conduct before the grand jury was at least reasonable.

We note that Nackson's counsel has requested that we adopt a rule of practice in the exercise of our supervisory power over grand juries, N.J.S.A. 2A:73A-3, to require prior court approval before an attorney is summoned before a grand jury. See *United States v. Klubock*, 639 F.Supp.117 (D.Mass.1986) (adopting rule requiring court approval prior to subpoenaing attorneys before grand jury). We have no sense from this record that this is anything but an isolated instance of client circumstances unlikely to recur. We see no current need for rulemaking. The principles of law are quite clear.

We agree with the court below that this record falls short of demonstrating either a substantive ground for piercing the privilege (on the basis that the address was not a client confidence or that it had been lost by the "crime or fraud" exception) or procedural compliance with the requirements of *In re Farber, supra*, 78 N.J. 259, prerequisites to piercing the privilege in the interests of justice.

The judgment of the Appellate Division is affirmed.

Notes from Mary:

1. Client is arrested for murder of Carol Jones, whose two children disappeared at the time of the killing. Client tells lawyer where Carol's body might be. Client tells lawyer "Satan killed Carol." When the lawyer asks, "What about the kids?" Client replies, "Jesus saved the kids."

If the lawyer believes that the children might still be alive, may he (*should* he? *must* he?) place an anonymous phone call to the police advising them of the possible whereabouts of the children? See *McClure v. Thompson*, 323 F.3d 1233 (9th Cir. 2003).

2. In *U.S. v. Doe*, 429 F.3d 450 (3rd Cir. 2005), the court stated:

> The [attorney-client] privilege is not lost if a client proposes a course of conduct which he is advised by counsel is illegal, but is extinguished when a client seeks legal advice to further a continuing or future crime.

3. In *People v. Navarro*, 131 Cal.app.4th 1326 (2005), the court wrote:

> A lawyer goes to the police, tells them her clients are committing a string of crimes, and also tells them where to look for evidence of those crimes. Based on that information — which the lawyer learned through her representation of the clients — the police obtain a search warrant and find the evidence, leading to criminal charges against the clients. Should the

search warrant be quashed and all evidence found through the warrant suppressed as a remedy for the lawyer's alleged breach of the attorney-client privilege? Because the government did not procure or induce the breach, we conclude the answer is no. * * * *

The attorney-client privilege, which authorizes a client to refuse to disclose, and prevent others from disclosing, confidential communications between lawyer and client, is considered a hallmark of our jurisprudence. The privilege is fundamental to our legal system and furthers the public policy of ensuring every person's right freely and fully to confer with and confide in his or her lawyer in order to receive adequate advice and a proper defense. Safeguarding a client's confidences is one of a lawyer's most basic obligations. Bus. & Prof.Code, § 6068, subd. (e)(1) [it is an attorney's duty to "maintain inviolate, and at every peril to himself or herself to preserve the secrets, of his or her client."]. The privilege applies even where the attorney has not actually been retained. When a person seeks legal assistance from an attorney in anticipation of hiring the lawyer to represent him, any information acquired by the lawyer is privileged even if actual employment does not result.

The Navarro appellants contend that because the Sheriff utilized privileged information in obtaining the warrant, the warrant should have been quashed and all evidence obtained through it should have been suppressed as the "fruit of the poisonous tree." The attorney-client privilege is a testimonial *privilege*. By itself, this privilege is merely a rule of evidence and does not supply a constitutional right. However, where the government intrudes into the attorney-client relationship to obtain privileged information, the Sixth Amendment right to counsel may be violated. This usually involves some type of government misconduct, such as infiltrating the defense by planting informants or intercepting confidential communications. However, the constitutional right to counsel does not attach until charges are actually brought. (*Moran v. Burbine* (1986) 475 U.S. 412 [initiation of judicial proceedings "fundamental to implication of Sixth Amendment"].

Because Elizabeth's alleged misconduct prompted the search warrant which thereafter led to charges being brought against the Navarro defendants, it is clear that her supposed breach of the attorney-client privilege came before charges were filed, and before the Sixth Amendment right to counsel attached. If the Navarro appellants were entitled to quash the search warrant and suppress the evidence, their right to such relief must come from some other source. * * * *

Although the right to counsel protections of the Sixth Amendment are limited to governmental misconduct occurring after charges have been brought, the due process protections of the Fifth Amendment may provide a remedy for misconduct by the government that occurs during the pre-indictment stage. * * *

A due process violation for breach of the lawyer-client privilege turns on whether the government helped instigate or orchestrate a breach of the privilege. * * * *

Synthesizing the federal decisions cited above, we conclude that in order to make out a Fifth Amendment due process violation against the government for obtaining a search warrant based on privileged lawyer-client information, a criminal defendant must show that: (1) the government objectively knew a lawyer-client relationship existed between the defendant and its informant; (2) the government deliberately intruded into that relationship; and (3) the defendant was prejudiced as a result. That the police are mere passive recipients of privileged information, then act on that information, is not enough to satisfy the second element of deliberate intrusion. Instead, some level of outrageous conduct, such as actively instigating or orchestrating a lawyer's breach of the attorney-client privilege, must occur.

Our review of the evidence given both in camera and in open court shows no government misconduct here.

UNITED STATES v. LOCASCIO
U.S. Court of Appeals, 2nd Circuit
6 F.3d 924 (1993)

ALTIMARI, CIRCUIT JUDGE:

Defendants-appellants John Gotti and Frank Locascio appeal from judgments of conviction entered on June 23, 1992 in the United States District Court for the Eastern District of New York.

Gotti and Locascio were convicted after a jury trial of substantive and conspiracy violations of the Racketeer Influenced Corrupt Organizations Act, 18 U.S.C. § 1962(c) and (d), and various predicate acts charged as separate counts. They were each principally sentenced to life imprisonment. The charges stemmed from their involvement with the Gambino Crime Family of La Cosa Nostra, an extensive criminal organization.

Background

On July 18, 1991, a grand jury in the Eastern District of New York returned a thirteen count superseding indictment against Gotti and Locascio. The indictment also named two other defendants, Salvatore Gravano and Thomas Gambino, who are not parties to this appeal. All four defendants were charged with violating the Racketeer Influenced and Corrupt Organizations Act ("RICO"), 18 U.S.C. § 1962(c)-(d), for unlawfully conducting and participating in the affairs of a criminal enterprise through a pattern of racketeering activity. The charged enterprise was the Gambino Organized Crime Family of La Cosa Nostra ("the Gambinos," "The Gambino Family," or "the Gambino Crime Family"). Gotti was charged as the head of the organization, and Locascio was accused of being the "underboss," or second-in-command.

Counts One and Two of the indictment charged Gotti and Locascio with the substantive and conspiracy violations of RICO. Many of the crimes charged as racketeering acts in the RICO counts were also the basis of separate counts in the indictment. Gotti was charged with the following predicate acts: the conspiracy to murder and the murder of Paul Castellano; the murder of Thomas Bilotti; the conspiracy to murder and the murder of Robert DiBernardo; the conspiracy to murder and the murder of Liborio Milito; and obstruction of justice at the Thomas Gambino trial. Gotti and Locascio were both charged with the following predicate acts: the conspiracy to murder and the murder of Louis DiBono; the conspiracy to murder Gaetano Vastola; conducting an illegal gambling business in Queens, New York; conducting an illegal gambling business in Connecticut; conspiracy to make extortionate extensions of credit; and obstruction of justice in the investigation of the Castellano murder. Gotti and Locascio were also charged in separate counts for a conspiracy to obstruct grand jury investigations, bribery of a public servant, and a conspiracy to defraud the United States.

Gotti and Locascio were tried before a sequestered anonymous jury. The government's proof to support the allegations that Gotti and Locascio had been in command of an extensive criminal enterprise was comprised mostly of lawfully intercepted tape-recorded conversations of the defendants-appellants and other alleged members of the Gambino Family. The government introduced tape recordings from four different locations over an eight-year period.

The most significant evidence consisted of conversations intercepted at 247 Mulberry Street in New York during the period from late 1989 until early 1990. The government had installed three listening devices in that building: in the Ravenite Social Club on the first floor, in a hallway behind the club's rear door, and in an apartment two stories above the club ("the Ravenite Apartment"). It was this last location that proved the most fruitful for the government, and the most damaging for the defendants-appellants. In the discussions in the Ravenite Apartment, Gotti, Locascio, and other Gambino Family members discussed various illegal acts. These discussions formed the core of the proof against the defendants-appellants at trial. Another major source of evidence was the testimony of Salvatore Gravano, who cooperated with the government following the indictment. As a high-level insider in the Gambino Family, Gravano's testimony was especially damaging.

The tape recordings, combined with Gravano's testimony, presented to the jury a picture of a large-scale enterprise involved in various criminal activities. The jury heard evidence on the structure and inner workings of the Gambino Family, and learned of the miscellaneous crimes with which Gotti and Locascio were charged: murders, obstruction of legal proceedings, conspiracies, gambling operations, and loansharking activities.

Following a six-week trial, the jury found Gotti guilty of all charges in the indictment. Locascio was found guilty of all charges except the count relating to a gambling operation in Queens, New York. Each defendant-appellant was sentenced by the district court to life in prison on the RICO and murder counts, and the statutory maximum prison terms on all remaining counts, with all sentences to run concurrently. * * * *

I. *Disqualification of Counsel*

Prior to trial, the district court disqualified attorneys for both Gotti and Locascio. Gotti and Locascio now contend that these disqualifications were unwarranted and violated their Sixth Amendment rights.

A. *Applicable Law*

The Sixth Amendment to the Constitution provides that "in all criminal prosecutions, the accused shall enjoy the right to have the Assistance of Counsel for his defence." The accused, however, does not have the absolute right to counsel of her own choosing. See *Wheat v. United States*, 486 U.S. 153, 159 (1988). As the Court stated in *Wheat*, while the right to select and be represented by one's preferred attorney is comprehended by the Sixth Amendment, the essential aim of the Amendment is to guarantee an effective advocate for each criminal defendant rather than to ensure that a defendant will inexorably be represented by the lawyer whom he prefers. Similarly, although a criminal defendant can waive her Sixth Amendment rights in some circumstances, that right to waiver is not absolute, since "federal courts have an independent interest in ensuring that criminal trials are conducted within the ethical standards of the profession and that legal proceedings appear fair to all who observe them." Id. at 160. The question of disqualification therefore implicates not only the Sixth Amendment right of the accused, but also the interests of the courts in preserving the integrity of the process and the government's interests in ensuring a just verdict and a fair trial.

In deciding a motion for disqualification, the district court recognizes a presumption in favor of the accused's chosen counsel, although this presumption can be overcome by a showing of an actual conflict or potentially serious conflict. We accord the district court's decision to disqualify an attorney "substantial latitude," and review the decision only for an abuse of discretion.

There are many situations in which a district court can determine that disqualification of counsel is necessary. The most typical is where the district court finds a potential or actual conflict in the chosen attorney's representation of the accused, either in a multiple representation situation, or because of the counsel's prior representation of a witness or co-defendant. Courts have also considered disqualification where the chosen counsel is implicated in the allegations against the accused and could become an unsworn witness for the accused, or where the chosen counsel is somehow unable to serve without unreasonable delay or inconvenience in completing the trial.

B. *Gotti*

1. *Background*

Bruce Cutler served as Gotti's attorney in previous criminal trials in federal court. Prior to trial, the government moved to disqualify Cutler from acting as Gotti's attorney. Although the motion also dealt with the disqualification of other Gotti attorneys, only the disqualification of Cutler has been challenged on appeal.

The district court granted the motion to disqualify on several grounds. Judge Glasser, in a thoughtful and well-reasoned opinion, found that Cutler had acted as "house counsel" to the Gambino Crime Family by receiving "benefactor payments" from Gotti to represent others in the criminal enterprise. The district court based this conclusion on excerpts from the government's taped transcripts, which left "little doubt that Gotti paid significant sums of money for legal services rendered to others."

The district court further determined that Cutler's participation in government-taped conversations at which illegal activity was discussed would impair his representation of Gotti. Specifically, the court noted that Cutler's mere presence at trial could make him an "unsworn witness" before the jury in explaining his own conduct and interpreting Gotti's conversations on the tapes. Even if Gotti waived the conflict, and even if the government did not intend to call Cutler as a witness, the district court found that Cutler's representation would still compromise the integrity of the proceeding.

Third, the district court found that Cutler's prior representation of Michael Coiro, a potential government witness, gave rise to a conflict of interest. The court reasoned that this conflict mandated disqualification both because Cutler was privy to events surrounding an obstruction charge, and because Cutler's cross examination of Coiro at trial would be circumscribed by the prior representation.

Finally, the district court also found disqualification warranted because of the implication by Gotti in taped conversations that he had paid Cutler money "under the table." This made Cutler a potential accomplice as well as a potential witness to Gotti's tax fraud.

In conclusion, the district court noted that it was mindful that disqualification is a drastic remedy for conflict problems, but that no less severe alternatives were viable. The court therefore held that "the grave peril the continued representation by Cutler poses to the integrity of the trial process" mandated disqualification.

Gotti now appeals the district court's ruling, arguing that the disqualification was an abuse of discretion. We disagree, and affirm the disqualification on two grounds: (1) Cutler's role as house counsel to the Gambino Crime Family; and (2) Cutler's anticipated role as an "unsworn witness" for Gotti had he been allowed to serve. We note that, importantly, Gotti does not challenge the effectiveness of his replacement trial counsel. Although the government cannot justify an otherwise unwarranted disqualification by arguing that the disqualification did not result in the accused receiving ineffective assistance of counsel, the fact that Gotti received more than competent representation is an additional consideration strongly supporting the district court's otherwise entirely correct ruling.

2. *Cutler's Role as House Counsel*

Gotti argues that the facts before the district court did not merit the conclusion that Cutler had acted as "house counsel" to the Gambino Crime Family. Rather, Gotti argues that Cutler was merely his personal attorney.

Ethical considerations warn against an attorney accepting fees from someone other than her client. As we stated in a different context, the acceptance of such "benefactor payments" "may subject an attorney to undesirable outside influence" and raises an ethical question "as to whether the attorney's loyalties are with the client or the payor." *In re Grand Jury Subpoena Served Upon John Doe*, 781 F.2d 238, 248 (2d Cir.1985). In this cotext, proof of house counsel can be used by the government to help establish the existence of the criminal enterprise under RICO, by showing the connections among the participants. See *United States v. Simmons*, 923 F.2d 934, 949 (2d Cir.) (holding that government can use evidence of benefactor payments to prove existence of enterprise); *United States v. Castellano*, 610 F.Supp. 1151 (S.D.N.Y.1985) (disqualifying attorney because attorney's acceptance of benefactor payments could be used to prove existence of enterprise).

Contrary to Gotti's assertions, there was sufficient evidence for the district court to determine that Cutler had acted as house counsel to the Gambino Crime Family. For example, the court cited one conversation in which Gotti, in the time-honored tradition of legal clients, complained about his legal fees:

> I gave youse $300,000 in one year. Youse didn't defend me. I wasn't even mentioned in none of these [expletive deleted] things. I had nothing to do with none of these [expletive deleted] people. What the [expletive deleted] is your "beef?" Before youse made a court appearance, youse got $40,000, $30,000 and $25,000. That's without counting [attorney] John Pollok. You standing there in the hallway with me last night, and you're plucking me. Tony Lee's lawyer, but you're plucking me. I'm paying for it. Where does it end? Gambino Crime Family? This is the Shargel, Cutler and who do you call it Crime Family.

Gotti thus demonstrated that he was incurring the legal fees for representation of others. As support for disqualification, the government indicated that it would introduce the testimony of Michael Coiro, who would testify that he had paid nothing to Cutler and another attorney for their services to him, presumably because Gotti paid for his defense.

Cutler's role as house counsel to the Gambinos raised a credible issue of the ethical propriety of his representation of Gotti in this case. An attorney cannot properly serve two masters, and the evidence before the district court indicated that Cutler had represented the Gambino Family as a whole. Moreover, Cutler's status as house counsel was potentially part of the proof of the Gambino criminal enterprise. We cannot say that the district court abused its discretion in disqualifying Cutler on this basis, considering the volume of proof of Cutler's proximity to the affairs of the Gambino Crime Family offered by the government in this case.

3. *Cutler's Role as an Unsworn Witness*

An even stronger basis for disqualification, however, was the possibility that Cutler would function in his representational capacity as an unsworn witness for Gotti. An attorney acts as an unsworn witness when his relationship to his client results in his having first-hand knowledge of the events presented at trial. If the attorney is in a position to be a witness, ethical codes may require him to withdraw his representation. See Model Code of Professional Responsibility DR 5-102(A) (1992).

Even if the attorney is not called, however, he can still be disqualified, since his performance as an advocate can be impaired by his relationship to the events in question. For example, the attorney may be constrained from making certain arguments on behalf of his client because of his own involvement, or may be tempted to minimize his own conduct at the expense of his client. Moreover, his role as advocate may give his client an unfair advantage, because the attorney can subtly impart to the jury his first-hand knowledge of the events without having to swear an oath or be subject to cross examination.

This is different from the situation in *Wheat*, since the conflict in *Wheat* — multiple representation — was a conflict inuring to the detriment of the accused. In such a case, waiver by the accused of the conflict can conceivably alleviate the constitutional defect, so long as the representation by counsel does not seriously compromise the integrity of the judicial process. When an attorney is an unsworn witness, however, the detriment is to the government, since the defendant gains an unfair advantage, and to the court, since the factfinding process is impaired. Waiver by the defendant is ineffective in curing the impropriety in such situations, since he is not the party prejudiced.

The district court disqualified Cutler partially on the ground that his representation of Gotti would place him in the role of such an unsworn witness. The clearest support for this finding was Cutler's presence during the Ravenite Apartment discussions taped by the government. The government was legitimately concerned that, when Cutler argued before the jury for a particular interpretation of the tapes, his interpretation would be given added credibility due to his presence in the room when the statements were made. This would have given Gotti an unfair advantage, since Cutler would not have had to take an oath in presenting his interpretation, but could merely frame it in the form of legal argument.

Gotti argues, however, that the district court erred in disqualifying Cutler where the government had no intention of calling Cutler. He also maintains that Cutler's presence and participation on the government's tapes could have been redacted to eliminate references to and statements by Cutler, thereby eliminating the unsworn witness problem. The first contention is meritless, since the district court explicitly and correctly noted that "whether the government will or will not call Cutler has no significance for this motion." The second contention is equally unavailing, since the district court explicitly found that redaction of the tapes would have eviscerated the government's case. We are not in a position to second-guess the district court's clearly supported factual findings on review. Moreover, we agree with the district court that the government's case should not be unfairly impaired so that an accused can continue with conflicted counsel.

The unsworn witness problem arises not only in relation to the Ravenite tapes, but to other grounds cited by the district court in support of disqualification. For example, the court found that Gotti's references to Cutler's acceptance of fees "under the table" were relevant to the government's case on the tax fraud count. Had Cutler argued Gotti's defense to that count, he would not only have had a conflict of interest but he would have been arguing as to events in which he was allegedly involved.

We are aware that disqualification is a drastic remedy to the unsworn witness problem. We are also, however, cognizant that this is an unusual case, in that Cutler had allegedly entangled himself to an extraordinary degree in the activities of the Gambino Crime Family: he is recorded on government tapes when discussions of allegedly illegal activity took place; he is allegedly involved in the tax fraud count against Gotti; his role as house counsel could be used to prove the criminal enterprise; and his representation of government witnesses caused a conflict with his representation of Gotti. Although we are cognizant of the right of the accused to secure representation, we are also conscious of the institutional interest in protecting the integrity of the judicial process. If an attorney will not perform his ethical duty, it is up to the courts to perform it for him. Bruce Cutler had no place representing John Gotti in this case, and the district court properly determined that he should be disqualified. * * * *

Having considering all of the defendants-appellants' contentions, we affirm the judgment of the district court.

Notes from Mary:

1. The court says that when Cutler accepted payments from Gotti to represent Mafia underlings charged with various crimes, he was "serving two masters". How so, exactly? Would Gotti want Cutler to do anything which was not in the best interests of those defendants?

2. Assuming that Cutler *was* somehow disloyal to the Mafia underlings he represented, so what? Does this mean that he would be disloyal *to Gotti*? If not, why did the court disqualify him from representing Gotti?

3. For a fascinating behind-the-scenes account of this case and motivations of the lawyers who represented John Gotti, see Dannen, "Defending The Mafia", *The New Yorker*, Feb. 21, 1994, p. 64.

PEOPLE v. SIMAC
Illinois Supreme Court
641 N.E.2d 416 (1994)

CHIEF JUSTICE BILANDIC

The sole issue in this appeal is whether appellant, David Sotomayor, an attorney licensed to practice law in this State, was properly found in direct criminal contempt of court. During a traffic proceeding in DuPage County, appellant substituted an individual other than defendant at counsel's table, without the court's permission or knowledge. The trial judge found that such conduct constituted direct criminal contempt, and fined appellant $500. The appellate court, with one justice dissenting, affirmed the finding of direct criminal contempt, but reduced the fine to $100.

The incident that gave rise to the contempt citation occurred during appellant's representation of defendant, Christopher Simac, for charges that arose from a car accident on March 20, 1990. Defendant was charged with driving with a revoked license and failure to yield while making a left-hand turn. After several delays, the case was called for trial on December 11, 1990. The State's only witness was Officer Ronald H. LaMorte. The complaining witness, Beth Nelson, never appeared at the trial.

Before trial, appellant seated David P. Armanentos, a clerical worker employed at his law firm, next to him at counsel's table. Defendant was seated at another location in the courtroom. Armanentos and defendant shared similar physical characteristics, in that they were both tall, thin, dark blond-haired men who wore eyeglasses. On the date of trial, Armanentos wore a white shirt with blue stripes, while defendant was dressed in a white shirt with red stripes.

Appellant did not ask the court's permission, or notify the court that he had substituted Armanentos in the customary place for a defendant at counsel's table. The State's Attorney also was not notified of the substitution. The court ordered all witnesses who were going to testify to come forth and be sworn. The clerk asked appellant, "Is your defendant going to be sworn?" Appellant replied, "No."

In the State's case in chief, Officer LaMorte testified regarding the automobile accident that he investigated on March 20, 1990, which resulted in injuries to a woman and her young child. He described the intersection where the accident occurred and the position of the cars. LaMorte testified that he asked defendant for identification; however, he believed that defendant was unable to produce his driver's license.

LaMorte identified Armanentos, who was seated next to appellant at counsel's table, as the person who was involved in the accident. The court noted LaMorte's identification of Armanentos as the defendant for the record. Appellant did not inform the court of the misidentification at this time or reveal that defendant was seated elsewhere in the courtroom.

After the State rested its case in chief, appellant made a motion to exclude witnesses. The motion was granted, and LaMorte left the courtroom. Appellant then called Armanentos, the person whom LaMorte previously identified, as a witness. Armanentos was sworn at this time, as he did not come forward to be sworn when the court called for witnesses at the beginning of the trial. When Armanentos stated his name for the record, the court received the first indication that a misidentification had occurred.

On direct examination, Armanentos testified that he was not driving a motor vehicle at the intersection in question on March 20, 1990. The defense then rested. Under cross-examination, Armanentos testified that he had never met defendant. He stated that he temporarily worked as a clerical employee in the appellant's law firm. It was his understanding that he was brought to court by appellant and instructed to sit at counsel's table to see whether the testifying officer would identify him as the defendant. Armanentos testified that he was told that he resembled defendant. He further admitted that he looked similar to defendant, as they were both tall, thin, and Caucasian. In response to the court's inquiry, Armanentos admitted that he did not approach the clerk to be sworn in as a witness before the commencement of the trial.

Appellant stated for the record that Armanentos never approached the bench. He was not sworn in, and was seated in the corner of the courtroom until appellant directed him to sit in the chair next to him. Appellant argued that no fraud was perpetrated on the court, for defendant was in open court as required. He asked that a directed finding of not guilty be entered in the traffic case based on the misidentification.

After appellant said that he did not intend to call any further witnesses, the State called defendant to testify. After taking the stand and stating his name for the record, defendant invoked his fifth amendment privilege and was excused. The court refused the State's request to call appellant as a witness. The State then asked that defendant take his position next to his attorney. The court replied: "He can sit any place he wants to in the courtroom. He is here." Over appellant's objection, the court allowed the State to recall LaMorte. LaMorte again misidentified Armanentos as the defendant. The court granted appellant's request for a directed finding of not guilty based upon the misidentification. In addition, the court entered an order for contempt of court against the appellant for placing the witness in such a manner as to mislead the State's Attorney and the arresting officer. The court stated that the person seated next to appellant did not look like co-counsel or anyone employed in an attorney's office. The court stated that appellant had seated Armanentos next to him to purposely mislead the court. The order prepared by the court stated that "defense attorney is held in direct contempt of court for having a person bearing the likeness of defendant sit at the counsel table with him in the location usually occupied by defendant." The court imposed a $500 fine on appellant for direct criminal contempt.

The next day, the court made the following supplemental findings concerning this episode:

> The court finds that it was the totality of the conduct of defense attorney in court in connection with this case that is the basis for the court's finding of criminal contempt for misrepresentation by inference, including the following findings: 1. That a person with the likeness of the defendant, a young, white male, was the only person with defense attorney at the counsel table when defense attorney came to the bench and said, "Here is my jury waiver." 2. That person was dressed in jeans and a shirt with no tie that is not the courtroom attire of an attorney or co-counsel, yet that person sat in the customary location of a defendant throughout the State's case. 3. That person was asked by the clerk to be sworn with other witnesses at the start of the trial, to which defense attorney said that said person was not going to testify. The obvious inference of this comment to the court and clerk was that the person was the defendant because witnesses were excluded except for defendant. 4. That person was identified as the defendant by the State witness police officer, and all of the foregoing resulted in the court's comment that the record could show that the defendant was identified for the record; there was no defense attorney response to this court's comment that advised of the court's impression and finding based on all that had occurred and that the court was misled as to the identity of the defendant. 5. That person's only apparent purpose in the courtroom, in a defendant's customary location with defense attorney, was to create an inference to the court that he was the defendant, and this was done with the knowledge of defense attorney. 6. That while there was no express misrepresentation by words, there was a misrepresentation by inference by the totality of the conduct of the defense attorney, and that was the basis of the criminal contempt of court finding.

On the same day that these supplemental findings were filed, appellant presented a motion to reconsider the order holding him in direct criminal contempt. In support of the motion, appellant stated that defendant was seated in the courtroom at the commencement of the trial. Appellant also stated that he made no representation to the court or State's Attorney concerning the identity of the person sitting next to him. Armanentos never approached the bench, nor did he take any affirmative action to falsely represent his identity. The motion to reconsider also described the six persons seated in the courtroom at the time of the misidentification. Appellant argued that his conduct did not embarrass, hinder or obstruct the court. He noted that the State was afforded every opportunity for the police officer to make an identification. The motion for reconsideration was denied. Appellant appealed the conviction of direct criminal contempt.

On appeal, a divided appellate court affirmed the judgment of direct criminal contempt, but reduced the fine from $500 to $100. * * * *

Analysis

It is well established law that all courts have the inherent power to punish contempt; such power is essential to the maintenance of their authority and the administration of judicial powers. This court has defined criminal contempt of court "as conduct which is calculated to embarrass, hinder or obstruct a court in its administration of justice or derogate from its authority or dignity, thereby bringing the administration of law into disrepute." People v. L.A.S. (1986), 111 Ill.2d 539, 543. Ill.2d 296, 299. A finding of criminal contempt is punitive in nature and is intended to vindicate the dignity and authority of the court. However, the exercise of such power is "a delicate one, and care is needed to avoid arbitrary or oppressive conclusions." *Cooke v. United States* (1925), 267 U.S. 517, 539. * * * *

I. *Intent*

In contending that the appellate court's holding violates principles of direct criminal contempt, appellant argues that the intent necessary to support a conviction of direct criminal contempt was not within the circuit court's personal knowledge and, therefore, his conviction must be overturned. In this regard, appellant argues that he has an ethical obligation to vigorously represent his client. Appellant asserts that, by placing a substitute at counsel's table, he merely intended in good faith to fulfill his ethical duties of zealous advocacy by testing the veracity of the State's identification testimony. Appellant argues that he was operating in unchartered waters, and that his intent was to facilitate rather than impede the administration of justice by preventing the conviction of a potentially innocent defendant based on a tainted in-court identification. He asserts that there was no evidence known to the court to establish an intent to obstruct the administration of justice or to derogate from the court's dignity or authority. Therefore, appellant asserts that, by its holding, the appellate court has improperly eliminated from the offense of direct criminal contempt the intent to embarrass, hinder, derogate, or obstruct the court.

Before citing one with contempt, a court must find that the alleged contemnor's conduct was willful. *People v. Ernest* (1990), 141 Ill.2d 412, 424. The alleged contemnor's state of mind, however, does not have to be affirmatively proven; the contemptuous state of mind may be inferred from the allegedly contemptuous conduct itself. The intent may be inferred from the surrounding circumstances and the character of the party's conduct. *Id.* at 424. "An attorney's zeal to serve his client should never be carried to the extent of causing him to seek to accomplish his purpose by a disregard of the authority of the court or by seeking to secure from a court an order or judgment without a full and frank disclosure of all matters and facts which the court ought to know." *People ex rel. Fahey v. Burr* (1925), 316 Ill. 166, 182.

In light of the aforementioned principles, we reject appellant's argument. We find that appellant's conduct clearly reveals that his intent was not merely to test the State's identification testimony. Rather, we find that appellant intended to cause a misidentification, thereby misleading not only the State and its witness but also the court itself. Appellant commissioned a clerical employee from his office to sit with him at the defendant's customary place at counsel's table. Appellant's employee resembled the defendant in important identification characteristics. Moreover, both the substitute and the defendant wore glasses and were similarly dressed. Under these circumstances, we find that appellant calculated to cause a misidentification.

Additionally, appellant's conduct before the court indicates appellant's intent to create a misapprehension and thereby cause a misidentification. It is evident to us that appellant's conduct was intended to deceive. For instance, appellant responded in the negative to the clerk's direct inquiry as to whether his defendant would be sworn. Appellant responded negatively even though, at the same time, he obviously anticipated that the substitute would eventually testify as a witness concerning the misidentification. Clearly, appellant was aware that the only inference the court could draw from the totality of these circumstances was that the person sitting next to appellant at counsel's table was the defendant and that the defendant was not going to testify at trial.

Most revealing of appellant's intent to deceive, however, was appellant's failure to correct the court and the record upon the court's erroneous statement for the record that the witness had identified the defendant. At this point, as an officer of the court, appellant had a responsibility to the court and the integrity of the proceedings to correct the court and the record. When the court made the erroneous statement for the record, appellant clearly knew that the court was laboring under a misconception as to the identity of the defendant, yet he took no action to correct the court's mistaken impression. If appellant had not calculated to cause such a misconception, he would have taken some action to clarify the defendant's identity.

As this court has stated, "An attorney's zeal to serve his client should never be carried to the extent of seeking to secure from a court an order or judgment without a full and frank disclosure of all matters and facts which the court ought to know." *Burr*, 316 Ill. at 182. The true identity of the defendant is clearly a fact "which the court ought to know" because it is the responsibility of the court to ensure the defendant's right to be present at all stages of the proceedings against him. Therefore, an attorney must not deceive the court as to the defendant's identity despite the attorney's obligation to vigorously represent his client. Such a deception prevents the court from fulfilling its obligation and derogates from the court's dignity and authority.

Furthermore, we reject appellant's claim that he merely intended in good faith to test the veracity of the State's identification testimony. Appellant could have easily achieved this purpose without resorting to deceptive and misleading practices. Many alternative methods are available to an attorney to test identification testimony. These available alternatives include conducting an in-court lineup, having defendant sit in the gallery without placing a substitute at counsel's table, or placing more than one person at counsel's table. It is readily apparent, therefore, that appellant could have achieved his goal as an advocate without misleading or deceiving the court, the State, and the witness and thereby remained within the bounds of his responsibilities as an officer of the court.

For the foregoing reasons, we conclude that there is sufficient evidence in the record to support appellant's conviction for direct criminal contempt. Appellant's actions derogated from the court's dignity and authority by causing the court to erroneously find for the record that the witness had identified the defendant, and his conduct delayed the proceedings. In view of appellant's actions and the surrounding circumstances, we find that appellant's conduct was calculated to and actually did embarrass, hinder, and obstruct the court and the proceedings.

II. *Professional Responsibility*

Appellant raises an additional argument that we will briefly address. Before us, appellant argues that requiring a defense attorney to give the court prior notice and obtain its permission before placing a substitute at counsel's table would violate principles of professional responsibility. Appellant contends that, in a bench trial such as this where the court also functions as the trier of fact, prior disclosure to the court of his concern regarding an identification issue would somehow influence the court's ability to render a just verdict based solely on evidence presented during the proceedings. Additionally, appellant argues that, since he cannot engage in ex parte communications with the court, he would also have to reveal his concern and strategy to the prosecution in violation of ethical obligations. Further, appellant contends that the prosecutor would then be placed in the ethical dilemma of deciding whether to inform the State's identification witness what to expect, or to seek a just result by refraining from influencing the identification witness' testimony.

We reject appellant's arguments. It is well established that, in a bench trial, the court is presumed to consider only competent evidence in making a finding. In order to overcome this presumption, the record must affirmatively demonstrate that the court's finding rests on a private investigation of the evidence or other private knowledge about the facts in the case. Furthermore, the court and prosecution are frequently made aware of defense concerns and potential strategies in situations involving motions *in limine*. Such pretrial motions occur on a daily basis. Defense attorneys who utilize this pretrial procedure do not violate their ethical obligations to their clients. Nor has the State ever indicated that such motion practice places it in an ethical dilemma. Many times in cases where the defense attorney's motion *in limine* has been granted, the prosecution is aware of evidence which it cannot use or allude to at trial. Nevertheless, the prosecution has been able to proceed with its function without violating its professional responsibilities. We find the practice of giving the court prior notice and obtaining its permission to place a substitute at counsel's table to be analogous to the filing and arguing of motions *in limine*. Therefore, we dismiss appellant's argument.

Before closing, we note that our determination in this case is supported by cases decided in other jurisdictions. These decisions have refused to allow the practice of placing a substitute at counsel's table without notifying the court of the attorney's intent to do so. For instance, in *United States v. Thoreen* (9th Cir.1981) 653 F.2d 1332, an attorney representing a defendant accused of violating a preliminary injunction against salmon fishing decided to test the witness' identification by placing at counsel's table another person who resembled the defendant. The substitute was dressed in outdoor clothing, while the defendant was dressed in a business suit and sat behind the rail in a row normally reserved for the press. Defense counsel neither notified the prosecutor nor asked the court's permission to arrange this substitution. On defense counsel's motion at the start of the trial, the court ordered all witnesses excluded from the courtroom. However, the substitute remained seated next to defense counsel. Throughout the trial, defense counsel did not correct any mistaken representation of the court when it expressly referred to the substitute as the defendant for the record. Two government witnesses misidentified the substitute as the defendant. Following the prosecutor's case in chief, defense counsel called the substitute as a witness and disclosed the substitution. The prosecutor was allowed to reopen his case. Defendant was identified by an agent who had cited him for two of the violations, and was ultimately convicted.

Based upon defense counsel's substitution of another individual for defendant at counsel's table, the district court found him in criminal contempt. On review, the Ninth Circuit rejected defense counsel's argument that his conduct was a good-faith tactic to aid cross-examination. The court held that the substitution crossed over the line from zealous advocacy to actual obstruction because it delayed the proceedings in the time taken for the witnesses' misidentification of the defendant. *Thoreen*, 653 F.2d at 1339. In addition, it violated the custom practiced in Federal and State courts of general jurisdiction to allow only counsel, parties, and others having the court's permission to sit at counsel's table. *Id.* at 1341. Most importantly, the defense counsel's subversive tactics impeded the court's ability to ascertain the truth. The *Thoreen* court noted that making misrepresentations to the court is inappropriate and unprofessional behavior. The guidelines promulgated in that State's code of professional responsibility to guide an attorney's conduct explicitly decree that an attorney's participation in the presentation or participation of false evidence is unprofessional and subjects him to discipline. *Id.* at 1340. In addition, the *Thoreen* court noted that substituting a person for the defendant in a criminal case without a court's knowledge has been noted as an example of unethical behavior by the American Bar Association Committee on Professional Ethics. *Id.* at 1340.

Similarly, in *Miskovsky v. State ex rel. Jones* (Okla.Crim.App.1978) 586 P.2d 1104, the defense counsel was found in direct contempt of court after he substituted another person at counsel's table, and seated his own client in the gallery. The reviewing court found that counsel's conduct consisted of knowingly implementing a plan of deception that would affect the witnesses, the District Attorney, and the court. The defense counsel's actions were designed to create that mistaken assumption. By resorting to deception and misrepresentation to protect his client's interests, the defense counsel showed a disrespectful attitude for the judicial process. The *Miskovsky* court reasoned that the contemptuous conduct was not merely the substitution of another person for the defendant, a tactic that may have been frequently employed in that area. Rather, the contempt finding was derived from defense counsel's substitution of an individual other than defendant at counsel's table without the knowledge of the court. *Id.* at 1108. The *Miskovsky* court also noted that that State's code of professional responsibility prohibited lawyers from engaging in conduct involving dishonesty, fraud, deceit or misrepresentation, or conduct that is prejudicial to the administration of justice. *Id.* at 1108. The court concluded that these standards justify a court's reliance upon the defense counsel to refrain from the type of misrepresentation perpetrated by the defense attorney. *Id.* at 1109. Similar to the *Thoreen* and *Miskovsky* courts, we conclude that appellant's conduct in the instant case constitutes direct criminal contempt.

For the reasons stated, the judgment of the appellate court, which affirmed the judgment of the circuit court in finding appellant guilty of direct criminal contempt but reduced the fine imposed to $100, is affirmed.

JUSTICE NICKELS, dissenting:

I do not agree that placing an individual in the defendant's customary place at counsel's table, without more, is a sufficient basis from which to infer an intent to hinder or obstruct the administration of justice or impugn the integrity of the court.

After a thorough review of the record, I believe that defense counsel was acting in good faith to protect his client from a suggestive in-court identification.

Criminal contempt is warranted for "conduct calculated to embarrass, hinder or obstruct a court in its administration of justice or to derogate from its authority or dignity, or bring the administration of law into disrepute." *In re Estate of Melody* (1969) 42 Ill.2d 451, 452. The usual protections of procedural due process do not apply to direct criminal contempt, which is punishable without notice or hearing, because the acts occur in the very presence of the judge. While universally recognized as essential to the administration of justice, such power is susceptible to abuse and must be closely examined. In particular, preserving the independence of the bar requires that a certain latitude be given to attorneys acting in good faith and on behalf of their clients. * * * *

At trial, the judge made two findings regarding the basis for the contempt charge. The first finding occurred after defense counsel asked the judge to state for the record the reason for the contempt. The judge responded, "You have brought a person in here to sit next to you as defendant, to mislead the State's Attorney and to mislead the police officer. That's my finding." I am not aware of a duty imposed upon a defense attorney to assist an eyewitness or the State by providing a suggestive identification setting. In refusing to assist the State's eyewitness, defense counsel's conduct is not calculated to embarrass, hinder or obstruct the court. Instead, counsel is merely requiring the State to prove its case. Thus, this finding is not sufficient to support the contempt charge.

On the trial record, the judge made a second statement to support his finding of direct criminal contempt. The judge stated, "You have not had a person sitting beside you that looked like your co-counsel or anyone that is an attorney from your office. And you have, I think, purposely done this to mislead the court." Similarly, the majority also finds that defense counsel intended to deceive the court by placing Armanentos in the defendant's customary place at counsel's table.

A contemptuous state of mind can be inferred from an act calculated to embarrass or obstruct the court. *People ex re. Kunce v. Hogan* (1977) 667 Ill.2d 55, 59–61 (finding an attorney's filing of a civil suit against the presiding judge in a criminal case before sentencing allows for a reasonable inference of contemptuous intent). However, not every questionable act can give rise to such an inference, particularly where the conduct involves a defense counsel's representation of a client. For example, in *People v. Miller* (1972) 51 Ill.2d 76, this court reviewed a direct contempt order imposed against a defense attorney for sarcastic comments made during a trial. This court found that although counsel was "improperly sarcastic" and "overzealous," his questionable conduct was committed in good-faith representation of his client and was therefore not contemptuous.

In determining whether the necessary contumacious intent can be inferred from a particular act, I agree with the majority that a reviewing court must look to the surrounding circumstances and the character of the action of the defendant. My examination of the record reveals that defense counsel's conduct was a good-faith attempt to protect his client from a suggestive in-court identification, and not an attempt to deceive or obstruct the court.

First, the surrounding circumstances show a good faith reason to test the State's ability to identify the defendant. The trial had been delayed by the State, the State had no complaining witness, and the entire case rested on the testimony of Officer

LaMorte. In addition, Officer LaMorte testified that he had not taken defendant's driver's license at the scene of the accident. Second, the character of defense counsel's conduct does not show disrespect for the court's authority or an attempt to disrupt the proceedings. Defense counsel showed respect to the court during the entire trial. At no point did defense counsel address the court in an inappropriate manner, disobey an order, or disrupt the proceedings. Immediately after the misidentification, defense counsel placed Armanentos on the stand in order to disclose his identity. Given the unreliability of an identification based only upon the placement of defendant at counsel's table, defense counsel acted in good faith and on behalf of his client. This is not conduct that evidences a contumacious design.

The majority finds that defense counsel intended to deceive the court and such conduct is sufficient to support a charge of contempt. In support of this conclusion, the majority relies on defense counsel's actions in telling the clerk that his defendant would not testify and the brief delay in alerting the court to the misidetification. However, my examination of the judge's order and the record do not support drawing this conclusion.

The judge's supplemental findings charge that defense counsel misrepresented to the court clerk that the person seated next to him was the defendant in the case. However, the record does not support a finding that any misrepresentation took place. The record discloses only that when witnesses were called to be sworn, the court clerk asked, "Is your defendant going to be sworn?" In reply, defense counsel answered, "No." The judge's findings state that "the obvious inference of this comment to the court and the clerk was that person was the defendant because witnesses were excluded."

However, because of the dangers inherent in summary contempt, this court has repeatedly stated that "it should be exercised with utmost caution and strictly restricted to acts and facts seen and known by the court, and no matter resting upon opinions, conclusions, presumptions or inferences should be considered." *People v. Loughran* (1954) 2 Ill.2d 258, 263.

In addition, the finding is factually incorrect. The record shows that no motion to exclude witnesses was made at the beginning of the trial when the witnesses were called to be sworn. The motion to exclude witnesses was not made until the State rested. Where the record of the proceedings is in conflict with the contempt order, the record of the proceedings controls. Even if made, the motion would not have applied to Armanentos, who would have only been called as a witness if he was misidentified as the defendant. Since the finding is based upon an inference and is factually incorrect, the finding cannot support the charge of contempt.

The supplemental findings also state that defense counsel's conduct caused the trial court to make a false finding and that counsel's silence in this circumstance misled the court. The majority also finds that defense counsel's silence directly after the misidentification evinces a contumacious intent to deceive the court.

I disagree. The finding entered into the record was based upon the testimony of Officer LaMorte and the court's own assumptions, not any misrepresentation by counsel. A defense attorney has no obligation to assist the State by alerting an identification witness as to defendant's location. Although defense counsel did not alert Officer LaMorte to his misidentification by immediately disclosing defendant's location, counsel did promptly place Armanentos on the stand after Officer LaMorte was excused to disclose his identity to the court. Defense counsel's silence was brief and lasted only as long as necessary to protect his client. In light of the seriousness of allowing an identification based only upon defendant's placement in the courtroom, defense counsel acted in good faith and on behalf of his client. Such conduct is insufficient to support a charge of contempt.

Under different circumstances, I agree that placing someone other than the defendant at counsel's table could evidence the contemptuous intent necessary to support a contempt charge. The *Thoreen* case relied upon by the appellate court and the majority provides an example. *United States v. Thoreen* (9th Cir.1981) 653 F.2d 1332. *Thoreen* involved the trial of a salmon fisherman for violating an injunction against salmon fishing. First, the character of the defense attorney's conduct in *Thoreen* showed an intent to mislead the court. The defense attorney in *Thoreen* actually disguised the person seated in defendant's place at counsel's table by dressing him in outdoor clothing, including heavy shoes, a plaid shirt and a jacket-vest. Unlike the contemnor below, the defense attorney in *Thoreen* actually gestured to the imposter as though he were the defendant and conferred with him during the trial. Second, there were no circumstances in *Thoreen* showing a need to test the reliability of the State's identification, as identification was not in issue. In using a disguise where identification was not in issue and gesturing to the defendant as his client, the attorney in *Thoreen* was not acting in good-faith representation of his client but was engaging in conduct calculated to obstruct the administration of justice.

I recognize that several jurisdictions which have considered the issue require counsel to inform the court before testing an in-court identification by placing someone other than defendant at counsel's table. See, e.g., *Thoreen*, 653 F.2d 1332; *Miskovsky v. State ex rel. Jones* (Okla.Crim.App.1978) 586 P.2d 1104. I agree with the majority that there are a variety of better ways to protect a defendant from such suggestive in-court identifications, including in-court lineups or other experiments done with the court's permission. The issue presented for review is not whether counsel made the best choice, but whether his specific conduct showed disregard for the court's authority and the administration of justice. A review of the record shows defense counsel was respectful at all times. Counsel did not misrepresent the identity of defendant in any way and attempted in good faith to test the veracity of the State's case. Under these facts, I believe counsel successfully charted a narrow pathway through a questionable course of conduct.

For the reasons stated, I would vacate the order finding defense counsel in direct criminal contempt of court. Therefore, I respectfully dissent.

Justices Harrison and McMorrow join in this dissent.

Notes from Mary:

1. Does defense counsel have an ethical duty to *tell the judge the law*?

Pavao was charged with sex offenses on a child. He signed a form waiving his right to a jury trial, and the judge tried the case, convicting Pavao on some charges. But the judge had not realized that an appellate decision required that, in order for a jury waiver to be effective, the judge must first engage in a "colloquy" with the defendant — to ensure that the waiver is knowing and voluntary. Nor did the prosecutor know this. But defense counsel did know of this requirement. However, "He chose not to bring the error to the attention of the court." Pavao appealed, arguing that the waiver was invalid because of the lack of colloquy. The Massachusetts Appeals Court held that there was error, but it was harmless, as the judge knew that Pavao had consulted with his lawyer about the waiver. The court also had a few words about the conduct of Pavao's lawyer:

> Acting under the belief that his strategy was justified by the exhortation of Canon 7 of Supreme Judicial Court Rule 3:07, the Canons of Ethics — "a lawyer should represent a client zealously within the bounds of the law" — Pavao's trial counsel deliberately failed to bring the omission of the colloquy to the court's attention, knowing that the judge and the prosecutor had improperly neglected it and with the anticipation that the oversight would afford him a ground of reversible error should Pavao be convicted. Both Pavao's trial and appellate counsel vigorously defended the professional propriety of this nonfeasance.

> We, however, deem such tactical silence to have exceeded the bounds of acceptably zealous representation. "It is not consistent with the purposes of justice, for a party knowing of a secret defect, to proceed and take his chance for a favorable verdict, with the power and intent to annul it, as erroneous and void, if it should be against him." *Commonwealth v. Cancel*, 394 Mass. 567, 571–572 (1985). * * * *

> Under those authorities, defense counsel's proper course was unequivocal: to alert the judge to the error so as to enable its immediate correction. To do so would have complied with long declared professional obligations without in any way inculpating the client, impairing his constitutional rights, prejudicing his legitimate defenses to the indictments, or impeding the ascertainment of the truth, which is the primary function and purpose of the adversary system. Failure to do so — thereby permitting the waste of judicial resources expended in a three-day trial whose viability was knowingly put in jeopardy, as well as compelling the waste of these very appellate proceedings, which would have been unnecessary had counsel correctly called for the colloquy — resulted in prejudice to the administration of justice.

> We accept that trial counsel's inaction here was sincerely based upon a common misconception that unremitting pursuit of a client's interest by any and all means short of active fraud is a lawyer's paramount obligation. It does not merit the opprobrious epithets invoked by the Commonwealth ("hoodwinking" and "sandbagging" the judge).

> Nonetheless, the bar must realize that an attorney's first duty is to further the administration of justice, which mandates candor toward the court. As the Supreme Judicial Court has recently stated: "As an officer of the court, an attorney is a 'key component of a system of justice' and is bound to uphold the integrity of that system by being truthful to the court and opposing counsel. Where this duty is in seeming conflict with the client's interest in zealous representation, the latter's interest must yield. Were we to condone any action to the contrary, the integrity of the judicial process would be vitiated. As stated by Justice Quirico, "The courts have emphasized an attorney's duty of candor, stemming from his role as an officer of the court. The more persuasive judicial decisions require an attorney to bring material facts to the attention of the court when

ignorance by the court is likely to produce an erroneous decision and not just when his opponent is and will remain ignorant." *In the Matter of Neitlich*, 413 Mass. 416, 423 (1992). Such limits upon advocacy are essential to preserve the adversary system itself, since it is a process in which the courts are almost wholly dependent on counsel to marshal and proffer the true facts and the accurate applicable law, so that correct conclusions that most closely approximate justice will emerge from the crucible of contending presentations. [*Commonwealth v. Pavao*, 658 N.E.2d 175 (1995)]

But the Supreme Judicial Court of Massachusetts reversed, holding that the colloquy requirement was meant to provide an appellate record which would make it unnecessary to look for an indirect indications that a waiver was knowing and voluntary. This "bright line" requirement "was just to preclude this kind of inquiry." Regarding counsel's conduct, the court said only this:

> We express no opinion on the propriety of defense counsel's inaction but do suggest to the Board of Bar Overseers and this court's committee on the new rules of professional conduct that they consider whether such conduct should be subject to an explicit disciplinary rule. [*Commonwealth v. Pavao*, 672 N.E.2d 531 (1996)]

2. Does defense counsel have an ethical duty *not to concede that defendant is guilty*?

In *Florida v. Nixon*, 543 U.S. 175 (2004), Nixon was charged with first degree murder. If found guilty in the "guilt" phase of the "bifurcated" trial, the jury would then decide in the "penalty" phase whether Nixon would receive the death penalty. Nixon's lawyer, Corin, conceded at the guilt phase that Nixon was guilty:

> Faced with the inevitability of going to trial on a capital charge, Corin turned his attention to the penalty phase, believing that the only way to save Nixon's life would be to present extensive mitigation evidence centering on Nixon's mental instability. Experienced in capital defense, Corin feared that denying Nixon's commission of the kidnaping and murder during the guilt phase would compromise Corin's ability to persuade the jury, during the penalty phase, that Nixon's conduct was the product of his mental illness. Corin concluded that the best strategy would be to concede guilt, thereby preserving his credibility in urging leniency during the penalty phase.

> Corin attempted to explain this strategy to Nixon at least three times. Although Corin had represented Nixon previously on unrelated charges and the two had a good relationship in Corin's estimation, Nixon was generally unresponsive during their discussions. He never verbally approved or protested Corin's proposed strategy. Overall, Nixon gave Corin very little, if any, assistance or direction in preparing the case, and refused to attend pretrial dispositions of various motions. Corin eventually exercised his professional judgment to pursue the concession strategy. As he explained: "There are many times lawyers make decisions because they have to make them because the client does nothing." * * *

> The guilt phase of the trial thus began in Nixon's absence. In his opening statement, Corin acknowledged Nixon's guilt and urged the jury to focus on the penalty phase:

In this case, there won't be any question, none whatsoever, that my client, Joe Elton Nixon, caused Jeannie Bickner's death. That fact will be proved to your satisfaction beyond any doubt. This case is about the death of Joe Elton Nixon and whether it should occur within the next few years by electrocution or maybe its natural expiration after a lifetime of confinement.

Now, in arriving at your verdict, in your penalty recommendation, for we will get that far, you are going to learn many facts about Joe Elton Nixon. Some of those facts are going to be good. That may not seem clear to you at this time. But, and sadly, most of the things you learn of Joe Elton Nixon are not going to be good. But, I'm suggesting to you that when you have seen all the testimony, heard all the testimony and the evidence that has been shown, there are going to be reasons why you should recommend that his life be spared. * * * *

During its case in chief, the State introduced the tape of Nixon's confession, expert testimony on the manner in which Bickner died, and witness testimony regarding Nixon's confessions to his relatives and his possession of Bickner's car and personal effects. Corin cross-examined these witnesses only when he felt their statements needed clarification, and he did not present a defense case. Corin did object to the introduction of crime scene photographs as unduly prejudicial, and actively contested several aspects of the jury instructions during the charge conference. In his closing argument, Corin again conceded Nixon's guilt, and reminded the jury of the importance of the penalty phase: "I will hope to argue to you and give you reasons not that Mr. Nixon's life be spared one final and terminal confinement forever, but that he not be sentenced to die." The jury found Nixon guilty on all counts.

At the start of the penalty phase, Corin argued to the jury that "Joe Elton Nixon is not normal organically, intellectually, emotionally or educationally or in any other way." Corin presented the testimony of eight witnesses. Relatives and friends described Nixon's childhood emotional troubles and his erratic behavior in the days preceding the murder. A psychiatrist and a psychologist addressed Nixon's antisocial personality, his history of emotional instability and psychiatric care, his low IQ, and the possibility that at some point he suffered brain damage. The State presented little evidence during the penalty phase, simply incorporating its guilt-phase evidence by reference, and introducing testimony, over Corin's objection, that Nixon had removed Bickner's underwear in order to terrorize her.

In his closing argument, Corin emphasized Nixon's youth, the psychiatric evidence, and the jury's discretion to consider any mitigating circumstances; Corin urged that, if not sentenced to death, "Joe Elton Nixon would never be released from confinement". The death penalty, Corin maintained, was appropriate only for "intact human beings," and "Joe Elton Nixon is not one of those. He's never been one of those. He never will be one of those." Corin concluded: "You know, we're not around here all that long. And it's rare when we have the opportunity to give or take life. And you have that opportunity to give life. And I'm going to ask you to do that. Thank you." After deliberating for approximately three hours, the jury recommended that Nixon be sentenced to death.

In accord with the jury's recommendation, the trial court imposed the death penalty. Notably, at the close of the penalty phase, the court commended Corin's performance during the trial, stating that "the tactic employed by trial counsel was an excellent analysis of the reality of his case." The evidence of guilt "would have persuaded any jury beyond all doubt," and "for trial counsel to have inferred that Mr. Nixon was not guilty would have deprived counsel of any credibility during the penalty phase."
* * * *

An attorney undoubtedly has a duty to consult with the client regarding "important decisions," including questions of overarching defense strategy. *Strickland*, 466 U.S., at 688. That obligation, however, does not require counsel to obtain the defendant's consent to "every tactical decision." *Taylor v. Illinois*, 484 U.S. 400, 417–418 (1988) (an attorney has authority to manage most aspects of the defense without obtaining his client's approval). But certain decisions regarding the exercise or waiver of basic trial rights are of such moment that they cannot be made for the defendant by a surrogate. A defendant, this Court affirmed, has "the ultimate authority" to determine "whether to plead guilty, waive a jury, testify in his or her own behalf, or take an appeal." *Jones v. Barnes*, 463 U.S. 745, 751 (1983). Concerning those decisions, an attorney must both consult with the defendant and obtain consent to the recommended course of action.

A guilty plea, we recognized in *Boykin v. Alabama*, 395 U.S. 238 (1969), is an event of signal significance in a criminal proceeding. By entering a guilty plea, a defendant waives constitutional rights that inhere in a criminal trial, including the right to trial by jury, the protection against self-incrimination, and the right to confront one's accusers. While a guilty plea may be tactically advantageous for the defendant, the plea is not simply a strategic choice; it is "itself a conviction," and the high stakes for the defendant require "the utmost solicitude". Accordingly, counsel lacks authority to consent to a guilty plea on a client's behalf; moreover, a defendant's tacit acquiescence in the decision to plead is insufficient to render the plea valid.

The Florida Supreme Court, as just observed, required Nixon's "affirmative, explicit acceptance" of Corin's strategy because it deemed Corin's statements to the jury "the functional equivalent of a guilty plea." We disagree with that assessment.

Despite Corin's concession, Nixon retained the rights accorded a defendant in a criminal trial. The State was obliged to present during the guilt phase competent, admissible evidence establishing the essential elements of the crimes with which Nixon was charged. That aggressive evidence would thus be separated from the penalty phase, enabling the defense to concentrate that portion of the trial on mitigating factors. Further, the defense reserved the right to cross-examine witnesses for the prosecution and could endeavor, as Corin did, to exclude prejudicial evidence. In addition, in the event of errors in the trial or jury instructions, a concession of guilt would not hinder the defendant's right to appeal. * * * *

Corin was obliged to, and in fact several times did, explain his proposed trial strategy to Nixon. Given Nixon's constant resistance to answering inquiries put to him by counsel and court, Corin was not additionally required to gain express consent before conceding Nixon's guilt. The two evidentiary hearings conducted by the Florida trial court demonstrate beyond doubt that Corin fulfilled his duty of consultation by informing Nixon of counsel's proposed strategy and its potential benefits. Nixon's characteristic silence each time information was conveyed to him, in sum, did not suffice to render unreasonable Corin's decision to concede guilt and to home in, instead, on the life or death penalty issue. * * * *

On the record thus far developed, Corin's concession of Nixon's guilt does not rank as a "failure to function in any meaningful sense as the Government's adversary." Although such a concession in a run-of-the-mine trial might present a closer question, the gravity of the potential sentence in a capital trial and the proceeding's two-phase structure vitally affect counsel's strategic calculus. Attorneys representing capital defendants face daunting challenges in developing trial strategies, not least because the defendant's guilt is often clear. Prosecutors are more likely to seek the death penalty, and to refuse to accept a plea to a life sentence, when the evidence is overwhelming and the crime heinous. In such cases, "avoiding execution may be the best and only realistic result possible." ABA Guidelines for the Appointment and Performance of Defense Counsel in Death Penalty Cases § 10.9.1, Commentary (rev. ed.2003), reprinted in 31 Hofstra L.Rev. 913, 1040 (2003).

Counsel therefore may reasonably decide to focus on the trial's penalty phase, at which time counsel's mission is to persuade the trier that his client's life should be spared. Unable to negotiate a guilty plea in exchange for a life sentence, defense counsel must strive at the guilt phase to avoid a counterproductive course. See Lyon, Defending the Death Penalty Case: What Makes Death Different?, 42 Mercer L.Rev. 695, 708 (1991) ("It is not good to put on a 'he didn't do it' defense and a 'he is sorry he did it' mitigation. This just does not work. The jury will give the death penalty to the client and, in essence, the attorney."); Sundby, The Capital Jury and Absolution: The Intersection of Trial Strategy, Remorse, and the Death Penalty, 83 Cornell L.Rev. 1557, 1589–1591 (1998) (interviews of jurors in capital trials indicate that juries approach the sentencing phase "cynically" where counsel's sentencing-phase presentation is logically inconsistent with the guilt-phase defense); id., at 1597 (in capital cases, a "run-of-the-mill strategy of challenging the prosecution's case for failing to prove guilt beyond a reasonable doubt" can have dire implications for the sentencing phase). In this light, counsel cannot be deemed ineffective for attempting to impress the jury with his candor and his unwillingness to engage in "a useless charade."

Renowned advocate Clarence Darrow, we note, famously employed a similar strategy as counsel for the youthful, cold-blooded killers Richard Loeb and Nathan Leopold. Imploring the judge to spare the boys' lives, Darrow declared: "I do not know how much salvage there is in these two boys. I will be honest with this court as I have tried to be from the beginning. I know that these boys are not fit to be at large." Attorney for the Damned: Clarence Darrow in the Courtroom 84 (A. Weinberg ed.1989); (Darrow's clients "did not expressly consent to what he did. But he saved their lives.").

To summarize, in a capital case, counsel must consider in conjunction both the guilt and penalty phases in determining how best to proceed. When counsel informs the defendant of the strategy counsel believes to be in the defendant's best interest and the defendant is unresponsive, counsel's strategic choice is not impeded by any blanket rule demanding the defendant's explicit consent. Instead, if counsel's strategy, given the evidence bearing on the defendant's guilt, satisfies the *Strickland* standard, that is the end of the matter; no tenable claim of ineffective assistance would remain.

In *U.S. v. Wellington*, 417 F.3d 284 (2nd Cir. 2005), at a bench trial, defense counsel Bach stipulated to every element of the charged offense, whereupon the court found Wellington guilty. The appellate court found that Wellington was not denied effective assistance of counsel:

In the instant case, defense counsel's stipulation on defendant's behalf, made in defendant's presence, to every element of the only charged offense — entered with a view to receiving a reduction in the computed offense level for acceptance of responsibility — coupled with his waiver of the right to claim such an adjustment after the USPO declined to recommend one, was an ill-advised and wholly ineffective trial strategy. There is, moreover, no doubt that the stipulation directly contributed to the resulting judgment of conviction. But defendant's counsel did not devise this strategy himself. He entered the stipulation and waived defendant's right to seek an offense-level adjustment because defendant instructed him to do so. Bach informed the Court that he did not necessarily agree with his client, but that defendant "has given a lot of thought to this and I advised him, and he's the boss."

Although defendant, represented by new counsel in this appeal, does not dispute at this juncture that his trial counsel was following his (defendant's) own instructions, he urges that he is nonetheless a victim of ineffective assistance because Bach "failed to subject the prosecution's case to meaningful adversarial testing." * * * *

It is the role of the lawyer to be a professional advisor and advocate, not to usurp his " 'client's decisions concerning the objectives of representation. * * * *

Accordingly, to the extent that defendant instructed his counsel to pursue a course of action that defendant now complains of, there was no abridgement — constructive or otherwise — of defendant's Sixth Amendment right to effective assistance of counsel.

3. Does defense counsel have an ethical duty *not to argue too much*?

In *McCann v. Municipal Court*, 221 Cal.App.4th 527 (1990), in the middle of defense counsel's closing argument, the prosecutor objected, claiming that certain arguments were not supported by the evidence. The judge sustained the objection. When defense counsel protested, the judge said, "Move on". Defense counsel replied, "I will not move on. I will not move on until you haul me away. This is the most important issue of the case and you're not going to convict my client." When the judge asked counsel to try to get control of himself, counsel replied, "You're not my mother." The judge held him in contempt and fined him $600. In affirming, the appellate court called counsel's comments "rude, obnoxious, offensive, and insulting."

This case presents an extreme in trial advocacy. It cannot be questioned that an advocate has the right to aggressively, respectfully and in good faith present contentions on behalf of his or her client. What seems to have been forgotten here is the imperative duty of an attorney to respectfully yield to the rulings of the court, *whether right or wrong*.

"HOW CAN YOU REPRESENT CRIMINALS?" — NEW ANSWERS TO OLD QUESTIONS
California Lawyer, June 2002, p. 72.
by Myron Moskovitz

It happens to every criminal defense lawyer. At a cocktail party, some Citizens learn that this Enemy of the People is present. They swarm around the culprit and launch the attack: "How can you represent those bums? How can you live with yourself knowing that you are putting criminals back on the street to rape, pillage, and plunder decent society?" And worse.

I've heard the usual answers, and I've seen the usual result. A well-rehearsed, well-expressed explanation — and an audience wholly unconvinced. The defenders might be excellent advocates for their clients, but when they try to represent themselves, they fall flat on their faces. The jury just doesn't buy it.

Perhaps a different perspective might persuade the skeptics to respect criminal defense lawyers — even if they'll never love them.

Let's put to one side two approaches that never work in this setting. First, the "True Believer" pitch: "I do it because I hate cops," "I do it because I love the downtrodden," and the like. If the goal is to convert the convertible rather than preach to the choir, these are hopeless. The audience doesn't have the experiences or values of the lawyer who gives these answers. Second, a lengthy exegesis on mistakes made by cops and prosecutors, how prisons don't rehabilitate and the death penalty doesn't deter murder, etc. probably won't be effective here. There just isn't enough time, and your audience will probably yawn and wander away before you get very far into it.

Here are the two short answers most commonly given to challengers. The first is Wrapping Yourself In The Constitution: "It's my job to protect The Constitutional Rights of the defendant. You believe in The Constitution, don't you? It's the Most Sacred Document Of Our Democracy, etc., etc." Well — thinks the skeptic — yes and no. I do believe in The Constitution — for decent citizens, but not for the slimeballs you represent. And what about the constitutional rights of victims — to be free to walk down the street without being attacked, robbed, etc.? (The Constitution places restrictions on government action, not private action, but not many non-lawyers know this — or care.) So this one doesn't work.

The other common answer is Everyone Needs Me: "Suppose you or a close friend or relative of yours is charged with a crime. Wouldn't you want a lawyer to vigorously protect their rights?" The listener thinks: "I won't ever be charged with a serious crime, and I don't hang out with people who are likely to get into that sort of situation." Another flop. They simply cannot identify with your clients.

Let's try a different approach: "I Help Convict The Guilty." *That* should catch their attention.

Skeptic: "What? I thought you try to get the guilty *off*!"

Lawyer: "I do. But most of the time I fail. And when I do, you can sleep soundly — knowing that the defendant truly *is* guilty, because I did my damndest to show he wasn't, but he was convicted anyway."

To flesh out this point, ask the skeptic to recall some recent newspaper story about some vicious crime.

Lawyer: If the police arrest someone for that crime, you'd like to see him convicted and punished, right?

Skeptic: Absolutely!

Lawyer: Suppose lawyers take your view and none of them is willing to represent him, so he goes to trial by himself. The police and the prosecutor strongly believe in their case, of course, so they think he is guilty, and they might not bother showing the jury and judge some evidence that might cast doubt on whether he is guilty. He says he is innocent, but because he doesn't know how to investigate the case or argue his points very well, he is convicted and sentenced to death or a long prison term. Are you comfortable with that?

Skeptic (weakening a bit): I'm not sure.

Lawyer: OK, then we'll move the clock ahead. Let's assume that this new "no-lawyer" system goes on for a while. It won't be long before some enterprising newspaper reporters look into these convictions and find evidence that some of these guys were in fact innocent. I'm willing to assume that the percentage might be small — maybe 10% or so. How do you feel about the next case? Can you sleep well knowing that there is a 10% chance that our society will be killing or imprisoning an innocent man?

The point here is to focus on *the system*, not the lawyer. The system punishes people only when a jury is convinced beyond a reasonable doubt that he is guilty. The system lets us all sleep well at night, knowing that there is very little chance that we have punished the innocent. But for this system to work, there must be some skilled person helping the defendant try to raise a reasonable doubt. That's the defense lawyer's role.

Now the skeptic is frowning and squirming — but not ready to quit. She moves on to another common question:

Skeptic: I see your point, I guess. But don't you *know* that he's guilty sometimes? How can you represent him when you *know* he's guilty?

The usual answer? "I don't decide guilt. That's for the jury." Doesn't work, because it's not really responsive to the question. You can know even if you don't decide. A bit of honesty might help, as in:

Lawyer: You're right. Sometimes I do know that he's guilty — because the evidence against him is overwhelming. Since there is almost no chance that he will be acquitted, I advise him to plead guilty. If he accepts my advice, he'll be convicted. But I do try to get the best deal I can for him to shorten his sentence. I can't *control* the sentence, however. That's up to the prosecutor and the judge.

Skeptic: But don't you sometimes defend him *at trial* even though you know he's guilty?

Lawyer: Yes, on occasion. He might reject my advice to plead guilty, because he has the right to decide what to do with his life. Or I might advise him that the prosecution's case is weak for some reason, so we should go to trial. And sometimes I "know" he's guilty because he told me. I can't tell anyone that he told me, because his communication with me is confidential. If it wasn't confidential, he wouldn't tell me anything, so I couldn't do my job of representing him.

Skeptic: But how can you stand to *get him off* when you know he's guilty?

Lawyer: I don't get him off. If he's acquitted, it's the jury or judge who does it, not me. All I do is deliver a message: the evidence or the law doesn't support a conviction. I'm not allowed to decide anything. If they like my message, they acquit. If not, they convict. I play a role, of course, but it's our system that gets him off, not me alone.

Skeptic: But don't you just use technicalities sometimes?

The usual answer to this one is: "Technicalities? You're talking about Our Hallowed Constitutional Rights — the 4th Amendment, the 5th Amendment, etc., etc." The Constitutional argument doesn't work, for reasons explained above. If you try to go further and *spell out* the exclusionary rule and the like, you just make it worse, because the average lay person can't see letting a crook go free because the cop screwed up a search or interrogation. This is a tough one. Let's try this:

Lawyer: Sure, I make the arguments, but they rarely work. Like you, judges and juries don't like technical arguments that would let a criminal go free — especially for a serious crime. And when they do work, it's usually because the cops or the prosecutor broke the law themselves rather flagrantly — like beating a guy up to get a confession. We can't allow that if we want people to respect our public servants.

And finally, the clincher:

Skeptic: So you're happy when your guilty client goes free?

When in doubt, tell the truth:

Lawyer: I confess: part of me is happy. I like to win — at sports, at cards, and at trial. But like any citizen, another part of me doesn't like criminals roaming the streets.

Skeptic: But you made that happen!

Lawyer: No, I didn't. The police made it happen by screwing up their investigation, or the prosecutor made it happen by presenting a lousy case. All I did was tell the judge and jury how they screwed up. I played a role, of course, but I'm not the one who decided the case. And I *helped* law enforcement convict *more* crooks *in the future*, because my victory showed them where they screwed up and how they should do it better next time. By the way, when I win a case for someone who is probably guilty, I go home and make sure my doors and windows are well locked.

Finally, after a few drinks, your interlocutor might throw a particularly nasty one at you: "OK, OK, I guess someone has to do it. But why *you*? Weren't you smart enough to get a real law job?"

Sorry, buddy — you're on your own.

Chapter 16

HABEAS CORPUS

"The Privilege of the Writ of Habeas Corpus shall not be suspended, unless when in Cases of Rebellion or Invasion the public Safety may require it."

U.S. Constitution, Article I, Section 9.

There are a number of extraordinary writs that might be sought at various stages in criminal cases: writs of prohibition, mandamus, coram nobis, coram vobis, and others. By far the most important is the writ of habeas corpus.

In its simplest form, a petition for this ancient "great writ" asks the court to order the petitioner released from custody. It is used in a wide variety of situations. A prisoner who contends that jailors are holding him despite expiration of his sentence might seek relief by a habeas petition. A prisoner who feels that he is being mistreated by his jailors might file a habeas petition asking for release or, in the alternative, an order compelling better treatment. And a defendant who contends that his conviction was obtained by a denial of due process might in some cases obtain a new trial via a habeas petition. (Indeed, many of the cases you have been reading in this course arose through petitions for habeas corpus.)

A habeas corpus proceeding is *an independent action*, i.e., a new lawsuit with a new case number. It is *separate* from any criminal action that caused the defendant's incarceration. This fact has important implications when seeking review of a conviction. Suppose that Dan has just been convicted of bank robbery. After trial and sentencing, Dan learns that his lawyer had a conflict of interest, or that a juror was not eligible for jury service, or that the prosecutor had hidden exculpatory evidence from him. Each of these might warrant a reversal on appeal, but for one serious problem: the evidence needed to show these things usually *does not appear in the trial court record*. On appeal, the appellate court will not look at evidence that is not in the trial court record. If the fact that Dan's lawyer also represented a prosecution witness is not in the record, Dan simply cannot raise this issue in his appeal. If, however, Dan files a separate habeas corpus action in the trial court, he may file an affidavit from the prosecution witness (or anyone else) setting out the facts Dan needs to support his argument. If the trial court denies Dan's habeas petition, Dan may then appeal *that* denial to the appellate court.

Habeas corpus is also used by defendants who seek *federal* court review of *state* court convictions (especially death penalty cases, where it is important for defense attorneys to invoke all avenues of relief). One may not normally *appeal* from state to federal court, but one may file a new, independent federal habeas petition, in limited circumstances. This chapter will explore some of those limitations. Watch for the tension between several competing interests, especially the need to give relief to defendants for constitutional violations versus the need for finality of state court judgments.

The history and importance of the writ is discussed in *Boumediene v. Bush*, 128 S.Ct. 2229 (2008).

Problem 16A

To: My law clerk

From: Natalie A. Tired, Esq.

Date: May 1

I just agreed to represent Dick Deadeye, a convict on death row, and I need your help. Here is what I know so far.

Deadeye was charged in State court with murder. His first trial resulted in a hung jury, so he was tried again. At trial, Winnie Winkle testified that while she was working at McGrease, a fast food outlet, she saw Deadeye and Ratzo Rizzo come in. Each pulled out a handgun, and they ordered Frenchy Fry, the manager, into the back room, where the day's receipts were kept. She then heard a shot. Deadeye and Rizzo ran out of the backroom and out of the store. Winkle went into the backroom, where she found the money missing and Fry dead of a gunshot wound.

Police Officer Carl Copp then testified that he was on patrol when he heard a report of the crime and that it had been committed by two white men. Copp said that he saw two white men coming from the direction of McGrease, about a block away, so he stopped and searched them, finding 2 guns on Deadeye and a McGrease bag full of money on Rizzo. When the prosecutor then tried to introduce the guns found on Deadeye into evidence, Deadeye's lawyer objected. The judge overruled the objection, relying on a State rule which required a motion to suppress evidence to be made before the trial begins. A state ballistics expert then testified that the bullet that killed Fry came from one of the guns found on Deadeye. Rizzo then testified that he and Deadeye held up McGrease together, and that Deadeye shot and killed Fry. Deadeye did not testify. The jury convicted Deadeye of first degree murder.

At the penalty phase of the trial, Deadeye took the stand and admitted that he and Rizzo held up the store. He said, however, that Rizzo killed Fry, and then handed the gun to Deadeye to carry so Rizzo could carry the money. On October 1, the jury gave Deadeye the death penalty.

On October 6, Deadeye's counsel filed a motion for new trial, alleging that on October 3 she learned for the first time that, soon after he was arrested, Rizzo had given the police a written statement admitting that he had killed Fry. The court denied the motion, citing a State rule that requires all motions for new trial to be filed within 5 days of any verdict.

Deadeye appealed, and the State Supreme Court affirmed both the guilty verdict and the death sentence.

I'd like to file a petition for habeas corpus in federal court. Please review the attached authorities and tell me what my chances are. If we need any more information, please let me know what it is.

Problem 16B

To: My law clerk

From: Natalie Attired, Esq.

Date: July 1

Well, we filed our petition for habeas corpus in federal district court (based on the grounds you advised me to assert), and the judge just denied it. Deadeye is scheduled to die next week, and I am desperately trying to think of a way to save him.

In preparing our habeas petition, I was so busy reviewing the record of the second trial that I didn't have time to read the record of the first trial. Now that I've had a chance to read it, I think I found something that we might be able to use.

The first trial lasted a month, but the jury had deliberated for only 2 hours when the judge declared a mistrial and dismissed the jury (without asking for the defendant's consent).

This doesn't seem right to me. Is there anything we can do with it? Please hurry.

UNITED STATES CODE, TITLE 28

§ 2254. State custody; remedies in Federal courts

(a) The Supreme Court, a Justice thereof, a circuit judge, or a district court shall entertain an application for a writ of habeas corpus in behalf of a person in custody pursuant to the judgment of a State court only on the ground that he is in custody in violation of the Constitution or laws or treaties of the United States.

(b)

(1) An application for a writ of habeas corpus on behalf of a person in custody pursuant to the judgment of a State court shall not be granted unless it appears that —

(A) the applicant has exhausted the remedies available in the courts of the State; or

(B)(i) there is an absence of available State corrective process; or (ii) circumstances exist that render such process ineffective to protect the rights of the applicant.

(2) An application for a writ of habeas corpus may be denied on the merits, notwithstanding the failure of the applicant to exhaust the remedies available in the courts of the State.

(3) A State shall not be deemed to have waived the exhaustion requirement or be estopped from reliance upon the requirement unless the State, through counsel, expressly waives the requirement.

(c) An applicant shall not be deemed to have exhausted the remedies available in the courts of the State, within the meaning of this section, if he has the right under the law of the State to raise, by any available procedure, the question presented.

(d) An application for a writ of habeas corpus on behalf of a person in custody pursuant to the judgment of a State court shall not be granted with respect to any claim that was adjudicated on the merits in State court proceedings unless the adjudication of the claim —

(1) resulted in a decision that was contrary to, or involved an unreasonable application of, clearly established Federal law, as determined by the Supreme Court of the United States; or

(2) resulted in a decision that was based on an unreasonable determination of the facts in light of the evidence presented in the State court proceeding.

(e)

(1) In a proceeding instituted by an application for a writ of habeas corpus by a person in custody pursuant to the judgment of a State court, a determination of a factual issue made by a State court shall be presumed to be correct. The applicant shall have the burden of rebutting the presumption of correctness by clear and convincing evidence.

(2) If the applicant has failed to develop the factual basis of a claim in State court proceedings, the court shall not hold an evidentiary hearing on the claim unless the applicant shows that —

(A) the claim relies on — (i) a new rule of constitutional law, made retroactive to cases on collateral review by the Supreme Court, that was previously unavailable; or (ii) a factual predicate that could not have been previously discovered through the exercise of due diligence; and

(B) the facts underlying the claim would be sufficient to establish by clear and convincing evidence that but for constitutional error, no reasonable factfinder would have found the applicant guilty of the underlying offense.

(f) If the applicant challenges the sufficiency of the evidence adduced in such State court proceeding to support the State court's determination of a factual issue made therein, the applicant, if able, shall produce that part of the record pertinent to a determination of the sufficiency of the evidence to support such determination. If the applicant, because of indigency or other reason is unable to produce such part of the record, then the State shall produce such part of the record and the Federal court shall direct the State to do so by order directed to an appropriate State official. If the State cannot provide such pertinent part of the record, then the court shall determine under the existing facts and circumstances what weight shall be given to the State court's factual determination.

(g) A copy of the official records of the State court, duly certified by the clerk of such court to be a true and correct copy of a finding, judicial opinion, or other reliable written indicia showing such a factual determination by the State court shall be admissible in the Federal court proceeding.

(h) Except as provided in § 408 of the Controlled Substances Act, in all proceedings brought under this section, and any subsequent proceedings on review, the court may appoint counsel for an applicant who is or becomes financially unable to afford counsel, except as provided by a rule promulgated by the Supreme Court pursuant to statutory authority. Appointment of counsel under this section shall be governed by § 3006A of title 18.

(i) The ineffectiveness or incompetence of counsel during Federal or State collateral post-conviction proceedings shall not be a ground for relief in a proceeding arising under § 2254. [As amended by the "Antiterrorism and Effective Death Penalty Act of 1996."]

§ 2255. Federal custody; remedies on motion attacking sentence

A prisoner in custody under sentence of a court established by Act of Congress claiming the right to be released upon the ground that the sentence was imposed in violation of the Constitution or laws of the United States, or that the court was without jurisdiction to impose such sentence, or that the sentence was in excess of the maximum authorized by law, or is otherwise subject to collateral attack, may move the court which imposed the sentence to vacate, set aside or correct the sentence. A motion for such relief may be made at any time. Unless the motion and the files and records of the case conclusively show that the prisoner is entitled to no relief, the court shall cause notice thereof to be served upon the United States attorney, grant a prompt hearing thereon, determine the issues and make findings of fact and conclusions of law with respect thereto. If the court finds that the judgment was rendered without jurisdiction, or that the sentence imposed was not authorized by law or otherwise open to collateral attack, or that there has been such a denial or infringement of the constitutional rights of the prisoner as to render the judgment vulnerable to collateral attack, the court shall vacate and set the judgment aside and shall discharge the prisoner or resentence him or grant a new trial or correct the sentence as may appear appropriate. * * * *

STONE v. POWELL
United States Supreme Court
428 U.S. 465 (1976)

Mr. Justice Powell delivered the opinion of the Court.

Respondents in these cases were convicted of criminal offenses in state courts, and their convictions were affirmed on appeal. The prosecution in each case relied upon evidence obtained by searches and seizures alleged by respondents to have been unlawful. Each respondent subsequently sought relief in a Federal District Court by filing a petition for a writ of federal habeas corpus under 28 U.S.C. § 2254. The question presented is whether a federal court should consider, in ruling on a petition for habeas corpus relief filed by a state prisoner, a claim that evidence obtained by an unconstitutional search or seizure was introduced at his trial, when he has previously been afforded an opportunity for full and fair litigation of his claim in the state courts. The issue is of considerable importance to the administration of criminal justice.

I

Respondent Lloyd Powell was convicted of murder in June 1968 after trial in a California state court. At about midnight on February 17, 1968, he and three companions entered the Bonanza Liquor Store in San Bernardino, Cal., where Powell became involved in an altercation with Gerald Parsons, the store manager, over the theft of a bottle of wine. In the scuffling that followed Powell shot and killed Parsons' wife. Ten hours later an officer of the Henderson, Nev., Police Department arrested Powell for violation of the Henderson vagrancy ordinance, and in the search incident to the arrest discovered a.38-caliber revolver with six expended cartridges in the cylinder.

Powell was extradited to California and convicted of second-degree murder in the Superior Court of San Bernardo County. Parsons and Powell's accomplices at the liquor store testified against him. A criminologist testified that the revolver found on Powell was the gun that killed Parsons' wife. The trial court rejected Powell's contention that testimony by the Henderson police officer as to the search and the discovery of the revolver should have been excluded because the vagrancy ordinance was unconstitutional. In October 1969, the conviction was affirmed by a California District Court of Appeal. Although the issue was duly presented, that court found it unnecessary to pass upon the legality of the arrest and search because it concluded that the error, if any, in admitting the testimony of the Henderson officer was harmless beyond a reasonable doubt under *Chapman v. California*, 386 U.S. 18 (1967). The Supreme Court of California denied Powell's petition for habeas corpus relief.

In August 1971 Powell filed an amended petition for a writ of federal habeas corpus under 28 U.S.C. § 2254 in the United States District Court for the Northern District of California, contending that the testimony concerning the.38-caliber revolver should have been excluded as the fruit of an illegal search. He argued that his arrest had been unlawful because the Henderson vagrancy ordinance was unconstitutionally vague, and that the arresting officer lacked probable cause to believe that he was violating it. The District Court concluded that the arresting officer had probable cause and held that even if the vagrancy ordinance was unconstitutional, the deterrent purpose of the exclusionary rule does not require that it be applied to bar admission of the fruits of a search incident to an otherwise valid arrest. In the alternative, that court agreed with the California District Court of Appeal that the admission of the evidence concerning Powell's arrest, if error, was harmless beyond a reasonable doubt.

In December 1974, the Court of Appeals for the Ninth Circuit reversed. The court concluded that the vagrancy ordinance was unconstitutionally vague, that Powell's arrest was therefore illegal, and that although exclusion of the evidence would serve no deterrent purpose with regard to police officers who were enforcing statutes in good faith, exclusion would serve the public interest by deterring legislators from enacting unconstitutional statutes. After an independent review of the evidence the court concluded that the admission of the evidence was not harmless error since it supported the testimony of Parsons and Powell's accomplices. * * * *

II

The authority of federal courts to issue the writ of habeas corpus *ad subjiciendum* was included in the first grant of federal-court jurisdiction, made by the Judiciary Act of 1789, with the limitation that the writ extend only to prisoners held in custody by the United States. The original statutory authorization did not define the substantive reach of the writ. It merely stated that the courts of the United States "shall have power to issue writs of Habeas corpus." The courts defined the scope of the writ in accordance with the common law and limited it to an inquiry as to the jurisdiction of the sentencing tribunal. See, e g., *Ex parte Watkins*, 7 L.Ed. 650 (1830) (Marshall, C. J.).

In 1867 the writ was extended to state prisoners. Under the 1867 Act, federal courts were authorized to give relief in "all cases where any person may be restrained of his or her liberty in violation of the constitution, or of any treaty or law of the United States." But the limitation of federal habeas corpus jurisdiction to consideration of the jurisdiction of the sentencing court persisted. And, although the concept of "jurisdiction" was subjected to considerable strain as the substantive scope of the writ was expanded, this expansion was limited to only a few classes of cases until *Frank v. Mangum*, 237 U.S. 309, in 1915. In *Frank*, the prisoner had claimed in the state courts that the proceedings which resulted in his conviction for murder had been dominated by a mob. After the State Supreme Court rejected his contentions, Frank unsuccessfully sought habeas corpus relief in the Federal District Court. This Court affirmed the denial of relief because Frank's federal claims had been considered by a competent and unbiased state tribunal. The Court recognized, however, that if a habeas corpus court found that the State had failed to provide adequate "corrective process" for the full and fair litigation of federal claims, whether or not "jurisdictional," the court could inquire into the merits to determine whether a detention was lawful. *Id.* at 333–336.

In the landmark decision in *Brown v. Allen*, 344 U.S. 443 (1953), the scope of the writ was expanded still further. In that case and its companion case, *Daniels v. Allen*, prisoners applied for federal habeas corpus relief claiming that the trial courts had erred in failing to quash their indictments due to alleged discrimination in the selection of grand jurors and in ruling certain confessions admissible. In *Brown*, the highest court of the State had rejected these claims on direct appeal, and this Court had denied certiorari. Despite the apparent adequacy of the state corrective process, the Court reviewed the denial of the writ of habeas corpus and held that Brown was entitled to a full reconsideration of these constitutional claims, including, if appropriate, a hearing in the Federal District Court. In *Daniels*, however, the State Supreme Court on direct review had refused to consider the appeal because the papers were filed out of time. This Court held that since the state-court judgment rested on a reasonable application of the State's legitimate procedural rules, a ground that would have barred direct review of his federal claims by this Court, the District Court lacked authority to grant habeas corpus relief.

This final barrier to broad collateral re-examination of state criminal convictions in federal habeas corpus proceedings was removed in *Fay v. Noia*, 372 U.S. 391 (1963).[10] Noia and two codefendants had been convicted of felony murder. The sole evidence against each defendant was a signed confession. Noia's codefendants, but not Noia himself, appealed their convictions. Although their appeals were unsuccessful, in subsequent state proceedings they were able to establish that their

---

[10] Despite the expansion of the scope of the writ, there has been no change in the established rule with respect to nonconstitutional claims. The writ of habeas corpus and its federal counterpart, 28 U.S.C. § 2255, "will not be allowed to do service for an appeal." *Sunal v. Large*, 332 U.S. 174, 178 (1947). For this reason, nonconstitutional claims that could have been raised on appeal, but were not, may not be asserted in collateral proceedings. *Id.* at 178–179. Even those nonconstitutional claims that could not have been asserted on direct appeal can be raised on collateral review only if the alleged error constituted "a fundamental defect which inherently results in a complete miscarriage of justice". *Id.* at 346.

confessions had been coerced and their convictions therefore procured in violation of the Constitution. In a subsequent federal habeas corpus proceeding, it was stipulated that Noia's confession also had been coerced, but the District Court followed *Daniels* in holding that Noia's failure to appeal barred habeas corpus review. The Court of Appeals reversed, ordering that Noia's conviction be set aside and that he be released from custody or that a new trial be granted. This Court affirmed the grant of the writ, narrowly restricting the circumstances in which a federal court may refuse to consider the merits of federal constitutional claims.

During the period in which the substantive scope of the writ was expanded, the Court did not consider whether exceptions to full review might exist with respect to particular categories of constitutional claims. Prior to the Court's decision in *Kaufman v. United States*, 394 U.S. 217 (1969), however, a substantial majority of the Federal Courts of Appeals had concluded that collateral review of search-and-seizure claims was inappropriate on motions filed by federal prisoners under 28 U.S.C. § 2255, the modern post conviction procedure available to federal prisoners in lieu of habeas corpus. The primary rationale advanced in support of those decisions was that Fourth Amendment violations are different in kind from denials of Fifth or Sixth Amendment rights in that claims of illegal search and seizure do not "impugn the integrity of the fact-finding process or challenge evidence as inherently unreliable; rather, the exclusion of illegally seized evidence is simply a prophylactic device intended generally to deter Fourth Amendment violations by law enforcement officers." 394 U.S. at 224.

Kaufman rejected this rationale and held that search-and-seizure claims are cognizable in § 2255 proceedings. The Court noted that "the federal habeas remedy extends to state prisoners alleging that unconstitutionally obtained evidence was admitted against them at trial," 394 U.S. at 225, and concluded, as a matter of statutory construction, that there was no basis for restricting "access by federal prisoners with illegal search-and-seizure claims to federal collateral remedies, while placing no similar restriction on access by state prisoners," 394 U.S. at 226. Although in recent years the view has been expressed that the Court should re-examine the substantive scope of federal habeas jurisdiction and limit collateral review of search-and-seizure claims "solely to the question of whether the petitioner was provided a fair opportunity to raise and have adjudicated the question in state courts," the Court, without discussion or consideration of the issue, has continued to accept jurisdiction in cases raising such claims.

The discussion in *Kaufman* of the scope of federal habeas corpus rests on the view that the effectuation of the Fourth Amendment, as applied to the States through the Fourteenth Amendment, requires the granting of habeas corpus relief when a prisoner has been convicted in state court on the basis of evidence obtained in an illegal search or seizure since those Amendments were held, in *Mapp v. Ohio*, 367 U.S. 643 (1961), to require exclusion of such evidence at trial and reversal of conviction upon direct review. Until these cases, we have not had occasion fully to consider the validity of this view. Upon examination, we conclude, in light of the nature and purpose of the Fourth Amendment exclusionary rule, that this view is unjustified. We hold, therefore, that where the State has provided an opportunity for full and fair litigation of a Fourth Amendment claim, the Constitution does not require that a state prisoner be granted federal habeas corpus relief on the ground that evidence obtained in an unconstitutional search or seizure was introduced at his trial.

III

The Fourth Amendment assures the "right of the people to be secure in their persons, houses, papers, and effects, against unreasonable searches and seizures." The Amendment was primarily a reaction to the evils associated with the use of the general warrant in England and the writs of assistance in the Colonies, and was intended to protect the "sanctity of a man's home and the privacies of life," *Boyd v. United States*, 116 U.S. 616, 630 (1886), from searches under unchecked general authority.

The exclusionary rule was a judicially created means of effectuating the rights secured by the Fourth Amendment. * * * *

Decisions prior to *Mapp v. Ohio*, 367 U.S. 643 (1961), advanced two principal reasons for application of the rule in federal trials. The Court in *Elkins v. U.S.*, 364 U.S. 206 (1960), for example, in the context of its special supervisory role over the lower federal courts, referred to the "imperative of judicial integrity," suggesting that exclusion of illegally seized evidence prevents contamination of the judicial process. But even in that context a more pragmatic ground was emphasized:

> The rule is calculated to prevent, not to repair. Its purpose is to deter to compel respect for the constitutional guaranty in the only effectively available way by removing the incentive to disregard it. [*Id.* at 217.]

The *Mapp* majority justified the application of the rule to the States on several grounds, but relied principally upon the belief that exclusion would deter future unlawful police conduct.

Although our decisions often have alluded to the "imperative of judicial integrity," they demonstrate the limited role of this justification in the determination whether to apply the rule in a particular context. Logically extended this justification would require that courts exclude unconstitutionally seized evidence despite lack of objection by the defendant, or even over his assent. It also would require abandonment of the standing limitations on who may object to the introduction of unconstitutionally seized evidence, and retreat from the proposition that judicial proceedings need not abate when the defendant's person is unconstitutionally seized. Similarly, the interest in promoting judicial integrity does not prevent the use of illegally seized evidence in grand jury proceedings. *United States v. Calandra*, 414 U.S. 338 (1974). Nor does it require that the trial court exclude such evidence from use for impeachment of a defendant, even though its introduction is certain to result in conviction in some cases. *Walder v. United States*, 347 U.S. 62 (1954). The teaching of these cases is clear. While courts, of course, must ever be concerned with preserving the integrity of the judicial process, this concern has limited force as a justification for the exclusion of highly probative evidence. The force of this justification becomes minimal where federal habeas corpus relief is sought by a prisoner who previously has been afforded the opportunity for full and fair consideration of his search-and-seizure claim at trial and on direct review.

The primary justification for the exclusionary rule then is the deterrence of police conduct that violates Fourth Amendment rights. Post-*Mapp* Decisions have established that the rule is not a personal constitutional right. It is not calculated to redress the injury to the privacy of the victim of the search or seizure, for any "reparation comes too late." *Linkletter v. Walker*, 381 U.S. 618, 637 (1965). Instead, "the rule is a judicially created remedy designed to safeguard Fourth Amendment rights generally through its deterrent effect." *United States v. Calandra, supra,* 414 U.S. at 348.

Mapp involved the enforcement of the exclusionary rule at state trials and on direct review. The decision in *Kaufman,* as noted above, is premised on the view that implementation of the Fourth Amendment also requires the consideration of search-and-seizure claims upon collateral review of state convictions. But despite the broad deterrent purpose of the exclusionary rule, it has never been interpreted to proscribe the introduction of illegally seized evidence in all proceedings or against all persons. As in the case of any remedial device, "the application of the rule has been restricted to those areas where its remedial objectives are thought most efficaciously served." *United States v. Calandra, supra,* 414 U.S. at 348. Thus, our refusal to extend the exclusionary rule to grand jury proceedings was based on a balancing of the potential injury to the historic role and function of the grand jury by such extension against the potential contribution to the effectuation of the Fourth Amendment through deterrence of police misconduct:

> Any incremental deterrent effect which might be achieved by extending the rule to grand jury proceedings is uncertain at best. Whatever deterrence of police misconduct may result from the exclusion of illegally seized evidence from criminal trials, it is unrealistic to assume that application of the rule to grand jury proceedings would significantly further that goal. Such an extension would deter only police investigation consciously directed toward the discovery of evidence solely for use in a grand jury investigation. We therefore decline to embrace a view that would achieve a speculative and undoubtedly minimal advance in the deterrence of police misconduct at the expense of substantially impeding the role of the grand jury. [414 U.S. at 351–352.]

The same pragmatic analysis of the exclusionary rule's usefulness in a particular context was evident earlier in *Walder v. United States, supra,* where the Court permitted the Government to use unlawfully seized evidence to impeach the credibility of a defendant who had testified broadly in his own defense. The Court held, in effect, that the interests safeguarded by the exclusionary rule in that context were outweighed by the need to prevent perjury and to assure the integrity of the trial process. The judgment in *Walder* revealed most clearly that the policies behind the exclusionary rule are not absolute. Rather, they must be evaluated in light of competing policies. In that case, the public interest in determination of truth at trial was deemed to outweigh the incremental contribution that might have been made to the protection of Fourth Amendment values by application of the rule.

The balancing process at work in these cases also finds expression in the standing requirement. Standing to invoke the exclusionary rule has been found to exist only when the Government attempts to use illegally obtained evidence to incriminate the victim of the illegal search. *Brown v. United States,* 411 U.S. 223 (1973). The standing requirement is premised on the view that the "additional benefits of extending the rule" to defendants other than the victim of the search or seizure are outweighed by the "further encroachment upon the public interest in prosecuting those accused of crime and having them acquitted or convicted on the basis of all the evidence which exposes the truth." *Alderman v. United States,* 394 U.S. at 174–175.

IV

We turn now to the specific question presented by these cases. Respondents allege violations of Fourth Amendment rights guaranteed them through the Fourteenth Amendment. The question is whether state prisoners who have been afforded the opportunity for full and fair consideration of their reliance upon the exclusionary rule with respect to seized evidence by the state courts at trial and on direct review may invoke their claim again on federal habeas corpus review. The answer is to be found by weighing the utility of the exclusionary rule against the costs of extending it to collateral review of Fourth Amendment claims.

The costs of applying the exclusionary rule even at trial and on direct review are well known: the focus of the trial, and the attention of the participants therein, are diverted from the ultimate question of guilt or innocence that should be the central concern in a criminal proceeding. Moreover, the physical evidence sought to be excluded is typically reliable and often the most probative information bearing on the guilt or innocence of the defendant. As Mr. Justice Black emphasized in his dissent in *Kaufman*:

> A claim of illegal search and seizure under the Fourth Amendment is crucially different from many other constitutional rights; ordinarily the evidence seized can in no way have been rendered untrustworthy by the means of its seizure and indeed often this evidence alone establishes beyond virtually any shadow of a doubt that the defendant is guilty. [394 U.S. at 237.]

Application of the rule thus deflects the truthfinding process and often frees the guilty. The disparity in particular cases between the error committed by the police officer and the windfall afforded a guilty defendant by application of the rule is contrary to the idea of proportionality that is essential to the concept of justice. Thus, although the rule is thought to deter unlawful police activity in part through the nurturing of respect for Fourth Amendment values, if applied indiscriminately it may well have the opposite effect of generating disrespect for the law and administration of justice. These long-recognized costs of the rule persist when a criminal conviction is sought to be overturned on collateral review on the ground that a search-and-seizure claim was erroneously rejected by two or more tiers of state courts.[31]

Evidence obtained by police officers in violation of the Fourth Amendment is excluded at trial in the hope that the frequency of future violations will decrease. Despite the absence of supportive empirical evidence, we have assumed that the immediate effect of exclusion will be to discourage law enforcement officials from

---

[31] Resort to habeas corpus, especially for purposes other than to assure that no innocent person suffers an unconstitutional loss of liberty, results in serious intrusions on values important to our system of government. They include "(i) the most effective utilization of limited judicial resources, (ii) the necessity of finality in criminal trials, (iii) the minimization of friction between our federal and state systems of justice, and (iv) the maintenance of the constitutional balance upon which the doctrine of federalism is founded." *Schneckloth v. Bustamonte*, 412 U.S. at 259.

We nevertheless afford broad habeas corpus relief, recognizing the need in a free society for an additional safeguard against compelling an innocent man to suffer an unconstitutional loss of liberty. But in the case of a typical Fourth Amendment claim, asserted on collateral attack, a convicted defendant is usually asking society to redetermine an issue that has no bearing on the basic justice of his incarceration.

violating the Fourth Amendment by removing the incentive to disregard it. More importantly, over the long term, this demonstration that our society attaches serious consequences to violation of constitutional rights is thought to encourage those who formulate law enforcement policies, and the officers who implement them, to incorporate Fourth Amendment ideals into their value system.

We adhere to the view that these considerations support the implementation of the exclusionary rule at trial and its enforcement on direct appeal of state-court convictions. But the additional contribution, if any, of the consideration of search-and-seizure claims of state prisoners on collateral review is small in relation to the costs. To be sure, each case in which such claim is considered may add marginally to an awareness of the values protected by the Fourth Amendment. There is no reason to believe, however, that the overall educative effect of the exclusionary rule would be appreciably diminished if search-and-seizure claims could not be raised in federal habeas corpus review of state convictions. Nor is there reason to assume that any specific disincentive already created by the risk of exclusion of evidence at trial or the reversal of convictions on direct review would be enhanced if there were the further risk that a conviction obtained in state court and affirmed on direct review might be overturned in collateral proceedings often occurring years after the incarceration of the defendant. The view that the deterrence of Fourth Amendment violations would be furthered rests on the dubious assumption that law enforcement authorities would fear that federal habeas review might reveal flaws in a search or seizure that went undetected at trial and on appeal.[35] Even if one rationally could assume that some additional incremental deterrent effect would be presented in isolated cases, the resulting advance of the legitimate goal of furthering Fourth Amendment rights would be outweighed by the acknowledged costs to other values vital to a rational system of criminal justice.

In sum, we conclude that where the State has provided an opportunity for full and fair litigation of a Fourth Amendment claim, a state prisoner may not be granted federal habeas corpus relief on the ground that evidence obtained in an unconstitutional search or seizure was introduced at his trial. In this context the contribution of the exclusionary rule, if any, to the effectuation of the Fourth Amendment is minimal, and the substantial societal costs of application of the rule persist with special force.

Accordingly, the judgments of the Courts of Appeals are reversed.

---

[35] The policy arguments that respondents marshal in support of the view that federal habeas corpus review is necessary to effectuate the Fourth Amendment stem from a basic mistrust of the state courts as fair and competent forums for the adjudication of federal constitutional rights. The argument is that state courts cannot be trusted to effectuate Fourth Amendment values through fair application of the rule, and the oversight jurisdiction of this Court on certiorari is an inadequate safeguard. The principal rationale for this view emphasizes the broad differences in the respective institutional settings within which federal judges and state judges operate. Despite differences in institutional environment and the unsympathetic attitude to federal constitutional claims of some state judges in years past, we are unwilling to assume that there now exists a general lack of appropriate sensitivity to constitutional rights in the trial and appellate courts of the several States. State courts, like federal courts, have a constitutional obligation to safeguard personal liberties and to uphold federal law. Moreover, the argument that federal judges are more expert in applying federal constitutional law is especially unpersuasive in the context of search-and-seizure claims, since they are dealt with on a daily basis by trial level judges in both systems. In sum, there is no intrinsic reason why the fact that a man is a federal judge should make him more competent, or conscientious, or learned with respect to the consideration of Fourth Amendment claims than his neighbor in the state courthouse.

Mr. Justice Brennan, with whom Mr. Justice Marshall concurs, dissenting.

* * * *

Today's holding portends substantial evisceration of federal habeas corpus jurisdiction, and I dissent. * * * *

Under *Mapp*, as a matter of federal constitutional law, a state court <u>must</u> exclude evidence from the trial of an individual whose Fourth and Fourteenth Amendment rights were violated by a search or seizure that directly or indirectly resulted in the acquisition of that evidence. As *United States v. Calandra*, 414 U.S. 338 (1974), reaffirmed, "evidence obtained in violation of the Fourth Amendment cannot be used in a criminal proceeding against the victim of the illegal search and seizure." When a state court admits such evidence, it has committed a *constitutional* error, and unless that error is harmless under federal standards, it follows ineluctably that the defendant has been placed "in custody in violation of the Constitution" within the comprehension of 28 U.S.C. § 2254. In short, it escapes me as to what logic can support the assertion that the defendant's unconstitutional confinement obtains during the process of direct review, no matter how long that process takes, but that the unconstitutionality then suddenly dissipates at the moment the claim is asserted in a collateral attack on the conviction.

The only conceivable rationale upon which the Court's "constitutional" thesis might rest is the statement that "the exclusionary rule is not a personal constitutional right. Instead, 'the rule is a judicially created remedy designed to safeguard Fourth Amendment rights generally through its deterrent effect.' " Although my dissent in *Calandra* rejected, in light of contrary decisions establishing the role of the exclusionary rule, the premise that an individual has no constitutional right to have unconstitutionally seized evidence excluded from all use by the government, I need not dispute that point here. For today's holding is not logically defensible even under *Calandra*. However, the Court reinterprets *Mapp*, and whatever the rationale now attributed to *Mapp's* holding or the purpose ascribed to the exclusionary rule, the prevailing constitutional *rule* is that unconstitutionally seized evidence *cannot be admitted* in the criminal trial of a person whose federal constitutional rights were violated by the search or seizure. The erroneous admission of such evidence is a violation of the Federal Constitution — *Mapp* inexorably means at least this much, or there would be no basis for applying the exclusionary rule in state criminal proceedings — and an accused against whom such evidence is admitted has been convicted in derogation of rights mandated by, and is "in custody in violation of" the Constitution of the United States. Indeed, since state courts violate the strictures of the Federal Constitution by admitting such evidence, then even if federal habeas review did not directly effectuate Fourth Amendment values, a proposition I deny, that review would nevertheless serve to effectuate what is concededly a constitutional principle concerning admissibility of evidence at trial.

The Court, assuming without deciding that respondents were convicted on the basis of unconstitutionally obtained evidence erroneously admitted against them by the state trial courts, acknowledges that respondents had the right to obtain a reversal of their convictions on appeal in the state courts or on certiorari to this Court. Indeed, since our rules relating to the time limits for applying for certiorari in criminal cases are nonjurisdictional, certiorari could be granted respondents even today and their convictions could be reversed despite today's decisions. And the basis for reversing those convictions would of course have to be that the States, in rejecting respondents' Fourth Amendment claims, had deprived them of a right in derogation of the Federal Constitution. It is simply inconceivable that that constitutional deprivation suddenly vanishes after the appellate process has been exhausted. And as between this Court on *certiorari*, and federal district courts on habeas, it is for *Congress* to decide what the most efficacious method is for enforcing *federal* constitutional rights and asserting the primacy of federal law. The Court, however, simply ignores the settled principle that for purposes of adjudicating constitutional claims Congress, which has the power to do so under Art. III of the Constitution, has effectively cast the district courts sitting in habeas in the role of surrogate Supreme Courts. * * * *

Federal habeas corpus review of Fourth Amendment claims of state prisoners was merely one manifestation of the principle that "conventional notions of finality in criminal litigation cannot be permitted to defeat the manifest federal policy that federal constitutional rights of personal liberty shall not be denied without the fullest opportunity for plenary federal judicial review." *Fay v. Noia*, 372 U.S. 391, 424 (1963). This Court's precedents have been "premised in large part on a recognition that the availability of collateral remedies is necessary to insure the integrity of proceedings at and before trial where constitutional rights are at stake. * * * * The threat of habeas serves as a necessary additional incentive for trial and appellate courts throughout the land to conduct their proceedings in a manner consistent with established constitutional standards. The availability of collateral review assures that the lower federal and state courts toe the constitutional line. * * * *

Enforcement of *federal* constitutional rights that redress constitutional violations directed against the "guilty" is a particular function of *federal* habeas review, lest judges trying the "morally unworthy" be tempted not to execute the supreme law of the land. State judges popularly elected may have difficulty resisting popular pressures not experienced by federal judges given lifetime tenure designed to immunize them from such influences, and the federal habeas statutes reflect the congressional judgment that such detached federal review is a salutary safeguard against Any detention of an individual "in violation of the Constitution or laws of the United States."

Federal courts have the duty to carry out the congressionally assigned responsibility to shoulder the ultimate burden of adjudging whether detentions violate federal law, and today's decision substantially abnegates that duty. The Court does not, because it cannot, dispute that institutional constraints totally preclude any possibility that this Court can adequately oversee whether state courts have properly applied federal law, and does not controvert the fact that federal habeas jurisdiction is partially designed to ameliorate that inadequacy. Thus, although I fully agree that state courts "have a constitutional obligation to safeguard personal liberties and to uphold federal law," and that there is no "general lack of appropriate sensitivity to constitutional rights in the trial and appellate courts of the several States," I cannot agree that it follows that, as the Court today holds, federal-court determination of almost all Fourth Amendment claims of state prisoners should be barred and that state-court resolution of those issues should be insulated from the federal review Congress intended. * * * *

In summary, while unlike the Court I consider that the exclusionary rule is a constitutional ingredient of the Fourth Amendment, any modification of that rule should at least be accomplished with some modicum of logic and justification not provided today. The Court does not disturb the holding of *Mapp v. Ohio* that, as a matter of federal constitutional law, illegally obtained evidence must be excluded from the trial of a criminal defendant whose rights were transgressed during the search that resulted in acquisition of the evidence. In light of that constitutional rule it is a matter for Congress, not this Court, to prescribe what federal courts are to review state prisoners' claims of constitutional error committed by state courts. Until this decision, our cases have never departed from the construction of the habeas statutes as embodying a congressional intent that, however substantive constitutional rights are delineated or expanded, those rights may be asserted as a procedural matter under federal habeas jurisdiction. Employing the transparent tactic that today's is a decision construing the Constitution, the Court usurps the authority vested by the Constitution in the Congress to reassign federal judicial responsibility for reviewing state prisoners' claims of failure of state courts to redress violations of their Fourth Amendment rights. Our jurisdiction is eminently unsuited for that task, and as a practical matter the only result of today's holding will be that denials by the state courts of claims by state prisoners of violations of their Fourth Amendment rights will go unreviewed by a federal tribunal. I fear that the same treatment ultimately will be accorded state prisoners' claims of violations of other constitutional rights; thus the potential ramifications of this case for federal habeas jurisdiction generally are ominous. The Court, no longer content just to restrict forthrightly the constitutional rights of the citizenry, has embarked on a campaign to water down even such constitutional rights as it purports to acknowledge by the device of foreclosing resort to the federal habeas remedy for their redress.

I would affirm the judgments of the Courts of Appeals.

Mr. Justice White, dissenting.

For many of the reasons stated by Mr. Justice Brennan, I cannot agree that the writ of habeas corpus should be any less available to those convicted of state crimes where they allege Fourth Amendment violations than where other constitutional issues are presented to the federal court. Under the amendments to the habeas corpus statute, which were adopted after *Fay v. Noia*, 372 U.S. 391 (1963), and represented an effort by Congress to lend a modicum of finality to state criminal judgments, I cannot distinguish between Fourth Amendment and other constitutional issues.

Suppose, for example, that two confederates in crime, Smith and Jones, are tried separately for a state crime and convicted on the very same evidence, including evidence seized incident to their arrest allegedly made without probable cause. Their constitutional claims are fully aired, rejected, and preserved on appeal. Their convictions are affirmed by the State's highest court. Smith, the first to be tried, does not petition for certiorari, or does so but his petition is denied. Jones, whose conviction was considerably later, is more successful. His petition for certiorari is granted and his conviction reversed because this Court, without making any new rule of law, simply concludes that on the undisputed facts the arrests were made without probable cause and the challenged evidence was therefore seized in violation of the Fourth Amendment. The State must either retry Jones or release him, necessarily because he is deemed in custody in violation of the Constitution. It turns out that without the evidence illegally seized, the State has no case; and Jones goes free. Smith then files his petition for habeas corpus. He makes no claim that he did not have a full and fair hearing in the state courts, but asserts that his Fourth Amendment claim had been erroneously decided and that he is being held in violation of the Federal Constitution. He cites this Court's decision in Jones' case to satisfy any burden placed on him by § 2254 to demonstrate that the state court was in error. Unless the Court's reservation, in its present opinion, of those situations where the defendant has not had a full and fair hearing in the state courts is intended to encompass all those circumstances under which a state criminal judgment may be re-examined under § 2254 — in which event the opinion is essentially meaningless and the judgment erroneous — Smith's petition would be dismissed, and he would spend his life in prison while his colleague is a free man. I cannot believe that Congress intended this result.

Under the present habeas corpus statute, neither Rice's nor Powell's application for habeas corpus should be dismissed on the grounds now stated by the Court. I would affirm the judgments of the Courts of Appeals as being acceptable applications of the exclusionary rule applicable in state criminal trials by virtue of *Mapp*.
* * * *

Notes from Natalie:

1. Many years ago, when I took Civil Procedure in law school, I learned that when a case is over, it's over, and the loser cannot file a new lawsuit challenging the result in the old one. I think they called this "res judicata" — Latin for "the thing has been adjudicated!" Isn't this still the law? If so, why should someone convicted of a crime *ever* be allowed to file a new lawsuit challenging his conviction? If he has any gripes about how he was convicted, let him raise them on *appeal*, just like civil litigants have to. *Stone v. Powell* seems to allow him to file a federal habeas petition challenging the conviction if he can show that the state procedure was not adequate to allow him to raise his claims. But couldn't *that* issue have been raised in his appeal? Isn't that what we would require of a *civil* litigant? Why give special favors to criminals?

2. As Justice White's dissent points out, a defendant who loses his state appeal may then petition the U.S. Supreme Court for *certiorari* to review the state decisions — *without* having to show that the state did not give him a full and fair hearing on his constitutional claim. Because of its heavy workload on other cases, however, the high court is unable to hear more than a tiny handful of these *certiorari* petitions. Doesn't federal habeas fill in this gap, allowing lower federal courts to act as a "surrogate", doing what the U.S. Supreme Court should do but doesn't have time to do? Should every convicted defendant have one opportunity to litigate his federal constitutional claims in federal court? Is *this* a sufficient justification for federal habeas? See Friedman, *Pas de Deux: The Supreme Court and the Habeas Courts*, 66 So.Cal.L.Rev. 2467, 2469 (1993). How does this square with footnote 35 of the *Stone* opinion?

WAINWRIGHT v. SYKES
United States Supreme Court
433 U.S. 72 (1977)

Mr. Justice Rehnquist delivered the opinion of the Court.

We granted certiorari to consider the availability of federal habeas corpus to review a state convict's claim that testimony was admitted at his trial in violation of his rights under *Miranda v. Arizona*, 384 U.S. 436 (1966), a claim which the Florida courts have previously refused to consider on the merits because of noncompliance with a state contemporaneous-objection rule. Petitioner Wainwright, on behalf of the State of Florida, here challenges a decision of the Court of Appeals for the Fifth Circuit ordering a hearing in state court on the merits of respondent's contention.

Respondent Sykes was convicted of third-degree murder after a jury trial in the Circuit Court of DeSoto County. He testified at trial that on the evening of January 8, 1972, he told his wife to summon the police because he had just shot Willie Gilbert. Other evidence indicated that when the police arrived at respondent's trailer home, they found Gilbert dead of a shotgun wound, lying a few feet from the front porch. Shortly after their arrival, respondent came from across the road and volunteered that he had shot Gilbert, and a few minutes later respondent's wife approached the police and told them the same thing. Sykes was immediately arrested and taken to the police station.

Once there, it is conceded that he was read his *Miranda* rights, and that he declined to seek the aid of counsel and indicated a desire to talk. He then made a statement, which was admitted into evidence at trial through the testimony of the two officers who heard it, to the effect that he had shot Gilbert from the front porch of his trailer home. There were several references during the trial to respondent's consumption of alcohol during the preceding day and to his apparent state of intoxication, facts which were acknowledged by the officers who arrived at the scene. At no time during the trial, however, was the admissibility of any of respondent's statements challenged by his counsel on the ground that respondent had not understood the *Miranda* warnings. Nor did the trial judge question their admissibility on his own motion or hold a factfinding hearing bearing on that issue.

Respondent appealed his conviction, but apparently did not challenge the admissibility of the inculpatory statements. He later filed in the trial court a motion to vacate the conviction and, in the State District Court of Appeals and Supreme Court, petitions for habeas corpus. These filings, apparently for the first time, challenged the statements made to police on grounds of involuntariness. In all of these efforts respondent was unsuccessful.

Having failed in the Florida courts, respondent initiated the present action under 28 U.S.C. § 2254, asserting the inadmissibility of his statements by reason of his lack of understanding of the *Miranda* warnings. The United States District Court for the Middle District of Florida ruled that *Jackson v. Denno*, 378 U.S. 368 (1964), requires a hearing in a state criminal trial prior to the admission of an inculpatory out-of-court statement by the defendant. It held further that respondent had not lost his right to assert such a claim by failing to object at trial or on direct appeal, since only "exceptional circumstances" of "strategic decisions at trial" can create such a bar to raising federal constitutional claims in a federal habeas action. The court stayed issuance of the writ to allow the state court to hold a hearing on the "voluntariness" of the statements.

Petitioner warden appealed this decision to the United States Court of Appeals for the Fifth Circuit. That court first considered the nature of the right to exclusion of statements made without a knowing waiver of the right to counsel and the right not to incriminate oneself. It noted that *Jackson v. Denno* guarantees a right to a hearing on whether a defendant has knowingly waived his rights as described to him in the *Miranda* warnings, and stated that under Florida law "the burden is on the State to secure a prima facie determination of voluntariness, not upon the defendant to demand it."

The court then directed its attention to the effect on respondent's right of Florida Rule Crim.Proc. 3.190(i),[5] which it described as "a contemporaneous objection rule" applying to motions to suppress a defendant's inculpatory statements. It focused on this Court's decisions in *Henry v. Mississippi*, 379 U.S. 443 (1965); *Davis v. United States*, 411 U.S. 233 (1973); and *Fay v. Noia*, 372 U.S. 391 (1963), and concluded that the failure to comply with the rule requiring objection at the trial would only bar review of the suppression claim where the right to object was deliberately bypassed for reasons relating to trial tactics.

The simple legal question before the Court calls for a construction of the language of 28 U.S.C. § 2254(a), which provides that the federal courts shall entertain an application for a writ of habeas corpus "in behalf of a person in custody pursuant to the judgment of a state court only on the ground that he is in custody in violation of the Constitution or laws or treaties of the United States." But, to put it mildly, we do not write on a clean slate in construing this statutory provision. Its earliest counterpart, applicable only to prisoners detained by federal authority, is found in the Judiciary Act of 1789. Construing that statute for the Court in *Ex parte Watkins*, 7 L.Ed. 650 (1830), Mr. Chief Justice Marshall said:

> An imprisonment under a judgment cannot be unlawful, unless that judgment be an absolute nullity; and it is not a nullity if the Court has general jurisdiction of the subject, although it should be erroneous.

In 1867, Congress expanded the statutory language so as to make the writ available to one held in state as well as federal custody. For more than a century since the 1867 amendment, this Court has grappled with the relationship between the classical common-law writ of habeas corpus and the remedy provided in 28 U.S.C. § 2254. Sharp division within the Court has been manifested on more than one aspect of the perplexing problems which have been litigated in this connection. Where the habeas petitioner challenges a final judgment of conviction rendered by a state court, this Court has been called upon to decide no fewer than four different questions, all to a degree interrelated with one another: (1) What types of federal claims may a federal habeas court properly consider? (2) Where a federal claim is cognizable by a federal habeas court, to what extent must that court defer to a

---

[5] Rule 3.190(i): "Motion to Suppress a Confession or Admissions Illegally Obtained. (1) Grounds. Upon motion of the defendant or upon its own motion, the court shall suppress any confession or admission obtained illegally from the defendant. (2) Time for Filing. The motion to suppress shall be made prior to trial unless opportunity therefor did not exist or the defendant was not aware of the grounds for the motion, but the court in its discretion may entertain the motion or an appropriate objection at the trial. (3) Hearing. The court shall receive evidence on any issue of fact necessary to be decided in order to rule on the motion."

resolution of the claim in prior state proceedings? (3) To what extent must the petitioner who seeks federal habeas exhaust state remedies before resorting to the federal court? (4) In what instances will an adequate and independent state ground bar consideration of otherwise cognizable federal issues on federal habeas review? * * * *

As to the role of adequate and independent state grounds, it is a well-established principle of federalism that a state decision resting on an adequate foundation of state substantive law is immune from review in the federal courts. *Fox Film Corp. v. Muller*, 296 U.S. 207 (1935). The application of this principle in the context of a federal habeas proceeding has therefore excluded from consideration any questions of state *substantive* law, and thus effectively barred federal habeas review where questions of that sort are either the only ones raised by a petitioner or are in themselves dispositive of his case. The area of controversy which has developed has concerned the reviewability of federal claims which the state court has declined to pass on because not presented in the manner prescribed by its *procedural* rules. The adequacy of such an independent state procedural ground to prevent federal habeas review of the underlying federal issue has been treated very differently than where the state-law ground is substantive. The pertinent decisions marking the Court's somewhat tortuous efforts to deal with this problem are: *Ex parte Spencer*, 228 U.S. 652 (1913); *Brown v. Allen*, 344 U.S. 443 (1953); *Fay v. Noia, supra*; *Davis v. United States*, 411 U.S. 233 (1973); and *Francis v. Henderson*, 425 U.S. 536 (1976).

In *Brown*, petitioner Daniels' lawyer had failed to mail the appeal papers to the State Supreme Court on the last day provided by law for filing, and hand delivered them one day after that date. Citing the state rule requiring timely filing, the Supreme Court of North Carolina refused to hear the appeal. This Court held that federal habeas was not available to review a constitutional claim which could not have been reviewed on direct appeal here because it rested on an independent and adequate state procedural ground.

In *Fay v. Noia*, respondent Noia sought federal habeas to review a claim that his state-court conviction had resulted from the introduction of a coerced confession in violation of the Fifth Amendment to the United States Constitution. While the convictions of his two codefendants were reversed on that ground in collateral proceedings following their appeals, Noia did not appeal and the New York courts ruled that his subsequent *coram nobis* action was barred on account of that failure. This Court held that petitioner was nonetheless entitled to raise the claim in federal habeas, and thereby overruled its decision 10 years earlier in *Brown v. Allen*: "The doctrine under which state procedural defaults are held to constitute an adequate and independent state law ground barring direct Supreme Court review is not to be extended to limit the power granted the federal courts under the federal habeas statute." 372 U.S. at 399.

As a matter of comity but not of federal power, the Court acknowledged "a limited discretion in the federal judge to deny relief to an applicant who had deliberately by-passed the orderly procedure of the state courts and in so doing has forfeited his state court remedies." *Id.* at 438. In so stating, the Court made clear that the waiver must be knowing and actual "an intentional relinquishment or abandonment of a known right or privilege." *Id.* at 439. Noting petitioner's "grisly choice" between acceptance of his life sentence and pursuit of an appeal which might culminate in a sentence of death, the Court concluded that there had been no deliberate bypass of the right to have the federal issues reviewed through a state appeal.

A decade later we decided *Davis v. United States, supra,* in which a federal prisoner's application under 28 U.S.C. § 2255 sought for the first time to challenge the makeup of the grand jury which indicted him. The Government contended that he was barred by the requirement of Fed.Rule Crim.Proc. 12(b)(2) providing that such challenges must be raised "by motion before trial." The Rule further provides that failure to so object constitutes a waiver of the objection, but that "the court for cause shown may grant relief from the waiver." We noted that the Rule "promulgated by this Court and, pursuant to 18 U.S.C. § 3771, 'adopted' by Congress, governs by its terms the manner in which the claims of defects in the institution of criminal proceedings may be waived," 411 U.S. at 241, and held that this standard contained in the Rule, rather than the *Fay v. Noia* concept of waiver, should pertain in federal habeas as on direct review. Referring to previous constructions of Rule 12(b)(2), we concluded that review of the claim should be barred on habeas, as on direct appeal, absent a showing of cause for the noncompliance and some showing of actual prejudice resulting from the alleged constitutional violation.

Last Term, in *Francis v. Henderson*, the rule of *Davis* was applied to the parallel case of a state procedural requirement that challenges to grand jury composition be raised before trial. The Court noted that there was power in the federal courts to entertain an application in such a case, but rested its holding on "considerations of comity and concerns for the orderly administration of criminal justice." 425 U.S. at 538–539. While there was no counterpart provision of the state rule which allowed an exception upon some showing of cause, the Court concluded that the standard derived from the Federal Rule should nonetheless be applied in that context since "there is no reason to give greater preclusive effect to procedural defaults by federal defendants than to similar defaults by state defendants." *Id.* at 542. As applied to the federal petitions of state convicts, the *Davis* cause-and-prejudice standard was thus incorporated directly into the body of law governing the availability of federal habeas corpus review.

To the extent that the dicta of *Fay v. Noia* may be thought to have laid down an all-inclusive rule rendering state contemporaneous-objection rules ineffective to bar review of underlying federal claims in federal habeas proceedings absent a "knowing waiver" or a "deliberate bypass" of the right to so object, its effect was limited by *Francis*, which applied a different rule and barred a habeas challenge to the makeup of a grand jury. Petitioner Wainwright in this case urges that we further confine its effect by applying the principle enunciated in *Francis* to a claimed error in the admission of a defendant's confession. * * * *

We therefore conclude that Florida procedure did, consistently with the United States Constitution, require that respondents' confession be challenged at trial or not at all, and thus his failure to timely object to its admission amounted to an independent and adequate state procedural ground which would have prevented direct review here. We thus come to the crux of this case. Shall the rule of *Francis v. Henderson*, barring federal habeas review absent a showing of "cause" and "prejudice" attendant to a state procedural waiver, be applied to a waived objection to the admission of a confession at trial?[11] We answer that question in the

---

[11] Petitioner does not argue, and we do not pause to consider, whether a bare allegation of a *Miranda* violation, without accompanying assertions going to the actual voluntariness or reliability of the

affirmative.

As earlier noted in the opinion, since *Brown v. Allen*, 344 U.S. 443 (1953), it has been the rule that the federal habeas petitioner who claims he is detained pursuant to a final judgment of a state court in violation of the United States Constitution is entitled to have the federal habeas court make its own independent determination of his federal claim, without being bound by the determination on the merits of that claim reached in the state proceedings. This rule of *Brown v. Allen* is in no way changed by our holding today. Rather, we deal only with contentions of federal law which were not resolved on the merits in the state proceeding due to respondent's failure to raise them there as required by state procedure. We leave open for resolution in future decisions the precise definition of the "cause"-and-"prejudice" standard, and note here only that it is narrower than the standard set forth in dicta in *Fay v. Noia*, 372 U.S. 391 (1963), which would make federal habeas review generally available to state convicts absent a knowing and deliberate waiver of the federal constitutional contention. It is the sweeping language of *Fay v. Noia*, going far beyond the facts of the case eliciting it, which we today reject.

The reasons for our rejection of it are several. The contemporaneous-objection rule itself is by no means peculiar to Florida, and deserves greater respect than *Fay* gives it, both for the fact that it is employed by a coordinate jurisdiction within the federal system and for the many interests which it serves in its own right. A contemporaneous objection enables the record to be made with respect to the constitutional claim when the recollections of witnesses are freshest, not years later in a federal habeas proceeding. It enables the judge who observed the demeanor of those witnesses to make the factual determinations necessary for properly deciding the federal constitutional question. While the 1966 amendment to § 2254 requires deference to be given to such determinations made by state courts, the determinations themselves are less apt to be made in the first instance if there is no contemporaneous objection to the admission of the evidence on federal constitutional grounds.

A contemporaneous-objection rule may lead to the exclusion of the evidence objected to, thereby making a major contribution to finality in criminal litigation. Without the evidence claimed to be vulnerable on federal constitutional grounds, the jury may acquit the defendant, and that will be the end of the case; or it may nonetheless convict the defendant, and he will have one less federal constitutional claim to assert in his federal habeas petition. If the state trial judge admits the evidence in question after a full hearing, the federal habeas court pursuant to the 1966 amendment to § 2254 will gain significant guidance from the state ruling in this regard. Subtler considerations as well militate in favor of honoring a state contemporaneous-objection rule. An objection on the spot may force the prosecution to take a hard look at its whole card, and even if the prosecutor thinks that the state trial judge will admit the evidence he must contemplate the possibility of reversal by the state appellate courts or the ultimate issuance of a federal writ of habeas corpus based on the impropriety of the state court's rejection of the federal constitutional claim.

---

confession, is a proper subject for consideration on federal habeas review, where there has been a full and fair opportunity to raise the argument in the state proceeding. See *Stone v. Powell*, 428 U.S. 465 (1976). We do not address the merits of that question because of our resolution of the case on alternative grounds.

We think that the rule of *Fay v. Noia*, broadly stated, may encourage "sandbagging" on the part of defense lawyers, who may take their chances on a verdict of not guilty in a state trial court with the intent to raise their constitutional claims in a federal habeas court if their initial gamble does not pay off. The refusal of federal habeas courts to honor contemporaneous- objection rules may also make state courts themselves less stringent in their enforcement. Under the rule of *Fay v. Noia*, state appellate courts know that a federal constitutional issue raised for the first time in the proceeding before them may well be decided in any event by a federal habeas tribunal. Thus, their choice is between addressing the issue notwithstanding the petitioner's failure to timely object, or else face the prospect that the federal habeas court will decide the question without the benefit of their views.

The failure of the federal habeas courts generally to require compliance with a contemporaneous-objection rule tends to detract from the perception of the trial of a criminal case in state court as a decisive and portentous event. A defendant has been accused of a serious crime, and this is the time and place set for him to be tried by a jury of his peers and found either guilty or not guilty by that jury. To the greatest extent possible all issues which bear on this charge should be determined in this proceeding: the accused is in the court-room, the jury is in the box, the judge is on the bench, and the witnesses, having been subpoenaed and duly sworn, await their turn to testify. Society's resources have been concentrated at that time and place in order to decide, within the limits of human fallibility, the question of guilt or innocence of one of its citizens. Any procedural rule which encourages the result that those proceedings be as free of error as possible is thoroughly desirable, and the contemporaneous-objection rule surely falls within this classification.

We believe the adoption of the *Francis* rule in this situation will have the salutary effect of making the state trial on the merits the "main event," so to speak, rather than a "tryout on the road" for what will later be the determinative federal habeas hearing. There is nothing in the Constitution or in the language of § 2254 which requires that the state trial on the issue of guilt or innocence be devoted largely to the testimony of fact witnesses directed to the elements of the state crime, while only later will there occur in a federal habeas hearing a full airing of the federal constitutional claims which were not raised in the state proceedings. If a criminal defendant thinks that an action of the state trial court is about to deprive him of a federal constitutional right there is every reason for his following state procedure in making known his objection.

The "cause"-and-"prejudice" exception of the *Francis* rule will afford an adequate guarantee, we think, that the rule will not prevent a federal habeas court from adjudicating for the first time the federal constitutional claim of a defendant who in the absence of such an adjudication will be the victim of a miscarriage of justice. Whatever precise content may be given those terms by later cases, we feel confident in holding without further elaboration that they do not exist here. Respondent has advanced no explanation whatever for his failure to object at trial, and, as the proceeding unfolded, the trial judge is certainly not to be faulted for failing to question the admission of the confession himself. The other evidence of guilt presented at trial, moreover, was substantial to a degree that would negate any possibility of actual prejudice resulting to the respondent from the admission of his inculpatory statement.

We accordingly conclude that the judgment of the Court of Appeals for the Fifth Circuit must be reversed, and the cause remanded to the United States District Court for the Middle District of Florida with instructions to dismiss respondent's petition for a writ of habeas corpus.

MR. CHIEF JUSTICE BURGER, concurring.

I concur fully in the judgment and in the Court's opinion. I write separately to emphasize one point which, to me, seems of critical importance to this case. In my view, the "deliberate bypass" standard enunciated in *Fay v. Noia* was never designed for, and is inapplicable to, errors even of constitutional dimension alleged to have been committed during trial. * * * *

The touchstone of *Fay* is the exercise of volition by the defendant himself with respect to his own federal constitutional rights. In contrast, the claim in the case before us relates to events during the trial itself. Typically, habeas petitioners claim that unlawfully secured evidence was admitted, but see *Stone v. Powell*, 428 U.S. 465 (1976), or that improper testimony was adduced, or that an improper jury charge was given, or that a particular line of examination or argument by the prosecutor was improper or prejudicial. But unlike *Fay* and *Zerbst*, preservation of this type of claim under state procedural rules does not generally involve an assertion by the defendant himself; rather, the decision to assert or not to assert constitutional rights or constitutionally based objections at trial is necessarily entrusted to the defendant's attorney, who must make on-the-spot decisions at virtually all stages of a criminal trial. As a practical matter, a criminal defendant is rarely, if ever, in a position to decide, for example, whether certain testimony is hearsay and, if so, whether it implicates interests protected by the Confrontation Clause; indeed, it is because "even the intelligent and educated layman has small and sometimes no skill in the science of law" that we held it constitutionally required that every defendant who faces the possibility of incarceration be afforded counsel. *Gideon v. Wainwright*, 372 U.S. 335, 345 (1963).

Once counsel is appointed, the day-to-day conduct of the defense rests with the attorney. He, not the client, has the immediate and ultimate responsibility of deciding if and when to object, which witnesses, if any, to call, and what defenses to develop. Not only do these decisions rest with the attorney, but such decisions must, as a practical matter, be made without consulting the client.[1] The trial process simply does not permit the type of frequent and protracted interruptions which would be necessary if it were required that clients give knowing and intelligent approval to each of the myriad tactical decisions as a trial proceeds.[2]

Since trial decisions are of necessity entrusted to the accused's attorney, the *Fay* standard of "knowing and intelligent waiver" is simply inapplicable. * * * *

---

[1] Only such basic decisions as whether to plead guilty, waive a jury, or testify in one's own behalf are ultimately for the accused to make. See ABA Project on Standards for Criminal Justice, The Prosecution Function and Defense Function § 5.2 (App.Draft 1971).

[2] One is left to wonder what use there would have been to an objection to a confession corroborated by witnesses who heard Sykes freely admit the killing at the scene within minutes after the shooting.

MR. JUSTICE STEVENS, concurring.

* * * *

In this case I agree with the Court's holding that collateral attack on the state-court judgment should not be allowed. The record persuades me that competent trial counsel could well have made a deliberate decision not to object to the admission of the respondent's in-custody statement. That statement was consistent, in many respects, with the respondent's trial testimony. It even had some positive value, since it portrayed the respondent as having acted in response to provocation, which might have influenced the jury to return a verdict on a lesser charge. To extent that it was damaging, the primary harm would have resulted from its effect in impeaching the trial testimony, but it would have been admissible for impeachment in any event, *Harris v. New York*, 401 U.S. 222. Counsel may well have preferred to have the statement admitted without objection when it was first offered rather than making an objection which, at best, could have been only temporarily successful.

Moreover, since the police fully complied with *Miranda*, the deterrent purpose of the *Miranda* rule is inapplicable to this case. Finally, there is clearly no basis for claiming that the trial violated any standard of fundamental fairness. Accordingly, no matter how the rule is phrased, this case is plainly not one in which a collateral attack should be allowed. I therefore join the opinion of the Court.

MR. JUSTICE BRENNAN, with whom MR. JUSTICE MARSHALL joins, dissenting.

Over the course of the last decade, the deliberate-bypass standard announced in *Fay v. Noia* has played a central role in efforts by the federal judiciary to accommodate the constitutional rights of the individual with the States' interests in the integrity of their judicial procedural regimes. The Court today decides that this standard should no longer apply with respect to procedural defaults occurring during the trial of a criminal defendant. In its place, the Court adopts the two-part "cause"-and-"prejudice" test originally developed in *Davis v. United States*, 411 U.S. 233 (1973), and *Francis v. Henderson*, 425 U.S. 536 (1976). As was true with these earlier cases, however, today's decision makes no effort to provide concrete guidance as to the content of those terms. More particularly, left unanswered is the thorny question that must be recognized to be central to a realistic rationalization of this area of law: How should the federal habeas court treat a procedural default in a state court that is attributable purely and simply to the error or negligence of a defendant's trial counsel? * * * *

Having created the bypass exception to the availability of collateral review, *Fay* recognized that intentional, tactical forfeitures are not the norm upon which to build a rational system of federal habeas jurisdiction. In the ordinary case, litigants simply have no incentive to slight the state tribunal, since constitutional adjudication on the state and federal levels are not mutually exclusive. Under the regime of collateral review recognized since the days of *Brown v. Allen*, and enforced by the *Fay* bypass test, no rational lawyer would risk the "sandbagging" feared by the Court.[5] If a constitutional challenge is not properly raised on the state level, the

---

[5] In brief, the defense lawyer would face two options: (1) He could elect to present his constitutional

explanation generally will be found elsewhere than in an intentional tactical decision.

In brief then, any realistic system of federal habeas corpus jurisdiction must be premised on the reality that the ordinary procedural default is born of the inadvertence, negligence, inexperience, or incompetence of trial counsel. The case under consideration today is typical. The Court makes no effort to identify a tactical motive for the failure of Sykes' attorney to challenge the admissibility or reliability of a highly inculpatory statement. While my Brother Stevens finds a possible tactical advantage, I agree with the Court of Appeals that this reading is most implausible: "We can find no possible advantage which the defense might have gained, or thought they might gain, from the failure to conform with Florida Criminal Procedure Rule 3.190(i)." Indeed, there is no basis for inferring that Sykes or his state trial lawyer was even aware of the existence of his claim under the Fifth Amendment; for this not a case where the trial judge expressly drew the attention of the defense to a possible constitutional contention or procedural requirement, or where the defense signals its knowledge of a constitutional claim by abandoning a challenge previously raised. Rather, any realistic reading of the record demonstrates that we are faced here with a lawyer's simple error.[6]

Fay's answer thus is plain: the bypass test simply refuses to credit what is essentially a lawyer's mistake as a forfeiture of constitutional rights. I persist in the belief that the interests of Sykes and the State of Florida are best rationalized by adherence to this test, and by declining to react to inadvertent defaults through the creation of an "airtight system of forfeitures." * * * *

Punishing a lawyer's unintentional errors by closing the federal courthouse door to his client is both a senseless and misdirected method of deterring the slighting of state rules. It is senseless because unplanned and unintentional action of any kind generally is not subject to deterrence; and, to the extent that it is hoped that a threatened sanction addressed to the defense will induce greater care and caution on the part of trial lawyers, thereby forestalling negligent conduct or error, the

---

claims to the state courts in a proper fashion. If the state trial court is persuaded that a constitutional breach has occurred, the remedies dictated by the Constitution would be imposed, the defense would be bolstered, and the prosecution accordingly weakened, perhaps precluded altogether. If the state court rejects the properly tendered claims, the defense has lost nothing: Appellate review before the state courts and federal habeas consideration are preserved. (2) He could elect to "sandbag." This presumably means, first, that he would hold back the presentation of his constitutional claim to the trial court, thereby increasing the likelihood of a conviction since the prosecution would be able to present evidence that, while arguably constitutionally deficient, may be highly prejudicial to the defense. Second, he would thereby have forfeited all state review and remedies with respect to these claims (subject to whatever "plain error" rule is available). Third, to carry out his scheme he would now be compelled to deceive the federal habeas court and to convince the judge that he did not "deliberately bypass" the state procedures. If he loses on this gamble, all federal review would be barred, and his "sandbagging" would have resulted in nothing but the forfeiture of all judicial review of his client's claims. The Court, without substantiation, apparently believes that a meaningful number of lawyers are induced into option 2 by *Fay*. I do not. That belief simply offends common sense.

[6] The likelihood that we are presented with a lawyer's simple mistake is not answered by respondent's stipulation to his trial counsel's competency. At oral argument it was made clear that Sykes so stipulated solely because of the position expressed by the habeas court that a challenge to his prior legal representation would require the return to the state courts and the further exhaustion of state remedies, a detour that respondent insisted on avoiding. Furthermore, in light of the prevailing standards, or lack of standards, for judging the competency of trial counsel, it is perfectly consistent for even a lawyer who commits a grievous error whether due to negligence or ignorance to be deemed to have provided competent representation.

potential loss of all valuable state remedies would be sufficient to this end. And it is a misdirected sanction because even if the penalization of incompetence or carelessness will encourage more thorough legal training and trial preparation, the habeas applicant, as opposed to his lawyer, hardly is the proper recipient of such a penalty. Especially with fundamental constitutional rights at stake, no fictional relationship of principal-agent or the like can justify holding the criminal defendant accountable for the naked errors of his attorney. This is especially true when so many indigent defendants are without any realistic choice in selecting who ultimately represents them at trial. Indeed, if responsibility for error must be apportioned between the parties, it is the State, through its attorney's admissions and certification policies, that is more fairly held to blame for the fact that practicing lawyers too often are ill-prepared or ill-equipped to act carefully and knowledgeably when faced with decisions governed by state procedural requirements. * * * *

In short, I believe that the demands of our criminal justice system warrant visiting the mistakes of a trial attorney on the head of a habeas corpus applicant only when we are convinced that the lawyer actually exercised his expertise and judgment in his client's service, and with his client's knowing and intelligent participation where possible. This, of course, is the precise system of habeas review established by *Fay v. Noia*. * * * *

Note from Natalie:

In *Teague v. Lane*, 489 U.S. 288 (1989), a black defendant was convicted by an all-white jury of murder, robbery, and aggravated battery. The convictions were affirmed on appeal in 1983. In his first federal habeas petition, he claimed that the prosecutor had used peremptory challenges to exclude blacks from the jury. The district court denied the petition, because then-controlling authority (*Swain v. Alabama*, 380 U.S. 202 (1965)) had held that peremptory challenges could be exercised on any basis (so long as the prosecutor was not trying to exclude blacks in every case). During his appeal of this ruling, the U.S. Supreme Court decided *Batson v. Kentucky*, 476 U.S. 79 (1986), which overruled *Swain*. The Court of Appeal affirmed, relying on *Allen v. Hardy*, 478 U.S. 255, where the Supreme Court had held that *Batson* would not be applied retroactively to cases which had become final (i.e., where direct appeals had been exhausted) before *Batson* was announced.

The Supreme Court affirmed the Court of Appeal. The Court adopted the view of former Justice Harlan: "new rules" should be applied retroactively to cases pending on "direct review" (i.e., on appeal) when the new rule is announced, but generally should *not* be applied retroactively to cases on "collateral review" (i.e., on habeas). A main purpose of federal habeas is to deter state courts from failing to apply existing law, and this purpose would not be served by granting habeas where state courts failed to anticipate *new* rules. Therefore, it is "sounder, in adjudicating habeas petitions, generally to apply the law prevailing at the time a conviction became final." The Court stated:

> Application of constitutional rules not in existence at the time a conviction became final seriously undermines the principle of finality which is essential to the operation of our criminal justice system. Without finality, the criminal law is deprived of much of its deterrent effect. The fact that life and liberty are at stake in criminal prosecutions shows only that conven-

tional notions of finality should not have as *much* place in criminal as in civil litigation, not that they should have *none*. * * * *

    In many ways the application of new rules to cases on collateral review may be more intrusive than the enjoining of criminal prosecutions, for it *continually* forces the States to marshal resources in order to keep in prison defendants whose trials and appeals conformed to then-existing constitutional standards. Furthermore, state courts are understandably frustrated when they faithfully apply existing constitutional law only to have a federal court discover, during a habeas proceeding, new constitutional demands. [*Id.* at 309–310.]

A "new rule" is one which "breaks new ground or imposes a new obligation on the States or the Federal government", i.e., where "the result was not *dictated* by precedent existing at the time the defendant's conviction became final". *Id.* at 301.

Justice Harlan had noted two exceptions to his general rule of non-retroactivity: (1) where the new rule places certain kinds of private conduct beyond the power of legislatures to proscribe, and (2) where the new rule requires procedures which are "implicit in the concept of ordered liberty" (such as the right to counsel at trial). The Court approved these exceptions, but held that neither applied to the present case. The second exception includes only "accuracy-enhancing" procedural rules which help assure that the innocent are not found guilty, and defendant's claim did not involve such a rule.

The Court noted that this defendant was not under sentence of death, and said that it did "not express any views as to how the retroactivity approach we adopt today is to be applied in the capital sentencing context." *Id.* at 313, fn. 2.

Teague has been heavily criticized. See, e.g., Brandes, *Taking Justice to its Logical Extreme: A Comment on Teague v. Lane*, 66 So.Calif.L.Rev. 2453 (1993); Rosenberg, *Kaddish for Federal Habeas Corpus*, 59 Geo.Wash.L.Rev. 362 (1991). It does, however, have its defenders. See, e.g., Higgenbotham, *Notes on Teague*, 66 So.Calif.L.Rev. 2433 (1993), which is discussed in Meltzer, *Habeas Corpus Jurisdiction: The Limits of Models*, 66 So.Calif.L.Rev. 2507 (1993).

McCLESKEY v. ZANT
United States Supreme Court
499 U.S. 467 (1991)

JUSTICE KENNEDY delivered the opinion of the Court.

The doctrine of abuse of the writ defines the circumstances in which federal courts decline to entertain a claim presented for the first time in a second or subsequent petition for a writ of habeas corpus. Petitioner Warren McCleskey in a second federal habeas petition presented a claim under *Massiah v. United States*, 377 U.S. 201 (1964), that he failed to include in his first federal petition. The Court of Appeals for the Eleventh Circuit held that assertion of the *Massiah* claim in this manner abused the writ. Though our analysis differs from that of the Court of Appeals, we agree that the petitioner here abused the writ, and we affirm the judgment.

I

McCleskey and three other men, all armed, robbed a Georgia furniture store in 1978. One of the robbers shot and killed an off duty policeman who entered the store in the midst of the crime. McCleskey confessed to the police that he participated in the robbery. When on trial for both the robbery and the murder, however, McCleskey renounced his confession after taking the stand with an alibi denying all involvement. To rebut McCleskey's testimony, the prosecution called Offie Evans, who had occupied a jail cell next to McCleskey's. Evans testified that McCleskey admitted shooting the officer during the robbery and boasted that he would have shot his way out of the store even in the face of a dozen policemen.

Although no one witnessed the shooting, further direct and circumstantial evidence supported McCleskey's guilt of the murder. An eyewitness testified that someone ran from the store carrying a pearl-handled pistol soon after the robbery. Other witnesses testified that McCleskey earlier had stolen a pearl-handled pistol of the same caliber as the bullet that killed the officer. Ben Wright, one of McCleskey's accomplices, confirmed that during the crime McCleskey carried a white-handled handgun matching the caliber of the fatal bullet. Wright also testified that McCleskey admitted shooting the officer. Finally, the prosecutor introduced McCleskey's confession of participation in the robbery.

In December 1978, the jury convicted McCleskey of murder and sentenced him to death. Since his conviction, McCleskey has pursued direct and collateral remedies for more than a decade. We describe this procedural history in detail, both for a proper understanding of the case and as an illustration of the context in which allegations of abuse of the writ arise.

On direct appeal to the Supreme Court of Georgia, McCleskey raised six grounds of error. A summary of McCleskey's claims on direct appeal, as well as those he asserted in each of his four collateral proceedings, is set forth in the Appendix to this opinion. The portion of the appeal relevant for our purposes involves McCleskey's attack on Evans' rebuttal testimony. McCleskey contended that the trial court "erred in allowing evidence of McCleskey's oral statement admitting the murder made to Evans in the next cell, because the prosecutor had deliberately withheld such statement" in violation of *Brady v. Maryland*, 373 U.S. 83 (1963). A unanimous Georgia Supreme Court acknowledged that the prosecutor did not furnish Evans' statement to the defense, but ruled that because the undisclosed evidence was not exculpatory, McCleskey suffered no material prejudice and was not denied a fair trial under *Brady*. The court noted, moreover, that the evidence McCleskey wanted to inspect was "introduced to the jury in its entirety" through Evans' testimony, and that McCleskey's argument that "the evidence was needed in order to prepare a proper defense or impeach other witnesses had no merit because the evidence requested was statements made by McCleskey himself." The court rejected McCleskey's other contentions, and affirmed his conviction and sentence. We denied *certiorari*.

McCleskey then initiated postconviction proceedings. In January 1981, he filed a petition for state habeas corpus relief. The amended petition raised 23 challenges to his murder conviction and death sentence. Three of the claims concerned Evans' testimony. First, McCleskey contended that the State violated his due process rights under *Giglio v. United States*, 405 U.S. 150 (1972), by its failure to disclose an agreement to drop pending escape charges against Evans in return for his cooperation and testimony. Second, McCleskey reasserted his *Brady* claim that the State violated his due process rights by the deliberate withholding of the statement he made to Evans while in jail. Third, McCleskey alleged that admission of Evans' testimony violated the Sixth Amendment right to counsel as construed in *Massiah v. United States*. On this theory, "the introduction into evidence of his statements to Evans, elicited in a situation created to induce McCleskey to make incriminating statements without the assistance of counsel, violated McCleskey's right to counsel under the Sixth Amendment to the Constitution of the United States."

At the state habeas corpus hearing, Evans testified that one of the detectives investigating the murder agreed to speak a word on his behalf to the federal authorities about certain federal charges pending against him. The state habeas court ruled that the ex parte recommendation did not implicate *Giglio*, and it denied relief on all other claims. The Supreme Court of Georgia denied McCleskey's application for a certificate of probable cause, and we denied his second petition for a writ of certiorari.

In December 1981, McCleskey filed his first federal habeas corpus petition in the United States District Court for the Northern District of Georgia, asserting 18 grounds for relief. The petition failed to allege the *Massiah* claim, but it did reassert the *Giglio* and *Brady* claims. Following extensive hearings in August and October 1983, the District Court held that the detective's statement to Evans was a promise of favorable treatment, and that failure to disclose the promise violated *Giglio*. The District Court further held that Evans' trial testimony may have affected the jury's verdict on the charge of malice murder. On these premises it granted relief.

The Court of Appeals reversed the District Court's grant of the writ. The court held that the State had not made a promise to Evans of the kind contemplated by *Giglio*, and that in any event the *Giglio* error would be harmless. The court affirmed the District Court on all other grounds. We granted *certiorari* limited to the question whether Georgia's capital sentencing procedures were constitutional, and denied relief.

McCleskey continued his postconviction attacks by filing a second state habeas corpus action in 1987 which, as amended, contained five claims for relief. One of the claims again centered on Evans' testimony, alleging the State had an agreement with Evans that it had failed to disclose. The state trial court held a hearing and dismissed the petition. The Supreme Court of Georgia denied McCleskey's application for a certificate of probable cause.

In July 1987, McCleskey filed a second federal habeas action, the one we now review. In the District Court, McCleskey asserted seven claims, including a *Massiah* challenge to the introduction of Evans' testimony. McCleskey had presented a *Massiah* claim, it will be recalled, in his first state habeas action when he alleged that the conversation recounted by Evans at trial had been "elicited in a situation created to induce" him to make an incriminating statement without the assistance of counsel. The first federal petition did not present a *Massiah* claim. The proffered basis for the *Massiah* claim in the second federal petition was a 21-page signed statement that Evans made to the Atlanta Police Department on August 1, 1978, two weeks before the trial began. The department furnished the document to McCleskey one month before he filed his second federal petition.

The statement related pretrial jailhouse conversations that Evans had with McCleskey and that Evans overheard between McCleskey and Bernard Dupree. By the statement's own terms, McCleskey participated in all the reported jail cell conversations. Consistent with Evans' testimony at trial, the statement reports McCleskey admitting and boasting about the murder. It also recounts that Evans posed as Ben Wright's uncle and told McCleskey he had talked with Wright about the robbery and the murder.

In his second federal habeas petition, McCleskey asserted that the statement proved Evans "was acting in direct concert with State officials" during the incriminating conversations with McCleskey, and that the authorities "deliberately elicited" inculpatory admissions in violation of McCleskey's Sixth Amendment right to counsel. *Massiah v. United States*, 377 U.S. at 206. Among other responses, the State of Georgia contended that McCleskey's presentation of a *Massiah* claim for the first time in the second federal petition was an abuse of the writ. 28 U.S.C. § 2244(b); Rule 9(b) of the Rules Governing § 2254 Cases.

The District Court held extensive hearings in July and August 1987 focusing on the arrangement the jailers had made for Evans' cell assignment in 1978. Several witnesses denied that Evans had been placed next to McCleskey by design or instructed to overhear conversations or obtain statements from McCleskey. McCleskey's key witness was Ulysses Worthy, a jailer at the Fulton County Jail during the summer of 1978. McCleskey's lawyers contacted Worthy after a detective testified that the 1978 Evans statement was taken in Worthy's office. The District Court characterized Worthy's testimony as "often confused and self-contradictory." Worthy testified that someone at some time requested permission to move Evans near McCleskey's cell. He contradicted himself, however, concerning when, why, and by whom Evans was moved, and about whether he overheard investigators urging Evans to engage McCleskey in conversation.

On December 23, 1987, the District Court granted McCleskey relief based upon a violation of *Massiah*. The court stated that the Evans statement "contains strong indication of an *ab initio* relationship between Evans and the authorities." In addition, the court credited Worthy's testimony suggesting that the police had used Evans to obtain incriminating information from McCleskey. Based on the Evans statement and portions of Worthy's testimony, the District Court found that the jail authorities had placed Evans in the cell adjoining McCleskey's "for the purpose of gathering incriminating information"; that "Evans was probably coached in how to approach McCleskey and given critical facts unknown to the general public"; that Evans talked with McCleskey and eavesdropped on McCleskey's conversations with others; and that Evans reported what he had heard to the authorities. These findings, in the District Court's view, established a *Massiah* violation.

In granting habeas relief, the District Court rejected the State's argument that McCleskey's assertion of the *Massiah* claim for the first time in the second federal petition constituted an abuse of the writ. The court ruled that McCleskey did not deliberately abandon the claim after raising it in his first state habeas petition. "This is not a case," the District Court reasoned, "where petitioner has reserved his proof or deliberately withheld his claim for a second petition." The District Court also determined that when McCleskey filed his first federal petition, he did not know about either the 21-page Evans document or the identity of Worthy, and that the failure to discover the evidence for the first federal petition "was not due to McCleskey's inexcusable neglect."

The Eleventh Circuit reversed, holding that the District Court abused its discretion by failing to dismiss McCleskey's *Massiah* claim as an abuse of the writ. The Court of Appeals agreed with the District Court that the petitioner must "show that he did not deliberately abandon the claim and that his failure to raise it in the first federal habeas proceeding] was not due to inexcusable neglect." Accepting the District Court's findings that at the first petition stage McCleskey knew neither the existence of the Evans statement nor the identity of Worthy, the court held that the District Court "misconstrued the meaning of deliberate abandonment." Because McCleskey included a *Massiah* claim in his first state petition, dropped it in his first federal petition, and then reasserted it in his second federal petition, he "made a knowing choice not to pursue the claim after having raised it previously" that constituted a prima facie showing of "deliberate abandonment." The court further found the State's alleged concealment of the Evans statement irrelevant because it "was simply the catalyst that caused counsel to pursue the *Massiah* claim more vigorously" and did not itself "demonstrate the existence of a *Massiah* violation." The court concluded that McCleskey had presented no reason why counsel could not have discovered Worthy earlier. Finally, the court ruled that McCleskey's claim did not fall within the ends of justice exception to the abuse of the writ doctrine because any *Massiah* violation that may have been committed would have been harmless error.

McCleskey petitioned this Court for a writ of certiorari, alleging numerous errors in the Eleventh Circuit's abuse of the writ analysis. In our order granting the petition, we requested the parties to address the following additional question: "Must the State demonstrate that a claim was deliberately abandoned in an earlier petition for a writ of habeas corpus in order to establish that inclusion of that claim in a subsequent habeas petition constitutes abuse of the writ?"

II

The parties agree that the government has the burden of pleading abuse of the writ, and that once the government makes a proper submission, the petitioner must show that he has not abused the writ in seeking habeas relief. Much confusion exists though, on the standard for determining when a petitioner abuses the writ. * * * *

Although our decisions on the subject do not all admit of ready synthesis, one point emerges with clarity: Abuse of the writ is not confined to instances of deliberate abandonment. * * * * A petitioner may abuse the writ by failing to raise a claim through inexcusable neglect. * * * *

The inexcusable neglect standard demands more from a petitioner than the standard of deliberate abandonment. But we have not given the former term the content necessary to guide district courts in the ordered consideration of allegedly abusive habeas corpus petitions. For reasons we explain below, a review of our habeas corpus precedents leads us to decide that the same standard used to determine whether to excuse state procedural defaults should govern the determination of inexcusable neglect in the abuse of the writ context.

The prohibition against adjudication in federal habeas corpus of claims defaulted in state court is similar in purpose and design to the abuse of the writ doctrine, which in general prohibits subsequent habeas consideration of claims not raised, and thus defaulted, in the first federal habeas proceeding. The terms "abuse of the writ" and "inexcusable neglect," on the one hand, and "procedural default," on the other, imply a background norm of procedural regularity binding on the petitioner. This explains the presumption against habeas adjudication both of claims defaulted in state court and of claims defaulted in the first round of federal habeas. A federal habeas court's power to excuse these types of defaulted claims derives from the court's equitable discretion. In habeas, equity recognizes that a suitor's conduct in relation to the matter at hand may disentitle him to the relief he seeks. For these reasons, both the abuse of the writ doctrine and our procedural default jurisprudence concentrate on a petitioner's acts to determine whether he has a legitimate excuse for failing to raise a claim at the appropriate time.

The doctrines of procedural default and abuse of the writ implicate nearly identical concerns flowing from the significant costs of federal habeas corpus review. To begin with, the writ strikes at finality. One of the law's very objects is the finality of its judgments. Neither innocence nor just punishment can be vindicated until the final judgment is known. "Without finality, the criminal law is deprived of much of its deterrent effect." *Teague v. Lane*, 489 U.S. 288, 309 (1989). And when a habeas petitioner succeeds in obtaining a new trial, the " 'erosion of memory' and 'dispersion of witnesses' that occur with the passage of time," *Kuhlmann v. Wilson*, *supra*, 477 U.S. at 453, prejudice the government and diminish the chances of a reliable criminal adjudication.

Finality has special importance in the context of a federal attack on a state conviction. Reexamination of state convictions on federal habeas "frustrates 'both the States' sovereign power to punish offenders and their good-faith attempts to honor constitutional rights.' " *Murray v. Carrier*, 477 U.S. at 487. Our federal system recognizes the independent power of a State to articulate societal norms through criminal law; but the power of a State to pass laws means little if the State cannot enforce them.

Habeas review extracts further costs. Federal collateral litigation places a heavy burden on scarce federal judicial resources, and threatens the capacity of the system to resolve primary disputes. Finally, habeas corpus review may give litigants incentives to withhold claims for manipulative purposes and may establish disincentives to present claims when evidence is fresh. *Wainwright v. Sykes*, 433 U.S. at 89.

Far more severe are the disruptions when a claim is presented for the first time in a second or subsequent federal habeas petition. If "collateral review of a conviction extends the ordeal of trial for both society and the accused," *Engle v. Isaac*, 456 U.S. at 126–127, the ordeal worsens during subsequent collateral proceedings. Perpetual disrespect for the finality of convictions disparages the entire criminal justice system. "A procedural system which permits an endless repetition of inquiry into facts and law in a vain search for ultimate certitude implies a lack of confidence about the possibilities of justice that cannot but war with the underlying substantive commands. There comes a point where a procedural system which leaves matters perpetually open no longer reflects humane concern but merely anxiety and a desire for immobility." Bator, *Finality in Criminal Law and Federal Habeas Corpus for State Prisoners*, 76 Harv.L.Rev. 441, 452 (1963). If re-examination of a conviction in the first round of federal habeas stretches resources, examination of new claims raised in a second or subsequent petition spreads them thinner still. These later petitions deplete the resources needed for federal litigants in the first instance, including litigants commencing their first federal habeas action. The phenomenon calls to mind Justice Jackson's admonition that "it must prejudice the occasional meritorious application to be buried in a flood of worthless ones." *Brown v. Allen*, 344 U.S. at 537 (Jackson, J., concurring). And if reexamination of convictions in the first round of habeas offends federalism and comity, the offense increases when a State must defend its conviction in a second or subsequent habeas proceeding on grounds not even raised in the first petition.

The federal writ of habeas corpus overrides all these considerations, essential as they are to the rule of law, when a petitioner raises a meritorious constitutional claim in a proper manner in a habeas petition. Our procedural default jurisprudence and abuse of the writ jurisprudence help define this dimension of procedural regularity. Both doctrines impose on petitioners a burden of reasonable compliance with procedures designed to discourage baseless claims and to keep the system open for valid ones; both recognize the law's interest in finality; and both invoke equitable principles to define the court's discretion to excuse pleading and procedural requirements for petitioners who could not comply with them in the exercise of reasonable care and diligence. It is true that a habeas court's concern to honor state procedural default rules rests in part on respect for the integrity of procedures "employed by a coordinate jurisdiction within the federal system," *Wainwright v. Sykes*, supra, 433 U.S. at 88, and that such respect is not implicated when a petitioner defaults a claim by failing to raise it in the first round of federal habeas review. Nonetheless, the doctrines of procedural default and abuse of the writ are both designed to lessen the injury to a State that results through reexamination of a state conviction on a ground that the State did not have the opportunity to address at a prior, appropriate time; and both doctrines seek to vindicate the State's interest in the finality of its criminal judgments.

We conclude from the unity of structure and purpose in the jurisprudence of state procedural defaults and abuse of the writ that the standard for excusing a failure to raise a claim at the appropriate time should be the same in both contexts. We have held that a procedural default will be excused upon a showing of cause and prejudice. *Wainwright v. Sykes, supra*. We now hold that the same standard applies to determine if there has been an abuse of the writ through inexcusable neglect.

In procedural default cases, the cause standard requires the petitioner to show that "some objective factor external to the defense impeded counsel's efforts" to raise the claim in state court. *Murray v. Carrier*, 477 U.S. at 488. Objective factors that constitute cause include " 'interference by officials' " that makes compliance with the state's procedural rule impracticable, and "a showing that the factual or legal basis for a claim was not reasonably available to counsel." *Ibid.* In addition, constitutionally "ineffective assistance of counsel is cause." *Ibid.* Attorney error short of ineffective assistance of counsel, however, does not constitute cause and will not excuse a procedural default. *Id.* at 486–488. Once the petitioner has established cause, he must show " 'actual prejudice' resulting from the errors of which he complains." *United States v. Frady*, 456 U.S. 152, 168 (1982).

Federal courts retain the authority to issue the writ of habeas corpus in a further, narrow class of cases despite a petitioner's failure to show cause for a procedural default. These are extraordinary instances when a constitutional violation probably has caused the conviction of one innocent of the crime. We have described this class of cases as implicating a fundamental miscarriage of justice. *Murray v. Carrier, supra*, 477 U.S. at 485.

The cause and prejudice analysis we have adopted for cases of procedural default applies to an abuse of the writ inquiry in the following manner. When a prisoner files a second or subsequent application, the government bears the burden of pleading abuse of the writ. The government satisfies this burden if, with clarity and particularity, it notes petitioner's prior writ history, identifies the claims that appear for the first time, and alleges that petitioner has abused the writ. The burden to disprove abuse then becomes petitioner's. To excuse his failure to raise the claim earlier, he must show cause for failing to raise it and prejudice therefrom as those concepts have been defined in our procedural default decisions. The petitioner's opportunity to meet the burden of cause and prejudice will not include an evidentiary hearing if the district court determines as a matter of law that petitioner cannot satisfy the standard. If petitioner cannot show cause, the failure to raise the claim in an earlier petition may nonetheless be excused if he or she can show that a fundamental miscarriage of justice would result from a failure to entertain the claim. Application of the cause and prejudice standard in the abuse of the writ context does not mitigate the force of *Teague v. Lane*, which prohibits, certain exceptions, the retroactive application of new law to claims raised in federal habeas. Nor does it imply that there is a constitutional right to counsel in federal habeas corpus. * * * *

Considerations of certainty and stability in our discharge of the judicial function support adoption of the cause and prejudice standard in the abuse of the writ context. Well-defined in the case law, the standard will be familiar to federal courts. * * * *

The cause and prejudice standard should curtail the abusive petitions that in recent years have threatened to undermine the integrity of the habeas corpus process. "Federal courts should not continue to tolerate — even in capital cases — this type of abuse of the writ of habeas corpus." *Woodard v. Hutchins*, 464 U.S. at 380. The writ of habeas corpus is one of the centerpieces of our liberties. "But the writ has potentialities for evil as well as for good. Abuse of the writ may undermine the orderly administration of justice and therefore weaken the forces of authority that are essential for civilization." *Brown v. Allen, supra*, 344 U.S. at 512 (opinion of Frankfurter, J.). Adoption of the cause and prejudice standard acknowledges the historic purpose and function of the writ in our constitutional system, and, by preventing its abuse, assures its continued efficacy.

We now apply these principles to the case before us.

IV

McCleskey based the *Massiah* claim in his second federal petition on the 21-page Evans document alone. Worthy's identity did not come to light until the hearing. The District Court found, based on the document's revelation of the tactics used by Evans in engaging McCleskey in conversation (such as his pretending to be Ben Wright's uncle and his claim that he was supposed to participate in the robbery), that the document established an ab initio relationship between Evans and the authorities. It relied on the finding and on Worthy's later testimony to conclude that the State committed a *Massiah* violation.

This ruling on the merits cannot come before us or any federal court if it is premised on a claim that constitutes an abuse of the writ. We must consider, therefore, the preliminary question whether McCleskey had cause for failing to raise the *Massiah* claim in his first federal petition. The District Court found that neither the 21-page document nor Worthy were known or discoverable before filing the first federal petition. Relying on these findings, McCleskey argues that his failure to raise the *Massiah* claim in the first petition should be excused. For reasons set forth below, we disagree.

That McCleskey did not possess or could not reasonably have obtained certain evidence fails to establish cause if other known or discoverable evidence could have supported the claim in any event. "Cause requires a showing of some external impediment *preventing* counsel from constructing or raising a claim." *Murray v. Carrier, supra,* 477 U.S. at 492. For cause to exist, the external impediment, whether it be government interference or the reasonable unavailability of the factual basis for the claim, must have prevented petitioner from raising the claim. Abuse of the writ doctrine examines petitioner's conduct: the question is whether petitioner possessed, or by reasonable means could have obtained, a sufficient basis to allege a claim in the first petition and pursue the matter through the habeas process, see 28 U.S.C. § 2254 Rule 6 (Discovery); Rule 7 (Expansion of Record); Rule 8 (Evidentiary Hearing). The requirement of cause in the abuse of the writ context is based on the principle that petitioner must conduct a reasonable and diligent investigation aimed at including all relevant claims and grounds for relief in the first federal habeas petition. If what petitioner knows or could discover upon reasonable investigation supports a claim for relief in a federal habeas petition, what he does not know is irrelevant. Omission of the claim will not be excused merely because evidence discovered later might also have supported or strengthened the claim.

In applying these principles, we turn first to the 21-page signed statement. It is essential at the outset to distinguish between two issues: (1) Whether petitioner knew about or could have discovered the 21-page document; and (2) whether he knew about or could have discovered the evidence the document recounted, namely the jail-cell conversations. The District Court's error lies in its conflation of the two inquiries, an error petitioner would have us perpetuate here.

The 21-page document unavailable to McCleskey at the time of the first petition does not establish that McCleskey had cause for failing to raise the *Massiah* claim at the outset. Based on testimony and questioning at trial, McCleskey knew that he had confessed the murder during jail-cell conversations with Evans, knew that Evans claimed to be a relative of Ben Wright during the conversations, and knew that Evans told the police about the conversations. Knowledge of these facts alone would put McCleskey on notice to pursue the *Massiah* claim in his first federal habeas petition as he had done in the first state habeas petition.

But there was more. The District Court's finding that the 21-page document established an *ab initio* relationship between Evans and the authorities rested in its entirety on conversations in which McCleskey himself participated. Though at trial McCleskey denied the inculpatory conversations, his current arguments presuppose them. Quite apart from the inequity in McCleskey's reliance on that which he earlier denied under oath, the more fundamental point remains that because McCleskey participated in the conversations reported by Evans, he knew everything in the document that the District Court relied upon to establish the *ab initio* connection between Evans and the police. McCleskey has had at least constructive knowledge all along of the facts he now claims to have learned only from the 21-page document. The unavailability of the document did not prevent McCleskey from raising the *Massiah* claim in the first federal petition and is not cause for his failure to do so. And of course, McCleskey cannot contend that his false representations at trial constitute cause for the omission of a claim from the first federal petition.

The District Court's determination that jailer Worthy's identity and testimony could not have been known prior to the first federal petition does not alter our conclusion. It must be remembered that the 21-page statement was the only new evidence McCleskey had when he filed the *Massiah* claim in the second federal petition in 1987. Under McCleskey's own theory, nothing was known about Worthy even then. If McCleskey did not need to know about Worthy and his testimony to press the *Massiah* claim in the second petition, neither did he need to know about him to assert it in the first. Ignorance about Worthy did not prevent McCleskey from raising the *Massiah* claim in the first federal petition and will not excuse his failure to do so.

Though this reasoning suffices to show the irrelevance of the District Court's finding concerning Worthy, the whole question illustrates the rationale for requiring a prompt investigation and the full pursuit of habeas claims in the first petition. At the time of the first federal petition, written logs and records with prison staff names and assignments existed. By the time of the second federal petition, officials had destroyed the records pursuant to normal retention schedules. Worthy's inconsistent and confused testimony in this case demonstrates the obvious proposition that fact-finding processes are impaired when delayed. Had McCleskey presented this claim in the first federal habeas proceeding when official records were available, he could have identified the relevant officers and cell assignment sheets. The critical facts for the *Massiah* claim, including the reason for Evans' placement in the cell adjacent to McCleskey's and the precise conversation that each officer had with Evans before he was put there, likely would have been reconstructed with greater precision than now can be achieved. By failing to raise the *Massiah* claim in 1981, McCleskey foreclosed the procedures best suited for disclosure of the facts needed for a reliable determination.

McCleskey nonetheless seeks to hold the State responsible for his omission of the *Massiah* claim in the first petition. His current strategy is to allege that the State engaged in wrongful conduct in withholding the 21-page document. This argument need not detain us long. When all is said and done, the issue is not presented in the case, despite all the emphasis upon it in McCleskey's brief and oral argument. The Atlanta police turned over the 21-page document upon request in 1987. The District Court found no misrepresentation or wrongful conduct by the State in failing to hand over the document earlier, and our discussion of the evidence in the record concerning the existence of the statement, as well as the fact that at least four courts have considered and rejected petitioner's *Brady* claim, belies McCleskey's characterization of the case. And as we have taken care to explain, the document is not critical to McCleskey's notice of a *Massiah* claim anyway. * * * *

We do address whether the Court should nonetheless exercise its equitable discretion to correct a miscarriage of justice. That narrow exception is of no avail to McCleskey. The *Massiah* violation, if it be one, resulted in the admission at trial of truthful inculpatory evidence which did not affect the reliability of the guilt determination. The very statement McCleskey now seeks to embrace confirms his guilt. As the District Court observed: "After having read the Evans statement, the court has concluded that nobody short of William Faulkner could have contrived that statement, and as a consequence finds the testimony of Offie Evans absolutely to be true, and the court states on the record that it entertains absolutely no doubt as to the guilt of Mr. McCleskey." We agree with this conclusion. McCleskey cannot demonstrate that the alleged *Massiah* violation caused the conviction of an innocent person.

The history of the proceedings in this case, and the burden upon the State in defending against allegations made for the first time in federal court some 9 years after the trial, reveal the necessity for the abuse of the writ doctrine. The cause and prejudice standard we adopt today leaves ample room for consideration of constitutional errors in a first federal habeas petition and in a later petition under appropriate circumstances. Petitioner has not satisfied this standard for excusing the omission of the *Massiah* claim from his first petition. The judgment of the Court of Appeals is affirmed.

JUSTICE MARSHALL, with whom JUSTICE BLACKMUN and JUSTICE STEVENS join, dissenting.

Today's decision departs drastically from the norms that inform the proper judicial function. Without even the most casual admission that it is discarding longstanding legal principles, the Court radically redefines the content of the "abuse of the writ" doctrine, substituting the strict-liability "cause and prejudice" standard of *Wainwright v. Sykes*, 433 U.S. 72 (1977), for the good-faith "deliberate abandonment" standard of *Sanders v. United States*, 373 U.S. 1 (1963). * * * * Because I cannot acquiesce in this unjustifiable assault on the Great Writ, I dissent. * * * *

Even if the fusion of cause-and-prejudice into the abuse-of-the-writ doctrine were not foreclosed by the will of Congress, the majority fails to demonstrate that such a rule would be a wise or just exercise of the Court's common-lawmaking discretion. In fact, the majority's abrupt change in law subverts the policies underlying § 2244(b) and unfairly prejudices the petitioner in this case.

The majority premises adoption of the cause-and-prejudice test almost entirely on the importance of "finality." At best, this is an insufficiently developed justification for cause-and-prejudice or any other possible conception of the abuse-of-the-writ doctrine. For the very essence of the Great Writ is our criminal justice system's commitment to suspending "conventional notions of finality of litigation where life or liberty is at stake and infringement of constitutional rights is alleged." *Sanders*, 373 U.S. at 8. To recognize this principle is not to make the straw-man claim that the writ must be accompanied by "a procedural system which permits an endless repetition of inquiry into facts and law in a vain search for ultimate certitude." *Ante* at 1461. Rather, it is only to point out the plain fact that we may not, "under the guise of fashioning a procedural rule, wipe out the practical efficacy of a jurisdiction conferred by Congress on the District Courts." *Brown v. Allen*, 344 U.S. 443, 498–499.

The majority seeks to demonstrate that cause-and-prejudice strikes an acceptable balance between the state's interest in finality and the purposes of habeas corpus by analogizing the abuse-of-the-writ doctrine to the procedural-default doctrine. According to the majority, these two doctrines "implicate nearly identical concerns flowing from the significant costs of federal habeas corpus review." And because this Court has already deemed cause-and-prejudice to be an appropriate standard for assessing procedural defaults, the majority reasons, the same standard should be used for assessing the failure to raise a claim in a previous habeas petition.

This analysis does not withstand scrutiny. This Court's precedents on the procedural-default doctrine identify two purposes served by the cause-and-prejudice test. The first purpose is to promote respect for a State's legitimate procedural rules. See *Sykes*, 433 U.S. at 87–90. As the Court has explained, the willingness of a habeas court to entertain a claim that a state court has deemed to be procedurally barred "undercuts the State's ability to enforce its procedural rules," *Engle v. Isaac*, 456 U.S. at 129, and may cause "state courts themselves to be less stringent in their enforcement," *Sykes, supra*, 433 U.S. at 89. The second purpose of the cause-and-prejudice test is to preserve the connection between federal collateral review and the general "deterrent" function served by the Great Writ. "The threat of habeas serves as a necessary additional incentive for trial and appellate courts throughout the land to conduct their proceedings in a manner consistent with established constitutional standards." *Teague v. Lane*, 489 U.S. 288, 306 (1989). Obviously, this understanding of the disciplining effect of federal habeas corpus presupposes that a criminal defendant has given the state trial and appellate courts a fair opportunity to pass on his constitutional claims. With regard to both of these purposes, the strictness of the cause-and-prejudice test has been justified on the ground that the defendant's procedural default is akin to an independent and adequate state-law ground for the judgment of conviction.

Neither of these concerns is even remotely implicated in the abuse-of-the-writ setting. The abuse-of-the-writ doctrine clearly contemplates a situation in which a petitioner (as in this case) has complied with applicable state-procedural rules and effectively raised his constitutional claim in state proceedings; were it otherwise, the abuse-of-the-writ doctrine would not perform a screening function independent from that performed by the procedural-default doctrine and by the requirement that a habeas petitioner exhaust his state remedies, see 28 U.S.C. §§ 2254(b), (c). Because the abuse-of-the-writ doctrine presupposes that the petitioner has effectively raised his claim in state proceedings, a decision by the habeas court to entertain the claim notwithstanding its omission from an earlier habeas petition will neither breed disrespect for state-procedural rules nor unfairly subject state courts to federal collateral review in the absence of a state-court disposition of a federal claim.

Because the abuse-of-the-writ doctrine addresses the situation in which a federal habeas court must determine whether to hear a claim withheld from *another* federal habeas court, the test for identifying an abuse must strike an appropriate balance between finality and review in that setting. Only when informed by *Sanders* does § 2244(b) strike an efficient balance. A habeas petitioner's own interest in liberty furnishes a powerful incentive to assert in his first petition all claims that the petitioner (or his counsel) believes have a reasonable prospect for success. *Sanders'* bar on the later assertion of claims omitted in bad faith adequately fortifies this natural incentive. At the same time, however, the petitioner faces an effective *disincentive* to asserting any claim that he believes does not have a reasonable prospect for success: the adverse adjudication of such a claim will bar its reassertion under the successive-petition doctrine, see 28 U.S.C. § 2244(b); whereas omission of the claim will not prevent the petitioner from asserting the claim for the first time in a later petition should the discovery of new evidence or the advent of intervening changes in law invest the claim with merit.

The cause-and-prejudice test destroys this balance. By design, the cause-and-prejudice standard creates a near-irrebuttable presumption that omitted claims are permanently barred. This outcome not only conflicts with Congress' intent that a petitioner be free to avail himself of newly discovered evidence or intervening changes in law, but also subverts the statutory disincentive to the assertion of frivolous claims. Rather than face the cause-and-prejudice bar, a petitioner will assert all conceivable claims, whether or not these claims reasonably appear to have merit. The possibility that these claims will be adversely adjudicated and thereafter be barred from relitigation under the successive-petition doctrine will not effectively discourage the petitioner from asserting them, for the petitioner will have virtually no expectation that any withheld claim could be revived should his assessment of its merit later prove mistaken. Far from promoting efficiency, the majority's rule thus invites the very type of "baseless claims," that the majority seeks to avert. * * * *

The majority concludes that McCleskey had no cause to withhold his *Massiah* claim because all of the evidence supporting that claim was available before he filed his first habeas petition. The majority purports to accept the District Court's finding that Offie Evans' 21-page statement was, at that point, being held beyond McCleskey's reach. But the State's failure to produce this document, the majority explains, furnished no excuse for McCleskey's failure to assert his *Massiah* claim "because McCleskey participated in the conversations reported by Evans," and therefore "knew everything in the document that the District Court relied upon to establish the ab initio connection between Evans and the police." The majority also points out that no external force impeded McCleskey's discovery of the testimony of jailer Worthy.

To appreciate the hollowness — and the dangerousness — of this reasoning, it is necessary to recall the District Court's central finding: that the State *did* covertly plant Evans in an adjoining cell for the purpose of eliciting incriminating statements that could be used against McCleskey at trial. Once this finding is credited, it follows that the State affirmatively misled McCleskey and his counsel throughout their unsuccessful pursuit of the *Massiah* claim in state collateral proceedings and their investigation of that claim in preparing for McCleskey's first federal habeas proceeding. McCleskey's counsel deposed or interviewed the assistant district attorney, various jailers, and other government officials responsible for Evans' confinement, all of whom denied any knowledge of an agreement between Evans and the State.

Against this background of deceit, the State's withholding of Evans' 21-page statement assumes critical importance. The majority overstates McCleskey's and his counsel's awareness of the statement's contents. For example, the statement relates that state officials were present when Evans made a phone call at McCleskey's request to McCleskey's girlfriend, a fact that McCleskey and his counsel had no reason to know and that strongly supports the District Court's finding of an *ab initio* relationship between Evans and the State. But in any event, the importance of the statement lay much less in what the statement said than in its simple *existence*. Without the statement, McCleskey's counsel had nothing more than his client's testimony to back up counsel's own suspicion of a possible *Massiah* violation; given the state officials' adamant denials of any arrangement with Evans, and given the state habeas court's rejection of the *Massiah* claim, counsel quite reasonably concluded that raising this claim in McCleskey's first habeas petition would be futile. All this changed once counsel finally obtained the statement, for at that point, there was credible, independent corroboration of counsel's suspicion. This additional evidence not only gave counsel the reasonable expectation of success that had previously been lacking, but also gave him a basis for conducting further investigation into the underlying claim. Indeed, it was by piecing together the circumstances under which the statement had been transcribed that McCleskey's counsel was able to find Worthy, a state official who was finally willing to admit that Evans had been planted in the cell adjoining McCleskey's.

The majority's analysis of this case is dangerous precisely because it treats as irrelevant the effect that the State's disinformation strategy had on counsel's assessment of the reasonableness of pursuing the *Massiah* claim. For the majority, all that matters is that no external obstacle barred McCleskey from finding Worthy. But obviously, counsel's decision even to look for evidence in support of a particular claim has to be informed by what counsel reasonably perceives to be the prospect that the claim may have merit; in this case, by withholding the 21-page statement and by affirmatively misleading counsel as to the State's involvement with Evans, state officials created a climate in which McCleskey's first habeas counsel was perfectly justified in focusing his attentions elsewhere. The sum and substance of the majority's analysis is that McCleskey had no "cause" for failing to assert the *Massiah* claim because he did not try hard enough to pierce the State's veil of deception. Because the majority excludes from its conception of cause any recognition of how state officials can distort a petitioner's reasonable perception of whether pursuit of a particular claim is worthwhile, the majority's conception of "cause" creates an incentive for state officials to engage in this very type of misconduct. * * * *

Note from Natalie:

In *Herrera v. Collins*, 506 U.S. 390 (1993), defendant's conviction and death sentence were affirmed on appeal. In his second federal habeas petition (filed more than 10 years after the conviction), defendant claimed to have "newly-discovered evidence" that his now-dead brother Raul had admitted committing the murders — one affidavit from an attorney who represented Raul and another from Raul's cellmate. The Supreme Court rejected the petition, holding that a claim of "actual innocence" was insufficient to support a habeas petition, because it alleged no violation of the Constitution.

Defendant argued that the 8th Amendment prohibition on cruel and unusual punishment forbids punishing the innocent. But the Court held that once defendant is convicted at a fair trial, he is presumed guilty, not innocent. A prior case, *Jackson v. Virginia*, 443 U.S. 307 (1979), had held that federal habeas is available to review a claim that the evidence at trial was insufficient to support the verdict, but the Court refused to stretch this rule to encompass defendant's situation, where the evidence at his trial was sufficient. A new trial for defendant would not necessarily ensure a more accurate verdict, because "the passage of time only diminishes the reliability of criminal adjudications."

Defendant also argued that punishing the "actually innocent" was a deprivation of *due process*. The Court rejected this too, holding that new trial motions based on newly-discovered evidence traditionally must be filed very soon after a verdict, and that the traditional remedy for *later* "newly" discovered evidence is the executive's power to grant *clemency*.

Justice Blackmun dissented, arguing that the question was not whether a new trial would be more reliable than the first, but whether, in light of the new evidence, the result of the first trial is "sufficiently reliable for the State to carry out a death sentence." He disagreed with the majority's reliance on clemency, which he viewed as a political "act of grace" which should not be considered by a Court that vindicates *rights*.

Question: What if Herrera now had *DNA* evidence that Raul had committed the murders, and DNA evidence was not available at the time of his trial? Would (or should) that have changed the Court's analysis?

WITHROW v. WILLIAMS
United States Supreme Court
507 U.S. 680 (1993)

JUSTICE SOUTER delivered the opinion of the Court.

In *Stone v. Powell*, 428 U.S. 465 (1976), we held that when a State has given a full and fair chance to litigate a Fourth Amendment claim, federal habeas review is not available to a state prisoner alleging that his conviction rests on evidence obtained through an unconstitutional search or seizure. Today we hold that *Stone's* restriction on the exercise of federal habeas jurisdiction does not extend to a state prisoner's claim that his conviction rests on statements obtained in violation of the safeguards mandated by *Miranda v. Arizona*, 384 U.S. 436 (1966).

I

Police officers in Romulus, Michigan learned that respondent, Robert Allen Williams, Jr., might have information about a double murder committed on April 6, 1985. On April 10, two officers called at Williams's house and asked him to the police station for questioning. Williams agreed to go. The officers searched Williams, but did not handcuff him, and they all drove to the station in an unmarked car. One officer, Sergeant David Early, later testified that Williams was not under arrest at this time, although a contemporaneous police report indicates that the officers arrested Williams at his residence.

At the station, the officers questioned Williams about his knowledge of the crime. Although he first denied any involvement, he soon began to implicate himself, and the officers continued their questioning, assuring Williams that their only concern was the identity of the "shooter." After consulting each other, the officers decided not to advise Williams of his rights under *Miranda*. When Williams persisted in denying involvement, Sergeant Early reproved him:

> You know everything that went down. You just don't want to talk about it. What it's gonna amount to is you can talk about it now and give us the truth and we're gonna check it out and see if it fits or else we're simply gonna charge you and lock you up and you can just tell it to a defense attorney and let him try and prove differently.

The reproof apparently worked, for Williams then admitted he had furnished the murder weapon to the killer, who had called Williams after the crime and told him where he had discarded the weapon and other incriminating items. Williams maintained that he had not been present at the crime scene.

Only at this point, some 40 minutes after they began questioning him, did the officers advise Williams of his *Miranda* rights. Williams waived those rights and during subsequent questioning made several more inculpatory statements. Despite his prior denial, Williams admitted that he had driven the murderer to and from the scene of the crime, had witnessed the murders, and had helped the murderer dispose of incriminating evidence. The officers interrogated Williams again on April 11 and April 12, and, on April 12, the State formally charged him with murder.

Before trial, Williams moved to suppress his responses to the interrogations, and the trial court suppressed the statements of April 11 and April 12 as the products of improper delay in arraignment under Michigan law. The court declined to suppress the statements of April 10, however, ruling that the police had given Williams a timely warning of his *Miranda* rights. A bench trial led to Williams's conviction on two counts each of first-degree murder and possession of a firearm during the commission of a felony and resulted in two concurrent life sentences. The Court of Appeals of Michigan affirmed the trial court's ruling on the April 10 statements, and the Supreme Court of Michigan denied leave to appeal. We denied the ensuing petition for writ of *certiorari*.

Williams then began this action pro se by petitioning for a writ of habeas corpus in the District Court, alleging a violation of his *Miranda* rights as the principal ground for relief. The District Court granted relief, finding that the police had placed Williams in custody for *Miranda* purposes when Sergeant Early had threatened to "lock him up," and that the trial court should accordingly have excluded all statements Williams had made between that point and his receipt of the *Miranda* warnings. The court also concluded, though neither Williams nor petitioner had addressed the issue, that Williams's statements after receiving the *Miranda* warnings were involuntary under the Due Process Clause of the Fourteenth Amendment and thus likewise subject to suppression. The court found that the totality of circumstances, including repeated promises of lenient treatment if he told the truth, had overborne Williams's will.

The Court of Appeals affirmed, holding the District Court correct in determining the police had subjected Williams to custodial interrogation before giving him the requisite *Miranda* advice, and in finding the statements made after receiving the *Miranda* warnings involuntary. The Court of Appeals summarily rejected the argument that the rule in *Stone v. Powell*, 428 U.S. 465 (1976), should apply to bar habeas review of Williams's *Miranda* claim. We granted *certiorari* to resolve the significant issue thus presented.

II

We have made it clear that *Stone's* limitation on federal habeas relief was not jurisdictional in nature, but rested on prudential concerns counseling against the application of the Fourth Amendment exclusionary rule on collateral review. We simply concluded in *Stone* that the costs of applying the exclusionary rule on collateral review outweighed any potential advantage to be gained by applying it there.

We recognized that the exclusionary rule, held applicable to the States in *Mapp v. Ohio*, 367 U.S. 643 (1961), "is not a personal constitutional right"; it fails to redress "the injury to the privacy of the victim of the search or seizure" at issue, "for any reparation comes too late." *Stone, supra,* 428 U.S. at 486. The rule serves instead to deter future Fourth Amendment violations, and we reasoned that its application on collateral review would only marginally advance this interest in deterrence. On the other side of the ledger, the costs of applying the exclusionary rule on habeas were comparatively great. We reasoned that doing so would not only exclude reliable evidence and divert attention from the central question of guilt, but would also intrude upon the public interest in "(i) the most effective utilization of limited judicial resources, (ii) the necessity of finality in criminal trials, (iii) the minimization of friction between our federal and state systems of justice, and (iv) the maintenance of the constitutional balance upon which the doctrine of federalism is founded." *Id.* at 491.

Over the years, we have repeatedly declined to extend the rule in *Stone* beyond its original bounds. In *Jackson v. Virginia*, 443 U.S. 307 (1979), for example, we denied a request to apply *Stone* to bar habeas consideration of a Fourteenth Amendment due process claim of insufficient evidence to support a state conviction. We stressed that the issue was "central to the basic question of guilt or innocence," *Jackson,* 443 U.S. at 323, unlike a claim that a state court had received evidence in violation of the Fourth Amendment exclusionary rule, and we found that to review such a claim on habeas imposed no great burdens on the federal courts.

After a like analysis, in *Rose v. Mitchell*, 443 U.S. 545 (1979), we decided against extending *Stone* to foreclose habeas review of an equal protection claim of racial discrimination in selecting a state grand-jury foreman. A charge that state adjudication had violated the direct command of the Fourteenth Amendment implicated the integrity of the judicial process, we reasoned, and failed to raise the "federalism concerns" that had driven the Court in *Stone*. Since federal courts had granted relief to state prisoners upon proof of forbidden discrimination for nearly a century, we concluded, "confirmation that habeas corpus remains an appropriate vehicle by which federal courts are to exercise their Fourteenth Amendment responsibilities" would not likely raise tensions between the state and federal judicial systems. *Ibid.*

In a third instance, in *Kimmelman v. Morrison*, 477 U.S. 365 (1986), we again declined to extend *Stone*, in that case to bar habeas review of certain claims of ineffective assistance of counsel under the Sixth Amendment. We explained that unlike the Fourth Amendment, which confers no "trial right," the Sixth confers a "fundamental right" on criminal defendants, one that "assures the fairness, and thus the legitimacy, of our adversary process." 477 U.S. at 374. We observed that because a violation of the right would often go unremedied except on collateral review, "restricting the litigation of some Sixth Amendment claims to trial and direct review would seriously interfere with an accused's right to effective representation." *Id.* at 378.

In this case, the argument for extending *Stone* again falls short. To understand why, a brief review of the derivation of the *Miranda* safeguards, and the purposes they were designed to serve, is in order.

The Self-Incrimination Clause of the Fifth Amendment guarantees that no person "shall be compelled in any criminal case to be a witness against himself."

U.S. Const., Amdt. 5. In *Bram v. United States*, 168 U.S. 532 (1897), the Court held that the Clause barred the introduction in federal cases of involuntary confessions made in response to custodial interrogation. We did not recognize the Clause's applicability to state cases until 1964, however, see *Malloy v. Hogan*, 378 U.S. 1, and, over the course of 30 years, beginning with the decision in *Brown v. Mississippi*, 297 U.S. 278 (1936), we analyzed the admissibility of confessions in such cases as a question of due process under the Fourteenth Amendment. Under this approach, we examined the totality of circumstances to determine whether a confession had been "made freely, voluntarily and without compulsion or inducement of any sort." *Haynes v. Washington*, 373 U.S. 503, 513. Indeed, we continue to employ the totality-of-circumstances approach when addressing a claim that the introduction of an involuntary confession has violated due process. *E.g., Arizona v. Fulminante*, 499 U.S. ___ (1991).

In *Malloy*, we recognized that the Fourteenth Amendment incorporates the Fifth Amendment privilege against self-incrimination, and thereby opened *Bram's* doctrinal avenue for the analysis of state cases. So it was that two years later we held in *Miranda* that the privilege extended to state custodial interrogations. In *Miranda*, we spoke of the privilege as guaranteeing a person under interrogation "the right 'to remain silent unless he chooses to speak in the unfettered exercise of his own will,'" *Miranda*, 384 U.S. at 460, and held that "without proper safeguards the process of in-custody interrogation contains inherently compelling pressures which work to undermine the individual's will to resist and to compel him to speak where he would not otherwise do so freely." 384 U.S. at 467. To counter these pressures we prescribed, absent "other fully effective means," the now-familiar measures in aid of a defendant's Fifth Amendment privilege:

> He must be warned prior to any questioning that he has the right to remain silent, that anything he says can be used against him in a court of law, that he has the right to the presence of an attorney, and that if he cannot afford an attorney one will be appointed for him prior to any questioning if he so desires. Opportunity to exercise these rights must be afforded to him throughout the interrogation. After such warnings have been given, and such opportunity afforded him, the individual may knowingly and intelligently waive these rights and agree to answer questions or make a statement. [*Id.* at 479.]

Unless the prosecution can demonstrate the warnings and waiver as threshold matters, we held, it may not overcome an objection to the use at trial of statements obtained from the person in any ensuing custodial interrogation.

Petitioner, supported by the United States as *amicus curiae*, argues that *Miranda's* safeguards are not constitutional in character, but merely "prophylactic," and that in consequence habeas review should not extend to a claim that a state conviction rests on statements obtained in the absence of those safeguards. We accept petitioner's premise for purposes of this case, but not her conclusion.

The *Miranda* Court did of course caution that the Constitution requires no "particular solution for the inherent compulsions of the interrogation process," and left it open to a State to meet its burden by adopting "other procedures at least as effective in apprising accused persons" of their rights. The Court indeed acknowledged that, in barring introduction of a statement obtained without the required warnings, *Miranda* might exclude a confession that we would not condemn as "involuntary in traditional terms," and for this reason we have sometimes called the *Miranda* safeguards "prophylactic" in nature. *E.g., Oregon v. Elstad*, 470 U.S. 298, 305 (1985).

As we explained in *Stone*, the *Mapp* rule "is not a personal constitutional right," but serves to deter future constitutional violations; although it mitigates the juridical consequences of invading the defendant's privacy, the exclusion of evidence at trial can do nothing to remedy the completed and wholly extrajudicial Fourth Amendment violation. 428 U.S. at 486. Nor can the *Mapp* rule be thought to enhance the soundness of the criminal process by improving the reliability of evidence introduced at trial. Quite the contrary, as we explained in *Stone*, the evidence excluded under *Mapp* "is typically reliable and often the most probative information bearing on the guilt or innocence of the defendant." 428 U.S. at 490.

Miranda differs from *Mapp* in both respects. "Prophylactic" though it may be, in protecting a defendant's Fifth Amendment privilege against self-incrimination *Miranda* safeguards "a fundamental *trial* right." *United States v. Verdugo-Urquidez*, 494 U.S. 259, 264 (1990) (emphasis added) (*Stone* does not bar habeas review of claim that the personal trial right to effective assistance of counsel has been violated). The privilege embodies "principles of humanity and civil liberty, which had been secured in the mother country only after years of struggle," *Bram*, 168 U.S. at 544, and reflects

> many of our fundamental values and most noble aspirations: our preference for an accusatorial rather than an inquisitorial system of criminal justice; our fear that self-incriminating statements will be elicited by inhumane treatment and abuses; our sense of fair play which dictates "a fair state-individual balance by requiring the government to leave the individual alone until good cause is shown for disturbing him and by requiring the government in its contest with the individual to shoulder the entire load;" our respect for the inviolability of the human personality and of the right of each individual 'to a private enclave where he may lead a private life;' our distrust of self-deprecatory statements; and our realization that the privilege, while sometimes "a shelter to the guilty," is often "a protection to the innocent." [*Murphy v. Waterfront Comm'n of New York Harbor*, 378 U.S. 52, 55 (1964).]

Nor does the Fifth Amendment "trial right" protected by *Miranda* serve some value necessarily divorced from the correct ascertainment of guilt. "A system of criminal law enforcement which comes to depend on the "confession" will, in the long run, be less reliable and more subject to abuses' than a system relying on independent investigation." *Michigan v. Tucker*, 417 U.S. at 448, (1964)). By bracing against "the possibility of unreliable statements in every instance of in-custody interrogation," *Miranda* serves to guard against "the use of unreliable statements at trial." *Johnson v. New Jersey*, 384 U.S. 719, 730 (1966); *cf. Rose v. Mitchell*, 443 U.S. 545 (1979) (*Stone* does not bar habeas review of claim of racial discrimination in selection of grand-jury foreman, as this claim goes to the integrity of the judicial process).

Finally, and most importantly, eliminating review of *Miranda* claims would not significantly benefit the federal courts in their exercise of habeas jurisdiction, or advance the cause of federalism in any substantial way. As one *amicus* concedes, eliminating habeas review of *Miranda* issues would not prevent a state prisoner from simply converting his barred *Miranda* claim into a due process claim that his conviction rested on an involuntary confession. Indeed, although counsel could provide us with no empirical basis for projecting the consequence of adopting petitioner's position, it seems reasonable to suppose that virtually all *Miranda* claims would simply be recast in this way.[5]

If that is so, the federal courts would certainly not have heard the last of *Miranda* on collateral review. Under the due process approach, as we have already seen, courts look to the totality of circumstances to determine whether a confession was voluntary. Those potential circumstances include not only the crucial element of police coercion, the length of the interrogation, its location, its continuity, the defendant's maturity, education, physical condition, and mental health. They also include the failure of police to advise the defendant of his rights to remain silent and to have counsel present during custodial interrogation. We could lock the front door against *Miranda*, but not the back.

We thus fail to see how abdicating *Miranda's* bright-line (or, at least, brighter-line) rules in favor of an exhaustive totality-of-circumstances approach on habeas would do much of anything to lighten the burdens placed on busy federal courts. We likewise fail to see how purporting to eliminate *Miranda* issues from federal habeas would go very far to relieve such tensions as *Miranda* may now raise between the two judicial systems. Relegation of habeas petitioners to straight involuntariness claims would not likely reduce the amount of litigation, and each such claim would in any event present a legal question requiring an "independent federal determination" on habeas. *Miller v. Fenton*, 474 U.S. at 112.

One might argue that tension results between the two judicial systems whenever a federal habeas court overturns a state conviction on finding that the state court let in a voluntary confession obtained by the police without the *Miranda* safeguards. And one would have to concede that this has occurred in the past, and doubtless will occur again. It is not reasonable, however, to expect such occurrences to be frequent enough to amount to a substantial cost of reviewing *Miranda* claims on habeas or to raise federal-state tensions to an appreciable degree. We must remember in this regard that *Miranda* came down some 27 years ago. In that time, law enforcement has grown in constitutional as well as technological sophistication, and there is little reason to believe that the police today are unable, or even generally unwilling, to satisfy *Miranda's* requirements. And if, finally, one should question the need for federal collateral review of requirements that merit such respect, the answer simply is that the respect is sustained in no small part by the existence of such review. "It is the occasional abuse that the federal writ of habeas corpus stands ready to correct." *Jackson*, 443 U.S. at 322. * * * *

[In Part III of its opinion, the Court held that the District Court erred by denying the state a hearing on the due process issue.]

The judgment of the Court of Appeals is affirmed in part and reversed in part, and the case is remanded for further proceedings consistent with this opinion.

---

[5] Justice O'Connor is confident that many such claims would be unjustified, but that is beside the point. Justifiability is not much of a gatekeeper on habeas.

JUSTICE O'CONNOR, with whom THE CHIEF JUSTICE joins, concurring in part and dissenting in part.

Today the Court permits the federal courts to overturn on habeas the conviction of a double-murderer, not on the basis of an inexorable constitutional or statutory command, but because it believes the result desirable from the standpoint of equity and judicial administration. Because the principles that inform our habeas jurisprudence — finality, federalism, and fairness — counsel decisively against the result the Court reaches, I respectfully dissent from this holding.

I

The Court does not sit today in direct review of a state-court judgment of conviction. Rather, respondent seeks relief by collaterally attacking his conviction through the writ of habeas corpus. While petitions for the writ of habeas corpus are now commonplace — over 12,000 were filed in 1990, compared to 127 in 1941 — their current ubiquity ought not detract from the writ's historic importance. "The Great Writ" can be traced through the common law to well before the founding of this Nation; its role as a "prompt and efficacious remedy for whatever society deems to be intolerable restraints" is beyond question. *Fay v. Noia*, 372 U.S. at 401–402.

Nonetheless, we repeatedly have recognized that collateral attacks raise numerous concerns not present on direct review. Most profound is the effect on finality. It goes without saying that, at some point, judicial proceedings must draw to a close and the matter deemed conclusively resolved; no society can afford forever to question the correctness of its every judgment. "The writ," however, "strikes at finality," *McCleskey v. Zant*, 499 U.S. ___ (1991), depriving the criminal law "of much of its deterrent effect," *Teague v. Lane*, 489 U.S. 288 (1989) and sometimes preventing the law's just application altogether. * * * *

II

In *Stone*, the Court explained that the exclusionary rule of *Mapp v. Ohio*, 367 U.S. 643 (1961), was not an inevitable product of the Constitution but instead "a judicially created remedy." By threatening to exclude highly probative and sometimes critical evidence, the exclusionary rule "is thought to encourage those who formulate law enforcement policies, and the officers who implement them, to incorporate Fourth Amendment ideals into their value system." *Stone*, 428 U.S. at 492. The deterrent effect is strong: Any transgression of the Fourth Amendment carries the risk that evidence will be excluded at trial. Nonetheless, this increased sensitivity to Fourth Amendment values carries a high cost. Exclusion not only deprives the jury of probative and sometimes dispositive evidence, but it also "deflects the truthfinding process and often frees the guilty." *Id*. at 490. When that happens, it is not just the executive or the judiciary but all of society that suffers: The executive suffers because the police lose their suspect and the prosecutor the case; the judiciary suffers because its processes are diverted from the central mission of ascertaining the truth; and society suffers because the populace again finds a guilty and potentially dangerous person in its midst, solely because a police officer bungled.

While that cost is considered acceptable when a case is on direct review, the balance shifts decisively once the case is on habeas. There is little marginal benefit to enforcing the exclusionary rule on habeas; the penalty of exclusion comes too late to produce a noticeable deterrent effect. *Id.* at 493.

Moreover, the rule "diverts attention from the ultimate question of guilt," squanders scarce federal judicial resources, intrudes on the interest in finality, creates friction between the state and federal systems of justice, and upsets the "constitutional balance upon which the doctrine of federalism is founded." *Id.* at 490. Because application of the exclusionary rule on habeas "offends important principles of federalism and finality in the criminal law which have long informed the federal courts' exercise of habeas jurisdiction," *Duckworth v. Eagan*, 492 U.S. at 208 (O'Connor, J., concurring), we held in *Stone* that such claims would no longer be cognizable on habeas so long as the State already had provided the defendant with a full and fair opportunity to litigate.

I continue to believe that these same considerations apply to *Miranda* claims with equal if not greater force. Like the suppression of the fruits of an illegal search or seizure, the exclusion of statements obtained in violation of *Miranda* is not constitutionally required. This Court repeatedly has held that *Miranda's* warning requirement is not a dictate of the Fifth Amendment itself, but a prophylactic rule. See, e.g., *McNeil v. Wisconsin*, 501 U.S. ___ (1991). Because *Miranda* "sweeps more broadly than the Fifth Amendment itself," it excludes some confessions even though the Constitution would not. *Oregon v. Elstad*, 470 U.S. 298 (1985). Indeed, "in the individual case, *Miranda's* preventive medicine often provides a remedy even to the defendant who has suffered no identifiable constitutional harm." *Id.* at 307.

Miranda's overbreadth, of course, is not without justification. The exclusion of unwarned statements provides a strong incentive for the police to adopt "procedural safeguards," *Miranda*, 384 U.S. at 444, against the exaction of compelled or involuntary statements. It also promotes institutional respect for constitutional values. But, like the exclusionary rule for illegally seized evidence, *Miranda's* prophylactic rule does so at a substantial cost. Unlike involuntary or compelled statements — which are of dubious reliability and are therefore inadmissible for any purpose — confessions obtained in violation of *Miranda* are not necessarily untrustworthy. In fact, because voluntary statements are "trustworthy" even when obtained without proper warnings, their suppression actually *impairs* the pursuit of truth by concealing probative information from the trier of fact. See *Elstad, supra*, 470 U.S. at 312 (loss of "highly probative evidence of a voluntary confession" is a "high cost for law enforcement").

When the case is on direct review, that damage to the truth-seeking function is deemed an acceptable sacrifice for the deterrence and respect for constitutional values that the *Miranda* rule brings. But once a case is on collateral review, the balance between the costs and benefits shifts; the interests of federalism, finality, and fairness compel *Miranda's* exclusion from habeas. The benefit of enforcing *Miranda* through habeas is marginal at best. To the extent *Miranda* ensures the exclusion of involuntary statements, that task can be performed more accurately by adjudicating the voluntariness question directly. And, to the extent exclusion of voluntary but unwarned confessions serves a deterrent function, "the awarding of habeas relief years after conviction will often strike like lightning, and it is absurd to think that this added possibility will have any appreciable effect on police training or behavior." *Duckworth, supra*, 492 U.S. at 211 (O'Connor, J., concurring).

Despite its meager benefits, the relitigation of *Miranda* claims on habeas imposes substantial costs. Just like the application of the exclusionary rule, application of *Miranda's* prophylactic rule on habeas consumes scarce judicial resources on an issue unrelated to guilt or innocence. No less than the exclusionary rule, it undercuts finality. It creates tension between the state and federal courts. And it upsets the division of responsibilities that underlies our federal system. But most troubling of all, *Miranda's* application on habeas sometimes precludes the just application of law altogether. The order excluding the statement will often be issued "years after trial, when a new trial may be a practical impossibility." *Duckworth*, 492 U.S. at 211 (O'Connor, J., concurring). Whether the Court admits it or not, the grim result of applying *Miranda* on habeas will be, time and time again, "the release of an admittedly guilty individual who may pose a continuing threat to society." *Ibid.*

III

The Court identifies a number of differences that, in its view, distinguish this case from *Stone v. Powell*. I am sympathetic to the Court's concerns, but find them misplaced nonetheless.

The first difference the Court identifies concerns the nature of the right protected. *Miranda*, the Court correctly points out, fosters Fifth Amendment rather than Fourth Amendment values. The Court then offers a defense of the Fifth Amendment, reminding us that it is "a fundamental trial right" that reflects "principles of humanity and civil liberty"; that it was secured "after years of struggle"; and that it does not serve "some value necessarily divorced from the correct ascertainment of guilt." The Court's spirited defense of the Fifth Amendment is, of course, entirely beside the point. The question is not whether *true* Fifth Amendment claims — the extraction and use of *compelled* testimony — should be cognizable on habeas. It is whether violations of *Miranda's* prophylactic rule, which excludes from trial voluntary confessions obtained without the benefit of *Miranda's* now-familiar warnings, should be. The questions are not the same; nor are their answers.

To say that the Fifth Amendment is a "fundamental trial right," is thus both correct and irrelevant. *Miranda's* warning requirement may bear many labels, but "fundamental trial right" is not among them. Long before *Miranda* was decided, it was well established that the Fifth Amendment prohibited the introduction of compelled or involuntary confessions at trial. And long before *Miranda*, the courts enforced that prohibition by asking a simple and direct question: Was "the confession the product of an essentially free and unconstrained choice," or was the defendant's will "overborne"? *Miranda's* innovation was its introduction of the warning requirement: It commanded the police to issue warnings (or establish other procedural safeguards) before obtaining a statement through custodial interrogation. And it backed that prophylactic rule with a similarly prophylactic remedy — the requirement that unwarned custodial statements, even if wholly voluntary, be excluded at trial.

Excluding violations of *Miranda's* prophylactic suppression requirement from habeas would not leave true Fifth Amendment violations unredressed. Prisoners still would be able to seek relief by "invoking a substantive test of voluntariness" or demonstrating prohibited coercion directly. The Court concedes as much. ("Eliminating habeas review of *Miranda* issues would not prevent a state prisoner from simply converting his barred *Miranda* claim into a due process claim that his conviction rested on an involuntary confession").

Excluding *Miranda* claims from habeas, then, denies collateral relief only in those cases in which the prisoner's statement was neither compelled nor involuntary but merely obtained without the benefit of *Miranda's* prophylactic warnings. The availability of a suppression remedy in such cases cannot be labeled a "fundamental trial right," for there is no constitutional right to the suppression of voluntary statements. Quite the opposite: The Fifth Amendment, by its terms, prohibits only *compelled* self-incrimination; it makes no mention of "unwarned" statements. U.S. Const., Amdt. 5 ("No person . . . shall be *compelled* in any criminal case to be a witness against himself" (emphasis added)). On that much, our cases could not be clearer. As a result, the failure to issue warnings does "not abridge the constitutional privilege against compulsory self-incrimination, but departs only from the prophylactic standards later laid down by this Court in *Miranda.*" *Michigan v. Tucker,* 417 U.S. at 446. If the principles of federalism, finality, and fairness ever counsel in favor of withholding relief on habeas, surely they do so where there is no constitutional harm to remedy.

Similarly unpersuasive is the Court's related argument that the Fifth Amendment trial right is not "necessarily divorced" from the interest of reliability. Whatever the Fifth Amendment's relationship to reliability, *Miranda's* prophylactic rule is not merely "divorced" from the quest for truth but at war with it as well. The absence of *Miranda* warnings does not by some mysterious alchemy convert a voluntary and trustworthy statement into an involuntary and unreliable one. To suggest otherwise is both unrealistic and contrary to precedent. As I explained above, we have held over and over again that the exclusion of unwarned but voluntary statements not only fails to advance the cause of accuracy but impedes it by depriving the jury of trustworthy evidence. In fact, we have determined that the damage *Miranda* does to the truth-seeking mission of the criminal trial can become intolerable. We therefore have limited the extent of the suppression remedy, see *Harris v. New York,* 401 U.S. 222, 224–226 (1971) (unwarned but voluntary statement may be used for impeachment), and dispensed with it entirely elsewhere, see *N.Y. v. Quarles, supra* (unwarned statement may be used for any purpose where statement was obtained under exigent circumstances bearing on public safety). Consequently, I agree with the Court that *Miranda's* relationship to accurate verdicts is an important consideration when deciding whether to permit *Miranda* claims on habeas. But it is a consideration that weighs decisively against the Court's decision today.

The consideration the Court identifies as being "most important" of all, is an entirely pragmatic one. Specifically, the Court "projects" that excluding *Miranda* questions from habeas will not significantly promote efficiency or federalism because some *Miranda* issues are relevant to a statement's voluntariness. It is true that barring *Miranda* claims from habeas poses no barrier to the adjudication of voluntariness questions. But that does not make it "reasonable to suppose that virtually all *Miranda* claims will simply be recast" and litigated as voluntariness claims. Involuntariness requires coercive state action, such as trickery, psychological pressure, or mistreatment. A *Miranda* claim, by contrast, requires no evidence of police overreaching whatsoever; it is enough that law enforcement officers commit a technical error. Even the forgetful failure to issue warnings to the most wary, knowledgeable, and seasoned of criminals will do. Given the Court's unqualified trust in the willingness of police officers to satisfy *Miranda's* requirements, its suggestion that their every failure to do so involves coercion seems to me ironic. If the police have truly grown in "constitutional sophistication," then certainly it is reasonable to suppose that most technical errors in the administration of *Miranda's* warnings are just that.

In any event, I see no need to resort to supposition. The published decisions of the lower federal courts show that what the Court assumes to be true demonstrably is not. In case after case, the courts are asked on habeas to decide purely technical *Miranda* questions that contain not even a hint of police overreaching. And in case after case, no voluntariness issue is raised, primarily because none exists. Whether the suspect was in "custody," whether or not there was "interrogation," whether warnings were given or were adequate, whether the defendant's equivocal statement constituted an invocation of rights, whether waiver was knowing and intelligent — this is the stuff that *Miranda* claims are made of. While these questions create litigable issues under *Miranda*, they generally do not indicate the existence of coercion — pressure tactics, deprivations, or exploitations of the defendant's weaknesses — sufficient to establish involuntariness. * * * *

In my view, *Miranda* imposes such grave costs and produces so little benefit on habeas that its continued application is neither tolerable nor justified. Accordingly, I join Part III of the Court's opinion but respectfully dissent from the remainder.

JUSTICE SCALIA, with whom JUSTICE THOMAS joins, concurring in part and dissenting in part.

The issue in this case — whether the extraordinary remedy of federal habeas corpus should routinely be available for claimed violations of *Miranda* rights — involves not jurisdiction to issue the writ, but the equity of doing so. In my view, both the Court and Justice O'Connor disregard the most powerful equitable consideration: that Williams has already had full and fair opportunity to litigate this claim. He had the opportunity to raise it in the Michigan trial court; he did so and lost. He had the opportunity to seek review of the trial court's judgment in the Michigan Court of Appeals; he did so and lost. Finally, he had the opportunity to seek discretionary review of that Court of Appeals judgment in both the Michigan Supreme Court and this Court; he did so and review was denied. The question at this stage is whether, given all that, a federal habeas court should now reopen the issue and adjudicate the *Miranda* claim anew. The answer seems to me obvious: it should not. That would be the course followed by a federal habeas court reviewing a federal conviction; it mocks our federal system to accord state convictions less respect. * * * *

Notes from Natalie:

1. Does the "right" to habeas corpus stem directly from the Constitution, or only from statute? What Congress giveth, can't Congress taketh away? And that is exactly what has been proposed by many members of Congress, over the years. These proposals are described and discussed in Yackle, *The Habeas Hagioscope*, 66 So.Cal.L.Rev. 2331 (1993), where the author states:

> The battle over habeas is driven, in the main, not by relatively sterile concerns for federalism and congested federal dockets, but by an ideologi-

cal resistance to the Warren Court's innovative interpretations of substantive federal rights. The objection in "conservative" circles is not so much that habeas petitions are heard by national tribunals that have better things to do, but that collateral litigation is undertaken at all, particularly in death penalty cases, and, accordingly, that criminal defendants may effectively upset their convictions and sentences. The rhetoric in political debates and judicial opinions often flags the delays associated with habeas practice and multiple federal petitions from the same prisoner. Yet the principal remedy proposed is not procedural reform, but the practical elimination of the federal courts' subject matter jurisdiction. [*Id.* at 2331–2332.]

Put another way, while Congresspeople have no power to overrule Supreme Court rulings declaring the meaning of the Constitution (such as *Mapp, Miranda,* etc.), they *do* have the power to cut off the Court's *ability to give relief* for violations of the Constitution — at least in habeas cases. "We can't change the water, but we can turn off the tap!"

And that is exactly what happened. In 1996, Congress enacted the Antiterrorism and Effective Death Penalty Act of 1996 ("AEDPA"), which added to 28 U.S.C. § 2254 (set out at the beginning of this Chapter) several provisions restricting the authority of federal courts to review state court convictions.

But the Supreme Court has (thus far) been unwilling to interpret these new restrictions as broadly as prosecutors would like.

In *Williams v. Taylor*, 120 S.Ct. 1479 (2000), the Court interpreted one of these new restrictions: § 2254(e)(2). The prosecutor argued that the petitioner could not bring a federal habeas petition if he "failed" *for any reason* to develop the factual basis for the claim in state court. The Court disagreed:

> In its customary and preferred sense, "fail" connotes some omission, fault, or negligence on the part of the person who has failed to do something. See, e.g., Webster's New International Dictionary 910 (2d ed.1939) (defining "fail" as "to be wanting; to fall short; to be or become deficient in any measure or degree," and "failure" as "a falling short," "a deficiency or lack," and an "omission to perform"); Webster's New International Dictionary 814 (3d ed.1993) ("to leave some possible or expected action unperformed or some condition unachieved"). See also Black's Law Dictionary 594 (6th ed.1990) (defining "fail" as "fault, negligence, or refusal"). To say a person has failed in a duty implies he did not take the necessary steps to fulfill it. He is, as a consequence, at fault and bears responsibility for the failure. In this sense, a person is not at fault when his diligent efforts to perform an act are thwarted, for example, by the conduct of another or by happenstance. Fault lies, in those circumstances, either with the person who interfered with the accomplishment of the act or with no one at all. We conclude Congress used the word "failed" in the sense just described. Had Congress intended a no-fault standard, it would have had no difficulty in making its intent plain. It would have had to do no more than use, in lieu of the phrase "has failed to," the phrase "did not."

* * * *

We are not persuaded by the Commonwealth's further argument that anything less than a no-fault understanding of the opening clause is contrary to AEDPA's purpose to further the principles of comity, finality, and federalism. There is no doubt Congress intended AEDPA to advance these doctrines. Federal habeas corpus principles must inform and shape the historic and still vital relation of mutual respect and common purpose existing between the States and the federal courts. In keeping this delicate balance we have been careful to limit the scope of federal intrusion into state criminal adjudications and to safeguard the States' interest in the integrity of their criminal and collateral proceedings.

It is consistent with these principles to give effect to Congress' intent to avoid unneeded evidentiary hearings in federal habeas corpus, while recognizing the statute does not equate prisoners who exercise diligence in pursuing their claims with those who do not. Principles of exhaustion are premised upon recognition by Congress and the Court that state judiciaries have the duty and competence to vindicate rights secured by the Constitution in state criminal proceedings. Diligence will require in the usual case that the prisoner, at a minimum, seek an evidentiary hearing in state court in the manner prescribed by state law. "Comity dictates that when a prisoner alleges that his continued confinement for a state court conviction violates federal law, the state courts should have the first opportunity to review this claim and provide any necessary relief." *O'Sullivan v. Boerckel*, 526 U.S. 838, 844 (1999). For state courts to have their rightful opportunity to adjudicate federal rights, the prisoner must be diligent in developing the record and presenting, if possible, all claims of constitutional error. If the prisoner fails to do so, himself or herself contributing to the absence of a full and fair adjudication in state court, § 2254(e)(2) prohibits an evidentiary hearing to develop the relevant claims in federal court, unless the statute's other stringent requirements are met. Federal courts sitting in habeas are not an alternative forum for trying facts and issues which a prisoner made insufficient effort to pursue in state proceedings. Yet comity is not served by saying a prisoner "has failed to develop the factual basis of a claim" where he was unable to develop his claim in state court despite diligent effort. In that circumstance, an evidentiary hearing is not barred by § 2254(e)(2).

And in a different *Williams v. Taylor*, 120 S.Ct. 1495 (2000), the Court interpreted another new restriction, § 2254(d)(1), which prohibits a federal court from granting habeas unless the state court proceedings "resulted in a decision that was contrary to, or involved an unreasonable application of, clearly established Federal law, as determined by the Supreme Court of the United States." The Court of Appeals held that "a federal court may issue habeas relief only if the state courts have decided the question by interpreting or applying the relevant precedent in a manner that reasonable jurists would all agree is unreasonable," but the Supreme Court disagreed:

In 1867, Congress enacted a statute providing that federal courts "shall have power to grant writs of habeas corpus in all cases where any person may be restrained of his or her liberty in violation of the constitution, or of any treaty or law of the United States. . . ." Over the years, the federal habeas corpus statute has been repeatedly amended, but the scope of that jurisdictional grant remains the same. It is, of course, well settled that the fact that constitutional error occurred in the proceedings that led to a state-court conviction may not alone be sufficient reason for concluding that a prisoner is entitled to the remedy of habeas. See, e.g., *Stone v. Powell*, 428 U.S. 465 (1976). On the other hand, errors that undermine confidence in the fundamental fairness of the state adjudication certainly justify the issuance of the federal writ. See, e.g., *Teague v. Lane*, 489 U.S. 288, 311–314. The deprivation of the right to the effective assistance of counsel recognized in *Strickland* is such an error.

The warden here contends that federal habeas corpus relief is prohibited by the amendment to 28 U.S.C. § 2254, enacted as a part of the Antiterrorism and Effective Death Penalty Act of 1996 (AEDPA). The relevant portion of that amendment provides:

"(d) An application for a writ of habeas corpus on behalf of a person in custody pursuant to the judgment of a State court shall not be granted with respect to any claim that was adjudicated on the merits in State court proceedings unless the adjudication of the claim —"

"(1) resulted in a decision that was contrary to, or involved an unreasonable application of, clearly established Federal law, as determined by the Supreme Court of the United States . . ."

In this case, the Court of Appeals read the amendment as prohibiting federal courts from issuing the writ unless:

(a) the state court decision is in square conflict with Supreme Court precedent that is controlling as to law and fact or (b) if no such controlling decision exists, the state court's resolution of a question of pure law rests upon an objectively unreasonable derivation of legal principles from the relevant Supreme Court precedents, or if its decision rests upon an objectively unreasonable application of established principles to new facts.

Accordingly, it held that a federal court may issue habeas relief only if "the state courts have decided the question by interpreting or applying the relevant precedent in a manner that reasonable jurists would all agree is unreasonable"

We are convinced that that interpretation of the amendment is incorrect. It would impose a test for determining when a legal rule is clearly established that simply cannot be squared with the real practice of decisional law. It would apply a standard for determining the "reasonableness" of state-court decisions that is not contained in the statute itself, and that Congress surely did not intend. And it would wrongly require the federal courts, including this Court, to defer to state judges' interpretations of federal law.

As the Fourth Circuit would have it, a state-court judgment is "unreasonable" in the face of federal law only if all reasonable jurists would agree that the state court was unreasonable. Thus, in this case, for example, even if the Virginia Supreme Court misread our opinion in *Lockhart*, we could not grant relief unless we believed that none of the judges who agreed with the state court's interpretation of that case was a "reasonable jurist." But the statute says nothing about "reasonable judges," presumably because all, or virtually all, such judges occasionally commit error; they make decisions that in retrospect may be characterized as "unreasonable." Indeed, it is most unlikely that Congress would deliberately impose such a requirement of unanimity on federal judges. As Congress is acutely aware, reasonable lawyers and lawgivers regularly disagree with one another. Congress surely did not intend that the views of one such judge who might think that relief is not warranted in a particular case should always have greater weight than the contrary, considered judgment of several other reasonable judges.

The inquiry mandated by the amendment relates to the way in which a federal habeas court exercises its duty to decide constitutional questions; the amendment does not alter the underlying grant of jurisdiction in § 2254(a). When federal judges exercise their federal-question jurisdiction under the "judicial Power" of Article III of the Constitution, it is "emphatically the province and duty" of those judges to "say what the law is." *Marbury v. Madison*, 2 L.Ed. 60, 1 Cranch 137, 177 (1803). At the core of this power is the federal courts' independent responsibility — independent from its coequal branches in the Federal Government, and independent from the separate authority of the several States — to interpret federal law. A construction of AEDPA that would require the federal courts to cede this authority to the courts of the States would be inconsistent with the practice that federal judges have traditionally followed in discharging their duties under Article III of the Constitution. If Congress had intended to require such an important change in the exercise of our jurisdiction, we believe it would have spoken with much greater clarity than is found in the text of AEDPA. * * * *

In sum, the statute directs federal courts to attend to every state-court judgment with utmost care, but it does not require them to defer to the opinion of every reasonable state-court judge on the content of federal law. If, after carefully weighing all the reasons for accepting a state court's judgment, a federal court is convinced that a prisoner's custody — or, as in this case, his sentence of death — violates the Constitution, that independent judgment should prevail. Otherwise the federal "law as determined by the Supreme Court of the United States" might be applied by the federal courts one way in Virginia and another way in California. In light of the well-recognized interest in ensuring that federal courts interpret federal law in a uniform way, we are convinced that Congress did not intend the statute to produce such a result.

2. A prisoner seeking postconviction relief by habeas corpus under 28 U.S.C. § 2254 has no automatic right to appeal a federal district court's denial of his petition. Instead, petitioner must first seek and obtain a "certificate of appealability" from the federal court of appeals. In *Miller-El v. Cockrell*, 123 S.Ct. 1029 (2003), the Court held:

A prisoner seeking a COA need only demonstrate "a substantial showing of the denial of a constitutional right." 28 U.S.C. § 2253(c)(2). A petitioner satisfies this standard by demonstrating that jurists of reason could disagree with the district court's resolution of his constitutional claims or that jurists could conclude the issues presented are adequate to deserve encouragement to proceed further.

Chapter 17

A COMPARATIVE PERSPECTIVE

We've been looking pretty closely at the "trees" of the American criminal justice system. Let's now stand back and look at the "forest" — whether the system as a whole does a good job of finding the truth in an efficient manner, whether other purposes interfere with those goals, and whether furthering those other purposes is worth the price.

A good way to examine a forest is to compare it with other forests.

The O.J. Inquisition: A United States Encounter With Continental Criminal Justice[1]

News Item: Due to pervasive public criticism of the United States "adversarial" criminal justice system, all parties have agreed to try the double murder trial in a neutral European nation, where the case will be handled under the "inquisitorial" legal system. When asked if it would be difficult to adjust to a new system in the short time remaining before trial, one of the attorneys replied, "No problem. There's probably a few minor differences between our systems, but we should be able to pick them up as we go along."

Scene I: A courtroom in Europe. Ms. Lark and Professor Schmrz sit at the prosecution table. Mr. Crane and Professor Grbzyk sit at the defense table. At another table sit the victims' families and their attorney, Ms. Smith. Behind the tables, guarded by bailiffs, stands the Accused, and behind him is a gallery packed with spectators. All face a long, raised bench.

Crane:	I must be nuts, letting you talk me into this. What now? They put my client on the rack and turn the screw 'til he talks?
Grbzyk:	*(laughing)* That went out in the 18th century. You Americans have the wrong impression of the inquisitorial system. It's probably the most widely used legal system in the world today. It was started by the Catholic Church, and after the French Revolution, it was further developed by the French and the Germans. It then spread to the rest of Europe, except for the British Isles. Many African, South American, and Asian countries have also adopted it. It's used much more today than your Anglo-American "adversarial" system. It's —

[1] Adapted from Moskovitz, 28 Vanderbilt Journal of Transnational Law 1121 (1995) (Reprinted with Permission). The article was preceded by an Editor's Note, which states in part: "October 3, 1995 marked the end of the O.J. Simpson double murder trial, which lasted 474 days and was billed 'the trial of the century.' After less than four hours of deliberation, the jury acquitted Mr. Simpson of all charges. The following article is a dramatization of how a case similar to the Simpson trial might be handled by a civil-law European criminal justice system."

Crane: Can the lecture, Professor. Here they come.

Grbzyk: *(whispering)* Straighten your robe.

Everyone stands. Nine people enter the courtroom from a side door. Three of them, wearing black robes, take the three center seats behind the bench. The other six wear red-and-white sashes, and they take the other seats. The man in the middle dons a red beret, then places a large book in front of him and opens it.

Presiding Judge: The People of the State of California versus Mr. Sampson. Are counsel ready?

Lark: Yes, your honor.

Crane: *(bowing)* Ready, your majesty.

Smith: Ready, your honor.

Lark: Excuse me, your honor. I don't know who this person is.

Smith: I'm Sally Smith, attorney for the families of the victims.

Lark: What are you doing here? This is my case, a criminal case, not a civil case. You don't belong here.

Presiding Judge: Ms. Lark, we allow the alleged victim to intervene and appear by counsel in our criminal trials. Who has a greater interest in seeing that justice is done than the victim?

Lark: The State does, your honor. I represent the State, she doesn't. That's how it's done in the United States.

Presiding Judge: But you haven't always done it that way. As I recall, in the early days of England and the United States, a criminal prosecution was usually brought by the victim, who also paid for it. Only recently, with the development of public prosecutors like yourself, has the status and the involvement of the victim withered away.

Lark: Maybe it's coming back. Some states now allow victims to take part in sentencing hearings.

Presiding Judge: In any event, we go further here, at least in trials of serious crimes. If the defendant is convicted, he might even be ordered to pay damages to the victim. You, of course, do represent the State, but the victim may also appear by counsel. Now let's get to work. I will call as the first witness —

Crane: Uh, excuse me, my lord.

Presiding Judge: Yes, Mr. Crane?

Crane: We seem to be forgetting something.

Presiding Judge: Forgetting?

Crane: Aren't we going to *voir dire* the jurors? You know, ask them a few questions to see if they're biased? Bounce a few out on peremptory challenges? That sort of thing. That comes first, doesn't it?

The Presiding Judge stares at Crane, then cracks up laughing. The whole courtroom joins in — except for Crane and Lark.

Presiding Judge: Very good joke, Mr. Crane. We will now call the first witness. Bailiffs, please bring the Accused forward.

Crane: *(sputtering)* The Accused? That — this man is my client! The defendant! You can't make him testify —

Presiding Judge: *(annoyed)* Sit down, Mr. Crane. If you don't understand our procedure, perhaps Professor Grbzyk can enlighten you during a recess. Now, Mr. Sampson, let me ask you —

Lark: Excuse me, judge.

Presiding Judge: Now what? Yes, Ms. Lark?

Lark: I believe it's the prosecution's duty to present the state's case. So if you don't mind, I'll question the witness.

Presiding Judge: *(frowning, slamming down his gavel)* We'll take a recess, so our U.S. friends may better acquaint themselves with continental procedure.

Scene II: A small cafe next to the courthouse. Crane and Grbzyk sit at one table drinking coffee. Lark and Schmrz sit at another table.

Crane: What are these people, animals? They've never heard of due process? No wonder they're always going to war. (Sipping some espresso and making a face.) Bitter, bitter, bitter.

Grbzyk: Sugar? Relax, Mr. Crane. You Americans didn't invent civilization, you know. There's more than one way to run a justice system.

Crane: You call this justice? I can't even *voir dire* my jurors.

Grbzyk: They're not jurors, at least not in the U.S. sense.

Crane: Those six people without the robes. Judges or jurors?

Grbzyk: Jurors, sort of. They're called lay assessors. They're ordinary people, like your jurors, selected at random from the population. The parties have no right to question them or to remove any of them, so long as they meet our minimal qualifications of age, citizenship, and the like. You don't need to, really, because they can't decide the case by themselves anyway.

Crane: What do you mean?

Grbzyk: The tribunal is a "mixed panel" of professional judges — the three people in the robes — and the lay assessors. The panel decides the case by a two-thirds majority.

Crane: Now just a minute. You're not telling me that the judges go into a room with these lay assessors and deliberate with them?

Grbzyk: I'm afraid I am. You seem shocked.

Crane: Of course I'm shocked. What kind of a jury do you have when judges vote with the jurors?

Grbzyk: Well, the jurors — as you insist on calling them — can outvote the judges. There are six jurors and only three judges.

Crane:	Look, Professor, I wasn't born yesterday. Jurors think judges walk on water. When a judge — when *three* judges — tell the jurors what they think, what juror is going to disagree?
Grbzyk:	I concede that it does not occur very often.
Crane:	Why not get rid of the jurors and be done with it? Be up front and let the judges decide the case.
Grbzyk:	This does happen in minor cases. But in major cases, we want some lay involvement. Also, we have the lay people vote before the judges vote, so the lay people will not be influenced by the judges' votes.
Crane:	But they know what the judges think anyway because they heard the judges during the pre-vote discussion.
Grbzyk:	I suppose this is so.
Crane:	Where does the judge instruct these lay assessors on the law? In open court or behind closed doors, in the deliberation room?
Grbzyk:	We have no formal jury instructions, as you do. During deliberations, the judge will explain the law to the assessors. I've seen your U.S. jury instructions. They are usually in the language of statutes or appellate court opinions. They may be legally correct, but they're very difficult for lay people to understand. Your judges are reluctant to depart from them by even a single word, for fear of reversal on appeal. In our system, the judge explains the law to the assessors in simple language. If they have trouble getting it, the judge may discuss it with them informally until they understand. This all happens in the deliberation room.
Crane:	Makes sense, I guess. I've often wondered how much U.S. jurors really understand when the judge reads them those long, legalistic instructions. But in your system, the lawyers have no idea what the judge is telling the jurors. Suppose he makes a mistake? How would I ever know about it?
Grbzyk:	After the tribunal decides the case, one of the judges will write the judgment. It is not a simple "guilty" or "not guilty" verdict, as you have. It will spell out what law the tribunal applied, in detail.
Crane:	But that's written after the tribunal already voted. Maybe the judge told the jurors something different from what he wrote in the judgment.
Grbzyk:	No European judge would do a thing like that, Mr. Crane.
Crane:	You sure seem to trust these guys.
Grbzyk:	I suppose we do. It's good to get an outsider's perspective on one's legal system, Mr. Crane. Perhaps we can learn a lot from each other.

* * * *

Lark:	I can't believe this. I schlepped all the way to Europe, and I can't even question a witness?
Schmrz:	Madame must have patience. Your turn will come.
Lark:	Oh yeah? When? After the verdict? It's my case to try, isn't it?

Schmrz:	Not exactly. Do you understand why our system is called "inquisitorial?"
Lark:	After the Spanish Inquisition?
Schmrz:	No, Madame. We have become a bit more civilized since then. It is inquisitorial because it is based on the tribunal's duty to inquire, to find the truth. In your adversarial system, the parties are responsible for presenting the evidence, pretty much in any way they see fit. The judge merely makes sure that everyone behaves, and the jury sits passively and listens. When the lawyers are done, the jury decides. Neither the jury nor the judge takes any active part in investigating the case, seeking out evidence, or otherwise finding out what happened. This is not so in the inquisitorial system. Here, our judges are responsible for finding the truth themselves.
Lark:	Do they do that in civil cases too?
Schmrz:	No. Our method of litigating civil disputes is different from yours, but it is built on the same basic premise: the state has very little stake in the outcome of civil litigation. In both Europe and the United States, the state provides a proper forum for the resolution of private disputes, but it cares little about who wins a particular case. True, the state establishes substantive rules of law, in order to cause certain results in society, and these rules are enforced partly through private litigation. But in a particular case, the state provides the playing field and the umpire, that's all. For example, if the parties choose to settle in the middle of a case — even on that which might seem unjust to an outsider — the judge will seldom hesitate to terminate the litigation. If the parties are satisfied, the state has no further interest in the matter. This is so in both of our systems. What seems odd to us, however, is that in the United States you treat *criminal* cases pretty much the same way, even though the state clearly has an interest in seeing that the guilty are convicted and the innocent are freed. In Europe, we operate openly on this principle. This is why the state inquires: the state itself cares about the outcome.
Lark:	So that's why the presiding judge does the questioning?
Schmrz:	Yes. When he is done, you and Mr. Crane will have a chance to ask additional questions.
Lark:	If there's anything left to ask about.
Schmrz:	I grant that this is unlikely, if the presiding judge is thorough.
Lark:	This is ridiculous. Why am I even in the courtroom? I might as well read a book or take a nap.
Schmrz:	Our prosecutors have been known to do both, on occasion.
Lark:	Look, Professor, you don't seem to realize what's at stake for me here. This is *my case*. If I lose, I'm back in Compton Muni Court prosecuting parking tickets.
Schmrz:	Lose? I don't understand.

Lark: What's to understand? Lose. You know, like the Super Bowl or the World Series. If you win, I lose.

Schmrz: . Ah, I see. The adversarial system is speaking. But in our system, prosecutors never lose.

Lark: Never lose? So the game is fixed?

Schmrz: No. There is no "game." Prosecutors never lose, but they never win, either. They simply don't think in terms of winning or losing. If the tribunal acquits the defendant, the prosecutor feels no sense of having lost the case. He has done his job, and the tribunal has done its job. His responsibility is to assist the tribunal in finding a just result, not to "win."

Lark: How "un-American."

Schmrz: Quite so, I'm afraid.

Lark: But what about the prosecutor's career? Doesn't he move up the ladder by winning his cases?

Schmrz: Our prosecutor is a civil servant, not a political figure. He advances by faithfully performing his duties. Whether the tribunal convicts or acquits the defendant is of no consequence.

Lark: It's certainly of consequence where I come from. My community fears crime, and they want convictions. If I don't get 'em, I'm out.

Schmrz: You are employed by your community, is that correct?

Lark: Sure. The county board of supervisors pays my salary.

Schmrz: So naturally you must please them. But our prosecutors do not work for local governments. All are employed by our central government in the capital. They are not unduly concerned with the ephemeral reactions of the communities in which they happen to be based. When a prosecutor is promoted, she will probably be transferred to another city anyway.

Lark: That certainly would affect how they see their cases.

Schmrz: Madame, you should stop thinking of "my case" and "their cases." The case belongs to the tribunal, not to the lawyers.

Lark: Very lofty, Professor, but let's get down to practicalities. I question witnesses because I *know* the case, backwards and forwards. I investigated the case and I prepared for trial, so I know what to ask and how to follow up answers with more questions. The judge can't do that, because he comes into court cold. He doesn't know the case.

Schmrz: This judge does.

Lark: How?

Schmrz: Did you notice the large book the presiding judge has been looking at?

Lark: Yes. I thought it was a law book.

Schmrz: Not quite. It is called a dossier. It contains the report of the examining magistrate.

Lark: Who's she?

Schmrz: The examining magistrate is another judge, who investigates the case before trial, after the police have completed their investigation. She interviews all witnesses and writes reports on what they said. She also sees that physical evidence is gathered and any needed scientific tests are performed. She then compiles all of these documents into the dossier, which she gives to the judge who will preside at the trial. This is the French system. Some countries, like Germany, have eliminated the examining magistrate, and the prosecutor prepares the dossier.

Lark: Hold on. You mean to tell me that before the trial even begins, the judges and jurors have read a whole report on the case?

Schmrz: Not all of them. Just the presiding judge and perhaps one other judge, who might be responsible for writing the judgment. The presiding judge needs the dossier in order to perform his job of questioning witnesses.

Lark: But he votes, and he can influence the others during deliberations. In the U.S. of A. we would never tolerate a judge or juror who had read a whole detailed report on the case before the trial even began. I'm no bleeding heart liberal, mind you, but even a slimeball criminal defendant is entitled to a fact-finder who hasn't already made up his mind.

Schmrz: Perhaps we trust our judges more than you trust yours.

Lark: It's not just a matter of trust. It's a matter of the limits of the human mind. While your presiding judge is questioning the witnesses, he is also supposed to be making up his mind on how to vote. How can anyone do both at the same time? Sure, he can throw out easy, softball questions to witnesses. But sometimes the best way to get to the truth is through tough, hardball cross-examination. That's often the best way to deal with a liar. How can a judge do that and still be a neutral fact-finder? I couldn't do it, and I don't think you could either. That's why it's better to have people like me and Crane cross-examine. We can be as tough or tricky as we want, and it doesn't matter, because we don't decide the case.

Schmrz: I see your point. Of course, keep in mind that we do allow the attorneys to question a witness when the presiding judge is done.

Lark: So they do the cross-examining?

Schmrz: Not in the way you describe. The presiding judge usually does such a complete job that there is little left to ask, and the attorneys don't want to offend the judge by implying that he was less than thorough. So at most, they might ask a question or two, usually very politely. Most of them have had little or no experience with U.S.-style cross-examination.

Lark: That must make it pretty easy for someone to lie in your courts — and get away with it.

Schmrz: The presiding judge is a very stern and prestigious figure. One would not lightly lie to him. And if the tribunal believes that the defendant has lied, that might well affect the sentence it imposes on the defendant.

Lark: In the United States, it's probably a little easier for a defendant to concoct a lie that sounds plausible, because he doesn't testify until after he's heard the prosecution case. Here, he can't do that, because he goes first.

Schmrz: He does go first, but he is nevertheless familiar with the prosecution case before he testifies. Before trial, we allow the defendant to see the complete dossier, which contains summaries of the testimony of each witness. However, those summaries might not be as detailed as the in-court testimony of witnesses, still yet to come. So our defendants might be taking a chance by inventing or embellishing stories.

Lark: You let him see the whole dossier?

Schmrz: We do. Both the prosecutor and the defense counsel may examine the dossier before trial. We believe in complete pre-trial discovery. There are no secrets.

Lark: Discovery is much more limited in the United States. We don't want to give the defendant a chance to adapt his story to what the prosecution witnesses are going to say, and we don't want him to intimidate or bribe prosecution witnesses.

Schmrz: But here the defendant has probably already told his story to the examining magistrate, as have the prosecution witnesses. They are not likely to change their stories much at trial, and if they do not appear, their written statements may be considered anyway.

Lark: Even though they're hearsay?

Schmrz: Hearsay? What is that?

Lark: Oh, boy. Toto, we're not in Kansas anymore.

* * * *

Crane: OK, Professor, I'm beginning to get a glimmer of how your system works, though I can't say I like it — yet. But how can they call the Accused as the first witness? Don't you have any privilege against self-incrimination here?

Grbzyk: In a way. After your client answers some general questions about his background, the presiding judge will advise him that he has the right not to answer questions about the crime itself. But defendants rarely assert that right.

Crane: Why not? I've had a lot of clients I'd never put on the stand. Why open them up to cross-examination and have their stories ripped apart?

Grbzyk: Remember, the presiding judge has read the dossier. He knows there is evidence that the defendant committed the crime, and he wants the defendant's response.

Crane: So he's presumed guilty, before the trial even starts?

Grbzyk: No. In former times, a conviction could be based on the dossier alone. Today, however, the tribunal may not convict the defendant unless the evidence produced at the trial firmly convinces the tribunal that the defendant is guilty. But let's be practical. The person who prepared the dossier — the examining magistrate or the prosecutor — is an experienced, unbiased government official. If she has determined that there is sufficient evidence to go forward with the trial, everyone knows there is a good chance the defendant is guilty. In the United States, you like to pretend otherwise, but that's just pretense, isn't it?

Crane: Well, maybe it is. I've always wondered if jurors really follow the judge's instruction to give no weight to the fact that the police have arrested the defendant and the prosecutor has brought the case to trial. I guess it's what you might call a "useful fiction."

Grbzyk: We believe in honesty.

Crane: Hmm. Before you get too cocky, Professor, answer this, if you will. Suppose I tell my client just to clam up when the judge questions him about the crime?

Grbzyk: If the defendant fails to respond, the judge will assume the worst. And the defendant knows it.

Crane: But that's using the defendant's silence against him. We don't allow that, at least not openly.

Grbzyk: We do. Who knows more about the crime than the defendant, and what good is served by his silence? In any event, there's another reason for him to talk.

Crane: Which is?

Grbzyk: In your system, the trial is about guilt, and only about guilt. Sentencing comes later. We don't do it that way. Our trials are about *both* guilt and sentencing. If the tribunal finds the defendant guilty, the judgment will also contain the sentence. So the presiding judge must develop evidence not only about whether the defendant committed the crime, but also about what sentence he deserves if he did it.

Crane: You're kidding! You mean that evidence about his prior record, his whole life — everything *we* consider in *sentencing* — comes in at his *trial*?

Grbzyk: Quite correct. Does that bother you?

Crane: Bother me? No, it *kills* me. How can you give a guy a fair trial on whether he committed *this* crime when you know that he has four priors, went AWOL from the Army, and stole two bits from the church collection box when he was a kid? In the United States, we call this stuff irrelevant and prejudicial and keep it out of the trial.

Grbzyk: I suppose we trust our tribunal more than you trust yours. With our judges deliberating along with the lay assessors, the judges will make sure that the assessors do not draw any improper inferences.

Crane: Yeah, I bet. Anyway, I see your point. At a U.S. sentencing hearing, it is better for the defendant to talk. He's already been found guilty, and if he won't cooperate now, the judge is likely to throw the book at him. If you guys *combine* guilt and sentencing into one trial, I have only one shot at showing the tribunal that the defendant isn't such a bad guy, so I'd better tell him to answer the judge's questions.

Grbzyk: You're learning fast, Mr. Crane.

Crane: I guess there's another reason to have him testify, or maybe a reason not to have him not testify. In the United States, if I allow my client to testify, the D.A. can then introduce his prior felony convictions to show that he's not a very credible witness. The judge will tell the jury not to think he's committed this crime just because he committed the priors, but I don't think most jurors can draw such fine lines. So lots of times I don't put him on the stand just because I don't want the jury to hear about the priors. Over here, the tribunal will hear about the priors anyway, whether he testifies or not. So I might as well put him on.

Grbzyk: Very astute. I hadn't thought of that.

Crane: Still, it doesn't seem fair to put a defendant in a position where he has to hang himself by talking. And if they think he's lying, they can try to nail him for perjury.

Grbzyk: That cannot happen.

Crane: You don't prosecute people for lying under oath?

Grbzyk: We do. But the accused is never put under oath. We want his testimony, but we feel that the threat of perjury would unfairly put too much pressure on him.

Crane: *(shaking his head)* Weird. You people are really weird.

Grbzyk: Perhaps when you see how all the pieces fit together, we will seem less weird.

Crane: What about *before* the trial? Can the police or the examining magistrate question the defendant, get a confession out of him, and then use it at the trial?

Grbzyk: Generally, yes. But whenever a suspect is to be questioned, he must first be advised of his right to silence and his right to counsel.

Crane: Sounds familiar.

Grbzyk: It should. Some countries have explicitly based these requirements on your *Miranda* decision.

Crane: Interesting. I've seen a few U.S. decisions cite European practices as authority for some new idea, but it's pretty rare.

Grbzyk: It should be rare. It's a dangerous thing to do. One shouldn't graft a feature from a different system until one fully comprehends how the entire system supports that feature.

Crane: I'm not sure I get what you're saying.

Grbzyk: You will, as you learn more about our system.

Crane:	So, do your defendants exercise their *Miranda* rights, or do they waive them?
Grbzyk:	Before the police, they often waive them, as do your defendants. But when the examining magistrate questions a defendant, usually she will not allow a waiver of the right to counsel.
Crane:	So once the guy gets a lawyer, the lawyer tells him not to answer the examining magistrate's questions, right?
Grbzyk:	Quite the contrary. The lawyer almost always advises him to answer.
Crane:	Even though his answers might be used against him in the dossier?
Grbzyk:	Yes. Don't forget, if he refuses to answer, he will be faced with the same questions at trial, and — as we discussed earlier — he will pretty much have to answer them then.
Crane:	So he might as well look cooperative from the get-go, to minimize his sentence.
Grbzyk:	Correct. And if he confesses before trial, there is not much point in refusing to confess again at the trial.
Crane:	Each aspect of this thing seems to support the other.
Grbzyk:	Quite so. And there is another reason for him to answer the examining magistrate's questions. The magistrate also has the power to decide whether the defendant is detained or released pending trial.
Crane:	So if he wants to stay out of the pokey, he'd better be nice.
Grbzyk:	You Americans are very practical, Mr. Crane.
Crane:	So are you Europeans. Your whole system seems designed to get a confession as soon as possible, even though you go through the motions of telling the guy he doesn't have to answer.
Grbzyk:	He does have the right not to answer. But we see no point in encouraging him to exercise that right, the way you Americans do. Our goal is to find the truth, and the defendant is in a very good position to help us accomplish that task. What is wrong with asking him to tell us what he knows?
Crane:	We've had some bad experiences with that, going back to the Star Chamber in England and "third degree" interrogations in the United States, with the police beating and threatening people if they won't talk.
Grbzyk:	So have we. Don't forget the Spanish Inquisition, and we did allow torture until the 19th century. But that is all behind us now, and torture and threats are illegal. So long as they are, why shouldn't we simply ask the defendant to tell what happened?
Crane:	It's just not right for the government to intrude into someone's mind, into his private thoughts.
Grbzyk:	But you intrude into private thoughts quite frequently, don't you? Any non-defendant witness may be compelled to testify about his thoughts, so long as they are relevant and no recognized privilege

applies. In this very case, police officers were compelled to testify about what they thought about many things, including probable cause to search and their beliefs about race and interracial marriage.

Crane: True, but a defendant in a criminal case is different. The government has many more resources than the defendant. They should have to prove the case without using him to help them.

Grbzyk: So in the adversary system, you handicap the prosecution in order to make the game fair, even if this detracts from finding the truth?

Crane: Look, the prosecution has plenty of ways to prove the truth. They have investigators, crime labs, the FBI, and the whole government apparatus when they need it. In the usual case, the defense has just one lawyer and, if you're lucky, maybe an investigator or two.

Grbzyk: Yes, but in a given case, all the government's resources might be insufficient. In this case, for example, the prosecution must prove its case by inference, with blood samples, DNA tests, and evidence of motivation and opportunity. But only one person who is still alive saw exactly what happened and knows exactly what his mental state was when (and if) he did it. That's the defendant himself. Why not allow the court to ask him?

Crane: Maybe it comes down to this. We don't think it's right to make people incriminate themselves with their own words.

Grbzyk: Strange. When European parents find cookies missing from the cookie jar and ask their child what happened, they do not expect the child to answer, "It's not right to ask me to incriminate myself." Are U.S. parents different?

Crane: Of course not, but criminal defendants aren't kids. A kid who steals cookies might be sent to his room for an hour, but a criminal defendant will be sent to a very small cell for a very long time, and maybe to the gas chamber. The parents are trying to help the kid learn how to behave. The government is *not* trying to help the defendant in any way, shape, or form. It's not the same.

Grbzyk: You seem to dislike our reliance on confessions, Mr. Crane. But U.S. attorneys advise most of their clients to confess, don't they?

Crane: We do?

Grbzyk: Yes. Isn't that what you do during your plea bargaining? You advise your client to plead guilty, in order to obtain the benefits of the bargain. Isn't that pretty much a confession?

Crane: I hadn't thought of it like that.

Grbzyk: So perhaps your system relies on confessions just as much as ours does.

Crane: Interesting. Even though our systems look really different on the surface, maybe there are similarities, once you look a little deeper.

Grbzyk: Possibly. But it is risky to assume that "we are all the same, at bottom." There might in fact be some real differences. And now we must return to court.

         They rise and begin walking, as do Lark and Schmrz.

Lark: Is the inquisitorial system the same throughout Europe, Professor?

Schmrz: Yes and no. There are fundamental features that do not vary much. Judges, not the parties, are responsible for developing the evidence. The judge receives a dossier before the trial begins. There are other common features I will explain when we have more time. There are variations, however. In smaller cases, what you call misdemeanors, the tribunal might consist of only one judge and two lay assessors. Some countries use tribunals where judges outnumber lay assessors. Germany, for example, uses three judges and two lay assessors in cases of serious crime. And some countries use no lay assessors at all except in major cases. The procedure you will see in this case is somewhat typical, but other countries might differ a bit. Italy has a sort of hybrid system.

Lark: Our adversary system also varies somewhat from state to state. I guess it's the same here.

Schmrz: Exactly. A very good analogy.

Scene III: The Courtroom

Presiding Judge: Thank you for your testimony, Mr. Sampson. We appreciate your candor. A truly amazing story. Oh, excuse me. Does counsel have any further questions for the accused?

Lark: I guess not, your honor. You seem to have asked everything I was going to ask.

Crane: Your astute questioning would put most U.S. lawyers to shame. No questions, your grace.

Presiding Judge: Why thank you, Mr. Crane. How very kind.

                                   * * * *

Presiding Judge: Detective Farmer, please tell us what happened when you went to the home of the accused.

Farmer: I went there to tell him his ex-wife had been killed. But his gate was closed, and no one answered the intercom. So I climbed over the gate. I found this glove on the driveway. (He displays a glove.) It matches a glove we found at the murder scene.

Crane: Objection, your honor. That glove was obtained in violation of the Fourth Amendment.

Presiding Judge: The what, Mr. Crane?

Crane: Sorry, Judge. Wrong country. We contend that Detective Farmer conducted an illegal search by hopping the gate without a warrant.

Presiding Judge: So?

Crane: So? So the glove can't be used in evidence.

Presiding Judge: Why not? It is relevant evidence, is it not?

Crane: That doesn't matter. If it was obtained by an illegal search, it goes out. Everyone knows that.

Presiding Judge: Not everyone in Europe knows that, Mr. Crane. We assume that the tribunal should consider all relevant evidence. We do not employ the exclusionary rule, as you call it in the United States, except in extreme cases.

Crane: Then how do you make your police behave?

Presiding Judge: All of our police work for the Ministry of Justice, which is part of our central government. When the Minister issues an order, every policeman in the country must obey it, or suffer demotion or termination of employment. In the United States, this cannot happen. You have many hundreds of independent cities, counties, and states, each running its own police department. The only institution you have for setting minimum standards of behavior for all policemen is your Supreme Court. And the only tool your Supreme Court has for enforcing those standards is to order that illegally-obtained evidence be excluded.

Crane: True, your honor, but even here in Europe, with a more transient population and an increase in crime, your cops will tend to feel the pressure to harass certain people. And the cops' bosses will tend to look the other way. That's why courts need to keep out illegally-seized evidence in order to deter the police from doing that kind of stuff.

Presiding Judge: The circumstances you describe have not afflicted Europe as much as the United States.

Crane: Times change, Judge.

Presiding Judge: You're quite right, Mr. Crane. Times do change. Some European countries have begun to experience more police abuses, and some have begun to apply an exclusionary rule to evidence obtained by certain acts, such as illegal wiretapping. As yet, none has gone so far as the United States. In our tradition, the goal of a criminal trial is to find the truth, not to serve other ends. But who knows what the future will hold?

* * * *

Presiding Judge: Detective Farmer, what did Mr. Crawford tell you about the activities of the accused that night?

Crane: Objection, your honor. That calls for hearsay.

Presiding Judge: Hearsay, counsel? We do not recognize such an objection.

Crane: What? I thought the point of an inquisitorial trial is to find the truth. In the United States, the key to making sure that witnesses tell the truth is cross-examination. Detective Farmer is here in court, so I can cross-examine him as to what he says he heard from Mr. Crawford. But Crawford isn't here, so if he was mistaken or lying about what he told the detective, I can't bring that out by cross-examining him. That's why we exclude hearsay, your honor, and you should too.

Presiding Judge:	You give good reasons for according less weight to hearsay, Mr. Crane, but why exclude it entirely? Isn't it worth something? It might help us to see the entire picture, and what's the harm in letting Mr. Farmer tell us what he heard?
Crane:	Jurors aren't well-trained and experienced enough to make the fine distinctions that you are making. They might not see the difference between hearsay and what the detective saw himself. They might give too much weight to the hearsay.
Presiding Judge:	But I will be there to help them make these distinctions. Don't forget: in our system, the judges and the lay assessors deliberate together.
Crane:	So you have no rules of evidence? Everything comes in?
Presiding Judge:	Not everything. Evidence must still be relevant to the case, and we do recognize certain privileges, as you do. A doctor may not testify as to what his patient told him, nor may a lawyer tell what his client told him. We want to encourage patients and clients to speak freely to professionals. But your stricter rules of evidence are built on the premise that untrained lay people, your jurors, might easily become confused or distracted if you did not limit what they could hear. We have no such problem, for we do not treat our lay assessors as a separate body.
Crane:	I think I'm starting to catch on to something. I can't just compare a feature of our system with a similar feature of your system. Each part is affected by other parts. I really have to consider the system as a whole.
Presiding Judge:	Quite so, Mr. Crane. People often look at an isolated aspect of a system, find it attractive, and assume that it may be transferred intact to another system. This is a mistake. Both the adversarial and the inquisitorial systems are integrated systems. Each piece is affected and supported by every other piece. Transfer a piece without its support system, and it will probably fail or distort some other features that you didn't intend to affect.

* * * *

Presiding Judge:	Ms. Bruin, did you ever see the Accused strike his ex-wife?
Crane:	Objection, your honor. Evidence of prior crimes or bad acts should be inadmissible to show that the defendant has a bad character.
Lark:	But it is admissible to show that he had a motive to kill, or a pattern of behavior that is consistent with the method of killing. That's what this evidence shows, your honor.
Presiding Judge:	An interesting dispute. I would expect you to make these arguments at the end of the trial, when you try to persuade the tribunal how much weight we should give to any evidence that he struck her. But why are you arguing this now?
Crane:	If I'm right, then the evidence is inadmissible. You and your fellow judges and jurors shouldn't even be hearing it. It's too prejudicial. Once you hear it, you might not be able to put it out of your minds.

Presiding Judge: Mr. Crane, in U.S. bench trials, your judges often hear evidence, rule it inadmissible, and then go on to decide the case. You trust *them* to disregard such evidence. Why don't you trust *me*?

Crane: Of course I trust *you*, your honor, but I'm not so sure about these lay jurors. They don't have your training and experience. They might convict just because this evidence shows that the defendant is a bad guy, not because he committed the killings.

Presiding Judge: Recall the response I made to your hearsay objection. I will be in the deliberation room to advise the lay assessors how to perform their jobs, and to prevent them from acting improperly. Your U.S. jurors are not so well monitored as ours. Objection overruled.

* * * *

Presiding Judge: Doctor, please tell us the results of your DNA testing on the hair samples.

Crane: Objection, your honor. We haven't heard any convincing evidence that DNA testing is scientifically valid.

Presiding Judge: Such evidence would be helpful, to be sure, but I am not aware of any statute that prevents us from hearing the doctor's testimony.

Crane: There's no statute, your honor, but I've got a case. In *People v. Glump*, the court held that a defendant was denied a fair trial when a technician testified about a breathalyzer test without evidence that the device they used was scientifically valid.

Presiding Judge: So?

Crane: So that case is precedent for my position, your honor. *Glump* seems to stand for the larger principle that —

Presiding Judge: Counsel, I do not care about *Glump*. We do not treat precedent as you do in the United States. In your common-law system, the law evolves through the application of the law to specific facts, so your published decisions are very important in determining what the law is. But in our system, the law is fixed by the Legislature, and it is changed by the Legislature, not by the courts. Evolution depends on changing values, and we leave the examination of values to our legislative bodies. So we have little need for case precedent.

Crane: All right, judge, here's my trump card: *Glump* was decided by the U.S. Supreme Court. Now will you pay a little more attention to it?

Presiding Judge: Not much, at least in the way you want me to use it. If I am unsure as to the meaning of certain terms used in a statute, I might find guidance in a reported decision, especially from such a prestigious body as the Supreme Court. But the facts of the case — breathalyzers, DNA, whatever — mean little or nothing to me. If you can show me something in this *Glump* decision that explains the meaning of a statute that applies to our case, I'll be happy to look at it, Mr. Crane.

Crane: Sorry, your honor, *Glump* doesn't do that.

Scene IV: On the Courthouse steps

Lark: I needed this break. My head is still spinning.

Schmrz: The adjustment must be difficult for you.

Lark: I guess I can handle it. If I can handle Crane, I can do any . . . Speak of the devil.

Crane and Grbzyk approach.

Crane: How you doin', Ms. D.A.?

Lark: Not bad, Counselor. Just ruminating over the peculiarities of this inquisitorial system. Do you understand it?

Crane: Perfectly. No problem at all. I'm a quick study.

Lark: Yeah, sure.

Crane: Now that you mention it, I might be a little shaky on a couple of nuances. I have to admit I'm having trouble predicting how this case is going to come out. It's hard enough to make predictions in our own courts. Here, with all these foreigners — well, it worries me.

Lark: I was thinking the same thing.

Crane: I don't want my client convicted of two first degree murders.

Lark: And I don't want to go back to Los Angeles with nothing but an acquittal to show for it.

They eye each other.

   Crane and Lark: *(together)* Let's deal!

They huddle.

Lark: Plead him guilty to just one first degree charge, and I'll drop the second charge.

Crane: Are you kidding? He'd still get life. One charge of involuntary manslaughter. That's my absolute top offer.

Lark: Very funny. How about —

Schmrz: Excuse me. What are you two doing?

Crane: We're plea bargaining.

Schmrz: Plea bargaining?

Lark: Yes. We do a little horse-trading, and maybe we can come to an agreement. I drop or reduce some charges, and perhaps agree to recommend a certain sentence. In return, he agrees to plead guilty.

Crane: If, of course, my client agrees.

Schmrz: In the United States, you bargain over justice like farmers bargain over horses? You consider this dignified?

Crane: Is it less dignified than pushing a guy to confess, Professor?

Grbzyk: At least our practice leads to the truth and a just result. Plea bargaining does just the opposite. According to the evidence we heard, your client is either guilty of two murders or guilty of no crime at all. How can you even consider a single manslaughter charge?

Lark: But that's what bargaining is all about. Each side gives up something. I want two murders, and he wants no crime at all. So we cut a deal.

Crane: And there's something you're overlooking. As I understand it, your sentences are pretty reasonable compared to ours. You mostly use fines, and when you do incarcerate people, it's usually for short terms. In the United States, our potential sentences are extremely high, and sometimes the legislature fixes the punishment and gives the judge no discretion to lower it for a particular defendant who doesn't deserve that much. So plea bargaining is our way of reaching a just result.

Lark: Why are your sentences so low? Don't you want to stop crime?

Schmrz: Of course we do. But we do it by curing the offender of his deviant ways and reintegrating him into society as soon as possible. The state assumes a parental role with the offender. By contrast, your system seems to be adversarial in more ways than one. Not only is the prosecutor the adversary of the defendant, so is the state itself. We prefer to see offenders as potentially decent citizens who have temporarily gone astray.

Lark: We used to see them that way, but at some point we gave up. These days, heavy criminals are treated as permanent outcasts. We don't see "reintegration" as a realistic possibility, so we pretty much lock 'em up and throw away the key.

Grbzyk: Do you think this is an effective way to reduce crime?

Lark: Sure. If they're in jail, they can't commit crimes — at least not on the law-abiding community.

Grbzyk: But they will eventually get out. When they are released, do their punishments make them less likely to commit more crimes?

Crane: No way. They'll be *more* likely to commit new crimes. We don't spend much effort trying to teach prisoners to adjust to society and earn their way honestly, so they just learn more about being criminals. And sentences being as long as they are, often these guys are pretty angry when they get out. We treat them as outcasts, so that's what they become.

Grbzyk: It seems odd. You punish your defendants more severely than we do, in order to reduce crime, and yet your crime rates are much higher than ours. What conclusions may we draw from this?

Crane: It's pretty obvious, isn't it? Harsh punishments don't work.

Lark: That's ridiculous. You could just as logically conclude that because of our high crime rates, we *need* harsher punishments to prevent them from going even higher.

Schmrz: One cannot infer causation just from correlation. High crime rates and high punishments often go together, but we cannot be sure whether either one has any causal impact on the other.

Grbzyk: Mr. Crane, earlier you seemed troubled by our quest for confessions. But a confession is an important step on the road to rehabilitation. Until the offender admits he did wrong, how can he change his ways? A good confession cleanses the soul.

Crane: So because we don't plan to do much to rehabilitate him, it doesn't matter much whether he confesses?

Lark: That's a bit of an overstatement. When a judge has discretion in sentencing, he will tend to go easier on a defendant who admits his crime. And the same is true of parole boards. So we do get a lot of confessions, at least after trial.

Grbzyk: Here in Europe, of course, the trial is about both guilt and sentencing, so he can't very well hold off confessing 'til after the trial. So it is important that he confess at trial.

Schmrz: I'd like to return to this plea bargaining for a moment. Once the lawyers arrive at a bargain, is that final? Does the judge have no say in whether the bargain does justice to the state and to the victim?

Lark: Well, the judge can reject the deal. But he's usually happy to accept it. It saves the court the expense and trouble of a trial.

Schmrz: But by reducing the charges you, the prosecutor, have effectively reduced the sentence. Is this proper? Are you trained in the sociological and psychological aspects of sentencing?

Lark: Not really, but neither are our judges. My guess is probably as good as theirs. And if they think I'm really off the mark, they can reject the deal.

Schmrz: In Europe, the prosecutor may recommend a certain sentence, but she does not make the final determination, even partially. That is for the court, not the prosecutor.

Grbzyk: This plea bargaining is legal in your country?

Lark: Legal? It's essential! In most places, less than twenty percent of our cases go to trial. The rest are plea bargained. If they weren't, we'd be up to our eyeballs in trials. We'd probably need five times more prosecutors, judges, jurors, courtrooms, bailiffs, and all the rest. Since every defendant has the right to a speedy trial, I'd have to dismiss a lot of cases if I couldn't plea bargain.

Grbzyk: I don't understand. If people in the United States really believe that the adversary trial is the best way to achieve justice, shouldn't they be more than willing to pay whatever it takes to try *every* case?

Lark: Tough question. I guess they're not *that* committed to the adversary trial. They may like the general idea of it, but when it comes to paying for it, they'd rather pay for more cops or more prisons, where they can *see* some effects on crime.

Schmrz: U.S. citizens are such a peculiar lot. Because they like the general idea of the adversary trial, they have made it so elaborate that they can afford to give it to only one out of every five defendants! Strange, very strange. Wouldn't it be better to make the trial less complex, so that more defendants could have a trial? That might make plea bargaining unnecessary.

Lark: I never quite looked at it that way. In any event, the way things are right now, we can't live without plea bargaining.

Schmrz: And we can't live with it. Here it is illegal.

Crane: Illegal? Why? If the parties agree to settle their case, why should that bother the court?

Schmrz: Because the case belongs to the court, not to the parties. The tribunal may not convict or sentence the defendant unless it first hears the evidence, and if the evidence shows that the defendant committed a certain crime, the tribunal may not reduce the crime just because the prosecutor agrees to it.

Lark: So every case goes to trial?

Schmrz: Every case, Madame. At least every major case.

Lark: But not if the defendant pleads guilty.

Schmrz: There is no such thing as a guilty plea in our system. That would be permitting the parties rather than the court to determine the truth, which is not permissible. Every case goes to trial. At the trial, the defendant might well admit that the charges are true, and many do so. But the tribunal must nevertheless hear evidence, in order to determine the sentence.

Lark: That must put a terrible burden on your courts. Trials can take weeks, even months in a murder case. It can take weeks just to pick a jury.

Grbzyk: You forget. Our "jurors" are picked without the lengthy *voir dire* and peremptory challenges that take so much time in your courts. Most of our trials do not take very long. Because the presiding judge questions the witnesses, we do not take up much time with lawyers' cross-examination and the like. We do not allow many objections to evidence, which may save us more time. We have no need for the lengthy pre-trial hearings on the admissibility of evidence that you have. And the defendant often confesses at trial, because he confessed earlier. Even if he didn't, the dossier usually contains rather strong evidence against him, and his denials, if seen as false, would affect his sentence, so often he confesses for that reason alone. Because he confesses, very little additional testimony is needed. Most of our trials are really about the sentence, not about guilt.

Crane: So it ends up looking somewhat like one of our sentencing hearings, which we must have whether or not there is a plea bargain.

Grbzyk: Yes, I suppose it does. However, I admit that we have been seeking ways to ease the burden on our system. As our crime rates rise, the volume of cases also rises, and some European countries have adopted devices that resemble your plea bargaining. But in most countries, such things are allowed only for misdemeanors, never for major felonies, such as the present case.

Lark: If your crime rates are rising, you might have to start dealing with organized crime, like we do. Plea bargaining really helps us with that. We bust the little guys, and give them plea bargains to get them to "cooperate" and help us get the big guys. Without plea bargains, we'd have nothing to offer them.

Grbzyk: I see. So U.S. prosecutors work closely with the police?

Lark: Absolutely. Our job is to help the cops fight crime. That's what the public expects of us.

Grbzyk: This is much less so in Europe. Our prosecutors see themselves as more closely allied with the judiciary than with the police. Some countries even allow prosecutors to become judges.

Crane: That must make your judges pro-prosecution.

Grbzyk: The reverse would be more accurate: our prosecutors tend to be "pro-judge," in the sense that they are out to secure justice, not to get convictions. For example, every prosecutor has a duty to present to the court all evidence that *favors* the defendant, and they readily do so.

Lark: Shocking.

Grbzyk: I'm speaking generally, of course. Individual prosecutors vary, and so do circumstances. Italy has had a serious problem with organized crime, and prosecutors there do work closely with the police and aggressively seek to convict Mafia leaders.

Crane: If your prosecutors tend to think like judges, why not give them the power to plea bargain? You said you trust your judges.

Schmrz: We trust our officials, so long as they do not have much discretion. We fear that discretion may be abused, as has occurred during periods of dictatorship. Perhaps a prosecutor would plea bargain because of political pressure from friends of the accused. We must protect ourselves from such a possibility, so the prosecutor is obliged to bring to trial every charge supported by the evidence and the law, at least in major cases. She has no discretion.

Crane: But you give your *judges* a lot of discretion.

Schmrz: No, we really don't. Under your common-law system, the law is always changing or "evolving," as you might put it. So your judges must have discretion to change the law slightly to adapt it to new situations, as society changes. This is not so in our "civil-law" system. Here, the law is fixed by the legislature, and the judge has no discretion to change it.

Lark: Look, we have a lot of statutes too, and our judges aren't supposed to change them. But they can *interpret* them, and when they do, they have plenty of discretion to plug in whatever policies they happen to like.

Schmrz:	I suppose our judges do the same on occasion.
Grbzyk:	But we pretend they don't! We prefer to imagine our judges as educated clerks, simply looking up the rules in the codes and telling us what they are. In truth, however, many of our statutes are quite vague, and the judge has some discretion in deciding what they mean. It is somewhat of a paradox.
Crane:	Or maybe a "useful fiction," Professor?
Grbzyk:	Quite useful, Mr. Crane.
Lark:	Anyway, we can't plea bargain, so it's back to the salt mines.

Scene V: At the cafe

The two lawyers and their consultants sit at one table, drinking cognac.

Lark:	Usually when I finish a trial, I'm exhausted. This time, I didn't even work up a sweat.
Crane:	That's because you didn't do anything. Neither did I. Just about every time we stood up, Judge Big Shot told us to sit down and watch *him* do everything. Who needs lawyers in this crazy system? What's there for us to *do*?
Lark:	We help decorate the courtroom. That's why they give us these snazzy black robes. We're not lawyers, we're fashion statements.
Grbzyk:	Ah, you feel that you are not as important as you are in the United States. I'm sorry. But you still have significant roles here. Defense counsel may summon witnesses not called by the tribunal, though this rarely occurs. And both counsel are expected to present final arguments to the tribunal, reviewing the evidence and the law, and arguing for a certain verdict and sentence. Both of you did a fine job, by the way, as did the victims' attorney.
Lark:	And now we wait for the verdict. I *hate* this part. It drives me batty.
Crane:	What will the verdict look like? Will it be short, like "not guilty" or "guilty, life imprisonment"?
Schmrz:	No, the tribunal's judgment will be quite long. It will set out the facts of the case, in detail, and the law that applies to the case, and explain why the tribunal came to its conclusion, both about guilt and about the sentence. It will discuss the testimony of each witness.
Lark:	Who writes it?
Schmrz:	Usually the presiding judge will assign this task to one of the other judges. It is never written by a lay assessor.
Lark:	Most U.S. courts require that the verdict be unanimous. Is that so here?
Schmrz:	No. A majority vote is sufficient in some countries. We require a two-thirds vote.
Crane:	Suppose one of the judges disagrees with the judge who writes the decision. Will he write a dissenting opinion?

Schmrz:	No. That would be unthinkable. It would tend to undermine the court's authority. The public must believe that every court decision is unanimous.
Crane:	Even if it wasn't?
Schmrz:	Even if it wasn't.
Crane:	So much for honesty, Professor. What are you afraid of? Do you think people won't obey the decision or respect your courts if they know someone disagreed with it? Are your institutions so fragile that they can't stand a little dissent?
Schmrz:	I admit, it is troubling.
Lark:	It should be. In the United States, some states allow less-than-unanimous votes by juries in some cases, and such votes must be announced in open court. In our appellate courts, judges often write dissents. We've had some very important Supreme Court cases decided on five to four votes, and people obey them. Dissent doesn't necessarily lead to anarchy.
Schmrz:	At the present time, even our highest courts never reveal that a judge dissented. I suppose a dissent implies either that the majority was incompetent, or that reasonable judges have the discretion to interpret the law in different ways. We do not want either message sent to the public.
Crane:	Look, this is all very interesting, but I'm having trouble concentrating, waiting for the verdict. I hate this part too. If I lose, it's all over.
Grbzyk:	Not quite, Mr. Crane. You still have your right of appeal.
Crane:	What's to appeal? The presiding judge seemed to know what he was doing. I don't think he made any mistakes. With virtually no rules of evidence, what mistakes are there to make, anyway? An appellate court would throw me out: no mistakes, no reversal.
Grbzyk:	You might argue that the judgment is not supported by the law or the evidence.
Crane:	But then I run up against presumptions, don't I? In the United States, the appellate court looks at the reporter's transcript of the trial and presumes that the jury resolved every credibility battle in favor of the judgment, so if the cop said one thing and my client said another, I'm out of luck. And the appellate court also presumes that the jury drew any reasonable inferences that support their verdict.
Grbzyk:	So even if the jury in fact did not do these things, the appellate court nevertheless presumes that they did?
Crane:	Exactly. I guess that's all our appellate courts can do, because the jury never explains their verdict, they just say "guilty." So the appellate court never knows how the jury really reasoned their way to the verdict.
Grbzyk:	But this is not so in our system. The judgment must fully explain the tribunal's reasoning, including why it believed one witness rather than another. So the appellate court sees what the tribunal actually

thought, not what it might have thought. And if the appellate court is not persuaded by such reasoning, it might well reverse the judgment.

Crane: You talk about the tribunal's reasoning. There are nine people on this tribunal, but the judgment is written by just one of them. Is it likely that nine people would have exactly the same reasoning, especially when three of them are professional judges and the others aren't?

Grbzyk: Probably not. Another "useful fiction," perhaps.

Crane: Do the appellate judges read the transcripts of the trial to see if they support the judgment?

Grbzyk: I'm afraid there are no transcripts, Mr. Crane. We have no court reporters at our trials.

Crane: But how do the appellate judges know if the judgment correctly summarizes the testimony? If I'm arguing a case on appeal, how can I show that the facts stated in the judgment are inaccurate?

Grbzyk: Our trial judges receive many hours of training in writing judgments, and I suppose we trust them to summarize the testimony honestly.

Crane: Amazing. Well, I hope this tribunal acquits my client, so I don't have to deal with one of your appeals.

Schmrz: Sorry, Mr. Crane, but an acquittal is no guarantee that you won't face an appeal. In our system, the prosecutor may appeal too. This is important to us, as it helps to ensure that the trial court follows the law. We strive for consistency in all of our courts. And if the appellate court reverses, your client may be tried again.

Lark: Really? In the United States, I think one or two states allow prosecutors to appeal, but only to get an advisory opinion on some important issue. And if the prosecutor wins, it doesn't affect the defendant. He can't be retried. That would violate his right against double jeopardy.

Schmrz: Here he may be retried. We do have concepts similar to your double jeopardy, but they have no application to an ongoing case. So the prosecution may appeal, and if the appellate court reverses, the defendant may be retried.

Crane: The way we see it, once a jury acquits him, that's it. A jury's verdict is sacred.

Schmrz: Sacred when it acquits, but not when it convicts? Why should you allow the defendant to appeal, but not the prosecution? How does that make sense?

Crane: We don't allow a conviction to stand if it doesn't square with the law. But if the jury acquits because the jury doesn't agree with the law, the verdict stands. The jury "nullifies" the law, just for that case. It doesn't happen often, but we view it as an outlet for public disagreement with a law that's not too popular, like laws against smoking a small amount of marijuana, for example.

Schmrz:	For us, the very notion of allowing a tribunal to nullify a law is inconceivable. We would never allow it, not even in a single case. As I said earlier, we do not tolerate discretion lightly, and this seems to be discretion run wild. It could never happen here, because judges sit with our lay assessors. Even if it did happen, the tribunal's written decision would reveal what they had done, and it would never stand up on appeal.
Crane:	There's another reason why we allow a retrial after a conviction, but not after an acquittal. The prosecution can afford another trial, but the defendant can't. Even if he has the money for another trial, or the state is paying his lawyer, it is just too difficult emotionally. And if the prosecutor could retry him once, why not two or three times? Eventually, they would wear him down to the point that he would probably rather take a plea bargain. So once there is an acquittal, that has to be the end of it.
Grbzyk:	Let's not forget the sentence. I believe your double jeopardy doctrine does not prevent prosecutors from appealing improper sentences. The same is true here. And the defense attorney, of course, may also appeal an improper sentence.
Crane:	Thanks a lot.
Grbzyk:	And even if you don't appeal, the prosecutor may appeal on the defendant's behalf.
Lark:	Why would I do a thing like that?
Schmrz:	Because it is your duty to do justice, Madame.
Crane:	Justice? She's never heard of it.
Lark:	This place is really weird.
Crane:	That's what *I* said.
Lark:	Do prosecutors really do that?
Schmrz:	Not often. If the trial court might have erred against the defendant, usually the defendant will appeal.
Grbzyk:	Of course, the defendant who appeals risks the imposition of further costs if he loses.
Crane:	You mean his attorney's fees?
Grbzyk:	Yes, of course, but not only that. Every losing defendant is assessed certain court costs, not including the prosecutor's costs. And if the victim intervened, the losing defendant must also pay the victim's attorney's fees.
Lark:	That's a lot more than most of our states require. I guess your system can discourage a defendant from dragging out the trial, or from appealing.
Grbzyk:	I suppose so, but that is not its purpose. We simply feel that it is just to compel a guilty person to make the state and the victim whole.
Lark:	Does it work the other way? If he is acquitted, does the state make him whole by paying his attorney's fees?

Grbzyk: Yes, as a matter of fact it does.

Lark: We don't do that in the United States.

Grbzyk: Perhaps that is because you sometimes acquit people not because they are innocent, but for extraneous reasons. You release the guilty where illegally seized evidence is excluded, and without such evidence you cannot obtain a conviction. This is not likely to happen in our system. If we acquit a man, he is probably truly innocent, so he should suffer no loss at all.

Crane: In the United States, none of this stuff would matter much, as the overwhelming majority of criminal defendants are indigent. They couldn't even pay for my lunch. In those cases, the state has to pay for their lawyers, usually public defenders.

Grbzyk: We do the same, at least in cases of serious crime. And indigent defendants cannot be required to pay any costs. In such cases, the issue of making the state and the intervenor whole is really moot.

Schmrz: Your client, of course, is not indigent, Mr. Crane. In fact, some have accused him of spending so much money on his defense that he is trying to "buy an acquittal."

Crane: Look, in the usual case, the prosecution uses or has access to many more resources than the defense. They have several lawyers available in the D.A.'s office, and they have their own investigators, plus the whole police department, a crime lab, and other agencies like the F.B.I. to turn to for help. And all this against a single defense lawyer with little investigative help. Do people accuse the prosecutors of trying to "buy convictions?" Of course not. In Mr. Sampson's case, the resources are almost equal for a change, so we have about as good a chance as the prosecutors to show the jury the whole story. That's not unfair. What's unfair is what happens in the other ninety-nine percent of the cases.

Schmrz: I hadn't thought of it that way.

Crane: In some cases, a U.S. defendant doesn't even have a lawyer. Our Supreme Court has held that a defendant has a constitutional right to represent himself, without a lawyer, if he's stupid enough to go that route. It's his case, so he can handle it as he likes. Do you allow this?

Schmrz: No. Every defendant must have counsel.

Lark: Why? It's the defendant's neck, isn't it?

Schmrz: Madame forgets. In our countries, the proceedings are held not for the benefit of the parties, but for the state. It is the duty of the tribunal to find the truth, and defense counsel is better qualified than the defendant to aid this effort.

Lark: Remarkable. Everything we talk about seems to keep coming back to the same fundamental concepts. Where do they come from? Why does the United States start with the notion that the parties run the trial, and Europeans start with the notion that the state runs it?

Grbzyk: An excellent question. Perhaps the United States has a very different attitude towards government and authority than we do.

Schmrz: I agree. To put it bluntly, Europeans trust authority, and Americans don't. Speaking generally, of course.

Crane: That's true about us. The easiest way to get elected to government office in the United States is to attack government, especially the central governments in Washington and the state capitals.

Grbzyk: But it goes well beyond campaign slogans. In the United States, you display your mistrust of authority by dividing it up. Europeans are not so afraid of concentrating it. Our judges have a great deal of power. They investigate the case before trial, examine all the witnesses during trial, and then deliberate right along with the lay assessors. Everyone else, the lawyers, the lay assessors, takes a back seat to the judges. This concentrates most of the power in one institution: the judges.

Crane: I don't think U.S. citizens would tolerate that.

Grbzyk: Quite so. Your judges may be respected, but in a trial of a major crime, they have very little power compared to European judges. But your fear of the concentration of power goes even further. In your system, *no one* individual has much power because you divide it into so many pieces. The prosecutor, not a judge, investigates the case. The lawyers, not the judge, present the evidence at trial. The judge sits primarily as an umpire, making sure that the lawyers obey the rules. And your jury, not the judge, decides who wins. But then the judge may set aside a verdict of conviction if he feels it is not supported by the evidence, and the judge, not the jury, sentences the defendant. But often your legislature has severely limited the judge's discretion in sentencing, so he has little to do except apply the legislature's predetermined formula. Then an appellate court decides if the whole thing was done properly. And your press keeps watch to tell the world if any of these actors has behaved improperly. Everyone — lawyers, jurors, judges, the legislature, reporters — has a little piece of the power. No one has it all, or even a major part of it.

Lark: You make us sound like a bunch of paranoids.

Schmrz: That's for you to decide. I'm merely stating the facts.

Crane: Perhaps this is why the U.S. system seems so complicated. Because we don't trust judges, we use a bunch of untrained amateurs: the jurors. But because we don't totally trust a bunch of amateurs we've never seen before, we have to take a lot of time questioning them and selecting them. Then we need complex rules of evidence to keep them from hearing stuff we don't think they can evaluate properly. Because we don't want too much power in judges, we have the lawyers investigate the case and examine and cross-examine the witnesses, which takes more time. And because our jurors don't know the law, the judge must spend time instructing the jury on the law. You don't have any of these things under your inquisitorial system.

Lark:	Our adversarial system doesn't seem very efficient.
Grbzyk:	No, it doesn't. Our trials usually take a fraction of the time yours take. One study showed that the average European trial for a serious crime takes about one day.
Crane:	Maybe so, Professor, but a monarchy is more efficient than a democracy. Kings can make decisions a lot quicker and cheaper than a bunch of quarrelsome legislators.
Grbzyk:	Touché, Mr. Crane. I catch your drift. Maybe our authoritarian mentality is showing. A vestige of the past, perhaps.
Lark:	And maybe ours is a case of democracy run amok.
Crane:	Wait a minute. Don't forget plea bargaining. Your trials might take less time than ours, but in your system every case goes to trial. Our trials are longer, but over 80% of our cases don't even go to trial. Plea bargained cases are handled at least as efficiently as your trials, maybe more so.
Grbzyk:	It seems ironic. You have this elaborate structure for your trials, no doubt for good reasons, but then you totally dispense with this structure in the great majority of your cases. Apparently, whatever reasons you have for your complex trial system are not good enough to persuade you to keep it for most of your cases. Is this not weird?
Lark:	Our "elaborate structure," as you call it, is mainly for the benefit of the defendant. If he's willing to waive it, that's his right. Nothing ironic about that. We respect the right of the individual to decide what's best for him.
Grbzyk:	And we view the features of our system as being there for the state, not the parties.
Schmrz:	I suspect that the jury is the fulcrum of your system. Suppose you just eliminated the jury, and all of your criminal cases were to be decided by judges. How would your citizens react?
Crane:	I'm not sure. The jury might be on the way out. In civil cases, especially business disputes, more and more cases are being handled by arbitrators. Most criminal cases are still tried by juries, but there have been changes that tend to make the jury somewhat less attractive, at least to defense attorneys. Traditionally, juries have been made up of twelve people, and their verdicts have had to be unanimous. But now some states allow juries of as few as six people, and some allow less than unanimous verdicts, like ten to two.
Lark:	Sure. It's cheaper with fewer people. And nonunanimous verdicts make a hung jury less likely, so we have to re-try cases less often. That saves money, as well as the burden on citizens called for jury duty.
Crane:	It also means you get more convictions, and that makes me a bit less eager to have a jury trial. What kind of a jury do I get? I used to be able to *voir dire* jurors pretty extensively, to find out what these strangers were really like. Now, in a lot of jurisdictions, the judge does most or all of the *voir dire*.

Lark:	That saves a lot of time.
Crane:	It sure does. The judge asks them "Can you be fair?" Then he gets the expected answer, and swears 'em in! When I did *voir dire*, I would try to draw out a juror's true feelings about whether they would automatically believe a cop's testimony, how they feel about the crime charged, and whether they could put aside their personal feelings and follow the judge's instruction on reasonable doubt.
Schmrz:	But you still have your peremptory challenges.
Crane:	Yes, but how can I exercise them intelligently if I don't know how the juror feels about these things? Sometimes I just have to go by what the juror looks like.
Lark:	Watch out with that one. You're treading on dangerous ground.
Crane:	Right. The courts have held that an attorney, criminal or civil, prosecution or defense, may not exercise a peremptory because of a juror's race or sex. So I can't go by what they look like, and I can't get into their heads. I'm flying blind.
Lark:	Come on. Don't you hire high-priced jury consultants?
Crane:	I have to, because I can't do much else. Consultants give me ideas about body language, jurors' occupations, and other things that indicate what these people are like. That's about all that's left for me to go on. But it's a rare case where I have a client that can afford a jury consultant. In most criminal cases, particularly where the defendant is indigent, the defense attorney has to pick jurors by the seat of his pants.
Lark:	It's no better for prosecutors. I live by the same rules you do. I need my *voir dire* and peremptories to get rid of flakes who might cause a hung jury. It's very expensive to re-try cases. It's well worth spending a little extra time and money up front to get a jury of sensible people, so we can try the case just once and get it over with.
Crane:	It's sad to see this weakening of the American jury. People used to view the jury as fundamental to our notion of individualism. A jury protects the accused from the government, and the judge is seen as part of the government.
Lark:	The prosecution needs protection too. In a lot of cases, I'd rather make my pitch to twelve ordinary citizens than to one judge, who might be some liberal appointed by a liberal governor.
Crane:	Come on. You know very well that most of them are ex-D.A.'s appointed by a conservative governor.
Lark:	Are you kidding? Let me tell you about a case I had in front of Judge. . . .
Schmrz:	An interesting dispute. It would not arise here.
Lark:	Why not?
Schmrz:	As you indicate, your judges are usually appointed by elected officials, and elected officials often have definite philosophies about crime, punishment, and the like. They will tend to select people with

a similar philosophy. And those people will have displayed their outlooks by their prior work. Most of them were former prosecutors, defense attorneys, personal injury lawyers, corporate lawyers. Whatever. Your governor has a pretty good idea how each of these specialists views the world, and he appoints accordingly.

Crane: And some of our judges are elected, usually after campaign battles over law and order.

Schmrz: Yes. These matters are relevant to the tasks your judges perform, which often involve much discretion in fact-finding, sentencing, and establishing the law. In our system, we try to minimize the judge's discretion, so her values are not important.

Lark: How do you pick your judges?

Grbzyk: In a way, we don't. They pick themselves. Let me explain. We do not have law schools as such, the separate post-graduate institutions that you have. Our law students are undergraduate university students, who study with the law faculty. At the end of their studies, they make a choice: to become lawyers or to become judges. If they wish to become lawyers, they must apprentice with a law office for a year or two, and then take a state examination. If they choose the judiciary path, they must pass a special state examination upon graduation. It is quite competitive, and very few are accepted. The candidate's political beliefs are wholly irrelevant to whether he or she is accepted.

Lark: Aren't they kind of young to be judges?

Grbzyk: Of course. But before they are allowed to handle cases, they must serve apprenticeships with experienced judges. Then they are assigned small civil and criminal cases. As they gain more experience and demonstrate their competence, they may be promoted to higher courts and be assigned more significant cases. Note that all three of the judges in our case are quite mature.

Lark: So politics has nothing to do with it?

Grbzyk: Nothing at all — we hope. Our judges are civil servants, not politicians. Each has political beliefs, of course, like any citizen does, and different judges might have different attitudes towards crime, sentencing, and the like. But a judge's political beliefs should have as little to do with her job as the court clerk's political beliefs affect his job.

Lark: Politics isn't necessarily a bad thing, you know. If a governor is elected on a tough-on-crime platform, he appoints tough-on-crime judges because that's what the people want.

Grbzyk: If our people choose to get tough on crime, they may elect legislators to enact statutes that do this. It is not the judge's place to make such choices.

Crane: So let's get to the bottom line, Professor. Which system is better?

Grbzyk: Better? Your question is very revealing, Mr. Crane. It displays a common assumption that a legal system may be appraised apart from the society it serves. But it can't. It cannot be constructed by experts and imposed from above. A nation's legal system emerges from the attitudes of its people. Asking which country's legal system is better is like asking which country's people are better.

Crane: So our system is complex and messy because we are complex and messy?

Lark: No. Our system breaks up power because Americans don't want power concentrated.

Schmrz: And our system concentrates power because this is more efficient, and because it does not particularly bother our people. We have had kings, queens, and other strong leaders for centuries, so perhaps our people have gotten used to it, even though they now claim to favor democracy. Also, as discussed earlier, we operate under the principle, or perhaps the illusion, that our judges have little discretion, that they merely apply the law mechanically.

Crane: Times change, Professor.

Schmrz: Indeed they do, Mr. Crane. Italy has recently changed its legal system. It is moving away from the inquisitorial system and toward your adversarial system. The Italians have retained their mixed panel, but they have taken away the power of judges to present the evidence, giving it to the lawyers.

Lark: Really? That's great! Why did they do it?

Schmrz: They say that they now realize that the adversarial system gives greater respect to the rights of the individual.

Crane: That's true. The parties have the most at stake, so their lawyers should control the presentation of the case.

Grbzyk: Of all Europeans, I think the Italians are most similar to the United States in your dislike of concentrations of power. They would rather spread it out.

Schmrz: These are the justifications given by the Italians, officially. But others suspect that something else is at work. For years, one of the most popular television programs in Italy has been your "Perry Mason," where a handsome trial lawyer always manages to win at the last moment. You know how Italians love a dramatic spectacle, like opera.

Lark: So we put on a better show than you do?

Grbzyk: That we must concede. U.S. trials have much better Nielsen ratings than European trials.

Crane: The adversarial system demands a lot more from lawyers than the inquisitorial system does. Are Italian lawyers up to it?

Schmrz: That remains to be seen. It will be difficult. Many Italian lawyers prepare for trial simply by reviewing their code books. They have no training in cross-examination, preparation of experts, and the like.

Crane: Those are the bread and butter tasks of U.S. lawyers. We take courses in those skills, read books on them, and practice them every day in court, for years. You can't learn them in a day.

Schmrz: The transition will not be easy.

Lark: I've never heard of a country grafting an important feature of one system onto another type of system, like the Italians are doing. Is it really possible?

Schmrz: A good question. I'm not sure that the Italians have thought that question through carefully enough. If and when their lawyers learn the U.S. style of trial advocacy, perhaps other aspects of their system will also have to change, or else they might have to give up the notion of letting lawyers control the evidence. I'm not sure that one can just plonk a major foreign feature into an existing system without radically altering the entire system.

Crane: Professor, you didn't like my question about which system is better. So let me rephrase it. Which system does a better job of finding the truth?

Grbzyk: You insist on pinning me down, eh? Well, let me begin by passing along a little saying I once heard: "An innocent defendant should prefer to be tried in Europe, while a guilty defendant should prefer to be tried in the United States."

Crane: Wonderful! A supreme compliment to the skills of U.S. defense lawyers — like me, naturally.

Lark: *(shaking her head)* Look at him. He's *proud* of it!

Crane: Just kidding, Counsel. Prosecutors have no sense of humor.

Grbzyk: The saying implies, of course, that the inquisitorial system does a better job of finding the truth.

Crane: Who said the saying, a European?

Grbzyk: This I must admit.

Schmrz: Let's examine the issue a little more closely. I suppose the key difference we should focus on is *who decides* what is the truth. You use lay jurors and we use professional judges, sometimes along with lay people. But as you pointed out, Mr. Crane, lay people tend to go along with judges. Isn't it rather obvious that professionals are better at their jobs than amateurs? Professionals have been selected for their aptitude, then they are trained, and then they spend much more time at their jobs than amateurs ever could. A research biologist stands a much better chance of finding the true cause of cancer than does some barber or baseball player. By the same token, judges are bound to be better at finding the truth at trial than jurors could ever hope to be.

Crane: Wait a minute. Judges are trained to know and apply *the law*. They don't take courses in law school on how to figure out who's telling the truth. And another thing: criminal trials aren't about finding the cure for cancer.

Schmrz:	Sometimes they seem like it. In the trial we just observed, several scientists testified about the accuracy of DNA evidence. It was very technical, and I must admit that I had some difficulty following it at times. Who was better able to understand it? Judges, all of whom have had university training and several years of listening to expert witnesses, or jurors, who might not have graduated from high school, and who might be seeing the inside of a courtroom for the first time?
Crane:	But this case isn't typical. Most criminal trials don't involve heavy scientific disputes. Most turn on a rather simple question: who's telling the truth and who's lying? A robbery victim points to the defendant and says, "That's the guy who robbed me," and the defendant testifies "I was home watching TV when the robbery occurred." A diploma in biology isn't going to help you figure out which one is right. And there's no reason a judge should be any better at it than a barber or a ballplayer.
Lark:	I'm not so sure about that. Judges hear defendants make up stories day in and day out. After a while, they get a pretty good ear for it. But some jurors are so naive they'll buy any cock-and-bull story.
Crane:	And some judges always believe the cops — or say they do, anyway. They have to work with the police every day, and they want to stay on good terms with them, especially if the judge is looking for an appointment to the next court up. Judges get more points for being pro-cop than being pro-defendant. And as for defendants making up stories, sure, some do. The judge hears a few of these and then decides that *all* defendants are probably lying. They get jaded. That's why we need jurors. They're not prejudiced, and they bring a fresh look to things.
Lark:	You mean they're more likely to fall for your tricks. A lot of defense lawyers make a career out of confusing jurors.
Crane:	Be nice to me, Ms. D.A. Without me, there's no you. An adversarial system with only one adversary is like the Dodgers showing up for the World Series with no opponent. There's not much point to it. Under this inquisitorial system, we're both out of work.
Schmrz:	Not quite, but your roles would be substantially diminished.
Lark:	That's true. I'd probably get more convictions here, not having to deal with juries and exclusionary rules and the like. But I wouldn't have much to do with getting them. It wouldn't feel like winning. Not as much fun.
Crane:	Ha! The truth comes out. You *like* battling me. See, we're *both* products of the adversarial system. Maybe U.S. prosecutors have more in common with U.S. defense lawyers than they do with European prosecutors.
Lark:	Perish the thought. Anyway, Professor, I see another problem with your view. Lots of times the "truth" we are looking for isn't just a "whodunnit." It involves values. The law says that murder should be reduced down to voluntary manslaughter if the defendant killed

because of some "reasonable provocation." So if the defendant kills because the victim recently molested the defendant's kid, we don't punish him as much as we would a Mafia hit man. But what a "reasonable" provocation is can be a tough question. Is it reasonable when someone says something racist to you? Is it reasonable if someone raped you last week? This isn't a question of "truth," it's a question of values. Twelve jurors might bring the values of the community into the decision better than one or even three judges could.

> **Schmrz:** But such "values" are never considered by our tribunals. These questions are decided by our legislatures, not our courts. We expect courts to apply the law, not to make it.

Lark: Our judges make law all the time. And I guess our juries also do it occasionally.

Crane: Jurors' experiences can be important even in a whodunnit case. I once had a Latino client who wouldn't look the judge in the eye when testifying because he came from a country where that was seen as a threat or an assertion of dominance. And you just don't do that with someone like a judge. The judge thought he was lying. But some of the jurors were Latino and knew about that, so they believed him, and they acquitted him.

Lark: I've had cases like that. Often twelve jurors have had experience with life that no one judge could have.

Crane: You know, some judges never get out of the courtroom. And when they do, they just hang out in country clubs with their buddies, other judges, a few doctors, and lawyers. They don't know much about real life on the streets, where most criminal defendants come from.

Schmrz: I suppose the same might be said of some of our judges.

Lark: It's more of a problem in the United States than here in Europe. We have a very diverse population, with racial and ethnic groups from all parts of the world. In Los Angeles, we probably have over fifty different language groups, just in one city. And these people have different cultures and customs. No single judge, no matter how much he gets out in the world, can possibly know as much about these cultures as twelve jurors.

Grbzyk: Perhaps our mixed tribunal obviates some of these difficulties. Our lay assessors may bring some real life into the tribunal's deliberations.

Lark: Sort of a compromise, isn't it? You have the benefit of professional judges running things, but you also get input from the public, through the lay assessors. Sounds like a good idea.

Grbzyk: Quite so. It satisfies both needs. Wouldn't such a compromise be an improvement over your jury system?

Crane: Maybe, but as we saw in court today, it would probably bring a lot of other changes along with it. No more hearsay rules, no jury instructions, no *voir dire*, and no peremptory challenges. And judges telling jurors how to vote. That's a lot of baggage to bring in just to get a mixed tribunal.

Lark: Baggage, or benefits? Many people see those things you mentioned as technicalities, well worth getting rid of.

Crane: Let's not overstate the amount of power our jurors have. Granted, they deliberate alone, without a judge with them, unlike the way you do it. But we limit them in a way you don't. Take that evidence of prior crimes which I tried to keep out. Your lay assessors would hear this evidence, and then in the deliberation room the judge might try to talk them out of misusing it. In our system, the judge would screen this evidence, and keep the jury from even hearing it at all if he felt it was only marginally relevant and too prejudicial.

Schmrz: Yes. I am quite struck by the amount of time you spend in the United States on objections and pre-trial motions involving whether jurors will be allowed to hear certain evidence. It seems to reflect a certain lack of confidence in their ability to find the truth.

Grbzyk: You know, this problem of finding the truth is not confined to criminal cases. We deal with it all the time in everyday life. An employer discovers money missing from the petty cash box. Does she just listen to the employee's explanations, or does she try to find out the truth herself?

Lark: Obviously, the latter. Are you suggesting that the inquisitorial system is more "natural" than the adversarial system?

Grbzyk: Perhaps.

Crane: It's more "natural" only if you see the state in a paternalistic role. Maybe you Europeans see the state as Big Daddy, but most in the United States don't.

Schmrz: Consider an institution many regard as quite paternalistic, the Catholic Church. The Church has had experience with both models when judging whether certain people were worthy of sainthood. The Church initially used the inquisitorial model, but this became too loose, sanctifying many candidates whose qualifications were questionable. So they changed to an adversarial system, establishing the office of Promoter of the Faith to argue against any proponents of a particular candidate.

Grbzyk: The proponents called the Promoter the "devil's advocate," didn't they?

Schmrz: Yes. Each side had its lawyers, and the case was tried before the Pope's representatives. It worked quite well for several centuries. But the whole process became so lengthy and cumbersome that it was recently abandoned. The process is now more inquisitorial.

Grbzyk: What about scientists? Do they seek the truth through an adversarial model, an inquisitorial model, or neither?

Schmrz: Probably through a blend of each. An individual scientist may act as an unbiased inquisitor, initially, but once he publicly proposes a new thesis, the process might well become somewhat adversarial, where he defends his thesis, other scientists attack it, and the remaining scientific community sits as the tribunal. It is a tribunal of professionals, of course, not lay people.

Crane: I think we're overlooking something here. Finding the truth, whatever that is, is important. But it's not the only thing. We have juries for other reasons as well.

Grbzyk: Such as?

Crane: Well, we talked earlier about how Americans don't really trust government that much. Criminal cases are about basic moral decisions, what the morals of a community are all about. Our communities want to be involved in making those decisions. They don't want to leave it all to the judges.

Grbzyk: Don't they elect the legislators who enact the criminal laws?

Crane: Yes, but that's not enough. The laws are abstract. A real case is concrete. It hits home.

Lark: I'm just trying to imagine what it would be like with no juries. People would probably think that all these judgments, both convictions and acquittals, were coming down from on high, from the top. I can just see the accusations of racism, sexism, classism, elitism, and other "isms" flooding the newspapers. When people see a case decided by fellow citizens, they are more likely to accept it.

Crane: Not always. Look at the riots resulting from the Rodney King case, when a California jury acquitted the white cops who beat up a black man.

Lark: True, but that was an aberration, an all-white suburban jury trying a case that should have been tried by a racially-mixed jury in Los Angeles. That proves my point. If a mixed Los Angeles jury had acquitted those cops, I don't think the riots would have happened.

Schmrz: Are you saying that even if your jury is more likely to be mistaken than our judges, the jury is still better because it makes the judicial system and its rulings more acceptable to your people?

Lark: Yes. Some things are more important than being right all the time.

Crane: And maybe we are saying only that it works better *for us*. In Europe, your local populations are not as diverse as ours. Perhaps it is less important to have a cross-section of the people deciding criminal cases. Maybe your judges are not all that different from the rest of the community, just a little better educated. So your people are more willing to accept judgments from judges.

Schmrz: Europe is changing. We now have more mobile populations, with more intermixing. So perhaps our needs will become similar to yours. Our crime rates are rising, and illegal drugs are becoming more of a problem, as they have been in your country for some time. Italy is changing, and it is also changing its legal system. Maybe other countries will follow suit.

Crane:	I'm beginning to see why my question about which system is better didn't make a lot of sense. Maybe there is no "better." It all depends on what a particular society wants and thinks it needs.
Schmrz:	We see another problem with juries. It is very important to us that the law be certain, consistent, and predictable, and that our officials be seen as having very little discretion. As an institution, the jury runs counter to these objectives. Because they are untrained novices, jurors are quite unpredictable and they appear to have wide discretion. Allowing them to return general verdicts, without explaining their reasons, tends to confirm this.
Lark:	I'm not sure that using judges is much better. True, an individual judge might be pretty predictable. An experienced local lawyer can usually tell you how Judge X will rule, if she's been on the bench for a while. But the lawyer will also predict that Judge Y will rule just the opposite. This seems to make "the law" not very predictable. It all depends on which judge the case is assigned to.
Schmrz:	That is not so much of a problem for us. As I explained earlier, our judges are not selected for their political philosophies. In addition, they are all trained in the same way, they are required to explain their decisions, and allowing both sides to appeal tends to ensure that they will follow the law. These features make judges consistent with each other and with their own prior rulings.
Lark:	The role of juries in U.S. law is important, but let's not overstate it. Except in death penalty cases, the jury usually has no say about what sentence the defendant receives. That's for the judge, and most of our jurisdictions do allow both the prosecution and the defense to appeal sentencing decisions. This helps to make the sentencing more consistent and predictable.
Crane:	I'm trying to imagine what it would be like if our juries did the sentencing. It could get pretty wild. Each jury is made up of twelve different people, most of whom have never decided a case before. If the law gave them a lot of leeway in sentencing, say one to ten years for armed robbery, some juries would give one and some would give ten.
Lark:	The same thing can happen with judges, as a group. One judge might give one year, and another ten. But at least a given judge will tend to be pretty consistent.
Crane:	Right. If the case has been assigned to a particular judge, the sentence becomes somewhat predictable. That's very important for plea bargaining. When I try to convince a client to accept a deal, he wants to know what will happen if he rejects the bargain and goes to trial. If I can't give him a pretty good idea of this, he's likely to take his chances and go to trial.
Lark:	So if sentencing were left to the jury, we'd probably have fewer plea bargains and more trials, which would require more resources.
Crane:	This all assumes, of course, that the legislature allows leeway in sentencing. These days, a lot of them don't.

Schmrz: Does it also assume that you will continue to bifurcate your trials, trying guilt and sentencing separately?

Crane: Yes. Even if we gave sentencing to the jury, we couldn't give it to them at the same time as the guilt issue. First, it would mean that evidence relating to sentencing would come in, maybe evidence of the defendant's prior criminal lifestyle, and you just can't trust a jury to decide guilt fairly when they've heard that stuff. Second, it's just too confusing for a bunch of lay people to decide more than one issue at a time. It would take them forever to come back with a verdict. And if we required a unanimous verdict, they'd probably never come back.

Lark: Your system of combining the two issues in one trial is probably more efficient than ours.

Schmrz: Yes, but it works only because we have professional judges deliberating with the lay assessors. I agree with Mr. Crane. It would never work if we used only the lay assessors.

Lark: So maybe our jury system is really a compromise. We use juries, for all the reasons we discussed, but we limit their input to only half the case: the question of guilt. They play no part in the sentencing half, which is just as important.

Crane: With one exception.

Lark: Yes, capital cases. There the penalty is so extraordinary that we don't want the state to impose it without the consent of the community, at least twelve of its members.

Grbzyk: Your comments on the truth intrigue me. Under your adversarial system, do lawyers *want* the tribunal to learn the truth?

Lark: I do. The truth is, the defendant is guilty.

Crane: There's an unbiased opinion for you.

Lark: Actually, it is. I spend a lot of time before trial talking to witnesses and examining the physical evidence. And I get to see a lot of evidence the jury probably *won't* see, such as illegally seized evidence and his prior record. These things might persuade me that he's guilty even if the jury later acquits him. But if what I see convinces me that he's innocent, I don't take the case to trial. I dismiss it. I don't want to convict an innocent man. So when I take a case to trial, I know he's guilty. For me, that *is* the truth.

Crane: Very noble, Counsel. But you don't always *know* someone is innocent or guilty. Suppose you aren't sure. Suppose some guy is accused of rape, he claims the woman consented, she denies it, and you aren't sure who's telling the truth. Do you take it to trial?

Lark: That's a tough one. A lot depends on whether I think I can get a conviction. I don't like to lose. It makes it harder for me to drive a tough plea bargain if people aren't afraid that I'll win if the case goes to trial. And losing isn't much of a career booster, quite frankly. So if I think he's guilty, but I'm not sure the evidence shows it beyond a reasonable doubt, I might dismiss or plea bargain instead of trying it. I have enough trouble finding time to prosecute the guys I know I can nail. I don't need to waste time with weak cases.

Crane: Don't dodge the issue. Suppose you have your doubts, but you're getting political pressure to prosecute — maybe from some women's group. Do you go to trial?

Lark: My inclination is to leave it to the jury. That's their job, not mine.

Crane: A clever way of covering your rear end. If you dismiss or plea bargain, the women's group will say you sold them out. But if you go to trial and lose, maybe they'll blame the jury and not you.

Grbzyk: Let me make sure I understand you, Ms. Lark. Even if you're not convinced he's guilty, in your role as an advocate you argue that he is? You try to persuade the jury that she's telling the truth and he isn't?

Lark: I guess I do. Once I get into trial, I want to win.

Grbzyk: In our system, no prosecutor would argue that the accused is lying if she did not in fact believe that he was.

Lark: When I get to trial, defense attorneys seem to bring out the worst in me.

Schmrz: What do you mean?

Lark: When I first look at a case, I'm very objective, seeing all sides of it pretty fairly. At that point, I might be willing to dismiss or settle. But as I get closer to trial, I become more of an advocate, and I hone down my arguments and my rebuttals to my opponent's arguments. But the odd thing is, I usually convince *myself* with my arguments. Sometimes I look back on how I felt when I first saw the case, when I was very dubious about it, and I can't figure out how I became so sure that the case should come out only one way. It's a strange transformation.

Crane: It's not peculiar to prosecutors. It happens to me too. It happens to all U.S. litigators, even in civil cases. There's nothing wrong with it. It's inherent in the adversary system. How can you persuade a jury if they don't feel that you believe what you're saying?

Schmrz: So U.S. lawyers are all actors, pretending to believe something they don't?

Lark: But you can't pretend. The jury will see through it. That's why you have to convince yourself first.

Grbzyk: A peculiar psychological task, isn't it?

Crane: It is, and a lot of people don't understand it. They just think lawyers are liars, saying things they don't believe just to win. It's not that simple.

Lark: Anyway, I don't feel so bad about it. Defense counsel will urge the jury to acquit the defendant, even when he *knows* the defendant is guilty. He's certainly not out for the truth.

Schmrz: I'm not convinced that *either* of you are out for the truth. I happened to read some newspaper reports that discussed some evidence that the Accused may have become agitated by something the victims did soon before the killings. This would tend to show that he did not premeditate the killing, which would have reduced the crime to second degree murder. If it showed a reasonable provocation, it might even have reduced it to voluntary manslaughter. And yet neither of you introduced this evidence. Why?

Crane: I took the position that the prosecution couldn't prove that he even committed the killings. I didn't want to confuse the jury with any arguments that assumed that he did commit them.

Lark: I charged him with first degree murder. So naturally I wouldn't want to put in any evidence that detracted from that.

Schmrz: So each of you, for different reasons, deceived the tribunal, correct?

Lark: That's putting it pretty strong. I think he premeditated, so why should I help him by putting on evidence that tends to show that he didn't?

Schmrz: *You* think he premeditated, but isn't it the *tribunal's* task to determine whether he did or not? And you deprived it of the opportunity to do so. This would never happen in our system. The prosecutor has a duty to present all evidence that is relevant to the case, no matter which side it seems to help. The task of the tribunal is to find the truth, not to decide which side has presented the better case.

Crane: I don't think I deceive the court when I don't put on evidence I know about. It's not the job of a defense attorney to help the court find the truth. My duty is to my client. I can't tell him to lie, and I can't put on false evidence. That *would* be deceiving the court.

Schmrz: A fine line, to be sure.

Crane: Is it? Is it much different from refusing to plead guilty when I know he's guilty? I do that when the prosecution has a weak case. I just try to poke holes in the prosecutor's case and hold her to her burden of proving the case beyond a reasonable doubt. If I succeed and get my client off, I've done my job well, even if he is actually guilty.

Schmrz: So his guilt has no effect on you?

Crane: I wouldn't say that. Like the prosecutor, I don't like to lose. And if I lose at trial, my client's sentence will be greater than it would be if I had gotten him a decent plea bargain. So if the prosecutor has a strong case, I'll probably advise my client to bargain.

Lark: Now who's dodging the issue? Suppose I have a weak case, but *you* know your client is guilty. You'll *still* urge the jury to acquit him. You know it and I know it.

Crane: Correct.

Schmrz: Morally, you have no problem with that, Mr. Crane?

Crane: Of course not. Look, I'm no different from any other decent citizen. I don't want a rapist running loose to threaten my wife or daughter.

As a citizen, I want this guy put away for a long time if he did it. But as his lawyer, I want him to walk.

Schmrz: How can you want two inconsistent results? And why put yourself in such a difficult position?

Crane: That's the same as asking me why I became a lawyer. I did it because I believe in our system, the adversary system. I think it works. Without me, or someone like me, doing what I do, the adversary system just couldn't work properly.

Schmrz: Many people feel that U.S. criminal defense lawyers are . . . how should I say it?

Crane: I'll say it for you. We're greedy shysters, manipulators, liars, out to get mass murderers off on technicalities, et cetera, et cetera. I've heard them all.

Schmrz: Do those accusations bother you?

Crane: I don't mind heat. I get plenty of it from prosecutors and judges, in court. That comes with the territory. But it does bother me when people don't understand how defense attorneys contribute to the rendering of justice. Basically, they just don't understand the adversary system.

Schmrz: Justice? Are you seeking justice when you urge a jury to free a guilty man?

Crane: See, that's the problem. You think *my* job is to find a just *result* and urge the jury to come back with that verdict. It isn't. Under the adversary system, it's the *system's* job to come up with a just result. That's not the job of *each player* in the system. Let's look at another player, the bailiff. His job is to take care of the jury. But he hears the evidence and arguments, and he might come to his own conclusions. When he escorts the jury into the deliberation room, is he supposed to tell them what he thinks is the just result? No way. That's not his role. Same with me.

Schmrz: So justice emerges from each player carrying out his or her limited role?

Crane: Yes, but only if every actor plays his role properly. Lark's role is to prosecute, my role is to defend, and the jury's rule is to decide who's right. If I play her role, or she plays mine, or either of us plays the jury's role, it doesn't work. We're sort of like an automobile engine. The pistons go up and down, the gears go from side to side, and some of the rods even go backwards. Everything seems to be going in a different direction, but when all of them work together properly, the whole car goes *forward*, just where you want it to go.

Schmrz: An attractive analogy, Mr. Crane. But the bailiff is not actively trying to free a man who might be guilty. You are. How can you expect the U.S. public to look kindly on you?

Crane: It's not easy. And we haven't done a very good job of explaining to the public how we help *them*. Look at it this way. There are two possibilities, my client will either be convicted or he'll be acquitted.

Either way, I help society. If he's convicted, the fact that I tried hard to get him acquitted lets us all sleep better, knowing that it's very unlikely we are punishing an innocent man, because I made sure the jury knew every weakness in the prosecution's case. And if my efforts help get him acquitted, we can be *sure* we're not punishing an innocent man.

Grbzyk: But sometimes your efforts have nothing to do with guilt or innocence. When you urge the court to exclude relevant evidence because the police forgot to obtain a search warrant, or to exclude a confession because the police forgot to read the defendant his *Miranda* rights, you seek to prevent the jury from finding the truth about guilt or innocence. Aren't these the sorts of technicalities the public complains about?

Crane: Look, my job is to make the arguments for my client, and that's all. I can't decide anything, and I can't make the rules. That's the court's job. If the public doesn't like the rules, they should blame the courts and the legislatures, not me. I'm just the messenger: I tell the court when the rules have been broken.

Grbzyk: That seems reasonable. But if people don't like the rules, I suppose they'll blame the first person that mentions them. You.

Crane: Right. The basic problem is that people don't appreciate why we have these rules. The exclusionary rule protects all of us from unreasonable searches and arrests, and the *Miranda* warnings make sure that the police don't coerce defendants into confessing. You can agree or disagree with these policies, but you can't fairly call them "technicalities." They're not like rules about what size paper your briefs have to be written on; they deal with fundamental rights. If they make it a little harder to find the truth in some cases, it's well worth the price. I just wish the public understood that.

Grbzyk: The U.S. public sometimes sees the arguments that lawyers present as rather fanciful. Shouldn't you take responsibility for the arguments you make?

Crane: I should, and I do. All good lawyers make creative arguments. The public doesn't realize that lawyers in an adversarial system have to push the envelope, to test the outer edges of the rules. That's part of our job. If we didn't, the law would never change, and we wouldn't be representing our clients to the fullest. And don't worry, if we cross the line between creative and fanciful, the judge won't hesitate to shoot us down.

Schmrz: Intellectually, you present a persuasive case, Mr. Crane, as one might expect from an intelligent lawyer. But let's talk about your *feelings* for a moment. I believe that's fashionable in California these days. How do you *feel* when a jury acquits a man you know to be guilty?

Crane: That doesn't happen often. But when it does, I don't lose any sleep. I just make doubly sure my doors are locked.

Schmrz: So you feel content?

Crane:	Content? When I win, I feel terrific!
Schmrz:	The verdict reinforces your belief in the system, I suppose.
Crane:	The system? When the jury walks through that door with a verdict, who's thinking about the system? Half the time, I'm not even thinking about my client! I'm thinking about one thing: *victory*. A lawyer in the adversarial system is like an athlete or a soldier, at least when we're caught up in the emotions of a trial. Who would think of asking a pro football player *why* he wants to win the game? We're the same way. I'm not sure whether we're born that way or the adversarial system makes us that way, but that's what happens.
Lark:	During trial, I feel the same thing. I might think about the rights and wrongs of it all before the trial begins, but once the judge bangs that gavel, I just want to win. Period.
Schmrz:	Of course, winning is profitable for both of you, is it not? Doesn't a good record enhance your careers?
Crane:	Sure it does. That's how I get clients and she gets promotions. But that's not what keeps us going during a trial. Then we're warriors, not career climbers. I'll balance my checkbook later.
Grbzyk:	Remarkable. I suppose this competitive drive is what creates the drama we spoke of earlier.
Lark:	Yes. We are very competitive, and most of our trial lawyers want to be Perry Mason, each in their own way.
Grbzyk:	I don't think our lawyers have these feelings, at least not to the degree you exhibit them.
Lark:	They don't know what they're missing. Say what you will about the adversarial system, but it sure is fun, at least for the lawyers.
Grbzyk:	Even when you lose?
Lark:	Of course not. But the thrill of winning makes you forget your losses, 'til the next one, anyway. It is pretty much like competitive sports, I suppose.
Grbzyk:	We Europeans think competition is more suited to the soccer field than our law courts. In the United States, you seem to treat the quest for justice as just a game.
Crane:	It's a game, all right, but it's not *just* a game. The competitive spirit is the gas that makes the car go. It's the energy that drives the adversarial system — a very good system, I might add. It gets to the truth, most of the time, while still serving other values we think are important.
Schmrz:	Does it? How can you have such faith in a system that might result in an acquittal of a client you know to be guilty? Doesn't that show that your adversarial system is faulty?
Crane:	Not necessarily. Maybe it just shows that humans aren't perfect. Until we develop an infallible lie detector machine, we'll have to rely on fallible people to decide whether other people are telling the

truth. And they won't always get it right. Do your judges always get it right?

Schmrz: Probably not, but when the defendant confesses, our judges are less likely to get it wrong. And we do get more confessions than you do.

Crane: But look at how you get them. As I said before . . .

Lark: Please, Crane. Once is enough.

Crane: Now wait a minute, Lark. I . . .

Schmrz: Pardon me for raising this, but I can't help noticing a certain tension between you two. Do you dislike each other?

Lark: Not at all. Crane and I get along pretty well, considering.

Schmrz: Considering?

Lark: Considering we're on opposite sides, of course.

Schmrz: Opposite sides? If Mr. Crane's analogy is correct, you are both parts of the same automobile engine, each working to move the car forward towards the same destination: a just result. Your goals are the same, aren't they? Why should there be any animosity at all between you?

Lark: Good question. I guess when you represent the same side over and over, you develop certain attitudes about crimes and cops. I have mine, he has his. And the two usually conflict.

Crane: And don't forget the emotions we talked about. When you get all worked up at trial a few times, always on the same side, it tends to worm its way inside you, and it stays there.

Lark: True. Also, different personality types are attracted to one side or the other. Prosecutors' offices tend to draw in people who are straight, orderly types.

Crane: So I'm crooked and disorderly?

Lark: Not necessarily. But you and your ilk do tend to be more like rebels. You're not too likely to pick prosecutors as your drinking buddies and vice-versa.

Crane: Conceded. We tend to distrust big government, cops, and the establishment generally. You don't. You wear pin stripes and wing-tips, and we wear flashy ties and pony tails.

Grbzyk: Could either of you switch sides?

Lark: Me? Defend criminals? Never in a million years.

Crane: Actually, I used to work as a prosecutor. But I couldn't do it now. I can't work for a bureaucracy. I'm just not the organization-man type. But I'm glad I did it. It taught me a lot about how the opposition operates.

Schmrz: The "opposition" — again. Is this healthy, this loyalty to one side only? And is it necessary to the adversarial system?

Lark: I never really thought about it. How could it be any different? You can't represent both sides.

| Schmrz: | British barristers do. A barrister might be retained by the prosecutor's office in one case, and then by the accused in the next case. Some tend to specialize in representing one side or the other, but many take each case as it comes. They are vigorous advocates in the particular case, put it behind them when it is over, and then become just as vigorous in the next case. It works, and no one has suggested that it diminishes the adversarial nature of British practice. |

| Grbzyk: | Maybe the United States should try this. |

| Crane: | Professor, didn't you warn me earlier against comparing one feature of another system with your own without looking at the whole system? I know a bit about the Brits. They separate their lawyers into solicitors and barristers. Solicitors tend to work one side of the street: either the prosecution or the defense, not both. They prepare the case for trial, just like our prosecutors and defense attorneys do. But then the solicitor brings in a barrister as a trial specialist to try it. So the lawyer with the most contact with the client, the solicitor, sticks to one side, just like our lawyers. |

| Grbzyk: | I stand corrected, Mr. Crane. |

| Lark: | Still, it's an intriguing idea, the more I think about it. Maybe each of us would have a little more respect for the other side if we took one of their cases occasionally. We could try it out, in some sort of test program. |

| Schmrz: | There is something else you might try: the inquisitorial system. Some American critics of your system have proposed this, believing that it would be much more efficient. Some have even pointed to the present case as an example of how expensive and inefficient the adversarial system can be. |

| Crane: | That might have had a chance a while ago, but not now. |

| Schmrz: | Why is that? |

| Crane: | Sentencing. In recent years, our sentences have gone through the roof. Mandatory minimums, consecutives, three-strikes-and-you're-out, truth-in-sentencing laws. It's getting worse all the time. |

| Schmrz: | I don't understand. I grant that your sentences are much higher than ours, but why would this preclude your adoption of the inquisitorial system? What is the connection? |

| Crane: | Let's forget about the lawyers for a moment and just think about the defendant. If you are charged with a crime in the United States, the prosecution is out to clobber you. They want to put you in a miserable place for a very long time, and sometimes they want to kill you. They might have good reasons for this. I appreciate people's frustrations about crime. But reasonable or not, it's clear that the prosecutors are not looking after *your* interests, so you have to do it yourself. It doesn't matter whether you're guilty or innocent. You're going to resist; it's human nature. And when you do, the government is going to fight even harder. So the system is inherently adversarial from the start — *with or without* lawyers and judges. All the |

lawyers and judges do is insist on some procedures that make the fight a little more civilized.

Lark: Makes sense, I guess. But I don't see how this explains the differences in systems. Doesn't the prosecution *always* want the defendant punished, even in the inquisitorial system?

Schmrz: It depends on how you are using the word "punish." When my child misbehaves, I punish him in order to reform his behavior and make him a better person, not to hurt him. I punish him because I love him.

Lark: Come on, Professor, tell the truth. When your kid wrecks the furniture, you punish him because you're angry at him, and also to cut down the expense of buying new chairs, don't you? It's not all just for him.

Schmrz: I confess, those motives are also present, along with the ones I mentioned. I want to help him, and I am also annoyed and want to protect my household. Is your decision to prosecute based on the same mixture of motives?

Lark: I guess not, at least for most major crimes. If I'm going after an adult armed robber, I try to satisfy my community's anger at people like him, and I want him off the streets for as long as possible. Usually, I'm not trying to help him at all.

Schmrz: Will he receive any help in prison?

Crane: Are you kidding? Years ago, we tried to rehabilitate prisoners: teach them to read and learn a trade, so they might get a job when they get out. In fact, rehabilitation was seen as one of the main purposes of punishment. But today people just want the two things Ms. Lark just mentioned: to hurt the guy and to get him out of the way. Any help he might get in prison is incidental, and most of them get very little.

Lark: I suppose it's true. Today, for most defendants, the sentence he receives has little to do with any notion of how long it might take to rehabilitate him.

Schmrz: You say "most." Are there exceptions?

Lark: Sure. If I have a young defendant without much of a record, I might give him a break, maybe get him into a diversion program to help him break a drug habit, or recommend a suspended sentence on condition he behaves himself and gets a job. If I don't have an angry victim pushing me, I might try to help him.

Grbzyk: This is the approach the inquisitorial system takes with almost all defendants. Perhaps I would not go so far as to say that we hurt them because we love them, as Professor Schmrz does his child. But we start with the assumption that they are redeemable.

Schmrz: Not all of them, of course. Terrorists who kill innocent people probably evoke the same response in our community that the average burglar does in yours.

Lark: Are you telling me that your defendants think the state is trying to help them by prosecuting them, so they don't have much incentive to fight?

Schmrz: I wouldn't go quite that far, but I would say this. The average robber would not feel that a state that fines him or sentences him to four or six months in prison hates him, even if it does not love him. On some level, he might believe that he did wrong and deserves some loss of freedom for a while. But if the state were to imprison him for ten years for the same crime, he might think that depriving him of a substantial part of his life was much more than just desserts.

Crane: It's worse than that. A ten-year sentence is society's declaration that he is worthless, that he has no chance for redemption, that his community *does* hate him. While a six-month sentence might conceivably reform him, there is little chance that a ten-year sentence will do so. He has effectively been declared an outcast for the rest of his life. He'll never see this as for his own benefit, and he won't take it without a fight. Any system that threatens him with this will necessarily be an adversarial system.

Grbzyk: Ms. Lark, you mentioned your occasional sympathy for young offenders. Wasn't your juvenile court system built on similar premises?

Lark: Yes. It was intended to punish juveniles like you punish your child: to protect society *and* to help the kids grow up to be good citizens. There was supposed to be an element of love in it, sort of.

Grbzyk: Did this approach affect the way juvenile court trials were handled?

Lark: Yes. They were set up to be pretty nonadversarial. No juries, no defense lawyers, and relaxed rules of evidence. The kid didn't need those things to protect him, because the court was out to help him, not to hurt him.

Crane: That was the idea, but it didn't work out that way. Kids were thrown into miserable detention homes, which were like jails, and often their "sentences" were set according to what they had done, not what they needed. It began to look so much like adult court that our Supreme Court required states to give them some of the same rights that adult defendants get, like defense lawyers. It became an adversarial proceeding because the state was trying to punish them, not help them. If the proceeding is based on hostility rather than concern, it will always be adversarial.

Schmrz: So, I see why you said that the nature of the sentence may affect the nature of the adjudicatory system.

Crane: Yes. Earlier, I compared a U.S. adversarial trial to a baseball game. Maybe for the lawyers it is. To us, it's mainly a game — a big game, but still a game. But the defendant has much more at stake. For him, it's more like a bullfight. The matador is trying to kill the bull, and the bull is fighting for his life. That's the essence of it. You can change the weapons, the costumes, or the players. You could even give the bull a lawyer. But if they're still trying to kill the bull, the adversarial nature of the contest won't change. The bull will never quietly accept an "inquisitorial" decision that he should die. He'll always fight back.

Schmrz: The bull is innocent, of course.

Crane: True, but that doesn't matter much. Even a guilty bull, or a guilty defendant, will resist when his enemy is trying to take his life or a substantial part of it. And he should. Even if you're guilty, that doesn't mean you deserve the penalty they're trying to inflict on you.

Schmrz: How would your bull-defendant react to an inquisitorial system, if the United States were to adopt it?

Crane: I can just imagine me telling him, "Joe, I won't bother cross-examining the key witnesses against you, because we can depend on the judge to try to get to the truth. You should just get up there and confess. Don't worry, you can trust the prosecutor and the court to look out for your interests." He'd say, "Counselor, are you nuts? Those guys are trying to put me away for twenty years. That is *not* in my interests, no matter what I did. If you won't fight back for me, I'll get a lawyer who will." See, the inquisitorial system just doesn't mesh with the high sentences.

Grbzyk: Are these harsh sentences wise? I understand that your communities are concerned about crime, but they might do more to stop crime if they directed their efforts more toward rehabilitation?

Lark: Rehabilitation is pretty tough to do. When you punish your child, you can do a lot to see that the punishment helps him, or at least doesn't hurt him, because you control most of his life. You make sure that he is well-fed and housed, that he does his homework, and develops a good character and work habits. You have some say over the company he keeps. The punishment might help him, because the rest of his life is in good shape. That's just not true of most criminal defendants in the United States. They live in rough neighborhoods where they hang out with criminals, they go to lousy schools, and they often have bad home situations. A prosecutor can't do anything about this. Neither can the judge, and neither can the prison warden. We can't take "the whole person" and help him the way you help your kid. So we punish to help us, not to help the defendant. That's all we can do.

Schmrz: In our villages, or in neighborhoods of our cities, there are often support systems that enable us to help wayward offenders, even adults. Couldn't your society do something to change the conditions you describe?

Lark: Maybe we could, but we don't. Those are political questions that are much larger than the question of whether we should have an adversarial or inquisitorial legal system. Some voters think we should do more for the poor, and others think it's hopeless or too expensive to try, and they're too angry with criminals to care about helping them. Right now, the second group seems to be having its way. But whatever the people decide, we in the legal profession are stuck with their decisions. We're just the tail, not the dog. Our criminal legal system is a symptom of how those larger political questions are handled. At the moment, U.S. prosecutors can't help the defendant much. So we try to hurt him. And when we do, he fights back.

Schmrz: Does it follow that you must give him the tools to fight with, like defense lawyers and juries?

Crane: It does follow. When you have a lot of cops and prosecutors trying to hurt people rather than help them, some are bound to make mistakes and commit abuses. So the defendant needs protections. You can't allow an aggressive prosecution without giving the defendant the power to defend himself.

Schmrz: Is there a consensus on that point among your citizens?

Crane: In the abstract, I'm not sure. But when just one case of serious injustice hits the newspapers, like an innocent guy getting railroaded, most people do insist that protections be built into the system.

Lark: Same thing happens on the other side. If just one man gets off or gets out and commits another serious crime, the public demands that we change the whole way we deal with criminal cases.

Crane: Yes. We've been talking as if our system is based on a careful weighing of all the things we've been talking about. But often we set policy by sound bites. Maybe that's why we sometimes seem so erratic. Somebody commits a crime the public sees as particularly heinous, and some politician gets a lot of mileage by pushing an increase in the penalty for that crime. Over time, this happens with *several* crimes, and gradually that changes the standard. So the sentences for *all* crimes get ratcheted up, even though we never sat down and decided that this would be a good idea for a coherent system.

Grbzyk: In Europe, where prosecutors are not so aggressively seeking long sentences, there is not as much need for protections for the defendant, which make up the heart of your adversarial system.

Crane: Right. Until we change to a sentencing approach that shows more concern for the defendant, I don't think we can change to an inquisitorial-type system.

Lark: But that doesn't mean we can't consider adapting certain features from the inquisitorial system that might improve our adversarial system.

Crane: Like what?

Lark: Well, for example, we might. . . .

A young man comes up to Grbzyk and whispers in his ear.

Grbzyk: A fascinating question, but we must defer it to another day. Now, we should return to court. The tribunal is ready to announce its judgment.

They all rise and begin walking.

Schmrz: So, my friends, you have learned much about our inquisitorial system?

Lark: Yeah. Thanks for the tips. But the funny thing is, something else happened, something I never expected. By looking at your system and comparing it with ours, I picked up some insights into *our* system. I've been an American lawyer for quite a while, and I thought I knew our system inside out. I do, in a way, but I've been so busy climbing the trees that I never had a good look at the forest. I just took juries, hearsay rules, and opponents like Crane for granted, without seeing how it all fit together. I guess a goldfish doesn't know what her bowl really looks like until she gets out and sees another bowl.

Crane: It's been an eye-opener, all right. I thought things like the jury trial, the exclusionary rule, and the privilege against self-incrimination were engraved in stone, like the Ten Commandments. They're not. You can have a just and civilized legal system without them. You do, and you don't seem to be savages, except for your coffee. Americans view those things as fundamental rights because. . . .

Lark: Just because they're American.

Grbzyk: And we do the same. We accept and expect certain features just because of who we are.

Schmrz: But people change. And when they do, maybe they can learn from other cultures.

All exit, into the courthouse.

- CURTAIN -

CUMULATIVE PROBLEMS

Here are two "cumulative" Problems, raising issues covered by *several* of the chapters you have read so far. Before writing answers, it will help if you try to *organize* the issues by writing *outlines* of your answers. When you finish, look at the sample outlines which appear after the Problems. (For some tips about how to *write an answer*, see the section "On Problem Analysis" in the Introduction.)

Problem A

To: My law clerk

From: Holly Moses, Esq.

I am handling appeals for Al Able (A) and Bob Baker (B). The record shows the following:

The federal grand jury transcript contains evidence that two men drove into Fort Bort army base, parked in front of the post exchange store, went into the store, pointed guns at store manager Mike Marsh, and forced him to give them about $5,000 in cash. The two men drove off. Military Police Captain Polly Patton (P) drove her car in front of the robbers' car. The robbers' car then ran into Patton's car, killing her. The two men abandoned the car and ran off. A bag of cocaine was found in the glove compartment of the car. The store manager later identified Able and Baker as the robbers, and Able and Baker were each arrested at home. The grand jury indicted both Able and Baker for (1) robbery on a military base[1], (2) assault on a federal law enforcement agent[2], and (3) possession of cocaine on a military base.[3]

Able and Baker retained attorney Larry Low (L) to represent them.

Low discussed the case with Assistant U.S. Attorney Felicia Fedd (F). He told her that Able claimed that he was not involved in any of the crimes charged, as he was at home watching TV when the crimes occurred, and has witnesses to prove it. Fedd said that if Able would plead guilty to robbery, she would have the other charges against him dismissed. Low said he would advise Able to decline the offer and stand trial. Fedd said that she thought that Able had murdered Patton, and the grand jury went too easy on him by indicting only for assault. She said that if Able did not accept her offer, she would go back to the grand jury and ask it to issue a new indictment for murder. Low advised Able to accept the offer, which he did. In court, Able told the judge that he did not commit any crime, but would plead guilty to robbery to avoid the other charges. The judge said that he had read the grand jury transcript. He advised Able of his rights, accepted the plea, and sentenced Able.

Baker went to trial. He testified that Able had forced him at gunpoint to drive Baker's car and help him commit the robbery. He also testified that while he did run into Patton's car, he did so only because he was unable to stop in time. He also

---

[1] "§ 234. *Robbery on Military Base.* Robbery is the taking and carrying away of personal property of another with the intent to steal, by force of fear. Robbery on a military base is a felony."

[2] "§ 345. *Assault on Federal Law Enforcement Officer.* Any person who intentionally assaults any federal law enforcement officer is guilty of a felony."

[3] "§ 456. *Possession of Cocaine on Military Base.* Any person who intentionally possesses cocaine on any military base is guilty of a felony."

testified that he did not know that there was cocaine in the glove compartment. The jury acquitted him of the robbery and assault charges, but convicted him of possession of cocaine.

After Baker's verdict, Able filed a motion to withdraw his plea of guilty to robbery. Fedd admitted that the above-described circumstances occurred, but the judge denied Able's motion.

Fedd then went back to the grand jury, which issued a new indictment against Baker, charging him with (1) involuntary manslaughter of Patton[4], and (2) bringing illegal drugs onto a military base[5]. Low moved to dismiss the indictment, claiming double jeopardy, but the judge denied the motion and set the case for trial.

During jury selection, Fedd asked the prospective jurors if any of them were in favor of legalization of drugs such as cocaine. John Jones, Mary Moore, and Sam Smith said that they were. Fedd exercised a peremptory challenge against each of them. Low objected, but the judge overruled the objection. Fedd exercised 9 of her 10 peremptory challenges.

Low exercised peremptory challenges against 8 prospective jurors. Fedd then stated, "Your honor, the jury commissioner gets names of some prospective jurors from voter registration lists, so both I and defense counsel know how these people are registered. Mr. Low has challenged 8 Republicans and no Democrats. I think this is improper." Low said, "Your honor, Republicans tend to be tougher on defendants in criminal cases." The judge disallowed Low's challenges.

Before the trial began, Baker spoke to Low in private and told him that he ran a stop sign and was driving about 60 miles per hour in a 35 MPH zone when his car hit Patton. Low said, "I had planned put on an expert to testify that your skid marks showed that you were going only 40. Now I can't ethically do that." Low did not put on the expert. Fedd put on 2 soldiers, who testified that Baker's car was traveling "pretty fast, over 50" when it hit Patton's car. Baker was convicted on both charges.

I am representing Able and Baker in appealing their convictions. Please advise me as to the best arguments I can make, and whether they are likely to succeed.

Problem B

To: My law clerk

From: Pandora Spocks, Esq.

I am representing Barry Beatty (B). I need your help on several questions I have.

On June 1, 1991, Beatty was indicted by a federal grand jury in San Francisco on two charges: (1) use of the mails to commit fraud[1], and (2) assault with a deadly

---

[4] "§ 567. *Involuntary Manslaughter on Military Base.* Any civilian who commits kills another person through gross negligence on a military base is guilty of a felony."

[5] "§ 678. *Bringing Illegal Drugs Into Military Base.* Any person who knowingly brings any illegal drug (including heroin, opium, cocaine, and barbiturates) onto any military base is guilty of a felony."

[1] "§ 123. Use of the mails to commit any fraud is a felony."

weapon on a federal officer[2].

The trial began on December 1, 1991. At trial, the main witness against Beatty was Fred Fedd (F). Fedd testified that he works as an inspector for the Savings & Loan Insurance Corporation, a federal agency that regulates savings and loan associations. On May 1, 1988, Fedd received a letter from Beatty, who was president of Jefferson Savings & Loan Co. The letter stated that Jefferson had assets of $100 million. Fedd suspected that this statement was false, and that it was based on an overestimate of the value of real estate that backed up loans Jefferson had made. Fedd went to see Beatty and told Beatty of his concerns. Beatty became very angry, and he picked up a letter opener and swung it at Fedd. Beatty left, did further investigation, and determined that Jefferson's assets were worth only $60 million.

Beatty testified in his own defense. He testified that when he sent the letter to Fedd, he believed that the assets of Jefferson were worth $100 million, based on appraisals furnished to him by independent appraisers. He now realizes that the appraisals were inaccurate, but he had no reason to believe that in 1988. He admitted that he picked up a letter opener while he was talking to Fedd, but claimed that he never swung it at Fedd. On cross-examination, Beatty admitted that he swung at Beatty with his fist.

The trial lasted a month. After deliberating for 2 hours, the jury returned. The foreman told the judge that the jury had voted to convict Beatty on the first charge (use of the mails to defraud), but was unable to get the unanimous vote needed to convict or acquit on the second charge. The judge entered the guilty verdict on the first charge and declared a mistrial on the second charge.

On March 1, 1992, the U.S. Attorney went back to the grand jury and obtained a new indictment against Beatty, charging him with (1) knowingly making a false statement to a federal agency in order to secure benefits,[3] and (2) assault on a federal officer.[4] The grand jury transcript shows that the sole evidence presented to the grand jury was the transcript of the trial described above. Trial has been set for July 1, 1992.

Question 1: I would like to file a motion to dismiss the new indictment, on double jeopardy grounds. What arguments can I make, and what is the likelihood that they will succeed?

Question 2: Both before and after the first trial, there was a lot of publicity in the media about this case. I would like to file a motion for change of venue, based on pretrial publicity. Please tell me how to package the motion, e.g., what should I look for in the publicity, what facts I need to find out, and what I should emphasize in my motion.

Question 3: I obtained a list of the jury venire (containing 60 names), and I had my investigator do some research on them.

40 of them have accounts in savings & loan institutions. I do not want any of

---

[2] "§ 234. Assault with a deadly weapon on a federal officer in the performance of his or her duties is a felony."

[3] "§ 345. Any person who knowingly makes a false statement to a federal agency in order to secure benefits from that agency is guilty of a felony."

[4] "§ 456. Assault on a federal officer in the performance of his or her duties is a misdemeanor."

these people on my jury, as they might fear loss of **their savings if the** activities described by the prosecution are allowed to go on. Of **the 40, five had accounts** with Jefferson, although all of those accounts were insured by the federal agency, so all of those five people will be reimbursed (after a bit of a wait).

Of the 60, eight work for the federal government (military, post office, Dept. of Veteran's Affairs, and the like). All eight happen to be women. As these people work for the same "person" who is prosecuting the case (the U.S. Government), I do not want them on my jury either.

I get only 10 peremptory challenges, so I would prefer to challenge these people for cause. Would challenges for cause be sustained? If not, would I have any problem using peremptory challenges against these people?

Outline of Issues in Problem A

I. Able. Was motion to withdraw plea properly denied?

A. Involuntary, because A claimed innocence? Not if there was "factual basis for plea".

B. Involuntary, because A's threat to obtain indictment for murder was vindictive? Might depend on whether F had probable cause for murder indictment. See *Bordenkircher v. Hayes*.

C. Was A denied effective assistance of counsel, because of conflict of interest?

II. Baker

A. Ineffective assistance of counsel, because of conflict?

B. Double jeopardy?

1. Involuntary manslaughter charge?

a. Under *Blockburger* test, this was not the "same offense" as assault on federal officer, as each crime requires elements other does not.

b. Collateral estoppel? No, as decided fact that A could not stop in time does not show that he did not commit gross negligence.

2. Bringing drugs charge?

a. Bringing cocaine in is probably the "same offense" as possession, under *Blockburger* test, because one could not bring it in without also possessing it.

b. Collateral estoppel? No, as D was *convicted* in first trial.

C. Sustaining F's peremptory challenges.

1. Are people in favor of legalization a "cognizable class"?

3. Was exclusion intentional?

D. Denying L's peremptory challenges.

1. Does *Batson* affect defense use of peremptories?

2. Are Republicans a "cognizable class"?

3. Was exclusion intentional?

E. Ineffective assistance of counsel, because of refusal to have expert testify?

    1. Would it be unethical to have expert testify?

    2. If not, was this below standard of "reasonably effective assistance"? *Strickland.*

    3. Prejudicial? *Strickland.*

Outline of Issues on Problem B

Question 1:

I. 1st Charge (Knowingly making false statement . . .)

    A. "Same offense", under *Blockburger* test? No.

    B. No collateral estoppel, as D was *convicted* at first trial.

II. 2nd Charge (Assault on federal officer).

    A. "Same offense", under *Blockburger* test? Seems so.

    B. Was D "put in jeopardy" for that offense? Yes, as jury was sworn in at first trial.

    C. Was there "manifest necessity" to declare mistrial in 1st trial? Consider facts that:

        1. Judge had alternative, such as asking jury to take more time to deliberate.

        2. No indication that D objected to mistrial.

Question 2:

Consider:

1. Size of community.

2. Extent of news broadcasting (newspaper circulation, TV & radio range).

3. Frequency of broadcasting.

4. Nature of news (type of crime, factual vs. opinion, detailed evidence, fact that first jury convicted D on one charge).

5. Passage of time since news coverage.

Question 3:

I. Prospective jurors with accounts in S&Ls.

    A. Challenge for cause?

        1. Would this fact alone prevent them from being fair?

        2. Is further *voir dire* necessary?

    B. Peremptory challenge?

      1. Cognizable class? It is quite large, but not suspect.

      2. Prima facie case?

      3. D's justification?

      4. Does *Batson* apply to defense counsel?

II. Prospective jurors with accounts at Jefferson.

    A. Challenge for cause?

      1. Would this fact alone prevent them from being fair?

      2. Is further *voir dire* necessary?

    B. Peremptory challenge?

      1. Cognizable class? It is quite large, but not suspect.

      2. Prima facie case?

      3. D's justification?

      4. Does *Batson* apply to defense counsel?

III. Prospective jurors who work for federal government.

    A. Challenge for cause?

      1. Would this fact alone prevent them from being fair?

      2. Is further *voir dire* necessary?

    B. Peremptory challenge?

      1. People who work for feds.

        a. Cognizable class? It is quite large, but not suspect.

        b. Prima facie case?

        c. D's justification?

      2. Women.

        a. Cognizable class?

        b. Prima facie case?

        c. D's justification?

TABLE OF CASES

[References are to pages]

A

Abbate v. United States 661
Acarino; United States v. 150
Accetturo; United States v. 612; 617
Adams v. Superior Court. 538
Adel; State v. 658
Aetna Ins. Co. v. Kennedy. 297
Agueci; United States v. 617
Agurs; United States v. 119; 131; 144; 157; 159;
168; 365
Akins v. Texas 501
Alabama; United States v. 474
Albernaz v. United States 665
Alderman v. United States 644; 978
Aleman; People v. 664
Alen; State v. 514
Alessi; United States v. 145
Alexander v. Louisiana. 500; 505
Allen v. Hardy 994
Allen v. McCurry. 647
Allen v. Thomas 401
Allen; U.S. v. 674
Alvarado v. Superior Court 140
Alvarado; United States v. 556
Alvernaz, In re. 882
Anaya v. Hansen. 434
Anders v. California 791; 819; 830
Anderson; State v. 206
Andis; United States v. 397, 398; 400
Andre; People v. 723
Andrews; United States v. 605
Angel; U.S. v. 550
Anzalone; United States v. 144
Apodaca v. Oregon. 409
Apprendi v. New Jersey. 746; 769; 771; 777
Argersinger v. Hamlin 833; 859
Arizona v. Washington 668; 671; 673
Arizona v. Fulminante. 804; 1012
Arizona v. Youngblood. 155; 329
Armstrong; United States v. 36; 47; 49–52
Arnett; U.S. v. 642
Ashe v. Swenson. 633; 642; 645; 649–651
Asher; U.S. v. 665
Auerbach; United States v. 320
Avery v. Georgia. 504

B

Bailey; People v. 846
Bailey v. State 521; 883
Bailey v. U.S. 367

Baker; State v. 490
Balfour; State v. 830
Ballard; State v. 480
Ballard v. United States. 419, 420; 430; 476
Ballew v. Georgia 409
Balog; Commonwealth v. 666
Baltes v. Doe I 938
Banks; United States v. 315
Barber v. Page 205
Barber v. Ponte. 426; 475
Barker v. Wingo . 293; 304; 318; 321; 322; 326; 327;
329; 331; 339–341
Barksdale v. Commonwealth. 532
Barnes v. State 401
Barnes; State v. 405
Barrett; U.S. v. 653
Barry; U.S. v. 432
Bartee; People v. 930
Bartkus v. Illinois. 661, 662
Bartlett; State v. 741
Bartolomucci; Commonwealth v. 668
Bass; United States v. 51
Basurto; United States v. . . 247; 253; 255; 279; 280
Batson v. Kentucky . . 453; 500; 519; 526; 541, 542;
545; 551–553; 558; 887; 893; 994
Beatrice Foods Co. v. United States. 255
Beavers v. Haubert. 318
Beck v. Alabama. 527
Bel-Mar Laboratories, Inc.; United States v. . . . 151
Bell; State v. 665
Bell v. U.S. 659
Bellomo; U.S. v. 85
Beltram; United States v. 244; 246
Benmuhar; U.S. v. 433
Bennett; People v. 198; 731
Benton v. Maryland 631; 633; 635, 636
Berger v. United States . . . 124; 135; 278– 280; 617
Berkow v. State 881
Bernstein; People v. 197
Berries; United States v. 39
Bettencourt; United States v. 256
Bey; State v. 387
Biddle v. District Court 196
Bieber; People v. 194–197
Bifield; United States v. 915
Bishop; U.S. v. 547; 549; 556
Black; People v. 774; 778
Blackburn v. Alabama 806; 808
Blackledge v. Allison. 375
Blackledge v. Perry 26

Blair v. United States 275

Blake, State ex rel. v. Hatcher. 845

Blakely v. Washington 767; 769; 771

Blasus; State v. 399

Blockburger v. United States . . .638; 649; 659; 665

Bloom; People v. 735

Bolden; Commonwealth v. 669, 670

Bollenbach v. United States 789

Bonin; People v. 446

Bonner; People v. 658

Bontkowski v. United States. 389

Booker; United States v. 769; 771; 776

Bordenkircher v. Hayes. . .25; 27; 31; 38; 386; 388; 390

Bosch; U.S. v. 874

Botero; United States v. 66

Boumediene v. Bush. 970

Bourjaily v. United States 204

Bousley v. U.S.. 367

Boyd; State v. 434

Boyd; U.S. v. .572

Boyd v. United States 977

Boykin v. Alabama 355; 357; 365; 386; 961

Braasch; United States v. 617

Bracy v. United States 256

Bradley; Commonwealth v. 670

Bradwell v. State 521

Brady v. Maryland. . .112; 131, 132; 143; 157; 168; 170; 274; 279; 365; 675; 820; 996

Brady v. United States .359; 365–367; 386; 388; 875

Brady; United States v. 429, 430

Bram v. United States 362; 1012, 1013

Braniff Airways, Inc.; United States v. 254

Branzburg v. Hayes 254

Braune; People v. 602, 603

Breed v. Jones 664

Breiner; State v. 358

Breinig; U.S. v. 603

Bridges v. State. 519

Brinkman; United States v. 138

Briscoe; United States v. 876

Broce; United States v. 366; 395

Brooks; People v. 597

Brooks v. Tennessee 859

Brown v. Allen. . .975; 987; 989; 1001, 1002; 1005

Brown v. Mississippi 1012

Brown v. Ohio 647; 660

Brown; People v. 137

Brown; State v. 665

Brown; U.S. v. 536

Brown v. United States 266; 281; 814; 978

Brown v. Walker 264

Bruce; U.S. v. 352

Brunn; U.S. v. 618

Bruton v. United States. . .579; 586; 587; 593; 600; 609; 614; 619; 621; 626; 800; 802; 810

Bryson v. United States 267

Bucci; U.S. v. .512

Buettner-Janusch; United States v. 143

Bufalino; United States v. 144

Buljubasic; United States v. 609; 616

Burch v. Louisiana. 409

Burgess; State v. 729

Burke; Commonwealth v. 123

Burks v. U.S.. . . . . .664; 675

Burr; U.S. v. 262; 481

Bushert; U.S. v. 396

Butera; United States v. 426

Butler; United States v. 299

C

Cafaro; United States v. 149

Calandra; United States v. . . 240; 254; 262; 263; 267; 269; 271; 275; 276; 280, 281; 977, 978; 981

Caldwell v. Mississippi 279

Caliendo; United States v. 609

California v. Green. 174

California v. Trombetta 157; 164, 165

Callahan; United States v. 152

Campbell v. Louisiana 511

Campbell; United States v. 879

Cancel; Commonwealth v. 958

Cannone; United States v. 145

Cantone v. Superintendent, New York Correctional Facility at Green Haven 143

Capaldo; United States v. 271

Carella v. California 814

Cariola; United States v. 879

Carnley v. Cochran. 297; 356

Carter; United States v. 506

Casamento; United States v. 610; 617

Castaneda v. Partida 436

Castellano; United States v. 945

Castello; United States v. 384

Castillo-Basa; U.S. v. 645

Cathey; United States v. 255

Chaffin v. Stynchcombe 715

Chambers v. Maroney 814

Chandler v. State. 794

Chanen; United States v. 254; 275

Chapman v. California . . . 189; 786; 800; 807; 809; 841; 866; 974

Chemical Foundation, Inc.; United States v. . . .38–40

Cherry; U.S. v. 154

Chiattello; United States v. 666

[References are to pages]

Chicago National League Ball Club, Inc. v. Thompson 33
Chidester; State v. 434
Chong; State v. 257
Ciambrone; United States v. 254; 280
Cigic; State v. 795
City of (see name of city) . . . .
Clark; United States v. 389; 394
Cleburne v. Cleburne Living Center 33; 541
Clemons v. Mississippi. 814
Clemons; U.S. v. 556
Cockrell v. Oberhauser. 584
Coleman v. Alabama. 181; 189; 206; 271; 814
Coleman v. Burnett. 178
Coleman v. Thompson. 340
Collins v. Commonwealth 673
Collins; State v. 373
Commonwealth v. (see name of defendant). . . . .
Conerly v. State 570
Contreras; State v. 657
Cooke v. United States. 951
Cooper; State v. 650
Cooper; U.S. v. 166; 800
Corona v. Superior Court 451
Correa; People v. 876
Correa v. Superior Court. 214
Corsi; State v. 597
Cortina; United States v. 254
Costello v. United States . . 184; 205; 228; 240; 245;
        246; 249; 256; 262, 263; 276; 278; 281
Costello; United States v. 230
Couch v. United States. 126
Coughlin, In re. 722
Counselman v. Hitchcock 263; 270
County of (see name of county). . . . .
Cox; U.S. v. 382
Craig v. Boren 521
Crane v. Kentucky 814
Craney; State v. 595
Crist v. Bretz 663
Cronic; United States v. 859
Crowley; United States v. 357; 879
Culombe v. Connecticut 812
Cunningham v. California 768
Cunningham v. Superior Court 23
Curtis; United States v. 915
Cuthrell v. Director. 879
Cuyler v. Sullivan 844, 845; 853; 855; 859; 860;
        863

D

Dahn; State v. 387

Daley v. United States 581
Daniels v. State. 844
Dansker; United States v. 474
Daubert v. Merrell Dow Pharmaceuticals, Inc. . . .86
Davenport; U.S. v. 654
Davis; State v. 492; 534; 536
Davis; U.S. v. 534-36; 538
Davis v. United States. 986–988; 992
Day; People v. 870
Deardorff; United States v. 153
Death of (see name of party) . . . .
DeBerry; United States v. 843
Deems; People v. 664
DeGross; United States v. 521
Del Carpio-Cotrina; United States v. 930
Del Muro; U.S. v. 847
Delaware v. Van Arsdall 814
DeLeo; United States v. 256
Delli Paoli v. United States 579; 621
DeMarco; United States v. 254
DeMond v. Superior Court. 197
Dennis; State v. 586
Dennis v. United States. 153; 472, 473
DePallo; People v. 927
Dias; Commonwealth v. 142
Diaz; United States v. 140; 614
DiGiacomo; United States v. 91
Dillard; U.S. v. 62
Dionisio; United States v. 263; 267; 269; 275
Dixon; United States v. 665
Doe; U.S. v. 940
Doe, In re. .937
Doggett v. United States. . .325; 334; 335; 336; 339
Dorsey v. State. 569
Douglas v. California 783; 791; 792; 828
Douglas; People v. 456
Downs-Morgan v. United States. 875
Duckworth v. Eagan 1016; 1017
Duncan v. Louisiana . .407; 419, 420; 749; 757; 818
Dunham, In re 722, 723
Dunnigan; United States v. 720
Duran de Amesquita; U.S. v. 513
Durbin v. U.S. 273
Duren v. Missouri. 426, 427; 429

E

Edmonson v. Leesville Concrete Co. 520
Edwards; People v. 21
EEOC v. Greyhound Lines, Inc. 552
Eid; People v. 213
Elkins v. U.S. 977

Ellerbee v. State 570
Engle v. Isaac. 819; 1000; 1006
Ernest; People v. 951
Erwin; People v. 212
Escalante; State v. 157
Eskridge v. Washington State Board. 792
Estelle v. Smith. 728
Estepa; United States v. 242; 278
Estes v. Texas. 438; 463
Ethington; State v. 398, 399
Evitts v. Lucey. 818
Ewell; United States v. 296; 308; 318
Ewing v. California 741
Ex parte (see name of relator). . . . .
Ex parte United States. 275
Ex rel. (see name of relator). . . . .

F

Fahey, People ex rel. v. Burr. 951, 952
Fahy v. Connecticut 787
Falter v. United States. 281
Farber, In re. 939, 940
Faretta v. California 833
Fay v. Noia . . . 975; 982, 983; 986, 987; 989; 1015
Fellerman v. Bradley 936; 938, 939
Feola; U.S. v. 143; 155
Ferguson; Commonwealth v. 669
Ferguson v. Georgia 859
Ferri; United States v. 473
Figueroa-Soto; U.S. v. 663
Fisher; People v. 581
Fletcher; People v. 594; 597
Florida v. Nixon 959
Ford; People v. 356
Foss, In re 739
Fox Film Corp. v. Muller 987
Frady; United States v. 1001
Francis v. Henderson. 987; 992
Frank v. Mangum 975
Franklin v. Anderson. 481
Freyre-Lazaro; U.S. v. 653
Frometa; Commonwealth v. 881
Frontiero v. Richardson. 521, 522
Fuller; State v. 537
Furey; U.S. v. 304

G

Gadson; People v. 927
Gale v. United States. 796
Gallardo-Mendez; U.S. v. 641
Gallo; United States v. 254; 610
Gamble v. Commonwealth. 488

Garcia; People v. 538
Garner; United States v. 613; 616
Garrett v. Morris. 556
Garrett v. U.S. 666
Gates; State v. 795
Gaughran; State v. 283
Gavilan; United States v. 879
Gaviria; United States v. 682
Gayther; People v. 738
Geders v. United States 859
Gelb; U.S. v. 537
George v. State. 795
Georgia v. McCollum 512; 520; 522; 527; 887
Gerstein v. Pugh. 205
Gideon v. Wainwright.787; 789; 809; 815; 827; 833;
                                            841; 859; 991
Giglio v. U.S. 113; 365; 996
Gilchrist v. State. 513
Gillis v. State. 661
Ginebra; State v. 876; 881
Glasser v. United States. . .419; 423; 789; 838, 839
Goba; U.S. v. 92
Gold; United States v. 254; 279
Goldman; United States v. 148
Gomillion v. Lightfoot. 46
Goodell, In re. 521
Goodspeed v. State. 872
Goodwin; United States v. 24; 38
Goss; People v. 641
Government of the Virgin Islands v. Dowling . .887;
                                                  896
Government of the Virgin Islands v.
    Weatherwax. 893
Government of Virgin Islands v. Fahie 123
Government of Virgin Islands v. Gereau 475
Grady v. Corbin 652
Grammatikos; United States v. 145
Grand Jury Subpoena Served Upon John Doe, In
    re 945
Grand Jury Subpoenas Served Upon Field, In re.938
Grand Jury Witness Ralph Altro, In re 371
Gravel v. United States. 275; 281
Gray v. Maryland. 586; 619
Gray; People v. 20
Grayson; United States v. 712; 719
Green v. United States 631; 636; 639; 649
Greer v. State. 657
Griffin v. California 786; 790, 791; 802
Griffin v. Illinois. 271; 792; 794; 823; 827
Grim; State v. 570
Grinnell Corp.; United States v. 622
Groban, In re. 266
Guevara; People v. 778

[References are to pages]

Guido; State v. 273

Gutierrez v. Superior Court 641

H

Hahn; U.S. v. 397

Hale v. Henkel 250; 253

Hall; U.S. v. 292

Hamilton v. Alabama. 789

Hannah v. Larche. 274

Harding; United States v. 682; 684

Hardwick; State v. 729

Harmelin v. Michigan 683; 741

Harmon v. State 653

Harrington v. California 622; 800; 816

Harris v. New York . . 266; 589; 625; 730; 915; 992; 1018

Harris; State v. .453

Harris; United States v. 184; 541; 685; 690

Hashem; Commonwealth v. 671

Hasting; United States v. 814

Hatten; Commonwealth v. 670, 671

Hawkins v. Superior Court 198; 206; 217; 219

Hayes; United States v. 334; 597

Haynes; U.S. v. 481

Haynes v. Washington. 789; 1012

Hazelton; State v. 654

Heath v. Alabama 662

Hedgpeth v. Pulida. 819

Heinz; People v. 879

Henderson; Commonwealth v. 166

Hendrix; United States v. 716

Henry v. Mississippi. 986

Hensley v. Municipal Ct. 97

Herbert v. Superior Court 206

Herman; United States v. 319

Hernandez v. N.Y. . . . 518; 544; 552; 556; 559; 564

Hernandez; People v. 778

Hernandez v. State 852; 853

Hernandez v. Texas. 430

Herrera v. Collins. 1008

Herring v. New York 753; 859

Herzog v. United States. 72

Hickman v. Taylor 127; 154

Hill v. Lockhart. 875; 878

Hill v. Texas 429

Hilliard v. Spalding 161

Hinds County School Bd; United States v. 43

Hischke; State v. 928; 930

Hoac; U.S. v. .595

Hoag v. New Jersey 634, 635

Hodge and Zweig; United States v. 937

Hoffa v. United States 115

Hoffman v. United States 269

Holland v. Illinois. 509; 526; 571

Holloway v. Arkansas. 718; 836; 846

Hollywood Motor Car Co.; United States v. 319, 320

Holt v. United States. 229, 230

Hopper v. Evans 814

Horn; U.S. v. 130; 131

Horning; State v. 390

Howard; Commonwealth v. 671

Howard v. Senkowski 533

Howard; State v. 487

Howell; State v. 665

Hoyt v. Florida. 421, 422

Hoyt; United States v. 682

Huante; People v. 881

Huey; U.S. v. 571, 572

Hugle, In re Grand Jury Investigation of. 275

Humes v. United States 716

Humphrey; People v. 737

Hunter v. District Court of Twentieth Judicial Dist. 193

Hurtado v. California. 218; 753

Huston; People v. 250

Hutchison v. United States. 879

I

Iannelli v. United States. 649

Ibarra, In re. 384, 385

Idaho v. Craig 204

Illinois v. Fisher 167

Illinois v. Perkins. 813

Illinois v. Somerville. 249

Imbler, In re 134

In re Estate of (see name of party) . . . .

In re (see name of party) . . . .

In re U.S. 122

In the Matter of (see name of party) . . . .

Inadi; United States v. 204

Ingram; State v. 657

Investigation of (see name of party). . . . .

Irvin v. Dowd. 438, 439; 441

Izazaga v. Superior Court 171

J

J.E.B. v. Alabama ex rel. T.B. . . 519; 532; 534; 538; 541, 542

Jackson v. Denno 355; 580; 806; 985

Jackson; People v. 850

Jackson; United States v. 363

Jackson v. Virginia. 803; 807; 1008; 1011; 1014

Jacqueline F., In re. 938
Jagodinsky; State v. 533
Janvier v. U.S.. 877
Javor v. U.S.. 870
Jencks v. United States. 125
Ji; State v. 433
Johnson v. California. 543
Johnson v. New Jersey. 1013
Johnson v. Pataki 10
Johnson; People v. 565; 803; 926
Johnson v. State. 141; 882
Johnson; State v. 403, 404; 665
Johnson v. Superior Court. 254
Johnson v. U.S.. 443
Johnson; U.S. v. 605; 729
Johnson v. Zerbst 270; 297; 879
Jones v. Barnes 888, 889; 961
Jones v. State. 569
Jones; State v. 665
Jones v. Superior Court. 194; 196
Jones v. United States. . . .401; 750; 757; 764; 771
Jones; United States v. 47; 488
Jorn; United States v. 649; 668; 670, 671
Joseph v. State. 537

K

Kail; People v. 32
Kamana'o; State v. 729
Kaminsky; United States v. 150
Kastigar v. United States. 263
Kaufman v. United States 976
Kelly; United States v. 610
Kelly, In re. 269
Kenny; United States v. 169
Kentucky v. Whorton. 807; 814
Kimmelman v. Morrison 1011
King v. State 473
King; State v.. 533
Kirby v. Illinois. 265; 270
Kivlin; Commonwealth v. 669
Kloper v. North Carolina. 293; 305
Klubock; United States v. 940
Knox; State v.. . . . . .512, 513
Knox; United States v. 267
Konefal; United States v. 150
Koon; U.S. v.. 662
Kopituk; U.S. v. 617
Korth; State v. 830
Kotteakos v. United States 135; 608; 613
Kozlov, In re. 935, 936
Krulewitch v. United States 581; 603
Kuhlmann v. Wilson 813

Kunce v. Hogan 955
Kyles v. Whitley 137; 365

L

L.A.S.; People v. 951
Lamb v. State. 530
Lambeth; People v.. 744
Lambright; State v.. 596
Lawson; United States v.. 279
Lee v. Hopper 878
Leffel v. Municipal Court. 20
Lefkowitz v. Turley 264
Leibengood v. State 437
Leibowitz; United States v. 245
Lemke, Ex Parte 374
Leroy; United States v.. 143
Lettley v. State 843
Levitt; People v. 735
Lilly v. Virginia 585
Lindh; U.S. v.. 16
Lindsey; State v. 116
Linkletter v. Walker 977
Lloyd, United States ex rel. v. Vincent 146
Locascio; United States v. 942
Locasio v. U.S.. 854
Lockett v. Ohio. 460
Lockhart v. McCree 489
Logan; State v.. 483
Long; United States v. 595; 925
Long Beach City Employees Assn. v. City of Long
    Beach. 23
Lopez v. People 776
Lopez; State v.. 660
Loraine v. United States 257
Los Angeles, County of v. Patrick 23
Loud Hawk; United States v.. . . .314; 327; 330; 340
Loughran; People v. 956
Lovasco; United States v. 305; 332
Lovell; U.S. v. 371
Lozano v. State 451; 452
Lumumba; United States v. 151
Lutwak v. United States 582
Lux v. Commonwealth. 849
Lynch, In re. 738; 741
Lynumn v. Illinois 789

M

MacDonald; United States v.. . . .316, 317; 320; 327
Mackey v. United States. 267
Maestas v. District Court, Colo.. . . . . . . 193; 195
Maguigan; Commonwealth v. 939

[References are to pages]

Mahan; U.S. v. 549
Main; People v.. 739
Maine v. Superior Court. 447
Majado; People v. 640
Malinski v. New York 621
Malloy v. Hogan 1012
Malloy; U.S. v. 86
Malofsky; United States v.. 245
Mancuso; United States v. 610
Mandujano; United States v.. . . . . . . .259; 275
Maness v. Meyers 126; 270
Mantel; People v. 35
Mapp v. Ohio 802; 976, 977; 1011; 1015
Mara; United States v. 265; 268
Marbury v. Madison 1023
Marion; United States v. . . 293; 307, 308; 310; 317;
                               321; 327; 330; 332
Marquez; People v.. 658
Marquez; U.S. v. 388
Marshak; United States v. 148
Martin v. Ohio. 751
Martin; People v.. 691
Martin; United States v. 254; 472
Martin Linen Supply Co; United States v. 809
Martinez v. Superior Court 446
Martinez-Salazar; U.S. v. 491
Masinia v. United States. 266
Mason; State v.. 661
Massiah v. United States 814; 816; 995; 998
Massino; United States v. 149
Mathews v. Eldridge. 724
Matthews; Commonwealth v. 435
McCann v. Municipal Court. 963
McCarthy v. United States. 879
McClellan; People v. 358
McCleskey v. Kemp 887
McCleskey v. Zant 995; 1015
McClure v. Thompson 940
McCollum; State v.. 570
McCoy v. Court of Appeals of Wis 822; 828
McCoy; People v. 431
McDaniels; United States v.. 506
McDole v. State 102
McDonough Power Equipment, Inc. v.
    Greenwood. 476
McDowell; State v.. 921
McGill; United States v.. 72
McIver; United States v.. 598
McKaskle v. Wiggins 815
McKeiver v. Pennsylvania. 409
McKenney; State v. 795
McKenzie; United States v. 254
McKinney v. Walker 506

McLawhorn v. State of North Carolina 139
McMann v. Richardson . . . 366, 367; 859, 860; 875
McMillan v. Pennsylvania 748; 753, 754
McMillan and Almendarez-Torres v. United
    States 753
McNamara; U.S. v.. 868
McNiece; People v. 734
McVeigh; U.S. v.. 457
Meaton v. United States 357; 879
Mechanik; United States v. 257
Meeks v. Bergen. 889
Mejia v. State. 515; 518
Melancon; United States v.. . . . . .374; 391
Melody, In re Estate of 955
Melvin, In re. 272
Meredith; People v. 647
Mezzanatto; U.S. v. 354
Michigan v. Tucker. 269; 730; 1013; 1018
Mickens v. Taylor 854
Midgett; U.S. v. 927
Miesner v. State 573
Miller v. Fenton. 806; 812; 1014
Miller; People v.. 955
Miller-El v. Cockrell 1023
Milton v. Wainwright. 808; 814; 816
Minetos v. City University of New York 556
Minniefield v. State 570
Miranda v. Arizona . . 259; 297; 362; 589; 625; 802;
                          808; 985; 1009; 1012; 1016
Miskovsky v. State ex rel. Jones. 954; 957
Misquadace; State v.. 401
Mistretta v. U.S. 679; 754
Mitchell; Commonwealth v.. . . . . .921; 929
Mitchell v. U.S. 728
Moen; State v.. 389
Moffett; Commonwealth v. 795, 796
Monia; United States v. 263
Montgomery v. Commonwealth. 488
Moody v. Daggett 311
Mooney v. Holohan. 112; 132; 279; 307
Moore v. Arizona. 304
Moore v. Hinton 357; 879
Moore v. Illinois. 134; 157; 662; 814
Moore v. Michigan. 370
Morales v. State 628
Moran v. Burbine. 591; 626; 941
Moreno; People v.. 737
Morey v. Commonwealth 649
Morissette v. United States 716
Morrissey v. Brewer 702
Morrow; United States v. 610
Moses; United States v. 21
Mosier v. Murphy 845

[References are to pages]

Motamedi; United States v. 71; 97
Mott v. State 876
Motton; People v. 508
Moussaoui; U.S. v. 141; 142
Mu'min v. Virginia. 443
Municipal Court; People v. 102
Murgia v. Municipal Court 20
Murphy v. Florida 437
Murphy; People v. 654
Murray v. Carrier 1001; 1003
Myers v. Commonwealth 197
Myers; U.S. v. 283

N

Nackson, In re 934
Napue v. Illinois 249
Nash; State v. 655
Nash; U.S. v. 644
Nash, In re 791; 793
Navarro-Botello; United States v. 391
Navarro-Vargas; U.S. v. 231
Neil; State v. 570
Neitlich, In the Matter of 959
Nelson v. O'Neil 584
Nelson; People v. 314; 722
Nelson; U.S. v. 481
Newberry; People v. 163
Newhouse v. Superior Court. 213
Newton v. Rumery 391; 393
Nichols v. Butler 896
Nichols; U.S. v. 730
Nickerson; U.S. v. 874
Nielsen, In re 650
Nix v. Whiteside 913; 922; 923
Nixon; United States v. 124; 262; 939
Nobles; United States v. 123; 154
Norris v. Alabama 502; 505
North Carolina v. Alford 357; 382; 388; 922
North Carolina v. Pearce. 649
Nuckols; United States v. 384; 386

O

O'Brien; United States v. 77; 87
O'Neill; U.S. v. 354
O'Shea; U.S. v. 230
O'Sullivan v. Boerckel 1021
Ocanas; United States v. 373
Odeneal; U.S. v. 426
Ogonowski v. State. 627
Ohio Bell Tel. Co. v. Public Utilities Comm'n . .297
Oliver v. U.S. 93

One Assortment of 89 Firearms; United States
v.. 726
Oregon v. Elstad 808; 1013; 1016
Oregon v. Hass. 730
Oregon v. Ice. 782
Orta; U.S. v. 78
Orta; United States v. 261
Ouber v. Guarino. 870
Owen; People v.. 22
Oyler v. Boles 11; 14, 15; 38; 40

P

Pacheco; United States v. 616
Padilla; People v. 876
Page; United States v. 274; 278
Paille; People v.. . . . . .194; 196
Parker v. North Carolina. 367
Parry v. Rosemeyer 358
Patane; United States v. 730
Patillo; United States v. 681
Patriarca; United States v.. 86
Patterson v. New York 751
Patton v. Yount 474; 486
Pavao; Commonwealth v. 959
Pavloyianis; U.S. v. 674
Payden; United States v. 150
Payne v. Arkansas. 787, 788; 807; 815
Payton; United States v. 245
Pearson; United States v.. 504
Pelullo; U.S. v.. 642
Pennsylvania v. Local Union 542 474
People v. (see name of defendant). . . . .
People ex rel. (see name of relator). . . . .
Percevault; United States v. 147–149
Perez; U.S. v. 373; 396; 667
Perkins v. LeFevre 143
Peters v. Kiff 419; 421; 431
Pfingst; United States v. 143; 148
Phillips; United States v.. 610
Phillips Petroleum Co.; United States v.. . .254; 279
Phipps; State v. 32
Pittsburgh Plate Glass v. U.S.. 225
Plessy v. Ferguson 511
Poindexter; United States v. 169
Pointer v. Texas. 580; 589; 800
Polichemi; U.S. v. 481
Polk v. Dixie Ins. Co. 556
Polk County v. Dodson 340
Pollard; U.S. v.. 387
Pollard v. United States 323
Pommerening; United States v. 267

[References are to pages]

Pope v. Illinois. 814
Pospisil; U.S. v. 549
Potter; United States v.. 436
Powell v. Alabama. 859
Powell v. Superior Court. 444
Powers v. Ohio. .510; 516; 520; 523, 524; 529; 571
Pozo; People v.. . . . . .874; 881
Price v. Johnston. 378
Puente; State v.. 434
Puglia; U.S. v. 283
Purkett v. Elem. 551; 556; 563
Putra; U.S. v.. 727

Q

Quintero v. U.S. 845

R

R. Enterprises; United States v. 275
Rainge; People v.. 597
Rambert; State v.. 657
Ramos; People v.. 732
Ramos v. State. 797
Randolph v. Commonwealth. 585
Raynor; U.S. v.. 396
Ready; U.S. v. 371; 374
Reardon v. Marlayne, Inc.. 936
Redmond; People v.. 719
Redondo-Lemos; U.S. v. 21
Redwine v. Zuckert. 357; 879
Reed v. Becka 373
Reed v. Reed. 521
Reed; United States v.. 278
Regalado; People v.. 743
Reid; People v.. 744
Respublica v. Shaffer. 277
Reyes; People v.. 742
Rhoden; People v.. 372
Riccobene; United States v. 608
Richards; People v.. 722
Richardson   v.   Communication   Workers   of
    America. 473
Richardson v. Marsh. .587; 594–596; 599, 600; 620;
                                      625; 627
Richardson, In re. 939
Rideau v. Louisiana. 438; 463
Riggins; State v.. 879
Riley v. Commonwealth. 531
Rimar; United States v. 597
Ring v. Arizona 766, 767; 769; 771
Rivera v. Illinois 818
Roberts; United States v.. 279
Robertson; U.S. v. 380

Robinson v. U.S.. 533
Robinson; United States v.. 502
Robson; Commonwealth v. 669
Rochin v. California 307
Rodriguez; People v.. 384
Rodriguez; U.S. v. 352; 723
Rogers v. Richmond 808
Rosa; United States v.. 400
Rosales-Lopez v. United States 472
Rose v. Clark. 814, 815
Rose v. Mitchell 1011; 1013
Rosenberg v. Fleuti. 184
Ross v. Moffitt 827
Ross v. Oklahoma 489; 819
Ross v. Sirica. 185; 189
Ross; State v.. 557
Rothgery v. Gillespie County 833
Roviaro v. United States 139; 140; 390
Rowan; United States v.. 597
Rubio v. Superior Court 436; 538, 539
Ruhbayan; U.S. v. 645
Ruiz; U.S. v.. 364
Rushen v. Spain 814
Russell; United States v.. 875
Rutan; United States v.. . . . . . .391, 392; 396; 400

S

Sacco; United States v.. 34
Sail'er Inn, Inc. v. Kirby 17
Salamone; United States v.. . . . . .469; 550
Salerno; U.S. v. 65; 83; 95
Samango; United States v.. . . . . .254; 279
Sanborn v. State 930
Sanchez v. State 795
Sanders v. United States 1005
Sandoval; People v.. 881
Santiago-Martinez; United States v.. 542
Santobello v. New York. 368; 374; 376
Satterwhite v. Texas 814
Scarborough v. State. 597
Scher; Commonwealth v.. . . . . .312; 314
Schiavo; United States v.. 72
Schmerber v. California 126
Schneckloth v. Bustamonte. 268; 979
Scott v. Illinois. 833
Scott; People v.. 652
Scott v. State. 928
Scott; U.S. v.. 93
Scott v. United States 716
Sealfon v. United States 635
Sellers v. United States 72
Selser, In re. 938

[References are to pages]

Senate of Puerto Rico v. United States Dep't of Justice 226

Serubo; United States v. 257; 280

Shannon; People v. 137

Shaw; United States v. 682

Shelton v. United States 345; 362

Sheppard v. Maxwell 438; 463; 789

Sherrick; People v. 396

Shockley v. State. 930

Shoher; United States v. 149

Short; U.S. v. 231

Shuttle v. Smith 840

Sidman; United States v. 597

Sigma Int'l, Inc.; United States v. 250; 251

Silva; People v. 23

Simac; People v. 948

Simmons; State v. 480

Simmons; United States v. 324; 945

Simons; Commonwealth v. 670

Simpson; People v. 743

Singer; People v. 851

Singer v. United States 30

Singleton; U.S. v. 61

Siragusa; United States v. 430

Smith v. Commonwealth. 797

Smith v. Hooey. 302, 303

Smith v. Illinois 141

Smith v. O'Grady 367

Smith; People v. 720; 733

Smith v. Phillips 473

Smith v. Robbins. 819

Smith v. Texas 419; 423

Smith v. U.S. 310; 364

Smith; U.S. v. 324

Snow, In re. 659, 660

Snyder v. Louisiana 558

Solano; State v. 381

Somerstein; U.S. v. 537

Soriano; People v. 876

Spann v. State 397

Spencer v. Texas. 589

Spencer, Ex parte. 987

Spicer v. Roxbury Correctional Institute 117

Spivey; State v. 434

Splunge v. Clark 556

St.Clair; People v. 790

Stack v. Boyle. 62; 72

Stagner; Commonwealth v. 405

Standefer v. U.S. 643

Stano v. Dugger 891

State v. (see name of defendant). . . . .

State ex rel. (see name of relator). . . . .

State of (see name of state) . . . .

Steele; United States v. 14

Steffes; State v. 166

Stemler v. City of Florence 13

Stephens v. Attorney Gen. 646

Stevens v. People. 587

Stirone v. United States 249

Stolar, In re. 937

Stone v. Powell . . 988; 991; 1009–1011; 1015; 1022

Strauder v. West Virginia 501; 502; 520; 524

Strickland; U.S. v. 595

Strickland v. Washington . .854; 855; 869; 871; 875; 878; 887; 890; 892; 894; 915; 920; 961

Stromberg v. California 789

Strunk v. United States. 302; 305

Stufflebean; State v. 487

Sudikoff; U.S. v. 114

Sugar; State v. 936

Sullivan v. Louisiana. 818

Sullivan, Pennsylvania ex rel. v. Ashe 715

Sunal v. Large 975

Superior Court of Alameda County; People v. . . . 17

Superior Court (Romero); People v. 697

Swain v. Alabama . . .474; 490; 492; 500; 508; 526; 568; 994

T

Tafoya v. State. 876

Takencareof; People v. 721; 746

Taylor v. Illinois. 961

Taylor v. Louisiana . . 418; 427; 431; 435; 501; 521; 528

Taylor; People v. 643

Taylor; State v. 627

Taylor v. Taylor 938

Teague v. Lane 994; 1000; 1006; 1015; 1022

Teague; U.S. v. 889

Tennessee v. Street. 590

Terry; People v. 595

Terry; U.S. v. 435

Test; United States v. 514

Thayer; United States v. 266

Thiel v. Southern Pacific Co. 420; 430; 474

Thomas v. Commonwealth. 488

Thomas; U.S. v. 456

Thompson; State v. 655

Thompson; United States v. 277

Thoreen; United States v. 953, 954; 957

Thurman v. State. 653

Tilley; People v. 197

Timmendequas; State v. 456

Timmreck; United States v. 880

Tollett v. Henderson 366

[References are to pages]

Tootick; U.S. v.................602

Torres v. Donnelly................933

Torres; U.S. v..................476

Tortora; United States v...........75; 88–92

Town of (see name of town)............

Trevino; People v.................515

Tucceri; Commonwealth v............137

Tucker; United States v...........556; 715

Tuitt; U.S. v....................45

Tumey v. Ohio.........787; 789; 809; 815

Turk; United States v...........609; 616

Turner v. Murray.................476

Turner v. State..................830

Turner; U.S. v....................44

U

U.S. v. (see name of defendant)...........

U.S. Dept. of Commerce, Bureau of the Census.515

Udziela; United States v..............252

Ullmann v. United States.............264

Umans; United States v...........245; 247

United States v. (see name of defendant).......

Uwaezhoke; U.S. v................547

V

Valenzuela-Bernal; United States v........157

Van Hemelryck; U.S. v..............595

Vasquez v. Hillery.......238; 487; 809; 815

Verdugo-Urquidez; United States v.......1013

Vermeulen; United States v............879

Vermont v. Brillon.................337

Villas; State v....................13

Vinal; State v...................602

Virgin Islands v. Weatherwax..........883

Vogt; U.S. v...................595

W

Waddy v. Davis...................879

Wade; United States v........162; 270; 802

Wainwright v. Sykes.....985; 1001; 1005, 1006

Wainwright v. Witt................474

Walder v. United States.......590; 977, 978

Walker v. Goldsmith...............435

Walker; State v...................570

Walker; United States v.............121

Wallace v. Morrison...............533

Wallace; United States v............147

Waller v. Florida.................648

Waller v. Georgia.............809; 815

Walters; United States v.............609

Walton v. Arizona............752; 754

Walton v. Aytch.................669

Ward v. State...................854

Wardlow; People v.................597

Warme; United States v.............148

Washington v. Clemmer.............184

Washington v. Davis...............546

Washington; People v..............801

Washington; State v...............506

Washington; U.S. v...............283

Watkins v. Sowders.............162; 590

Watkins, Ex parte.............975; 986

Watson; State v..................597

Watson; United States v.........331; 541

Watts v. Indiana.................268

Watts; U.S. v...................726

Wayte v. United States..........33; 39

Weatherford v. Bursey.............365

Weaver; People v.................352

Weaver v. State..................883

Welch v. Texas Highways and Public Transp. Dept..................809

Wellington; Commonwealth v..........876

Wellington; U.S. v................963

Wells; United States v.............254

Wende; People v.................820

West; State v...................513

West, Commonwealth ex rel. v. Rundle.....356

Whalen v. U.S..................656

Wheat v. United States.........572; 944

Wheeler; People v......508; 543; 566, 567; 570

White; People v.................877

White, State ex rel. v. Gray...........384

Whitman v. Superior Court of Santa Clara County.............199; 209, 210; 212

Whitus v. Georgia................789

Wiggins; United States v............391

Wilcox, United States ex rel. v. Johnson.....930

Williams; Commonwealth v...........668

Williams v. Florida........125; 409; 501

Williams v. Illinois................272

Williams v. New York....714, 715; 717; 719; 750

Williams; People v................352

Williams v. State.............847; 881

Williams; State v................435

Williams v. Taylor..........1020; 1021

Williams; United States v.......238; 240; 273

Willis; United States v.............151

Wilson v. Mitchell...............335

Wilson v. State..........194; 196; 207

Wilson; United States v.......146; 318; 668

Wimberly; People v..............209

Winkler v. Keane................845

[References are to pages]

Winship, In re 163; 748, 749; 753

Winter; United States v. 266

Wisconsin v. Mitchell 760

Witherspoon v. Illinois 417; 430

Withrow v. Williams 1009

Witsell; State v. 674

Wood v. Bartholomew 138

Wood v. Georgia. 217; 276; 281; 846

Wood v. United States 268

Wood; United States v. 489

Woodard v. Hutchins 1002

Woodford v. Municipal Court 643

Woods; United States v. 841

Woodson v. North Carolina 867

Wrenn v. Sheriff 194; 196

Wright; U.S. v. 364; 387

Wright v. United States 879

Y

Yaccarino, In re 937

Yarborough v. Gentry 870

Yick Wo v. Hopkins 15; 17; 38; 46

York, In re 96

Z

Zafiro v. United States 598

Zimmerman & Schwartz, P.C.; United States v. . 277

INDEX

[References are to pages.]

A

ABA (See AMERICAN BAR ASSOCIATION (ABA))

ADVERSARIAL LEGAL SYSTEM
Inquisitorial system compared . . . 1025

AMERICAN BAR ASSOCIATION (ABA)
Model Code of Professional Responsibility . . . 904
Standards for Criminal Justice
    Decision to prosecute (See DECISION TO PROSECUTE)
    Effective assistance of counsel, right to (See EFFECTIVE ASSISTANCE OF COUNSEL, RIGHT TO)
    Ethical obligations of defense attorneys (See ETHICAL OBLIGATIONS OF DEFENSE ATTORNEYS)
    Plea bargaining . . . 347
    Sentencing . . . 691

ANDERS V. CALIFORNIA
Appeals, Federal Rules of Criminal Procedure, Rule 52 . . . 791

APPEALS
Generally . . . 783
Federal Rules of Criminal Procedure, Rule 52
    Generally . . . 786
    Anders v. California . . . 791
    Arizona v. Fulminante . . . 804
    Chapman v. California . . . 786
    Harrington v. California . . . 800
    Smith v. Robbins . . . 819

APPRENDI V. NEW JERSEY
Sentencing, California Rules of Court . . . 746

ARIZONA V. FULMINANTE
Appeals, Federal Rules of Criminal Procedure, Rule 52 . . . 804

ARIZONA V. YOUNGBLOOD
Jencks Act, effect of . . . 155

ASHE V. SWENSON
Double jeopardy issue in . . . 633

ATTORNEYS
Effective assistance of counsel, right to (See EFFECTIVE ASSISTANCE OF COUNSEL, RIGHT TO)
Ethical obligations of criminal defense attorneys (See ETHICAL OBLIGATIONS OF DEFENSE ATTORNEYS)
Peremptory challenge, attorneys' view of . . . 494
Sentencing, attorneys' role in . . . 691

B

BAIL (See PRETRIAL RELEASE)

BARBER V. PONTE
Exclusion from venire, USC Title 28 . . . 426

BARKER V. WINGO
Right to speedy trial, Federal Rules of Criminal Procedure, Rule 48 . . . 293

BARNES V. STATE
Plea bargaining, Federal Rules of Criminal Procedure, Rule 11 . . . 401

BATSON V. KENTUCKY
Jury panels . . . 500

BLACKLEDGE V. ALLISON
Plea bargaining, Federal Rules of Criminal Procedure, Rule 11 . . . 375

BOYKIN V. ALABAMA
Plea bargaining, Federal Rules of Criminal Procedure, Rule 11 . . . 355

BRADY V. MARYLAND
Jencks Act, effect of . . . 112

BRADY V. UNITED STATES
Plea bargaining, Federal Rules of Criminal Procedure, Rule 11 . . . 359

BROWN V. OHIO
Double jeopardy issue in . . . 647

BRUTON V. UNITED STATES
Joinder and severance, Federal Rules of Criminal Procedure, Rules 8, 13, and 14 . . . 579

C

CHAPMAN V. CALIFORNIA
Appeals, Federal Rules of Criminal Procedure, Rule 52 . . . 786

COLEMAN V. BURNETT
Preliminary hearings, Federal Rules of Criminal Procedure, Rules 5 and 5.1 . . . 178

COMMON LAW AND CONTINENTAL SYSTEMS COMPARED
Simpson case, analysis using case similar to . . . 1025

COMMONWEALTH V. BALOG
Double jeopardy issue in . . . 666

COSTELLO V. UNITED STATES
Grand juries, Federal Rules of Criminal Procedure, Rule 6 . . . 228

CUNNINGHAM V. CALIFORNIA
Sentencing, California Rules of Court . . . 768

D

DECISION TO PROSECUTE
ABA Standards for Criminal Justice
    Generally . . . 4
    Oyler v. Boles . . . 11
    People v. Kail . . . 32
    People v. Superior Court [and Cynthia Hartway] . . . 17

DECISION TO PROSECUTE—Cont.
ABA Standards for Criminal Justice—Cont.
    United States v. Armstrong . . . 36
    United States v. Bass . . . 51
    United States v. Goodwin . . . 24
    United States v. Steele . . . 14
Oyler v. Boles . . . 11
Prosecutor, role of . . . 1

DISCOVERY
Civil and criminal discovery distinguished . . . 101
Federal Rules of Criminal Procedure . . . 105
Jencks Act
    Generally . . . 111
    Arizona v. Youngblood . . . 155
    Brady v. Maryland . . . 112
    United States v. Agurs . . . 131
    United States v. Brinkman . . . 138
    United States v. Feola . . . 143
    United States v. McDade . . . 168
    United States v. Nobles . . . 123

DOGGETT V. UNITED STATES
Right to speedy trial, Federal Rules of Criminal Pro-
    cedure, Rule 48 . . . 325

DOUBLE JEOPARDY
Generally . . . 631
Ashe v. Swenson . . . 633
Brown v. Ohio . . . 647
Commonwealth v. Balog . . . 666
Stephens v. Attorney General of California . . . 646

E

**EFFECTIVE ASSISTANCE OF COUNSEL,
    RIGHT TO**
Generally . . . 833
ABA Standards for Criminal Justice
    Generally . . . 873
    *Government of the Virgin Islands v. Weather-
      wax* . . . 883
    Johnson v. State . . . 882
    People v. Pozo . . . 874
Holloway v. Arkansas . . . 836
Strickland v. Washington . . . 855

**ETHICAL OBLIGATIONS OF DEFENSE AT-
    TORNEYS**
Generally . . . 901
ABA Model Code of Professional Responsibility
    . . . 904
ABA Standards for Criminal Justice
    Generally . . . 908
    Matter of Nackson . . . 934
    Nix v. Whiteside . . . 913
    People v. Simac . . . 948
    United States v. Locascio . . . 942
Representation of criminals, justification of
    . . . 964

F

**FEDERAL RULES OF CRIMINAL PROCE-
    DURE**
Appeals, as to (See APPEALS)
Discovery, as to . . . 105

**FEDERAL RULES OF CRIMINAL
    PROCEDURE**—Cont.
Grand juries, as to (See GRAND JURIES)
Joinder and severance, as to (See JOINDER AND
    SEVERANCE)
Plea bargaining, as to (See PLEA BARGAINING)
Preliminary hearings, as to (See PRELIMINARY
    HEARINGS)
Speedy trial, applicability to right to (See SPEEDY
    TRIAL, RIGHT TO)

G

**GOVERNMENT OF THE VIRGIN ISLANDS V.
    WEATHERWAX**
Right to effective counsel, ABA Standards for
    Criminal Justice . . . 883

GRAND JURIES
Generally . . . 217
Federal Rules of Criminal Procedure, Rule 6
    Generally . . . 222
    Costello v. United States . . . 228
    United States v. Basurto . . . 247
    United States v. Estepa . . . 242
    United States v. Mandujano . . . 259
    United States v. Udziela . . . 252
    United States v. Williams . . . 273

GRAY V. MARYLAND
Joinder and severance, Federal Rules of Criminal
    Procedure, Rules 8, 13, and 14 . . . 619

H

HABEAS CORPUS
Generally . . . 969
United States Code, Title 28
    Generally . . . 971
    McCleskey v. Zant . . . 995
    Stone v. Powell . . . 973
    Wainwright v. Sykes . . . 985
    Withrow v. Williams . . . 1009

HARRINGTON V. CALIFORNIA
Appeals, Federal Rules of Criminal Procedure, Rule
    52 . . . 800

HOLLOWAY V. ARKANSAS
Right to effective assistance of counsel in . . . 836

HUNTER V. DISTRICT COURT
Preliminary hearings, Federal Rules of Criminal Pro-
    cedure, Rules 5 and 5.1 . . . 193

I

INQUISITORIAL LEGAL SYSTEM
Adversarial system compared . . . 1025

J

J.E.B. V. ALABAMA
Cognizable groups in . . . 519

JENCKS ACT
Discovery (See DISCOVERY)

[References are to pages.]

JOHNSON V. STATE
Right to effective counsel, ABA Standards for
   Criminal Justice . . . 882

JOINDER AND SEVERANCE
Generally . . . 577
Federal Rules of Criminal Procedure, Rules 8, 13,
   and 14
      Generally . . . 579
      Bruton v. United States . . . 579
      Gray v. Maryland . . . 619
      Richardson v. Marsh . . . 587
      United States v. Andrews, et al. . . . 605
      Zafiro v. United States . . . 598

JURIES
Grand jury (See GRAND JURIES)
Jury venire (See JURY VENIRE)
Panels (See JURY PANELS)
Reconsideration of . . . 574

JURY PANELS
Generally . . . 467
Challenges for cause
      Generally . . . 469
      State v. Logan . . . 483
      United States v. Salamone . . . 469
Cognizable group
      Generally . . . 512
      J.E.B. v. Alabama . . . 519
      United States v. Santiago-Martinez . . . 542
Peremptory challenges
      Generally . . . 492
      Batson v. Kentucky . . . 500
      Cognizable group (See subhead: Cognizable
        group)
      Courts' view of . . . 492
      Impropriety of challenge, proof of (See sub-
        head: Proof of impropriety of challenges)
      Reconsideration of . . . 573
      Remedies . . . 569
      Trial attorneys' view of . . . 494
Proof of impropriety of challenges
      Generally . . . 543
      Purkett v. Elem . . . 551
      Snyder v. Louisiana . . . 558
Reconsideration of . . . 574

JURY VENIRE
Generally . . . 407
Exclusions from venire
      Generally . . . 418
      Barber v. Ponte . . . 426
      Taylor v. Louisiana . . . 418
      Walker v. Goldsmith . . . 435
Pretrial publicity
      Generally . . . 437
      Murphy v. Florida . . . 437
      Powell v. Superior Court . . . 444
United States Code, Title 28
      Generally . . . 411
      Exclusions from venire (See subhead: Exclu-
        sions from venire)
      Pretrial publicity (See subhead: Pretrial public-
        ity)

L

LAWYERS (See ATTORNEYS)

M

MATTER OF NACKSON
Ethical obligations of defense attorneys, ABA Standards for Criminal Justice . . . 934

MCCLESKEY V. ZANT
Habeas corpus, USC Title 28 . . . 995

MOORE V. ARIZONA
Right to speedy trial, Federal Rules of Criminal Procedure, Rule 48 . . . 304

MURPHY V. FLORIDA
Pretrial publicity, USC Title 28 . . . 437

N

NIX V. WHITESIDE
Ethical obligations of defense attorneys, ABA Standards for Criminal Justice . . . 913

O

OYLER V. BOLES
Decision to prosecute in . . . 11

P

PEOPLE V. BENNETT
Sentencing, California Rules of Court . . . 731

PEOPLE V. KAIL
Decision to prosecute in . . . 32

PEOPLE V. MCNALLY
Sentencing, California Rules of Court . . . 734

PEOPLE V. POZO
Right to effective counsel, ABA Standards for
   Criminal Justice . . . 874

PEOPLE V. REYES
Sentencing, California Rules of Court . . . 742

PEOPLE V. SIMAC
Ethical obligations of defense attorneys, ABA Standards for Criminal Justice . . . 948

PEOPLE V. SMITH
Sentencing, California Rules of Court . . . 720

**PEOPLE V. SUPERIOR COURT [AND CYNTHIA
HARTWAY]**
Decision to prosecute in . . . 17

PEOPLE V. TAKENCAREOF
Sentencing, California Rules of Court . . . 721

PEOPLE V. WIMBERLY
Preliminary hearings, Federal Rules of Criminal Procedure, Rules 5 and 5.1 . . . 209

PLEA BARGAINING
Generally . . . 343
ABA Standards for Criminal Justice . . . 347

[References are to pages.]

PLEA BARGAINING—Cont.
Federal Rules of Criminal Procedure, Rule 11
    Generally . . . 349
    Barnes v. State . . . 401
    Blackledge v. Allison . . . 375
    Boykin v. Alabama . . . 355
    Brady v. United States . . . 359
    Santobello v. New York . . . 368
    State v. Solano . . . 381
    United States v. Melancon . . . 391

POWELL V. SUPERIOR COURT
Pretrial publicity, USC Title 28 . . . 444

PRELIMINARY HEARINGS
Generally . . . 173
Federal Rules of Criminal Procedure, Rules 5 and 5.1
    Generally . . . 176
    Coleman v. Burnett . . . 178
    Hunter v. District Court . . . 193
    People v. Wimberly . . . 209
    Whitman v. Superior Court . . . 199

PRETRIAL RELEASE
Generally . . . 54
Bail Reform Act of 1984
    Generally . . . 56
    Stack v. Boyle . . . 62
    United States v. Botero . . . 66
    United States v. Motamedi . . . 71
    United States v. Patriarca . . . 86
    United States v. Tortora . . . 75
Importance of . . . 53

PROSECUTORS
Decision to prosecute by . . . 1

PURKETT V. ELEM
Impropriety of peremptory challenge, proof of . . . 551

R

RICHARDSON V. MARSH
Joinder and severance, Federal Rules of Criminal Procedure, Rules 8, 13, and 14 . . . 587

S

SANTOBELLO V. NEW YORK
Plea bargaining, Federal Rules of Criminal Procedure, Rule 11 . . . 368

SENTENCING
Generally . . . 677
ABA Standards for Criminal Justice . . . 691
California, in . . . 690
California Penal Code sections regarding . . . 694
California Rules of Court
    Generally . . . 703
    Apprendi v. New Jersey . . . 746
    Cunningham v. California . . . 768
    People v. Bennett . . . 731
    People v. McNally . . . 734
    People v. Reyes . . . 742
    People v. Smith . . . 720
    People v. Takencareof . . . 721

SENTENCING—Cont.
California Rules of Court—Cont.
    United States v. Grayson . . . 712
Determinate sentencing system . . . 678
Federal sentencing guidelines
    Generally . . . 679
    United States v. Patillo . . . 681
Indeterminate sentencing system . . . 678
Judge's role in . . . 677
Lawyer's role in . . . 691

SEVERANCE OF TRIAL (See JOINDER AND SEVERANCE)

SIMPSON CASE
Common law and continental systems comparison based on case similar to . . . 1025

SMITH V. ROBBINS
Appeals, Federal Rules of Criminal Procedure, Rule 52 . . . 819

SNYDER V. LOUISIANA
Impropriety of peremptory challenge, proof of . . . 558

SPEEDY TRIAL, RIGHT TO
Generally . . . 285
Federal Rules of Criminal Procedure, Rule 48
    Generally . . . 292
    Barker v. Wingo . . . 293
    Doggett v. United States . . . 325
    Moore v. Arizona . . . 304
    Strunk v. United States . . . 302
    United States v. Loud Hawk . . . 314
    United States v. Lovasco . . . 305
    Vermont v. Brillon . . . 337
Speedy Trial Act . . . 287

STACK V. BOYLE
Pretrial release issue in . . . 62

STATE V. LOGAN
Challenging jurors for cause in . . . 483

STATE V. SOLANO
Plea bargaining, Federal Rules of Criminal Procedure, Rule 11 . . . 381

STEPHENS V. ATTORNEY GENERAL OF CALIFORNIA
Double jeopardy issue in . . . 646

STONE V. POWELL
Habeas corpus, USC Title 28 . . . 973

STRICKLAND V. WASHINGTON
Right to effective assistance of counsel in . . . 855

STRUNK V. UNITED STATES
Right to speedy trial, Federal Rules of Criminal Procedure, Rule 48 . . . 302

T

TAYLOR V. LOUISIANA
Exclusion from venire, USC Title 28 . . . 418

[References are to pages.]

U

UNITED STATES V. AGURS
Jencks Act, effect of . . . 131

UNITED STATES V. ANDREWS, ET AL.
Joinder and severance, Federal Rules of Criminal
Procedure, Rules 8, 13, and 14 . . . 605

UNITED STATES V. ARMSTRONG
Decision to prosecute in . . . 36

UNITED STATES V. BASS
Decision to prosecute in . . . 51

UNITED STATES V. BASURTO
Grand juries, Federal Rules of Criminal Procedure,
Rule 6 . . . 247

UNITED STATES V. BOTERO
Pretrial release issue in . . . 66

UNITED STATES V. BRINKMAN
Jencks Act, effect of . . . 138

UNITED STATES V. ESTEPA
Grand juries, Federal Rules of Criminal Procedure,
Rule 6 . . . 242

UNITED STATES V. FEOLA
Jencks Act, effect of . . . 143

UNITED STATES V. GOODWIN
Decision to prosecute in . . . 24

UNITED STATES V. GRAYSON
Sentencing, California Rules of Court . . . 712

UNITED STATES V. LOCASCIO
Ethical obligations of defense attorneys, ABA Standards for Criminal Justice . . . 942

UNITED STATES V. LOUD HAWK
Right to speedy trial, Federal Rules of Criminal Procedure, Rule 48 . . . 314

UNITED STATES V. LOVASCO
Right to speedy trial, Federal Rules of Criminal Procedure, Rule 48 . . . 305

UNITED STATES V. MANDUJANO
Grand juries, Federal Rules of Criminal Procedure,
Rule 6 . . . 259

UNITED STATES V. MCDADE
Jencks Act, effect of . . . 168

UNITED STATES V. MELANCON
Plea bargaining, Federal Rules of Criminal Procedure, Rule 11 . . . 391

UNITED STATES V. MOTAMEDI
Pretrial release issue in . . . 71

UNITED STATES V. NOBLES
Jencks Act, effect of . . . 123

UNITED STATES V. PATILLO
Federal Sentencing Guidelines in . . . 681

UNITED STATES V. PATRIARCA
Pretrial release issue in . . . 86

UNITED STATES V. SALAMONE
Challenging jurors for cause in . . . 469

UNITED STATES V. SANTIAGO-MARTINEZ
Cognizable groups in . . . 542

UNITED STATES V. STEELE
Decision to prosecute in . . . 14

UNITED STATES V. TORTORA
Pretrial release issue in . . . 75

UNITED STATES V. UDZIELA
Grand juries, Federal Rules of Criminal Procedure,
Rule 6 . . . 252

UNITED STATES V. WILLIAMS
Grand juries, Federal Rules of Criminal Procedure,
Rule 6 . . . 273

V

VERMONT V. BRILLON
Right to speedy trial, Federal Rules of Criminal Procedure, Rule 48 . . . 337

W

WAINWRIGHT V. SYKES
Habeas corpus, USC Title 28 . . . 985

WALKER V. GOLDSMITH
Exclusion from venire, USC Title 28 . . . 435

WHITMAN V. SUPERIOR COURT
Preliminary hearings, Federal Rules of Criminal Procedure, Rules 5 and 5.1 . . . 199

WITHROW V. WILLIAMS
Habeas corpus, USC Title 28 . . . 1009

Z

ZAFIRO V. UNITED STATES
Joinder and severance, Federal Rules of Criminal
Procedure, Rules 8, 13, and 14 . . . 598